LIBRARY

OF

USEFUL KNOWLEDGE.

NATURAL PHILOSOPHY.

I.

OBJECTS, ADVANTAGES, AND PLEASURES OF SCIENCE.
MECHANICS.
HYDROSTATICS.
HYDRAULICS.
PNEUMATICS.
HEAT.
OPTICS.
DOUBLE REFRACTION AND POLARISATION OF LIGHT.

WITH

AN EXPLANATION OF SCIENTIFIC TERMS,

AND

AN INDEX.

LONDON:

BALDWIN AND CRADOCK, PATERNOSTER-ROW.

MDCCCXXIX.

CONTENTS.

	Page
I. PRELIMINARY TREATISE: Objects, Advantages, and Pleasures of Science.	
II. MECHANICS: On Mechanical Agents, or Prime Movers	1—32
III. ———— Elements of Machinery	1—64
IV. ———— Friction and Rigidity of Cordage	1—32
V. HYDROSTATICS	1—32
VI. HYDRAULICS	1—32
VII. PNEUMATICS	1—32
VIII. HEAT	1—64
IX. OPTICS*	1—68
X. DOUBLE REFRACTION AND POLARISATION OF LIGHT	1—64
XI. Glossary.	
XII. Index.	

* The four last pages of the Treatise on Optics will be found in the Second Part of Optical Instruments, and must be taken from that Number to be bound in this Volume.

COMMITTEE.

Chairman—H. BROUGHAM, Esq., F.R.S., M.P.   *Vice Chairman*—LORD JOHN RUSSELL, M.P.

Treasurer—WILLIAM TOOKE, Esq., F.R.S.

Rt. Hon. J. Abercrombie, M.P.
W. Allen, Esq., F.R.S.
Lord Althorp, M.P.
Rt. Hon. Lord Auckland.
W. B. Baring, Esq., M.P.
Capt. F. Beaufort, R.N., F.R.S.
C. Bell, Esq., F.R.S., L. & E.
T. F. Buxton, Esq., M.P., F.R.S.
R. Otway Cave, Esq., M.P.
John Conolly, M.D.
William Coulson, Esq.
Wm. Crawford, Esq.
Fred. Daniell, Esq., F.R.S.
T. Denman, Esq.
Hon. G. A. Ellis, M.A., M.P.
T. F. Ellis, Esq., M.A.
I. L. Goldsmid, Esq., F.R.S.
B. Gompertz, Esq., F.R.S.
H. Hallam, Esq., F.R.S., M.A.

M. D. Hill, Esq.
Rowland Hill, Esq.
E. Hill, Esq.
Leonard Horner, Esq., F.R.S.
David Jardine, Esq.
Henry B. Ker, Esq., F.R.S.
J. G. S. Lefevre, Esq., F.R.S.
Edward Lloyd, Esq., M.A.
James Loch, Esq., M.P., F.G.S.
J. W. Lubbock, Esq., M.A.
Dr. Lushington, D.C.L., M.P.
Sir J. Mackintosh, M.P., F.R.S.
B. H. Malkin, Esq., M.A.
Rev. Ed. Maltby, D.D., F.R.S.
James Manning, Esq.
F. O. Martin, Esq.
J. Marshall, Esq., M.P.
John Herman Merivale, Esq.
James Mill, Esq.

James Morrison, Esq.
Right Hon. Lord Nugent, M.P.
Sir H. Parnell, Bart., M.P.
Professor Pattison.
T. Spring Rice, Esq., M.P., F.A.S.
Dr. Roget, Sec. R.S.
C. E. Rumbold, Esq., M.P.
J. Smith, Esq., M.P.
William Sturch, Esq.
Right Hon. Lord Suffield.
Dr. A. T. Thompson, F.L.S.
William Eyton Tooke, Esq.
A. N. Vigors, Esq., F.R.S.
H. Warburton, Esq., M.P., F.R.S.
H. Waymouth, Esq.
J. Whishaw, Esq., M.A., F.R.S.
Mr. Serjeant Wilde.
John Wood, Esq., M.P.
John Wrottesley, Esq., M.A.

Ashburton—J. F. Kingston, Esq.
Birmingham Local Association.
  Rev. John Currie, *Chairman*.
  Paul Moon James, Esq., *Treasurer.*
  Thos. Clarke, Esq.
  T. Eyre Lee, Esq. } *Hon. Secs.*
  Jos. Parkes, Esq. }
Bristol—J. N. Sanders, Esq., *Chairman.*
  J. Reynolds, Esq., *Treasurer.*
  J. B. Estlin, Esq., F.L.S., *Sec.*
Cambridge—Rev. James Bowstead, M.A.
  Rev. Professor Henslow, M.A., F.L.S. & G.S.
  Rev. Leonard Jenyns, M.A., F.L.S.
  Rev. John Lodge, M.A.
  Henry Malden, Esq., M.A.
  Fred. Malkin, Esq., M.A.
  Rev. George Peacock, M.A., F.R.S. & G.S.
  Marmaduke Ramsay, Esq., M.A., F.L.S.
  Rev. Professor Sedgwick, M.A., F.R.S. & G.S.
  Professor Smyth, M.A.
  Rev. C. Thirlwall, M.A.
Derby—Joseph Strutt, Esq.
Devonport—C. Greaves, Esq.

Dublin—Hon. Thomas Vesey.
Edinburgh—R. Greville, LL.D.
  D. Ellis, Esq., F.R.S.
  Captain Basil Hall, R.N., F.R.S.L. & E.
  Francis Jeffrey, Esq.
  Professor Napier, F.R.S.E.
  Rev. A. Thomson, D.D.
  W. Thomson, Esq.
Etruria—Jos. Wedgwood, Esq.
Exeter—Rev. J. P. Jones.
  J. Tyrrell, Esq.
Glasgow—K. Finlay, Esq.
  D. Bannatyne, Esq.
  Robert Grahame, Esq.
  Professor Mylne.
  Alexander McGrigor, Esq.
  C. Macintosh, Esq., F.R.S.
  Mr. T. Atkinson, *Hon. Sec.*
Hull—Daniel Sykes, Esq., M.P.
Keighley, Yorkshire—Rev. T. Dury, M.A.
Launceston—Rev. J. Barfitt.
Leamington Spa—Dr. Loudon.
Leeds—Benjamin Gott, Esq.
  J. Marshall, Jun., Esq.
Lewes—J. W. Woollgar, Esq.
Liverpool Local Association.
  Dr. Traill, *Chairman.*
  J. Mulleneux, Esq., *Treasurer.*
  Rev. W. Shepherd.

  J. Ashton Yates, Esq.
Maidenhead—R. Goolden, Esq., F.L.S.
Manchester Local Association.
  G. W. Wood, Esq., *Chairman.*
  B. Heywood, Esq., *Treasurer.*
  T. W. Winstanley, Esq., *Hon. Sec.*
  Sir George Philips, Bart., M.P.
Newcastle—James Losh, Esq.
  Rev. W. Turner.
Newport—Ab. Clarke, Esq.
  T. Cooke, Jun., Esq.
  R. G. Kirkpatrick, Esq.
Newport Pagnell—James Millar, Esq.
Norwich—Richard Bacon, Esq.
Plymouth—George Harvey, Esq., F.R.S.
Portsmouth—E. Carter, Esq.
  G. Grant, Esq.
  D. Howard, Esq.
  Rev. Dr. Inman, Nav. Col.
Sheffield—J. H. Abraham, Esq.
Tavistock—Rev. William Evans.
  John Rundle, Esq.
Truro—William Peter, Esq.
Waterford—Sir John Newport, Bart., M.P.
Wolverhampton—J. Pearson, Esq.

THOMAS COATES, *Secretary.*

TREATISES PREPARING FOR PUBLICATION.

* Optical Instruments.
* Strength of Materials.
* Plane Geometry.
* Solid Geometry.
* Algebra.
* Algebraic Geometry.
* Conic Sections.
* Dynamics.
* Hydrodynamics.
* Physical Astronomy.
* *Observatories.
* *Astronomical Instruments.
* *Gunnery and Fortification.
* *Land Surveying.
* *Navigation.
* Heat—(2 *Treatises*).
* *Thermometer and Pyrometer.
* *Steam Engine.
* Affinity.
* Chemical Apparatus and Processes.
* Definite Proportions.
* Electro-Chemistry.
* Objects of Chemistry—(4 *Treatises*).
* Geology.—(2 *Treatises*).
* Chemical Functions of Animals.
* Chemical Functions of Vegetables.
* Meteorology.
* *Dyeing.
* *Bleaching.
* *Assaying.
* Structure of Plants.
* Functions of Plants.
* Diseases of Plants.
* Geography of Plants.
* Arrangement of Plants.
* Uses of Plants.
* General Principles of Agriculture.
* Agricultural Buildings and Machinery.
* Management of a Farm.
* Breeding of Cattle.
* Fattening of Cattle.
* Diseases of Cattle.
* *Farriery.
* *Hop-planting.
* *Sheep-farming.
* *Dairy-farming.
* *Woods and Timber.
* *Potatoes, Cabbage, and Spade Husbandry.
* Account of the PRINCIPIA.
* ————— OPTICS.
* ————— MECHANIQUE CELESTE.
* ————— NOVUM ORGANUM.
* ————— DE DIGNITATE ET AUGMENTIS.

INTELLECTUAL PHILOSOPHY.

Fundamental Principles of Human Knowledge.
Association of Ideas and Habit.
Signs of Thought (natural and arbitrary).
Grammar and Language.
Judgment and Reasoning.
Evidence and Belief; and the conduct of the Understanding.

ETHICAL PHILOSOPHY.

Pains and Pleasures.
Motives.
Classification of Human Actions.
Human Obligations.

POLITICAL PHILOSOPHY.

Objects of Government, and its means.
  Legislative,
  Judicial, and
  Administrative powers.
Jurisprudence, Civil.
——————, Criminal.
——————, Preliminary (Police).
Political Economy.

HISTORY OF SCIENCE.

Mathematics.	Chemistry.	Ethics.
Natural Philosophy.	Anatomy.	Religion.
Astronomy.	Metaphysics.	Law.

HISTORY OF ART.

Useful Arts. Navigation. Commerce.
Fine Arts. War. Manufactures.

HISTORY OF NATIONS.

Greece. The Low Countries. Spanish America.
Rome. Switzerland. Portuguese America.
England. Italy. British America.
Scotland. Northern States. Egypt.
Ireland. Russia. Western Asia.
France. United America. British India.
Germany. West Indies. China.
Spain and Portugal.

HISTORY OF INDIVIDUALS.

Patriots.

Bruce. Hampden. Lord Falkland.
De Witt. Sydney. Washington.
William Tell. Russell. Paoli.

Warriors.

Black Prince. Wolfe. Rodney.
Gustavus Adolphus. Abercrombie. Nelson.
Marlborough. Blake. St. Vincent.
Turenne. De Ruyter. Duncan.

Discoverers.

Galileo. Kepler. Black.
Copernicus. Newton. Cavendish.
Bacon. Leibnitz. Priestley.
Tycho Brahe. Hervey. Lavoisier.

Self-exalted Men.

Franklin. Rennie. Arkwright.
Sir Christopher Wren. Watt. Smeaton.

Moral Philosophers.

Locke. Berkeley. Turgot.
Malbranche. Grotius. Smith.

Navigators.

Columbus. Vasco di Gama. Cook.
Drake. Anson. La Perouse.

Statesmen.

Wolsey. Sully. Somers.
Burleigh. O. Cromwell. Chatham.

The foregoing List is not to be considered as comprising every subject belonging to each class, but principally those which it is intended shall be first treated of.

SOCIETY
FOR THE
DIFFUSION
OF
USEFUL KNOWLEDGE.

The object of the Society is strictly limited to what its title imports, namely, the imparting useful information to all classes of the community, particularly to such as are unable to avail themselves of experienced teachers, or may prefer learning by themselves.

The plan proposed for the attainment of this object, is the periodical publication of Treatises, under the direction and with the sanction of a superintending Committee.

As numerous Societies already exist for the dissemination of Religious Instruction, and as it is the object of this Society to aid the progress of those branches of general knowledge which can be diffused among all classes of the community, no Treatise published with the sanction of the Committee shall contain any matter of Controversial Divinity, or interfere with the principles of revealed Religion.

1. Each Scientific Treatise will contain an Exposition of the Fundamental Principles of some Branch of Science—their proofs and illustrations—their application to practical uses, and to the explanation of facts or appearances.

2. For this purpose, the greater Divisions of Knowledge will be subdivided into Branches; and if one of these Subdivisions or Branches cannot be sufficiently taught in a single Treatise, it will be continued in a second.

3. When any part of a subdivision is of sufficient practical importance to require being minutely pursued in its details, an extra or separate Treatise upon this part will be given, without interrupting the Series; and care will be taken, as far as possible, to publish those Treatises first that relate to subjects the knowledge of which is necessary for understanding those which follow.

4. Thus the great division of Natural Knowledge, commonly called Natural Philosophy, will be subdivided into different Branches, as Elementary Astronomy—Mechanical Powers—Application of these to Machinery—Hydrostatics—Hydraulics—Pneumatics—Optics—Electricity—Magnetism. Separate Practical Treatises will be given on Dialling—Millwork—Optical Instruments; and Treatises on Geometry, Algebra, and Trigonometry will be published before extending Natural Philosophy to its higher branches of Dynamics, Hydrodynamics, and Physical Astronomy,—the object being thus to furnish the means of acquiring, step by step, the whole of any department or Science, to the study of which interest or inclination may lead.

5. To each Treatise will be subjoined a reference to the works or parts of works in which the same subject is discussed more at large, with suggestions for enabling the student, who may feel so disposed, to prosecute his studies further.

6. Each Treatise will consist of about thirty-two pages Octavo, printed so as to contain the quantity of above one hundred ordinary octavo pages, with neat Engravings on Wood, and Tables. It will be sold for Sixpence; and one will appear on the 1st and 15th of each Month. Reading Societies, Mechanics' Institutions, and Education Committees, in the Country, will be furnished with supplies at a liberal abatement in price.

7. The first Treatise, being an INTRODUCTORY DISCOURSE UPON THE OBJECTS, ADVANTAGES, AND PLEASURES OF SCIENTIFIC PURSUITS, will be published on the 1st of March, by

Messrs. BALDWIN, CRADOCK, & JOY, London.

The following are *among* the subjects which the plan of the Work embraces, and will follow each other in regular succession, though not exactly in the order here exhibited. The *extra* Treatises are thus marked *.

NATURAL PHILOSOPHY.

Elementary Astronomy.
Mechanical Powers.
Practical Mechanics.
Mechanical Anatomy.
Hydrostatics.
Hydraulics.
Pneumatics.
Optics.
Electricity.
Magnetism.
* Dialling.
* Millwork.

The practical means for ensuring steady adherence to the object of of the Society, and for most efficaciously securing a due execution of the plan proposed, with all such improvements of detail as experience may from time to time dictate, will be found in the following Rules for the establishment and continuance of the Society, under the conduct of an efficient Committee.

RULES.

I. The Society to consist of all such individuals as may be induced to contribute the sum of Ten Pounds or upwards, in one payment, or One-Pound or upwards, annually.

II. Every Annual Subscription to be considered as made on the preceding 1st of January, and to fall due again on the following 1st of January, in each year.

III. Every Subscriber, on having paid his Subscription for the current year, to be entitled to a copy of each Tract as soon as published, and to have the privilege of purchasing twelve, or any greater number, at a considerable reduction from the publication price, for gratuitous distribution.

IV. The business of the Society to be transacted by a Committee, not less than thirty in number, consisting, in the first instance, of the following Subscribers:—

Hon. J. ABERCROMBIE, M.P.
WM. ALLEN, Esq., F.R.S.
Rt. Hon. Lord ALTHORP, M.P.
Rt. Hon. Lord AUCKLAND.
Capt. FRANCIS BEAUFORT, R.N., F.R.S.
C. BELL, Esq., F.R.S.
H. BROUGHAM, Esq., M.P., F.R.S.
T. F. BUXTON, Esq., M.P., F.R.S.
J. CARTER, Esq. M.P.
R. OTWAY CAVE, Esq. M.P.
WM. CRAWFORD, Esq.
T. DENMAN, Esq., Common Sergeant of the City of London.
ROBERT FORSTER, Esq.
I. L. GOLDSMID, Esq.
Dr. OLINTHUS GREGORY, Royal Academy, Woolwich.
H. HALLAM, Esq., F.R.S.

Capt. BASIL HALL, R.N., F.R.S.
M. D. HILL, Esq.
ROWLAND HILL, Esq.
BELLENDEN KER, Esq.
JAMES LOCH, Esq.
Dr. LUSHINGTON, D.C.L., M.P.
Sir J. MACKINTOSH, M.P., F.R.S.
Rev. EDW. MALTBY, D.D., F.R.S.
J. MARSHALL, Esq. M.P.
JOHN MARTIN, Esq., M.P.
JAMES MILL, Esq.
JAMES MILLAR, Esq.
Rt. Hon. Lord NUGENT, M.P.
Sir H. PARNELL, Bart., M.P.
GEORGE PHILIPS, Esq., M.P.
T. SPRING RICE, Esq., M.P., F.A.S.
Rt. Hon. Lord JOHN RUSSELL, M.P.
J. SMITH, Esq., M.P.

W. STURCH, Esq.
Rt. Hon. Lord SUFFIELD.
DAN. SYKES, Esq., M.P.
Dr. A. THOMSON, F.L.S.
WILLIAM EYTON TOOKE, Esq.
H. WARBURTON, Esq., M.P., F.R.S.

Treasurer—WILLIAM TOOKE, Esq., F.R.S., V.P. Soc. Arts.

LEO. HORNER, Esq., F.R.S. L. & E., Edinburgh.
J. MARSHALL, Jun., Esq., Leeds.
Prof. NAPIER, F.R.S.E., Edinburgh.
FRAS. JEFFREY, Esq., Edinburgh.
D. ELLIS, Esq., F.R.S., Edinburgh.
R. GREVILLE, LL.D., Edinburgh.
Rev. A. THOMSON, D.D., Edinburgh.
T. EYRE LEE, Esq., Birmingham.
JAMES LOSH, Esq., Newcastle.
JOS. PARKES, Esq., Birmingham.
JOS. WEDGWOOD, Esq., Etruria.
J. ASHTON YATES, Esq., Liverpool.
J. H. ABRAHAM, Esq., Sheffield.
GEO. W. WOOD, Esq., Manchester.
AB. CLARKE, Esq., Newport.
T. COOKE, Jun., Esq., Newport.
R. G. KIRKPATRICK, Esq., Newport.
Dr. TRAILL, Liverpool.
E. CARTER, Esq., Portsmouth.
D. HOWARD, Esq., Portsmouth.
Rev. Dr. INMAN, Naval College, Portsmouth.
G. GRANT, Esq., Portsmouth.
Rev. W. SHEPHERD, Liverpool.
Rev. W. TURNER, Newcastle.
J. TYRRELL, Esq., Exeter.
JOS. REYNOLDS, Esq., Bristol.

Secretary—Mr. THOMAS COATES.
Collector—Mr. KENNELL.

V. The Committee to have the entire conduct of the affairs of the Society, and disposal of its Funds towards the attainment of the proposed object.

VI. The Committee to elect from time to time, from their own body, a Chairman, Deputy Chairman, and Treasurer.

VII. The Committee also to engage convenient Apartments, and a Secretary or Clerk, and Collector, taking security from the latter for the faithful discharge of his duty, with power to allow Salaries to them; and to engage, suspend, or discharge such officers as the Committee may think fit.

VIII. The Committee to add to their number and supply vacancies occurring in their own body, by ballot, from among the Subscribers; the person proposed being nominated and seconded at one Meeting in ordinary, and not to be ballotted for until the next following ordinary Meeting of the Committee—notice being given in the summons for such Meeting of the name of the person proposed, and by whom nominated and seconded.

IX. No person deriving any emolument directly or indirectly from the funds of the Society, shall be eligible to be a Member of the Committee.

X. The Committee shall meet the first Monday in every Month, without summons, or oftener, if necessary, upon special summons, under the direction of the Chairman, Deputy Chairman, or Treasurer.

XI. The ordinary business of the Committee to be transacted as soon as five Members shall assemble, and in the absence of the Chairman, Deputy Chairman, or Treasurer, the person who shall have first come to preside; and such Chairman shall thereupon sign the Minutes of the preceding Meeting.

XII. On any election of Officers, ten Members at the least to be present.

XIII. The Committee to have liberty to appoint Sub-Committees from their own Members, for particular objects, with power for any three to act.

XIV. All questions to be decided by a majority of the Members actually present, the Chairman having only a casting vote in case of equality of numbers.

XV. In the event of any Member of the Committee not having attended one Meeting during the year, he shall be considered as having tendered his resignation.

XVI. For the conduct of their business, the Committee may, from time to time, make such regulations of detail as they shall deem expedient, and may alter or repeal such regulations as often as circumstances shall require, provided they be not inconsistent with these fundamental Rules.

XVII. That the Committee shall promote the establishment of Local and Provincial Committees throughout the United Kingdom, for extending the object of the Society, and facilitating the attainment of it by every means of co-operation which may be suggested for that purpose; and that Members of such Local Committees shall have the privilege, when in town, of attending, but not voting, at Meetings of the London Committee.

XVIII. That every person who shall have gratuitously contributed a Tract, which shall have been published under the sanction of the Committee, shall immediately be considered an Honorary Member of the Society, and eligible on the Committee.

XIX. The Treasurer to receive all monies on account of the Society; and from time to time to invest the amount in Exchequer

Bills, except a competent sum for current expenses. The Treasurer to pay all demands upon the Society as often as he shall be authorised to do so by a Minute of the Committee: he shall also make up his Accounts half-yearly, and lay the same before Auditors to be nominated by the Committee; and such Accounts, when passed and verified by the Auditors, shall be signed, and the balance in hand declared by a Minute to be entered on the proceedings of the Committee. The Treasurer, however, to be at liberty to disburse sums for current expenses not exceeding 20*l.* at one time; subject, however, to be checked by the Auditors on passing each half-yearly Account.

XX. The Secretary or Clerk shall keep the Minute-books of the Committee, enter the Reports and Proceedings of all Sub-Committees, send written or printed notices to Members of the Committee to meet at the times and places fixed; and act and correspond as such Committees may direct, in furtherance of the views of the Society; and, in general, perform all the other duties which are understood to belong to the office of Secretary.

XXI. The Collector to act as Messenger, as there may be occasion; and to render such assistance in the office, from time to time, as may be required of him by the Committee, Treasurer, or Secretary; and to be paid such salary or poundage as may be agreed on, he giving security duly to account for all monies which may come to his hands.

XXII. No alteration to be introduced into these Rules, or any new one proposed, unless the same shall have been moved and seconded, in writing, at an ordinary Meeting, and entered on the Minutes for the purpose of being considered at the next Meeting, which shall consist of not less than ten Members; the subject being specially noticed in the summons, and not to be carried into effect until confirmed at a following Meeting.

⁎⁎* All Communications to the Society; offers of literary assistance, with the Terms, &c., to be addressed to Mr. Coates, the Secretary, No. 7, Furnival's Inn, Holborn; and, *if from the Country*, under cover to any of the Committee who may be in Parliament.

Orders for the Publications to be addressed to Messrs. Baldwin & Co.

London: Printed by William Clowes, Stamford Street.

A DISCOURSE

OF THE

OBJECTS,

ADVANTAGES, AND PLEASURES

OF

SCIENCE.

LONDON:
BALDWIN, CRADOCK, AND JOY,

MDCCCXXVII.

COMMITTEE
OF THE
SOCIETY FOR THE DIFFUSION
OF
USEFUL KNOWLEDGE.

Hon. J. ABERCROMBY, M.P.
WM. ALLEN, Esq., F.R.S.
Rt. Hon. Lord ALTHORP, M.P.
Rt. Hon. Lord AUCKLAND.
Capt. FRANCIS BEAUFORT, R.N., F.R.S.
C. BELL, Esq. F.R.S.
H. BROUGHAM, Esq., M.P., F.R.S.
T. F. BUXTON, Esq., M.P., F.R.S.
J. CARTER, Esq., M.P.
R. O. CAVE, Esq., M.P.
WM. CRAWFORD, Esq.
T. DENMAN, Esq., Common Sergeant of the City of London.
ROBERT FOSTER, Esq.
I L. GOLDSMID, Esq.
Dr. OLINTHUS GREGORY, LL.D.
Capt. BASIL HALL, R.N., F.R.S.
M. D. HILL, Esq.
ROWLAND HILL, Esq.
JAMES LOCH, Esq.
Dr. LUSHINGTON, D.C.L., M.P.
J. MARSHALL, Esq., M.P.
JOHN MARTIN, Esq., M.P.
JAMES MILL, Esq.
JAMES MILLER, Esq.
Sir J. MACKINTOSH, M.P., F.R.S.
Rev. EDWARD MALTBY, D.D., F.R.S.
Rt. Hon. Lord NUGENT, M.P.
Sir H. PARNELL, Bart., M.P.
GEORGE PHILIPS, Esq., M.P.
T. SPRING RICE, Esq., M.P., F.A.S.
Rt. Hon. Lord JOHN RUSSEL, M.P.
J. SMITH, Esq., M.P.
Rt. Hon. Lord SUFFIELD.
Dr. A. T. THOMPSON, F.L.S.
WILLIAM TOOKE, Esq., F.R.S.
WILLIAM EYTON TOOKE, Esq., F.R.S.
H. WARBURTON, Esq., M.P., F.R.S.

OBJECTS, ADVANTAGES, AND PLEASURES

OF

SCIENCE.

INTRODUCTION.
I. MATHEMATICAL SCIENCE.
II. DIFFERENCE BETWEEN MATHEMATICAL AND PHYSICAL TRUTHS.
III. NATURAL OR EXPERIMENTAL SCIENCE.
IV. APPLICATION OF NATURAL SCIENCE TO THE ANIMAL AND VEGETABLE WORLD.
V. ADVANTAGES AND PLEASURES OF SCIENCE.

IN order fully to understand the advantages and the pleasures which are derived from an acquaintance with any Science, it is necessary to become acquainted with that science, and it would therefore be impossible to convey a complete knowledge of the benefits conferred by a study of the various sciences which have hitherto been chiefly cultivated by philosophers, without teaching all the branches of them. But a very distinct idea may be given of those benefits, by explaining the nature and objects of the different sciences; it may be shown by examples how much use and gratification there is in learning a part of any one branch of knowledge; and it may thus be inferred, how great reason there is to learn the whole.

It may easily be demonstrated, that there is an advantage in learning, both for the usefulness and the pleasure of it. There is something positively agreeable to all men, to all at least whose nature is not most grovelling and base, in gaining knowledge for its own sake. When you see any thing for the first time, you at once derive some gratification from the sight being new; your attention is awakened, and you desire to know more about it. If it is a piece of workmanship, as an instrument, a machine of any kind, you wish to know how it is made; how it works; and what use it is of. If it is an animal, you desire to know where it comes from; how it lives; what are its dispositions, and, generally, its nature and habits. This desire is felt, too, without at all considering that the machine or the animal may ever be of the least use to yourself practically; for, in all probability, you may never see them again. But you feel a curiosity to learn all about them, because they are new and unknown to you. You accordingly make inquiries; you feel a gratification in getting answers to your questions, that is, in receiving information, and in knowing more,—in being better informed than you were before. If you ever happen again to see the same instrument or animal, you find it agreeable to recollect having seen it before, and to think that you know something about it. If you see another instrument or animal, in some respects like, but differing in other particulars, you find it pleasing to compare them together, and to note in what they agree, and in what they differ. Now, all this kind of gratification is of a pure and disinterested nature, and has no reference to any of the common purposes of life; yet it is a pleasure—an enjoyment. You are nothing the richer for it; you do not gratify your palate or any other bodily appetite; and yet it is so pleasing that you would give something out of your pocket to obtain it, and would forego some bodily enjoyment for its sake. The pleasure derived from science is exactly of the like nature, or, rather, it is the very same. For what has just been referred to is in fact Science, which in its most comprehensive sense only means *Knowledge*, and in its ordinary sense means *Knowledge reduced to a System*; that is, arranged in a regular order, so as to be conveniently taught, easily remembered, and readily applied.

The practical uses of any science or branch of knowledge are undoubtedly of the highest importance; and there is hardly any man who may not gain some positive advantage in his worldly wealth and comforts, by increasing his stock of information. But there is also a pleasure in seeing the uses to which knowledge may be applied, wholly independent of the share we ourselves may have in those practical benefits. It is pleasing to examine the nature of a new instrument, or the habits of an unknown animal, without considering whether they may be of use to ourselves or to any body. It is another gratification to extend our inquiries, and find that the instrument or animal is useful to man, even although we have no chance ourselves of ever benefiting by the information: as, to find that the natives of some distant country employ the animal in travelling;—nay, though we have no desire of benefiting by the knowledge; as, for example, to find that the instrument is useful in performing some dangerous surgical operation. The mere gratification of curiosity; the knowing more to-day than we knew yesterday; the understanding what before seemed obscure and puzzling; the contemplation of general truths, and the comparing together of different things,—is an agreeable occupation of the mind; and, beside the present enjoyment, elevates the faculties above low pursuits, purifies and refines the passions, and helps our reason to assuage their violence.

It is very true, that the fundamental lessons of philosophy may to many at first sight wear a forbidding aspect, because to comprehend them requires an effort of the mind somewhat, though certainly not much, greater than is wanted for understanding more ordinary matters; and the most important branches of philosophy, those which are of the most general application, are for that very reason the less easily followed, and the less entertaining when apprehended, presenting as they do few particulars and individual objects to the mind. In discoursing of them, moreover, no figures will be at present used to assist the imagination; the appeal is made to reason, without help from the senses.

But be not therefore prejudiced against the doctrine, that the pleasure of learning the truths which philosophy unfolds is truly above all price. Lend but a patient attention to the principles explained, and giving us credit for stating nothing which has not some practical use belonging to it, or some important doctrine connected with it, you will soon perceive the value of the lessons you are learning, and begin to interest yourselves in comprehending and recollecting them; you will find that you have actually learnt something of science, while merely engaged in seeing what its end and purpose is; you will be enabled to calculate for yourselves, how far it is worth the trouble of acquiring, by examining samples of it; you will, as it were, taste a little to try whether or not you relish it, and ought to seek after more; you will enable yourselves to go on, and enlarge your stock of it; and after having first mastered a very little, you will proceed so far as to look back with wonder at the distance you have reached beyond your earliest acquirements.

The Sciences may be divided into three great classes: those which relate to *Number and Quantity*, those which relate to *Matter*, and those which relate to *Mind*. The first are called the *Mathematics*, and teach the properties of numbers and of figures; the second are called *Natural Philosophy*, and teach the properties of the various bodies which we are acquainted with by means of our senses; the third are called *Intellectual* or *Moral Philosophy*, and teach the nature of the mind, of the existence of which we have the most perfect evidence in our own reflections; or, in other words, the moral nature of man, both as an individual and as a member of society. Connected with all the sciences, and subservient to them, though not one of their number, is *History*, or the record of facts relating to all kinds of knowledge.

I. The two great branches of the *Mathematics*, or the two mathematical sciences, are *Arithmetic*, the science of number, from the Greek word signifying *number*, and *Geometry*, the science of figure, from the Greek words signifying *measure of the earth*,—land measuring having first turned men's attention to it.

When I say that 2 and 2 make 4, I state an arithmetical proposition, very simple indeed, but connected with many others of a more difficult and complicated kind. Thus, it is another proposition, somewhat less simple, but still very obvious, that 5 multiplied by 10, and divided by 2 is equal to, or makes the same number with, 100 divided by 4—both results being equal to 25. So, to find how many farthings there are in 1000*l*., and how many minutes in a year, are questions of arithmetic which we learn to work by being taught the principles of the science one after another, or, as they are commonly called, the *rules* of addition, subtraction, multiplication, and division. Arithmetic may be said to be the most simple, though among the most useful of the sciences; but it teaches only the properties of particular and known numbers, and it only enables us to add, subtract, multiply, and divide those numbers. But suppose we wish to add, subtract, multiply, or divide numbers which we have not yet ascertained, and in all respects to deal with them as if they were known, for the purpose of arriving at certain conclusions respecting them, and among other things, of discovering what they are; or, suppose we would examine properties belonging to all numbers; this must be performed by a peculiar kind of arithmetic, called *universal* arithmetic, or *Algebra*.* The common arithmetic, you will presently perceive, carries the seeds of this most important science in its bosom. Thus, suppose we inquire what is the number which multiplied by 5 makes 10? this is found if we divide 10 by 5—it is 2; but suppose that, before finding this number 2, and before knowing what it is, we would add it, whatever it may turn out, to some other number; this can only be done by putting some mark, such as a letter of the alphabet, to stand for the unknown number, and adding that letter as if it were a known number. Thus, suppose we want to find two numbers, which, added together, make 9, and multiplied by one another make 20. There are many, which added together, make 9; as 1 and 8; 2 and 7; 3 and 6; and so on. We have, therefore, occasion to use the second condition, that multiplied by one another they should make 20, and to work upon this condition before we have discovered the particular numbers. We must, therefore, suppose the numbers to be found, and put letters for them, and by reasoning upon those letters, according to both the two conditions of adding and multiplying, we find what they must each of them be in numbers, in order to fulfil or answer the conditions. Algebra teaches the rules for conducting this reasoning, and obtaining this result successfully; and by means of it we are enabled to find out numbers which are unknown, and of which we only know that they stand in certain relations to known numbers, or to one another. The instance now taken is an easy one; and you could, by considering the question a little, answer it readily enough; that is, by trying different numbers, and seeing which suited the conditions; for you plainly see that 5 and 4 are the two numbers sought; but you see this by no certain or general rule applicable to all cases, and therefore you never could work more difficult questions in the same way; and even questions of a moderate degree of difficulty would take an endless number of trials or guesses to answer. Thus, if a ship, say a smuggler, is sailing at the rate of 8 miles an hour, and a revenue cutter, sailing at the rate of 10 miles an hour, descries her 18 miles off, and gives chase, and you want to know in what time the smuggler will be overtaken, and how many miles she will have sailed before being overtaken; this, which is one of the simplest questions in algebra, would take you a long time, almost as long as the chase, to come at by mere trial and guessing (the chase would be 9 hours, and the smuggler would sail 72 miles;) and questions only a little more difficult than this, never could be answered by any number of guesses; yet questions infinitely more difficult can easily be solved by the rules of algebra. In like manner, by arithmetic you can tell the properties of particular numbers; as, for instance, that the number 348 is divided by 3 exactly, so as leave nothing over: but algebra teaches us that it is only one of an infinite variety of numbers, all divisible by 3, and any one of which you can tell the moment you see it; for they all have the remarkable property, that if you add together the figures they consist of, the sum total is divisible by 3. You can easily perceive

* Algebra, from the Arabic words signifying the *reduction of fractions;* the Arabs having brought the knowledge of it into Europe.

this in any one case, as in the number mentioned, for 3 added to 4 and that to 8 make 15, which is plainly divisible by 3; and if you divide 348 by 3, you find the quotient to be 116, and nothing over. But this does not at all prove that any other number, the sum of whose figures is divisible by 3, will itself also be found divisible by 3, as 741; for you must actually perform the division here, and in every other case, before you can know that it leaves nothing over. Algebra, on the contrary, both enables you to discover such general properties, and to prove them in all their generality.*

By means of this science, and its various applications, the most extraordinary calculations may be performed. We shall give, as an example, the method of *Logarithms*, which proceeds upon this principle. Take a set of numbers going on by equal differences; that is to say, the third being as much greater than the second, as the second is greater than the first; thus, 1, 2, 3, 4, 5, 6, and so on, in which the common difference is 1; then take another set of numbers, such that each is equal to twice or three times the one before it, or any number of times the one before it; thus, 2, 4, 8, 16, 32, 64, 128; write this second set of numbers under the first, or side by side, so that the numbers shall stand opposite to one another thus,

1	2	3	4	5	6	7
2	4	8	16	32	64	128

you will find, that if you add together any two of the upper or first set, and go to the number opposite their sum, in the lower or second set, you will have in this last set the number arising from multiplying together the numbers of the lower set corresponding to the numbers added together. Thus, add 2 to 4, you have 6 in the upper set, opposite to which in the lower set is 64, and multiplying the numbers 4 and 16 opposite to 2 and 4, the product is 64. In like manner, if you subtract the upper numbers, and look for the lower numbers opposite to their difference, you obtain the quotient of the lower numbers opposite the number subtracted. Thus, take 4 from 6 and 2 remains, opposite to which you have in the lower line 4; and if you divide 64, the number opposite to 6, by 16, the number opposite to 4, the quotient is 4. The upper set are called the *logarithms* of the lower set, which are called *natural numbers*: and tables may, with a little trouble, be constructed, giving the logarithms of all numbers from 1 to 10,000 and more; so that, instead of multiplying or dividing one number by another, you have only to add or subtract their logarithms, and then you at once find the product or the quotient in the tables. These are made applicable to numbers far higher than any actually in them, by a very simple process; so that you may at once perceive the prodigious saving of time and labour which is thus made. If you had, for instance, to multiply

---

* Another class of numbers divisible by 3 is discovered in like manner by algebra. Every number of 3 places, the figures (or digits) composing which are in arithmetical progression, (or rise above each other by equal differences,) is divisible by 3: as, 123, 789, 357, 159, and so on. The same is true of numbers of any amount of places, provided they are composed of 3, 6, 9, &c. numbers rising above each other by equal differences, as 289, 299, 309, or 148, 214, 280, 346, or 307142085345648276198756, which number of 24 places is divisible by 3, being composed of 6 numbers in a series whose common difference is 1137.

7,543,283 by itself, and that product again by the original number, you would have to multiply a number of seven places of figures by an equally large number, and then a number of 14 places of figures by one of seven places, till at last you had a product of 21 places of figures—a very tedious operation; but working by logarithms, you would only have to take three times the logarithm of the original number, and that gives the logarithm of the last product of 21 places of figures, without any further multiplication. So much for the time and trouble saved, which is still greater in questions of division; but by means of logarithms many questions can be worked, and of the most important kind, which no time or labour would otherwise enable us to solve.

Geometry teaches the properties of figure, or particular portions of space, and distances of points from each other. Thus, when you see a triangle, or three-sided figure, one of whose sides is perpendicular to another side, you find, by means of geometrical reasoning respecting this kind of triangle, that if squares be drawn on its three sides, the large square upon the slanting side opposite the two perpendiculars, is exactly equal to the two smaller squares upon the perpendiculars, taken together; and this is absolutely true, whatever be the size of the triangle, or the proportions of its sides to each other. Therefore, you can always find the length of any one of the three sides by knowing the lengths of the other two. Suppose one perpendicular side to be 10 feet long, the other 6, and you want to know the length of the third side opposite to the perpendiculars, you have only to find a number such, that if multiplied by itself, it shall be equal to 10 times 10, together with 6 times 6, that is 136. (This number is between $11\frac{4}{7}$ and $11\frac{5}{7}$.) Now only observe the great advantage of knowing this property of the triangle, or of perpendicular lines. If you want to measure a line passing over ground which you cannot reach—to know, for instance, the length of one side covered with water of a field, or the distance of one point on a lake or bay from the opposite side—you can easily find it by measuring two lines perpendicular to one another on the dry land, and running through the two points; for the line wished to be measured, and which runs through the water, is the third side of a perpendicular-sided triangle, the other two sides of which are ascertained. But there are other properties of triangles, which enable us to know the length of two sides of any triangle, whether it has perpendicular sides or not, by measuring one side and also measuring the inclination of the other two sides to this side, or what is called the two angles made by those sides with the measured side. Therefore you can easily find the perpendicular line drawn or supposed to be drawn from the top of a mountain through it to the bottom, that is the height of the mountain; for you can measure a line on level ground, and also the inclination of two lines, supposing them drawn in the air, and reaching from the ends of the measured lines to the mountain's top; and having thus found the length of the one of those lines next the mountain, and its inclination to the ground, you can at once find the perpendicular, though you cannot possibly get near it. In the same way, by measuring lines and angles on the ground, and near, you can find the length of lines at a great distance, and which you cannot get near: for instance, the length and breadth of a field on the opposite side of a lake or sea; the distance of two islands; or the space between the tops of two mountains.

Again, there are curve-lined figures as well as straight, and geometry teaches the properties of these also. The best known of all the curves is the circle, or a figure made by drawing a string round a fixed point, and marking where its other end traces, so that every part of the circle is equally distant from the fixed point or centre. From this fundamental property, an infinite variety of others follow by steps of reasoning more or less numerous, but all necessarily arising one out of another. To give an instance; it is proved by geometrical reasoning, that if from the two ends of any diameter of the circle you draw two lines to meet in any one point of the circle whatever, those lines are perpendicular to each other. Another property, and a most useful one is, that the sizes, or areas, of all circles whatever, from the greatest to the smallest, from the sun to a watch-dial-plate, are in exact proportion to the squares of their distances from the centre; that is, the squares of the strings they are drawn with: so that if you draw a circle with a string 5 feet long, and another with a string 10 feet long, the large circle is four times the size of the small one, as far as the space or area enclosed is concerned; the square of 10 or 100 being four times the squares of 5 or 25. But it is also true, that the lengths of the circumferences themselves, the number of feet over which the ends of the strings move, are in proportion to the lengths of the strings; so that the curve of the larger circle is only twice the length of the curve of the lesser.

But the circle is only one of an infinite variety of curves, all having a regular formation and fixed properties. The *oval* or *ellipse* is, perhaps, next to the circle, the most familiar to us, although we more frequently see another curve line formed by the motions of bodies thrown forward. When you drop a stone, or throw it straight up, it goes in a straight line; when you throw it forward, it goes in a curve line till it reaches the ground; as you may see by the figure in which water runs when forced out of a pump, or from a fire-pipe, or from the spout of a kettle or tea-pot. The line it moves in is called a *parabola*; every point of which bears a certain fixed relation to a certain point within it, as the circle does to its centre. Geometry teaches various properties of this curve; for example, that if the direction in which the stone is thrown, or the bullet fired, or the water spouted, be half the perpendicular to the ground, that is, half way between being level with the ground and being upright, the curve will come to the ground at a greater distance than if any other direction whatever were given, with the same force. So that to make the gun carry furthest, or the fire-pipe play to the greatest distance, they must be pointed, not as you might suppose, level or point blank, but about half way between that direction and the perpendicular. If the air did not resist, and so somewhat disturb the calculation, the direction to give the longest range ought to be exactly half perpendicular.

The *oval*, or *ellipse*, is drawn by taking a string of any certain length, and fixing, not one end as in drawing the circle, but both ends, and then carrying a point, as a pencil or chalk, round inside the string, always keeping it stretched as far as possible. It is plain, that this figure is as regularly drawn as the circle, though it is very different from it; and you perceive that every point of its curve must be so placed, that the straight lines drawn from it to the two points where the string was fixed, are, when added together, always the same; for they make together the length of the string. Among various properties belonging to this curve, in relation to the straight lines drawn within it, is one which gives rise to the construction of the *trammels* or elliptic compasses used for making figures and ornaments of this form; and also to the construction of lathes for turning oval frames, and the like.

If you wish at once to see these three curves, take a sugar-loaf, and cut it any where clean through in a direction parallel to its base or bottom; the outline or edge of the loaf where it is cut will be a *circle.* If the cut is made so as to slant, and not be parallel to the base of the loaf, the outline is an *ellipse,* provided the cut goes quite through the sides of the loaf all round ; but if it goes slanting, and parallel to the line of the loaf's side, the outline is a *parabola ;* and if you cut in any direction not through the sides all round, but through the sides and base, and not parallel to the line of the side, the outline will be another curve of which we have not yet spoken, but which is called an *hyperbola.* You will see another instance of it, if you take two plates of glass, and lay them on one another ; then put their edge in water, holding them upright and pressing them together; the water, which, to make it more plain, you may colour with a few drops of ink or strong tea, rises to a certain height, and its outline is this curve; which, however much it may seem to differ in form from a circle or ellipse, is found by mathematicians to resemble them very closely in many of its most remarkable properties.

These are the curve lines best known and most frequently discussed; but there are an infinite number of others all related to straight lines and other curve lines by certain fixed rules; for example, the course which any part, as the nail in the felly of a wheel rolling along takes through the air, is a curve called the *cycloid,* which has many remarkable properties; and, among others, this, that it is, of all lines possible, the one in which any body not falling perpendicularly, will descend from one point to another the most quickly.

II. You perceive, if you reflect a little, that the science which we have been considering in both its branches, has nothing to do with matter ; that is to say, it does not at all depend upon the properties or even upon the existence of any bodies or substances whatever. The distance of one point or place from another is a straight line; and whatever is proved to be true respecting this line, as, for instance, its proportion to other lines of the same kind, and its inclination towards them, what we call the angles it makes with them, would be equally true whether there were any thing in those places, at those two points, or not. So if you find the number of yards in a square field, by measuring one side, 100 yards, and then, multiplying that by itself, which makes the whole area 10,000 square yards, this is equally true whatever the field is, whether corn or grass, or rock or water; it is equally true if the solid part, the earth or water, be removed, for then it would be a field of air bounded by four walls or hedges; but suppose the walls or hedges were removed, and a mark only left at each corner, still it would be true that the space enclosed or bounded by the lines supposed to be drawn between the four marks was 10,000 square yards in size. But the marks need not be there; you only want them while measuring one side; if they were gone, it would be equally true that the lines, supposed to be drawn from the places where the marks had been, enclose 10,000 square yards of air. But if there were no air, and consequently a mere void, or empty space, it would be equally true that this space is of the size you had found it to be by measuring the distance of one point from another, of one of the space's corners or angles from another, and then multiplying that distance by itself. In the same way it would be true, that if the space were circular, its size, compared with another circular space of half its diameter, would be four times larger; of one third its diameter, nine times larger, and of one fourth sixteen times, and so on always in proportion to the squares of the diameters; and that the length of the circumference, the number of feet or yards in the line round the surface, would be twice the length of a circle whose diameter was one half, thrice the circumference of one whose diameter was one third, four times the circumference of one whose diameter was one fourth, and so on, in the simple proportion of the diameters. Therefore every property which is proved to belong to figures belongs to them without the smallest relation to bodies or matter of any kind, although we generally see figures in connection with bodies; but all those properties would be equally true, if no such thing as matter or bodies existed; and the same may be said of the properties of number, the other great branch of the mathematics. When we speak of twice two, and say it makes four, we affirm this without thinking of two horses, or two balls, or two trees; but two of any thing and every thing equally. Nay, this branch of mathematics may be said to apply still more extensively than even the other; for it has no relation to space, which geometry has; and, therefore, it is applicable to cases where figure and size are wholly out of the question. Thus you can speak of two dreams, or two ideas, or two minds, and can calculate respecting them just as you would respecting so many bodies; and the properties you find belonging to numbers, will belong to those numbers when applied to things that have no outward or visible or perceivable existence, and cannot even be said to be in any particular place, just as much as the same numbers applied to actual bodies which may be seen and touched.

It is quite otherwise with the science which we are now going to consider, *Natural Philosophy*. This teaches the nature and properties of actually existing substances, their motions, their connections with each other, and their influence on one another. It is sometimes also called *Physics*, from the Greek word signifying *Nature*, though that Greek word is more frequently, in common speech, confined to one particular branch of the science, concerning the bodily health.

We have mentioned one distinction between Mathematics and Natural Philosophy, that the former does not depend on the nature and existence of bodies, which the latter entirely does. Another distinction, and one closely connected with this, is, that the truths which Mathematics teach us are *necessarily* such,—they are truths of themselves, and wholly independent of facts and experiments,—they depend only upon reasoning; and it is utterly impossible they should be otherwise than true. This is the case with all the properties which we find belong to numbers and to figures—2 and 2 must of *necessity*, and through all time, and in every place, be equal to 4; those numbers must *necessarily* be always divisible by 3 without leaving any remainder over, which have the sums of the figures they consist of divisible by 3; and circles must *necessarily*, and for ever and ever, be to one another in the exact proportion of the squares of their diameters. It cannot be otherwise; we cannot conceive it in our minds to be otherwise. No man can in his own mind suppose to himself that 2 and 2 should ever be more or less than 4; it would be an utter impossibility—a contradiction in the very ideas. The other properties of number, though not so plain at first sight as this, are proved to be true by reasoning, every one step of which follows from the step immediately before, as a matter of course, and so clearly and unavoidably, that it cannot be supposed or even imagined to be otherwise; the mind has no means of fancying how it could be otherwise: the final conclusion from all the steps of the reasoning or demonstration, as it is called, follows in the same way from the last of the steps, and is therefore just as evidently and necessarily true as the first step, which is always something self-evident, as that 2 and 2 make 4, or that the whole is greater than any of its parts, but equal to all its parts put together. It is by this kind of reasoning, step by step, from the most plain and evident things, that we arrive at the knowledge of other things which seem at first not true, or at least not generally true; but when we do arrive at them, we perceive that they are just as true, and for the same reasons, as the first and most obvious matters; that their truth is absolute and necessary, and that it would be as absurd and self-contradictory to suppose they ever could, under any circumstances, be not true, as to suppose that 2 added to 2 could ever make 3, or 5, or 100, or any thing but 4; or, which is the same thing, that 4 should ever be equal to 3, or 5, or 100, or any thing but 4. To find out these reasonings, to pursue them to their consequences, and thereby to discover the truths which are not immediately evident, is what science teaches us; but when the truth is once discovered, it is as certain and plain by the reasoning, as the first truths themselves from which all the reasoning takes its rise, on which it all depends, and which require no proof because they are self-evident at once, the instant they are understood.

But it is quite different with the truths which Natural Philosophy teaches. All these depend upon matter of fact; and that is learnt by observation and experiment, and never could be discovered by reasoning at all. If a man were shut up in a room with pen, ink, and paper, he might by thought discover any of the truths in arithmetic, algebra, or geometry; it is possible, at least; there would be nothing absolutely impossible in his discovering all that is now known of these sciences; and if his memory were as good as we are supposing his judgment and conception to be, he might discover it all without pen, ink, and paper, and in a dark room. But we cannot discover a single one of the fundamental properties of matter without observing what goes on around us, and trying experiments upon the nature and motion of bodies. Thus, the man whom we have supposed shut up could not possibly find out beyond one or two of the very first properties of matter, and those only in a very few cases; so that he could not tell if these were general properties of all matter or not. He could tell that the objects he touched in the dark were hard and resisted his touch; that they were extended and were solid; that is, that they had three dimensions, length, breadth, and thickness. He might guess that other things existed beside those he felt, and that those other things resembled what he felt in these properties, but he could know nothing for certain, and could not even conjecture much beyond this very limited number of qualities. He must remain utterly ignorant of what really exists in nature, and of what properties matter in general has. These properties, therefore, we learn by experience; they are such as we know bodies to have; they happen to have them—they are so formed by Divine Providence as to have them—but they might have been otherwise formed; the great Author of Nature might have thought fit to make all bodies different in every respect. We see that a stone dropped from our hand falls to the ground; this is a fact which we can only know by experience; before observing it, we could not have guessed it, and it is quite *conceivable* that it should be otherwise: for instance, that when we remove our hand from the body it should stand still in the air; or fly upward, or go forward, or backward, or sideways; there is nothing at all absurd, contradictory, or inconceivable in any of these suppositions; there is nothing impossible in any of them, as there would be in supposing the stone equal to half of itself, or double of itself; or both falling down and rising upwards at once; or going to the right and the left at one and the same time. Our only reason for not at once thinking it quite conceivable that the stone should stand in the air, or fly upwards, is, that we have never seen it do so, and have become accustomed to see it do otherwise. But for that, we should at once think it as natural that the stone should fly upwards or stand still, as that it should fall. But no degree of reflection for any length of time could accustom us to think 2 and 2 equal to any thing but 4, or the whole to be equal to a part.

After we have once by observation or experiment ascertained certain things to exist in fact, we may then reason upon them by means of mathematics; that is, we may apply mathematics to our experimental philosophy, and then such reasoning becomes absolutely certain, taking the fundamental facts for granted. Thus, if we find that a stone falls in one direction when dropped, and we further observe the peculiar way in which it falls, that is, quicker and quicker every instant till it reaches the ground, we learn the rule or the proportion by which the quickness goes on increasing; and we further find, that if the same stone is pushed forward on a table, it moves in the direction of the push, till it is either stopped by something, or comes to a pause, by rubbing against the table, and being hindered by the air. These are all facts which we learn by observing and trying, and they might all have been different if matter and motion had been otherwise constituted; but supposing them to be as they are, and as we find them, we can, by reasoning mathematically from them, find out many most curious and important truths depending upon these facts, and depending upon them not accidentally, but of necessity. For example, we can find, in what course the stone will move, if, instead of being dropped to the ground, it is thrown forward: it will go in the curve already mentioned, the parabola, and it will run through that curve in a peculiar way, so that there will always be a certain proportion between the time it takes and the space it moves through, and the time it would have taken, and the space it would have moved through had it fallen from the hand to the ground. So we can prove, in like manner, what we before stated of the relation between the distance at which it will come to the ground, and the direction it is thrown in; the distance being greatest of all when the direction is nearly half way between the level or horizontal and the upright or perpendicular. These are mathematical truths, derived by mathematical reasoning upon physical grounds; that is, upon matter of fact found to exist by actual observation and experiment. The result, therefore, is necessarily true, and proved to be so by reasoning only, provided we have once ascertained the facts; but taken altogether, the result depends partly on the facts learned by experiment or experience, partly on the reasoning from these facts. Thus it is found to be true by reasoning, and necessarily true, that *if* the stone falls in a certain way when unsupported, it must when thrown forward go in the curve called a parabola: this is a necessary or mathematical truth, and it cannot possibly be otherwise. But when we state the matter without any supposition,—without any "*if*,"—and say, a stone thrown forward goes in the curve called a parabola, we state a truth, partly fact, and partly drawn from reasoning on the fact; and it might be otherwise if the nature of things were different. It is called a proposition or truth in Natural Philosophy; and as it is discovered and proved by mathematical reasoning, it is sometimes called a proposition or truth in the *Mixed Mathematics*. The man in the dark room could never discover this truth unless he had been first informed, by those who had observed the fact, in what way the stone falls when unsupported, and moves along the table when pushed. These things he never could have found out by reasoning: they are facts, and he could only reason from them after learning them, by his own experience, or taking them on the credit of other people's experience. But having once so learnt them, he could discover by reasoning merely, and with as much certainty as if he lived in daylight, and saw and felt the moving body, that the motion is in a parabola, and governed by certain rules. As experiment and observation are the great sources of our knowledge of Nature, and as the judicious and careful making of experiments is the only way by which her secrets can be known, Natural and Experimental Philosophy mean one and the same thing; mathematical reasoning being applied to certain branches of it, particularly those which relate to motion and pressure.

III. *Natural Philosophy*, in its most extensive sense, has for its province the investigation of the laws of matter; that is, the properties and the motions of matter; and may be divided into two great branches. The first and most important (which is sometimes on that account called

Natural Philosophy, but more properly *Mechanical Philosophy*,) investigates the sensible motions of all bodies. The second investigates the constitution and qualities of all bodies, and has various names, according to its different objects. It is called *Chemistry*, if it teaches the properties of bodies with respect to heat, mixture together, weight, taste, appearance, and so forth : *Anatomy* and *Animal Physiology*, if it teaches the structure and functions of living bodies, especially the human, for when it shows those of other animals, we term it *Comparative Anatomy: Medicine*, if it teaches the nature of diseases, and the means of preventing them and of restoring health: *Zoology*, (from the Greek words signifying *to speak of animals*,) if it teaches the arrangement or classification and the habits of the different lower animals: *Botany*, if it teaches the arrangement or classification and habits of plants : *Geology*, (from the Greek words meaning *to speak of the earth*,) including *Mineralogy*, if it teaches the arrangement of minerals, the structure of the masses in which they are found, and of the earth composed of those masses. The term *Natural History* is given to the three last branches taken together, but chiefly as far as relates to the classification of different things, or the observation of the resemblances and differences of the various animals, plants, and inanimate and ungrowing substances in nature.

But here we may make two general observations. The *first* is, that every such distribution of the sciences is necessarily imperfect ; for one runs unavoidably into another. Thus, Chemistry shows the qualities of plants with relation to other substances, and to each other ; and Botany does not overlook those same qualities, though its chief object be arrangement. So Mineralogy, though principally conversant with classifying metals and earths, yet regards also their qualities in respect of heat and mixture. So, too, Zoology, beside arranging animals, describes their structures, like Comparative Anatomy. In truth, all arrangement and classifying depends upon noting the things in which the objects agree and differ ; and among those things, in which animals, plants, and minerals agree, must be considered the anatomical qualities of the one and the chemical qualities of the other. From hence, in a great measure, follows the *second* observation, namely, that the sciences mutually assist each other. We have seen how Arithmetic and Algebra aid Geometry, and how both the purely Mathematical Sciences aid Mechanical Philosophy. Mechanical Philosophy, in like manner, assists, though, in the present state of our knowledge, not very considerably, both Chemistry and Anatomy, especially the latter ; and Chemistry very greatly assists both Physiology, Medicine, and all the branches of Natural History.

The first great head, then, of Natural Science, is Mechanical Philosophy ; and it consists of various subdivisions, each forming a science of great importance. The most essential of these, and which is indeed fundamental, and applicable to all the rest, is called *Dynamics*, from the Greek word signifying *power* or *force*, and it teaches the laws of motion in all its varieties. The case of the stone thrown forward, which we have already mentioned more than once, is an example. Another, of a more general nature, but more difficult to trace, and far more important in its consequences, and of which, indeed, the former is only one particular case, relates to the motions of all bodies, which are attracted (or influenced, or drawn) by any power towards a certain point, while they are, at the same time, driven forward by some push given to them at first, and continuing to act on them while they are drawn towards the point. The line in which a body moves while so drawn and so driven, depends upon the force it is pushed with, the direction it is pushed in, and the kind of power that draws it towards the point; but, at present, we are chiefly to regard the latter circumstance, the attraction towards the point. If this attraction be uniform, that is, the same at all distances from the point, the body will move in a circle, and the point to which it is constantly drawn will be the centre of the circle. Thus, a stone in a sling, when whirled round the hand, moves for this reason in a circle, while it remains in the sling; the force that draws it towards the hand being always the same, and the hand either stopping after setting the stone a-whirling, in which case it is the centre of the circle, or going round in a smaller circle, in which case the point is the centre of the two circles, the one the stone whirls round in, and the one the hand moves round in. (Of course we speak not now of the line the stone moves in after leaving the sling; that is a parabola, as before stated.) If the force that draws the moving body changes at different distances, so as to make the body move quicker, by drawing it more strongly towards the point, the nearer it is to that point, then the body will move, not in a circle, but in other curve lines of various kinds, according as the proportion of the force to the distance varies, and according also to the direction of the forward push, and the force with which it was originally given. If the force drawing towards the point is such, that, at two feet from the point, it is four times less than at one foot; at three feet, nine times less; at four feet, sixteen times less; and so on, always lessening in the same proportion, that is, as the squares of the distances increase; and if the body is pushed forward with a particular degree of force; the line in which it moves will go round the point, but it will not be a circle; it will be an oval or ellipse; the curve described by means of a cord fixed at both ends, in the way we have already explained; the point of attraction will be nearer one end of the ellipse than the other, and the time the body will take to go round, compared with the time any other body would take, moving at a different distance from the same point of attraction, but drawn towards that point with a force which bears the same proportion to the distance, will bear a certain proportion, discovered by mathematicians, to the average distances of the two bodies from the point of common attraction. If you multiply the numbers expressing the times of going round each by itself, the products will be to one another in the proportion of the average distances multiplied each by itself, and that product again by the distance. Thus, if one body take two hours, and is five yards distant, the other, being ten yards off, will take something less than five hours and forty minutes.

Now, this is one of the most important truths in the whole compass of science; for it does so happen, that the force with which bodies fall towards the earth, or what is called their *gravity*, the power that draws or attracts them towards the earth, varies with the distance exactly in the proportion of the squares, lessening as the distance increases: at two miles from the earth, it is four times less than at one mile; at three miles, nine times less; and so forth. It goes on lessening, but never is destroyed, even at the greatest distances to which we can reach, and there can be no doubt of its extending indefinitely beyond. But, by astronomical observations made upon the motion of the heavenly bodies, upon that of the moon for instance, it is proved that her movement is slower and quicker at different parts of her course, in the same manner as a body's motion on the earth would be slower and quicker, according to its distance from the point it was drawn towards, provided it was drawn by a force acting in the proportion to the squares of the distance, which we have frequently mentioned; and the proportion of the time to the distance is also observed to agree with the rule we have referred to. Therefore, she is shown to be attracted towards the earth by a force that varies according to the same proportion in which gravity varies; and she must consequently move in an ellipse round the earth, which is placed in a point nearer the one end than the other of that curve. In like manner, it is shown that the earth moves round the sun in the same curve line, and is drawn towards the sun by the same force; and that all the other planets in their courses, at various distances, follow the same rule, moving in ellipses, and drawn towards the sun by the same kind of power. Three of them have moons like the earth, only more numerous, for Jupiter has four, Saturn seven, and Herschel six, so very distant that we cannot see them without the help of glasses; but all those moons move round their principal planets, as ours does round the earth, in ovals or ellipses; while the planets, with their moons, move in their ovals round the sun, like our own earth with its moon. But this power, which draws them all towards the sun, and regulates their path and their motion round him, and which draws the moons towards the principal planets, and regulates their motion and path round those planets, is the same with the gravity by which bodies fall towards the earth, being attracted by it. Therefore, the whole of the heavenly bodies are kept in their places, and wheel round the sun, by the same influence or power that makes a stone fall to the ground.

It is usual to call the sun, and the planets which with their moons move round him, (twelve in number, including the four lately discovered, and the one discovered by Herschel,) the *Solar System*, because they are a class of the heavenly bodies far apart from the innumerable fixed stars, and so near each other as to exert a perceptible influence on one another, and thus to be connected together. The *Comets* belong to the same system, according to this manner of viewing the subject. They are bodies which move in elliptical paths, but far longer and narrower than the curves in which the earth, and the other planets and their moons roll. Our curves are not much less round than circles; the paths of the comets are long and narrow, so as, in many places, to be more nearly straight lines than circles. They differ from the planets and their moons in another respect; they do not depend on the sun for the light they give, as our moon plainly does, being dark when the earth comes between her and the sun; and as the other planets do, those of them that are nearer the sun than we are, being dark when they come between us and him. But the comets give light always of themselves, being apparently vast bodies heated red-hot by coming in their course far nearer the sun than the nearest of the planets ever do. Their motion is much more rapid than that of the planets: they both approach the sun much nearer, retreat from him to much greater distances, and take much longer time in going round him than any of the planets do. Yet even these comets are subject to the same great law of gravitation, which regulates the motions of the planets. Their year, the time they take to revolve, is in some cases 75, in others 135, in others 300 of our years; their distance is a hundred times our distance when furthest off, and not a hundred and sixtieth of our distance when nearest the sun; their swiftest motion is above twelve times swifter than ours, although ours is a hundred and forty times swifter than a cannon ball's; yet their path is a curve of the same kind with ours, though longer and flatter, differing in its formation only as one oval differs from another by the string you draw it with having the ends fixed at two points more distant from each other; consequently the sun, being in one of those points, is much nearer the end of the path the comet moves in, than he is near the end of our path. The motion, too, follows the same rule, being swifter the nearer the sun; the attraction of the sun varies according to the squares of the distances, being four times less at twice the distance, nine times less at thrice, and so on; and the proportion between the times of revolving and the distances is exactly the same, in the case of those remote bodies, as in that of the moon and the earth. One law prevails over all, and regulates their motions as well as our own: it is the gravity of the comets towards the sun, and they, like our own earth and moon, wheel round him in boundless space, drawn by the same force, acting by the same rule, which makes a stone fall when dropped from the hand.

The more full and accurate our observations are upon these heavenly bodies, the better we find all their motions agreeing with this great doctrine; although, no doubt, many things are to be taken into the account beside the force that draws them to their different centres: thus, while the moon is drawn by the earth, and the earth by the sun, the moon is also drawn directly by the sun; and while Jupiter is drawn by the sun, so are his moons; and both Jupiter and his moons are drawn by Saturn: nay, as this power of gravitation is quite universal, and as no body can attract or draw another without being itself drawn by that other, the earth is drawn by the moon, while the moon is drawn by the earth; and the sun is attracted by the planets which he draws towards himself. These mutual attractions give rise to many deviations from the simple line of the ellipse, and produce many irregularities in the simple calculation of the times and motions of the bodies that compose the system of the universe. But the extraordinary powers of investigation applied to the subject by the modern improvements in Mathematics, have enabled us at length to reduce even the greatest of the irregularities to order and system; and to unfold one of the most wonderful truths in all science, namely, that by certain necessary consequences of the simple fact upon which the whole fabric rests,—the proportion of the attractive force to the distances at which it operates,—all the irregularities which at first seemed to disturb the order of the system, and to make the appearances depart from the doctrine, are themselves subject to a certain fixed rule, and can never go beyond a particular point, but must begin to lessen when they have slowly reached that point, and then lessen until they reach another point, when they begin again to increase; and so on, for ever. Thus, the planets move in ovals, from gravity, the power that attracts them, towards the sun, combined with the original impulse they received forwards; and the disturbing forces are continually varying the course of the curves or ovals, making them bulge out in the middle, as it were, on the sides, though in a very small proportion to the whole length of the ellipse. The oval thus bulging, however, its length never alters, only its breadth, and that breadth increases by a very small quantity yearly and daily; after a certain number of years it becomes as great as it ever can be; then the alteration takes a contrary direction, and the curve gradually flattens as it had bulged; till, in the same number of years which it took to bulge, it becomes as flat as it ever can be, and then it begins to bulge again, and so on for ever; and so of every other disturbance and irregularity in the system. What at first appears to be some departure from the rule, when more fully examined, turns out to be only a consequence of it, or a result of a more general arrangement springing from the principle of gravitation; an arrangement of which the rule itself, and the apparent or supposed exception, form parts.

The power of gravitation, which thus regulates the whole system of the universe, is found to rule each member or branch of it separately. Thus, it is demonstrated, that the tides of the ocean are caused by the gravitation which attracts the water towards the sun and moon; and the figure both of our earth and of such of the other bodies as have a spinning motion round their axis, is determined by gravitation; they are all flattened towards the ends of the axis they spin upon, and bulge out towards the middle.

The great discoverer of the principle on which all these truths rest, Sir Isaac Newton, certainly by far the most extraordinary man that ever lived, concluded by reasoning upon the nature of motion and matter that this flattening must take place in our globe: every one before his time had believed the earth to be a perfect sphere or globe, chiefly from observing the round shadow which it casts on the moon in eclipses; and it was many years after his death that the accuracy of his opinion was proved by measurements on the earth's surface, and by the different weight and attraction of bodies at the equator, where it bulges, and at the poles, where it is flattened. The improved telescopes have enabled us to ascertain the same fact with respect to the planets Jupiter and Saturn.

Beside unfolding the general laws which regulate the motions and figures of the heavenly bodies forming our solar system, Astronomy consists in calculations of the places, times, and eclipses of those bodies, and their moons or *satellites*, (from a Latin word, signifying an *attendant*;) and in observations of the fixed stars, which are innumerable assemblages of bodies, not moving round the sun as our earth and the other planets do, nor receiving the light they shine with from his light; but shining, as the sun and the comets do, with a light of their own; and placed, to all appearance, immovable, at immense distances from our world, that is, from our solar system. Each of them is probably the sun of some other system like our own, composed of planets and their moons, or satellites; but so extremely far off from us, that they all are seen by us like one point of faint light, as you see two lamps, placed a few inches asunder, only like one, when you view them a great way off. The numbers of the fixed stars are prodigious; even to the naked eye they are very numerous, about 3000 being thus visible; but when the heavens are viewed through the telescope, stars become visible in numbers wholly incalculable: 2000 are discovered in one of the small collections of a few visible stars called *Constellations*; nay, what appears to the naked eye only a light cloud, as the *Milky Way*, when viewed through a telescope, proves to be an assemblage of innumerable fixed stars, each of them in all likelihood a sun and a system like the rest, though at an immeasurable distance from ours.

The size, and motions, and distances of the heavenly bodies are such as to exceed the power of ordinary imagination, from any comparison with the smaller things we see around us. The earth's diameter is nearly 8000 miles in length; but the sun's is above 880,000 miles, and the bulk of the sun is above 1,300,000 times greater than that of the earth. The planet Jupiter, which looks like a mere speck, from his vast distance, is nearly 1300 times larger than the earth. Our distance from the sun is above 95 millions of miles; but Jupiter is 490 millions, and Saturn 900 millions of miles distant from the sun. The rate at which the earth moves round the sun is 68,000 miles an hour, or 140 times swifter than the motion of a cannon-ball; and the planet Mercury, the nearest to the sun, moves still quicker, nearly 110,000 miles an hour. We, upon the earth's surface, beside being carried round the sun, move round the earth's axis by the rotatory or spinning motion which it has; so that every 24 hours we move in this manner near 14,000 miles, beside moving round the sun above 1,600,000 miles. These motions and distances, however, prodigious as they are, seem nothing compared to those of the comets, one of which, when furthest from the sun, is 11,200 millions of miles from him; and when nearest the sun, flies at the amazing rate of 880,000 miles an hour. Sir I. Newton calculated its heat at 2000 times that of red-hot iron; and that it would take millions of years to cool. But the distance of the fixed stars is yet more vast: they have been supposed to be 400,000 times further from us than we are from the sun, that is 38 millions of millions of miles: so that a cannon-ball would take between four and five millions of years to reach one of them, supposing there was nothing to hinder it from pursuing its course thither.

Astronomers have, by means of their excellent glasses, aided by Geometry and calculation, been able to observe not only stars, planets, and their satellites, invisible to the naked eye, but to measure the height of mountains in the moon by observations of the shadows which these eminences cast on her surface; and they have discovered volcanoes, or burning mountains, on the same body.

The tables which they have by the same means been enabled to form of the heavenly motions, are of great use in navigation. By means of the eclipses of Jupiter's satellites, and by the tables of the moon's motion, we can ascertain the position of a ship at sea; for the observation of the sun's height at mid-day gives the *latitude* of the place, that is, its distance from the equinoctial or equator, the line passing through the middle of the earth's surface; and these tables, with the observations of the satellites, or moons, give the distance east and west of the observatory for which the tables are calculated; what is called the *longitude* of the place: consequently the mariner can thus tell nearly in what part of the ocean he is, how far he has sailed from his port of departure, and how far he must sail, and in what direction, to gain the port of his destination. The advantage of this knowledge is therefore manifest in the common affairs of life; but it sinks into insignificance compared with the vast extent of those views which the contemplations of the science afford, of numberless worlds filling the immensity of space, and all kept in their places, and adjusted in their prodigious motions by the same simple principle, under the guidance of an all-wise and all-powerful Creator.

We have been considering the application of Dynamics to the motions of the heavenly bodies, which forms the science of *Physical Astronomy*. The application of Dynamics to the calculation, production, and direction of motion, forms the science of *Mechanics*, sometimes called *Practical Mechanics*, to distinguish it from the more general use of the word, which comprehends every thing that relates to motion and force. The fundamental principle of the science upon which it mainly depends, flows immediately from a property of the circle already mentioned, and which, perhaps, appeared at the moment of little value, that the lengths of circles are in proportion to their diameters. Observe how, upon this simple truth, nearly the whole of those contrivances are built by which the power of man is increased, as far as solid matter assists him in extending it; and nearly the whole of those doctrines, too, by which he is enabled to explain the voluntary motions of animals, as far as those depend upon their own bodies. There can be nothing more instructive in showing the importance and fruitfulness of scientific truths, however trivial and forbidding they may at first sight appear. For it is an immediate consequence of this property of the circle, that if a rod of iron, or beam of wood, or any other such solid material, be placed on a point or pivot, so that it may move as the arms of a balance do round its centre, or a see-saw board does round its prop, the two ends will go through parts of circles, each proportioned to that arm of the beam to which it belongs; the two circles will be equal if the pivot is in the centre or middle point of the beam; but if it is nearer one end than the other, say three times, that end will go through a circular space, or arch, three times shorter than the circular space the other end goes through in the same time. If, then, the end of the long beam goes through three times the space, it must move with three times the swiftness of the short beam's end, since both move in the same time; and therefore any force applied to the long end must overcome the resistance of three times that force applied at the opposite end, since the two ends move in contrary directions; hence one pound placed at the long end would balance three placed at the short end. The beam we have been supposing is called a *Lever*, and the same rule must evidently hold for all proportions of the lengths of its beams. If, then, the lever be 17 feet long, and the pivot, or *fulcrum*, (as it is called, from a Latin word signifying *support*,) be a foot from one end, an ounce placed on the other end will balance a pound placed on the near end; and the least additional weight, or the slightest push or pressure on the far end, so loaded, will make the pound weight on the other move upwards. If, instead of an ounce, we place upon the long end the short end of a second beam or lever supported by a fulcrum, one foot from it, and then place the long end of this second lever upon the short end of a third lever, whose fulcrum is one foot from it; and if we put on the end of this third lever's long arm an ounce weight, that ounce will move upwards a pound on the second lever's long arm, and this moving upwards will cause the short arm to force downwards 16 pounds at the long end of the first lever, which will make the short end of the first lever move upwards, though 256 pounds be laid on it; the same thing continuing, a pound on the long end of the third lever will move a ton and three quarters at the short end of the first lever; that is, will balance it so that the slightest touch or pressure with the finger, or a touch from a child's hand will move as much as two horses can draw. The Lever is called on this account a *mechanical power*; and there are five other mechanical powers of which its properties form the foundation; indeed they may be resolved into combinations of levers. Thus the wheel and axle is only a lever moving round an axle, and always retaining the effect gained during every part of the motion, by means of a rope wound round the butt end of the axle; the spoke of the wheel being the long arm of the lever, and the half diameter of the axle its short arm. By a combination of levers, wheels, pullies, so great an increase of force is obtained, that, but for the obstruction from friction, and the resistance of the air, there could be no bounds to the effect of the smallest force thus multiplied; and to this fundamental principle, Archimedes, one of the most illustrious mathematicians of ancient times, referred, when he boasted, that if he only had a pivot or fulcrum whereon he might rest his machinery, he could move the earth. Upon so simple a truth, assisted by the aid derived from other means, rests the whole fabric of mechanical power, whether for raising weights, or cleaving rocks, or pumping up rivers from the bowels of the earth; or, in short, performing any of those works to which human strength, even augmented by the help of the animals whom Providence has subdued to our use, would prove altogether inadequate.

The application of Dynamics to the pressure and motions of fluids, constitutes a science which receives different appellations according as the fluids are heavy and liquid like water, or light and invisible like air. In the former case it is called *Hydrodynamics*, from the Greek words signifying *water* and *power*, or *force*; in the latter *Pneumatics*, from the Greek word signifying *breath* or *air*; and Hydrodynamics is divided into *Hydrostatics*, which treats of the weight and pressure of liquids, from the Greek words for *balancing* of *water*, and *Hydraulics*, which treat of their motion, from the Greek name for certain musical instruments played with *water* in *pipes*.

The discoveries to which experiments, aided by mathematical reasoning, have led, upon the pressure and motion of fluids, are of the greatest importance, whether we regard their application to practical purposes, or to the explanation of the appearances in nature, or their singularity as the subjects of scientific contemplation. When it is found that the pressure of water upon any surface that contains it, is not in the least degree proportioned to its bulk, but only to the height at which it stands, so that a long small pipe-full, containing a pound or two of water, will give the pressure of twenty or thirty ton; nay, of twice or thrice as much, if its length be increased, and its bore lessened, without the least regard to the quantity of the liquid: we are not only astonished with so extraordinary and unexpected a property of matter, but we at once perceive one of the great agents employed in the vast operations of nature, in which the most trifling means are used to work the mightiest effects. We likewise learn to guard against many serious mischiefs in our own works, and to apply safely and usefully a power calculated, according as it is directed, either to produce unbounded devastation, or to render the most beneficial service.

Nor are the discoveries relating to the Air less interesting in themselves, and less applicable to important uses. It is an agent, though invisible, as powerful as water, both in the operations of nature and of art. Experiments of a simple and decisive nature show the amount of its pressure to be between 14 and 15 pounds on every square inch; but, like all other fluids, it presses equally in every direction; so that, though on our hand there is a pressure downwards of above 250 pounds, yet this is exactly balanced by an equal pressure upwards, from the air pressing round and getting below. If, however, the air be removed below, the whole pressure from above acts unbalanced: hence the ascent of water in pumps, which suck out the air from a barrel, and allow the pressure upon the water to force it up 32 or 33 feet, that body of water being equal to the weight of the atmosphere; hence the ascent of the mercury in the barometer but only 28 or 29 inches, mercury being between 13 and 14 times heavier than water. Hence, too, the motion of the steam-engine; the piston of which is pressed downwards by the weight of the atmosphere from above, all air being removed below it by first filling it with steam, and then suddenly cooling and converting that steam into water. Hence, too, the power which some animals possess of walking along the perpendicular surfaces of walls, and even the ceilings of rooms, by squeezing out the air between the inside of their feet and the surface of the wall, and thus being supported by the pressure of the air against the outside of their feet.

The science of *Optics*, (from the Greek word for *seeing*,) which teaches the nature of light, and of the sensation conveyed by it, presents, of itself, a field of unbounded extent and interest. To it the arts, and the other sciences, owe those most useful instruments which have enabled us at once to examine the minutest parts of the structure of animal and vegetable bodies, and to calculate the size and the motions of the most remote of the heavenly bodies. But as an object of learned curiosity, nothing can be more singular than the fundamental truth discovered by the genius of Newton,—that the light, which we call white, is in fact composed of all the colours, blended in certain proportions; unless, perhaps, it be that astonishing conjecture of his unrivalled sagacity, by which he descried the inflammable nature of the diamond, and its belonging, against all appearance of probability, to the class of oily substances, by observing that it stood among them, and far removed from all crystals, in the degree of its action upon light; a conjecture turned into certainty by discoveries made a century afterwards.

To a man who, for original genius and strong natural sense, is not unworthy of being named after this illustrious sage, we owe the greater part of *Electrical* science. It treats of the peculiar substance, resembling both light and heat, which, by rubbing, is found to be produced in a certain class of bodies, as glass, wax, silk, amber; and to be conveyed easily or *conducted* through others, as wood, metals, water; and it has received the name of *Electricity* from the Greek word for *amber*. Dr. Franklin discovered that this is the same matter which, when collected in the clouds, and conveyed from them to the earth, we call *lightning*; and whose noise, in darting through the air, is *thunder*. The observation of some movements in the limbs of a dead frog gave rise to the discovery of *Animal Electricity or Galvanism*, as it was at first called from the name of the discoverer; and which has of late years given birth to improvements that have changed the face of chemical philosophy; affording a new proof how few there are of the processes of nature, incapable of repaying our labour, bestowed in patiently and diligently examining them. It is to the results of the remark accidentally made upon the twitching in the frog's leg, not, however, hastily dismissed and forgotten, but treasured up and pursued through many an elaborate experiment and calculation, that we owe our acquaintance with the extraordinary metal, liquid like mercury, lighter than water, and more inflammable than phosphorus, which forms when it burns, by mere exposure to the air, one of the salts best known in commerce, and the principal ingredient in saltpetre.

In order to explain the nature and objects of those branches of Natural Science more or less connected with the mathematics, some details were necessary, as without them it was difficult at once to perceive their importance, and, as it were, relish the kind of instruction which they afford. But the same course needs not be pursued with respect to the other branches. The value and the interest of Chemistry is at once perceived, when it is known to teach the nature of all substances, the relations of simple substances to heat and to one another, or their combinations together; the composition of those which nature produces in a compound state, and the application of the whole to the arts and manufactures. Some branches of philosophy, again, are chiefly useful and interesting to particular classes, as surgeons and physicians. Others are easily understood by a knowledge of the principles of Mechanics and Chemistry, of which they are applications and examples; as those which teach the structure of the earth and the changes it has undergone; the motions of the muscles, and the structure of the parts of animals; the qualities of animal and vegetable substances; and that department of Agriculture which treats of soils, manure, and machinery. Other branches are only collections of facts, highly curious and useful indeed, but which any one who reads or listens, perceives as clearly, and comprehends as readily, as the professed student. To this class belongs Natural History, in so far as it describes the habits of animals and plants, and its application to that department of Agriculture which treats of cattle and their management.

IV. But, for the purpose of further illustrating the advantages of Philosophy, its tendency to enlarge the mind, as well as to interest it agreeably, and afford pure and solid gratification, a few instances may be given of the singular truths brought to light by the application of mathematical, mechanical, and chemical knowledge to the habits of animals and plants; and some examples may be added of the more ordinary and easy, but scarcely less interesting observations, made upon those habits, without the aid of the profounder sciences.

We may remember the curve line which mathematicians call a cycloid. It is the path which any point of a circle, moving along a plane, and round its centre, traces in the air; so that the nail on the felly of a cart-wheel moves in a cycloid, as the cart goes along, and as the wheel itself both turns round its axle, and is carried along the ground. Now this curve has certain properties of a peculiar and very singular kind with respect to motion. One is, that if any body whatever moves in a cycloid by its own weight or swing, together with some other force acting upon it, it will go through all distances of the same curve in exactly the same time; and, accordingly, pendulums are contrived to swing in such a manner, that they shall describe cycloids, or curves very near cycloids, and thus move in equal times, whether they go through a long or a short part of the same curve. Again, if a body is to descend from any one point to any other, not in the perpendicular, by means of some force acting on it together with its weight, the line in which it will go the quickest of all will be the cycloid, not the straight line, though that is the shortest of all lines which can be drawn between the two points; nor any other curve whatever, though many are much flatter, and therefore shorter than the cycloid—but the cycloid, which is longer than them, is yet of all curves or straight lines which can be drawn, the one the body will move through in the shortest time. Suppose the body is to move from one point to another, by its weight and some other force acting together, but to go through a certain space, as a hundred yards, the way it must take to do this in the shortest time possible, is by moving in a cycloid; or the length of a hundred yards must be drawn into a cycloid, and then the body will descend through the hundred yards in a shorter time than it could go the same distance in any other path whatever. Now, it is believed that birds which build in the rocks, drop or fly down from height to height in this course. It is impossible to make very accurate observations on their flight and path; but there is a general resemblance certainly between the course they take and the cycloid, which has led ingenious men to adopt this opinion.

If we have a certain quantity of any substance, a pound of wood, for example, and would fashion it in the shape to take the least room, we must make a globe of it; it will in this figure have the smallest surface. But suppose we want to form the pound of wood, so that in moving through the air or water it shall meet with the least possible resistance, then we must lengthen it out for ever, till it becomes not only like a long-pointed pin, but thinner and thinner, longer and longer, till it is quite a straight line, and has no perceptible breadth or thickness at all. If we would dispose of the given quantity of matter so that it shall have a certain length only, say a foot, and a certain breadth at the thickest part, say three inches, and move through the air or water with the smallest possible resistance which a body of those dimensions can meet, then we must form it into a figure of a peculiar kind, called the *Solid of least resistance*, because of all the shapes that can be given to the body, its length and breadth remaining the same, this is the one which will make it move with the least resistance through the air, or water, or other fluid. A very difficult chain of mathematical reasoning, by means of the highest branches of algebra, leads to a knowledge of the curve, which by revolving on its axis makes a solid of this shape, in the same way that a circle by so revolving makes a sphere or globe; and the curve certainly resembles closely the face or head part of a fish. Nature, therefore, (by which we always mean the Divine Author of nature,) has fashioned these fishes so, that, according to mathematical principles, they swim the most easily through the element they live and move in.

Suppose upon the face part of one of these fishes a small insect were bred, endowed with faculties sufficient to reason upon its condition, and upon the motion of the fish it belonged to, but never to have discovered the whole size and shape of the face part, it would certainly complain of the form as clumsy, and fancy that it could have made the fish so as to move with less resistance. Yet if the whole shape were disclosed to it, and it could discover the principle on which that shape was preferred, it would at once perceive, not only that what had seemed clumsy was skilfully contrived, but that if any other shape whatever had been taken, there would have been an error committed; nay, *that there must of necessity* have been an error; and that the very best possible arrangement had been adopted. So it may be with man in the Universe, where, seeing only a part of the great system, he fancies there is evil; and yet, if he were permitted to survey the whole, what had seemed imperfect might appear to be necessary for the general perfection, insomuch that any other arrangement, even of that seemingly imperfect part, must needs have rendered the whole less perfect. The common objection is, that what seems evil might have been avoided; but in the case of the fish's shape it *could not* have been avoided.

It is found by optical inquiries, that the rays or particles of light, in passing through transparent substances of a certain form, are bent to a point where they make an image or picture of the shining bodies they come from, or of the dark bodies they are reflected from. Thus, if a pair of spectacles be held between a candle and the wall, they make two images of the candle upon it; and if they be held between the window and a sheet of paper when the sun is shining, they will make a picture on the paper of the houses, trees, fields, sky, and clouds. The eye is found to be composed of several natural magnifiers which make a picture on a membrane at the back of it, and from this membrane there goes a nerve to the brain, conveying the impression of the picture, by means of which we see it. Now, white light was discovered by Newton to consist of different-coloured parts, which are differently bent in passing through transparent substances, so that the lights of different colours come to a point at different distances, and thus create an indistinct image. This was long found to make our telescopes imperfect, insomuch that it became necessary to make them of reflectors or mirrors, and not of magnifying glasses—the same difference not being observed to affect their reflection. But another discovery was about fifty years afterwards made by Mr. Dollond, that by combining different kinds of glass in a compound magnifier, the difference may be greatly corrected; and on this principle he constructed his telescopes. It is found, too, that the different natural magnifiers of the eye are combined upon a principle of the same kind. Thirty years later, a third discovery was made by Mr. Blair, of the greatly superior effect which combinations of different liquids have in correcting the imperfection; and, most wonderful to think, when the eye is examined, we find it consists of different liquids, acting naturally upon the same principle which was thus recently found out in Optics by many ingenious mechanical and chemical experiments.

Again, the point to which any magnifier collects the light is more or less distant as the magnifier is smaller or rounder, so that a small globe of glass or any transparent substances makes a microscope. And this property of light depends upon the nature of lines, and is purely of a mathematical nature, after we have once ascertained by experiment, that light is bent in a certain way when it passes through transparent bodies. Now birds flying in the air, and meeting with many obstacles, as branches and leaves of trees, require to have their eyes sometimes as flat as possible for protection; but sometimes as round as possible, that they may see the small objects, flies and other insects, which they are chasing through the air, and which they pursue with the most unerring certainty. This could only be accomplished by giving them a power of suddenly changing the form of their eyes. Accordingly, there is a set of hard scales placed on the outer coat of their eye, round the place where the light enters; and over these scales are drawn the muscles or fibres by which motion is communicated; so that, by acting with these muscles, the bird can press the scales, and squeeze the natural magnifier of the eye into a round shape when it wishes to follow an insect through the air, and can relax the scales, in order to flatten the eye again when it would see a distant object, or move safely through leaves and twigs. This power of altering the shape of the eye is possessed by birds of prey in a very remarkable degree. They can see the smallest objects close to them, and can yet discern larger bodies at vast distances, as a carcass stretched upon the plain, or a dying fish afloat on the water.

A singular provision is made for keeping the surface of the bird's eye clean, for wiping the glass of the instrument, as it were, and also for protecting it, while rapidly flying through the air and through thickets, without hindering the sight. Birds are, for these purposes, furnished with a third eyelid, a fine membrane or skin, which is constantly moved very rapidly over the eyeball by two muscles placed in the back of the eye. One of the muscles ends in a loop, the other in a string which goes through the loop, and is fixed in the corner of the membrane, to pull it backward and forward. If you wish to draw a thing towards any place with the least force, you must pull directly in the line between the thing and the place; but if you wish to draw it as quickly as possible, and do not regard the loss of force, you must pull it obliquely, by drawing it in two directions at once. Tie a string to a stone, and draw it straight towards you with one hand; then, make a loop on another string, and running the first through it, draw one string in each hand, not towards you, but side-ways, till both strings are stretched in a straight line: you will see how much swifter the stone moves than it did before when pulled straight forward. Now this is proved, by mathematical reasoning, to be the necessary consequence of forces applied obliquely: there is a loss of power, but a great increase of velocity. The velocity is the thing required to be gained in the third eyelid, and the contrivance is exactly that of a string and a loop, moved each by a muscle, as the two strings are by the hands in the case we have been supposing.

A third eyelid of the same kind is found in the horse, and called the *haw*; it is moistened with a pulpy substance (or mucilage) to take hold of the dust on the eyeball, and wipe it clean off, so that the eye is hardly ever seen with any thing upon it, though greatly exposed from its size and posture. The swift motion of the haw is given to it by a gristly, elastic substance, placed between the eyeball and the socket, and striking obliquely, so as to drive out the haw with great velocity over the eye, and then let it come back as quickly. Ignorant persons when this haw is inflamed from cold and swells so as to appear, which it never does in a healthy state, often mistake it for an imperfection, and cut it off: So nearly does ignorance produce the same mischief as cruelty! They might as well cut off the pupil of the eye, taking it for a black spot.

If any quantity of matter, as a pound of wood or iron, is fashioned into a rod of a certain length, say one foot, the rod will be strong in proportion to its thickness; and, if the figure is the same, that thickness can only be increased by making it hollow. Therefore, hollow rods or tubes, of the same length and quantity of matter, have more strength than solid ones. This is a principle so well understood now, that engineers make their axles and other parts of machinery hollow, and therefore stronger with the same weight, than they would be if thinner and solid. Now the bones of animals are all more or less hollow; and are therefore stronger with the same weight and quantity of matter than they otherwise would be. But birds have the largest bones in proportion to their weight; their bones are more hollow than those of animals which do not fly; and therefore they have strength without having to carry more weight than is absolutely necessary. Their quills derive strength from the same construction. They have another peculiarity to help their flight. No other animals have any communication between the air-vessels of their lungs and the hollow parts of their bodies; but birds have; and by this means they can blow out their bodies as we do a bladder, and thus make themselves lighter when they would either make their flight towards the ground slower, or rise more swiftly, or float more easily in the air. Fishes possess a power of the same kind, though not by the same means. They have air-bladders in their bodies, and can puff them out, or press them closer, at pleasure: when they want to rise in the water, they fill out the bladder, and this lightens them. If the bladder breaks, the fish remains at the bottom, and can only be held up by the most laborious exertions of the fins and tail. Accordingly, flat fish, as skaits and flounders, which have no air-bladders, seldom rise from the bottom, but are found lying on banks in the sea, or at the bottom of sea rivers.

If you have a certain space, as a room, to build up with closets or little cells, all of the same size and shape, there are only three figures which will answer, and enable you to fill the room without losing any space between the cells; they must either be squares, or figures of three equal sides, or figures of six equal sides. With any other figures whatever, space would be lost between the cells. This is evidently true upon considering the matter; and it is proved by mathematical reasoning. The six-sided figure is by far the most convenient of these three shapes, because its corners are flatter, and any round body placed in it has therefore more space, there being less room lost in the corners. Likewise, this figure is the strongest of the three; any pressure either from without or from within will hurt it less, as it has something of the strength of an arch. A round figure would be still stronger, but then room would be lost between the circles, whereas none at all is lost with the six-sided figure. Now, it is a most remarkable fact, that *Bees* build their cells exactly in this shape, and thereby save both room and materials beyond what they could save if they built in any other shape whatever. They build in the very best possible shape for their purpose, which is to save all the room and all the wax they can. So far as to the shape of the walls of each cell; but the roof and floor, or top and bottom, are built on equally true principles. It is proved by mathematicians, that to give the greatest strength and save the most room, the roof and floor must be made of three square planes meeting in a point; and they have further proved by a demonstration belonging to the highest parts of Algebra, that there is one particular angle or inclination of those planes to each other where they meet, which makes a greater saving of materials and of work than any other inclination whatever could possibly do. Now, the bees actually make the tops and bottoms of their cells of three planes meeting in a point, and the inclination or angle at which they meet is precisely the one found out by the mathematicians to be the best possible for saving wax and work. Who would dream for an instant of the bee knowing the highest branches of Mathematics—the fruits of Newton's most wonderful discovery—a result, too, of which he was himself ignorant, one of his most celebrated followers having found it out? This little insect works with a truth and correctness which are quite perfect, and according to the principles at which man has only arrived, after ages of slow improvement in the most difficult branch of the most difficult science. But the mighty and all wise Creator, who made the insect and the philosopher, bestowing reason on the latter, and giving the former to work without it—to Him all truths are known from all eternity, with an intuition that mocks even the conceptions of the sagest of human kind.

It may be recollected, that when the air is exhausted or sucked out of any vessel, there is no longer the force necessary to resist the pressure of the air on the outside; and the sides of the vessel are therefore pressed inwards with violence: a flat glass would thus be broken, unless it were very thick; a round one, having the strength of an arch, would resist better; but any soft substance, as leather or skin, would be crushed or squeezed together at once. If the air was only sucked out slowly, the squeezing would be gradual, or, if it were only half sucked out, the skin would only be partly squeezed together. This is the very process by which *Bees* reach the fine dust and juices of hollow flowers, like the honeysuckle, and some kinds of long fox-glove, which are too narrow for them to enter. They fill up the mouth of the flower with their bodies, and suck out the air, or at least a large part of it; this makes the soft sides of the flower close, and squeezes the dust and juice towards the insect as well as a hand could do, if applied to the outside.

We may remember this pressure or weight of the atmosphere as shown by the barometer, the sucking-pump, and the air-pump. Its weight is near 15 pounds on every square inch, so that if we could entirely squeeze out the air between our two hands, they would cling together with a force equal to the pressure of double this weight, because the air would press upon both hands; and if we could contrive to suck or squeeze out the air between one hand and the wall, the hand would stick fast to the wall, being pressed on it with the weight of above two hundred weight, that is, near 15 pounds on every square inch of the hand. Now, by a late most curious discovery of Sir Everard Home, the distinguished anatomist, it is found that this is the very process by which *Flies* and other insects of a similar description are enabled to walk up perpendicular surfaces, however smooth, as the sides of walls and panes of glass in windows, and to walk as easily along the ceiling of a room with their bodies downwards and their feet over head. Their feet, when examined by a microscope, are found to have flat skins or flaps, like the feet of web-footed animals, as ducks and geese; and they have towards the back part or heel, but inside the skin or flap, two very small toes so connected with the flap as to draw it close down upon the glass or wall the fly walks on, and to squeeze out the air completely, so that there is a vacuum made between the foot and the glass or wall. The consequence of this is, that the air presses the foot on the wall with a very considerable force compared to the weight of the fly; for if its feet are to its body in the same proportion as ours are to our bodies, since we could support by a single hand on the ceiling of the room (provided it made a vacuum) more than our whole weight, namely, a weight of fifteen stone, the fly can easily move on four feet in the same manner by help of the vacuum made under its feet. It has likewise been found that some of the larger sea animals are by the same construction, only upon a greater scale, enabled to climb the perpendicular and smooth surfaces of the ice hills among which they live. Some kinds of lizard have the same power of climbing, and of creeping with their bodies downwards along the ceiling of a room; and the means by which they are enabled to do so are the same. In the large feet of these animals, the contrivance is easily observed, of the two toes or tightners, by which the skin of the foot is pinned down, and the air excluded in the act of walking or climbing; but it is the very same, only upon a larger scale, with the mechanism of a fly's or a butterfly's foot; and both operations, the climbing of the sea-horse on the ice, and the creeping of the fly on the window or the ceiling, are performed exactly by the same power, the weight of the atmosphere, which causes the quicksilver to stand in the weather-glass, the wind to whistle through a key-hole, and the piston to descend in a steam-engine.

Although philosophers are not agreed as to the peculiar action which light exerts upon vegetation, and there is even some doubt respecting the decomposition of air and water during that process, one thing is undeniable, the necessity of light to the growth and health of plants; and accordingly they are for the most part so formed as to receive it at all times when it shines on them. Their cups, and the little assemblages of their leaves before they sprout, are found to be more or less affected by the light, so as to open and receive it. In several kinds of plants this is more evident than in others; their flowers close entirely at night, and open in the day. Some, as the Sunflower, and a tribe of the like description, constantly turn round towards the light, following the sun, as it were, while he makes or seems to make his revolution, so that they receive the greatest quantity possible of his rays. Plants of this kind require more light than others for their growth, and this is the provision made for supplying them.

The lightness of inflammable gas is well known. When bladders, of any size, are filled with it, they rise upwards, and float in the air. Now, it is a most curious fact, that the fine dust, by means of which plants are impregnated one by the other, is composed of very small globules, filled with this gas—in a word, of small air balloons. These globules thus float from the male plant through the air, and striking against the females, are detained by a glue prepared on purpose to stop them, which no sooner moistens the globules than they explode, and their substance remains, the gas flying off which enabled them to float. A provision of a very simple kind is also made to prevent the male and female blossoms of the same plant from breeding together, this being found to hurt the breed of vegetables, just as breeding in and in does the breed of animals. It is contrived that the dust shall be shed by the male blossom before the female is ready to be affected by it, so that the impregnation must be performed by the dust of some other plant, and in this way the breed be crossed. The light gas with which the globules are filled is most essential to this operation, as it conveys them to great distances. A plantation of yew trees has been known, in this way, to impregnate another several hundred yards off.

The contrivance by which some creeper plants are enabled to climb walls, and fix themselves, deserves attention. The *Virginia creeper* has a small tendril, ending in a claw, each toe of which has a knob, thickly set with extremely small bristles; they grow into the invisible pores of the wall, and swelling stick there as long as the plant grows, and prevent the branch from falling; but when the plant dies, they become thin again, and drop out, so that the branch falls down. The *Vanilla* plant of the West Indies climbs round trees likewise by means of tendrils; but when it has fixed itself, the tendrils drop off, and their place is supplied by leaves.

It is found by chemical experiments, that the juice which is in the stomachs of animals, (called the *gastric* juice, from a Greek word signifying *the belly*,) has very peculiar properties. Though it is for the

c

most part a tasteless, clear, and seemingly a very simple liquor, it nevertheless possesses extraordinary powers of dissolving substances which it touches or mixes with; and it varies in different classes of animals. In one particular it is the same in all animals: it will not attack living matter, but only dead; the consequence of which is, that its powers of eating away and dissolving are perfectly safe to the animals themselves, in whose stomachs it remains without ever hurting them. This juice differs in different animals according to the food on which they subsist: thus, in birds of prey, as kites, hawks, owls, it only acts upon animal matter, and does not dissolve vegetables. In other birds, and in all animals feeding on grass, as oxen, sheep, hares, it dissolves vegetable matter, as grass, but will not touch flesh of any kind. This has been ascertained by making them swallow balls with meat in them, and several holes drilled through, to let the gastric juice reach the meat: no effect was produced upon it. We may further observe, that there is a most curious and beautiful correspondence between this juice in the stomach of different animals and the other parts of their bodies, connected with the important operations of eating and digesting their food. The use of the juice is plainly to convert what they eat into a fluid, from which, by various other processes, all their parts, blood, bones, muscles, &c. are afterwards formed. But the food is first of all to be obtained, and then prepared by bruising, for the action of the juice. Now birds of prey have instruments, their claws and beak, for tearing and devouring their food, (that is animals of different kinds,) but those instruments are useless for picking up and crushing seeds: accordingly, they have a gastric juice which dissolves the animals they eat; while birds which have only a beak fit for pecking, drinking, and eating seeds, have a juice that dissolves seeds, and not flesh. Nay more, it is found that the seeds must be bruised before the juice will dissolve them: this you find by trying the experiment in a vessel with the juice; and accordingly the birds have a gizzard, and animals which graze have flat teeth, which grind and bruise their food before the gastric juice is to act upon it.

We have seen how wonderfully the *Bee* works, according to rules discovered by man thousands of years after the insect had followed them with perfect accuracy. The same little animal seems to be acquainted with principles of which we are still ignorant. We can, by crossing, vary the forms of cattle with astonishing nicety; but we have no means of altering the nature of an animal once born, by means of treatment and feeding. This power, however, is undeniably possessed by the bees. When the queen bee is lost, by death or otherwise, they choose a grub from among those which are born for workers; they make three cells into one, and placing the grub there, they build a tube round it; they afterwards build another cell of a pyramidal form, into which the grub grows: they feed it with peculiar food, and tend it with extreme care. It becomes, when transformed from the worm to the fly, not a worker, but a queen bee.

These singular insects resemble our own species, in one of our worst propensities, the disposition to war; but their attention to their sovereign is equally extraordinary, though of a somewhat capricious kind. In a few hours after their queen is lost, the whole hive is in state of confusion. A singular humming is heard, and the bees are seen moving all over the surface of the combs with great rapidity. The news spread quickly, and when the queen is restored, quiet immediately succeeds. But if another queen is put upon them, they instantly discover the trick, and, surrounding her, they either suffocate or starve her to death. This happens if the false queen is introduced within a few hours after the first is lost or removed; but if twenty-four hours have elapsed, they will receive any queen, and obey her.

The labours and the policy of the *Ants* are, when closely examined, still more wonderful, perhaps, than those of the *Bee*. Their nest is a city consisting of dwelling-places, halls, streets, and squares, into which the streets open. The food they principally like is the honey which comes from another insect found in their neighbourhood, and which they, generally speaking, bring home from day to day as they want it. Later discoveries have shown that they do not eat grain, but live almost entirely on animal food and this honey. Some kinds of ant have the foresight to bring home the insects on whose honey they feed, and keep them in particular cells, where they guard them to prevent their escaping, and feed them with proper vegetable matter which they do not eat themselves. Nay, they obtain the eggs of those insects, and superintend their hatching, and then rear the young insect until he becomes capable of supplying the desired honey. They sometimes remove them to the strongest parts of their nest, where there are cells apparently fortified for protecting them from invasion. In those cells the insects are kept to supply the wants of the whole ants which compose the population of the city. It is a most singular circumstance in the economy of nature, that the degree of cold at which the ant becomes torpid is also that at which this insect falls into the same state. It is considerably below the freezing point; so that they require food the greater part of the winter, and if the insects on which they depend for food were not kept alive during the cold in which the ants can move about, the latter would be without the means of subsistence.

How trifling soever this little animal may appear in our climate, there are few more formidable creatures than the ant of some tropical countries. A traveller who lately filled a high station in the French government, Mr. Malouet, has described one of their cities, and, were not the account confirmed by various testimonies, it might seem exaggerated. He observed at a great distance what seemed a lofty structure, and was informed by his guide that it consisted of an ant hill, which could not be approached without danger of being devoured. Its height was from 15 to 20 feet, and its base 30 or 40 feet square. Its sides inclined like the lower part of a pyramid, the point being cut off. He was informed that it became necessary to destroy these nests, by raising a sufficient force to dig a trench all round, and fill it with fagots, which were afterwards set on fire; and then battering with cannon from a distance, to drive the insects out and make them run into the flames. This was in South America; and African travellers have met with them in the same formidable numbers and strength.

The older writers of books upon the habits of some animals abound with stories which may be of doubtful credit. But the facts now stated respecting the Ant and Bee, may be relied on as authentic. They are the result of very late observations, and experiments made with great accuracy by several most worthy and intelligent men, and the greater part of them have the confirmation arising from more than one observer having assisted in the inquiries. The habits of *Beavers* are equally well authenticated, and, being more easily observed, are vouched by a greater number of witnesses. These animals, as if to enable them to live and move either on land or water, have two web feet like those of ducks or water dogs, and two like those of land animals. When they wish to construct a dwelling-place, or rather city, for it serves the whole body, they choose a level place with a stream running through it; they dam up the stream so as to make a pond, and perform the operation as skilfully as we could ourselves. They drive into the ground stakes of five or six feet long in rows, wattling each row with twigs, and puddling or filling the interstices with clay which they ram close in, so as to make the whole solid and water-tight. This dam is likewise shaped on the truest principles;* for the upper side next the water slopes, and the side below is perpendicular; the base of the dam is 10 or 12 feet thick: the top or narrow part two or three, and it is sometimes as long as 100 feet. The pond being thus formed and secured, they make their houses round the edge of it; they are cells, with vaulted roofs, and upon piles; they are made of stones, earth, and sticks; the walls are two feet thick, and plastered as neatly as if the trowel had been used. Sometimes they have two or three stories for retreating to in case of floods, and they always have two doors, one towards the water, and one towards the land. They keep their winter provisions in stores, and bring them out to use; they make their beds of moss; they live on the bark of trees, gums, and crawfish. Each house holds from twenty to thirty, and there may be from ten to twenty-five houses in all. Some of their communities are therefore larger than others, but there are seldom fewer than two or three hundred inhabitants. In working they all bear their shares: some gnaw the trees and branches with their teeth to form stakes and beams; others roll the pieces to the water; others diving make holes with their teeth to place the piles in; others collect and carry stones and clay; others beat and mix the mortar; and others carry it on their broad tails, and with these beat it and plaster it. Some superintend the rest, and make signals by sharp strokes with the tail, which are carefully attended to; the beavers hastening to the place where

---

* If the base is 12, and the top 3 feet thick, and the height 6 feet, the face must be the side of a right-angled triangle, whose height is 8 feet. This would be the exact proportion which there ought to be, upon mathematical principles, to give the greatest resistance possible to the water in its tendency to turn the dam round, provided the materials of which it is made were lighter than water in the proportion of 44 to 100. But the materials are probably more than twice as heavy as water, and the form of so flat a dike is taken, in all likelihood, in order to guard against a more imminent danger, —that of the dam being carried away by being shoved forwards. We cannot calculate what the proportions are which give the greatest possible resistance to this tendency, without knowing the tenacity of the materials, as well as their specific gravity. It may very probably be found that the construction is such as to secure the most completely against the two pressures at the same time

they are wanted to work, or to repair any hole made by the water, or to defend themselves or make their escape, when attacked by an enemy.

The fitness of different animals, by their bodily structure, to the circumstances in which they are found, presents an endless subject of curious inquiry and pleasing contemplation. Thus, the *Camel* which lives in sandy deserts has broad spreading hoofs to support him on the loose soil; and an apparatus in his body by which water is kept for many days, to be used when no moisture can be had. As this would be useless in the neighbourhood of streams or wells, and as it would be equally so in the desert, where no water is to be found, there can be no doubt that it is intended to assist in journeying across the sands from one watered spot to another. There is a singular and beautiful provision made in this animal's foot, for enabling it to sustain the fatigues of journeys under the pressure of its great weight. Beside the yielding of the bones and ligaments, or bindings, which gives elasticity to the foot of the deer and other animals, there is in the camel's foot, between the horny sole and the bones, a cushion, like a ball, of soft matter, almost fluid, but in which there is a mass of threads extremely elastic, interwoven with the pulpy substance. The cushion thus easily changes its shape when pressed, yet it has such an elastic spring, that the bones of the foot press on it uninjured by the heavy body which they support, and this huge animal steps as softly as a cat.

Nor need we flee to the desert in order to witness an example of skilful structure in the foot: the *Horse's* limbs display it strikingly. The bones of the foot are not placed directly under the weight; if they were in an upright position, they would make a firm pillar, and every motion would cause a shock. They are placed slanting or oblique, and tied together by an elastic binding on their lower surfaces, so as to form springs as exact as those which we make of leather or steel for carriages. Then the flatness of the hoof which stretches out on each side, and the frog coming down in the middle between the quarters, adds greatly to the elasticity of the machine. Ignorant of this, ill-informed farriers nail the shoe too far back, fixing the quarters, and causing permanent contraction—so that the contracted hoof loses its elasticity; every step is a shock; inflammation and lameness ensue.

The *Rein-deer* inhabits a country covered with snow the greater part of the year. Observe how admirably its hoof is formed for going over that cold and light substance, without sinking in it, or being frozen. The under side is covered entirely with hair, of a warm and close texture; and the hoof, altogether, is very broad, acting exactly like the snow-shoes which men have constructed for giving them a larger space to stand on than their feet, and thus to avoid sinking. Moreover, the deer spreads the hoof as wide as possible when it touches the ground; but, as this breadth would be inconvenient in the air, by occasioning a greater resistance while he is moving along, no sooner does he lift the hoof than the two parts into which it is cloven fall together, and so lessen the surface exposed to the air, just as we may recollect the birds doing with their bodies and wings. The shape and structure of the hoof is also well adapted to scrape away the snow, and enable the animal to get at the particular kind of moss (or *lichen*) on which he feeds.

This plant, unlike others, is in its full growth during the winter season; and the rein-deer, accordingly, thrives from its abundance, notwithstanding the unfavourable effects of extreme cold upon the animal system.

There are some insects, of which the males have wings, and the females are grubs or worms. Of these, the *Glow-worm* is the most remarkable: it is the female, and the male is a fly, which would be unable to find her out, creeping, as she does, in the dark lanes, but for the shining light which she gives, to attract him.

There is a singular fish found in the Mediterranean, called the *Nautilus*, from its skill in navigation. The back of its shell resembles the hulk of a ship; on this it throws itself, with two of its feet raised in the air, and over these two spreads a thin membrane to serve for a sail, paddling itself on with the other two feet as oars.

The *Ostrich* lays and hatches her eggs in the sands; her form being ill adapted to that process, she has a natural oven furnished by the sand, and the strong heat of the sun. The *Cuckoo* is known to build no nest for herself, but to lay in the nests of other birds; but late observations show that she does not lay indiscriminately in the nests of all birds; she only chooses the nests of those which have bills of the same kind with herself, and therefore feed on the same kind of food. The *Duck*, and other birds breeding in muddy places, have a peculiar formation of the bill: it is both made so as to act like a strainer, separating the finer from the grosser parts of the liquid, and it is more furnished with nerves near the point than the bills of birds which feed on substances exposed to the light; so that it serves better to grope in the dark stream for food, being more sensitive. The bill of the *Snipe* is covered with a curious net-work of nerves for the same purpose; but a bird, (the *Toucan* or *Egg-sucker*,) which chiefly feeds on the eggs found in birds' nests, and in countries where these are very deep and dark, has the most singular provision of this kind. Its bill is very broad and long; when examined, it is completely covered with branches of nerves in all directions; so that, by groping in a deep and dark nest, it can feel its way as accurately as the finest and most delicate finger could. Almost all kinds of birds build their nests of materials found where they inhabit, or use the nests of other birds; but the *Swallow of Java* lives in rocky caverns on the sea, where there are no materials at all for the purpose of building. It is therefore so formed as to secrete in its body a kind of slime with which it makes a nest, much prized as a delicate food in eastern countries.

Plants, in many remarkable instances, are provided for by equally wonderful and skilful contrivances. There is one, the *Muscipula, Fly-trap*, or *Fly-catcher*, which has small prickles in the inside of two leaves, or half leaves, joined by a hinge; a juice or syrup is provided on their inner surface, and acts as a bait to allure flies. There are three small spines or prickles standing upright in this syrup, and upon the only part of each leaf that is sensitive to the touch. When the fly therefore settles upon this part, its touching as it were the spring of the trap occasions the leaves to shut and kill and squeeze the insect; so that its juices and the air arising from their rotting serve as food to the plant.

In the West Indies, and other hot countries, where rain sometimes does not fall for a great length of time, a kind of plant called the

Wild-pine grows upon the branches of the trees, and also on the bark of the trunk. It has hollow or bag-like leaves so formed as to make little reservoirs of water, the rain falling into them through channels which close at the top when full, to prevent it from evaporating. The seed of this useful plant has long threads, by which, when carried through the air, it catches any tree in the way, and falls on it and grows. Wherever it takes root, though on the under side of a bough, it grows straight upwards, otherwise the leaves would not hold water. It holds in one leaf from a pint to a quart; and although it must be of great use to the trees it grows on, to birds and other animals its use is even greater. Another tree, called the *Water-with*, in Jamaica, has similar uses; it is like a vine in size and shape, but growing in very parched districts, is yet so full of clear sap or water, that on cutting a piece two or three yards long, and merely holding it to the mouth, a plentiful draught is obtained. In the East there is a plant somewhat of the same kind, called the *Bejuco*, which grows near other trees and twines round them, with its end hanging downwards, but so full of juice, that on cutting it, a plentiful stream of water spouts from it; and this, not only by its touching the tree so closely must refresh it, but is a supply to animals, and to the weary herdsman on the mountains.

V. After the many instances or samples which have now been given of the nature and objects of Natural Science, we might proceed to a different field, and describe in the same way the other grand branch of Human Knowledge, that which teaches the properties or habits of *Mind* —the *intellectual faculties* of man; that is to say, the powers of his understanding, by which he perceives, imagines, remembers, and reasons;—his *moral faculties*, that is to say, the feelings and passions which influence him;—and, lastly, as a conclusion or result drawn from the whole, his *duties* both towards himself as an individual, and towards others as a member of society; which last head opens to our view the whole doctrines of *political science*, including the nature of governments, of policy, and generally of laws. But we shall abstain at present from entering at all upon this field, and shall now take up the subject, more particularly pointed at through the course of the preceding observations, and to illustrate which they have been framed, namely,—the use and importance of scientific studies.

Man is composed of two parts, body and mind, connected indeed together, but wholly different from one another. The nature of the union—the part of our outward and visible frame in which it is peculiarly formed—or whether the soul be indeed connected with any particular portion of the body, so as to reside there—are points as yet wholly hid from our knowledge, and which are likely to remain for ever concealed. But this we know, as certainly as we can know any truth, that there is such a thing as the mind; and that we have at the least as good proof of its existence, independent of the body, as we have of the existence of the body itself. Each has its uses, and each has its peculiar gratifications. The bounty of Providence has given us outward senses to be employed, and has furnished the means of gratifying them in various kinds, and in ample measure. As long as we only taste those pleasures according to the rules of prudence and of our duty, that is, in moderation for our own sakes, and in harmlessness towards our neighbours, we fulfil rather than thwart the purposes of our being. But the same bountiful Providence has endowed us with the higher nature also—with understandings as well as with senses—with faculties that are of a more exalted nature, and admit of more refined enjoyments, than any the bodily frame can bestow; and by pursuing such gratifications rather than those of mere sense, we fulfil the highest ends of our creation, and obtain both a present and a future reward. These things are often said, but they are not therefore the less true, or the less worthy of deep attention. Let us mark their practical application to the occupations and enjoyments of all branches of society, beginning with those who form the great bulk of every community, the working classes, by what names soever their vocations may be called—professions, arts, trades, handicrafts, or common labour.

The first object of every man who has to depend upon his own exertions must needs be to provide for his daily wants. This is a high and important office; it deserves his utmost attention; it includes some of his most important duties, both to himself, his kindred, and his country; and although in performing this office he is only influenced by his own interest, or by his necessities, yet it is one which renders him truly the best benefactor of the community to which he belongs. All other pursuits must give way to this; the hours which he gives to learning must be after he has done his work; his independence, without which he is not worthy to be called a man, requires first of all that he should have ensured for himself, and those dependent on him, a comfortable subsistence before he can have a right to taste any indulgence, either of his senses or of his mind; and the more he learns—the greater progress he makes in the sciences—the more will he value that independence, and the more will he prize the industry, the habits of regular labour, whereby he is enabled to secure so prime a blessing.

In one view, it is true, the progress which he makes in science may help his ordinary exertions, the main business of every man's life. There is hardly any trade or occupation in which useful lessons may not be learnt by studying one science or another. The necessity of science to the more liberal professions is self-evident; little less manifest is the use to their members of extending their knowledge beyond the branches of study, with which their several pursuits are more peculiarly conversant. But the other departments of industry derive hardly less benefit from the same source. To how many kinds of workmen must a knowledge of Mechanical Philosophy prove useful! To how many others does Chemistry prove almost necessary! Every one must with a glance perceive that to engineers, watch-makers, instrument-makers, bleachers, and dyers, those sciences are most useful, if not necessary. But carpenters and masons are surely likely to do their work better for knowing how to measure, which Practical Mathematics teaches them, and how to estimate the strength of timber, of walls, and of arches, which they learn from Practical Mechanics; and they who work in various metals are certain to be the more skilful in their trades for knowing the nature of those substances, and their relations to both heat and other metals, and to the airs and liquids they come in contact with. Nay, the farm-servant, or day-labourer, whether in his master's employ, or tending the concerns of his own cottage, must derive great practical benefit,—must be both a better servant, and a more thrifty, and therefore comfortable, cottager, for knowing something of the nature of soils and manures, which Chemistry teaches, and something of the habits of animals, and the qualities and growth of plants, which he learns from Natural History and Chemistry together. In truth, though a man be neither mechanic nor peasant, but only one having a pot to boil, he is sure to learn from science lessons which will enable him to cook his morsel better, save his fuel, and both vary his dish and improve it. The art of good and cheap cookery is intimately connected with the principles of chemical philosophy, and has received much, and will yet receive more, improvement from their application. Nor is it enough to say, that philosophers may discover all that is wanted, and may invent practical methods, which it is sufficient for the working man to learn by rote without knowing the principles. He never will work so well if he is ignorant of the principles; and for a plain reason:—if he only learn his lesson by rote, the least change of circumstances puts him out. Be the method ever so general, cases will always arise in which it must be varied in order to apply; and if the workman only knows the rule without knowing the reason, he must be at fault the moment he is required to make any new application of it. This, then, is the *first* use of learning the principles of science: it makes men more skilful, expert, and useful in the particular kinds of work by which they are to earn their bread, and by which they are to make it go far and taste well when earned.

But another use of such knowledge to handicraftsmen and common labourers is equally obvious: it gives every man a chance, according to his natural talents, of becoming an improver of the art he works at, and even a discoverer in the sciences connected with it. He is daily handling the tools and materials with which new experiments are to be made; and daily witnessing the operations of nature, whether in the motions and pressures of bodies, or in their chemical actions on each other. All opportunities of making experiments must be unimproved, all appearances must pass unobserved, if he has no knowledge of the principles; but with this knowledge he is more likely than another person to strike out something new which may be useful in art, or curious or interesting in science. Very few great discoveries have been made by chance and by ignorant persons—much fewer than is generally supposed. It is commonly told of the steam-engine that an idle boy being employed to stop and open a valve, saw that he could save himself the trouble of attending and watching it, by fixing a plug upon a part of the machine which came to the place at the proper times, in consequence of the general movement. This is possible, no doubt; though nothing very certain is known respecting the origin of the story; but improvements of any value are very seldom indeed so easily found out, and hardly another instance can be named of important discoveries so purely accidental. They are generally made by persons of competent knowledge, and who are in search of them. The improvements of the Steam-engine by Watt resulted from the most learned investigation of mathematical, mechanical, and chemical truths. Arkwright devoted many years, five at the least, to his invention of Spinning jennies, and he was a man perfectly conversant in every thing that relates to the construction of machinery : he had minutely examined it, and knew the effects of each part, though he had not received any thing like a scientific education. If he had, we should in all probability have been indebted to him for scientific discoveries as well as practical improvements. The most beautiful and useful invention of late times, the Safety-lamp, was the reward of a series of philosophical experiments made by one thoroughly skilled in every branch of chemical science. The new process of Refining sugar, by which more money has been made in a shorter time, and with less risk and trouble, than was ever perhaps gained from an invention, was discovered by a most accomplished chemist,* and was the fruit of a long course of experiments, in the progress of which, known philosophical principles were constantly applied, and one or two new principles ascertained. But in so far as chance has any thing to do with discovery, surely it is worth the while of those who are constantly working in particular employments to obtain the knowledge required, because their chances are greater than other people's of so applying that knowledge as to hit upon new and useful ideas : they are always in the way of perceiving what is wanting, or what is amiss in the old methods; and they have a better chance of making the improvements. In a word, to use a common expression, they are in the way of good luck ; and if they possess the requisite information, they can take advantage of it when it comes to them. This, then, is the *second* great use of learning the sciences : it enables men to make improvements in the arts, and discoveries in philosophy, which may directly benefit themselves and mankind.

Now, these are the *practical* advantages of learning ; but the *third* benefit is, when rightly considered, just as practical as the other two— the pleasure derived from mere knowledge, without any view to our own bodily enjoyments ; and this applies to all classes, the idle as well as the industrious, if, indeed, it be not peculiarly applicable to those who have the inestimable blessing of time at their command. Every man is by nature endowed with the power of gaining knowledge, and the taste for it: the capacity to be pleased with it forms equally a part of the natural constitution of his mind. It is his own fault, or the fault of his education, if he derives no gratification from it. There is a satisfaction in knowing what others know—in not being more ignorant than those we live with : there is a satisfaction in knowing what others do not know—in being more informed than they are. But this is quite independent of the pure pleasure of knowledge—of gratifying a curiosity implanted in us by Providence, to lead us towards the better understanding of the universe in which our lot is cast, and the nature wherewithal we are clothed. That every man is capable of being delighted with extending his information upon matters of science will be evident from a few plain considerations.

Reflect how many parts of the reading, even of persons ignorant of all sciences, refer to matters wholly unconnected with any interest or

* Edward Howard, brother of the Duke of Norfolk.

advantage to be derived from the knowledge acquired. Every one is amused with reading a story: a romance may please some, and a fairy tale may entertain others; but no benefit beyond the amusement is derived from this source: the imagination is gratified; and we willingly spend a good deal of time and a little money in this gratification, rather than in rest after fatigue, or in any other bodily indulgence. So we read a newspaper, without any view to the advantage we are to gain from learning the news, but because it interests and amuses us to know what is passing. One object, no doubt, is to become acquainted with matters relating to the welfare of the country; but we read the occurrences which do little or not at all regard the public interests, and we take a pleasure in reading them. Accidents, adventures, anecdotes, crimes, and a variety of other things amuse us, independent of the information respecting public affairs, in which we feel interested as citizens of the state, or as members of a particular body. It is of little importance to inquire how and why these things excite our attention, and wherefore the reading about them is a pleasure: the fact is certain; and it proves clearly that there is a positive enjoyment in knowing what we did not know before; and this pleasure is greatly increased when the information is such as excites our surprise, wonder, or admiration. Most persons who take delight in reading tales of ghosts, which they know to be false, and feel all the while to be silly in the extreme, are merely gratified, or rather occupied, with the strong emotions of horror excited by the momentary belief, for it can only last an instant. Such reading is a degrading waste of precious time, and has even a bad effect upon the feelings and the judgment. But true stories of horrid crimes, as murders, and pitiable misfortunes, as shipwrecks, are not much more instructive. It may be better to read these than to sit yawning and idle—much better than to sit drinking or gaming, which, when carried to the least excess, are crimes in themselves, and the fruitful parents of many more. But this is nearly as much as can be said for such vain and unprofitable reading. If it be a pleasure to gratify curiosity, to know what we were ignorant of, to have our feelings of wonder called forth, how pure a delight of this very kind does Natural Science hold out to its students? Recollect some of the extraordinary discoveries of Mechanical Philosophy. How wonderful are the laws that regulate the motions of fluids! Is there any thing in all the idle books of tales and horrors more truly astonishing than the fact, that a few pounds of water may, by mere pressure, without any machinery, by merely being placed in a particular way, produce an irresistible force? What can be more strange, than that an ounce weight should balance hundreds of pounds, by the intervention of a few bars of thin iron? Observe the extraordinary truths which Optical Science discloses. Can any thing surprise us more, than to find that the colour of white is a mixture of all others—that red, and blue, and green, and all the rest, merely by being blended in certain proportions, form what we had fancied rather to be no colour at all, than all colours together? Chemistry is not behind in its wonders. That the diamond should be made of the same material with coal; that water should be chiefly composed of an inflammable substance; that acids should be almost all formed of different kinds of air, and that one of those acids, whose strength can dissolve almost any of the metals, should be made of the self-same ingredients with the common air we breathe; that salts should be of a metallic nature and composed, in great part, of metals, fluid like quicksilver, but lighter than water, and which, without any heating, take fire upon being exposed to the air, and, by burning, form the substance so abounding in saltpetre and in the ashes of burnt wood: these, surely, are things to excite the wonder of any reflecting mind—nay, of any one but little accustomed to reflect. And yet these are trifling when compared to the prodigies which Astronomy opens to our view: the enormous masses of the heavenly bodies; their immense distances; their countless numbers, and their motions, whose swiftness mocks the uttermost efforts of the imagination.

Akin to this pleasure of contemplating new and extraordinary truths, is the gratification of a more learned curiosity, by tracing resemblances and relations between things, which, to common apprehension, seem widely different. Mathematical science to thinking minds affords this pleasure in a high degree. It is agreeable to know that the three angles of every triangle, whatever be its size, howsoever its sides may be inclined to each other, are always of necessity, when taken together, the same in amount: that any regular kind of figure whatever, upon the one side of a right-angled triangle, is equal to the two figures of the same kind upon the two other sides, whatever be the size of the triangle: that the properties of an oval curve are extremely similar to those of a curve, which appears the least like it of any, consisting of two branches of infinite extent, with their backs turned to each other. To trace such unexpected resemblances is, indeed, the object of all philosophy; and experimental science in particular is occupied with such investigations, giving us general views, and enabling us to explain the appearances of nature, that is, to show how one appearance is connected with another. But we are now only considering the gratification derived from learning these things. It is surely a satisfaction, for instance, to know that the same thing, or motion, or whatever it is, which causes the sensation of heat, causes also fluidity, and expands bodies in all directions; that electricity, the light which is seen on the back of a cat when slightly rubbed on a frosty evening, is the very same matter with the lightning of the clouds;—that plants breathe like ourselves, but differently by day and by night;—that the air which burns in our lamps enables a balloon to mount, and causes the globules of the dust of plants to rise, float through the air, and continue their race;—in a word, is the immediate cause of vegetation. Nothing can at first view appear less like, or less likely to be caused by the same thing, than the processes of burning and of breathing,—the rust of metals and burning,—an acid and rust,—the influence of a plant on the air it grows in by night, and of an animal on the same air at any time, nay, and of a body burning in that air; and yet all these are the same operation. It is an undeniable fact, that the very same thing which makes the fire burn, makes metals rust, forms acids, and causes plants and animals to breathe;

that these operations, so unlike to common eyes, when examined by the light of science, are the same,—the rusting of metals,—the formation of acids,—the burning of inflammable bodies,—the breathing of animals,—and the growth of plants by night. To know this is a positive gratification. Is it not pleasing to find the same substance in various situations extremely unlike each other;—to meet with fixed air as the produce of burning,—of breathing,—and of vegetation;— to find that it is the choak-damp of mines,—the bad air in the grotto at Naples,—the cause of death in neglected brewers' vats,—and of the brisk and acid flavour of Seltzer and other mineral springs? Nothing can be less like than the working of a vast steam-engine, and the crawling of a fly upon the window. We find that these two operations are performed by the same means, the weight of the atmosphere, and that a sea-horse climbs the ice-hills by no other power. Can any thing be more strange to contemplate? Is there in all the fairy tales that ever were fancied any thing more calculated to arrest the attention and to occupy and to gratify the mind, than this most unexpected resemblance between things so unlike to the eyes of ordinary beholders? What more pleasing occupation than to see uncovered and bared before our eyes the very instrument and the process by which nature works? Then we raise our views to the structure of the heavens; and are again gratified with tracing accurate but most unexpected resemblances. Is it not in the highest degree interesting to find, that the power which keeps this earth in its shape, and in its path, wheeling round the sun, extends over all the other worlds that compose the universe, and gives to each its proper place and motion; that this same power keeps the moon in her path round our earth, and our earth in its path round the sun, and each planet in its path; that the same power causes the tides upon our earth, and the peculiar form of the earth itself; and that, after all, it is the same power which makes a stone fall to the ground? To learn these things, and to reflect upon them, fills the mind, and produces certain as well as pure gratification.

But if the knowledge of the doctrines unfolded by science is pleasing, so is the being able to trace the steps by which those doctrines are investigated, and their truth demonstrated: indeed you cannot be said, in any sense of the word, to have learnt them, or to know them, if you have not so studied them as to perceive how they are proved. Without this you never can expect to remember them long, or to understand them accurately; and that would of itself be reason enough for examining closely the grounds they rest on. But there is the highest gratification of all, in being able to see distinctly those grounds, so as to be satisfied that a belief in the doctrines is well founded. Hence to follow a demonstration of a grand mathematical truth—to perceive how clearly and how inevitably one step succeeds another, and how the whole steps lead to the conclusion—to observe how certainly and unerringly the reasoning goes on from things perfectly self-evident, and by the smallest addition at each step, every one being as easily taken after the one before, as the first step of all was, and yet the result being something not only far from self-evident, but so general and strange, that you can hardly believe it to be true, and are only convinced of it by going over the whole reasoning—this operation of the understanding, to those who so exercise themselves, always affords the highest delight. The contemplation of experimental inquiries, and the examination of reasoning founded upon the facts which our experiments and observations disclose, is another fruitful source of enjoyment, and no other means can be devised for either imprinting the results upon our memory, or enabling us really to enjoy the whole pleasures of science. They who found the study of some branches dry and tedious at the first, have generally become more and more interested as they went on; each difficulty overcome gives an additional relish to the pursuit, and makes us feel, as it were, that we have by our work and labour established a right of property in the subject. Let any man pass an evening in listless idleness, or even in reading some silly tale, and compare the state of his mind when he goes to sleep or gets up next morning with its state some other day when he has passed a few hours in going through the proofs, by facts and reasoning, of some of the great doctrines in Natural Science, learning truths wholly new to him, and satisfying himself by careful examination of the grounds on which known truths rest, so as to be not only acquainted with the doctrines themselves, but able to show why he believes them, and to prove before others that they are true—he will find as great a difference as can exist in the same being; the difference between looking back upon time unprofitably wasted, and time spent in self-improvement: he will feel himself in the one case listless and dissatisfied, in the other comfortable and happy; in the one case, if he do not appear to himself humbled, at least he will not have earned any claim to his own respect; in the other case, he will enjoy a proud consciousness of having, by his own exertions, become a wiser and therefore a more exalted creature.

To pass our time in the study of the sciences, in learning what others have discovered, and in extending the bounds of human knowledge, has, in all ages, been reckoned the most dignified and happy of human occupations; and the name of Philosopher, or Lover of Wisdom, is given to those who lead such a life. But it is by no means necessary that a man should do nothing else than study known truths, and explore new, in order to earn this high title. Some of the greatest philosophers, in all ages, have been engaged in the pursuits of active life; and an assiduous devotion of the bulk of our time to the work which our condition requires, is an important duty, and indicates the possession of practical wisdom. This, however, does by no means hinder us from applying the rest of our time, beside what nature requires for meals and rest, to the study of science; and he who, in whatever station his lot may be cast, works his day's work, and improves his mind in the evening, as well as he who, placed above such necessity, prefers the refined and elevating pleasures of knowledge to the low gratification of the senses, richly deserves the name of a True Philosopher.

One of the most gratifying treats which science affords us is the knowledge of the extraordinary powers with which the human mind is endowed. No man, until he has studied philosophy, can have a just idea of the great things for which Providence has fitted his understanding, the extraordinary disproportion which there is between his natural strength and the powers of his mind, and the force which he derives from those powers. When we survey the marvellous truths of Astronomy, we are first of all lost in the feeling of immense space, and of the comparative insignificance of this globe and its inhabitants. But there soon arises a sense of gratification and of new wonder at perceiving how so insignificant a creature has been able to reach such a knowledge of the unbounded system of the universe—to penetrate, as it were, through all space, and become familiar with the laws of nature at distances so enormous as baffle our imagination—to be able to say, not merely that the Sun has 329,630 times the quantity of matter which our globe has, Jupiter $308\frac{9}{10}$, and Saturn $93\frac{1}{2}$ times; but that a pound of lead weighs at the Sun 22 lbs. 15 ozs. 16 dwts. 8 grs. and $\frac{3}{4}$ of a grain; at Jupiter 2 lbs. 1 oz. 19 dwts. 1 gr. $\frac{29}{43}$; and at Saturn 1 lb. 3 ozs. 8 dwts. 20 grs. $\frac{1}{11}$ part of a grain; and what is far more wonderful, to discover the laws by which the whole of this vast system is held together and maintained through countless ages in perfect security and order. It is surely no mean reward of our labour to become acquainted with the prodigious genius of those who have almost exalted the nature of man above its destined sphere; and, admitted to a fellowship with those loftier minds, to know how it comes to pass that by universal consent they hold a station apart, rising over all the Great Teachers of mankind, and spoken of reverently, as if NEWTON and LAPLACE were not the names of mortal men.

The highest of all our gratifications in the contemplations of science remains: we are raised by them to an understanding of the infinite wisdom and goodness which the Creator has displayed in all his works. Not a step can we take in any direction without perceiving the most extraordinary traces of design; and the skill everywhere conspicuous is calculated in so vast a proportion of instances to promote the happiness of living creatures, and especially of ourselves, that we can feel no hesitation in concluding, that if we knew the whole scheme of Providence, every part would be in harmony with a plan of absolute benevolence. Independently, however, of this most consoling inference, the delight is inexpressible of being able to follow, as it were, with our eyes, the marvellous works of the Great Architect of Nature, to trace the unbounded power and exquisite skill which are exhibited in the most minute, as well as the mightiest parts of his system. The pleasure derived from this study is unceasing, and so various, that it never tires the appetite. But it is unlike the low gratifications of sense in another respect: it elevates and refines our nature, while those hurt the health, debase the understanding, and corrupt the feelings; it teaches us to look upon all earthly objects as insignificant, and below our notice, except the pursuit of knowledge and the cultivation of virtue—that is to say, the strict performance of our duty in every relation of society; and it gives a dignity and importance to the enjoyment of life, which the frivolous and the grovelling cannot even comprehend.

Let us, then, conclude, that the pleasures of Science go hand in hand with the solid benefits derived from it; that they tend, unlike other gratifications, not only to make our lives more agreeable, but better; and that a rational being is bound by every motive of interest and of duty, to direct his mind towards pursuits which are found to be the sure path of virtue as well as of happiness.

MECHANICS.

TREATISE I.

ON THE MECHANICAL AGENTS OR FIRST MOVERS.

CHAPTER I.—*Introduction.*

(1.) WHATEVER communicates or tends to communicate motion to a body, is called a *force*. The object of MECHANICS, in the most extended sense of that term, is the investigation of the effects of forces on bodies.

If a body which is absolutely at rest be submitted to the action of two or more forces, one of two effects must ensue; either the body must continue in its state of rest, or it must commence to move in some determinate direction, and with some determinate force. If the body continue at rest, it necessarily follows, that the forces which act upon it are so related as to their directions and intensities, that they neutralise each other, or mutually destroy each other's effects. Under such circumstances, the body is said to be in a state of *equilibrium*,* and we also commonly apply the same term *equilibrium* to the forces which act upon the body.

It is, therefore, a very important problem, or rather class of problems, to assign in every particular case that relation between the intensities and directions of the forces acting upon a body under given circumstances, which will keep the body in a state of equilibrium. By the solution of such a problem, we shall always be able to predict whether a body urged by given forces shall receive any motion or not.

If the forces which act upon the body be not so related as to neutralise each other's effects, motion must ensue, and the body will be urged with some determinate force in some determinate direction. To assign the force with which the body will thus be moved, and the direction of its motion, the intensities and directions of the forces impressed on the body being given, is another important class of problems, and of a nature altogether distinct from the former.

(2.) These considerations suggest the division of the science into two parts. In the first, which is called *statics*,* bodies are considered as submitted to the influence of forces which are in equilibrium.

(3.) In the second part, which is called *dynamics*,† bodies are considered as submitted to the action of forces which are not in equilibrium. In the former, therefore, bodies are considered at rest, and in the latter as in motion.

(4.) Although this be unquestionably the most philosophical division of the subject, and that which should be adopted in a treatise designed for the use of certain classes of students; yet, considering the objects which we have in view in the present series of works, and the persons for whose instruction they are intended, we think it expedient to pursue a different course, and do not hesitate to sacrifice system to utility.

In all the various changes which the raw productions of nature must undergo in order to adapt them to supply the wants of civilized life, *motion* is the principal agent. The wool which is shorn from the sheep, requires a rotatory motion to form it into threads. These threads must be submitted to a variety of other motions, in order to produce that arrangement which gives them the form of cloth; and cloth when woven must pass through many other processes, in all of which motion is the chief agent, before it is prepared for use. To obtain these motions, we avail ourselves of the forces which we find actually existing in nature, such as the falling of water, the force of wind, the strength of animals, and numerous others. As, however, the forces and motions which are required for the various manufactures, are generally different in many respects from those forces with which nature has supplied us, it is

---

* *Equilibrium* is originally a Latin word signifying *balance*, the forces, as it were, balancing each other.

* From a Greek word στατος, *statos*, signifying *standing still*.
† From the Greek word δυναμις, *dunamis*, signifying *force*.

necessary that means should be contrived of modifying them so as to suit them to our wants. It may so happen that we have at our command a natural force of variable intensity, when it is necessary to apply to the work which we design to execute one of a perfectly uniform intensity. We are, therefore, compelled to contrive some means by which, in transmitting the force from the natural mechanical agent, whatever it be, to the working point, it may be so modified as to be rendered uniform in its action. Again, the natural force may act constantly in one direction, as for example, a running stream, or a perpendicular fall of water, or a current of air, when it may be required that the force on the working point should be alternate or reciprocating, as for example, that which is necessary to work the piston of a common pump. In such cases, therefore, some apparatus must be interposed between the natural agent and the working point, which is capable of converting the one species of motion into the other. Such a contrivance is called a *machine*, and the natural force which it is designed to modify is called its *first mover*; that part of the machine at which the required modification is produced, being generally called the *working point*.

In that part of Mechanics which is confined to the consideration of the nature and principles of machinery, there are two objects intimately related each to the other, and each of which strongly demands our attention; first, the natural *mechanical agents* or *first movers*; secondly, *machines*, or the means whereby these powers are modified and rendered applicable to our purposes. We propose in this *first* treatise to confine the attention of the reader to the explanation of the nature and laws of those powers in nature which furnish first movers, and to the properties of motion and force in general. In conformity with this method, we shall devote the *second treatise* to the *elements of machinery*.

CHAPTER II.—*On the composition and resolution of Motion and Force.*

(5.) IF two equal forces act upon the same point of a body, in directions immediately opposite, they will keep that body at rest. Such forces, then, are the most simple example of equilibrium, and the truth of this principle is self-evident.

Thus, if to a point P two threads be attached, and that two wheels C D, turning on fixed centres, and having grooves on their edges, be so placed that when the strings are passed over them the parts P C and P D shall be in the same straight line, equal weights A and B suspended from the strings will draw the point P equally in the opposite directions P C and P D, and they will thus evidently neutralise each other, and the body P will be in equilibrium.

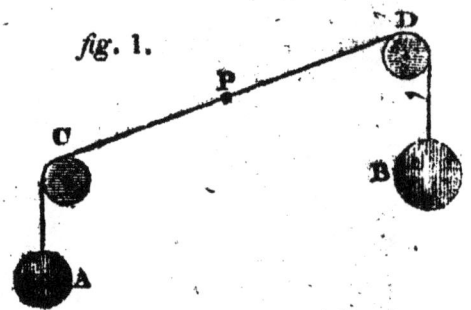

fig. 1.

(6.) But now let us suppose that the weight B is greater than the weight A. In that case the point P will be drawn in the direction P D with a greater force than that which draws it in the opposite direction P C, and it will evidently have a tendency to move in the direction P D. But what tendency? To what amount, or, in other words, with what force is P pulled in the direction P D? This is easily determined. Suppose that the weight B is divided into two parts, one of which is equal to A; the other part will be evidently equal to the difference of the weights A and B, or to the excess of the weight B above the weight A. Call this excess E, and let the apparatus assume the form *fig.* 2. Now, it appears

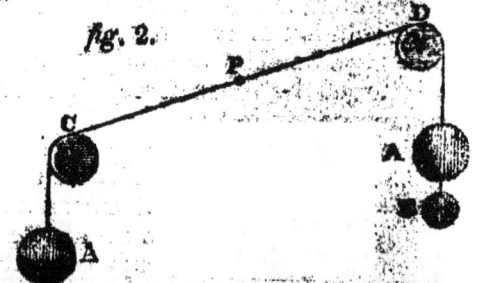

fig. 2.

by (5.), that the weight A acting in direction P C, exactly balances weight A acting in the direction P so that the combined effect of t weights is nothing. The consequ is, that the point P is pulled in direction P D only by the force E the excess of the greater weigh above the lesser weight A.

Hence we may, in general, infer,

when a body is drawn in directions immediately opposite by two unequal forces, it is affected exactly in the same manner as if it were drawn by a single force equal to the difference between the two forces, and acting in the direction of the greater force.

(7.) This single force, whose action is equivalent to the combined action of two or more forces, is called their *resultant*; and the process by which a single force equivalent in its effect to two or more other forces is found, is called the *composition of force*.

(8.) On the other hand, two or more forces may be found whose combined effects are equivalent to that of a single given force; the process by which these are determined is called *the resolution of force*; and the two or more forces which are equivalent to the single force, are called its *components*.

(9.) Having considered the simpler instance in which the directions of the forces are in the same straight line, let us now examine the more complex case in which two forces act on the same

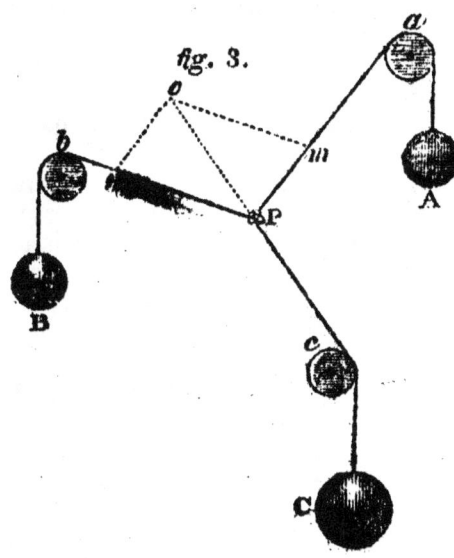

fig. 3.

point in different directions. Let P (*fig.* 3.) be a fixed point to which three strings are attached; and let the strings P*a* and P*b* be passed over fixed grooved wheels as before, and let any weights A and B be suspended from them. The point P is now drawn by two forces A and B, in the directions P*a* and P*b*. The question is, what single force would produce the same effect upon it? Take lengths P*m* and P*n* on the strings, so that they shall be in the same proportion as the weights A and B, that is, so that P*m* : P*n* :: A : B; and upon the board to which the wheels *a*, *b* are supposed to be attached, draw the parallelogram P*m o n*. Draw the diagonal P*o*. A single force acting in the direction of the diagonal P*o*, and having the same ratio to the weight A or B as the diagonal P*o* has to the side P*m* or P*n* of the parallelogram, will produce the same pressure on the point P as the combined actions of A and B produced. To prove this, let a third wheel *c* be so placed that the thread P*c* shall, when stretched over it, be in a direction immediately opposite to P*o*, and suspend from it a weight C which shall have the same proportion to A or B as the diagonal P*o* has to P*m* or P*n*. If the point P, hitherto supposed to be fixed, be disengaged and left free to move, it will be found to maintain its position and remain at rest. Hence it follows, that the weight C neutralises the effects of A and B, and keeps them in equilibrium. But it would also keep in equilibrium a force equal to C in the direction P*o* (5.); from whence it follows, that a force equal to C in the direction P*o* is equivalent to the united actions of the forces A and B, in the directions P*m* and P*n*. Hence we derive the following important theorem:*—

If two forces acting on the same point in the directions of the sides of a parallelogram be proportional in their intensities to these sides, their united effects will be equivalent to that of a single force acting on the same point in the direction of the diagonal of that parallelogram, and whose intensity is proportional to the diagonal.

This single force in the direction of the diagonal is therefore their resultant.

(10.) It will very easily appear that two forces have but one resultant; for, if the force C be in the least degree altered, either in its magnitude or in its direction, the point P, when disengaged, will no longer maintain its position, but will move until it settles into such a position that the magnitudes of the diagonal and sides of the corresponding parallelogram shall be proportional to those of the forces A B C.

(11.) We can now extend our investigation to the combined action of three or more forces on the same point. Let P, (*fig.* 4.) as before, be a fixed point to which several strings are attached, and

---

* This theorem admits of rigorous demonstration independently of the experimental proof which we have given. The demonstration is, however, of too complex a character, and requiring the aid of mathematical reasoning of a kind which we cannot properly introduce here.

passing these strings over wheels $a\,b\,c\,d$, let weights A B C D be suspended from them.

Take any part Pm on the string Pa, and from m on the board to which the apparatus is attached, draw a line parallel to the string Pb, and take a part mn upon that parallel, such that Pm : mn :: A : B. Again, through n draw a parallel to the string Pc, and on that parallel take a part no, such that mn : no :: B : C. In like manner draw op

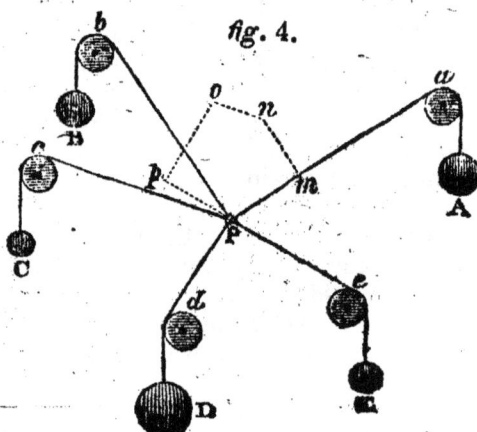

fig. 4.

parallel to Pd, and such that $no:op$ :: C : D. Finally, join the points p and P by a right line. A single force, acting in the direction of the line Pp, and having the same ratio to each of the other forces as the line Pp has to the side of the polygon, which is parallel to that other force, will produce a pressure on the fixed point P equivalent to the combined actions of the forces A B C D. This may be established by the same means as were used in the former case. Let a string, attached to the fixed point P, be carried over a wheel e, so that the string Pe shall be the continuation of the line pP, and let a weight E be suspended from it which shall have the same proportion to the weights A B C D, as the side Pp has to the sides of the polygon parallel to the strings respectively. If the point P be then disengaged from the board, it will be found to maintain its position, and remain at rest; so that the force E in the direction Pe, immediately opposite to Pp, counteracts the combined effects of the forces A B C D; and it would also counteract the effect of a force equal to E, in the direction of the line Pp (5.) Hence such a force is equivalent to the combined effects of A B C D, and is therefore their resultant. From whence we infer the following general theorem:—

If several forces act on the same point parallel and proportional to all the sides of a polygon taken in order except one, a single force proportional to, and in the direction of, that one side will be their resultant.

It may be proved that this is the only resultant, in the same manner as in the former case; for if either the direction of the string Pe, or the magnitude of the weight E, or both, be in any way changed, the point P, when disengaged, will no longer maintain its position, but will move until it settles into that position in which the sides of the corresponding polygon are proportional to the weights suspended from the strings to which they are parallel.

(12.) Hitherto we have supposed that the forces applied to the point are in the same plane. This, however, is not at all necessary, and the same principles exactly will apply when the forces act in different planes.

(13.) It must be evident from the reasoning in the preceding articles, that if any number of forces acting on a point, be proportional to the sides of a polygon which are severally parallel to the direction of the forces, and that the forces are in the directions of the sides, taken successively in the same order, the point will be kept at rest, and the forces will be in equilibrium, and will neutralise each other's effects.

Since any one side of a triangle or polygon is always less than the sum of all the remaining sides, it follows that a mechanical effect will always be more economically produced by a single force acting in the proper direction, than by a number of forces acting in different directions.

(14.) All that we have established respecting the composition of forces or pressures, also applies to the composition of motions. Two impulses, which separately communicated, will cause a body to move over the sides of a parallelogram in the same time, would, if communicated at the same instant, cause the body to move over the diagonal of the parallelogram in that time. This may be submitted to actual experiment.

Let a level table, A B C D (*fig.* 5.), in the form of a parallelogram, be provided, furnished with a ledge to prevent a ball from rolling off; and let two spring guns G G′, be placed at one of the corners A, so that when G strikes the ball X, it shall move along the side A B in a certain time, and that when G' strikes the ball it shall move along AD in the same time. Now, if both the guns strike X at the same instant, it will be found to move along the diagonal, and to do so

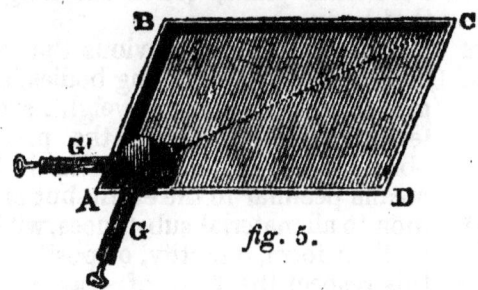

fig. 5.

exactly in the same time as, by the impulse of each gun separately it moved along the sides. In order that the ball X should move along the sides A B and A D in the same time, it is necessary that the force of the springs should be proportional to the lengths of the sides. In constructing such a table it is usual to make it square, and, therefore, to make the springs of equal force.

In like manner, if several impulses, which, communicated separately to a body, would make it move parallel to the several sides of a polygon taken in order, the last side alone excepted, and with velocities proportional to those sides, be communicated to it at the same instant, it will move in the direction of the last side, with a velocity proportional to that side.

There are numerous effects, familiar to every one, which are examples of the composition and resolution of motion. If, in walking along one side of a street, we desire to reach a distant point at the opposite side; the direct method would be to pass in a straight line to the point, moving diagonally across the street; but wishing to be for as short a space as possible off the foot-path, we first pass across the street in a direction perpendicular to the foot-path, and then pass down the opposite side to the desired point. This is, in fact, nothing more than a resolution of the diagonal motion first mentioned into its two components, viz. the sides of the parallelogram.

Again, if a boat be rowed directly across a river, when there is no current, it will pass over in a straight line, perpendicular to the banks. But, if there be a current, the boat will be carried by the current parallel to the banks, while it is impelled by the oars in a direction perpendicular to the banks: the consequence will be, that it will pass across in a diagonal direction, arriving at the other bank not at the point immediately opposite to where it started, but at a point considerably below it: it moves, in fact, in the diagonal of a parallelogram, one side of which is a straight line drawn across the river from the point where it started perpendicular to the banks; and the other side is so much of the bank itself measured from the point where it started as the current moved with the boat down the river in the time taken to cross it. This, therefore, is an example of the composition of motion, as the former was of its resolution.

The facility with which many of the feats of horsemanship exhibited in the circus are performed may be accounted for on this principle. When the man and horse are moving with great speed, it sometimes excites surprise, that when the man leaps directly upward, the horse does not pass from under him, and that he does not, in descending, alight upon the ground perpendicularly under the point at which he sprang from the saddle. But it should be considered, that, on leaving the saddle, the body of the rider has the same velocity as that of the horse: the spring which he takes perpendicularly upward in no degree diminishes this velocity; so that, while he is ascending from the saddle, he is still advancing with the same speed as the horse, and continues so advancing until his return to the saddle. In this case, the body of the rider describes the diagonal of a parallelogram, one side of which is in the direction of the horse's motion, and the other perpendicularly upward, in the direction in which he makes the leap.

In the common feat of jumping through a hoop, and alighting again on the saddle, an inexperienced rider would be likely to project his body forward in the same manner as he would do in leaping through the same hoop from the ground. In such a case, instead of alighting on the saddle, he would alight either before the horse or on his head or neck; for he would, in fact, then advance forward more rapidly than the horse, his body having, besides the speed of the horse, in which it always partakes, the additional speed derived from the muscular exertion by which the rider projects his body forward. All that is requisite to execute this feat is, to leap directly up wards from the saddle, to a sufficient height to clear the lower part of the hoop with the feet. By the speed which the rider has in common with the horse, his body will, without any exertion on his part, pass through the hoop, and he will alight again in the saddle, on the other side, in his descent. These are striking instances of the composition of motion.

Chapter III.—*On the Force of Gravity.*

(15.) ALTHOUGH the force of gravity cannot be considered, properly speaking, as itself a first mover or mechanical agent, yet it is the means of producing and giving effect to so extensive a class of first movers, that it becomes necessary to explain the laws which regulate its action, in order to render the agency of some of the principal first movers intelligible.

The earth which we inhabit is a mass of matter, nearly, but not exactly, of a globular form, the diameter being about 8000 miles in length. This enormous mass possesses the property of attracting towards its centre all smaller bodies placed near its surface; so that if they be perfectly free to move and opposed by no obstacle, they will move in straight lines towards the centre of the globe, and will continue so to move until they reach the surface. If the part of the surface which they meet be solid, or even a liquid specifically heavier than the descending bodies, their further approach to the centre will be obstructed; but in that case the attraction towards the centre will be manifested by the force with which the bodies press upon the resisting surface. If the bodies thus supposed to have met the surface in their approach towards the centre happen to meet a liquid, as the sea, and be specifically heavier than it, they will still continue to approach the centre, moving through the liquid until, in fine, they be stopped either by a liquid heavier than themselves or a hard surface. All lines which are drawn from points without a globe to its centre are evidently perpendicular to its surface; and hence bodies, in moving towards the centre of the earth, attracted by its influence, move perpendicularly to its surface; and when their progress is obstructed by that surface they press on it perpendicularly with a force equal to that with which they are attracted towards the centre.

This attraction which the earth exerts upon all bodies placed near its surface is called *terrestrial gravity:* and the force with which any body drawn towards the centre is pressed upon an horizontal plane, called the *weight* of that body.

It must be very obvious that all the common effects of falling bodies, and of pressures produced by weight, are perfectly accounted for in the preceding observations. This attraction is by no means peculiar to the earth, but is common to all material substances, whatever be their form, quantity, or position. In this respect the force of gravity differs from magnetism, and other attractions which are only resident in substances of particular species. If the earth were a large magnet, those peculiar substances only which are affected by the loadstone would have weight, or would fall to the surface when unsupported. All other bodies would rest indifferently in any position in which they might happen to be placed, and would move upwards just as readily as downwards. But every material substance is susceptible of the attraction of gravity, and what is more, it is susceptible of this in the exact proportion of its mass. Thus, if the mass of the earth were doubled, it would exert a double attraction on all bodies placed near it, and consequently the weights of all bodies would in that case be doubled. If its mass were tripled, the weights of all bodies would be tripled, and so on. In general, therefore, the attraction which the earth exerts on a body in its vicinity is proportional to its mass.

We have stated that gravity is an attraction common to all material substances; if so, then it may be asked why do not the various bodies placed near the earth's surface attract the earth towards them? If a body be disengaged at any height from the surface, it will be drawn by the attraction of the earth, and will consequently descend in a straight line perpendicular to the surface; but since the body attracts the earth, why does not the surface *ascend* towards the body, being drawn by the attraction of the body on the earth; in which case, the surface of the earth and the body would meet at some place intermediate between their first positions? We answer that, in fact, this very effect takes place. The surface of the earth *does* approach the descending body, and that descending body not only attracts the mass of the earth towards it, but attracts it with exactly as much force as that by which the earth attracts the descending body. Why then, it will be asked, is not the rapid approach of the earth to meet the descending body perceptible? To explain this we must go into some details.

(16.) If two bodies A and B be moving with the same velocity, the forces with which they move will be equal provided their masses or quantities of matter be equal, but not otherwise. If the mass of A be greater than the mass of B its force will be greater in the same proportion. This will be very evident if we consider the forces with which they would strike any obstacle opposed to them. If B be a musket-ball and A be a cannon-ball of one hundred times the weight, both being projected with the same speed, A will strike any obstacle with one hundred times the force with which B would strike it. In general, then, "when the velocities with which bodies are moved are the same, their forces are proportional to their masses or quantities of matter."

Now, let us suppose that the masses of the bodies A and B are equal, but that they move with unequal velocities; that is, that they move through different spaces in the same time. Let the space described in one second by the body A be a, and let the space described in the same time by the body B be b; these spaces are called the velocities of the bodies. The equal bodies thus moving with different velocities will move with different forces. It is evident that the body which has the greater velocity will have the greater force; and that also in the same proportion as its velocity is greater. If two equal bullets be successively projected from the same gun, but with different charges of powder, that which is projected by the stronger charge will strike the mark with a proportionally greater force. But in this case the only difference in the motions of the bullets is, that one has a greater velocity than the other. Hence we perceive that "when equal masses are in motion their forces are proportional to their velocities."

(17.) We have thus separately considered the cases in which unequal masses are moved with equal velocities, and in which equal masses are moved unequal velocities; and we have seen that the forces are, in the one case, proportional to the masses, and in the other, to the velocities. Now, if unequal masses be moved with unequal velocities, it is natural to expect that we should, in comparing the forces, take into account both the velocities and the masses. It appears that the moving force of a body may be increased or diminished by increasing or diminishing either its mass, or its velocity, or both. In fact, if the number representing the mass be multiplied by the number representing the velocity, the product thus obtained will represent the moving force. Thus, if the masses of two bodies A and B be in the ratio of the numbers 8 and 5, and the velocities of these bodies be in the ratio of the numbers 7 and 3, their moving forces are as the product of 8 and 7 to the product of 5 and 3, that is, as 56 to 15. It appears, therefore, that in this instance the force of A bears a much higher ratio to the force of B than either the mass of A bears to the mass of B, or the velocity of A to the velocity of B; the reason of which is, that the mass and velocity conspire in imparting to A a superior moving force. In general, then, we conclude, "that the moving forces of bodies are proportional to the products of their masses and their velocities."

(18.) Since then the moving force of a body depends conjointly on its mass and its velocity, it necessarily follows that if, while we increase its velocity in any proportion, we diminish its mass in the same proportion, its moving force will be the same; for it will lose as much force by the diminution of its mass as it gains by the increase of its velocity. In like manner, if, while we increase its mass, we diminish, in the same proportion, its velocity, the moving force will be unaltered; for as much will be lost by the diminished velocity as will be gained by the increased mass.

(19.) The several theorems which we have just expressed, relative to the forces of bodies in motion, do not rest entirely upon reasoning, but may very easily be submitted to the test of actual experiment.

Let two strings be attached to the centre C of a graduated arch X Y; and let two balls A B, formed of clay or any other inelastic substance, be suspended so as to hang in contact at the middle of the arch. Let us first suppose that the balls are equal: if they be separated, moved from the middle of the arch in opposite directions towards its extremities, and permitted to descend from any distance to the lowest point 0, they will, when they meet there, have velocities proportional to the arches through which they have descended.* Now, if the equal balls be permitted to descend through equal arches, they will, therefore, impinge each upon the other with equal velocities; and they will be found, after impact, to remain quiescent, each having destroyed the force of the other. This proves that, when equal masses have equal velocities, they have equal forces; for if their forces were not equal in this case, the united masses would, after impact, move in the direction of that which had the greater force.

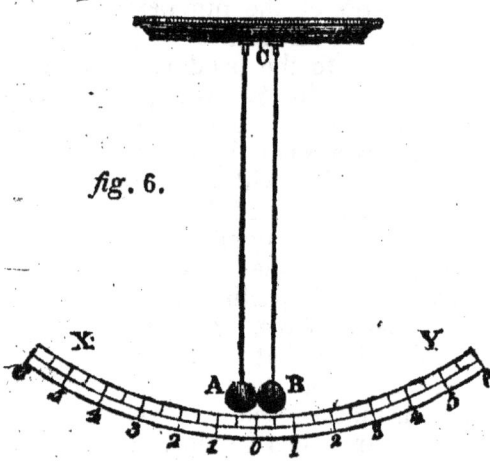

fig. 6.

(20.) Now suppose that the ball A (fig. 6.) is double the weight of the ball B; let A be raised towards X to the division 3, and let B be raised towards Y to the division 6; when allowed to descend from those positions their velocities will be as 3 to 6, but their masses are as 2 to 1, and therefore their forces ought to be as 2×3 to 1×6; that is, as 6 to 6, or equal. We accordingly find, that after impact they will be quiescent; the equal and opposite forces having destroyed each other. In like manner, if balls, whose weights are as 2 to 3, fall from distances which are as 6 and 4, their forces being as 2×6 to 3×4, or as 12 to 12, will be equal, and after impact the united masses will be quiescent.

In the same manner, however the experiment may be varied, it will be found that the product of the numbers

---

* Strictly, the velocities are as the chords of the arches; but as the arches used in this case are small compared with the radius, they may be considered to be nearly proportional to their chords. It is another property of this apparatus, that, from whatever distance from the middle of the arch the balls fall, they will arrive at the middle in the same time. This, however, like the property just mentioned, is only true when the arches used are small compared with the radius.

representing the mass and velocity always truly represents the moving force.

(21.) To return, then, to the case of the earth and a body near its surface, they attract each other with equal forces; and, therefore, in their consequent approach to each other, the earth must have a velocity as many times less than that of the falling body, as the mass of the earth is greater than that of the falling body. Since all bodies which can be submitted to these circumstances must be infinitely smaller than the earth, the space through which the earth approaches them in their fall must be infinitely smaller than the space which they fall through.

To take a very improbable and extreme case: suppose a ball of earth of a diameter equal to the tenth part of a mile were to be placed at an height above the surface equal to the tenth part of a mile; let us consider what space the earth would move through to meet it. The earth's diameter being about 8000 miles, and spheres being as the cubes of their diameters, the mass of the earth would have to the mass of the ball the ratio of 512,000,000,000,000 to 1; consequently, if the tenth part of a mile were divided into 512 millions of millions of equal parts, one of these parts would be pretty nearly the space through which the earth would move towards the falling body. In the tenth part of a mile there are somewhat less than 6400 inches: if this were divided into 512 millions of millions of parts, each part would be the eighty millionth part of an inch; it is therefore through a space less than this that the earth would move, under the circumstances which we have supposed.

It is, therefore, quite evident that, with respect to falling bodies, the earth is to be considered at rest.

(22.) We have stated that bodies attract each other in proportion to their quantities of matter. Hence the earth attracts different bodies with different forces. A piece of lead contains a considerably greater quantity of matter in the same bulk than a piece of cork, and accordingly we find that the earth attracts it with a proportionally greater force; in other words, it has greater weight. It is for this reason that *weight* is justly assumed as the measure, or exponent of the quantity of matter in any substance, whatever, in other respects, be the species or qualities of that substance.

(23.) But it is not *alone* the masses of

bodies which determine their mutual attractions. Their distances from each other affect this force. It is found that the force of attraction decreases as the distance is increased, but in a still greater proportion. Thus, for example, a body placed upon the surface of the earth, at the distance of 4000 miles from its centre, is attracted with a certain force towards that centre. At double that distance, or at 4000 above the surface, it would be only attracted with the fourth part of that force, and it would, in fact, lose three-fourths of its weight.

We shall not, however, pursue this investigation further, since it more properly belongs to another department of the science. The motions to which we shall have to call the attention of the student, all take place upon the surface of the earth, or so near it that the change in the intensity of the force of gravity arising from the difference of distance is altogether insignificant. We shall, therefore, consider gravity as a uniform force, that is, as an attraction which affects the same body in the same degree, whatever its position may be, and which affects equal bodies equally.

(24.) The earth being globular, or nearly so, it follows, that the lines in which its attraction acts converge towards its centre, and that at different parts of the earth the lines in which falling bodies descend are not parallel, but are such as, if continued, would intersect at the centre. In considering, however, the action of gravity on bodies, at places not far distant on the surface of the earth; we may assume, without sensible error, that the directions in which it acts are parallel, and that they are all perpendicular to the same horizontal plane. A distance so great as one mile will only produce a deviation from parallelism amounting to less than one minute, or the sixtieth part of a degree.

(25.) If a body be put in motion by an impulse, the consequence would be, that it would continually move in the direction of that impulse, with the same uniform velocity with which it commenced its motion, provided that it were free from resistances, such as those of friction, air, &c. The force of gravity, or any other attraction, differs essentially from an impulse. An impulse acts instantaneously, and produces all its effect at once, and time does not change that effect. On the other hand, attraction, such as gravity, requires *time* to produce any effect at all, and the effect produced increases exactly in the same ratio as the time of producing it. When a body, suspended at any height above the surface of the earth, is first disengaged, it commences to move with an infinitely small velocity, but, by the continual action of the attraction of the earth, that velocity is increased, and is constantly increasing during the descent of the body. This peculiar species of motion is therefore called *accelerated motion*, and the force which produces it is called an *accelerating force*.

(26.) To explain the uniformity of the attraction of the earth upon a falling body, let us suppose that, at the end of the first second of the fall, the body has received a certain velocity. At the end of the first two seconds it will be found to have received twice that velocity; at the end of the first three seconds, three times that velocity, and so on, the velocity continually increasing, and in the same ratio, as the time from the commencement of the descent increases.

There will, therefore, be no difficulty in calculating arithmetically the velocity which a falling body will acquire in any time from the commencement of its fall. Let g express the velocity which it would acquire in one second, and let T be the number of seconds from the commencement of its fall, and V be the velocity acquired. From what we have stated, it must be evident that V is as many times g as there are seconds in T. Hence, expressing this algebraically, we have $V = g T$.

(27.) We have stated that the earth's attraction acts on all bodies in proportion to their quantities of matter; in fact, it would seem that it impressed a separate force upon each particle of a body, and equal forces on all the particles. Thus, if it impress a certain force on a solid body, that force is made up of the forces which it impresses on all its several parts, so that if the solid body be broken into small pieces, each piece will be attracted as strongly by gravity as it was when united in one solid mass with the other pieces. From this a very remarkable, and, apparently, false consequence follows: viz. that all bodies whatever, large and small, heavy and light, must descend with the same speed. We know, however, that under ordinary circumstances, a feather and a piece of gold will not fall with the same speed; and we know further, that some bodies, an inflated balloon for example, will, instead of falling, actually rise.

These examples appear to contradict the conclusion to which our reasoning has conducted us, but they *only* appear to do so. It is perfectly true, that gravity, as far as its attraction is concerned, accelerates the descent of all bodies equally; but when bodies fall under ordinary circumstances, another force opposed to gravity is produced, which is the resistance of the air on the surface of the descending body. Now this resistance, unlike the force of gravity, is *not* proportional to the weight or quantity of matter in the body, but depends on the surface which the body happens to oppose to the air. A feather exposes, in proportion to its weight, a much greater surface to the air than a piece of gold does, and therefore suffers a much greater resistance to its descent. That it is the weight of the air prevents the descent, and causes the ascent of the balloon, will be seen by reference to the sixth chapter of our treatise on Pneumatics, art. (51.)

(28.) It may, however, be satisfactory to establish, by immediate experiment, the theorem that gravity, acting independently of other forces, causes all bodies to descend with the same velocity.

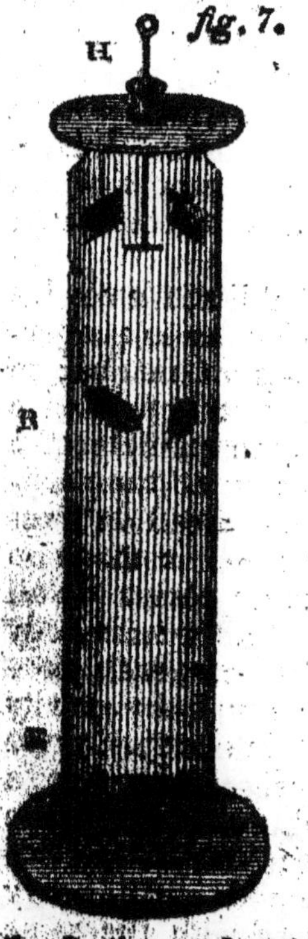

fig. 7.

On the plate E (*fig.* 7.) of the air pump, place a tall glass receiver R, open at the top. On the top place a brass cover, fitting it air-tight. Through this cover let a wire pass, air-tight also, and bearing a small stage, on which a feather and a piece of metal are placed, the stage being so contrived as to fall when the wire is turned by the hand at H. This being arranged, let the receiver be exhausted by the pump, which having been effected, turn the wire at H, so as to let the stage, on which the feather and metal are placed, fall. It will be found that the feather and metal strike the pump plate E at the same instant.* If we could construct a small balloon of materials strong enough to resist the elastic force of the gas, which would tend to burst it when placed in the exhausted receiver, we should find not only that it would not remain at the top, but that it would fall as rapidly as a piece of lead.

(29.) Having shown that the velocity acquired by a falling body is proportional to the time, it is natural to inquire whether any rule can be obtained by which we may compute the spaces through which a body will fall in any given time. Such a rule may be easily derived by mathematical reasoning from the rule already given for the velocity, but the reasoning cannot be properly introduced here.* The rule itself, however, is easily understood. If a falling body descend through a certain space in the first second of its fall, it will descend through four times that space in the first two seconds, nine times that space in the first three seconds, sixteen times that space in the first four seconds; and in general, to find the space it will fall through in any given number of seconds, multiply the space through which it falls in one second by the square† of the number of seconds in the time of the fall.

Thus if m be the space through which a body would fall in one second, $m\,T^2$ is the space through which it will fall in the number of seconds expressed by T; and if S be this space, we have $S = m\,T^2$. We, therefore, commonly say, that the spaces through which a body falls, are as the squares of the times from the beginning of its fall.

(30.) We shall find the space through which a body falls in the second *second* of its descent, by subtracting the space fallen through in the first second from that fallen through in the first two seconds. The former being expressed by m, the latter is $4\,m$ and the difference is $3\,m$. Again, the space it falls through in the third second will be found by subtracting the space described in the first two seconds which is $4\,m$, from that described in the first three seconds which is $9\,m$, and the difference $5\,m$ is the space described in the third second. In the same way we shall find that $7\,m$, $9\,m$, $11\,m$, &c. are the spaces which it

* This experiment is called the "guinea and feather experiment," a guinea having been commonly used for the piece of metal.

* Let S be the space described by the falling body. $V = \frac{dS}{dT} = gT$. Hence, $dS = gT\,dT$, which being integrated gives $S = \frac{1}{2} g . T^2$.

† The square of a number is the number found by multiplying the proposed number by itself, thus 2×2 or 4 is the square of 2, 3×3 or 9 is the square of three, and so on.

falls through in the fourth, fifth, sixth seconds, &c. respectively. The spaces, therefore, through which a body falls in the successive seconds, or any other equal portions of time, are as the odd integers, 1, 3, 5, 7, &c.

(31.) From these investigations it appears, that the calculation of the velocity which a falling body acquires in any given time, depends on that which it acquires in one second, which, therefore, it is absolutely necessary to know in order to be able to compute any other velocity. In like manner, in order to be able to compute the space through which a body will fall in any given time, it is necessary to know the space through which a body would fall in one second. The velocity acquired in one second, and the space fallen through in one second, are therefore the fundamental elements of the whole calculation, and are all that are necessary for the computation of the various circumstances attending the phenomena of falling bodies.

(32.) But even these two elements are not independent. If we knew either, we should immediately detect the other. This circumstance arises from a very remarkable relation which is found to subsist between the space through which a body falls in any time, and the velocity which it acquires in that time. If, after a body has fallen by the action of the force of gravity for any time, say one second, the action of the soliciting force were suddenly suspended, what would be the consequence? No further velocity would be communicated to the body, since the cause from which its constant accession of velocity proceeded is suspended; but, on the other hand, the body will not lose that velocity which it has already acquired. It will consequently continue to fall, but instead of descending with an accelerated motion, it will descend with the velocity which it has acquired, continued uniform through the whole of its descent, describing equal spaces in equal times. In this case, it will be found that the space through which it falls in each second after the first will be exactly equal to twice the space through which it fell in the first second by the force of gravity.* Now if the velocity be estimated by the space described uniformly in one second, it will follow that the velocity acquired in one second is equal to twice the space through which a body will fall freely by the action of gravity in one second. Thus the space which we have expressed by m is equal to half of that which we have expressed by g.

(33.) The two formulæ expressing algebraically the relation between the space, time, and the velocity acquired, become therefore $V = g\,T$, $S = \tfrac{1}{2} g\, T^2$, where g represents the velocity acquired in one second; or $V = 2\,m\,T$, $S = m\,T^2$, where m represents the space through which a body falls freely in one second.

The following TABLE exhibits the relation of the spaces, velocities, and times, conformably to the laws which we have just laid down. The space fallen through in the first second is taken as the unit of length:

Seconds from the beginning of the descent.	Velocity acquired at the end of that time.	Space fallen through in that time.	Space fallen through in the last second of the fall.
1	2	1	1
2	4	4	3
3	6	9	5
4	8	16	7
5	10	25	9
6	12	36	11
7	14	49	13
8	16	64	15

and, in the same manner, the table might be continued to any extent.

(34.) To submit the several laws which we have now explained, as governing the descent of heavy bodies, to direct experiment, would be attended with considerable difficulties. A body will fall, in a single second, through the height of about sixteen perpendicular feet.* In two seconds it will therefore fall through sixty-four feet; and in four seconds through about 256 feet. Thus if our experiments are limited to four seconds, it would be necessary that we should command an height of 256 feet. But further; in observing the velocity, considerable difficulty would arise from its magnitude. The velocity acquired in one second would be one of 32 feet per second; and, therefore, the velocity acquired in four

---

* By art. (26.) we found $V = g\,T$; and in note on art. (29.) we obtained $S = \tfrac{1}{2} g\, T^2$. Eliminating g by these equations, we obtain $S = \tfrac{1}{2} V T$. But $V T$ is the space which would be described with the uniform velocity V in the time T, and is, therefore, twice the space S, through which the body falls in the time T.

* Accurately 16 feet and one inch or 193.09 inches in the latitude of London.

seconds would be 128 feet per second, or 7680 feet per minute.

Independently of these difficulties, the resistance which the atmosphere would offer to such rapid motions, would be so considerable as to produce a great discordance between the effects observed, and the laws which have been laid down on the supposition that all resistances to the free descent of the body are removed.

(35.) Nevertheless, the truth of these laws can be established by the most rigorous experiments; and although the impediments to which we have just alluded cannot be directly removed, they may be evaded. It occurred to Mr. George Attwood, that, if a force of *the same kind* with the force of gravity, but of a much less intensity, could be obtained, the descent of bodies, actuated by such a force, while it would be regulated by the *same laws* as the descent of heavy bodies by the force of gravity, would be so slow that the resistance of the air would produce no sensible effect, and at the same time all the particulars of space, time, and velocity might be deliberately observed, and accurately measured. To realize this conception, he passed a fine silken thread over a groove in the edge of the rim of a wheel which turned freely on an horizontal axle, and from the ends of the thread he suspended equal weights. In this state, the weights were necessarily in equilibrium. To one of the weights he added a small quantity, so as to give it a slight preponderance. It consequently commenced to descend, causing the lighter weight to ascend. Setting aside the effects of the friction of the wheel on which the string connecting the weights rested, the descent of the weight was, in this case, one of uniform acceleration, similar exactly to the descent of a heavy body, but differing in this, that the acceleration might be rendered as slow as might be thought necessary for the purposes of convenient and accurate observation, by diminishing to any degree the preponderancy given to the heavier weight.

(36.) As we have stated that light and heavy bodies are equally accelerated by gravity, it might be supposed, that, since the equal weights first suspended from the thread counterpoise each other, the additional weight suspended from one end should descend with as great velocity as it would have by the immediate action of gravity. This, in fact, would be the case were the force which gravity exerts upon it wholly spent in producing its descent; but it should not be forgotten that the ascent of the weight at the opposite end of the thread is to be accomplished; and since the original weight placed upon the descending end is only sufficient to counterpoise it, it can have no share in raising it. Its elevation, therefore, is entirely effected by the force which gravity impresses on the additional weight placed at the descending end of the string; and all the force thus spent in drawing up the opposite weight is necessarily subtracted from the force with which the additional weight at the descending end falls. The additional weight has also to draw down the descending weight, and to give it as much moving force in its descent as it gives to the ascending weight in its ascent. Hence it follows, that the smaller this additional weight is in comparison with the equal weights originally suspended, the slower will be the rate of its descent.

It still remained, however, to remove the effects of the friction of the wheel, on which the thread connecting the weights turned. Mr. Attwood accomplished this, by an ingenious combination of wheels, called friction-wheels, by which the axle of the wheel carrying the thread, instead of turning in cylindrical holes, rested on the edges of other wheels, by which means, the friction against the inner surface of the holes in which the axle turned, was entirely avoided; and, if all friction was not removed, as far as it affected the motion of the weights, it was so far diminished as to produce no sensible effect upon the motion of the weights in the experiments for which the apparatus was used.

(37.) A representation of this beautiful and useful contrivance is given in *fig.* 8, (and on an enlarged scale in *fig.* 9,) bcd is the rim of the wheel over which the thread sustaining the weights passes. The ends of the axle of this wheel rest upon the rims of two pairs of wheels, as is represented in the figure, and already described. The stand carrying the apparatus is supported by a strong pillar, and immediately under this stand is placed an upright shaft CD, divided to inches, half inches, and tenths, for the purpose of measuring the rate of descent. A and B are two equal cylindrical weights suspended from the ends of the thread, which rests in a groove on the edge of the wheel *b c d*. S is a small stage which can be screwed upon the graduated shaft, at any particular division at which it is designed to stop the descent of the weight. G is a clock, attached to the principal pillar, which beats seconds, in order to mark the rate of descent.

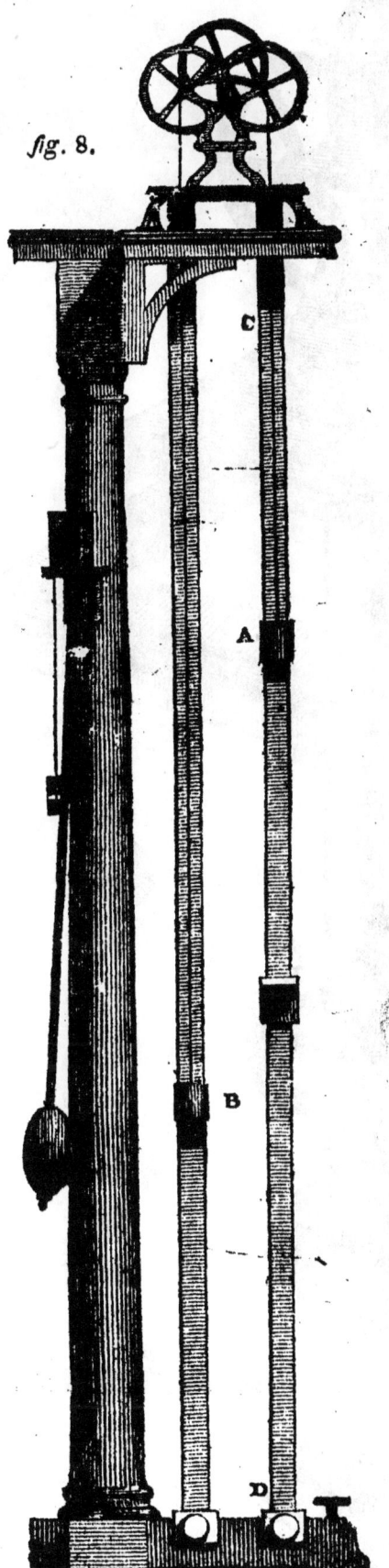

fig. 8.

The weights A B are, commonly, so adjusted, that, by placing on the top of the cylindrical weight A a weight O of a quarter of an ounce, the weight A will descend through three inches in one second. Thus we have obtained an accelerating force, which is sixty-four times less than that of gravity, and yet which retains all the characteristic peculiarities of that force. In fact it is the force of gravity correctly represented in miniature.

(38.) We shall now show how this machine is applied to establish by experiment the laws which regulate the descent of heavy bodies, and which have been already explained.

Ex. 1. To establish these laws by experiment, a ring R is provided, attached to a block E, which can be fixed by a screw to any division of the graduated shaft. A bar of metal *f* is also provided, weighing a quarter of an ounce, and longer than the diameter of the ring R. Let the ring R be fixed by the screw to any division of the scale, and let the stage S be so fixed, that when the weight A rests upon it, the top of the weight will be six inches exactly below the ring R. This done, let the weight A be elevated by drawing down the weight B until the top of the weight A is exactly three inches above the ring R. Holding the weight A in this position, let the bar F be placed upon it, and observing the beats of the clock, let the weight A commence its descent with any beat. It will be found that the stroke of the bar F on the ring R will exactly coincide with the next beat, and that the stroke of the weight A on the stage S will coincide precisely with the succeeding beat. It will be observed that the accelerated motion of the weight A for the first second, and before the bar strikes the ring, is entirely owing to the action of the force of gravity on the bar (36). When the bar is taken off the weight A by the ring at the end of the first second, this cause of acceleration ceases, the action of gravity is suspended, and the weight A moves on to the stage S with the velocity which it

fig. 9.

had acquired at R. Now we have seen that this velocity was such that it moved through six inches in one second.

Ex. 2. Again, let the stage be placed so that when the weight A rests upon it, the top of the weight will be twelve inches from the ring R, and let the weight B be depressed until the top of the weight A is twelve inches above the ring R. This done, let the bar F be placed on the weight A, and let that weight be disengaged at the moment of any beat of the clock; it will be observed that the stroke of the bar F upon the ring R will coincide exactly with the third beat, the descent through twelve inches being made in two seconds, and that the stroke of the weight A upon the stage S will coincide precisely with the fourth beat, the weight moving through the twelve inches below the ring with the velocity it has acquired in two seconds.

Ex. 3. Now let the stage S be once more removed, and placed so that, when the weight A stands upon it, the top of the weight will be eighteen inches below the ring R. Let the weight B be depressed until the top of the weight A is twenty-seven inches above the stage S. Let the bar F be then placed upon the weight A as before, and permitting the weight to commence its descent with the first beat of the pendulum, the bar will strike the ring R with the fourth beat, and the weight A will strike the stage S with the fifth beat. The weight, therefore, descends through twenty-seven inches with an accelerated motion in three seconds, and at the end of that time has acquired such a velocity, as to move through eighteen inches in a second.

(39.) Now let us review the results of these three experiments. By the first it appears, that the velocity acquired in one second is such as to make the weight A move at the rate of six inches per second. By the second experiment it appears, that the velocity acquired in two seconds is twelve inches per second; and by the third experiment it appears, that the velocity acquired in three seconds is eighteen inches per second. Thus the velocities acquired in one, two, and three seconds, are as six, twelve, and eighteen, which numbers are as one, two, and three. Hence the law before explained, that "the velocities acquired are as the time of acquiring them," is verified.

In the first experiment the weight fell through three inches in one second; in the second experiment it fell through twelve inches in two seconds, and in the third it fell through twenty-seven inches in three seconds. Now the numbers three, twelve, and twenty-seven are as one, four and nine, which are the squares of one, two, and three. Hence the law already explained, that "the spaces fallen through are proportional to the squares of the times," is verified.

In the first experiment it was shown that the velocity acquired in falling through three inches, was such as would carry the weight in the same time through six inches when continued uniform and without further increase. In the second experiment it was shown that with the velocity acquired in falling through twelve inches in two seconds, the weight A would move through twelve inches in one second, and it would, therefore, move through twenty-four inches in two seconds. In like manner, in the third experiment, it appeared that with the velocity acquired in falling through twenty-seven inches in three seconds, the weight A moved through eighteen inches in one second; and, therefore, would move through fifty-four inches in three seconds. Each of these experiments, therefore, verifies the law, that, "with the velocity which a body acquires in any time, it would, if that velocity were continued uniform, move through twice that space in the same time."

Also by the first experiment it appeared that the space fallen through in the first *second* of the descent was three inches. By the second experiment it appeared, that the space fallen through in the first two seconds was twelve inches. It consequently follows, that the space fallen through in the second *second* must have been nine inches. By the third experiment the space fallen through in three seconds was twenty-seven inches. Taking from this the space fallen through in the first two seconds, which is twelve inches, the remainder, fifteen inches, is the space fallen through in the third second. Thus the spaces described in the first, second, and third seconds of the fall are three, nine, and fifteen inches respectively, which are as the numbers one, three, and five. This verifies the law before explained, that "the spaces described by a falling body in the successive equal intervals are as the odd integers."

Since the heights from which bodies

fall are proportional to the squares of the times of the fall (29.), and the times themselves are proportional to the velocities (26.), it follows that the heights are proportional to the squares of the velocities. That a body may acquire a double velocity, it is requisite that it should fall from a fourfold height, and so on.

CHAPTER IV.—*On the Centre of Gravity.*

(40.) WE have stated that, at a given place upon the surface of the earth, the force of gravity acts on all bodies in lines which are parallel to each other, and perpendicular to an horizontal, or level plane. When it acts upon a single body, it does not act, as it were, by a single effort, but impresses a separate force upon each particle of the body; and its total effect is composed of the sum of all its effects thus produced upon the particles. Now there is in the body a certain point, at which, if the attraction of gravity impressed a single force, equal in intensity to the sum of all its separate actions on the component parts of the body, the ultimate effect would be the same as it is under the system of separate action which really obtains. This point, the existence of which we shall prove experimentally, is called the *centre of gravity*.

(41.) If the attraction of gravity were confined in its action to one particular point, there are certain effects which would very evidently ensue.

First, if that point were supported or fixed, the body would rest in any position whatever in which it should be placed. For the only cause which we suppose to affect it so as to produce motion, acts upon a point which we suppose fixed.

Secondly. If the body be perfectly free to move, the point on which the attraction acts will commence to move in the direction of that attraction, and in this case will, therefore, commence to move in a line perpendicular to an horizontal plane.

Thirdly. If the body be suspended by any point different from that at which alone the attraction of gravity is supposed to act, it will only remain at rest in two positions, viz. when the attracted point is immediately under or immediately over the point of suspension. If the attracted point be in any other position, the body will move round the point of suspension, all its parts describing circles round that point, until the attracted point settles directly under the point of suspension.

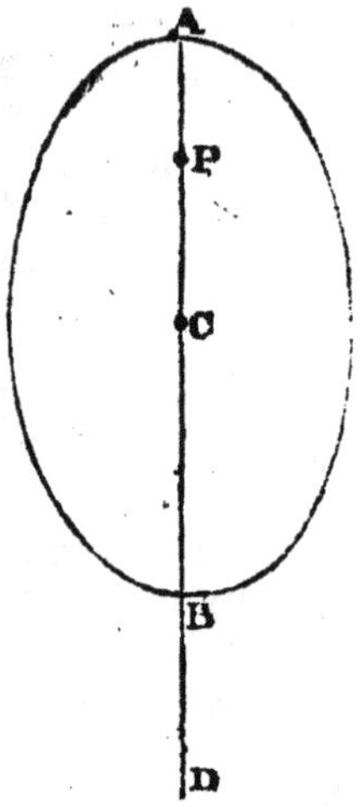

These effects will be evident from a little consideration. Let A B be the body, and P the point at which it is suspended, and round which it is capable of moving. Let C be the point at which the whole attraction of gravity is supposed to act.— First, suppose this point to be placed in a line P D, vertically under the fixed point P. The attraction then acting in the direction of the line C D, will only produce a *pull* on the point P, which will resist it, and no motion will ensue.

fig. 10.

fig. 11.

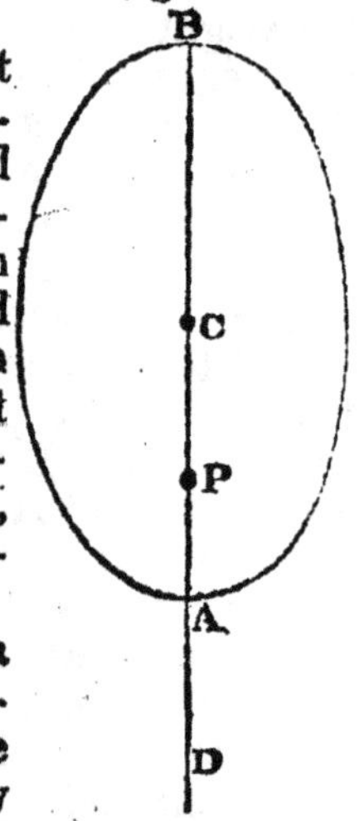

Next, let the point C be in a line vertically *above* the fixed point P. The whole attraction will now act in the direction C D, and will therefore produce a *pressure* on the point P, which will be resisted by that point, and no motion will ensue.

Lastly, let C be in a position neither directly *above* nor *below* the fixed point P. Draw C D′ perpendicular to an horizontal plane, and parallel to C D, and taking

fig. 12.

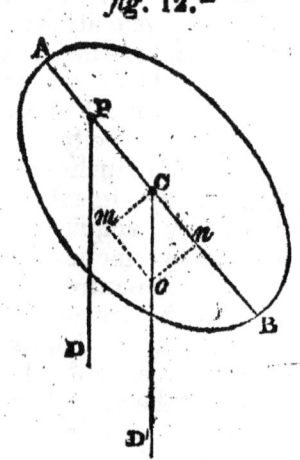

any portion C *o* from C, draw the

parallelogram C n o m, the sides n o and m C being perpendicular to P C B.

By (9.) it appears, that if C o, (*fig.* 13), be taken to represent the whole attraction on the point C, it is equivalent

fig. 13.

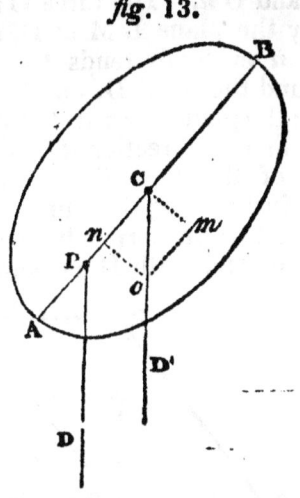

to two separate attractions represented in intensity and direction by the lines C n and C m, and its effect is the same as the united effects of these two would be. Now it is obvious, that a force acting from C, in the direction C n, would have no effect in producing motion, but would be resisted by the fixed point P, against which it would press, while the other force C m, perpendicular to C P, would tend to turn the body round C P, so as to bring the point C to the line P D, directly below the point of suspension P, in which position, after some oscillations, it would rest.

(42.) From this investigation, it follows, that if the parallel actions of the force of gravity on the particles of a body be capable of being represented by an equivalent force, acting at a single point, that point may be determined by the properties which we have just explained. Let a body which is bounded by two parallel planes, be suspended from any point taken at pleasure in it. It will be found that there is but one position in which it will hang steadily at rest, and without swinging. To the point of suspension let a plumb line be attached, and let the line in which it touches the plane surface of the suspended body be marked. Let the body be now suspended from some other point in its plane surface, and let another line be drawn upon it in the direction of the plumb line. This process being applied to any number of different points in the surface of the body, and a number of such lines being drawn upon it in the direction of the plumb line, it will be found that all these lines will intersect each other in the same point. It follows, therefore, that this point has the property mentioned in (41.), of settling itself vertically under the point of suspension when the body is in equilibrium.

Next let the point thus determined be made the point of suspension, and it will be found that the body will rest in any position in which it may be placed, and that it will not, under any circumstances, vibrate or swing.

Again, let the body be suspended by any point different from that which we have here determined, and let it be so placed that this point shall be placed vertically over the point of suspension. It will be found that the body will remain in equilibrium so long as its position is not changed; but upon the least impulse which moves the point in question from its position, it will turn round the point of suspension, and settle, after some vibrations, into the position directly under the point of suspension.

The point, the existence and properties of which are thus established, is then the *centre of gravity*.

In the preceding experiment, we have selected a body bounded by parallel planes, for the purpose of simplifying the experimental process. Strictly speaking, the centre of gravity is not at the intersection of the lines determined by the plumb line on the plane surface, but, if a line be drawn perpendicular to the plane surface through the body, it will be at the middle point of this line.

If we could conveniently pierce the dimensions of a body by straight lines, the centre of gravity of any body, whatever be its figure, could be found experimentally by the same process. If it be successively suspended by several points, and pierced by straight lines, in each case passing in a vertical direction through the point of suspension, it would be found that, however numerous these lines might be, they would all intersect in one point, which would be the centre of gravity of the body.

(43.) By these properties of the *centre of gravity*, mechanical problems respecting the effects of the weights of bodies are susceptible of considerable simplification; for, instead of taking into consideration the separate effects of the attraction of gravitation on the several particles of which a body is composed, it will be

c

sufficient to consider a single force equal to the sum of all these separate attractions, drawing the centre of gravity in a line perpendicular to an horizontal plane, which line is called the *line of direction*. In this line the centre of gravity will always either move, or endeavour to move, and *it will always assume the lowest position which the circumstances under which the body is situated will admit of.*

(44.) If by the application of external force a body be so adjusted, that the centre of gravity be placed in the *highest* position which the circumstances under which the body is situated permit, the body will remain at rest so long as it be perfectly undisturbed; but, as in the case of suspension already mentioned, the slightest disturbance will cause the centre of gravity to descend to the lowest position. Of these two positions in which it is possible for the body to rest, the former is called *instable*, and the latter *stable*, equilibrium.

(45.) If a body be placed upon a plane, its stability will be determined by the position of the *line of direction* with respect to the base.

Let A B C D (*fig.* 14.) be a body resting on the level plane L M. Let O be

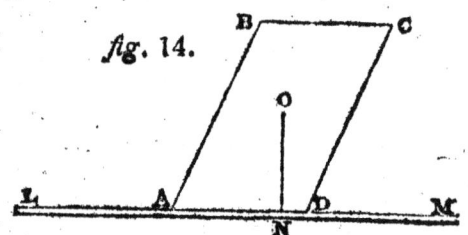

its centre of gravity, and O N the line of direction falling within the base A D. Since the whole force which gravity exerts upon the body may be conceived to be applied at O, in the direction O N, that force will be supported or resisted by the plane L M, and the body will stand firm.

But if the line of direction O N (*fig.* 15.) fall *without* the base A D, the case will

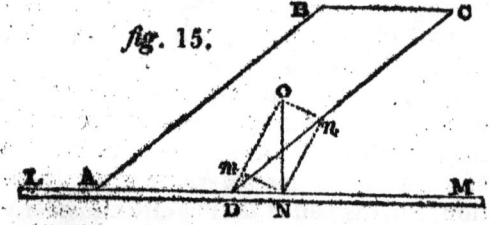

be different. The force of gravity will now act upon the body, so as to make it turn over the edge D, and fall upon the side D C. For draw O D, and from N draw N m perpendicular to D O, and complete the parallelogram N m O n. The diagonal N O being taken to represent the whole force of gravity, it may be resolved (9.) into two forces, represented by O m and O n. The force O m is resisted by the plane L M at D, and the force O n evidently tends to turn the body round the point D, and to make it fall upon the plane towards the point M.

If the line of direction fall upon the edge D of the base, the body is in a state of instable equilibrium. For let O D (*fig.* 16.) be perpendicular to the plane L M, and with D as centre, and

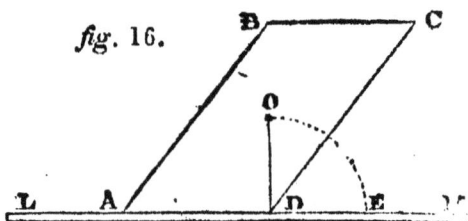

the distance or radius D O, describe a quadrant of a circle. It is evident that if the point O be moved towards M, it will move through a part of the circular arc O E, and every part of this arc is nearer to D M than O, and, therefore, the point O must descend. The slightest disturbance in this case will make the body fall towards M.

(46.) In general, the higher the centre of gravity of a body is, compared with the extent of its base, the more easily will it be overturned. This will be easily explained. Let A B C D, (*fig.* 17.) be

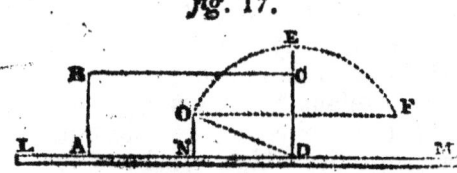

a body resting on the horizontal plane L M, and on the base A D. Let O be the centre of gravity, and O N the line of direction. Draw O D, and with D as centre, and the radius D O, let the circular arch O F be described. In order that the body A B C D should turn over the edge D, it will be necessary that the edge A be lifted off the plane L M to such an height, that the point O shall be raised through the arch O E, beyond the point E.

Now let us suppose that, by placing a load G K, (*fig.* 18.) over A B C D, the centre of gravity be raised from O to O', it will be only necessary to raise the centre of gravity O' through the arch O' E, in order to turn the body over the edge D.

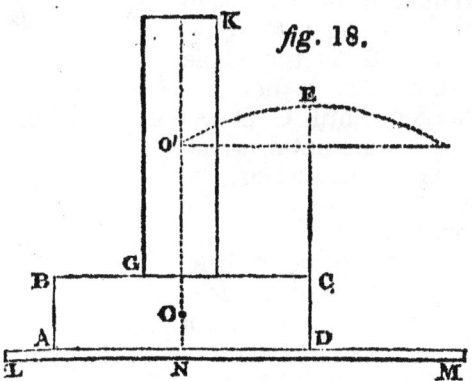
fig. 18.

It is evident that a much less elevation of the edge A will effect this, than that which would be necessary to raise the centre O through the arch O E in the former case.

The danger of loading carriages heavily at the top, when the lower parts of the vehicle are comparatively unloaded, is accounted for in this way, and also the danger arising from persons standing up in a boat. In these cases, the centre of gravity is raised, and the facility with which the vehicle may be overturned is proportionally increased.

If it be attempted to support a body upon a sharp point, considerable difficulty will be felt owing to the practical impossibility of keeping the centre of gravity of the body vertically over the point on which it is sustained. If, however, a motion of rotation be communicated to the body, and it be made to spin on the point, it will be found to be balanced with comparative ease. In this case, the centre of gravity in each revolution of the body assumes every possible position round the point, and has an equal tendency to make the body incline in all directions round it. Consequently, its tendency to make the body incline in any one direction, is after half a revolution counteracted by an equal tendency to make it incline in the opposite direction; and provided the motion of rotation be sufficiently rapid, these opposite tendencies follow in such quick succession, that they counteract each other as effectually as if they acted simultaneously.

CHAPTER V.—*On Water considered as a Mechanical Agent.*

(47.) WHEN water descends from any level to a lower one, its weight during the descent may be used as a mechanical agent. That this may be possible, it is only necessary that there should be a sufficient supply of water at the superior level, and that there should be means of carrying it off after its descent, so as to prevent, by its accumulation, the equalization of the two levels. The most usual means of giving motion to machinery by this power is a wheel, on the circumference of which the weight of the water is made to act in its descent, in a direction as nearly as possible at right angles to the radii; this pressure, however, acting only at one side of the wheel. Wheels driven by this power are of two kinds, the *overshot wheel* and the *breast-wheel*.

The diameter of an overshot wheel is nearly equal to the difference of the levels of the water by which it is moved. A section of such a wheel at right angles to its axle is represented in *fig.* 19. The

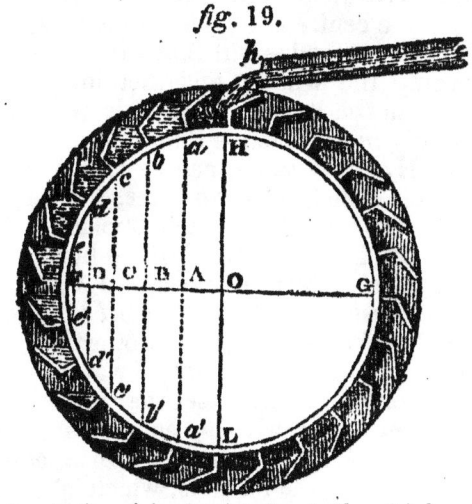
fig. 19.

rim is furnished with buckets which receive the water as it descends from the superior level h. The buckets from the top H of the wheel to the end F of the horizontal diameter F G are constantly full of water, while those from F to a point a', where the side of the bucket becomes level or horizontal, are only partially filled; those from a' to the lowest point L being empty. It is evident that the buckets on the other side, G, of the vertical diameter H L, will be all empty.

In this state the wheel will be turned round by the weight of the water in the buckets, since that weight acts entirely on one side, H F L, of the wheel, and is not counterpoised by an equal weight on the other side; and the wheel will continue to be turned so long as a supply of water sufficient for the purpose is received from the superior level h.

The weights of the water in the several buckets, however, are not equally effective in turning the wheel; this will be easily perceived. If any water were contained in the highest bucket H, its weight would press upon the axle O in the direction H O. This weight would be entirely sustained by the supports of the wheel, and would contribute in no degree to its motion. From the several buckets $a\ b\ c$, &c., conceive the lines aA, b B, cC, &c. drawn perpendicular to the horizontal diameter F G. The weight of the water in the bucket a has the same effect in making the wheel revolve as if that weight acted at A, by the arm or lever A O. In the same way the weights of the water in the several buckets $b\ c\ d$ and e have the same effect as if they acted at the points B C D E. Now it is very evident, that the more remote from the centre O a given weight acts, the more effective will that weight be in turning the wheel; and therefore, the water in the buckets near F is proportionally more effective than that in those near H. The same may be said of the buckets $e'\ d'\ c'$. As, however, the water begins to flow from each bucket as it descends from the end F of the horizontal diameter, these buckets, $e'\ d'\ c'$, produce a less effect than those $e\ d\ c$ immediately above them, in proportion as they contain a less weight of water.

In order to increase the power of overshot water-wheels, engineers have given considerable attention to the construction of the buckets, which should be so shaped as to retain as much of the water as possible until they reach the lowest point L, but to retain *none* after they pass that point: in fact, each bucket should be empty on arriving at the lowest point L, but should remain filled until it come as near as possible to that point: to attain this, various forms of buckets have been suggested. That which has been generally considered best is represented in fig. 21.

This bucket is formed of three planes; A B is in the direction of the radius of the wheel, and is called the *start*, or *shoulder*; B C is called the arm, and C H the *wrist*. These buckets are so constructed, that when A B makes an angle of 35° with the vertical diameter of the wheel, the line A D is horizontal; and the area of the figure A D C B is equal to that of F C B A; so that as much water is retained in the bucket in this position as would fill F C B A: the whole of the water is not discharged until C D becomes horizontal, which takes place when the line A B is very near the lowest point.

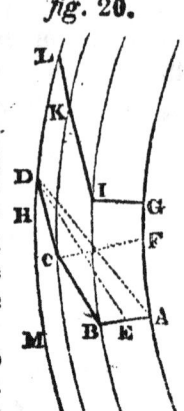

fig. 20.

In attempting to keep *all* the descending buckets filled, it should not be forgotten, that the increased pressure upon the supports of the axle produces an increased resistance from friction; and therefore, that there is necessarily a certain distance from the highest and lowest point, within which a weight in a descending bucket is a positive impediment to the motion of the wheel. This will be readily understood by commencing with the extreme cases of the highest and lowest buckets themselves. If these be filled, the weight of the water which they contain will, as we have before stated, have no effect whatever in turning the wheel, but will press on the supports of the axle with its entire force; the friction, being proportional to the perpendicular pressure, will therefore be increased; and hence an additional resistance to the effect of the water in the descending buckets will be created: thus it appears, that water in the highest and lowest buckets is a positive resistance to the motion of the wheel. Now, suppose the buckets $a\ a'$ near the highest and lowest points be filled, two effects will then be produced: an additional pressure on the axle; and therefore an increased resistance will be created on the one hand, and a moving force with the leverage A O will be brought into action on the other hand: but when the buckets $a\ a'$ are very near the highest and lowest points, the leverage A O will be very small, while the increased pressure on the axle will be very great. Thus the increased resistance may be greater than the moving force which is gained; and therefore, on the whole, a loss of power will ensue.

From this reasoning, it is apparent that there is a certain distance from the highest and lowest points at which the momentum, or moving power of the water in the buckets is only equal to resistance arising from friction, which its own weight creates; and it is very plain, that, within this distance from the highest and lowest points, a full bucket occasions a positive loss of power, and even beyond this limit, but near it, very little advantage can be gained.

There is a certain velocity with which an over-shot wheel should move, in order to produce the greatest effect. This will be evident from considering two extreme cases. If the wheel be so loaded as to render the weight of water insufficient to move it, the velocity becomes nothing; and it is evident that the effect becomes nothing. If, on the other hand, the wheel be supposed to turn as rapidly as the water would fall freely, it is evident that the effect of the weight of the water in the buckets will be nothing, since they descend as fast as the water itself would. Between these limiting cases there is an intermediate velocity, which will give the best possible effect.

Mr. Smeaton concludes from experience, that the best general rule for the velocity of the circumference of an over-shot wheel is three feet per second; and he considers that this equally applies to large and small wheels. In deviating, however, from this rule, he considers that high wheels lose less of their effect, in proportion to their whole power, than smaller ones.

(48.) In cases where the height of the fall is considerable, and the supply of water very limited, a contrivance of the kind represented in *fig.* 21 is frequently used.

An endless chain, carrying a series of buckets C F E D, is made to revolve on two wheels A B, called *rag-wheels*. The water flows into the highest bucket at N; and when it descends, the next bucket D takes its place, and is likewise filled, and thus every bucket on the side C is filled, while those on the side E, being inverted, are empty; the chain of buckets is therefore constantly car-

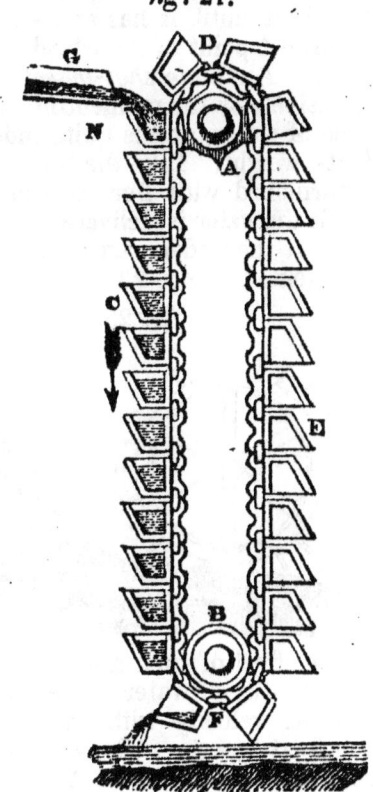

fig. 21.

ried round in the direction C F E D by the weight of the water.

(49.) The *breast-wheel* is another means by which the weight of water is applied as a mechanical agent. This wheel is furnished at its edge or rim with flat boards, called *float-boards*, the planes of which are at right angles to the plane of the wheel, and in the direction of the radii. The water is delivered at some point near the end of the horizontal diameter. The float-boards are fitted to the mill-course, as represented in *fig.* 22, so as to leave only as much play as is absolutely necessary for the free motion

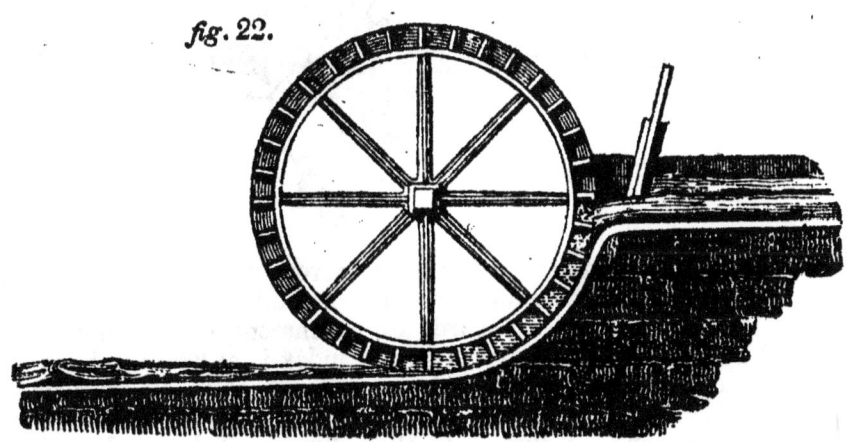

fig. 22.

of the wheel, so that the water may be retained between the float-boards and the mill-course, and that it may act by its weight until it has arrived nearly at the lowest point of the wheel.

(50.) An *undershot-wheel* is driven exclusively by the momentum or moving force of water, and is quite independent of its weight. Like the breast-wheel it is furnished with float-boards, against which the water is delivered by a sloping canal at the under part of the wheel, as represented in *fig.* 23.

fig. 23.

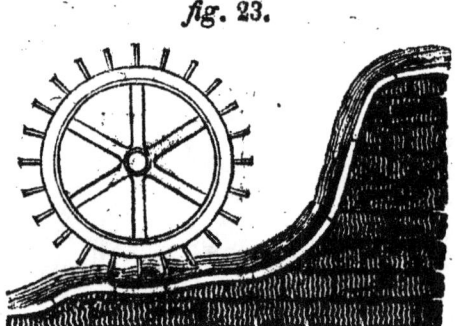

The effect of such a wheel depends on the quantity of water in the mill-course, and the velocity with which it strikes the float-boards. The velocity will depend on the height of the fall, which therefore should be as much increased as the peculiar circumstances of the situation will admit.

Much difference of opinion has subsisted among mechanical writers respecting the best number of float-boards in undershot-wheels. Bossut shows, that when the velocity of the wheel is given, there is a certain number of float-boards, which produces the greatest effect.

The rule of Bossut, however, is not simple enough to be of use to the practical mechanic. In general, it may be observed that the wheel may be furnished with as great a number of float-boards as the strength of the rim to which they are attached will conveniently admit, care being taken at the same time not to overload the wheel by their weight. The injury arising from having too limited a number of float-boards is much greater than any which could possibly arise from the opposite error.

(51.) In estimating the power of a stream on an undershot-wheel, it is frequently necessary to measure the velocity of the stream, and the quantity of water which flows through its bed. Various methods have been suggested of measuring the velocity of a stream. One of the most simple is to stretch two strings across it, each perpendicular to its course, and at as great a distance one from the other as may be found convenient. Let a light floating body be flung into the stream, above the higher string, and let the moment of its passing under each string be observed by a clock which beats half or quarter seconds. The time of the passage of the floating body from the one string to the other, will thus be obtained, and by measuring the distance between the two strings, the *rate* at which it was carried along by the stream will be found, which will be the velocity of the stream.

A more accurate method of determining the velocity of a stream is, by a small wheel, furnished with float-boards as represented in *fig.* 24. This wheel is

fig. 24.

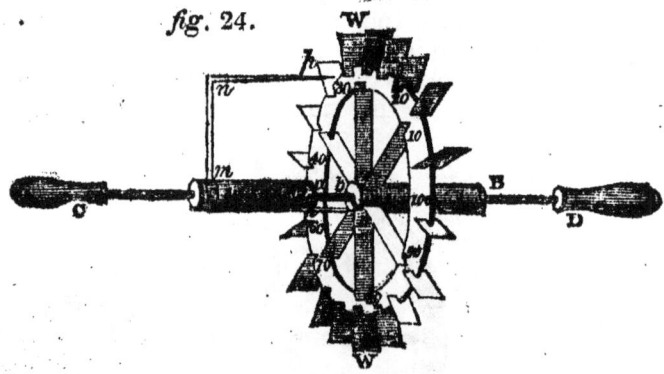

about one foot in diameter, and moves upon a fine screw *a b*, passing through its axle B *b*. When the float-boards are impelled by the stream, the axle B *b* will be turned upon the screw *a b*, and will approach toward D, each revolution moving it through one thread of the screw. An index *o h* is fixed to the movable axle at *h*, and when the wheel commences its motion, the point of the index is at 0 on the fixed scale *m a*. As the wheel moves towards D, each revolution moves the index *o h* over one division of the graduated scale, so that the number of revolutions of the wheel performed in a given time may be thus found. Another rectangular index $m\,n\,p$ shows the parts of a revolution. At the commencement of the motion, the point p is directed to 0 on the graduated rim of the wheel.

Having found by this instrument the number of revolutions and fractional parts of a revolution which have been performed in a given time; multiply the circumference of the wheel by that number, and we shall then find the velocity with which the circumference of the wheel moves.

(52.) The third property, in virtue of which water becomes a mechanical agent, is that power which, in common with all fluids, it possesses of transmitting pressure equally in every direction. If water be confined in any vessel, and a pressure to any amount be exerted on a square inch of that water, a pressure to an equal amount will be transmitted to every square inch of the surface of the vessel in which the water is confined.

One of the most remarkable instances of the employment of this property as a mechanical agent, is in Bramah's hydrostatic press, the theory of which is extremely simple. A large solid plug or piston A B (*fig.* 25.) is constructed so as to move water-tight in a cylinder C D. The space beneath the piston is filled with water, and communicates by a pipe E F with a small forcing-pump, worked by the piston G, and by which the water is forced into the chamber of the cylinder

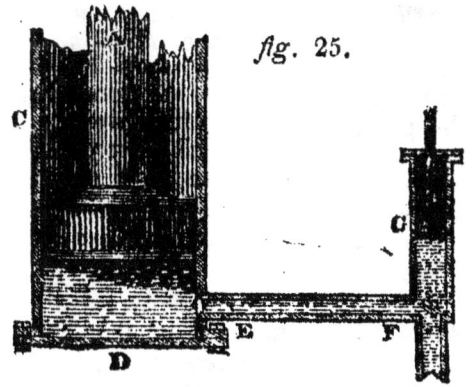

fig. 25.

C D below the great piston. Let us now suppose the entire space between the two pistons to be filled with water, and a pressure of one pound exerted on the water by means of the piston G of the forcing-pump. Let us also suppose that the diameter of the piston G is a quarter of an inch, and that the diameter of the piston B is one foot. In that case, the base of the piston B, which is pressed by the water, is 2304 times the base of the piston G, which presses the water, and in virtue of the power of transmitting pressure to which we have already alluded, a pressure of one pound will be transmitted to every part of the base of the greater piston which is equal to the base of the less. Thus an urging pressure of one pound on the base of the lesser piston G will produce a pressure of 2304*lbs.* against the base of the greater piston B. This property of fluids, therefore, seems to invest us with a power of increasing the intensity of a pressure exerted by a comparatively small force, without any other limit than that of the strength of the materials of which the engine itself is constructed.

This property of liquids also enables us with great facility to transmit the motion and force of one machine to another, in cases where local circumstances preclude the possibility of instituting any ordinary mechanical connexion between the two machines. Thus merely by means of water-pipes the force of a machine may be transmitted to any distance, and over inequalities of ground, or through any other obstructions.

CHAPTER VI.—*Air considered as a Mechanical Agent.*

(53.) AIR may become a mechanical agent by means of its four properties, weight, inertia, fluidity, or power of transmitting pressure, and its elasticity.

In our treatise on PNEUMATICS, Chapter III., it was proved, that a column of air, whose base is one square inch, and whose height is that of the atmosphere, weighs about fifteen pounds. Consequently, it follows, that an horizontal surface sustains a weight or pressure amounting to fifteen times as many pounds as there are square inches in its extent. If then we have a solid substance with an horizontal surface, for example, a piston placed in a vertical cylinder, and that we are able by any means to remove all resistance from *below* it, it will be forced down by a mechanical pressure of fifteen times as many pounds as there are square inches in its upper surface, and in this way a mechanical agent of a power limited only by the magnitude of the piston will be obtained.

But peculiar difficulties in giving efficacy to this power arise from two other properties of air, its fluidity and its elasticity. By the former it transmits the pressure arising from the weight of the incumbent atmosphere equally in every direction, so that it is not only an horizontal surface which sustains the pressure of 15lbs. per inch, but surfaces in all possible directions and positions suffer the same pressure. Also, by reason of air being an elastic fluid, it expands itself, so as to fill every open space not actually occupied by other bodies, whether solid or fluid. Consequently in the case we have supposed, air must occupy the space in the cylinder below the piston as well as above it, and if so, the fluidity of the air will transmit the pressure arising from the weight of the atmosphere to the lower surface of the piston with undiminished force, and thus we shall have the piston pressed upwards and downwards with equal forces, and consequently no mechanical advantage will be obtained.

(54.) It appears, therefore, that before the weight of the atmosphere, whether acting immediately downwards, or transmitted laterally, obliquely, or upwards, by means of its fluidity, can be used as a mechanical agent, it is indispensably necessary that the air be removed from the other side of the body on which this weight or pressure is designed to act. Recurring to the example of a piston in a cylinder, it is necessary to remove the air from one side of the piston before its weight or pressure can take effect upon the other side. Now if this removal, as is often the case, be effected by mechanical means, it must, on the slightest consideration, be quite apparent that it will require exactly as much force to remove the air from one side of the piston, as will be subsequently gained by the pressure of the atmosphere on the other side. Suppose, for example, that from two feet in length of the cylinder below the piston, the air which it originally contained be withdrawn by mechanical force. To effect this will require a force of at least 15lbs. for every square inch in the section of the cylinder, acting through the space of two feet, and after it has been effected the piston will be forced into the vacuum with exactly the same force.

It appears, therefore, that in order to render the atmospheric pressure an available mechanical agent, a vacuum, or a partial vacuum, must always be produced; and further, that if this vacuum, or rarefaction, be produced by mechanical means, no power will be gained, since it will always require as much force to accomplish this, as will be exerted by the atmospheric pressure when it has been accomplished. In the use of mechanism, however, the gaining of power is not always the end to be attained. It is frequently a matter of great convenience, and, in a certain sense, of great mechanical advantage, to be able, by a power which acts in some particular manner, to obtain another *equal* power, whose mode of action may be different, and better suited to the purpose to which mechanical agency is to be applied. This is, in fact, the case in every instance in which the atmospheric pressure is obtained by mechanical rarefaction, and in every such case the atmospheric pressure should not be looked upon as the prime mover, but rather as an intermediate agent deriving its entire efficacy from that power, whatever it may be, which is used to produce the rarefaction. A most obvious instance of this may be observed in the common suction-pump, described in our Treatise on Pneumatics, Art. 40. This machine is introduced into that treatise, not because it owes its original mechanical efficacy to the pneumatical principle of atmospheric pressure, but because this principle is involved in the detail of its operation. In this machine, the first mover is the power, whatever it be, which works the piston. This power, at the commencement of the operation, produces a rarefaction in the space between the piston and the surface of the water in the well. The weight of the atmosphere acting upon the external surface of the water in the well forces into the pump-barrel just so much water as the power applied to the pump-rod would have been capable of lifting, were it immediately applied to that purpose. This appears very evident from the investigation contained in Art. 42. PNEUMATICS.

What we have observed of the suction-pump may be applied in general to all cases where the atmospheric pressure receives its efficacy from mechanical rarefaction. Strictly speaking, we cannot consider the atmospheric pressure as a first mover at all; the first mover is the cause, whatever it be, whether mechanical or otherwise, which produces the rarefaction.

(55.) By that quality called inertia, air, when in motion, exerts a force upon any solid body, which obstructs its course. (PNEUMATICS, Art. 9.) This force is used as a first mover, by means analogous to water-wheels, viz. by flat surfaces exposed to the impact of the wind, by that impact made to revolve on a centre. When this rotatory motion is once produced, it may be easily transmitted, and modified by machinery, and applied to any required purpose.

If the sails of a windmill be constructed in a manner analogous to the float-boards of an undershot-water-wheel, the plane of the wheel must be in the direction of the wind; and it is evident that one half of the wheel must be sheltered from the action of the wind, for otherwise equal forces would tend to turn the wheel in opposite directions, and no motion would ensue. Besides this, the wind would act with very little advantage on those sails whose planes are nearly in its own direction. For this reason windmills of this construction are not generally used. On the other hand, the arms which carry the sails revolve in a plane facing the wind. In this arrangement, if the sails were in the same plane with the arms, the wind would fall perpendicularly upon them, and merely press the arms against the building perpendicular to the plane in which they are designed to move. If, on the other hand, the sails were perpendicular to the plane in which the arms move, their edges would be presented to the wind, and would, therefore, offer no resistance, and there would be no motion. In order to make the arms revolve, the sails must, therefore, be placed in some direction intermediate between those of the wind and the plane in which the arms revolve.

The most accurate experimentalists and the most profound mathematicians have instituted inquiries, practical and theoretical, to determine that position which should be given to sails of windmills, in order to produce the best effect. Most of the theoretical calculations on this difficult subject have been vitiated by conditions and hypotheses, which are inadmissible in practice. The angle which *Parent* and others deduced from mathematical calculation to be the best at which the planes of the sails could be inclined to the axis of motion or the direction of the wind, was found to be one of the worst in Mr. Smeaton's experiments. The position determined by *Parent*, was the best at the beginning of motion, but his calculation proceeded on the supposition, that the wind struck the sail *at rest*; and was, therefore, inapplicable to the continuance of its action.

When the wind acts upon the sail in motion, it is necessary to take into account the velocities both of the sail and the wind. For if the sail moved before the wind with a speed equal to that of the wind itself, no effect would be produced. The effect will depend on the difference of the velocities, that being the velocity with which the wind strikes the sail. Now as the obliquity of the sail to the wind should depend on the force with which the wind acts upon it, and as those parts of the sail which are nearer to the centre of motion move more slowly than those which are more remote, it follows that the position of the sail should vary at different distances from the centre of rotation. From several experiments executed on a large scale, Mr. Smeaton concluded the following positions to be among the best.* Let the radius be conceived to be divided into six equal parts, and let the first part, beginning from the centre, be called 1; the second 2, and so on; the extreme part being 6.

No.	Angle with the axis.	Angle with the plane of the motion.
1	72°	18°
2	71	19
3	72	18
4	74	16
5	77½	12½
6	83	7

(56.) The last property, in virtue of which we have stated that air becomes a mechanical agent, is its *elasticity*. The nature of this property, and the laws by which it acts, have already been explained in our treatise on PNEUMATICS, Chap. IV. When this property is considered as a mechanical agent, it is subject to nearly the same observations as we have already applied to the weight and pressure of the atmosphere. To give effect to the elastic force of air, it is necessary that it should predominate over the weight of the atmosphere, a pressure to which, as we have before stated, all bodies in their ordinary state

---

* The general resemblance which the best form of windmill sails bears to the arrangement of the feathers in the wings of birds is very striking, and one of those beautiful instances of the truly mathematical principles on which the works of the creation are constructed.

are subject. If increased elasticity be communicated to air by mechanical means, it must be by compression or condensation. It is evident, that in this case, no power whatever will be gained, in as much as it will require exactly as much power to produce a given degree of condensation in a given quantity of air, as is equal to the increased elasticity with which that condensed air will be endued. However, in this case, as in that of the ordinary use of atmospheric pressure, although no power be gained by mechanical condensation, yet considerable advantage may be derived from this as a method of transmuting one power into another, and as means of accumulating the effects of a small intermitting power, so as to convert it into a severe or continued pressure.

We have already seen an instance of this in the air-gun. (PNEUMATICS, Art. 52.) If we attempted, by mere manual force, to project a bullet, we should find our efforts attended with but a small effect; but if it were possible to unite in one impulse the combined force of a vast number of separate impulses, we should produce the desired effect. The air-gun, then, is nothing more than a contrivance, by which a great number of separate exertions of our strength are accumulated and combined, and made to act simultaneously. The process of condensing the air is conducted by a number of successive muscular exertions; and the elastic force which the condensed air thus receives, is exactly equal to the sum of these several exertions of human strength, and may, therefore, be considered as a magazine in which these separate exertions are contained in such a manner, that their combined intensity may be, at any moment, applied to the ball or other missile to be projected.

In this instance, the object to be attained is the production of a severe but instantaneous effect. The elastic property of air is also sometimes used to convert an intermitting or reciprocating action into a continued and uniform one. The fire-engine, described in our treatise on PNEUMATICS, Art. 48, is an instance of this. The force which works the pistons is intermitting or reciprocating, while the pressure of the condensed air in the air-vessel, produced by that intermitting force, is continuous in its action. Its total action, however, must be precisely equal to the sum of the forces which depress the pistons.

The force of condensed air may be applied to produce a severe and continued pressure, on a principle similar to that of Bramah's hydrostatic press, already described. Let B (*fig.* 26.) be a

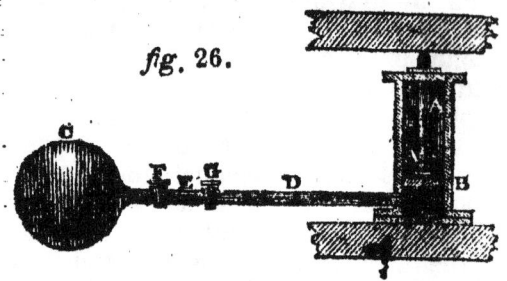

fig. 26.

large cylinder, in which a solid piston or plunger moves air-tight. Let D E be a small tube, having a stop-cock at G, and terminated in a screw at E. Let C be a strong metal ball, capable of bearing an intense bursting pressure, having a small tube, terminated by a screw at E, by which it may be connected occasionally with the tube D E, or with a condenser, (PNEUMATICS, Art. 38,) and also furnished with a stopcock at F.

By means of a condenser screwed upon E, the stopcock F being opened, let air be forced into the ball C, until it presses against the cock F, when closed, with a force of more than one ton. The condenser being then removed from E, the air cannot escape, the cock F being closed. Let the ball and tube C F E be then screwed upon the tube D E, and the cocks F and G both opened. The condensed air will expand through the tube D, and fill the part of the cylinder below the piston. If, after this expansion, the elastic force of the compressed air is such that it would press on the stopcocks with a force exceeding that of the atmosphere by one ton, there will be an effective pressure against the piston A, of as many tons as the number of times that the section of the tube D is contained in that of the piston. Suppose the section of the tube to be a quarter of an inch in diameter, and the piston to be one foot, the pressure on the piston will then be equal to 2304 tons.

In this case, like all the former, air is only used as a convenient means of accumulating mechanical force; and ought not, properly speaking, to be looked upon as the prime mover. As in using the weight or pressure of the atmosphere, we consider that cause, whatever it be, that produces the vacuum, or the rarefaction, to be properly the prime mover, so also in using the elastic force of the air as a mechanical agent, we consider the means whereby the necessary degree of elasticity is imparted to it, whatever those means may be, as the real prime mover. We shall see hereafter that, for this reason, *heat* assumes an important rank in the class of first movers.

CHAPTER VII.—*Of Animal Strength.*

(57.) ONE of the most obvious, and therefore one of the earliest, although, perhaps, the least efficient of the prime movers, is *animal strength.*

From our ignorance of the nature and principle of animal life, it is evident that we cannot attempt to explain, on scientific principles, the laws which regulate animal strength: and, on the other hand, owing to the very fluctuating nature of this force, the various physical causes which produce differences in its manifestations in different individuals, and even in the same individual, at distances of time by no means great, considerable difficulties obstruct the investigation and development of these laws by the process of actual observation and experiment. The whole analogy of nature, the beauty, order, and singular harmony of all her works, however, convince us that this force, like every other, is regulated by fixed laws.

To simplify our investigations, we shall consider every exertion of animal strength to be represented by that which is necessary to carry a load or weight. It is not difficult to imagine that, in whatever way strength be used, we can find a certain load carried with a certain speed, which may be considered as an equivalent exertion.

In estimating the exertion of animal strength in this way, one law is very obvious, which is, that as the load is increased (all other things being the same), the velocity of the animal must necessarily be diminished. But then, it becomes a more difficult matter to determine in what proportion the velocity should be diminished with a given increase of load, in order that the expenditure of animal labour should be the same. Different formulæ have been suggested, each agreeing more or less with experience, and we shall here attempt to explain in a popular way that formula which seems to represent the results of experiments most accurately.

There are two extreme cases of animal exertion. There is a certain speed at which the animal can carry no load, and can barely move its own body; let this speed be called X. There is some load so great that the animal can barely sustain it, without being able to move it; call this load L. What is technically called the *useful effect* depends on two things—the *load* which is borne, and the speed or velocity with which it is carried. The useful effect is, in fact, estimated by multiplying the load by the speed. This will be easily understood by an example. Suppose one horse carry two hundred weight six miles an hour, and another carry three hundred weight four miles an hour. The load of the former is two, and the speed six; the product or useful effect being twelve. The load of the latter is three, and the speed four; the useful effect being twelve. The propriety of considering the useful effect to be equal in these two cases, will appear very evidently, if we consider both horses to be employed in transporting weights between two places, distant one mile asunder, for six hours. The first horse will carry in the six hours 72 hundred weight between the two places, for he will make thirty-six turns, travelling for six hours at six miles an hour, and at each turn he will carry two hundred weight. The other horse will make but twenty-four turns, since he travels only four miles an hour; but then, in each turn, he will carry three hundred weight; and, therefore, he will also transport in the given time 72 hundred weight between the two places. Thus the useful effects of these horses are equal, and hence the propriety of estimating the useful effect by the product of the numbers which express the load and the speed with which that load is carried.

Recurring now to the load L, and the speed X, it is apparent that, with the load L, the useful effect is nothing, because there is no speed; and again, with the speed X, the useful effect is nothing, because there is no load. But with a load less than L there will be a speed less than X; and therefore, there will be an useful effect. These, then, are two limiting cases, in which the useful effect vanishes, approaching which it diminishes, and at some point between which it is a *maximum*. To determine where this maximum lies, it is necessary that we should know in what proportion the velocity diminishes as the load increases.

Let l be any load less than L, and let x be the greatest speed with which this load can be carried. The useful effect will be $l \times x$; that is, the load multiplied by the speed. The rule which seems best to agree with experience is that the load l increases in the same ratio as the square of the difference between the greatest velocity X, with which the animal can move unloaded, and the greatest velocity x with which it can move the load; that is, l increases as $(X - x)^2$. Assuming this rule, therefore, it follows, that the useful effect is represented by the product $(X - x)^2 \times x$. This will probably be more easily understood by reducing it to an arithmetical table. Let us suppose that the number 15 represents the greatest unloaded speed, and that the square of 15, or 225, represents the greatest load which can be sustained without moving. The signification of the units which compose the number 15, will be found, by dividing the space through which the animal would move in a given time, suppose one hour, into 15 equal parts: each of these parts will be expressed by an unit of the number 15, which expresses the greatest unloaded speed; and the signification of the units of 225 will be found, by dividing the greatest load which can be sustained without moving, into 225 equal parts: one of these parts will be expressed by an unit of the number 225, which expresses the greatest load. The following Table gives for each degree of speed from 1 to 15, the corresponding load and useful effect.

Speed	0	1	2	3	4	5	6	7	8	9	10	11	12	13	14	15
Load	225	196	169	144	121	100	81	64	49	36	25	16	9	4	1	0
Useful effect	0	196	338	432	484	500	486	448	392	324	250	176	108	52	14	0

From the inspection of this Table it appears that a much greater useful effect is to be attained by the slower motions with heavier loads than by the quicker motions with lighter loads. The greatest useful effect is produced by the speed 5 with the load 100; that is, with a velocity which is one-third of the greatest unloaded speed, and a load which is four-ninths of the greatest load which can be sustained without moving. We shall find this result, whatever be the number we take, to represent the greatest speed.*

Thus, if the greatest unloaded speed of a horse be 15 miles an hour, and that the greatest weight which he is capable of sustaining without moving be divided into 225 equal parts, his labour will be most advantageously employed if he be loaded with 100 of these parts, and travels at the rate of 5 miles per hour. If he be thus employed, it will be found that he will carry a greater weight through a given distance in a given time than under any other circumstances.

The average value of human strength considered as a mechanical agent, has been variously estimated. Desaguliers considers that a man can raise the weight of 550 lbs. 10 feet high in a minute, and continue to do so for 6 hours. Smeaton considers that this is too high an average, and thinks that six good English labourers will be required to raise 21,141 solid feet of sea-water to the height of four feet in four hours. In this case they will raise very little more than six cubic feet of fresh water each, 10 feet high in a minute. The labourers whom Smeaton supposes capable of executing this work he considers to be equal to twice the number of ordinary men. It would, therefore, perhaps, be a fair average value of a man's work to estimate it, for a continuance, at half an hogshead of water raised through 10 feet in a minute.

The efforts of men differ with the manner in which these efforts are employed. It has been shown by Mr. R.

---

* The mathematical investigation is not difficult. Let u be the *useful effect*. Then by the empirical formula already explained we have $u = (X-x)^2 x$. Differentiating this we obtain

$$\frac{du}{dx} = (X - x)^2 - 2(X-x)x.$$

Supposing this $= 0$ we shall obtain the value of x, which corresponds to a maximum or minimum value of u. This gives the equation,

$$(X-x)(X-3x) = 0$$

the roots of which are

$$x = X \qquad x = \frac{1}{3}X.$$

For $x = X$ the load and useful effect are each $= 0$. This root, therefore, corresponds to a minimum; and for $x = \frac{1}{3}X$ $l = (X - \frac{1}{3}X)^2 = \frac{4}{9}X^2$; that is, the load corresponding to one-third of the greatest speed is $\frac{4}{9}$ of the greatest load; for $L = X^2$. That this is a *maximum* is easily shown by taking the second differential, which gives

$$\frac{d^2 u}{dx^2} = -3(X - x) - (X - 3x)$$
$$= -4X + 6x$$

in which, if we substitute $\frac{1}{3}X$ for x, we find

$$-4X + 2X = -2X,$$

which, being negative, shows that the value $\frac{1}{3}X$ corresponds to a maximum value of u.

Buchanan that the same quantity of human labour employed in working a pump, turning a winch, ringing a bell, and rowing a boat, are as the numbers 100, 167, 227, and 248.

The most advantageous manner of applying human strength is in the act of rowing.

The most useful of quadrupeds, as a mechanical agent, is the *horse*. The relative values of the labour of a horse and man are variously stated. Some estimate them as five to one, some six to one, and some seven to one. Perhaps the medium may be nearest to the true average, and that we may generally consider six men equivalent to one horse.

The most advantageous method of using the strength of the horse is in the act of *drawing*. The worst method in which this animal can be employed is in *carrying* a weight up a steep hill; while, on the other hand, the peculiar disposition of the limbs of a man, renders him well-fitted for this species of labour. It has been observed that three men climbing a hill, loaded with 100lbs. each, will ascend with greater speed than one horse carrying 300lbs.

CHAPTER VIII.—*On the Mechanical Agents depending on Heat.*

(58.) IN order to explain the several ways in which heat is rendered subservient to the production of mechanical agency, it will be necessary, in the first instance, to offer a few observations on its properties, and particularly those properties which have relation to that quality of matter called *cohesion*. The necessity of entering into very minute details on this subject, however, is superseded by our treatise on *heat*, to which we refer the reader who desires to proceed with the subject beyond the general view of it which we shall give.

There is supposed to exist between the particles of matter, whatever be their form or situation, a certain mutual attraction, by which, if it be unresisted by any opposing force, they have a tendency to approach each other, to collect together, and to form themselves into solid concrete masses. *Heat*, or *caloric*, is supposed to be a subtle and highly elastic fluid, which transfuses itself through the dimensions of bodies in a greater or less degree, and by its intense elasticity has a tendency to force the particles asunder. Whatever be the nature of heat, however, and whether it be *material* or not, it is an undisputed fact, that it is a *cause*, which produces an effect exactly opposite to the effects of cohesion, and that, in proportion as it pervades any body, it gives the particles of that body a tendency to repel each other and fly asunder, which tendency, in some cases, prevails over the cohesive force and actually produces that effect.

When we find a body in the solid state, we therefore conclude, that the cohesive force by which its particles attract each other greatly predominates over the repulsive energy of the caloric which may pervade its dimensions, and that, consequently, the particles cohere with a force equal to the difference between these cohesive and repulsive forces. If, then, by the external application of fire, we transfuse through the dimensions of the body an increased quantity of heat, we naturally expect that, the repulsive effect of the caloric being increased, the particles which compose the body will be more separated, and will retire from each other to increased distances, so as to enlarge the dimensions of the body.

This effect we find actually to obtain; for if a cylindrical bar of metal, C D, be gauged by means of a flat piece of metal *b*, (*fig.* 27.) furnished with a

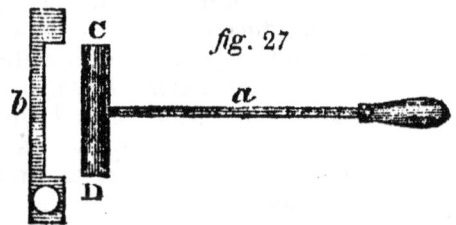

circular hole, in which the bar exactly passes, and having a notch in its side, corresponding to the length of the bar, it will be found that, after the bar is heated, its length and thickness will be so much increased that it will no longer fit in the notch, nor pass through the circular aperture.

In general, when heat is communicated to solids, their bulk is increased from the cause which we have assigned; but this effect is more perceivable in metals than other solids.

This effect of heat, however, is not confined to solids, but is observable in liquids, and still more in aëriform substances. The thermometer is an instrument in which the expansion of a fluid by heat is used as an indication, or measure, of the degree of heat to which the instrument is exposed (see HEAT, Chap. IV.), and the fluid which is used in thermometers may be either liquid or aëriform, although most frequently the former.

(59.) Bodies whether solid, liquid, or aëriform, exert a certain degree of mechanical force, in the process of enlarging their dimensions, on receiving an accession of heat; and any obstacle which opposes this enlargement sustains an equivalent pressure. This force is frequently used as a mechanical agent, and has this to recommend it, that it may be produced to almost any degree of intensity, without the expenditure of any other mechanical force in its production. In this respect it has the advantage over the mechanical agency of air, arising from its pressure and condensation, (53, 54.)

A remarkable instance of the use of the power with which solids expand by heat, occurred in Paris some years since, in a method which was used to force together the walls of a gallery in the Abbey of *St. Martin*, now the *Conservatoire des Arts et Métiers*. The weight of the roof was forcing the walls of this building asunder, and they were restored to their perpendicular position by the following method:—Holes were made at opposite points, in several parts of the walls, through which strong iron bars were introduced, so as to extend across the building, and so that their extremities should extend beyond the walls. Large nuts were placed upon their ends, and screwed up so as to press upon the walls. Every alternate bar was then heated by powerful lamps, so that its length increased by expansion, and the nuts, before in close contact with the walls, retired to some distance from them. The nuts were then screwed up to the walls, and the bars cooled. The process of cooling restored the length of the bars to what it had been before the heat had been applied, and the nuts were drawn together by an irresistible force, and consequently the walls drawn towards each other. The same process being repeated with the intermediate bars, and this being continued, the walls of the building were gradually restored to their perpendicular position.

In the processes of shoeing wheels, and hooping barrels, the same force is used mechanically. The iron hoop, or rim, is put on hot, and made to fit the wheel or the barrel exactly, and being then cooled, it contracts and binds the parts of the wheel or the barrel together with immense force.

It is evident, however, that these forces of expansion and contraction of bodies by heat and cold, act through spaces so limited that they can be used as mechanical agents but very rarely, and under peculiar circumstances.

(60.) Heat is productive of mechanical agents of much greater power, by the influence which it has upon the form of bodies, than by its power of enlarging their dimensions. We have stated that, in a solid body, the cohesive force of the particles predominates over the repulsive influence of the caloric which pervades its dimensions. Supposing the cohesive force to continue unincreased, what will be the effect if we transfuse through its dimensions, by the application of fire, such an abundant portion of caloric that the repulsive force of it will become equal, or nearly equal, to the cohesive force of the particles? We should evidently anticipate that the particles, having no tendency, or very little, to cohere, they would move freely among each other, and fall asunder by their own weight, unless they were prevented by the sides of the vessel which might contain them; in fact, we should predict that, by the application of such a quantity of heat, as we have supposed, the *solid* would become a *liquid*. And such we find to be the case: solids liquefy by exposure for a sufficient time to the action of fire.

It would appear, therefore, that the solid and liquid forms in which we find bodies, are maintained by the proportion which subsists between the force of cohesion peculiar to the particles, and the repulsive force of the caloric which pervades them, the former greatly predominating in solids, and these forces being nearly in equilibrium in liquids.

We accordingly find, by experience, that if a sufficient portion of heat be withdrawn from a liquid it becomes solid, the cohesive force of its particles receiving a sufficient predominance over the repulsive force of the caloric, by diminishing the quantity of the latter.

(61.) This, however, is not the only, nor the most important, change of form in bodies, which depends on the proportion which subsists between these two forces.

In a liquid, as we have already explained, the repulsive energy of the caloric nearly balances the cohesive force of the particles. Now, if we increase the quantity of caloric considerably, its repulsive effect will predominate over the cohesive attraction of the particles; and instead of being nearly in a state of indifference as to mutual attraction, we may expect to find that they strongly repel each other, and that the liquid will assume a form in which it will be necessary that it should be closely confined in order to prevent its total dissipation by the dispersion of the particles owing to this repulsive effect.

Accordingly we find that if a liquid be exposed for a considerable time to the action of fire, it will be gradually converted into steam; a fluid totally differing in its mechanical character from a liquid. If the liquid be inclosed in any vessel, it will press with no other force upon the surface which confines it, than with those pressures which are produced by its weight; but when the same liquid is converted into vapour and confined in a close vessel, it will press on the confining surface with its elastic force, which is quite independent of its gravity, and arises from the effort which its particles exert to repel each other; and which, therefore, exert a bursting pressure on the inner surface of the vessel which contains it.

The degree of elasticity or the pressure which confined steam exerts upon the surface of the vessel which contains it, will, according to our theory, and which is confirmed by experience, increase with the heat which is communicated to the steam; and, on the other hand, according as the temperature of the steam is lowered, the elastic pressure will be proportionally diminished.

The evaporation of liquids, however, is effected by a force, whose effects are not sensible in the liquefaction of solids. The atmospheric pressure has an effect in binding together the particles of a liquid; and, therefore, conspires with the cohesive force in opposing the effects of the caloric. When the caloric has been communicated to a body in such a quantity as to form a balance for the cohesive force; the body, according to our theory, ought to be in a state in which the slightest increase of caloric would convert it into an elastic vapour. Under these circumstances, however, the atmospheric pressure opposes the change, and is the means, and the only means, by which the particles are bound together and retained in a state of liquidity. In proof of this, we have only to remove the atmospheric pressure, and many bodies which are now held in the liquid state, by the mechanical action of that pressure, will evaporate.

Let water at 180° of temperature, or alcohol, or ether, be placed under the receiver of an air-pump, and they will boil and evaporate on removing or rather diminishing, by rarefaction, the pressure of the air on their surfaces. Indeed, ether will evaporate if exposed to the atmosphere without any diminution of pressure.

On the other hand, it would follow from this theory, that if the pressure be increased, the evaporation will be resisted by it; and such, in fact, we find to be the case. Water under the atmospheric pressure, when the barometer is at 30 inches, will boil and vaporize at 212° of Fahrenheit's thermometer; but if the same water be submitted to increased pressure, it will not boil or evaporate until it has reached much higher temperatures.

If a sufficient quantity of heat be withdrawn from the vapour which has been raised from a liquid, it will be restored again to its liquid form; and it is a very important fact, that, in this case, its bulk is reduced in a very high ratio. A cubic inch of water, when converted into steam at the usual atmospheric pressure, will form a cubic foot of steam; and it follows, therefore, that if the caloric be withdrawn from a cubic foot of such steam, by application of cold bodies, or otherwise, it will be reconverted into a cubic inch of water. Now this property is rendered subservient to the production of a very important mechanical agent. If a cubic foot of steam be inclosed in a vessel, and that the vessel be cooled until the steam be *condensed* or reconverted into water, we shall have 1727 cubic inches of empty space or vacuum; for the steam, which, before condensation, filled a cubic foot, or 1728 cubic inches, will, after condensation, be reduced to one cubic inch, leaving 1727 cubic inches void of any material substance.

The condensation of vapour, or its reconversion into the liquid state, is thus rendered an easy and effectual method of producing a vacuum, and is free from the objections to the mechanical method of producing the same effect alluded to in Chap. VI., inasmuch as a vacuum may thus be obtained without the expenditure of any mechanical force.

This was the principle from which the earlier steam-engines derived their efficacy. In the engine constructed by Savery, about the year 1700, the atmospheric pressure was used for elevating water into a tube, in which a vacuum was produced by first blowing the air out by means of hot steam; and when the tube was filled with pure steam, and the air had been completely expelled through a valve which opened outwards, the steam was condensed by cooling the external surface of the vessel which contained it. A vacuum was thus produced, into which the air was prevented from entering, by the circumstance of the valve opening *outwards*; and, consequently, the pressure of the atmosphere on the surface of the water in the well or reservoir, forced it up into the vessel or tube.

Shortly after this, Newcomen used the same means of producing a vacuum in his atmospheric steam-engine, but availed himself of the atmospheric pressure in another way. He provided a cylinder and a piston moving steam-tight in it. He connected the piston rod with the end of a great beam turning on a centre, the other end of which was connected with pump-rods, which he proposed to work. The weight of the pump-rods was sufficient to draw the piston to the top of the cylinder. He then filled the cylinder with steam, by which the air was blown out. Upon cooling the cylinder, the steam was condensed, and a vacuum was produced beneath the piston; and, consequently, the atmospheric pressure taking effect above it, forced it down and drew up the pump-rod at the opposite end of the beam, and so the process was continued.

In this case, the direct or elastic force of steam was not employed, the atmospheric pressure being the effective agent, but receiving its efficiency from the vacuum produced by the condensation of the steam. At a much earlier period, however, the mechanical agency of steam, arising from its elasticity, was suggested as a power, whose extent was almost unlimited. In 1663, the then MARQUESS OF WORCESTER asserts that he constructed a machine which raised a great quantity of water to a considerable height, and which was more powerful than the atmospheric pressure, inasmuch as this could only act through a limited space: whereas the elastic force of steam "hath no other bounder than the strength of the vessels which contain it."

In modern times, the improved steam-engines, commonly called *low pressure engines*, employ both the powers of steam which we have mentioned. A piston is moved in a cylinder, and the elastic force of steam acts on one side of it, while a vacuum is produced by the condensation of steam on the other side, and thus the piston is urged forward.

In *high pressure engines*, the elastic force of steam is used to urge a piston against the atmospheric pressure on the opposite side. The advantage which this has over the low pressure engine is, that all the apparatus for condensing the steam, in order to produce a vacuum, is dispensed with, and the machine is consequently cheaper and lighter. On the other hand, it is attended with the disadvantage, that all the elastic force of the steam which is expended in balancing the atmospheric pressure is lost, since that pressure must be overcome before motion is produced; and, consequently, it becomes necessary to use steam of a very high temperature and pressure in these engines, which increases the expense of fuel, and renders the operation more dangerous.

Having once obtained, in any of the ways which we have mentioned, the power of moving a piston in a cylinder, it will be no difficult matter to apply that power by a working-beam, or various other ways, to any mechanical purpose.

In this *First Treatise*, we have merely attempted to give the reader a succinct account of the most important properties of motion and force, and to offer a rapid sketch of the principal mechanical agents, or first movers. Our design being that the treatise should be adapted for the more popular purposes, we have not entered into any mathematical details on the subject; and in the same popular form, we propose, in the *Second Treatise*, to give an account of the *Elements of Machinery*, or the means whereby the natural powers which we have explained here, may be rendered available for mechanical purposes. In that treatise, the MECHANIC POWERS will hold a prominent part

MECHANICS.

TREATISE II.

ELEMENTS OF MACHINERY.

CHAPTER I.—*Machines—Power and weight—Principle of virtual velocities—Simple Machines or Mechanic Powers.*

(1.) NATURE has placed at the disposal of man various mechanical agents, endued with different kinds and degrees of power. The weight of solid bodies, and their momentum when in motion; the weight and pressure of liquids; the weight and pressure of air and other gases; the elastic force of vapour raised from liquids by heat; the elasticity of springs, and the muscular strength of animals, furnish striking examples. In applying these forces to overcome resistances, or to communicate motion to bodies, it seldom happens that, without some previous modification, they are capable of accomplishing the end we desire to attain. The power which we may happen to have at our disposal may not act in the proper direction, or may not have that velocity or intensity which suits our purpose; and some contrivance must be found by which, in transmitting it to the working point, its direction, velocity, or intensity, may be regulated in such a manner as to be suitable to the purpose to which it is to be applied. Such a contrivance is called a *Machine*.

(2.) Notwithstanding the infinite variety of ways in which machinery is employed, and the great diversity of ends which it appears to attain, yet it will be found that every machine, whether simple or complex, can only be designed to produce one or more of the three following effects: 1. To change the *direction* of the moving power so as to accommodate it to overcome a given resistance, or to produce in some body to which it is applied a given species of motion. 2. To render a power which has a certain *velocity* capable of producing a *different velocity* in the work to be performed or the body to be moved. 3. To render a power of a certain *intensity* capable of overcoming a resistance or of exerting a force upon the body to be moved of a *different intensity*, and frequently of a much greater intensity.

(3.) In order to simplify the development of the nature and properties of Machinery, we shall consider the moving power, as well as the resistance to be overcome, as represented by equivalent weights; that weight which is taken to represent the moving force being technically called the *power*, and that which represents the resistance being called the *weight*. It is easy to conceive that, whatever species of force the moving power and the resistance may be, weights equivalent to them can be assigned. Thus, if the moving power be the elastic force of steam pressing upon a piston, we familiarly say that the pressure amounts to so *many pounds* per square inch, meaning that it produces the same effect in forcing the piston through the cylinder as a weight of so many pounds laid upon the piston would produce. Again, if the resistance be that which timber offers to the wedge which splits it, there is no difficulty in conceiving a weight acting against the wedge so as to offer an equal resistance. We shall therefore henceforward express the moving power and the resistance to be overcome, whatever be their nature, by the terms *power* and *weight*.

(4.) In transmitting the influence of the *power* to the *weight* through the intervention of a machine, it has various resistances to encounter which oppose its action, and which impair its effects. Such are, for example, the roughness of surfaces which move in contact, the stiffness of cordage, the yielding or flexibility of bars, and numerous others. If the calculation of the effects of these forces were introduced into the elements of the science, and constituted a part of our first investigations of the properties of machines, the investigations would become extremely complex, and present difficulties which most students

would be deterred from encountering. To avoid this, it is usual, in the first instance, to omit the consideration of these obstructions to the action of the power, and to consider a machine as free from them. Surfaces are considered as perfectly smooth, cords as perfectly flexible, bars and levers as perfectly inflexible, and so on. Although these suppositions are absolutely false, yet they are found to be, in the end, the shortest road to truth. For having determined what would be the relation between the power and weight in any machine, were there no friction or rigidity, it will be easy to correct the result when the effects of these forces are subsequently ascertained, and the process is found to be, on the whole, not only more simple and intelligible to the student, but more expeditious in actual practice by taking this course, than if the real state of the machine were taken under consideration in the first instance.

These observations apply more or less to every part of physical science. The results which we obtain are rather to be considered as constant approximations to truth, than truth itself. In our first essays, false suppositions are ever mixed up with true ones, and our first conclusions are more or less tainted with the errors of the source from which they flow. Being, however, aware of the deviations from the truth in our primitive hypotheses, we are enabled to perceive the consequences which they produce and the errors which they entail upon our results, and we gradually remove these errors as they are detected, and our conclusions thus constantly come nearer to that truth which is the great end of all our researches. Thus the progress of the mind in the acquisition of the knowledge of physical science resembles that of an artist in the production of a picture or statue; the first rude attempt bears but a remote and uncouth resemblance to the original, while every successive stroke of the pencil or the chisel removes some deviation from perfect similitude, and the work gradually approximates to a faithful copy of nature.

(5.) Viewing a machine, then, divested of those considerations to which we have alluded, the problem which first presents itself is the determination of the *power*, which by its means would be capable of supporting a given weight. Now it happens, that notwithstanding the great variety of machines which have actually been constructed, and the infinitely greater variety which it is possible for human invention to produce, there is one great principle, simple in itself and easily intelligible, which applies indifferently to all, and by which the power, which is capable of supporting a given weight, may be determined. The power being connected with the weight so as to act upon it by means of the machine, if any motion be given to it, the weight will receive a corresponding motion, and a certain proportion will be found to subsist between the velocity with which the power descends in the vertical direction, and that with which the weight ascends in the vertical direction; which proportion depends entirely on the nature and construction of the machine. But whatever proportion this may be, in order that the power may be capable of sustaining the weight, it is only necessary that it should have to the weight the same ratio as the velocity of the weight just mentioned has to the power; or, to express the same condition in other words, THE POWER MULTIPLIED BY THE SPACE THROUGH WHICH IT MOVES IN THE VERTICAL DIRECTION MUST BE EQUAL TO THE WEIGHT MULTIPLIED BY THE SPACE THROUGH WHICH IT MOVES IN THE VERTICAL DIRECTION.*

This great principle, which is known under the name of "the principle of virtual velocities," may be considered as the *golden rule* of mechanics. Indeed, we may say that it implicitly contains the whole science, statics and dynamics; and equally includes the resolution of all problems respecting bodies and systems of bodies in equilibrium and in motion: for it applies immediately and most evidently to all questions respecting equilibrium or *statical problems*, and by means of another principle, known by the name of *D'Alembert's principle*, the whole region of dynamics is brought under its dominion. We cannot pretend, in a short popular treatise like the present, to make the full value of this principle apparent, nor even to offer a general demonstration of it; not because it is incapable of rigorous proof, nor because its results are few or unimportant, but because its general proof requires the aid of algebraic investigations of too difficult a

---

* The principle of virtual velocities is much more general than that which is announced above; but we shall not have to apply it in its full generality.

nature to be introduced here; and its most striking results are spread over departments of physical science, far beyond the necessary limits of this treatise. Nevertheless, even within our narrow limits, the student will have numerous instances of the truth and power of this principle.

(6.) Every machine, however complex it be, must consist of some combination of the following simple machines, which are commonly called the *mechanic powers*:—

1. THE LEVER,
2. THE WHEEL AND AXLE,
3. THE PULLEY,
4. THE INCLINED-PLANE,
5. THE WEDGE,
6. THE SCREW.

This classification of the ELEMENTS OF MACHINERY, although very simple when considered with respect to the extent and power of the results which spring from it, may be still further simplified; not because any of the six machines which we have just enumerated admits of being resolved into more simple parts, but because some of them are identical in principle, and different only in appearance. We shall show hereafter that the wheel and axle is in fact a lever, and that the wedge and screw are only modifications of the inclined plane; so that it follows, that all the varieties of simple machines may be reduced to three:—

1. THE LEVER,
2. THE PULLEY,
3. THE INCLINED-PLANE.

CHAPTER II.—*Of the Lever.*

(7.) A LEVER is sometimes defined "an inflexible right line, void of gravity, and turning on a certain point as a centre." It is also defined "an inflexible bar or rod resting upon a fulcrum or prop, on which it is capable of turning as on a centre." We shall, however, take a more general view of this machine, and consider it as any solid body having a fixed axle on which it is capable of turning, and round which all its parts describe circles. In considering such a machine as applicable to mechanical purposes, we usually conceive its axis to be placed at right angles to the plane in which the power and weight or resistance act. In order, also, to simplify the investigation, we shall, in the first instance, omit the weight of the machine itself, or, what will amount to the same effect, we will consider the fixed axle as passing through the centre of gravity of the machine, which will therefore rest indifferently in any position. (*Treatise* I. 42.)

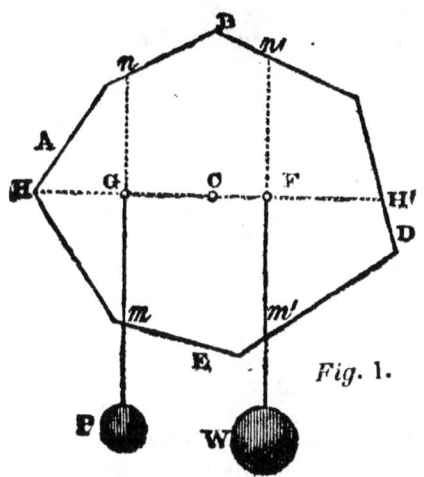

Fig. 1.

Let us suppose that AB D E (*fig.* 1.) is the section of a solid body, moveable on a fixed axis, and taken in a plane perpendicular to that fixed axis; and suppose the axis passes through the plane of the section at C. The axis being supposed horizontal, the section A B D E will be vertical. Through C suppose the horizontal line H C H' to be drawn, and let the weight W, to be sustained, be applied at F, and the power P which supports it be applied at G. Let us consider, then, under what conditions P can support W, conformably to the principle of *virtual velocities*. If the machine be put in motion round the centre C, so that P shall descend and W ascend; the points G and F, to which the power and weight are applied, will commence to move through similar circular arcs, having C as their common centre, and C G and C F as their radii. These arcs, if taken of small magnitudes, will then be the spaces through which the power and weight will move in the vertical direction; and whatever be their magnitudes, they will be proportional to the vertical motions of these weights. But these arcs being similar, are proportional to their radii; and hence follows, what indeed is otherwise abundantly evident, that the perpendicular descent of P is to the corresponding ascent of W, as the distances C G and C F of the points, at which these forces are applied, from the centre C. These distances C G and C F may be taken to represent the vertical velocities of the power and weight; and if C G and C F be called p and w, the condition on which the power P shall support the weight W, will, according to the principle of virtual velocities, be

$$P : W :: w : p,$$
$$\text{or } P \times p = W \times w.$$

The meaning of which is, that the power will sustain the weight in equilibrium, provided that the number of ounces in the power, multiplied by the number of inches in its distance from the centre, shall be equal to the number of ounces in the weight, multiplied by the number of inches in its distance from the centre. It is evident, that any other denominations of weight and measure besides ounces and inches may be used, provided the *same denomination* be used both with respect to the weight and power.

(8.) Such is the condition of equilibrium resulting from the principle of virtual velocities, and which it is very easy to submit to the test of experiment. Let a weight W, amounting to any number of ounces, be suspended at the point F, and let the number of inches in C F be exactly measured. Suppose that 12 ounces are suspended, and that C F is 8 inches. Now take any distance C G on the other side, and suppose that distance 32 inches, and that a weight of three ounces be suspended, it will be found, that equilibrium shall be preserved, and that the power shall exactly balance the weight; and, accordingly, the product of 3 and 32 is exactly equal to the product of 12 and 8.

Again, if instead of 32 inches C G is 24 inches, it will then be found to require a power of 4 ounces to balance the same weight. The product of 4 and 24 is 96, as before. In the same way, however we may change the distance of the power from the centre, it will be necessary to change its amount, so that the product of the number of ounces in it, by the number of inches in the distance, shall be equal to 96, in order that it shall exactly balance the weight. If in any case the product exceed 96, the power will preponderate; and if the product be less than 96, the weight will preponderate.

It appears, therefore, that the same weight W, at the same distance C F from the centre, may be balanced by innumerable different powers. In fact, a power of any magnitude whatever, great or small, may balance it, provided that the distance of that power from the centre be so regulated, that when multiplied by the power itself, the product shall be equal to the product of the weight multiplied by *its* distance from the centre.

It is evident, that the efforts which the power and weight make to turn the machine round the centre C, will be the same, to whatever point in the lines G m or F m', the strings supporting the power and weight may be attached, or even though they be attached to points in the lines G n and F n' above the points G and F. Thus it appears, that in estimating the distances of the power and weight from the centre, we are not to take the distances of the points of suspension; but the perpendiculars drawn from the centre C to direction $n\,m$ and $n'\,m'$ in which the power and weight act. Thus, if the power and weight were suspended from n and m', we should still consider C G and CF to be their distances from the centre.

In like manner, the directions of the power and weight may not happen to be parallel, as in the example we have taken; but still their distances from the centre of motion are estimated by perpendiculars from that point upon their directions.

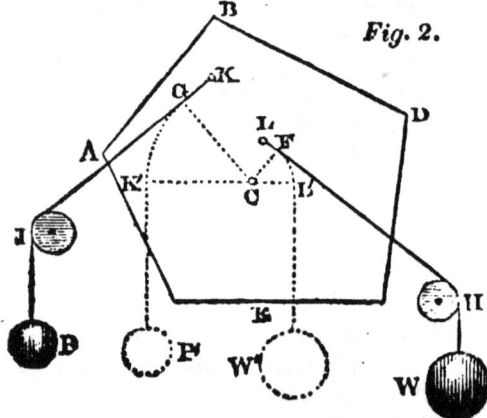

Fig. 2.

Let the point of application of the weight be L (*fig.* 2.) and let the string by which the weight acts pass over a wheel H; and in like manner let the power act by a string at K passing over a wheel I. In this case, L H is the direction of the weight, and K I that of the power. Suppose the perpendicular C F and C G drawn upon their directions; the condition of equilibrium will still be the same; viz. that the product of the power P, and the perpendicular C G shall be equal to the product of the weight W and the perpendicular C F. This may easily be established experimentally.

From all that we have stated, it follows, that the effort of any force to turn a body round an axis, is to be measured by multiplying the force by the perpendicular from the axis on its direction. The product thus obtained is called the *moment* of the force round that axis. This is a principle of such extreme importance, that we shall develop it somewhat further.

(9.) To establish satisfactorily the proposition, that the efficacy of a force to turn a machine round an axis is measured by its *moment*, we ought to prove, that if the moment be doubled or halved, or increased, or decreased, in any proportion, the efficacy of the force in turning the machine round the axle is doubled or halved, or increased or decreased in exactly the same proportion: this may be very easily proved by experiment.

Let the weight W act perpendicularly to the line C F. We shall assume as a self-evident truth, that if the weight W be doubled or halved, or increased or decreased in any proportion, its effort to turn the machine round C will be doubled or halved, or increased or decreased in the same proportion.

Let the power P at the distance C G balance the weight W at the distance C F. Hence the product P × C G must be equal to W × C F. Now, suppose that the power P, or its distance C G from the centre, or both, be so increased, that the moment P × C G shall be doubled, it is evident, that, in order to preserve equilibrium, it will be necessary that the moment W × C F shall be also doubled; and if the distance C F be preserved, this can only be done by doubling W. Hence the double moment P × C G will balance a double weight acting at the same distance C F, and therefore must have a double effect in turning the machine round its centre. In the same manner exactly it may be proved, that in whatever manner the moment P × C G may be varied by the change of the power P, or the distance C G, or both, the weight W must suffer a proportional change, the distance C F remaining unaltered: but the effort to turn the machine round the centre is in this case proportional to the weight W.

(10.) We therefore conclude that the effort of any force to turn a machine round its axis, is rightly measured by the moment of that force round that axis.

Hence, if several forces tend to turn any body round its axis, they will sustain it in equilibrium *if the sum of the moments of those forces which tend to turn it round in one direction, be equal to the sum of the moments of the forces which tend to turn it round in the other direction.* For then, according to what we have just proved, the sum of the efforts which tend to turn the body round in one direction, will be exactly equal to the sum of the efforts which tend to turn it round in the other direction.

This, which is the most general view which can be taken of the lever, may be illustrated by experiment as follows:—

Let a circular board be placed with its plane vertical, and turning upon an horizontal axle C (*fig.* 3.) and let strings

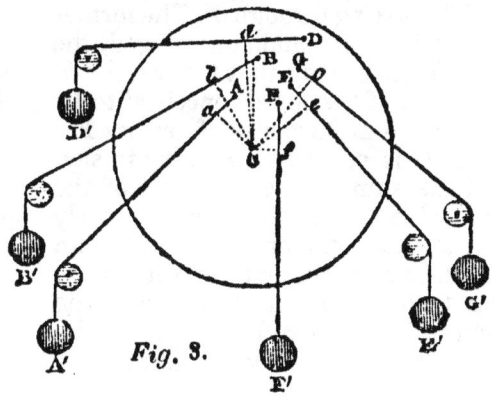

Fig. 3.

be attached to pins A, B, D, E, F; and let these strings be drawn by weights in different directions, passing over fixed wheels as represented in the figure. Let the board drawn by these strings settle itself until it come to a state of equilibrium. Then draw from the centre C perpendiculars C*a*, C*b*, C*d*, C*e*, &c. on the directions of the strings, and measure the lengths of these lines. Multiply the weights A', B', D' by the perpendiculars C*a*, C*b*, C*d*, and the products A' × C*a*, B' × C*b*, D' × C*d*, will express the effort of each weight to turn the board round in one direction. Multiply the weights E', F', G', by the perpendiculars C*e*, C*f*, C*g*, and the products E' × C*e*, F × C*f*, G' × C*g*, will express the effort of each of these weights to turn the board round in the other direction. Now, it will be found that the sum of the former products is equal to the sum of the latter; that is,*

---

* We have endeavoured, as far as possible, in these treatises on MECHANICS, to give the various conditions in a popular form, and divested of geome

$A \times Ca + B' \times Cb + D' \times Cd = E' \times Ce + F' \times Cf + G' \times Cg$; that is, that the sum of the efforts to turn the board round in one direction, is equal to the sum of the efforts to turn it round in the other direction.

(11.) We have hitherto neglected to consider the weight of the machine itself, the axis being always supposed to pass through the centre of gravity. If this be not the case, we have only to consider the weight of the machine itself as one of the weights or forces which are applied to it, and that this force is applied in a vertical direction at the centre of gravity. Thus, for example, in the last experiment, let us suppose the weights A', B', D', E', G' to be the forces which act upon the board. Let F be the centre of gravity of the board, and let F' be its weight acting in the vertical line F F' passing through F. The former investigation will remain unchanged, the only difference being that the weight F' is now that of the board conceived to be concentrated at its centre of gravity F.

(12.) It is scarcely necessary to say, that if the sum of the moments of the forces which tend to turn the body round in one direction, be greater than the sum of the moments of the forces which tend to turn it in the opposite direction, the body will move round its centre in the direction of the former.

CHAPTER III.—*Straight Levers—three kinds—Lever bearing several Weights—Beam bearing a Weight and resting on two Props—Pressure on the Fulcrum of a Lever—Load borne on Poles.*

(13.) A LEVER considered as a bar or rod, supported on a prop or fulcrum, is of three kinds, according to the position of the power and weight with respect to the prop.

If the prop be in the middle, the lever is said to be of the *first kind;* if the weight be in the middle, it is of the *second kind;* and if the power be in the middle, it is a lever of the *third kind.*

(14.) A lever of the first kind is represented in *fig.* 4. If we neglect in

---

trical reasoning or algebraical notation. The student, however, will find his progress most materially facilitated by the acquisition even of a very small portion of the first elements of Geometry and Algebra. For students who only seek this limited knowledge of these sciences, there are perhaps no treatises which can be read with more advantage than DARLEY's *Popular Geometry and Algebra.*

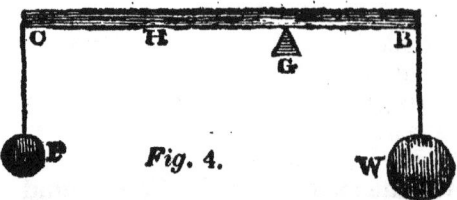

Fig. 4.

the first instance, the weight of the bar itself, or suppose the centre of gravity to be placed immediately over the prop G, the efforts of the power and weight to turn the lever in opposite directions are $P \times p$ and $W \times w$, p and w being C G and B G; and in order that equilibrium should subsist, these must be equal (7.) that is $P \times p = W \times w$.

A lever of the second kind is represented in *fig.* 5; and one of the third kind

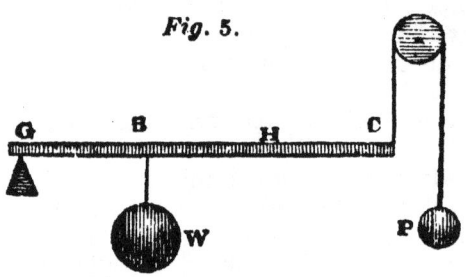

Fig. 5.

in *fig.* 6. What we have just observed respecting the power and weight

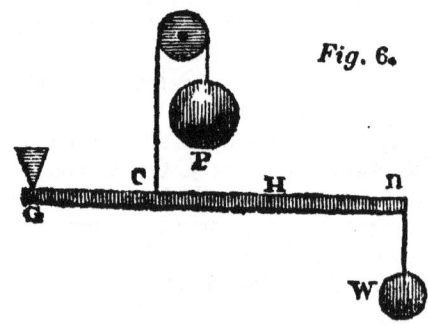

Fig. 6.

in levers of the first kind, also applies to those of the second and third kinds.

(15.) The condition of equilibrium in the straight lever being that the product $P \times p$ should be equal to $W \times w$, it follows, that the power P may be diminished indefinitely by increasing its distance p from the prop indefinitely, for what the magnitude of the product $P \times p$ loses by the diminution of P, it will gain by the increase of p.

There is another way in which the power which supports a given weight by means of a lever may be indefinitely diminished, and yet its distance from the prop may be preserved. Let the distance w of the weight from the prop be diminished until the product $W \times w$ becomes equal to $P \times p$.

Thus the mechanical efficacy of this machine increases as the distance of the power from the prop is increased, and as the distance of the weight from the prop is diminished.

(16.) It is evident on inspection, that in a lever of the *second kind*, the power must necessarily be less than the weight, since it must be farther from the fulcrum; and in a lever of the *third kind* it must be greater than the weight because it is nearer to the fulcrum.

It appears also, that in a lever of the first kind the power and weight act in the *same direction*, both acting downwards; while in those of the second and third kinds they act in opposite directions.

In the lever of the third kind there is a mechanical disadvantage, the power being greater than the weight, and therefore, this species of lever is never used except in cases in which velocity, and not power, is wanted; for it will be remembered that the velocities of the power and weight are as their distances from the prop (7).

(17.) If the centre of gravity of the bar itself be not over the prop, the weight of the bar must be taken into account. Let this be G, and let the distance of the centre of gravity from the prop be g. The moment of this is $G \times g$. If this force tend to turn the lever in the same direction with the power, the condition of equilibrium is

$$P \times p + G \times g = W \times w.$$

But if it conspire with the force of the weight, the condition is

$$P \times p = W \times w + G \times g.$$

If the lever be of uniform thickness, its centre of gravity will be at its middle point. In a lever of the first kind, the whole length is equal to $p + w$; and therefore, if H (*fig.* 4.) be the centre of gravity, C H is equal to $\frac{1}{2} p + \frac{1}{2} w$; but H G or g is equal to C G − H C = $p - \frac{1}{2} p - \frac{1}{2} w = \frac{1}{2} p - \frac{1}{2} w$. Hence, $g = \frac{1}{2} (p - w.)$ That is, the distance of the centre of gravity from the prop is equal to half the difference of the arms.

In levers of the second and third kinds, when they are of uniform thickness, the distance of the centre of gravity from the prop is half the length of the arm, the lever being supposed to extend only on one side of the prop. If it extend on both sides, the distance is the same as in the last case.

(18.) If the arms of the lever be not straight but curved, as in *fig.* 7, the distances p and w are the perpendicu-

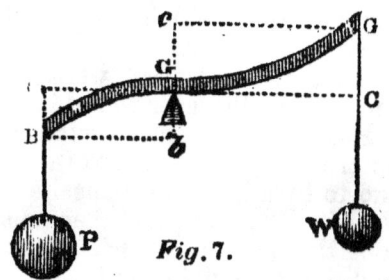

Fig. 7.

lars G B, G C, drawn from the prop upon the directions of the power and weight. But still the condition of equilibrium remains the same, $P \times p = W \times w.$ (7.)

(19.) Also, if the power and weight be not parallel, as in *fig.* 8, the dis-

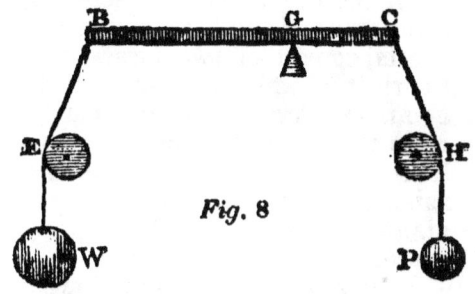

Fig. 8

tances p and w are the perpendiculars drawn from the prop upon the directions of the strings which act upon the lever, and which are drawn by the power and weight.

(20.) If several weights act upon different sides of the prop, as in *fig.* 9,

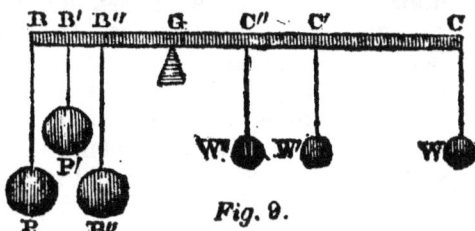

Fig. 9.

or in different directions on the same side, the condition of equilibrium is immediately derived from (10.); viz. the

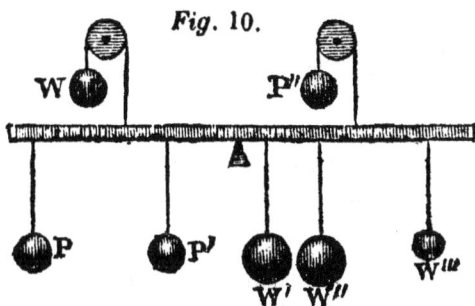

Fig. 10.

sum of the moments of those which tend to turn the machine round in one direction is equal to the sum of moments of those which tend to turn it round in the other.

Thus, if the several weights which tend to turn the lever round in one way be P, P', P'', and their distances from the prop be p, p', p''; and those which tend to turn it in the opposite way be W, W', W'', W''', and their distances from the prop be w, w', w'', w'''; the condition of equilibrium is

$$P \times p + P' \times p'' + P'' \times p'' = W \times w + W' \times w' + W'' \times w'' + W''' \times w'''.$$

If the centre of gravity be not over the prop, the moment $G \times g$ must be added to whichever of these the weight of the machine conspires with.

(21.) Of levers of the first kind there are numerous instances. Scissars, pincers, snuffers, and all similar instruments, consist of two levers, of which the rivet by which they are united is the common fulcrum. A crow-bar used to raise stones and for other purposes, is a lever of the first kind. A poker used for raising the coals in the grate is an instance of this, the bar of the grate being the fulcrum.

Levers of the second kind are not so frequent, yet several instances of them occur. The oar of a boat is an instance. In this case, the water against which the blade presses is the fulcrum, the boat is the weight, and the hand of the rower is the power. The rudder is another instance of the same kind. A door turning on its hinges, or the lid of a desk, are also examples; the hinges being the fulcrum; the door, acting at the centre of gravity, is the weight. A chipping-knife is also an example. This instrument is fixed at one end, the fulcrum; the substance to be cut is placed under it, and the power is applied at the other extremity.

Levers of the third kind, having a mechanical disadvantage, as we have already proved, are the least common. They are used only in cases where despatch is more an object than the exertion of great force. The most striking instance of the use of levers of this kind is in the structure of the limbs of animals, in which the bones are so connected at the joints as to form levers of this kind. In this case their use is peculiarly well adapted to the convenience of the animal, for in almost every case facility and despatch is rather an object than the exertion of intense force. Tongs are also an instance of this species of lever; and shears for shearing sheep.

In elevating a ladder, it is first a lever of the second and afterwards of the third kind. While the centre of gravity is between the hands that raise it and the end on which it rests, it is a lever of the second kind, and when the hands pass the centre of gravity it becomes a lever of the third kind.

(22.) A bar supporting a weight by two props acts on the principles of a lever. Suppose the prop B removed

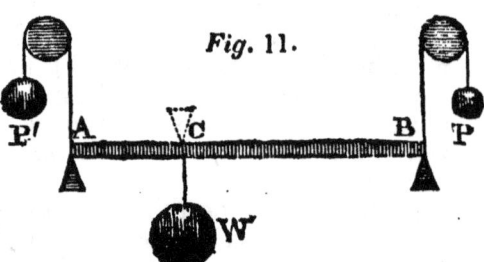

Fig. 11.

and replaced by a power P, as represented in the figure; that power will evidently represent the pressure of the weight W on the prop B. Now, by the principles already established are

$$P \times AB = W \times AC,$$

and therefore,

$$P = W \times \tfrac{AC}{AB};$$

and in exactly the same manner, if P' represent the pressure on the prop A, we find

$$P' = W \times \tfrac{BC}{AB}.$$

The pressure on each prop is therefore a certain fractional part of the weight, viz. that fraction whose numerator is the distance of the weight from the other prop, and whose denominator is the distance between the props.

It follows from this that the sum of the pressures is equal to the weight, and that the weight is distributed between the props in the *inverse* proportion of its distances from them.

(23.) It easily follows from this, that the pressure upon the fulcrum of a lever of the second or third kind is equal to the *difference* between the power and weight. For if A be considered as the fulcrum, W the weight, and P the power; the lever will be of the second kind, and P' will be the pressure on the fulcrum; and by what we have already proved, P' is the difference between W and P. If P be considered as the weight, and W as the power, it is a lever of the third kind, and the same observation applies.

If at C a fulcrum be placed presented downwards, and the weight W be removed, and in place of the props A and

MECHANICS.

B, the weights P′ and P act at those points, the pressure on the fulcrum C will evidently be equal to the weight W which was removed. But W is equal to the sum of P′ and P, and in this case the lever is one of the first kind. Hence, in a lever of the first kind, the pressure on the fulcrum is equal to the sum of the power and weight.

(24.) In (22) we supposed that the bar which sustains the weight rests on the props in a horizontal position. But the conclusions which we have deduced are equally true if the bar be inclined to the horizon and the weight is distributed between the props precisely in the same proportion. For let A B (*fig.* 12.) be the beam, and, as before, let the prop B be replaced by a weight P acting over a wheel, and let the vertical line in which the string

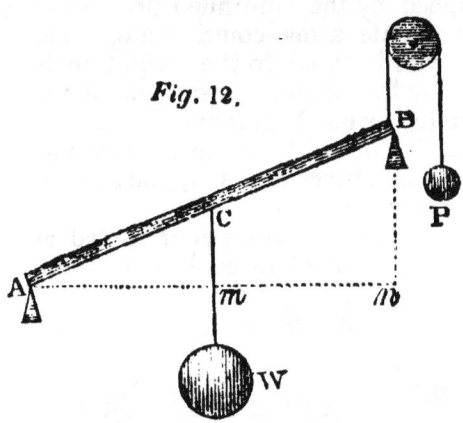

Fig. 12.

from B acts be B n, and let C W be the direction of the weight. This is a lever of the second kind, and by (14) it follows that

$$P : W :: A m : A n.$$

But since C m and B n are parallel, it follows by the principles of geometry that A m : A n :: A C : A B. Hence

$$P : W :: A C : A B$$

or $P = W \times \frac{AC}{AB}$

which is the same value as we obtained for the pressure on the prop B when we supposed the beam A B to be horizontal.

Hence it appears that, whether the beam be horizontal or inclined, the weight is distributed between the props in the same proportion.

From what we have established in (22) it follows, that when the weight is placed at the middle point of the beam, it is equally distributed between the props, each prop bearing half of it.

(25.) When two men bear a weight on poles, the proportion sustained by each is to be determined on the principles which we have just established, and when it is, as is usual, placed in the centre between them, each bearer carries half the load. If the centre of gravity of the load be in the plane of the poles which support it, this equal distribution of the load continues whether the bearers move on a level plane or on a declivity. If, however, the centre of gravity be above or below the poles, the load is not equally distributed if the bearers are on an ascent or descent. In this case let G (*fig.* 13.) be the centre of

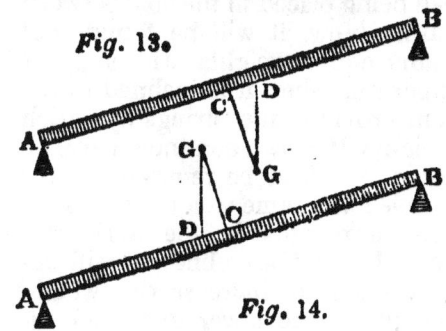

Fig. 13.

Fig. 14.

gravity of the load below the poles A B, and through G draw the vertical line G D. Since the weight acts as if it were collected at the centre of gravity, it must produce the same effect as if it were suspended from D, and consequently is distributed between the bearers A and B in the proportion of B D to A D, and consequently it presses more severely on the upper bearer B.

But if, on the other hand, the centre of gravity be *above* the beam, the weight, acting as if it were placed at D (*fig.* 14.), is distributed between the bearers A B in the proportion B D to A D, and therefore presses more severely on the lower bearer A.

This may be proved experimentally by providing two straight bars, A B, A′B′, (*fig.* 15.) and attaching them to the sides

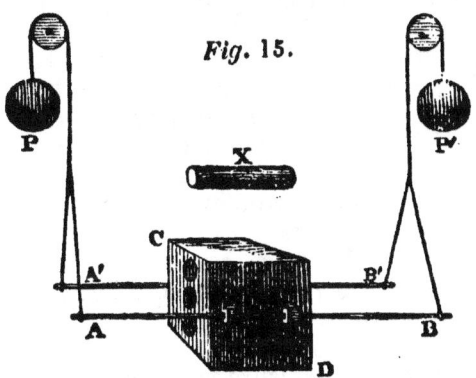

Fig. 15.

of a block of wood C D, which is pierced with three holes, in any of which may be placed a cylindrical piece of lead X. Let the apparatus be so adjusted that when the lead is put into the hole between the bars, the centre of gravity will be between them, and that the centre of gravity will be below or above them when the lead is put into the hole which is below or above the bars. Let strings be attached to the extremities of the bars, and passing them over wheels as represented in the figure, let the whole apparatus be supported in the horizontal position by equal weights, P and P', the lead being placed in the hole between the bars. Now, it will be found that the same equal weights will support the apparatus when it is inclined to the horizon, provided the strings by which the weights P P' act continue parallel. Let, then, the lead be removed to the upper hole; the same weights will support the apparatus in the horizontal position; but if it be inclined, it will become necessary to increase the weight which supports the lower end, and diminish that which supports the upper end. On the other hand, if the lead be placed in the lower hole, when the apparatus is inclined, it will be necessary to increase the weight which supports the upper end, and to diminish that which supports the lower end.

Throughout these experiments the strings which support the weights should be kept parallel.

Mechanical writers have sometimes investigated this problem erroneously.

CHAPTER IV.—*Compound Levers— Rectangular Lever—Weighing Machine — All simple and complex Machines reducible to equivalent Levers.*

(26.) THE power may act upon the weight through the intervention of a series of levers, in which case the apparatus is called a *composition of levers*, or a *compound lever*. There is one general condition which applies to every combination of levers, viz. that "When the system is in equilibrium, the power multiplied by the continued product of the alternate arms commencing from the power, is equal to the weight multiplied by the continued product of the alternate arms beginning from the weight." This will be more easily understood by observing its application to the following examples.

The system of levers represented in *fig.* 16 consists of three levers of the first kind. The power acting at B exerts a certain pressure at B'. Let

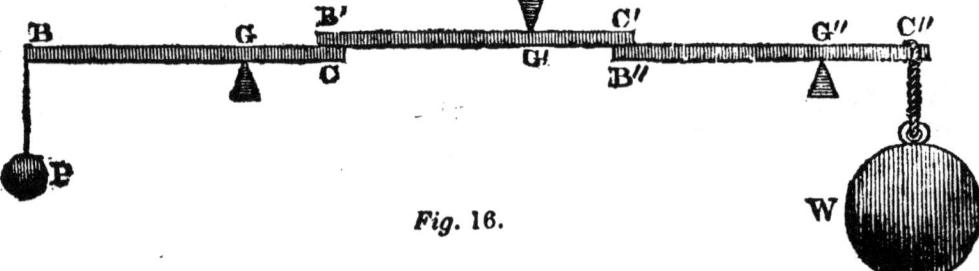

Fig. 16.

this pressure be called x. Again, the pressure x by means of the lever B' C' produces a pressure, which we call y, at C', and the pressure y at C' supports the weight W at C''.

Let the alternate arms B G, B' G', B'' G'', commencing from the power, be called p, p' and p''; and let the alternate arms C'' G'', C' G', C G, commencing from the weight, be w'', w', and w. Now, since the power P equilibrates with the pressure x, we have

$$P p = x \cdot w.$$

Also, since the pressure x equilibrates with the pressure y, we have

$$x\, p' = y\, w';$$

and since the pressure y equilibrates with the weight W, we have

$$y\, p'' = W \cdot w''.$$

Since $P p$, $x p'$, and $y p''$ are respectively equal to $x w$, $y w'$, and $W w''$, it follows that, if the former be multiplied together, they will be equal to the latter multiplied together. Hence we have

$$P\, p\, x\, p'\, y\, p'' = x\, w\, y\, w'\, W\, w''.$$

In these equal products, by omitting the common multipliers x and y, we obtain

$$P \cdot p\, p'\, p'' = W\, w\, w'\, w'';^*$$

that is, *the power multiplied by the continued product of the alternate arms commencing from the power, is equal to the weight multiplied by the continued product of the alternate arms commencing from the weight.*

Those students who are not sufficiently masters of the signification of the alge-

---

* See DARLEY's *Algebra*, p. 61.

braic notation to follow the preceding very simple proof, may easily be satisfied of the truth of the result by actual experiment.

Let us suppose that the arms p, p', p'', are 4, 6 and 8 inches respectively, and that w, w', w'' are 1, 2 and 3 inches; it will be found that a power of two ounces at B will sustain a weight of 64 ounces at C″. In this case we have the product $2 \times 4 \times 6 \times 8$ equal to 384, and the product $64 \times 1 \times 2 \times 3$ also equal to 384; and the same would be found to be true of any power and weight which would balance each other.

The demonstration which we have given above of the condition of equilibrium will be found to apply equally to any system of compound levers. *Fig.* 17 is a system of levers of the second kind.

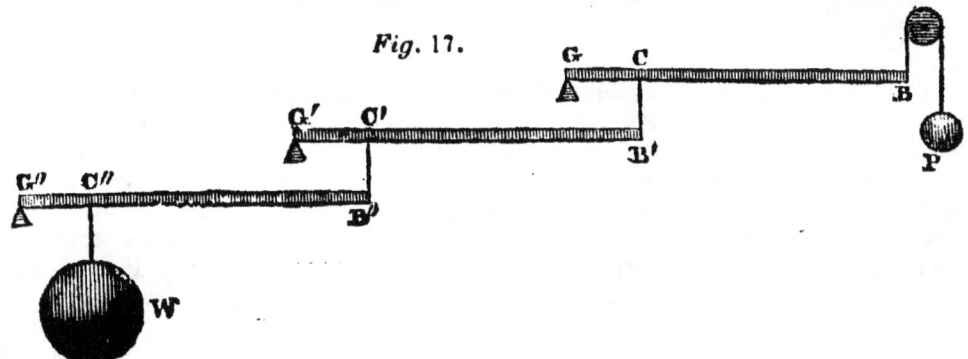

Fig. 17.

The alternate arms, beginning from the power, and those beginning from the weight, are marked by the same letter as in *fig.* 16.

In *fig.* 18, we have represented a system of mixed levers, some of the first, and some of the second, kind. The same condition establishes the equilibrium.

(27.) A rectangular lever is a form

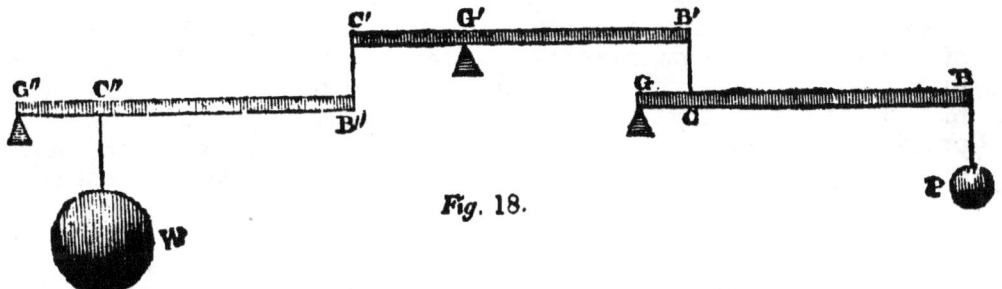

Fig. 18.

not unfrequently used, and is governed by the same condition of equilibrium as other levers. Such a lever is represented in *fig.* 19. The weight W is

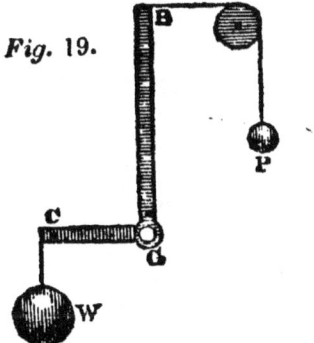

Fig. 19.

suspended from the shorter arm G C or w, and the power P from the longer G B, or p: the condition of equilibrium is evidently

$$P p = W w.$$

When a hammer is used for drawing a nail it is a lever of this kind, G C being the claw and G B the handle. In this and all the other cases which we have now noticed, we consider the axis, or fulcrum, to pass through the centre of gravity of the lever, and therefore we have not attended to the effect of the weight of the bar itself.

The condition of equilibrium in the rectangular lever may be verified by experiment in a manner similar to the other cases, by suspending such weights as will produce equilibrium, and multiplying them by the lengths of the arms by which they respectively act, and showing that $P p = W w$.

(28.) The rectangular lever may form part of a compound system, as in *fig.* 20; but the general condition of equilibrium established in (7.) will still be applicable.

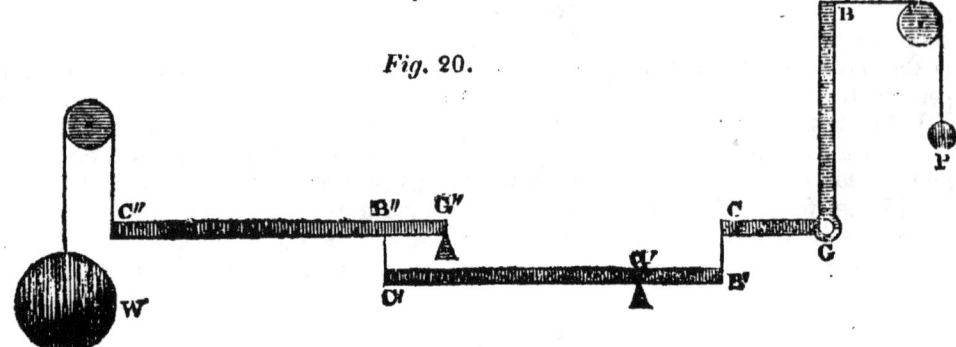

Fig. 20.

(29.) The *weighing-machine* is formed of a composition of levers. This machine may be used in any case where considerable weights are to be determined, and is commonly used at turnpikes in weighing wagons, to ascertain that they are not loaded beyond what is allowed by law to the breadth of their wheels.

A system of levers is placed in a horizontal position in a box about a foot deep, so that a platform supported by the levers shall be on a level with the road; the wagon to be weighed being rolled upon the platform, the power which, through the intervention of the combination of levers, is capable of sustaining it, becomes an indication of its weight. The advantage of this is, that a very small weight becomes the measure of a very great one, and the practical process of weighing is thereby expedited.

Fig. 21 is a ground plan of the system of levers in such a machine as this*. In the middle of the box is a fulcrum-pin, $l\,k$, formed like the nail of

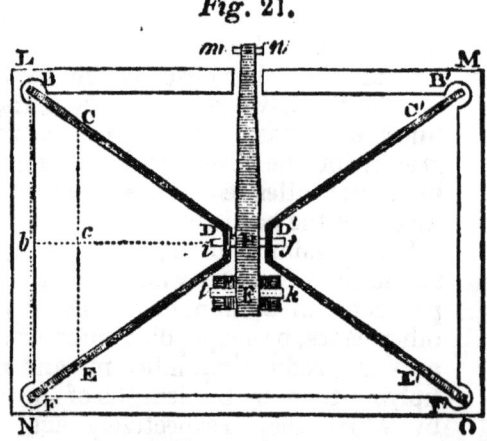

Fig. 21.

a balance, which rests with its edge on arches of hardened steel firmly fastened to the bottom of the box. This lever goes through one side of the box, and is furnished at its extremity with a hard steel pin $m\,n$, also formed to an edge below. In the centre of the box a nail of hard steel $i\,j$ passes through the lever just mentioned at P, and presents a hard edge upwards. In the four corners L M N O of the box are firmly fixed small blocks of hard steel, having hollow hemispherical cavities or cups in their upper surfaces. B C D E F represent the upper edge of a strong iron bar, having hard steel studs on its lower surface at B and F, which rest in the cups or cavities of the steel blocks just mentioned. There is also a hard edge immediately under D which rests on the edge of $i\,j$ and at right angles to it. At C E are fixed studs of pointed steel presented upwards. On the other side of the lever is a similar arrangement marked by the same letters accented.

We have, then, four pointed studs presented upwards, and which are so adjusted as to be in the same horizontal plane. On these studs the platform rests on which the body to be weighed is placed.

Now, suppose that a wire or rod be connected with the end $m\,n$ of the lever F P, and be carried upwards perpendicularly to the plane of the box L M O N, and finally, be connected with the end of another lever, from the other arm of which the counterpoise or power is suspended; the amount of that power or counterpoise will be the indication of the weight upon the platform. To determine the proportion of this counterpoise to the weight on the platform, let the arms B C, F P, and the arm of the final lever with which $l\,m$ is connected be w, w' and w'' respectively, and let B D, F m and the arm of the final lever on which the power acts be p, p', and p'' respectively. The four levers B' D', B D,

---

* For a more detailed account of this machine, see Gregory's *Mechanics*, vol. ii. p. 553.

FD, F′D′, being perfectly equal and similar, the effect of the weight distributed amongst them is the same as if the whole weight rested upon any one. Hence the condition of equilibrium is
$$P \times p\, p'\, p'' = W \times w\, w'\, w''.$$
Thus, if w and w' be each one foot, and that p and p' be each 10 feet, and if w'' be one inch, and p'' be one foot; we have
$$P \times 10 \times 10 \times 1 = W \times 1 \times 1 \times \tfrac{1}{12}$$
$$\text{or } 100\, P = \tfrac{W}{12}$$
that is $1200\, P = W$.
In which case the weight would be 1200 times the counterpoise, and thus a weight of one pound would balance 1200 lbs.

By a proper adjustment of the levers, the indicating weight might be made to have any convenient relation to the weight to be ascertained. Thus one ounce might correspond to one hundred weight. This would be effected if w and w' were each one foot, and p were 8 feet, p'' 16 feet, and w'' one inch, and p'' 14 inches: for then we should have
$$P \times 8 \times 16 \times \tfrac{14}{12} = W \times 1 \times 1 \times \tfrac{1}{12}$$
$$\text{or } 1792\, P = W\ ;$$
that is, the weight is 1792 times the counterpoise; and since there are 1792 ounces in one hundred weight, it follows, that one ounce will balance an hundred weight.

(30.) The *mechanical efficacy* of a machine depends on the ratio of the weight to the power, and is said to be greater or less according as this ratio is greater or less. It might be well at once to define the mechanical efficacy to be the numerical quota arising from the division of the weight by the power. Thus, if the weight be ten times the power, the mechanical efficacy is ten. If three times the weight is equal to twenty times the power, the mechanical efficacy is $\tfrac{20}{3}$ or $6\tfrac{2}{3}$. It follows, therefore, that when this quantity is a proper fraction, what in ordinary cases is mechanical efficacy, becomes a mechanical disadvantage, as when the weight is half the power. We have already seen when the power on the lever is between the weight and prop, the machine acts in this way under a mechanical disadvantage.

(31.) The same lever admits of having its mechanical efficacy varied at pleasure, by changing the positions of the power and weight with respect to the prop, so that it may be made to act with any given mechanical efficacy, or even with any mechanical disadvantage. This is a property in which it is distinguished from most other simple machines, and one which renders it a convenient standard or modulus for representing all other machines. Whatever be the proportion of the power and weight in any machine, a lever may be assigned in which the power and weight will have the same proportion, and which, therefore, we call an *equivalent lever*.

As all simple machines may be represented by equivalent simple levers, so all complex machines may be represented by equivalent systems of compound levers. To effect this, it is only necessary to determine the proportion of the power to the weight in all the simple component machines, which, in the complex machine under consideration, are interposed between the weight and the power, and take a series of levers whose alternate arms, beginning from the power, bear the same proportions to the remaining arms respectively. Such a system of levers will be *mechanically equivalent* to the complex machine.

Hence, and from the result of (26) it follows, that in any complex machine, the proportion of the power to the weight may be easily assigned, provided the proportions of the power to the weight in the simple component machines are known. For let these proportions be $w : p$, $w' : p'$ and $w'' : p''$; then the proportion of the power and weight in the complex machine will be determined by
$$P . p\, p'\, p'' = W, w\, w'\, w''.$$
When we say that a lever or a system of levers can always be found which are *mechanically equivalent* to any given machine, we would be understood to mean only, that the same power will sustain the same weight in each, but by no means implying that all the mechanical functions of each species of machine can be discharged by a system of levers.

Chapter V.—*The Balance—common Balance with equal Arms—its requisites—sensibility—Method of detecting a fraudulent Balance—Steel-yard—Danish Balance—bent lever Balance—Brady's Balance.*

(32.) The balance is an instrument used for determining the weights of bodies, by showing their relation to the weights of some other bodies which are known, or which are assumed as general standards of weight. This is one of the most interesting and generally useful applications of the lever, and assumes various forms, according to the nature and magnitude of the substances whose weights are to be determined, and to the degree of accuracy which is required in the result.

The most usual form of the balance is that of a lever of *the first kind* with equal arms; so that the substance to be weighed being suspended from one arm, and the weights assumed as standards of comparison being suspended from the other, the equilibrium will necessarily be established when these weights are equal (14).

This, however, is only the general principle of the *common balance*. In its construction there are various circumstances to be attended to which are of considerable importance.

(33.) The lever which forms the balance, and which is called the *beam*, should be so constructed that its centre of gravity should be immediately *under* the axis or centre of motion. For if the centre of gravity were itself the centre of motion, the beam would rest indifferently in any position; whereas the equality of the weights is determined by its assuming the horizontal position. If the centre of gravity were above the centre of motion, the least disturbance would cause the beam to upset. (*Treatise I.* chap. iv.)

The centre of gravity being, by the construction of the beam, beneath the centre of motion, the line joining it with the centre of motion will, when the beam is unloaded, always settle itself so as to be in a vertical direction.

(34.) The substance to be weighed, and the weights with which it is compared, are placed in dishes suspended from points at the extremities of the beam, called the *points of suspension*. These points should be so placed, that a straight line drawn joining them shall be perpendicular to the straight line which is drawn joining the centres of

Fig. 22.

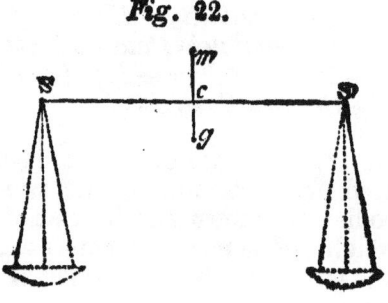

gravity and motion, and so that it shall be divided by that line into two equal parts.

That is, if S and S' (*fig.* 22.) be the **points of suspension**, m the centre of motion, and g the centre of gravity of the beam; the lines S S' and $m\,g$ should intersect at c at right angles, and S c should be equal to S' c.

The beam being thus constructed, the point g will, by the properties of the centre of gravity explained in *Treatise I.* settle itself vertically below m, so that $m\,g$ shall be perpendicular to an horizontal plane. The line S S', being perpendicular to $g\,m$, will in that case be horizontal.

(35.) In order to exhibit, in using the balance, the direction of the line $m\,g$ (*fig.* 23.) a needle or index is attached to the beam, which sometimes plays upon a graduated arch; and when it is directed to that point of the arch which is in a vertical line passing through the centre of motion, the line S S' will be horizontal, and the line $m\,g$, which is the direction of the index, will be vertical. This, as we shall presently see, is the position of the balance which indicates the equality of the weights suspended from S and S'.

Fig. 23.

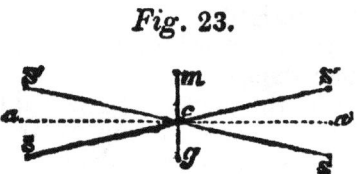

(36.) The practical determination of all these circumstances in a beam is not difficult. Under any circumstances, the line $m\,g$, when the beam is at rest, will be vertical. In order to determine whether S S' is in that case horizontal or perpendicular to $m\,g$, let the beam be suspended against a vertical plane, and mark the points on the plane at which S and S' are placed. Then lift the beam off its centre and reverse it. If it be found that S' exactly takes the place of S, and S of S', then the line S S' is horizontal, and at right angles to $m\,g$, but otherwise not. To explain this more clearly, let us suppose, that the line S S' is, in the first instance, not perpendicular to $m\,g$, but that it deviates from the perpendicular $a\,c$ by the angle S $c\,a$. Let the position of the points S and S' on the vertical plane against which the beam is suspended be marked, and let the beam be reversed. When reversed, it will assume the position represented by the faint line, the arm S'c being as much above the horizontal line ac as it was when on the other side above the horizontal line a'c; but that is evidently as much as the arm Sc was below the horizontal line ac. Hence, it is quite apparent, that if the positions of the points S and S' below and above the line ac before and after reversion be noted, half the angle S'cS will be the deviation of the line Sc or SS' from the perpendicular aa'.

(37.) A process somewhat similar to this serves to determine the deviation of the index from the direction of the line gm (fig. 24.) Suppose that the previous adjustment has been made, and that the line SS' is perpendicular to gm; but

Fig. 24.

still that the index mv deviates from the direction of gm by the angle bmv. It is necessary to determine practically whether any such deviation exists, and if so, to what amount.

As before, suppose the beam suspended against a vertical plane, and the position of the point v marked. Let the beam be reversed, and the index will assume the position mv', deviating as much to the left side of the true direction mb as it before deviated to the right. The point v' being then marked, the angle v'mv will be twice the deviation of the index from its true position.

The common commercial balance is usually sustained upon a loop of metal on which the beam rests by a knife edge. In this case, when the beam is unloaded, the index ought to settle exactly between the sides of the loop, and it should always be in this position when equal weights are suspended from S and S'.

(38.) The several adjustments which we have now described being made, it will be evident that, when equal weights are suspended from SS', the beam will maintain its horizontal position. For the perpendicular distances of the vertical lines through S and S', which are the directions in which the weights act are equal, being, in fact, Sc and Sc'. Hence these distances, when multiplied by the equal weights, will give equal products, and therefore the weights will have equal tendencies to turn the machine in opposite directions round the centre of motion m, and, consequently, they will mutually destroy each other's effects, and the instrument will maintain the position it had when unloaded.

But let us consider what would be the consequence if unequal weights were suspended from S and S'. Let W be suspended from S, and W' from S', and let W be the greater. Let the common length of the arms Sc and S'c be a.

The tendency of the weight W to depress the arm Sc is measured by the product of this weight, and the length a of the arm Sc or W × a; and the tendency of the weight W' to resist this is the product of the weight W' and the arm S'c, or W' × a. Now, as W is greater than W', the product of W and a must be greater than the product of W' and a, and therefore the tendency of W to depress the arm Sc is greater than the tendency of W' to resist that, and therefore the arm Sc will fall and S'c will rise.

It appears, therefore, that if the balance be properly constructed, and the several adjustments which we have pointed out be attended to, it will only maintain that position in which the beam is horizontal, and the index vertical, when loaded with equal weights; but that if either weight be greater than the other, it will always incline in the direction of the greater weight.

The *sensibility* of a balance is measured by the smallness of the difference of weights which turns the index from its unloaded position mo, and by the greatness of the deviation vmo from the unloaded position which that difference produces. To explain this more fully, let us suppose that, W being greater than W', the beam rests in equilibrium in the position represented in *fig.* 25.

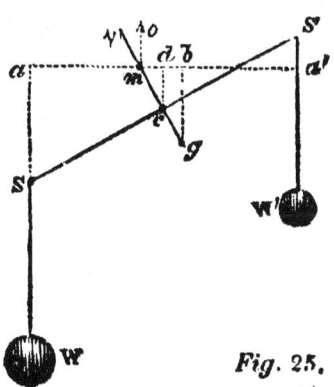

Fig. 25.

Let the weight of the entire beam be G. Through m let a line $a\, m\, a'$ be conceived to be drawn perpendicular to the directions of the weights, and therefore horizontal. Through c draw $c\, d$ perpendicular to $a\, a'$, and therefore parallel to $S\, a$ and $S'\, a'$, and parallel to the same lines let $g\, b$ be drawn. The machine is thus maintained in equilibrium on its centre m by three weights, viz. W in the direction $a\, S$, W' in the direction $S'\, a'$, and G acting at the centre of gravity (*Treatise I.* chap. iv.) of the beam, and in the direction $b\, g$. The weight W tends to turn the system round in one direction, and the weights G and W' tend to turn it round in the other direction; and since these tendencies mutually counteract each other, the product $W \times a\, m$, of the weight W and its leverage $a\, m$ must be equal to $(W' \times a'\, m + G \times b\, m)$ the sum of the products of the weights W' and G multiplied into their respective leverages $a'\, m$ and $b\, m$.

Since c is the middle point of the line $S\, S'$, and since $S\, a$, $c\, d$, and $S'\, a'$ are parallel, d must be the middle point of the line $a\, a'$, and therefore $a\, m$ will be obviously less than $a'\, m$, and therefore, in the present position of the beam, W acts with a less leverage than W'. A little attention to the figure will show that, as the weight W depresses the beam, it continually loses its leverage, and that, on the other hand, W' is continually gaining leverage on W. Besides this, the weight of the beam G, which, in the unloaded position, had no leverage, gains leverage continually as W depresses S, and conspires with W' in resisting the descent of S by the force of the heavier weight W. This being the state of the forces, they must come to equilibrium after the beam has turned from its unloaded position. Now, the greater the deviation of the beam from its unloaded position, when it attains the state of equilibrium, the greater will be its *sensibility*, the difference of the weights being the same. The sensibility then, it is evident, will be increased by diminishing those causes which resist the deflection of the beam from its unloaded position by the heavier weight W. One of the principal of these causes is the weight of the beam G acting with the leverage $b\, m$. Hence it follows, that, all other things being the same, the sensibility of a balance will be increased by diminishing the weight of the beam, and by diminishing also the distance $m\, g$ between the centres of gravity and motion, for that will evidently diminish the leverage $m\, b$.

Another cause which resists the effect of W is the relatively increased leverage of W'. This will be diminished by diminishing $m\, d$ (d being the middle point of $a\, a'$) or $c\, m$, that is, by diminishing the distance of the line which joins the points of suspension from the centre of motion.

(40.) To those students who have attained a slight knowledge of the most elementary parts of mathematical science, the following investigation of the circumstances which regulate the sensibility of the balance will be more satisfactory than the popular explanation which we have just attempted to give. Those students who are not familiar with elementary mathematics will pass over this article.

Let the angle $o\, m\, v$, by which the index is deflected from the vertical position, be D. Let $g\, m = d$, $c\, m = b$, and $S\, c$ or $S'\, c = a$. Since the angles $m\, c\, d$ and $m\, g\, b$ are each equal to D, by the parallels, and the angles d and b are right, we have $d\, m = b \sin D$ and $b\, m = d \sin D$. Also, since the angles formed by the lines $S\, S'$ and $a\, a'$ are equal to that formed by $m\, v$ and $m\, o$, which are respectively perpendicular to the former, that angle is equal to D, and since the angles at $a\, a'$ are right, we have $S\, S' \times \cos D = a\, a'$, or $a\, a' = 2\, a \cos D$, and therefore $a\, d = a \cos D$. But $a\, m = a\, d - m\, d = a \cos D - b \sin D$, and $a'\, m = a\, d + m\, d = a \cos D + b \sin d$.

Now, suppose that the weight W consists of two parts, one equal to W', and therefore the other E to the difference between W and W': the combined effect of that part of W which is equal to W', and of W' itself, will be the same as if 2 W' acted at the middle point c of the beam, and with the leverage $m\, d$. Hence the condition of equilibrium will be

$$E \times a\, m = 2\, W' \times m\, d + G \times m\, b, \text{ or}$$
$$E\, (a \cos D - b \sin D) = 2\, W'\, b \sin D + G\, d \sin D.$$

Dividing this entire equation by $\cos D$, observing that $\dfrac{\sin D}{\cos D} = \tan D$

we have $E\,(a - b \tan D) = 2\, W'\, b \tan D + G\, d \tan D.$

$\therefore \tan D \left\{ (E + 2\, W')\, b + G\, d \right\} = E\, a.\quad \therefore \dfrac{\tan D}{E} = \dfrac{a}{G\, d + (2\, W' + E)\, b}.$

The first member of this equation may be taken as the measure of the sensibility.

(41.) From the result of this investigation, the student will find no difficulty in drawing the following conclusions:—

1. That all other things being the same, the sensibility of a balance is increased by increasing the lengths of its arms.
2. That all other things being the same, the sensibility is increased, diminishing the weight of the beam.
3. That the sensibility is increased by diminishing the distance between the centres of gravity and motion.
4. That the sensibility is increased by diminishing the distance of the line, joining the points of suspension from the centre of motion.
5. That the sensibility is greater when the load is smaller.

We cannot here pursue this subject further, although numerous other interesting consequences might be deduced. We have supposed that the line joining the points of suspension is below the centre of motion. This is not always the case, and when it is above it, the formula which we have obtained for the sensibility becomes

$$\frac{\tan. D}{E} = \frac{a}{G\,d - (2\,W' + E)\,b}.$$

We leave the mathematical student to pursue the effects of this modification on the sensibility.

(42.) In the practical construction of a balance of a high degree of sensibility for philosophical purposes, there are many circumstances to be attended to, which are properly enough neglected in balances used for commercial purposes.

Fig. 26. is a representation of a very sensible philosophical balance, by which very minute differences of weight may be determined. The beam S S' has arms of equal length, and of perfectly equal and similar figures. It is very accurately placed upon knife-edges at *m*, which rest upon highly-polished plates of hardened steel. The beam is only allowed to rest upon the plates when in use. Two forks are placed under its arms at G G', supported by vertical pillars, which when raised by screws which are represented at the foot of each pillar, will lift the beam from the plates on which the knife-edges rest. By this, the wear arising from the continued pressure of the edges on

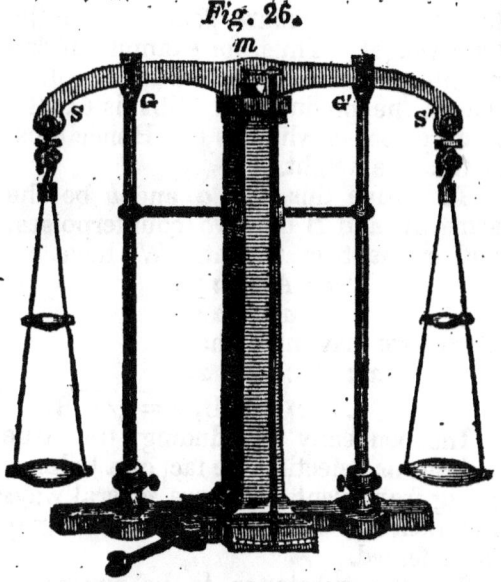

Fig. 26.

the plates is avoided. A needle or index is attached to the centre *m* and plays upon a graduated arch below, and points to zero on the arch when there is exact equilibrium. A balance such as this is generally inclosed in a glass case, and only opened sufficiently to introduce into the dishes the weights and substances to be weighed.

(43.) Commercial balances are frequently misconstructed for fraudulent purposes, by making the arm, from which the substance to be weighed is suspended, longer than that from which the counterpoise is hung, thereby giving the substance to be weighed a greater leverage and enabling it to support a counterpoise proportionally greater than itself. The end to be attained by the use of such a balance may be defeated in several ways. If the object be merely to detect the fraud, it will be sufficient, after equilibrium has been established between the substance to be weighed and the weights, to transpose them, and put the substance to be weighed in the dish in which the weights were, and *vice versâ*. If the balance be honestly constructed, the equilibrium will be undisturbed; but if it be fraudulent, the substance to be weighed will preponderate, since, after the transposition, it will have the greater leverage. But if the object be not alone to detect the fraud, but to ascertain the true weight of the substance, let the counterpoise which will produce equilibrium after transposition be found, and let this and the former counterpoise be reduced to the same denomination of weight, and let the two counterpoises thus expressed be multiplied together, and the square root of the product extracted; that square root will be the true weight. Thus, for example, if one counterpoise be 7lbs., and the other 9¼lbs., the product 7 × 9¼lbs. is 64, the square root of which is 8. Hence 8lbs. is the true weight.

To prove this, let a and b be the arms, A and B the two counterpoises, and x the true weight. We have
$$x : A :: a : b.$$
$$B : x :: a : b.$$
Hence we may infer, that
$$x : A :: B : x.$$
$$\therefore x^2 = AB, x = \sqrt{AB}.$$

Independently of finding the true weight, or detecting the fact of a balance being fraudulent, there are several ways in which the design of the vender may be defeated.

Let the substance to be purchased be bought in two quantities nominally equal, and let these be weighed in different dishes; the result will be, that the buyer will always get more than the just quantity, in proportion as the balance is more fraudulent. Thus, suppose that the arms of the balance were in the proportion of 11 to 12, and that two pounds of any substance be weighed in different dishes, the counterpoise in each case being just a pound: in the one case the buyer will receive eleven-twelfths of a pound, and in the other twelve-elevenths; so that in one portion he will receive one-twelfth less than one pound, and in the other he will receive one-eleventh more than a pound. Now, one-eleventh being more than one-twelfth, he will, on the whole, receive more than the just quantity, by the difference between an eleventh and a twelfth, or by $\frac{1}{132}$ of a pound.

In general, let $a\ b$ be the arms, W the counterpoise, and x and y the two portions, nominally equal,
$$x : W :: a : b \therefore x = W \cdot \frac{a}{b}$$
$$y : W :: b : a \therefore y = W \cdot \frac{b}{a}$$
Hence we find,
$$x + y = W \left(\frac{a}{b} + \frac{b}{a} \right)$$

Now, the sum of a number and its reciprocal is always greater than 2, and therefore $x + y$ is greater than 2 W.

But the best way of ascertaining the true weight of a substance with a fraudulent balance, or indeed with any common balance, is to place the substance in one dish, and accurately counterpoise it with fine sand in the other. Then take out the substance to be weighed, and replace it by the weights with which it is to be compared; and the equilibrium being produced by them, the true weight will thus be determined, independent of all imperfection of the instrument.

(44.) Besides the common balance with equal arms, there are various other modifications of the lever used for determining the weights of bodies. We have already described one (the *Weighing Machine*,) for ascertaining very great weights. Those which we shall now describe are suited to ascertain the weights of smaller quantities.

The *Roman balance*, or the *common steel-yard* (*fig.* 27.) consists of a beam or a bar of iron resting upon knife-edges or

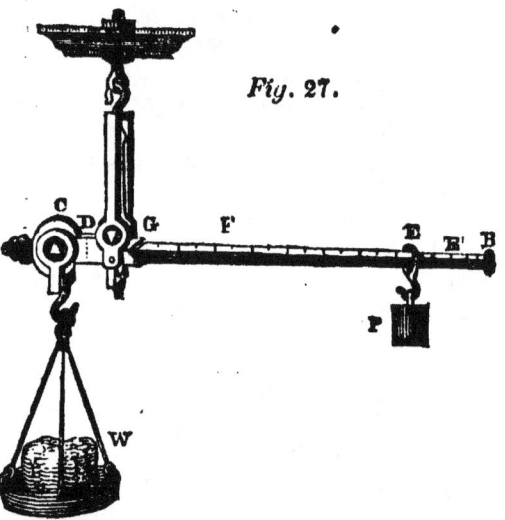

Fig. 27.

a pivot, and having one arm much longer than the other. We shall first suppose, that the shorter arm is rendered so heavy as to balance the longer arm when the instrument is unloaded, and that in that state the beam is horizontal. A hook is fixed upon the shorter arm, from which the substance to be weighed is to be suspended, and a determinate and moveable weight P slides on the longer arm. Equilibrium is established by moving the sliding-weight P from the centre G until it acquires such a leverage that it supports the weight W. The arm G B is graduated, so that it indicates the amount of the weight W at the point where the sliding-weight supports it.

The principle of this machine, and the method of graduating it, are very simple. By the general property of the lever, the condition of equilibrium is, that the weight W multiplied by its distance w from the fulcrum, is equal to the counterpoise P multiplied into its distance p from the fulcrum, or W × w

$= P \times p$. Now, since the distance w of the weight from the fulcrum always remains the same, and since the counterpoise P is not changed, it follows, that in whatever proportion W is increased or diminished, p must be increased or diminished in exactly the same proportion, in order to sustain the equality of the products we have just mentioned; that is, if W be doubled or trebled, p must be likewise doubled or trebled, and so on.

If, then, it be required to graduate the steel-yard so as to indicate to the exactness of ounces, let one ounce be suspended from C, and let the counterpoise P be moved towards G until the beam rests in the horizontal position. Then let two ounces be suspended from C, and move the counterpoise P from G until the beam rests as before. Having marked two divisions at the two positions of the counterpoise thus obtained, let the whole length of the arm G B be divided into equal divisions at the same distance, and the number of any division, beginning from that which is nearest to G, will give the number of ounces which the counterpoise P placed at that division will sustain.

If the centre of gravity of the beam be not at or under the fulcrum, the graduation must be effected differently. First, let us suppose that the centre of gravity of the beam is at D at the same side of the fulcrum with the weight. In that case the end C of the beam will preponderate when unloaded. Let F be the place at which the counterpoise P must be suspended in order to keep the unloaded beam horizontal, and let G F be called f. As before, let the steel-yard be graduated to ounces. The counterpoise P being placed at F, let one ounce be suspended from C, and a division having been marked at F, let the counterpoise be moved from G until equilibrium is established. Let the second division be marked at that position. After this, let the divisions towards B be continued at equal distances, and the number of any division beginning from F will be the number of ounces which the counterpoise P placed at that division will sustain: for let the distance D G be d, and let g be the weight of the steel-yard: the whole weight acting at D, its effort to depress the arm C G is measured by the product $g \times d$. Also, the effort of W to depress the arm is measured by the product $W \times w$. These two efforts are counteracted by the effort of P to depress the arm G B, which effort is measured by the product of P, and the distance of P from G. Let the distance of P from F be p, and its distance from G will be $p + f$, and the product just mentioned is $P \times (p+f,)$ or the sum of the products $P \times p$ and $P \times f$. Thus, we have
$$W \times w + g \times d = P \times p + P \times f.$$
But it was before stated, that P, at the distance f, balanced the unloaded beam; and therefore $P \times f$, which measures the effort of P to depress the arm G B, is equal to $g \times d$, which measures the effort of the weight of the beam to depress the arm C G. Hence the equals $g \times d$ and $P \times f$ being taken from the former equals, we have remaining
$$W \times w = P \times p.$$
Hence, in whatever proportion W is increased or diminished, p must be increased or diminished; but p is the distance of the counterpoise P from F, that position in which it balances the unloaded beam. From that point F, therefore, the graduation must commence.

If the centre of gravity be in the longer arm, the graduation will commence from that point in the shorter arm at which the counterpoise will balance the unloaded beam. For, suppose this position to be D, and the centre of gravity of the beam to be F, the distances G D and G F being denominated as before, suppose the counterpoise first suspended at D; a weight W being suspended from C, let the counterpoise be moved towards G until equilibrium is established. First let this take place, when P is between D and G, and let the distance of P from D be p. Then we have
$$W \times w + P \times (d-p) = g \times f,$$
or $W \times w + P \times d - P \times p = g \times f$; adding to both these equals $P \times p$, we obtain
$$W \times w + P \times d + P \times p - P \times p = g \times f + P \times p,$$
or $W \times w + P \times d = g \times f + P \times p$.

But, since the product $P \times d$ represents the effort of the counterpoise at D to depress the arm C G, and $G \times f$ represents the effort of the weight of the beam to depress the arm G B, and these efforts are equal, it follows that the products $P \times d$ and $g \times f$ are equal. These then being taken from the last equals, there remains
$$W \times w = P \times p.$$
Hence, in whatever proportion W is increased, p must be increased in the same

proportion; and since p is measured from D, the graduation must commence from that point.

The same will be true if the counterpoise be on the longer arm; but our limits compel us to leave the further investigation to the student.

It is evident that there is a limit to the weight which can be determined by this machine. When the counterpoise has been brought to that division which is nearest to B, it sustains the greatest weight which it is capable of determining. There are two ways of estimating greater weights than this, either by using a heavier counterpoise, or by having another point of suspension on the shorter arm nearer to the fulcrum. It is evident that either will have the desired effect.

(45.) The *Danish balance* is a steelyard, in which the counterpoise is fixed in one position, but the fulcrum is moveable. It is represented in *fig.* 28.

Fig. 28.

Let C be the centre of gravity of the unloaded beam, and let the distance C G be x. The effort of the weight g of the beam to depress the arm is then $g \times x$. The effort of W to depress the other arm is $W \times AG$, or $W \times (AC - GC)$. Now, let AC be called a, and the condition of equilibrium will be

$$g x = W a - W x$$
or $$g x + W x = W a$$
$$\therefore x = \frac{W a}{g + W}$$

(46.) Hence may be deduced the method of graduation. The divisions must obviously commence from C, since when the loop is there it poises the unloaded beam. If it be required to be graduated for pounds, let the weight of the instrument g be expressed in pounds, and let a, the distance C A, be expressed in inches. First, suppose W to be one pound, and we have

$$x = \frac{a}{g+1}$$

If we suppose W to be successively 2, 3, 4, &c. pounds, we have

$$x = \frac{2a}{g+2}$$
$$x = \frac{3a}{g+3}$$
$$x = \frac{4a}{g+4} \ \&c.$$

For example, let a be 18 inches, and g be 6 lbs.—the distances of the divisions corresponding to 1, 2, 3, and 4 lbs. from x, will be

$$x = \frac{18}{6+1} = \frac{18}{7} = 2\tfrac{4}{7} \quad x = \frac{36}{8} = 4\tfrac{1}{2}$$
$$x = \frac{54}{9} = 6 \quad x = \frac{72}{10} = 7\tfrac{1}{5};$$

these several numbers expressing in inches the distances of the several divisions from C.

This instrument may be graduated experimentally by suspending from A successively 1, 2, 3, &c. pounds, and finding by trial the position of the fulcrum which will produce equilibrium.

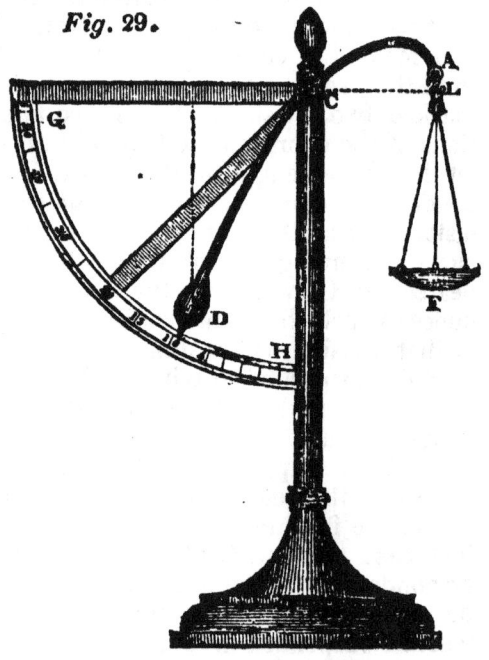

Fig. 29.

(47.) The *bent lever balance* is represented in *fig.* 29. The substance to be weighed is placed in a dish F, suspended from the arm of a bent lever at L. The other arm C D is terminated in a heavy knob, which plays upon a graduated arch G H. As the weight depresses the arm C A, it is so constructed, that the leverage of W is constantly diminished; and since D is moved up the arch, its leverage is constantly increased. When D acquires such a position that it counterpoises the weight, the division to which the index points on the graduated arch expresses the amount of the weight.

To graduate this instrument, let the first division be placed at the position which the index assumes when the dish F is unloaded. Then let the dish be successively loaded with 1, 2, 3, &c. pounds or ounces, or whatever denomination of weight it is designed that the divisions should indicate; and the successive positions of the index will determine the divisions.

A method of graduating the arch may be derived from mathematical investigation, independently of experiment, but we cannot introduce it here.

(48.) We shall conclude this chapter with the description of a more modern instrument, somewhat similar to the bent lever balance. Brady's balance is represented in *fig.* 30. B C D is an

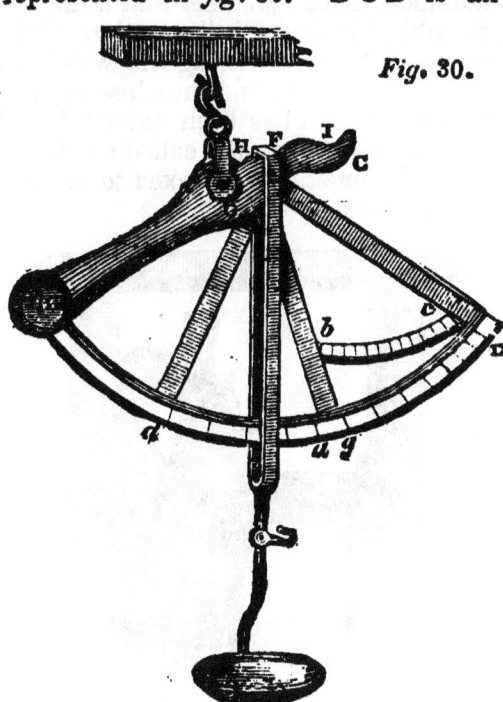

Fig. 30.

iron frame, being much thicker and heavier towards B than in the other parts. It is supported upon a fulcrum G, and F is a moveable suspender to which a scale or hook is attached to receive the substance to be weighed. There are three distinct positions, H F I, in which this suspender may be placed, and for which there are three distinct graduated scales. When a weight is suspended from the hook, or placed in the dish, the machine is turned round the fulcrum G, and the side C descends until equilibrium is established, and the weight is read off from that scale which corresponds to the position of the suspender.

One scale shows the weights of bodies not exceeding two pounds, and is graduated to ounces; another determines weights not exceeding eleven pounds, and is graduated to two ounces; and the third determines weights not exceeding thirty pounds, and is graduated also to four ounces.

CHAPTER VI. *The Axle in the Wheel—Methods of applying the Power—Windlass—Capstan—Pressure on the Pivots—Defects of this Machine—Methods of removing them—Method of Regulating the Variation of a Power or Resistance.*

(49.) When a very severe force, acting through a small space, is required to be produced by a comparatively small power, the common lever, whether simple or complex, is a machine well adapted to produce the effect. But the defect of this engine is, that, under all circumstances, it works through a very limited space, and that the action of the power is almost necessarily intermitting. Thus if a weight is to be raised by a lever, the prop or fulcrum is generally placed somewhat above the point at which the working end of the lever is to be applied to the weight. The end to which the power is applied is, therefore, above the fulcrum. On depressing that extremity, the weight is raised until the end at which the power is applied is a little below, and that which sustains the weight a little above the fulcrum. The weight must then be supported by some other means until the fulcrum be raised above it, and another similar exertion of the power be made.

(50.) To remove this inconvenience a modification of the lever, called *the axle in the wheel*, is used. This ma-

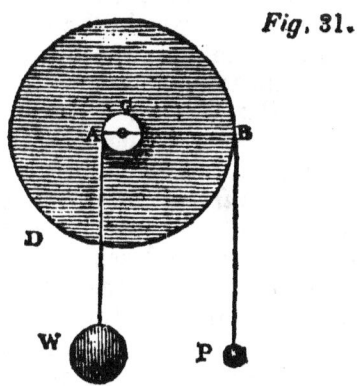

Fig. 31.

chine consists of a cylinder A C, and a wheel B D, having the same axis, at the extremities of which are points on which the whole may turn.

Fig. 31 is a section of this machine, taken in the plane of the wheel; and *fig.* 32 is a projection on a plane at right angles to the wheel. The power P is applied at the circumference of the wheel, and generally in the direction B P of the tangent. A cord is wrapped about the cylinder, and is the means by which the weight is to be raised, or the resistance overcome.

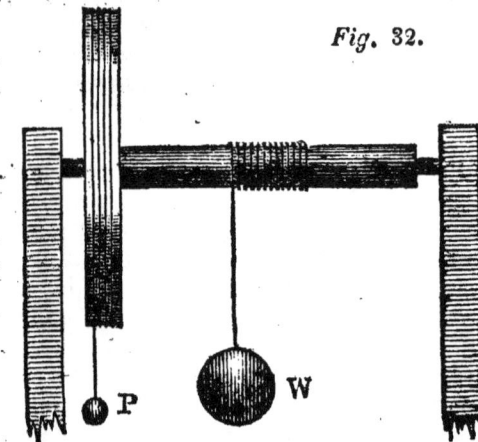

Fig. 32.

It is evidently only a modification of the lever, as will appear by reference to (7,) and the condition of its equilibrium immediately follows from the general principle there established. Let R be the radius of the wheel, and r that of the axle, and the condition of equilibrium is $P \times R = W \times r$; that is, *the power multiplied by the radius of the wheel is equal to the weight multiplied by the radius of the axle.*

Thus, if the power be two pounds, and the radius of the wheel 12 inches, and the weight 8 pounds, and the radius of the axle 3 inches, there will be equilibrium, each product being 24.

This condition is sometimes expressed otherwise; thus, that the power must have to the weight the same ratio as the radius of the wheel has to the radius of the axle, or

$$P : W :: r : R.$$

(51.) It is easy to perceive that this machine furnishes an instance of the *principle of virtual velocities* already alluded to (5.) In one revolution of the wheel, the power descends to a space equal to the circumference of the wheel, and the weight is raised through a space equal to the circumference of the axle. Hence, the velocity of the power is to the velocity of the weight, as the circumference of the wheel is to the circumference of the axle. But the circumferences of circles are as their radii, and therefore the velocity (V) of the power is to the velocity (v) of the weight as the radius of the wheel is to that of the axle, that is

$$V : v :: R : r.$$

By what has been already proved, the weight is to the power in the same proportion, and therefore we have

$$W : P :: V : v.$$
$$\text{or } P \times V = W \times v;$$

that is, *the power multiplied by the velocity of the power is equal to the weight multiplied by the velocity of the weight.*

(52.) The axle in the wheel has been not improperly called the continual or perpetual lever, because the motion which it communicates to the weight is constant and not intermitting, as we have explained to be the case in the common lever. In order that it may be possible to suspend the action of the power without suffering the weight to descend or recoil, and thus lose the advantage which has been gained by its elevation, a contrivance called a *ratchet-wheel* is sometimes annexed to the cylinder or axle.

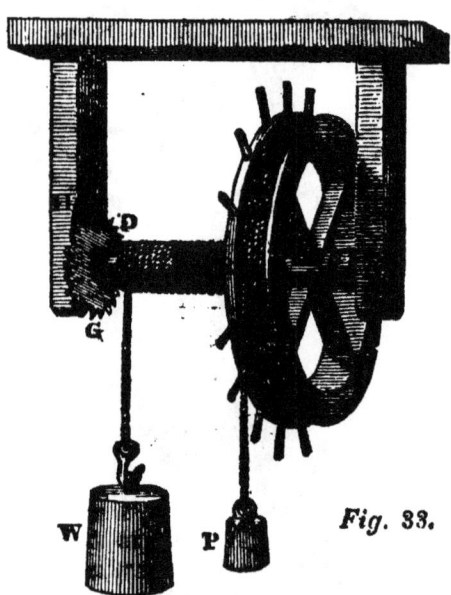

Fig. 33.

In *fig.* 33, this apparatus is represented at G D. It is a wheel furnished with teeth upon its edge. The teeth are not presented directly from the centre, but are curved and all bent in one direction, which is that direction in which the rope is coiled upon the cylinder. A curved bolt or catch working on a pivot at H, falls by its weight between the teeth of the wheel; and the effect is, that the wheel and cylinder to which it is attached, are suffered to revolve in that direction in which the weight is raised, but are not permitted to revolve in the other direction. So that the weight can never descend unless the bolt H be prevented from acting on the wheel G D. By such an apparatus the action of the power may be suspended at pleasure, and yet the effects of its past action maintained.

(53.) There are various ways in which the power is applied to the wheel; and the weight suspended by the rope which we have used is only to be understood as a general representation of the mechanical effect of the power, however it be applied.

Sometimes pins are placed at equal distances round the circumference of the wheel, by which the hand may be applied as the power. (See *fig.* 33.) An instance of this manner of applying the power will be seen in the wheel used to work the rudder of a ship.

Sometimes there is no wheel, but a number of long levers are inserted in the axle, and diverge from it like spokes from the box of a wheel, and the operator moves the axle by these levers. (See *fig.* 35.)

Frequently, as in the windlass, there is not either a wheel or diverging spokes, but simply holes, in which the workman inserts the end of a strong bar of considerable length, by which, as a lever, he turns the axle and raises the weight. He removes the bar as he works, from one hole to another, the weight being sustained by the action of the ratchet-wheel in the interim.

The windlass is frequently wrought by a winch, as represented in *fig.* 34.

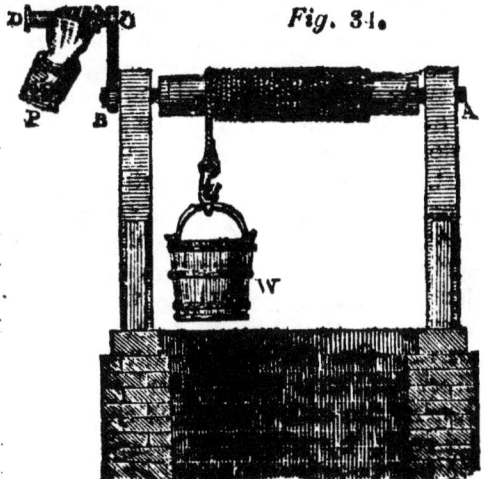

Fig. 34.

The cylinder is fixed upon the axle A B, and at right angles to this axle a lever B O is fixed, and from O another arm O D extends, to which the hands of the operator are applied. By means of this simple contrivance, the operator can work upon the machine through the entire of each revolution, although not in every part with equal effect. In this case the ratchet-wheel is less necessary than in any of the former.

(54.) The axle is sometimes horizontal and sometimes vertical. In the *windlass* it is horizontal, also in most kinds of *cranes*. In the *capstan* (*fig.* 35.) it is vertical. The advantage of its vertical position in the capstan is very evident. The

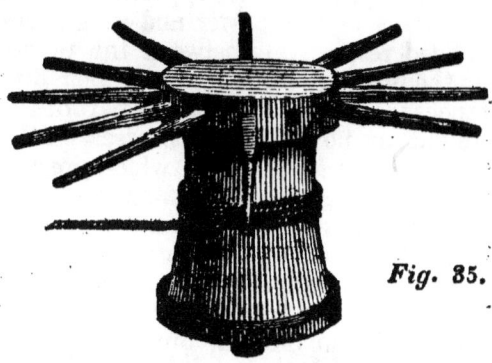

Fig. 35.

workmen insert levers in holes made to receive them, and walk round the axle, pushing the levers before them. In this manner a great number of men may work together, and there is no intermission of the power even when different men succeed each other.

(55.) When several forces act at the same time at different parts of the circumference of the same wheel, and all perpendicular to the radii, their combined effect is to be estimated in the same manner as if they all acted at the same point.

But if they act with different levers, each power is to be multiplied by the lever by which it acts, and the sum of these products is to be taken as the total effect. (10.)

(56.) In estimating the effect of the resistance or weight when the rope by which it acts has any considerable thickness, half the thickness of the rope is to be considered as a part of the radius of the cylinder, as the force is considered to be transmitted through the centre or axis of the rope.

The same may be said of the power, when it acts by a rope of any considerable thickness.

(57.) In order to determine the strength necessary to be given to the pivots which support the wheel and axle, it is necessary to determine the pressures to which they are liable.

If the axle be horizontal, the weight of the machine will press upon the pivots; and if its centre of gravity be equally distant from the pivots, its pressure will be equally distributed between them, half the weight of the machine pressing upon each pivot. If, however, the axis be vertical, the whole weight will rest on the point of the lower pivot.

The manner in which the pressures of the power and weight are divided between the pivots, may be determined by the principles established in Chap. iii. By these principles it appears, that the pressures of the power and weight are divided respectively between the pivots in the inverse proportion of their distances from them; that is, the part of the weight or power which presses on the one pivot, is to the part which presses on the other as the distance of the weight or power from the latter pivot is to its distance from the former.

In this investigation it should be remembered, that we do not consider the machine as in motion, but merely that the power sustains the weight.

(58.) In the simple wheel and axle, whatever be its form or peculiarity, its *mechanical efficacy* depends on the ratio of the radius of the wheel to the radius of the axle, or, to speak more generally, the length of the lever by which the power acts, to the radius of the cylinder on which the rope which raises the weight is coiled. There are then two, and only two, ways, in which this efficacy may be increased; viz. by increasing the leverage of the power, or by diminishing the radius of the cylinder which supports the weight. Now, although, in a theoretical view, there is no limit to our power of increasing this efficacy, since we can conceive the leverage of the power increased without limit, or the thickness of the cylinder diminished without limit, yet there is a practical limit to the increase of the mechanical efficacy of this engine.

If we attempt to increase this efficacy by giving to the power a considerable leverage, the machine will become unwieldy; the power will work through a most inconveniently great space, and the practical disadvantages which will arise, will more than counterbalance any thing which can be gained by the increased power.

If, on the other hand, we attempt to increase the efficacy by diminishing the thickness of the axle, we diminish the strength of that part of the machine which must support the weight; and the cases in which this great efficacy is required are precisely those cases in which the greatest weights are to be raised, or resistances to be overcome, and, therefore, where the greatest strength in those parts of the machine on which the weight or resistance acts are indispensably necessary.

In cases, therefore, where great resistances are to be overcome, it is a problem of considerable importance to assign a method, by which, without rendering the machine more complex, sufficient strength may be preserved by preserving the thickness of the axle, the machine may not be rendered unwieldy by increasing very much the leverage of the power, and a high degree of power may be gained.

(59.) All these ends are attained by the simple modification of the wheel and axle in *fig.* 36. The axle or cylinder

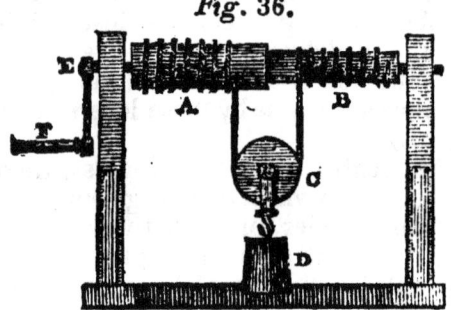

Fig. 36.

A B consists of two parts, the diameter of one part being less than that of the other. A wheel and block C is attached to the weight, and round the wheel the rope which elevates the weight is passed, and is coiled in the *same direction* on the thicker and thinner parts of the axle. The elevation of the weight is thus effected: upon turning the axle in such a direction that the rope shall be coiled upon the thicker part, it will necessarily be rolled off the thinner part. Upon every revolution of the wheel, therefore, a portion of the rope equal to the circumference of the thicker part will be *drawn up;* but, at the same time, a portion, equal to the circumference of the thinner part, will be *let down.* On the whole, therefore, the effect of one revolution will be to shorten the entire length of that part of the rope, by which the weight is suspended, by a length equal to the difference between the circumferences of the thicker and thinner parts of the axle; consequently, half that portion of the rope will be shortened by half the difference between these circumferences. But half that part of the rope by which the weight is suspended, is evidently equal to the distance of the wheel to which the weight is attached from the cylinder. Hence, we perceive that every revolution of the cylinder raises the weight through a space equal to half the difference between the circumferences of the thicker and thinner parts of the axle.

To determine the conditions of equilibrium in this engine, we shall refer to *fig.* 37.

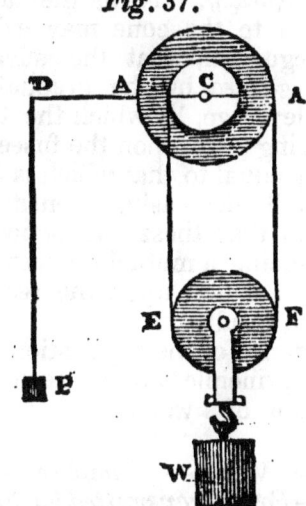

fig. 37, which is a section of the apparatus taken perpendicular to the cylinder, of which C is the centre, C B the radius of the thinner and C A of the thicker part, and C D the lever by which the power P acts. As the weight W hangs from the rope, which passes round the wheel E F, the parts E B and F A of the string are equally concerned in supporting the weight; and, consequently, half the weight is the force which hangs from each part of the string. If, then, the lever by which the power acts be R, and that r be the radius C A, and r' be C B, the condition of equilibrium, conformably to the principle laid down in (10), is

$$P \times R + \tfrac{1}{2} W \times r' = \tfrac{1}{2} W \times r;$$

that is, if the power be multiplied by its leverage, and half the weight by the radius of the thinner part of the cylinder, and these two products be added together, their sum will be equal to the product found by multiplying half the weight by the radius of the thicker part of the cylinder. Or, what amounts to the same thing, we have,

$$P \times R = \tfrac{1}{2} W \times r - \tfrac{1}{2} W \times r',$$
$$\text{or } P \times R = W \times \tfrac{1}{2}(r - r');$$

that is, *the power multiplied by the lever by which it works is equal to the weight multiplied by half the difference of the radii of the thicker and thinner parts of the cylinder.*

This condition may also be expressed thus: *the weight is to the power, as the lever by which the power works is to half the difference of the radii of the cylinder;* i. e.

$$W : P :: R : \tfrac{1}{2}(r - r').$$

From considering this condition, it is plain that, where the mechanical efficacy depends on the proportion of the lever of the power to half the difference of the radii of the cylinder, this efficacy may be increased, without any limit, by merely diminishing the difference of the radii of the cylinder, without either increasing the leverage of the power or diminishing the thickness of the cylinder. Thus, by this contrivance, the power will act through a convenient space; there will be nothing unwieldy in the construction of the apparatus; and all the requisite thickness and strength may be given to the cylinder.

A capstan, constructed upon the same principle, is represented in *fig.* 38.

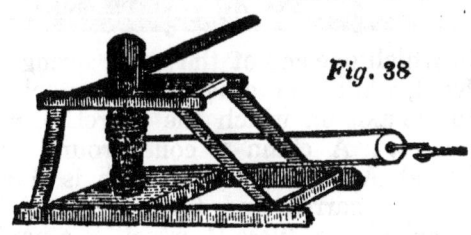

Fig. 38

A great advantage attending this machine is, that there is no recoil upon the weight upon the remission of the power, and, therefore, the use of the *ratchet-wheel* and *catch* (5?) is superfluous.

Almost the only disadvantage attending it is, that a considerable quantity of rope is requisite to raise the weight through a very small height; but still much less than what is requisite in any machine of the same power in which rope is employed.

Dr. Gregory states, that although this invention is generally ascribed to *George Eckhardt,* who probably invented it without being aware that it had been previously used; yet that there is a figure of it in some Chinese drawings, more than a century old, from which Dr. Gregory took the sketch, *fig.* 36. See *Gregory's Mechanics,* vol. ii. p. 3.

(60.) The principle of varying the diameter of the cylinder while the leverage of the power remains unvaried, is sometimes used to accommodate an uniform power to a varying resistance. We may state this principle still more generally. If a power, varying under any given conditions, be required to overcome a resistance which varies according to some other given conditions, the one may always be accommodated to the other by producing a variation in the leverage by which one or both acts, which will modify the effect of the power so as to make it conformable to the variation in the resistance to be overcome.

This will probably be better understood by an example. Suppose that the power is a spiral spring of tempered steel, (*fig.* 39.) placed in a barrel A, (*fig.* 40.)

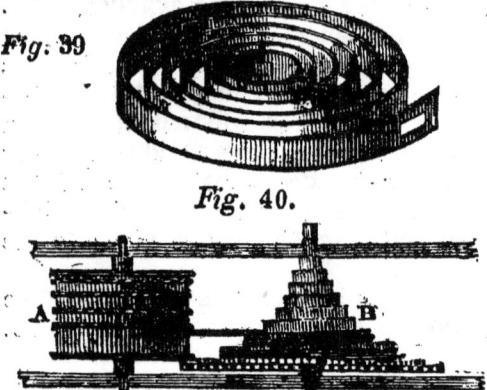

Fig. 39

Fig. 40.

to which one end of the spiral spring is fixed, while the other end is attached to the axis on which the barrel A revolves. A chain is coiled round the barrel A, one end of which is fixed on the barrel, and the other end is attached to a *fusee* B, which is a conical figure, also capable of turning on an axle, and on which a spiral channel or thread is cut to receive the chain after it has been rolled off from the barrel A. Let us suppose that the resistance, whatever it be, is uniform, and that it is applied to the axle of the fusee, or to a wheel connected with that axle; and that when the chain is rolled upon the spiral thread of the fusee, the spring within the barrel A is stretched to its utmost intensity. It is this which gives the barrel A a tendency to recoil, which tendency is communicated by the chain to the fusee B, and acts in turning the fusee by the leverage of the highest part of the conical figure. With this leverage the tension of the chain acts upon the resistance, and its effect is to be estimated by multiplying the tension of the chain, or, what is the same, the intensity of the spring, by the radius of that part of the cone on which the chain acts. As the fusee revolves, and the chain rolls *off* the fusee B and *on* the barrel A, the spring gradually loses its intensity; and consequently the tension by which the chain acts upon the fusee is gradually diminished, while the resistance to be overcome by that tension remains the same. It is, however, to be considered, that as the chain is rolled off the fusee, the part on which it acts, coming nearer to the base of the cone, becomes constantly thicker. The tension of the string, therefore, acts by a constantly increasing leverage, and therefore with a constantly increasing *mechanical efficacy*. Now, the tapering form given to the cone may evidently be so regulated, that the advantage which is *gained* by the gradually increasing leverage, by which the tension of the string acts upon the fusee, shall be exactly equal to that which is *lost* by the gradually decreasing intensity of the spring; so that these two opposite effects producing a mutual compensation, an uniform action upon the resistance will be the result.

An instance of the application of this beautiful principle will be seen in the construction of a watch.

CHAPTER VII. — *Complex Wheel-work—Force transmitted by Friction—Straps—Tooth and Pinion—Shape of Teeth — their number — Lantern and Trundles—Spur, Crown, and bevelled Gear.*

(61.) IT does not always happen that the end to be accomplished can be attained with convenience by the simple wheel and axle; and it frequently becomes necessary to transmit the effect of the power to the resistance, through a system of wheels and axles mutually acting upon each other. As the wheel and axle is only a modification of the lever, so a system of such machines acting one upon another is only another form of the compound lever, and the conditions of equilibrium are exactly the same in both.

In complex wheel-work, the power is applied to the circumference of the first wheel, which transmits its effect to the circumference of the first axle. This circumference is made to act, by various means, which we shall presently explain, upon the circumference of the second wheel, which again transfers the effect to the circumference of the second axle, which acts upon the circumference of the third wheel, and this in the same way transmits the effect to the circumference of the third axle; and thus the transmission of the force is continued, until it has arrived at the circumference of the last axle to which the weight or resistance is applied.

Each separate wheel and axle being a lever, the effect of such a combination as we have described is the same as that of a series of levers, whose longer arms are respectively equal to the radii of the several wheels, and whose shorter arms are equal to the radii of the several axles, and therefore the condition of equilibrium is that the power multiplied by the product of the radii of all the wheels is equal to the weight multiplied by the radii of all the axles. Thus if R, R', R'' be the radii of the wheels, and r, r', r'' those of the axles, we have

$$P \times R\, R'\, R'' = W \times r\, r'\, r''.$$

(62.) The force of these observations will more readily appear, by considering the combination of wheels and axles in *fig.* 41. The radius of the wheel on which the power acts being R, and

Fig. 41.

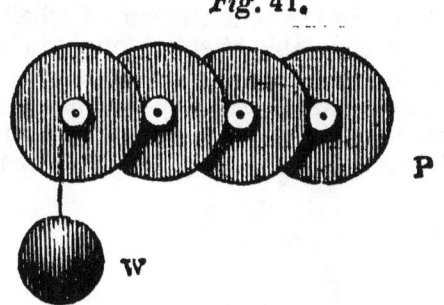

that of the axle r, it is equivalent to a lever of the first kind, whose fulcrum is its centre. The first axle acts on the circumference of the second wheel with the leverage of its radius r, and the second wheel is also a lever of the first kind, the fulcrum being the centre. The radius r of the first acts upon the radius R' of the second wheel, which depresses the radius r' of the second axle, and thereby depresses the radius R'' of the third wheel, which raises the radius r'' of the third axle, and thereby raises the weight.

(63.) In this case the wheels and axles are supposed to work by the friction of their surfaces. In light work, where the pressure on the machinery is not very considerable, this method of connecting the wheel-work is often adopted with advantage. The friction of the surfaces is increased by cutting the wood so that the grains of the surfaces in contact shall run in opposite directions. Also by glueing upon the surfaces of the wheels and axles buffed leather. A saw-mill in which the wheels act by friction has been used at Mr. Taylor's, of Southampton, for nearly twenty years, and is found to work well.

(64.) There are, however, other ways of transmitting the force of each axle to the circumference of the succeeding wheel. A very common method is by ropes or straps passing round the circumferences of the wheel and axle, which act one upon the other. The action is in this manner transmitted by the tension of the rope or strap, and rendered effective by friction with the circumferences on which it is rolled. This

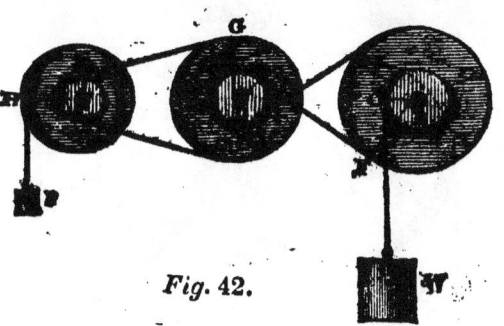

Fig. 42.

method of connecting wheels and axles is represented in *fig.* 42. When the wheel and the axle from which it receives motion are intended to revolve in the same direction, the strap is not crossed, but applied as between the axle B and the wheel G. But when the wheel is to revolve in a direction contrary to the revolution of the axle, the strap is crossed as between the axle D and the wheel F. This latter method of applying the strap has the advantage of having more surface to act upon, and therefore having more friction.

(65.) But by far the most usual way of transmitting the action of the axles to the succeeding wheels, is by means of teeth or cogs raised on their surfaces. When this is the case, the cogs on the surface of the wheel, are generally called *teeth*, and those on the surface of the axle are called *leaves*; the axle itself is in this case called a *pinion*.

As the *leaves* of the pinion successively pass between the *teeth* of the wheel, they are perfectly equal and similar to them. Hence the circumferences of the wheels and pinions are proportional to their respective numbers of *teeth* and *leaves*; and since the circumferences are as the radii, it follows, that the numbers of teeth or leaves are proportional to the radii. Hence, in the condition of equilibrium determined in (61.), we substitute the number of teeth and leaves for the radii of the wheels and axles. Thus, then, the condition of equilibrium is, that the power multiplied by the product of the numbers of teeth in all the wheels is equal to the weight multiplied by the product of the number of leaves in all the pinions. Or, if N, N′, N″ be the numbers of teeth in the several wheels, and n, n', n'' the numbers of leaves in all the pinions, the condition of equilibrium is

$$P \times N N' N'' = W \times n n' n''.$$

A system of tooth and pinion-work is represented in *fig.* 43. In this case the

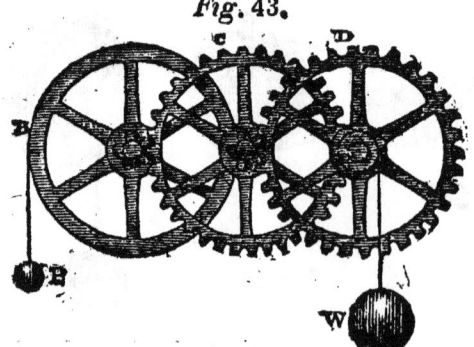

Fig. 43.

power acts upon the first wheel by a rope; but in submitting it to the above condition of equilibrium, it is only necessary to calculate how many teeth the circumference would contain, and use that number in the condition.

(66.) It will be easy to show, that complex wheel-work obeys the law of virtual velocities (5); for since the teeth are equal, the circumference of each wheel moves with the same velocity as that of the circumference of the pinion by which it is driven, which is equally evident if they be connected by straps or work by friction. Now, since each wheel revolves in the same time with its axle, the velocities of their circumferences are as their circumferences, or, what is the same, as their radii or number of teeth. Hence, the velocity of the power, or the velocity of the circumference of the first wheel, is to that of the first axle as their radii. But the velocity of the circumference of the first axle is equal to the velocity of the circumference of the second wheel, which is to that of the second axle as their radii; and by continuing this reasoning, we shall find that the velocity of the power is to that of the weight, as the product of the radii of the wheels to the product of the radii of all the axles; and, therefore, that the power multiplied by the velocity of the power is equal to the weight multiplied by the velocity of the weight.

This will be better understood by an example. Let the number of teeth in the first wheel be 100, and the leaves in the first pinion 9; and let the teeth in the second and third wheels be 120 and 130, and the leaves in the respective pinions be 7 and 11. The velocity of the circumference of the first wheel being expressed by 1, that of the circumference of the second wheel will be $\frac{9}{100}$. This velocity is to that of the circumference of the second pinion or third wheel, as 120 is to 7; and therefore the velocity of the circumference of the third wheel is $\frac{9 \times 7}{100 \times 120}$. Again, this velocity is to that of the circumference of the last axle as 130 to 11. This velocity is therefore $\frac{9 \times 7 \times 11}{100 \times 120 \times 13}$; which verifies what we have just advanced.

(67.) In the construction of wheel-work considerable attention ought to be paid to their shape, as much of the efficiency and permanency of the work depends on this. Suppose that the teeth were found as in *fig.* 44. The tooth

Fig. 44.

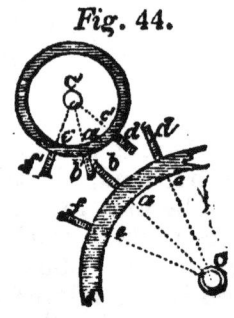

$a\,b$ in driving $a'\,b'$ would be moved round the centre C, in a direction perpendicular to $C\,a\,b$, and would therefore press on the tooth $a'\,b'$ obliquely to the radius $C'\,a'\,b'$; whereas, to produce the best effect, the pressure should be directed perpendicularly to that radius. Besides this, the whole pressure of the wheel is thrown upon one tooth, by which the chances of fracture are much increased, and the wear materially augmented. Another defect which appears manifest is, that during the motion the direction of the pressure of $a\,b$ on $a'\,b'$ is constantly changing while the teeth are in contact; and since the leverage by which the wheel C′ is turned by $a\,b$ is therefore variable, it is turned with an unequable force. In the motion, the corner of the tooth $a\,b$ scrapes or rubs the surface of the tooth $a'\,b'$; and the machine suffers a jolt when the tooth $a'\,b'$, finally slipping from the tooth $a'\,b'$, falls into the angle formed at the point where the tooth $a'\,b'$ springs from the circumference of the wheel.

The teeth should, therefore, be so formed as to remove these defects; for which purpose it would be necessary that they should act in such a manner, that,

1st. The teeth of one wheel should press in a direction perpendicular to the radius of the other wheel; or, in other words, the pressure should be *tangential* to the wheel which is driven.

2d. As many teeth as possible should be in contact at the same time, in order to distribute the pressure amongst them, and thereby to diminish the pressure upon each tooth. This arrangement will diminish the wear, and the chances of fracture.

3rd. During the entire action of one tooth upon another, the direction of the pressure should be the same, in order that, acting with the same leverage, the effect may be uniform.

4th. The surfaces of the teeth in working should not rub one upon another, and should suffer no jolt either at the commencement or termination of their mutual contact.

Various forms have been suggested for the teeth, with a view to the accomplishment of some or all of these advantages; but that which seems best calculated to attain the desired ends is the following:

Suppose that F H I, *fig.* 45, is the circumference of the wheel on which it is proposed to raise teeth, and let H

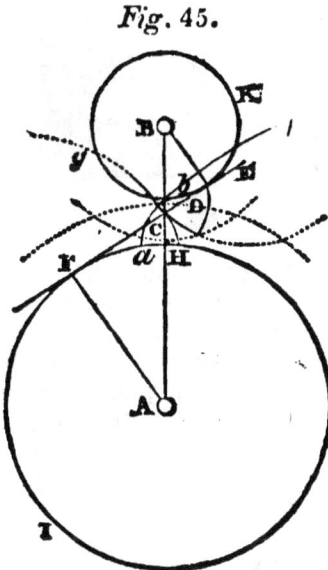

Fig. 45.

be one of the points from which the side of a tooth is to spring. Suppose a string is attached to the circumference of the wheel as at I, and applied to the circumference I F, and terminated at H carrying a pencil at its extremity. Let the string, being constantly stretched tight, be rolled off, so that that part of it, F C, which has been at any time disengaged from the circumference of the wheel shall be in a straight line, touching the circumference at F, and in this way let the pencil describe the curve* H C g. Let *a* H be the breadth of the tooth at the circumference of the wheel; and attaching a string in like manner to the other side of the wheel, and rolling it on in the opposite direction, so that its extremity bearing the pencil shall be at *a*, let a similar curve be described. These two curves will include a space which will represent the form of a tooth which will accomplish all the purposes and possess all the advantages we have mentioned.

The teeth of the pinion, of course, are to be formed in the same manner.

It is a remarkable property of these curves that a line F E which touches both circles will pass through the point of contact of the teeth, and not only of one pair of teeth, but of every pair which are in contact: and this line will be perpendicular to the direction of the surfaces of the teeth at the point of their mutual contact. Thus the pressure of the pinion on the wheel is exerted tangentially to both, and therefore acts always with the same leverage and to the greatest advantage.

Further, during the whole period of the contact of any two teeth, the pressure acts in the same direction and with the same force, and therefore when it is uniform, it necessarily produces an uniform effect.

During the motion, the surface of one tooth does not *rub* or *scrape* against the surface of the other, but the one *rolls* upon the other, thereby removing nearly all the effects of friction, and diminishing considerably the wear of the machinery, and the waste of the power.

Several teeth are in contact at the same time, and all working with equal power, so that the stress is equally distributed among them, and the chances of fracture are greatly diminished.

Thus this form of tooth has all the advantages which can be desired.

(68.) In regulating the number of teeth in the wheel and the pinion which works it, it should be so contrived that the same teeth should be engaged as

---

* This curve is called the *involute of the circle.*

seldom as possible, in order to avoid inequality of wear. For example, let us suppose that the number of teeth in a wheel were exactly ten times the number of leaves in the pinion; each leaf in the pinion would engage every tenth tooth of the wheel, and would work inevitably on the same ten teeth every revolution of the wheel. If it were possible that all the teeth and leaves could be constructed with mathematical precision, and perfect and absolute similitude, and that no accidental difference, owing to any want of uniformity in the material of which they are formed, could exist, this would be a matter of no consequence, and the wear would still be even and equable. But as these perfections never can exist, the inevitable inequalities incident, as well to the nature of the material of which wheels are constructed as to the forms they derive even from the most perfect mechanical construction, must be compensated by making the teeth and leaves work, so that each leaf shall successively engage with all the other teeth of the wheel before it engages a second time with any one of them.

This is accomplished by making the number of teeth and the number of leaves *prime* to each other, that is, such that no integer divides both exactly. The manner in which this is commonly done, is by making the number of teeth such, that it is just one more than a number which is exactly divisible by the number of leaves. This is what millwrights call making a *hunting cog*. Thus, suppose that there are ten leaves, and that the diameter of the wheel is about six times that of the pinion. If this were the exact ratio, there would be just sixty teeth, and after each revolution of the wheel the same teeth and leaves would be continually engaged, each leaf taking every sixth tooth. But if the diameter of the wheel be made somewhat greater than six times that of the pinion, so as to admit sixty-one teeth: then, after six revolutions of the pinion, the first leaf will be engaged with the tooth immediately before that in which it had worked at the commencement, and after six more revolutions it will be engaged with the tooth before that, or the second tooth from that at which the motion commenced. Thus, it is evident, that the wheel must revolve 61 times, and the pinion 6 × 61, or 366 times before the same teeth will be again engaged. By these means, the inequalities of wear arising from inequalities of form and material will compensate each other.

(69.) The teeth of the wheel, instead of working in the leaves of a pinion, are made to act upon a form of wheel called a *lantern*, as represented at *fig.* 46. The

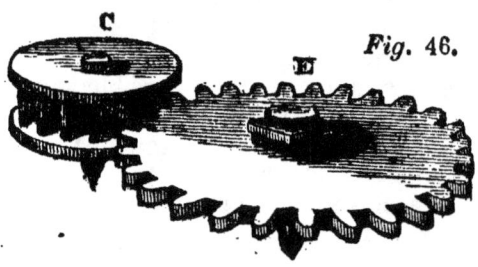

Fig. 46.

cylindrical teeth or bars of the lantern are called *trundles* or *spindles*. However, notwithstanding the various forms of wheel-work, the principles which we have already explained will always determine the relation between the power and resistance.

(70.) Wheels are denominated *spur*, *crown*, or *bevel gear*, according to the position or direction of the teeth. If the teeth be perpendicular to the axis of the wheel, and in the direction of radii, as in the wheel E, *fig.* 46. it is called a *spur-wheel*. If the teeth be parallel to the axis of the wheel, and therefore perpendicular to its plane, it is called a *crown-wheel*. Two spur-wheels, or a

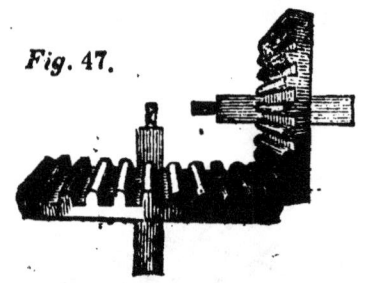

Fig. 47.

spur-wheel and pinion which work in one another, are always in the same plane, and have their axis parallel. But when a spur and crown-wheel are in connection, their planes and axis are at right angles. By this means, therefore, rotatory motion may be transferred from a horizontal to a vertical plane, or *vice versâ*.

When the teeth are oblique to the plane or axis wheel, it is called a bevelled-wheel. Two wheels of this kind are represented in *fig.* 48. In this case, the surfaces on which the teeth are raised are parts of the surfaces of two cones. The manner in which these wheels act, and the principles on which

Fig. 48.

their formation depends, may be conceived by imagining two cones to be applied side to side, as in *fig.* 49. If their surfaces have sufficient friction,

Fig. 49.

and one of them be turned upon its axis by a mechanical force, it will compel the other to revolve; and if the bases of the cones be equal, each will revolve in the same time; as in *fig.* 49. But if the diameter of the base of one be equal to any number of times the diameter of the base of the other, as in *figs.* 48 and 50, then the lesser cone will

Fig. 50.

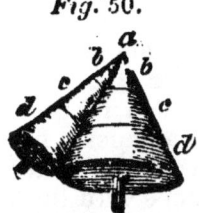

revolve as many times in one revolution of the greater. It is evident that what we have observed of the entire cones, will be equally true of any parts of them, *a, b, c,* &c. equally distant from their common vertex, and therefore would be true of wheels, the edges of which are parts, *c d,* of the conical surfaces.

If the friction of the conical surfaces be insufficient to transmit the force, the surfaces may be fluted, as in *fig.* 51;

Fig. 51.

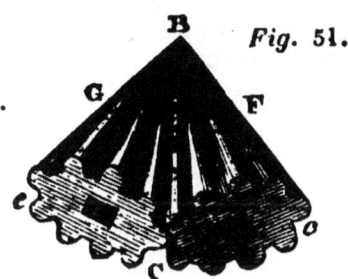

and if the conical surfaces be incomplete, the breadth being F *c,* they will become *bevelled-wheels.*

It will be easily perceived that the use of bevelled-wheels is to produce a rotatory motion round one axis by means of a rotatory motion round another which is oblique to it; and, provided that the two axes are in the same plane, this may always be accomplished by two bevelled-wheels. A system of wheels of this kind is represented in *fig.* 52.

Fig. 52.

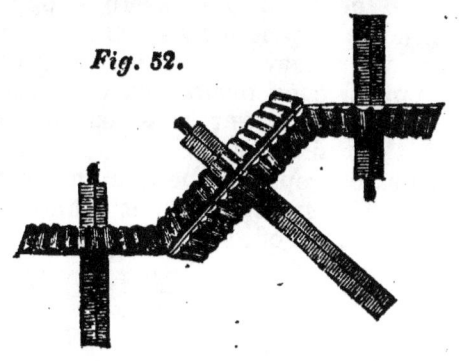

CHAPTER VIII.— *Of the Pulley— Fixed Pulley—Single moveable Pulley— Spanish Burtons — Systems with a single Rope—their defects— White's Pulley — Systems with several Ropes.*

(71.) THE machines, the theory of which has been explained in the preceding chapters, derive their whole efficacy from the supposed inflexibility of the materials of which they are constructed. The effect of weights acting on a lever is to bend it over the fulcrum, and if the lever yields to this, and suffers itself to be bent, it loses its mechanical efficacy. The same observation may be applied to all the machines which we have hitherto described. It may be said that there are no materials of which such machines can be constructed which are perfectly inflexible. This is true; but we have before observed, that the most easy method of teaching the science, is to suppose, in the first instance, this perfect inflexibility, and subsequently to apply to the results *corrections* which will adapt them to cases where small degrees of flexibility are found, at least to those cases where the flexibility produces any effect sufficiently great to affect the practical accuracy of the result.

On the other hand, the machine to whose properties we are now to call the attention of the student, is one whose efficacy depends on the perfect flexibility of the material. On this supposition our theory will necessarily be founded, and in cases where this supposed flexibility is not found, it will be necessary to apply *corrections* to our results to render them practically applicable.

(72.) A perfectly flexible rope, or thread, is a machine which, independently of the usual advantage attending the use of machines, of enabling us, by the aid of fixed points, to support a considerable weight by a small power, offers what may be considered great mechanical convenience, even in cases in which the power is equal to the weight or resistance.

A flexible rope may be used in transmitting force from one point to another in the direction of its length. Thus the force of the weight W (*fig.* 53.) is transmitted by the string *a* to the hook H, and presses on the hook in the same manner as if it were immediately suspended from it without the intervention of the rope *a*. This power of transmitting pressure in the direction

Fig. 53.

of its length, is not owing to the flexibility of the rope, but to its *inextensibility*. This quality the rope enjoys in common with an inflexible bar, which would also transmit the force of the weight to the hook in the same way. An inflexible bar, however, has the advantage of the flexible rope in transmitting force in the direction of its length; for, although a flexible rope will transmit a force applied at one end to the other end when that force is directed *from* the end to which it is to be transmitted, it will totally fail if the force be directed *towards* the other, in which case the inflexible bar will be effectual. Thus, if the weight acted towards the hook H, which would be the case if it were below W, the string *a* will fail to transmit the force, but if it were an inflexible bar it would do so.

(73.) One of the greatest conveniences attending the use of a flexible rope, is that by its means a force in any one direction may be made to balance an equal force in any other direction. Thus, if it be necessary to sustain the weight W, (*fig.* 54.) acting vertically downwards, by a power which acts in the direction P H, let a point P be assumed directly over the weight, and in the line P H, and let a flexible string be attached to the weight, passed through a ring at P, and connected with the power at H, and the object will be evidently accomplished. For if the rope be supposed to be perfectly flexible and smooth, it will suffer no resistance either from rigidity or friction, in passing through the ring at P, and the string will be stretched by the same force in its entire length, that tension being equal to the weight W.

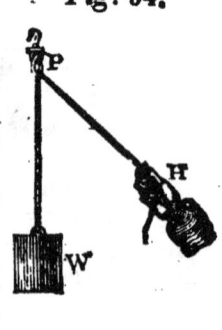

Fig. 54.

But since it is impossible in practice to obtain ropes which are perfectly smooth and flexible, nor to construct rings whose surfaces are free from all asperities, it is usual, instead of passing the rope through a ring, to pass it over a grooved wheel which turns freely on an axle, or on pivots, as in *Fig.* 55

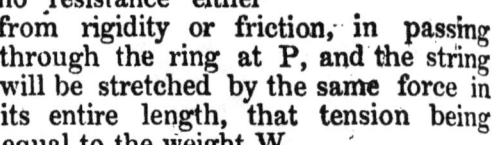

Fig. 55.

The substitution of the wheel for the ring is attended in practice with two obvious advantages: first, it removes in a great degree the effects of the friction of the rope with the surface of the ring, for instead of the surface of the rope sliding on the surface of the wheel, that surface turns with it. Secondly, it diminishes very much the effects of the imperfect flexibility of the rope, which instead of being suddenly and sharply bent, as over the ring, is gradually deflected upon the curvature of the rim of the wheel.

The wheel, therefore, is not used to impart any *mechanical advantage* properly speaking to the machine, nor is it at all necessary to be taken into account in the theory in which the perfect smoothness and flexibility, the want of which it is introduced to remedy, are pre-supposed.

The wheel thus used is called a *pulley*, and hence that name has been given to the machine itself, and its various modifications. Some writers have even ascribed to the wheel thus used, the whole mechanical virtue of the machine, and have established the conditions of equilibrium by considering it as a lever. That such investigations are founded on wrong principles, although their results happen to be true, appears from this, that if we suppose the wheels and blocks abandoned, and the ropes merely to pass through rings, but to be perfectly flexible and to act without friction, all the properties of the pulley may be established.

In our diagrams of pulleys, we shall always represent the cords as acting in the usual way over wheels; but our demonstrations will be founded only on the supposed flexibility of the string, and its perfect power of transmitting force by its tension.

(74.) The mechanical efficacy of every system of pullies may be immediately derived from this single principle, that the same flexible string must always suffer the same tension in every part of its length. Thus, if the weight W (*fig.* 56) be supported by the string A B, the parts of the string A and B will be equally stretched, and consequently the two hooks are equally engaged in sustaining the weight. Hence, each part A and B of the string must sustain half the weight. In this case we suppose the string to be perfectly free in passing through the ring, and the parts A and B to be parallel.

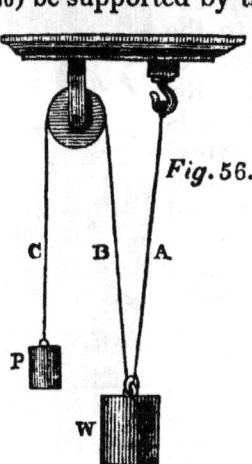

Fig. 56.

(75.) Pulleys are *fixed* and *moveable*. A fixed pulley has no *mechanical advantage*, since the power and weight are equal. This apparatus is represented in *fig.* 55. It is, however, very convenient in accommodating the direction of the power to that of the resistance. Thus, by *pulling downwards*, we are able to draw a weight *upwards*. It has been already observed, that by means of this simple machine, a power in any direction whatever may be opposed to a resistance in any other direction.

(76.) The *single moveable pulley*, sometimes called a *runner*, is represented in *fig.* 57. In this machine the same rope extends from the power P to the fixed point E, and has the same tension throughout its whole length.

It is evident that this tension is equal to the power, for in that part P B of the rope, between the power and the fixed pulley, the power is supported by this tension. The weight W is supported by the parts C A and D E of the string, and

Fig. 57.

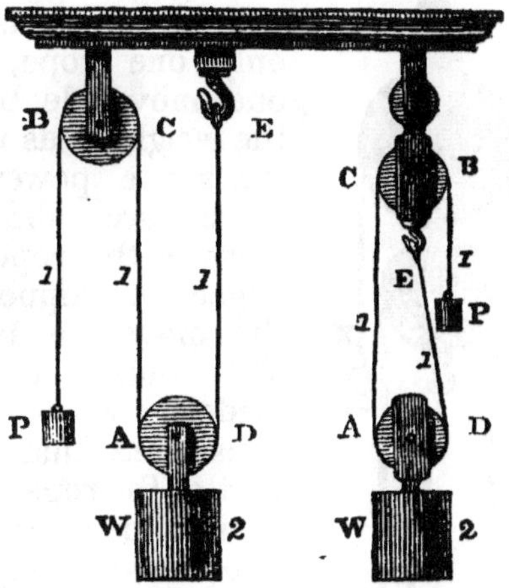

must be equal to the sum of the tensions, that is, to twice the tension of the rope, or to twice the power. In this machine, therefore, a power is capable of opposing a resistance of twice its own amount.

We have not noticed the effect of the weight of the pulley A. If this be taken into account, it is only necessary to add it to the weight. The single moveable pulley may also be so constructed that the weight will be three times the power. This is evidently the case in the arrangement in *fig.* 58.

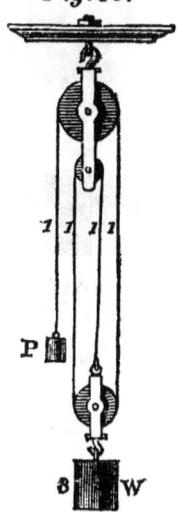

Fig. 58.

(77.) There are several systems of pullies worked by a single rope. In all these there is one moveable block, in which *wheels* or *sheaves* are fixed, over which the rope runs, and to which the weight is attached. In estimating the mechanical effect, the moveable block is to be considered as a part of the weight. Since the same rope is successively passed over all the wheels, it must have in every part the same tension; and since the part K sustains the power, this tension must be equal to the power. The weight (including the weight of the block to which it is attached) is supported equally by each part of the rope, which passes between it and the fixed block. In *fig.* 59, the weight is distributed equally among four ropes, each of which is stretched by the force of the power.

D

Fig. 59.

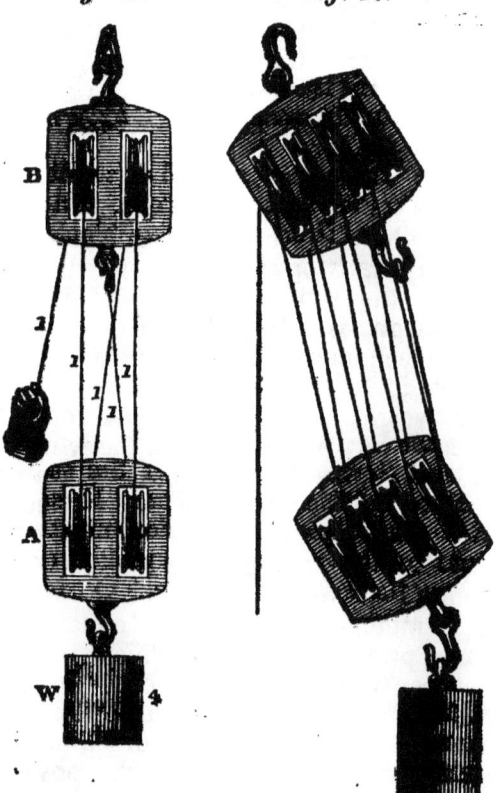

Fig. 60.   Fig. 61.

Fig. 62.

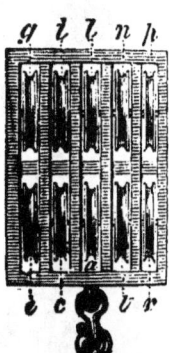

Hence, in this case, the weight is four times the power.

In general, in systems of pullies having only one rope, and one moveable block, the weight is as many times the power, as there are different parts of the rope engaged in supporting the moveable block. This must be very evident, when it is considered that each part of the rope which passes between the two blocks is equally engaged in sustaining the weight.

In the system represented in *fig*. 59, if the rope, instead of being finally attached to the fixed block, were passed over a third wheel in that block, and finally attached to the lower block, the weight would be five times the power.

(78.) In these systems the wheels move on separate axles. They are sometimes placed side by side on the same axle, as represented in *fig*. 60. But the proportion of the power to the weight is the same in all.

In this arrangement of the sheaves it is difficult to keep the strings parallel, and to prevent the effect of the power and weight deranging the position of the blocks in the manner represented in *fig*. 61.

To remedy this inconvenience the ingenious and powerful arrangement represented in *fig*. 62, has been suggested. To prevent confusion in the figure, the rope has been omitted, but its course may be easily traced. Suppose one extremity attached to the hook at the bottom of the upper block: the rope from this point is brought under the wheel a, over b, under c, over d, under e, over f, and so on according to the order of the letters, until it finally passes over the wheel u, and is then attached to the power. In this case there can be no derangement in the position of the blocks, as in *fig*. 61, since the power acts immediately over the weight. The weight is here sustained by the ropes, which pass over *ten* wheels, and therefore is distributed between twenty parts of the rope, so that the weight is twenty times the power.

(79.) All systems of pullies of this kind, however, have still great defects. The great number of wheels requisite when much power is required increases the quantity of friction prodigiously; for each wheel has not only the friction on its axle, but also the friction against the side of the block in which it revolves. Besides this, they are liable to great inequality of wear, owing to the circumstance of revolving on their axles with different velocities. Suppose that, by the action of the power, the lower block in *fig*. 62 is moved one foot towards the upper block; it is evident that the several parts of the rope between the blocks will be each shortened by one foot. Hence it appears that one foot of that part of the rope which extended from the hook in the upper block to the wheel *a* must pass over that wheel: this foot of rope must evidently also pass over the wheels *b*, *c*, and all the succeeding wheels. But the part of the rope which extended from the wheel *a* to the wheel *b* is also shortened by one foot. This foot of rope must therefore pass over the wheel *b* and all the succeeding wheels *c*, *d*, &c. Hence one foot of rope passes the wheel *a* in the ascent, and two feet pass *b*. By continuing this reasoning, we shall find that three feet of rope pass *c*, four pass *d*, and so on. Now the velocities with which the wheels revolve (their diameters being the same) is justly measured by the quantity of rope which passes over them in the same time. Hence, while the wheel *a* revolves once, *b* revolves twice, *c* three times, *d* four times, and so on. Hence arises that inequality of wear which we have already mentioned.

If we attempt to remove this defect by fixing all the wheels on the same pivots so as to compel them to turn with the same velocity, we shall introduce another source of friction and cause of wear much greater than the former; for since the rope passes over the wheels with different velocities, while they revolve with the same velocity, it must necessarily scrape or slide more or less on the grooves of all of them, one excepted.

The great object, therefore, in the construction of such a system of pullies would be to make them all revolve on their axles in the same time, so as to avoid unequal wear; and yet that their grooves or circumferences should have different velocities equal to those of the rope in passing over them.

(80.) These ends were all attained by a pulley invented by Mr. *James White*. In order that the successive wheels should revolve in the same time, he constructed them of different magnitudes; and so that their several circumferences would be equal to the length of rope which passes over them in the same time. This will be easily understood by recurring to *fig.* 62. Suppose the circumference of the wheel *a* to be one foot: it makes one revolution, while the lower block is raised through one foot towards the upper block. In this time three feet of rope pass over the circumference of the wheel *c*. If then the circumference of this wheel be three feet, it will revolve once during the supposed ascent of the weight. In like manner, the wheel *e* will revolve once if its circumference be five feet, and so on. Thus, then, in general it follows, that the several wheels will revolve in the same time, if their circumferences be as the numbers 1, 3, 5, &c.; and in the same way it may be proved, that the wheels in the upper block will revolve in the same time with each other, and with the wheels in the lower block, if their circumferences be as the numbers 2, 4, 6, &c., or, what is the same, as the successive integers 1, 2, 3, &c.

The circumferences of circles are proportional to their diameters, and, therefore, by constructing the several wheels *a*, *b*, *c*, *d*, &c. with diameters proportional to the successive integers 1, 2, 3, &c., equality of wear would be obtained.

But still the multiplied friction of a great number of different wheels would

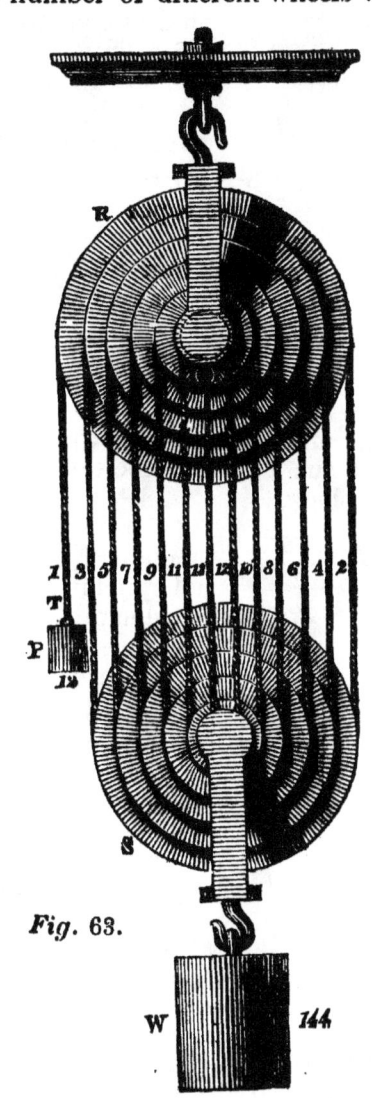

Fig. 63.

Fig. 64.

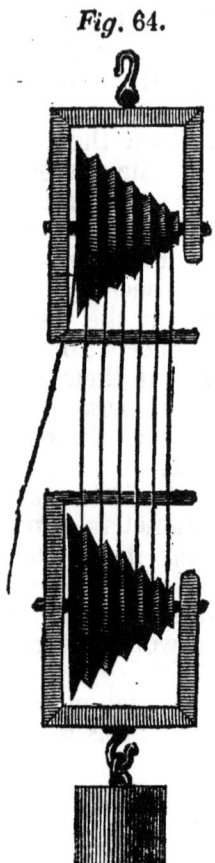

remain, as well the friction on their axles or pivots, as the lateral friction of their surfaces with the blocks. To remove this defect, Mr. White conceived the notion of reducing all the wheels in the same block to one; or rather, instead of using separate wheels, to cut several circular grooves, with the diameters we have already described upon the *same wheel*. Thus, all the friction was reduced to that of the pivots, and the lateral friction of *one wheel*.

This pulley is represented in *figs*. 63, 64, and it will be easily understood from the preceding observations. In this, like every other system in which there is a single rope, the weight is as many times the power as there are ropes sustaining the lower block.

(81.) The condition of equilibrium in all such systems may be mathematically expressed thus:—

$$W = nP;$$

where n signifies the number of parts of the rope which sustain the lower block, and where W expresses the weight sustained and the weight of the lower block.

Fig. 65.

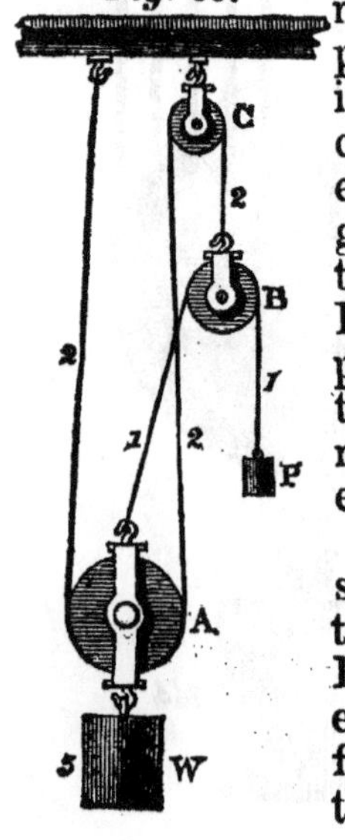

(82.) We have now mentioned the principal systems of pullies in which there is but one rope. Much power, however, may be gained by increasing the number of ropes. In *figs*. 65, 66, are represented systems with two ropes and two moveable pullies, called *Spanish burtons*.

In the system represented in *fig*. 65, the tension of the rope P B is equal to the power, and this rope being finally attached to the pulley which sustains the weight, supports a part of the weight equal to the power. The rope from C to B balances the united tensions of both parts of the rope extending from B to the weight and power, and therefore its tension is twice the power, and being brought under the pulley which sustains the weight, and finally attached to the fixed point, it sustains a part of the weight equal to four times the power. Thus, the whole weight must be equal to five times the power. The power being taken as the unit, the number placed at each rope expresses the part of the weight which it sustains.

The system represented in *fig*. 66 has also two ropes, but is not so powerful as the former. The tension of the rope extending from the power to the fixed point is equal to the power, and the tension of that extending from the pulley B to the weight is obviously equal to twice the power.— Thus, the weight is four times the power. The tensions are here, also, expressed by the figures placed at the ropes.

Fig. 66.

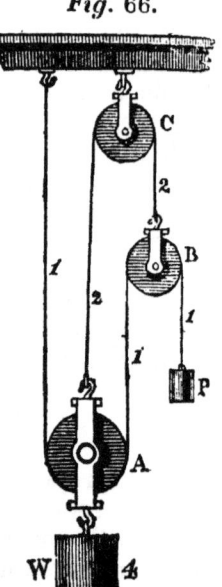

In both these systems the weight of the pulley B assists the power, and that of A opposes it. In the system represented in *Fig*. 65, if the weight of the pulley B be half that of A, the weights of the two pullies will balance one another; but if the weight of B be more than half of A, the power will be assisted, and a less power than the fifth part of the weight will sustain equilibrium. If the weight of B be less than half of A, a contrary effect will take place.

In the system represented in *Fig*. 66, if the weight of B be equal to that of A, it will exactly balance it. If it be greater or less, it will assist or oppose the power.

(83.) In *fig*. 67, a system of pullies is represented with four ropes, in which the weight is sixteen times the power; for the tension of the rope D E is evidently equal to the power, because it sustains it. D, being a moveable pulley, must sustain a weight equal to twice the power; but the weight which it sustains is the tension of the second rope D C,

MECHANICS.

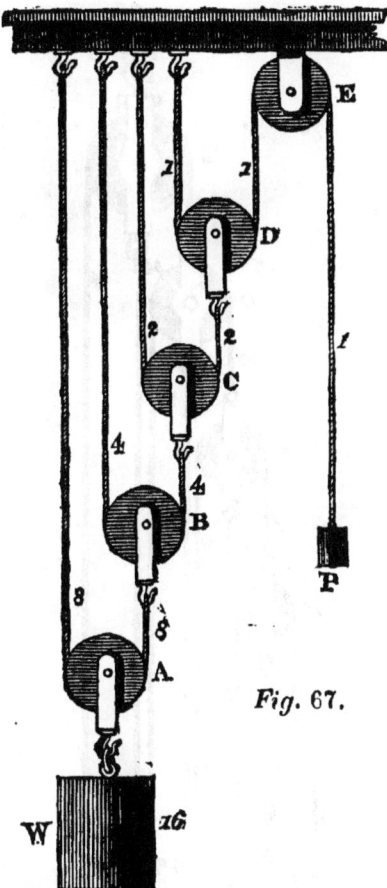

Fig. 67.

Hence the tension of the second rope is twice that of the first: in like manner, the tension of the third rope is twice that of the second, and so on, the weight being equal to twice the tension of the last rope. If then, as in the present instance, there be four ropes, the tension of the first is P, that of the second 2 P, that of the third 2×2 P or 4 P, that of the fourth $2 \times 2 \times 2$ P or 8 P, and therefore the weight W will be 16 P.

It is obvious that each rope, which is added to such a system, will double its effect, and that the condition of equilibrium expressed mathematically will be

$$W = 2^n P;$$

n expressing the number of distinct ropes.

In this case the effect of the weights of the pullies themselves is neglected; but it is evident that they act against the power, and therefore that it requires a certain power to sustain them, even when unloaded.

(84.) The power of this system may be greatly increased without increasing the number of ropes, by substituting fixed pulleys for the hooks to which each rope is finally attached. This method was applied to a single moveable pulley in *fig.* 58, and *fig.* 68 exhibits a series of such pulleys. By *fig.* 58, it follows that the tension of the second rope is three times that of the first, which is equal to the power. The tension of the third is three times that of the second, or nine times that of the

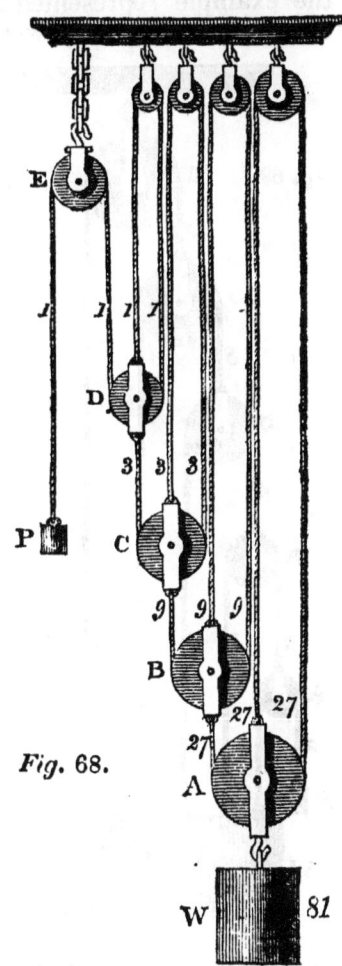

Fig. 68.

first, and so on, the weight being three times the tension of the last rope.

In the present example there are but four ropes, and the weight is 81 times the power. The relation between the power and weight in such a system may be expressed mathematically thus:

$$W = 3^n P;$$

n being the number of distinct ropes.

The effect of the weights of the pulleys themselves in this case is also in opposition to the power, and robs the machine of part of its efficacy.

(85.) A powerful system is represented in *fig.* 69. In this system each rope is finally attached to the weight. The first rope sustains a part of the weight which is equal to the power. The tension of the second rope is twice that of the first, and therefore it sustains a part of the weight equal to twice the power. In like manner the third sustains a part equal to four times the power, and so on, the part sustained by each rope being double that which is sustained by the preceding one.

In this case the weight is equal to the sum of the tensions of all the strings, and in the example represented in *fig.* 69, it is thirty-one times the power.

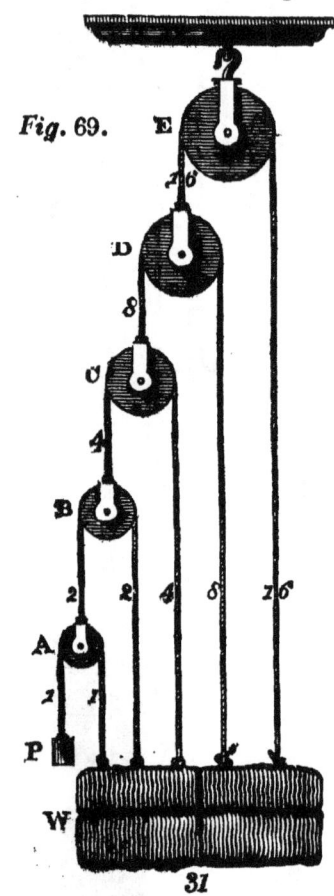

Fig. 69.

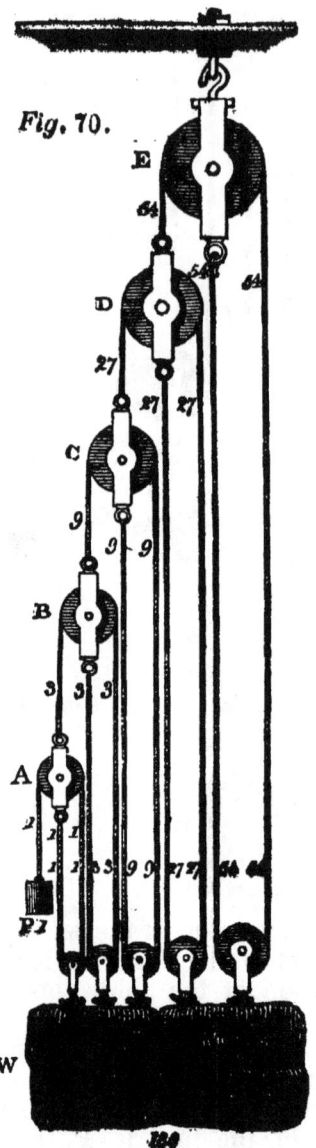

Fig. 70.

It is not difficult to give a general mathematical investigation of the relation between the power and weight. The tensions of the several ropes by which the weight is sustained are P, 2 P, 2^2 P, 2^3 P, &c. and if n be the number of ropes, the tension of the last is 2^{n-1} P. So that we have

$$W = P . (1 + 2 + 2^2 + 2^3 + \ldots 2^{n-1})$$

But the series within the parentheses being in geometrical progression*, its sum is $2^n - 1$. Hence we have

$$W = (2^n - 1) P.$$

(86.) Such a system may be rendered much more powerful without increasing the number of ropes, by passing each rope round a pulley, and finally attaching it to the moveable pulley over which it first passed, as in *fig.* 70. The numbers placed upon the several ropes express the parts of the weight which they respectively support, the power being the unit. In the system in the figure the weight is 188 times the power.

The general mathematical investigation of the relation between the power and weight is similar to that in (85.) The parts of the weight supported by each successive rope is 2 P, 6 P, 18 P, 54 P, &c. and that which is supported by the last rope, the number being n, is $2 . 3.^{n-1}$ P. Hence we have

$$W = 2 P (1 + 3 + 3^2 + 3^3 + \ldots 3^{n-1}).$$

Summing the geometric series within the parentheses, we have

$$W = (3^n - 1.) P.$$

(87.) The various systems of pullies which we have here described are not offered to the student as machines which he will frequently find adopted in practice, but rather as an exercise in the combination of these engines, and as the best means of impressing upon

* See Darley's *Popular Algebra*, p. 97

the memory the general principles upon which the mechanical agency of pullies is to be investigated.

Like all other machines, the pulley obeys the principle of *virtual velocities;* that is, the ascent of the weight is as many times less than the simultaneous descent of the power as the weight itself is greater than the power.

Thus in the single moveable pulley represented in *fig.* 57, if the power descend through two feet, two feet of the rope C A D E will pass over the fixed pulley B C. Hence, that part of the rope will be shortened by two feet, and therefore, each of the parts C A and D E will be shortened by one foot. Thus the weight ascends through one foot while the power descends through two feet, that is, the velocity of the power is twice that of the weight. But by (76) it appears that the weight is equal to twice the power.

In the same manner it may be proved that in *fig.* 58, while the power descends through three feet, the rope extending from the fixed pulley to that end which is attached to the pulley which supports the weight is shortened by three feet, and therefore, each of the three parts engaged in supporting the weight is shortened by one foot. Hence, it appears, that the velocity of the power is three times that of the weight; by (76) it was proved that the weight is three times the power.

In general, in all systems of pullies in which there is but one rope, the space through which the power descends is equal to the entire length by which the rope extending from the pulley next the power to its extremity is shortened. But this length is distributed equally between all the parts of the rope which are engaged in supporting the weight. Hence each part will be shortened by a quantity as many times less than the descent of the power as there are parts of the rope engaged in supporting the weight. But the number of these parts expresses the proportion of the weight to the power.

This reasoning will be easily applied to the systems represented in *figs.* 59, 60, 63, &c. We shall not pursue this investigation to the other systems. By adopting a similar method of reasoning, the student will find no difficulty in perceiving that it is applicable to all of them, and that universally as we gain great mechanical efficacy, that is, raise a very great weight with a very small power, we invariably lose just as much in velocity as we gain in force.

(88.) We have hitherto supposed that the ropes by which the pulleys are sustained are all in the vertical direction. When this is not the case, the several results which we have obtained are not applicable. In *fig.* 71 the power sustains the weight by the tension of a rope, in which the parts are not parallel. Let E F (*fig.* 71.) be the vertical line

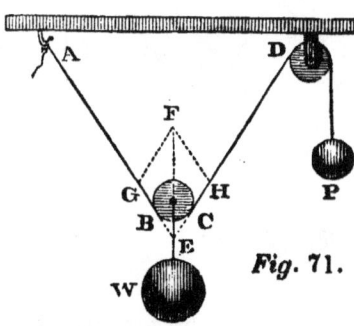

Fig. 71.

through which the centre of gravity of the weight passes, and from F draw F G and F H parallel to D C and A B. At the point E three forces may be considered as acting, which are in equilibrium, viz. the tensions in the directions E H and E G, and the weight W. Hence, by Treatise I. (9), these forces must be represented by the lines E H, E G, and E F. But, since the tension of every part of the rope is the same, and equal to the power P, the sides E H and E G of the parallelogram must be equal, and therefore the diagonal E F must divide the angle G E H into two equal parts. Hence, it follows that the weight will always settle itself into that position in which the two parts A B, D C of the rope will be equally inclined to the vertical line, and it will have to the power the same ratio as E F to E H.

Those who are conversant with trigonometry will perceive, that if the angle A E D, at which the parts of the suspending rope are inclined, be called E, we have

E F : E H : : Sin. E : Sin. ½ E.
But Sin. E = 2 Sin. ½ E Cos. ½ E.
Hence
E F : E H : : 2 Sin. ½ E Cos. ½ E : Sin. ½ E.
  E F : E H : : 2 Cos. ½ E : 1
∴ W : P : : 2 Cos. ½ E : 1
   W = 2 P Cos. ½ E;

that is, twice the power, multiplied by the cosine of half the angle under the ropes, is equal to the weight.

(89.) In the same way the effect of the obliquity of the ropes may be determined, whatever be the system of pulleys. In *fig.* 72, the system of pullies described in (83) is represented with the ropes oblique. The tension of the first rope, P A″, (*fig.* 72.) is equal to

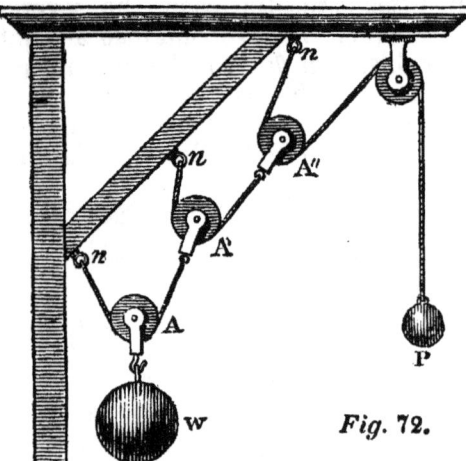

Fig. 72.

the power. Let the tension of the second rope be t. Then by (88) we have
$$t = 2 \text{ P Cos. } \tfrac{1}{2} \text{ A}''$$,
A″ being the angle under the parts of the first rope.

In like manner, if t' be the tension of the rope A A′, we have
$$t' = 2 t \text{ Cos. } \tfrac{1}{2} \text{ A}'$$,
and in the same way
$$\text{W} = 2 t' \text{ Cos. } \tfrac{1}{2} \text{ A}.$$
Multiplying these three equations together, we have
$$\text{W } t' t = \text{P } t' t \text{ Cos. } \tfrac{1}{2} \text{ A Cos. } \tfrac{1}{2} \text{ A}' \text{ Cos. } \tfrac{1}{2} \text{ A}''.$$
Omitting the common multipliers $t' t$, we have
$$\text{W} = 8 \text{ P Cos. } \tfrac{1}{2} \text{ A Cos. } \tfrac{1}{2} \text{ A}' \text{ Cos. } \tfrac{1}{2} \text{ A}''.$$

It is easy to see how a similar investigation may be extended to any case in which the ropes are oblique.

(90.) Friction has always been a great source of waste of power in pullies. This, however, has been in a great degree removed by an ingenious contrivance of Mr. Garnet, called *friction-rollers*. They not only save expense and labour, but also considerably diminish the wear of the machine. The principle is this: between the axis on which the wheel turns, and the concave cylinder or box in which that axis is placed, a hollow space is left to be filled by solid equal rollers, nearly touching each other. These are furnished with axles, inserted in a circular ring at each end, by which their relative distances are preserved, and they are kept parallel by means of wires fastened to the rings between the rollers, and which are rivetted to them.

CHAPTER IX.—*On the Inclined Plane.*

(91.) THE INCLINED PLANE is a machine formed, as the name imports, by a plane surface, supposed to be perfectly hard and inflexible, and which is always inclined obliquely to the weight or the resistance to be overcome.

Let the line L H (*fig.* 73.) be horizontal, and let L M be a perfectly hard and smooth plane, forming, with the horizontal plane, the angle M L H, called the *elevation* of the plane. The line L M is called its *length*, M H its *height*, and L H its *base*.

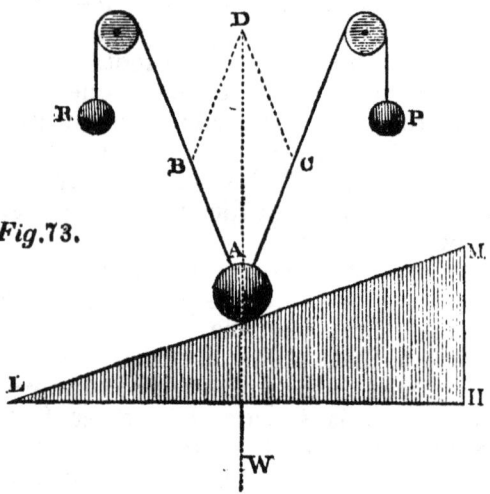

Fig. 73.

Let A be a weight placed upon this plane, and sustained by a power in any direction, as A C. The body A is kept at rest by three forces acting at its centre of gravity: 1°, the force of gravity, W acting in the vertical direction, A W; 2°, the power P acting in the direction A C; and 3°, the resistance R of the plane acting in the direction A B perpendicular to the plane. Now, since the weight W, in the direction A W, resists the forces P and R, in the directions A C and A B, it must be equal and opposite to the resultant of these two forces. (Treatise I. Chap. II.) Suppose A D drawn directly upward, in the direction W A, and from any point D draw D C and D B, parallel to A B and A C respectively, and it follows that the weight, the power, and the resistance of the plane will be proportional to the lines A D, A C, and A B. This may easily be verified by experiment. On a vertical plane behind the power and weight, draw the line A D vertical, and from any point D in it draw D C in a direction at right angles to the plane. Upon measuring the lines A D and A C, they will be found to have exactly the same proportion as the weight W and the power P. The quantity of the resistance may be determined, experimentally, in the same manner. Let a string be attached to the weight, and brought in a direction A B, over a fixed pulley, and let a weight R be suspended from it, which will bear the same ratio to W and P, as the line A B or D C bears to the lines A D and A C. Upon removing the plane, it will be found that the weight A will remain suspended, undisturbed in its position. Hence, it appears that the tension of the string A C, which is a force equal to the weight R, supplies the place of the plane, and produces the same mechanical effect. The force R, therefore, is the amount of the pressure of the weight upon the plane*.

Since all equiangular triangles have their sides proportional†, it follows that if any triangle be drawn, whose angles are equal to those of a triangle, one side of which is vertical, another perpendicular to the plane, and the third in the direction of the power, the sides of that triangle will always be proportional to the power, the weight, and the pressure upon the plane. This relation between the power, weight, and pressure may be very simply expressed mathematically. Let the angle formed by the vertical line A D, (*fig.* 73.) and the perpendicular A B to the plane be A, and let the angle B D A, formed by the vertical line A D, and the direction A C of the power be D; and the angle under the direction of the power A C, and the perpendicular to the plane, viz. D B A be B. Since the sides of triangles are proportional to the sides of the opposite angles, we have

$$\frac{P}{W} = \frac{\text{Sin. A}}{\text{Sin. B}} \quad \frac{R}{W} = \frac{\text{Sin. D}}{\text{Sin. B}}$$

(92.) In the preceding investigation of the proportion of the power, weight, and pressure, we have conceived the power to act in any direction whatever. If it act in the direction of the plane, the triangle whose sides will determine its proportion to the weight, will be A C B, (*fig.* 74.) in which B C is the direction of the power, A B of the weight, and A C of the pressure. This triangle

---
* The experiments which we have thought it advisable to describe, in verification of the theory, are not those which are the most easily executed, but those which we conceive to be best adapted to render the theory intelligible, independent of much mathematical reasoning.

† See DARLEY's *Popular Geometry*, Art. 112.

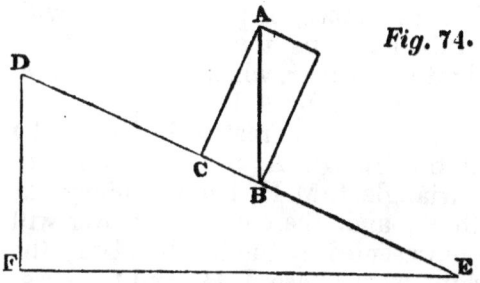
Fig. 74.

is evidently similar to the triangle F D E, formed by the height, length, and base of the plane. Hence, in this case, the height D F of the plane represents the power, the length, the weight, and the base of the pressure.

This may be verified experimentally. Let a thread, attached to the weight A, be brought parallel to the plane, and passed over a fixed pulley at D; let

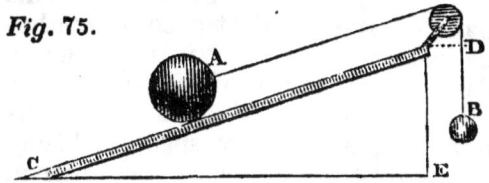
Fig. 75.

such a weight P be suspended from it, as will bear the same proportion to A as the height D E bears to the length D C, and it will be found to sustain the weight. The amount of the pressure may be shewn to be represented by the base C E in a manner exactly similar to that explained in *fig.* 73.

This may be expressed mathematically thus: let E be the elevation of the plane

$$\frac{P}{W} = \frac{D E}{D C} = \text{Sin. E} \qquad \frac{R}{W} = \frac{C E}{C D} = \text{Cos. E.}$$

(93.) If the power act in a horizontal direction, or parallel to the base of the plane, its proportion to the weight will be that of the height of the plane to the base. For, in *fig.* 76, let A B be ver-

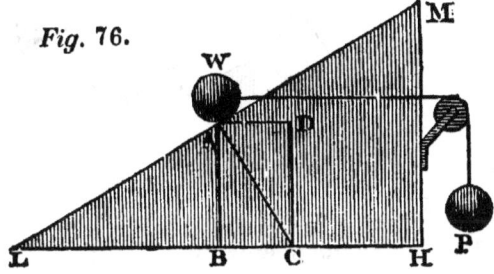
Fig. 76.

tical, and, therefore, in the direction of the weight; and let A D, parallel to the base, be in the direction of the power, and A C, perpendicular to the plane, will be in the direction of the resistance.

The resistance, or pressure A C, will, in this case, be the resultant of the weight and power, which will, therefore, be represented by A D and A B, or by B C and A B.—(Treatise I. Chap. II.) But the triangle A B C is similar to the triangle L M H, being equiangular with it; and, therefore, the power will be represented by the height M H, the weight by the base L H, and the pressure by the length L M.

To express this mathematically, we have

$$\frac{P}{W} = \frac{MH}{LH} = tan.\ E.\quad \frac{R}{W} = \frac{LM}{LH} = \frac{1}{Cos.\ E} = Sec.\ E.$$

(94.) It is easy to see that the power acts to greatest advantage, when its direction is parallel to the plane. This may be established at once by mathematical reasoning; but it is sufficiently plain, from considering, that if the power be directed *above* the plane, as in *fig.* 73, it is partly spent in lifting the weight from the plane, or rather in diminishing the pressure, and only partly in drawing it *up* the plane. If, on the other hand, it be directed *below* the plane, as in *fig.* 76, it is spent partly in pressing the weight against the plane, and only partly in drawing the weight *up* the plane. This will be very evident to the student, who has attended to what has been said of the composition of force in Chap. II. of our first Treatise. But if, on the other hand, the power acts parallel to the plane, its whole effect will be spent in drawing the weight up the plane.

(95.) If a weight on one inclined plane be supported by a power on another, their proportion will be that of the

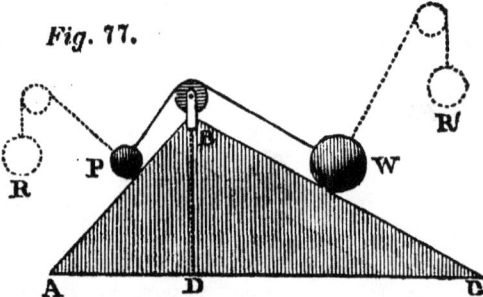

Fig. 77.

lengths of the planes on which they rest. In this case we may consider P and W (*fig.* 77.) as two weights, sustained on two inclined planes, A B and C B, by the tension of the string which unites them, and which is the common power which sustains both, and which supports each in a direction parallel to the planes on which they respectively rest. Considering only the inclined plane A B, the power, that is the tension of the string, the weight P and the pressure are represented by B D, B A, and A D, respectively (92). In like manner, considering only the plane B C, the power or tension of the string, the weight W and the pressure are represented by B D, B C, and C D, respectively. The power, or tension of the string, being the same for both planes, it follows that the weights P and W are as the lengths B A and B C, and that the pressures are as the lines A D and C D.

This may be submitted to the test of experiment, by ascertaining the power P, which supports any given weight W, and measuring the lengths of the planes. They will always be found to be in the same proportion. To determine the proportion of the pressures, let threads be attached to P and W, and brought in directions perpendicular to the planes over fixed pulleys, and let weights R' and R be suspended from them, which shall have the same proportion to P and W, as the lines A D and C D have to B A and B C, and upon removing the planes from beneath the weights, they will retain their positions undisturbed.

(96.) The principle of virtual velocities may be easily applied to the inclined plane. In *fig.* 75, suppose that at the commencement of the motion the weight is at the foot C of the plane, and the power is at the top D of the altitude. Let the power then descend until the weight shall arrive at the top of the plane. It will have descended through a space equal to the length of rope which has passed over the pulley, that is, equal to the length of the plane, and at the same time the weight will have ascended through a space equal to the height of the plane; so that the perpendicular spaces, through which the weight and power move in the same time, are the height and length of the plane, and these are, therefore, the proportion of their velocities. But the proportion of the weight to the power is that of the length to the height. Hence, the power and weight are reciprocally as their vertical velocities, which is conformable to the principle of virtual velocities.

It would not be difficult to show the application of this principle to the other modifications of the inclined plane; but this instance will serve our present purpose.

MECHANICS.

(97.) In the inclined plane, therefore, like every other mechanical power, we lose velocity in proportion as we increase the force. In some instances, however, this is an advantage. For instance, in an inclined plane constructed for launching a ship. Here the plane is slightly inclined, and the power which would sustain the vessel on the plane (allowing the effects of friction) is equal to the force with which the vessel descends, which, owing to the small elevation, is comparatively trifling.

CHAPTER X.—*On the Wedge.*

(98.) A WEDGE is a solid figure, which is called in geometry a *triangular prism*. Its two ends are equal and similar triangles, and its three sides are rectangular parallelograms. This figure is represented in *figs*. 78, 79.

The wedge is very generally used in

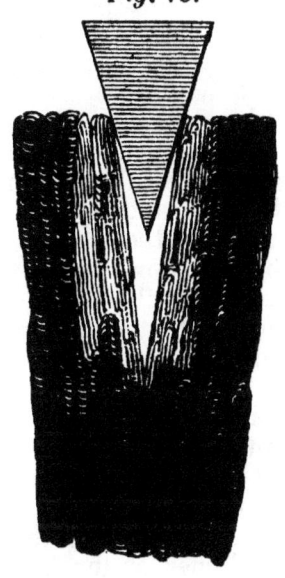

Fig. 78.

cleaving timber, in which case its edge is introduced into a cleft already made to receive it, and it is urged at the

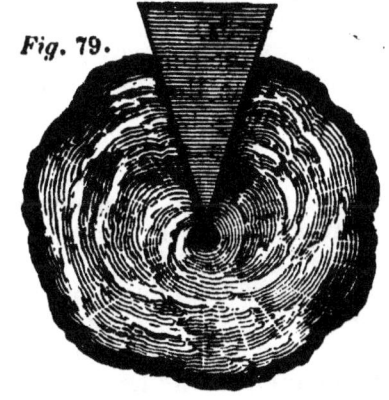

Fig. 79.

back by percussion. The friction of the faces of the wedge with the timber ought to be sufficient to prevent its recoil.

The wedge may be considered as formed by two inclined planes placed base to base, their altitudes forming the back of the wedge. The power being generally applied perpendicularly to the back will be parallel to the common base. But it is a more difficult matter to say in what direction the resistance is to be considered as acting against the face of the wedge.

In the theory of the wedge, there are introduced so many conditions, which are perfectly inapplicable in practice, so many gratuitous assumptions and suppositions so inconsistent with practical truth, that the whole doctrine has little or no value.

One of the circumstances, which creates the greatest difficulty in the theory of the wedge, is the very heterogeneous nature of the resistance, and the force or power by which it is overcome. The resistance is generally that modification of force called *pressure*. The power, which is opposed to this resistance, is commonly that species of action called *percussion*. These are modifications of force so totally different as not even to admit of comparison. It has been generally thought that there is no *blow* or *impact*, however slight, which will not overcome a pressure or resistance however great. From which it would seem to follow, that an infinitely small impact is equivalent to an infinitely great pressure. Be this as it may, however, the great difference between these modifications of force, is sufficiently evident to demonstrate the total impossibility of establishing the condition of equilibrium of a machine in which the weight or resistance is a force of the one, and the power is a force of the other species.

Nothing, therefore, can more plainly demonstrate the inutility of the theory of the wedge than that, in this theory, the power is supposed to be a pressure exerted on the back of the wedge, which is supposed to be capable of balancing the effect of the resistance in producing the recoil of the wedge. In all cases, where the wedge is practically used, the friction of its faces with the resisting substance, is sufficient to prevent the recoil; so that, strictly speaking, no force whatever is necessary to sustain the machine in equilibrium, and to move it, pressure is never resorted to, inasmuch as the slightest percussion is far more effective.

The only general theoretical principle respecting the wedge, which obtains always in practice is, that its power is increased by diminishing the angle.

All cutting instruments, as knives, swords, hatchets, chisels, planes, &c. are wedges. In these cases, the harder, in general, the substance to be divided is, the greater will be the angle of the wedge. Thus, chisels for cutting soft woods are sharper than those used for the harder species, and these, again, are sharper than chisels used for cutting metals.

In the preceding observations on the wedge, we have not attempted to explain its theory, conceiving, that a theory, which is utterly inapplicable in practice, is better omitted in the "Library of Useful Knowledge."

CHAPTER XI.—*On the Screw—Hunter's Screw — Perpetual Screw — Micrometer Screw.*

(99.) THE screw is a machine of great mechanical power, and is applied to various purposes; but is most generally used in cases where an intense pressure is to be exerted. This machine is a modification of the inclined plane. Let an inclined plane (*fig.* 80.) be placed with

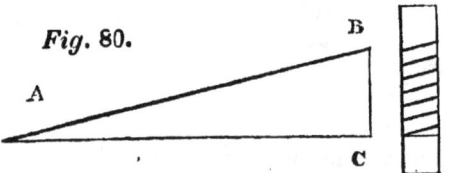

Fig. 80.

its altitude B C parallel to the axis of a cylinder, and placing the altitude B C on the side of the cylinder, let the plane, supposed flexible, be rolled round it. The length A B of the plane will trace upon the cylinder a spiral thread, which is called the thread of the screw.

A perspective view of this machine is given in *fig.* 81. If any body be placed between two threads, and the screw be turned once round, the body so placed not being permitted to turn with it, it is plain that this body will be moved from its first position to a similar place on the thread next above that on which it was first placed. In fact, it will be elevated through an height equal to the distance between two contiguous threads. By this process the body is forced up the inclined plane, which is wrapped upon the cylinder, and the power being

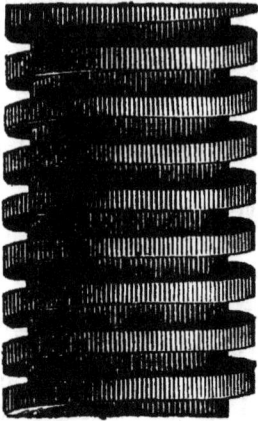

Fig. 81.

supposed to be applied at the circumference of the screw acts parallel to the base of the plane.

In this case, the proportion of the power to the weight is that of the height of the plane to its base (93). But in one revolution of the screw, the body, which is placed between the threads, is moved up an inclined plane, whose height is the interval between two contiguous threads, and whose base is the circumference of the screw. Hence, it follows that the power is to the weight or resistance as the interval between the threads is to the circumference of the cylinder on which the thread is raised.

The energy of the power on the screw is transmitted by means of a concave cylindrical screw, on the inner surface of which a spiral channel is cut, corresponding exactly to the thread raised upon the cylinder, so that by turning the one within the other the convex screw will pass through the concave screw, and will advance every revolution through a space equal to the distance between two contiguous threads.

A section of the convex and concave screw, by a plane through the axis, is represented in *fig.* 82. If the concave screw be fixed, so as to be incapable either of revolving or moving in the direction of its length, it is evident that the convex screw will gradually penetrate it, advancing through the space between two contiguous threads every revolution. If, on the other hand, the convex screw be incapable of moving in the direction of its length, it will, by its rotatory motion, force the concave screw in the direction of its length, through a space equal to the interval between two contiguous threads, every revolution.

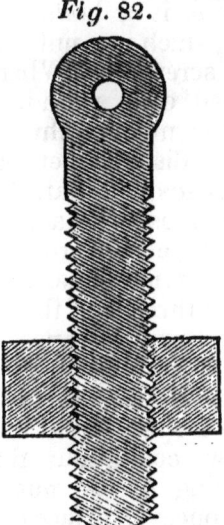

Fig. 82.

The convex screw is generally called the *screw*, and the concave screw is denominated the *nut*.

(100.) We have here considered the power to be applied at the circumference of the screw; and if we consider the screw as a simple machine, we must suppose it thus applied. But, in practice, the screw never is used as a simple machine, and the power is always applied to a lever at the head of the screw, in the same manner as it is applied in the wheel and axle, and as represented in *fig.* 83. In this case the machine is really complex, being composed of a lever and a screw. The proportion of the power to the weight is easily investigated. Let P be the power, and let x

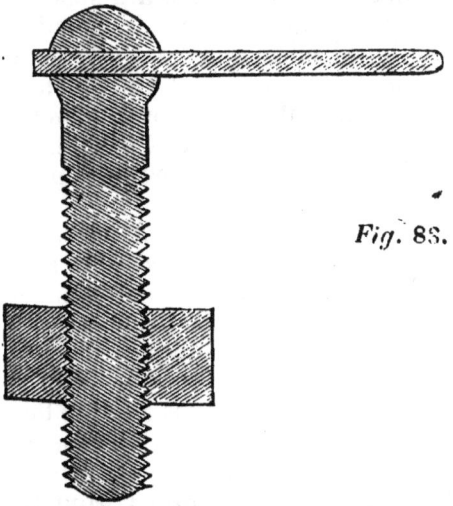

Fig. 83.

be the effect of this power at the circumference of the screw. Let R be the arm of the lever by which the power acts, and let r be the radius of the section of the screw, at right angles to its length. By the principles established in Chap. III., we have

$$P \times R = x \times r,$$
$$\text{or } P : x :: r : R.$$

But the radii of circles are as their circumferences. Let C be the circumference described by the power, and whose radius is R, and c the circumference of the screw, whose radius is r.

$$r : R :: c : C$$

Hence, we have

$$P : x :: c : C,$$
$$\text{or } P \times C = x \times c.$$

But, by (99),

$$x : W :: D : c,$$

where D signifies the distance between the threads. Hence, we have

$$x \times c = W \times D \therefore P \times C = W \times D$$
$$\text{or } P : W :: D : C.$$

That is, "the power, multiplied by the circumference which it describes, is equal to the weight or resistance, multiplied by the distance between two contiguous threads;" or, "The power is to the weight, as the distance between two contiguous threads is to the circumference described by the power."

It frequently happens, that the lever by which the power acts is attached to the nut, and the screw is capable only of a longitudinal motion. Thus, in the press represented in *fig.* 84, the board

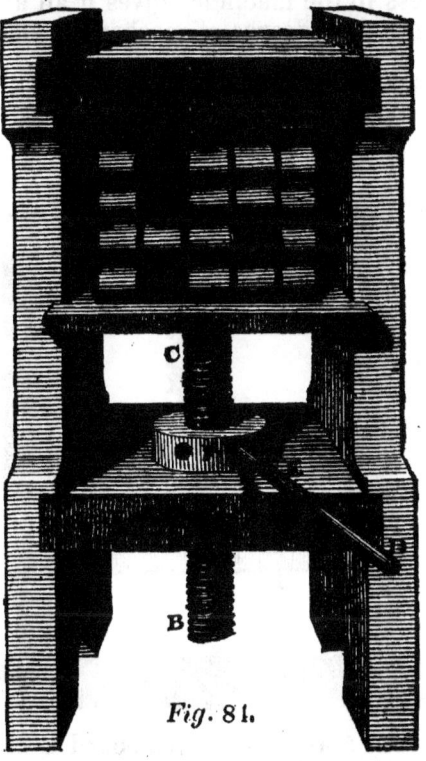

Fig. 84.

C, moveable between the sides of the frame, is urged by the screw C B, capable of moving directly upwards or downwards, but not of revolving. The nut F is worked by the lever D E. Every complete revolution of the nut urges the screw upward, through a space equal to the distance between two contiguous threads.

The proportion of the weight to the power, or the mechanical efficacy of the screw, depends on the proportion of the circumference described by the power, to the distance between two contiguous threads. Hence, it is evident that the efficacy of the screw may be increased, either by increasing the length of the lever by which the power acts, or by diminishing the distance between the threads. To both of these there are, however, practical limits, similar to those mentioned in the case of the wheel and axle (58.)

If the leverage of the power be very much increased, the power will work through an inconveniently great space, and the machine will become unwieldy. If, on the other hand, the thread of the screw be made very small and fine, it will be torn off by a great resistance in passing through the nut.

These inconveniences have been obviated by a contrivance of Mr. Hunter, the Surgeon, which, while it preserves all the requisite strength and compactness in the machine, gives it an almost unlimited degree of mechanical efficacy.

A perspective drawing of this contrivance is given in *fig.* 85: E E is a

Fig. 85.

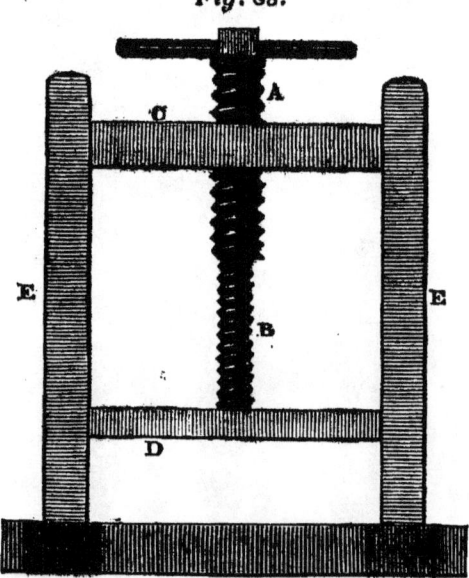

strong frame in which a board D moves, so that when it is forced towards the bottom, it will exert a pressure on any substance placed between it and the bottom. To this moveable board D is attached a cylinder B, on which the thread of a screw is raised. C is a fixed nut through which a screw A plays. The screw A is a hollow cylinder, the interior of which is a nut adapted to receive the screw B. When the screw A is turned once round, it advances through the nut C, through a space equal to the distance between two contiguous threads; so that, if the screw B were not supposed to act, the board D would advance towards the bottom, through a distance equal to the distance between the threads of the screw A. But while the screw A advances through the nut C by its revolution, the very same cause makes the screw B move towards C through a space equal to the distance between two contiguous threads of B; or, by turning A, the nut contained in the inner concave surface of A is turned upon the screw B. Now, if the threads of the two screws A and B were perfectly equal, the effect of these two motions would be, that the board D would retain its position, inasmuch as the effect of one screw, in moving it *downwards*, would be exactly equal to the effect of the other screw in moving it *upwards*.

But if we suppose the interval between the threads of the screw B to be somewhat less than the interval between the threads of the screw A, the effect will be different. In this case, one revolution will move the screw A *downwards*, through a space equal to the interval between its threads, while the screw B will be moved within the screw A and *upwards*, through a space equal to the interval between *its* threads. The combined effect will be, that the screw B, and the board C to which it is attached, will be moved *downwards* through a space equal to the difference of the distances between the threads of the two screws.

Thus, if the screw A have twenty threads in an inch, and the screw B have twenty-one; in one revolution, A is moved downwards through the twentieth of an inch. Suppose that the nut A did not, in this motion, turn on B, it is plain, then, that B and the board C would be moved down through the $\frac{1}{20}$th of an inch. Suppose, then, that the screw B was turned round once within the nut A, the screw B and the board C would be raised through the $\frac{1}{21}$th of an inch. Its position would then be below its original position by the excess of $\frac{1}{20}$th of an inch above $\frac{1}{21}$th of an inch; that is, by $\frac{1}{420}$th of an inch.

To render the explanation clearer, we have here supposed things to happen in succession, which really happen together. The same motion which advances the screw A downwards, draws the screw B upwards; but the final effect is the same as if these two motions took place in succession.

It is plain, therefore, that the effect of this machine is the same as that of a simple screw in which the distance between the threads is equal to the difference of the distances between the threads of the two screws A and B; and, therefore, that the ratio of the power to the weight is the difference between the distances of the threads of the two screws to the circumference described by the power.

The mechanical efficacy is, therefore, increased by diminishing the difference of the distance between the threads of the screws. If the circumference described by the power be 20 inches, and one screw have twenty threads to an inch, and the other twenty-one, the power will be to the weight as the difference between $\frac{1}{20}$ and $\frac{1}{21}$, or $\frac{1}{420}$ to 20, or as 1 to 8400. If, however, one screw have 30 threads and the other 31 to an inch, then the power is to the weight as the difference between $\frac{1}{30}$ and $\frac{1}{31}$, or $\frac{1}{930}$ to 20, or as 1 to 18600.

The threads of each screw may be constructed of any size and strength which may be required, and yet so very nearly equal, that any degree of power may be imparted to the machine. Thus, by the preceding investigation, it appears that two screws, constructed with 30 and 31 threads in a foot, are equivalent to a single screw with 930 threads in a foot.

(101.) The thread of the screw, instead of urging forward the nut, sometimes is made to act upon the teeth of a wheel, as in *fig.* 86. In this case it is called a *perpetual screw*. The machine in this figure is complex, being composed of the screw and the axle in the wheel. The relation between the

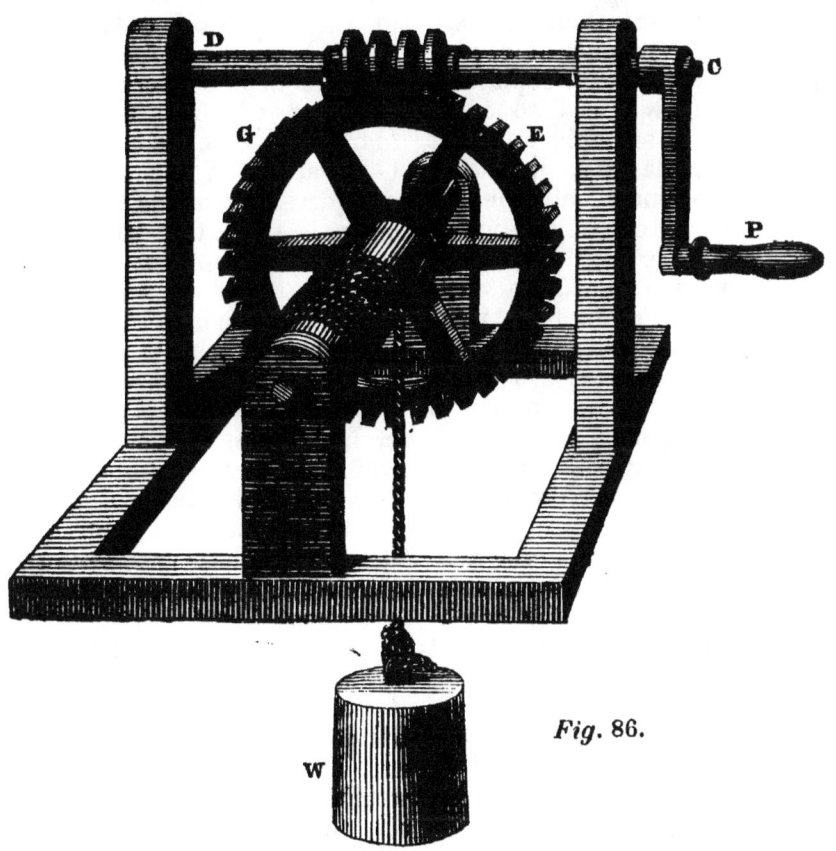

Fig. 86.

power, and the weight is easily investigated. Let P be the power, and let x be its effect on the wheel G E. Let R be the radius of the wheel, D the distance between the threads of the screw, r the radius of the axle, and W the weight or resistance; and let C be the circumference described by the power. By what we have established respecting the screw,

$$P \times C = x \times D$$
and by the properties of the wheel and axle established in (50),
$$x \times R = W \times r$$
Multiplying these equalities, we have
$$P \times C \times x \times R = x \times D \times W \times r$$
Omitting the common multiplier x, we have
$$P \times C \times R = W \times D \times r$$
or $P : W :: D \times r : C \times R$; that is, "the power is to the weight as the distance between the threads multiplied by the radius of the axle to the circumference described by the power, multiplied by the radius of the wheel."

The condition of equilibrium of this machine has been mistaken by some writers, and the error seems to have crept from one treatise to another. Instead of the circumference described by the power, the radius is used which gives the machine only about a sixth of its true efficacy.

(102.) The very slow motion which may be imparted to a screw by a very considerable motion in the power, renders it an instrument peculiarly well adapted to the measurement of very minute spaces. The manner of applying it to this purpose is easily explained. Suppose that a screw is cut so as to have fifty threads in an inch, and that round its head is placed a graduated circle, on which an index, attached to the screw, plays. In one revolution of the screw its point, or anything moved by its point, is moved through a space equal to the fiftieth part of an inch. The circle on which the index plays may be easily divided into 100 equal parts, and it follows that the motion of the index through one of these parts corresponds to one-hundreth part of a complete revolution: since, in a complete revolution, the screw moves through the fiftieth part of an inch, it follows, that when the index moves over one division of the circle, the screw moves through the five-thousandth part of an inch.

A screw constructed for this purpose is called a micrometer screw: it is used with great effect in astronomical instruments, where very minute portions of degrees or divisions on graduated instruments are to be ascertained. The limit of accuracy of any divided instrument adapted for measuring spaces or distances is primarily the magnitude of the smallest division on it. If it be required to determine the distance from any given division to a point which is placed somewhere between two divisions, it is easy to conclude that the distance sought is greater than a certain number of divisions, and less than a number greater than that by one. But how much greater than the one or less than the other, the mere graduation of the instrument does not indicate. Now, suppose that a micrometer screw is placed on the instrument, its length being parallel to the graduated face, and that the point of the screw, or rather, a wire which is moved by the point of the screw, is brought exactly opposite to one of those divisions between which the point, whose exact position is to be determined, lies. If the screw be turned until the wire is moved by its point from coincidence with the adjacent division till it coincides with the point, the number of turns of the screw, and parts of a turn, will indicate exactly the distance of the point from the adjacent division.

We may give an example of the application of the screw to this purpose in the steel-yard (44). If the loop which bears the sliding weight P carries inserted in it a micrometer screw, the point of which is adjusted so as to mark the place on the graduated arm G B, at which the weight P is to be considered as acting; and suppose the screw is such, that in sixteen turns its point would move over one division of the arm, which we will suppose graduated for pounds,—let us suppose that when the weight W is counterpoised, the point of the screw is between the tenth and eleventh division of the arm G B. It is evident, then, that the weight is more than ten pounds, and less than eleven pounds. Let the screw be turned until its point moves from the intermediate position to the tenth division, and note the number of turns—suppose it seven: that would be equivalent to seven-sixteenths of a division, or seven-sixteenths of a pound, that is, seven ounces. The weight is, therefore, ten pounds seven ounces. In like manner, if there had been but $5\frac{1}{2}$ turns, the weight would be 10 pounds $5\frac{1}{2}$ ounces, and so on.

Hunter's screw is peculiarly well adapted to micrometrical purposes, because it gives an indefinitely slow motion, without requiring a very exquisitely fine thread, which the simple screw would require in this case.

CHAPTER XII.—*Methods of regulating Machinery—Nature of a Fly-Wheel—its power of regulating force—its power of accumulating force—Instances—Nature and Properties of the Governor.*

(103.) IN applying force to impel machinery, for the purposes of manufacture, the mere transmission of the effect of the power to the working point is not the only end to be attained. It is most frequently necessary that the action of the working point should be steady and uniform, and not subject to irregular or desultory changes, occasioning jolts in the machinery, and sudden inequalities in the work. The want of uniformity, in the performance of a machine, may arise from either of three causes. *First*, a want of uniformity in the action of the power, or *first mover*, which impels the machine. Thus, for instance, in the single-acting steam-engine, where the elastic force of steam acts upon the piston during its descent, but which action is suspended during the ascent. *Secondly*, a want of uniformity in the resistance, or load upon the machine; and, *thirdly*, because the machine, in the different positions which its parts assume during the motion, transmits the impelling power to the working point with greater or less effect.

One of the most simple and effectual methods of equalizing these irregularities, is by the use of a FLY-WHEEL. A FLY-WHEEL is a heavy disc, or hoop balanced on its axis, and so connected with the machinery, as to turn rapidly round with it, and so as to receive its motion from the impelling power. Let us suppose a case in which the impelling power is perfectly uniform, but the resistance or load is irregular and intermitting. Thus, suppose an overshot water-wheel, (Treatise I. Chap. V.) urged by a regular and uniform fall of water, applied to work a common suction-pump. (PNEUMATICS, 40.) Here the impelling power is constant and uniform, but the resistance only acts during the ascent of the piston, and the machine is unloaded during its descent. As the impelling power during the descent of the piston has nothing to overcome except the inertia of the machine, and the friction of the parts, it will urge the piston down with a rapidly accelerated force, so that at the end of the stroke the piston will have acquired a considerable velocity. But, in the ascent of the piston, the impelling power is opposed by the column of water which the piston has to raise. (PNEUMATICS, 40.) This continually retards the wheel, and when the piston has reached the summit of the stroke, all its former acceleration is destroyed, and the same hobbling, irregular motion is continued. If a FLY-WHEEL be attached to such a machine, almost all this irregularity will be removed. When the heavy mass of the fly-wheel has been put in rapid motion by the impelling power, it will produce two very obvious effects: by virtue of its inertia, it will oppose a considerable resistance to any sudden acceleration, and also to any sudden retardation of its motion; that is, it has a disposition to continue the motion which has been imparted to it, and to resist the reception of more. By this, on the ascent of the piston, the weight of the column of water is dragged up, not alone by the energy of the prime mover as before, but by the moving force which has been imparted to the fly-wheel, and which that wheel endeavours to keep. On the other hand, when the piston descends unloaded, the action of the prime mover upon it, which before caused its sudden and rapid acceleration, is now intercepted by the fly-wheel, which, by its great inertia, refuses to receive that rapid degree of acceleration which had been before produced.

The power of a fly-wheel to resist acceleration is proportional to the square of its diameter, and, therefore, by sufficiently increasing its size and weight, we may be enabled to equalize the most desultory and irregular motions in the machinery.

In the example which we have just given, there was a variable resistance opposed by an uniform power. The reverse of this often happens, and a variable power is opposed to a constant resistance. Thus, in the single-acting steam-engine already alluded to, when the piston has been forced down by the pressure of steam, it is usually drawn up again by a weight suspended from the opposite end of the beam. In this case the mover is very unequal and desultory, and would never serve any purpose in which uniformity of action is necessary. But, if a fly-wheel be attached to the machine, the momentum which it acquires during the de-

E

scent of the piston, it will retain, by virtue of its inertia, during the suspension of the power in the ascent; and this force will drive the machinery, or act against the resistance, whatever it be, in the intervals of the intermission of the power.

Even where both the impelling power and the resistance are uniform, the one may not be uniformly transmitted to the other. Suppose that piston P, working in a cylinder C, is connected with the end B of a beam, which works on the centre A. The other end, B', of the beam, is connected by a rod, B'D, with a crank F G H I K, which is turned

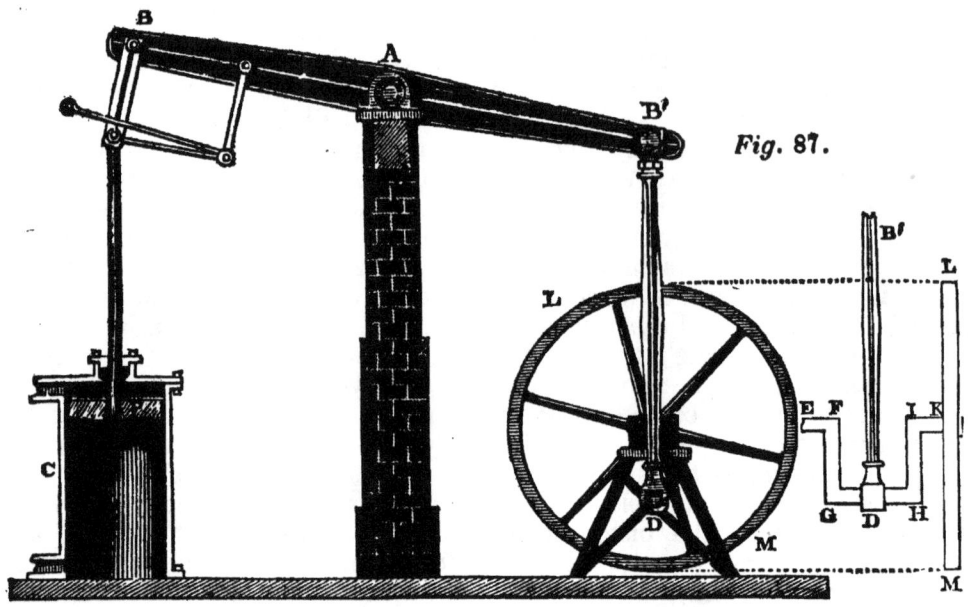

Fig. 87.

round the axis E F I K. The piston being supposed to be pressed both upwards and downwards by steam, suppose it at the top of the cylinder, as in *fig*. 87. The end B of the beam will then be in the highest position, and the end B' in the lowest, and therefore, the crank G H in the lowest position. In this position, let us suppose the pressure of steam to urge the piston P downwards. It is evident, that the piston and beam have no power whatever in turning the crank. The piston being pressed downwards, draws the connecting rod, B'D, directly upwards. But since, in the present position, the rods B'D, E F, F G, G H, H I, and I K, are all in the same vertical plane, the upward force of B D is resisted by the pivots E K, of the axis of the crank, and there is no leverage to enable the force of B'D to turn the crank. The machine is, therefore, placed in that mechanical dilemma in which the impelling power loses all influence in moving it. But if we suppose the crank moved a little out of this position, the rod B'D and crank cease to be in the same vertical plane, and the rod acquires a small leverage on the crank, by which it turns it. This leverage continues to increase until the plane of the crank F G H I becomes perpendicular to the connecting rod, as represented in *fig*. 88. In this case, the power of the connecting rod over the crank is at its maximum, and when the crank is further raised, the leverage constantly

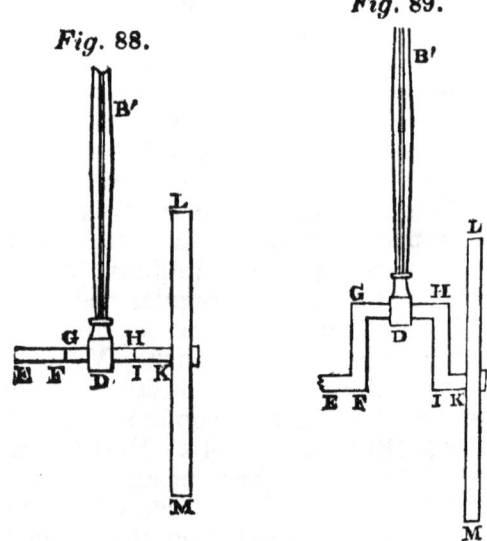

Fig. 88. Fig. 89.

diminishes, until the piston reaches the bottom of the cylinder, and the crank attains its highest position, as in *fig*. 89. Here, again, the impelling power loses all influence on the crank. Suppose the pressure of steam to urge the piston *upwards;* the connecting rod B'D would thereby be pressed downwards; but since the crank and rod are now in the same vertical plane, the pressure of the rod will be entirely spent on the pivots, and, having no leverage, cannot turn the crank. Thus, it appears that when a machine is constructed in this way, an uniform action of the first mover will be modified, and rendered desultory and variable, and at certain moments totally destroyed by the nature of the machinery by which it is transmitted to the working point. If, however, on the axis of the crank a FLY-WHEEL (L M, *fig.* 87) be fixed so as to turn with the crank, this inconvenience will be completely removed. The moving force of the fly-wheel will extricate the machine from the dilemmas in which it is involved at those moments at which the impelling force loses its power over the crank, and it will equalize the effects of the varying leverage by which the first mover acts on the crank.

A very remarkable instance of the use of a fly occurs in the engine constructed by Mr. Vauloue, for driving the piles of Westminster bridge. In this machine, a heavy mass is elevated by horse-power acting upon it through the intervention of a rope and wheel-work, and when it has reached a considerable height it is disengaged, and permitted to fall upon the pile which is to be driven. Now the moment this mass is disengaged, the machine having no resistance, and the horses being relieved from the weight they before encountered, would immediately fall forward. This is prevented by connecting the wheel-work with a heavy fly, the inertia of which opposes the strength of the animals when they are suddenly relieved from the weight of the elevated mass.

The advantages of a fly-wheel are sensibly perceptible when a man acts upon a *winch* (*fig.* 34). In this case the action of the power is very unequal: its effect is greatest when he pulls upwards from the height of his knee, and least when, the handle being in a vertical position, he thrusts from him in an horizontal direction. The force is increased when, pressing the handle downwards, he is assisted by his own weight. If a fly be placed upon the axis of the winch, all these unequal effects run into one another, and the force becomes uniform.

Besides the use of a fly, in regulating the action of machinery, it is employed for the purpose of accumulating or collecting together successive exertions of a power, so as to produce a much more forcible effect by their aggregation than could possibly be done by the separate and successive actions. In this respect a fly-wheel serves the same purpose as condensed air (Treatise I. 56). If a small force be repeatedly applied in giving rotation to a fly-wheel, and be continued until the wheel has acquired a very considerable velocity, such a quantity of force will be at length accumulated in its circumference as to overcome resistance and produce effects utterly disproportionate to the immediate action of the original force. Thus it would be very easy in a few seconds, by the mere action of a man's arm, to give to the circumference of a fly-wheel a force which would give an impulse to a musket ball equal to that which it receives from a full charge of powder.

The same principle explains the force with which a stone may be projected from a sling. The thong is swung several times round by the force of the arm, until a considerable portion of force is accumulated, and then it is projected with all the collected force.

If a heavy leaden ball be attached to the end of a strong piece of cane or whalebone, it may easily be driven through a board: by taking the end of the rod remote from the ball in the hand, and striking the board a smart blow with the end bearing the ball, such a velocity may easily be given to the ball as will drive it through the board.

Much of the efficacy of a fly depends on the position assigned to it in the machinery. If it be used as a regulator of force, it should be placed near the prime mover; but if, on the other hand, it be used as a magazine of power, it should be nearer to the working point. No general rules can, however, be given for its exact position.

The accumulating power of the fly has led some persons into the error of supposing that it adds force to the machine, besides what is received from the first mover. That this is not the case is very plain, from considering the perfect inactivity of matter, and its incapability of possessing any force that it has not received from some effective agent. On the contrary, the fly never retains all the force communicated to it by the first mover, for the resistance of the air and the effects of friction rob it of a certain part of this force.

A fly-wheel is not the only regulator of force, and, even in cases where it is used, we are sometimes obliged to have recourse also to other contrivances. In manufactures it generally happens that there is one certain and determinate velocity with which the machinery should be moved, and which, if increased or diminished, would render the machine unfit to perform the work it is designed to execute. The application of a perfectly-uniform power, aided by a fly, will not effect this. For suppose, as very frequently happens, the resistance is changed by some of the machines, which are worked, being thrown out of gear or an increased number put on, the moving power having the resistance thus diminished or increased, will impart a greater or a less velocity to the machinery, and all the fly-wheel can do in this case is to maintain the velocity uniform after it has been so increased or diminished.

To maintain an uniform velocity with a varying resistance, one of the most beautiful contrivances ever used is the *governor*, an instrument used in mill-work, but the application of which is most conspicuous in the steam-engine, when that machine is applied to manufacturing purposes. The principle on which the efficacy of this instrument depends, is easily explained.

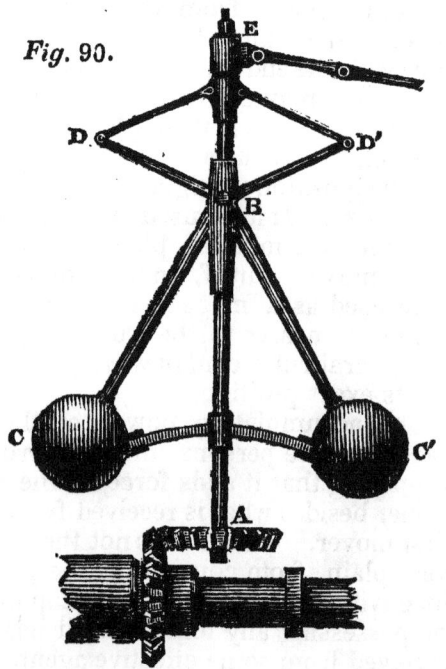

Fig. 90.

Let A B be a vertical axis, which is made to revolve by the bevelled wheel A, acted on by the other parts of the machinery, and so that it always revolves with a velocity proportional to that of the fly-wheel. Two heavy balls C C' are attached to metal rods, which work on a pivot at B, so that they are capable of receding from the axis A B. As they recede from the axis, the joints D D' recede from one another, and the joint E is drawn down. This joint E is connected with the end of a lever or a system of levers, the action of which we shall presently explain.

Now, by the revolution of the spindle or axis A B, the balls C C' acquire an obvious tendency to fly off from the axis, and this tendency is resisted by their weight, so that, when the instrument is revolving with a certain velocity, the balls will remain suspended. The property, from which this apparatus derives its whole efficacy, is, that at whatever distance or in whatever position the balls remain suspended, and neither move to or from the axis, the spindle A B must be revolving with the *same velocity*. A greater velocity would cause the balls to fly farther off, and a lesser velocity would cause them to fall towards the axis*.

If the action of the levers with which the joint E is connected, be directed upon the first mover, in such a manner, that its energy is diminished when E is depressed, and increased when E is elevated, it is plain that the uniformity of velocity which is sought may be obtained. Let us suppose that the levers on which E works communicate with a valve which admits steam to the piston of a steam-engine to which this governor is applied; and suppose that, when E is raised, and the balls C C' rest in their seats, the valve is fully open, so as to allow the steam to flow in a full stream to the piston; but that according as E is depressed the levers gradually close the valve, so as to admit the steam in a constantly diminished quantity. Now, suppose that the engine has been working twenty printing presses, and that the action of ten of them is suddenly suspended. The engine thus loses half its load, and would, if the same power of steam continued to be admitted, move with about twice its former velocity. But the moment an increased velocity is perceived

---

* This is strictly true only when the range of the balls is small compared with the length of the rods to which they are attached, which, however, is always the case in practice.

in the machine, the balls C C' recede from the axis, draw down the joint E, partially close the valve, and check the supply of steam to the cylinder. The impelling power is thus diminished; and if it be diminished in exactly the same degree as the load, the machine will move with its former velocity; but if it should, at first, be more diminished, the velocity will be less than its former velocity, and the balls will again move towards the axis and open the valve, and will, at length, settle into that position in which the steam admitted to the cylinder is exactly proportioned to the load on the machine; and the proper velocity will thus be restored.

By this exquisite contrivance, therefore, however the load or resistance may from time to time be varied, the velocity will be constantly the same, the impelling power being varied in exactly the same proportion as the resistance.

There are various other contrivances for regulating the motion of machinery, amongst which the pendulum of a clock may be mentioned. Our limits preclude us from prosecuting this interesting subject further in this place. We may refer the reader to the second volume of Dr. Brewster's edition of Ferguson's Mechanics for some valuable information on this subject; as also to the second volume of Dr. Gregory's Mechanics, article "SCAPEMENTS."

CHAPTER XIII.—*On Mechanical Contrivances for Modifying Motion.*

(104.) WE have frequently stated, that one of the great ends to be attained by machinery is the change, or modification of motion. Our impelling power may be rectilinear when a circular motion may be required in the working point, or the impelling power may be alternate, or reciprocating, when the force required at the working point is continuous. In a word, the motion of the impelling power may be of any one species, and that required at the working point may be of any other species. It is, therefore, a very important problem to assign the nature of the machinery which should be interposed between a given impelling power and the working point, so as to produce at that point the effect required.

This problem, in its most general form, it is evidently impossible to solve; nor is it easy to enumerate all the different motions which the impelling power may have, nor the various motions which these may be required to produce at the working point. Generally speaking, however, the motions which we meet with in the use of machinery may be resolved into *rectilinear* and *circular*, that is, one in which the points of the moving part describe parallel straight lines, or one in which they move in circles round a common centre or axis. These, again, may be divided into *continued* and *alternate*, or *reciprocating*. That is, the point which moves in a straight line may move continually in the same direction, or it may move backwards and forwards, or upwards and downwards, its range being limited by two points on the straight line in which it moves. Again, if the point move in a circle, it may move constantly round the centre in the same direction with a continued rotatory motion; or, on the other hand, it may only move over an arc of the circle in one direction, and then return through that arc in the opposite direction, and so on alternately, having a vibrating or reciprocating motion in the circular arc.

The motions which we have to consider may then be resolved into the four following:—

1. Continued rectilinear motion.
2. Reciprocating rectilinear motion.
3. Continued circular motion.
4. Reciprocating circular motion.

We shall devote the present chapter to explain some of the contrivances by which each of these may be modified or converted one into another.

(105.) *To convert continued rectilinear motion in any one direction into continued rectilinear motion in any other direction.*

If the directions of the two motions be in the same plane, this may evidently be effected by a fixed pulley. But if the directions be in different planes, two fixed pulleys will be requisite, one being in the plane of the direction of one motion, and the other in the plane of the direction of the other motion.

In *fig.* 91, a contrivance is represented, by which a rectilinear motion in one direction is made to produce a rectilinear motion in a direction at right angles to the former. The inclined plane or wedge A B, is moved under C D, which is connected by *guides* with the pillars of the frame. It is evident, that as A B advances from A towards B, C D rises in the vertical direction.

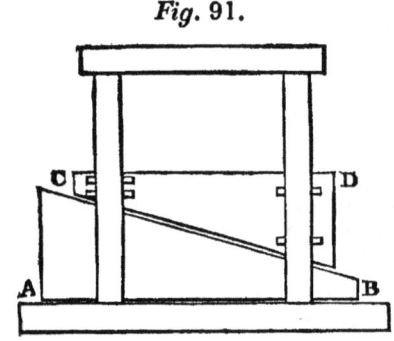

Fig. 91.

The wind acting on the sails of a ship in one direction gives the vessel a rectilinear motion in another direction.

(106.) *To convert continued rectilinear motion into reciprocating rectilinear motion.*

Let A B be a chain furnished with wipers *m, n, o*. Let B be a frame loaded with weights and furnished with a wheel C, and let the frame be so fixed

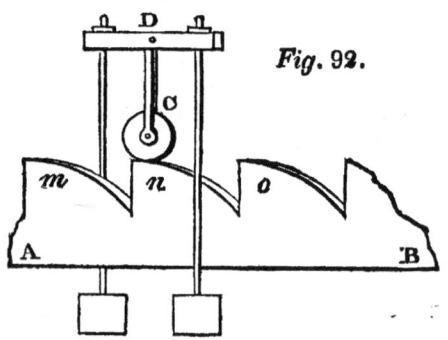

Fig. 92.

that it is incapable of any but a vertical motion. As the chain is moved continually in the direction A B, the wheel C running up the surfaces of the wipers will be elevated, and when it passes the point of each wiper it will fall into the space between that and the succeeding one, and thus the frame B will acquire a rectilinear motion upwards and downwards.

(107.) *To convert a continued rectilinear motion into a continued circular, or vice versâ.*

There are various methods of effecting this. The wheel and axle is an obvious instance where the continued rotation of the power produces the continued rectilinear ascent of the weight, or if the weight be permitted to descend, its continued rectilinear descent will give a continued rotation to the wheel.

This may also be effected by a toothed wheel working in a rack. A rack is a straight bar on which teeth are raised. If such a bar be placed in connexion with a wheel on which similar teeth are raised, the continued rectilinear motion of the rack will produce continued circular motion in the wheel, and *vice versâ*.

A strap, or belt, passing round a wheel, and turning it by its friction with the surface or groove in which it works, will attain the same end where the resistance is not very great. An endless strap may be used, in which case two wheels will be necessary.

But in cases where much resistance is to be overcome, the friction of the strap with the surface of the wheel would not be sufficient to transmit the force. In this case, however, a chain and rag-wheel may be used. The chain sometimes lays hold of pins or hooks in the wheel, as represented in *fig.* 93, and

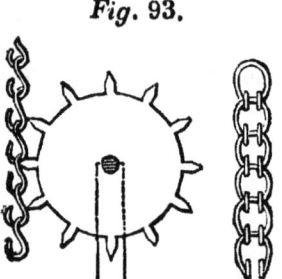

Fig. 93.

sometimes carries pins upon it, which enter notches in the circumference of the wheel, as in *fig.* 94.

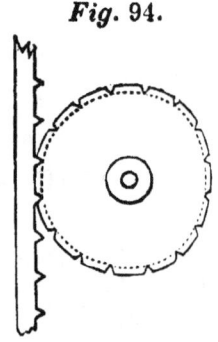

Fig. 94.

A common screw offers an instance of the conversion of continued circular motion into continued rectilinear.—The power applied to the head of the screw moves with continued circular motion, and the screw itself advances with continued rectilinear motion.

The paddle-wheels of a steam-boat and an undershot water-wheel are examples of a continued rectilinear motion produced by a continued circular, and of a continued circular produced by a continued rectilinear.

An overshot or breast-wheel is an instance of continued rectilinear motion producing continued circular; also the wind, acting on the arms of a windmill, is another example of the same effect.

The screw of Archimedes is an instance of a continued circular motion producing a continued rectilinear one. (See *Hydraulics*, chap. ii.)

Barker's mill is a remarkable instance of a continued rectilinear motion producing a continued circular one.

(108.) *To convert a continued rectilinear motion into a reciprocating circular motion, or vice versâ.*

Fig. 95.

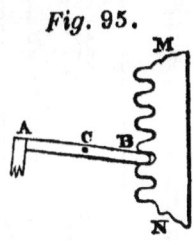

One method of effecting this is by a rack M N, (*fig.* 95.) in the teeth of which the end B of a lever A B works. As the rack M N descends, the end of the lever falls from one tooth to another, and the end A moves alternately up and down in a small circular arc.

A method of producing either a reciprocating circular motion from a continued rectilinear motion, or a continued rectilinear from a reciprocating circular motion, is represented in *fig.* 96. A B C D is a double rack, fur-

Fig. 9

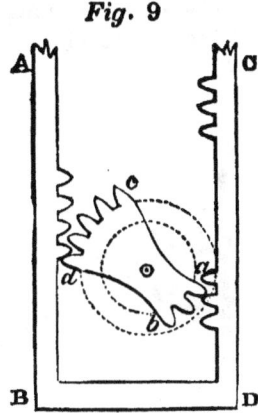

nished with teeth at intervals, the parts of A B, which bear teeth, being opposite to those parts of C D which are free from them; *a b c d* is a wheel bearing teeth, corresponding to those of the rack. Suppose the rack in its highest position, and the first tooth *b* of the wheel engaged with the lowest tooth on the rack C D. As the rack descends, the teeth *b a* are successively engaged with the corresponding teeth of the rack, and the wheel revolves until the last tooth *a* is passed by the last tooth of the first set on the rack C D. At this moment the lowest tooth *d* on the other side of the wheel is seized by the lowest tooth of the first set on the rack A B; and after this, the teeth *d c* are successively engaged by those of the rack, and the wheel is turned in the direction contrary to its former motion. As the rack continues to descend, the same reciprocating circular motion continues to be produced in the wheel.

The motion may be continued without limit by using two chains, bearing teeth at intervals, working on two pair of rag-wheels.

The *lever of La Garousse* is a contrivance by which a reciprocating circular motion produces a continued rectilinear one. M N (*fig.* 97.) is a fixed

Fig. 97.

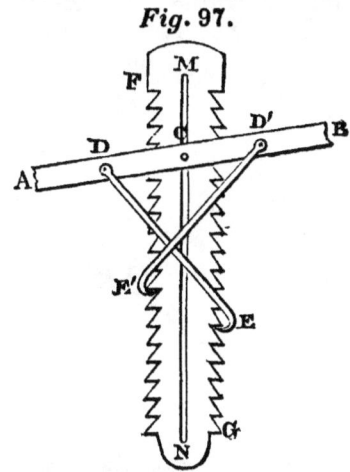

shaft, in which a centre is placed at C, on which the lever A B works. F G is a rack, which is capable of being raised in the vertical direction. This is effected by two bars D E, D′ E′, placed on joints at D, D′. When the extremity A descends, the point D′ rises, and the hook E′, being engaged with a tooth of the rack, draws it up. The hook E in this process falls from one tooth of the rack to the tooth immediately under it. When B is depressed, and D rises, the same effects take place, but on different sides of the rack.

Thus, the reciprocating circular motion of the lever A B produces a continued rectilinear motion in the rack F G. The term *continued* rectilinear motion here means rectilinear motion which is always in the same direction; for, strictly speaking, the motion is not *continued*, since it is *intermitting*.

(109.) *To convert reciprocating rectilinear motion, in one direction and with one velocity, into reciprocating rectilinear motion in another direction and with another velocity.*

If the velocities of the two motions were equal, and the directions in the same plane, this might be effected by a strap passing over a wheel, the part of the strap on one side of the wheel being in one of the given directions, and that on the other side in the other given direction. If friction were insufficient, a rag-wheel and chain might be used, and if the directions be in different planes two wheels will be necessary.

If, however, the velocities be different, other means must be resorted to. If the two directions be in the same plane, two racks may be worked by the sectors of two wheels moving on the same axle, the magnitudes of the sectors being proportional to the two velocities. Such an apparatus is represented in *fig.* 98. If, however, the two directions

Fig. 98.

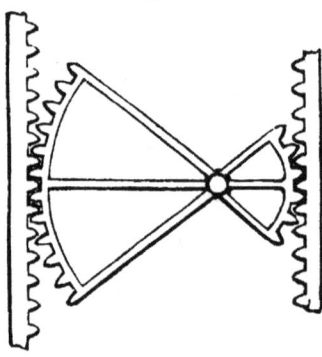

be in different planes, the motion must be transmitted from the one rack to the other by the aid of bevelled wheels.

Rag-wheels and chains may evidently be used in these cases for racks.

(110.) *To convert a reciprocating rectilinear motion into a continued circular motion, and vice versâ.*

The methods of producing these effects are very numerous. A continuous circular motion will produce a reciprocating rectilinear one, if a wheel having wipers on its circumference be placed in connection with a vertical beam or stamper, on which a projecting shoulder or pin is raised, by which the beam is lifted by each wiper, and falls, when disengaged from it, by the revolution of the wheel: it is then lifted by the next wiper, and so on.

Also, if a vertical beam be terminated in a rack which is connected with a wheel which has teeth only on a part of its circumference. While the toothed part of the wheel is engaged with the rack, the beam will be raised, and the moment the last tooth of the wheel passes the rack, it will fall. It will be again raised when the teeth engage the rack, and so motion is continued.

In this case, the motion of the rack in one direction is produced by its weight, or that of the beam, or stamper, with which it is connected. It is easy to make the wheel itself produce both motions in the rack. In *fig.* 99 is repre-

sented a double rack, worked by a wheel partially furnished with teeth. As the wheel P is turned in the direction of the arrow, its teeth, being previously disengaged from those of the rack, B D, will commence to work in those of A C, and will evidently press the rack down. When the last tooth of the wheel has passed the rack A C, this downward motion will cease, and the teeth will become engaged with those of the rack B D, and the rack will accordingly be raised; and by continuing the rotation of the wheel P in the same direction, the rack will be alternately elevated and depressed.

Fig. 99.

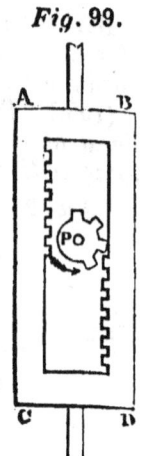

This may also be effected by a simple method, represented in *fig.* 100, where M N is a beam moving in guides *c d* and *e f*: *a b* is a bar moving on joints, or pivots, at *a* and *b*, and A is a wheel turned by a winch A H, or otherwise.

Fig. 100.   *Fig.* 101.

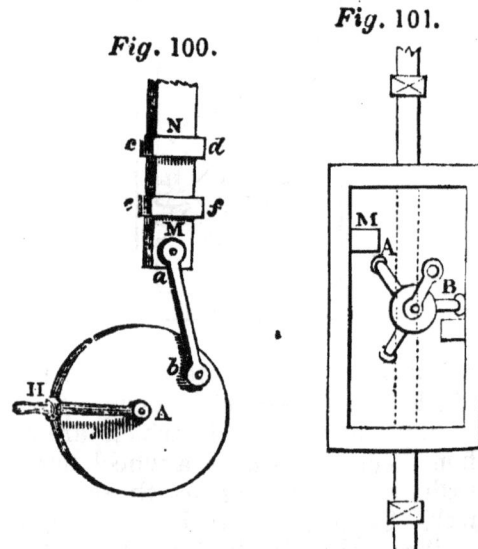

As the wheel revolves, the bar *a b* is evidently alternately pressed upwards, and drawn downwards, and by this the beam M N is moved alternately upwards and downwards between the guides.

In *fig.* 101 is represented a method similar to that shown in *fig.* 99, but each rack is furnished with but one tooth. In this case the pins or teeth of the wheel alternately raise and depress the rack, in the same manner as in *fig.* 99.

A very ingenious contrivance, for

producing the same effect is represented in *fig.* 102. When the pinion

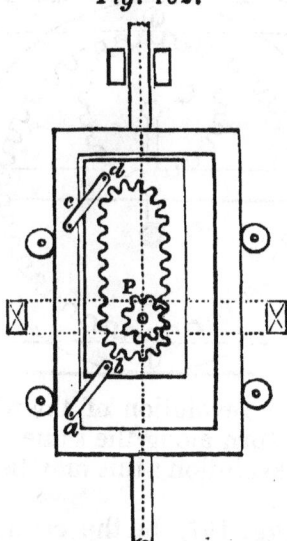

Fig. 102.

P has worked in one side of the rack, it acts upon the teeth in the semi-circular end, by which it gives the rack a slight lateral motion, which is permitted by the joints *a b* and *c d*. The pinion then engages the teeth of the rack on the contrary side, and moves it in the opposite direction, and so the process is continued.

In *fig.* 103 is represented a contri-

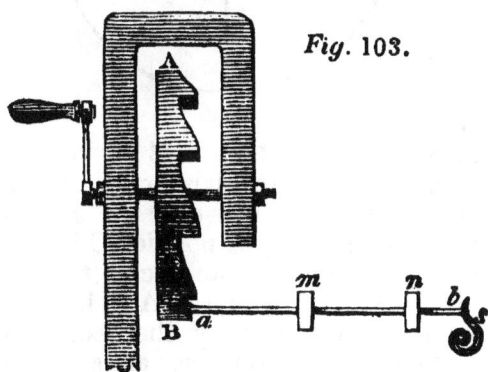

Fig. 103.

vance for producing an alternate rectilinear motion, by a continued circular. A B is a wheel turned by a winch or otherwise, and bearing, in the manner of a crown-wheel, teeth, the form of which may be adapted to the circumstances of the case. A rod, *a b*, plays in guides *m n*, and has one end bearing on the teeth of the wheel, while the other end presses against a spring *s*. As the wheel is turned, the rod is forced in the direction *a b* by the teeth; and as it passes the top of each tooth, it is forced back in the direction *b a* by the spring. Thus the rod *a b* has a reciprocating rectilinear motion. This machine has been applied by *M. Zureda* for pricking holes in leather, for making cards, and has also been employed in the manufacture of fishing nets.

M. Zureda has also contrived a very ingenious piece of mechanism for converting a continued circular into a reciprocating rectilinear motion. A cylinder rests in a fixed frame, on pivots, and is turned by a winch, or otherwise, round its axis. On the surface of this cylinder a spiral groove is cut, similar to the thread of a screw. This spiral groove, when it reaches the end of the cylinder, meets another similar groove, which traverses the cylinder in the opposite direction, and which runs into the first-mentioned groove at the opposite end of the cylinder. A pin is passed through a groove, cut through and through a straight beam, which is placed over the cylinder, and parallel to its length. The end of this pin falls into the spiral groove in the cylinder. As the cylinder is turned round its axis, the pin is moved along the spiral groove, so as to be urged from one end of the straight beam to the other, moving in the groove cut through that beam. When it arrives at the end of the cylinder, it passes from the spiral groove, in which it moved, into that which traverses the cylinder in the opposite direction; and the pin is thus moved back towards the opposite end of the straight beam, and so the process is continued.

In *fig.* 104, a very simple contrivance

Fig. 104.

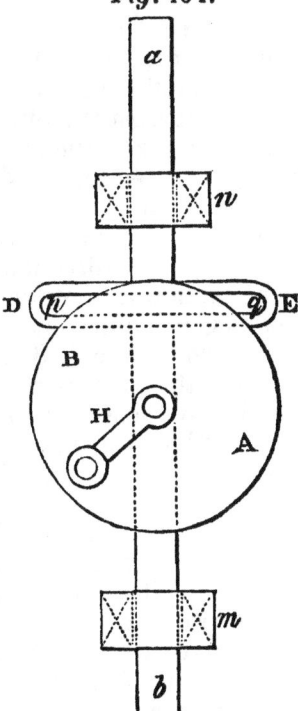

for attaining the same end is represented. A B is a wheel turned by a winch H or otherwise; *a b* is a beam, which moves through the guides *m n*. Attached to this beam is a cross-piece D E, having a groove *p q* cut in it. This groove receives a pin *c*, which projects from the wheel A B. As the wheel revolves, the pin *c* moves in the groove from *p* to *q* and from *q* to *p* alternately, and evidently raises and depresses the beam *a b* through the guides *m n*. The vertical action of the pin *c* on the sides of the groove *a b* is variable, and gives the beam *a b* an unequable motion. This defect may be removed by forming the sides of the groove into proper curves, so that the action of the pin may be rendered perfectly equable.

Another very ingenious contrivance is represented in *fig.* 105. A B is a double

Fig. 105.

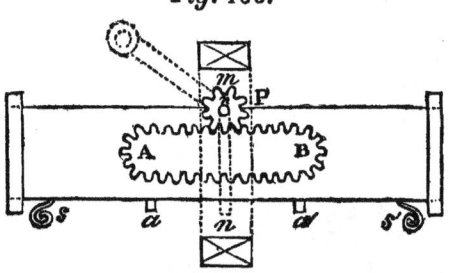

rack, with circular ends fixed to a beam, capable of moving in the direction of its length. This rack is driven by a pinion P, which moves in a groove *m n* cut in the cross-piece. When the pinion has moved the rack and beam until it comes to the end B, the projecting piece *a* meets the spring *s*, and the rack is pressed against the pinion. The pinion, then, working in the circular end of the rack, will be forced down the groove *m n* until it works in the lower side of the rack, and moves the beam back in the opposite direction; and in this way the motion is continued.

Another elegant contrivance is represented in *fig.* 106, where A B is a wheel having teeth in the inner part of its rim. This wheel is fixed so as not to revolve; C is a wheel of half the diameter of the former, and having teeth on its outer edge, which work in the teeth of the fixed wheel. As the wheel C is turned on its axis, it traverses the inner circumference of the wheel A B, the centre C describing a circle round the centre of the fixed wheel. Now it may be proved geometrically, that any point on the circumference of the wheel C will move along a diameter of the wheel

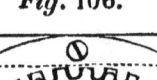

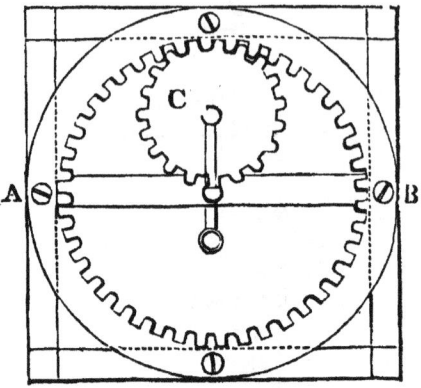

A B in one revolution of the wheel C, and will return along the same diameter the next revolution: this may be proved as follows:—

Let C, *fig.* 107, be the centre of the

Fig. 107.

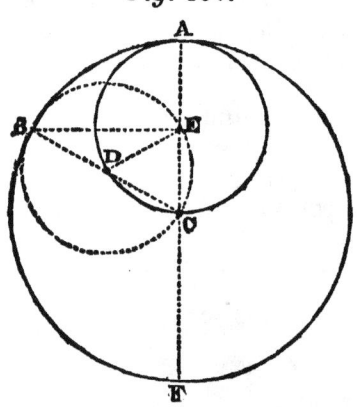

fixed wheel, and let A C be the initial position of the revolving one. Let the revolving wheel roll over the arc A B, so as to assume the position C B. It is evident, then, that an arc of the lesser circle, which is equal to A B, has rolled over A B. But by the established principles of geometry, an arc of the lesser circle, equal to the arc A B, subtends at its centre an angle which bears to the angle A C B the same proportion as the diameter of the greater circle bears to that of the lesser, that is, two to one. Hence, the arc of the lesser circle, which has rolled over A B, subtends at the centre of the lesser circle an angle equal to twice the angle ACB. To the point where the lesser circle in the position A B intersects C A, draw the line B E, and from the centre of the lesser circle draw D E. The angle B D E is equal to twice the angle B C A[*], and therefore the arc B E of the lesser circle is equal to the arc B A of

---

[*] DARLEY's *Popular Geometry*, Art. 71.

the greater circle. Hence, the arc B E is that which has rolled over B A, and E is the point of the lesser circle, which at the beginning of the motion was at A, and it is now found on the line A B. In the same manner it may be proved that this point is found on the diameter A, F in every position of the lesser circle. When the lesser circle has rolled over a quadrant of the greater, the point is found at the centre C; and when it has rolled over a semicircle, it is found at the other extremity, F, of the diameter. While the lesser rolls over the other semicircle, the point returns along the diameter F A to A. Thus the point alternately moves from A to F, and from F to A.

A very simple and obvious contrivance for producing a reciprocating rectilinear motion by a continued circular one, is by a crank wrought by a winch. A rope attached to the crank, and passed over a fixed pulley, from which a weight is suspended, will attain the desired end. As the crank revolves, the weight will evidently ascend and descend in a straight line.

If a connecting rod be carried from the crank and connected by a joint with a straight bar or beam, which moves in guides, this bar will receive a reciprocating rectilinear motion. In this way the piston of any species of pump may be wrought by a continued circular motion. Such a contrivance as this is used in the apparatus for condensing gas, in the portable gas manufacture.

The common apparatus, called an eccentric, may be made to produce a similar effect. This contrivance consists of a circular metallic ring, the inner surface of which is perfectly smooth. This ring is connected by a shaft and a joint, with a straight rod or beam moving in guides. Within the ring is fitted a circular metallic plate, capable of turning freely within the ring, the surfaces in contact being perfectly smooth, and lubricated with oil or grease. This circular plate revolves, but not on its centre. It turns, in fact, on an axis at some distance from its centre, the effect of which is, that the ring within which it turns is moved alternately in opposite directions, and through a space equal to twice the distance of the axis from the common centre of the ring, or circular plate. This communicates, through the shaft and joint, an alternate rectilinear motion to the rod which works in the guides.

(111.) *To convert a reciprocating rectilinear motion into a reciprocating circular one, or vice versâ.*

This is one of the most useful and important changes of motion which can be effected by machinery, and merits the greatest attention.

A beam, having an arched head at one end, bearing teeth, which work in a rack, the opposite end being moved alternately in a circular arc, will move the rack alternately in a straight line.

Also, if a weight be suspended by a chain which hangs on the arched head of a beam, the other end of the beam being alternately moved in a circular arch, the weight will alternately ascend and descend in a vertical straight line.

An example of this will be observed in the atmospheric steam-engine, and of the former contrivance in the earlier double-acting steam-engines of Watt.

A very neat method of accomplishing this change is represented in *fig.* 108. A B is a lever turning on the

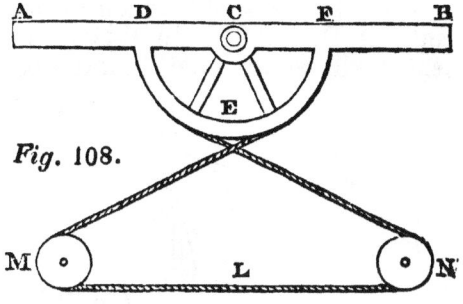

Fig. 108.

centre C. D E F is a half-wheel, to which, at the extremities, D F, a rope or strap is attached, and is passed, as represented in the figure, round the wheels or sheaves MN. A reciprocating circular motion, in the ends A B of the lever, will produce a reciprocating rectilinear motion in any point L, on or connected with the rope, and *vice versâ*.

A common bow used by watchmakers and other artists for drilling holes, is another example of this. The bowstring is rolled once round a small sheaf or wheel carrying the piercer, and an alternate rectilinear motion in the bow produces an alternate circular motion in the wheel.

But by far the most remarkable method of converting an alternate rectilinear motion into an alternate circular one, is that known by the name of the *parallel motion*, and invented by Watt for his double-acting steam-engine.

In this machine the piston is urged

upwards and downwards, in a very exact straight line, and any force which deflects it from this straight line will injure or destroy the operation of the machine. The end of the beam, on the other hand, with which the piston-rod is to be connected, moves alternately in a circular arc. It became then a difficult problem to connect these in such a manner that a perfectly smooth motion, and free from strain, should be imparted from the one to the other. In the first instance, Watt placed a rack on the end of the piston-rod, which worked in teeth raised upon the circular head of the beam. It was found, however, that this gave an uneven jolting motion, and was liable to rapid wear. He soon substituted for it his *parallel motion*.

The beam turns on the centre C, and its end B moves alternately in a circular arc, of which C is the centre; a rod FE plays on fixed centre F, and the end E moves in a circular arc, with that point F as centre. The end E of the rod FE is connected with a point D on the arm BC by a rod which moves on joints at D and E. In this arrangement it will be observed, that the points

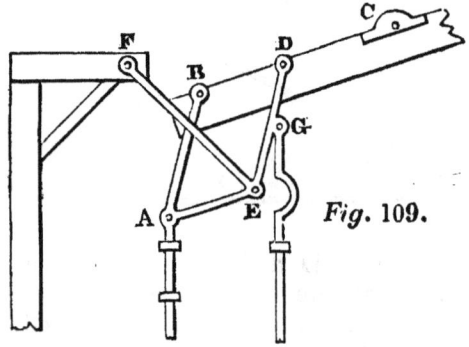

Fig. 109.

D and E each move alternately in circular arcs. Now, it is found that the middle point G of the bar DE moves alternately upwards and downwards in a straight line, and, therefore, a piston rod attached to the point G will be moved upwards and downwards in a straight line*.

Jointed at E is another rod, AE, equal to BD, and another, AB, equal to DE, jointed at A and B. The figure ABDE is evidently a parallelogram, and the point A moves in a line similar and parallel to that described by G, but longer than it, in the proportion of BC to DC.

It is usual, in the steam-engine, to attach the great piston of the cylinder to the point A, and the piston of the air-pump to the point G.

The most common proportion of the several rods forming the parallel motion is as follows: D is at the middle point of BC; FE is equal to DC, or half of BC. Great latitude is allowed in the length of DE. There are, however, various proportions which may be given to these rods, and for which we refer to works on the Steam-engine.

Another contrivance for this purpose is represented in *fig.* 110. AB is a wheel capable of moving round an axis or spindle, and also capable of moving

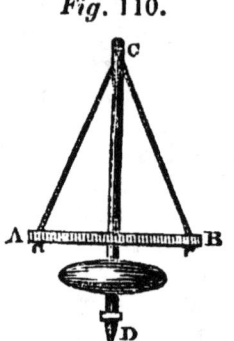

Fig. 110.

longitudinally on it. A rope is attached to A, and passing through a hole at the top, C, of the spindle, or axis, it is fastened at B, the opposite end of the diameter of the wheel which passes through A. By turning the wheel, the rope is twisted round the spindle, and the wheel drawn up towards C; and as the rope is again untwisted, the wheel descends to its former position. Or, if the wheel be incapable of a longitudinal motion, but the spindle CD be capable of moving longitudinally through it, a similar effect will be produced. This apparatus may be used for drilling or boring with the point D.

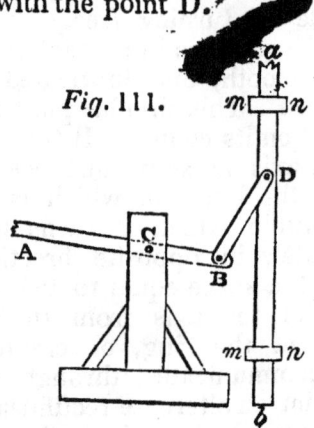

Fig. 111.

---

* Strictly speaking, the path of the point G is not a straight line, but is a curve of a high order. That part of the curve, however, which is included within the range of the piston-rod lies at equal distances on each side of a point of inflection. The radius of curvature is, therefore, infinite, and the curve differs imperceptibly from a straight line.

Another contrivance for the same purpose is exhibited in *fig*. 111. A B is a lever working on the centre C. B D is jointed at B to the extremity of this lever, and at D to a beam *a b*, which moves in guides *m n*. It is evident that a reciprocating circular motion at A will produce a reciprocating rectilinear motion in the beam *a b*, and *vice versâ*.

(112.) *To convert a continued circular motion into another continued circular motion.*

In a motion of continued rotation, two things are to be considered; the axis round which the rotation is made, and the velocity, or the number of revolutions performed in a given time.

If, by a rotation round one axis, it be required to produce a rotation round another axis parallel to it, the problem may be solved thus: place two wheels on the two axes, so that they shall be in the same plane at right angles to the given axes. Let these wheels act one upon the other either by the friction of their edges or by a strap, or chain, or, finally, by teeth. If they act either by friction or by teeth, the rotation round the two axes will be made in contrary directions; but if they act by a strap or chain, the rotation will be in the same direction if the strap be crossed; but otherwise in opposite directions.

The rotation may be produced in the same direction when the wheels act by teeth, or friction, by interposing a third wheel between those which are placed upon the given axes. There is an advantage in the use of a strap, in cases where the two axes are at a considerable distance one from the other; as it does not render the multiplication of wheels necessary.

In cases where the resistance is too great for the use of a strap, rotation may be transmitted to a number of parallel shafts by means of bevelled wheels on a shaft at right angles to them. This method of giving rotation to several parallel shafts is represented in *fig*. 112.

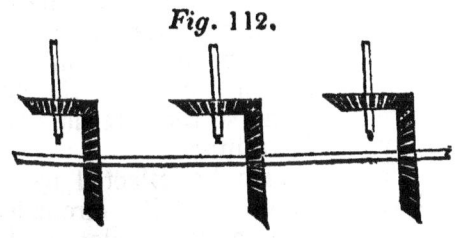

Fig. 112.

When the velocity of rotation is to be the same as that of the shaft from which it is received, the wheels by which it is transmitted, whether by friction, straps, or teeth, are to be of equal diameters; and in whatever proportion the velocity is to be increased or diminished, the diameter of the wheel must be diminished or increased exactly in the same proportion.

We have here supposed that the shafts through which the rotation is transmitted are parallel. Suppose they are not parallel, but their directions intersect; the rotation may then be transmitted by bevelled wheels placed upon the shafts, as represented in *fig*. 47 (70.); and if the velocity of rotation be required to be changed, the cones, from which the bevelled wheels are formed, must have different angles, as explained in (70.)

If the shafts be at a considerable distance one from the other, the bevelled wheels placed upon them cannot conveniently act one upon the other immediately. In this case a third shaft must be used, bearing two bevelled wheels, as represented in *fig*. 113, through which the motion is transmitted.

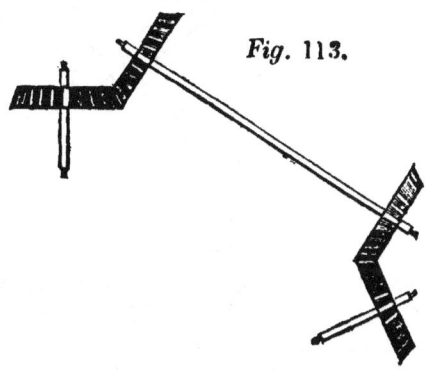

Fig. 113.

This method of connecting the shafts by a third shaft will also serve when the two given shafts are not in the same plane.

When the shafts, between which the motion is to be transmitted, are at right angles, two bevelled wheels, such as are represented in *fig*. 47, are most frequently used. A crown and spur wheel would, however, serve the same purpose, and are sometimes resorted to. This arrangement is represented in *fig*. 114.

Rotation round an axis may be transferred to an axis at right angles to it by means of a perpetual screw working in a toothed wheel, as represented in *fig*. 86. In this figure the axis of the wheel is represented parallel to the horizon; but it is plain that the same effect will be produced at whatever angle it is inclined to the horizon, provided it be perpendicular to the axis of the screw.

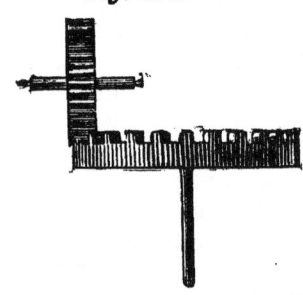

Fig. 114.

Hooke's universal joint is a very simple and effectual method of transferring rotation from one axis to another.

The *single universal joint* is represented in *fig.* 115. A and B are the

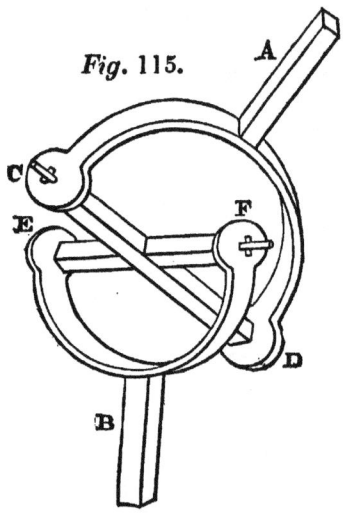

Fig. 115.

shafts, between which the rotation is transmitted; C D, E F is a cross of metal, the ends of which turn freely in bushes placed in the extremities of two diameters in which the shafts terminate.

From considering this arrangement, it is evident that, when the shaft A is turned round, the shaft B will receive a similar motion. If, however, the angle under the shafts A and B be less than 140°, this will fail to act.

In this case, the *double universal joint* must be resorted to. This is represented in *fig.* 116. There are here two crosses, the extremities of which move on pivots, like the former. This will serve when the angle contained by the shafts is less than 140°.

These joints may also be constructed with four pins, fastened at right angles upon the circumference of a hoop, or solid ball. They are of considerable use in cotton mills, where the tumbling shafts extend to a great distance from

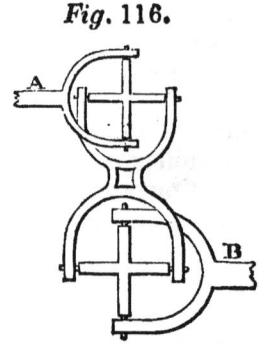

Fig. 116.

the impelling power; for, by applying an universal joint, the shaft may be cut into convenient lengths, and be thus enabled to overcome a greater resistance.

(113.) *To convert a continued circular motion into a reciprocating circular motion, or vice versâ.*

There are various methods of making this change. One of the most common is by a crank, connected by a rod with the end of a working beam, or lever, as represented in *fig.* 87. Here the end of the rod connected with the crank moves with a continued circular motion round the axis of the crank, while the other end, connected with the beam, moves alternately in a circular arc.

Another contrivance for this purpose is represented in *fig.* 117, where B and

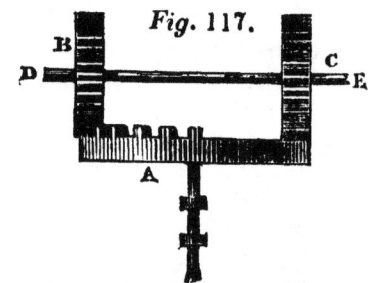

Fig. 117.

C are two spur-wheels on the same shaft, and A is a crown-wheel, which is only partially furnished with teeth, and placed on a shaft at right angles to D E. The shaft D E, being turned constantly in the same direction, so long as the teeth of the wheel A are engaged with those of B, the shaft of A is turned in one direction; but when they begin to be acted upon by those of C, it is turned back in the opposite direction, and so the alternate rotatory motion is continued.

It may also be effected by a wheel having wipers on its circumference, which raise a lever placed at right angles to the plane of the wheel, the lever descending by its own gravity.

In *fig.* 118 the wipers are represented

Fig. 118.

as lifting a forge hammer, which falls on the anvil by its own weight.

Another contrivance is represented in *fig.* 119, somewhat similar to that represented in *fig.* 103, but instead

Fig. 119.

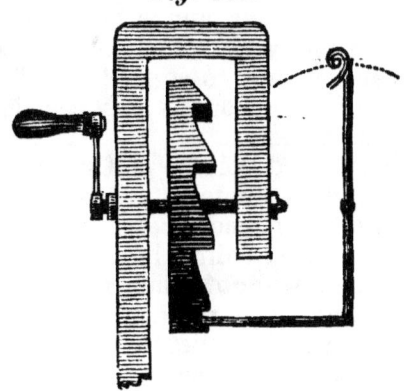

of the wipers acting on a rod moving in guides, they act on a lever working on a centre. The end of the lever is pressed against the wipers by a spring.

The *sun and planet wheel*, invented by Watt for his earlier double-acting steam-engines, is another example of this. To the end of a vibrating beam, a connecting rod, A B, is attached, on

Fig. 120.

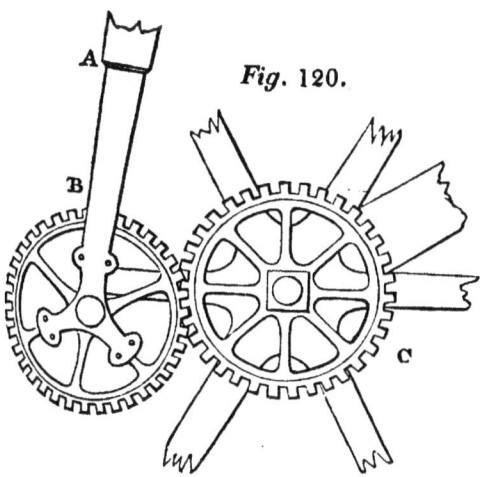

the lower end of which is fixed a toothed wheel, incapable of turning on its centre. This wheel works in the teeth of another, C, which turns freely on the centre, so that, as the one wheel is carried round the other by the connecting rod, it gives to the other a continued rotatory motion. The alternate circular motion of the end of the beam is thus made to communicate a continued rotatory motion to the wheel.

In *fig.* 121 is represented a contri-

Fig. 121.

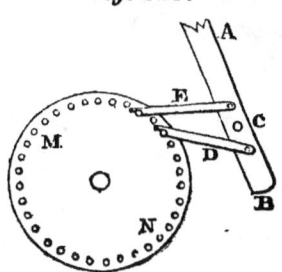

vance on nearly the same principle as the *lever of La Garousse*. M N is a wheel having teeth, or spindles, projecting from it in the manner of a crown-wheel: A B is a lever working on the centre C; D and E are two rods turning on pins in the lever, and the opposite ends of which are so formed, as to press against the spindles, and turn the wheel round. When the end B of the lever is pressed towards the wheel, the rod D presses the spindle, and urges the wheel round its centre. By the same motion, the rod E, and the spindle on which it rests, are separated, and the rod E falls upon the next spindle of the wheel. The end B being then moved from the wheel, the rod E presses upon the spindle, and urges the wheel round its centre; while the rod D, and the spindle on which it rests, are separated, and the rod D falls upon the next spindle. In this way the alternate circular motion of the lever A B produces a continued circular motion in the wheel M N.

The various kinds of escapements which are used in clock-work, are instances of the same effect. The pendulum has a reciprocating circular motion, and the wheel in connection with it, and which it regulates, has a continued circular motion.

(114.) *To convert a reciprocating circular motion into another reciprocating circular motion.*

The means of accomplishing this are numerous and obvious. If the two vibrations be round the same axis, it is evident it may be done by fixing upon the axes two arms or levers, presented from the centre in the directions in which the motions are to be made, and of lengths proportional to the circular arcs through which their extremities are to vibrate.

If the motions be not on the same axis, the two axes may be connected by almost any of the methods used in transferring continued circular motion from one axis to another.

In *fig.* 122 is represented a contrivance of *M. Camus*, for the purpose of moving

Fig. 122.

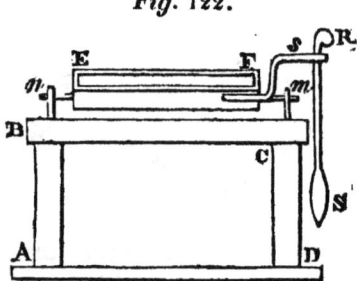

sieves. A B C D is a table, on which is a plank E F, capable of revolving on the pivots *m n*. To an arm, *s*, attached to one of the pivots, a pendulum, R S, is suspended. The first mover gives the pendulum an alternate circular motion, and this gives the plank a vibrating motion on the pivots.

There are numerous other contrivances for accomplishing this change, but our limits preclude us from prosecuting this subject further.

Chap. XIV.—*Works on Mechanics.*

The treatises which have been published on this subject, not to mention innumerable detached pieces which have been printed in the transactions of learned societies, scientific periodicals, &c., &c., are so numerous, that we cannot pretend to insert here any catalogue of them. Nevertheless, we may refer the student, who is desirous of extending his inquiries on the subject, to sources where he may find ample materials for the extension and improvement of his mechanical knowedge.

To those who are not very familiar with mathematical science, we should recommend Dr. Brewster's edition of Ferguson's Mechanics. In the second volume of this work, more especially, a vast quantity of valuable information is collected and explained with admirable clearness and simplicity. This volume is entirely from the pen of Dr. Brewster, and is by far the best part of the work. The student should be cautious not to consult the old editions of Ferguson, as they contain numerous errors.

The second volume of Dr. Gregory's Mechanics contains a great quantity of interesting and useful practical information, explained in a very familiar style, and without much mathematical reasoning. The mathematical student will be greatly benefitted by the study of the first volume of this excellent work.

For those who seek an acquaintance with the mathematical theory of Mechanics, there is a very numerous class of English authors, amongst whom we may mention Bridge, Desaguliers, Emerson, Gravesande, Playfair, Robison, Whewell, Wood, Young, &c.

The foreign authors, on this subject, are also very numerous:—Laplace, Lagrange, Prony, Poisson, Belidor, Biot, Venturoli, &c. &c.

MECHANICS.

THIRD TREATISE.

ON FRICTION AND THE RIGIDITY OF CORDAGE.

CHAPTER I.—*Of resisting Forces in general.*

(1). WHATEVER is capable of putting a quiescent body in motion, of increasing, or diminishing, the quantity of motion in a moving body, or finally, of destroying the motion of a moving body, and reducing it to a state of rest, is denominated *a force*. There are two kinds of forces, distinguished one from the other by the effects they are capable of producing. The first species are those which are capable of communicating motion to a body which is quiescent. Such forces will manifestly be also capable of producing, under different circumstances, all the other effects enumerated in the above definition of the word *force*. Thus it is quite evident, that the same force which would give motion to a body at rest, would, if applied in the proper direction to a body in motion, increase the quantity of motion, and if applied in the opposite direction would diminish it. Also, it is clear that if such a force, first applied to a body at rest give it motion in a certain direction, and be afterwards applied to the same body in the opposite direction, it will destroy the motion which it had communicated, and will again reduce the body to a state of rest. This species of force may be denominated *active force*, and all those forces, the properties of which we investigated in our first treatise, and which are prime movers, come under this class.

The second species of forces are those which are capable of diminishing the quantity of motion in a moving body, or of totally destroying it, and reducing the body to a state of rest; but which are entirely incapable either of producing motion in a quiescent body, or of increasing the motion of a moving body. Such forces may be denominated *passive* or *resisting forces*. Examples of such forces are numerous, and indeed it may be truly asserted, that no motion ever takes place on the surface of the earth without the manifestation of the effect of *resisting forces*. The resistance which fluids, both elastic and inelastic, oppose to the motion of bodies through them, are, perhaps, the most common and striking examples of the effects of these forces. The resistance which a projectile suffers in its passage through the air, and a solid body in descending through water, are familiar examples. As, however, the resistance of fluids properly belongs to another branch of the science, we shall not notice it particularly here, but shall confine ourselves to those resisting forces which arise from friction, and the rigidity of cordage.

(2). It requires but little consideration to perceive of how great importance the knowledge of the effects of these resistances is in mechanical science. In our first treatise, we explained the nature and laws of the active forces, or those mechanical agents which are commonly employed in giving motion to machinery. In our second treatise, we explained the nature, construction, and properties of the machinery, which was destined to receive motion from these active forces just mentioned. But in this investigation, in order to disembarrass the subject of its complexity, and present it to the student in the most simple and intelligible form, we considered that the machines by which the active forces were transmitted to the working points were absolutely free from all resistances; that the surfaces which moved in contact were perfectly polished, and acted without friction; that axles and pivots were mathematical lines and points; that ropes were perfectly flexible; and in a word, that the effect of the prime mover was absolutely undiminished by any resistance whatever in its transmission through the machine to the working point. None of these suppositions, however, really obtain in the practical application and use of machinery; the various surfaces which move in contact are never perfectly smooth: axles are of sensible thickness, and move in sockets never perfectly polished; ropes, so far from being perfectly flexible, have considerable rigidity, and this rigidity is generally great in proportion to their strength. Art may do, and has done, much to diminish the effects of these resistances; surfaces have been produced of high polish, and various means have been adopted to give them additional smoothness, but still they continue to be studded with small asperities, which, coming constantly in opposition during their motion one upon another, obstruct that motion, offer a considerable resistance to the action of the prime mover, and robbing that power of a great part of its efficacy, send it with proportionally diminished intensity to the working point. It is clear, therefore, that if we would estimate the real practical efficacy of a machine, we should possess the means of calculating the amount of these resistances, and when so found, we should subduct it from the effect computed on the theoretical principles laid down in our second treatise, where no regard was had to these resisting forces. The overplus of force after this deduction is the only part of the effect of the first mover, which can be considered as practically available in any application of the machine.

(3). Passive or resisting forces produces very different effects in *Statics* and *Dynamics*, that is, in machines in a state of equilibrium, and in a state of motion. If the machine be in a state of equilibrium, the resisting forces are said to *assist the power*. The meaning of this is, that in a real machine having those resistances, a less power will be sufficient to support a given weight than would be necessary to support it were those resistances removed. As an example, suppose that a weight of two pounds were placed upon an inclined plane, of which the length is twice the height. If there were no friction between the surfaces of the weight and the plane, a power of one pound acting parallel to the plane would be necessary to sustain the weight in equilibrium. But if we suppose, what always really obtains, that the surfaces of the weight and plane are subject to friction, this friction conspires with the power in resisting the descent of the weight, and consequently the power requisite to sustain the weight will be less than before by the amount of the friction.

Again, suppose a weight suspended from a single moveable pulley, the amount of the weight and pulley together being two pounds. If the rope had no rigidity, and passed without friction over the wheels, the wheels themselves also moving without friction, either with the blocks or on their axles, the power necessary to sustain the weight would be one pound. But if on the other hand, the rope have a stiffness which requires a certain force to bend it over the wheels; if also, in passing over the wheels, the roughness of its surface, and that of the wheel produce a resistance from friction; and lastly, if the wheel rubs against the block, the surfaces not being perfectly smooth, and also is subject to friction in its motion on its axis; then all these resistances require a considerable portion of the weight to overcome them, and, consequently, they conspire with the power in supporting the weight, so that the power which will accomplish this, will be less than in the former case, by the total effect of the several resistances.

In cases of equilibrium, therefore, and in the sense we have explained, the power is said to be *assisted* by the resisting forces. The very opposite effect obtains in dynamics, or when the power is used not merely to *sustain* the weight, but to *move* it. Here the resisting forces obviously *oppose* the power, and deprive it of a part of its efficacy.

Let us take the same examples. Suppose a weight of two pounds placed upon an inclined plane, whose length is twice its height. If there be no friction, any power exceeding one pound will be sufficient to draw the weight up the plane. But this will not be true, if there be, as there always is, friction. For a power of one pound being only sufficient to sustain the body on the plane without moving it when there is no friction, if a small quantity be added to this, that quantity may not exert sufficient force to overcome the friction, and to put the weight in motion. In fact, the weight will not commence to move up the plane, until such a quantity be added to the power of one pound, as is commensurate to the friction. When this quantity precisely has been added, the weight will still be at rest, but will be with respect to its motion *up* the plane, in the same situation as if there were no friction, and the least accession which the power receives will draw up the weight. Thus it appears, that when there is friction, a less power is necessary to *sustain* a given weight on an inclined plane, and a greater power is necessary to *move* it up the plane than would be necessary were there no friction.

In like manner, in the case of the single moveable pulley, if there were none of the resistances already mentioned, any power exceeding one pound would draw up the weight. But if the resistances be supposed to exist before motion can ensue, we must add to the power a sufficient quantity to balance all the resistances. The least addition to the power after that will produce motion.

We, therefore, infer in general, that when a machine of any kind is used simply to sustain a weight, or to balance a resistance, the resisting forces act in conjunction with the power, and are of mechanical advantage. In many instances the resisting powers constitute the whole power and efficacy of the instrument. Thus, when screws are used to bind together the parts of any structure, the friction of the screw with the substances in which it is inserted prevents its return, and constitutes its whole efficacy. In like manner, in the use of nails, which are nothing but narrow wedges, the friction prevents the recoil of the instrument, and gives it all its binding power.

The ordinary use of the wedge itself presents at once an instance of the statical advantage, and the dynamical disadvantage, of a resisting force. When a wedge is used for any purpose, as to split timber, the great friction which is produced between its faces and the surface of the timber, opposes a considerable resistance to the effect of the force of percussion applied to the back of the wedge to urge it forward, and it accordingly advances with much less force and effect than it would if the friction were removed. But after it *has* advanced, this same friction prevents its recoil, in the interval between two successive strokes on its back. In this case, therefore, were it not for the effect of friction, we should be compelled to urge the wedge by pressure instead of the far more efficacious force of percussion. Much more power is gained here by the effect of the friction in preventing the recoil during the intermission of the force, than is lost by its resistance to the advance of the wedge.

(4). The laws which govern resisting forces are derived wholly from experiment, nor have we any simple and general principles from which they can be deduced by mathematical reasoning. It is to be regretted, that even among the best-conducted experiments which have been instituted, some considerable discrepancies are observable, and differences of opinion subsist between the most respectable authorities respecting many particulars connected with the properties and laws of these forces. We shall give a general account of those properties in which philosophers have most generally agreed, stating those cases distinctly in which the results of different systems of experiments are materially at variance.

Although, as we have just stated, the laws of resisting forces are derived wholly from experiment, yet even here the general principles of the science are far from being useless. They serve as a guide in the selection of the experiments best calculated to develop those laws which are the subject of inquiry, as well as to shew the inconclusiveness of some experiments on which we might otherwise be induced to rely; and they also enable us to deduce from the results of experimental inquiry numerous useful practical results.

We shall commence with the consideration of *friction*, by far the most important of those resisting forces which we shall have to investigate.

CHAPTER II.—*Of the Friction of one Surface sliding over another.*

(5). FRICTION necessarily supposes the surface of one body moving or tending to move upon the surface of another. It also necessarily supposes the one surface to be urged against the other with some sensible degree of pressure. Under these circumstances, the cause of friction is the want of perfect smoothness, or polish in the surfaces which are in contact. The small asperities which are spread over each surface, become, when the surfaces are in contact, inserted, as it were, among each other; and upon any effort to move the surfaces one upon the other, these asperities and inequalities oppose each other, and resist the tendency to motion. The manner in which this effect is produced, may be conceived by placing two brushes with the points of the hairs presented towards each other, and in this position pressing them together in the direction of the hairs, so that the hairs of each brush insert themselves between those of the other. Any attempt to move the one brush upon the other in a direction at right angles to the hairs, will be found to be opposed by a considerable resistance. The inequalities with which surfaces subject to friction are covered, act upon one another in the same manner as the hairs of the brushes; and as it is obvious, that the greater the force with which the brushes are pressed together, the greater the lateral resistance, so also it is invariably found that the greater the pressure with which surfaces are urged one against the other, the greater will be the friction.

(6). There are three species of friction, or, to speak more properly, there are three ways in which one surface can move upon another, in each of which the friction acts differently. The first is, when one body resting on a plane base, *slides* upon the plane surface of another body. The second is, when one body being cylindrical, *rolls* upon the surface of another body. The third is, when a solid cylinder is inserted in a hollow cylinder of a greater diameter, and being pressed in any direction with a certain force revolves within it. We shall consider successively friction acting in these several ways.

(7.) That under the same circumstances the friction of one surface moving upon another is proportional to the pressure with which the surfaces are urged together, seems to be a law pretty satisfactorily established by experiment. Considering then, for the present, this law as exact, we shall explain the nature of the experiments by which it may be established.

Let A B (*fig.* 1,) be a perfectly level plane, the surface of which is one of those whose friction is to be examined. Let CD be a piece of the substance, the lower surface of which it is proposed to move in contact with that of the plane, this surface and that of the plane being those between which the friction is to be examined. The upper part of C D is adapted to receive weights, so as to vary at pleasure the pressure of C D on the plane A B. Attached to C D, at D, is a thread, which is carried parallel to the plane over a fixed pulley, P, and

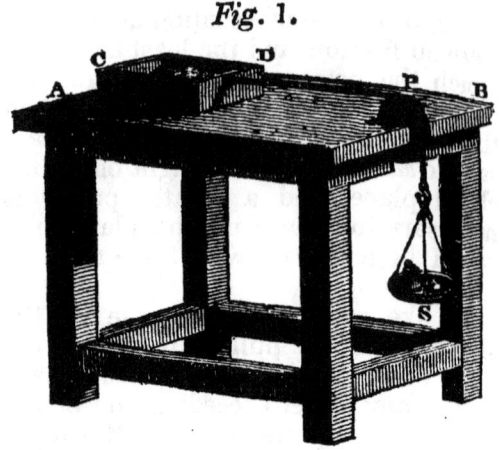

Fig. 1.

has a dish, S, suspended from it, adapted to receive weights, the effect of which will be to draw C D along the plane. Now, let C D be loaded so that the weight of itself and its load shall be one pound. Let fine sand flow into the dish, S, until it is of just sufficient weight to move C D. The weight of the sand, including that of the dish, will then represent the friction. Suppose that this is half a pound. Now let C D be loaded with another pound, so that the pressure upon the plane will be twice its former amount. It will be found that it will require half a pound more to be placed in the dish, S, in order to put C D in motion. Thus, when the pressure is doubled, the friction is also doubled. Again, let a third, fourth, and fifth pound be successively added to C D, it will be found to be necessary to add a third, fourth, and fifth half pound to the weight in S, in order to overcome the friction. And in the same manner the experiment may be continued, demonstrating that in whatever proportion the pressure is increased, the friction will be increased in exactly the same proportion.

Such is the result of the experiments of *Coulomb* and *Ximenes*, instituted on a large scale, and submitted to a great variety of trials. There was, however, in an extreme case, found to be a slight deviation from this law. For when the pressures used were extremely intense, it was found that the friction did not increase in quite so great a proportion as the pressure. The deviation from the law, however, was so very inconsiderable, and happened only in such extreme cases, that it might for the most part be neglected.

The friction being then considered to be proportional to the pressure when the surfaces are given, a very remarkable consequence follows, which is, that however the magnitude of the surface of contact may vary, the friction will remain the same so long as the pressure is unchanged. Thus, suppose the body, C D, to be a flat block of wood, the face of which is sixteen square inches in magnitude, and the edge of which is equal to only one square inch, it will have the same friction with the plane, A B, whether it be placed upon its face or upon its edge. To explain this, let us suppose the weight of the block to be sixteen ounces; and let us suppose that when the body rests upon its edge, the amount of the friction, determined in the manner already explained, be eight ounces; it therefore follows that then the friction of every square inch of surface is equal to half the pressure on that square inch. Now let the block be placed upon its face, and let us suppose that the magnitude of the face is sixteen square inches; the whole weight of the block is sixteen ounces, and therefore the pressure on each square inch will be one ounce. When the pressure on a square inch was sixteen ounces, the friction was eight ounces; and since by hypothesis, the friction is proportional to the pressure, it follows that in the present case, in which the pressure is one ounce on each square inch of surface, the friction of each square inch of surface must be half an ounce; and since there are sixteen square inches, the total friction will be sixteen half ounces, or eight ounces, which is exactly equal to the friction when the block rested upon its edge.

It is evident that the same result would be obtained had we supposed the surfaces of any other magnitudes, and the pressure of any other amount. It may be satisfactory, however, to those who are a little conversant with algebraic notation, to see a general proof of this remarkable property.

*[Supposing the unit of surface to be one square inch, and the unit of pressure to be one pound, let P be the pressure upon a square inch of surface, expressed in pounds or parts of a pound. Let S be the number of square inches in the surface of contact; then S P will be the total pressure. Let f be the friction which one pound of pressure would produce on one square inch of surface; then f P will be the friction produced by the pressure, P, on one square inch of surface, and f S P will be the friction produced by the pressure, S P, upon the surface, S. If F be this total friction, we shall have $F = f S P$. But S P is the total pressure or weight of the block. Calling this W, we have $F = f W$, which is independent of the magnitude of the surface of contact.]

The result which we have here obtained as a consequence of the proportionality of the friction to the pressure, is fully confirmed by the experiments of *Coulomb* and *Ximenes*. They found that when a block of any substance has several faces of different magnitudes, the friction will be the same on whatever face it is placed; as in the former instance there is an extreme case which forms an exception to this law; for when the pressure is very small, and the surface of contact very much increased, the friction is found to be somewhat greater than it would be with a smaller surface.

(8.) There is another method of proving, experimentally, the proportion of the friction to the pressure, which depends on a property of the inclined plane. Let the body W (*fig.* 2), be placed

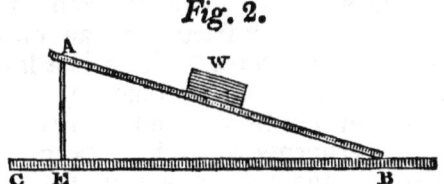

Fig. 2.

upon a plane, A B, which is hinged to an horizontal plane, C B, so that it can be raised to any proposed elevation. Now let the plane, A B, be slowly raised, until it acquires such an elevation that the force of the body down the plane is just sufficient to overcome the friction, and that the body will therefore commence to move. In this case, therefore, the force down the plane will be equal to the friction. If the length of the plane, A B, be taken to represent the whole weight, W, the height, A E, will represent the force down the plane, and the base, B E, will represent the pressure of the weight, W, upon the plane. The proportion of the friction to the pressure will then be that of A E to B E. Now let the weight be successively doubled, trebled, &c.; and it will be found that the same elevation of the plane will continue to overcome the friction, and put the body

---

* Those readers not familiar with mathematical reasoning will omit the paragraphs included within brackets.

in motion. Hence the proportion between the weight, friction, and pressure continues to be the same; a double or treble pressure always produces a double or treble degree of friction, and so on.

[The constant proportion which is found to subsist between the friction and the pressure may be expressed in reference to the angle, A B E, which gives a force down the plane equal to the friction. Let this angle be called X, let F be the friction, and P the pressure. By what has been already proved, we have

$$F : P :: A E : B E$$
$$\text{but } A E : B E :: \tan. X : 1$$
$$\therefore F : P :: \tan. X : 1$$
$$\therefore F = P \tan. X.$$

Thus it appears that the tangent of this angle always expresses the ratio of the friction to the pressure.]

What we have already stated as to the independence of the friction on the magnitude of the surface of contact, may also be established experimentally by the inclined plane. For on whatever side the body W, is placed upon the plane, the angle X, will be found to be the same; and therefore the proportion of the friction to the pressure will be the same.

(9.) Another law deduced from experiment is, that "friction is an uniformly retarding force." This is a law respecting which no difference of opinion whatever subsists; and the results of all experiments which have been instituted on the subject are in perfect accordance.

It will be recollected, than an uniformly accelerating force, as explained in our first treatise on *Mechanics*, is one which produces an increase of velocity in the moving body, which is proportional to the time of its motion; and the motion of a body excited by such a force is characterized by several remarkable properties, such as " that the spaces described from the beginning of motion are proportional to the squares of the times of describing them; the spaces described in equal successive intervals are as the odd numbers," &c. Now an uniformly retarding force, on the other hand, is one which destroys a portion of the velocity of the moving body; and the quantity thus destroyed is proportional to the time of the motion.

If a body be urged at the same time by two forces, the greater an uniformly accelerating force, and the lesser an uniformly retarding force, it is evident that the effect will be, that the body will move with an uniformly accelerating force which is equal to the *difference* of the two forces to which it is subjected. But if the force which retards the body be not uniform, while the force which accelerates it *is* so, then the *difference* of these forces, with which the body will move, will not be an uniformly accelerating force, since the want of uniformity in the retarding force will plainly affect the difference of the two forces. If, therefore, a body move with an uniformly accelerated motion, being urged by two forces, an accelerating and a retarding force, we are warranted in concluding, that if the accelerating force be uniform, the retarding force must also be uniform, for otherwise, according to what has just been explained, the motion of the body would not be uniformly accelerated.

These observations being premised, we are now prepared to explain the experiments by which friction is proved to be an uniformly retarding force.

(10.) An apparatus such as has been described in (7), is provided, the horizontal plane, A B, being of considerable length. The body, C D, is placed near the extremity, A, and a weight is suspended at S, sufficient to move the body along the plane from A towards B. The descent of the weight, S, is measured by a graduated vertical scale, similar to that used in Atwood's machine (First Treatise, p. 13), and the rate noted by a clock in exactly the same manner. In moving along the plane from A to B, the body, C D, is affected by two forces, one of which, viz. the force with which the weight, S, would draw it, independently of friction, is an uniformly accelerating force; the other, is the retarding force arising from the friction. According to what we have proved (9), it will immediately follow, that the friction is an uniformly retarding force, if we can shew by experiment that the motion of the body is uniformly accelerated. For since the entire urging force of the weight, S, is an uniformly accelerating force, and the motion which actually obtains is also uniformly accelerated, the retarding force must be uniform (9). Let the body, C D, commence its motion with a beat of the clock, and let a stage be adjusted by successive trials upon the vertical scale, so that the weight, S, will strike it with the second beat. The space through which C D will move in one second will thus be determined. By the same process we may find the spaces described in two, three, four seconds, or in as great a number of seconds as the length of the plane, A B, will permit. If these spaces be found to be in the same proportion as the squares of the numbers 1, 2, 3, 4, &c., then the motion of the body, C D, is uniformly accelerated, and otherwise not. (Treatise I.) In a series of very accurately conducted experiments, instituted by the late Professor *Vince* of Cambridge, this law was found to be observed with the utmost exactness.

Hence we infer, that " friction is an uniformly retarding force."

The same conclusion might be established by experiments on the inclined plane. If the plane be elevated to such an height as to cause the body to descend, it will be found that the descent is uniformly accelerated. Since the force down the inclined plane, independent of friction, is an uniform force, it follows, upon the same principle as before, that friction must be an uniformly retarding force.

(11.) The law which we have explained of the proportionality of the friction to the pressure under given circumstances, was derived from very extensive and varied experiments instituted by several philosophers, but particularly by *Coulomb* and *Ximenes*; nor was it ever called in question until the late Professor *Vince* of Cambridge renewed the inquiry, and instituted experiments, the results of which led him to conclude that this law does not obtain, or at least not accurately. We shall now explain the manner in which Professor *Vince* conducted the experiments from which he deduced results differing from those of Coulomb.

When the body, C D, is moved along the plane, A B, by the effect of the weight, S, omitting the consideration of the friction, the accelerating force with which it would move would depend on the proportion of the weights of C D and S. It follows, therefore, that if C D and S be both increased in the same proportion, the accelerating force, independent of the friction, will remain unchanged. If the friction be proportional to the pressure, it will be increased in the same proportion as the weight of C D; but then the weight C D, which it retards, is proportionally increased, and therefore the degree of retardation which it produces must be the same. Hence it follows, that since, by increasing the weights of C D and S in the same proportion, the two forces which affect C D, viz. the accelerating and retarding force, remain unaltered, their difference, which is the actual accelerating force with which C D is moved, will remain unaltered. Thus, it follows that, granting the proportionality of the friction to the pressure, no change should be produced in the rate of motion of C D, when both C D and S are doubled, or trebled, or increased or decreased in any other proportion.

[A rigorous mathematical investigation of this may be satisfactory to some readers. Let m be the quantity of matter in C D, and m' that in S; let g be the accelerating force of gravity, and f the constant ratio of the friction to the pressure; $m'g$ is the moving force which draws the combined masses m and m'. Therefore, the accelerating force with which they would be moved, independently of friction, would be $\dfrac{m'g}{m+m'}$, since the accelerating force is equal to the moving force divided by the quantity of matter. But fm expresses a moving force, which is equal to the friction of C D with the plane; and as this force acts in retarding the combined masses m and m', the corresponding retarding force is $\dfrac{fm}{m+m'}$. The actual accelerating force being the difference between this and the former, is $\dfrac{gm' - fm}{m + m'}$.

This being put under the form

$$\frac{g - f\dfrac{m}{m'}}{\dfrac{m}{m'} + 1}$$

it is evident that its value does not depend on the absolute values of m and m', but only on their *ratio*; and that so long as that ratio remains the same, the accelerating force with which C D moves along the plane will remain unaltered.

If, upon experiment, it were found that, by increasing the weights of C D and S in the same proportion, the accelerating force with which C D is moved *does not* continue the same, but is increased, what is to be inferred? That part of the accelerating force which is independent of the friction, depends entirely on the proportion of the weights of C D and S, as has been already explained; and therefore the *increase* of the accelerating force with which C D is moved, must necessarily proceed from a *decrease* in the retarding force arising from the friction. But again, this retarding force depends on two things: 1st, on the proportion of the friction to the pressure; and 2d, on the proportion of the weights of C D and S. The latter remains unaltered, and therefore we are compelled to infer, that the former must be diminished; that is, that the friction does not increase in proportion to the pressure, but in a less ratio.

[To express this mathematically, let the accelerating force with which C D is actually moved be C. We have then

$$C = \frac{gm' - fm}{m + m'} = \frac{g}{\frac{m}{m'}+1} - \frac{f\frac{m}{m'}}{\frac{m}{m'}+1}$$

Let us suppose that upon increasing m and m', in the same ratio C is increased. The first part $\frac{g}{\frac{m}{m'}+1}$ of the value of C, evidently remains of the same value as before. Hence, the second part $f\frac{\frac{m}{m'}}{\frac{m}{m'}+1}$ must necessarily be diminished. But the factor $\frac{\frac{m}{m'}}{\frac{m}{m'}+1}$ remains the same, and therefore f must be diminished. But f expresses the ratio of the friction to the pressure, which would, therefore, under these circumstances, be diminished.]

(12.) Such are the principles upon which Professor *Vince* founded his experiments. He found that when he doubled and trebled the weights of C D and S, the accelerating force with which C D was moved, was continually increased. Thus, when C D was 10 oz., and S = 4 oz., the space moved through in two seconds, was 51 inches. Upon making C D = 20 oz., and S = 8 oz., the space described in two seconds was 56 inches; and when C D = 30 oz., and S = 12 oz., the space was 53 inches. Numerous other experiments were made, all producing similar results.

Professor *Vince* therefore concluded, "that although the friction increased with the increase of pressure, yet that it increased in a somewhat less proportion." Thus, when the pressure was doubled, the friction was not quite twice its former amount; also, when the pressure was trebled, the friction was less than three times its former amount; and so on.

Having established this conclusion, at variance with former received doctrines, a consequence immediately followed from it, also inconsistent with what had been considered as an established property of friction. We have shewn, that if the friction be proportional to the pressure, it will be independent of the magnitude of the surface of contact, and that on whatever face a body is placed, the friction will be the same. If, however, according to the results of Professor *Vince*, the friction increase in a less proportion than the pressure, it will follow that, with the same pressure, the friction will increase when the surface of contact is increased.

To explain this, let us suppose, as in the former case, that a block weighing sixteen ounces, has a face whose magnitude is sixteen square inches, and an edge whose magnitude is equal to one square inch. When the block is placed upon its face, there will be a pressure of sixteen ounces upon a surface of sixteen square inches; let the whole friction be equal to eight ounces. Hence, on each square inch there will be a pressure of one ounce, producing friction equal to half an ounce. Now suppose the block to be placed upon its edge. There will be in this case a pressure of sixteen ounces upon a surface of one square inch. The pressure of one ounce upon a square inch producing a friction of half an ounce, and the friction increasing in a less proportion than the pressure, it follows that a pressure of sixteen ounces upon one square inch will produce a quantity of friction less than eight ounces. Hence the friction, when the block rests upon its face, is greater than when it is placed upon its edge. In the same way, it follows generally, that, under the same pressure, the friction is increased when the surface of contact is increased.

This conclusion being, like the former, contrary to the previously-received opinions, Professor *Vince* submitted it to the test of experiments conducted upon the same principle as we have already explained, and obtained results from numerous trials, which fully confirmed the consequence he had deduced. He found that the motion of C D on the plane, produced by a given weight, S, was always more accelerated as the surface of contact was diminished, the pressure being the same; from whence it followed, on the principles already explained, that the friction was diminished.

For example, a body was taken, whose face was to its edge in the ratio of 22 to 9. The same weight, S, which moved it through $33\frac{1}{2}$ inches in two seconds, placed upon its face, moved it through 47 inches in the same time, when placed upon its edge.

Again, when the face was to the edge as 32 to 3, the spaces through which it was moved in two seconds were 32 inches and $37\frac{1}{2}$ inches. Numerous other experiments were instituted, and attended with similar results.

(13.) Most of the experiments by which the proportionality of the friction to the pressure had been established, were conducted on a principle different from that adopted by *Vince*. In these the friction was generally measured by the force necessary to put the body C D in motion, being placed at rest upon the horizontal plane. *Vince*, however, makes several objections to this method of measuring the friction. In the first place, he objects, that the force necessary to *put the body in motion* must be necessarily *greater* than the friction. This objection, in strict theory, is undoubtedly valid, but, practically considered, will, we conceive, be found to have but little weight. It is very true that the force which is equal to the friction, is that weight which exactly keeps the friction in equilibrium, and without putting the body in motion, puts it in a state in which the smallest additional force imaginable will produce motion. If the experiment be nicely executed, therefore, the weight which is found just to produce motion will exceed the friction by a quantity so small as to produce no sensible effect on the results of the investigation.

It is further objected by *Vince*, that the force which opposes the motion of the body from a state of rest is not friction alone, but friction and cohesion conjointly, the latter in general greatly predominating over the former. In confirmation of this, he instituted several experiments, by which he proved that the force necessary to put a body in motion was much greater than the force which is necessary to continue that motion uniform; assuming that the latter must be the true measure of the friction.

That the resistance which a body resting upon another offers to a force tending to put it in motion, is greater than the friction of the same body when moving on the other, is a fact which was distinctly noticed, and very accurately investigated by *Coulomb*. But this resistance is ascribed by him entirely to *friction*, and accordingly one of the principles which he lays down as established by experiment is that the friction of bodies at rest is *greater* than the friction of the same bodies in motion.

Coulomb found that this friction of bodies at rest (we shall call it friction for the present), is increased to a certain limit with the duration of their contact. That is to say, when one body rests upon another, the friction of their surfaces increases for a certain length of time, until it reaches its greatest value; after this, it remains constant; and whatever length of time the bodies are permitted to rest in contact, the friction is not increased. The length of time in which the friction reaches its greatest amount was found to be different in different bodies. When the bodies are both wood, it is one or two minutes; when they are both metal, it is so short as not to be perceptible. When wood is placed upon a metallic surface, the friction continues to increase for several days.

It is, therefore, agreed on all hands, that the resistance of bodies at rest is much greater than the friction when one body moves upon another; and the only question to be decided is, whether this resistance be entirely friction, or the mixed effects of friction and cohesion; and if so, what proportion the cohesion bears to the friction. Professor *Vince's* reasoning on these points appears to be far from conclusive. He gratuitously assumes in the first place that the resistance of bodies at rest is the mixed effect of friction and cohesion. Thus far we should be inclined to go with him; because, if we grant the existence of such a force as cohesion, we can scarcely deny that it must be mixed more or less with friction in resisting the motion of the one body upon the other. But then another difficulty arises respecting the results of *Vince's* own experiments.

Does the motion of one body upon the other altogether destroy the cohesion? If not, why should the resistance of bodies in motion be entirely ascribed to friction, while the resistance of the same bodies at rest is ascribed to the united effects of friction and cohesion? We shall not, however, pursue this objection.

Vince next assumes that all that quantity by which the resistance of bodies at rest exceeds the friction of the same bodies when moving one upon the other, is the effect of cohesion. It is evident, that in this there is a tacit assumption that the friction of bodies at rest is equal to the friction of bodies in motion; for the whole resistance of bodies at rest arises from the sum of the effects of their friction and cohesion; and he assumes that if from this sum the *friction in motion* be subtracted, the remainder will be the *friction at rest*.

If the proportion of the parts of the resistance which are to be assigned to friction and cohesion be introduced into the investigation at all, it would have been desirable that experiments should be instituted to determine this. We would be led expect from such experiments a very different result from that assumed by *Vince*, and should anticipate that in most cases the cohesion would be found to bear a very small proportion to the friction; and that, therefore, the *friction at rest* would still be found to be much greater than the *friction in motion*.

The quantity of cohesion might, we conceive, be thus determined:—Let a string be attached to the body, which rests upon the plane at a point immediately over its centre of gravity, and let this string be carried in a vertical direction over a fixed pulley, and let a weight be suspended from it exactly equal to the weight of the body which rests upon the plane. This weight will equilibrate with that of the body, and the force with which the body will then be attached to the plane will be that of the cohesion alone. Now, let small weights or fine sand be added to the weight which equilibrates that of the body, until the body be just lifted from the plane. This additional weight may be taken as the measure of the cohesion; and if it be subtracted from the weight which just moves the body upon the plane acting in a direction parallel to the plane, the remainder will evidently be the true value of the friction at rest. We have not had an opportunity of instituting experiments on this principle, but are strongly disposed to predict that in most cases the cohesion would be found to bear a very small ratio to the friction.

That the duration of the contact should increase the friction is not difficult to conceive, inasmuch as the effect of the pressure acting for a certain time is to make various asperities and inequalities of the surfaces insert themselves among each other more effectually than they could if one surface were moving over the other. We may illustrate this as in a former instance, by two brushes placed one upon the other. If a weight be placed upon the upper brush, the pressure will cause the hairs of the one to insinuate themselves and descend between the hairs of the other. This process will, however, proceed gradually; and, after the lapse of a certain interval, will cease. A considerable force will then be requisite to put the one brush in motion over the other; but when in motion, the same pressure will fail to produce so great an intermixture of the hairs, since in no one position of the brushes will sufficient *time* be given to produce so great an effect. These effects, if minutely examined, will be found to have the most exact analogy and correspondence with the properties of friction, as determined by the experiments of *Coulomb*; and they illustrate, if not explain, the phenomenon of the *friction at rest* being greater than the *friction in motion*.

The experiments of *Coulomb* were not, however, confined to the investigation of the quantity of the friction when the bodies under examination are put in motion from a state of rest. He also examined the friction of bodies in motion, and determined that friction is an uniformly retarding force, in nearly the same manner as Professor *Vince*. He also examined, in different substances, the proportion between the *friction at rest* and the *friction in motion*, and found that this proportion is different with different bodies. In woods, the *friction at rest* he found to amount to half the pressure, while the *friction in motion* only amounts to an eighth of it. Between wood and metal, the *friction at rest* was found to be one-fifth of the pressure, and the *friction in motion* one-twelfth of it. Between metals, there was no sensible difference observed between the two frictions.

(14.) From the circumstance of friction being an uniformly retarding force, it follows that it is independent of the velocity, for it is found to continue the same while the velocity is continually increased. In this result all the experiments agree very nearly.

(15.) From all that we have stated, the reader will easily perceive that much still remains to be discovered respecting the nature and properties of friction. The experiments of *Coulomb* and *Vince* seem to be executed with equal precision, and governed by scientific principles equally just, and yet we find them differ considerably concerning the leading and important principle of the proportionality of the friction to the pressure. *Coulomb* is, however, uniformly supported in his results by the experiments of *Ximenes* and various others; and *Vince*, we believe, stands alone in his conclusions, at variance with these. The experiments of *Ximenes* are subject to some little discordance with each other, and those of *Coulomb*, owing to his not having noticed the circumstance of the *friction at rest* depending on the time of contact, and having put the bodies in motion without having waited for the friction to reach its *maximum*.

(16.) Besides the results which we have mentioned, there are other particulars which were developed in the experiments of *Coulomb*, which it may not be useless to state.

Friction varies in general with the *quality* of the surfaces: in new wood planed, it amounts to half the pressure; in metals, to one-fourth; and in wood and metals, to one-fifth.

As the surfaces are worn by attrition, the friction is generally diminished; but this has a limit, and the friction soon reaches its *minimum*. In woods, from being half the pressure, it is reduced by attrition to a third.

Between woods the friction is less when the grains cross each other than when they are placed in the same direction. It is, in the former case, one-fourth of the pressure; and, in the latter, half the pressure.

In general, friction is greater between surfaces of the same kind than between surfaces of different kinds.

While the attrition continues to diminish the friction it is not an uniformly retarding force, and, therefore, until this effect ceases it will not be found to be independent of the velocity.

Friction diminishes as the smoothness of the surfaces of contact is increased. However, by carrying the polish of the surface too far, we shall produce a considerable resistance from cohesion.

Friction is diminished by anointing the surfaces of contact with some unctuous substances, as tallow, oil, grease, &c. *Coulomb* considers that the greater the consistency of the ointment, the greater will be the advantage. Fresh tallow diminishes the friction by one-half.

According to *Vince's* results, it would appear that friction is diminished by diminishing the surface of contact. But even admitting this as a general principle, it has an obvious limit in practice, for if the one surface be small and the other soft, a groove will be ploughed by one surface in the other, and thus the friction will be produced.

CHAPTER III.—*Of the Friction of one Body rolling over the Surface of another.*

(17.) WHEN one body rolls upon another, it is very obvious that friction produces much less resistance to the motion than when it slides, as described in the last Chapter. In this case the parts of the one surface are, in some degree, successively *lifted* from off the other, and the asperities act in a manner totally different from the case of sliding, already considered. One, at least, of the bodies must, in this case, be bounded by a curved surface, and therefore the surface of contact must necessarily be very small, which is another cause of the diminution of the friction. If the rolling body be cylindrical, the points of contact of the surfaces will form a straight line upon the surface of the cylinder, the surface on which the cylinder rolls being either that of another cylinder having its axis parallel to that of the former, or a plane. But if the rolling body be a sphere, a spheroid, or any similar shape, the surface of contact will be reduced to a single point.

To explain the manner of investigating experimentally the properties of this species of friction, let us suppose two perfectly plane tables, A B, C D, (*fig*. 3,) placed exactly in the same horizontal plane. On these let a cylinder, E F, be placed with its axis at right angles to their length. At the middle of the interval between the tables, let a flexible string be passed across the

Fig. 3.

cylinder, having dishes of exactly equal weight suspended at its extremities. By placing equal weights in these dishes, any required pressure may be produced upon the table. If, then, fine sand be poured into either scale until its preponderance just gives motion to the cylinder, this additional weight will be equal to the friction.

In this way the diameter and material of the cylinder, as well as the pressure it exerts against the plane, may be varied at pleasure. In making experiments, it would be useful, in each trial, to pour the sand successively in each scale, so as just to make the cylinder move in each direction. If the weights which produce the motion differ by a small quantity, a mean between may be taken to represent the friction.

(18.) The results of numerous experiments instituted in this way by *Coulomb* were as follow:—

1. With the same cylinder the friction is proportional to the pressure.

2. With cylinders of the same substance, having different diameters, but equal pressures, the friction is inversely as the diameters.

3. With cylinders of the same substance, differing both in diameter and pressure, the friction is directly as the pressures, and inversely as the diameters; or in a ratio compounded of the direct ratio of the pressures and the inverse ratio of the diameters.

To explain the last two results to those who are not conversant with mathematical phraseology:—Suppose that two cylinders, one of two and the other of five inches diameter, exerted equal pressures on the tables, it would be found that the friction of the two-inch cylinder would be greater than that of the five-inch cylinder, in the proportion of five to two.

Again, suppose that the two-inch cylinder exerts a pressure of three pounds, and the five-inch cylinder a pressure of seven pounds,—it will be found that the friction of the two-inch cylinder will be to that of the five-inch cylinder in the proportion of the produce of five and three to the product of two and seven, or as fifteen to fourteen.

It was found that greasing the surfaces does not at all diminish this species of friction.

When a cylinder of mahogany, whose diameter was about three inches, was rolled upon a plane of oak, the friction was about one-sixteenth of the pressure; and when it rolled upon a plane of elm, the friction was only one hundredth of the pressure.

It is evident, therefore, that between the same substances this species of friction is much less than that of sliding.

The string used in these experiments should be so flexible, that its rigidity or stiffness shall produce no sensible effect upon the results.

CHAPTER IV.—*On the Friction of one Surface revolving in contact with another, without rolling.*

(19.) IF a body, having any round figure, be made to revolve while it is pressed with any force against any surface, and at the same time is prevented from rolling along that surface, a species of friction will be produced different from any which we have yet considered. This species of friction seems to partake of the nature of each of those which we have considered in the last two Chapters. As in the former, the surfaces *slide* one over the other, and as in the latter, the surface of contact is reduced to a line; we accordingly find the degree of this friction, under similar circumstances, holding an intermediate place between the other two, being less than the *friction of sliding*, and greater than the *friction of rolling*.

To explain this friction, and the experiments by which its properties may be determined, let us suppose a solid cylindrical axis, A B, (*fig. 4*,) inserted in an hollow cylinder, of a diameter, C B, somewhat greater than A B, so as to permit the hollow cylinder, B C, to turn round it, A B. Let the cylinders be

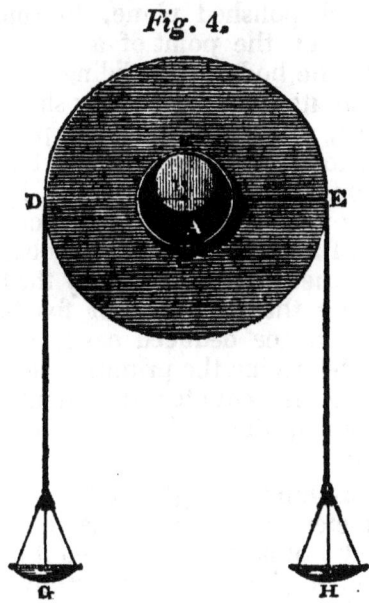

Fig. 4.

placed with their axes horizontal, and let the hollow cylinder be the centre or box of a wheel, D E. Let an extremely flexible string be passed over the edge of this wheel, in a grove formed to receive it, and let scales, G H, be appended to its extremities. In consequence of the form of the axle and hollow cylinder, and the manner in which the weight of the wheel acts, the points of contact of the axle and the cylinder will be in a straight line, formed by the intersection of a vertical plane passing through the axis of the cylinder, with the surface of the cylinder. In fact, if from the point of contact, B, a line be conceived to be drawn perpendicular to the plane of the paper, along the inner surface of the cylinder, the axle and the cylinder will touch in that line, and in no other points. It appears, therefore, that if the hollow cylinder be supposed to revolve round the axle, as happens in a carriage wheel, every part of the surface of the hollow cylinder is successively exposed to the effect of friction; while no part of the axle suffers this effect, except the side which passes through the point, B, of its section. If,

on the contrary, as sometimes happens, the axle revolve within the cylinder, the opposite effects are produced. The entire surface of the axle is successively exposed to the effects of friction, while these effects are confined to one line upon the surface of the hollow cylinder.

By loading the dishes G H with any equal weights, the axle may be submitted to any proposed pressure. If, when they are equally loaded, some fine sand be poured into one of the dishes until its weight just gives motion to the wheel, the weight of the sand will be sufficient to determine the quantity of friction.

The preponderating weight is not, however, in this case, the immediate measure of the friction. It is to be considered that the wheel is turned round its centre, I; that the friction which resists this motion acts at B, and therefore with the leverage B I; while the preponderating weight which overcomes the friction acts with the leverage E I. Let the friction be F, and the preponderating weight be W; then by the established properties of the lever we have

$$F : W :: E I : B I$$
$$\therefore F = W \frac{E I}{B I};$$

that is, the friction is equal to the additional weight which produces the motion, multiplied by the radius of the wheel, and divided by the radius of the hollow cylinder which plays upon the axle.

Thus, it appears that the friction is greater than the preponderating weight in the proportion of the radius of the wheel to the radius of the cylinder.

As, in the experiments to determine the *friction of rolling*, so here also each experiment should be tried in both dishes, and the mean of the results taken.

To determine whether the friction be an uniformly retarding force, a weight must be placed in one of the dishes greater than that which is necessary to overcome the friction. This will cause the dish to descend with an accelerated motion, and by placing a graduated vertical scale near it, the rate of its acceleration may be ascertained. If it be found that the spaces through which it descends, in one, two, or three seconds, &c. are as the numbers 1, 4, 9, &c.; in other words, if the spaces be as the squares of the times, the motion is uniformly accelerated. Hence it may be inferred, that the friction is an uniformly retarding force, on exactly the same principles as have already been fully developed in (9) and (10).

The string used in these experiments, like those described in the last Chapter, should be so flexible as that its stiffness shall produce no sensible effect on the results.

(20.) By a series of experiments conducted as we have described, *Coulomb* found that, like the other modifications of friction, the law of the proportionality of the friction to the pressure obtained, also in this case, subject however to the exception before mentioned, that in very great pressures the friction is somewhat less in proportion.

He also found, that, as in the *friction of sliding*, great advantage was gained by greasing the surfaces. In general, fresh tallow diminishes the friction by one-half. It increases as the grease is wasted away. This effect is, however, more slow than in the friction of sliding.

This species of friction is also an uniformly retarding force, and is therefore independent of the velocity.

Like the other species of friction, the quantity of this depends on the quality of the surfaces. If iron revolve in contact with brass, the friction is one-seventh of the pressure. When both surfaces are wood, the friction is one-twelfth of the pressure.

In general, the same observations which were made respecting the friction of sliding, will also apply to the species of friction which we have considered in this Chapter.

(21.) The friction of bodies turning on pivots seems to come within the species we are now considering. This was also examined by Coulomb, and a memoir on the subject was published by him in the Memoirs of the French Academy in 1790. A very succinct and clear account of this is given by Dr. Gregory in the second volume of his *Mechanics*, from which we extract the following particulars:—

"Bodies which are made to turn upon pivots are usually suspended by means of a cheek, socket, or collar, of very hard matter. The collar has its cavity of a conic form, and terminated at its summit by a little concave segment, whose radius of curvature is very small. The point of the pivot which is sustained by this collar forms at its summit a little convex surface, whose radius of curvature should be still smaller than that of the extremity of the cheek. Experience evinces that the curvature of the bottom of the socket is irregular, and that the friction of a collar of agate on which a pivot turns, is frequently five or six times more considerable than the *momentum of friction* of a well-polished plane of agate on which the same pivot turns.

"These considerations induced M. Coulomb to employ in the course of his experiments, not a cheek or a socket, but a well-polished plane, to support the body on the point of a pivot. To prevent the body from sliding, he took care that its centre of gravity should be very low, with respect to the point of suspension: he then made the body to whirl or spin about its pivot, by impressing upon it a rotatory motion. By means of a seconds watch, he observed exactly the time employed by the body in making the first four or five turns, and he thence deduced easily a mean turn to determine the primitive velocity: after this he counted the number of turns which the body made before it stopped.

"Coulomb took a glass bell of 48 lines in diameter and 60 lines in height, which weighed 5 ounces. He placed it on the point of a pivot; and after giving it successive degrees of velocity about that pivot, he observed very exactly the time that it employed to make the first turn, which gave him for the mean velocity that which answered to the half of such first turn. He then estimated the number of turns made by the bell before it stopped: the results were as below—

"*1st Trial.* The bell made one turn in $4''$, and came to rest after $34\frac{1}{10}$ turns.

"*2d Trial.* The bell made one turn in $6\frac{1}{4}''$, and stopped after $14\frac{1}{10}$ turns.

"*3d Trial.* The bell made one turn in $11''$, and stopped after $4\frac{6}{10}$ turns.

["Now if b denote the primitive velocity, X the space described between the commencement and the end of the motion, A the constant momentum of the retarding force; $\int \frac{\mu r^2}{a}$ the sum of the products of every particle μ, by the square of its distance r from the axis of rotation, divided by the quantity a, measuring the distance from the axis of rotation to the point whose primitive velocity is b, it is easy to find the following analytical expression for the constant momentum of the *vis retardatrix*, viz.

$$A = \frac{b^2}{2x} \int \frac{\mu r^2}{a}.$$

"But, because in the three preceding trials, the same bell was employed, the quantity $\int \frac{\mu r^2}{a}$ is the same; $\frac{b^2}{x}$ must therefore be a constant quantity if A be constant, and reciprocally. But in each trial there was reckoned the time employed by the apparatus in performing an entire revolution. The mean velocity, or the velocity due to the half of each first revolution, will, therefore, be measured by the circumference run over. The space described up to the end of the motion, will be measured by the number of turns run through from the instant where the mean velocity was determined until the end of the motion. Thus by computing from the data furnished by the three trials, we may form the following table:—

"1st Trial. 1 turn in 4″, stops at $34\frac{1}{10}$ turns, whence results $\frac{b^2}{x} = \frac{1}{547}$

2d Trial. . . . $6\frac{1}{4}″$ . . . $14\frac{1}{10}$ . . . . $= \frac{1}{550}$

3d Trial. . . . $11″$ . . . $4\frac{6}{10}$ . . . . $= \frac{1}{557}$

"This experiment, then, shows unequivocally that the quantity $\frac{b^2}{x}$, and consequently the quantity A which expresses the momentum of friction, are constant quantities, whatever be the primitive degree of velocity; and that, consequently, the velocity has not any influence upon the *resistance* due to the friction of pivots, which from this experiment is necessarily proportional to a function of the pressure.

"When this experiment is made in a vacuum, a much less heavy body may be employed, and of any form whatever, and the same result will be obtained.

"In other experiments, Coulomb bent a brass wire of 9 inches in length; the parallel branches were 24 lines distant from one another: the part of the wire curved in the form of a semicircle which joined the two branches was about 3 inches long; and the two vertical and parallel branches were also each 3 inches long. To the extremity of each vertical branch was attached by means of wax a piece of metal, and there was fixed, in like manner, in the middle of the concave part of the wire, to serve for the cheek or bush, a small well-polished plane of different substances on which the friction of the point of the pivot was to be determined: finally, there was fixed to the summit of a support a little needle of tempered steel, and whose point it was necessary to render more or less fine, rounded, or obtuse, according to the nature of the cheeks, and to the pressure which they were to experience. The extremity of the needle first used by Coulomb, appeared, when examined by a microscope, to form a conic angle of 18 or 20 degrees. The friction of this needle against well-polished planes of granite, agate, rock crystal, glass, and tempered steel respectively, was tried; and the result, taking in each experiment the mean quantity represented by $\frac{b^2}{x}$ (a quantity which was always found to vary between very narrow limits), gave the momentum of friction of the point of the needle against the planes of granite, agate, &c. respectively, in the ratio of the fractions $\frac{1}{1028}, \frac{1}{847}, \frac{1}{784}, \frac{1}{579}, \frac{1}{487}$: so that the momentum of friction of the plane of granite being represented by unity, we shall have for the momentum of the friction of rotation relative to the other substances as below:—friction of granite, 1; of agate, 1·214; of rock crystal, 1·313; of glass, 1·777; of steel, 2·257.

"Coulomb likewise employed himself during these experiments, in determining the more or less acute form which should be given to the points of the pivots. To this end he caused to be successively rounded into cones of greater or less acuteness, the extremity of a steel needle, that it might thence appear whether the change of figure had any influence upon the friction. Thus he found that, under a certain charge, the point of the pivot being shaped to 45 degrees, the quantity $\frac{b^2}{x}$ was, for granite, $\frac{1}{2500}$; agate, $\frac{1}{2100}$; glass, $\frac{1}{1100}$; tempered steel, $\frac{1}{1000}$.

"Coulomb then gave to the point a more acute form, so that the angle of the cone which terminated it could not be more than 6 or 7 degrees; and he found, still retaining the same charge or pressure as before, that the quantity $\frac{b^2}{x}$ was, for agate, $\frac{1}{500}$; glass, $\frac{1}{150}$; tempered steel, $\frac{1}{150}$.

"Comparing from these, and other experiments, the momentum of friction of rotation of the point of different pivots against a plane of agate, he found that the quantity $\frac{b^2}{x}$ which varies as that momentum, was, for a pivot of 45°, $\frac{1}{3100}$; a pivot of 15°, $\frac{1}{1200}$; a pivot of 6°, $\frac{1}{800}$.]

"After this, Coulomb varied the charge in his experiments, and determined the relative momentum of friction of pivots under different pressures. But without going further into detail, we may give the following as the principal deductions from the whole.

"1. That the friction of pivots is independent of the velocities, being merely as a function of the pressure.

"2. That the friction of granite is less than that of glass.

"3. That the figure of the point of the pivot, as to acuteness, affects the quantity of friction; in such manner that when we cause to whirl, upon the point of a needle, a body weighing more than 5 or 6 drachms, the most advantageous angle for that point appeared to be from 30° to 45°; under a less pressure, the angle might be progressively diminished, without the friction being perceptibly augmented: it may even without great inconvenience be reduced to 10° or 12° with good steel, when the charge does not exceed 100 grains,—an important consideration in the suspension of light bodies upon cheeks or sockets.

"These rules may be useful to the makers of chronometers."

CHAPTER V.—*On the Rigidity of Cordage.*

(22.) IN considering the effects of cordage in our second treatise, we assumed that it possessed perfect flexibility. In cases where experiments are instituted on a small scale, with light weights and moderate tensions, fine silken threads, or even thin packthread, may be used, without any consideration of their rigidity, because in these cases the flexibility is so great that no sensible effect is produced by stiffness. But in most cases which occur in actual practice, where great resistances are to be overcome, or considerable weights to be elevated, ropes are used whose thickness and strength necessarily produce considerable rigidity; and if we would know the real and practical power of the machines we use, it is necessary to be able to determine the effects of the stiffness of the cordage with which we work.

Although the theory of the rigidity of cordage is much more satisfactory and more conformable to experiment than any which has yet been invented respecting friction, yet it is more difficult to explain it in a simple and popular manner. The stiffness of a rope depends on the elements by which it is determined in a manner which is very easily explained to one that is familiar with the elements of algebra, but extremely difficult to express in ordinary language.

To explain the manner in which the rigidity of a rope obstructs the action of a machine, let the equal weights A, B, (*fig.* 5,) be supposed to be connected by

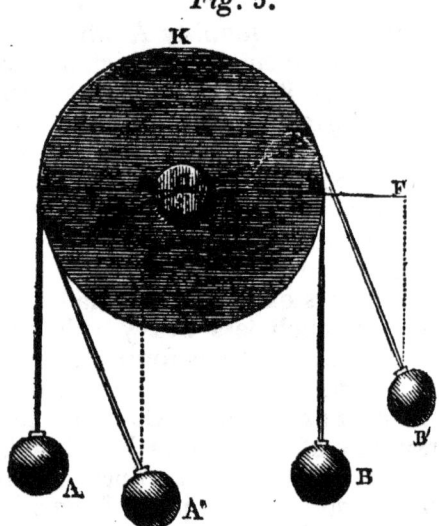

Fig. 5.

a rope ACDB passing over a fixed pulley, O. By adding a small weight to A, the wheel will be turned in the direction DKC. That part of the rope which has been applied to the semicircle DKC will, by reason of its rigidity, have a tendency to retain the semicircular form, and to resist any effort to disturb that form. Let us suppose that it actually retains that form during a small motion of the wheel. The part DCK of the rope will then continue to be applied to the wheel, but the points C and D will be moved to the position C', D'. For the same reason that the part DCK of the rope endeavours to retain its semicircular form, the parts DB and CA will endeavour to retain their rectilinear form, and also *their position with respect to the part* DCK. Let us also suppose that during the small motion already mentioned, they actually do maintain both their figure and relative position, and that, consequently, at the end of the motion the rope and weights are in the position A′C′D′B′, which would, in fact, be the case if the rope were *perfectly rigid*, and the friction with the wheel sufficient to prevent it from sliding in the groove. In this position the weight added to A, instead of acting against B with an equal leverage CO, would act with the diminished leverage EO against B resisting with the increased leverage FO, (the lines A′E and B′F being drawn perpendicular to CD and its production.) Thus it appears that if the rope were *perfectly rigid*, any power which would commence to turn the wheel would very soon bring the apparatus into such a position, the opposing weight or resistance gaining leverage, while on the other hand the moving power would be losing its leverage, that the machine would come to equilibrium, and no further motion would ensue.

Now let us suppose, what is generally the case, that the rope, without being absolutely and perfectly rigid, has a certain degree of stiffness. First, suppose the apparatus to assume the position represented in the last figure. The weights A′ and B′, acting upon the partially flexible ropes A′C′C and B D′, will evidently bend them into curves such as represented in *fig.* 6. From A′

Fig. 6.

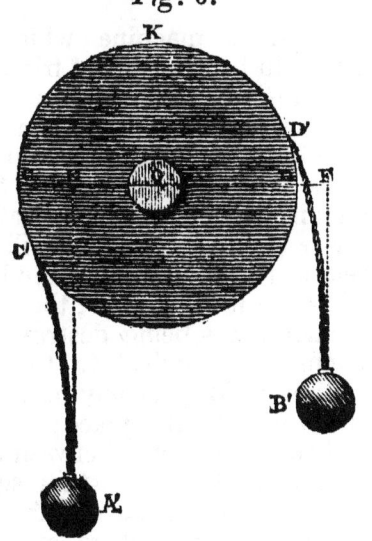

and B′, as before, draw the perpendiculars A′E and B′F, and it is obvious that the increase of weight given to A′ works with a diminished leverage EO, while the unaltered weight B′ receives an increased leverage FO. If the weight which is added to A′ multiplied by EO be not greater than the weight B′ multiplied by FO, no motion can ensue; and thus, owing to the effect of the rigidity of the rope, a fixed pulley may be loaded with unequal weights, and yet continue in equilibrium.

If we consider the effects which the weights A′ and B′ produce upon the rope as the wheel revolves, we shall find them very different. The weight B continually bends the rope B′D, so as to give it at the point D′ a curvature equal to that of the groove of the wheel. On the other hand, the weight A′ is employed in destroying the curvature which the rope had when resting in the groove, and even in giving it a curvature in the opposite direction. The effort which the rope in this case makes to retain its curvature at C tends to diminish the leverage by which A′ acts, but the effect of A′ in giving curvature to the rope in the *opposite direction* below C′ counteracts this effect, and has a tendency to increase the leverage of A′; the difference between these effects is what produces the diminution of the leverage of A′. On the other hand, the resistance which the rope B′D offers to flexure is opposed to the effect of B′; and this resistance, undiminished by any other cause, is wholly effective in increasing the leverage of B′. We may, therefore, anticipate that the increase DF of the leverage of B′ is much greater than the diminution CE of the leverage of A′. This effect, which is found by actual experiment to obtain, is of some importance in simplifying the theory of rigidity. For we find, in general, that the effect of the weight A′ upon the rope is so considerable that the diminution CE of its leverage, owing to the rigidity of the rope on the side C, is so small that it may be entirely neglected, and that in our investigations we may, without sensible error, consider the weight A′ as acting with the leverage OC, or the radius of the wheel.

On the contrary, for the reasons just assigned, the increase DF of the leverage of B′, owing to the rigidity of the rope D B′, is considerable, and forms an important element in the determination of the effects of rigidity.

[Let x express the weight which must be added to A′, in order just to put the wheel in motion, and we have by the principles of the lever,

$$(x+A')\ r = B'\ (r+b),$$

where r expresses the radius of the pulley and b = DF. Hence,

$$xr + A'r = B'r + B'b;$$

but since A′ = B′, therefore A′r = B′r. Taking these equals from both, we find

$$xr = B'b \therefore x = B'\frac{b}{r}.$$

Thus, if b were known, the effect of the rigidity corresponding to any given weight or pressure would be known. It appears also, that in order to allow for the rigidity of ropes in any machine, it is only necessary to suppose the leverage by which the resistance acts to be greater than it is by a certain quantity.

To complete the theory of rigidity, it will then be necessary to determine this quantity b; and in explaining how this is done, we shall perhaps be compelled to use more algebraical principles and notation than most of our readers are familiar with. The quantity b evidently depends altogether on the curvature of the rope B′D′, *fig.* 6. It is easy to perceive the several elements on which this curve depends; 1st, on the tension of the rope or the weight B′ with which it is loaded; let this be called w: 2nd, on the materials of the rope, and the manner in which they have been manufactured; let a express the quantity by which this affects the rigidity: 3rd, on the diameter of the rope; let this be d: 4th, on the radius r of the wheel.

The empirical formula

$$x = \frac{d^n}{r}(a+mw)$$

is assumed to represent x. By an *empirical* formula is meant one that is conceived or invented without any analysis or demonstration, and the truth (or rather probable truth) of which can only be established by shewing that it is verified by experiment.

In this formula the letters m and n represent indeterminate numbers, the values of which, as well as that of a, can only be found by experiment. To determine these let four pulleys be taken whose radii are r, r', r'', and r'''. The rope whose rigidity is under examination being successively laid over these, let it be stretched by weights equal to w, w', w'', and w''', and let the weights which in each case just give motion to the wheels be x, x', x'', and x'''. Substituting these in the formula already mentioned, we obtain

$$\left. \begin{array}{l} x = \dfrac{d^n}{r}(a+mw) \\[4pt] x' = \dfrac{d^n}{r'}(a+mw') \\[4pt] x'' = \dfrac{d^n}{r''}(a+mw'') \\[4pt] x''' = \dfrac{d^n}{r'''}(a+mw''') \end{array} \right\} (A)$$

From any three of these four equations the values of a, m, and n may be deduced. These being known, we have

$$x = w \cdot \frac{b}{r} \therefore b = \frac{x}{w} \cdot r;$$

and hence

$$b = \frac{d^n}{w}(a+mw);$$

thus we obtain the increase of leverage which should be allowed to the resistance when the diameter of the rope and its tension are known.

In order to verify the empirical formula just mentioned, or to prove it as far as it is capable of proof, it is only necessary to eliminate the quantities a, m, and n by the four equations (A,) and if the result be an identity, that is, an equation whose members are perfectly the same, the four equations are consistent. This species of proof may be strengthened by multiplying the experiments, and using different values of x, w, and r; and if an elimination of a, m, and n, from every combination of four equations, the certainty of the proof is all but equal to that of demonstration.]

CHAPTER VI.— *Of the Modification which Friction and other Resistances produce upon the Conditions of Equilibrium.*

(23.) IN a machine which is conceived to be divested of friction and all other resisting forces, there is one certain and determinate power which will equilibrate with a given weight, the methods of determining which have been explained in our second Treatise. Any power greater than this will cause the weight to ascend, and any less power will allow it to descend; the equilibrium in such cases being destroyed. If the machine be subject to the effects of friction, rigidity, or any resisting forces, this will not take place; and we shall find that any power between two determinate limits will sustain equilibrium. This circumstance arises from that peculiarity in the nature of resisting or passive forces, that in whatever direction motion, or a tendency to motion, is produced, they assume the direction immediately opposed to that tendency. If the power has a tendency to raise the weight by being increased beyond the value due to equilibrium, by the principles established in Treatise II., the friction, &c., oppose that tendency; and if then the weight be increased so as to predominate and tend to raise the power, the resisting forces immediately change their direction and oppose the effect of the weight. Let us suppose that P is the power which by any machine would equilibrate with W, independently of friction or any resisting force, according to the principles established in Treatise II. If P be increased, it will have a tendency to raise W; but that tendency will be opposed by the resistances. Let the effect of these resistances on P be R, then it will be necessary to increase P by a quantity greater than R, in order that W should be raised. Again, if P be diminished, W would have a tendency to descend, but this tendency is opposed by the resisting forces; and, in fact, W cannot descend unless P be diminished by a quantity greater than R. Thus it appears, that in order to raise the weight, the power must be greater than $P+R$; and in order to prevent the descent of the weight, the power cannot be less than $P-R$. Hence every power whose value is between the limits $P+R$ and $P-R$, will sustain the weight in equilibrium. The powers $P+R$ and $P-R$ will sustain the weight in equilibrium also, but it will be in a state *bordering on motion*, the least imaginable increase of the one or diminution of the other necessarily producing the ascent or descent of the weight.

The increase R of the power which balances the resisting forces is not necessarily equal to these forces themselves, because the increase R generally acts upon the resistances, through the intervention of the machine or some part of it. To explain the methods of determining the quantity R, even in the several simple machines, would require more mathematical investigation than would be suitable to the objects of the present Treatise. We shall, however, explain some of the more simple cases.

(24.) If a lever rest upon a knife-edge like a balance, the friction will be imperceptible; but if it turn upon a cylindrical axle, this is not the case. Let f be the absolute quantity of the friction on the axle, determined in the manner explained in the preceding chapters; let r be the radius of the axle, W the weight, and w its leverage, and let p be the leverage of the power. In order to raise the weight, the power will have to overcome the friction f acting with the leverage r, and the weight W acting with the leverage w. The moment of the power which would exactly balance these would be

$$Ww + fr.$$

Let the power sought be P'; hence

$$P'p = Ww + fr \therefore P' = \frac{Ww + fr}{p}.$$

This power will just balance the weight and friction, and any greater power will raise the weight.

If the weight be supposed to descend, it will be opposed by the friction f acting with the leverage r, which will thus assist the power. Let P'' be the power which will just prevent the descent of the weight, and we evidently have

$$P''p = Ww - fr \therefore P'' = \frac{Ww - fr}{p}$$

Any power less than P'' will permit the weight to descend, and these powers P' P'', and all intermediate ones, will sustain the weight in equilibrium.

Since P, the counterpoise for W when there is no friction, is equal to $\frac{Ww}{p}$, we have

$$P' = P + \frac{fr}{p} = P + R$$

$$\therefore R = \frac{fr}{p}$$

which is the limit of the increase or decrease of the power consistently with equilibrium.

This investigation applies also to the wheel and axle as is evident. In that case, however, the rigidity of the rope must be allowed for, conformably to the principles established in the last Chapter; and the same may be observed with respect to the pulley.

(25.) Let a body W be placed upon an horizontal plane, and f express

Fig. 7.

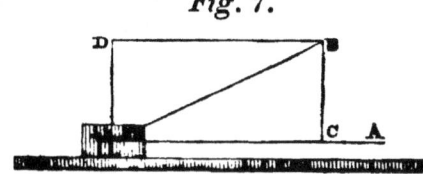

the proportion of the friction to the pressure. If a force draw it in the direction W A, parallel to the plane, the force which will put it in motion will be equal to the friction, and is, therefore, W f. Let us now suppose that it is drawn along the plane by a force which constantly acts in the direction W B, forming with the horizontal line always the same angle B W A. This force produces a twofold effect. Draw the lines B C and B D so as to form the parallelogram W D B C. The force W is equivalent to two forces expressed in quantity and direction by the sides W D and W C. The part W D tends to raise the body W from the plane, and, therefore, to diminish the pressure and the friction, while the part W C tends to move the body along the plane.

By the obliquity of the draught advantage is gained and lost. Advantage is gained, because the friction which is to be overcome is diminished by the effect of that element W D of the draught, which acting upwards, lessens the pressure upon the plane. Advantage is lost, because the element W C of the draught, which is effective in advancing the body on the plane, is less than the whole draught W B, which would be effective if it acted parallel to the plane. It is found, however, that provided the angle (B W C) of draught does not exceed a certain limit, an advantage on the whole is gained by the obliquity, that is to say, a less force will put the body in motion, and continue that motion than would do so acting parallel to the plane.

It becomes, therefore, an important problem to determine what that angle of draught is which affords the greatest possible advantage, or with which the smallest power will move the body along the plane. This is very easily solved analytically; we shall, however, attempt to explain it by geometrical construction, being a more elementary process, though not the most expeditious.

Let the drawing force as already explained, be represented by W B, and suppose it just sufficient to put the body in motion. The element W C must then be equal to the friction. Let W A represent the quantity of friction which would be produced by the whole weight

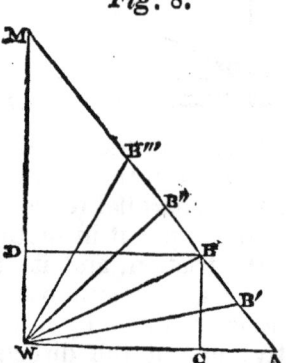

Fig. 8.

of the body pressing on the plane, that is Wf (7). Since W C represents the quantity of friction which remains after the pressure is diminished by the upward element WD, it follows that CA must represent the quantity of friction which would be produced by the pressure DW or BC; and since f expresses the proportion of the friction to the pressure generally, we have

C A : C B :: f : 1.

It will be recollected, that we have already shewn (pp. 5, 6) that if the plane W A were elevated until the body W B would just be moved down it, the proportion of the height of the plane to its base would be that of the friction to the pressure. Hence, in this case, the height of the plane would have the same ratio to its base as the line C A has to C B; and, consequently, the right-angled triangle included by the height and base of the plane is similar to the triangle A C B, and, therefore, the angle A B C is equal to the elevation of the plane, which would just give motion to the body. The angle B A C is the complement of this angle. Now since W A represents the whole friction of the body undiminished by the obliquity of the draught, and the angle B A W depends on the proportion of the friction to the pressure, these quantities are both independent of the direction, or length of the line W B, which represents the drawing force, and will, therefore, remain unaltered, however that drawing force be changed in its direction or length.

Thus we have obtained a very elegant geometrical construction, by which the force which is just sufficient to move the body at each angle of draught may be determined. From any point W on the plane draw a perpendicular W M, and take any parts, W A and W M, on the plane and the perpendicular which have the ratio of the friction to the pressure, that is, so that

WA : WM :: f : 1.

Then if WM be supposed to represent the weight, WA will represent the friction due to the pressure of the entire weight, and the angle WMA will be equal to that elevation, X (p. 6), of the plane at which the force of the weight down the plane would be equal to the friction. We will suppose WM to be taken of such a length that the number of inches in it is equal to the number of pounds in the weight. Then the number of inches in WA will be the number of pounds which would overcome the friction due to the entire weight, or which acting parallel to the plane WA would just put the weight in motion. But we desire to know the power which acting at any given angle with WA would just move the weight. Draw the line WB″ in the direction of the required power, and terminated in AM; the number of inches in WB″ will be the number of pounds which, acting in the direction WB″, will just move the weight. Again, it may be required to assign the direction in which a given power must act in order just to move the weight. To determine this let a line of as many inches as there are pounds in the required power be inflected from W on the line AM. If WB′ be this line, WB′ will be the required direction.

To determine the best angle of draught, is then only to assign the least line which can be drawn from the point W on the line AM, which is, as is well known, a perpendicular to it. Let WBA be a right angle, and the angle BWA is, therefore, the best angle of draught. The right-angled triangles WBA and BCA are similar, (Euc. VI. prop. 8,) and, therefore, the angle BWA is equal to the angle CBA. But this last is equal to the angle to which the plane should be elevated, in order that the body should just move down it.

(26.) [We may obtain this result analytically thus. Let x be the angle of draught, P the drawing force, and X the elevation at which the body just moves down the plane. The elements into which P is resolved are $P \cos x$, and $P \sin x$. The pressure on the plane is consequently $W - P \sin x$, and the corresponding friction

$$(W - P \sin x) \tan X.$$

This is balanced by $P \cos x$; therefore, we have

$$(W - P \sin x) \tan X = P \cos x.$$

The question then is to determine the value of x, which renders P a maximum. Differentiating considering P and x as variables, we have

$$-P \cos x \tan X\, dx - \sin x \tan X\, dP = \cos x\, dP - P \sin x\, dx.$$

Let $dP = 0$, and omit dx, and we obtain

$$-P \cos x \tan X = -P \sin x.$$

$\therefore \tan X = \tan x \therefore x = X$,

which is the conclusion obtained geometrically above.]

(27.) Hence, if a body be required to be drawn upon a plane subject to friction, the best direction for the traces is to be inclined to the plane at that angle, at which the plane itself should be inclined to the horizon, in order to make the body move down it without any drawing force.

In the construction already instituted, the angle of draught corresponding to the direction WM is 90°. In this case the whole drawing force is spent in diminishing the pressure on the plane, the element in the direction of the plane gradually diminishing as the angle of draught increases, and at length altogether disappearing. The line WM ought then to represent as it does the weight of the body, the pressure being in this case absolutely destroyed.

(28.) In the preceding investigation of the best angle of draught, we have supposed that the plane upon which the load is drawn is horizontal. If, however, it be not so but inclined, the process of investigation will be somewhat modified, but the final result will be the same, the best angle of the draught being in all cases equal to that elevation of the plane, at which the body would just move down without any drawing force.

Let FI (*fig*.9.) be the inclined plane on which the body is placed, and let its length FI, expressed in inches, represent the weight of the body, expressed in pounds.

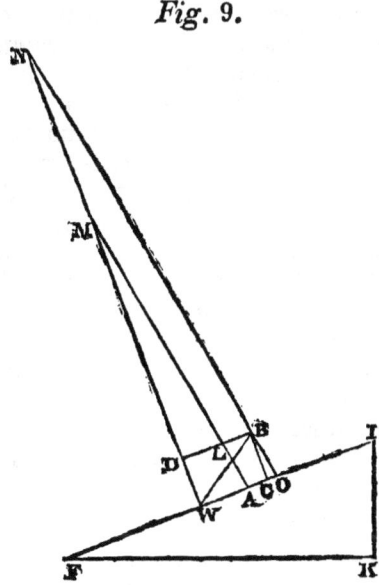

Fig. 9.

Hence, its base FK will represent the pressure on the plane, and its height KI the force down the plane. (Second Treatise). Draw WM perpendicular to FI and equal to FK, and draw MA, making the angle WMA equal to the angle of elevation, which would just make the force of the body down the plane equal to the friction. Hence, as we have already explained, M W is to W A as the pressure to the friction. But M W represents the pressure on the plane, and, therefore, W A represents the corresponding friction. Let W D be the element of the drawing force which is perpendicular to the plane, and which therefore diminishes the pressure. Since W M is the undiminished pressure, and W D the quantity by which the drawing force diminishes it, the effective pressure will be M D. Through D draw D L parallel to W A. The triangles M D L and M W A are similar, and therefore,

M W : W A :: M D : D L.

And since W A is the friction corresponding to the pressure M W, D L must be the friction corresponding to the effective pressure M D. This then is one part of the force which is to be overcome by the element of the drawing force which is parallel to the plane. The other part is the force of the body down the plane, which is represented by K I. From A take A O equal to K I, and draw O B parallel to A M, and to meet D L produced at B. Then in the parallelogram A L B O, the side A O is equal to the opposite side L B. Hence, L B represents the force of the body down the plane. This added to the friction D L, gives the whole force D B, which is to be balanced by the element of the drawing force in the direction of the plane. Hence, if W B be drawn, and also B C parallel to D W, it is plain that W B must represent the drawing force, since W C (which is equal to D B), and W D are its elements in the direction of the plane and perpendicular to it. The number of inches in the several lines we have here drawn, is equal to the number of pounds in the forces or pressures which they severally represent.

(29.) Such is the analysis of the problem when the plane is inclined, and from which it appears, that the drawing force, corresponding to any angle of draught, may be found by drawing a line from W in the direction of the draught, and terminated in the line O B, or its production. The length of this line will represent the quantity of the drawing force. And on the other hand, if the angle of draught corresponding to any given drawing force be required, it is only necessary to inflect from W a line equal to the given drawing force on the line O B, and the direction of this line will be that of the corresponding draught.

To find the best angle of draught, it is only necessary to find when the drawing force is the least possible, which is evidently done by drawing a perpendicular, W B, from W, on O B. This will be the least line which can be drawn from W to O B. Also, since the triangles W C B and B C O are similar, the angle B W O is equal to the angle C B O; and since B C is parallel to M W, and B O to M A, the angle C B O is equal to W M A; therefore the angle B W O is equal to W M A; but this last angle is equal to the elevation at which the body would just move down the plane.

(30.) [The same may be analytically investigated as follows:—

Let e be the elevation of the plane. The force down the plane is $W \sin. e$, and the pressure is $W \cos. e$; the friction due to this pressure is

$W \cos. e \tan. X$.

The element of the drawing force perpendicular to the plane is

$P \sin. x$,

and the diminution of the friction due to this is

$P \sin. x \tan. X$.

Hence the effective friction is

$(W \cos. e - P \sin. x) \tan. X$;

and the entire force to be balanced by the element $P \cos. x$ of the drawing force, in the direction of the plane, is the sum of this friction, and the force $W \sin. e$ down the plane. Hence we have the equation,

$W \sin. e + (W \cos. e - P \sin. x) \tan. X = P \cos. x.$

Considering P and x variable, let this equation be differentiated, and we obtain

$- P \cos. x \tan. X dx - \sin. x \tan. X dP = \cos. x dP - P \sin. x dP.$

This is the same differential equation as was obtained in p. 21, and therefore gives the same result $x = X$.]

(31.) We shall now investigate the limits of the value of the power which is capable of sustaining in equilibrium a given weight upon an inclined plane, subject to the effects of friction. Let us first suppose that the power acts in the direction of the plane.

If the elevation of the plane be not greater than that at which the body will just move down the plane, and which we shall in general call X, it is evident that the power necessary to sustain the weight in equilibrium has no *minor limit*, because, without the assistance of any power, the friction alone is sufficient to prevent the descent of the weight. If the weight be represented by the length of the plane, the pressure is represented by its base B. Let the proportion of the friction to the pressure, as usual, be $f:1$. Hence Bf is the friction. The force of the weight down the plane is represented by the height H. Hence the force to be overcome by the power in order just to produce motion, is $H + Bf$, which is therefore the *major limit* of the power which is capable of sustaining equilibrium. Any power greater than this will draw the weight up the plane.

This may be easily represented by geometrical construction. Let AB (*fig.*10.) be the inclined plane which represents the weight, AC represents the pressure,

Fig. 10.

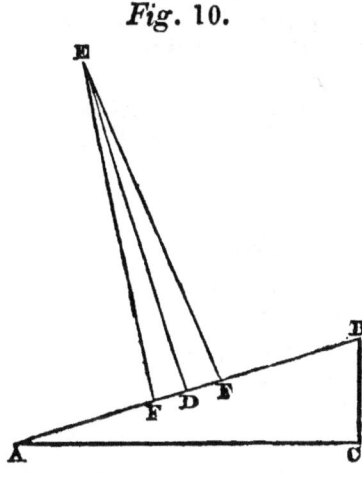

and BC the force down the plane. Take AD, equal to BC, and from D draw DE perpendicular to the plane, and equal to AC, and from E draw EF, making the angle DEF, equal to the angle X. Hence
$$DF : DE :: f : 1;$$
that is, as the friction to the pressure; and since DE represents the pressure, DF represents the friction. Since AD represents the force of the body down the plane, and DF represents the friction, AF represents a force equal to the combined effects of these, and which would keep them in equilibrium. Any force greater than AF, therefore, will draw the weight up the plane. Hence AF represents the greatest power which can act upon the weight, consistently with equilibrium.

If we suppose the elevation BAC of the plane to be greater than the angle X, the power necessary to sustain the weight will have a *minor limit;* for in this case the friction alone is insufficient to prevent the descent of the weight. Upon the principles already explained, the height H expresses the force down the plane, and Bf is the friction which will resist the descent of the weight; hence the actual tendency to descend is $H - Bf$, which is therefore the minor limit of the power. If P′ and P″ be used in the sense explained in (24), we therefore have
$$P' = H + Bf$$
$$P'' = H - Bf;$$
or, following the construction in *fig.* 10, draw EF′, making the angle DEF′ equal to X, and DF′ will be equal to the friction, and we shall have
$$P' = AF, \qquad P'' = AF'.$$

(32.) Let us next suppose that the direction of the power is inclined to the plane.

The power which acting at any given angle with the plane would just overcome the weight and the friction, was determined by the analysis and construction instituted in (28). Hence, if FI, *fig.* 9, represent the weight, and WB the direction of the power, the length of the line WB, will express the magnitude of the power which will just overcome the weight and friction; so that any power greater than WB acting in that direction would move the weight up the plane. Hence P′ = WB.

To assign the minor limit of the power will be easy, by a slight modification of the construction.

In the process described in (28), instead of making the angle WMA equal to X towards the top I of the plane, let it be made, as in *fig.* 11, towards the foot F. Then, as before, WD (*fig.* 11.) representing the element of the drawing force perpendicular to the plane, DL will represent the friction. Take AO equal to IK, and through O draw a parallel to AM to meet LD produced at B. The force with which the weight has a tendency to descend on the plane will be the difference between the part LB of the weight resolved in the direction of the plane and the friction LD, which is DB. This line DB must then be equal to the element of the power in the direction of the plane; and since WD is the element perpendicular to the plane, the power must be WB.

(33.) Divesting the construction of

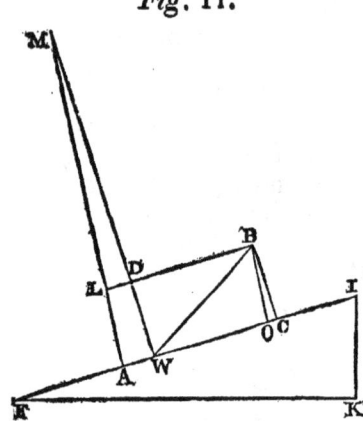

Fig. 11.

those lines which are merely introduced to supply the links of the analysis, the two limits of the power may be thus determined. Let WB be the direction of the power. Take WA and WA', (*fig.* 12.) each equal to the friction due to the pressure of the weight upon the plane, the weight being supposed not to be affected by any power. Take A O and

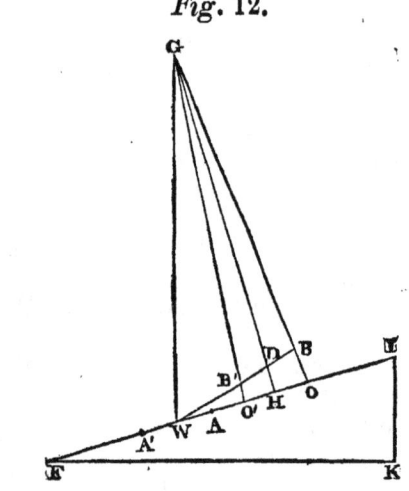

Fig. 12.

A'O', each equal to IK, and through O and O' draw lines each inclined to OO' at an angle equal to the complement of X, and produce the direction of the power to intersect these lines at B' and B. Then WB' will be the least power which can prevent the descent of the weight, and WB will be the greatest power which can be applied without causing its ascent. All intermediate powers will produce equilibrium.

The construction which we have given not only exhibits in every case the two limiting values of the equilibrating power, but also shows what the single value of this would be if there were no friction. Let D be the point where WB'B intersects the perpendicular GH from G on OO'; WD is the value of the power which would sustain the weight were there no friction. For the element of this, which is in the direction of the plane, is WH; but since O'GO is isosceles, H must be the middle point of OO', but A'O' is equal to AO: take AO' from both, and the remainders, AA' and OO', are equal; and therefore WA, which is half of the one, is equal to HO, which is half of the other; add to both AH, and WH is equal to AO, which by construction is equal to KI, or the force down the plane. Hence, the element of WH in the direction of the plane would be equal to the force down the plane, and WG is, therefore, the equilibrating power.

(34.) From considering this construction it appears that if the direction of the power be that of the line WG passing through the intersection of the lines drawn through O' and O, the two limits of the power become the same, the points B' and B coincide, and there is but one power, WG, which will keep the weight in equilibrium; every greater power will cause its ascent, and every lesser one will permit its descent. This may be easily accounted for, and is in fact what might be expected. Since WA = HO and WA is the friction due to the weight, HO is equal to this friction; and since HGO is the complement of HOG, it is equal to the angle X, and therefore HO is to HG as the friction to the pressure; but HO is the friction due to the weight, and, therefore, GH is the pressure. But since WG is the power, HG is its element perpendicular to the plane. Hence the part of the power which tends to diminish the pressure is equal to the entire pressure. The pressure being thus destroyed, there is no friction; and hence it is that the two limits of the power become equal, their difference, which is always twice the effect of the friction, having vanished.

Since GH is equal to FK, and WH to IK, and the angles at H and K are right, it follows that WG is equal to FI, and that the angle GWH is equal to FIK, and, therefore, that WG is parallel to IK. Thus it appears that this is the case, in which the direction of the power is vertical, and is, therefore, equal to the weight, and sustains it independently of the plane.

(35.) [The preceding results may very easily be obtained analytically, and the formulæ thus found are better fitted for calculation than the geometrical constructions which we have given in the text.

Retaining the notation which we have used in pp. 21, 22, the effect of the friction in resisting either the ascent or descent of the weight is—
$$(W \cos. e - P \sin. x) \tan. X.$$
This must be added to the element $W \sin. e$ of the weight, in the direction of the plane, in order to obtain the force which is to be balanced by the element of P' in the direction of the plane, and must be subtracted from it in order to obtain the element of P'' in the direction of the plane. Hence we have—

$$W \sin. e + (W \cos. e - P' \sin. x) \tan. X = P' \cos. x.$$
$$W \sin. e - (W \cos. e - P'' \sin. x) \tan. X = P'' \cos. x.$$

Multiplying both members of each equation by $\cos. X$, and observing that $\tan. X \cos. X = \sin. X$, we find—

$$W (\sin. e \cos. X + \sin. X \cos. e) - P' \sin. x \sin. X = P' \cos. x \cos. X$$
$$W (\sin. e \cos. X - \sin. X \cos. e) + P'' \sin. x \sin. X = P'' \cos. x \cos. X$$
$$\therefore W (\sin. e \cos. X + \sin. X \cos. e) = P' (\cos. x \cos. X + \sin. x \sin. X)$$
$$W (\sin. e \cos. X - \sin. X \cos. e) = P'' (\cos. x \cos. X - \sin. x \sin. X)$$

But, by trigonometry,
$$\sin. e \cos. X \pm \sin. X \cos. e = \sin. (e \pm X)$$
$$\cos. e \cos. X \pm \sin. e \sin. X = \cos. (e \mp X)$$

Hence we obtain,
$$W \sin. (e + X) = P' \cos. (x - X)$$
$$W \sin. (e - X) = P'' \cos. (x + X)$$
$$\therefore P' = W \cdot \frac{\sin. (e + X)}{\cos. (x - X)}$$
$$P'' = W \cdot \frac{\sin. (e - X)}{\cos. (x + X)}$$

which formulæ are adapted for computation.

Let us examine under what conditions the two limiting values P', P'' of the equilibrating power will become equal. If this be the case we must have—
$$\frac{\sin. (e + X)}{\cos. (x - X)} = \frac{\sin. (e - X)}{\cos. (x + X)}$$
$$\therefore \sin. (e + X) \cos. (x + X) = \sin. (e - X) \cos. (x - X)$$
$$\therefore 2 \sin. (e + X) \cos. (x + X) = 2 \sin. (e - X) \cos. (x - X)$$

But by trigonometry,
$$2 \sin. (e + X) \cos. (x + X) = \sin. (e + x + 2X) + \sin. (e - x)$$
$$2 \sin. (e - X) \cos. (x - X) = \sin. (e + x - 2X) + \sin. (e - x)$$

Omitting the common quantity $\sin. (e - x)$ in these equals, we have,
$$\sin. (e + x + 2X) = \sin. (e + x - 2X)$$

Hence the angles within the parentheses must be either equal or supplemental.

1st. Suppose them equal,
$$e + x + 2X = e + x - 2X$$
$$\therefore X = 0$$
the case in which there is no friction, and therefore but one value of P.

2nd. Suppose them supplemental,
$$e + x + 2X = 180^\circ - e - x + 2X$$
$$\therefore 2e + 2x = 180^\circ;$$
$$\text{or, } e + x = 90^\circ$$
$$\therefore x = 90^\circ - e$$

Hence the angle x, which the direction of the power makes with the plane, is equal to the complement of the elevation e. This is the same result as was obtained in (34.) geometrically.

It is very easy to shew that the geometrical construction in *fig.* 12, exhibiting the value of P' and P'', might be derived from the formulæ for these quantities which we have just found, or, *vice versâ*, that the formulæ may be derived from the construction.

In *fig.* 12, W G is equal to F I, or to W; the angle W G H is equal to K F I, or e; and the angle H G O or H G O′ is equal to X. Hence W G B′ is equal to W G H − H G O′, or $(e - X)$; and W G B is equal to W G H + H G O, or $e + X$. Also, G W B is equal to G W H − B W H, or G W H − x. But

$$GWH = 90° - WGH = 90° - e.$$

Hence,
$$GWB = 90° - (e + x).$$
$$GB'B = GWB' + WGB'$$
$$= 90° - (e + x) + e - X$$
$$= 90° - (x + X).$$

Also G B W = G B′ W − B′ G B;
but B′ G B = 2 X.

Hence,
$$GBW = 90° + (x + X) - 2X,$$
$$\text{or } GBW = 90° - (x - X).$$

By trigonometry we have—

$$WB : WG :: \sin. WGB : \sin. WBG$$
$$\text{or } P' : W :: \sin. (e + X) : \cos. (x - X)$$
$$WB' : WG :: \sin. WGB' : \sin. WB'G = \sin. GB'B$$
$$\text{or } P'' : W :: \sin. (e - X) : \cos. (x + X)$$

Hence we find,
$$P' = W \cdot \frac{\sin. (e + X)}{\cos. (x - X)}$$
$$P'' = W \cdot \frac{\sin. (e - X)}{\cos. (x + X)}$$

which are the formulæ already determined analytically, and by reversing this process, the construction may be deduced from the formulæ.

If the power be parallel to the plane $x = o$, and the formulæ become—

$$P' = W \cdot \frac{\sin. (e + X)}{\cos. X}$$
$$P'' = W \cdot \frac{\sin. (e - X)}{\cos. X}.]$$

(36.) It is evident that all the preceding reasoning will be applicable, whether the body slide or roll, or be moved on wheels. The only difference will be that the proportion of the friction to the pressure, or the value of f or WA will be different in each case.

CHAPTER VII.—*Tables of the Results of Experiments on Friction and Rigidity of Cordage.*

(37.) SINCE no theory of friction and the rigidity of cordage has been yet established on perfectly satisfactory principles, and all our knowledge respecting it must be derived immediately from experiment, we shall lay before the student some tables containing the results of experiments instituted by *Coulomb*, and by comparing these results with the principles which have been deduced from them, the degree of validity to be allowed to these principles will be apparent.

The following tables are extracted from *Dr. Gregory's Treatise on Mechanics.*

TABLE I.—*Friction of Woods, the Directions of the Fibres being the same, and the pressure being Unity.*

	Value of f.
Oak against oak	0.43
Oak against fir	0.65
Fir against fir	0.56
Elm against elm	0.47

Friction of Woods, the Directions of the Fibres being at Right Angles.

Oak against fir	0.158
Fir against fir	0.167
Elm against elm	0.100

TABLE II.—*Friction of Rollers of Lignum-vitæ of six inches and two inches diameter. Pressure = 1.*

Charge of the rollers, their weight being comprised.	Weights which produce an extremely slow motion, the diameter of their rollers being	
	6 inches	2 inches
100lbs.	0.6	1.6
500	3.0	9.4
1000	6.0	18.0

"We shall next present the results of Coulomb's experiments upon the rigidity of cords, and different rollers between 2 and 12 inches in diameter; the deduction for the friction is stated in the table, and a comparative column exhibits the rigidity deduced from the experiments made with the apparatus of Amontons. The cords were of three kinds: No. 1, of 6 threads in a yarn, or 2 in a strand, the circumference 12½ lines, and weight of a foot in length 4½ drachms. No 2, of 15 threads in a yarn, or 5 in a strand, circumference 20 lines, weight of a foot in length 12½ drachms. No. 3, of 30 threads in a yarn, or 10 in a strand, circumference 28 lines, weight of a foot in length 24½ drams.

TABLE III.—*Rigidity of Cords.*

No. of Experiments.	Cords used in the experiments.	Kinds of wood, diameter and weight of the rollers.	Weights hung on each side the roller in lbs.	Additional weight to surmount friction of roller and stiffness of cords.	Total charge of the rulers which support the roller.	Friction of the roller.	Stiffness of the Cord.	
							Valued by Coulomb's apparatus.	Valued by Amonton's apparatus.
1	Cord No. 3. of 30 threads in a yarn.	Elm 12 inches diameter, weight 110 lbs.	100	5lbs	315	1.5	3.5	4.4
			300	11	721	3.6	7.4	10.4
			500	20	1130	5.6	14.4	16.4
2	Idem.	Elm 6 inches diameter, weight 25 lbs.	200	18	443			
3	Idem.	Guiacum 6 inches diameter, weight 50 lbs.	200	16	466	2.8	13.2	14.8
4	Idem.	Guiacum 2 inches diameter, weight 42½ lbs.	25	11	65½			
			200	52	456½			
5	Cord No. 2. of 15 threads in a yarn.	Guiacum 6 inches diameter, weight 50 lbs.	25	1¼	101¼			
			100	6	256			
			200	11	461	2.8	8.2	7.6
			500	24	1074	6.4	17.6	17.8
6	Cord No. 1. of 6 threads in a yarn.	Idem.	100	3	253			
			200	6	456	2.7	3.3	3.1

"From this table it will be seen that the method of Amontons and that of Coulomb furnish nearly the same results: M. Coulomb ascribes the differences, where greatest, to the circumstances of the cords having been more used previous to their being taken for one kind of experiment, than for the other."

Table of Friction.

No. of experiments.	Kind of cord used.	Kind of greasing.	Weight used to bend the cord over the pulley.	Weight hung on each side of the pulley.	Additional weight to move the pulley.	Motion of the weight suspended on each side of the pulley.	Pressure on the axis.	Friction reduc. to surface of axis.	Ratio of friction to the pressure.
1	Very flexible thread of 3 lines circumference.	Friction without greasing.	0.0	103	6	Slow and irregular.	226	42	0.186
2	Cord No. 1. of 6 threads in a yarn.	Idem.	1.5	200	10.5 / 13.5	Slow and irregular. The first 3 feet fallen through in 6″, the last 3 in 3″.	424	65	0.153
3	Idem.	Idem.	3.0	400	21 / 28 / 39	Slow but continual. The first 3 feet described in 5″.5, the last 3 in 2″.5. First 3 feet described in 3″, the last 3 in 1½″.	825	130	0.156
4	Very flexible thread of 2 lines circumference.	Tallow.	0.0	100	2.5	Slow but continual.	216.5	17.5	0.808
5	Cord No. 1. of 6 threads in a yarn.	Idem.	1.5	200	6 / 6.5	The first 3 feet described in 3″.5, the last 3 in 1″.5. Slow but continual.	420	36	0.086
6	Idem.	Idem.	3.0	400	10.0 / 13 / 18	The first 3 feet described in 3″.5, the last 3 in 1″.5. Slow and continual. The first 3 feet described in 5′.5, the last 3 in 2′.	827	72	0.087
7	Thread of 2 lines in circumference.	Cart-grease.	0.0	50	24 / 2.5	First 3 feet in 3″. Last 3 feet in 2″. Slow and continual. Idem.	117 / 218	17.5 / 26	0.15 / 0.119

MECHANICS.

Table of Friction, &c.—continued.

No. of experiments.	Kind of cord used.	Kind of greasing.	Weight used to bend the cord over the pulley.	Weight hung on each side of the pulley.	Additional weight to move the pulley.	Motion of the weight suspended on each side of the wheel.	Pressure on the axis.	Friction reduc. to surface of axis.	Ratio of friction to the pressure.
8	Thread of 2 lines in circumference.	Cart-grease.	0.0	100	3.7	Slow and continual.	320	40	0.125
9	Idem.	Idem.	0.0	150	5.7	Slow and uncertain.	218	26	0.119
10	Cord No. 1. of 6 threads in a yarn.	Idem.	0.7	100	{4.3, 9}	{first 3 feet in 3″, last 3 feet in 1⅜″.}			
.						Uncertain.	422	50	0.119
11	Idem.	Idem.	1.5	200	{8.5, 14}	{first 3 feet in 4″, last 3 feet in 2″.} all 6 feet in 3″.5.			
						Uncertain.	831	101	0.121
12	Idem.	Idem.	3.0	400	{20, 17, 22, 28}	{first 3 feet in 6″.5, last 3 feet in 2′.5. first 3 feet in 4″, last 3 feet in 1″.5.}			
13	....	The cart-grease of prec. exp. wiped, the pores of the metal remained unctuous.	....	....	....	....	From 200 to 1200 lbs.	....	0.127
14	....	The surface fresh done with oil.	....	....	....	....		....	{0.127, 0.133}
15	....	The greasing not renewed of a long time, though the machine had been much used.	....	....	....	....		....	0.133

"The preceding Table contains the results of experiments on the friction of axes of iron in boxes of copper. The axis used was 19 lines in diameter, and had a play of 1.75 lines in the copper box; the pulley was 144 lines in diameter, and weighed 14 lbs.

"The chief object in these experiments was to determine the friction of axis *in motion*. Coulomb, therefore, caused the weights to run over a space of six feet, and measured separately by half seconds, the time employed to run over the first and last three feet.

"The weights employed to bend the cord, and which are contained in the fourth column, were calculated from the tensions expressed in the fifth column, by means of the formulæ already given, and the results of some previous experiments. These weights being subtracted from those of the sixth column, which put the system in motion, leave the weights employed in overcoming the friction. These latter weights acting at a distance from the centre of rotation equal to the sum of the radii of the pulley and the cord: the friction which is exerted upon the axis, and which, in the case of a very slow motion, may be considered as making an equilibrium with those weights, is therefore equal to the product of those weights into the ratio of the sum of the radii of the pulley and the cord, to the radius of the axis, which ratio is very nearly 7 to 1, when the weight is suspended by a thin packthread, and nearly 7·2 to 1, when it is suspended by the cord No. 1. From these considerations the ninth column was calculated. The weights comprised in the eighth column are composed, 1. Of the weight of the pulley or cylinder; 2. Double the corresponding weight in the fifth column; 3. The weights contained in the sixth column; for the sum of these evidently compose the pressure upon the axis. Hence, to find the ratio of the friction to the pressure, as expressed in the tenth column, it is only to divide any number in the ninth column by the corresponding one in the eighth."

"M. Coulomb has likewise endeavoured to ascertain the friction of axes of rotation made of the different kinds of wood which are commonly found in rotatory machines. To render the friction more sensible, he used pulleys of 12 inches mounted upon axes of 3 inches: sometimes the axes were immoveable; at others, they moved, but in both cases the friction was the same: the proper precautions were adopted to smoothen the surfaces in contact, and thence to avoid the uncertainty and irregularity which might otherwise have attended the results.

TABLE V.—"*Kinds of Wood used in the Experiments.*

	Ratio of friction to pressure.
Axis of holm-oak, box of lignum vitæ, coated with tallow	0.038
Ditto the coating wiped, the surface remaining oily	0.06
Axis and box as before, but used several times without having the coating refreshed	0.06 / 0.08
Axis of holm-oak, box of elm, coated with tallow	0.03
Ditto, both axis and box wiped, surfaces remaining oily	0.05
Axis of box-tree, box of lignum vitæ, coated with tallow	0.043
Ditto, the coating wiped, the surfaces remaining oily	0.07
Axis of box-tree, box of elm	0.035
Ditto, the coating wiped off	0.05
Axis of iron, box of lignum vitæ, the coating wiped off, and the pulley turned for some time	0.05

"The velocity does not appear to influence the friction in any sensible manner, except in the first instants of motion: and in every case the friction is least, not when the surfaces are plastered over, but when they are merely oily.

"The experiments on the stiffness of cords already described, were made in cases of motions nearly insensible; but M. Coulomb inquired whether with a finite velocity the resulting effect of the stiffness of the cord were augmented or diminished. For this purpose he took a pulley and box of copper, and an axis of iron done over with tallow: the diameter of the pulley was 144 lines, and that of the axis 20¼ lines, and the cord was one of 30 threads to a yarn, or No. 3, of which the stiffness with respect to insensible velocities was determined by some of the foregoing experiments. The ensuing table shows the results of the experiments: the weights were made to run over a distance of 6 feet, and the times of describing the first three and the last three feet were measured by a half-second pendulum.

"TABLE VI.

No. of experiments.	Weight hung on each side the pulley.	Additional weight to move the pulley.	Part of weight to overcome friction and rigidity.	Motion of the weights hung upon the pulley.	Pressure on the axis in lbs.	Weight acting at extremity of pulley, balancing the friction.	Stiffness of the cord deduced from the weights which move the pulley.	Stiffness of the cord estimated from its tension and former experiments.
	lbs.	lbs.	lbs.		lbs.	lbs.	lbs.	lbs.
1	100	7.5	7.5	Slow and continued.	221	2.6	4.9	4.0
		12	7.6	first 3 feet in 3″ / last 3 feet in 1½″				
		15	7.6	first 3 feet in 2″ / last 3 feet in 1½″				
2	200	11	11	Slow and uncertain.	425	4.9	6 1	6.6
		15	12.9	first 3 feet in 6″ / last 3 feet in 3″				
		19	12.2	first 3 feet in 3½″ / last 3 feet in 1½″				
3	400	20.5	20.5	Slow and uncertain.	834	9.7	10.8	11.8
		24	19.9	first 3 feet in 6″ / last 3 feet in 3″				
		31	17.6	first 3 feet in 3″ / last 3 feet in 2″				
4	600	31.5	31.5	Doubtful & continued.	1235	14.5	17.0	17.0
		37	31.5	first 3 feet in 6″ / last 3 feet in 3½″				

" It appeared in the Table III., that to bend the cord No. 3, of 30 threads in a yarn, about a roller of 12 inches diameter, and with a tension of 500 lbs., would require a weight of 14.4 lbs.; of which weight the constant part due to the fabrication of the cord is about 1.4 lbs: this value may be retained, but it will be here proper to reduce the part due to the tension of the cord by the quintal to $\frac{1}{5}(14.4-1.4) = \frac{1}{5} \times 10 = 3.6$ lbs. From these data the last column to the right of the above table was computed."

CHAPTER VIII.—*Works on Friction and the Rigidity of Cordage.*

(38.) On the subjects of friction and the rigidity of cordage, we are not able to direct the student's attention to any except those to which we have occasionally referred in the preceding treatise. The most extensive investigations on the subject are those of *Coulomb*, contained in the tenth volume *des Memoires des savans étrangers.*

A memoir on friction by *Ximenes* (*Terria e Pentica delle Resist. de sol ne' loro Attr. Pisa,* 1782), may also be consulted.

In the second volume of the *Petersburgh Transactions*, there is a memoir on friction, by *Bulfinger*.

In the transactions of the *French Academy*, 1769, there is a paper on friction by *Perronet*.

The memoirs by Professor *Vince*, with his theory of friction, will be found in the 75th vol. of the *Philosophical Transactions*, and also in *Tilloch's Philosophical Magazine*, Nos. 65, 66.

In the latter of these numbers will be found an account of a series of experiments instituted by Mr. John Southern, of Birmingham, an ingenious engineer. These experiments were instituted with mills turning grindstones, and the object was to corroborate the principle, that friction is an uniformly retarding force. "These experiments," says Dr. *Gregory*, "are the more worthy of notice, as they were made on *heavy* machinery with considerable variation of velocity of the rubbing surface, and great spaces rubbed over: the weight which caused the friction being upwards of 33 cwt., the velocity of the rubbing surfaces four feet per second at the greatest, and the length of surface rubbed over about 1000 feet at a medium. These experiments seem to confirm the opinion, that friction is an uniform resistance, at least, where the rubbing surface moves with a velocity of from nine inches to four feet per second; and Mr. *Southern* concludes from them, that in favourable cases, it does not exceed the fortieth part of the pressure or weight that occasions it."

A memoir by *Coulomb*, on the friction of pivots, will be found in the *Memoirs of the French Academy* for 1790.

A very instructive digest of all that has been done towards establishing a theory of friction, will be found in the second volume of *Dr. Gregory's Treatise on Mechanics*.

HYDROSTATICS.

CHAPTER I.

Definitions—Nature of Fluids.

HYDROSTATICS is the science which treats of the pressure of watery or liquid fluids; *Hydraulics* treats of their motion; and *Pneumatics* treats of the pressure and motion of the air and other light elastic fluids of a similar kind. These words are derived from the Greek tongue, which being well fitted to combine words together, and thereby to express the union and the difference of ideas, has been very generally used for scientific names. *Hydrostatics* comes from two Greek words which signify the *stopping* or *balancing* of *water*; *hydraulics* from two words signifying *water* and a *pipe*, referring to the movement of water in certain musical instruments used by the Greeks; and *Pneumatics* from a word denoting *breath* or *air*; and these three branches of science are intimately connected with each other. The whole science of liquids, or watery fluids, comprehending both Hydrostatics and Hydraulics, is sometimes called *Hydrodynamics*, from the Greek words for *water* and *power* or *force*.

When we make the division of fluids into watery or liquid, and aëriform, or air-like, we arrange them more accurately than if we used the old distinction of non-elastic and elastic; for though the aëriform fluids are much more elastic than the watery, the latter are by no means without elasticity. It was at one time believed that they were wholly without it; and could not be compressed, or made to occupy a smaller space by being squeezed. A society of scientific men in Tuscany (the *Academia del Cimento* of Florence) made an experiment which was for a long while supposed to prove this. They filled a hollow ball of thin beaten gold with water, and placing it in a press or vice, they applied a great force to squeeze it: by altering the shape of the ball, the pressure made the water ooze through the pores of the gold, and stand in drops on its surface. But although this only proved that the water was not easily compressible, it did not shew that no force could change its bulk; and Mr. Canton afterwards proved that liquids are in some degree compressible, and therefore elastic. His experiment was very simple, and quite decisive. He observed the height at which water, previously well boiled, and some other liquids, stood in a glass tube, in the air; and then, by means of an air pump, he removed the air: he found the liquid rose in the tube, so that the weight of the air must before have compressed the liquid, or made it fill a smaller space. It was found that the weight of the air compresses rain water about 1-22000th of its bulk, or makes it shrink about one part in 22000; olive oil, about one part in 21000; spirit of wine, one part in 15000, and mercury only one part in 33000.

By Mr. Perkins's late experiments, it should seem that water is more compressible than those older observations indicate. It had always been remarked, that when a bottle, filled with water, and corked tight, was plunged to a great depth in the sea, the water in the bottle tasted salt on bringing it up, as if the cork had been forced in when it was under water. He therefore constructed an instrument to ascertain how far the cork is forced in. He made a hollow cylinder of brass, water-tight, with a rod moving in the top through an air-tight and water-tight hole, and on this rod he put a spring ring, which remained fixed at any point at which it was placed. Over the whole he screwed a cover or cap, to protect the rod, but drilled with holes to let in the water; he filled the cylinder with water, and plunging it five hundred fathoms deep, he found that the ring, when the instrument was brought up, stood eight inches high on the rod. The rod therefore had been forced eight inches into the water in the cylinder, when at the deepest. The pressure upon the rod was about thirteen hundred pounds; the surface of the end of the rod about one-ninth of the surface of the water in the cylinder, and the cylinder two feet long; the water must therefore have been forced by the rod into a space less than its whole bulk when uncompressed by $\frac{8}{216}$, or one twenty-seventh part of that bulk.

That watery fluids have some elasticity is indeed so plainly proved by every day's experience, and by simple facts, as to occasion some wonder at the contrary ever having been asserted upon the authority of any one experiment, especially when that was of a somewhat complicated nature, and in itself far from conclusive. The common play of making ducks and drakes, that is, throwing a flat stone in a direction nearly horizontal against a surface of water, and thus making it rebound, proves the water to be elastic; and a musket-ball when so fired flies up in like manner, after striking the water. But you have only to pour water into an empty basin to be convinced of its elasticity; the first water that falls sparks about, flying up from the basin, and then what falls on the surface of the water which has been poured in will not fly so much up, because the water is much less elastic than the basin; and on a glass it will fly still more, glass being the most elastic body we know. But a piece of suet or putty, or any other non-elastic body, will not rebound even from glass.

Chapter II.

Fundamental Principle of equal Pressure.

All the particles of fluids are so connected together, that they press equally in every direction, and are equally pressed upon: each particle presses equally on all the particles that surround it, and is equally pressed upon by these; it equally presses upon the solid bodies which it touches, and is equally pressed upon by those bodies. From this, and from their gravity, it follows, that when a fluid is at rest, and left to itself, all its parts rise or fall, so as to settle at the same level, no part standing above or sinking below the rest. Hence if we pour water or any other liquid into a tube (or pipe) bent like a U, it will stand at the very same height in both limbs. Nor does it make any difference if one limb is wider than the other. For suppose we knock off the bottoms of a quart bottle and of a phial, and plunge them upright in a trough of water, A B C D (fig. 1.); the water will enter both the phial and the bottle, and stand at the same level in both, being the same with the level of the water, F G, outside the glass, or of the water in the trough before the bottle and phial were placed in it. Suppose we join the bottoms of the two by a tube, K, passing from one to the other in the water, and inclosing so much water; this will make no difference in the level of the water either in the bottles or in the trough generally. So if we solder this connecting tube to the two upright ones, so as to make the joinings water-tight, and thus to form one vessel, H K I, this can make

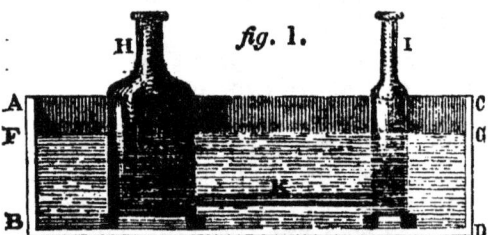

no difference on the level, F G, of the water: then, if we remove the vessel thus formed from the trough, the water must stand in it exactly as it did when in the trough, because it is manifestly impossible that it should make any difference to the water inside the bottle, whether there be water on the outside, or only air; and the water will stand as high in the wide bottle as in the narrow phial. In like manner, if, instead of filling the bottles by plunging them in the full trough, we pour water into them when empty, and standing in the empty trough, and at the same time we pour water into the trough, the water will stand equally high in both bottles: and so if we only pour it into the bottles, and not into the trough at all, or into the bottles without any trough; because it can make no difference to the water inside the glass, whether there be any outside or not, there being no communication whatever between the inside and outside. Generally, then, and in every case, if there be two tubes or limbs of a tube connected together, how-

HYDROSTATICS.

ever different their width may be, a fluid poured into them will stand at the same level, and thus a portion of fluid, however small, as B D, (*fig*. 2.) will re-

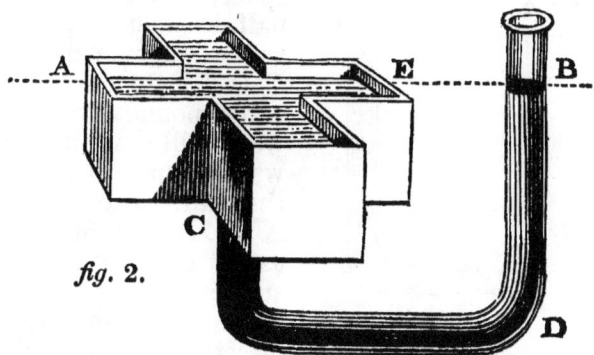

fig. 2.

sist the pressure of a portion, however large, as A C E, and balance it; for if the small did not balance the large portion, it would be forced upwards and rise above B, so as to run over the mouth of the tube, and be higher than the level, A B. Neither the shape nor the size of the two portions make any difference; the mass, A E C, will be supported by the mass, B D, however unequal in bulk, and however unlike in form, the line A E B being the level. Thus, if A B (*fig*. 3.) a small upright tube, C D a large one also upright,

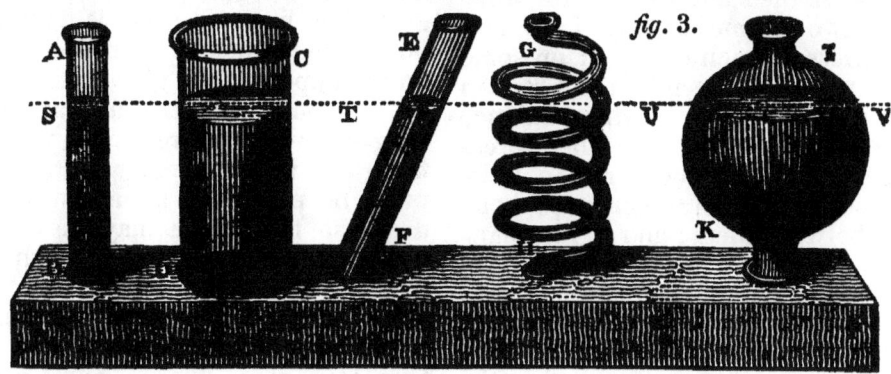

fig. 3.

E F a slanting one, G H a crooked one, and a globular one I K, are all fixed in the vessel W P, so as to communicate with it, and by means of it, with each other, water or any other liquid, being poured into them, will stand at the same height in them all, or have the same level line, S T U V.

From these considerations two most important conclusions follow, derived both from reasoning, and from innumerable facts of daily occurrence. The one is, that water, though, when unconfined, it never can rise above its level at any point, and never can move upwards, will yet, by being confined in pipes or close channels of any kind, rise to the height from which it came, that is, as high as its source; and upon this principle depend all the useful contrivances for conveying water by pipes, in a way far more easy, cheap, and effectual than those vast buildings, called aqueducts, by which the ancients carried their supplies of water in artificial rivers over arches for many miles. It is evident that the stream must have been running down all the way, and consequently that a fountain could in this manner never supply any place at the same or nearly the same height with itself. The other conclusion is not less true, but far more extraordinary, and indeed startling to our belief, if we did not consider the reasoning upon which it is founded: it is, that the pressure of the water upon any object against which it comes, any vessel which contains it, or any space upon which it rests, is not at all in proportion to the body or bulk of the water, but only to the size of the surface on or against which it presses, and its own height above that surface.

This follows immediately from the foregoing explanation and reasoning. For, suppose the communication between the two limbs of the tube, G D I, is cut off at F (*fig*. 4.), the body of water may be raised to G H in the limb G K, while it remains at B in the other limb; turn the stop-cock F, and the water will sink a little in the wide limb,

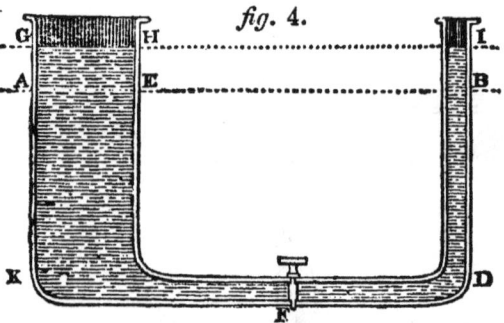
fig. 4.

and rise to the same level, I, in the narrow one: in like manner, while the obstruction remains, you may raise the water to I, and if it be removed, it will fall in B D, while in A K it will rise till it is equally high in both. So that the small quantity I B balances the large quantity G A E H, because both press on the same space at F, and both are of the same height: for whether the two volumes of water I D F and G E F press on each other, or on some surface placed between them at F, can make no difference; if they balance each other it is because they press equally: they therefore press equally on the same plate or other solid body placed between them; and in like manner two volumes of water quite unconnected and standing upon different bodies, whatever the bulk of water may be, press upon an equal extent of surface, with a weight proportioned to the height, and not at all to the bulk of the water. Hence the general rule for estimating the pressure of any fluid is, to multiply the height of the fluid by the extent of the surface on which it stands, and the product gives a mass which presses with the same weight as the fluid standing on that surface, however shallow it may be, provided any portion is supported at the height by a tube. If A B (*fig.* 5.), a tube twenty feet high,

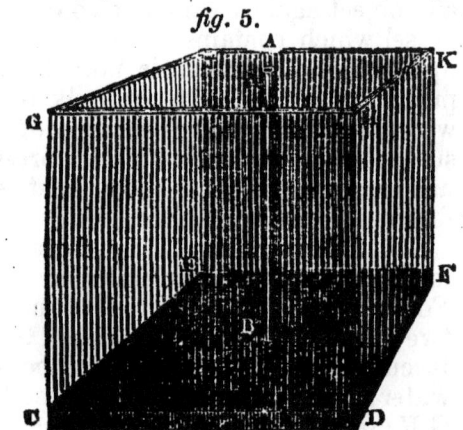
fig. 5.

and one inch in bore (or diameter), be filled with water, and plunged into a space, C D E F, three feet square and half an inch deep, likewise filled with water, there will stand in A B and C D F E together only about thirty-seven pounds troy of water; yet this water will press in all directions, downwards, upwards, and sideways, with the same force as if the whole space A D C B were filled with water, that is, as if there were five tons of water standing on B C.

The equal pressure of fluids in every direction, is illustrated by many very simple experiments. If a weight of a pound or two is placed upon a thin plate of glass, it breaks through the glass immediately, because all the pressure is from above; but if the glass is laid on a flat surface sufficiently strong to support it, the weight will not break the glass, provided it be laid gently on, because there is a resistance on the under side equal to the pressure on the upper. If the glass plate is made the bottom of a cistern, and a sufficient weight of water poured in, it will break the glass in the same way; but if the plate be placed in a cistern, however deep, so that there may be water on both sides of it, however thin the glass may be, it will not be broken. Suppose the glass is a foot square, and is placed twelve feet deep, and is as thin as a piece of the finest cambric paper, so that the weight of a few grains would break through it in the air; it will support a weight of twelve cubic feet of water, or nearly seven hundred weight, without being broken, crushed, or cracked; or if the cistern be filled with mercury, the film of glass will support a weight of above four tons and a half without any injury. This could only happen by the pressure of the fluid being exactly the same upwards and downwards, and in all directions. So if a force is applied to the water for the purpose of pressing it, however great the force may be which is thus conveyed through the liquid to the solid plunged in it, though that solid be an egg, or an egg-shell filled with water, or a piece of the finest spun glass, or a spider's web, the shape will remain wholly unchanged by the pressure applied. This is sometimes illustrated still further by a curious experiment. An egg and a piece of very soft wax are placed in a bladder filled with water, and this is placed in a box, so as to touch its sides and bottom; then a brass plate is laid loosely upon the bladder, and a hundred pounds weight or more is laid upon the plate; the wax and the egg though pressed by the water with this weight, yet being pressed equally in all directions, are not in the least either crushed, or altered in shape.

CHAPTER III.

Consequences of the Principle—Hydrostatic Paradox—Levelling.

It is a consequence, or rather another example of the same principle, that if you poise in a balance a pitcher full of water, by loading the opposite scale, and then hold in the pitcher a block of wood, or any other substance nearly the size of the pitcher, but so that it shall not touch its sides or bottom, although almost all the water will thus have been made to run over the sides, and only a spoonful may remain, yet the scales will continue balanced; and this without any regard to the weight of the body plunged into the water, and though you hold it entirely clear of the pitcher, so that it touches it in no place; for the effect will be the same if what you plunge in be scooped hollow, and made water-tight, so as to displace the greater part of the water. A bladder blown up, and tied fast, for example, and held down in the water, so as to leave only a spoonful surrounding it, will keep the scales balanced just as well as a block of lead the same size. Thus if E F (*fig.* 6.) be a balance with two scales E and F, you may put a jar of water A in one of the scales F, and balance it with weights in the other scale E. Then pour out

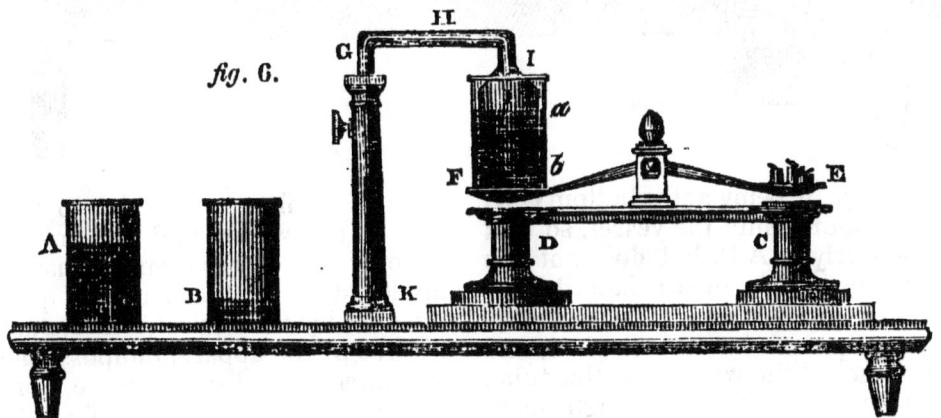

fig. 6.

all the water but an inch or two at the bottom, so that it stands at B instead of A, as in the jar B; the weights in E will be much too heavy for it: now take a crooked piece of wood G H I, and place it so that the thick part I is plunged to near the bottom of the jar, and make the water rise from *b* to *a*, as high as it stood before in the full jar A; the scale F will again balance the weights in the scale E, although there is only the small quantity of water in it that surrounds the block. And this does not depend on the weight of the block I, which is entirely supported by the stand G K; for whether it be made of wood or lead or card, the water, if it stands as high round it, balances the same weight as before. An easy way of trying this is, by putting a tumbler full of water in one scale, and balancing it with weights in the other, then pouring out all but two or three tablespoonsfull; the scale with the weights will of course sink; but if you now put a smaller empty tumbler in the other, so as to make the water rise round it to the brim, still holding it when immersed, the balance will be restored; and the small tumbler will not make the scale weigh heavier if it be filled with lead-shot; nor will it make the scale lighter, if, instead of glass, the smaller tumbler is made of thin wood or card.

There is yet another way of illustrating the effects of this property of fluids. We have seen how the displacing of any portion of a fluid by a fixed solid, whatever be the weight of the solid, produces no difference in the weight of the fluid. provided it stands at the same height as before, and how, raising the height of the fluid by plunging a solid into it, increases its pressure, or apparent weight. If the fluid is raised by pressing or forcing it upwards, in however thin a column, provided the vessel be kept full, and closed in all directions, the pressure of the fluid will be increased, and the apparent weight of the vessel will be increased, although nothing whatever, either solid or fluid, is added to it. The cylindrical vessel A B C D, (*fig. 7.*) has a tube H closely fitted into its top, and a rod E K fixed to a plate F G, moving up and down, water-tight, in the vessel, which is supposed fixed to the frame

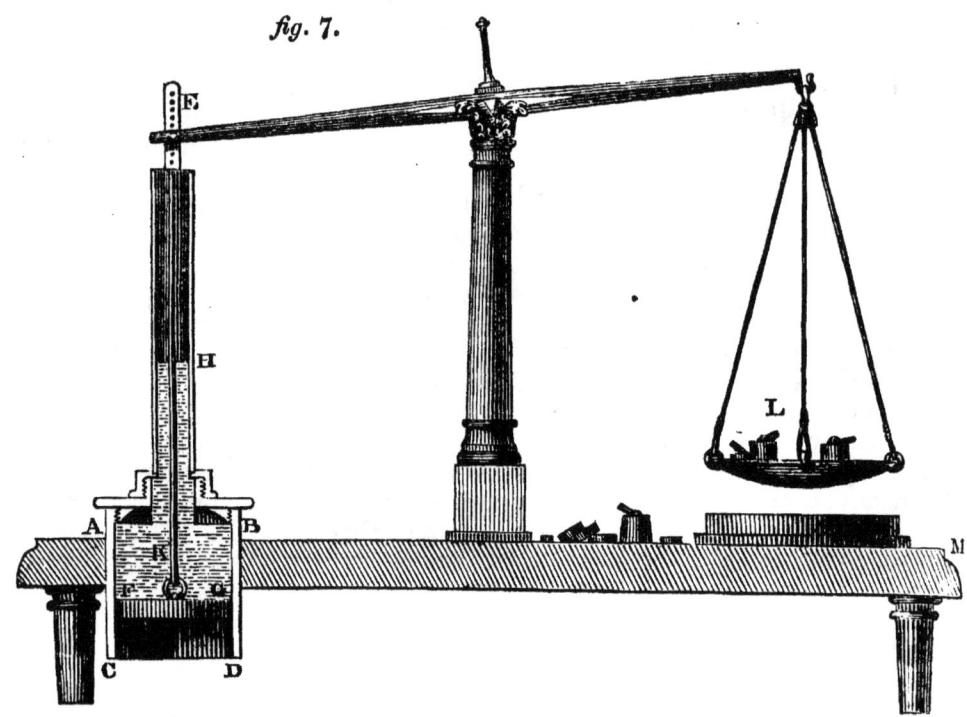

fig. 7.

A M. The plate being at the bottom C D, water is poured into the vessel, so that it rises nearly to A B. but does not rise in the tube. It is then balanced by a weight in the scale L. If the rod E K is drawn up so as to raise the plate, and force some of the water into the tube, the water will seem to weigh more than it did; and to restore the balance, more weight must actually be put into the scale L. If the vessel is three inches diameter, every inch that the water rises in the tube will require more than four ounces to be added to the weight, whatever be the bore of the tube; for the pressure of the water in all directions will be increased by the weight of a body of water, whose height is the height of the water in the tube, and whose base is the extent of the surface of the water pressing on the top A B of the vessel. Now the top being three inches diameter, its surface is about $7\frac{1}{15}$ square inches; and a portion of water one inch high, and $7\frac{1}{15}$ square inches broad, is $7\frac{1}{15}$ cubic inches of water, which weigh about four ounces. Thus, raising the rod a foot will add three pounds to the apparent weight of the water.

This principle, from its extraordinary illustrations, is called the *Hydrostatical paradox; paradox* being a word from the Greek, and signifying something, which, though true, appears when first considered to be untrue. When we are told that any quantity of water, however small, may be so employed as to balance any quantity of water, however great, we are at first startled by the apparent impossibility of the statement. But when we come to examine it more closely, we find it to be accurately true; for the small tube in the foregoing figures may be made ever so narrow, and to hold ever so little water, while the wide tube communicating with it may be made ever so large, and holding ever so much water; and the level at which the water stands in both tubes will be the same. So in the scales you may plunge as large a body as you please into the vessel of water, and leave as little water in the vessel as possible; still, if what you leave stands as high as the whole quantity stood, it will, by weight and pressure together, produce as much effect as the whole quantity of fluid.

Every thing, under these circumstances, depending upon the height and the surface, and very little upon the bulk of the fluid, we may easily perceive what mischief may be done by a very small quantity of water, if it happens to be applied or distributed, so as to stand high, in however thin a body or column, and to spread over a wide but confined and shallow space. Suppose that, in any building, a very small quantity of water has settled, and is confined to the extent of a square yard on the ground near the foundation, and suppose it to fill up the whole vacant space or crevice of no more than half an inch deep, between the ground and some part of the masonry; if you take a tube, however slender, of twenty feet long, and thrust it down into the water, and then fill it with water from above, you apply a force or pressure of above five tons under a space of only a yard square of the building, and destroy it as easily as if you had mined it with gunpowder. This may be easily tried with a hogshead or butt of water, or any other liquid, by fixing a small strong pipe in the bung-hole, and pouring water through it; when the water rises in the pipe to a sufficient height (and this will be more or less according to the strength of the barrel), the barrel will burst, although but a very small quantity of water may have been poured into the pipe; for the pipe may be of an extremely small bore, its width being wholly immaterial. One, twenty feet long, was found to burst a hogshead with great violence.

The same effect may be produced naturally by the rain falling into and filling some long narrow chink that may have been left in the walls of a building, or may be made by its decay in the course of time; and whether the chink be equally wide throughout, or vary in its size, and whether it be straight like a pipe, or crooked, makes no difference: provided it is water-tight, so as to get full of the rain, the pressure will always be in proportion to its perpendicular height, and not to its length if it winds. The same process in nature may produce the most extensive devastation; it may cause earthquakes, and split or heave up mountains. Suppose, in the bowels of some mountain, (*fig.* 8.) there should be an empty space of ten yards square, and only an inch deep on an average, in which a thin layer of water had lodged so as to fill it entirely; and suppose,

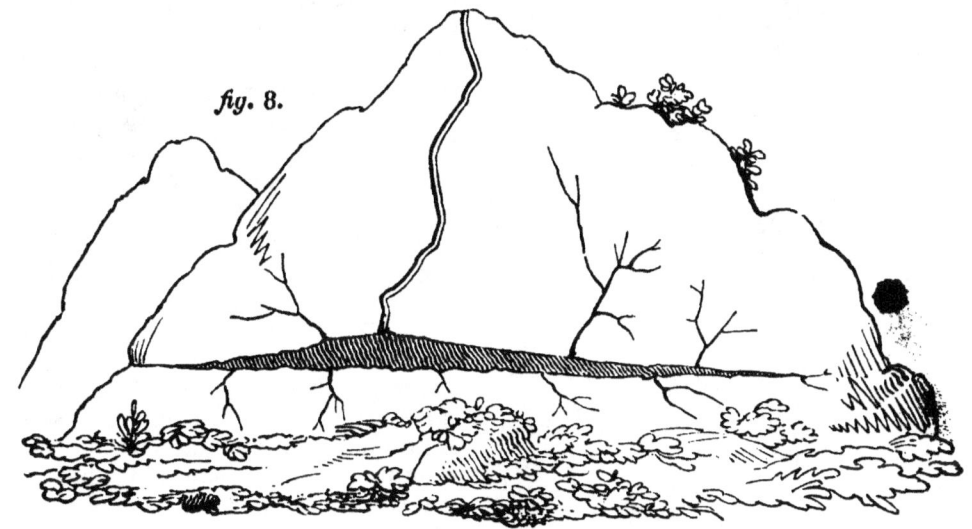

fig. 8.

that, in the course of time, a small crack of no more than an inch in diameter should be worn from above, 200 feet down to the layer of water; if the rain were to fill this crack, the mountain would be shaken, perhaps rent in pieces with the greatest violence, being blown up with a force equal to the pressure of above 5022 tons of water, though only about 2½ tons altogether had been actually applied. The same thing would happen if any one on the spot where there is such a layer of water below ground should bore down in sinking a well, or seeking for a spring, and then fill the tube with water; it is impossible to fix the limits to the convulsion which might ensue. This prodigious power however may be employed safely, and even beneficially. In the operations of nature, it is probably an important agent, though it has not been sufficiently attended to by philosophers in their attempts to explain natural appearances; and it is capable of being applied advantageously in the operations of art. It may plainly be used with great effect in mining. On a smaller scale, and as a power in machinery, it may certainly be employed far more extensively than it has hitherto been. A tube of a yard long, acting on a cavity of a yard square, will give a pressure equal to the weight of ¾ of a ton avoirdupois, if used with water; but quicksilver may be employed instead of water, and as it is between thirteen and fourteen times heavier, we shall have a power of ten tons, by the use of a tube and a few pounds of mercury; and in like manner the power of a ton weight may be obtained within the space of a square foot in breadth, by a tube a little less than three feet long, and of the bore of a common goose quill.

The instrument, or rather plaything, called the *Hydrostatic Bellows*, is constructed upon the same principle. It consists of two boards attached to one another by leather, going all round them, and making the space within water-tight; there is no valve as in the air-bellows, but instead of it, a hole is bored in the upper board, and a pipe inserted, through which water is poured so as to fill the space between the boards. If the boards be a foot and a half long, and sixteen inches broad, and you load the upper one with three hundred weight, a quarter of a pound of water poured through the tube, and rising only three feet in it, will raise the whole weight as high as the leather allows. In this way it will raise two stout men; and if, instead of pouring water into the pipe, the two men stand upon the upper board, and one of them blows into the pipe, the pressure thus made upon the water being conveyed in every direction, will produce the same effect, and raise them both. The smaller the bore of the pipe, the easier will they be raised, and by stopping it with the finger immediately after blowing, so as to keep in the air, they may keep themselves raised up. So when water is poured in, if the pipe be ever so small, and contain ever so little water, provided it be long enough, the weight will be raised by it.

A more striking as well as accurate manner of exhibiting this experiment was contrived by Ferguson, a man of great genius, who from the humble condition of a shepherd's boy raised himself to rank with the most useful philosophers of his age, and composed a work upon the different branches of Natural Philosophy that still holds a high place among the books which treat of those sciences, although he never had any further education from teachers than three months' reading and writing. A tube A B* (*fig.* 9.) is fixed upright in the end of a box C D E F, open at the top and on one side. The tube is bent at B,

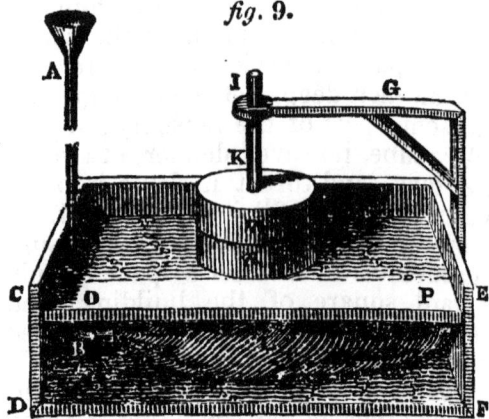

fig. 9.

and inserted in the neck of a bladder L, upon which is laid a board O P, and upon the board different weights *m n*, through a hole in each of which the pin I K, fixed in the board, passes; an arm G I, passes from the box to steady the pin; water is then poured through A B till it fills the bladder, and the bladder is stretched, and raises the board, as soon as the water rises in the tube, although the weights may be above sixteen pounds, and the water in the tube not a quarter of an ounce.

The uses to which this power may be applied are of great variety and extent; and this branch of art appears as yet to be in its infancy. There has, however, been a most valuable and ingenious application of it by the late Mr. Bramah, in what is called the *Hydrostatic Press*, by which a prodigious force is obtained, strictly upon this principle, with the greatest ease, and within a very small compass; so that a man shall, with a machine the size of a common teapot, standing before him on the table, cut through a thick bar of iron as easily as he could clip a piece of pasteboard with a pair of shears. The machine as most commonly used is thus constructed. E F (*fig.* 10.) is a solid mass of wood or masonry, rendered steady by its weight, or by being fixed in the ground. B represents a strong horizontal board, moveable up and down in grooves of the two uprights; and any substance to be pressed or broken, is placed in the space above it. The piston A, on which B rests, moves up and down in the hollow cylinder L, and fits the neck N, so as to be water-tight. From the cylinder runs a tube, of much less bore

---

* As the tube A B could not have sufficient length without encroaching too much upon the page, it is represented as if a part of it betwixt the extremites had been removed.

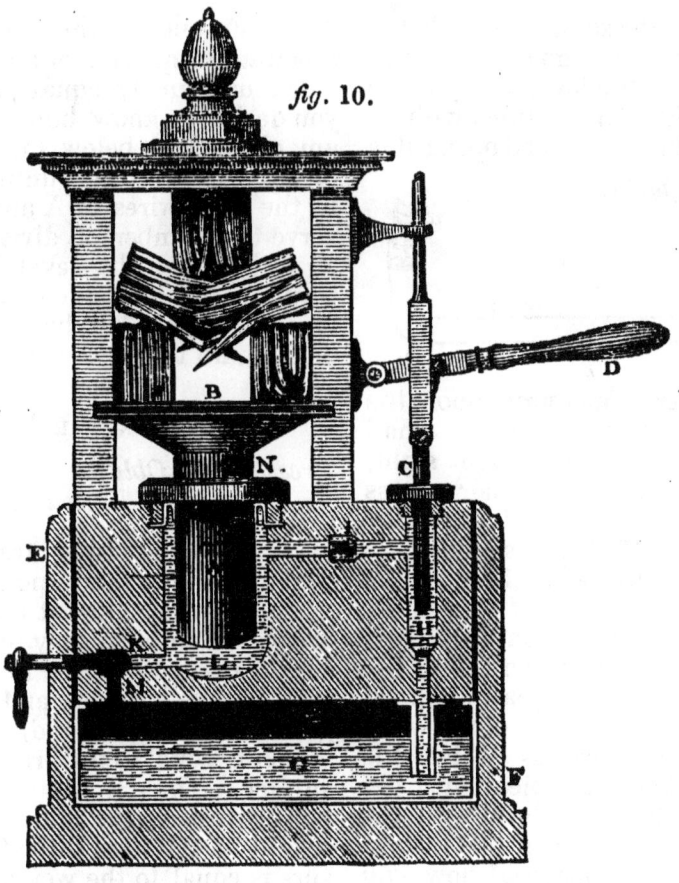

fig. 10.

than the cylinder L, having at the part I a valve opening towards the cylinder; and D is the handle of a forcing pump C H, by means of whose piston water can be forced under the piston A. K represents another valve which, relieved from the pressure of the adjacent screw, allows the water to flow back again through the pipe M into the reservoir G, when the solid A is required to descend. The pressure upon the bottom of the piston at L, will be to the pressure upon the water in H, by means of the piston rod C, as the size of the under surface of A, to the size of the surface H, or as the section of that part of the cylinder occupied by the respective pistons. It is therefore as if we had to compare the pressure of water of the same depth, but on different surfaces; and this is in proportion to the surfaces. If the piston H is half an inch diameter, and the cylinder A one foot, the pressure of the water on the bottom of the cylinder will be to the pressure of the smaller piston on the water at H, as a square foot to a quarter of a square inch (the areas of circles being as the squares of their diameters), that is, as 144 square inches to a quarter of a square inch, or as 576 to 1; and therefore if the pressure of a ton weight be given by means of the lever D, the cylinder A will be moved upwards, and be forced or pressed against whatever is placed in the space above it, with the weight of 576 tons. It is evident that this power may be increased without any other bounds than the strength of the materials, either by machinery, which will increase the force upon the water in the pump C H; or by increasing the disproportion between the diameters of the two pistons, or by both. Thus, if a pressure of two tons be given by a pump of only a quarter of an inch, and the cylinder be a yard in diameter, the pressure upwards will be equal to the weight of 41472 tons; and this prodigious effect will be produced by the agency of less than a pound of water. Such a force is much too great for the strength of any materials which we can employ. But within the space of nine or ten inches square and a foot high, a force of 5 or 600 tons may easily be brought to bear upon any substance which it is wished to press, to tear up, to cut in pieces, or to pull asunder.

Upon the tendency of all the parts of fluids to dispose themselves in a plain or level surface, depends the making of *levelling* instruments, or instruments for ascertaining whether any surface is level, or any line horizontal; for finding what point is on the same level with any given point, and how much any point is above or below the level of any other point. A B (*fig.* 11.) is a tube, with its two ends, *d, c*, turned up, and open; it is

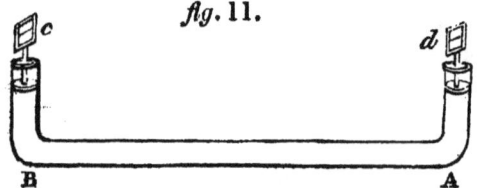

fig. 11.

filled with water or mercury: upon the fluid at *d* and at *c* are placed small floats, each carrying an upright sight, or square with a wire or hair across it; and the sights are placed across the direction A B. If the instrument is placed on any surface, or held in the hand, whether level or not, on looking through the sight *c* you find the cross wire of *c* cover the cross wire of *d*, because the fluid stands equally high at both ends; and if the two cross wires cover any object towards which the sights are pointed, that object must necessarily be on the same level with the instrument. In the use of this instrument it is quite immaterial how you place or hold it, whether level or not. The common spirit-level is a tube filled with spirit of wine, excepting a small space, in which there is a bubble of air left; and then the tube is hermetically sealed, or closed by being melted with a blow-pipe. When the tube is laid on a level surface, the air-bubble stands in the very middle of the tube; when the surface slopes, the bubble rises to the higher end. A B (*fig.* 12.) is the spirit-level, and

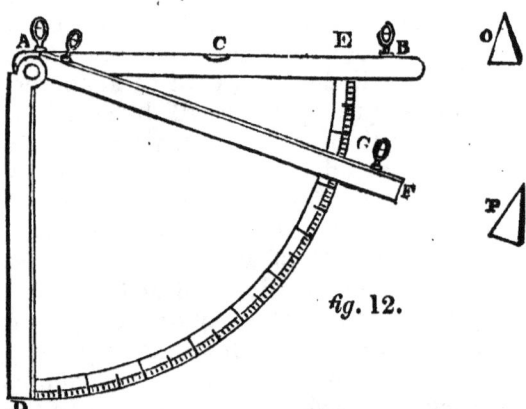

fig. 12.

sights being fixed at A and B, when A B is so placed that the bubble C stands at the middle point, any object O covered by the two cross wires of the sights A and B, is on the same level with the surface where A B is placed. Then there is a limb A F, with sights at A and F, and moving round A, on a quadrant or quarter of a circle D E divided into ninety equal parts. When you desire to know how many degrees any object P is below the level of A B, or of O, you turn A F until P is covered by the cross wires of A and F, and observe the number of divisions in E G. If P is above the level of A B, you turn up the instrument, and raise the arm A F above A B, by turning it round on A, until the cross wires cover P.

Chapter IV.

Pressure on Oblique Surfaces—Centre of Pressure.

Hitherto we have treated of the pressure of any fluid upon a horizontal or level surface; and it is always easily found. You have only to multiply the height or depth of the fluid by the extent of the surface, and the product gives the bulk of fluid, the weight of which is equal to the pressure upon the surface. Thus if the surface is three feet by two, or six square feet, and the height of the fluid three feet, the pressure is equal to the weight of eighteen cubic or solid feet of the fluid. If it is water, a cubic foot of which weighs $62\frac{1}{2}$ pounds, the pressure is equal to 1125 pounds.

But if the surface is not horizontal, a different rule must be applied; for then the pressure is equal to the weight of a bulk of fluid found by multiplying the extent of the surface into the depth of the centre of gravity of the surface; that is, of the point, which, being supported, the whole surface remains balanced or at rest. If A B (*fig.* 13.) is the surface of the

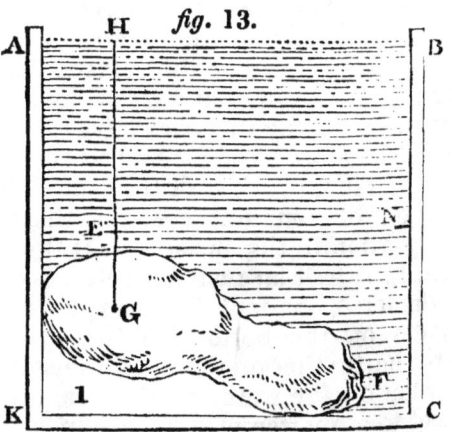

fig. 13.

fluid, and E F I the sloping surface upon which it presses, G its centre of gravity, and G H the depth of G; the pressure on E F I is the weight of a body of the fluid equal to E F I multiplied by G H;

HYDROSTATICS.

or a body or column of the fluid, whose base is E F I, and height G H. Thus if the surface E F I be removed, and the vessel A B C K be a cube, or one with bottom and sides, A K, K C, and B C, equal to each other; the centre of gravity of the sides being in the middle point N, the pressure upon each side is that of the body of fluid found by multiplying K C and N B together, or half the whole fluid in the vessel; while the pressure on the bottom is equal to the weight of the whole fluid.

In this manner we can easily find the pressure upon a dam, whether it is upright or sloping in the water. We have only to take half the depth of the water, and multiply it by the superficial extent of the dam; this gives the bulk of water whose weight is the pressure on the dam. Suppose the water to be four feet deep, and twelve broad; the dam, if perpendicular, is forty-eight square feet; the centre of gravity being at half the depth, or two feet, the pressure is equal to ninety-six cubic feet of water, or 6000 pounds exactly; about two tons and three-quarters.

The pressure against the upright sides of a cylinder filled with water, such as a pipe, or well, or the cylinder of a steam-engine, may be found in the same way. Multiply the curve surface under water by the depth of its centre of gravity, which is half the depth of the water. If the water stands twenty feet high, and the diameter or bore of the cylinder is four feet; the curve surface being about $251\frac{1}{3}$ square feet, and the centre of gravity 10 feet deep, the pressure is equal to the weight of above 2513 cubic feet of water, or above 70 tons[*].

It is convenient in practice to bear in mind, that the pressure of fresh water, the fluid most commonly the subject of calculation, is always about thirteen pounds upon every square inch of level bottom, at the depth of 30 feet, whatever the form or position of the sides may be; and so in proportion for greater or lesser depths; and that if the sides are perpendicular, whatever may be their shape, that is, provided the width of the vessel or pond is the same all the way down, the pressure on every square inch of the sides is nearly thirteen pounds at the depth of 30 feet; and so in proportion for greater or lesser depths.

The same rule extends to finding the pressure upon surfaces, whatever be their shape, whether plain or curve; whatever be their position, horizontal, perpendicular, or slanting: It is always the pressure of a body of water equal to the product of the surface by the depth of its centre of gravity. Thus, if you would find the pressure upon the sloping side of a pond; drop a line from the water to the middle point of the sloping side between the water's edge and the bottom, and multiply the length of the plum-line under water by the extent of the side covered with water. If the plum-line is ten feet, there will be upon every six feet square of that side a pressure of about ten tons. So if you would find the pressure on a hemispherical vessel, or half globe, just covered by the water, multiply half the depth of the water by the curve surface of the vessel. If the diameter is a yard, the surface will be about $14\frac{2}{15}$ feet; consequently the pressure is equal to $10\frac{3}{5}$ cubic feet of water, or nearly six hundred weight.

The pressure upon a number of surfaces is, in like manner, equal to the pressure of a body of fluid, found by multiplying the whole extent of the surfaces into the depth of their common centre of gravity below the surface of the fluid; and thus the finding the pressure is in every case reduced to finding the centre of gravity.

The increase of pressure in proportion to the depth of the fluid proves the necessity of making the sides of pipes or masonry, in which fluids are to be contained, stronger the deeper they go; and shows that it is a superfluous expense to make them equally thick and strong from the top downwards. If they are thick enough for the great pressure below, they will be thicker than is required for resisting the smaller pressure above. The same remark applies to floodgates, dams, and banks. If the pipes or cylinders placed upright have the same bore all the way down, their walls may taper from the bottom upwards, provided the thickness has been ascertained which is sufficient to resist the pressure at the greatest depth. So in a dam or flood-

---

[*] The circumference of the circle is to its diameter nearly as 3.14159, (or a little less than $3\frac{3}{20}$) to 1. The surface of the sphere or globe is in the same proportion to the square of its diameter. The curved surface of the cylinder is in the same proportion to the product of its length multiplied by its bore or diameter.

gate, one side being perpendicular, the other may slant towards the top. In constructing a bank of a given quantity of materials, against whose sloping side the water presses, it is found by mathematical reasoning, that it will just resist the water, if the square of its thickness at the base (that is, the thickness multiplied by itself) is to the square of its perpendicular height, as the weight of a given bulk of water, say a cubic foot, is to the weight of the same bulk of the material the bank is made of, increased by twice the aforesaid weight of the given bulk of water. Thus if the bank is of common stone, which is 2 times heavier than water; the thickness at the base should be to the height nearly as 1 to 2. Therefore, a bank of 3 feet base and 6 feet height, will answer the purpose. If the bank be of fir timber, which is little more than half the weight of water, the base being a yard, the height should be about 4 feet 9 inches. These proportions correspond to an equilibrium; but if stability be the object, the base must always have a greater ratio to the height than is here assigned. If the height and thickness be to each other as 10 to 7, stability is always ensured, whatever be the specific gravity of the materials.

If a fluid presses upon a surface, there is a point of that surface at which if a force be applied in the same line with the pressure of the fluid, and equal to the whole of that pressure, but in a contrary direction, it will exactly balance or counteract the whole pressure of the fluid; and this point is called the *centre of pressure*. If the water in the upper part of the vessel A O C D Q H F (*fig.* 14.) presses against the surface B C D E, there is a

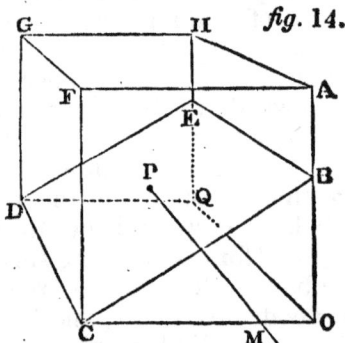

fig. 14.

point P, in that surface, against which, if a force be applied in the opposite direction P M, and equal to the whole pressure of the water upon B C D E, it will support B C D E, and prevent the pressure from turning it or moving it in any way. It is here supposed that there is no water below the surface B C D E, but that, if unsupported, the water above would press it down. If the opposite force were applied to any other point than P, the centre of pressure, the water would make the surface turn round upon that point.

To find this point often becomes of great importance. It may be the best means of propping a floodgate or other surface from behind against the pressure of water upon its face. The position of the point varies according to the figure of the surface and its depth under water. If the surface is a rectangle of any kind, as a square, standing upright, and the water rises to its upper edge, the centre of pressure is two-thirds down the line, dropped perpendicularly from the middle of that upper edge. If the surface is a triangle, whose point is at the surface of the water, the centre of pressure is three-fourths down the perpendicular dropped from the point; and if both sides of the triangle are equal, the centre is in that perpendicular. If the sides are unequal, but the triangle is rightangled at the base, the centre of pressure is three-fourths down the perpendicular side, and three-eighths of the base distant from that side.

Thus if A M (*fig.* 15.) is the surface of the water, A C D M the upright

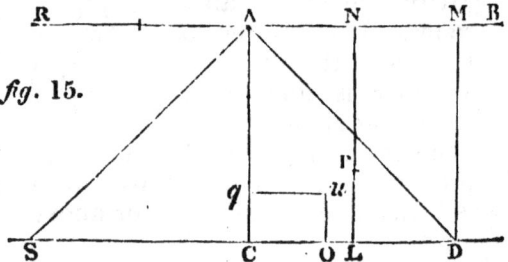

fig. 15.

and square surface against which the water presses, N, the middle point of A M, and N L a perpendicular from N to the base of the surface, N P being two-thirds of N L, P is the centre of pressure upon A C D M. If A S D be a triangle, and A S equal to A D, q being taken at three-fourths down A C, is the centre of pressure on the triangle A S D. If A C D be a triangle, rightangled at C, A q being three-fourths of A C, and $q\,u$ or C O three-eighths of C D, u is the centre of pressure upon A C D. Therefore, if a force be applied on the opposite side of A C D M at P, of A S D at q, and of A C D at u, equal to the pressure of the water on these surfaces respectively, and perpendicular to them, the whole surface in each case will be supported. Now we have found before that the whole pressure upon any rectangular figure upright in the water, is the weight of a bulk of water equal to the surface, multiplied by half its depth below water. We can, therefore, see at once the force required to balance the water, and the point where it must be applied. Multiply the height of the surface by its breadth, and the product by half the height, (the water being supposed to stand as high as the upper edge of the surface;) then apply a force or a resistance equal to this weight of water, in a horizontal line against a point situated two-thirds down the perpendicular, from the middle point of the upper edge of the surface, the whole pressure of the water will be balanced. Suppose the height and breadth of the sluice or floodgate are equal, it being a square of six feet; the pressure on it will be 108 cubic feet of water, or about three tons. A force of this amount, then, applied on the back of the sluice, in the middle line, and four feet from the top, will be sufficient to counteract the pressure of the water, without any assistance from the hinges or sides of the gate.

The strain which the water exerts upon the hinges of the floodgate is the pressure to make it turn round on its lower side; and it is found by multiplying one-sixth of the breadth of the gate into the cube of the height, and taking a bulk of water equal to the product. The pressure which the water exerts to open the gate, or make it move round on its hinges, is found by multiplying one-fourth of the square of the height into the square of the breadth, and taking a bulk of water equal to the product. The proportions of these two pressures may therefore be easily found. They are to one another as one-sixth of the breadth multiplied by the cube of the height, to one-fourth of the squares, of height and breadth multiplied together; that is, as one-sixth of the height to one-fourth of the breadth, or as twice the height to thrice the breadth. When, therefore, the gate is a square, the height and breadth being equal, the pressures are as two to three; and the same gate at the same time has half as much more force exerted to make it open on its hinges, as to make it turn over on its base; supposing that there were either no resistance from the hinges, or that there were hinges at the base. Thus, if the gate is a square of six feet, the pressure to turn it on its bottom is one-sixth of 1296 cubic feet of water, or 216 feet; and to turn it on its hinge, one-fourth of 1296, or 324 feet. Therefore there will be a force of six tons pressing it round on its bottom, and nine tons pressing it open on its hinges.

Chapter V.

Specific Gravity—The Hydrometer and Areometer.

When a solid body is plunged in any liquid, it must displace a quantity of that liquid exactly equal to its own bulk. Hence, by measuring the bulk of the liquid so displaced, we can ascertain precisely the bulk of the body; for the liquid can be put into any shape, as that of cubical feet or inches, by being poured into a vessel of that shape, divided into equal parts; or the vessel in which the body is plunged may be of that shape, and so divided. If the width of the vessel is four inches by three, or twelve square inches, and divided on the upright side into twelfths of an inch—when a body of an irregular shape, as a bit of rough gold or silver, is plunged in it, every division that the water rises will show that one-twelfth of twelve cubic inches, or one cubic inch of water, has been displaced; so that if it rises two divisions, the body contains exactly two solid inches of metal. And this is by far the easiest way of measuring the solid contents of irregular bodies.

When a body is so plunged, it will remain in whatever place of the fluid it is put in, if it be of the same weight with the fluid, that is, if the bulk of the body weighs as much as the same bulk of the fluid; for in this case it will be the same thing as if the fluid were not displaced; and as an equal quantity of the fluid would have remained at rest there, being equally pressed on all sides, so will the solid body: it will be pressed from below with the same weight of fluid as from above. But if the body be heavier than the fluid, bulk for bulk, this balance will be destroyed, and the weight of the fluid pressing from above, will be greater than that pressing from below, by the weight of the solid body, which will therefore sink to the bottom. So if it be lighter than an equal bulk of the fluid, it will rise through the fluid to the surface. But if a solid, heavier than the fluid, be plunged to a depth as many times greater than its thickness, as the solid is heavier than the fluid, and there protected by any means from the pressure of the fluid above, it will float, notwithstanding its weight, because the pressure from below being in proportion to the depth, will counterbalance the weight of the body, and there will be no pressure from above, except the weight of the body. Thus, lead is somewhat above eleven times heavier than water. If a cube of lead be placed so as to press closely against the bottom of a wooden pipe one foot square, closed at the top, and plunged twelve feet deep, and held upright, it will there swim; the water pressing it upwards with a force greater than its weight, and there being no pressure from the water downwards. So if a body lighter than water, as cork, be placed at the bottom of a vessel, and so smoothly cut that no water gets between its lower surface and the surface of the bottom, it will not rise, but remain fixed there, because it is pressed downwards by the water from above, and there is no pressure from below to counterbalance that from above.

It follows from these principles, that if any body be weighed in the air, and then weighed in any liquid, it will seem to lose as much as an equal bulk of the liquid weighs. Not that the body really loses its weight, but that it is pressed upwards by a force equal to the weight of the liquid the place of which it fills. Thus, if a piece of lead weigh an ounce before being plunged in water, that is, requires an ounce weight on the opposite scale to balance it; if you hang it by a thread from its own scale, and let it be plunged so that the water in a full jar covers it, a quantity of water equal to the bulk of the lead will run over the sides of the jar, and a number of grains equal to the weight of this quantity of water must be taken out of the opposite scale, to restore the balance; for the lead is now pressed downwards in the water with a force not equal to its own weight, but to the difference between its own weight and that of an equal bulk of the water. And in this manner we can determine the relative weights of all bodies, or the proportion which they bear to each other in weight; which is called their *specific gravity:* that is, their weight in kind, and sometimes their *relative gravity*, that is, their weight compared with the weight of other bodies. By weighing a known bulk, as a cubic foot or a cubic inch of any two substances, we can find their specific gravity; or their gravity as compared with each other: if, for instance, we found a cubic inch of iron weighed 1948 grains, and a cubic inch of lead 2858, we should say, that the specific gravities of the two substances were in the proportion of 3 to $4\frac{2}{3}$ nearly; and so we might find the specific gravity of a solid substance, as compared with that of a liquid, by weighing an equal bulk of each. But this operation is extremely difficult, because it requires the substances compared to be fashioned accurately into the same shape and size; and when we are not allowed to change their figure, the comparison cannot be made at all. Thus we could not ascertain the specific gravity of precious stones, crystals, metallic ores, or animal and vegetable substances, without in effect destroying them. But the *Hydrostatic Balance*, upon the principles now explained, affords a perfectly easy and most accurate method of comparing all substances, solid and fluid. We have only to weigh any substance first in air, and then in water; the difference of the weights is the weight of a bulk of water equal to the bulk of the substance; and by comparing any other substance with water, in like manner, we ascertain its specific gravity, as compared with that of the first substance. And this operation may be performed with substances lighter than water, either by fixing them to a stiff pin, attached to the bottom of the scale, taking care to trim the balance before the pin is plunged into the water; or by loading the substance with a known weight of something heavier than water, and making an allowance for the load's difference of weight in air and water.

It is evident also that the same principle enables us to ascertain the specific gravities of different fluids. For if the same substance be weighed in two fluids, the weight which it loses in each is as the specific gravity of that fluid. Thus a cubic inch of lead loses 253 grains when weighed in water, and only 209 grains when weighed in rectified spirits; therefore a cubic inch of rectified spirit weighs 209 grains, an

HYDROSTATICS.

equal bulk of water weighing 253; and so the specific gravity of the water is about a fourth greater than that of the spirit.

Upon this principle the *Hydrometer* is constructed: its name is derived from two Greek words signifying *measure of water*. There are various kinds of hydrometers. One is a glass or copper ball with a stem, on which is marked a scale of equal parts or degrees. The point to which the stem sinks in any liquid being ascertained, and marked on this scale, we can tell how many degrees any other liquid is heavier or lighter, by observing the point to which the stem sinks in it. Another and a very simple Hydrometer is formed by preparing a number of hollow glass beads of different weights, but the proportions of which are known, and the beads marked accordingly; they are then successively dropped in the fluid to be examined, until one is found which neither sinks nor comes up to the surface, but remains at rest, wherever it is placed in the liquid. You thus ascertain that the liquid is of the same specific gravity with this bead. If the same bead be dropt into another liquid, and sinks, that liquid must be lighter than the first; if the bead comes to the top, the second liquid is heavier than the first; and by trying the liquid with the other beads until one is found which neither sinks nor floats, you ascertain the relative weight of the liquid by the number of the bead.

A Hydrometer of great delicacy and peculiarly useful for measuring the specific gravity of different waters, and thereby ascertaining their degrees of purity, consists of a ball of glass three inches diameter, with another joining it and opening into it, of one inch diameter, B and C, (*fig.* 16.) and a brass neck *d*, into which is screwed a wire *a o*, about ten inches long and 1-40th of an inch diameter, divided into inches and tenths of an inch. The whole weight of this instrument is 4000 grs. when loaded with shot in the lower ball.

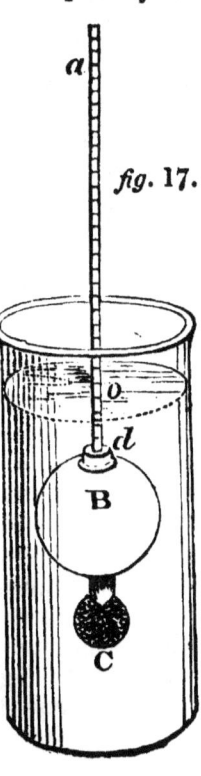

fig. 17.

It is found that when plunged into water in the jar, a grain laid upon the top *a* makes it sink one inch; therefore a tenth of a grain sinks it a tenth of an inch. Now it will stand in one kind of water a tenth of an inch lower than in another, which shows that a bulk of one kind of water equal to the bulk of the instrument weighs one-tenth of a grain less than an equal bulk of the other kind of water; so that a difference in specific gravity of one part in forty thousand is thus detected. This weight of 4000 grs. is convenient for comparing water; but the quantity of shot in the lower ball may be varied, so as to make it lighter or heavier, and so adapt it to measure the specific gravities of lighter or heavier liquids. It will always be an accurate and very delicate measure for liquids of nearly the same weight. Indeed its delicacy is so great, that an impurity too slight to be detected by any ordinary test, or by the taste, will be discovered by this instrument.

The *Areometer* invented by M. De Parcieux of Paris, and so named from two Greek words, signifying *measure of weight*, is more simple and affords a very accurate comparison of different liquids. It is only a different form of the instrument just described. A glass phial, about two inches or two inches and a half in diameter, and seven or eight long, with a plane or round bottom, is corked tight, and into the cork is fixed a perfectly straight wire of about 1-12th inch diameter, and thirty inches long. The phial is loaded with shot, so as to make it sink in the heaviest liquid to be examined, leaving the wire just below the surface. There is a cylinder of glass, about three or three and a half inches diameter, and three or four feet long, with a scale of equal parts on the side. The liquor to be tried is put in this; and the scale marks the point to which the top of the wire sinks. This instrument is so sensible, that if it stands at any point in water of the common temperature, and the sun's rays fall upon the water, the wire will sink several inches, from the slight increase of heat causing an increase of bulk, and consequently a diminution of relative weight in the water; and it will rise again when carried into the shade. A pinch of salt or sugar thrown in makes it rise some inches, and a little spirits poured in makes it sink. With one of these instruments, weighing somewhat less than twenty-four ounces, and plunged in water, there is a fall or rise of above half an inch for every 1-17424th part of the water displaced; so that a difference of the hundred-thousandth part is easily perceived.

The principal use of the Hydrometer is to ascertain the specific gravity of spirits, and to detect adulteration or mixture of water with it. But it is equally applicable to find the specific gravity of any other fluids. Thus milk is about 1-31 part heavier than water; and therefore the instrument will easily shew if water has been mixed with it. Accordingly, in Switzerland and the North of Italy, where the peasants all bring their milk every evening to a common dairy, and having it measured each time, are allowed a portion of cheese at the end of the season, according to the quantity of the milk carried in the books to the credit of their account, a Hydrometer is used to detect any mixture of water, which would make the milk lighter.

By means of the same kind we can ascertain the adulteration of solid substances, as metals, mixed with others of different specific gravity. An instrument upon this principle was constructed by Mr. Bradford, calculated to shew how much alloy there was in the gold coin, and also whether that alloy was silver or a lighter metal.

The proposition which forms the foundation of this branch of Hydrostatics, that a solid plunged in a fluid displaces a quantity of the fluid equal to its bulk, was discovered by Archimedes, one of the greatest mathematicians of ancient times, in consequence of Hiero, king of Syracuse, his friend and patron, and himself an eminent philosopher, and, it needs hardly be added, a virtuous and patriotic prince, having set him a problem to solve upon the adulteration of metals. Hiero had given a certain quantity of gold to an artist to make into a crown, and suspecting, from the lightness of the crown, that some silver had been used in making it, he begged Archimedes to investigate the matter. It is said that while this great man was intent upon the question, he chanced to observe, in bathing, the water which ran over the sides of the bath; and immediately perceiving that, as the water was equal to the bulk of his body, this would furnish him with the means of detecting the adulteration, by trying how much water a certain weight of silver displaced, how much a certain weight of gold, and how much a certain mixture of the two, he rushed out of the chamber, exclaiming, "*I have found it! I have found it!*"

But no test of this kind can ever be accurate either with respect to solids or liquids, unless we have previously ascertained by experiment that the substances mixed do not enter into such a chemical union as alters their internal structure; for in many cases this takes place, and the specific gravity of the parts in composition is thus different from their specific gravity when separate. A piece of gold, in which there should be a hollow space filled with silver, could, by the process of weighing in water, be accurately proved; for we should thus ascertain that a given bulk fell short of the requisite weight by a certain quantity. But if the two metals were melted together, and chemically united, they might very possibly form such a compound as should have its specific gravity greater or less than the medium of the specific gravities of the gold and silver; and so of fluids. Before, therefore, the Hydrostatic Balance or the Hydrometer can be relied on as proofs of admixture, trials must be made with the simple substances, and their compounds in known proportions; and the effects of the mixture being thus ascertained in these cases, the weight becomes an accurate test of the degree of adulteration; because we have learnt what allowance to make for the effects of chemical combination.

But there is one circumstance which must, in all trials for ascertaining specific gravity, be taken into the account; and that is, the Heat or temperature of the substances at the time of the experiment. The effect of heat is to increase the bulk of all bodies; consequently to make them specifically lighter, by making the same quantity of matter fill a larger space; and different substances are expanded in different degrees by it. Thus water, when heated from 60 degrees of Fahrenheit's thermometer to 100, is increased in bulk 1-167th part, mercury not above 1-243; consequently, a cubic inch of water weighs about a grain and a half lighter (the 167th part of 253, the weight of the cubic inch, when of the ordinary heat of 60 degrees). A cubic inch of mercury, equally heated, weighs 14 grs.

less, which bears a considerably smaller proportion to its former weight of 3415 grs. The comparative trials are generally made at a temperature of 60, at which rain-water weighs 1000 ounces avoirdupois, or 62½ pounds, by the cubic foot, or 253 grs. by the cubic inch. Spirits expand and become lighter by means of heat, in a greater proportion; consequently they are heaviest in winter. A cubic inch of brandy has been found by many trials to weigh 10 grs. more in winter than in summer, the difference being between 4 drs. 32 grs. and 4 drs. 42 grs. Of this, liquor-merchants are often found to take advantage, making their purchases in winter rather than in summer, because they get in reality a greater quantity in the same bulk, buying by measure.

If two liquids of different specific gravities are poured into a bent tube, so as to meet at the bottom or middle point, they will balance each other, and each keep its own side of the tube, if they are in height inversely as their specific gravity; the heaviest being the lowest. Thus mercury, being thirteen times and a half heavier than water, if you pour in so much mercury as will stand 2 in. high, and so much water as will stand 27, they will balance each other, and meet at the bottom; thus, in the tube A B, (*fig.* 18.) D I being the mercury, and E I the water, and C the middle point, if E G, the perpendicular from the surface of the water to the level at G is thirteen and a half times D F, the perpendicular from the surface of the mercury to the horizontal line F G, passing through the contiguous surfaces of the water and mercury, the water will balance the mercury. Nor will this depend at all upon the figure of the tube, or the quantity of the two fluids: for whatever be the shape or inclination of the branches A C and B C, the balance will be kept, provided the heights E G and F D are in the same proportion. Thus, the part E C K in the tube A C D, (*fig.* 19.)

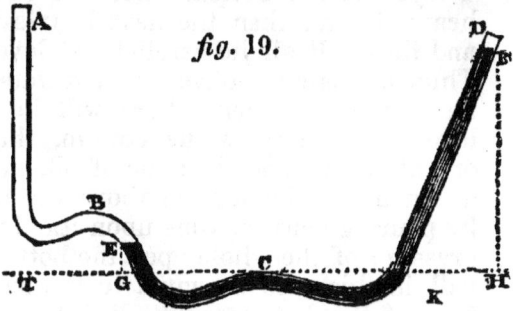

fig. 19.

may contain as much or more mercury than K F does water; still the water will balance the mercury, the height F H of its surface being thirteen times and a half the height E G of the mercury. Nor is it at all necessary that the branches of the tube should be of the same bore; for the one with the mercury (*fig.* 20.) may be much wider than the one with the water;

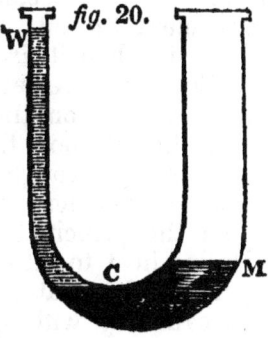

fig. 20.

and the smaller weight of water will balance the greater weight of mercury, provided the water stand thirteen times and a half higher than the mercury. But if the tube has both branches perpendicular, an easy method is furnished of comparing the specific gravity of liquids. We have only to divide the upright branches into equal parts, and observe at what height above the common level the two fluids stand in them when they are balanced (*fig.* 21.); their specific gravities are inversely as the heights: if oil, for instance, stands at 10 in one branch, while water stands at nine in the other, we infer that the specific gravity of the oil is to that of the water as nine to ten.

If there are various liquids of different specific gravities, and which do not mix together, all poured into the same vessel, they will arrange themselves so that the heaviest will make a layer at the bottom, then the next heaviest, and then the next heaviest; and they will all lie parallel and level. Thus if mercury, olive oil, and water, be poured together, there will be a layer of mercury at the bottom, then one of water, and then one of oil, and a fourth may be formed above the oil by pouring spirit of wine upon it. The pressure of the whole upon the bottom will in this case be equal to the surface of the bottom multiplied, by the sum of the products of each layer's depth into its specific gravity.

If the lighter fluid be poured in first, and then the heavier, the lighter will rise through it and float on the top; and if any thing be done to alter the weight of the lower layer, it will rise through the upper one. Thus, while the oil is floating on the water, if, by heating the bottom of the vessel you heat the water, it becomes lighter and rises through the oil, until the oil too gets heated, when it rises through the water. So when a vessel containing any liquid is placed on the fire, the parts of the liquid next the fire get heated, and rise up through the colder parts which are heavier: and this is found to be the principal manner of communicating heat to all the parts of a liquid; for if the heat is applied at the top, it can only with great difficulty be conducted through the liquid either sideways or downwards; but when applied below, the parts as they are heated become enlarged and lighter: they rise up to the top, and they heat the others in their progress, while those others, being still somewhat heavier, sink down and are heated fully in their turn. By degrees the whole liquid gets so hot that the parts next the bottom are converted into steam or vapour, which rises through the rest of the liquid in bubbles to the top, and there flies off till the whole liquid is evaporated. This is the common process of *Boiling*.

When a solid body floats in a liquid, its weight is equal to the weight of liquid which the body displaces: but in order that it may float at rest, and not roll round, its centre of gravity must be in the perpendicular, which runs through the centre of gravity of the part of the liquid displaced by it; for the pressure upwards of the liquid is in this line, and unless that pressure is in a direction running through the body's centre of gravity, it cannot support the centre, and when the centre is not supported, the body is not at rest, but must fall; or if the centre is kept up by the fluid, the body must still turn round when the upward pressure bears on some other part of it. When the line which joins the centre of gravity of the whole body and the centre of gravity of the part under water, is perpendicular to the surface of the water, the body will float at rest in the water. In order, therefore, to make a body of any figure float steadily, and, as it were, balance itself in the water, with a certain proportion of its bulk under water, the depth to which it must be sunk must be ascertained by the proportion of its specific gravity to that of the water, and the position must be ascertained by making the centre of gravity of the whole body and the part under water be in the plumb-line or line perpendicular to the upper surface of the water.

Chapter VI.

Specific Gravities of Bodies.

By experiments with hydrostatic balances, and with hydrometers of different kinds, the comparative gravities of bodies have been ascertained with great nicety. The following Table exhibits in one connected view the results of those trials, collected from a great variety of sources, and reduced to one common measure.

In consulting it, this may further be borne in mind; that water is taken as the unit for solids and liquids; atmospheric air for gases. Thus water is 1.000; mercury, at the common temperature, 13.58: whence we conclude, that mercury is between 13 and 14 times heavier than water. So common air is 1.000; chlorine (or oxymuriatic acid) 2.500; and hydrogen 0.069. Whence we conclude, that chlorine is two and a half times heavier, and hydrogen between fourteen and fifteen times lighter than common air. Again: one cubic foot of water weighs 1000 ounces; therefore all the numbers in the

HYDROSTATICS.

Table for solids and liquids represent the absolute weight of a cubic foot of each; if we remove the decimal point, and add a cypher where there are only two decimals — thus a cubic foot of mercury weighs 13580 ounces and a cubic foot of bar-iron 7788 ounces.

To ascertain, in like manner, the absolute weight of the gases, we have only to observe that 100 cubic inches of common air weigh 30.50 grs.; and as there are 1728 cubic inches in a cubic foot, the simple method of calculation will stand thus: — As $100 : 30.50$ grs. :: $1728 : 527.04$ grs., the weight of a cubic foot of common air.

In order to ascertain the weight of a cubic foot of any other kind of gas, it is necessary merely to observe its specific gravity in relation to that of common air; for instance, chlorine has a specific gravity $= 2.5$: hence a cubic foot of chlorine will weigh 2.5 times as much as the same bulk of common air; thus $527.04 \times 2.5 = 1317.60$ grs. the weight of a cubic foot of chlorine.

If we wish to know the weight of a cubic foot of any gas lighter than common air, we also compare their specific gravities. Thus the specific gravity of ammoniacal gas is 0.5, and that of atmospheric air being $= 1$; then $1728 \div 2 = 864$ grs. will be the weight of a cubic foot of ammoniacal gas. And so on for all other gaseous bodies.

TABLE OF SPECIFIC GRAVITIES.

Acid, Acetic	1.062
Arsenic	3.391
Arsenious	3.728
Benzoic	0.667
Boracic, crystallized	1.479
Do. fused	1.803
Citric	1.034
Formic	1.116
Fluoric	1.060
Molybdic	3.460
Muriatic	1.200
Nitric	1.271
Do. highly concentrated	1.593
Phosphoric, liquid	1.558
Do. solid	2.800
Sulphuric	1.850
Agate	2.590
Alcohol, absolute	0.797
Do. highly rectified	0.809
Do. of commerce	0.835
Alum	1.714
Amber from 1.065 to	1.100
Ambergris from 0.780 to	0.926
Amethyst, common	2.750
oriental	3.391
Amianthus from 1.000 to	2.313
Ammonia, aqueous	0.875
Arragonite	2.900
Azure-stone	2.850
Barytes, Sulphate of, from 4.000 to	4.865
Do. Carbonate of, from 4.100 to	4.600
Basaltes from 2.421 to	3.000
Beryl, oriental	3.549
Do. occidental	2.723
Blood, human	1.053
Do. crassamentum of	1.245
Do. serum of	1.030
Borax	1.714
Butter	0.942
Camphor	0.988
Caoutchouc, or India rubber	0.933
Carnelian, speckled	2.613
Chalcedony, common, from 2.600 to	2.65
Chalk, from 2.252 to	2.657
Chrysolite	3.400
Chrystalline Lens of the Eye	1.100
Cinnabar, from Almaden	6.902
Coals from 1.020 to	1.300
Copal	1.045
Coral, red from 2.630 to	2.857
white from 2.540 to	2.570
Corundum	3.710
Cyder	1.018
Diamond, oriental, colourless	3.521
Do. coloured varieties, from 3.523 to	3.550
Do. Brazilian	3.444
Do. coloured varieties, from 3.518 to	3.550
Dolomite from 2.540 to	2.830
Dragon's Blood (a resin)	1.204
Ether, Acetic	0.866
Muriatic	0.729
Nitric	0.908
Sulphuric from 0.632 to	0.775
Emerald from 2.600 to	2.770
Euclase from 2.900 to	3.300
Fat of Beef	0.923
Hogs	0.936
Mutton	0.923
Veal	0.934
Felspar from 2.438 to	2.700
Flint, black	2.582
Gamboge	1.222
Garnet, precious, from 4.000 to	4.230
Garnet, common, from 3.576 to	3.700
Gases, — Atmospheric Air	1.000
Ammoniacal	0.590
Carbonic Acid	1.527
Carbonic Oxide	0.972
Gases, Carburetted Hydrogen	0.972
Chlorine	2.500
Chlorocarbonous Acid	3.472
Chloroprussic Acid	2.152
Cyanogen	1.805
Euchlorine	2.440
Fluoboric Acid	2.371
Fluosilicic Acid	3.632
Hydriodic Acid	4.340
Hydrogen	0.069
Muriatic Acid	1.284
Nitric Oxide	1.041
Nitrogen	0.972
Nitrous Acid	2.638
Nitrous Oxide	1.527
Oxygen	1.111
Phosphuretted Hydrogen	0.902
Prussic Acid	0.937
Sub-carburetted Hydrogen	0.555
Sub-phosphuretted ditto	0.972
Sulphuretted do.	1.180
Sulphurous Acid	2.222
Glass, crown	2.520
green	2.642
flint from 2.760 to	3.000
plate	2.942
Granite from 2.613 to	2.956
Gum arabic	1.452
cherry-tree	1.481
Gunpowder, loose	0.836
shaken	0.932
solid	1.745
Gypsum, compact, from 1.872 to	2.288
crystallized, from 2.311 to	3.000
Heliotrope, or Bloodstone from 2.629 to	2.700
Honey	1.450
Honeystone, or Mellite, from 1.560 to	1.666

Material	Specific Gravity
Hornblende, common, from 3.250 to	3.830
basaltic, from 3.160 to	3.333
Hornstone from 2.533 to	2.810
Hyacinth from 4.000 to	4.780
Jasper from 2.358 to	2.816
Jet	1.300
Indigo	1.009
Ironstone from Carron	3.281
Do. Lancashire	3.573
Isinglass	1.111
Ivory	1.825
Lapis Nephriticus	2.894
Lard	0.947
Lead, Glance or Galena from Derbyshire, from 6.565 to	7.786
Limestone, compact, from 2.386 to	3.000
Magnesia, native, Hydrate of	2.330
Do. Carbonate of, from 2.220 to	2.612
Malachite, compact, from 3.572 to	3.994
Marble, Carrara	2.716
white Italian	2.707
black veined	2.704
Parian	2.560
Mastic, (a resin)	1.074
Melanite, or black Garnet, from 3.691 to	3.800
Metals, Antimony	6.702
Arsenic	5.763
Bismuth	9.880
Brass, from 7.824 to	8.396
Cadmium	8.600
Chromium	5.900
Cobalt	8.600
Columbium	5.600
Copper	8.900
Gold, cast	19.25
Do. hammered	19.35
Iridium, hammered	23.00
Iron, cast at Carron	7.248
Do. bar-hardened, or not	7.788
Lead	11.35
Manganese	8.000
Mercury, solid, 3° below 0 of Fahr.	15.61
Do. at 32° of Fahr.	13.61
Do. at 60° of Fahr.	13.58
Do. at 212° of Fahr.	13.37
Molybdenum	8.600
Nickel, cast	8.279
forged	3.666
Osmium and Rhodium, alloy of	19.50
Palladium	11.80
Platinum	21.47
Potassium at 59° Fah.	0.865
Rhodium	10.65
Selenium	4.300
Silver	10.47
hammered	10.51
Sodium at 59° Fahr.	0.972
Steel, soft	7.833
tempered	7.816
Metals, Steel, hardened	7.840
tempered and hardened	7.818
Tellurium, from 5.700 to	6.115
Tin, Cornish	7.291
Do. hardened	7.299
Tungsten	17.40
Uranium	9.000
Zinc from 6.900 to	7.191
Mica from 2.650 to	2.934
Milk	1.032
Mineral Pitch, or Asphaltum, from 0.905 to	1.650
Mineral Tallow	0.770
Myrrh (a resin)	1.360
Naphtha from 0.700 to	0.847
Nitre	1.900
Obsidian from 2.348 to	2.370
Oils, Essential—Amber	0.868
Anise-seed	0.986
Carraway-seed	0.904
Cinnamon	1.043
Cloves	1.036
Fennel	0.929
Lavender	0.894
Mint, common	0.898
Turpentine	0.870
Wormwood	0.907
Expressed—Sweet Almonds	0.932
Codfish	0.923
Filberts	0.916
Hempseed	0.926
Linseed	0.940
Olives	0.915
Poppyseed	0.939
Rapeseed	0.913
Walnuts from 0.923 to	0.947
Whale	0.923
Opal, precious	2.114
Do. common, from 1.958 to	2.114
Opium	1.336
Orpiment from 3.048 to	3.500
Oyster-shell	2.092
Pearl, Oriental, from 2.510 to	2.750
Pearlstone	2.340
Peat from 0.600 to	1.329
Peruvian Bark	0.784
Phosphorus	1.770
Pitchstone from 1.970 to	2.720
Plumbago or Graphite, from 1.987 to	2.400
Porcelain from China	2.384
Sèvres	2.145
Porphyry from 2.452 to	2.972
Porphyry, Seltzer	1.003
Proof-spirit	0.923
Pumice-stone from 0.752 to	0.914
Quartz from 2.624 to	3.750
Realgar from 3.225 to	3.338
Rock-crystal, from 2.581 to	2.888
Ruby, Oriental	4.283
Sal Gem	2.143
Sapphire, Oriental, from 4.000 to	4.200
Sardonyx from 2.602 to	2.698
Scammony of Smyrna	1.274
Aleppo	1.235
Schorl from 2.922 to	3.452
Serpentine from 2.264 to	2.999
Shale	2.600
Silver Glance, from 5.300 to	7.208
Slate (drawing)	2.110
Smalt	2.440
Spar, Fluor, from 3.094 to	3.791
Do. calcareous, from 2.620 to	2.837
Do. double refrg. from Castleton	2.724
Spermaceti	0.943
Spodumene or Triphane, from 3.000 to	3.218
Stalactite from 2.323 to	2.546
Steatite from 2.400 to	2.665
Steam of water	0.481
Stilbite from 2.140 to	2.500
Strontian, Sulphate of, from 3.583 to	3.958
Do. Carbonate of, from 3.658 to	3.675
Stone, Bristol, from 2.510 to	2.640
cutlers'	2.111
grinding	2.142
hard	2.400
paving, from 2.415 to	2.708
Portland	2.496
Rotten	1.981
Sugar	1.606
Sulphur, native	2.033
fused	1.990
Talc, from 2.080 to	3.000
Tallow	0.941
Topaz from 4.010 to	4.061
Tourmaline from 3.086 to	3.362
Turquoise, from 2.500 to	3.000
Ultramarine	2.360
Uranite	2.190
Vesuvian from 3.300 to	3.575
Vinegar from 1.013 to	1.080
Water, distilled	1.000
Sea	1.028
Water, of Dead Sea	1.210
Wax, Bees'	0.964
White	0.968
Shoemakers'	0.897
Whey, Cows'	1.019
Wine, Bourdeaux	0.993
Burgundy	0.991
Constance	1.081
Malaga	1.022
Port	0.997
White Champagne	0.997
Wood, Alder	0.800
Apple-tree	0.793
Ash	0.845
Bay-tree	0.822
Beech	0.852
Box, French	0.912
Dutch	1.328
Brazilian, Red	1.031
Campeachy	0.913
Cedar, Wild	0.596
Palest	0.613

HYDROSTATICS.

Wood, Cedar, Indian	1.315	Wood, Hazel	0.600	Wood, Plum-tree	0.785
Americ.	0.561	Jasmin, Spanish	0.770	Pomegranate-tree	1.351
Cherry-tree	0.715	Juniper-tree	0.556	Poplar-tree	0.883
Citron	0.726	Lemon-tree	0.703	Do. White Spanish	0.529
Cocoa-wood	1.040	Lignum Vitæ	1.333	Quince-tree	0.705
Crab tree	0.765	Linden-tree	0.604	Sassafras	0.482
Cork	0.240	Mastick-tree	0.849	Vine	1.327
Cypress, Spanish	0.644	Mahogany	1.063	Walnut	0.681
Ebony, American	1.331	Maple-tree	0.750	Willow	0.585
Do. Indian	1.209	Medlar	0.944	Yew, Dutch	0.788
Elder-tree	0.695	Mulberry, Spanish	0.897	Spanish	0.807
Elm-tree	0.671	Oak-heart, 60 yrs. old	1.170	Knot of 16 years old	1.760
Filbert-tree	0.600	Olive-tree	0.927	Woodstone	from 2.045 to 2.675
Fir, Male	0.550	Orange-tree	0.705	Zeolite	from 2.073 to 2.718
Do. Female	0.498	Pear-tree	0.166	Zircon	from 4.385 to 4.700

CHAPTER VII.

The Syphon—Intermitting Springs.

IF a bent tube with equal branches, like the letter U, be filled with water, and placing the thumbs upon its two openings, you turn it upside down, and place it in a basin of water, the liquid will stand in it. Let one of the branches

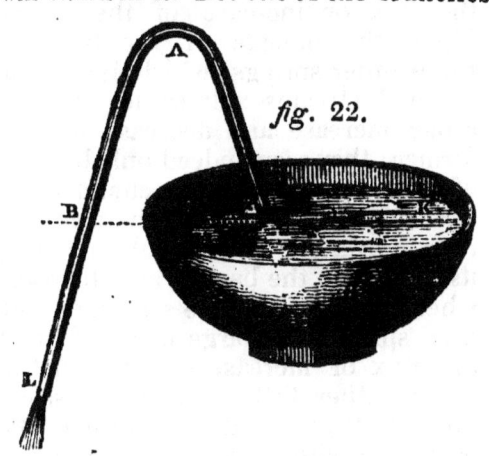

fig. 22.

A B (*fig.* 22.) be brought out of the water, and over the edge of the vessel; the pressure upon the mouth of the branch at B is equal to the pressure on the mouth at G; for it is in both cases the weight of the air which presses on the surface of the water I K, and makes the water remain in the tube A G, and which also presses against the water in the tube A B; and the weight of the air meets with the same weight of water to balance it in both branches, because the height of both is equal. Therefore the water will not run through the tube. But if the branch A B be lengthened to L, then there being a greater weight of water in A B L than in G A, it will overcome the pressure of the air at L; the water will flow out of the tube, and the water in the basin will be forced up through A G until the basin is emptied, if the arm A G is held to the bottom, and the bottom is higher than the mouth L of the tube. This kind of tube is called a *Syphon*, and is very conveniently used for decanting liquors from casks or other vessels, when it is wished to draw them off without shaking, or when there is a sediment at the bottom which it is wished to leave.

The strange appearance of intermitting springs, or springs which run for a time, and then stop altogether, and after a time run again, and then stop, is entirely occasioned by the channels in which the water flows being formed like syphons. Thus if A B C (*fig.* 23.) represents a hill or mountain, in which there is a hollow E F G, and a channel bent like a syphon F H B leading out of it. The water collected from the rills *d, d, d*, will fill the hollow, and as soon as it rises to the line O P, of the same height with H, it will rise to H in the channel, and then flow out through B, till the whole runs off to the level of F. It will then cease to flow until the hollow is again filled to the level O P, when it will flow again, and so on. Some springs, called *variable* or *reciprocating*, do not cease to flow, but only discharge a much smaller quantity of water for a certain time, and then give out a greater quantity. This may be owing to another hollow situated higher up, which has a common runner going to join the stream below the bend H; for this runner keeps the stream always supplied to a certain degree, and when the lower hollow, which feeds the syphon runner F H, is filled up to O H, both the common runner and the syphon runner feed the stream together, until the lower hollow is drained. Or it may be owing to another runner I K, from the same hollow, situated lower down, and going into the syphon runner F H B; for, if the lower runner be too

HYDROSTATICS.

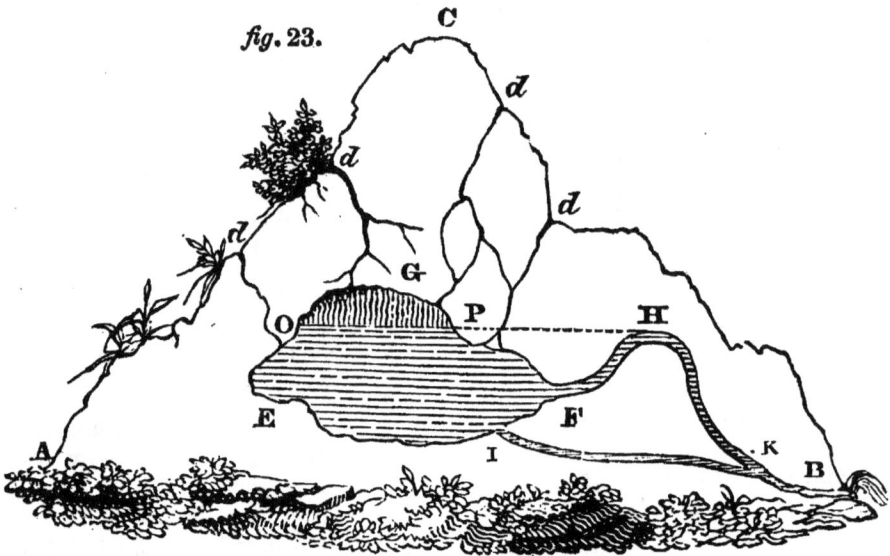

fig. 23.

small to carry off the supply from the rills *d, d, d*, the water, as soon as it sinks to F, and the syphon stops, will begin to rise again; and it will, therefore, never descend to the level of I; and, consequently, the runner I K will flow without ceasing, either augmenting the syphon stream when it runs, or running by itself when that stops.

In some places the most absurd tales are told, and believed by ignorant people, respecting such springs; their flowing and ceasing are ascribed to witchcraft; and designing men have sometimes taken advantage of the credulity of others, and gained credit for themselves, by foretelling the return of the spring after it had ceased, or pretending to stop it when it was running. Some notions connected with superstitions of this kind are adverted to in the account given of an intermitting or rather a variable spring, at Laywell, near Torbay, in Devonshire, by Dr. Atwell, the first person who distinctly explained these appearances by the nature of the syphon. "It is a long mile (says he) distant from the sea, upon the north side of a ridge of hills lying between it and the sea, and making a turn or angle near this spring. It is situated in the side of those hills, near the bottom, and seems to have its course from the S.W. towards the N.E. There is a constantly running stream which discharges itself near one corner, into a basin, about eight feet in length, and four feet and a half in breadth, the outlet of which is at the furthest end from the entrance of the stream, about three feet wide, and of a sufficient height. This I mention, that a better judgment may be made of the perpendicular rise of the water in the basin at the time of the flux or increase of the stream. Upon the outside of the basin are three other springs, which always run, but with streams subject to a like regular increase and decrease with the former: they seem indeed only branches of the former, or rather channels discharging some parts of the constantly running water, which could not empty itself all into the basin; and, therefore, when, by means of the season or weather, springs are large and high, upon the flux or increase of this fountain, several other little springs are said to break forth, both at the bottom of the basin and without it, which disappear again upon the ebb or decrease of the fountain. All the constant running streams put together, at the time I saw them, were, I believe, more than sufficient to drive an overshot mill, and the stream running into the basin might be one-half of the whole. I had made a journey, purposely to see it, in company with a friend; when we came to the fountain, we were informed by a man, working just by the basin, that the spring had flowed and ebbed about twenty times that morning, but had ceased doing so about half an hour before we came. I observed the stream running in the basin for more than an hour, by my watch, without perceiving the least variation in it, or the least alteration in the height of the surface of the water in the basin; which we could observe with great nicety, by means of a broad stone laid in a shelving position in the water. Thus disappointed, we were obliged to go and take some little refreshment at our inn, after which we intended to come back and spend the rest of our time by the fountain, before we returned home. They told us in the house that many had been disappointed in this manner, and the common people superstitiously imputed it to I know not what influence which the presence of some people had over the fountain; for which reason they advised, that, in case it did not flow and ebb when we were both present, one of us should absent himself, to try whether it would do so in the presence of the other. Upon our return to it, the man, who was still at work, told us that it had begun to flow and ebb about half an hour after we went away, and had done so ten or twelve times in less than a minute. We saw the stream coming into the basin, and likewise the others on the outside of the basin begin to increase, and to flow with great violence, upon which the surface of the water in the basin rose an inch and a quarter perpendicularly, in near the space of two minutes; immediately after which, the stream began to abate again to its ordinary course, and in near two minutes time the surface was sunk down to its usual height, where it remained two minutes more; then it began to flow again as before, and in the space of twenty-six minutes, flowed and ebbed five times; so that an increase, decrease, and pause, taken together, were made in about five minutes, or a little more. I could observe, by the mark upon the stones, that the surface of the water in the basin had rose before we came, at least three-quarters of an inch perpendicularly higher than we saw it; and I thought that I could perceive some very little abatement each turn, both in the height, and in the time of its sinking; but the time of the pause, or standing on the surface at its usual height, or equable running of the stream, was lengthened, yet so as to leave some abatement in the time of the rising, sinking and pause taken together."—(*Phil. Trans.* No. 424.)

It should seem that, in the hill from which this stream comes, there are three hollows, or reservoirs, of different sizes, and connected by syphons of different widths. The times of the increase and decrease lengthening, arises from the water sinking in one of the reservoirs, which makes it flow more slowly than when it is full.

In some places there are springs which run freely in summer, or in dry weather, and almost stop in winter, or in wet weather. This is owing to a hollow in the hill being fed by runners, but having beside the vent through which the spring flows out, a waste pipe F L G like a syphon, which carries off the water another way as soon as the space is filled high enough. Thus if the cavern is fed with water by the runners E, E, E, (*fig.* 24.) and these, from the drought, are not sufficient to raise its level as high as I K, the syphon outlet F L G cannot act at all; but the stream H will flow constantly. But if, during wet weather, the runners feed the cavern faster than the stream H can empty it, the water will rise to the level

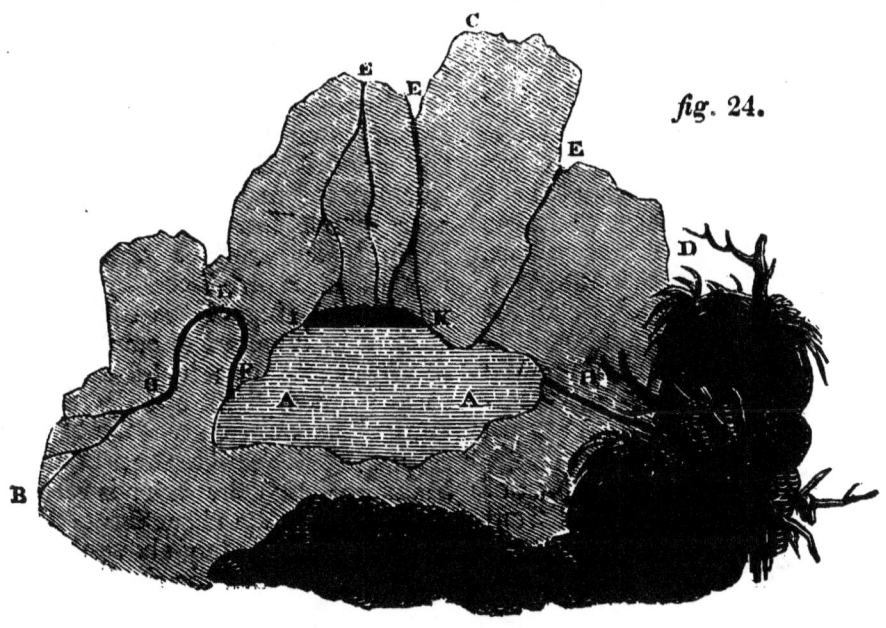

fig. 24.

of L K, and the syphon outlet will begin to act, which, together with the stream of the spring, may soon reduce the water to the level of H, or below it; and, consequently, the spring will cease to run. If now the syphon drain off as much as the runners supply, and the aperture F be lower than H, the water will not rise to H, nor, of course, the spring flow; but when, in consequence of the drought, the runners E, E, E, lessen their supply, the syphon gains on them, and at length, sinking the water to F, stops. There being now no water draining from the cavern it rises to H, through which it will continue to run again until the return of wet weather once more brings the syphon into action. The less L ascends above the level of H, and the less F descends beneath it, the more easily these phenomena are produced, and the more closely they follow the changes of weather.

Chapter VIII.
Capillary Attraction.

HITHERTO we have seen no exception to the general rule, that all the parts of a liquid stand always at the same height if left to themselves, and that consequently no liquid can of itself rise higher in the inside of a tube, than it stands on the outside. But there is an exception, or rather an apparent exception, to this rule, which must now be explained.

If a drop of water, or any liquid of a like degree of fluidity, be pressed upon a solid surface, it will wet that surface, and stick to it, instead of keeping together, and running off when the surface is held sloping. This shows that the parts of the liquid are more attracted by the parts of the solid than by one another. In the same manner, if you observe the edge of any liquid in a vessel, as wine in a glass, and note where it touches the glass, you will see that it is not quite level close to the glass, but becomes somewhat hollow, and is raised up on it, so as to stand a little higher at the edge than in the middle and other parts of its surface. It appears, therefore, that there is an attraction at very small distances from the edge, sufficient to suspend the part of the fluid near it, and prevent it from sinking to the level of the rest. Suppose the wine-glass to be diminished so as to leave no room for any of the wine in the middle, which lies flat and level, but only to leave room for the small rim of liquor raised up all round on the side of the glass; in other words, suppose a very small tube, placed with its lower end just so as to touch the liquor; it is evident that the liquor will stand up somewhat higher in the tube than on the outside; and if the tube be made smaller and smaller, the liquor will rise higher, there being always less weight of liquid to keep it from rising and counterbalance the attraction of the glass.

Tubes of this very small bore are called *Capillary*, from a Latin word, signifying *hair*, because they are small like hairs. Generally, any tube of less than the twentieth of an inch diameter in the inside is called a *capillary* tube; and if it is placed so as to touch the surface of water, the water will rise in it to a height which is greater the smaller the bore of the tube is. If the diameter of the tube is the fiftieth part of an inch, the water will rise to the height of $2\frac{1}{2}$ inches; if it be the hundredth part of an inch, the water will rise 5 inches; if the two hundredth part of an inch, the water will rise 10 inches, and so on in proportion as the bore is lessened. Now the quantity of water raised in these tubes is in proportion to the square of the diameter, multiplied by the height it rises to, because cylinders are to one another as the squares of their diameter multiplied by their lengths; therefore, the height being inversely as the diameter, it follows, that the quantity of water raised is in proportion to the diameter; and the circumferences of the tubes being also in the proportion of the diameter, it is plain that the quantity of water raised is in proportion to the circumference of the tube, or the quantity of matter in the ring of the tube which first touches the water. From hence arises a probability that this effect is produced by the attraction of the ring of the tube. But the subject is involved in considerable obscurity; and although philosophers have thrown much light upon it by mathematical reasoning, great doubt remains respecting the explanation of the fact. Some hold that the water is raised and supported by the attraction of the ring of glass immediately above the water's surface; but then the ring immediately below the surface ought to draw it down as much as the ring immediately above draws it up. Others hold, that the first ring of glass which meets the water, that is, the bottom of the tube, attracts it, there being no ring below to draw it down. But this seems not very well to explain how this ring pushes the water up past it; for it ought naturally to draw it back as much as the second ring draws it up; and still less how the water remains suspended without running out at the top, when you break off the tube below the point to which it rises. However, the fact of the water rising higher the smaller the tube is, cannot be doubted, and there are some other facts equally well ascertained.

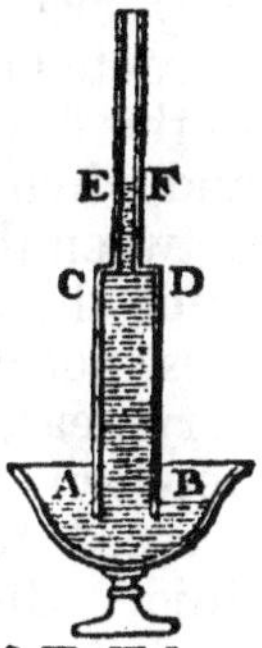

If a tube have, in different parts, two bores, as A D the larger, and E F the smaller, the water, if raised by suction or otherwise, will stand at the same height E, at which it would have stood if the small tube E F were continued down to the surface of the water A B; and this will take place whatever be the bore or shape of A B D C, provided E F be a capillary tube, and the experiment be not made in vacuo: so that the water will stand in the larger tube, or in any vessel ending in a capillary tube, as well as if it were closed at the top; and if the tube or vessel be turned upside down, the water will stand as high as it would have done in the smaller tube alone.

fig. 25.

If a capillary tube, like the one above, composed of two, or a tube tapering to one end, be filled with liquid, and placed horizontally, the liquid will run towards the narrow part, and leave the wide part towards the mouth empty.

If a capillary tube be bent into the form of a syphon, the water will rise as high as if it were straight, and so may reach the middle of the bend, but it will not run over through the other leg. If the syphon, however, is filled in both legs, and one is made so much longer as to counterbalance the attraction which keeps it in the other, it will flow over, and will thus bring the water from one place to another.

If a plate of glass be placed with its upright edge against another plate, and kept in a slanting position towards it, at an inclination to it of about 1-36th part perpendicular, (that is, at an angle of about 1½ deg.), and the lower edges of both plates be placed in any watery liquid, the liquid will rise between the plates, and it will rise higher the nearer it is to the upright edge; that is, the smaller the space is between the two plates; so that the liquid will form itself into a curve line. Thus, if the plates A B D C and A E F C (*fig*. 26.) meet in

fig. 26.

the edge A C, and are held very near each other, but not touching, except in A C, the liquid in which they are placed will rise between them, and stand in the form of D I G L; the height of the liquid at any point G, that is G H, being greater in proportion as its distance from A is less. So that, if C K is twice as long as C H, I K, will be half as long as G H. This curve is well known to mathematicians under the name of *hyperbola*. It is the same line which is made by cutting a cone through its sides and base, in a direction perpendicular to its base. When water is the liquid, it rises to the height of 2½ inches at the point where the two plates are 1-100th of an inch asunder, and so in proportion, the height being 1¼ inch where the distance is 1-50th, or 5 inches where the distance is 1-200th of an inch. And if the plates are held parallel to one another, and very near, the upper edge of the liquid will be a straight line. This rise is plainly owing to the same attraction which acts in capillary tubes; for the two plates may be considered as an assemblage of an infinite number of capillary tubes of bores always diminishing till at A B the bore is nothing. So if a number of capillary tubes, each one smaller than the next, be placed upright in a row and resting upon a liquid, it will rise in them to different heights; and if the bores of the tubes diminish in proportion as they are nearer the end of the row, the liquid will stand in them at different heights, so that its heights in the different tubes will be in the same curve line as the upper edge of the liquid between the plates.

The height to which water rises in the tube, we have seen, is $2\frac{1}{2}$ inches when the diameter of the tube is 1-50th of an inch, and it rises between the plates to the same height when they are twice as near, or only 1-100th inch asunder. But this difference is what might be expected, upon the supposition that the rise is owing to the attraction of the glass; for in the tube there is glass all round, and it may be supposed to be a small square, each of the four sides acting on the water; whereas the plates have only two sides acting, and therefore little more than half the power.

The action of the tubes or plates upon liquids depends upon the nature of the solid substances of which they are made. If the glass is smeared with grease so that water will not stick to it, that liquid will not rise at all; nor will it rise between two cakes of wax or of grease. So different liquids rise to different heights in the same tube; but not according to their specific gravity; for oil of turpentine, which is one-seventh lighter than water, only rises one-fourth as high; and aqueous ammonia, which in the table of specific gravities appears to be about a tenth lighter than water, and consequently heavier than oil of turpentine, rises higher than water by nearly a fifth, and consequently nearly five times higher than oil of turpentine. Spirit of wine, somewhat lighter than oil of turpentine, rises nearly twice as high, or about $\frac{2}{3}$ as high as water. Mercury does not rise at all, either between the plates or in the tubes, unless they have been completely deprived of moisture by repeated boilings of the mercury in them, and then the mercury ascends like water: on the contrary, it usually sinks considerably lower than its level outside the tube or plate. In a tube of 1-5th inch bore, it sinks 1-11th of an inch; and in a tube of 1-10th inch bore, it sinks about 1-5th of an inch; so that the sinking is in the same proportion to the bore of the tubes in mercury as the rising in watery fluids, being inversely as the diameters; and melted lead is found to sink in the same manner, and according to the same rule. Again, it is observable that mercury, (and probably melted lead,) which sinks in this way, has always a round surface, and never stands up at the edge of the vessel containing it, unless the vessel be made of silver, or tin, or some other substance with which mercury has a strong chemical affinity. Watery fluids sink instead of rising in tubes, or between plates, which are oiled or waxed. The thickness of liquors seems to have but little influence on their capillary attraction, nor has their heat; for white varnish, which is exceedingly thick and viscid, rises nearly as high as spirit of wine, and hot and cold water stand at nearly the same height, the hot, however, standing lower of the two.

It is one consequence of capillary attraction, that when light bodies, capable of being wetted by any liquid, float upon it, and come very near each other, they are drawn together as if they attracted one another; but this is owing to the fluid being raised on their sides, and when very near it becomes raised between them and attracts them. The same thing happens when two light bodies, not capable of being wetted, float very near, for they make the fluid sink between them, and the bodies are pressed together by the surrounding fluid. But when one body is capable of being wetted, and the other not, they are driven back one from the other, because the fluid being raised by the wetted body, on one side of the dry body, and sunk on the other, the dry body is, as it were, on a slope, and falls away from the other.

Capillary attraction performs many important offices in nature. Probably the distribution of moisture in the earth is regulated by it; and there is no doubt that the distribution of the juices in plants depends principally upon it. The rise of the sap and its circulation is performed in the fine capillary tubes of the wood and bark, which are the arteries and veins of vegetables. Any one may perceive how this process is performed, by twisting together several threads of cotton or worsted, and wetting them. If they are then put in a glass of any coloured fluid, as red wine or ink, and allowed to hang down to the plate on which the glass stands, the fluid will soon be perceived to creep up, and colour the whole of the threads, red or black, as the case may be; and in a short time the whole contents of the glass will come over into the plate. Capillary tubes may in this manner carry juices upwards, and distribute them through plants. The juice, it is true, cannot be so carried from a lower to a higher level in a capillary tube, and flow out from the top; but it may be carried upwards in one, and forwards into others, partially oblique, and from these it may be carried upwards again in a third set of tubes.

Spongy bodies act in all probability on liquids in the same manner, by means of a great number of extremely small capillary tubes, of which their substance is entirely composed.

The attraction, by means of which capillary tubes and plates nearly touching, act on fluids, may be seen very easily by placing a drop of water upon any surface which, from being oiled, or from any other cause, cannot be easily wetted. It assumes a roundish form. If over this you hold any flat surface, easily wetted, you will perceive that, when it is brought near, but not touching, the upper part of the drop rises to meet it, and by moving the surface to a greater distance the drop becomes lengthened out, broader on the two surfaces, and narrow in the middle. If the second surface, instead of being held parallel to the first, is placed upright upon it, and brought near the side of the drop, the water is drawn towards it, and stands up against it in the corner with a hollow surface; as in a glass containing any liquid formerly mentioned. And in this manner, when any vessel is nearly full, but not overflowing, the liquor may be made to run over, by placing any body upon the top and leaning over the edge, so that it touches the liquor and raises it to that edge.

Chapter IX.

Mathematical Illustrations.

1. Let A B C D (*fig.* 27.) be the section of a vessel filled with any liquid; the pressure of the liquid upon the base B C, is measured by the area of the base multiplied into the altitude A B. Thus if the figure is a cube, the pressure is the weight of a bulk of the liquid equal to the cube of B C: if a rectangular parellelo-

---

* The foregoing Chapters contain the science adapted to readers who are unacquainted with the Mathematics. These may pass over this concluding Chapter.

ped, the presssure is equal to B C² × A B the depth of the liquid: if a

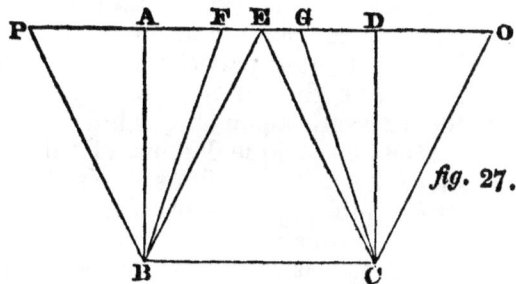

fig. 27.

cylinder, it is B C² × .7854 × A B: if a cone, whose base and altitude are the same with those of the cylinder, the pressure is the same: if the frustrum of a cone F G B C, or B C O P, the pressure on B C is still the same as that of the cylinder A B C D, as long as B C, the base, and B A, the altitude, continue the same.

2. If there are two vessels of the same figure but of different depths and bases, and filled with different fluids, let D and d be the depths, B and b the area of the bases, G and g the specific gravities of the fluids; then the pressure upon B is to that upon b as D × B × G to d × b × g.

3. If in any vessel there be strata of the thickness $F F' F''$, &c. of fluids, whose densities are D, D', D'', &c., the pressure of the whole strata on the area B of the bottom, is equal to B × $(D × F + D' × F' + D'' × F'' +$, &c.)

4. Let there be a perpendicular-sided vessel, that is, a vessel whose sides, if planes, are at right angles to the base, and if curvilinear surfaces, have all their tangents in planes at right angles to the base, and let the vessel be filled with any liquid; if a be the height of the liquid, p the perimeter of the vessel; the pressure on the whole perpendicular sides, that is, the whole perpendicular surface, is the weight of a rectangular prism of the liquid whose base is $a \times \frac{p}{2}$ and altitude is a; therefore the pressure is $\frac{a^2 p}{2}$. If the vessel be a cube, the whole lateral pressure is $2 a^3$, and the pressure on each side $\frac{a^3}{2}$, or half the pressure on the base. If it be a cylinder, whose diameter is d, the lateral pressure is $a^2 d \times 1.57079$, and that on the bottom $a d^2 \times .78539$.

5. As the pressure on any particle of fluid at rest is equal to the weight of a column of that fluid whose base is the particle, and whose altitude is the depth of the particle below the surface; if we call those particles p, p', p'', &c., and the depths d, d', d'', &c. respectively, the pressure upon the whole of any vertical or oblique lamina of the fluid on each side of it, will be a weight of the fluid equal to $p \cdot d + p' \cdot d' + p'' \cdot d'' +$, &c., and this is also the pressure with which the lamina next to the vertical side weighs upon that side. But if D be the distance of the centre of gravity of all the particles from the horizontal surface of the liquid, it is a property of this point that $D \times (p + p' + p'' +$, &c.$)$ is equal to $p \cdot d + p' \cdot d' + p'' \cdot d'' +$, &c.; and as $p + p' + p'' +$, &c. is the area of the plane or surface formed by all the p, p', p'', &c. therefore the pressure upon the whole area, whether vertical, oblique, or horizontal of any surface under water, is equal to D times that area, or the area multiplied by the distance of its centre of gravity, below the plane of the fluids' surface.

6. It follows from hence that the pressure upon the sides, whose breadth is b, of a rectangular vessel, as a cube or paralellopiped, at different depths D, D', D'' is as $b \times D \times \frac{D}{2}$, $b \times D' \times \frac{D'}{2}$, $b \times D'' \times \frac{D''}{2}$; or as D^2, D'^2, D''^2; that is, as the squares of the depths. Hence, if a conic parabola be described, whose axis is the upper edge of the vessel AB, (*fig.* 28.) and conjugate the depth BM'', the pressure upon the whole of the side AP'' above P, will be as the ordinate PM; upon

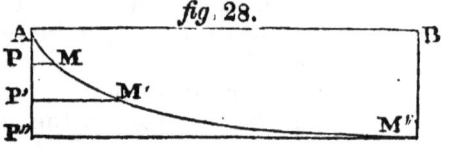

fig. 28.

the portion above P', P'M'; upon the portion above P'', P''M''.

7. If a body, whose specific gravity is S, be plunged in two fluids of different specific gravities, G and G', the heavier being G', it will float in equilibrio, if the part P in the lighter be to the part P' in the heavier, as $G'-S$ is to $S-G$. For the weight of the whole body is $S \times (P + P')$, the weight of the fluid displaced by P is $G \times P$, and that displaced by P' is $G'P'$; and because the body floats, and its weight is suspended; $G \times P + G' \times P' = S \times (P + P')$; therefore $P \times (S - G) = P' \times (G' - S)$ and $P : P' :: G' - S : S - G$. It follows also that $P : P + P' :: G' - S : G' - G$, or the part in the lighter is to the whole body as the difference between the specific gravities of the solid and the heavier fluid to the difference between the specific gravities of the two fluids. When that difference is very great, G may be neglected as evanescent in the last term of the proportion; or the part of the body out of water is to the whole body, as the difference between the specific gravities of the body and water to the specific gravity of water; or (because neglecting G, $P' : P + P' :: S : G'$) the part plunged is to the whole as the specific gravity of the solid to that of the fluid; and, in like manner, neglecting G in the former proportion, $P : P' :: G' - S : S$; or the part out of water is to the part plunged, as the difference of the specific gravities of the solid and fluid to the specific gravity of the solid.

8. The centre of pressure of any triangle A B C (*fig.* 29.) placed vertically at the depth C W, below the surface W R of the water is found thus. Let $AS = SB$, and $GS = \frac{1}{3} CS$; G will be the centre of gravity of A B C; and GM being perpendicular to W R, the pressure on A B C will be equal to a column of water whose base is A B C and altitude G M; that is, equal to $CP \times$

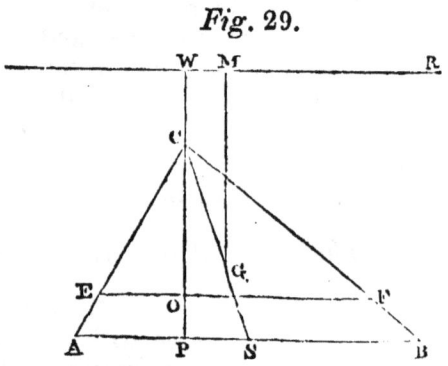

Fig. 29.

$AB \times \frac{GM}{2} \times g$; g being the specific gravity of water.

Draw E F parallel to A B, and let $WO = x$, $CW = a$, $CP = b$, $AB = c$, $GM = m$. Then $CO = x - a$; $EF =$ (by similar triangles) $\frac{c}{b}(x - a)$, and the pressure upon $ABC = \frac{bc}{2} \times mg$. And by the property of the centre of percussion, the distance of the centre of percussion of C E F below W R is equal to the fluent $\int \frac{c}{b} \times (x-a) x^2 \dot{x}$ divided by the product of the triangle E C F into the distance of its centre of gravity from W R; and finding the fluent, we have $\frac{c}{b} \left(\frac{x^4}{4} - \frac{a x^3}{3} \right) + C$, a constant quantity; which constant quantity (as the fluent vanishes at C, or when $x - a = 0$, that is $x = a$) is $\frac{c a^4}{12 b}$; so that the whole fluent is $\frac{c}{b} \times \left(\frac{x^4}{4} - \frac{a x^3}{3} + \frac{a^4}{12} \right)$: and if we take this for the whole triangle A B C, where $x = a + b$; we have to substitute this for x, and to divide by A B C $\times$ G M, that is, by $\frac{m b c}{2}$. Let $a + b = d$; the expression becomes

$$\frac{2}{m b^2} \times \left(\frac{d^4}{4} - \frac{a d^3}{3} + \frac{a^4}{12} \right).$$

Therefore the centre of percussion, is in the line found E F. But if the triangle were to revolve in a plane perpendicular to its own round W R, and strike against a plane passing through E F, its motion would be destroyed, the motions on the opposite sides of that line balancing each other; therefore the pressure of the fluid on the triangle being counteracted by an equal and opposite pressure on the line E F, the triangle must be supported; that is, the centre of pressure is in E F.

If the vertex of the triangle be situated at W, the surface of the water, then $a = 0$, $d = b$, and $m = \frac{2}{3} b$, and the expression becomes $\frac{3}{4} b$; or the centre of pressure is at three-fourths of the depth of the water.

The point of the line E F, which is the centre of pressure, that is, the distance of that centre from C P, may be found by a similar process. It is equal to

$$\frac{2 \tan. \varphi}{m b^2} \times \left(\frac{d^4}{4} - \frac{1}{3} a d^3 - \frac{m a b^2}{2} + \frac{a^4}{12} \right)$$

φ being the angle P C G. When, therefore, the triangle is isosceles, and the centre of gravity is in C P, this quantity vanishes, and the centre of pressure is in O, the intersection of C P and E F; and when the vertex of the triangle touches the surface W R, the expression becomes $\frac{3}{4} b \times \tan. \varphi$.

Of the two expressions, for the distance of E F from W R, and for the distance of the centre from C P, it may be remarked that, in the former, c disappears at one of the steps of the analysis. Wherefore the distance of E F from W R does not depend on the line A B: in other words, all triangles of the same altitude, and in the same depth of water, have the centre of pressure at the same depth below the surface, whatever be their bases. But the latter expression involving the angle φ, the horizontal distance of the centre of pressure from the vertical line depends upon the base of the triangle, because that determines the position of G, the centre of gravity.

To apply this analysis to other figures, the line E F $= n$ must be found in terms of x, or of the given quantities, and substituted in the fluxional expression $\frac{n x^2 \dot{x}}{m}$: and the fluent being found, it must be divided by the expression for the figure. This gives the depth of the line E F below W R.

To find the distance of the centre from C P on E F, when C G S bisects all the ordinates, we must substitute for n (or E F) its value in terms of x as before, in the expression

$$\frac{\tan. \varphi}{m} \times \int n (x^2 - m a) \dot{x};$$

and then having found the fluent, (regarding m under the integral sign as constant or independent of x), divide it by the expression for the figure.

Thus, if the figure is a rectangle, whose sides are equal to b, and base equal to c; and if the upper edge is at the surface of the water, so that $a = 0$, the first fluxional expression becomes

$$\frac{\frac{c}{b} \times x^2 \dot{x}}{2}$$

whose fluent is $\frac{2 c x^3}{3 b}$ and dividing this by $b c$, the area of the figure, we have

$$\frac{2 x^3}{3 b^2}$$

which, for the whole rectangle, when

$x = b$, becomes $\frac{2}{3} b$. The second fluxional expression $= 0$ because the centre of gravity is in the axis and $\varphi = 0$.

If the figure be a Conic Parabola, whose parameter is p, and vertex at the surface of the water $n = 2\sqrt{px}$, $m = \frac{3}{5} b$, and the area $= \frac{2}{3} bc$; the fluxional expression, therefore, for the depth, is

$$\frac{2\sqrt{px}\, x^2\, \dot{x}}{\frac{3}{5} b} = \frac{10\sqrt{p}}{3b} \times x^{\frac{5}{2}}\, \dot{x}$$

whose fluent is $\frac{20}{21 b} \times \sqrt{px}\, x^3$; and when $x = b$, and dividing by $\frac{2}{3} bc$, it becomes $\frac{10}{7}\, \frac{b\sqrt{pb}}{c}$ or, as $\sqrt{pb} = \frac{c}{2}$, it becomes $\frac{5}{7} b$; and therefore is wholly independent of the breadth of the base, or the value of the parameter. Consequently, if an infinite number of parabolas be drawn through any point as a vertex, their common centre of pressure will always be a point 5-7ths of the axis distant from the vertex.

The same calculus may be applied to, and the same proposition shewn to hold of, parabolas of all orders.

$$y^e = p^{e-1} x$$

for here $n = 2 x^{\frac{1}{e}} p^{\frac{-1}{e}}$; $m = \frac{e+1}{2e+1} b$; and the area to divide by $= \frac{2 e p^{\frac{e-1}{e}} b^{\frac{1}{e}+1}}{1+e}$ and the fluxional expression being

$$\frac{2(1+2e)\, p^{\frac{e-1}{e}}\, x^{\frac{1}{e}+2}\, \dot{x}}{(1+e)\, b}$$

finding the fluent, substituting, and reducing, we have $\frac{1+2e}{1+3e} \times b$ for the depth of the centre of pressure, an expression wholly independent of the parameter, or of the breadth of the figure.

CHAPTER X.

BOOKS UPON THIS BRANCH OF SCIENCE.

Hydrostatics in general.

Rowning's Natural Philosophy, vol. 2nd, 8vo. (published 1765.)
'SGravesande's Natural Philosophy, vol. 2nd, 4to. (1749.)
Abbé Nollet's Lectures on Experimental Philosophy.
Ferguson's Lectures on Mechanics, &c., vol. 2nd, (Brewster's Edition, 1806.)
Desaguliers's Course of Experimental Philosophy, vol. 2, 4to. Sect. 108, (1763.)
Muschenbroëk's Natural Philosophy, 2 vols. 8vo. (1744.)
Dr. T. Young's Lectures on Natural Philosophy, 2 vols. 4to. (1807.)
Professor Millington's Epitome of Natural Philosophy, 8vo.

(These eight works give a very popular view of Hydrostatics, under that head, which forms a division of each work; and Dr. T. Young's contains the best selected catalogue ever published.)

Dr. Olinthus Gregory's Mechanics, 3 vols. 8vo., gives (vol. i.) a much more full and profound view of the subject.
Professor Playfair's Outlines of Natural Philosophy, vol. i. 8vo. (1804.)
Dr. M. Young's Outlines of Natural Philosophy, 8vo. (1800.)
Robison's Mechanical Philosophy, vol. ii.
Leslie's Elements of Natural Philosophy, vol. i. 8vo. (1823.)

(These four works give the heads of lectures on this subject among others of Natural Philosophy; but they are not sufficiently full or explicit for the mere beginner.)

Two Papers of Mr. Boyle, in Phil. Trans. for 1665 and 1669, on Hydrostatics.
Pascal's Treatise on the Equilibrium of Liquids, (1664.)
Mariotte on Hydrostatics.—Mem. Roy. Acad. of Paris, i. 69.
On the Equilibrium of Fluids.—*Ibid.* ii. 78.
Euler's Principles of Hydrostatics.—Mem. of Acad. of Berlin, 1755, p. 217.
Gulielmini on Hydrostatics.—Mem. Acad. of Bologna, i. 545.
Euler on Equilibrium of Fluids.—New Comments. of Acad. of Petersburgh, vols. xiii. xiv. and xv.
Matucci's Principles of Statics and Hydrostatics.—Mem. Acad. of Bologna, vi. 286,
Delangers, Statics of Semi-fluids.—Mem. of the Italian Society, iv. 329.
Hydrodynamics; in Dr. Brewster's Encyclopedia, treats the subject of Hydrostatics very learnedly and satisfactorily, and with minute references to all the works upon this subject. It is a most valuable Treatise.
Fontana on the Pressure of Fluids.—Mem. Italian Society, ii. 142.
Cotes's Hydrostatical Lectures, (1747.)
Emerson's Hydrostatics.
Parkinson's Hydrostatics, (1789.)
Bossut's Hydrodynamics, 2 vols. 8vo. (1771.)

Statics of Floating Bodies.

Bernouilli on the Equilibrium of Floating Bodies.—Comment. of Petersburgh Acad. vols. x. and xi.

Parent on Floating Bodies.—Mem. Acad. of Paris, (1700.)
Bouguer's Oscillation of Floating Bodies—*Ibid.* (1755.)
Pilot's Theory of Working of Ships.—*Ibid.* (1731.)
Paul Horti's Theory of the Construction of Ships, (1696.)
Euler's Complete Theory of the Construction and Working of Ships, 1790. (English Translation.)
Bossut's Hydrodynamics, vol. i. chap. 12, 13, and 14.
Atwood's Paper.—Phil. Trans. 1796, p. 46.

Capillary Attraction.

Pascal, Equilibrium of Liquids.
Rohault's Physics, part i. chap. 22, sec. 69, and seq. 9.
De la Hire.—Mem. Acad. Paris, vol. ix. p. 152.
Carrè's Experiments on Capillary Tubes.—*Ibid.* (1705,) p. 241.
D. Bernouilli.—Com. Acad. Petersburgh, (1727,) p. 246.
Marriotti, Motion of Fluids, vol. ii. p. 105.
Cotes's Hyd. Lectures, s. xi.
Lord C. Cavendish, in Phil. Trans. 1776, p. 382.
Monge.—Mem. Acad. Paris, (1787,) p. 506.
Wilson.—Edin. Trans. vol. iv. p. 144.
La Place Mechanique Celeste, 10th Book, Supplement.
La Place's Supplement to the Theory of Capillary Attraction, 1807.
Biot's Treatise on Physics, vol. i. chap. 22, (1816.)

Hydrostatic Instruments.

Homberg on Specific Gravities.—Acad. Paris, vol. x. p. 257.
Irwin on Weighing Bodies.—Phil. Trans. (1721,) p. 223.
Fahrenheit on Specific Gravity.—*Ibid.* (1724,) p. 114.
Schmeisser's Instrument.—*Ib.* (1793,) p. 165.
Professor Robison's Article in Ency. Brit. on Specific Gravity.
Montigny on Areometers.—Mem. Acad. Paris, (1768,) 435.
Le Roy on the same subject.—*Ibid.* (1770,) 526.
Brisson's Areometer.—*Ibid.* (1788,) 512.
San Martini on the Areometer.—Mem. Italian Society, vii. 79.
On the Hydrometer.—Phil. Trans. (1790,) p. 342.

HYDRAULICS.

Introduction.

As *Hydrostatics* is that branch of Natural Philosophy which treats of the weight, pressure, and equilibrium of water, and all such fluids as are non-elastic; so *Hydraulics* has for its object the investigation of the motions of such fluids, the means by which such motions are produced, the laws by which they are regulated, and the force or effect they exert against themselves, or against solid bodies which may oppose them. To avoid repetition, whenever fluids are mentioned in this treatise, they must always be understood to be inelastic, a character which not only belongs to water, but to oils, spirits, and all the visible and tangible fluids, to such an extent that, although they may vary in their bulk by change of temperature, yet they yield in so slight a degree to mechanical compression, as to have obtained the character of being non-elastic, notwithstanding which it does not *perfectly* apply to them, as will be found explained at the commencement of the Treatise on Hydrostatics.

Fluids are characterized by a want of cohesion among their parts: hence they are incapable of assuming any particular form without external support, but always accommodate themselves to the shape of the vessel which contains them. This same cause influences the motions of fluids, and produces the difference that exists between their pressure and motion and that of solids: for a solid, if it moves, must move altogether, and can only produce a pressure downwards, which will be equivalent to its weight or gravitating force; but a part of a mass of fluid may be in motion while other parts of the same mass may be perfectly quiescent; and although a mass of fluid can in no case produce a greater downward pressure than is equivalent to its weight, yet, at the same time, its want of cohesion among its particles will permit it to exert a lateral pressure, or tendency to spread horizontally, which will be exerted against the sides of the vessel that contains it, without altering or affecting its weight; and this constitutes the chief difference between the motions of solids and fluids. The investigation of this subject very naturally divides itself into three distinct heads. 1st, The effects which take place in the natural flowing of fluids through the various ducts or channels which convey them. 2ndly, The artificial means of producing motion in fluids, and destroying their natural equilibrium by means of pumps and various hydraulic engines and machines; and 3rdly, the force and power which may be derived from fluids in motion, whether that motion be produced naturally or artificially: and these several subjects will accordingly be separately considered in the following distinct chapters.

Chapter I.

On the Motion of Fluids through various Channels, Pipes, and Orifices.

Whatever may be the shape or conformation which the ultimate or original particles of fluids possess, they are found to flow over or amongst each other with less friction and impediment to motion than when they have to pass over solid substances. And as each individual particle is under the influence of gravitation, so it follows that no quantity of homogeneous fluid can be in a state of rest and perfect equilibrium, unless every part of its surface is on a level, by which we are not to understand a level plane, but a surface that is convex upwards to such an extent, that every one of its points may be equidistant from the earth's centre, to which fluids in common with all other matter gravitate. This equally applies to all masses of fluid, whether they are contained in a cup, in the ocean, or in any number of tubes or vessels which communicate with each other; for in this latter case the aggregate quantity of fluid must be considered as one mass. If, therefore, any one part of the surface is made higher than another, that high part may be conceived to be composed of a pillar or column of particles, and of course a greater number of particles will be necessary to constitute this high column than the shorter ones which surround it: consequently, the high column will gravitate with greater force, and by pressing downwards will remove such particles as are opposed to its descent until an equilibrium of pressure is produced; and this equilibrium can never exist until the whole mass of fluid is operated upon by the same force, an effect that occurs only when the surface is truly level. In the same manner, if one perpendicular column of fluid is conceived to be shorter than the others that surround it, it will contain fewer particles, and hence will be lighter than them; the consequence of which will be that the heavier surrounding columns will press upon and buoy up that which is lighter, until an equilibrium of pressure is produced by their becoming equal or level.

As the particles of all fluids gravitate, so will any vessel whatever, that contains a quantity of water or other fluid, be drawn towards the earth with a power equivalent to the weight of the fluid it contains; and if the quantity of the fluid be double, triple, or increased in any other proportion, so will the weight or gravitating influence be doubled, tripled, or increased in like proportion; from which we learn an important hydraulic corollary, that the weight or pressure of fluids at rest is simply as their quantities or heights: so that if a perpendicular pipe three inches diameter, and three feet high, contains nine pounds of water, that pressure of nine pounds will be exerted upon a valve or stopper of any description, and three inches diameter, placed in the bottom of the pipe; and if the pipe is made twice as high, or six feet long, the pressure will be eighteen pounds, if three times as high, twenty-seven pounds—the pressure increasing in the same ratio as the altitude of the column, while the valve or orifice below remains the same,—a circumstance which is of great consequence to be known in the construction of pumps and engines for raising water.

Water not only gravitates with the vessel that contains it as in the last case, but independently of it; and thus, if the containing vessel is supposed stationary and a hole is bored in its bottom, the contained water will flow out and descend through the air for the purpose of obtaining a lower situation than it before occupied; and, in so flowing out, those particles of fluid which were over, or in immediate contact with the hole, will be discharged first. Their motion will of course cause a momentary vacuum or void space above the hole, and from the ease with which the particles of fluids slide over each other, and thereby press in all directions alike, it is not a perpendicular column of particles, equal in their base to the area of the hole that will be set in motion, but particles will flow in all directions towards the hole, and thus put the whole mass of fluid into motion; and if the water so flowing out falls perpendicularly, its descent will be accelerated in the same proportion, and its motion will be regulated by the same laws as apply to the falling of solid bodies. When water flows in a current or stream, as in rivers or channels, it does so in consequence of the end of the channel towards which it is flowing being lower than that from which it proceeds, in which case its motion is referrible to that of solids descending inclined planes; but, from the want of cohesion among the particles of fluids, their motions are much more irregular than those of solids, and they involve a number of intricacies of very difficult solution, and which are rendered still more uncertain in their investigation, by the few experiments that have accurately been tried on a large scale to furnish data for calculation. The friction that occurs between a solid and the surface upon which it moves can be accurately ascertained, but not so with a fluid; for in this, while one part may be moving rapidly, another may be quite stationary, moving slowly, or even moving in a contrary direction. This is particularly observable in rivers, where the central part or main current will always be found flowing with much greater rapidity than either side; and experiment proves that the same effect occurs when water flows through pipes, for that water which is in contact with the side of the pipe moves with much more resistance than that at the centre, whereby the calculated discharge of any given pipe of considerable length becomes much less than is due to its magnitude. The term 'friction' is applied to this obstruction to the passage of fluids, in the same manner as it is to solids, and it exists to such an extent as to become an object of considerable inconvenience in practice. It can only be obviated by making the conveying-pipe of much larger dimensions than would otherwise be necessary, so as to allow the free passage of a sufficient quantity of fluid through the centre of the pipe, while a ring or hollow cylinder of water is considered to be nearly at rest all around it. Other circumstances besides friction likewise tend to diminish the quantity of fluid which would otherwise pass through pipes, such as the existence of sharp or right-angled turns in them, and permitting eddies or currents to be formed, or not providing for the eddies or currents that form naturally by suiting the shape of the pipe to them. It follows therefore that, whenever a bend or turn is necessary in a water-pipe, it should be made in as gradual a curve or sweep as possible, instead of the form of an acute or even right angle; that the pipe should not only be sufficiently capacious to afford the necessary supply, but should be of an equal bore throughout, and free from all projections or irregularities, against which the water can strike and form eddies or reverberations, since these will impede the progress of the fluid as effectually as the most solid obstacles. These subjects have been particularly investigated and examined by Newton, Bernoulli d'Alembart, De Buat, Robison, Venturi, Dr. Young, and many others; and the following important practical results obtained from their labours are highly worthy of attention: 1st. The friction of water in rivers or channels increases as the square of the velocity. 2nd. Although the sides of a pipe must in every case produce a certain degree of friction, yet that defect is frequently overbalanced by a duly-proportioned size of pipe properly fixed, giving a moving direction to the fluid which it would not otherwise obtain, and by which a greater quantity of discharge is produced than could otherwise take place. Thus, for example, a vessel or reservoir, having a thin bottom of tin, with a smooth circular hole formed therein, might be supposed most capable of parting rapidly with its water, because the fluid in running out has no continued length of substance to rub against, and consequently it might be imagined that very little friction could be generated; but M. Venturi found by his experiments, that such a vessel did not discharge its water so rapidly as another containing the same height of water and area of hole to which a short pipe of the same diameter as the hole was applied, and by varying the length of pipe he ascertained, that when its length was equal to twice its diameter it produced the most rapid discharge, for being so circumstanced it discharged eighty-two quarts of water in 100 seconds, while the simple hole, without the pipe, discharged but sixty-two quarts in the same time. Pursuing the same experiments, he found that if the pipe, instead of being applied to the bottom of the reservoir, so as to be flat and even with it, was made to project some distance into it as at *p*, in the vessel A, *fig.* 1, it had the effect of diminishing the flow of water even to less than issued through the simple hole without any pipe. This phenomenon of a pipe and hole, of similar area, discharging various quan-

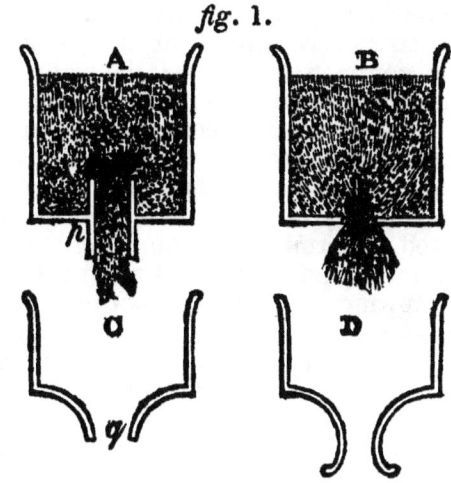

fig. 1.

tities of water under different circumstances, while the head or pressure remain the same, is sufficiently accounted for by the cross or opposing currents in which all fluids move, when the conducting pipes or vessels are formed so as to oppose or divert the assisting currents that would otherwise form: thus currents will form from the top and sides of the containing vessels towards the orifice of discharge, as indicated by the direction of the long dots, drawn within the vessel shown in section at B, *fig.* 1. The direction of these dots do not, however, stop at the discharging orifice, but, from the inertia of water, are constrained to cross each other and pass beyond it; hence to a certain extent they tend to stop or shut up the orifice against the passage of that water that is descending more perpendicularly, and by their contending influence cause the water that issues to run in a screw-like form. This effect is in a great measure counteracted and destroyed by the application of a short tube below the hole, but if that tube projects into the vessel as at A, the dots assume a new form, and those columns which descend from near the outsides of the vessel, by turning up again to reach the discharging orifice, are thrown into a more direct opposition to the motion of the central descending columns, at the same time that they are themselves constrained to turn suddenly in opposition to their inertia before they can enter the pipe; and thus the discharge is more effectually impeded than if it were proceeding from a mere hole through a thin bottom.

Sir Isaac Newton investigated the curves in which a fluid will proceed from the interior of a reservoir to a discharging orifice in its bottom, and found that the solid figure produced by the streams flowing from all parts to one common centre, viz. the orifice of discharge as indicated by the dots in B, was an Hyperboloid of the fourth order; and Venturi, from finding the great difference of discharge through the same area of opening as before stated, determined on applying a discharging-pipe of this, the natural form of flowing water, to the bottom of a reservoir as shown at C, when he found that although the bottom orifice q was the same as before, the quantity discharged was increased to ninety-eight quarts in the same period of time: and conceiving that the curve which water naturally assumes in running was continued beyond the point of discharge, he likewise enlarged the lower or discharging end of the delivering pipe by making it bell or trumpet mouthed in the same curve, as at D; and from this form he obtained the maximum quantity of water that could be delivered through a given orifice.

It will be evident that these examples do not refer to extended lengths of pipe, but merely to the rapid discharge of water from reservoirs, and they are merely given here to show by what simple means the flow of water may be impeded or increased in practice.

As water in descending is actuated by the same laws as falling bodies, it follows that its motion will become accelerated: therefore, in rivers or open channels, the velocity and quantity discharged at different depths would be as the square roots of those depths, did not the friction against the bottom of the channel interfere and check the rapidity of flow which would otherwise take place at that part, but by which a uniform, straight-forward velocity is produced. Thus, in *fig*. 2, if A B C D represents a reservoir of water, and B C G I a canal leading therefrom, and sloping from the prolonged horizontal line A B H, the bottom water at C

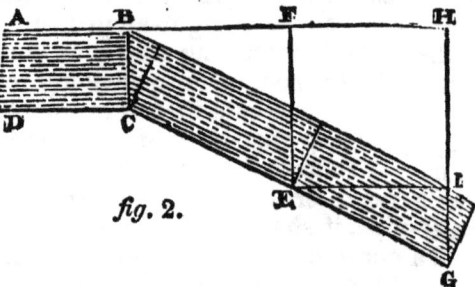

fig. 2.

would have a velocity as the square root of the depth B C. The water at E would flow with a velocity proportioned to the square root of the depth F E, and that at G as $\sqrt{\mathrm{H\,G}}$, while the top water at I would have a less velocity, or one only equal to the bottom water at E; because the point E is the same depth as the point I from the level line A B H. The same law holds good with respect to the spouting or flowing of water through jets or adjutages. Thus, if D is a hole made in the side of the vessel of water A, *fig*. 3, the water

fig. 3.

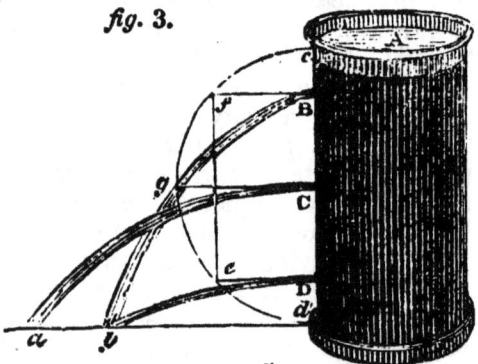

at D would only be pressed by the simple weight of the perpendicular column of water from A to D; but when the orifice D is opened and the water is permitted to spout out, its motion throws the whole column into effect, and it will now press upon and discharge the water from D, with the same force as if the water had been a solid, descending from A to D, *i. e.* as the square root of the height A D; and, for the same reason, any water issuing from other orifices, as C and B, would run in quantities and velocities proportionate to the square root of the depths of such orifices below the surface of the fluid. Now the quantity of water spouting from any hole in a given time, must necessarily be as the velocity with which it flows; and if, therefore, the hole D is supposed to be four times as deep below the surface A, as the hole B is, it follows that D will discharge twice the quantity of water, that can flow from B in the same time, because 2 is the square root of 4. So in like manner, if D had been nine times the depth of B, three times the quantity of water would issue from it, 3 being the square root of 9.

From the above law of spouting fluids, if a semicircle cgd be drawn from the central height of the column of fluid as at C, so that cCd may be the perpendicular diameter, and c the top of the fluid, while d is its bottom, any parallel lines drawn from that semicircle to the diameter, and at right angles to it, as at fB, gC, and eD, will be proportionate to the horizontal distances to which the fluid will spout from holes made at the points B C D where those lines cut the diameter; and as gC is the longest line that can be drawn within the semicircle, so we learn that a hole made in the centre of the column at C will project its water to the greatest horizontal distance or range ad, and that range (if in vacuo) would be equal to twice the length of the diameter cd. In like manner two jets of water spouting from B and D would be thrown to the same distance and meet in the point b, because the lines fB and eD proceeding from the respective jets are equal to each other. The path of the fluid in so spouting will in every case be a parabola, because it is impelled by two forces, the one being horizontal, while the other (gravitation) is perpendicular. The velocity of the jet will not be affected by its direction, because fluids press equally in all directions, and that velocity may be found by multiplying the square root of the head in feet by $8\frac{1}{44}$, so that a four-feet head would produce a velocity of discharge of rather more than 16 feet in a second. If the water, instead of flowing out at small holes, as in the figure, had been permitted to run from a long slit, or opening, of equal width throughout, it is evident from the laws above stated, that the discharge from the top and bottom would be very different, but the general velocity of the whole stream will be two-thirds of that at the lowest point. Hence if the head be not kept up to one height by a fresh supply, the initial velocity will soon be lost, and the discharge become very languid, which is the reason why canal locks, or reservoirs, are so long filling, although the process at first proceeds most rapidly. M. De Buat has given the best practical rule for calculating the velocity of rivers when the sectional area and inclination in a certain distance are known; that is, to suppose the whole quantity of water to be spread on a horizontal surface, equal in extent to the bottom and sides of the river, when the height at which the water would so stand is called the hydraulic mean depth. This found, the square of the velocity will be jointly proportional to this depth, and to the fall in a given length. The fall in such length must, therefore, be ascertained, and the square of the velocity in a second will be very nearly equal to the product of this fall multiplied by the hydraulic mean depth: the velocity thus given will, however, be a trifle too great, particularly if the river is very crooked. For practical purposes, the usual process is to take the sectional area of the stream in superficial feet by soundings, and to measure off ten, twenty, or any number of feet on the banks, and then to ascertain by a stop-watch the mean time that slices of turnip (or any other body of nearly the same weight as the water, and which will therefore float, but not float on the surface) thrown into different parts of the stream, take to pass through this measured distance, from which the number of cubic feet of water flowing through the stream in a given time can be pretty accurately determined.

Pipes must be considered in the same light as small rivers, taking the mean depth as one-fourth of the diameter, and a sufficiently accurate determination of the velocity will be obtained by supposing the height of the head of water from its surface to the discharging orifice to be diminished in the same proportion as the diameter of the pipe would be increased by adding to it one-fiftieth part of its length, and finding the whole velocity corresponding to four-fifths of this height. Thus, if the diameter of the pipe was one inch, and its length 100 inches, we must suppose the effective height to be reduced to one-third by friction, and the discharge must be calculated from a height four-fifths as great as this. If the pipe had been two inches, the head would only have been supposed to be reduced to one-half by the friction, and such a pipe would therefore discharge five times as much water as the former, although only twice the diameter; a circumstance that requires the serious attention of all such as are practically concerned in the construction of pumps, or distribution of water through pipes for any purposes.

Chapter II.

Of the various Pumps, Engines, and Machines for raising Water.

Having, in the preceding Chapter, laid down the fundamental principles upon which the motions of fluids depend, and shown how they are acted upon by the natural effects of gravitation, the next object will be, to show how their gravitation may be overcome with the greatest advantage; and how water may be raised, and made to move in various directions, to supply the wants of man. This division of the subject is of the greatest practical utility, as embracing an account of the various pumps, engines, and machines, which have, from time to time, been invented and constructed for this purpose; and numerous as they may appear to be, yet it will be found that they are all comprehended under four general heads; viz. those machines in which water is lifted in vessels, by the application of some mechanical force to them; those, in which it is raised by the pressure of the atmosphere; those which act by compression on the water, either immediately, or by the intervention of condensed air; and those which act by the weight and momentum of the water, of which they raise a part.

The earlier hydraulic machines appear to have been constructed on the first or simplest principle, with the exception of the pump of Ctesebes of Alexandria, who flourished about one hundred and twenty years before Christ, but respecting the particular construction of which little appears to be known. Probably, the first process resorted to, was the common bucket and rope, either raised by the hands, or drawn up by a windlass, as in our common draw-wells; but as such a process is very tedious in deep wells, and even expensive, if performed by manual labour, it would easily be improved by the employment of animal strength to a greater load, such as using several buckets, at different heights, on the same rope or chain; which approximates very closely to the more modern bucket-engine and chain-pump. Accordingly, two of the most ancient hydraulic engines are on this principle; viz. the Persian Wheel, and the Archimedian Screw.

The *Persian Wheel*, shown at *fig.* 4, must be of greater diameter, than the height to which it may be necessary to raise the water, and must stand in the stream or reservoir from which the water is to be taken; it consists of a rim or circle of wood, supported by arms or spokes from the central axis or gudgeon *m*, upon which the wheel revolves in a vertical direction. Upon its circumference a number of buckets or boxes, as *n, o, p,* and *q*, are hung by iron loops upon round iron bolts, in such a manner, that these boxes may constantly hang upright as the wheel revolves, and since the lower boxes *n n* are constrained, by the motion of the wheel, to dip into the water *r*, they will become filled, and will carry up their charge of water as at *o o o*, until at length arriving at the highest point *p*, they all in succession come into contact with the cistern *s*, by which they are tilted up, and discharge their contents into it, and having passed over it, they descend on the opposite side *q q* in an empty state, and are ready to be filled again by dipping into the water. Motion may be given to this wheel, either by the power of animals, or, if *r* is a running stream with sufficient water to spare, by equipping the circumference of the wheel itself with vanes or float-boards similar to those of the wheel of any water-mill, in which case it will raise up a portion of that water by which it is itself driven round. Small springs *t t* are fixed to each of the buckets, at that part which comes into contact with the side of the cistern *s*, for the double purpose of breaking the violence of the blows which the buckets would otherwise give to the cistern, and likewise for more effectually tilting the buckets to enable them to completely discharge their contents. Simple as this machine may appear to be, yet it is one of the most cheap and effectual that can be put up for irrigating land for farming or gardening purposes, where it may be necessary to raise a part of the water of a running stream into a higher situation. It requires no care or attendance while working, and as it moves incessantly while the stream runs, it will carry up a very considerable quantity of water,

HYDRAULICS.

fig. 4.

even if its buckets are but small, and the smaller they are the less power will be required to give motion to the wheel. It likewise requires none of that nicety in its construction which is usually necessary in millwork, but will act if made in the roughest manner. It may likewise be applied in many cases with advantage to the tail stream of a water-mill, when water is scarce, so as to work by the water after it has passed the mill-wheel, in order to raise and return a portion of it, instead of letting it all run to waste.

Nearly allied to the Persian Wheel, but much more elegant in its contrivance, is *The Cochlion*, or *Screw o Archimedes*, a machine invented and used by this philosopher, for raising water and draining land in Egypt, about 200 years before the Christian æra. The Cochlion consists of a succession of buckets or recesses to be filled with the water to be raised; but instead of their being separate and detached, as in the last-described machine, they are formed by the lower parts of the hollow thread of a screw, and their motion and succession are brought about by turning that screw. This will be better understood by referring to *fig.* 5, which is a representation of this machine, and in which $vuwx$ shows a flexible tube or pipe, wound in a screw-like form round a solid cylinder yy, the two extreme ends of which are equipped with pivots, so that the cylinder, with its encircling screw-formed tube, may be made to revolve on its axis by the force of running water, or any other power applied to its upper or lower end. Lastly, this machine must be supported by its two pivots, so as to make an angle with the horizon, as shown in the figure. If now the lower end v of the tube be supposed to be covered with water, that water will flow to its own level within the tube, and will occupy the lowest bend v; and if now the cylinder yy be turned round by its handle, in a direction from left to right, the lower end of the spiral tube will become elevated above the surface of the water in the reservoir, and that water which had entered into the tube will have no opportunity of escaping, but, by the motion of the screw-tube, will flow within it, until, at the end of the first revolution, it will be

HYDRAULICS.

fig. 5.

found in the second lower bend u. In the mean time, the lowest extreme end of the tube will have made a second dip into the water of the reservoir, and will receive a second charge, which, in like manner, will be transferred to u at the next revolution, while the water lately at u will be elevated to w; until at length, when the cylinder has made as many revolutions as there are turns of the tube round it, each lower bend will become filled with water, whatever may be the length of the cylinder $y\,y$; and, as the extreme upper end a of the tube becomes depressed, in each revolution, into the situation of a lower bend, it will there discharge its water into an elevated cistern b placed to receive it. The quantity of water raised by this machine will depend upon the capacity of the screw-pipe, and the angle above the horizon at which it is placed to work; but it will be seen by the figure, that there is room to dispose several pipes parallel to each other, round the same cylinder, when they will all work simultaneously; or the whole cylinder itself may be made into a hollow screw, by merely placing a thin, screw-formed diaphragm or partition round its central axis, which is the most usual form of the machine in practice. On a small scale, it may be constructed by wrapping one or more flexible lead pipes round a solid cylinder of wood, which forms a useful machine for raising water to small heights. It was formerly much used; but owing to its liability to become choked by mud, weeds, and other impediments, and the great difficulty of cleaning it out, it is seldom met with. It has, from its specious appearance of seeming to throw the entire weight of water that it is raising upon its axles, and the little friction with which these may be made to move by friction rollers, had astonishing powers ascribed to it; but if investigated, it will be found that the water is merely made to flow up an inclined plane; and whether water, or any other weight be drawn up a fixed inclined plane, or it be stationary until moved by an inclined plane being forced under it, as is the case with the quantities of water contained in the several bends v, u, w, x, &c. the mechanical effort will be the same; consequently, this machine possesses no other mechanical advantage over other constructions of pumps, except that its motions are attended by less friction than belongs to most of them.

The principle of the Archimedian Screw is occasionally adopted in the wheel-form, by making the spokes or radii hollow and curved, as shown at $c\,c\,c$ (fig. 4.): but in this way the water cannot be raised higher than the centre or axis of the wheel; for the hollow spokes being open at the circumference of the wheel, dip into the water and receive their supply, which, from the wheel's motion, and their peculiar form, is carried to the axis; which may either be hollow to receive and carry away the water, or a cistern may be placed under it to receive the water from the arms,

HYDRAULICS.

The *Bucket-Engine* and *Chain-Pump* are but modifications of the above-described machines, and are very useful in particular situations. The chain-pump is shown at *fig.* 6, and consists of a number of flat plates or discs of wood or metal *d d d*, which are usually square, and are connected together through their centres by an iron rod, with joints

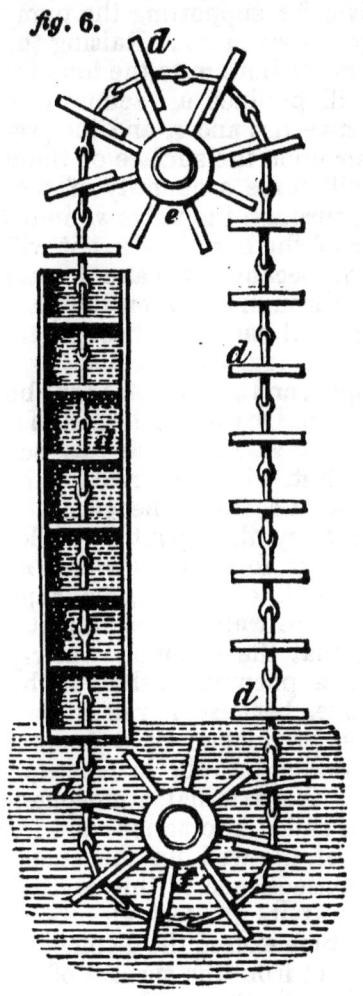

fig. 6.

between each board, so as to permit them to turn with nearly the same freedom as if they were connected by a chain. The chain of plates so formed is supported and kept in its place by two wheels *e* and *f*, each being furnished with double projecting arms to lay hold of, and support the plates in succession, and in such manner, that if the upper wheel *e* is turned by a winch, it will cause the whole chain to move, one side of it passing upwards, while the other descends continually in the same direction. The ascending side of the chain is made to pass through a considerable length of square box or trunk which, by fitting pretty closely to the plates, forms the pump. The lower wheel *f*, as well as the lower end of the trunk, must be under water, and the chain of plates passing upwards through the trunk, produces a succession of chambers or cavities that become filled with water, which is eventually discharged from the top. From the formation of this pump, it requires to work in deep water, and consequently cannot drain a reservoir to the bottom; but it has the advantage of not being liable to choke, and will even bring up mud, stones, and such weeds and chips, as would entirely destroy the operations of a more perfect machine; and notwithstanding it may be supposed to lose much of its power, owing to the plates not fitting very accurately into the trunk, yet as an upper chamber can only leak into one that is below, and the motion of the plates is very rapid, it will, when properly constructed, bring up a very considerable quantity of water; and it is, on this account, more frequently used than any other sort of pump, in draining the water from foundations, in the construction of bridges, docks, and large works. If the top and bottom wheels *e* and *f* are supposed to be retained, while the trunk is taken away, and a number of buckets, similar to those upon the wheel (*fig.* 4.), are attached to the chain, instead of the square plates *d d d*, then the machine becomes a bucket-engine, which is but another form of the Persian wheel already described. There are many more machines of this class for raising water, but the examples already given embrace the principles of most of them, and it would be quite beyond the limits of this work to attempt to describe the whole of them.

The *Rope-Pump* of Vera, described in most books on Hydraulics, consists likewise of an upper and lower pulley, formed in the ordinary manner, but with several grooves in each, in which endless ropes of very loosely spun horsehair or wool are made to move with great rapidity by a multiplying wheel connected with the upper pulley. The lower pulley, together with a great part of the rope, moves in the water, which is merely brought up by adhering to the ropes and the rapidity of their motion. This, therefore, is but a very imperfect and rude kind of bucket-pump, and is by no means deserving the place it has so long held in the catalogue of Hydraulic machines.

The second class of contrivances for raising water, or that in which they act by atmospheric pressure, comprises all those machines to which the name of *pump* is more particularly applied. Of pumps there are several varieties; but the simplest and most common is *the ordinary lift*, or *Household Pump*, which depends chiefly on the pressure of the atmosphere for its action. This useful machine is one of great antiquity, its invention being ascribed by Vitruvius to Ctesebes of Alexandria, before-mentioned; but the principles upon which it acts were not understood until long afterwards, as appears by the very lame explanation of them that is attempted by Galileo towards the beginning of the seventeenth century. The nature of atmospheric pressure was not, however, at this time at all understood; and it is a curious fact, that the experiments made upon this now common machine should have led to the invention of the barometer, by which the variations of the atmosphere have since been so accurately investigated.

The form and construction of the common lift-pump is shown in section at *fig.* 7, in which mm is the cylinder or

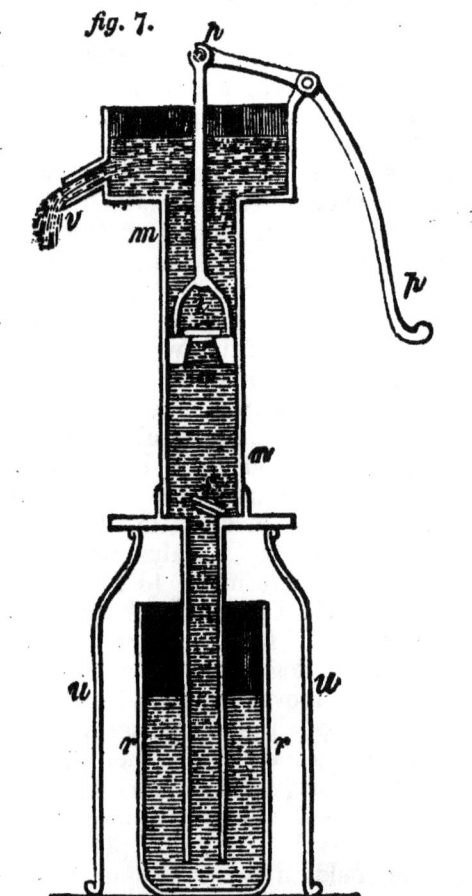

fig. 7.

barrel, n an air-tight piston, which moves or works within it, by means of the piston-rod o, moved by the lever pp, or any other contrivance; q is the suction or feeding pipe, descending into the jar of water rr, which would be a well or other reservoir in an actual pump, s a valve at the bottom of the barrel covering the top of the feeding-pipe, and t a valve in the piston, both which valves open upwards; uu is an open-topped receiver for supporting the pump above the jar of water rr. Raising the piston n from the bottom to the top of the barrel, will produce a vacuum in the barrel between n and s, and the pressure of the air upon the surface of the water at rr, will force a quantity of that water up q, through the valve s, into the interior of the barrel, where it will be retained, because it cannot pass back again through s; when the piston n is lowered, it can pass through the water previously raised, because its valve t will open, and thus it gets to the bottom of the barrel. On raising the piston a second time, the water, which has so passed through it, will be carried up by it into the cistern o, from whence it will be discharged by the spout v, while a new vacuum is forming between n and s, which will, of course, be supplied as before with water; and thus it will appear, that the common water-pump is rather a pneumatic, than an hydraulic machine, because it raises water only by the production of a vacuum within the working barrel; in consequence of which, the external atmospheric pressure is called into action, and forces the water of the well up the suction-pipe. The consequence of this is, that if the piston, at its greatest elevation, should at any time exceed the distance of thirty-three feet from the surface of the water in the well, the working of the pump may not produce a sufficiently perfect vacuum to raise the water.

It may not be amiss to notice a frequent error in the construction of pumps, which is very detrimental to their action, namely, making the feeding-pipe, or that pipe which proceeds from the water to be raised, to the bottom of the working barrel, of too small a capacity, under a notion, that if this pipe is large, the piston in ascending will have to raise and draw after it a much thicker column of water, and consequently a much greater load than is necessary. The fallacy of this supposition is clearly shown in the Treatise upon Hydrostatics; for whether a column of water be pressing downwards upon a piston, or be underneath an ascending piston, and is drawn upwards by it, as is the case in a pump, the circumstances of pressure will always remain the same, and will be regulated only by the perpendicular height and horizontal sectional area of the column. The working barrel of the pump, or the piston that works in it, will therefore always determine the area of the column; and whether the pipe that carries the water up into it, or upwards from it, be greater or less, the effective force to work the pump will be the same, friction only excepted.

Notwithstanding the common lifting pump is incapable of raising water from more than 33 feet (or rather 30 feet) below the place where it may be fixed, yet it may be made to deliver water at almost any required height above its piston by the application of a continued straight pipe instead of the cistern-head shown at $o\,v$ in the last figure. Thus if that cistern-head and spout be supposed to be taken away, and 20 or 30 feet of close iron pipe to be added to the top of the working-barrel $m\,m$, since the water once raised cannot pass downwards again through the valve t in the piston or bucket $t\,n$, it must continue to rise with each stroke of the pump, until at length it will flow over the top of the pipe, or through a spout inserted in any part of its side. In this case atmospheric pressure has nothing to do with the elevation above the piston, consequently it may be carried to any height that the strength of the pump will admit of, but the handle $p\,p$ (or any other contrivance by which the pump is worked) must be fixed above the top of this pipe, and the piston-rod o must be equal in length to the pipe in order to keep the working-barrel within the limits of atmospheric pressure, which makes this arrangement of pump inapplicable to very great depths on account of the bending of the piston-rod. Where cast-iron pipes are used, this may be in a great measure prevented by placing small pieces with projecting arms of sufficient length to touch the inside of the pipe at each joint of the piston-rod, or about 10 or 12 feet asunder, when this pump may be used for considerable depths with advantage.

In using pumps to draw muddy or sandy water, it is always advisable to set the bottom of the pump in a close wicker basket or other strainer, because sand and small stones very soon destroy the leather and working parts of any pump; and when pumps are used for hot liquors, which is the case in many manufactories, thick hempen canvass must be substituted for leather, unless the valves and piston are made entirely of metal.

As the above-described pump acts entirely by atmospheric pressure, and is therefore incapable of drawing water from a greater depth than from 30 to 33 feet, it will at once appear that it is inapplicable to mines, or those situations in which it may be necessary to bring water from great depths, or to raise it to great elevations. Whenever this requires to be done, the third class of pumps or machines must be resorted to, or those which act by mechanical force or compression, instead of atmospheric pressure alone; and all pumps of this description are very properly denominated *Forcing-pumps*. Although atmospheric pressure is not necessary to the construction of forcing-pumps, yet it is in most cases resorted to for raising the water in the first instance into the body of the pump where the forcing action commences and takes place; and when so constructed, such pumps are generally called lift and force pumps, and in all the machines of this description the water may be raised to any required height without limit, provided there is sufficient power to work the pump, and the pipes and materials of the machine are strong enough to bear the pressure of the perpendicular column of water.

Forcing-pumps do not differ materially in construction from the common lifting or household pump already described; indeed that pump, by a mere inversion of its parts, may be made into a forcing-pump, that is to say, placing the piston below, and the stop-valve and delivering pipe above, as shown at *fig.* 8, where $h\,h$ shows the inverted working barrel, and i the inverted piston and rod with a valve opening upwards; k is the stop-valve placed at the top, instead of the bottom of the barrel, and also opening upwards into the rising pipe $l\,l$, which may be continued to any required height; the lower end of the working-barrel is quite open, and must stand in, and be covered with the water it has to raise, so that no suction or feed pipe is necessary to this pump, and the piston i may be worked by a handle and series of levers m, n, o, or in any other convenient manner. After the description already given of the common lift-pump, it will be needless to say any thing on the action of this machine, as it is presumed the figure will render it suffi-

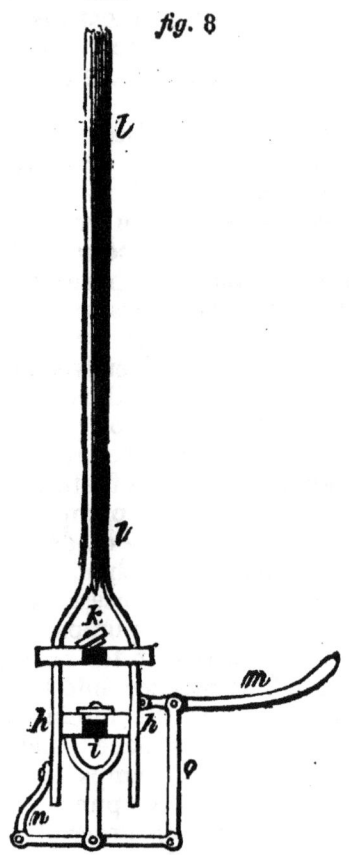

fig. 8

ciently obvious; while the lower end of the working-barrel hh is immersed in water, and the piston i moves upwards and downwards, the barrel will be filled through the piston-valve at each down-stroke, and at each up-stroke its contents will be expelled through the stop-valve k into the ascending pipe ll; and whatever the diameter of this pipe may be, still its resistance will constantly be equal to the weight of a column of water of the size of the working-barrel, and of a height equal to the *perpendicular* altitude of the water in the ascending pipe; for this pipe may be placed horizontally or obliquely so as materially to alter its length, but it is the perpendicular height between the surface of the water to be raised and its point of discharge, which must alone be taken into account in estimating the load upon a pump, since increase of length, without height in the pipe, produces no other resistance than that of friction, which is easily overcome by increasing the capacity of the pipe.

It may appear that the above pump is applicable to every purpose and to every situation, such as raising water from mines and the deepest places; but this is not the case, owing to the almost imperceptibly small elasticity of water, and the effects of the *vis inertiæ*, which belongs to fluids in common with solid matter. In working the pump shown in the last figure, if we presume the pipe ll to be full of water, that water has not sufficient elasticity to permit the barrel hh to discharge its contents through the valve k without putting all the water contained in ll into motion, while, when the piston descends, that motion will be at an end. The water in ll will therefore be in an alternate state of rest and motion; and if the column is long, and its quantity great, the *vis inertiæ* will be very considerable, that is to say, it will require a considerable exertion of force to get it from a state of rest into motion; and when it has once begun to move, it will have no immediate tendency to return again to rest, but might be continued in its motion with less force than that which was originally employed to move it. The descent of the piston, however, allows sufficient time for all the motion that was communicated to be completely lost; and hence in working this pump we not only have the weight of the column to overcome, but the natural inertia to combat with at every stroke. This may in great measure be removed by keeping two, or what is still better, three pumps constantly at work by what is called a triple or three-throw crank; and accordingly this expedient is generally resorted to in all small engines for throwing water to a great height: for by this means the water is never permitted to stand still in the pipes, but a constant flow or stream is maintained. The triple crank is an axle of iron, bent into the form shown at *fig.* 9, so as to form three elbows $v\,u\,w$, to each of which the piston-rod of a

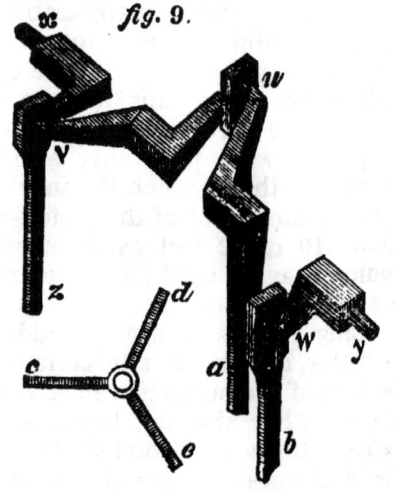

fig. 9.

pump is attached by a swivel-joint, while the whole revolves on two end-bearings or pivots $x\,y$. The consequence of this is, that while the piston-rod b connected to the crank w is at the very lowest point or bottom of its stroke, the piston-rod a with its crank u is very nearly at its greatest height, but the rod z and the crank v are horizontal and in the middle of their stroke: the pump connected with v would therefore be the only active one in the present state of things, but if the crank is supposed to be in motion, before the rod z gets to the bottom, b will have begun its ascending and a its descending stroke, so that by this contrivance one pump is always brought into effective action just before another ceases to act, and thus a constant stream is produced. To give the triple crank its most perfect action, the three cranks or arms should make angles of 120 degrees with each other, or, when viewed from either end x or y, should stand like the three radii $c\,d\,e$ drawn separately under the last figure.

In most cases of raising water, the forcing-pump may be resorted to with advantage, particularly when the pump is of large dimensions, and the height to which the water is to be raised is great, for this might endanger the distortion or breaking of the crank above-described. The forcing-pump is likewise generally used in conjunction with an air-vessel, or strong metallic box to contain condensed air, the spring or elasticity of which enables this pump to produce all the beneficial effects of a constant current with one, or at most two working-barrels, instead of the three that are necessary with the triple crank, and thus a considerable portion of friction is avoided.

The forcing-pump is made in two forms, suited to the situation and circumstances under which it has to work. The simplest and best construction is shown at *fig.* 10. It consists of a truly-bored cylindrical working-barrel ff, the top of which is quite open to admit the solid piston i, which works in it in a perfectly air and water tight state, by means of the lever or handle $g\,g$, or any other or more convenient application of power: h is the feeding-pipe, dipping into the water to be raised as in any other pump, and this pipe may of course be made of any length under 33 feet; k is the stop-valve, covering the top of the feed-pipe, and permitting water to rise into the working-barrel as the piston ascends, but not permitting it to return again: so that whenever the

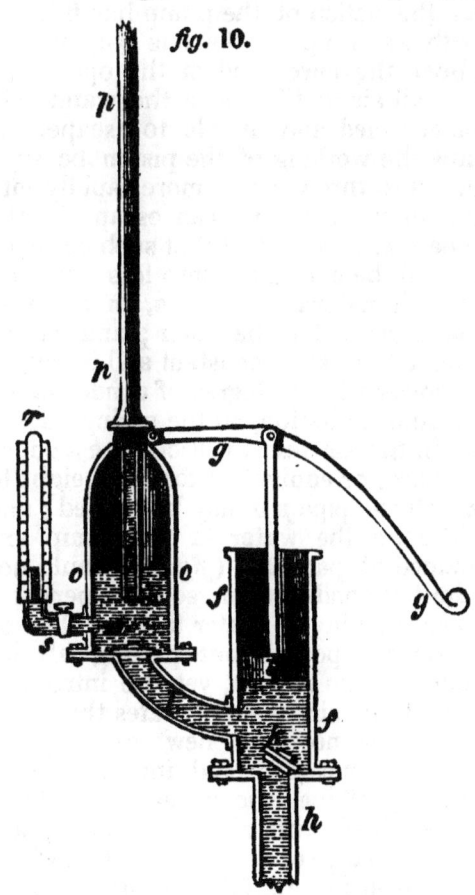

fig. 10.

piston is raised by its handle g, the barrel will be filled with water forced up the pipe h by atmospheric pressure; and when the piston descends again, since there is no valve in it to permit the water to pass through it, it will be forced up the lateral pipe l (opening into the bottom of the working-barrel,) and through the valve m, which prevents its returning back again, so that it is constrained to find its way up the rising pipe $p\,p$ fixed above the valve m, and this pipe may be continued to any required height without regard to the pressure of the atmosphere, since the ascent of the water does not depend upon its action, but upon the mechanical force that is applied to the handle g to depress the piston. While the piston rises to fill the working-barrel, the valve m will be shut, and of course all motion of the fluid in the pipe $p\,p$ will cease, and hence the use of the air-vessel n; for it will be seen that the pipe $p\,p$ is not joined on immediately above the valve m, but that it passes through the top of an air-tight copper or other hollow vessel n, and proceeds nearly to the bottom of it. Air being a lighter fluid than water will of course occupy the upper part of this vessel, and as soon as the action of the pump has filled it with water up to the line *o o*, or just above the lower end of the open pipe *p p*, all air that is above the water will be confined and unable to escape. If now the working of the piston be supposed to throw water more rapidly into the air-vessel than it can escape by the pipe *p p*, it is evident that such confined air will be condensed into less compass than it naturally occupies, in order to make room for the water; and as the elasticity of air is constant and increases in power with its degree of condensation without limitation, so the spring of the air in the air-vessel will become a counterpoise, or equivalent for any height to which the pipe *p p* may be carried; and although the water in the pump explained at page 12, (*fig.* 8.) would not admit of condensation, so as to permit a fresh quantity of water to enter the ascending pipe without putting all its contents into motion, yet the introduction of the air-vessel obviates this difficulty, for now the new quantity of water is not delivered into a former quantity of inelastic water, but into a vessel filled with air which readily allows a change of dimensions; and while the piston *i* (*fig.* 10.) is rising and projecting no water, the previously condensed air in *n* has time to re-expand into its former volume, by expelling an equivalent quantity of water up the pipe *p p*, and thus, if the air-vessel is large enough, a constant and equable current may be maintained.

Fig. 11 shows the other form of the forcing-pump, though this construction is generally called *The Lift and Force-pump*. Its formation is the same as the last-described figure, except that the piston is not solid, but is perforated, and covered by a valve opening upwards, as in the common lifting-pump: the piston-rod *q* likewise moves in an air-tight manner, through a stuffing-box, or collar of leather, on the top of the working-barrel, which in this case is closed; and the lateral delivering-pipe with its air-vessel proceeds from the upper, instead of the lower, part of the working-barrel. This pump not only has the stuffing-box, but three valves, instead of two as in the last example. It is consequently rather more intricate and expensive in its construction, with no other advantage than that it is rather more cleanly in its working; for if the piston of the former pump is not quite water-tight, a quantity of water may flow over the

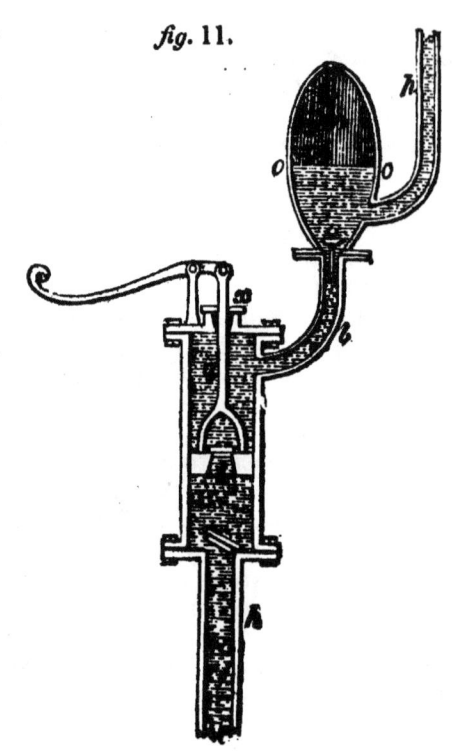

fig. 11.

open top of its working-barrel, which cannot be the case in this pump if well made. Their action is very nearly alike, for this last pump raises water through the suction-pipe *h* by the elevation of the piston *i*: on depressing the piston, that water passes through it by its valve, and gets above it to fill the upper part of the working-barrel; on the re-ascent of the piston, the water, being unable to escape at the top of the barrel on account of the cover and stuffing-box *x*, is forced up the lateral pipe *l* into the air-vessel, and from thence passes away by the ascending pipe *p* as before. The first pump raises water by the down and this by the up stroke; but this is easily changed if required, by adopting a lever of the first, instead of one of the second kind, as shown in the figures.

The air-vessel, shown in this figure, likewise differs from that in *fig.* 10, because the delivering pipe *p* of the first passes through the top, and the latter through the bottom of the air-vessel; but they both proceed from near the bottom, and in either case, when the water has risen to the dotted line *o o*, so as to cover the lower end of this pipe, the air will be confined, and their operations must be alike. The air-vessel must be suited in its capacity to the magnitude of the pump or pumps that deliver water into it, (for several pumps are frequently made to open into one common air-vessel,) and ought in all cases to contain at least six or eight volumes of the pump, in order that the increasing expansive force of the air may not influence the motion of the piston during a single stroke: but for this no precise rule can be given, as the relative dimensions may vary to suit the circumstances of the case. These forcing-pumps with air-vessels are now very generally adopted in Water-Works for supplying cities or towns; and the height at which the water is at any time delivering may be very nearly estimated if the air-vessel is large, and the supply equable, by examining the degree of condensation of the air within it. This is very conveniently done by a gauge, consisting of a glass tube with a close top, applied by a stop-cock to the lower part of the air-vessel, or that which is always filled with water: thus, $r s$ (*fig.* 10.) represents such a tube, and as it has an open communication with the air-vessel when the cock s is open, the air in the top of the tube will suffer the same condensation as that within the vessel. The height of the space occupied by air within the tube must be measured; and as the air, at its ordinary density, will balance a column of water 33 feet high, so if confined air is loaded with the weight of such a column, it will shrink or be condensed into half its former bulk. Whenever, therefore, the air contained in the tube r is diminished to half its original length, the condensation within the air-vessel must be equal to two atmospheres, or, what is the same thing, the water in the pipe $p p$ must stand at the elevation of 33 feet. If the water in $p p$ is raised to twice 33 feet, or 66 feet, then the condensation within the air-vessel must be equal to three atmospheres, and the air within it, as well as within the tube, will be diminished to one-third of its original bulk. One-fourth of the bulk will indicate four atmospheres of condensation, and be equal to the elevation of the water column to 132 feet, and so on, more or less, as the barometer may vary.

That useful machine, the *Fire-engine*, or engine for extinguishing fires, is nothing more than two forcing-pumps of the construction shown at *fig.* 10, working into one common air-vessel placed between them, and from which the spouting pipe for directing the water upon the fire proceeds. The handles are so disposed, that while the piston of one pump is up the other is down; and they are elongated for the purpose of enabling a great number of men to work them at the same time, for the purpose of throwing a very large quantity of water, which is rendered a continuous stream by the action of the air-vessel. It is curious that the most ancient pump we are acquainted with, namely, that of Ctesebes, at least as it is handed down to us, very closely resembles the present fire-engine, for it consists of two forcing-pumps, disposed as just described; but instead of discharging their contents into an air-vessel, they merely deliver them into an intermediate close cistern, from which the water ascends by a perpendicular pipe, and in which nothing is wanting but the condensation of air*. It must, however, be observed, that both the pumps shown at *figs.* 10 and 11, would be forcing-pumps without their respective air-vessels; and though they act much more advantageously with them, they are sometimes constructed without these useful appendages.

A pump, the invention of M. de la Hire, produces the full effect of two pumps with the friction of one only, for it is a lift and force pump that raises an equal quantity of water by its up and down stroke. But few instances of its adoption occur, and considering its advantages, it is surprising that it is not more frequently put into practice. It is shewn in section at *fig.* 12, $t\,t$ being the working barrel, in which the solid piston v moves up and down, u is the feeding-pipe, and w the stop-valve upon it; x is a lateral pipe proceeding upwards from the bottom of the working barrel, until it terminates in the under part of the air vessel y, such termination being closed by a valve opening upwards into the air-vessel, from which z is the discharging-pipe. So far this pump precisely resembles that shewn and described by *fig.* 10, both in construction and action; but in the present pump, instead of the working-barrel $t\,t$ being open at its top, it is closed by a cap, and the piston rod $a\,a$ works in an air-tight manner through the stuffing-box b, consequently when the piston is depressed to expel the water out of the lower part of the working-barrel into

---

* See Ctesebes's Pump, article "Pump," in **Dr.** Hutton's Mathematical Dictionary, vol. ii. p. 304.

HYDRAULICS.

the air-vessel through the pipe x, a vacuum will be formed in the upper part

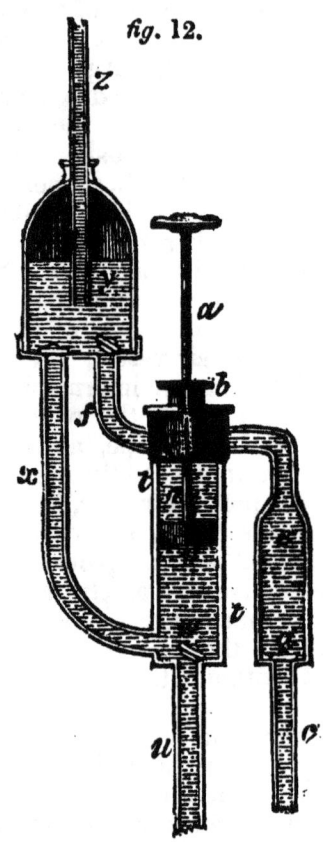

fig. 12.

of the working-barrel, and this is supplied by water through a second feeding-pipe c also descending into the well, and having a stop-valve d applied to it in a chamber or cavity e formed for that purpose; the upper part of this second suction-pipe opens into the top of the working-barrel above the greatest height to which the piston can ascend, and thus by its descent is that part of the barrel which is above the piston completely filled with water, while the lower part of it is emptying; and when the piston ascends again, all the water that has been so deposited above it, is forced up the pipe f into the same air-vessel y. The pipe f is likewise closed at its upper end by a valve opening upwards to prevent the return of the water when the piston descends, and thus by the alternate action of a piston moving in one barrel the beneficial effects of two pumps produced with the friction of only one.

Since it is impossible, when a pump is well made and is in good order, that its piston can move without displacing the water that is above or below it, according to the circumstances of its construction, so in all pumps that consist of cylindrical working-barrels and pistons, nothing more is necessary to ascertain the quantity of water they will deliver, than to calculate the solid or cubical contents of that part of the barrel in which the vacuum is produced, and to reduce it to some standard measure, and then to multiply this by the number of strokes made in a given time: thus if a pump is nine inches diameter, and makes an effective stroke of about eighteen inches, such a cylinder will be found to contain about 1134 cubic inches, and as $277\frac{1}{4}$ cubic inches make an imperial gallon, so four gallons will be equal to 1109 cubic inches; consequently such a barrel will contain and throw out rather more than four gallons at every stroke, and supposing this pump to make ten strokes in a minute, it would yield above forty gallons in a minute, or sixty times that quantity in an hour, and so on. This rule applies in every case, whether the water is sent to a small or great elevation, because the piston cannot move without displacing the water in the barrel; but a small allowance must be made for leakage or waste, because some water will constantly pass the piston and escape, or be otherwise lost and wasted.

This mode of calculation, as before observed, only applies to such pumps as have cylindrical working-barrels and pistons, but sometimes pumps are otherwise constructed, of which the fire-engine of the late Mr. Bramah, and the excentric pump are instances. In the former of these contrivances, the working-barrel, instead of being an entire cylinder, is a semi-cylinder, and lies horizontally, while the place of a piston is supplied by a parallelogram of the same radius and length as the semi-cylinder moving by an iron bar passing through its axis, and properly packed at its exterior edges. This parallelogram is made to vibrate through about 170 degrees by its handles, while its outer edges keep in contact with the interior surface and ends of the semi-cylinder, and two feeding and two delivering valves are placed upon the flat top or covering of the whole. This pump, therefore, in effect is the same as that of M. de la Hire last described, though quite different in form, and its mode of operation is nearly allied to *The Excentric Pump*, a section of which is shewn at *fig.* 13. It consists of a hollow drum or cylinder of metal $a\,d$, in the interior of which a solid cylinder b, of the same length, but of only half the diameter or

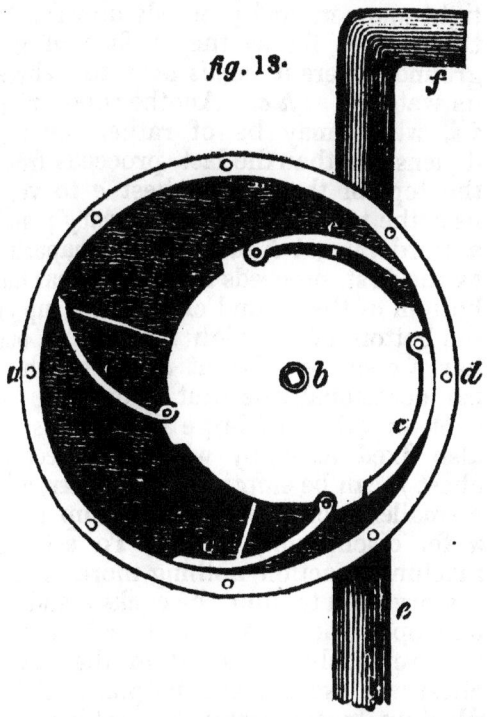

fig. 13.

thereabouts, is made to revolve by its axles passing through water-tight stuffing boxes in the sides of the larger and exterior cylinder. The internal cylinder does not revolve in the centre of the large cylinder, but is so placed that one of its convex exterior edges may come into close contact with some one part of the concave or internal surface of the larger cylinder, as shown in the figure; and the circular exterior surface of the small cylinder is equipped with four metal flaps or valves $cccc$, turning on hinges, and partaking of its own curvature, so that when they are shut down or closed, they form no projections, but appear as parts of the same cylinder. These flaps are made to open either by springs placed underneath them, or, what is still better, by two cross wires, sliding through the internal cylinder in such manner that they may cross each other exactly in its centre, by which their operation will be rendered equable in every part of their revolution. From the formation of this machine, when one of these flaps is brought by the revolution of the internal cylinder between itself and the external one, it will be pressed down close and will shut, but as the inner cylinder moves, it will be carried into a continually widening space until it arrives at a opposite to the last-mentioned situation, when the cavity formed between it and the smaller and larger cylinder will have so far increased as to form a vacuum, which is filled with water by the feeding pipe e. This cavity is no sooner so increased to its largest dimensions than it is diminished by a continuation of the revolution, in consequence of which the water being pent up and squeezed into less compass, makes its escape by the delivering pipe f; and as each of the flaps performs the same operation in its turn, this pump affords a very equable and constant supply of water. The greatest difficulty in its construction is, that of keeping the sides of the flaps so packed as to maintain a perfect contact with the sides of the large cylinder without unnecessary friction, a fault which equally holds good in Mr. Bramah's fire-engine, in all excentric pumps, and in all the rotatory steam-engines that have yet been invented. The Excentric Pump is of the lift and force variety, since it will deliver water to an indefinite height above its working cylinders.

The fourth class or division of pumps, or rather hydraulic machines for raising water, consists of such engines as act either by the gravity or weight of a portion of the water they have to raise, or of any other water that can be used for such purpose, or by its centrifugal force, momentum, or other natural powers; and this class, therefore, includes some very beautiful and truly philosophical contrivances, too numerous to be described in these limits: but the Hungarian machine, the Centrifugal Pump and the Water-Ram offer interesting examples of the general nature and construction of the machines which are placed under this division.

The Hungarian machine, so called from its having been employed in draining a mine at Chemnitz, in Hungary, produces its action by the condensation of a confined portion of air produced by the descent of a high column of water contained in a pipe, and therefore acts with a force proportionate to the weight of such column. Its general form is shown at fig. 14, by which will appear that it is an exceedingly simple and useful machine, admitting of many modifications and applications, but it can be used only in hilly countries, or situations where the source of water by which it is to be worked is as much above the top of the well, as the water to be raised is underneath it. In this figure a is supposed to be a well or the shaft of a mine, from the bottom of which it is necessary to raise the water standing

fig 14

at the level bb. cc' is the surface of the ground at the top of the well or shaft, at which the discharged water must have an opportunity of escaping, either by running to waste or being converted to some useful purpose; and d is the spring or other elevated source from whence the supply of water for working the machine may be obtained. The machine itself consists of three cisterns, chests, or reservoirs, two of which at e and f must be made very strong, and perfectly air-tight, while the third at d may be weaker and open at the top, as it is merely for collecting and retaining the spring, rain, or other water for working the machine. The lowest close chest or reservoir e must be sunk below the surface bb of the water in the shaft or well a, but must not come into contact with its bottom, otherwise the water would be prevented entering the chest by the valve g, which opens inwards for its admission. An open pipe hh passes from very near the bottom of this chest, through its top, in an air-tight manner, and proceeds upwards in the shaft as far as the surface of the ground, where it bends over to deliver its water as at hc. Another open pipe ii, which may be of rather smaller dimensions than the last, proceeds from the top of the lower chest e to very near the top of the second chest f; and a third pipe, kl, of the same capacity as the first, proceeds from very near the bottom of the second close chest, up to the bottom of the high reservoir d, but has a cock or valve at l, by which it can occasionally be shut or opened. A cock or valve, of large dimensions, is also fixed at m, by which the second chest f can be emptied of its water, and a smaller cock is fixed higher up as at n for discharging its air. To set the machine in action nothing more is necessary than to shut the cocks l and m, and open the cock n, from which the air previously contained in the lower chest will escape, and its place will be filled up by the water bb, which will pass through the valve g, until the chest e is completely filled. That done, the air cock n is to be shut, and the water cock l opened, when a column of water, equal to the full height and pressure of the cistern d, will rush down the pipe kl, and by filling the chest f will expel its air, which has no other opportunity of escaping but by the open pipe ii, down which it will pass, and produce a pressure on the surface of the water in the lower chest, equal to the entire height of the column kl; and the air thus thrown into the chest e, being in a condensed state, will force the water previously in that chest up the pipe hh, from whence it will be discharged at c. The lower chest e will now be filled with air, while the upper chest f will be occupied by water: therefore, the cock l must be shut, and that at m opened, when the whole of the water from f will be discharged at c', and will give the air in e an opportunity of returning again into f through the pipe ii; and as the air from e escapes, its place will be occupied by a new charge of water, which will rise through the valve g, and again fill the lower chest e, and prepare it for a second discharge. All, therefore, that is necessary to keep the machine in action is to open the cocks l and m alternately, that is to say, to keep the cock l open as long as any water flows

HYDRAULICS.

from the discharging pipe at *h c*, and as soon as the efflux ceases, to shut the cock *l*, and open *m* to discharge the water from *f*, and permit the lower chest *e* to fill, which will be effected whenever water ceases to flow from *m*. The cock *m* must then be shut, and *l* opened, and so on alternately, which may easily be done mechanically, and without superintendence, by using a part of the impelling water from *d*, or that which has been discharged from *h c*, and which may be employed to turn a small water-wheel, or to fill two small cisterns in which floats are made to act. Mr. John W. Boswell devised a contrivance for answering this same purpose, which will be found fully detailed in the second volume of Dr. Gregory's excellent Treatise on Mechanics, where this simple machine is described under several forms and modifications.

It must not be supposed that filling the middle vessel *f* with water will discharge the whole of the water out of *e*, otherwise disappointment in its effects will ensue; because, although water is nearly incompressible, air is highly elastic, and the air in *e* will be compressed into less than its natural bulk, or will be condensed with a force equivalent to the pressure of the perpendicular column of water *h h*, which it has to overcome; and as atmospheric pressure was shown, when speaking of the pumps under the second head or division, to be only equal to the support of a column of water about 33 feet in height, so if we imagine this to be the height of the pipe *h h*, that column of water would require one of double atmospheric elasticity to support it, and hence the air in *e* would be condensed to half its former volume, and, therefore, discharge but half the volume of water, although *f* should be completely filled.

Dr. Gregory further describes a curious phenomenon which takes place in the working of this machine, and which never fails to create surprize in the strangers who visit it, and to whom it is usually shown. That is, when the efflux at *h c* has stopped, if the cock *n* be opened, the water and air rush out together with prodigious violence, and the drops of water are changed into hail or lumps of ice, issuing with such force as frequently to pierce a hat, if held against them, like pistol bullets. This rapid congelation is a remarkable instance of the general fact, that air, by suddenly expanding, generates cold, its capacity for heat being increased.

The *Centrifugal Pump* has several different forms, one of the most simple of which is shown at *fig.* 15, in which *g h* represents an upright spindle, so fixed, that rapid rotatory motion

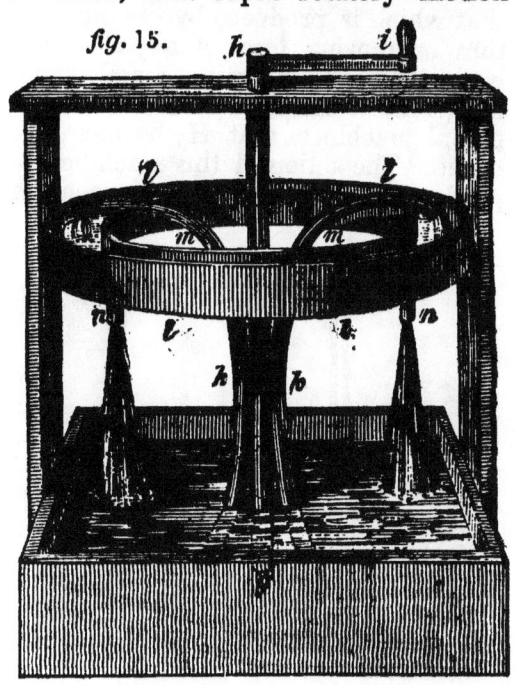

fig. 15.

may be communicated to it by the winch *i*, and *k m* represent any number of curved pipes (each of which contains one valve opening upwards) so disposed and fixed to the spindle, that their lowest ends may be near to it, and be covered by the water to be raised; and their upper ends, which are quite open, are extended to a considerable distance from the centre of motion, and finally bent downwards to prevent the dispersion of the water. The several curved pipes must be filled with water, which will be retained in them by their bottom valves, and are then put into rapid motion by turning the winch, when the higher ends *m m* of the pipe will describe a much larger circle than the ends below, and consequently such a centrifugal force, or tendency to fly off and empty the pipes, will be induced at the upper ends as will produce a vacuum, capable of raising a column of water. *l l l l* is a circular pan or reservoir to receive the upper ends of all the pipes and the water they deliver, which runs off by spouts at *n n*. This machine, according to theory, should deliver water with a velocity nearly equal to that with which the upper ends of the pipes move, but in practice it has failed of producing very advantageous effects.

The *Water Ram* or *Bélier Hydraulique*, as it was called by its inventor, M. Montgolfier, of Paris, is a highly useful and simple machine, for the purpose of raising water without the expenditure or aid of any other force than that which is produced by the momentum or moving force of a part of the water that is to be raised; and is one of the most simple and truly philosophical machines that Hydraulics can boast. The action of this machine depends entirely upon the momentum that is generated whenever a body is put into motion, and its effect is so great as to give the apparatus the appearance of acting in defiance to the established laws of Hydrostatic equilibrium; for a moving column of water of small height is made to overcome and move another column much higher than itself.

The form and construction of the Water-ram is shown at *fig.* 16. Suppose *o* to represent a cistern or reservoir, or the source of a spring which is constantly overflowing and running to waste, by means of a chan-

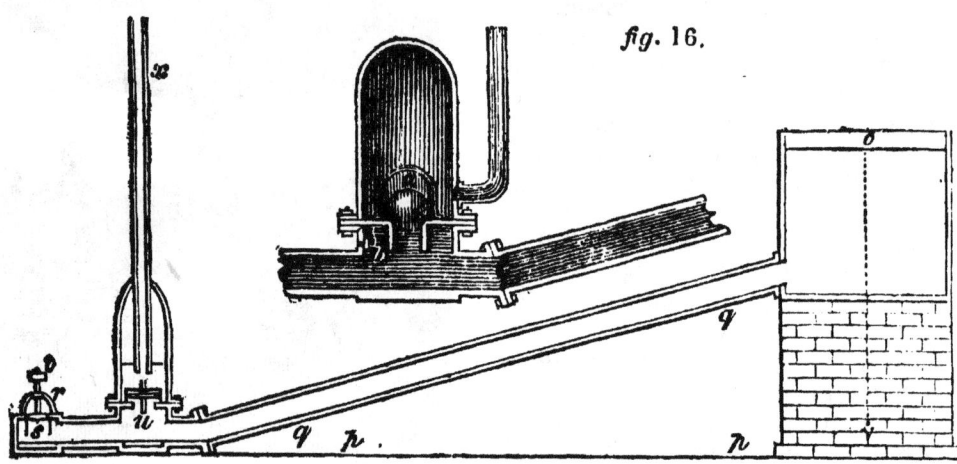

fig. 16.

nel a few feet lower than itself, as at the level line *p p*. Instead of permitting the water to run over the sides of *o*, let it be conducted to the level *p p*, by means of iron or other pipes *q q* connected with the side of the reservoir, and terminating by an orifice *r*, in which a conical or other valve *s*, is placed so as to be capable of effectually closing the pipe when such valve is drawn upwards; *t* is an adjustable weight fixed on to the spindle of the valve *s*, by means of which the valve is kept down and open; any water therefore that is in the cistern *o* will flow down the pipe *q q*, and escape at the orifice *r*, so long as the valve remains down, but the instant it is raised and shut, all motion of the water is suspended. Thus situated, the adjustment of the weight *t* must take place, and by adding to or subtracting from it, it must be made just so heavy as to be capable of sinking or forcing its way downwards, against the upward pressure of the water, the force of which will depend upon the perpendicular distance from the surface of the water in *o*, to its point of discharge at *r*, (represented by the dotted line *o v*). But the water by moving acquires momentum and new force, and consequently is no longer equal to the column *o v*, to which the valve has been adjusted, but is superior to it, by which it is enabled to overpower the resistance of the weight *t*, and it carries the valve up with it, and closes the orifice *r*. This is no sooner done than the water is constrained to become stationary again, by which the momentum is lost, and the valve and weight once more become superior, and fall, thus re-opening the orifice and permitting the water to move again; and as the pressure of the water and the weight of the valve each become alternately superior, the valve is kept in a constant state of vibration, or of opening and shutting without any external aid whatever. Such is the principle upon which the motion of the water in the pipe *q q* is produced: but the momentum generated cannot be instantly annihilated; and it is not only of sufficient power to raise the valve *s*, but likewise to burst open the lower end of the pipe *q q*, unless a sufficient vent be provided by which this accumulated force can escape. Accordingly a second valve *u* is placed near the lower end of the pipe *q q*, and is made to open upwards into an air-vessel, having a discharging pipe *x*; and consequently whenever the valve *s* is closed, the water, which otherwise would have flowed from the orifice *r*, now opens the valve *u* and enters the air-vessel, until the spring of the contained air overcomes the gradually decreasing force of the momentum, when the valve *u* closes, and that at *s* opens to permit the water to make a second blow or pulsation, and in this way the action of the machine continues unceasingly without any external aid so long as it is supplied with water and remains in repair. A small running stream is necessary for this machine, as the water at *o* should be kept at one constant elevation to insure the perfection of its action. A much greater quantity of water likewise escapes at the orifice *r*, between the pulsations, than can be raised in the delivering pipe *x*, particularly if it extends to any considerable height, for the comparative quantity of water discharged through *x*, and permitted to run to waste at *r*, must always depend upon the respective perpendicular heights of the pressing column *o v*, and the delivered or resisting column *u x*, and the rapidity of the pulsations will likewise depend on the same circumstances. A very insignificant pressing column *o v* is capable of raising a very high ascending column *u x*, so that a sufficient fall of water may be obtained in almost every running brook, by damming up its upper end to produce the reservoir *o*, and carrying the pipes *q q* down the natural channel of the stream until a sufficient fall be obtained, for a considerable length of descending pipes from *o* to *r* is necessary to insure the certain effect of the machine, since, if the column *q q* is not of sufficient length, its water will be thrown back into the reservoir, instead of entering the air-vessel, which requires to be replenished with air, and this is admitted into it by the self-acting shifting valve, shown at *b* in the shaded part of (*fig.* 16), which is an enlarged view of the air-vessel in an improved form; its valve is made by a ball at *a*, having a metal bridle over it to prevent its rising too high.

In taking the height to which water is to be raised by a pump, *perpendicular height alone* is to be regarded, and not lateral extension, because fluids press according to their perpendicular height. Thus, if a pipe 100 feet long is six feet higher at one end than at the other, the six feet only are to be regarded as the height to which the water must be raised, and the 100 feet may be disregarded, except so far as it produces friction detrimental to the motion of the water. The height of a lift of water must be taken from the surface of the water which is to be lifted to the surface of the cistern, or reservoir, or end of the pipe that is to receive or deliver it, and not from the bottom of the suction-pipe, because that pipe may descend any distance below the surface of the water to be raised without affecting the measurement, since the water will always rise to its own level within that pipe, without the aid of any exertion of force by the pump. Be careful, likewise, to introduce no right-angled or short turns into pipes, if they can be avoided; but let every such turn be a regular curved sweep, and the larger and more regular that sweep is made, the less impediment it will offer to the passage of the water.

In order to determine the force or power necessary to work a pump of any description, the height to which the water is to be raised must always be taken into account; for, according to what has been before stated, (col. i. page 11), this height multiplied into the area of the piston, and reduced to any of the usual denominations of weight, will give the amount of resistance to be overcome (friction of the pump only excepted). The size of the pipe containing the water is quite immaterial, as before noticed, provided it be large enough to prevent friction and unnatural velocity in the water; and the entire perpendicular height from the surface of the water raised to the point where it is delivered, whether occupied by suction or feeding-pipe, or delivering-pipe from a forcing-pump, must be added together and considered as the height of the lift: so that if a lift and force-pump of four inches in diameter in the working-barrel, has ten feet of three-inch suction-pipe below its piston, and twenty feet of two-inch delivering-pipe (including the length of the working-barrel) above it, the column to be lifted will be equal to thirty feet of four-inch-pipe filled with water. The contents in gallons of thirty feet of four-inch-pipe must therefore be found, and as each Imp. gallon of water weighs 10 lbs. avoirdupois, the weight or load upon the pump will be immediately found, to which must be added, from one-tenth to one-sixth, according to the construction of the pump for friction. The load upon an excentric or any other pump may be found by the same rule if the effective horizontal area of the piston, or its substitute, be found, and this be in like manner multiplied into the height of the lift. It therefore becomes important to know the weight and quantity of water which a certain length of pipe of any given diameter will contain, and a tolerably close approximation to this may be obtained by squaring the diameter of any pipe in inches, and cutting off the last figure of the product by a decimal point, which will nearly give the contents in ale gallons of one yard in length of such pipe. Thus, for example, if a pipe is six inches in diameter, 6 times 6 make 36, and introducing the decimal point would reduce this number to 3.6, so that one yard of such pipe would contain three gallons and six-tenths. If a three-inch pipe had been taken, then $3 \times 3 = 9$; consequently, there remains but one figure to cut off. The gallons' place must therefore be supplied by a cipher, thus 0.9, and the yard of such pipe would contain but nine-tenths of a gallon.

For greater certainty, however, the following table and rules are introduced. They are extracted from "Brunton's Compendium of Mechanics;" a recent little work, published at Glasgow, and which is so replete with useful information, that no working mechanic should be without it.

TABLE
Of the contents of a pipe one inch diameter for any required height.

Feet high.	Quantity in Cub. In.	Weight in Avoir. Oz.	Gallons, Wine Mea.
1	9.42	5.46	0.0107
2	18.85	10.92	.0816
3	28.27	16.38	.1224
4	37.70	21.85	.1632
5	47.12	27.31	.2040
6	56.55	32.77	.2423
7	65.97	38.23	.2448
8	75.40	43.69	.3264
9	84.82	49.16	.3671
10	94.25	54.62	.4080
20	188.49	109.24	.8160
30	282.74	163.86	1.2240
40	376.99	218.47	1.6300
50	471.24	273.09	2.0400
60	565.49	327.71	2.4480
70	659.73	382.33	2.8560
80	753.98	436.95	3.2640
90	848.23	491.57	3.6700
100	942.48	546.19	4.0800
200	1884.96	1092.38	8.1600

Although the above Table only gives the contents of a pipe one inch in diameter, it will serve as a standard for pipes of any other size, by observing the following

RULE.—Multiply the numbers found in the table against any height, by the square of the diameter of the pipe, and the product will be the number of cubic inches, avoirdupois ounces, and wine gallons of water, that the given pipe will contain.

EXAMPLE.—How many wine gallons of water are contained in a pipe six inches diameter, and sixty feet long?

$2.4480 \times 36 = 88.1280$ wine gallons.

The wine gallon contains 231 cubic inches, and the new imperial gallon 277.274 cubic inches; therefore, to reduce the wine to the imperial gallon, divide by 1.20032; and for a like reduction of the ale gallon, which contains 282 cubic inches, divide by 0.98324.

CHAPTER III.

Of the Force and Power to be derived from Fluids in Motion.

HYDRAULICS contemplates not only the construction and action of machines for raising water above its level, such as those that have been last described; but likewise the means by which motion and power may be obtained from the motion and other properties of fluids. Accordingly a brief examination of the various mill or water-wheels and other contrivances, by which motion is given to machinery, will form the conclusion of the present essay.

Motion is generally obtained from water, either by exposing obstacles to the action of its current, as in water-wheels, or by arresting its progress in movable buckets or receptacles which retain it during a part of the progress of its descent. Thus, if we suppose the action of the Persian wheel shown at *fig.* 4, to be the reverse of what it has been described to be, viz. that instead of the buckets $n\ o\ p$ receiving their water from the stream $r\ r$, and delivering it into the elevated cistern s, we imagine the cistern s to be supplied by the stream, and that the several buckets $o\ o\ o\ n$ shall become filled with water instead of emptied by passing the cistern s, the side $o\ o\ o$ of the wheel will become heavier by the weight of all the water that the buckets contain, than the opposite side $q\ q$, in which the buckets are supposed to remain empty. The consequence of this will be that the wheel will revolve in the direction of the letters p o n, and if the buckets q q are filled as they get to the top, and those at o n emptied by some contrivance when they reach the bottom, the motion of such a wheel will be continuous; and it will revolve with a force and velocity dependent on the weight of the buckets of water, their distance from the centre, and the velocity with which they are filled: in fact, such an arrangement is a very close approximation to what is called the over-shot water-wheel, which will be presently described.

Water-wheels have three denominations, depending on their own particular construction, on the manner in which they are set or used, and on the manner in which the water is made to act upon them; but all water-wheels consist in common of a hollow cylinder or drum revolving on a central axle or spindle from which the power to be used is communicated, while their exterior surface is covered with vanes, float-boards, or cavities, upon which the water is to act. Thus *fig.* 17 is a side view of an under-shot, tide, or stream wheel, which was

fig. 17.

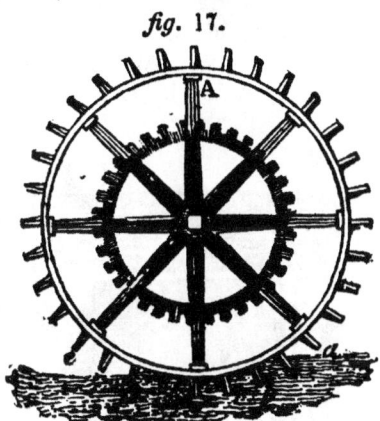

the most common and is by far the oldest construction in use. As this kind of wheel requires no other fall in the water than that which is necessary to produce a rapid progressive motion in it, and as it acts chiefly by the momentum of the water, its positive weight being scarcely called at all into action, it is only fit to be used when there is a profusion of water always in motion. It has however the advantage of being the cheapest of all water-wheels; and as it does not require a very considerable fall of water, it is more applicable to rivers in their natural state than any other form. It likewise works equally well whether the water acts upon the one or the other side of its float-boards, which renders it particularly applicable to tide-rivers, where the current is sometimes running in one direction, and at others in an opposite course. There are however some practical disadvantages attendant upon this form of wheel, particularly when made of small diameter: for if the float-boards stand radiantly round it, or pointing to the centre, as *a b c d e*, although the central floats *b c d* stand in good positions to produce the greatest effect, being all nearly at right angles to the direction in which the water moves, yet the float *a* enters the water so obliquely as to meet with great resistance to its passage, at the same time that the retiring float *e* leaves the water under circumstances that are equally disadvantageous, in being obliged to plough or throw up a portion of water before it, which tends very materially to retard the motion and impede the power. This appears to be partly obviated by giving the float-boards a different figure, or placing them so as not to point to the centre of the wheel, as shown at *fig.* 18. In this case, the ascending float-board *f* is nearly at right angles to the water at the time of leaving it, and rises almost perpendicularly out of it, being thus placed in a much more beneficial position than in the last figure. But, although the retiring float is thus improved, the entering one *g* is much more disadvantageously placed, for now it will come down almost parallel to the

fig. 18.

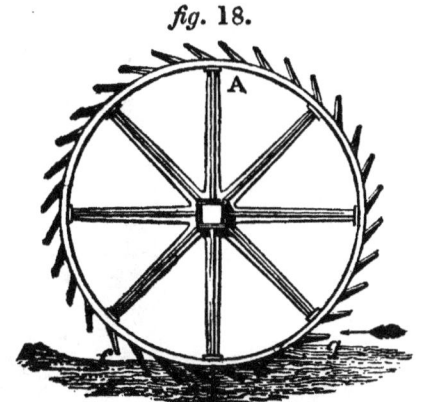

surface of the water, and thus the advantage that is gained at one side of the wheel is lost at the other. It does however appear that there is a small practical advantage in giving the float-boards a slight inclination from the centre, but it must not be carried by any means so far as shown in the above figure.

As action and re-action are always equal, but in contrary directions, of course it is the same thing whether the power of the moving water be applied to the float-boards of a wheel which revolves in a fixed building, or whether any extraneous force be applied to the axis of a wheel to cause it to move in still water: in the first case the power of the water will be transferred to the axle of the wheel, and is applicable to the driving or moving of machinery; while, in the second case, the power applied to the axle will be resisted by the quiescent water, and will be converted into so much power for moving the building or boat in which the wheel is placed; and upon this principle depends the action of those steam-boats which are impelled through the water by means of water-wheels driven round by the power of steam-engines applied to their axles, instead of permitting the water to move the float-boards and transfer its power to the axis.

Whenever the weight and motion of water can be made use of, as well as its momentum, much greater effects can be produced than the last described machine is capable of, and with a much less lavish expenditure of the fluid, for then its utmost powers of action are brought into play at once; and accordingly those water-wheels that are distinguished by the names of breast-wheels, and over-shot wheels, will produce much greater power with a much less supply of water than the under-shot wheel already described. Both these wheels however require a considerable fall in the stream upon which they are placed, and consequently destroy it for the purposes of navigation, unless that ingenious Hydraulic contrivance the *Canal Lock* be resorted to, by means of which barges or vessels of any magnitude may be transported from one level to another without difficulty, and with very little loss of time. The *Over-shot Water-Wheel*, which of all others gives the greatest power with the least expense of water, requires a fall in the stream equal to rather more than its own diameter, therefore it is customary to give this description of wheel a greater length in proportion to its height than is given to any other, by which an equality of power is obtained. In the construction of the over-shot wheel a hollow cylinder or drum that is impervious to water is first prepared, and hung upon a proper central axis. A number of narrow troughs, or cells, generally formed of thin plates of metal, extending from one end of the drum to the other, are next fixed round the outside of the wheel so as to give a transverse section through the middle of the wheel, the appearance shown at *fig.* 19. The water is conducted by a level trough of

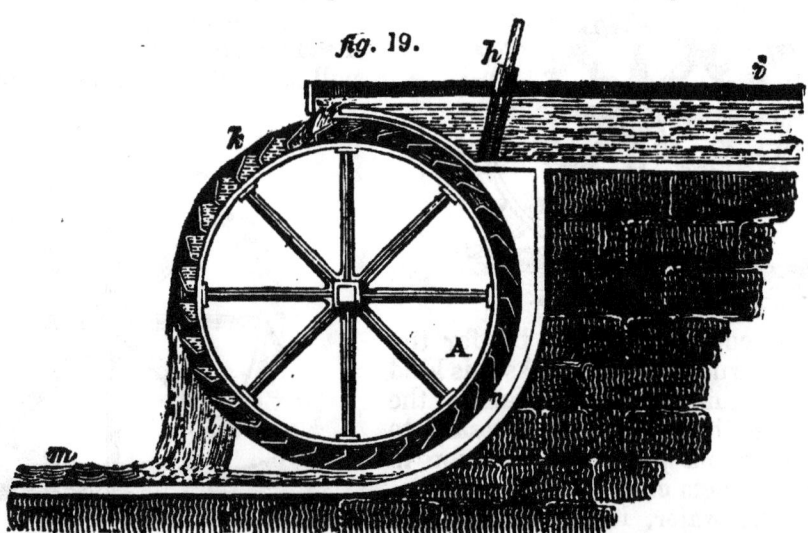

fig. 19.

the same width as the wheel over its top, as at $h\,i$, and is discharged into the buckets or cells placed round the wheel to receive it, as at $k\,l$; from the particular form of these buckets they retain the water thus thrown into them, until by their motion they descend towards the point l, when their mouths being turned downwards they discharge their contents into the tail-stream m, where the water runs to waste. The buckets on the opposite side n of the wheel descend with their mouths downwards, and thus remain empty, until they arrive under the end h of the water-trough to be refilled; at h there is a penstock or sluice for regulating the quantity of water and preventing waste, since, if the water was permitted to flow too rapidly, it would splash out of the buckets near *k* instead of filling them, and would run down over the surface of the wheel without producing its proper effect. To prevent this the water is seldom permitted to run upon the wheel in a stream of more than from half an inch to an inch in thickness, and when well regulated there is scarcely a drop of water ineffectually wasted. The over-shot wheel therefore acts by the gravity or weight of the water contained in the buckets for nearly one-third of its circumference, and from the experiments of Mr. Smeaton, which were made with great accuracy, it appears that the dimensions, quantity of water, and height of fall being the same, the over-shot wheel will produce double the effect of the under-shot.

The *Breast Wheel* is by far the most common; and may be considered as a mean between the two varieties before mentioned. In this, the water, instead of passing over the top of the wheel, or entirely beneath it, is delivered about half way up it, or rather below the level of the axis, and the race or brickwork upon which the water descends is built in a circular form, having the same common centre with the wheel itself, so as to make it parallel to the exterior edges of the flat-boards or extreme circumference of the wheel. This construction is shown at *fig.* 20, where *o p q* is a side-view of a wheel, formed with float-boards in the same manner as

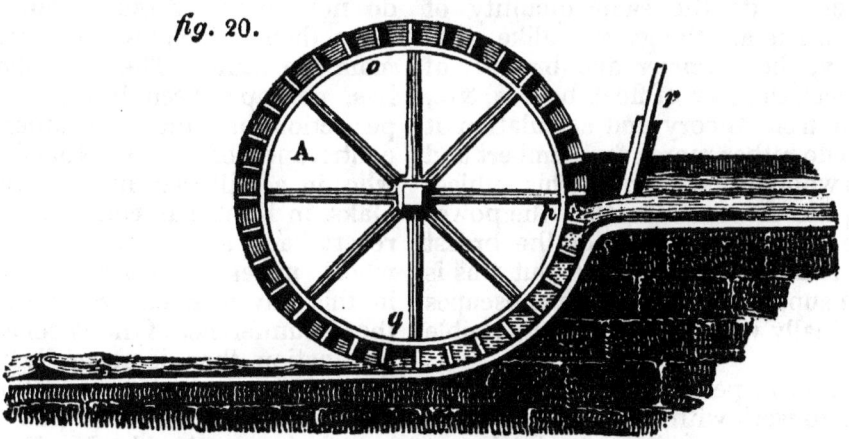

fig. 20.

the under-shot wheel; but instead of the water acting upon its lower part *q*, it is introduced upon it at *p*, by the sluice or penstock *r*, which, by rising or falling, permits a greater or less quantity of water to act on the wheel: and as the float-boards are made to fit as accurately as possible without contact, into the circular hollow *s t* of brickwork, no water can escape past the wheel without producing its proportionate effect.

Mr. Smeaton makes no observations on the nature of Breast Wheels in his valuable Papers,[*] except to state that all wheels by which the water is prevented from descending, unless the wheel moves therewith, are to be considered of the nature of over-shot wheels, having power in proportion to the perpendicular height from which the water descends; while all those that receive the impulse or shock of the water, whether in an horizontal, perpendicular or oblique direction, are to be considered as under-shots. The breast wheel is nearly allied to the over-shot: for notwithstanding it has only float-boards instead of buckets, yet as the mill course is made concentric to the outside of the wheel, and is not only there, but at the two sides, made as close as convenient, so as to prevent the escape of water as effectually as possible, the spaces between one float-board and another become buckets for the time being and retain the water, and thus the breast wheel is not only impelled by the weight of water, but by its impetus or momentum also, for the water is so confined as to be incapable of splashing or being lost, and consequently its moving force may be exerted to great advantage. Notwithstanding this apparent superiority, still the breast wheel is, in effect, vastly inferior to the over-shot wheel, not only on account of the smaller height at which the water is supplied, but from the waste with which it must always be attended, even under circumstances of the most perfect workman-

---

[*] Experimental Inquiry concerning the natural powers of the Wind and Water to turn Mills and other Machines, by John Smeaton, F.R.S., 1 vol., 8vo. London, 1796.

ship. When well constructed and closely built in, its effect, according to Mr. Smeaton, should be the same as an under-shot wheel, whose head of water is equal to the difference of level between the surface of the stream and the point where it strikes the wheel, added to the effect of an over-shot wheel, whose height is equal to the distance from the striking point, to the tail-water of the mill, or that which runs to waste. This is however on the presumption that the wheel receives the impulse of the water at right angles to its radii, and that every thing is constructed to the best advantage. In practice it is found that the breast wheel just consumes about double the quantity of water that the over-shot wheel requires, to do the same quantity of work, when all things are alike, that is to say, the diameter and breadth of the wheel, number of float-boards, &c., though from theory and calculation it should do rather more; for Lambert and others who have written on this subject attempt to demonstrate, that the power of the over-shot to that of the breast wheel is as thirteen to five; but this is upon a supposition that no water escapes ineffectually which is utterly impossible in practice.

In order to permit any of the above wheels to work with freedom, and to the greatest advantage, it is absolutely necessary that the tail-water, as it is called, or that which is discharged from the bottom of the wheel after it has produced its effect, should have an uninterrupted passage to run away, for whenever this is not the case, it accumulates, and forms a resistance to the float-boards, and consequently abstracts considerably from the velocity and power of the wheel, sometimes indeed to so great an extent as to prevent its working altogether. One of the simplest and most effectual means of removing this inconvenience is by an expedient not much known or practised, and which consists of forming two drains or tunnels through the brickwork or masonry at each side of the water-wheel, whatever may be its construction, so as to permit a portion of the upper water to flow down into the tail or lower stream immediately in front of the wheel. The water thus brought down with great impetuosity drives the tail-water before it, in such a manner as to form a basin or hollow place, in which the wheel can work free from interruption, even if the natural state of the water were such as might produce a tailing of from twelve to eighteen inches without this assistance. And since the tailing of mill-streams only occurs in the winter seasons, or at times when there is a profusion of water, so the quantity that is thus thrown away without operating upon the wheel can be spared without inconvenience. Each of the drains or tunnels is furnished with a sluice-gate or penstock at its upper end, by which the quantity and impetus of the water can be regulated at pleasure, or the whole be shut off whenever water happens to be scarce.

The three varieties of water-wheels already noticed are the only ones generally admitted into practice, and they do not admit of much improvement, since their principles must always remain the same. The over-shot wheel has, perhaps, been brought nearer to perfection than any of the others, by the contrivance of Peter Nouaille, Esq., who, in a mill that he has near Seven Oaks, in Kent, has caused the water to revert back again from the top of the wheel, instead of passing over it, and in this way a much greater portion of the circumference of the wheel is brought into action than is generally the case. Other improvements or variations in the form and construction of water-wheels, have been contrived by Mr. Besant, Mr. Smart, Mr. Perkins, and others, which will be found described in the *Transactions of the Society for the Encouragement of Arts, Manufactures, and Commerce;* the object of them principally being to obtain as much force as possible from the water, by arranging the forms of the buckets or float-boards in such manner that they may receive the impulse of, or retain the greatest quantity of water, which is of great importance, particularly in the construction of under-shot wheels, which act by the impulse of the water alone. The over-shot wheel depends entirely on the weight of the water delivered into its buckets, which ought therefore to be as capacious as they can conveniently be made, not only that they may contain as much water as possible, but allow ample room for the discharge of the air that will be thrown into them with the water, as well as for the delivery of that water when done with. From the nature of a water-wheel it will be evident, that if it had no work to perform or resistance to overcome, it would move with the same velocity as the stream that drives it; while, on the contrary, if it was loaded with a quantity of resistance equal to the power of the stream, it could not move at all: hence, every degree of resistance between these extremes will produce its proportionate retardation of the wheel; and from accurate experiments which have been tried, it has been determined that an undershot wheel does its maximum quantity of work when its circumference moves with between one-half and one-third of the velocity of the stream that drives it. The overshot wheel cannot be so influenced by the velocity of the water, because it requires all its buckets or cells to be filled in succession; and Mr. Smeaton has determined that the best velocity to effect the above purpose is three feet in a second. Having therefore previously determined the quantity of water which the stream will deliver in a given time, it becomes a matter of easy calculation to determine the length and capacity of the buckets which shall be capable of carrying off the whole of the water at that velocity. Thus, for example, if the stream is found to deliver ninety-six gallons per second, and it is determined to make the buckets on the wheel six inches apart from one partition to another, and fifteen inches deep, then six such buckets will be contained in every three feet of the wheel; therefore ninety-six gallons must be divided by six buckets, which gives sixteen gallons for the contents of each. It will therefore only remain to be determined, how long a vessel of six inches wide and fifteen inches deep must be to contain sixteen gallons, and this will of course give the necessary width of the wheel, while the number of buckets must depend upon the circumference, which is always limited by the diameter, being the extreme height (if necessary) that can be obtained in the fall of water; for the larger the wheel, the greater will be the power derived from it, provided a due velocity can be maintained at the same time; because the power of water on wheels is directly as the height it falls through. The power of every wheel, of course, depends upon the quantity of water thrown upon it, and the height from which it has to fall; but as every bucket must be filled, or every floatboard struck by the water in succession, so, of course, if the wheel is too large, it will move too slowly for the purpose for which it is intended; and in this case the speed must be raised by cog-wheels within the mill, which, on the common principles of mechanics, must dissipate the power intended to be gained by the magnitude of the water-wheel. Hence, great attention should be paid in the construction of mills, to let the size of the water-wheel be well proportioned not only to the velocity of the stream, but to the speed of the work it is required to perform; and this may always be accomplished without waste or difference of power, by using a wider wheel of small diameter where rapid speed is necessary, or a narrow wheel of great diameter when this is not essential. In every case the full power of a stream should be taken advantage of in the first erection of a mill, because it is a troublesome and expensive operation to increase the power of a mill when once built, and power is always valuable.

Mr. Banks, in his excellent *Treatise upon Mills*, gives many useful practical rules; from amongst which the following is selected. Being simple, it may prove useful for determining the quantity of water that will flow through a sluice or penstock upon a wheel, with sufficient accuracy for most purposes, because the whole motion of a stream must not be taken when it is principally dammed or stopped, and only permitted to flow through a small orifice to produce mechanical effect.

Rule.—Measure the depth, from the surface of the water to the centre of the orifice of discharge, in feet, and extract the square root of that depth: multiply it by 5.4, which will give the velocity in feet per second, and this, multiplied by the area of the orifice (also in feet), will give the number of cubic feet of water which will flow through in a second. From knowing the quantity of water discharged, and the height of fall, not only the size of the wheel, but its extent of power may be calculated; for, in the undershot wheel the power is to the effect nearly as 3 : 1; while in the overshot wheel it is double, or as 3 to 2.

In the connexion of the work to be performed with a water-wheel, some attention is necessary to mechanical principles, which are frequently grossly neglected; and it is on this account that the teeth or cogs of wheels, or even shafts themselves, are broken, through the unnecessary strain that may, by this means, be thrown upon them. It is well known that the pendulum, when swinging, has but one point in which its whole moving force is concentrated, and which point must be stopped, if it is required to make the pendulum stop instantly, in a completely dead manner, or without communicating vibration or a strain on any one part, in particular. This point is called its centre of oscillation. So likewise in a stick or sword: if it is desired to strike the most powerful blow that can be given by such a weapon, it must not be made with the point nor near the hand, but at a certain distance between the two, where the point of percussion exists; and this, if the stick is of equal size and weight throughout, will be at two-thirds of its length from the centre upon which it turns, or the hand that wields it; but if it tapers, or becomes lighter at the end, the point of percussion will be moved nearer to the hand. The same reasoning applies to water-wheels, and indeed to all other wheels and bodies in circular motion; for if such a wheel had no rim or periphery, its arms might be considered as so many sticks whirling round one common centre. But having such a rim, which is of considerable weight in respect to the arms, the point of percussion, or of greatest effect, (which, in revolving bodies, is called *the centre of gyration*,) will be moved further from the centre to near the external weight or rim; and in the circle described by these points should the power be taken, in order to equalize the strain upon every part of the water-wheel as well as its shaft. Placing cogs, therefore, on one of the rings of a water-wheel, or using a driving wheel of the same diameter as itself, is an injudicious application, as thereby the natural momentum of the wheel will be considerably checked; and, on the contrary, if too small a driving wheel is used upon the water-wheel shaft, the outside of the water-wheel will have a constant tendency to run faster than its central part, which will be very likely to break its shaft.

To ascertain the circle of gyration in a water-wheel, its radius must be taken, and the weight of its arms, rim, shrouding, and float-boards, as well as the weight of water acting upon it. Thus, for example, in a wheel twenty-four feet diameter, the arms of which weigh two tons, the shrouding and rim four tons, and the water in action two tons; call the weight of the rim R, which must be multiplied by the square of the radius, and the product be doubled, because the rim exists on both sides of the centre, when the new product may be carried out. Next, the weight of the arms called A, must be multiplied by the square of the radius, and be doubled and carried out as before. Then the weight of the water in action called W, must be multiplied in like manner and carried out, without doubling, because the water only acts on one side of the wheel. Then double the weight of the rim and the arms, and add the weight of the water to them, which will give a sum by which the sum of the former products carried out are to be divided; and the square root of the quotient so obtained, will be the radius of the circle of gyration, or circle of greatest power; and putting down the foregoing operations in figures, they will assume the following form:—

$$R = 4 \text{ Tons} \times 12^2 = 576 \times 2 = 1152$$
$$A = 2 \text{ Tons} \times 12^2 = 288 \times 2 = 576$$
$$W = 2 \text{ Tons} \times 12^2 = 288$$
$$2 \times \overline{4+2+2} = \frac{2016}{16} = 126,$$

the square root of which, 11.225 feet, will be the radius of the circle of gyration. The heavier the rim and load of water are in respect to the arms, the nearer will this circle coincide with the size of the wheel; while, if they are light, it will approach nearer the centre: but power may always be safely derived from a water-wheel, at about one-fourth of the radius from the circumference.

The power from a water-wheel ought likewise to be taken as nearly as possible at the point that is opposite to where the water is producing its greatest action upon the wheel; otherwise a great and, in some cases, very unequal strain will be thrown upon different parts of its shafts and bearings, and such a one as, if it does not cause their fracture, will require unnecessary strength in them, and cannot fail to produce waste and unequal wear of the brasses or other bearings upon which they are supported. Thus, for example: let it be supposed that the power is communicated from an undershot-wheel, as at (*fig*. 17.) by a toothed-wheel, or pinion, placed directly under the main shaft upon which that wheel turns: then, since the power of the water acts under the bottom of the wheel a little lower than where the power is taken from, it will be evident that both the strains will be on the under side of the shaft without any thing above to balance them; and as the power derived is in most cases nearly equal to that of the wheel, and in almost all cases superior to its weight, the effect will be to produce a constant tendency to raise the wheel out of its bearings; while, if the power had been derived from the point A on the top of the cog-wheel, the water would be driving the wheel forward in the direction of the current, while the derived power would act in a directly opposite direction with nearly equal force; and as the one acts below while the other acts above, it follows that they must nearly balance each other, and thus produce no impediment to the steady revolution of the wheel. What has been stated with respect of the undershot-wheel equally applies to all others; for in the breast-wheel, the power should be derived from the point opposite to that on which the water is acting, and so of the overshot-wheel, where the power should be taken behind the wheel nearly in its horizontal diameter as at A in (*figs*. 19 and 20.)

The varieties of water-wheels above described comprehend all those that are generally used in Great Britain; but in America and some parts of Europe, horizontal water-wheels, or wheels with oblique floats, acting on the principles of the smoke-jack by oblique impulse, are very common and very simple in their construction; but as they are less efficient in mechanical power and advantage, it is needless to describe them here: the reader is therefore referred to page 46 of the fourth volume of the *Quarterly Journal of Science and the Arts*, edited at the Royal Institution, where a short but comprehensive account is given by Mr. Adamson of all the various contrivances, on this principle, which have from time to time been used, together with a particular description of one of the best forms of this kind of water-mill.

The best mode of obtaining the utmost power out of a small stream of water, when it happens to be in an elevated situation, and there is an opportunity of discharging the waste water in an intermediate position between that which is to be raised and that employed to produce the effect, as in the Hungarian machine, is what is called the *Water-pressure Engine*, being, in fact, a steam-engine, worked by water instead of steam, and possessing the powers of Bramah's hydrostatic press. This kind of engine is particularly applicable to pumping, or any other purpose, in mines which have the advantage of an adit level, and in which there also happens to be a small stream of running water at the surface. Such a stream is most frequently applied to turning a water-wheel and then runs to waste; but, by the application of this machine, it may be converted to highly useful purposes. The form and operation of the water-pressure engine will be understood by referring to *fig.* 21, in which *a b* is a metal cylinder, truly bored, closed at its

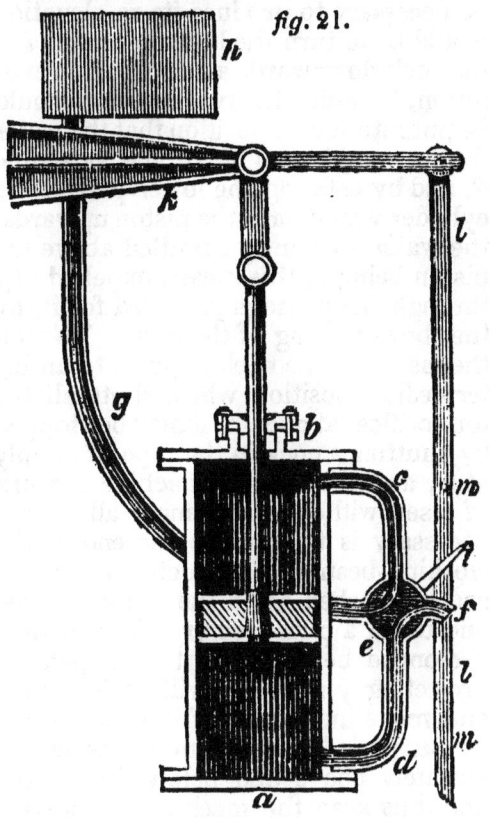

fig. 21.

two ends, and having an air-tight piston and piston-rod working through a stuffing-box, precisely in the same way as if prepared and made for a steam-engine. The cylinder has, likewise, the same nozzles and side pipes as the steam-engine, which are united in a common four-way (or rather double passage) cock at *e*. The operation of this kind of cock is too well known to need particular description. It presents four external openings, and has the effect of permitting two opposite currents to pass through it at the same time, the direction of which may be reversed by turning the cock a quarter round, although the supply is constantly delivered in at the same orifice. Thus, as the cock is shown in the figure, any water that may be conveyed from the elevated reservoir *h* through the pipe *g*, which is connected with one of the orifices in the cock at *e*, would find an immediate passage up the side-pipe *c* into the upper part *b* of the cylinder, and would therefore press upon the top of the piston and force it downwards; while, at the same time, any air or other fluid that might be contained in the cylinder below the piston could escape through the ascending side-pipe *d*, and would flow out from the cock at the external orifice *f*, thus permitting the piston to descend without impediment. Having done so, all that would be necessary to produce its re-elevation would be to turn the lever or handle *i* of the cock downwards a quarter of a revolution, by which the two passages would be put into such a position that the water from *e* would pass down the side-pipe *d*, and by entering the lower part of the cylinder would force the piston upwards, the water previously admitted above the piston being by this means expelled at *f* through the passage prepared for it, by the above turning of the cock. To stop the machine, the cock is put into an intermediate position, which shuts all the four orifices at once, or it may be stopped by shutting a cock in the pipe of supply at *g*; and to cause the machine to work of itself without attendance, all that is necessary is to prolong the end of the working-beam *k*, to which the piston-rod is attached as in the steam-engine, and to fix a plug-tree or rod *l l* to such prolonged beam, when the tappets or projecting pins *m m* will strike upon and move the lever *i* of the cock at the proper periods for sending the water alternately above and below the piston, and thus keep the machine in constant action.

This machine is dependant on the principles of Hydrostatic pressure, and is in every respect similar in operation to the hydrostatic bellows or Bramah's water-press, described in the *Treatise on Hydrostatics*. In that treatise it is shown that the pressure of fluids is according to the area or surface upon which they press, and the perpendicular height of the column, without any regard to the quantity of water employed, consequently, whatever may be the size of the pipe *g* which conveys the water, the effect of that water will be as the area of the piston or the cylinder. The pipe *g* needs therefore be no larger than what is necessary to convey a sufficiently speedy supply into the cylinder *a b*, for if it was twice or thrice as large, the rapidity of the working alone, and not the power of the machine, would be affected. And since a column of water about thirty-three feet high is equivalent to atmospheric pressure, or fifteen pounds upon the square inch, so if we suppose the pipe *g* to be thirty-three feet long from the surface of the water in the reservoir *h*, down to the medium point of the cylinder as at *e*, then that column of water will exert a power to move the piston upwards or downwards equal in force to fifteen pounds multiplied by the number of square inches the piston may contain, without any deduction except what is necessary for the friction of the machine. Now a cylinder only twelve inches diameter, will contain 113 square inches upon its piston, which multiplied by 15 pounds gives no less than 1715 pounds pressure upon so small a machine; and as both the height of column and magnitude of the cylinder may be greatly increased without inconvenience, it will be seen that this is a most excellent and simple machine, affording disposable power applicable to any purpose, whenever the two requisites for its construction can be obtained, viz., a sufficiently elevated supply to work the piston, and a convenient discharge for the waste water to escape after it has performed its duty.

So far, the weight and moving impetus of water have alone been noticed as capable of producing power to work machinery; but a similar effect may also be obtained from the re-action and centrifugal force of water in machinery properly constructed for the purpose of obtaining it, and the present account of hydraulic machines shall therefore be concluded by a description of a curious machine invented by Dr. Barker towards the close of the seventeenth century, and which is generally known by the name of *Barker's Centrifugal Mill*. In this the water does not act by its weight or momentum, but by its centrifugal force and the re-action that is produced by the flowing of the water on the point immediately behind the orifice of discharge. Its general construction is shown at *fig.* 22, in which *v u* is a metal pipe of considerable height, its top *v* being widened or extended into a funnel shape. The pipe is maintained in its vertical position, as shown in the figure, by resting on a pointed steel pivot turning into a brass box *w* at the lower extremity, while the upper part has a cylindrical steel axis passing through the top *y y* of a frame which supports it: the pipe *v u* is consequently free to move round upon its

HYDRAULICS.

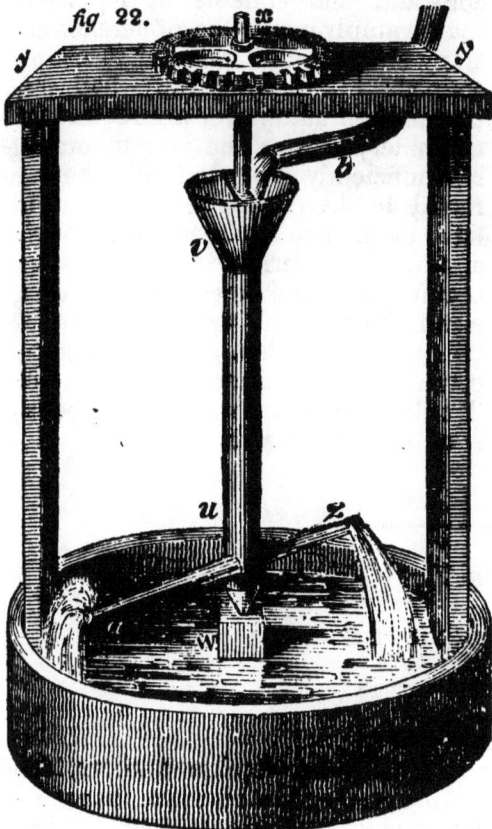

fig. 22.

own axis, which it does with very little friction. Towards the lower extremity of the pipe $v\,u$, and at right angles to its axis, two or more smaller pipes or arms with closed external ends are inserted, as at $z\,a$, and an adjustable orifice is made at the side of each of these small pipes as near as possible to its end, and placed on opposite sides of such pipes, so that water issuing from them may spout horizontally and in opposite directions, as shown at the letters z and a. One end of a pipe b communicates with a supply of water which it delivers into the funnel head v, without touching it in any part, and the supply of this pipe must be so regulated by a cock or otherwise, that it may constantly keep the pipe $u\,v$ filled with water without running over, at the same time that the discharge is going on from the orifices $z\,a$, which will deliver their water with a force proportionate to the perpendicular height of the column of water contained in $u\,v$; and since the holes $z\,a$ are in opposite directions, the water in passing from them will generate such a resistance or re-action as to throw the pipe $u\,v$, with its arms and axis x, into rapid rotatory motion, and this axis may communicate its motion and power to wheel-work or machinery, or even to a millstone connected with its upper end. This machine is described and highly spoken of in almost all the books that treat of hydraulic machinery, but it does not appear to have been carried into practical effect in England. Euler enters into an elaborate description of the theory and importance of this machine in the memoirs of the Academy of Berlin for 1751, and agrees with Bernouilli, at the close of his Hydraulics, in saying that it excels all other methods of employing the force of water to obtain motion. The power of this machine does not depend altogether on the perpendicular height of the water in the pipe $u\,v$, but on the centrifugal force that is generated in the arms $z\,a$, by which a much more rapid and violent discharge of the water takes place than would occur from the elevation of head alone, and by which a proportionate velocity of motion is also produced. In Rozier's *Journal de Physique*, August 1775, there is an account of an improvement of this machine by M. Mathon de la Cour, in which the water is made to ascend instead of descend into the pipe $u\,v$, by means of a close ground joint: in this way any height of water can be conducted by close pipes to operate on the machine without increasing the height and consequent weight of the revolving pipe, which makes the machine much more compact and free from friction. Mr. Waring describes a machine of this description, on M. Mathon de la Cour's construction, from his own inspection, in the 3d vol. of the Transactions of the American Philosophical Society, and of which he gives the following dimensions. The radius of the arms from the centre pivot to the centre of the discharging holes forty-six inches; inside diameter of the arms three inches; diameter of the supplying pipe two inches; height of the working head of water twenty-one feet above the points of discharge. This, though a great fall, is evidently a very small consumption of water, since it was all supplied by a two-inch pipe; and when the machine was not loaded, and had but one discharging orifice open, it made 115 turns in a minute. This gives a velocity of forty-six feet in a second for the orifice of discharge, which is nine feet and five-sixths in a second faster than the water would flow out under the simple pressure of a twenty-one feet head, which great excess of velocity can only be attributed to the prodigious centrifugal force generated in the arms, and upon which this machine, in a great measure, depends for its action. Barker's mill is a machine which is very warmly recommended to practice by all the eminent mechanics who have investigated the subject; and considering the high respectability of their names, and the simplicity and cheapness of the machine, it cannot but be matter of surprise that no attempts at its construction on a large scale have been made in Great Britain, where the motive power of water has been more extensively used than in any other part of the world, and has in no small degree contributed to that pre-eminent excellence which our country is acknowledged to have obtained in her various manufacturing processes. The application of water to the driving of machinery is so simple, so cheap, so constant, and equable in its action, that it amply merits the preference constantly shown to it whenever it can be obtained: but it frequently happens, that motion and power are required for machinery, where the stream may not be sufficiently powerful all the year round to drive a large wheel; and in that case, two smaller water-wheels are to be preferred to one large one; because the one wheel may be driven when there is not water enough for both; besides which, it affords an opportunity of repairing one wheel while the other may be at work, and possesses other practical advantages.

Chapter IV.

BOOKS UPON THIS BRANCH OF SCIENCE.

Hydraulics in general.

The principal books on these subjects are chiefly by foreign authors, and were, till lately, in foreign languages. Amongst the most conspicuous are:—

Architecture Hydraulique, par M. Bélidor, 4 vols. 4to. Paris, (1782.)
Nouvelle Architecture Hydraulique, par M. Prony. Paris, (1796.)
Principes d'Hydraulique, par Du Buat, 2 vols. 8vo. Paris, (1786.)
Hydrodynamica, sive de Viribus et Motibus Fluidorum, Commentarii, Dan. Bernoullii. 4to. Strasburg, (1738.)
Opera Hydraulica de Joh. Bernoullii, vol. 4. Lausanne, (1742.)
Traité élémentaire d'Hydrodynamique, par Bossut, 2 vols. 8vo. Paris, (1771.)
Jacob Leupold, Theat. Machinarum hydraulicarum, (1724, 1725.)

(Among the best English works, and translations on the subjects generally, are):—

A Treatise of Mechanics, by Olinthus Gregory, LL.D., Prof. Math. in the Roy. Mil. Acad., Woolwich, 2 vols. 8vo. London, (1826.)
Lectures on Natural Philosophy, by Thomas Young, M. D., 2 vols. 4to. London, (1807.)
The Works of Vitruvius, translated from Latin, by Newton, 2 vols. fol., (1791.)
Emerson's Principles of Mechanics, 4to. London, (1758.)
Ency. Brit., Art. *Hydraulics* and *River*.—Many valuable detached articles throughout the Trans. of the Society of Arts—The Repertory of Arts—Nicholson's Phil. Journal—The Philosophical Magazine.

Particular Subjects.

Experimental Inquiry on the Power of Mills, by John Smeaton, F. R. S., 1 vol. 8vo., London, (1796.) Also, Smeaton's Reports, 3 vols. 4to. (1812.)
A Treatise on Mills, by John Banks, 1 vol. 8vo., (1815.) also, by the same, on the Power of Barker's Mill, Westgarth's Engine, &c., 1 vol. 8vo., (1803.)
Practical Essays on Mill-work, by R. Buchanan, 2 vols. 8vo., (1823.)
Experimental Inquiry concerning the Motion of Fluids, by J. B. Venturi, translated by W. Nicholson, 1 vol. 8vo., London, (1799.)
A Treatise on Rivers and Torrents, by P. Frisi, translated by Maj.-Gen. John Garstin, 1 vol. 4to., London, (1818.)

PNEUMATICS.

Chapter I.

Division of Bodies—Subject of Pneumatics.

(1.) MATERIAL SUBSTANCES, in reference to their mechanical properties, are divided into *solids* and *fluids*.

Wood, stone, metal in its ordinary state, are instances of solids. One of the most striking mechanical peculiarities of this class is that, if to such a body any force be applied, the whole mass will be moved without suffering any change in its figure or shape.

Water, quicksilver, melted metal, air, steam, are instances of fluids. This class of bodies differ essentially in their mechanical properties from the former. That cohesion of parts which is the cause of the preservation of the figure of a solid, notwithstanding the application of a force tending to change the figure, has here no existence whatever. The parts of a fluid are perfectly free to move among each other, and immediately yield upon the application of the smallest force. Fluids easily allow solid bodies to pass through them, and their surfaces always compose themselves into a perfect level. On the other hand, the cohesion of the parts of solids do not permit the passage of another body through them unless extraordinary force be used, and their surfaces maintain any position with respect to a level or horizontal plane in which they may happen to be placed.

(2.) Fluids are divided into two very distinct classes, denominated, from their characteristic mechanical properties, *elastic* and *inelastic*.

If a strong cylindrical vessel, of which A B (*fig.* 1.) is a section, be filled to the height C with water, and a piston or plug D, accurately fitting the vessel, and capable of moving water-tight in it, be introduced over the surface of the water, and a pressure be exerted on that surface by means of the piston, it will be found that no pressure which can be produced will force the surface of the water lower in the vessel than its original height C.

fig. 1.

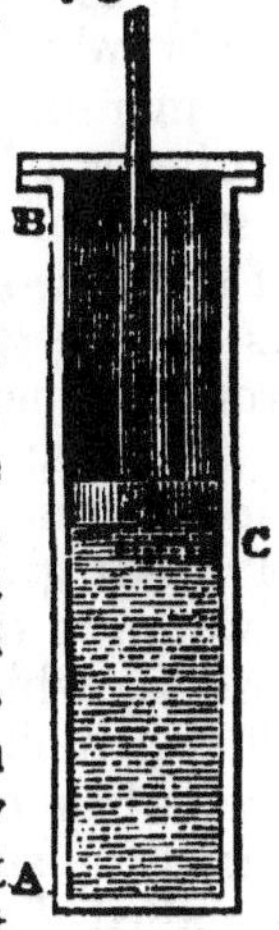

Now let us suppose the water discharged from the vessel A B, and its place occupied by common air. Let the piston, as before, be introduced into the cylinder, fitting it so that no air can escape between the piston and the cylinder. A pressure being now exerted on the piston it will immediately descend; but the moment the pressure is removed, it will again ascend, and resume its first position.

(3.) The property, in virtue of which the water resisted the descent of the piston and would not admit of a diminished bulk, is called *incompressibility*; and, on the other hand, the property by which the air admitted the descent of the piston and was forced into a less bulk, is called *compressibility*. Again, the property manifested by the air in forcing back the piston when the pressure was removed, and resuming its original bulk, is called *elasticity*.

It appears, therefore, that elasticity supposes compressibility, and a body which is incompressible must necessarily be also inelastic. Hence water is an inelastic, air an elastic fluid.

Strictly speaking, neither water, nor any other liquid which we know of, is perfectly incompressible or inelastic. It was long supposed that water possessed neither of these properties; but accurate experiments have shown, that it and other liquids are both compressible and elastic. A pressure of 15lbs. on each square inch of surface, reduces the bulk of water by one part in 21740. The degrees of compressibility, however, which

B

are found in liquids, are so inconsiderable, that the quality of compressibility in these substances is rather to be looked upon as a *philosophical fact*, than as a property to be taken into account in mechanical investigations. Accordingly, in all mechanical treatises, liquids and aëriform bodies are considered to be distinguished as we have already explained; and when their properties are expressed mathematically, the formulæ for the one are founded on the supposition of their being inelastic, and for the other of their being elastic.

The same property of incompressibility which we have just explained in water, is common to all that class of fluids which are called liquids, such as mercury, alcohol, &c.; and the property of elasticity explained in the instance of air is common to all fluids of the gaseous or vaporous form, such as all the gases, steam raised by heat from all species of liquids, &c.

This manifest and important mechanical distinction between the two classes of fluids gives rise to a corresponding division in that part of mechanical philosophy which treats of their properties. That which treats of the mechanical properties of elastic fluids, and which forms the subject of the present treatise, is called *Pneumatics*, from the Greek word πνυμα, *(pneuma,)* which signifies *breath* or *air*.

(4.) The various elastic fluids differ one from another in many respects. One of the most striking distinctions is, that some are permanently elastic, and others not. Those which are incapable by any known means of being converted into a liquid are called *permanently elastic fluids*. Such, for example, is *air*. On the other hand, those which, by being submitted to pressure or exposed to cold, are reduced to liquids, are not permanently elastic, and are generally called *vapours*. Such, for example, is *steam*. Besides this, there are many other distinctions between elastic fluids, arising out of their chemical properties. It will not, however, be necessary here to inquire into these, since the mechanical properties which we shall have to consider in the present treatise are common to all elastic fluids, whatever be their differences as to permanent elasticity or any other properties. The elastic fluid with which we are most familiar is *atmospheric air*, and it possesses all the mechanical properties which we shall have to notice in any elastic fluid. For this and other reasons it will be convenient to adopt it as the representative of elastic fluids in general, and there will be no difficulty in applying to them the conclusions to which we may arrive.

Chapter II.

Air possesses the universal Properties of Matter—Impenetrability, Inertia, Mobility, and Weight.

(5.) Air being apparently an invisible, intangible substance in which we freely move, it may at first be doubted whether it be matter or not. It should be observed, that the properties of substances, even those with which we are most habitually conversant, do not always offer themselves immediately to the observation of the senses, and that in noticing them our senses must often be guided by philosophical considerations. Not that these philosophical considerations add any thing to the certitude derived from the senses, but rather that they direct the senses to the proper objects of attention. Let us then consider how we should use the senses in deciding the question, whether *air* be material or not? We know that there are certain properties which any thing must have in order to be material, and that having these properties it is necessarily one of that class of beings which we denote by the term *matter*. Air, then, will be material or not, according as it is found to possess or not these requisite qualifications. The principal of these properties are, *impenetrability, inertia, mobility,* and *weight*.

(6.) *Impenetrability* is that property by which a body occupies any space to the exclusion of every other body, or so that no other body can fill that space until the other deserts it.

(7.) *Air* is *impenetrable*.

There are various experimental proofs of this proposition. Let A B (*fig* 2.) be a glass receiver, or cylindrical vessel, containing water to the level B, and let C D (*fig*. 3.) be a smaller vessel of the same kind empty, and having an aperture in the bottom furnished with a stop-cock at F. Let a cork or other light body be placed floating on the surface of the water at G, and the stop-cock F being closed, let the vessel C D be inverted over the cork G, (as at *fig* 4.) and let its mouth D be pressed into the water to any convenient depth. It will

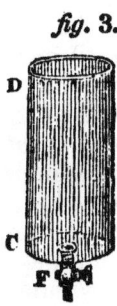
fig. 3.
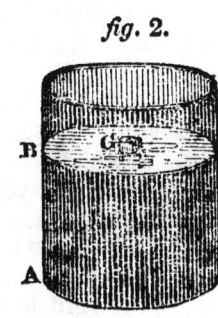
fig. 2.
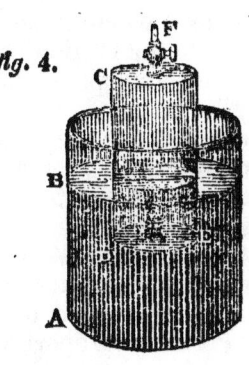
fig. 4.

be found that the water will not enter the inverted receiver, except to a very limited height as E, as will be made visible by the cork floating on the surface and seen through the glass. Thus the air in the receiver which occupies the space C E excludes the water. That this is the cause of its exclusion will be rendered apparent by opening the stopcock F, by which the air which hitherto prevented the ascent of the water beyond the level E will escape, and the water will immediately rise until it assumes the same level in both receivers.

Again, if the piston described in (2.) be forced against the air confined in the cylinder, it will be found that no force whatever will compel it to reach the bottom; however strong the apparatus may be, it will burst or break before this can happen.

(8.) In both of these experiments it might seem that the air was partially penetrable, since in the former the water entered the cylinder to the height E, and in the latter, although the piston could not be forced to the bottom, yet it was found to approach it. These effects, however, were not produced by the penetration of the air contained in the respective vessels, but by its compression. The air in both cases yielded to the body, which entered the cylinder and contracted itself into a smaller space.

It would be very easy to multiply proofs of the existence of this property in air, but it is the less necessary, as additional proofs of it will be perceived in many of the experiments which we shall have to describe for other purposes. The same, indeed, may be said of all the other properties of air which we are about to establish, and such is ever the nature of principles established by philosophical investigation. They are continually reappearing and soliciting our notice when we are not seeking them, and we recognise fresh proofs of them in investigations apparently the most remote from those in which they first originated.

The quality in *air* which we have called *impenetrability*, is sometimes called *solidity*, and *air* is said to be *solid*. There is, however, an objection to the use of this term in this sense. *Solid* has already been used in opposition to *fluid*, and *air* is of the latter class. The word *solid* would thus be used in two different senses, which should be avoided. We have, therefore, in the present instance, thought it better to express that universal property of all species of matter by which it refuses admission of other matter to the space it fills until it has deserted it, by the negative term *impenetrability*.

(9.) *Air* is *inert* and *moveable*.

The quality of inertia which is known as an universal property of matter, is that in virtue of which it requires a certain effort or force to produce motion in matter if it be at rest, and to destroy or modify any motion which it has if not at rest.

That *air* possesses inertia we have numerous and familiar proofs. *Wind* is nothing but air in motion. Any obstacle which opposes this motion sustains a considerable pressure, and must exert a proportionate resistance, otherwise it will be carried forward with the body of moving air. Such are the effects of wind on balloons and other bodies floating in the atmosphere. Also on ships and all bodies floating on water which present sufficient surfaces in opposition to the wind, such as sails. Nay, we find, notwithstanding the extreme thinness of the atmosphere which surrounds us, that it is capable of exerting very powerful degrees of force when it acquires sufficient velocity: witness the effects of hurricanes in agitating the waters of the ocean, in tearing up by the roots the largest trees, in overthrowing buildings, &c. These effects establish beyond question the great force which is necessary to destroy or modify the motion of air.

If the atmosphere be quiescent and there be no wind, there is a resistance opposed by it to the passage of any body through it. This resistance is produced by the force exerted by the body so passing through it in displacing the air in its progress. When the motion is slow, and the surface of the body which faces the direction of the motion not very great in proportion to the whole body, this resistance is perhaps not sensibly felt. But if the motion be accelerated or the surface much enlarged, it is instantly perceived. In walking at a moderate pace on a calm day we do not easily feel the resistance of the air, but if we increase our speed and run, we find the same effect as if a wind were blowing in our face; this effect increases in proportion to the speed, and is very obvious when riding or driving rapidly.

If a large fan or an open umbrella be moved slowly against the calm air, the resistance will be instantly felt, and a considerable exertion will be necessary to sustain the motion.

(10.) *Air* has *weight*.

If our object be merely to establish the *fact* that air is heavy, the most direct method is to weigh it by the usual means, a balance. But if it be required to ascertain with great nicety its degree of weight or *specific gravity*, other less direct but more accurate means must be resorted to. In the present instance we shall be content with establishing the *fact* that air has weight.

There are some very obvious effects which plainly indicate this. It is shown in our treatise on Hydrostatics, that when a lighter body is placed in a fluid it ascends in it, and that if it so ascend it must be lighter than the fluid in which it moves. Now there can be no doubt that a *balloon* has weight, and yet it ascends in the atmosphere. The atmosphere must then, bulk for bulk, be heavier than the balloon. Besides this, the clouds which we see floating in the atmosphere are generally composed of water, as is proved by their frequently falling in rain. They have therefore weight, but yet must be lighter than the atmosphere in which they are suspended.

If a piston move in a cylinder so as to be air-tight and be provided with a valve which opens upwards, upon pressing the piston to the bottom of the cylinder, the air contained in the cylinder will be forced through the valve in the piston. Let us then suppose the piston in close contact with the bottom and sides of the cylinder, all air having been excluded: upon attempting to draw the piston up, it will be found that very considerable force will be necessary; and that when sufficient effort has been used, and the piston has been brought to the top of the cylinder, if it be disengaged from the agent which drew it up, it will descend with great force and strike the bottom. This effect plainly indicates the weight of the air pressing on the upper surface of the piston. This is what is vulgarly called *suction*; as if there were some force within the cylinder which drew the piston to the bottom. But within the cylinder is nothing but empty space, and it is plainly unreasonable to ascribe to empty space any mechanical influence.

That it is the weight of the incumbent atmosphere pressing on the upper surface of the piston which forces it to the bottom of the cylinder, is still further proved by the fact, that if the upper surface of the piston be increased, the force which presses it down will be also increased, and what is more, will be increased in precisely the same proportion as the surface of the piston. In fact, it is found that when all air or other elastic fluid has been expelled from beneath the piston, there will be a pressure amounting to about fifteen pounds on every square inch of the upper surface of the piston; from which we may infer that a column of air, having a square inch for its base, and which extends from the surface of the earth to the top of the atmosphere, weighs about fifteen pounds*. The atmospheric engine is a machine whose efficacy depends on the principle which we have been just explaining. In this machine the weight of the atmosphere is used as a first mover in pressing a piston to the bottom of a cylinder†.

---

* Its weight varies within narrow limits, as will appear hereafter. Fifteen pounds may be considered an average in round numbers.

† In calculating the atmospheric pressure on any surface, it is necessary to determine the number of square inches in the surface. As it often happens that the surface thus to be measured is circular, it may be useful to have a short and easy rule, by which the number of square inches in a circle of a given diameter may be found. The following rule will be found to serve this purpose:—

Let half the diameter of the circle expressed in inches be found, and its square taken, and let this square be multiplied by the number 3.1415, *and the*

But there is a still more conclusive argument that it is the weight of the atmosphere which presses down the piston. If, by a valve in the bottom of the cylinder, the air be admitted *below* the piston, it will no longer be pressed down, or rather it will be pressed both upwards and downwards by equal forces, and will be indifferent as to its ascent or descent, except so far as the weight of the piston itself will produce the effect. This is owing to a property of air, by which it presses equally in every direction, which we shall explain more fully hereafter. (13.)

The most direct proof, however, that air is a heavy substance is, that it can be directly *weighed*.

Let a phial be provided, containing not less than two quarts, and having a stop-cock screwed upon its neck. By means of the air-pump or exhausting syringe, which will be described hereafter, the air may be withdrawn from this vessel. When this has been done, and the stop-cock closed, let it be suspended from one arm of a very accurate balance, and an exact counterpoise placed in the opposite scale-pan. The empty phial is thus balanced. When the beam ceases to vibrate and becomes steady, open the stop-cock and admit the air into the phial. It will immediately preponderate, and it will be found that to restore the equilibrium a weight must be placed in the opposite pan, at the rate of about 523 grains for every cubic foot of air contained by the bottle. Since there are 1000 ounces in a cubic foot of water, it follows that, bulk for bulk, water is about 840 times the weight of air.

(11.) Many effects with which we are familiar, and which often excite our curiosity, are accounted for by the gravitation of the atmosphere. If the nozzle and the valve-hole of a pair of bellows be stopped, it will be found that a very considerable force will be necessary to separate the boards. This is owing to the air not being permitted to enter at the usual apertures, to resist the pressure of the atmosphere on the external surfaces of the boards. Shell-fish which adhere to rocks, snails, and other animals, have a power by muscular exertion of expelling the air from between the surface of the rock and the surface which they apply to it, in consequence of which they are pressed upon the rock by the atmosphere with a force of about fifteen pounds for every square inch in the surface of contact. The same cause enables flies and other animals to walk on a perpendicular plane of glass or on the lower surface of an horizontal plane, apparently suspended by their feet, and with their bodies downwards. This has lately been proved to arise from a power of expelling the air from between their feet and the surface on which they tread, so as to obtain a pressure from the atmosphere proportionate to the magnitude of the soles of their feet.

Chapter III.

Of the Weight of the Atmosphere—The Barometer.

(12.) Having in the last chapter considered in a general way those properties which elastic fluids have in common with every species of matter, we shall now examine more particularly the weight of the atmosphere and the methods of measuring it. It will be necessary first, however, to mention a quality of all fluids, whether elastic or inelastic, to which we shall have occasion to allude.

(13.) One of the most striking properties by which fluids are distinguished from solids, and that indeed which has been adopted in mechanical science as the definition of a fluid, is the quality by which it is capable of *transmitting pressure equally in every direction*.

To explain this, let us suppose a vessel of any shape completely filled with a fluid and closed at every part, so that

---

product will be the number of square inches in the circle.

This rule will give the area of the circle to within one 10,000th part of the square of half its diameter. The following example will serve to show the application of this rule. Let the diameter of the circle be 24 inches. The square of half this is $12 \times 12 = 144$. Hence the area will be found thus:

$$\begin{array}{r} 144 \\ 3.1415 \\ \hline 720 \\ 144 \\ 576 \\ 144 \\ 432 \\ \hline 452.3760 \end{array}$$

which expresses the number of square inches in the circle to within one hundred and forty-four 10,000th of an inch.

The area may be found without decimals by the following rule: *Let the diameter of the circle be squared, and its square divided by 14. If the quote be multiplied by 11, the product will be the area nearly.* Thus, in the preceding example, the diameter is 24, the square of which is 576; this, divided by 14, gives $41\frac{2}{7}$, which, being multiplied by 11, gives $452\frac{3}{7}$.

the fluid is confined within it, and has no opening through which it can escape. Let a hole be cut any where in this vessel of any proposed magnitude, as a square inch, and let the piece cut out be imagined to be replaced by a solid piston fitting the hole, so that the fluid cannot escape between it and the sides of the hole. We shall suppose the fluid inelastic. Let a pressure equal to one pound weight urge the piston inwards. Such is the peculiar nature of fluidity, that a pressure of one pound will be exerted on every square inch of the inner surface of the vessel, so that by an actual pressure amounting to one pound, an effective pressure of as many pounds as there are square inches on the inner surface of the vessel will be thus produced. This perfect power of transmitting pressure is the specific attribute of fluids whether elastic or inelastic, and it is the mechanical property which forms the basis of all mathematical treatises on the theory of fluids.

(14.) We shall now enter more minutely into the consideration of the weight of the atmosphere.

Let A B (*fig.* 5.) be a glass tube upwards of thirty-two inches in length, open at one extremity A, and closed at the other, B. The tube having been carefully cleaned on the inside, let a quantity of mercury (quicksilver,) well cleansed and purged of air by boiling, be provided. Turning the closed end B of the tube down, let it be filled with the mercury through the open end A. Let a small cistern C D be also provided, and filled with mercury to the height C D. Placing the finger firmly on the end A, so as to prevent the mercury from escaping out of the tube, let it be inverted, and the open end A plunged in the vessel of mercury. When the mouth A of the tube is below the surface C D of the quicksilver in the cistern, let the finger be removed from the aperture A, the mercury in the tube will then be observed to fall to the height E, about twenty-nine or thirty inches above the surface C D, and there, after a few vibrations, it will rest.

It must no doubt excite inquiry, why the column F E of mercury remains suspended in the tube, and why, as might naturally be expected, the surface E does not fall to the level D C of the mercury in the cistern? A little consideration will, however, solve this difficulty. It will be remembered, that the tube being closed at B, the space B E is a perfect void, in which there is neither air nor any other fluid. The column of mercury E F therefore presses with nothing but its own weight on the level C F D of the mercury in the cistern; for in this pressure the weight of the atmosphere has no part, since it is excluded from above the surface of the mercury E. The pressure thus exerted at F, by the weight of the column E F, is, by the property of the liquid mercury described in (13), transmitted to the exterior surface C F of the mercury in the cistern, and gives that surface a tendency to rise with an equivalent force. That this surface *would rise* is certain, were it not resisted by a force accurately equal and opposite to that we have just mentioned. This force is the weight of the atmosphere itself resting on the surface C F. Thus, then, it appears that the atmosphere must necessarily press on the surface C F with a force exactly equal to that with which the weight of the column of mercury F E presses on the level F.

If we were to suppose the base of the column F E to be equal to a square inch, it would therefore follow that the atmosphere presses on every square inch of the surface of the mercury in the cistern C D, with a force equal to the

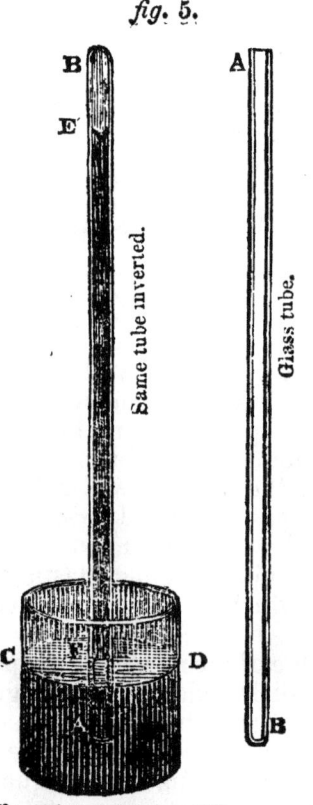

fig. 5.

Glass cistern filled to C D with quicksilver.

weight of a column of mercury, whose base is a square inch and whose height is F E.

It might appear, that in this experiment the weight of the column of mercury F E suspended in the tube must be equal to the *total pressure* on the surface of the mercury in the cistern, and that, therefore, (supposing, as before, the base of the column in the tube to be equal to a square inch,) this pressure being distributed over as many square inches as are in the surface of the mercury in the cistern, the proportion of pressure by which the ascent of each square inch must be resisted, is as many times *less* than the weight of the column F E, as the surface of the mercury in the cistern is *greater* than the base of the column. This, however, is not the case; for it is the peculiarity of fluids, not merely to transmit pressure equally in every direction, but to transmit whatever pressure is exerted on any one part of its surface, undiminished, to every part equal in magnitude with the first.

(15.) If a scale be adapted to the tube A B, in the apparatus which we have just described, suited to indicate the height of the column of mercury F E, it will become a *barometer**, which is an instrument constructed to determine the weight of the atmosphere. It should be observed, that the height of the mercury in the barometric tube will be the same, whatever be the bore of the tube. Thus it is the *height* of the column, and not its absolute weight, which measures the weight of the atmosphere.

That it is the weight of the atmosphere which, pressing on the surface of the mercury in the cistern, sustains the column of mercury in the tube, will be made manifest by breaking the upper end B of the tube, and admitting the air to press on the mercury E. The consequence will be, that the mercury in the tube will fall to the level F of the mercury in the cistern.

There is another very satisfactory proof that the weight of the atmosphere is the cause which sustains the mercury in the tube. If a tube of more than thirty-four feet long be immersed in a cistern of water, and the air be withdrawn from it, by means which shall be hereafter explained, the water will rise according as the air is expelled; but the ascent of the water will be limited to about thirty-two perpendicular feet: at the same time it will be found that the column of mercury suspended in the barometric tube will be about twenty-eight perpendicular inches. If, then, the weight of the atmosphere be the cause which sustains both the water and the mercury, we may expect to find that a column of water thirty-two feet high, and a column of mercury twenty-eight inches high, ought to have the same weight when they have the same base. To determine whether this be the case, let equal measures of mercury and water be accurately weighed, and it will be found that the mercury is about thirteen and a half times heavier than the water. Hence we perceive, that a column of water, whose base is a square inch and whose height is thirteen inches and a half, will have the same weight as a column of mercury whose base is a square inch and whose height is one inch. Hence it appears that columns of water and mercury, with equal bases, will have equal weights, if the column of water be thirteen and a half times the height of the mercury. In the present instance, the height of the water is 32 feet, or 384 inches; and that of the mercury is 28 inches. If 384 be divided by $13\frac{1}{2}$, the quotient will be nearly 28 inches.

If similar experiments be tried upon other fluids of different specific gravities, it will be found that they will be sustained at different altitudes in their respective tubes; but that if the weights of the several columns be determined as above, they will be found to be equal.

When the barometric column is thirty inches, the atmosphere presses with about 15 lbs. av. on the square inch; and, therefore, in general, we may estimate the pressure nearly by allowing 1 lb. for every two inches in the column.

(16.) In the construction of a barometer which will give an exact measure of the atmospheric pressure, there are many circumstances to be attended to, the details of which would be unsuitable to the present treatise. It may not, however, be uninteresting, and certainly not uninstructive, in a general way, to state some of the most important precautions to be taken in the construction of this instrument.

In order that the weight of the column suspended in the tube should be exactly equal to that of a column of the atmosphere, of an equal base, it is evidently necessary that the space in the tube

---

* From two Greek words, βαρος (baros), *weight*, and μετρον (metron), *measure*.

above the mercury should be a perfect vacuum; for if it be occupied by any fluid, this will press on the surface of the mercury in the tube, and the real weight of the atmosphere will be equal to that of the mercury suspended in the tube, together with the pressure of the fluid above it.

To prevent the existence of any air or other fluid in this space, two precautions are necessary: first, the mercury must be well purified before it is introduced into the tube; and, secondly, the interior of the tube itself must be rendered perfectly clean.

Mercury, in its ordinary state, generally contains a quantity of air incorporated with it, or fixed in it: by boiling it, this air is rendered highly elastic, and it accordingly disengages itself, and escapes at the surface. If this air were permitted to remain in the mercury when introduced into the tube, it would escape from it when the mercury would be relieved from the atmospheric pressure by inverting the tube in the cistern, and would rise in bubbles at the top, and thus would occupy the part of the tube above the mercury, and exert a pressure on its surface—an effect which is particularly to be avoided.

Particles of moisture and air are apt to adhere to the interior surface of the tube: these are also removed by heat. On introducing the cleansed mercury into the tube, it will even contribute to the perfection of the instrument to boil it in the tube: this, which can be done without much difficulty, will at once disengage from it the particles of air and moisture which may remain either in the mercury itself or on the tube.

(17.) In estimating the weight or pressure of the atmosphere by a barometric tube thus prepared, it is necessary to measure the height E of the mercury in the tube, above the surface F of the mercury in the cistern. Therefore, the graduation of the scale by which this height is measured, should be taken from the surface of the mercury in the cistern. It is found that the weight of the atmosphere is subject to very irregular changes, being at one time capable of sustaining a greater column of mercury than at another; and one of the most common and interesting uses of the barometer is to mark these changes. The weight of the atmosphere is never less than what sustains a column of mercury of twenty-eight inches, nor greater than what supports one of thirty-one inches. Thus, supposing the barometric tube to be perpendicular, the surface of the mercury in it has a range of three inches.

This variation of the height of the mercury in the tube, united with the necessity of measuring the column from the surface of the mercury in the cistern, suggests a circumstance which should be attended to in the construction of a barometer.

As the surface E of the mercury *falls* in the tube, the surface C F of the mercury in the cistern must necessarily *rise*; since the mercury, which is discharged from the tube, is thrown into the cistern: and, on the other hand, when the surface E of the mercury in the tube *rises*, that C F of the mercury in the cistern must *fall*. Thus the two surfaces move always together, and in opposite directions. It must, therefore, be evident, that if the scale, by which the distance between these surfaces is measured, be fixed, two observations would be necessary to determine the height of the column. To avoid this, the cistern is usually constructed of very considerable dimensions in comparison with those of the tube; so that the cubic quantity of mercury contained in three inches of the tube, can produce a very inconsiderable change in the level of the mercury in the cistern.

(18.) Such a barometer, although sufficient for the more popular purposes, does not give all the accuracy requisite for some more scientific investigations. Accordingly, contrivances have been adopted for regulating the level of the mercury in the cistern, among which the following is worthy of notice:

The glass tube is enclosed in another of brass, in which, however, a longitudinal aperture D E (*fig.* 6.) is cut, extending from the lowest to beyond the highest altitude of the mercury; so that the whole play of the barometer is included between D and E. The cylindrical cistern A B, in which the tube is plunged, has a bottom B moveable by a screw V; so that it may be raised and lowered at pleasure, and a corresponding motion given to the level of the mercury in the cistern. An ivory index is attached to the top of the cistern, with a fine point P, which marks the level from which the divisions of the scale CF are measured. When the height of the barometric column is to be observed, the screw V is to be turned, until the point P meets the surface of the mercury, the tube being placed in a truly vertical position, the altitude then denoted by the scale C F will be the height of the barometer.

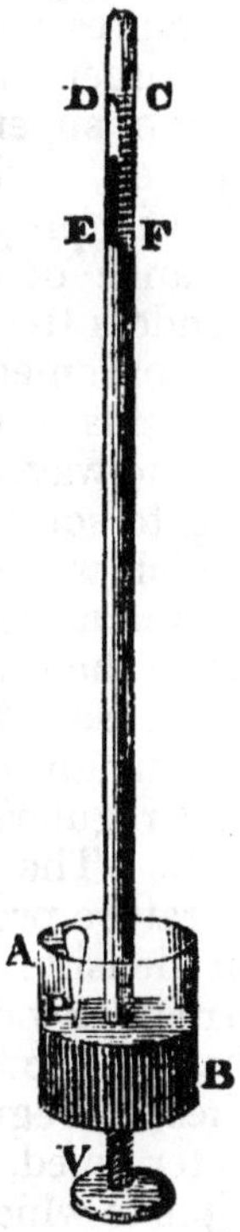

To the scale C F a *vernier* or *nonius* may be attached, to give greater accuracy to the observation, by which the divisions can be read to the one-hundredth part of an inch.

(19.) In order to compare barometric observations made at different times or places, it is necessary to observe the temperature of the mercury which composes the barometric column. For mercury, like all other bodies, is dilated by heat; so that at different temperatures the same weight of mercury stands at different heights in the tube. Tables are accordingly constructed, and rules given, by which the heights of the mercury in the barometer may be reduced to what they would be, if the temperature of the mercury had been fixed, and the same as that of melting ice.

(20.) The entire play of the mercury in the barometer not exceeding three inches, minute variations in the weight of the atmosphere will produce so small a change in the altitude of the column, that the observation of it is attended with considerable difficulty. Various contrivances have been suggested to increase the range of the mercury in the tube, and render small changes perceptible: one of the most obvious would be to use a lighter fluid, instead of mercury; but to this there are various practical objections. The following contrivances for enlarging the scale may be mentioned:—

(21.) The *diagonal barometer* is one in which the tube A B (*fig.* 7.) is bent from the vertical position, at a point C less than twenty-eight inches from the level A of the mercury in the cistern; and the inflected part of such a length, that the perpendicular altitude of its extremity B above A, shall exceed 31 inches. To determine the relation between the scale of such a barometer and the common vertical one, let the line A C be continued upwards from C, until it meet the horizontal line B D, drawn

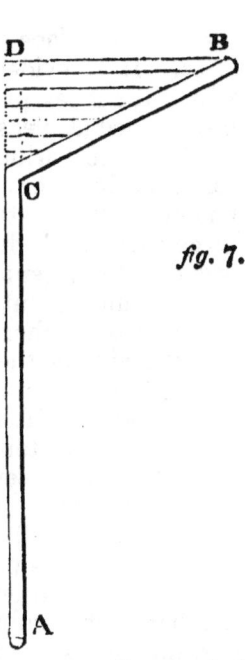

fig. 6.

through B. Let the scale C D be then made as for the vertical barometer, and parallels to BD, from its points of division, will give the scale for C B. It is evident that the divisions will thus be enlarged, in proportion as the tube C B is deflected from the vertical position C D.

(22.) Another contrivance for increasing the scale, is the *wheel-barometer*. This instrument consists of a bent tube A B C (*fig.* 8.) closed at A, and so that the distance C A shall not be less than about thirty-one or thirty-two inches: the end C being open, the tube is filled with mercury. The mercury will subside in the leg A B until the difference of the levels E F will be equal to the height of a column of quicksilver which balances the pressure of the atmosphere, and every change in the level of E will be accompanied by an equal change, but in the opposite direction, in the surface F; so that the change in the height of the barometric column, is double the change of the level F. On the level F there floats a small iron ball, to which a string is attached, which is passed over a pulley P, and to which a weight W less than that of the ball P is suspended. The axis of the pulley P passes through the centre of a large graduated circular plate G, and carries an hand or index H, which revolves when the pulley is turned.

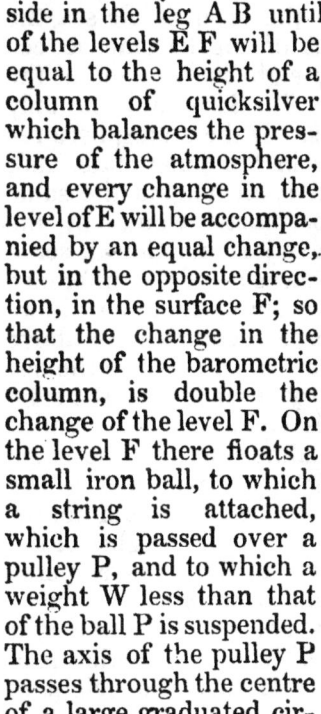

fig. 7.

fig. 8.

In this apparatus, when the mercury E rises, and F falls, the floating ball, not being completely balanced by W, falls with it. The string being pressed by the weights on the wheel P, turns it, and with it the index which plays on the graduated circular plate. The contrary effect takes place when E falls and F rises. It is evident that the scale on which the index plays may, in this case, be enlarged at pleasure.

There are various other contrivances for enlarging the scale of the barometer, and other circumstances connected with its construction, which we feel ourselves precluded from entering on, by our necessary limits; but the student who is desirous of further information on the subject, will find them treated of at large in most works on mechanical science. See *Gregory's Mechanics*, vol. ii. 119; *Biot, Physique*, tom. i. p. 69.

(23.) As we ascend to greater heights it is natural to expect that the atmospheric pressure will be diminished, there being a much less portion of atmosphere above us; and therefore the altitude of the barometric column should be proportionably lessened. And this we find in fact to be the case. If a barometer be carried to the top of high mountains, or taken up in a balloon, the level of the mercury in the tube will be observed to fall as the elevation of the instrument increases. At the level of the sea the medium height of the barometric column is twenty-eight inches, and at the top of Mount St. Bernard it is only fourteen inches. If the atmosphere remained always in the same state, and, like water, had at all heights the same density, the barometer would, by the property we have just mentioned, serve as an accurate measure of the difference of levels of two stations, or the difference of their perpendicular heights above the level of the sea. For since the column of mercury suspended in the tube at each place is equal to the weight of the column of atmosphere of the same base, extending from that place to the top of the atmosphere, it would follow that the difference of the heights of the columns (reduced to the same temperature (27.)) would be equal to the weight of a column of atmosphere, whose height is equal to the difference of the levels of the two places. If then the height of a column of air, corresponding to that of a column of one inch of mercury, be known, it would only be necessary to multiply this height by the number of inches by which the barometric altitudes at the two places differ, to obtain the difference of levels.

But the density of the air is not the same at different heights. Air being elastic, each inferior stratum suffers compression from the incumbent weight of all the superior strata, and by this compression its density is increased. As we ascend in the atmosphere the quantity of superior strata is gradually diminished, and the compressing force and density proportionately diminished. This change of density from level to level renders the computation of heights by the barometer somewhat more complex; but this would throw but little difficulty in the way, if the density varied according to some fixed and known law, and which would probably be the case if the temperature of the air at all elevations were the same. This, however, is not the case. The temperature decreases as the height of the station increases; but not regularly, nor according to any fixed rule. The irregular variation in temperature produces an irregular variation in density, and therefore produces an irregular variation in the change of the barometric column. Notwithstanding these irregularities, rules have been determined, founded mainly on the principle to which we have alluded, by which the difference of levels of two places may be computed, when the heights of the barometer and thermometer at the two places are known.

(24.) The changes in the altitude of the mercury in the barometer which we have just been considering, have proceeded from the change in the altitude of the barometer itself, with respect to the earth's surface. But, besides this, even when the place of the instrument is not changed, when it remains suspended in the same chamber, the surface of the mercury, as we have stated, is subject to rise and fall. This effect proceeds from a change in the state of the atmosphere, and being continually observed in connexion with the state of the weather, it has been attempted to establish rules, by which changes of the weather may be predicted from the variations in the altitude of the barometric column. Hence the barometer is also called a *weather-glass*. It is proper, however, to observe, that even the best established rules for determining changes of the weather by the barometer, are very far from being either general or certain. The rule which seems most generally to obtain is, that the mercury is low in high winds; but even this frequently fails. It is scarcely necessary to observe, that the words *rain, fair, changeable*, &c. engraved on the plates of common barometers, are entitled to no attention. The changes of weather are not so much indicated by the actual height of the mercury as by its variations in height. The following rules may, in a certain degree, be relied on, as corresponding generally to the concomitant changes in the barometer and the weather:—

1. *Generally*, the rising of the mercury indicates the approach of fair weather; the falling of it that of foul weather.

2. In hot weather the fall indicates thunder.

3. In winter the rise indicates frost, and in frost the fall indicates thaw, and the rise snow.

4. If fair or foul weather *immediately* follows the rise or fall, little of it is to be expected.

5. If fair or foul weather continue for some days, while the mercury is falling or rising, a continuance of the contrary weather will probably ensue.

6. An unsettled state of the mercury indicates changeable weather.

By these rules it will be seen that the words engraved on the plate are frequently calculated to mislead the observer. Thus, if the mercury be at *much rain*, and rise to *changeable*, fair weather is to be looked for. Again, if it be at *set fair*, and fall to changeable, foul weather may be expected.

Chapter IV.

Of the Elasticity of Air.

(25.) We have already mentioned the property which fluids in general possess of transmitting pressure (13.) Air and other elastic fluids possess this quality as perfectly as liquids, but there are some circumstances attending the manner in which they exert it which must be attended to. If we suppose the closed vessel A B C D E F G H (*fig.* 9.) described in (13,) to be filled with air instead of water, while the air is of the same density as the free external air, let the piston P be laid upon the aperture *a b* so as to confine the air, but not compress it or reduce its bulk.

From the aperture *a b* let a cylinder, open at both ends, enter the vessel to any distance *c d*. Upon urging the piston with any pressure, as one pound, it will enter the cylinder to a certain distance *a' b'* (*fig.* 10.) at which its further progress will be arrested by the increased resistance of the confined air becoming equal to the urging pressure. In this state of the apparatus, every part of the inner surface of the vessel will sustain a bursting pressure amounting to one pound on every square inch, supposing that to be the magnitude of the aperture *a b*. Thus the air or other elastic fluid has the same extraordinary facility in transmitting pressure as we already ascribed to liquids or inelastic fluids. The only difference between the cases is, that the elastic fluid yields to the incumbent pressure, and suffers itself to be driven into a diminished space, while it transmits the incumbent pressure to the inner surface of the vessel in which it is confined.

(26.) The next property of air which calls our attention is its *elasticity*, a property intimately connected with the last-mentioned, though not dependent

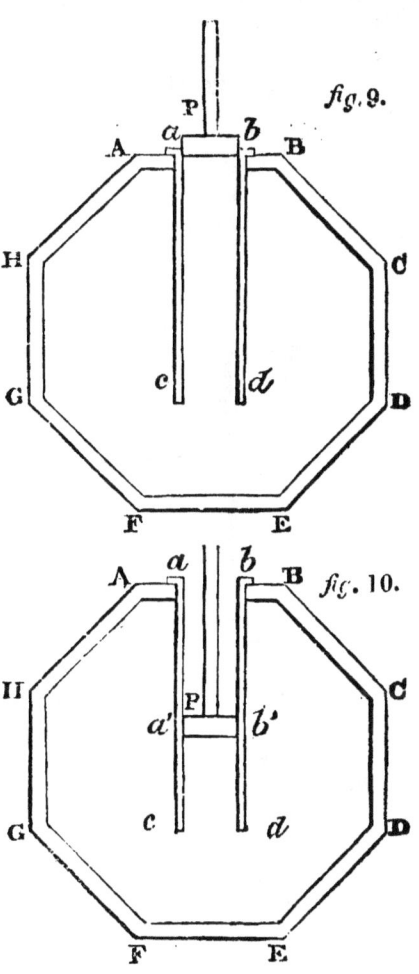

on it. This, as we have already stated, is the line of distinction between gaseous fluids and liquids.

In the apparatus which has been just described, the air confined in the vessel yielded to the pressure which urged the piston P, so as to allow the piston to enter the cylinder; but the pressure on the piston continuing the same, the progress is stopped at a certain point $a'b'$. The resistance which thus arrests the motion of the piston, is the increased elastic force of the air, owing to its having been driven by the piston into a diminished space. It is worthy of notice, that an uniform law governs this increase of elastic force, arising from the diminished bulk of the air, which is, that *the elastic force, or the pressure exerted by the air against the sides of the vessel which contains it, is increased in precisely the same proportion as the space which it occupies is diminished.* To establish this remarkable law some further explanation will be necessary.

Let a syphon tube A B C (*fig.* 11.), open at both ends, be filled to the level xy with mercury. The air which fills the tube will then have the same density, and be in all other respects

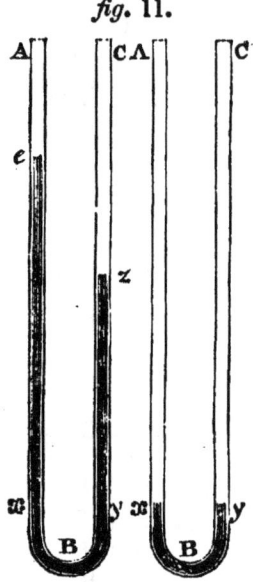

fig. 11.

similar to the external atmosphere. Let the end C be now closed, so as to prevent the escape of air, and let the level y of the mercury in the closed leg be marked on the exterior surface of the tube. Let mercury be then poured in at the open end A; as this fills the leg A B, it will press with its entire weight upon the mercury x B y, and force it up in the tube B C. The air in this tube will then be reduced in bulk, or condensed. Let the mercury be poured in at A, until the mercury in B C rises to half the height y C, so that its surface being at z, C z will be half of C y. The air which originally filled the space C y is now confined to half that space C z. It exerts a pressure on the surface z, which supports a column of mercury, whose height is equal to the difference between the levels e and z, together with the weight of the atmosphere pressing on the surface e. Now, in its original state, before any mercury had been poured in at A, it supported *only* the weight of the atmosphere on x. If the difference of the levels z and e be now measured, it will be found to be exactly equal to the height of the barometer, thereby indicating that the force which presses on the surface z, is equal to twice the weight of the atmosphere. Thus it appears, that when air is condensed into half the bulk which it occupies when free, it exerts double the pressure. In like manner, if mercury be poured in at A, until the air in C y is reduced to one-third of its bulk, it will be found to exert three times its original pressure; and so on. Hence we may in general infer, that the elastic force with which confined air presses against the sides of the vessel which encloses it, is equal to the force which was necessary to condense it; and that both of these increase in precisely the same ratio as the space occupied by the air is diminished. Since the density of any fluid increases in the same proportion as the space it occupies is diminished, it follows also that *the elastic force of air or other fluid is proportional to its density*.

This law, though generally true, is not found to be exact in extreme cases, both of condensation and rarefaction. When a high degree of condensation is required, a greater degree of compressing force is found to be necessary than that which would result from the above law. If an external pressure of 15 lbs. on each square inch be sufficient to confine atmospheric air in its ordinary state, it would only require a pressure of 150 lbs. on the square inch to confine it when reduced to one-tenth of its bulk by compression, but it is found to require a somewhat greater force. In other words, when a great degree of condensation is effected, the elasticity of air increases in a somewhat higher ratio than the density.

In like manner we find, that in high degrees of rarefaction the law is also not precise, highly rarefied air having a less degree of elasticity than that which would be consistent with the law. This, indeed, is a necessary consequence of the former, or rather it may be considered as another way of expressing the same fact.

(27.) Throughout all this process, however, we have supposed that the temperature of the air remains the same. For if the temperature be elevated, an increase of elasticity will ensue, without any change in the density; nay, even with a diminution of the density. For if a flaccid bladder be secured at the mouth so as to stop the transmission of air, and be then heated, the air within it will expand by its increased elastic force, and at length the bladder will be perfectly filled, and have a tendency to burst. In this instance, the increased space occupied by the air in the bladder, proves that its density is diminished; notwithstanding which, its elastic force is increased.

(28.) Liquids transmit pressure only when some mechanical force produces a corresponding pressure on some part of their surface. Elastic fluids, however, exert a pressure quite independently of this. To explain this more fully, let A B (*fig.* 12.) be an horizontal tube, filled with a liquid, and closed at both ends. If we set aside the tendency of the fluid to fall out at the ends by its weight, the ends sustain no pressure from it. If any pressure be exerted at

fig. 12.

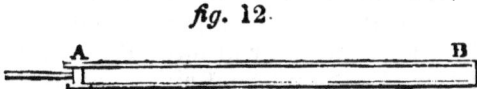

one end A by a piston, the other end B will sustain an equal pressure; but upon removing the pressure at A, the other end B will be immediately relieved from it. Now, if, instead of a liquid, we suppose the tube filled with air, the case will be quite otherwise; for each end will then sustain a pressure *outwards*, by reason of the *elasticity* of the air, and which will be equal exactly to the weight of the atmosphere, if the air in the tube have the same density and temperature as the external air. That there *is* this outward pressure must be evident, when we consider, that if there *were not*, the pressure of the atmosphere would force the ends A B *inwards*, with a force equal to its weight. We can, however, give more direct proofs of this pressure of air against the inner surface of any vessel in which it is contained, and show the means whereby the amount of this pressure may be ascertained.

(29.) Let a flaccid bladder, containing a small quantity of air, be placed under an inverted glass receiver, and let the air be withdrawn from the receiver by means of the air-pump. As the air is gradually withdrawn, the bladder will apparently become inflated, and will at length assume the same appearance as if a quantity of air had been forced into it. But no air has been introduced into it, nor does it, when thus apparently inflated, contain more air than it did when in its flaccid state. What then, it will be asked, produces the apparent inflation? On the removal of the air from the receiver by means of the pump, its pressure on the external surface of the bladder is removed; the elastic force of the air contained in the flaccid bladder is then no longer opposed by the resisting pressure of the external air, and it accordingly takes effect; and its pressure on the inner surface of the bladder swells it in the same manner as if, while the pressure of the external air remained, the pressure of the confined air had been increased by the introduction of an additional quantity. In this case, the inflation or swelling of the bladder is produced by a very different cause from that which produced it when heated. (27.) In that case, while the pressure of the atmosphere on the external surface remained the same, the elastic force pressing on the interior surface was increased by heat. On the other hand, in the present instance, the elastic force of the air contained in the bladder is *less* after it has swelled, and apparently filled, than it was when flaccid. For the air it contains continues of the same temperature, while the space it occupies is increased. Its density, and therefore its elastic force (26.), are thus diminished. The cause of apparent inflation is the diminution of the external pressure of the atmosphere by the pump; so that although the elastic force of the air in the bladder be diminished, yet it is not so much diminished as the pressure of the external air, and so predominates and swells the bladder.

(30.) This experiment merely establishes the fact, that air without condensation *does* press on the inner surface of the vessel which encloses it. We shall now, however, describe a method of measuring this pressure:

Let A B (*fig.* 13.) be a cylindrical glass bottle, containing a quantity of mercury to the level F. Let a glass tube C D, open at both ends, and upwards of thirty-two inches in length, be introduced at the neck E of the bottle, so that the lower end D shall be nearly in contact with the bottom; and thus placed, let it be secured at E, so as not to permit the escape of the air which fills the part of the bottle above the surface of the mercury, and which is thus of the same density and temperature as the atmosphere. Let the whole apparatus thus arranged be introduced under the receiver of an air-pump, and let the air be gradually withdrawn. The pressure of the air on the surface of the mercury in the tube C D being gradually diminished, the elasticity of the air in A E, pressing on the surface F, will force the mercury to ascend in the tube; and the height of the mercury thus pressed into the tube, will increase as the pressure of the air in the receiver is diminished by rarefaction. The column of mercury suspended in the tube, at any period of the process, will evidently indicate the excess of the elasticity of the air in E F, or of the external air above the elasticity of the rarefied air in the receiver.

fig. 13.

Now suppose another tube G H (*fig. 14.*), open at both ends, and exactly similar to the former, be made to communicate at one end G with the receiver R; and let the other end H be plunged in a cistern of mercury, open at the top, and exposed to the atmospheric pressure. As the rarefaction proceeds, the pressure of the air in the tube G H being gradually diminished, the weight of the atmosphere pressing on the surface I, will force the mercury up in the tube G H; and the altitude of the column, at any stage of the process, will indicate the excess of the weight of the atmosphere above the elastic force of the rarefied air in the receiver.

fig. 14.

Now, upon comparing the altitudes of the columns in the two tubes G H and C D, in every stage of the process it will be found that the columns of mercury suspended in them, above the levels of the mercury in their respective cisterns, are accurately equal. From whence it follows, that the weight of the atmosphere pressing on the surface L, and its elastic force pressing on the surface F, exceed the elastic force of the rarefied air in the receiver by the same quantity; and, therefore, that the *weight or pressure of the atmosphere is exactly equal to its elasticity*.

(31.) There are many familiar effects, which are only consequences of the elasticity of air. Beer or ale, bottled, contains in it a quantity of air, the elastic force of which is resisted by the pressure of the condensed air between the cork and the surface of the liquid in the bottle. On removing the cork the liquid, and the air which it contains, are relieved from this intense pressure. The liquid itself not being elastic, is not affected by this; but the elastic force of the condensed air which has been fixed in it, having no adequate resistance, it immediately escapes, and rises in bubbles to the surface, and produces the frothy appearance consequent upon opening the bottle.

If a shrivelled apple be placed under the receiver of an air-pump, and the air be withdrawn, it will have its coat distended by the internal air, so as to present a perfectly smooth appearance. Also, if a thin glass bottle, with atmospheric air confined in it, be placed under a receiver, it will burst by the elasticity of the enclosed air when a sufficient exhaustion has been produced.

Chapter V.

On the Air-Pump.—Condenser.

I. *The Air-Pump.*

(32.) In philosophical investigations it frequently becomes necessary that the substances which are the subjects of experiment should be removed from the influence, whether mechanical or chemical, of the atmosphere. For this purpose it is desirable, that we should possess the means of withdrawing the air from a glass vessel called a *receiver*, in which the substance is placed, and through which the changes which it suffers may be observed. The space under the glass vessel after the air has been withdrawn from it is called a *vacuum*, and the machine by which the air is withdrawn is called an *air-pump*.

We shall devote the present chapter to explain the construction of this instrument, and the principles which govern its action.

(33.) The air-pump is exhibited under various forms, each of which is attended with particular advantages and disadvantages, according to the purposes to which it is applied. There are, however, some general principles in which all modifications of this interesting machine agree, and which we shall first explain.

Let R (*fig.* 15.) be the section of a glass vessel closed at the top T, but open at the bottom, and having its lower edge ground smooth, so as to rest in close contact with a smooth brass plate, of which S S is a section. When the receiver R is thus placed upon the plate S S it will, with the assistance of a little unctuous matter previously rubbed on the edge of the glass, be in air-tight contact. In the plate is a small aperture A, which communicates, by a tube A B, with a cylinder in which a solid

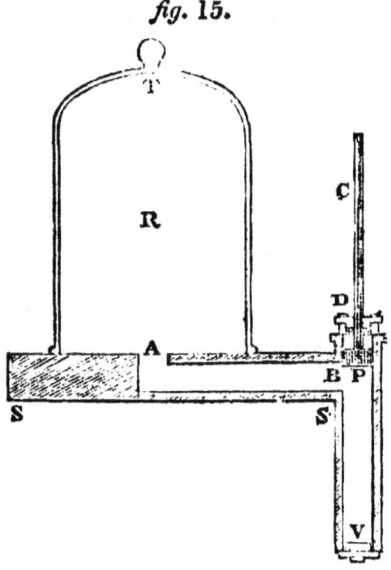

fig. 15.

piston P is moved. The piston-rod C moves in an air-tight collar D, and a valve V is placed in the bottom of the cylinder opening outwards.

Let the air in the receiver R, the exhausting tube A B, and the barrel S V be first supposed to have the same density as the external air. Upon depressing the piston, after it has passed the aperture B, the air in the barrel S V will be compressed by the piston. Its density, and therefore its elasticity, will be increased, and will become greater than that of the external air. This superior elastic force will open the valve V, through which as the piston descends, the air in the barrel will be driven into the atmosphere. When the piston has reached the bottom of the cylinder, the valve V will be closed by a spring or otherwise, and will be pressed into its seat also by the atmospheric pressure.

When the piston has thus arrived at the bottom of the barrel, the air which before filled the receiver R and the exhausting tube A B, will have expanded by its elastic property, and diffused itself also through the barrel above the piston. But upon again raising the piston it will be forced back into its former bounds, until the piston has passed the aperture B. As the piston ascends, it leaves beneath it a vacuum, into which the external air is prevented from entering by the valve V. When, therefore, the piston has been raised beyond the aperture B, the air in the receiver R and the exhausting tube A B will expand once more, and also fill the barrel S V.

Upon a second depression of the piston the air which fills the barrel will be discharged, and similar effects will follow its ascent, and so the process may be continued at pleasure.

It will be perceived that this instrument depends for its efficacy entirely on the elastic quality in the air, by which, while there is any portion of air in the receiver and exhausting tube, that portion, however small, will expand and diffuse itself equally through the barrel in addition to the space it before filled. It must be pretty evident, with very little consideration, that by this process a *perfect vacuum* can never be produced under the receiver. For *some* air, however small the quantity be, *must* remain after every depression of the piston. Let us, however, examine how nearly we may approach to a vacuum, or more properly speaking, let us determine what degree of rarefaction may be effected, supposing the mechanical construction of the instrument we have described to be perfect, and no obstructions to arise from circumstances merely practical.

At the commencement of the process the air which fills the receiver, exhausting tube, and barrel, is of the density of the external air; let its entire quantity in this state be called *one*. Let the capacity of the barrel S V bear any proposed proportion to that of the receiver and tube; suppose that it is one-third of their united magnitudes, and therefore that it contains one-fourth of the air contained within the valve V in the entire apparatus. Upon the first depression of the piston this fourth part will be expelled, and three-fourths of the original quantity will remain. One-fourth of this will in like manner be expelled upon the second depression of the piston, which is equivalent to three-sixteenths of the original quantity, and consequently there remains in the apparatus nine-sixteenths of the original quantity. Calculating in this way, that one-fourth of what is contained in the apparatus is expelled at every descent of the piston, the following Table will be easily computed.

No. of Strokes.	Air expelled at each Stroke.		Air remaining in the Receiver and Barrel.	
1.	$\frac{1}{4}$		$\frac{3}{4}$	
2.	$\frac{3}{16}$	$= \frac{3}{4 \times 4}$	$\frac{9}{16}$	$= \frac{3 \times 3}{4 \times 4}$
3.	$\frac{9}{64}$	$= \frac{3 \times 3}{4 \times 4 \times 4}$	$\frac{27}{64}$	$= \frac{3 \times 3 \times 3}{4 \times 4 \times 4}$
4.	$\frac{27}{256}$	$= \frac{3 \times 3 \times 3}{4 \times 4 \times 4 \times 4}$	$\frac{81}{256}$	$= \frac{3 \times 3 \times 3 \times 3}{4 \times 4 \times 4 \times 4}$
5.	$\frac{81}{1024}$	$= \frac{3 \times 3 \times 3 \times 3}{4 \times 4 \times 4 \times 4 \times 4}$	$\frac{243}{1024}$	$= \frac{3 \times 3 \times 3 \times 3 \times 3}{4 \times 4 \times 4 \times 4 \times 4}$

The method by which the computation might be continued is obvious. The air expelled at each stroke is found, by multiplying the air expelled at the preceding stroke by 3 and dividing it by 4; and the air remaining after each stroke is also found by multiplying the air remaining after the preceding stroke by 3, and dividing it by 4.

It appears by this computation, that after the fifth stroke, the air remaining in the receiver is *less than* one-fourth of the original quantity. Less than one-fourth of this will remain after the next five strokes, that is, less than one sixteenth part of the original quantity. If we calculate that every five strokes extract three-fourths of the air contained in the apparatus, we shall then *underrate* the rapidity of the exhaustion; and yet, even at this rate, after thirty strokes of the pump, the air remaining in the receiver would be only one 3096th part of the original quantity. The pressure of this would amount to about the sixteenth part of an ounce upon the square inch. It is evident that by continuing the process any degree of rarefaction which may be desired can be obtained. For all practical purposes, therefore, a *vacuum* may be considered to be procured; but, in fact, we are as far from having a real vacuum in the receiver as ever, for such is the infinite expanding power of air, that the smallest particle will as completely fill the receiver and barrel as the most dense substance could; that is to say, no part of the receiver or barrel, however small, will be found absolutely free from air, however long the process of exhaustion may be continued.

(34.) In the uses to which the air-pump is applied, various degrees of exhaustion are necessary, and it becomes very desirable to have some exact and obvious *indicator* of the degree of rarefaction which has been produced within the receiver at any stage of the process. We find in the barometer a simple and most accurate means of measuring this effect.

Let a glass tube, open at both ends, be inserted into the exhausting tube A B (*fig.* 16.), or into any other part of

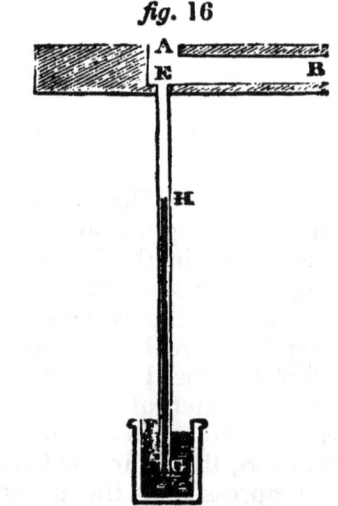
fig. 16

the apparatus, so as to communicate freely with the receiver; and being placed in a vertical position, let the other end G be immersed in a cistern of mercury. As the rarefaction proceeds, the air in the receiver losing a part of its elastic force no longer balances the pressure of the atmosphere at F, and consequently the mercury rises in the tube E G. The weight of the column of mercury suspended in this tube, together with the elastic force of the air in the receiver which presses on its surface at H, are the forces which balance the atmospheric pressure at F. They are, therefore, together equal to the atmospheric pressure; and hence it follows that the column of mercury in the tube is always equal to the excess of the atmospheric pressure above the elastic force of the air in the receiver.

Since the column of mercury suspended in the common barometer is always a measure of the atmospheric pressure, it is evident that the difference between this column and that suspended in the *gauge* E G of the pump will be the exact measure of the pressure of the rarefied air remaining in the receiver.

(35.) By a gauge of this form (and it is the usual one for standing air-pumps) the elastic force of the rarefied air can only be known by comparison with a barometer. A gauge might, however, be very easily constructed which would give the amount of the pressure immediately. Let C (*fig.*17.) be a cistern containing mercury, and closed at the top, communicating

fig. 17.

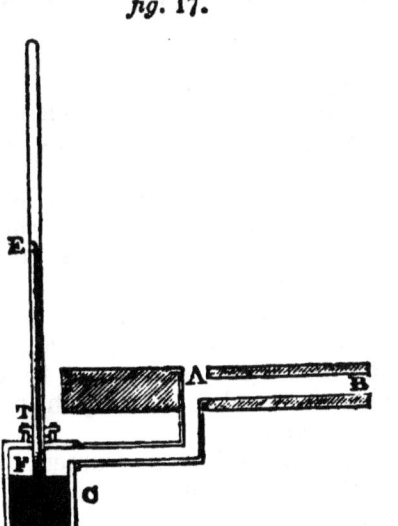

with the exhausting tube A B, or in any other convenient manner with the receiver. In the top of this let a barometer-tube filled with mercury be inserted, so as to be air-tight at T. The atmospheric pressure at F sustains as usual the barometric column. But upon rarefying the air in the receiver by means of the pump, this pressure will be diminished, and the mercury at E will accordingly fall, and the column which will be sustained will measure the elastic force of the rarefied air.

Such a gauge, although simpler in principle than the common one, would not however be attended with the same practical advantages.

(36.) Such is the general theory of the *Air-pump*. The varieties of its construction are very considerable, and it would not be consistent with our plan to enter into details respecting them. We shall, therefore, conclude this chapter with a description of the air-pump which is in most general use.

A sectional drawing of this apparatus, with some trifling transposition of parts to bring them all into view, is given in the annexed *fig.* 18. R is the glass receiver placed on the pump-plate S S, T T T is the exhausting tube communicating with two pump barrels B B′, and furnished with a cock C by which the communication between the receiver and barrels may be cut off at pleasure.

V V′ are parchment valves in the bottoms of the pump-barrels, opening upwards, so that air may pass through them from the tube T T, into the barrel, but cannot return.

P P′ are two pistons, fitting, air-tight, in the barrels, and furnished with valves similar to V V′, which also open upwards. The piston-rods are furnished with racks E E′, which are wrought by a toothed wheel W. This wheel is turned, in the usual way, by a winch D, and by alternately turning it in opposite directions, the pistons are elevated and depressed.

G is the barometer gauge, communicating with the receiver at H.

Let us now suppose the piston P ascending, and P′ descending. Since the valve in P opens upwards, no air can pass from above through it; as it ascends, therefore, the air in P V, expanding into the space deserted by the piston, becomes rarefied, and presses with diminished force on the valve V. The superior elasticity of the air in the receiver and tube will force open the valve V, and will continue to pass through that valve until its elasticity exceeds that of the air in the barrel P V, by a force less than that which is requisite to raise the valve V.

In the meantime the piston P′ has been descending, and the air in P′ V′ is

c

PNEUMATICS.

fig. 18.

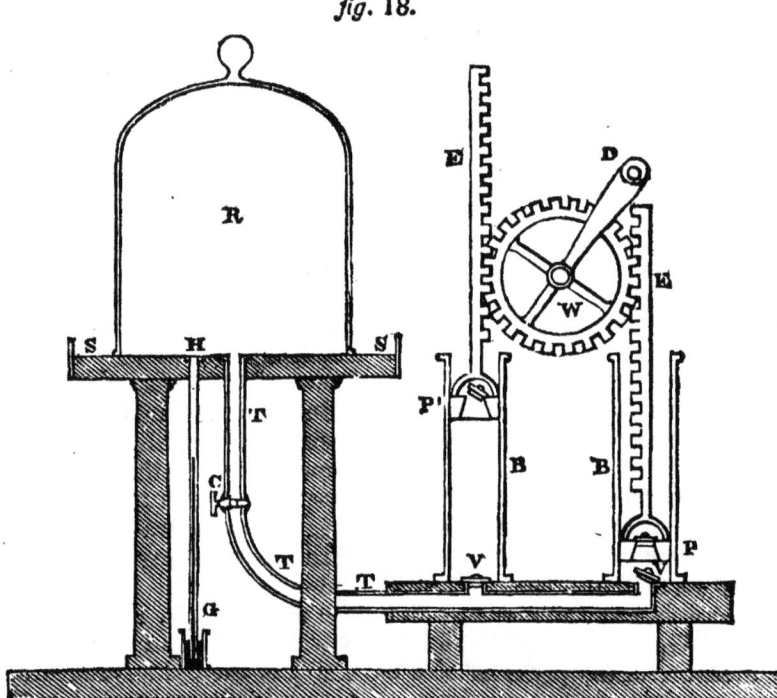

compressed; for since the valve V' opens *upwards*, it cannot pass through it. As soon as it is so far condensed, that its elasticity exceeds the atmospheric pressure, by a force sufficient to raise the valve in the piston P, it will pass into the atmosphere through that valve, and will continue to pass into it, until the piston P (*fig.* 19.) strikes the bottom of the barrel.

fig. 19.

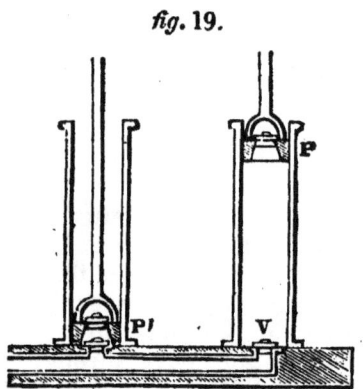

The pistons now have assumed the position (*fig.* 19.): the wheel W is turned in the opposite direction, so that P will descend and P' will ascend. In this motion, the atmospheric pressure acts on each piston, against the inferior force of the rarefied air in the barrel, and therefore resists the ascent; and the resistance increases as the rarefaction proceeds. These resistances are, however, not felt by the operator, since they balance each other through the medium of the wheel and racks; and this, independently of the increased speed of the process of rarefaction, is one of the advantages of the double barrel.

As the piston P descends, the rarefied air in P V is condensed; and as soon as its elasticity exceeds the atmospheric pressure by a force sufficient to open the valve in the piston P, it will pass into the atmosphere, and will be all discharged when the piston shall arrive at the bottom.

While the piston P has been descending and discharging the air below it, the piston P' has been ascending and drawing more air from the receiver, through the valve V'. For as P' ascends, it leaves a vacuum below it; the elasticity of the air in the receiver and tubes encountering no resistance above the valve V', opens it, and continues to pass through until its elasticity exceeds that of the air in the barrel, by a less force than that which is sufficient to raise the valve V'. And in this way the process is continued*.

(37.) In such an instrument there is a very obvious limit to the degree of rarefaction. When the elasticity of the air in the receiver is no longer sufficient to open the valves V, V', it is clear that no further rarefaction can be effected. Besides, it is to be considered, that the

---

* *Fig.* 20. (*see next page*) is a perspective view of this important instrument, which, though its parts are somewhat differently arranged, is exactly the same in principle, and marked with the same letters of reference.

PNEUMATICS.

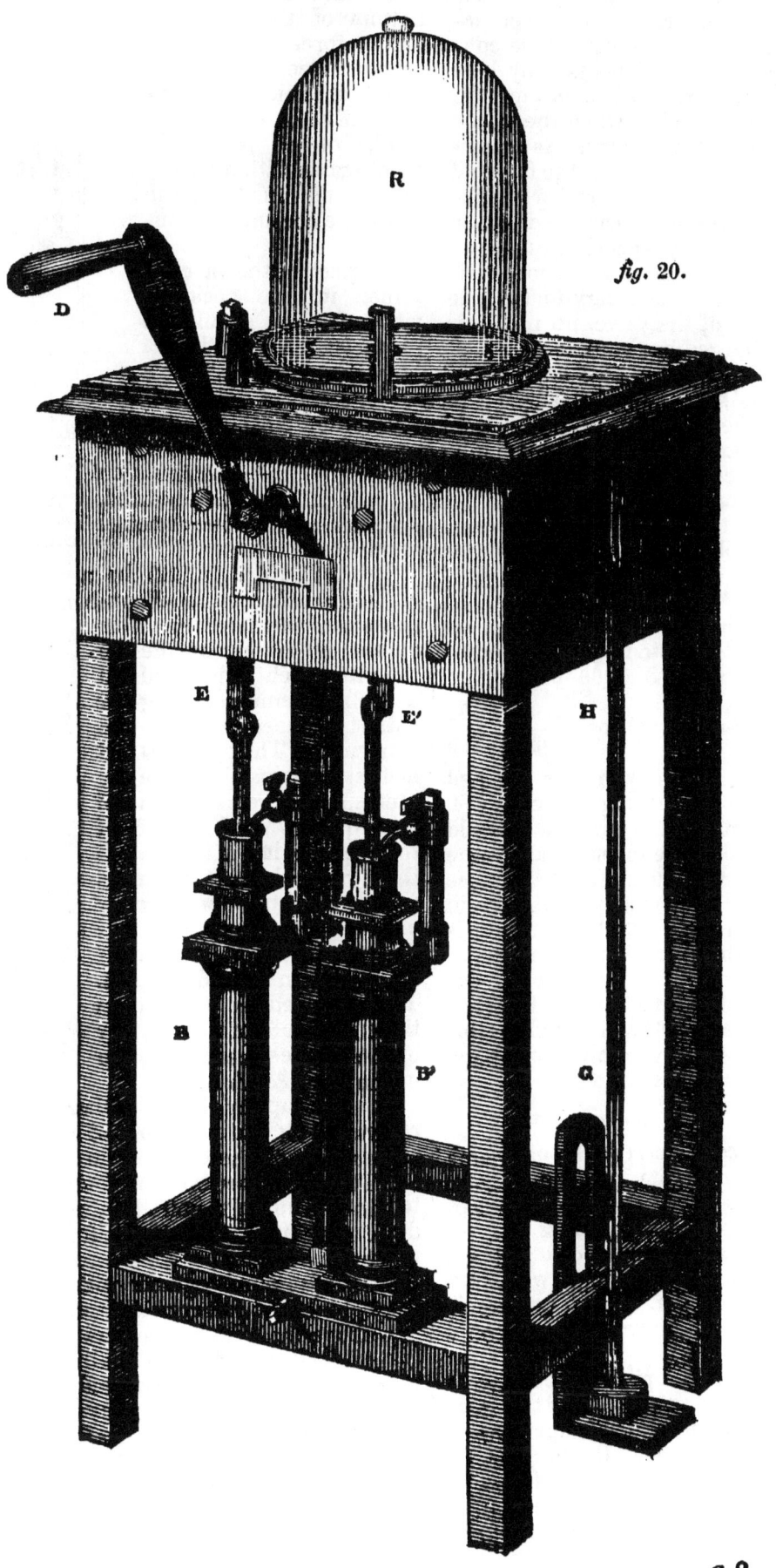

fig. 20.

piston valves are opened against the atmospheric pressure, and however accurately the barrels and pistons be constructed, yet there will necessarily be a certain space, capable of containing air, below the piston valve, when the piston is at the bottom of the barrel. As soon as the rarefaction has proceeded so far, that the air which filled the barrel when the piston was at the top, being reduced to this last-mentioned space, acquires an elasticity, exceeding the atmospheric *only* by the force necessary to balance the resistance of the valve, no more air can be discharged by the piston.

To calculate the power of such a pump, let us suppose the space below the valve, when the piston is at the bottom of the barrel, to be the 1000th part of the whole capacity of the barrel; and let the force of the piston valve be the 100th part of the atmospheric pressure. If the atmospheric density be 1000, the density of the air under the piston valve, when at the bottom of the cylinder, at the extreme limit of exhaustion, will be 1010. When the piston has been raised, this will be rarefied 1000 times, and therefore its density will be $\frac{1010}{1000}$ or $\frac{101}{100}$ = 1.01. The elasticity of this rarefied air resists the exhausting valves V, V'. Let the density of the air which would open these valves be the same as for the piston valves, viz. 0.01. Hence the force which resists the elasticity of the air in the receiver, is $1.01 + 0.01 = 1.02$. This number will therefore express the density of the air in the receiver, at the extreme limit of rarefaction, that of the atmosphere being 1000. The same principles will evidently apply when any other numbers are selected.

II. *The Condenser.*

(38.) The *condenser*, as the name implies, is the opposite of the air-pump. R (*fig.* 21) is a receiver, with a valve V in the neck, opening *inwards*. C is a stop-cock in a tube connected with a barrel in which a solid piston without a valve plays air-tight. B is a small orifice to admit air below the piston when it is drawn above B.

Suppose now the piston above B and air filling all the apparatus, of the same density as the atmosphere: upon pressing the piston down, the air in the pump-barrel will be compressed after the piston passes B, and will force open the valve V; and when the piston shall have arrived at the bottom of the barrel it will be forced into the receiver, except that part which occupies the neck C. Every succeeding stroke of the piston will be attended with a similar effect, and thus the air in R will be continually condensed.

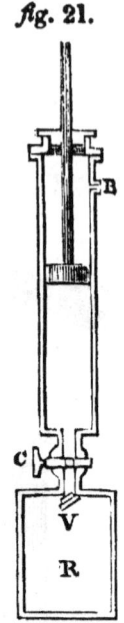

fig. 21.

Neglecting the air contained in the neck C, which is very small, the portion forced into the receiver at each stroke is the contents of the barrel B C at the atmospheric density.

(39.) To indicate the degree of condensation which has been obtained, a *gauge* may be attached to the condenser.

Let A B (*fig.* 22) be a glass tube communicating at E with a vessel C containing mercury. This vessel is closed at the top, in which is inserted a tube communicating with the receiver of the condenser. The tube A B at first contains air of the atmospheric pressure, and consequently the level of the mercury in the tube is the same as in the cistern C. Let the tube be now closed at the top A, so as to be air-tight, and let the condensation be produced. The increased pressure on the surface of the mercury in C will force mercury up in the tube A B.

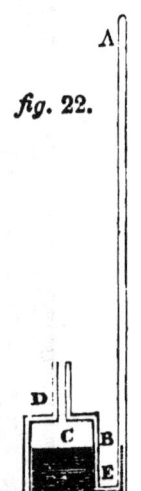

fig. 22.

Let us suppose that the mercury is raised to half the height of A above the surface of the mercury in the cistern. The air in the tube will thus be reduced to half its bulk, and will therefore exert double the pressure, or a force equal to twice the atmospheric pressure. (30.) This pressure, together with that of the column of mercury in the tube A B, above the level C, balances the pressure of the condensed air in C. Hence the pressure of the condensed air in this case will be equal to that of a column of mercury whose height is found by adding the height of the mercury in A B, above the level C, to twice the height of the barometer. There will be no difficulty in generalizing this principle.

PNEUMATICS. 21

CHAPTER VI.—*Of Pumps and Syphons—Air-balloon and Air-gun.*

I. *The common Suction-Pump.*

(40.) The suction-pump consists of two hollow cylinders A B, B C, (*fig.* 23.) placed one under the other, and communicating by a valve V which opens upwards. The cylinder B C is called the suction-tube, and has its lower end C immersed in the well or reservoir from which the water is to be raised. In the upper cylinder, A B, a piston P is moved, having a valve in it which opens upwards; this piston should move air-tight in the cylinder. At the top of the cylinder A B is a spout S, for the discharge of the water.

fig. 23.

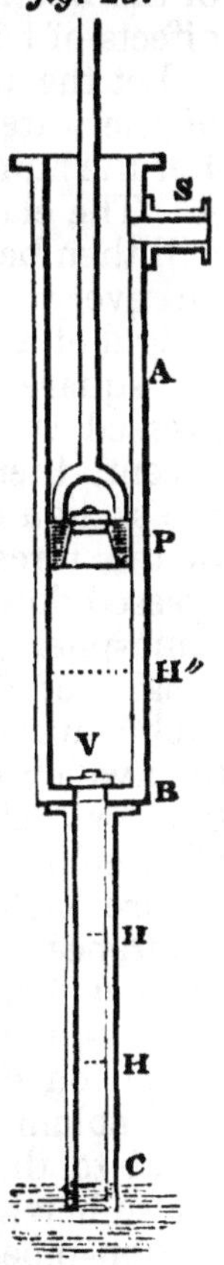

We will first suppose the piston to be at the bottom of the cylinder A B, and in close contact with the valve V. Upon elevating it, the piston valve is kept closed by the atmospheric pressure, and if the valve V were not permitted to rise, a vacuum would be produced between it and the piston, the elevation of which would then require a force equal to about 15 lbs., multiplied by as many square inches as are in the section of the piston. But this is not the case. The moment the piston begins to ascend, the elasticity of the air in B C opens the valve V, and the air rushing in through it, balances part of the atmospheric pressure on the piston. Now, if the water at C were not permitted to rise, the air between the piston and the surface C would be rarefied by the ascent of the piston. It would therefore press against the lower surface of the water with a force less than the atmosphere. But the entire force of the atmosphere presses on the surface of the water in the well. The diminished elasticity of the air in the suction-pipe not being a counterpoise for this, the water is necessarily pressed up into that pipe. Let us consider to what height it will rise.

If the surface of the water in the suction-pipe rest at H, and rise no higher, there is a compound column of air and water pressing on the level C'; viz. the column of water C H, and the elastic force of the air in B H. These two together balance the atmospheric pressure on the external surface of the water in the well. It consequently follows, that the air in B H must be rarefied, since its elasticity falls short of the atmospheric pressure by the pressure of the column of water C H. As a column of water, about thirty-four feet in height, balances the atmosphere, it follows, that the elastic force of the air in B H is equal to the pressure of a column of water whose height is the excess of thirty-four feet above B H.

Upon the descent of the piston, the air compressed between it and the valve V, escapes through the piston valve in the same manner as we have described in the air-pump; and upon the succeeding ascent, the elastic force of the air in B H, raising the valve V, passes into the space in which the piston would otherwise leave a vacuum. The air in B H being thus rarefied, its elastic pressure on the surface H of the water in the suction-pipe is diminished; and, therefore, when added to the pressure of the column of water C H, is no longer equivalent to the atmospheric pressure on the external surface of the water in the well. This pressure must therefore force more water up in the suction-pipe, and will continue to do so, until the pressure of the increased column C H', added to the elasticity of the air in B H', is an exact balance for the atmospheric pressure on the external surface. Upon the principle already explained it follows, that the elastic pressure of the air in B H', is equal to the pressure of a column of water, whose height is equal to the excess of thirty-four feet above the height C H'.

While the water is rising in the suction-pipe B C, the machine is in fact an air-pump, the suction-pipe itself acting the part of receiver. The air which originally filled the suction-pipe B C, is gradually pumped out, and its place is in part filled by the water which is forced in by the pressure of the external air. Now, upon the principles already established, respecting the action of the air-pump, it is quite apparent that a perfect exhaustion can never be effected in the suction-pipe B C; and therefore a column of water can never be raised, whose pressure is equal to that of the atmosphere; and hence we deduce a consequence of the most vital importance, *that the height of the valve* V, *at the top of the suction-pipe, above the level of the water in the reservoir, must always be less than thirty-four feet**.

Let us then suppose that the height B C is less than thirty-four feet, and that the exhaustion has been carried so far, that the water has risen in the suction-pipe, and that a portion of it, B H″, has been forced by the atmospheric pressure through the valve V. Upon the next descent of the piston, the water in H″ B will be forced through the valve in the piston, and will be above the valve when the piston has reached V. Since the piston-valve opens upwards, this water cannot return through it, and upon the next ascent of the piston, the atmospheric pressure forces more water through V. The next descent and ascent are attended with like effects. By continuing this process, a column of water is collected above the piston, which is lifted every ascent, and receives an addition to its quantity every descent. Near the top of the pump-barrel a spout S is provided for the discharge of the water, and when the elevation of the column of water on the piston reaches the level of this spout, it ceases to accumulate; whatever addition of water is received through the piston-valve on the descent, being discharged at the spout S on the ascent.

It should be observed, that if the piston in its descent do not reach the bottom of the barrel B, the space between it and the bottom B will never be reduced to a vacuum, and can only be rarefied to a certain extent. In this case the suction-pipe B C should be much less than thirty-four feet, for otherwise the water can never rise to the valve V, since it has the elastic force of the air in P B to oppose its ascent.

(41.) From this description of the common pump, it appears that two distinct forces are engaged in the elevation of the water. The pressure of the atmosphere, acting on the surface of the water in the well, raises it through the valve V. After what has thus been lodged in the chamber above V, has passed through the piston-valve, it is then lifted by the mechanical force, whatever that be, which works the pump-rods.

(42.) Let us now consider the force which is required in each stage of the process, to elevate the piston, exclusive of the weight of the piston-rods and the effects of friction.

Let the piston be at V, and the level of the water in the suction-pipe at H. Let the number of feet in C H be called h. The elastic force of the air in B H will then be such as to exert a pressure on every square inch, equal to the weight of a column of water, whose base is a square inch, and whose height, expressed in feet, is $34 - h$*. In its ascent, therefore, each square inch of the section of the piston is pressed up by this force. It is, on the other hand, pressed down by the whole force of the atmosphere, which is equal to the weight of thirty-four feet of water on each square inch. The effective force then which resists the ascent of the piston, for each square inch, is the weight of a column of water, whose base is a square inch and whose height is the difference between thirty-four feet and $34 - h$ feet; that is, h feet. Thus it appears, that it requires a force to lift the piston exactly equal to the weight of a column of water, whose base is equal to the section of the piston, and whose height is that of the water in the suction-pipe, above the level of the water in the well.

It follows, therefore, that as the water rises in the suction-pipe, the force required to lift the piston is proportionally increased.

Let us next consider the force requisite to lift the piston, in the second part of the process; viz. when the water raised has passed through the piston valve.

Let the piston be at V, and the level of the water at H″; the downward pressure sustained by the piston in this case, is evidently the weight of the incumbent water B H″, together with the weight of the atmosphere. Let h be the number of feet in the height B H″, and $34 + h$ † will express the number of feet in a column of water, whose base is equal to the section of the piston, and whose weight is equal to the whole

---

* Thirty-four feet is here used as the height of a column of water equal to the atmospheric pressure. This pressure, as we have already stated, is variable, and its lowest value in these countries is about 14 lbs. to the square inch. This is equal to the pressure of a column of water of about 32¼ feet high. When the barometer is at 28 inches this is the pressure. When it is at 30 inches the pressure is equal to a column of water 34½ feet high.

* $34 - h$ means the remainder, obtained by subtracting the number which h represents from 34.

† $34 + h$ means the sum obtained by adding the number expressed by h to 34.

downward pressure sustained by the piston.

On the other hand, the upward pressure is produced by the weight of the atmosphere pressing on the water in the reservoir, and transmitted through the column C B, to the lower surface of the piston. But as this pressure has to support the column B C, we must subtract from it the weight of this column, in order to obtain the effective upward pressure on the piston. From a column of water, thirty-four feet in height, and with a base equal to the section of the piston, subtract as many feet as there are in B C, and we shall obtain a column whose weight is equal to the upward pressure. This must be taken from the downward pressure, and the remainder will give the force required to lift the piston. If from $34 + h$ feet we subtract 34 feet, the remainder is h feet; but in doing this, we have subtracted more than enough by the number of feet in B C; this number must, therefore, be added, and the whole column whose weight is lifted, has the height $h + BC$; that is, $H''B + BC$, or $H''C$.

(43.) Thus it appears, that the force necessary to lift the piston is the weight of a column of water, whose height is that of the level of the water in the pump, above the level of the water in the well, and whose base is equal to the section of the piston. This force, therefore, from the commencement of the process, continually increases, until the level of the water rises to the discharging spout S, and thenceforward remains uniform.

(44.) To compute the actual force necessary to work a pump, (exclusive of the pump-rods,) therefore, let the height of the discharging spout S, above the level C of the water in the well, be expressed in feet, and let the number which expresses it be h. Let half the diameter of the piston, expressed in parts of a foot, be r; the section of the piston, expressed in parts of a square foot, will then be $r \times r \times 3.14$. (*note, p.* 4.) If this be multiplied by the number of feet h in the height, we shall obtain the number of cubic feet of water which it is necessary to lift at each stroke. This is $h \times r \times r \times 3.14$. Each cubic foot of water weighs about 1000 oz. av., or $62\frac{1}{2}$ lbs.; this, multiplied by $h \times r \times r \times 3.14$, will give, in pounds av., the force required at each stroke to lift the piston.

The quantity of water discharged at each stroke, is equal to a column of water, whose base is the section of the piston, and whose altitude is the length of the stroke. This quantity may, therefore, be found in cubic feet, by multiplying $r \times r \times 3.14$ by the number of feet in the length of the stroke. The weight of the water discharged may be ascertained in pounds avoirdupois, by multiplying this by $62\frac{1}{2}$, and the number of imperial gallons by dividing the number of pounds by 10.

II. *The Lifting-Pump*

(45.) This pump also consists of an hollow cylinder A B (*fig.* 24.) immersed in the reservoir from which the water is to be raised. A valve opening upwards is fixed in this cylinder at V, a little below the level L of the water in the reservoir. A piston P, having also a valve opening upwards, is moved in this cylinder by a frame F F F F, connected with the end of the piston-rod P H. At the top of the cylinder is a spout S to discharge the water elevated.

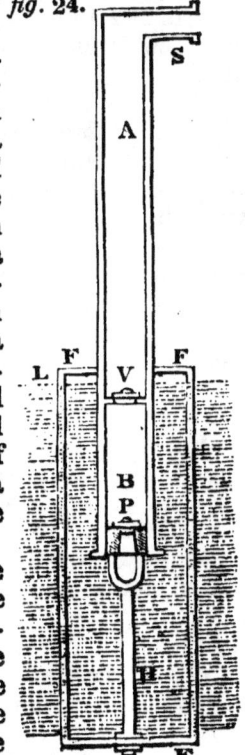

fig. 24.

Let us suppose the piston P at the bottom B of the cylinder. The pressure of the water in the reservoir, will force water through the piston-valve, until the water rises in the cylinder to the valve V, or to about the level of the water in the reservoir. It would rise to the exact level, but for the weights of the valves. Upon elevating the piston P, the water not being permitted to pass through the piston-valve will be pressed against the valve V, and opening it, will pass into the upper chamber V A of the cylinder; from whence it is not allowed to return, since the valve V opens upwards. As the piston rises in B V, the pressure of the water in the reservoir forces water after it into the cylinder; and upon its descent, this water passes through the piston-valve. The next ascent forces water again through V; and so on.

The water thus continually forced through V, every ascent of the piston accumulates in the cylinder above the valve V, and its height increases until it reaches the spout S, where it is discharged.

To find the force necessary to raise the piston, we are to consider that the water in the reservoir balances the water in the cylinder from the bottom B to the level L. The piston, therefore, has only to lift the column from L, to the level of the water in the cylinder. After a few strokes, this level rises to S, and continues permanently at that level afterwards. If, then, the number of feet in S L be called h, and half the diameter of the section of the piston, expressed in parts of a foot, be called r, the number of cubic feet of water which presses on the piston, will be expressed by $h \times r \times r \times 3.14$. This, multiplied by $62\frac{1}{2}$, will express the pressure on the piston in pounds; and if to this the weight of the piston and rod, together with the effects of friction, be added, the whole force necessary to lift the piston will be obtained.

The quantity of water discharged is found in the same manner as for the suction-pump.

III. *The Forcing-Pump.*

(46.) A cylinder A B C (*fig.* 25.) is placed with its lower end C in the reservoir. It has a fixed valve at V opening upward, and a solid piston without a valve playing air-tight in the upper barrel A B. It is connected with another barrel D E by a valve V' opening upwards and outwards. The tube D E is brought to whatever height it may be necessary to elevate the water.

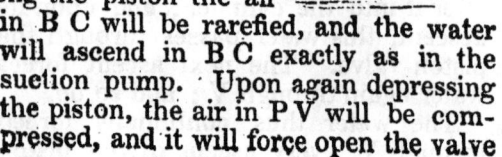

Let us suppose that the solid piston P is in contact with the valve V, and that the water in the lower barrel is at the same level C with the water in the reservoir. Upon raising the piston the air in B C will be rarefied, and the water will ascend in B C exactly as in the suction pump. Upon again depressing the piston, the air in P V will be compressed, and it will force open the valve V', and escape through it. The process, therefore, until water is raised through V into the upper barrel, is precisely the same as for the suction-pump, the valve V' taking the place of the piston-valve in that machine.

Now, let us suppose that water has been elevated through V, and that the space P V is filled with it. Upon depressing the piston, this water not being permitted to return through V, is forced through V', and ascends in the tube D E. By continuing the process, water will accumulate in the tube D E, until it acquires the necessary elevation and is discharged.

The force requisite to elevate the piston in this pump until the water reaches it, is computed in exactly the same manner as for the suction-pump, and, exclusive of the weight of the piston and its rods and the effects of friction, it is equal to the weight of a column of water whose base is the section of the piston, and whose height is the distance of the level of the water in the barrel A C above the level in the reservoir. It is evident also from what has been said on the suction-pump, that the valve V should be less than thirty-four feet above the level of the water in the reservoir. If the P express in pounds av. the weight of the piston and its rods, r be half the diameter of a section of the piston expressed in parts of a foot, and h be the number of feet in A C, the force in pounds necessary to lift the piston will be

$h \times r \times r \times 3.14 \times 62.5 + P.$

Let us now examine the force necessary to depress the piston. Let the level of the water in E D be M. The atmospheric pressure on M will be balanced by the same pressure on the piston by the power of transmitting pressure peculiar to fluids. This force may, therefore, be neglected; also the P V' will balance the part N D of the column M D, which is equal to it in height, and that whether their sections be equal or not. (*See Hydrostatics.*) Hence it appears, that the pressure exerted by the water in P V on the lower surface of the piston is equal to the weight of a column of water whose base is equal to the section of the piston, and whose height is M N. This, therefore, is the force to be overcome in the descent of the pistons and the weight P of the piston and it, rods assist in overcoming it. Let h' be the number of feet in M N, and the mechanical force necessary to be applied to depress the piston will be expressed in pounds by

$$h' \times r \times r \times 3.14 \times 62.5 - P.$$

From these observations, it appears that the weight of the piston and its rods assist the *forcing-power* of the machine, but oppose its *suction-power*. These effects, therefore, on the whole, neutralize each other.

The entire force used in raising the water will be found by adding the force necessary to elevate the piston to that which is necessary to depress it. As in this case the weight of the piston and rods increases the one by as much as it diminishes the other, the entire force will be the weight of a column of water whose base is the section of the piston, and whose height is P C + M N, that is the height of the level of the water in the forcing-pipe above the level of the water in the reservoir, and expressed in pounds, this is

$$(h+h') \times r \times r \times 3.14 \times 62.5.$$

(47.) It appears, therefore, that other circumstances being the same, the power of the forcing-pump has the advantage over that of the suction-pump by the weight of the piston and its rods.

In the suction-pump the elevation of the water is entirely effected by the ascent of the piston: during its descent the engine, mechanically speaking, is inactive. It would, therefore, require that the power applied to the piston-rod should be an intermitting one, for otherwise a waste would take place on every descent of the piston. On the other hand, in the forcing-pump, the elevation is partly produced in the ascent and partly in the descent of the piston, and the power must be continued, but proportionally less intense. Thus a single-acting steam-engine, or an atmospheric engine, would be suitably applied to raise water by the suction-pump, and a double-acting engine by the forcing-pump.

In the forcing-pump, however, the forces required to effect the elevation and depression of the piston are not always equal, and it is in many cases desirable that they should be so; for it generally happens that the power applied to elevate and depress is uniform, as for example, in the steam-engine. Let us consider how the powers of elevation and depression could be equalized.

We have proved that the power of elevation is equal to the weight P, together with that of the column of the height h, and with a base equal to the section of the piston. The power of depression is equal to the weight of a column whose height is h', *diminished by* the weight P. Now the difference of these two forces is twice the weight P, together with the weight of the column h diminished by the weight of the column h'. This, expressed algebraically, is

Elevating force . . . . $h \times r \times r \times 3.14 \times 62.5 + P$
Depressing force . . . $h' \times r \times r \times 3.14 \times 62.5 - P$
Difference . . . . $(h-h') \times r \times r \times 3.14 \times 62.5 + 2P$
Or $(2P + h \times r \times r \times 3.14 \times 62.5) - h' \times r \times r \times 3.14 \times 62.5$

This difference will evidently be nothing, and the elevating and depressing forces will be equal when

$$2P = (h'-h) \times r \times r \times 3.14 \times 62.5$$

that is, when the weight of the column M N exceeds that of the column P C by twice the weight of the piston and rods. The position of the spout should, therefore, be regulated by these considerations; and it is evident that, in order to an uniformity of action, if P C is nearly thirty-four feet, the piston rods should always be loaded with a sufficient weight to balance a column of water, whose base is the section of the piston, and whose height is the excess of the height of the spout from the level of the water in the cistern above sixty-eight feet.

It must be evident from this account of the forcing-pump, that the discharge from the spout can only take place on the descent of the piston, and is therefore intermitting. One method of remedying this is the application of an air-vessel to the apparatus. At the top of the forcing-pipe D E (*fig.* 26.) instead of a spout place a close vessel E F communicating with the force-pipe by a valve in the bottom opening upwards at E. A tube T T' is introduced at the top of this vessel, and fitted so as to be air-tight, and extending nearly to the bottom, furnished with a stop-cock G. The stop-cock being closed and water forced in through the valve, the air contained in the vessel will be condensed, and will exert a proportionate pressure on the surface of the water in the vessel, so as to force it up in the tube which is terminated with the stop-cock G. If then the stop-cock be opened, the water will be forced out in a continued stream.

The force with which the water issues from the tube T T' is easily determined. Let us suppose that one-half of the air-vessel is filled with water. The air it contains is therefore reduced to half its original bulk, and therefore (26) exerts twice its original pressure. It is therefore forced from the tube T T', with a force equal to the weight of thirty-four feet of water, for the atmospheric pressure balances one-half of the force with which it is pressed up the tube. Again, suppose the vessel is three-fourths filled, the air is then reduced to one-fourth of its original force, and therefore exerts four times its original pressure. Once its pressure being balanced by the atmosphere, an effective force is obtained equal to three times the pressure of the atmosphere, or to 132 feet of water, and so on.

It is proved in Hydrostatics, that water pressed out of a vertical tube will ascend to nearly the height of a column of water of equivalent pressure, setting aside the resistance of the air. Hence we may easily infer, that in the cases just stated, except so far as the resistance of the air is stated, a jet or fountain would rise to the heights already mentioned.

By screwing on the tube T T', jets pierced with apertures in various directions, ornamental fountains may be constructed.

It should be observed, that by thus introducing the elastic force of the air no additional force is gained, nor is the *mechanical efficacy* of the apparatus, properly speaking, increased; for the force used in the depression of the piston in compelling the water to enter the air-vessel is exactly equal to the elasticity of the compressed air. This elastic force is as it were a number of accumulated strokes of the piston, stored up or

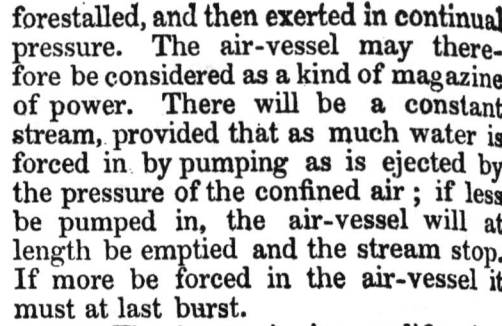
fig. 26.

forestalled, and then exerted in continual pressure. The air-vessel may therefore be considered as a kind of magazine of power. There will be a constant stream, provided that as much water is forced in by pumping as is ejected by the pressure of the confined air; if less be pumped in, the air-vessel will at length be emptied and the stream stop. If more be forced in the air-vessel it must at last burst.

(48.) The *fire-engine* is a modification of the forcing-pump.

A B (*fig.* 27.) are two forcing pumps, whose pistons P are wrought by a beam whose fulcrum is at F. V V are valves which open upwards from a suction-tube T, which descends to a reservoir; *t* are force-pipes which communicate by valves V' V' opening into an air-vessel M. A tube L is inserted in the top of this vessel, terminating in a leathern tube or hose, through which the water is forced by the pressure of the air confined in M, as described in (47.)

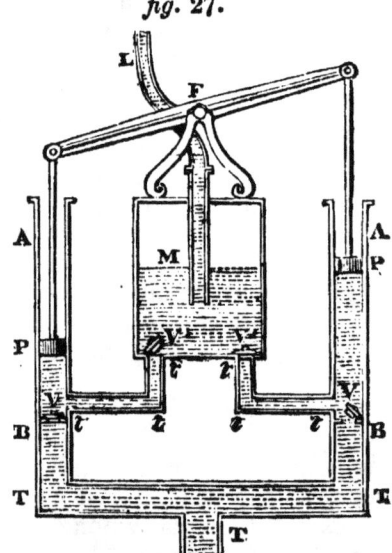
fig. 27.

By the double pump wrought by the same lever, the process is expedited and the power economised. It is not necessary to enter into further particulars respecting this machine, after what has been said on the forcing-pump. There are many varieties in fire-engines, but most of them are governed by the same principles.

IV. *The Syphon.*

(49.) The *syphon* is a bent tube with one leg, A B (*fig.* 28.) shorter than the other, used for transferring a liquid from one vessel to another.

This is effected by exhausting the syphon of the air it contains, or at least so rarefying it, *fig. 28*. that the pressure of the atmosphere on the surface D will force the liquid up the tube beyond the point B, and until it descends in the leg BC below the level D′ of the water D in the vessel. It will then descend by its weight, and flow continually from the tube at C.

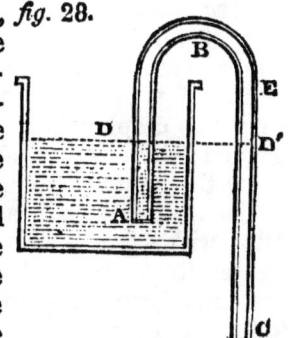

The principle of the syphon is easily understood. Suppose the suction of the mouth or a syringe applied at C so as to produce a considerable rarefaction of the air in A B C. The elasticity of the rarefied air in the syphon pressing on the surface of the water in the leg B A will then be unable to balance the atmospheric pressure acting on the surface D. The liquid will therefore be forced up the leg B A. After passing B into the leg B C, its descent is still opposed by the resistance of the air, and it will be necessary to keep up the rarefaction until the liquid passes the level D′. For, suppose that at any point above D′, as E, the rarefaction were discontinued, the atmosphere would then press the surface E upwards with its whole force. This pressure would, however, be resisted by the weight of the liquid B E; the atmospheric pressure diminished by the weight of B E would then be the effective force which presses the surface E *upwards*. The pressure of the atmosphere on D is transmitted through the liquid to E (see *Hydrostatics*); but this pressure is diminished by the weight of the column D B which it sustains. Hence the effective force which urges the surface E *downwards* is the atmospheric pressure diminished by the weight of the column D E. So long, therefore, as B E is less than D E, the force which urges E *upwards* will be greater than that which presses it *downwards*, and it will therefore return into the vessel D.

The rarefaction must therefore be continued until the liquid has been drawn below the level of D. After that the force downward will exceed the force upward by the weight of the liquid in BC below the level D′.

Since the liquid is raised in D B by the atmospheric pressure, the leg B D must be shorter than a column of the liquid whose pressure is equal to that of the atmosphere; that is, less than thirty-four feet for water, thirty inches for mercury, &c.

It is evident, that the power of the syphon is limited to merely decanting a liquid, but it will not raise it above the level of the liquid in the original vessel. Neither will it continue to act after the level of the vessel into which it is decanted becomes equal to that from which it is drawn off.

Instead of exhausting the syphon, which is sometimes a difficult process, it may be inverted and filled with water; then stopping each end, and placing it with the shorter leg immersed in the water to be drawn off, remove the stops, and it will immediately begin to flow from the longer leg.

When the syphon is large, this process is, however, not easy. In this case, an aperture may be made in the highest point B of the inflected leg of the syphon, and, each end being plugged, the syphon may be filled through the aperture. This aperture being then plugged, and the plugs removed from the ends, the liquid will flow through it. In cases where the syphon is used to carry water over an elevation or a hill, this method is often adopted.

(50.) A syphon, in which the extremities of the legs are turned upwards, called the *Wirtemburg syphon*, may be kept constantly filled. The open ends D and E (*fig. 29.*), are at the same level,

fig. 29.

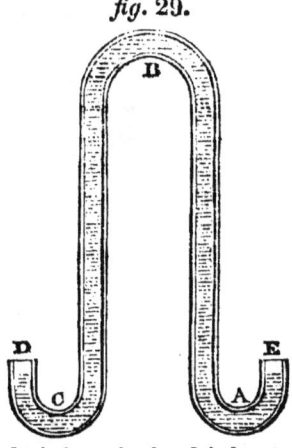

and the height of the highest point B, above this level should be less than the height of a column of the liquid, whose pressure is equal to that of the atmosphere. If the leg D be immersed in a liquid, it will flow out of E, until its level is reduced to D: for the pressure of the liquid above the level D, exerted on the surface of the liquid in the syphon, is transferred by it to the end E, where, being unresisted by any equivalent pressure, the liquid is forced out. It should be remembered, that the atmospheric pressure on the surface E, is resisted by an equivalent pressure on the surface of the liquid in the vessel in which the leg D is immersed. After the level of the liquid in that vessel has fallen to D, the liquid will cease to flow from the syphon, which, therefore, remains full, and may be hung up by a loop at B, till again required for use.

V. *Of Aërostats, or Air-balloons.*

(51.) Aërostats, or air-balloons, are machines, constructed so as to be able to rise in the atmosphere, and float in it at considerable heights, bearing with them, in a car suspended from them, the *aëronaut.*

The principle of the air-balloon is exactly the same as that which governs the ascent of a piece of cork from the bottom of a vessel of water to its surface. If any body is placed in a fluid, whether elastic or inelastic, a gas or a liquid, it will rise or sink, according as it is lighter or heavier, bulk for bulk, than the fluid.

Let A B (*fig.* 30.) represent a level plane, and let C D represent the highest

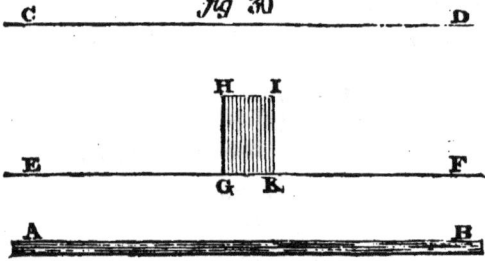

stratum of the atmosphere, and E F any inferior stratum. Every part of the level E F must be equally pressed by the weight of the incumbent atmosphere; and, by the general property of fluids, the pressure to which it is submitted, it transmits equally in every direction; so that a square inch of the level E F, is equally pressed upwards and downwards by a force equal to the weight of a column of the atmosphere whose base is a square inch at the level E F, and whose height is the difference of the levels E F and C D. Now, if a body G H I K, whose base is a square inch, be placed with its base on the level E F, it will take the place of as much air as is equal to its own bulk. If it be lighter than the air it has displaced, it will press on the level E F with a less force; but the level E F will press on it with the same force as before; and, therefore, being pressed upwards with a greater force than downwards, it will rise. If, on the other hand, it be heavier than the air it displaces, it will fall; and, finally, if it be equal in weight with the air it has displaced, it will remain suspended: these last cases being established by the same reasoning as the first.

The air-balloon is a light silken bag filled with a gas, which, bulk for bulk, is lighter than air, so that when inflated, the machine becomes considerably lighter than the air which it displaces. It will therefore ascend in the atmosphere with a force equal to the difference between its own weight and that of the air it displaces. This difference, if the balloon be sufficiently large, is so considerable, that it is enabled to carry up with it one or two persons in a car attached to it.

As it ascends, the air becoming less dense (23.), the difference between its weight and that of the air displaced by it, is gradually diminished, until it attains such an height, that the air it displaces is so rare as to be only equal in weight to the balloon. This, therefore, must be the limit of its ascent.

The aëronaut can descend by permitting some of the gas to escape through a valve, and thereby diminishing the bulk of the balloon. By this means the air it displaces is diminished, and the weight of the balloon is made to exceed that of an equal bulk of air; and therefore it falls until it comes to a lower and denser stratum, in which the weight of the air, bulk for bulk, is equal to that of the balloon, and here again it is suspended.

To be enabled to rise, the aëronaut is provided with ballast, composed of bags of sand; upon throwing out some of these he lightens the machine, and accordingly rises. By these means, as long as a sufficient quantity of gas remains in the balloon, he can ascend and descend at pleasure.

VI. *Of the Air-gun.*

(52.) The air-gun is an instrument for projecting balls, or other missiles, by the elastic force of condensed air.

The principle of the air-gun is easily understood. By means of a condenser, such as has been described in (38.), air is highly condensed in a strong receiver, provided for the purpose, having a valve in it which opens inwards. This receiver, or magazine of compressed air, is screwed upon the stock of the air-gun, so that a communication can be made between the barrel and the compressed air, by opening the valve by proper mechanism provided for that purpose. A bullet being placed in the barrel, and the valve opened, the condensed air will press it forward, and this pressure will continue until the bullet leaves the mouth of the barrel.

The best construction of the air-gun is *Martin's*. It has a lock, stock, barrel, ramrod, &c., similar to a common fowling-piece. The magazine for condensed air is a strong hollow copper ball, in which air is condensed by a syringe. If the air be highly condensed, a ball will be projected by this instrument to the distance of sixty or seventy yards. A number of balls may be discharged in rapid succession, without requiring any further condensation in the magazine.

Chapter VII.—*On Sounds.*

(53.) Sound is the sensation produced in the mind, when the organs of hearing are affected by peculiar motions, transmitted to them through the medium of the air or other bodies.

To enter into any details on the theory of sound, would require a much more extended discussion than would be consistent with the limits which our plan necessarily prescribes to the present Treatise. We shall, therefore, in this chapter, confine ourselves to the statement and explanation of a few of the most important properties connected with the propagation of sound.

When an elastic body is struck, it acquires a tremulous or vibratory motion; this motion is communicated to the air which surrounds the body, and produces in it corresponding undulations, by which, the ear being affected, the sensation of sound is produced. The air being thus the most usual medium by which we receive the sensation of sound, this part of physical science has been generally considered as a branch of pneumatics, but under the separate name of *Acoustics*.

(54.) That it is the air surrounding the sonorous body which transmits the sound to the ear may easily be proved.

Let a small bell be suspended in the moveable receiver of an air-pump. Before the process of rarefaction commences let the receiver be shaken, so that the bell may ring, and the sound will be distinctly heard. As the rarefaction proceeds, the sound of the bell will be gradually weakened, and the process may be continued until it become perfectly inaudible. Upon allowing the air to return gradually into the receiver, the bell will become gradually louder, until as much air be admitted as was withdrawn.

Air, however, although the most usual, is neither the only nor the best conductor of sound. Other elastic fluids, as vapours and gasses, have this property in common with air, as may be proved by introducing them into the exhausted receiver in place of the air which has been withdrawn from it. Inelastic fluids or liquids also conduct sound. If two stones be struck together under water the sound will be heard, the ear being placed under the same water. Solid bodies also conduct sound. If a beam of wood, of considerable length, be struck at one end, the sound will be audible to an ear placed close to it at the other end, although the same sound would be perfectly inaudible to an ear at the same distance, in any other direction, from the striking body.

(55.) The propagation of sound is not instantaneous; that is to say, the sensation is not produced at the same instant as the motion in the sonorous body which causes it. If a gun or piece of ordnance be discharged at a considerable distance, the flash will be first seen, and after a considerable interval has elapsed, the explosion will be heard. In like manner, lightning always precedes thunder by an interval of some seconds. It thus appears, that sound is propagated through the air with a certain velocity; and to determine experimentally this velocity has been considered an interesting physical problem.

By a comparison of the most accurate experiments which have been made on the subject, we may conclude that the atmosphere, in its ordinary state, conducts sound at the rate of 1130 feet per second. The velocity is subject to some slight variation, owing to the change of temperature, the moisture suspended in the air, and other causes; but 1130 feet may be taken as an average rate. This rate also supposes the atmosphere to be perfectly calm. If there be a wind, its velocity must be added to the velocity already mentioned, when it blows from the sounding body to the ear; and subtracted from it when it blows in a contrary direction.

Different bodies conduct sound with different velocities. A beautiful experiment was lately instituted at Paris, to illustrate this fact, by Biot. At the extremity of a cylindrical tube, upwards of 3000 feet in length, a ring of metal was placed, of the same diameter as the aperture of the tube; and in the centre of this ring, in the mouth of the tube, was suspended a clock-bell and hammer. The hammer was made to strike the ring and the bell at the same instant, so that the sound of the ring would be transmitted to the remote end of the tube, through the conducting power of the matter of the tube itself; while the sound of the bell would be transmitted through the medium of the air included within the tube. The ear being then placed at the remote end of the tube, the sound of the ring, transmitted by the metal of the tube, was first distinctly heard; and after a short interval had elapsed, the sound of the bell, transmitted by the air in the tube, was heard. The result of several experiments was, that the metal of the tube conducted the sound with about ten and a half times the velocity with which it was conducted by the air; that is, at the rate of about 11,865 feet per second.

(56.) Sound is reflected from hard and smooth surfaces, according to laws similar to those which govern the reflection of light; and, similar to light, it is propagated in right lines.

Let A (*fig.* 31.) be the position of a sounding body, and let B C be a smooth

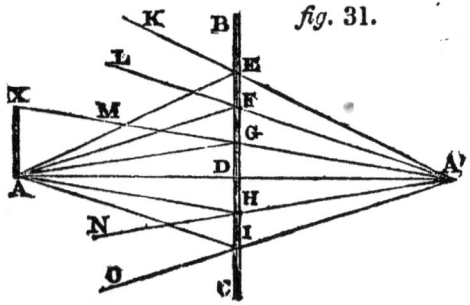

fig. 31.

and hard surface at the distance A D, the line A D being perpendicular to B C. The sound is propagated in right lines diverging from A, and the rays of sound strike the surface B C at the points E, F, G, H, I, &c. They are then reflected from the surface B C, at angles equal to those at which they strike it; that is, the angle D E A is equal to B E K, D F A is equal to B F L, D G A to B G M, &c. Now, if this be the case, by a well-known geometrical theorem, the lines K E, L F, M G, N H, &c., if continued back in the directions K E, L F, &c., will all meet in a point A', as far behind the surface B C, as A is before it; so that A D = A'D. The rays of sound, E K, F L, G M, &c., will therefore proceed, as if they emanated from a sounding body placed at A'. These rays of sound will therefore affect an ear placed any where within their range, as at X, exactly as if the sounding body were placed at A'; and if a sufficient number of these reflected rays meet the ear at X, the reflected sound will be heard. But the sound of A will be first heard in the direction of the line A X, so that a repetition or *echo* will be the effect. The line X A being less than X A, the direct sound in the line X A will be first heard; and after an interval, equal to the time which sound takes to move through a space equal to the difference between the distances X A and X A', the echo will be heard.

When there is but one reflecting surface, it seldom happens that a sufficient number of rays of sound meet the ear to produce sensation, in which case no echo will be perceived. But if the ear be placed at the sounding body, and if smooth and hard surfaces be placed in various directions round this centre, they will severally reflect back the sound. In order, however, that sensation should be produced, it will be necessary that a number of these reflections should reach the ear at the same instant. This will necessarily be the case if a number of the reflecting surfaces are at equal distances from the ear and the sounding body. If, then, the place of the ear and the sounding body be the centre of a circle, and if in the circumference of this circle and at right angles to lines drawn from the centre, a number of plane reflecting surfaces be placed, the rays of sound proceeding from the centre will be reflected back to the centre, so as to produce a distinct perception of the sound or an echo. The number of seconds between the production of the sound and its echo may be found by dividing twice the number of feet in the radius of the circle by 1130.

Let C (*fig.* 32.) be the place of the auditor, and A, B, D, E, F be plane reflecting surfaces placed in the circumference of the same circle. The sound produced at C moves along C A, and being reflected at A, returns along A C, and arrives at C after as many seconds as 1130 feet are contained in twice A C. Since the lines A C, B C, D C, E C, F C are equal, the sound is reflected from the surfaces B, D, E, F in exactly the same time as from A. Now, al-

PNEUMATICS.

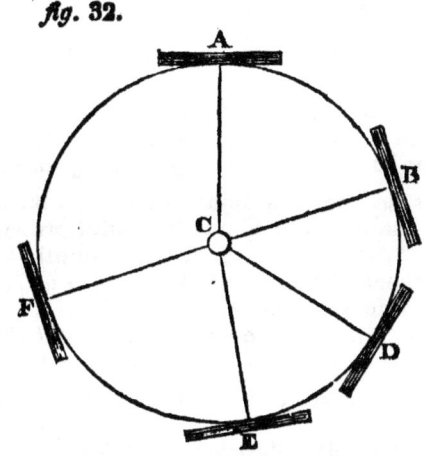

fig. 32.

though one of these reflections might be insufficient to render the echo perceptible, yet their combined effect cannot fail to do so.

When accident or design has placed surfaces in such a position, an echo will therefore be the consequence, and it may even happen that the same point C will be the centre of several concentrical circles of reflecting surfaces, in which case there will be as many reverberations of the sound.

If the sound be produced at one point, and the auditor be placed at another, the reflecting surfaces must be placed in an ellipse, of which those two points are the *foci*. This will be easily understood by the aid of the known properties of this curve.

Let S (*fig.* 33.) be the place of the sounding body, and A the place of the auditor, and with these points as foci, let an ellipse B, C, D, &c. be described. Let B, C, D, E, &c. be plane surfaces, coinciding at the points B, C, D, E, &c. with the curve, or, more strictly speaking, tangents, to the curve at these points. By the established properties of this curve, the sums of the distances of each point in it from the foci A S are the same; that is, A B + B S = A C + C S = A D + D S, &c. Also the angles which each pair of these lines make with the respective tangents are equal; that is, the angle A B a is equal to the angle S B b, A C c = S C d, &c. Hence it follows, that sounds proceeding from S in the direction S B will be reflected

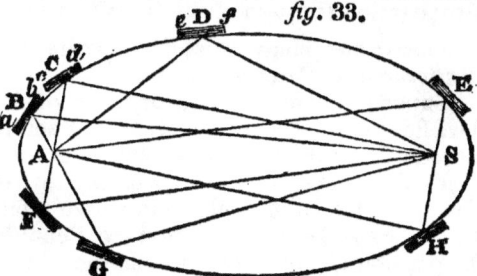

fig. 33.

from B in the direction B A; also the sound from S to C will be reflected from C to A; and in the same manner the rays of sound proceeding from S and striking on D, E, F, &c. will also be reflected to A. And since the spaces through which these several rays have to move, viz. S B + B A, S C + C A, S D + D A, &c. are equal, they will all arrive at A at the same instant, and will consequently be sufficient to produce sensation. The sound of S will, therefore, be first heard directly along S A, and afterwards by the reflections just described. If it happen that there are a sufficient number of reflecting surfaces in several ellipses having the same points S A as foci, there will be several repetitions of the echo.

Chapter VIII.

Works upon this Branch of Science.

Gravesande's Mathematical Elements of Natural Philosophy, book II, part III.
Furguson's Lectures on Select Subjects, Lect. VI.

These two works give a popular exhibition of the science; and describe fully the experiments which illustrate it, and the machines to which it is applied. Rowning's Natural Philosophy gives an easy and somewhat more superficial account of it.

The heads of the subject, but only as heads for lecturing from, are to be found more learnedly given in Prof. Playfair and Dr. M. Young's Outlines of Natural Philosophy.

History of the Fundamental Discovery

Galileo's Dialogues. The rise of fluids in tubes by suction is ascribed to nature's horror of a vacuum, but some of the experiments by which the weight of air is shewn are described.

Pascal—Nouvelles Expériences touchant le Vuide. This was first published before 1643, the date of the Torricellian Experiment, and Pascal adopts Galileo's notion. After 1643 he followed Torricelli, and caused the experiment of Puy de Dome to be made on the fall of the mercury as we mount in the atmosphere; and repeated it in a church at Paris.

Des Cartes, Letters III., p. 111, 1631, explains the rise of Mercury in close tubes by the weight of the atmosphere.

Stevinus, 1585, published in Flemish his Mechanics, and one chapter is entitled 'On the Weight or Statics of Air.' Montucla (History of Mathem. II. 180), had never seen it; the Latin translator of Stevinus's works, published 1608, having omitted this part, he seems to suspect that it only discussed the force of air impinging on sails, &c. Montucla (II. 203) gives the history of the Torricellian Discovery in a very striking manner.

The Theory of the Resistance of Elastic Fluids, to bodies moving in them, a branch of Dynamics rather than Pneumatics, is given in some profound and beautiful propositions of the Principia: see lib. II., props. 34 and 35, 37 and 38, 40, and the scholium to it, in which Sir Isaac relates his admirable experiments on bodies falling in the air, and among others the experiments on bodies falling from the roof of St. Paul's (220 feet) made in June 1710. Props. 43, 47, 48, and 49, contain the theory of pulses, and their propagation through elastic media, and consequently the theory of sound.

There are many valuable papers on subjects connected with Pneumatics in the *Philosophical Transactions** :—

Experiments on the Compression of Air by Water.—Dr. Halley on the Barometer.—Dr. Papin, on Air rushing into a Vacuum.—Hauksbee, on Sound propagated in condensed and rarefied Air.—Hauksbee, on the Density and Temperature of Air.—Desaguliers Experiments on Bodies falling in Air. (This last set of experiments is described by Sir I. Newton in the Scholium above referred to. He appears to have assisted and taken the times.)—Derham, Motion of Pendulums in Vacuo.—Darwin, on the Mechanical Expansion of Air.—Edgeworth, on the Resistance of Air.—On the Motion of Air.—Dr. Young's Paper on Sound and Light.

The Air-Pump.—Smeaton's proposed Air-Pump.—Nairne's Experiments with that and other Pumps.—Cavallo's Air Pump.—(There are in the older volumes some papers on the same subject, beginning with the proposals by Dr. Beale and Mr. Boyle, of several experiments to be made with the " Pneumatic Engine.")—Mr. Boyle's New Pneumatical Experiments about Respiration—(all in the *Philosophical Transactions*.)

Boyle's Treatise on the Spring and Weight of Air, Oxford 1663.
Boyle, on the Rarity and Density of Air.—Marriotte sur la Nature de l'Air, 1676.
Homberg on the Spring of Air in Vacuo. Mem. of the French Acad. of Sciences, I. 105.
La Hire on the Condensation and Dilatation of Air, *ib.* 1705, p. 110.
Carré on the Spring of Air, *ib.* 1710, p. 1.
Richmann on the Compression of Air by Ice. Nova Comment. Petropolitana, II. 162.
Nollet on Pneumatic Experiments. Mem. French Acad. 1740, pp. 385, 567—1741, p. 338.
Fontana on the Elasticity of Gases. Mem. Societa Italiana, I. p. 83.

The Barometer.—Traité des Barometres. Amsterdam, 1686.—Mercurial and Water Barometers compared. Mem. Fr. Acad. I. 234.—Amontons on Barometers, *ib.* II. 23.—Huygens on a New Barometer, *ib.* X. 375.—La Hire on Barometers, *ib.* 1706, p. 432.—Franceschini on the Height of the Barometer. Mem. Soc. Ital. V. 294.—Dalton on Barometrical Observations. Manchester Mem. V. 666.

Barometrical Measurements.—Halley, Barometrical Observations on Snowden.—Halley on Barometrical Measurements.—Derham on the Height of the Barometer on Mountains.—Desaguliers Contrivance for taking Levels.—Scheuchzer's Barometrical Method of Measuring the Height of Mountains.—Deluc, Barometrical Observations on the Depth of Mines.—Sir G. Shuckburgh.—Gen. Roy on Measurement of Heights—(all in the *Philosophical Transactions.*)

Euler on Barometrical Measurements. Mem. Acad. Berlin, 1753, p. 114.
Lavoisier on Weight of Air. Mem. French Acad. 1774, p. 364.
Morozzo on the Constitution of the Atmosphere. Mem. Soc. Ital. VI. 221.
Playfair on the Causes which affect the accuracy of Barometric Measurements. Edin. Trans. I. 87.

Acoustics, or Doctrine of Sound

Perrault on Hearing. Mem. Fr. Acad. I. 158.—Nollet on the Hearing of Fishes, *ib.* 1743, p. 199.—Anderson on the same subject, *ib.* 1748, p. 149.—Hunter on the same subject. Phil. Trans. 1782, p. 379.—La Hire on Sound. Mem. Fr. Acad. 1716, p. 262.—Cassini on Sound, *ib.* 1738, p. 128.—Lagrange on Sound. Mem. Acad. Turin, I. II.—Euler on the Propagation of Pulses. Nov. Com. Petropol. I. 67.—Euler on the same subject. Mem. Acad. Berlin, 1765, p. 335.—J. Gough on Sound. Manchester Mem. V. 622.

---

* The pages referred to in the Philosophical Transactions will be easily found by consulting the Index to the *Abridgement*, want of space preventing their insertion here.

HEAT.

Chapter I.

General Remarks, upon the Agency of Heat, and its connexion with Chemical Science.

In all our excursions over the surface of this globe, innumerable objects excite our admiration, and contribute to inspire delight. But whether our gratitude is awakened by the verdure of the earth, the lustre of the waters, or the freshness of the air, it is to the beneficial agency of *Heat* (under Providence) that we are indebted for them all. Without the presence and effects of heat, the earth would be an impenetrable rock, incapable of supporting animal or vegetable life; the waters would be for ever deprived of their fluidity and motion; and the air of its elasticity and its utility together.

Heat animates, invigorates, and beautifies all nature. Its influence is absolutely necessary to enable plants to grow, put forth their flowers, and perfect their fruit. It is closely connected with the powers of life; since animated beings lose their vitality when heat is withdrawn.

Such is the universal influence of this powerful agent in the kingdoms of nature; nor is this influence diminished in the provinces of art. It is with the aid of heat that rocks are rent, and the hidden treasures of the earth obtained. Matter is modified ten thousand ways by its agency, and rendered subservient to the uses of man; furnishing him with useful and appropriate instruments, warm and ornamental clothing, wholesome and delicious food, needful and effectual shelter.

Increase of temperature facilitates the operations of chemistry in various ways; but chiefly by heightening the attractive forces which the particles of matter exert for each other, and thus enabling them to combine together. In many instances the particles which enter into the composition of compound bodies may remain in close contact without uniting, unless the temperature is raised, and then the combination proceeds with rapidity.

The term *Caloric* was introduced by Lavoisier to distinguish the cause of heat from the sensation which we call by the same name; but the terms *caloric* and *calorific fluid* seem to imply the material nature of heat, which has not yet been proved. The *heat* of the sun's rays is a common form of expression; it seems to convey just as clear an idea as the *caloric* of the sun's rays; and is more conformable to common modes of speech: the *heat* which we feel is another equally common form of expression, which applies to the sensation produced, while the former use of the word marks the cause, whatever it be, that produces the sensation. The common usage has long been, it thus appears, to apply this term both to heat, and to the sensation which heat produces; and it is still so applied in the works of the most scientific writers; the meaning of the expression in which it is used being considered sufficient to prevent any ambiguity or confusion. The author of this treatise does not, therefore, consider himself bound to adhere to the term *caloric*, although he may sometimes find the use of it convenient.

Chapter II

Of the Nature or Cause of Heat.

Whoever is employed in examining refined and powerful natural agencies, must speedily be convinced that the causes of such agencies still continue unknown; notwithstanding the patient and persevering efforts of learned men, through many ages of investigation. This is strictly true with regard to heat or caloric; concerning which it cannot be determined whether its phenomena are occasioned by a subtile fluid, capable of entering into bodies and of being emitted from them, or by motion, vibration, or rotation excited among the particles of matter. The arguments which have been adduced, and the experiments which have been made, are inconclusive, however varied and ingenious they may be.

Pictet suspended a thermometer in an exhausted receiver; and, finding that it was capable of undergoing changes of temperature while in that situation, he regarded this as a proof that heat is material, on account of its capability of passing through a vacuum.

Count Rumford proved the passage of heat through a Torricellian vacuum; that is, the space left at the top of a barometer by the mercury falling. He placed a thermometer in such a vacuum, and submitting the whole apparatus to changes of temperature, the thermometer was affected by every change. The Count imagined that the very subtile vapour which arises from quicksilver, and occupies the space called the Torricellian vacuum, is too rare to transmit caloric by its vibrations in a short time; and concluded, therefore, that heat being able to pass through such a space, without the aid of any vibrating elastic fluid, must be material.

The strongest argument in favour of the material nature of heat is probably that which is derived from its radiation. When a heated body is exposed in the atmosphere, a portion of its heat gradually quits it, and passes rapidly through space in straight lines: this heat may be reflected by mirrors and condensed by lenses; and always produces effects upon bodies exposed to its influence.

Attempts were made by Buffon, Roebuck, and Whitehurst, to ascertain if the weight of bodies, to which heat is applied, is increased: but their experiments have been considered deficient in philosophical accuracy.

A very remarkable result was obtained by Dr. Fordyce in an experiment to determine the weight of latent heat, described in the 75th vol. of the Philosophical Transactions. He put about 1700 grains of water into a glass globe, three inches in diameter, and sealed it hermetically; it then weighed $2150\frac{31}{32}$ grains; its temperature having been reduced to 32° by being plunged in a freezing mixture. When its weight was ascertained, it was again submitted to the freezing mixture for twenty minutes, until a part of the water was frozen. Its weight was ascertained, after it had been very carefully dried, and it was found to have gained $\frac{1}{50}$th part of a grain.

This process was repeated five times, more of the water being frozen each time, and an increase of weight obtained. When all the water had become solid, the weight gained was $\frac{3}{15}$ of a grain; the temperature of the globe and the ice which it contained having been reduced to 12° of Fahrenheit's scale. The beam used was a very delicate one, and the temperature of the room during the experiment was 37°.

Similar experiments were made by Morveau and Chausier, with similar results; sealed glass vessels containing water becoming heavier when they were frozen. In one experiment, two pounds of sulphuric acid lost three grains of its weight when it became fluid, after having been frozen.

Were the results of these experiments satisfactorily established, they would prove that bodies become heavier on the discharge of caloric; and consequently, that the combination of caloric with a body renders it lighter.

A fallacy in determining the results of these experiments may be ascribed to overlooking the fact, that the air above the scale being cooled down, by the frozen body in it, to a lower degree than the other parts of the atmosphere of the room, that portion of it below the scale would necessarily be displaced, and the scale preponderate. But other philosophers have tried experiments of the same kind, without obtaining corresponding results.

The weight of frozen and liquid sulphuric acid was tried by Fontana, without finding any difference.

Lavoisier took a thin glass flask containing a pound of water, and having hermetically sealed it, weighed it very accurately, and then submitted it to the usual cooling process, by which the water was frozen; but the flask weighed exactly the same when its contents were solid as when they were fluid. In another experiment the same philosopher put six grains of phosphorus upon a small capsule, within a very strong glass flask, which he closed securely; he then weighed it, with great care, and afterwards inflamed the phosphorus, by directing upon it the rays of the sun through a burning glass. No difference of weight was discovered when the vessel was weighed again after becoming cold; nor, indeed, could any be expected from such an experiment.

Count Rumford made an experiment which seemed to confirm the result obtained by Dr. Fordyce and others; but on varying the same experiment, he concluded differently. He put equal weights of water and quicksilver into two bottles, very much alike, and suspended them to the arms of a delicate balance, until they acquired the temperature of the room, 61°: he then submitted them to the influence of an atmosphere at 34° for twenty-four hours, without effect, as the weights remained precisely the same; although it is certain, from the respective capacities of the two fluids, that the water must have given out much more heat than the quicksilver.

In making other experiments with bottles containing different fluids, he found that difference of temperature in the bottle, when weighed, occasioned an apparent difference of weight, as he supposed from the vertical currents which they occasioned in the atmosphere, when heated or cooled in it; or from the unequal quantities of moisture condensed upon their surfaces, or from both causes operating together.

The hypothesis, or supposition, by which caloric is considered a subtile material fluid, the particles of which mutually repel each other, appears to give a plausible explanation of most of the phenomena dependant upon heat, as the expansion, fusion, and vaporisation of bodies, on the supposition that the particles of caloric when interposed between the particles of bodies, in sufficient quantity, produce these effects. It is natural to suppose, when a body is enlarged in bulk, that the enlargement is occasioned by the introduction of the particles of other matter, by which the particles of the expanded body are repelled to a greater distance from one another; and this repulsion becomes so great, in consequence of the introduction of a large quantity of heat, as to enable the particles of solid bodies to assume the fluid or aëriform states.

The communication of heat from one body to another is also accounted for by this hypothesis,—on the supposition that bodies have the power of attracting this refined matter. According to the same hypothesis, we may account for the unequal effects produced by equal quantities of heat, upon different bodies, by supposing them to exert different degrees of attraction for caloric. The cold which is occasioned by the conversion of solid substances into fluids or gases, and the great increase of temperature which attends the condensation of gases or fluids, admits of satisfactory elucidation upon this hypothesis, the matter of heat or caloric being absorbed, it is supposed, in the former case, and set free in the latter.

There are phenomena, however, which are not easily reconciled to this hypothesis;—the high degree of heat occasioned by the explosion of gunpowder, where large quantities of gaseous matter are disengaged;—the heat which results from the decomposition of euchlorine gas, although it is resolved into gases of greater volume;—and the production of heat by friction or percussion.

Dr. Murray was of opinion that there is a strong analogy between the usual mode of exciting electricity and the production of heat by friction, and that the phenomenon may be explained consistently with the hypothesis alluded to.

According to this author, the particles of bodies are made to vibrate or oscillate by friction, percussion, or other mechanical impulse, and that during this state of motion they must ultimately approach to and recede from each other: when the particles approach, part of the caloric interposed between these particles must be forced out; and when they recede from each other, caloric must be absorbed. A part of the caloric set free at every vibration is evolved; and it is supposed that its loss is supplied by other bodies, with which the body operated upon may be in contact, in consequence of the strong tendency of caloric to maintain an equilibrium, in the same way as electricity is supplied to an electrical machine in action and in contact with the earth.

The caloric that is continually evolved raises the temperature of the substance undergoing friction, or percussion, which bears some analogy to the charging of an electrical conductor, with the electricity given out by the action of the electrical machine.

It has been proved by Berthollet that there is a close connexion between the heat produced by percussion, and the reduction of bulk which the body operated upon undergoes. Pieces of gold, silver, copper and iron, alike in size, were submitted to the stroke of a coining press, by this philosopher, and the heat produced by each stroke was ascertained by throwing the pieces into water; the relation existing between the degree of heat imparted to the water, and the heat previously existing in the metal, having been found by experiment. In this manner he was enabled to determine how much the temperature of each piece had been raised; and the important fact resulting from these experiments is this, that the heat produced was greatest at the first stroke to which each piece was subjected, less at the second, and less still at the third. After the third stroke, the temperature was but very little raised. The following numbers are the degrees of heat according to the Centigrade scale which the strokes of the press occasioned in two pieces of copper

1st Stroke	First Piece	. .	9.60
	Second Piece	. .	11.56
2nd Stroke	First Piece	. .	4.06
	Second Piece	. .	2.09
3rd Stroke	First Piece	. .	1.06
	Second Piece	. .	0.81

The other metals gave similar results.

The quantities of heat here measured by the Centigrade scale, may easily be estimated according to the scale of Fahrenheit, on recollecting that one degree of the former is equal to one eight-tenths of the latter, or that $10°$ of the Centigrade scale are equal to $18°$ of Fahrenheit.

It appears, therefore, from these experiments, that the degree of heat produced is always in proportion to the degree of condensation. The specific gravity of a piece of copper before the first stroke was 8.8529, after it 8.8898; and after the second stroke 8.9081. The specific gravity of silver before the operation was 10.4667, and after it 10.4838.

The other hypothesis which has prevailed with regard to the cause of heat is, that it consists in motion among the particles of bodies.

The invention of this hypothesis is usually ascribed to Lord Bacon, who having observed, in some instances, a connexion between rise of temperature and increase of motion, concluded that motion is always the cause of rise of temperature, or, as expressed by himself, that "heat arises from violent motion in the internal parts of bodies." This hypothesis was adopted by Boyle, and the opinions which Newton maintained also corresponded with it.— He believed "that heat consists in a minute vibratory motion in the particles of bodies, and that this motion is communicated through an apparent vacuum, by the undulations of a very subtile elastic medium, which is also concerned in the phenomena of light."

The production of heat by friction is known to some of the least-civilized races of men, who light their fires by rubbing two pieces of wood together. It has been considered as furnishing the strongest argument against the materiality of heat; and consequently in favour of the hypothesis of motion.

It occurred to Count Rumford, who had observed the great heat produced in the operation of boring cannon, that the heat occasioned by friction might be ascertained by a similar process. He took an unbored cannon, with the large projecting piece "two feet beyond its muzzle," which is usually cast with cannon to ensure solidity: this projecting piece was bored, and reduced to the form of a hollow cylinder, attached to the cannon by a small neck: the whole apparatus being wrapped in flannel, was made to revolve upon its axis by the power of horses, and a blunt steel borer was pressed against the bottom of the cylinder. The whole mass of metal at the commencement of the operation being at the temperature of $60°$, the force with which the borer was pressed against the cylinder was estimated at about 10,000 pounds avoirdupois, and the surface of contact between the borer and the bottom of the cylinder was about two square inches. The cylinder had made 960 turns in half an hour; the apparatus was then stopped, and the heat which had been produced ascertained, by introducing a mercurial thermometer into a perforation of the cylinder extending from the circumference to the axis, by which it was found that its temperature was raised to $130°$, which was considered to be a correct indication of the mean temperature of the cylinder. The particles of iron abraded during the operation weighed 837 grains, being about $\frac{1}{948}$th part of the whole weight of the cylinder.

The experiment was varied by the same philosopher. He fixed a cylinder of brass, partly bored, in a box containing eighteen pounds of water, excluding the water from the bore of the cylinder by oiled leathers. The borer was made to revolve, by machinery, thirty-two times in a minute. The temperature, which at the commencement was $60°$, rose in an hour to $107°$; and in two hours and a half the water boiled. The whole apparatus, weighing fifteen pounds, was raised to the same temperature. In estimating the quantity of heat produced in this experiment

Count Rumford considered it to be equal to that of nine wax candles, each three-quarters of an inch in diameter, burning the same length of time.

In searching for the source of heat in this experiment, it could not be found in any change of capacity, as the borings continued of the same capacity as the metal from which they were abraded. The air of the atmosphere having been excluded in the process, no part of the heat could be ascribed to its agency; the water used underwent no chemical change, and could not, therefore, have contributed any portion of the heat, nor could any part of the heat have been derived from surrounding bodies, as they rather received heat from the matter exposed to friction.

The Count considered it proved by these experiments that heat may be obtained, without limitation, by subjecting metal to friction; and concluded that what can be obtained from insulated bodies without limitation cannot be material, and believed it impossible to account for such phenomena upon any other hypothesis than that of motion among the particles of bodies.

It had been before proved by Boyle that friction in vacuo produces heat, he having obtained this result by making two pieces of brass rub against each other in the exhausted receiver of an air-pump. The same fact was proved by Pictet, who found that the introduction of a soft substance, such as cotton, between the rubbing surfaces, increased the heat. He conjectured that electricity is concerned in the production of heat by friction.

Sir H. Davy made various experiments illustrative of this subject. He insulated an apparatus for occasioning friction, by placing it on ice in vacuo, in which situation heat was produced. Two pieces of ice, similarly circumstanced, being made to rub against each other, heat enough was produced to melt them. The heat produced in this experiment could not arise from any diminution of capacity, as the water resulting from the melting of the ice has the greater capacity for heat. It seemed to be satisfactorily shown also, that it could not be derived from air, and the same conclusion was drawn from these experiments that Count Rumford drew from his, namely, that heat is produced by motion among the particles of bodies.

Having thus detailed the most remarkable experiments favourable to both of the prevailing hypotheses as to the cause of heat, and having stated the conclusions drawn from them, it may be useful to quote the opinions of two philosophers who think differently on the subject, and place them in opposition to each other.

Dr. Murray, (*System of Chemistry, third edition,* vol. i. page 468,) after describing the hypothesis upon which heat is supposed to be material, proceeds to speak of the other in the following words:—" The opposite opinion, that caloric is motion, placing it on the same ground, or considering it as an hypothesis, does not afford an explanation of those phenomena equally satisfactory. The most general effect arising from the operation of caloric, is expansion; but if caloric is mere motion, or vibration of the particles of the heated body, how is this effect produced? Vibration is the alternate approximation and retrocession of the particles; but from this state it is evident that no permanent and uniform increase of volume can take place. Still less can this cause account for the augmentation of volume which accompanies fluidity and vaporisation. When water is converted into vapour, it occupies 1800 times the space which it did while in the liquid form. Suppose vibration increased to any intensity, it cannot be shown how it can permanently separate the particles of a body to such distances. The deficiencies of this opinion are likewise evident in its application to other phenomena. The laws of its propagation through bodies are different from the established laws of motion. Were they the same, the propagation of caloric ought to be momentary through elastic bodies, and should be more or less rapid through others, according to their elasticity, which is far from being the case. Neither is any cause pointed out why it should be so slowly transmitted through liquids or airs. We are equally unable to account for its distribution in bodies, and the quantities of it required to produce given temperatures in different substances, or the portions of it absorbed when bodies change their forms, on any laws it could observe, supposing it to be any species of motion."

Dr. Young (in his *Lectures on Natural Philosophy,* vol. i. page 653,) proceeds thus with the discussion of the nature of heat, "a subject," says he, "upon which the popular opinion seems to have been lately led away by very superficial considerations. The facility with which the mind conceives the existence of an independent substance, liable to no material variations, except those of its quantity and distribution, especially when an appropriate name, and a place in the order of the simplest elements has been bestowed on it, appears to have caused the most eminent chemical philosophers to overlook some insuperable difficulties attending the hypothesis of caloric." In another part of the same passage he remarks, that "the circumstances which have already been stated, respecting the production of heat by friction, appear to afford an unanswerable confutation of the whole of this doctrine. If the heat is neither received from the surrounding bodies, which it cannot be, without a depression of their temperature; nor derived from the quantity already accumulated in the bodies themselves, which it could not be, even if their capacities were diminished in any imaginable degree; there is no alternative, but to allow that heat must be actually generated by friction: and if it is generated out of nothing, it cannot be matter, nor even an immaterial or semi-material substance. The collateral parts of the theory have also their separate difficulties: thus, if heat were the general principle of repulsion, its augmentation could not diminish the elasticity of solids and of fluids; if it constituted a continued fluid, it could not radiate freely through the same space in different directions; and if its repulsive particles followed each other at a distance, they would still approach near enough to each other, in the focus of a burning-glass, to have their motions deflected from a rectilinear direction."

In page 656, the same author, having drawn a parallel between the production of heat and sound, observes that "all these analogies are certainly favourable to the opinion of the vibratory nature of heat, which has been sufficiently sanctioned by the authority of the greatest philosophers of past times, and of the most sober reasoners of the present. Those, however, who look up with unqualified reverence to the dogmas of the modern schools of chemistry, will, probably, long retain a partiality for the convenient, but superficial and inaccurate, modes of reasoning, which have been founded on the favourite hypothesis of the existence of caloric as a separate substance; but it may be presumed that, in the end, a careful examination of the facts, which have been adduced in confutation of that system, will make a sufficient impression on the minds of the cultivators of chemistry, to induce them to listen to a less objectionable theory." The question, therefore, remains undetermined; and it is fortunate that, most of the phenomena connected with the operation of heat, may be explained equally well upon either theory.

Chapter III.

Of the Expansion of Bodies by Heat.

The most general effect produced by heat upon bodies to which it is applied, is the enlargement of their bulk. Solids, fluids, and airs, all expand on being heated, and contract when they are cooled. Some useful processes of art and several important operations of nature depend upon this law.

The expansion of solids may readily be proved by simple and convincing experiments.

Ex. A cylindrical piece of brass *a*, (*fig.*1,) having a handle adapted to it, is fitted to a flat piece *b*, so that it may just pass through the large notch lengthwise, and by its ends go through the round hole: when heated in the fire it will be too long to pass in one direction, and too thick to pass in the other. Having become cold, it will again fit and pass through, as before.

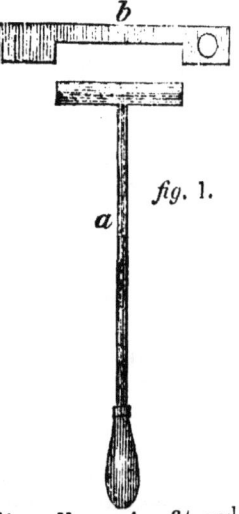

fig. 1.

Ex. An iron ball, adapted to a ring of the same metal, so as to pass through when cold, will be too large to pass when heated; when cooled again it will pass as before.

If the relative degrees of expansion which different bodies undergo at low temperatures, are to be ascertained, the instrument (*fig.* 2) called a pyrometer, or some similar one must be used.

Ex. A rod of any metal or other

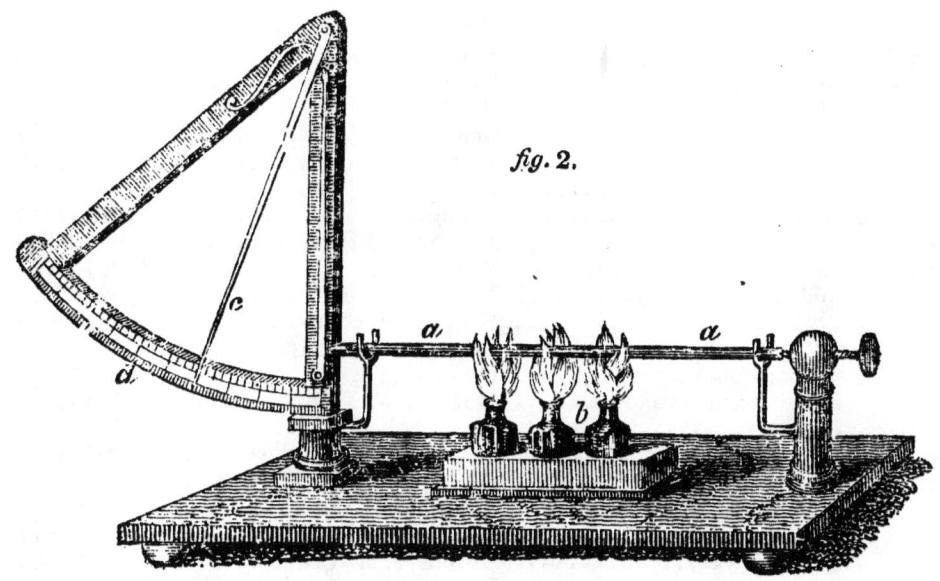

fig. 2.

substance, *a*, the expansion of which is to be tried, is laid upon the rest, touching an immoveable screw at one end, and the moveable index at the other; as soon as the heat of the spirit-lamp *b* is applied, the substance, if it is a very expansible one, will begin to expand, and its comparative degree of expansibility will be shown by the distance to which the index *c* moves along the graduated part of the instrument *d*. In comparing different substances together with this instrument, it will be necessary to make all the rods of the same size, and to apply the heat of the lamp the same length of time to each.

The following TABLE of the "linear dilatation of solids by heat," is taken from Dr. Ure's *Dictionary of Chemistry*, and is probably the most correct extant.

Dimensions which a bar takes at 212° whose length at 32° is 1.000000.

Substance	Authority	Value	Dilatation in vulga fraction.
Glass tube	Smeaton	1.00083333	
Do.	Roy	1.00077615	
Do.	De Luc's mean	1.00082800	$\frac{1}{1\,1\,3}$
Do.	Dulong and Petit	1.00086130	$\frac{1}{1\,1\,4\,5}$
Do.	Lavoisier and Laplace	1.00081166	$\frac{1}{1\,1\,3\,3}$
Plate glass	Do. do.	1.000890890	$\frac{1}{1\,1\,4\,3}$
Do. crown glass	Do. do.	1.00087572	$\frac{1}{1\,1\,4\,2}$
Do. do.	Do. do.	1.00089760	$\frac{1}{1\,0\,9\,5}$
Do. do.	Do. do.	1.00091751	
Do. rod	Roy	1.00080787	
Deal	Do. as glass		
Platina	Borda	1.00085655	
Do.	Dulong and Petit	1.00088420	$\frac{1}{1\,1\,3\,1}$
Do.	Troughton	1.00099180	
Do. and glass	Berthoud	1.00110000	
Palladium	Wollaston	1.00100000	
Antimony	Smeaton	1.00108300	
Cast-iron prism	Roy	1.00110940	
Cast iron	Lavoisier by Dr. Young	1.00111111	
Steel	Troughton	1.00118990	
Steel rod	Roy	1.00114470	
Blistered steel	Phil. Trans. 1795, 428	1.00112500	
Do.	Smeaton	1.00115000	
Steel not tempered	Lavoisier and Laplace	1.00107875	$\frac{5}{5\,2\,7}$
Do. do. do.	Do. do.	1.00107956	$\frac{5}{5\,2\,8}$
Do. tempered yellow	Do. do.	1.00136900	
Do. do. do.	Do. do.	1.00138600	
Do. at a higher heat	Do. do.	1.00123956	$\frac{5}{8\,0\,7}$
Steel	Troughton	1.00118980	
Hard steel	Smeaton	1.00122500	

Table—(continued.)

Material	Authority	Value	
Annealed steel	Muschenbrock	1.00122000	
Tempered steel	Do.	1.00137000	
Iron	Borda	1.00115600	
Do.	Smeaton	1.00125800	
Soft-forged iron	Lavoisier and Laplace	1.00122045	
Round iron, wire-drawn	Do. do.	1.90123501	
Iron wire	Troughton	1.00144010	
Iron	Dulong and Petit	1.00118203	$\frac{1}{848}$
Bismuth	Smeaton	1.00139200	
Annealed gold	Muschenbroek	1.00146000	
Gold	Ellicot, by comparison	1.00150000	
Do. procured by parting	Lavoisier and Laplace	1.00146606	$\frac{1}{682}$
Do. Paris standard unannealed	Do. do.	1.00155155	$\frac{1}{645}$
Do. do. annealed	Do. do.	1.00151361	$\frac{1}{661}$
Copper	Muschenbroek	1.0019100	
Do.	Lavoisier and Laplace	1.00172244	$\frac{1}{581}$
Do.	Do. do.	1.00171222	$\frac{1}{584}$
Do.	Troughton	1.00191880	
Do.	Dulong and Petit	1.00171821	$\frac{1}{582}$
Brass	Borda	1.00178300	
Do.	Lavoisier and Laplace	1.00186671	
Do.	Do. do.	1.00188971	
Brass scale, supposed from Hamburgh	Roy	1.00185510	
Cast brass	Smeaton	1.00187500	
English plate brass, in rod	Roy	1.00189280	
Do. do. in a trough form	Do.	1.00189190	
Brass	Troughton	1.00191880	
Brass wire	Smeaton	1.00192000	
Brass	Muschenbroek	1.00216000	
Copper 8, tin 1	Smeaton	1.00181700	
Silver	Herbert	1.00189000	
Do.	Ellicot, by comparison	1.0021000	
Do.	Muschenbroek	1.00212000	
Do. of cupel	Lavoisier and Laplace	1.00190971	$\frac{1}{524}$
Do. Paris standard	Do. do.	1.00190868	$\frac{1}{524}$
Silver	Troughton	1.0020826	
Brass 16, tin 1	Smeaton	1.00190800	
Speculum metal	Do.	1.00193300	
Spelter solder; brass 2, zinc 1	Do.	1.00205800	
Molacca tin	Lavoisier and Laplace	1.00193765	$\frac{1}{516}$
Tin from Falmouth	Do. do.	1.00217298	$\frac{1}{462}$
Fine pewter	Smeaton	1.00228300	
Grain tin	Do.	1.00248300	
Tin	Muschenbroek	1.00284000	
Soft solder; lead 2, tin 1	Smeaton	1.00250800	
Zinc 8, tin 1, a little hammered	Do.	1.00269200	
Lead	Lavoisier and Laplace	1.00284836	$\frac{1}{351}$
Do.	Smeaton	1.00286700	
Zinc	Do.	1.00294200	
Zinc, hammered out half inch per foot	Do.	1.00301100	
Glass from 32° to 212°	Dulong and Petit	1.00086130	$\frac{1}{1161}$
Do. from 212° to 392°	Do. do.	1.00091827	$\frac{1}{1089}$
Do. from 392° to 572°	Do. do.	1.000101114	$\frac{1}{987}$

Note.—"The last two measurements by an air thermometer."

"To obtain the expansion in volume, multiply the above decimal quantities by 3, or divide the denominators of the vulgar fractions by 3; the quotient in either case is the dilatation sought."

"We see that a condensed metal, the particles of which have been forcibly approximated by the wire-drawing process, expands more, as might be expected, than metals in a looser state of aggregation."

It would appear from the foregoing table, that in many instances there is a relation between the expansion or enlargement of metals and their fusibility, or disposition to melt, as, in general, those which are most fusible are also the most expansible.

Advantage is taken by some artizans of the expansion of solid bodies by heat. The parts of large vessels for holding fluids, such as are used by brewers and other manufacturers, are firmly bound together by strong iron hoops; these hoops, which are at first made too small to fit, are heated until they are sufficiently enlarged; they are then driven on, and suddenly cooled, by throwing water upon them; the contraction of the iron, which ensues on cooling, brings the parts of the vessels into closer contact than they could easily be brought by other means, and fixes the hoops firmly round them.

The parts of carriage wheels are bound together in a similar way; the iron band, or tire, is made a little smaller than the circumference of the wooden part of the wheel: being put on while it is enlarged by heat, it is suddenly cooled, and by its contraction binds the parts of the compound wheel together with great force.

The force with which metals expand when heated, and contract when cooled, is capable of overcoming powerful resistance. This may be illustrated in regard to contraction, by an experiment which succeeded some years since at the *Conservatoire des Arts et Metiers*, in Paris. The two side walls of a gallery at that place, having been pressed outwards by the weight of the floors and roof, M. Molard proposed making several holes in the walls, opposite to each other, through which strong iron bars were introduced so as to cross the apartment, their ends projecting outside the walls. Strong circular plates of iron were screwed on to these projecting ends. The bars were then heated, by which their ends were made to project farther beyond the walls, permitting the circular iron plates to be advanced, which they were until they again touched the walls. The bars, on cooling, contracted, and drew the walls which were receding from each other, closer together. This process being several times repeated, the walls were made to re-assume their proper perpendicular position, and might easily have been curved inwards, by the application of the same means.

The sudden expansion of bodies by heat occasions some effects which require to be guarded against. Thus, glass is very liable to break when heat is applied to it, on account of the unequal expansion which is occasioned. Glass being a bad conductor of heat, when one surface of any vessel or plate of this substance has its temperature suddenly raised, that surface is expanded, but the heat not being able to pass quickly through to the other surface, that part is not at all or but very little expanded, and the unequal expansion of the two surfaces occasions the glass to break. From what has been said, it will appear that there is most danger where the glass is very thick: boiling water may be poured into a very thin glass vessel without danger, because the heat passes through thin glass in time to make both its surfaces stretch equally. Looking-glasses have often been broken by heating one surface with a candle or lamp; and electrical-machine plates have many times been destroyed by setting them before a fire, one surface being expanded by the heat of the fire, while the other is probably contracted by a current of cold air rushing towards the fire; the inequality of temperature producing inequality of expansion, occasions the glass to crack with considerable noise. So cold showers of rain and warm sunshine succeeding each other, occasion loss in sky-light windows.

Other brittle substances are liable to similar accidents from the same cause; heated plates of cast iron are very liable to be broken by suddenly pouring cold water upon them.

The expansion and contraction occasioned by variations of temperature in the metals forming the pendulums of clocks, and the balance-wheels of watches, have been found to occasion great irregularities in the movements of these machines. The rate of going, in common clocks, depends upon the length of the pendulum. When the pendulum is lengthened, by heat or any other cause, the clock goes slower; and when it is shortened the motion is quickened. The ball of a pendulum that vibrates seconds, being lowered one hundredth part of an inch, the clock will lose ten seconds in twenty-four hours. By the foregoing table of expansion, it may be found that a seconds pendulum, the length of which is 39.13929 inches, will be lengthened by an increase of temperature equal to 30° of Fahrenheit's scale, $\frac{1}{128}$th part of an inch, which will occasion an error of eight seconds in twenty-four hours. Various contrivances have been introduced for the purpose of remedying these defects, by making the expansibility of some metals counteract that of others.

The first of these was the invention of

Graham, and consisted in substituting for the usual bob of the pendulum, a glass cylinder, about six inches deep, holding about ten or twelve pounds of mercury. When the suspending steel rod expanded by heat so as to lengthen the pendulum, the mercury, by its expansion, raised the centre of oscillation as much as the increased length of the steel rod occasioned it to be depressed. But the plan most usually adopted for clocks, is the invention of Harrison, and is called the *gridiron pendulum*; it consists of a combination of bars, three of which are of steel, and two compounded of zinc and silver. These are so arranged, and the weight is suspended in such a way, that the expansion occasioned by heat in the steel is counteracted by the expansion of the other metal, so as to keep the pendulum always of the same length.

The contrivance applied by Arnold to watches, for the purpose of preventing the injurious effects of expansion and contraction, is upon the same principle, and is called the *compensation balance*, in the construction of which, interrupted concentric rings of different metals are joined together, so that the expansion of one counteracts the expansion of the other.

The expansibility of fluids by heat is still greater than that of solids, and the differences which they exhibit among themselves are more striking. Mercury does not expand so much as water, water not so much as spirit of wine, and spirit of wine is not so expansible as ether.

The following TABLE *of the expansions produced in liquids by being heated from 32° to 212° is from* Dr. Ure's Dictionary of Chemistry.

Liquid	Observer	Expansion	Fraction
Mercury	Dalton	0.020000	$\frac{1}{50}$
Do.	Lord Charles Cavendish	0.018870	$\frac{1}{53}$
Do.	Deluc	0.018000	$\frac{1}{55}$
Do.	General Roy	0.017000	$\frac{1}{59}$
Do.	Shuckburgh	0.01851	$\frac{1}{54}$
Do.	Lavoisier and Laplace	0.01810	$\frac{1}{55.22}$
Do.	Haellstroem	0.0181800	$\frac{1}{55}$
Do.	Dulong and Petit	0.0180180	$\frac{1}{55.50}$
Do.	Do. from 212° to 392°	0.0181331	$\frac{1}{55.22}$
Do.	Do. from 392° to 572°	0.0188700	$\frac{1}{53}$
Do.	Do. in Glass from 32° to 212°	0.015432	$\frac{1}{64.8}$
Do.	Do. Do. from 212° to 392°	0.015680	$\frac{1}{63.75}$
Do.	Do. Do. from 392° to 572°	0.0158280	$\frac{1}{62.18}$
Water	Kirwain, from 39° its maximum density	0.04332	$\frac{1}{23.33}$
Muriatic Acid (sp. gr. 1.137.)	Dalton*	0.0600	$\frac{1}{17}$
Nitric Acid (sp. gr. 1.40)	Do.	0.1100	$\frac{1}{9}$
Sulphuric Acid (sp. gr. 1.85)	Do.	0.0600	$\frac{2}{7}$
Alcohol	Do.	0.1100	$\frac{1}{9}$
Water	Do.	0.0460	$\frac{1}{22}$
Water saturated with common salt	Do.	0.0500	$\frac{1}{20}$
Sulphuric Æther	Do.	0.0700	$\frac{1}{14}$
Fixed Oils	Do.	0.0800	$\frac{1}{125}$
Oil of Turpentine	Do.	0.0700	$\frac{1}{41}$
Water, saturated with common salt	Robison	0.05198	$\frac{1}{19}$

Ex. The expansion of a liquid may be strikingly shown, by filling a glass bulb, having a long tube attached to it, with the liquid, so that it may rise a small part of the way upwards in the tube; the bulb being set upon a stand, and heat applied under it, the bulk of the liquid will be enlarged, as will be seen by its rising higher in the tube. This effect is produced notwithstanding the expansion of the glass which occasions its capacity to be enlarged.

Ex. Or the expansion of water may be shown by partly filling a bulb and tube, like that described in the last experiment, with coloured water: immersion in a jar of hot water will occasion the water contained in the bulb and tube to expand and ascend higher. *(Fig. 3.)*

Those liquids are the most expansible which require the least heat to make them boil.

Ex. Equal quanties of heat applied to liquids do not occasion equal degrees of expansion: this may be shown by ap-

---

* The quantities given by Mr. Dalton are, probably, too great, as is certainly the case with Mercury; his experiments being, perhaps, modified by his hypothetical notions.

HEAT.

fig. 3.

plying the heat of a spirit lamp to a liquid contained in a bulb, such as described in the last experiment, differing only in having its tube divided into a number of equal parts. The number of divisions past which the liquid rises in the first five minutes having been observed, the same heat applied during five minutes more will occasion a greater expansion; and, consequently, the liquid rising in the tube will pass by a greater number of divisions in the second than it did in the first five minutes. Every successive portion of heat applied produces an increased effect, until the water arrives at the boiling point. In explaining this fact, it is said that the particles of the fluid have existing among them a certain force of cohesive attraction, which resists the expansive effects of heat; the first portions of heat applied having most of this resistance opposed to them, their effects are proportionably lessened; while succeeding quantities, having less resistance to overcome, produce increased degrees of expansion. The irregularities in the expansion of quicksilver are less than those of any other fluid.

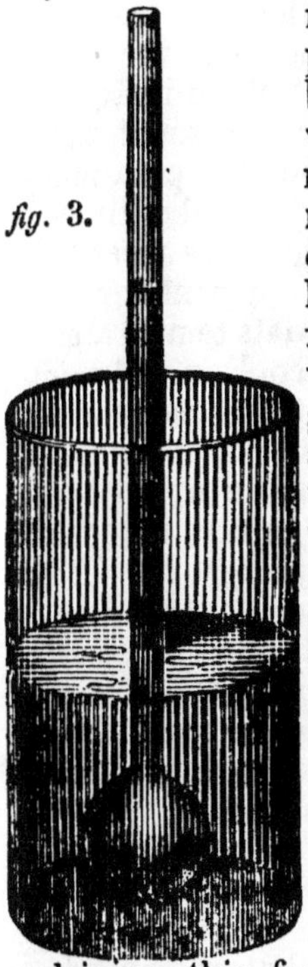

Count Rumford ascertained the contraction of water for every $22\frac{1}{2}°$ in cooling from 212° to 32°, the results being as follows:—

In Cooling $22\frac{1}{2}°$ from 212° or to $189\frac{1}{2}$ 18 parts.
"   " $189\frac{1}{2}$ "   167   16.2 "
"   "   167   " $144\frac{1}{2}$ 13.8 "
"   " $144\frac{1}{2}$ "   122   11.5 "
"   "   122   " $99\frac{1}{2}$ 9.3 "
"   " $99\frac{1}{2}$ "   77   7.1 "
"   "   77   " $54\frac{1}{2}$ 3.9 "
"   " $54\frac{1}{2}$ "   32   0.2 "

The very great irregularity at the bottom of the table will be adverted to in considering the remarkable peculiarity of water by which it is occasioned. It appears by the above table, that the expansion occasioned by heating water $22\frac{1}{2}°$ nearest the boiling point is almost five times as great as is produced by the heating it $22\frac{1}{2}°$ from about the natural medium temperature.

De Luc tried the relative expansibilities of a number of different liquids, by putting them into thermometer tubes: the scale which he used was that of Reaumur, upon which 80° indicates the boiling point of water, and 0° the melting point of ice. The results are expressed in the following TABLE, to which are added, by Dr. Ure, the corresponding indications according to the Centigrade and Fahrenheit Thermometers.

| Mercury. | | | Olive Oil. | Es. Oil of Chamomile. | Oil of Thyme. | Alcohol. | Brine. | Water. |
R.	Cent.	Fahr.						
80°	100°	212°	80°	80°	80°	80°	80°	80°
75	$93\frac{3}{4}$	$200\frac{3}{4}$	71.6	71.7	74.3	73.8	74.1	71
70	87.5	$189\frac{1}{2}$	69.4	69.5	68.8	67.8	68.4	62
65	81	$178\frac{1}{4}$	64.4	64.3	63.5	61.9	62.6	53.5
60	75	167	59.3	59.1	58.3	56.2	57.1	45.8
55	$68\frac{1}{4}$	$155\frac{3}{4}$	54.2	53.9	53.3	50.7	51.7	38.5
50	$62\frac{1}{2}$	$144\frac{1}{2}$	49.2	48.8	48.3	45.3	46.6	32
45	$56\frac{1}{4}$	$133\frac{1}{4}$	44.0	43.6	43.4	40.2	41.2	26.1
40	50	122	39.2	38.6	38.4	35.1	36.3	20.5
35	$43\frac{3}{4}$	$110\frac{3}{4}$	34.2	33.6	33.5	30.3	31.3	15.9
30	$37\frac{1}{2}$	$99\frac{1}{2}$	29.3	28.7	28.6	25.6	26.5	11.2
25	$31\frac{1}{4}$	$88\frac{1}{4}$	24.3	23.8	23.8	21.0	21.9	7.3
20	25	77	19.3	18.9	19.0	16.5	17.3	4.1
15	$18\frac{3}{4}$	$65\frac{3}{4}$	14.4	14.1	14.2	12.2	12.8	1.6
10	$12\frac{1}{2}$	$54\frac{1}{2}$	9.5	9.3	9.4	7.9	8.4	0.2
5	$6\frac{1}{4}$	$43\frac{1}{4}$	4.7	4.6	4.7	3.9	4.2	0.4
0	0	32	0.0	0.0	0.0	0.0	0.0	0.0
5	$6\frac{1}{4}$	$20\frac{3}{4}$				−3.9	−1.8	
−10	$12\frac{1}{2}$	$9\frac{1}{2}$				−7.7	−8.1	

There are a few partial exceptions to the expansion of bodies by heat, and their contraction by cold, of which water presents the most remarkable. This fluid contracts in cooling until it arrives at a certain point, and then expands as if heat were applied. This property of water was first observed by the Florentine Academicians, in cooling a thermometer glass, filled with water, by immersion in a mixture of ice and salt; but De Luc afterwards investigated the subject, and considered the greatest density of the water to be attained when it arrived at 40°, as it ceased to contract from that point, although the cooling process continued; on the contrary, expansion was found to result both from the addition and the abstraction of heat, after the water arrived at the above-mentioned temperature. Sir Charles Blagden and Mr. Gilpin discovered that De Luc had omitted to make the proper correction for the expansion of the glass; which, when they had done, they found that water arrives at its greatest density on being cooled to 39° of Fahrenheit. Dr. Hope considers the greatest density to be at 39° 5', and the French chemists at 40°. Taking the temperature at which the greatest density occurs to be 40°, the density of water at 48° and 32° will be the same.

It was ascertained by the experiments of Sir Charles Blagden, Mr. Dalton, and M. Gay-Lussac, that the expansion of water continues below 32°, when it is cooled lower than that temperature without freezing; and it was expanded as much in some of the experiments alluded to, as it would have been if heated to 75°.

The enlargement of bulk occurring in water as it cools, from 40° to the freezing point, was ascribed by Hooke, and afterwards by Dalton, to the contraction of the glass vessels which contain the water used in the experiments. That the bulb of a thermometer used in such experiments does contract by being cooled, contributing in some measure to raise the liquid in the tube, cannot be doubted, but from other experiments and considerations yet to be stated, it appears certain that water expands on cooling, independently of the contraction of the vessel in which it is contained.

Dr. Hope filled a glass jar, 8½ inches deep and 4½ inches wide, with water at 32°; one thermometer was suspended nearly in the axis, with its bulb about half an inch from the bottom, and another at the same distance from the surface of the fluid. The jar being exposed to a temperature of 60°, gradually rose to 38°, during which increase of temperature the lower thermometer was at least one degree higher than the thermometer at the surface, which indicated that the density of the water must have increased along with its temperature; for if the water had expanded with the increase of heat, it would have ascended to the surface, and the uppermost thermometer would have had its temperature the most raised. In cooling water to 32°, the temperature of the thermometer near the bottom of the jar was still found to be higher than the upper one. While water is cooling to 40°, its coldest particles are always at the bottom; but when it arrives at 40°, it remains there until the whole of the fluid arrives at the same point; and then in cooling lower, the colder particles collect at the surface, those at the bottom being four degrees warmer.

These experiments of Dr. Hope prove that water is most dense at a considerable number of degrees above the freezing point, and that it expands as it cools to that point.

The expansive force of water on freezing is well known, as water-pipes and vessels filled with it are often burst by its force. Even in our bed-rooms, in very cold weather, water-bottles are frequently broken, if they be quite full of water, and have such narrow necks as to prevent the free expansion of the fluid in freezing. The flat stones of pavements are frequently raised out of their places by the freezing of the water beneath them, trunks of trees are split, and rocks are rent asunder by the same force. The agency of frost is very beneficial in occasioning the substance of rocks and of soils to moulder to powder, thereby fitting them better for the purposes of vegetation. A strong brass globe, the cavity of which was only one inch in diameter, was used by the Florentine Academicians, for the purpose of trying the expansive force of congelation, by which it was burst, although the force required was calculated to exceed 27,720lbs. Experiments were tried by Major Williams, at Quebec, in one of which an iron plug, nearly 3lbs. in weight, was projected from a bomb-shell to the distance of 415 feet; and in another, the shell was burst by the freezing of the water which it contained.

Several attempts have been made to

explain the expansion of water in freezing; the most plausible of which is, that given by De Mairan, who supposed that the particles when they crystallize and assume the solid state, have a tendency to unite by certain sides in preference to others, arranging themselves so as to form right lines at determinate angles. This arrangement of the particles requiring more space, and leaving numerous vacuities, the bulk of the whole must necessarily be enlarged.

The most important effects result from the remarkable property of water which has been described. If the density of water continued to decrease until it arrived at the freezing point, ice would be heavier than water, and as soon as formed would subside to the bottom in successive flakes, until the whole of the water, however deep, should become solid. The effects of such an arrangement can easily be conceived. Climates which, according to the present state of things, are the delightful abodes of innumerable animated beings, would be rendered unfavourable to their existence, and must inevitably become dreary and desolate. On the contrary, since water expands previously to its freezing, ice is lighter than water, and floats upon its surface, protecting the water below from the influence of frost.

Aëriform bodies in their expansion differ from solids and fluids, in being uniformly affected by the same quantities of heat applied to them at all temperatures, which is thus explained. The attractive force that exists in solids and fluids resisting the expansive effect of heat, the first portions applied have most of this resistance opposed to them, and therefore produce less expansion than succeeding portions, which have less resistance to contend with; but as there is no cohesive attraction existing among the particles of aëriform bodies, there is no resistance opposed to the expansive power of heat upon them; and consequently all of them undergo the same degrees of expansion with the same degrees of heat; and the same effect is produced upon all of them by equal quantities of heat applied at all different temperatures.

The following TABLE gives the changes of bulk produced upon 100,000 parts of air, by every additional degree of Fahrenheit, from 32° to 100; and by every additional ten degrees afterwards to 210°.

Temp.	Bulk.	Temp.	Bulk.
32	100,000	73	108,528
33	100,208	74	108,736
34	100,416	75	108,944
35	100,624	76	109,152
36	100,833	77	109,360
37	101,040	78	109,568
38	101,248	79	109,776
39	101,459	80	109,984
40	101,666	81	110,192
41	101,872	82	110,400
42	102,080	83	110,608
43	102,290	84	110,816
44	102,496	85	111,024
45	102,708	86	111,232
46	102,916	87	111,440
47	103,124	88	111,648
48	103,333	89	111,856
49	103,536	90	112,064
50	103,749	91	112,272
51	103,952	92	112,480
52	104,166	93	112,388
53	104,368	94	112,896
54	104,576	95	113,104
55	104,791	96	113,312
56	104,992	97	113,520
57	105,200	98	113,728
58	105,408	99	113,936
59	105,616	100	114,144
60	105,824	110	116,224
61	106,032	120	118,304
62	106,210	130	120,384
63	106,448	140	122,464
64	106,656	150	124,544
65	106,864	160	126,624
66	107,072	170	128,704
67	107,280	180	130,784
68	107,488	190	132,864
69	107,696	200	134,944
70	107,904	210	137,024
71	108,112	212	137,440
72	108,320		

Ex. The expansion of air may be pleasingly illustrated by a simple apparatus, such as is shown at *fig.* 4.

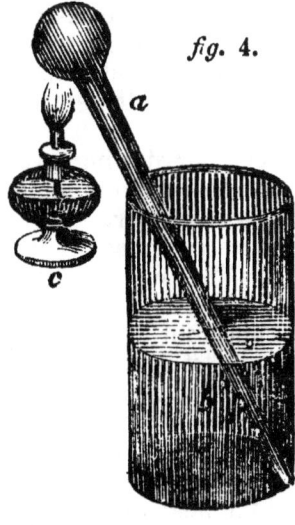

fig. 4.

The bulb with the long tube *a*, full of air, has its open end plunged in the jar of water *b*; the heat of the spirit lamp *c* being applied, the air will be expanded by the heat, and a portion of it will be expelled; it will rise through the water of the jar and escape: the lamp being removed, as soon as the remaining air cools, it will contract to its original bulk, and the pressure of the air on the surface of the water in the jar will force water up into the bulb with great velocity, and the quantity of water that enters the bulb will be equal in bulk to the air expelled.

Convincing demonstrations of the power, wisdom, and goodness of Providence are obtained by watching the silent, and often unobserved, but irresistible agency of heat, in the distribution of temperature over the globe. Some examples of this may be adduced.

The surface of the earth in many parts of the world would be excessively and injuriously heated by the sun's rays, if means were not provided for withdrawing portions of this heat. The transparent air not being heated in the same degree by the influence of the sun, and there being a strong tendency to an equilibrium in heat, the stratum of air nearest to the earth receives a portion of its excessive heat; in consequence of which it is expanded, and rendered lighter than the less heated air above, and must therefore ascend, since it is a law of nature that light fluids ascend through heavier; another portion of colder air descends to the surface of the earth, and is warmed, and made to ascend. Thus the earth is cooled, and refreshed by the agency of air, the heated particles of which are, by the principle of expansion, enabled to ascend into the higher regions of the atmosphere; from whence they are wafted away to colder climates, to mitigate the extremes of the seasons there.

Again, cold air flowing over the surface of the ocean, from polar regions towards the equator, is very much warmed in its progress; if it were not, the climate that we inhabit would be less genial than it is. As the water of the ocean does not freeze, except in very high latitudes, it is considerably warmer than the air which passes over it. On account of the strong tendency to an equilibrium, before mentioned, the air which is nearest to the water receives a portion of the heat which the water contains, above that of the air: the portions of air so heated ascend, while the portions of water, which are lowered in temperature, contract in bulk, become heavier, and descend; other warmer portions of water ascend to the surface, and other colder portions of air descend; and this process goes on as long as the water is warmer than the air.

But, perhaps, some readers may find difficulty in believing that such small differences in the relative weights or specific gravities of different portions of the same fluid, should enable some to ascend, and others to descend, producing such important effects in the economy of nature. A few experiments may tend to impress conviction on their minds.

Ex. Fill a tall glass with hot water, and take up in a dropping tube a little cold water, slightly coloured with litmus, or any other dye, that it may be better seen, and let it fall gently into the hot water, the end of the dropping tube being held below the surface, and the coloured water will fall to the bottom, because being cold its specific gravity is rather greater than that of the hot water.

Perhaps it may be objected to this experiment, that the colouring matter added to the cold water must tend to increase its weight. Any error arising from this cause may easily be guarded against by making the two fluids, while cold, of the same specific gravity: the difference between cold and hot will still be found to produce the same effect.

Ex. Fill a small glass bulb, having a narrow neck, with port wine, or with a mixture of water with a small quantity of spirit of wine, coloured with tincture of litmus, and put the bulb so filled into a tall, narrow, glass jar, which must then be filled up with cold water; immediately an ascending current will be seen proceeding from the bulb, the coloured fluid will accumulate on the surface of the water in the jar, while colourless water will be seen accumulating at the bottom of the bulb. By close inspection, the descending current may also be observed; and it will be obvious that the coloured and the colourless liquids pass each other in the narrow neck of the bulb, without mingling. In a short time the whole of the coloured liquid will have ascended, and the bulb will be entirely filled with clear water.

It is proved by this experiment that a very small difference in the specific gravities, in two portions of a fluid, enables the light portion to ascend, and the heavier to descend. As spirit of wine is considerably lighter than water, an admixture of it, in any proportion, produces a fluid lighter than water; but the quantity of spirit required in this experiment is very small, and therefore the difference of specific gravity must be very small also. It is very remarkable, that so minute a difference should not only enable the one portion to ascend, and the other to descend; but also to pass each other in the very narrow neck of the bulb without mingling.

Chapter IV.

Application of the Doctrine to Thermometers.

The expansion of bodies by heat and their contraction by cold, afford the means of measuring degrees of temperature. The instrument used for this purpose, and which acts upon these principles, is called a *thermometer*, and was originally invented by an Italian physician of the seventeenth century, named Santorio; who used air as a measure of the variations of temperature. This instrument is now called an *air-thermometer*, and consists of a glass vessel or bottle, with a broad base, and narrow neck, containing a coloured liquid *a* (*fig.* 5); a long tube having a glass bulb blown at one end *b*; the other extremity of the tube being open, and plunged in the coloured liquid; and a scale of equal parts *c*. Heat is applied to the bulb to expel a part of the air, which permits a portion of the coloured fluid to rise in the tube: this fluid column indicates the slightest changes of temperature by rising when it is diminished, and falling when it is increased; because every increase of temperature expands the air in the bulb, occasioning it to press upon the fluid column and force it down, while any decrease of temperature contracts the bulk of the air, and permits the fluid to rise. This instrument is not capable of measuring variations of temperature through any very considerable range, and it is liable to other objections; yet, notwithstanding, it is still applicable, from its great delicacy, to many purposes.

The members of the *Academia del Cimento* substituted spirit of wine, coloured, instead of air; and, to prevent any effect from being produced by the variations of atmospheric pressure, the tube was hermetically sealed. Dr. Halley and Sir Isaac Newton used mercury as the thermometric fluid, which is now most generally employed; but spirit-thermometers are also in use. The mercurial is better adapted for high, the spirit for low temperatures.

Whichever fluid is used, the shape of the instrument is the same, consisting of a tube, having a bulb blown at one end of a globular or cylindrical shape, the latter being considered the best. *Fig.* 6 represents a mercurial thermometer, with part of its scale moveable. The tube ought to have an equal bore throughout; but as tubes of this kind can rarely if ever be obtained, it is necessary to ascertain the inequalities of the tube, that they may afterwards be adapted to the scale. To divide the tube into spaces of equal capacity, it is dipped into quicksilver, until a column about half an inch in length enters the bore; this is removed to about two inches from the end, at which the bulb is to be made; then marking the tube with a file or diamond, it is laid upon the brass, ivory, or wood, which is to form the scale intended to be applied, so that the lower end of the mercurial column may correspond with the lower end of the scale, the upper end of the column being marked with a fine point upon the scale; the tube is to be a little inclined and gently shaken, until the lower part of the mercurial column stands exactly where the upper part was before; the place of the upper part must then be marked upon the scale, and the process must be continued until the tube is divided to a sufficient height.

A bulb having been blown upon the instrument in the usual way, with the aid of a blow-pipe, in order to fill it with quicksilver, a piece of paper is tied over the open end of the tube in the manner of a funnel, into which a quantity of quicksilver is put; the bulb is heated over a lamp to expel the air, and when the portion of air which remains cools, the quicksilver descends and partly fills the bulb; heat is again applied until the quicksilver boils,—this occasions the more effectual expulsion of the air; on cooling a larger quantity of the fluid metal is made to enter into the instrument. A sufficient quantity having been introduced, and the whole having been properly boiled, heat is applied until the mercury begins to overflow at the extremity of the tube, previously drawn to a fine point; flame is urged upon it by a blow-pipe, and it is hermetically sealed, or melted and joined to exclude the air.

To regulate whatever scale may be applied to the instrument, it is necessary to ascertain the points in the tube at which the mercurial column stands when cooled to the freezing, and heated to the boiling, of water. For this purpose, the instrument is immersed in melting ice or snow, and permitted to remain there for some time, until the quicksilver becomes stationary at one place, which is the freezing point; a mark is made at that point upon the glass. By allowing the instrument to remain for some time in boiling water, the mercury, after having ascended through a large proportion of the tube, becomes stationary at one place, which is the boiling point; if the calibre, or bore, of the tube is equal throughout, the space between these two points upon the scale, to be applied, according to Fahrenheit, is divided into 180 equal parts, thirty-two of the same equal divisions being placed below the freezing point. In other words, the scale invented by Fahrenheit, which is in general use in this country, commences at 32° below the freezing point of water, and has the boiling point at 212°. It is believed that Fahrenheit took his *zero* or commencement of his scale from the degree of cold produced by mixing snow and common salt, that being the greatest degree of cold known in his time; although a considerably greater degree of cold may be produced by mixing the same or other ingredients. If the tube is unequal in the bore, use must be made in the graduation of the scale, of points obtained by dividing the tube into parts of equal capacity, in the manner already described.

The scale called Reaumur's, which has been much used on the Continent, commences at the freezing point of water which is marked 0, between which and the boiling point are eighty equal divisions or degrees, the point at which water boils being at the 80th degree. Each degree of Fahrenheit's scale being equal to $\frac{4}{9}$ of a degree of Reaumur's, to find the correspondence between these scales, it is only necessary to multiply the number of degrees of Fahrenheit, above or below the freezing point, by 4, and divide by 9; the sum obtained will indicate the number of degrees upon Reaumur's scale.

Fahrenheit.   Reaumur.
$50° - 32 = 18 \times 4 = 72 \div 9 = 8°$.
$185° - 32 = 153 \times 4 = 612 \div 9 = 68°$.

To make those of Reaumur correspond with Fahrenheit, the rule is to multiply by 9 and divide by 4.

Reaumur.   Fahrenheit.
$8° \times 9 = 72 \div 4 = 18 + 32 = 50°$.
$68° \times 9 = 612 \div 4 = 153 + 32 = 185°$.

Another scale, which is now extensively used, particularly in France, is that of Celsius, and is more simple than any: it begins at the freezing of water, between which and the boiling of the same fluid there are 100 equal divisions upon the scale; so that the boiling point is at the 100th degree. This instrument is now called the Centigrade Thermometer, and is by many preferred to the others, the divisions on its scale being considered the most natural. The graduation of Fahrenheit, however, has some important advantages over the others: its divisions being small, there is the less necessity for stating fractional parts; and its commencement being low, it is seldom required to state negative degrees.

The degrees on Fahrenheit's scale, being each equal to $\frac{5}{9}$ of a degree, on the Centigrade scale, to find the correspondence of the degrees of the former with those of the latter, multiply the degrees, above or below the freezing of water, by 5 and divide by 9, thus:—

Fahrenheit.   Centigrade.
$86° - 32° = 54 \times 5 = 270 \div 9 = 30°$.
$176° - 32° = 144 \times 5 = 720 \div 9 = 80°$.

To reduce the degrees of the Centigrade scale to those of Fahrenheit, multiply by 9 and divide by 5.

Centigrade.   Fahrenheit.
$30° \times 9 = 270 \div 5 = 54 + 32 = 86°$.
$80° \times 9 = 720 \div 5 = 144 + 32 = 176°$.

HEAT.

The following TABLE gives the correspondence between the degrees of the different scales mentioned, without the trouble of calculation.

Fahr.	Reaum.	Centi.
212	80	100
211	79.5	99.4
210	79.1	98.8
209	78.6	98.3
208	78.2	97.7
207	77.7	97.2
206	77.3	96.6
205	76.8	96.1
204	76.4	95.5
203	76	95
202	75.5	94.4
201	75.1	93.8
200	74.6	93.3
199	74.2	92.7
198	73.7	92.2
197	73.3	91.6
196	72.8	91.1
195	72.4	90.5
194	72	90
193	71.5	89.4
192	71.1	88.8
191	70.6	88.3
190	70.2	87.7
189	69.7	87.2
188	69.3	86.6
187	68.8	86.1
186	68.4	85.5
185	68	85
184	67.5	84.4
183	67.1	83.8
182	66.6	83.3
181	66.2	82.7
180	65.7	82.2
179	65.3	81.6
178	64.8	81.1
177	64.4	80.5
176	64	80
175	63.5	79.4
174	63.1	78.8
173	62.6	78.3
172	62.2	77.7
171	61.7	77.2
170	61.3	76.6
169	60.8	76.1
168	60.4	75.5
167	60	75
166	59.5	74.4
165	59.1	73.8
164	58.6	73.3
163	58.2	72.7
162	57.7	72.2
161	57.3	71.6
160	56.8	71.1
159	56.4	70.5
158	56	70
157	55.5	69.4
156	55.1	68.8
155	54.6	68.3
154	54.2	67.7
153	53.7	67.2
152	53.3	66.6
151	52.8	66.1
150	52.4	65.5
149	52	65
148	51.5	64.4
147	51.1	63.8
146	50.6	63.3
145	50.2	62.7
144	49.7	62.2
143	49.3	61.6
142	48.8	61.1
141	48.4	60.5
140	48	60
139	47.5	59.4
138	47.1	58.8
137	46.6	58.3
136	46.2	57.7
135	45.7	57.2
134	45.3	56.6
133	44.8	56.1
132	44.4	55.5
131	44	55
130	43.5	54.4
129	43.1	53.8
128	42.6	53.3
127	42.2	52.7
126	41.7	52.2
125	41.3	51.6
124	40.8	51.1
123	40.4	50.5
122	40	50
121	39.5	49.4
120	39.1	48.8
119	38.6	48.3
118	38.2	47.7
117	37.7	47.2
116	37.3	46.6
115	36.8	46.1
114	36.4	45.5
113	36	45
112	35.5	44.4
111	35.1	43.8
110	34.6	43.3
109	34.2	42.7
108	33.7	42.2
107	33.3	41.6
106	32.8	41.1
105	32.4	40.5
104	32	40
103	31.5	39.4
102	31.1	38.8
101	30.6	38.3
100	30.2	37.7
99	29.7	37.2
98	29.3	36.6
97	28.8	36.1
96	28.4	35.5
95	28	35
94	27.5	34.4
93	27.1	33.8
92	26.6	33.3
91	26.2	32.7
90	25.7	32.2
89	25.3	31.6
88	24.8	31.1
87	24.4	30.5
86	24	30
85	23.5	29.4
84	23.1	28.8
83	22.6	28.3
82	22.2	27.7
81	21.7	27.2
80	21.3	26.6
79	20.8	26.1
78	20.4	25.5
77	20	25
76	19.5	24.4
75	19.1	23.8
74	18.6	23.3
73	18.2	22.7
72	17.7	22.2
71	17.3	21.6
70	16.8	21.1
69	16.4	20.5
68	16	20
67	15.5	19.4
66	15.1	18.8
65	14.6	18.3
64	14.2	17.7
63	13.7	17.2
62	13.3	16.6
61	12.8	16.1
60	12.4	15.5
59	12	15
58	11.5	14.4
57	1.1	13.8
56	10.6	13.3
55	10.2	12.7
54	9.7	12.2
53	9.3	11.6
52	8.8	11.1
51	8.4	10.5
50	8	10
49	7.5	9.4
48	7.1	8.8
47	6.6	8.3
46	6.2	7.7
45	5.7	7.2
44	5.3	6.6
43	4.8	6.1
42	4.4	5.5
41	4	5
40	3.5	4.4
39	3.1	3.8
38	2.6	3.3
37	2.2	2.7
36	1.7	2.2
35	1.3	1.6
34	0.8	1.1
33	0.4	0.5
32	0	0
31	−0.4	−0.5
30	−0.8	−1.1
29	−0.3	−1.6
28	−1.7	−2.2
27	−2.2	−2.7
26	−2.6	−3.3
25	−3.1	−3.8
24	−3.5	−4.4
23	−4	−5
22	−4.4	−5.5
21	−4.8	−6.1
20	−5.3	−6.6
19	−5.7	−7.2
18	−6.2	−7.7
17	−6.6	−8.3
16	−7.1	−8.8
15	−7.5	−9.4
14	−8	−10
13	−8.4	−10.5
12	−8.8	−11.1
11	−9.3	−11.6
10	−9.7	−12.2
9	−10.2	−12.7
8	−10.6	−13.3
7	−11.1	−13.8
6	−11.5	−14.4
5	−12	−15
4	−12.4	−15.5
3	−12.8	−16.1
2	−13.3	−16.6
1	−13.7	−17.2
0	−14.2	−17.7
−1	−14.6	−18.3
−2	−15.1	−18.8
−3	−15.5	−19.4
−4	−16	−20
−5	−16.4	−20.5
−6	−16.8	−21.1
−7	−17.3	−21.8
−8	−17.7	−22.2
−9	−18.2	−22.7
−10	−18.6	−23.3
−11	−19.1	−23.8
−12	−19.5	−24.4
−13	−20	−25
−14	−20.4	−25.5
−15	−20.8	−26.1
−16	−21.3	−26.6
−17	−21.7	−27.2
−18	−22.2	−27.7
−19	−22.6	−28.3
−20	−23.1	−28.8
−21	−23.5	−29.4
−22	−24	−30
−23	−24.4	−30.5
−24	−24.8	−31.1
−25	−25.3	−31.6
−26	−25.7	−32.2
−27	−26.2	−32.7
−28	−26.6	−33.3
−29	−27.1	−33.8
−30	−27.5	−34.4
−31	−28.4	−35
−32	−28	−35.5
−33	−28.8	−36.1
−34	−29.3	−36.6
−35	−29.7	−37.2
−36	−30.2	−37.7
−37	−30.6	−38.3
−38	−31.1	−38.8
−39	−31.5	−39.4
−40	−32	−40

Dr. Murray proposed a scale which he believed would combine all the advantages of other scales, without their disadvantages; his plan is to make the extreme points of his scale at the freezing and boiling of mercury, and to divide the space between into 1000 degrees.

As mercury expands more uniformly than any other fluid, and as there is a wider range between its freezing and boiling points, mercurial thermometers are most generally useful; but, when low degrees of temperature are to be measured, a thermometer containing coloured alcohol is the best adapted to the purpose, since it has not been found possible to make this fluid solid by any reduction of temperature yet effected.

Dr. Halley, Dr. Brook Taylor, Dr. Black, and other philosophers, have made numerous experiments to ascertain whether the expansion and contraction of mercury is the same at every temperature, for equal portions of heat applied or withdrawn. The experiment most generally made by them was to take a thermometer with a perfectly cylindrical tube, and having plunged it in hot water, to mark the stationary point of the fluid; they then observed where the fluid stood when plunged into an equal weight of cold water; and, lastly, they mixed the two portions of water together, and tried the temperature of the mixture: if the temperature indicated was the mean between the temperatures of the two fluids, they considered the indications of the thermometer, as to changes of temperature, to be correct. Many sources of error were to be guarded against in this experiment, and different conclusions were arrived at; De Luc's opinion was, that the thermometric fluids do not expand equally, with equal quantities of heat applied. The least deviation from regularity was observed in mercury. Equal weights of water at 200·7° and 45° being mixed together, the temperature was 2·5° lower than the arithmetical mean, and experiments tried with other temperatures gave similar results.

De Luc thought that experiments of the kind just stated could not be relied upon, as they rested on an assumption that the capacity of water for heat is the same throughout the whole range of temperature operated upon, while he believed that the capacity increased along with the temperature. On mixing two quantities of water at different temperatures, a diminution of capacity would therefore result, and heat would consequently be given out, which would occasion the temperature of the mixture to appear higher than it ought to do.

Dr. Crawford, in order to obviate this objection, exposed a thermometer equally to air cooled by snow to 32°, and heated by steam to 212°: the resulting temperature at which the instrument remained stationary fifteen minutes, was 121°, only one degree lower than the mean; and he thought that this deviation should be reduced, by admitting a correction for the effect of temperature on the quantity of fluid in the stem.

Experiments of a still greater accuracy have been made by Dr. Ure, and by MM. Dulong and Petit, which prove that the slight degree of inequality in the expansion of mercury in thermometer-tubes is compensated by the expansion of the glass, and also by the lessening mass of mercury remaining in the bulb as the temperature rises; so that the mercurial thermometer may be considered as an accurate indicator of changes of temperature.

Various modifications of the air thermometer have been introduced, of which Mr. Leslie's is considered the most useful*. It is called the differential thermometer, and consists of a long glass tube, twice bent at right angles, having a bulb at each extremity; the tube contains a quantity of sulphuric acid tinged with carmine. The original adjustment of this fluid is rather difficult, and requires care and dexterity. The instrument is furnished with a scale of 100 equal parts, and is fixed upon a wooden support. Both the bulbs of the instrument being exposed to the same temperature, it is not in the least affected; but as soon as one of the bulbs is exposed to a higher temperature than the other, the difference between them is delicately shewn by the falling of the coloured fluid below the bulb which is most heated. This instrument not being affected by the variations of atmospherical pressure, nor by fluctuations of temperature in the atmosphere, it is admirably fitted for experiments on radiant heat; its form is shewn at *fig*. 7.

Another modification of this instrument was introduced by Dr. Howard,

---

* Experimental Inquiry into the Nature and Propagation of Heat.

(*Journal of Science*, No. XVI.) which he considers more convenient. One of the

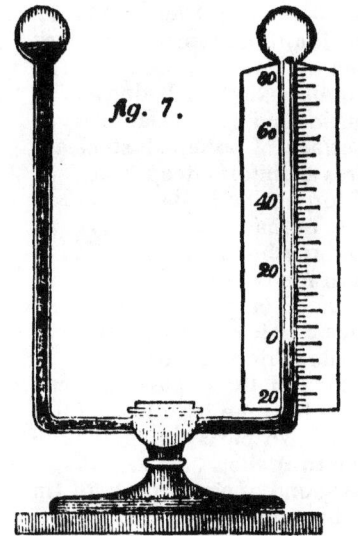

bulbs is made to stand higher than the other, and the included liquid is alcohol or ether coloured, which is made to boil for the purpose of excluding the air, previous to the closing of the instrument by the blow-pipe. (*Fig.* 8.)

Several instruments have been made, to indicate changes of temperature, upon the principle of the unequal expansion of different metals. Mr. Crichton of Glasgow, has combined small oblong plates of steel and zinc: the compound bar thus produced, is firmly secured at one end to a board; the other end is applied to a moveable index, so that the whole of the bending occasioned by the superior expansibility of the zinc over that of the steel, is exercised in moving the arms of the index along a graduated arc, and leaves them at the greatest deviation to the right or left of any observed temperature.

"An exquisite instrument," says Dr. Ure, "on the same principle has been invented by M. Breguet, member of the Academy of Sciences, and Board of Longitude of France. It consists of a narrow metallic slip, about $\frac{1}{100}$ of an inch thick, composed of silver and platina soldered together; and is coiled in a cylindrical form. The top of this spiral tube is suspended by a cross arm, and the bottom carries, in a horizontal position, a very delicate golden needle, which traverses as an index on a graduated circular plate. A steel stud rises in the centre of the tube, to prevent its oscillations from the central position. If the silver be on the outside of the spiral, then the influence of increased temperature will increase the curvature, and move the appended needle in the direction of the coil; while the action of cold will relax the coil, and move the needle in the opposite direction." The principle of these last-mentioned contrivances is clearly the same as that of Arnold's compensation balance, already alluded to.

Various modifications of the thermometer have been introduced, for the purpose of adapting it to particular purposes, which cannot here be described.

Of the contrivances for measuring high degrees of temperature, that of Wedgewood has been the most in use: its indications depend upon the contraction of pure clay when much heated. This reduction of bulk is first observed when the clay acquires a red heat, and continues to increase until vitrification ensues; the contraction of volume being permanent, and amounts, in the whole, to about one fourth. In order to take advantage of this property of clay, Mr. Wedgewood constructed a guage of brass, consisting of two straight pieces, two feet long, fixed upon a plate, a little nearer to each other at one end than at the other; the space between them at the widest end being five-tenths of an inch, and at the narrowest three-tenths. The converging pieces were divided into inches and tenths of inches. The pieces of clay, the contractions of which were to be measured, were of a cylindrical form, flattened on one side, and of such a size as to be exactly adapted to the wider end of the guage, so that it might slide farther in, in proportion, to the degree of heat applied to it.

The indications of this instrument, which he called the *Pyrometer*, from two Greek words signifying *measure of fire*, gave the comparative degrees of heat produced in different processes; but to obtain the utmost information which the instrument was capable of affording, it seemed absolutely necessary to apply a scale to it, the degrees on which should bear some certain proportion to the degrees on the scale of Fahrenheit.

Mr. Wedgewood observed that the heat which raised the temperature of Fahrenheit's thermometer from 50° to 212°, expanded a piece of silver from 0° to 8° of a certain scale, and that a heat which expanded the silver from 0° to 66° of its scale, corresponded to 2¼° of the clay or Wedgewood's scale. By these and similar experiments, he found that each degree of his Pyrometer is equal to 130° of Fahrenheit's scale. The temperature of a red heat, visible by daylight, which was found to correspond to 1077½°, was taken as the commencement of Wedgewood's scale.

The following TABLE, pointing out the effects upon bodies of different degrees of heat according to this and Fahrenheit's scales is taken from Murray's *System of Chemistry*.

	Wedg.	Fahren.
Extremity of the Scale of Wedgwood's Thermometer	240°	32277°
Greatest heat of an air furnace, 8 inches in diameter, which neither melted nor softened Nankin porcelain	160	21877
Chinese porcelain softened, best sort	156	21357
Cast iron, thoroughly melted	150	20577
Hessian crucible, melted	150	20577
Bristol porcelain, not melted	135	18627
Cast iron begins to melt	130	17977
Greatest heat of a common smith's forge	125	17327
Plate glass furnace, strongest heat	124	17197
Bow porcelain, vitrifies	121	16807
Chinese porcelain, softened, inferior sort	120	16677
Flint glass furnace, (strongest heat)	114	15897
Derby porcelain vitrifies	112	15637
Chelsea porcelain vitrifies	105	14727
Stone ware baked in	102	14337
Welding heat of iron (greatest)	95	13427
Worcester porcelain vitrifies	94	13297
Welding heat of iron (least)	90	12777
Cream-coloured ware baked in	86	12257
Flint glass furnace (weak heat)	70	10177
Working heat of plate glass	57	8487
Delft ware baked in	41	6407
Fine gold melts	32	5237
Settling heat of flint glass	29	4847
Fine silver melts	28	4717
Swedish copper melts	27	4587
Silver melts (Dr. Kennedy)	22	3937
Brass melts	21	3807
Heat, by which enamel colours are burnt on	6	1857
Red heat, fully visible in day-light		1077
Iron red hot in the twilight		884
Heat of a common fire		790
Iron bright red in the dark		752
Zinc melts		700

	Fahren.
Quicksilver boils (Irvine)	672
———————— (Dalton)	660
———————— (Crichton)	655
Lowest ignition of iron in the dark	635
Linseed oil boils	600
Lead melts (Guyton, Irvine)	594
Sulphuric acid boils (Dalton)	590
The surface of polished steel acquires a uniform deep blue	580
Oil of turpentine boils	560
Sulphur burns	—
Phosphorus boils	554
Bismuth melts (Irvine)	476
The surface of polished steel acquires a pale straw-colour	460
Tin melts (Crichton, Irvine)	442
A mixture of three parts tin and two of lead melts; also a mixture of two parts tin and one of bismuth melts	334
A compound of equal parts of tin and bismuth melts	283
Nitric acid boils	242
Sulphur melts	226
A saturated solution of salt boils	218
Water boils (the barometer being at 30 inches); also a compound of five of bismuth, three of tin, and two of lead melts	212
A compound of three parts of tin, five of lead, and eight of bismuth, melts rather below	210
Alcohol boils	174
Bees' wax melts	142
Spermaceti melts	133
Phosphorus melts	100
Ether boils	98
Heat of the human blood	98
Medium temperature of the globe	50
Ice melts	32
Milk freezes	30
Vinegar freezes at about	28
Strong wine freezes at about	20
A mixture of one part alcohol and three parts water freezes	7
A mixture of alcohol and water in equal quantities freezes	−7
A mixture of two parts alcohol and one part water freezes	−11
Melting point of quicksilver (Cavendish)	−39
Liquid ammonia crystallizes (Vauquelin)	−42
Nitric acid sp. gr. about 1.42 freezes (Cavendish)	−45
Sulphuric æther congeals (Vauquelin)	−47
Natural temperature observed by Mr. Hutchins at Hudson's Bay	−50
Ammoniacal gas condenses into a liquid (Guyton)	−54
Nitrous acid freezes	−56
Cold produced from diluted sulphuric acid and snow, the materials being at the temperature of 57	−78
Greatest artificial cold yet measured (Walker)	−91

It has been asserted by Guyton de Morveau*, that the indications of Wedgewood's pyrometer are not so high as they are made to appear; but he has certainly erred, in supposing that the red heat, at which Wedgewood commences his scale, is no higher than 517° of Fahrenheit; since oil and mercury are both capable of indicating higher degrees of heat, without exhibiting the least appearance of redness.

In Guyton de Morveau's pyrometer†, platina is used to measure high degrees of heat. The instrument alluded to, is formed of a mass of highly-baked white clay, having a groove in it for the purpose of receiving a rod or plate of platina, which, resting on the clay at one end, at the other presses against it the end of a bended lever, the longest arm of which is made, by the expansion occasioned by increased heat, to traverse a graduated arc, and thus indicates the rise of temperature.

Dr. Ure (*Chemical Dictionary*, p. 657) is of opinion that high degrees of heat may be measured by the expansion of air. "Since dry air augments in volume 3-8ths for 180 degrees, and since its progressive rate of expansion is probably uniform by uniform increments of heat, a pyrometer might easily be constructed on this principle. Form a bulb and tube of platinum of exactly the same form as a thermometer, and connect, with the extremity of the stem at right angles, a glass tube of uniform calibre, filled with mercury, and terminating below in a recurved bulb, like that of the Italian barometer. Graduate the glass tube into a series of spaces equivalent to 3-8ths of the total volume of the platina bulb, with 3-4ths of its stem. The other fourth may be supposed to be little influenced by the source of heat. On plunging the bulb, and 2-3rds of the stem into a furnace, the depression of the mercury will indicate the degree of heat. As the movement of the column will be very considerable, it will be scarcely worth while to introduce any correction for the change of the initial volume by barometric variation. Or the instrument might be made with the recurved bulb sealed, as in Professor Leslie's differential thermometers. The glass tube may be joined by fusion to the platinum tube. Care must be taken to let no mercury enter the bulb. Should there be a mechanical difficulty in making a bulb of this metal, then a hollow cylinder half an inch in diameter, with a platinum stem, like that of a tobacco pipe, screwed into it, will suit equally well."

Having considered the expansion of bodies by heat, and the various means of measuring that expansion, it seems to be required, in order to give a complete view of the subject, that the effects capable of being produced by reducing bodies below their usual temperatures, and the artificial modes by which this is effected, should be noticed in this place; but it is believed that a still more appropriate opportunity of entering into this discussion will be found in a more advanced part of this treatise.

Chapter V.
Of the different powers of bodies in conducting heat.

To prove in a simple and convincing way that heat passes through different bodies with very different degrees of velocity, it is only necessary to take slender cylinders of different substances, as, for example, silver, glass, and charcoal, and while holding one end of each in the hand, let the other end be held in the flame of a candle; the silver will soon become too hot to hold, the glass will be much longer in being heated, and the charcoal will be ignited (or red-hot) at one end, long before any sensation of heat is felt at the other. The substances that become hot soonest at the end farthest from the flame, are said to be the best *conductors* of caloric.

The densest bodies are generally the best conductors; but there is no invariable relation existing between the density of a body and its conducting power; as the densest of the metals, platinum, is one of the worst of metallic conductors. Earthy substances are much inferior to metals in their conducting power; wood is still more so; but the solid substances that have the least conducting power, are those which constitute the coverings of animals, as wool, hair, and feathers. Hence the great use of even small portions of such substances in preventing the heat of animals from being carried off by the cold air; in other words, keeping them warm.

Ex. The difference between the conducting powers of metal and wood may be strikingly shown, by taking a smooth cylindrical tube, or still better a solid

---

* Guyton on Wedgewood's Thermometer, *Ann. de Chimie*, xxxi. 171.
† Guyton's Metalline Thermometer of Platina, *Repertory*, ii. III. 459.

piece of metal, about one and a half inch in diameter, and eight inches long; wrapping a piece of clean writing paper round the metal, so as to be in close contact with its surface, and then holding the paper in the flame of a spirit lamp: it may be held there for a considerable time, without being in the least affected. Wrap a similar piece of paper round a cylindrical piece of wood of the same diameter, and hold it in the flame; it will very speedily burn. When the paper is in close contact with the metal, the heat which is applied to it in one particular part cannot accumulate there; but enters into the metal, and is equally diffused through its substance, so that the paper cannot be burned or scorched until the metal becomes very hot: but when paper is wrapped round wood, the heat that is applied in one particular part, not being able to enter into the wood with facility, accumulates, in a short time, in sufficient quantity to burn the paper.

Sand conducts heat so slowly, that the red hot balls used at Gibraltar in repelling the attack of the Spaniards, were conveyed from the furnaces to the bastions, in wooden wheelbarrows, having only a layer of sand between them and the balls.

Solid substances conduct heat in all directions, upwards, downwards, and sideways, with nearly equal facility.

A set of experiments was made by Richman, with a view to ascertain if any relation existed between the conducting powers of bodies and their other properties. He took hollow balls of the metals, equal in size to each other, and having the bulb of a mercurial thermometer inclosed in each. The balls having been immersed in boiling water until each thermometer attained the same temperature, they were then exposed to the air, and the times of their cooling observed: the differences in this respect were considered as marking their differences of conducting power. The metals which appeared to have the greatest power of retaining heat were brass and copper; then iron, tin; and lead the least of all. The decrements of temperature in a given time, in the metals above mentioned, being as follows: lead, 25; tin, 17; iron, 11; copper, 10; brass, 10,—he considered himself justified in inferring, from his experiments, that the increments and decrements (or increases and decreases) of temperature in the bodies upon which he experimented, are not in the inverse ratio of their density, of their hardness, of their cohesion, nor in any compound ratio of these.

Rods of different metals, of the same length and diameter, were dipped by Ingenhouz into melted wax, by which they acquired a coating of that substance. When cold, they were plunged to the depth of about two inches into heated oil, and the conducting power was inferred from the length of wax coating melted in a given time. Silver, according to these experiments, is the best conductor; then gold, tin, copper, platinum, steel, iron, and lead. These experiments, however, are not considered as perfectly accurate. The experiments of Meyer, of Erlangen, by which he endeavoured to ascertain the conducting powers of different kinds of wood, appear to be subject to so many causes of error, that the results obtained by them can scarcely be depended upon.

The following TABLE gives the results which he obtained; the conducting power of water being made the standard.

	Conducting Power.	Specific Gravity.
Water	10	1.000
Ebony wood	21.7	1.054
Apple tree	27.4	0.639
Ash	30.8	0.831
Beech	32.1	0.692
Hornbeam	32.3	0.690
Plum tree	32.5	0.687
Elm	32.5	0.616
Oak	32.6	0.668
Pear tree	33.2	0.603
Birch	34.1	0.608
Silver fir	37.5	0.495
Alder	38.4	0.484
Scotch fir	38.6	0.408
Norway spruce	38.9	0.447
Lime	39.0	0.408

Experiments were made by Count Rumford, for the purpose of investigating the fitness of various substances, as articles of warm clothing. That philosopher suspended a thermometer in a cylindrical glass tube, the end of which had been blown into a bulb, $1\frac{6}{10}$ inch in diameter, placing the bulb of the thermometer in the centre of the larger bulb, surrounded with the substance, the conducting power of which was to be ascertained. Prepared in this way, the apparatus was heated by being plunged into boiling water, and afterwards cooled by being plunged in a mixture of pounded ice and water; and the number of seconds was accurately marked, which the thermometer required in each experiment to cool from $70°$ to $10°$ of Reaumur.

Surrounded with	Seconds.
Air, (it cooled in)	576
16 grs. of raw silk	1284
,, Ravellings of taffety	1169
,, Sewing silk, cut	917
,, Wool	1118
,, Cotton	1046
,, Fine lint	1032
,, Beaver's fur	1296
,, Hare's fur	1315
,, Eider-down	1305
,, Charcoal	937
,, Lamp black	1117
,, Wood-ashes	927

The worst conductors, as hares' fur and eider-down, involve a large quantity of air among the parts of which they consist, to which, it is believed, they chiefly owe the power of resisting the passage of heat. The same substance is found to have different conducting powers, in proportion to the closeness or openness of its texture, as will be seen by reference to the experiments on silk, the twisted silk having the greatest conducting power.

The substances which form the warmest articles of clothing are those which have the longest nap, fur, or down, on account of the air which is involved resisting the escape of the natural warmth of the body. The imperfect conducting power of snow arises from the same cause; and is of the greatest utility in preventing the surface of the earth from being injuriously cooled in many parts of the world. It is affirmed, that while the temperature of the air in Siberia has been 70° below the freezing point, the surface of the earth, protected by its covering of snow, has seldom been colder than 32°.

Advantage is taken of the imperfect conducting powers of bodies for the purpose of confining heat: furnaces are frequently surrounded by a thick coating of clay and sand for some purposes; the interposition of a layer of charcoal, or of a stratum of air, is very effectual in preventing the escape of caloric. Double windows may be seen at Kensington Palace, and in many houses in and about London, upon the same principles. The air inclosed between the two windows opposes great resistance to the escape of the heat which is produced within the house in winter.

Loose clothing is warmer than such as fits close, on account of the quantity of imperfectly conducting air confined around the body, resisting the escape of heat. The same substances that prevent the escape of heat, will be equally effectual in preventing its admission; and ice-houses are constructed upon this principle.

The very different sensations which we experience on touching substances of different kinds, as ivory, marble, glass, wood, are occasioned by the differences of conducting powers in these bodies. A piece of wood, for example, being touched in cold weather, does not seem so cold by very much as a piece of iron in the same place, although they are exactly of the same temperature, as may be proved by the application of a thermometer to them. The iron feels colder, because, being a good conductor of caloric, the heat existing in the hand over that of the iron, has a tendency to enter into the iron, that an equality of temperature may be produced between them, and the rapid abstraction of caloric occasions the sensation alluded to; but wood, being a slow conductor, it does not take away heat from the hand so rapidly, and therefore does not feel so cold. For the same reason, when the iron and the wood are at high temperatures, the former seems the hottest, because it imparts heat most readily.

Operators who have frequently to touch substances hotter or colder than is agreeable, find it very convenient to wear gloves of worsted, that substance being a very bad conductor of heat.

Count Rumford illustrated, by numerous experiments, the very imperfect conducting power of fluids: indeed, he supposed it proved by his experiments that they are absolutely non-conductors of caloric. This opinion has been successfully controverted, and fluids are now generally admitted to have a very small degree of conducting power. It has been proved that water may be made to boil in the upper part of a tube, without imparting much heat to the lower portions: that water may be brought to the boiling point within one fourth of an inch of ice without producing immediate liquefaction; and that ice is melted eighty times slower, when it is fixed at the bottom of a cylindrical vessel, with warm water above it, than when it floats upon the surface of warm water.

Dr. Murray, who was the most successful opponent of Count Rumford's theory, selects the following as one of the most unobjectionable of the Count's experiments. Over a piece of ice, frozen in the bottom of a cylindrical glass jar, and having a small projection of ice rising from the centre of it, he poured olive oil, at 32°, to the height of three inches above the surface of ice, surrounding the under part of the jar with pounded ice, and water. A solid cylinder of iron, 1¼ inch in diameter, and 12 inches long, to which a sheath of thick paper to preserve its heat was adapted, being heated to 210° by immersion in water, it was introduced into the sheath, and suspended in the jar in such a manner, that the middle of its lower extremity was directly above the pointed projection of ice, and distant from it only $\frac{2}{10}$ths of an inch. If any heat had descended through the thin stratum of oil, interposed between the hot iron and the projection of ice under it, it must have been apparent, by the melting of the ice. But this was not the case; the ice did not appear to be diminished, or otherwise affected by the hot iron. When mercury was substituted instead of oil, the hot iron was placed at the distance of ¼-inch from the ice without affecting it.

Dr. Murray remarks, that all the arrangements in this experiment are such as to occasion waste of heat, and to prevent the conducting power of the fluid, if it had any, from being apparent. Instead of using a little oil only, the ice was covered to the height of three inches, and this oil was kept as nearly as possible at 32° during the whole of the experiment. The heated cylinder being suspended in the oil, the portions of oil nearest to its surfaces would be heated, and expanded, and would therefore ascend; other portions would successively come in contact with the iron, and similar effects would be produced upon them; and this circulation would continue as long as the iron continued to impart caloric to the oil; the ascending current being in the middle of the jar, and the descending current keeping near to the sides. By this circulation it is obvious that no caloric could be communicated to the ice, until the whole of the liquid arrived at a higher temperature than 32°. The rise of temperature of the liquid in the jar must have been greatly retarded by its being surrounded with ice and water. In addition to this it has been remarked, that this mode of detecting the communication of caloric, by the melting of ice, is unfavourable; since in that operation, a large quantity of caloric is absorbed, and a portion might be actually communicated to the ice, and yet might not be able to melt a sufficient quantity to render its effects apparent.

The results of experiments by many different philosophers, are hostile to the assertion of Count Rumford, that fluids are absolutely non-conductors of caloric.

Dr. Hope applied heat to the surface of water in a vessel eleven inches in diameter, and at the same time contrived that a stream of water should circulate on the outside, to prevent the conducting power of the sides of the vessel from affecting the result; heat was conducted downwards, as appeared by the indications of a thermometer placed at some depth below the surface of the fluid. Dr. Hope also mixed portions of hot and cold water, and, after agitating them, permitted them to remain at rest for a time: no separation took place of the hot from the colder portions, but the whole had attained one uniform temperature, which is considered to be inconsistent with the theory of Rumford. Similar facts were ascertained by Thomson, Nicholson, and Dalton; but the most satisfactory and conclusive experiment was made by Dr. Murray of Edinburgh, the original account of which was published in *Nicholson's Journal, 8vo. Vol. I. page* 241. It appeared to him that all the precautions which had previously been taken to obviate errors, arising from the conducting powers of the vessels in which the experiments were performed, were insufficient for that purpose; and a more effectual method was invented by him. Since ice cannot have its temperature raised above 32°, it occurred to him that a vessel of that substance would answer well for holding fluids, the conducting power of which is intended to be tried; for whatever degree of heat may be applied to it above, it cannot conduct the heat downwards, the melting of a part of the ice being the only effect which it would be capable of producing. Heat being applied to the surface of a fluid, under such circumstances, if that fluid should have its temperature increased below, it may be with certainty inferred that such increase is owing to the conducting power of the fluid itself, and not to that of the vessel in which it is contained.

Mr. Murray gives the following account of this experiment in his *System of Chemistry, third edition, Vol. I. page* 305. "In a hollow cylinder of ice, a thermometer was placed horizontally, at the depth of one inch, its bulb being in the axis of the cylinder, and the part of the stem to which the scale was attached, entirely without. As water could not be employed at the temperature at which it is requisite to make the experiment in this apparatus, on account of the property it possesses of becoming more dense in the rise of its temperature from 32° to 40°, oil was first used. A quantity of almond oil at the temperature of 32° was poured into the ice cylinder, so as to cover the bulb of the thermometer ¼ inch. A flat-bottomed iron cup was suspended, so as nearly to touch the surface of the oil, and two ounces of boiling water were poured into it. In a minute and a half, the thermometer had risen from 32° to 32¾°, in three minutes to 34½°, in five minutes to 36¼°, in seven minutes to 37½°, when it became stationary, and soon began to fall. When more oil was interposed between the bottom of the cup and the bulb of the thermometer, the rise was less; but even when its depth was three-quarters of an inch, the rise was perceptible, amounting to 1½ degree. With Mercury the same results were obtained, the thermometer rising, only with much more rapidity, from the mercury being a better conductor than the oil."

Dr. Trail (*Nicholson's Journal, Vol. XII. page* 127) ascertained the relative conducting powers of different fluids, by finding the length of time required to raise the temperature of a mercurial thermometer three degrees of Fahrenheit's scale, when placed in each liquid, heat being applied by means of a cylinder of iron one inch in diameter, heated to 212°, and suspended in the liquid at the distance of half an inch from the bulb of the thermometer; and that the conducting power of the vessel might influence the results as little as possible, it was made of wood. The thermometer placed in

	Minutes.	Seconds.
Mercury, required	0	15
Saturated Solution of Sulphate of Soda	6	30
Water	7	5
Proof Spirit	8 nearly	
Solution of one part of Sulphate of Iron, in five parts of Water	8	0
Water of Potassa	8	15
Milk of a Cow	8	25
Saturated Solution of Sulphate of Alumine	9	40
Alcohol Lond. Pharm.	10	45
Saturated Solution of Sulphate of Soda, but the liquid not touching the iron cylinder by 0.1 inch, or nearly so	19	20

The great difficulty opposed to the progress of caloric downwards, and the motion of the particles by which heat is conveyed through water upwards, may be further illustrated by a few experiments.

Ex. Pour into a glass tube about ten inches long and one inch in diameter, a little water tinged with litmus; then fill up gradually and carefully with colourless water: heat being applied near the top, the coloured liquid will remain stationary at the bottom, which it could not do if it were heated and thus expanded or made lighter; but when heat is applied at the bottom, the coloured portion will ascend and be diffused through the whole.

Ex. Secure a circular piece of ice to the bottom of a cylindrical glass jar, about twelve inches deep and four wide; cover the ice to the depth of two or three inches with water at 32°: on the surface of this water place, so that it may float, a wooden box perforated with minute holes in its sides only; then pour, gently and gradually, boiling water into the box, until the jar is nearly full—the ice will remain unmelted for a very considerable time; but if a similar piece of ice is placed upon the surface, it will very quickly be melted.

The slow conducting power of water may be illustrated by the arrangement represented at *fig.* 9. A small air-thermometer, capable of shewing very minute alterations of temperature, being plunged in the water of the jar, so that the bulb may be a little below the surface ether may be inflamed on the surface of the water, without affecting the thermometer in any considerable degree.

The cooling of water is very much impeded by a mixture of starch, mucilage, or other substances with it, on account of the difficulty thus opposed to the ascending motion of its particles, by which the heat is prevented from reaching its surface. Thus compounds, such as soups, require much longer time to cool than pure water.

Ex. The circulation of the particles of fluid is very pleasingly shewn by heating water in a tube similar to that in the last experiment but one, the water having some particles diffused in it of amber or other light substance not soluble in water.

From these and similar experiments, it appears that the reason why heat is so slowly diffused through liquids in a downward direction, is, that the heated particles being expanded are rendered specifically lighter than those immediately above them, and therefore immediately ascend, without having had time to impart heat to the particles below.

Count Rumford also endeavoured to prove that the gases are non-conductors of caloric: the truth of this conclusion, however, is not admitted, but the experiments prove that whatever obstructs the motion of the particles of air, renders the propagation of heat slower.

The facility with which an air thermometer shews changes of temperature, was adduced by Berthollet, to shew that air must be a good conductor of heat; and he refers to the fact that in air-balloons the gas has been found to expand suddenly when the sun became unclouded. In explaining this effect, it appeared to him impossible that the particles of the gas within the balloon could be so quickly heated by coming individually and successively into contact with its sides. He infers, therefore, that the heat must have been conducted by the gas itself. He accounts for the effect which, it is acknowledged, confined air has in retarding the communication of heat, by supposing it to depend upon a degree of compression by which its expansion is prevented, a solution not very satisfactory.

It has been ascertained by Mr. Leslie, that bodies require different times to cool in different gases. In hydrogen the process of cooling goes on rapidly, not so quick in atmospheric air, and much slower in carbonic acid gas.

In describing the effects produced by expansion, the agency of air in distributing heat has already been adverted to. The expansion and consequent ascension of successive portions of air from heated parts of the earth's surface, occasions a current of air to flow from the poles towards the equator, near the surface of the earth; a superior current from the equator towards the poles, modifying and regulating temperature over the globe.

The agency of water is of equal importance. Cold air passing over the water of the sea, from the polar regions, is much warmed in its progress, by heat derived from the water. Count Rumford affirms, that one cubical foot of water, in cooling one degree, gives out a sufficient quantity of heat to raise the temperature of a stratum of air over it, forty-four times as thick as the water, ten degrees. The Count entertained an opinion that the water which imparts its heat, and which descends, in consequence of its increased specific gravity, flows towards the equator, occasioning a current at the surface, in an opposite direction; tending, like the currents in the air, to moderate the extremes of temperature.

It is impossible to consider these, and similar silent and unobtrusive, but extensive and most useful operations, without being deeply affected by a sense of the wisdom and power by which they were contrived and carried into effect.

Chapter VI.

Radiation of Heat.

When heated bodies are exposed to the air, they lose portions of their heat by projection, in right lines into space, from all parts of their surfaces. The investigations by which this interesting property of caloric has been made fully known are of recent date, although it was not entirely unknown at an earlier period. In 1682 it was mentioned by Marriotte, in the Memoirs of the Academy of Sciences of Paris; he pointed out the fact, that the heat of a fire, which is rendered sensible in the focus of a burning mirror, ceases to be sensible when a glass is interposed. Having found that substances may be inflamed at a distance of twenty or twenty-four feet, by burning charcoal placed between two concave reflectors, Lambert, in order to ascertain if any part of the effect was occasioned by light, collected the light of a clear fire by a large lens, but could scarcely discover any heat in its focus.

In the celebrated Treatise on Air and Fire, by Scheele, similar experiments are detailed, with important additions; the term *Radiant Heat*, or heat flying off like light in *rays*, originated with him, as did also the knowledge that it passes through the air, without heating it; and that its direction is not changed by a current of air. He observed that glass, which permits the light of a fire to pass through, intercepts the heat; that a glass mirror reflects the light without the heat, absorbing the latter; while a metallic mirror reflects both heat and light, so that it is not quickly warmed, unless its surface be blackened, which occasions it to absorb the heat.

The experiments of Lambert were repeated, and varied by Saussure and Pictet. They used two concave reflectors, of polished tin plate, one foot in diameter, with a focal length of four inches and a half; they placed these twelve feet two inches distant, and exactly opposite to each other. In the focus of one reflector they placed a ball of iron, two inches in diameter, heated so as not to appear luminous in the dark, and in the focus of the other they placed the ball of a mercurial thermometer, (*fig.* 10.) The temperature of the thermometer

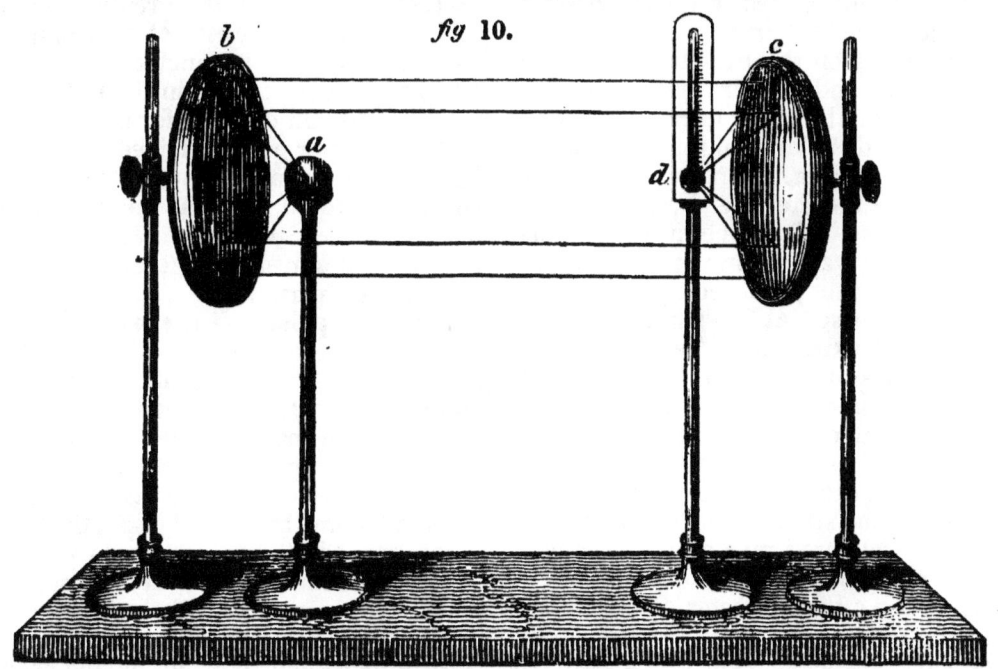

fig 10.

began to increase as soon as the ball was put in its place, and continued rising from 4° of Reaumur's scale to 14¼°, which it did in six minutes. Another thermometer, at the same distance from the heated ball, but out of the focus of the reflector rose only from 4° to 6½°.

The heated ball *a*, (*fig.* 10,) in the focus of one reflector, *b*, projects heat from every part of its surface; those rays that proceed towards the reflector are intercepted by it, and in consequence of its shape, they are again projected into space, in straight lines, towards the other reflector *c*, by which they are reflected, and brought to a focus at the point where the thermometer *d* is placed: the heat, thus accumulated, affects the thermometer *d*, and makes it rise.

To prove that the thermometer is not affected by heat proceeding directly from the ball, a plate of glass may be held between it and the reflector *b*, which will prevent any effect from being produced upon the thermometer; or the plate of glass may be held between the reflector *c*, and the thermometer *d*: in either case the instrument will remain unaffected. An air, or differential thermometer, (*fig.* 5. or *fig.* 7.) answers much better for this experiment.

Whatever hot substance may be used as the source of heat, the effect is the same, and is always in proportion to the temperature of the body used.

Pictet made other experiments, some of which approached near to the discovery of the different radiating powers of different surfaces. When he used a glass concave mirror behind the ball, instead of a metallic one, very little effect was produced upon the thermometer. A glass plate covered with amalgam on one side, having its coated part presented to the hot body, and the uncoated glass surface to the thermometer, produced the effect of 3.5; the glass surface being turned to the hot body, and the metallic surface towards the thermometer, the effect was only as 0.5. When the metallic side was blackened and presented to the heated body, 9.2 marked the heating power. A still greater effect, equal to 18°, was produced, when the surface of the glass, next to the source of heat, was blackened, the metallic coating being entirely removed.

Endeavouring to discover the velocity with which radiant heat moves through space, Pictet placed two concave metallic reflectors opposite to each other, at the distance of sixty-nine feet apart: he interposed a thick screen, a few inches distant from the focus of the mirror in which the heated body was to be placed, and an air thermometer in the focus of the other mirror; the ball, heated a little below ignition, being introduced, the screen was removed, and instantly the thermometer began to show an increase of temperature. When the screen was again suddenly interposed, the effect produced upon the thermometer ceased at the same moment; from which experiments he inferred that radiant heat moves with such velocity, as to require no perceptible interval of time to enable it to traverse sixty-nine feet of space. Sir William Herschel, in his investigation concerning the constitution of the sun's rays, found that the different coloured rays of the prismatic spectrum produced different degrees of effect upon a thermometer, the red occasioning the greatest rise of temperature, the violet the least. The heat of the red rays, compared with that of the green, was considered to be as 55 to 26, and with that of the violet rays as 55 to 16. In ten minutes a thermometer, placed in the full red rays, rose 7° of Fahrenheit's scale, and beyond the red ray the increase, in the same time, appeared to be nine degrees. These experiments were repeated and verified by Sir H. Englefield. He discovered also that invisible heating rays exist beyond the coloured rays, and imagined that the greatest degree of heat was produced at the distance of half an inch beyond the red rays. Other philosophers have confirmed the existence of these invisible heating rays, but M. Berard affirms that the greatest heating effect is produced within the red ray. The experiments of M. Berard on the sun's rays, (*Annales de Chimie, March,* 1813, and *Annals of Philosophy, September,* 1813) were conducted with the aid of *a heliostate,** by which he was enabled to obtain an immovable coloured spectrum. In the different coloured rays, of which this spectrum is composed, he suspended delicate thermometers, and ascertained their different heating powers with accuracy. The greatest heating effect was produced upon a thermometer, when its bulb was entirely covered by the red ray; the instruments being placed beyond the red ray, in the space where Sir W. Herschell imagined the greatest degree of heat to exist, the rise of temperature was only one-fifth as much as that which had been produced within the red rays.

The same philosopher formed a prism of Iceland spar, which divided a beam of light, made to pass through it, into two similar coloured spectra, the properties of which were the same as those of the spectrum obtained by decomposing light with a glass prism.

He also polarized a portion of the light by receiving it upon glass; this polarized portion being intercepted by a second glass which was made to revolve, the rays were then collected by a mirror, and directed upon a thermometer, and it was found that as long as light was reflected from the second glass, the temperature of the thermometer was raised; but when the position of the second glass was such, that all the light was transmitted, the whole of the heat was transmitted along with it, as the thermometer ceased then to be affected. The experiments and discoveries of Herschell, which have been alluded to, are published in the Philosophical Transactions for 1800, as were also the accounts of other experiments, by the same philosopher, yet to be mentioned.

Having ascertained, from the phenomena of the prismatic spectrum, the refraction of the heating rays accompanying light in the beam, he determined to try if the calorific rays projected from a heated body were also subject to refraction. He placed a lens near to a burning candle, having first interposed a screen, with an aperture nearly of the same size as the lens; the rays from the candle passing through this aperture, were refracted by the lens to a focus, and in three minutes raised the temperature of a thermometer two and a half degrees.

Experiments of the same kind were made upon the rays projected from a common fire, and from a mass of iron not quite heated to redness, and they were found to be equally subject to the

---

* From two Greek words signifying the *standing still* of the *sun;* because, by machinery, the image of the sun is kept stationary upon a wall or sheet of paper.

laws of refraction. A remarkable difference however was discovered between the radiant heat of the sun's rays and that proceeding from a fire, the former passing much more easily through a glass than the latter. Two equally delicate thermometers were exposed to the rays of the sun, one being uncovered, and the other covered with very transparent glass, having a bluish white tinge; in five minutes the temperature of the uncovered thermometer was raised from 67° to 73°, and the covered one from 67° to 71½°; by which it appears that one fourth part of the radiant heat falling upon the thermometers, was intercepted by the glass which covered one of them. When the thermometer was covered with flint glass, 2½ tenths of an inch thick, the uncovered thermometer rose 5½° in five minutes, and the covered one 5°, so that fewer of the rays were intercepted by flint glass, than by the glass used in the first experiment. The thermometers were then exposed, under the same circumstances, to the rays of a lighted candle; in five minutes the one which was covered with the same bluish glass used in the first experiment, rose from 59¼ to 60⅝, while the uncovered one rose from 59⅜ to 62⅔: in this last experiment more than half the heating rays proceeding from the candle were stopped by the glass of the covered thermometer. A similar effect was produced when the thermometer was covered with flint glass. It is shown by these experiments, that the heating rays which accompany the sun's light, are able to pass through glass with greater ease, than the heating rays which proceed from a burning body.

Lest the results of the foregoing experiments should have been affected by the light accompanying the heat, the experiments were varied so as to render the introduction of error in this way impossible. Covered and uncovered thermometers, as before, were exposed to the influence of the invisible heating rays of the prismatic spectrum; in five minutes the covered one rose from 47° to 48⅝°, and the uncovered one from 48° to 49¾. When the flint glass was used, the increase of temperature indicated by both thermometers was nearly equal. Experiments were also tried on heat projected from bodies not luminous; and it was found that the results were very nearly the same when light was absent as when it was present.

It was further ascertained by Herschel, that the different coloured rays into which light is separated by the prism, pass through different substances with different degrees of facility; that the invisible calorific rays, when separated from light, pass through more readily than when accompanied by light; and that coloured glass intercepts more of the rays than colourless glass.

The differential thermometer invented by Mr. Leslie, and which has already been described and represented (fig. 7,) was of great use in his researches on radiant heat. The apparatus used by him in his experiments, consisted of the above-named thermometer, a highly-polished concave reflector of tinned iron, and hollow cubes of tin, from three to ten inches, for the purpose of holding hot water. One of these cubical vessels, filled with boiling water, being placed at the distance of a few feet from the reflector, and one of the bulbs of the differential thermometer in the focus of the mirror (fig. 11), an instantaneous rise of temperature is indicated by the instrument. By this method of conducting the experiment, great facilities are afforded for trying the radiating powers of different surfaces. Mr. Leslie covered one side of a six-inch cubical vessel with lampblack, another side with writing-paper, a third side with glass, and left the fourth side without a covering. The vessel being filled with boiling water, and its black side being turned towards the reflector, the fluid in the thermometer, which was placed in the focus of the reflector, indicated a rise of temperature equal to 100°: the papered side being presented to the reflector occasioned a rise of 98°; the glass side 90°; and the metallic side only 12°: the relative radiating powers of these surfaces being as the numbers expressing the effects which they produced.

The *reflecting* powers of different surfaces were also tried by Mr. Leslie. He coated the ball of the thermometer placed in the focus of the reflector with tin foil, and then exposed it to the radiant heat of the blackened surface; the rise of temperature produced, instead of being 100°, as it was before the ball was coated with tin foil, amounted only to 20°; and when the metallic surface of the tin vessel was turned to the reflector, the thermometer increased in temperature only 2½°, instead of 12°, as

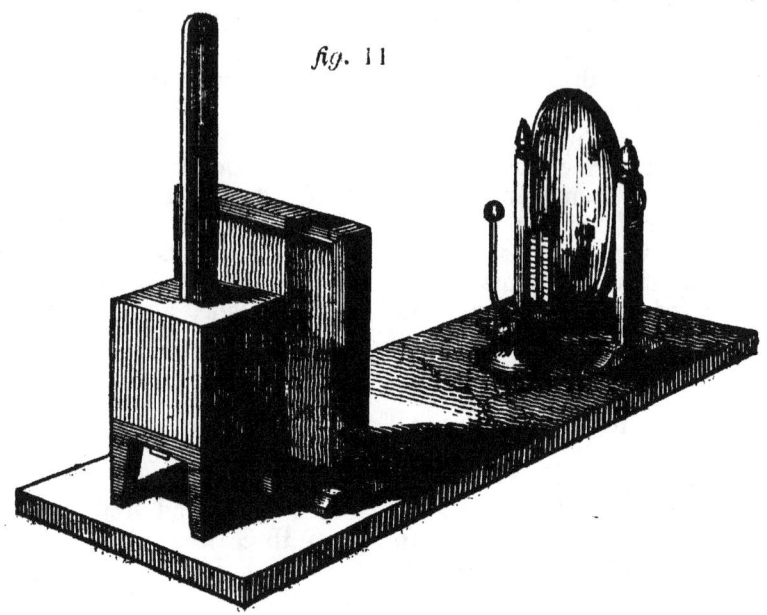
fig. 11

in a former experiment. Thus it is shown that the metallic covering of the ball reflects the greatest portion of heat falling upon it, and therefore that the temperature of the instrument cannot be much raised.

A glass mirror being substituted for the metallic one, and an uncovered thermometer placed in its focus, when the black surface of the cubical vessel was presented, so little of the heat was reflected by the glass, that the thermometer was affected in a very small degree; and when the mirror was covered with a thin coating of China ink, no perceptible effect was produced upon the thermometer, all the heat being absorbed by the blackened glass. But when the surface of the mirror was covered with tin foil, the thermometer was ten times as much affected as it was by the heat reflected from the uncovered glass mirror.

It will appear from the foregoing experiments, that bodies which radiate heat most effectually, absorb it in the same proportion; and those which are the best reflectors of heat have the least radiating power.

Mr. Leslie made an extensive series of experiments on the powers of different bodies to intercept radiant caloric. A frame similar to that represented at fig. 10, being adapted to receive various substances, it is placed, when each substance is applied, in the manner of a screen, between the tin vessel and the reflector. When a sheet of tin foil was attached to the frame, and placed at the distance of two inches from the blackened surface of the tin cannister, no effect was produced on the thermometer in the focus of the reflector; nor was the result at all affected by altering the distance of the screen from the tin vessel; the whole of the heat being intercepted at whatever place the screen might be situated between the source of heat and the thermometer. The same effect was produced by gold leaf, although it is 600 times thinner than the tin foil. A plate of glass being interposed at the distance of two inches from the tin vessel, the thermometer shewed an increase of temperature equal to 20°, eighty degrees of the effect, capable of being produced by the blackened surface, being intercepted. The rise of temperature when paper was interposed was about three degrees greater.

Mr. Leslie explains the effect resulting from radiant heat, by an hypothesis peculiar to himself. He believes air to be the sole agent concerned in conveying heat in these experiments. A portion of air coming into contact with the heated surfaces is suddenly expanded, and communicates the impulse which is thus imparted to it, along with a portion of its newly-acquired heat; and the particles continuing to be thus acted upon in succession, the heat is conveyed through space, with the swiftness of sound, by a series of undulations or wavering motions so produced. These undulations being extended to the mirror, they are reflected and brought to a focus. He contends that when glass or paper is interposed, the effect produced upon the thermometer is not produced by portions of radiant heat passing through these substances, but by the undulations before mentioned, which convey a portion of the heat given out from the tin vessel; and the screen being heated by this process, it also gives out heat, occasioning new undulations on the side nearest to the reflector, by which heat is conveyed to it, and finally to the bulb of the thermometer in its focus.

This view of the subject is supported by other experiments. Mr. Leslie found that when a thin sheet of ice, which cannot have its temperature raised, was interposed, no heat was imparted to the thermometer.

Two panes of glass were coated on one side with tinfoil. When they were both placed in the screen, with the tinfoil inwards, so that one of the uncovered surfaces of the glass was next the source of heat and the other towards the reflector, the thermometer was elevated in temperature 18°; but when the plates of glass were so placed in the screen as to have their uncovered surfaces inwards, and their metallic surfaces presented to the cubical vessel and the reflector, no effect whatever was produced upon the thermometer.

Mr. Leslie contends, that since the resistance opposed to the passage of radiant heat in both these experiments was precisely the same, the effect must be accounted for in some other way than by supposing a portion of heat capable of passing through. In the first experiment with the compound screen, surfaces were presented which had the power of receiving and emitting heat; the screen was heated, therefore, by the undulatory process, and the heat which was emitted was conveyed to the reflector in the same way. But when the metallic surfaces of the compound screen were exposed, heat could not be received readily, and if it had been received, it could not readily have been imparted: the effects of the undulations could not, therefore, extend beyond the screen.

It is not necessary, however, to adopt Mr. Leslie's theory in explaining these experiments, as they admit of an equally plausible explanation according to the usual theory of radiant heat. Admitting the possibility of the undulations supposed by Mr. Leslie, it is difficult to imagine by what agency caloric is transferred so rapidly from particle to particle; especially as the propagation of heat through elastic fluids is usually so slow. This theory is at variance with the results obtained by the experiments of Herschel and Berard. It is an essential part of the hypothesis alluded to, that these pulsatory undulations are incapable of existing in a vacuum, and consequently that heat cannot pass through a vacuum, as its propagation depends upon the agency of air.

The experiments of MM. Dulong and Petit, are hostile to this part of the theory, the overthrow of which must destroy the whole; and an experiment of Sir H. Davy, now to be described, seems quite conclusive against it. A piece of platinum-wire was heated by voltaic electricity within a receiver (*fig*. 12,) containing concave reflectors

fig. 12.

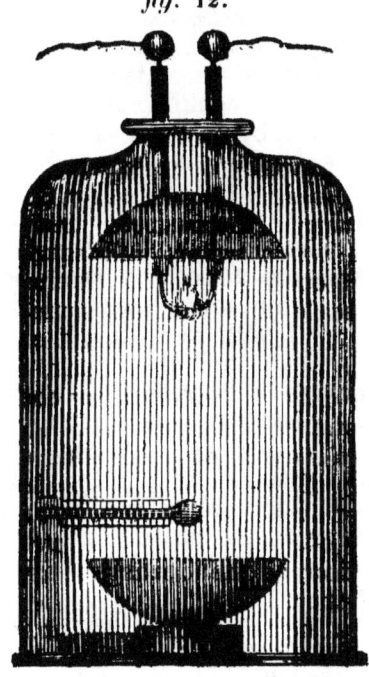

with a thermometer in the focus of one of them, the heated wire being in the focus of the other. The effect was first tried in air of the natural density, and then repeated when the receiver was exhausted to $\frac{1}{125}$th part of what it contained before; the temperature of the thermometer was three times as much raised when the receiver was thus exhausted, as when it contained air in its natural state. A similar result was obtained by the ignition of charcoal under the same circumstances.

Mr. Leslie, Count Rumford, and others, have made numerous experiments on the cooling of bodies under different circumstances, illustrative of the radiation of heat.

Count Rumford found that a thermometer suspended in a Torricellian vacuum, required ten minutes twelve seconds to cool from 190° of Fahrenheit to 68°. When surrounded with atmospheric air confined in a vessel, having the same extent of space as the vacuum, it required only six minutes eleven seconds: proving that the air facilitates refrigeration.

Two hollow tin globes, one of which was painted with lamp-black, and the other left bright, were filled with warm water and exposed by Mr. Leslie to the influence of air, in different states of motion. A gentle breeze occasioned the bright globe to lose half its heat in 44 minutes, the painted one lost the same quantity in 35 minutes. Exposed to a strong breeze, the times of cooling were 23 minutes and 20¼ minutes; and a vehement breeze occasioned them to cool in 9½ minutes and 9 minutes. The influence of currents of air in accelerating the cooling of bodies, is clearly shown by these experiments.

Mr. Leslie filled a hollow globe of tin, having a thermometer inserted in it with warm water, and marked its time of cooling, from 35° of the centigrade scale to 25° of the same scale, to be 150 minutes; when the globe was covered with lamp-black, it required only 81 minutes to cool the same number of degrees.

A tin vessel, covered with a thin coating of isinglass, lost its heat by radiation much more rapidly, and the rapidity of the cooling was greater in proportion, as the coating of isinglass was thicker.

When heated bodies are immersed in water, the nature of their surfaces does not affect their rates of cooling, because radiation does not take place under the surface of that fluid.

The times of cooling heated bodies was found to be different in different gases. Mr. Dalton shows that a thermometer immersed in

	Seconds.
Carbonic acid gas, (cooled in)	112
Sulphuretted hydrogen and nitrous oxide	100
Olefiant gas	100
Common air, azotic, and oxygen gas	100
Nitrous gas	90
Coal gas	70
Hydrogen	40

The times of cooling are different, also, according to the degree of density of the gas in which a body is immersed, the cooling proceeding most slowly when the density is least. Mr. Leslie ascribes the different rates of cooling in the different gases, to the different conducting powers of these gases.

The radiating power of different substances in atmospheric air, are stated by the same philosopher as follows.

	Seconds.
Lamp-black	100
Writing-paper	98
Sealing-wax	95
Crown-glass	90
China-ink	88
Ice	85
Red-lead	80
Plumbago	75
Isinglass	75
Tarnished lead	45
Clean lead	19
Iron, polished	15
Tin-plate	12
Gold, silver, and copper	12

Several important suggestions arise from a review of the doctrines of radiant heat. Whenever it is necessary to the complete success of any operation that the heat of a fluid should be retained for a considerable length of time, the vessel containing that fluid should have bright metallic surfaces, as such surfaces have least radiating power: thus, water in bright metallic coffee or tea pots will be more effectual in extracting the strength of tea and coffee than it would be if contained in vessels of any other kind.

In heating an apartment with steam, it would be absurd to use black pipes for conveying the steam; because, in that case, much of its heat would escape by radiation, before it arrived at its place of destination: the pipes should be of bright metal. It would be equally absurd to make the pipes, intended to distribute heat to the air of the apartment, bright, because such pipes would defeat the object in view by retaining the heat; black pipes would here answer the best.

Vessels intended to receive heat in the operation of cookery and in those of the arts, should not be bright, because bright surfaces reflect and do not absorb heat; and it may be considered as a useful property of the fuel which we generally use, that it blackens the surfaces of metallic vessels in heating them.

The properties of different colours in absorbing, reflecting, and radiating heat are well worthy of attention in regulating our summer and winter clothing. Since dark colours have been proved by the experiments of Dr. Franklin, Mr. Leslie, Sir H. Davy, and others, to absorb heat in a much greater degree than the lighter colours, it does not seem advisable to use dark-coloured clothes, particularly black, as summer clothing, on account of the power that such dark colours have of absorbing the heat of the sun's rays. Since those surfaces that absorb heat most abundantly, also radiate most freely, the propriety of using dark-coloured clothes in winter, may admit of being questioned.

If, instead of the heated body in the arrangement shown at *fig*. 10, we substitute a mass of ice, the effect will be the reverse of what it was before, the temperature of the thermometer being rapidly reduced: this used to be called the radiation of cold, and was ascribed to the effect of a *frigorific* or cooling principle, the existence of which has long ceased to be believed. Considerable difficulty has, however, been experienced in giving a perfectly satisfactory explanation of this remarkable phenomenon. Mr. Leslie explains it in accordance with his theory of pulsatory undulations in the air, by supposing that a portion of heat being abstracted by the cold body from the air nearest to it, the air so cooled is suddenly contracted, which occasions the commencement of a series of pulsations accompanied with a discharge of heat to the cold surface. Explanations intended to agree with the usual theory of radiant heat have been given by Pictet, Prevost, and Martin. The prevailing opinion is, that the phenomenon may be explained by supposing that it arises from radiation of heat in an opposite direction; the thermometer in this case being the hotter body. Bodies exposed to the air are all supposed to radiate heat, at whatever temperatures they may be; and their temperatures are raised when they receive more than they radiate, and depressed when they radiate more than they receive. Both the ice and the thermometer radiate towards the reflectors, before which they are placed; but the temperature of the ice being lower than that of the thermometer, it radiates less towards the thermometer, than that does towards the ice; consequently, the temperature of the thermometer is reduced.

Chapter VII.

Of Specific Caloric and of the different Capacities of Bodies for Heat.

The first experiments in the investigation of this subject were made by Fahrenheit, at the desire of Boerhaave. Equal quantities of the same fluid, such as water, oil, or alcohol, being mingled together at different temperatures, a common temperature resulted: half the excess of heat contained in one portion being speedily imparted to the other, until both became hot alike: but, when fluids of different kinds were mingled together, at different temperatures, very different effects were observed. Water and quicksilver, in equal bulks, added to each other, the water being hottest, gave a mixture, the heat of which was higher than the medium between the two: when the quicksilver was most heated before mixture, the resulting temperature was lower than the medium. Three parts by volume of quicksilver mixed with two of water, at different temperatures, gave a mean temperature; as when equal volumes of water heated to different degrees are mixed together.

Boerhaave judged from these experiments that heat is not distributed through bodies in proportion to their quantity of matter, since the effect produced by a quantity of mercury in raising temperature is considerably less than that of the same bulk of water, although the former is thirteen times heavier than the latter.

Another inference was most inaccurately drawn, by Boerhaave, from these experiments. Convinced that heat is not distributed among different bodies in proportion to the quantity of matter in each, he concluded, in opposition to the very experiments from which he drew the conclusion, that heat is distributed in proportion to the space occupied by each body; and the same opinion was adopted, without examination, by Muschenbroeck.

The labours of Black, Wilcke, Irvine, Crawford, Lavoisier, Gadolin, and other philosophers, were applied to this difficult department of science, and the result obtained tended to prove that equal weights or volumes of different bodies contain unequal quantities of caloric at any given temperature.

D

The experiments by which this has usually been determined, are similar to those already mentioned. Equal portions of the same fluid at different temperatures being mingled together, the mean temperature results; but when two bodies of different kinds are used, the resulting temperature is never the mean between the two; as, when a pound of water heated to 156° is mixed with one pound of quicksilver at 40°, the temperature produced is 152° instead of 98°, the exact mean.

In this experiment the water loses four degrees of temperature, and the quicksilver gains one hundred and twelve degrees; by which it is proved that the quantity of caloric which is capable of raising one pound of quicksilver from 40° to 152° is the same as that which is required to raise one pound of water from 152° to 156°; or, in other words, that the same quantity of heat which raises the temperature of one pound of water four degrees, raises the same weight of quicksilver one hundred and twelve degrees. On this account it is said that the capacity of water for heat is to the capacity of quicksilver for the same, as 28 to 1.

The experiment being reversed by mixing one pound of quicksilver, heated to 156°, with one pound of water at 40°, the resulting temperature will be 44°; the water acquiring an increase of 4°, while the quicksilver loses 112°.

A pound of gold heated to 150° was quickly added to a pound of water at 50°, by Dr. Black; the temperature of the whole became 55°, the gold losing 95° and the water gaining 5°, making the capacity of the gold, compared with that of the water, as 1 to 19.

The general rule given for finding, by calculation combined with experiment, the relative capacities of different bodies is as follows:—

"Multiply the weight of each body by the number of degrees between its original temperature and the common temperature obtained by their mixture: the capacities of the bodies will be inversely as the products." Or, if the bodies be mingled in unequal quantities, "the capacities of the bodies will be reciprocally as the quantities of matter multiplied into their respective changes of temperature."

If we compare the quantities of caloric which are necessary to raise equal volumes of different substances to any given temperature, they will also be found different: water requires more than twice as much caloric to raise its temperature any given number of degrees, as the same volume of mercury requires.

A variety of different methods have been used for the purpose of ascertaining the capacities of bodies, by finding the comparative quantities of caloric which they contain at different temperatures. The method of Wilcke, who operated on solid substances, was to suspend given weights of them, by threads, in boiling water, until they acquired the same temperature; they were then suspended in cold water, and the quantity of heat imparted to the water carefully calculated.

It also occurred to him that the specific heat or comparative quantities of caloric existing in bodies at given temperatures, might be ascertained by the quantities of ice or snow capable of being melted by each; but this method proved unsatisfactory, chiefly on account of the great difficulty in determining how much of the water produced remained adhering to the unmelted portions of ice or snow.

An instrument called a *Calorimeter* was invented, and used in similar investigations, by Lavoisier and La Place. In this instrument there are three vessels within one another, the innermost of which a, (*fig.* 13) is of open wire-work, and is for holding the body on which experiments are to be made: it is figured upon a larger scale at $a\,2$: it rests upon bars of iron, which communicate with the interior of the middle vessel b: into this vessel the ice is put, broken small, that it may be more readily acted upon by the heat of the body placed in the interior cage; the water produced passes through a grating at the bottom, and is conveyed by the pipe d into a vessel e placed to receive it. The third vessel c is intended to hold ice and water, to prevent the temperature of the atmosphere from affecting the experiment by surrounding the ice to be operated upon by a temperature of 32°. The cage has its own cover f; and, in addition, the whole apparatus is furnished with a double cover g, capable of holding pounded ice.

The instrument being prepared, a heated body, the temperature of which is ascertained, is put into the cage, where it remains until it is cooled to 32°; the heat given out by the body is then estimated by the quantity of water produced.

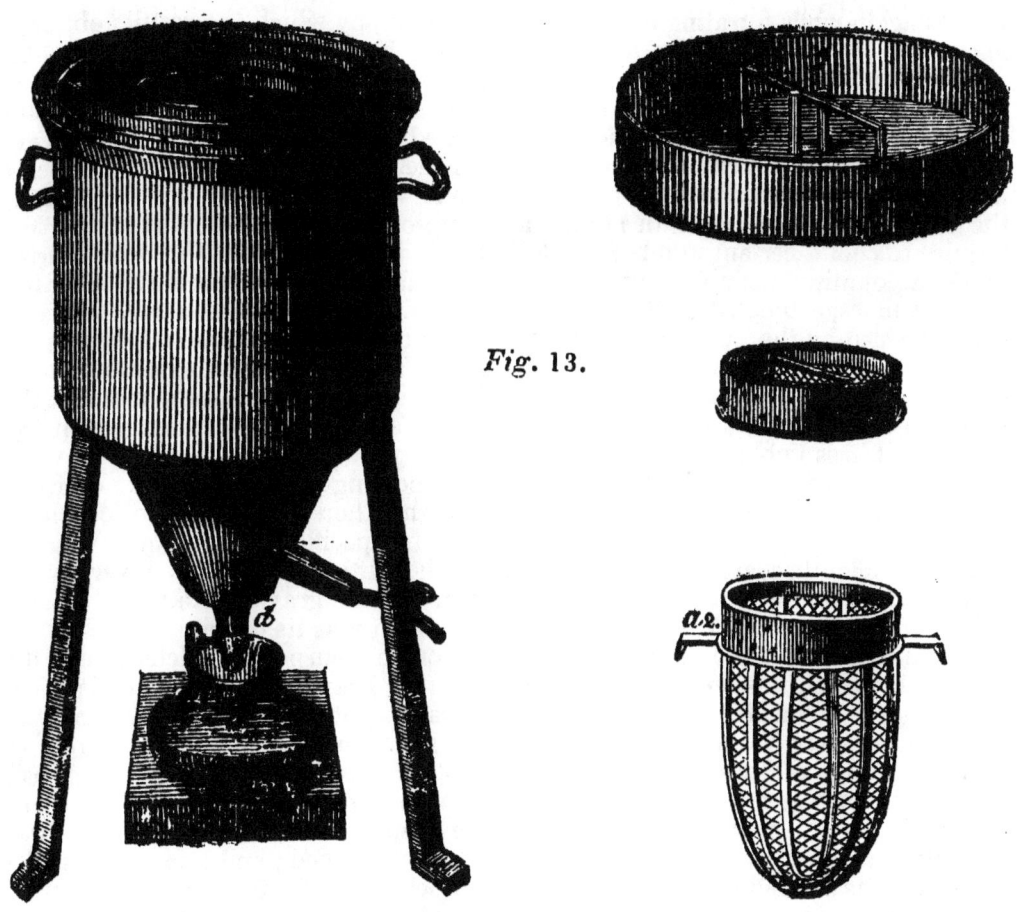

Fig. 13.

According to Lavoisier and La Place, as much heat is absorbed by one pound of ice in melting, as would raise the temperature of the same weight of water 135° of Fahrenheit's scale. By numerous experiments with this apparatus, they ascertained the comparative quantities of caloric evolved by different bodies in passing from one temperature to another, by which the comparative quantities contained were also made known.

When a liquid was operated upon, it was put into a glass mattrass, allowance being made for the effects of the glass, and suspended in the wire cage; and when gases were subjected to experiment, they were made to pass through a spiral tube enclosed within the wire cage, the tube being furnished with a thermometer at each end.

To prevent the contents of the outer vessel from being frozen in experiments made with this apparatus, it is necessary that the temperature of the external air should be a little above 32°; for, if the outer vessel should be cooled below that point, it would absorb heat from the middle vessel, and thus interfere with the result of the experiment; but the temperature should not be more than ten or twelve degrees higher than the freezing point; for, in that case, the air within the apparatus being heavier than the external air, it would descend and escape by the water-tube at the bottom, occasioning a current of air to pass through the instrument, which would melt a portion of the ice, independently of the heat intended to melt it.

Mr. Wedgewood pointed out two sources of inaccuracy in the use of this apparatus; one of which arises from a portion of the water produced by the melting of the ice being retained by capillary attraction, among the pores of the unmelted ice, making the quantity obtained less than it ought to be. Endeavouring to remedy this source of error, Lavoisier and La Place exposed the pounded ice, for some time, to the atmosphere, before the experiment began, that the pores might be filled with water. It was also shown by Wedgewood, that while the process of thawing is going on in the upper part of the middle vessel, the water freezes again while filtrating through the ice in the lower part of it; a circumstance very unfavourable to the accuracy of the experiment.

It occurred to Meyer, that the comparative quantities of caloric existing in bodies may be ascertained, by marking the times which equal quantities of them require to cool a certain number of degrees, accounting their capacities to be as these times, estimated by the volume; or, if divided by the specific gravity of the substance, giving the capacity as estimated by the weight. This plan has been used by Leslie and Dalton, who consider it less liable to objection than any of the preceding, although it might easily be shown that its accuracy is very doubtful.

Great difficulties are opposed to the investigation of the comparative quantities of caloric belonging to elastic fluids at different temperatures. The method by which this investigation has been most frequently pursued, is to watch the degrees of heat imparted, by given portions of these elastic fluids, cooling through a certain range of temperature; and, notwithstanding the difficulties alluded to, Dr. Crawford is believed to have made near approximations to truth, in his numerous delicate and ingenious experiments.

Mr. Leslie proposed to ascertain the capacities of elastic fluids by the following method :—The capacities of elastic fluids for heat being increased by rarefaction, he proposed to exhaust a receiver, by the air-pump, of a portion of its air; the receiver having a delicate thermometer suspended within it, and the apparatus being allowed to acquire the temperature of the room, more air is admitted, which occasioning the condensation of the rarefied air, its capacity is reduced, and heat consequently set free. By repeating the experiment several times, with common air, and then by comparing the effect produced upon other gases, with that produced upon common air, Mr. Leslie thinks that the capacities of elastic bodies in general might be ascertained. This plan has been strongly objected to by M. Gay Lussac, who believes it to be incapable of accuracy.

It appears from the experiments of the last-named philosopher, that a part of the heat in Mr. Leslie's process is derived from the gas that is permitted to enter into the receiver after the rarefaction, by which the results obtained would be materially affected. It also appeared to M. Gay Lussac, that some unknown circumstances must have misled Mr. Leslie in judging of his experiments, since similar experiments made with great care by the French philosopher gave different results. Mr. Leslie inferred, from the experiments alluded to, that the specific heats of hydrogen gas and common air, in equal volumes, are the same. Gay Lussac, in operating upon these elastic fluids according to Mr. Leslie's method, observed a considerable difference in the effects produced upon them; and, without coming to a positive decision, thought there is reason to conclude, that the specific heat of equal volumes of the different gases is inversely as their specific gravity; and of the same gas directly as its density.

For the purpose of determining the specific heats of elastic fluids, Gay Lussac contrived that a hot current of one gas should meet a cold current of another gas, in the centre of a small reservoir containing a thermometer: the temperature of the mixture was then ascertained; and knowing also the temperature of each before they were permitted to mix, it was easy to infer the ratio between their respective specific heats.

The capacities of numerous gaseous bodies have been calculated by Mr. Dalton upon a plan peculiar to himself, and which is founded upon the supposition that the ultimate particles of all elastic fluids contain the same quantity of heat under the same pressure and temperature. The following TABLE gives his results:—

Hydrogen gas	9.382
Azotic gas	1.866
Atmospheric air	1.759
Ammonia	1.555
Olefiant gas	1.555
Oxygen	1.333
Carburetted hydrogen	1.333
Aqueous vapour	1.166
Vapour of ether	0.818
Nitrous gas	0.777
Oxide of carbon	0.777
Vapour of alcohol	0.586
Sulphuretted hydrogen	0.583
Nitrous oxide gas	0.519
Vapour of nitric acid	0.491
Carbonic acid	0.491
Muriatic acid	0.424

Berard and Delaroche caused a uniform current of any gas, the specific heat of which was to be ascertained, to issue from a gasometer, and pass through a pipe forty inches long, which was inclosed in a larger pipe, constantly filled with the steam of boiling water, by which it was heated; and its temperature being determined, it was made to pass slowly through a spiral tube, immersed in a quantity of cold water; the cylindrical vessel containing the water, and the spiral tube, being called the calorimeter. When the gas issued from this tube, its temperature was indicated by a thermometer at the extremity, to be always the same as the water in the calorimeter; and the specific heat of the gas operated upon was judged of by the degree of heat which it imparted to the water in being cooled to the same temperature.

An extract from a translation of the memoir in which the researches alluded to were made known, will assist in giving a clear idea of the methods by which Berard and Delaroche estimated the specific heats of different gases. Speaking of their calorimeter, they say, "Now, let us conceive a thin copper cylinder, six inches long, and three in diameter, filled with distilled water, and traversed by a serpentine of about five feet in length, forming eight spiral turnings, the two ends of which open without the vessel, the one at the top and the other at the bottom. If we make a regular current of gas traverse this serpentine, maintained before its entrance at an elevated and constant temperature, this current may be considered as an uniform source of heat, and the water in the cylinder as the body heated. Of course, if we repeat the same experiment upon each of the gases, each current will raise the temperature of the cylinder to a fixed point, where it will remain stationary: and it follows from the principles announced above, that, reckoning from this point, the excess of the temperature of the cylinder above that of the ambient air, will be proportional to the quantity of heat given out by the current of gas that passed through the cylinder. Hence, we shall obtain by this method, with great exactness, the relative specific heats of the gases subjected to this kind of experiment. There are likewise two methods of comparing them with water. The first consists in subjecting the cylinder which we call the calorimeter to the action of a current of water, perfectly regular, and so slow that it will hardly produce a greater effect than the current of the different gases. The second method consists in determining by calculation the real quantity of heat which the calorimeter, come to its stationary temperature, can lose in a given time; for since, after it reaches this point, it does not become hotter, though the source of heat continues to be applied to it, it is evident that it loses as much heat as it receives." *Annals of Philosophy*, vol. ii. page 212.

The ingenious and delicate arrangement used by Delaroche and Berard in the experiments, is shown at *fig.* 14: *a* is the vessel for containing the water, so contrived, that an uniform

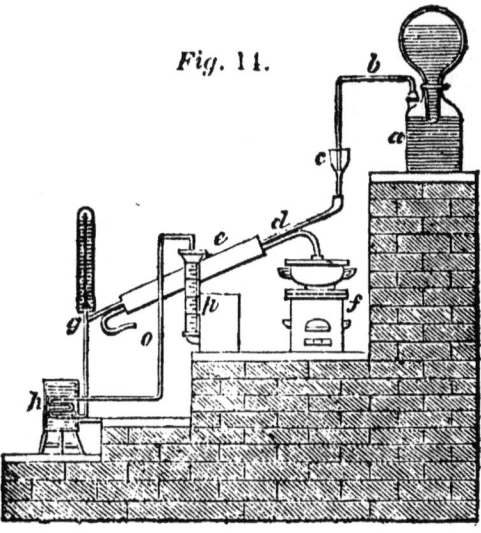

Fig. 14.

supply is made to pass through the syphon tube b, into the funnel c, and thence into the tube d, which is enclosed in a larger one supplied with steam from the furnace f: the water, passing through the tube g, imparts its temperature to the thermometers placed in it; it then enters at the bottom of the calorimeter h, and traversing the spiral tube passes out by the tube o, and drops into the graduated tube p.

The results obtained by Delaroche and Berard are contained in the following Table, the specific heat of atmospheric air being considered 1.000 :—

	Equal Volumes.	Equal Weights.	Specific Gravity.
Air	1.0000	1.0000	1.0000
Hydrogen	0.9033	12.3401	0.0732
Carbonic acid	1.2583	0.8280	1.5196
Oxygen	0.9765	0.8848	1.1036
Azote	1.0000	1.0318	0.9691
Oxide of azote	1.3503	0.8878	1.5209
Olefiant gas	1.5530	1.5763	0.9885
Carbonic oxide	1.0340	1.0805	0.9569

The specific heats of the gases included in the foregoing table being each compared with that of an equal weight of water, the following numbers are obtained :—

Oxygen	0.2361
Azote	0.2754
Water	1.0000
Air	0.2669
Hydrogen gas	3.2936
Carbonic acid	0.2210
Oxide of Azote	0.2369
Olefiant gas	0.4207
Carbonic oxide	0.2884
Aqueous vapour	0.8470

With the exception of hydrogen, which has a greater degree of specific heat than any other body, all the gases mentioned in the preceding table have less specific heat than water, and more than any of the metals.

The results of these experiments are hostile to the theory invented by Irvine, adopted by Crawford, Leslie, and others, that the evolution of heat, when bodies combine together, arises from a diminution of the specific heat of the bodies combined. One of their strongest arguments against this theory is derived from a comparison of the specific heat of water obtained by experiment with that of the constituent parts, deduced by calculation, which they state as follows:

Water (composed of 0.87 oxygen and 0.13 hydrogen).
Its specific heat by calculation ... 0.6335
By experiment 1.0000

By which it appears, that the specific heat of the constituents of water is increased by their combination.

The specific heat of oxygen compared with that of water is 0.2361; that of carbonic acid being $0.2210 \tfrac{23}{1000}$ parts less than that of oxygen. "Let us suppose a pound of charcoal consumed. From Lavoisier's experiments, it appears that the heat evolved is sufficient to melt $96\tfrac{1}{4}$ lbs. of ice. Now, this (supposing Mr. Cavendish's estimate correct) is equal to $1.3027\tfrac{1}{2}$ degrees of heat. The oxygen consumed amounts to 28lbs. nearly; so that each lb. of oxygen, when changed into carbonic acid, must have given off 3428 degrees. Here a change in the specific heat amounting only to $\tfrac{23}{1000}$, or not quite $\tfrac{1}{43}$ of the whole, occasioned the escape of 3428 degrees. Such a conclusion can only be adopted, if we suppose the absolute quantity of heat in the oxygen gas to amount to 147.404 degrees. This supposition exceeds the estimate of Dr. Crawford nearly 100 times; and it is more than ten times greater than that adopted by Dalton. No person can believe that oxygen gas contains so much heat. Of course, the supposition that the heat evolved during combustion is owing to a change of capacity merely, cannot be defended. If heat be a fluid, it must enter into chemical combination with certain bodies; and the decomposition of these bodies must be the cause of heat evolved during combustion." *Annals of Philosophy*, Dec. 1813.

Experiments have frequently been made to ascertain specific heats by suspending bodies heated to a given degree in a cool and uniform medium, until their temperature descends through a certain part of the thermometric range, marking the times which different substances require to cool the same number of degrees, all of them being exposed under the very same circumstances; their specific heats are considered to be directly as the times of their cooling

The method by which Dulong and Petit ascertained the specific heats of metals was by reducing them to very fine filings, which were close pressed into a thin and small cylindrical vessel of silver, having the bulb of a thermometer in its axis, the vessel containing about

460 grains of the substance, heated to about 12° of Fahrenheit above the surrounding air, was suspended in the centre of a vessel which was blackened on the inside, and exhausted of air, to make the cooling slower; the time required being generally about 15 minutes, although the exhausted vessel was surrounded with melting ice.

The specific heats of metals thus obtained are as under, that of water being considered 100:—

Bismuth	0.0288
Lead	0.0293
Gold	0.0298
Platinum	0.0314
Tin	0.0514
Silver	0.0557
Zinc	0.0927
Tellurium	0.0912
Copper	0.0949
Nickel	0.1035
Iron	0.1100
Cobalt	0.1498
Sulphur	0.1880

From the statements which have been made respecting the capacities of bodies for heat, and the specific heat of bodies, it will be evident that a very close connection exists between these, so close, that one of the terms is frequently used for the other without occasioning confusion: the former means the relative powers of bodies in receiving and retaining heat in being raised to any given temperature, some bodies receiving and retaining much more than others; the latter term applies to the actual quantities of heat so received and retained.

Whatever may be the cause of the different capacities of bodies for heat, it appears to be greatly influenced by the state of density in which bodies exist; although not so regularly as to admit of being considered as an invariable relation: hydrogen, the lightest of all bodies, having the greatest capacity, and metals, the heaviest of bodies, having the least. The same body may have its capacity enlarged by the decrease of its density; thus, the intense cold existing in the higher regions of the atmosphere has been accounted for on the supposition of the increased capacity of the air for heat. On the contrary, by increasing the density of a body, its capacity for heat is diminished; a quantity of heat is therefore set free, and produces sensible effects; as in the sudden condensation of air, the rapid reduction of which to one-fifth of its volume occasions the evolution of heat in sufficient quantity to inflame tinder; and if the condensation be effected in a glass tube in a dark place, a flash of light may be seen at the same time.

Supposing caloric to consist of material particles, the tendency of which is to diffuse themselves equally over space, it seems natural that they should be introduced in largest quantity into those bodies, the particles of which are at the greatest distance from each other. On this account, bodies which have the least density may have the greatest capacity for heat; and, as the particles of different bodies probably attract heat with different degrees of force, which, it is imagined, may account for the different quantities of heat retained by different bodies at any given temperature; although by this attraction no intimate union be occasioned as if chemical attraction were exerted, the particles of heat still retaining all their properties unaltered.

Chapter VIII.

Of the absolute quantity of Heat which any Body contains at any given Temperature.

All bodies, it is obvious, must contain limited quantities of heat; but since it is not in our power to deprive them of it entirely, it is exceedingly difficult to determine how much any body continues to possess after we have reduced its temperature as much as possible. While Dr. Irvine was engaged in the investigation of the capacities of bodies for heat, it occurred to him, that, if the quantities of heat contained in bodies be in proportion to their capacities, a knowledge of the capacity of a body in its different states, together with the quantities of heat which it absorbs or gives out when it undergoes a change of form, may enable us to infer the amount of the whole quantity existing in the body: as for example, the capacity of water to that of ice being as 10 to 9. Water at the temperature of 32 will contain one-tenth more heat than ice at the same temperature. Before ice can assume the state of water, it must give out this tenth part, which may then be measured. Dr. Black estimated the quantity at 140° of Fahrenheit, that is to say, ice requires as much heat to liquefy it as would raise the temperature of the same weight of water 140°: this number multiplied by 10 will give the whole quantity of heat contained in water at 32°; namely, 1400°, which points out the actual zero, at which no heat would remain.

The theorem of Dr. Irvine for calculating the real zero of bodies is thus stated by Dr. Murray: "The capacities of the solid and liquid being as the whole quantities of caloric they contain, it will follow, that the difference between the numbers which express their capacities, is, to the number which expresses the capacity of the liquid, as the difference between the quantity of heat which each contains, measured according to the capacity of the liquid, is to the number of degrees which will express the quantity of caloric it contains from zero." The above expression will not, it is suspected, challenge admiration on account of its clearness; what succeeds is less objectionable: "The following general formula, therefore, may be given for the calculation. Multiply the number which expresses the quantity of caloric absorbed when the body passes from the solid to the liquid, or given out when it passes from the liquid to the solid state, by the number denoting the capacity of the liquid. Divide the product by the number which expresses the difference in the capacities of the body in its two forms; the quotient will be the number of degrees of temperature between the freezing point of the liquid, and zero measured according to the capacity of the liquid."

Dr. Robison, speaking of Dr. Irvine's ingenious method of determining the point of absolute privation of heat, and quoting his own words, says his fundamental proposition was, that "the heat which appeared in mixing vitriolic acid and water is the difference between the sum of the absolute heats of the two ingredients, and the absolute heat of the mixture; while the heats, which each of them separately required for an equal variation of temperature, had the proportion of their respective absolute heats." Therefore, having discovered by such experiments the difference and the ratio of the absolute heats of the ingredients, we can find those absolute heats, and the temperature at which those heats commence, or in which the ingredients contain no heat at all.—*Black's Lectures, by Robison*, page 505.

It was considered that the degrees of temperature are the same in all bodies, although different bodies require different quantities of heat to produce these degrees. So that if the distance of water at 32° be 1400° from zero, all other bodies at the same temperature will be at the same distance from zero; the distance of each body being measured by degrees according to its own capacity.

Many different philosophers have engaged in this difficult investigation, and have obtained from various experiments very discordant results.

Dr. Crawford calculating from the capacities of the constituents of water, and the circumstances attending their combination, states that the absolute zero of water is 1532° below its freezing point.

Gadolin measured the capacity of sea-salt and of its solutions, in given quantities of water, and having observed the degrees of cold produced by the solutions, he calculated from these, and brought out the zero at 1432° below the freezing of water. The same philosopher deduced a variety of numbers from other experiments on the mixture of sulphuric acid and water, and on the mixture of snow and salt; the lowest of which for the zero was 1510°, and the highest 3230°.

The results obtained by Lavoisier and La Place are difficult to reconcile with one another, and with those obtained by other philosophers. From experiments on the mixture of quicklime and water, the apparent zero was 3460° below the freezing point; experiments on sulphuric acid and water brought out the zero at 7294° lower than the freezing point; and it was made to appear by experiments on a mixture of nitric acid and quicklime to be 23,837° above the same point.

Mr. Dalton deduced different numbers from different experiments, all of the numbers expressing the distance of the zero in degrees of Fahrenheit's scale below the freezing of water: from the mixture of $5\frac{3}{4}$ parts of sulphuric acid with one part of water 6400°; from a mixture of three parts of lime with one of water 4260°; from seven parts of nitric acid and one of lime 11,000°; from the combustion of hydrogen 5400°, and from the combustion of oil, wax, and tallow 6900°.

MM. Clement and De Sormes state the absolute zero at 448° of Fahrenheit; while MM. Dulong and Petit fix it at infinity. It is almost superfluous to remark, after what has been stated, that the results hitherto obtained in this difficult research are not such as to engage our confidence, or to admit of being made the basis of other calculations.

Chapter IX.

Of Latent Heat, including Fluidity, Steam, Evaporation, and Distillation.

The honour of having made the important discovery that large quantities of heat must enter into bodies, and be concealed to enable them to pass from the solid to the fluid state, or from the fluid state to that of vapour, is universally ascribed to Dr. Black. His first decisive experiment was made in December, 1761, at Glasgow, where he was then professor of chemistry. This experiment consisted in comparing the length of time which a given weight of water required to raise its temperature one degree, with the length of time which the same weight of ice required for its liquefaction, an equal heat being applied in both cases; and also reversing the experiment, he compared the length of time required to depress the temperature of a given weight of water one degree with the length of time required to freeze the same quantity: he was thus enabled to determine that the quantity of heat necessary to enable a given weight of ice to assume the fluid form, is equal to that which would raise the temperature of the same weight of water 140°. He also found that an equal quantity of heat is set free from water when it assumes the solid form. Since the increased quantity of heat, thus proved to be essential to the fluid state, is not capable of being detected by the touch, or by the application of a thermometer, Dr. Black called it concealed or latent heat.

He was led to this discovery by noticing what takes place in some natural operations, particularly the melting of ice and snow. Portions of these being brought into a warm room, gradually attain the temperature of 32°, if previously below that point; they then begin to melt, and continue at the same temperature until the whole is melted; all the heat which enters into the melting ice or snow being converted into latent heat, to promote the liquefaction: when the whole is liquefied the temperature again rises, and continues to do so until it becomes the same as that of the room. The slow manner in which ice melts in ice-houses, and in which ice and snow, where they are accumulated in large quantities, assume the fluid state, were observed by Dr. Black; and he described in his lectures the effects which would happen if large quantities of heat were not necessary to enable ice and snow to liquefy. In that case, he affirmed, that torrents and inundations would be irresistible and dreadful, tearing up and sweeping away every thing so suddenly, as scarcely to permit the human inhabitants of those districts to escape from the ravages.

Dr. Black put five ounces of pure water into each of two thin globular glass vessels, about the same size and weight; the water in one of the vessels was completely frozen by immersion in a mixture of snow and salt; the vessel was then set on a wire ring attached to a reading-desk, in a large hall, where it remained until it was entirely melted. The other vessel containing the same quantity of water cooled to 33°, and, having a delicate thermometer suspended in it, was placed in a similar situation. In about half a minute the thermometer assumed the temperature of the water, after which the increase of temperature was observed every five or ten minutes during half an hour, at the end of which time the degree of heat indicated was 40° of Fahrenheit. When the glass containing the ice was taken out of the freezing mixture, it was four or five degrees colder than melting snow; when it arrived at the freezing point, and was just beginning to melt, the time was noted, and the glass was then left undisturbed ten hours and a half. At that time a small spongy mass of the ice remained unmelted in the upper part of the water, although that part of the water which was near the sides of the vessel had attained the temperature of 40°. In a few minutes more the whole of the ice had become liquid. Thus it appears that the same quantity of heat which was capable of raising the temperature of the water-glass seven degrees in half an hour, required ten hours and a half, or twenty-one half hours, to raise the ice-glass to the same temperature; so that 21 multiplied by 7, will give the number of degrees of heat.

The temperature to which the two glasses were exposed, under precisely the same circumstances, was 47°. The water-glass attained the temperature of 40° in half an hour, being an increase of 7°; the ice-glass, after being exposed twenty-one half hours, attained the same temperature. It is obvious that the ice-glass must have received, during every half hour, nearly the same quantity of heat which the water-glass did, while its temperature was being raised 7°; so that the whole quantity of heat imparted to the ice-glass will be found by multiplying 21 by 7, or 147°. In other words, the quantity of heat received by the ice-glass would have raised the temperature of water 147°, but only eight degrees of this quantity were to be detected in the water by a thermometer; consequently the remaining 139° or 140° must have been absorbed to enable the ice to liquefy.

Another method of ascertaining the same thing occurred to Dr. Black, by submitting ice to the action of warm water. Having prepared a piece of ice of a shape fit for his purpose, and weighing 59½ drachms, he plunged it into a quantity of water at the temperature of 190°, weighing 67½ drachms; the whole of the ice was liquefied in a few seconds, and the temperature of the fluid was immediately found to be 53°. Thus the heat of the water used in this experiment was reduced from 190° to 53°, as was the glass vessel which contained the water: it had been previously ascertained that the power of the vessel to heat bodies was not more than half that of water; the weight of the vessel was eight drachms, but on account of its less power of heating, the eight drachms are taken in the calculation as four of water. The temperature of 67½ drachms of water, together with four drachms of water capable of exerting the same heating power, was reduced, in this experiment, 137°; the whole of which quantity being communicated to 59½ drachms of ice, at 32°, raised its temperature only 21°; although, according to the relative proportions of hot and cold matter, it ought to have elevated the temperature of the ice 86°. A quantity of heat, therefore, was suddenly lost, equal to 65°, which, it was calculated, would have been sufficient to have raised the temperature of a quantity of water equal in weight to the ice 143°.

Dr. Black simplified the experiment by putting a lump of ice into an equal weight of water at 176°; the ice was melted, and the temperature of the whole was reduced to 32°.

Ex. This experiment will succeed more satisfactorily, if to a pound of new-fallen snow we add a pound of water at 172°; the snow will be liquefied, and 32° will be the resulting temperature.

Thus it appears that heat entering into bodies enables them to assume the fluid state by counteracting in some degree the influence of cohesive attraction, which holds the particles together, repelling them to greater distances, and permitting them to have freedom of motion among each other. It is believed, however, that something more is necessary to this freedom of motion than weakness of cohesive attraction. Professor Robison supposed, that while a substance remains in the solid state, the particles attract each other more strongly in one direction than another, on which account they will assume particular positions, and oppose more or less resistance to any force tending to change these positions; but when these particles enter into the fluid state, it is supposed that they attract each other equally in all directions, which would enable them to move with the smallest impulse, although the attraction between them should scarcely be diminished in force.

It has often been asserted, that a state of solidity is the natural state of all bodies: but the propriety of this assertion is doubtful, as examples might easily be adduced of substances which continue in different states according to the heat of the climate in which they may happen to be placed: thus sulphuric ether, which is permanently liquid in this climate, would always remain solid in the coldest parts of the arctic regions; and the state of elastic gas would be the only state in which it could exist near the Equator.

Fluidity.

All liquids, with the exception of alcohol, have been reduced to the solid state; and it is generally believed that this also would become solid if we were able to reduce its temperature sufficiently: the same opinion is entertained respecting elastic fluids. All solids that do not suffer decomposition at low temperatures may be converted into fluids, and most of them into vapour, by the intense heats produced by modern ingenuity. When bodies that remain fluid at the usual temperature of the air become solid, we say they are frozen;

and when bodies that are usually solid become fluid, in consequence of the addition of caloric, it is said they are melted, or fused. The transition of water and of metals from a solid to a fluid state being produced by the same cause, we may consider water as melted ice, with as much propriety as we do the fluid state of metallic substances melted metals.

It is not possible, under usual circumstances, to melt numerous compound substances, chiefly of animal or vegetable origin, on account of the decomposition which they suffer at comparatively low temperatures; but Sir James Hall, by subjecting several substances of this kind, as coal and limestone, to heat, under a great degree of pressure, so as to prevent the escape of their gaseous parts, succeeded in fusing them.

Ice cannot be raised higher than the temperature of 32° without melting; but water may, under certain circumstances, be cooled much lower without freezing. Mr. Dalton succeeded in reducing it to 5° of Fahrenheit before it solidified. Agitation is unfavourable to this experiment, occasioning the water to freeze instantly, and its temperature to rise to the freezing point. It was proved by Dr. Black that water which has been deprived of air by boiling freezes more readily than unboiled water, on account, as he supposed, of a slight agitation upon its surface, occasioned by the attraction of air. Whatever particles impair the transparency of water, when mixed with it, produce the same effect; but the most effectual method of determining the congelation of water which is colder than the freezing point, is to introduce a particle of ice or snow; crystallization instantly commences. Sir Charles Blagden exposed to the atmosphere two vessels containing distilled water, when the temperature was about 20° and the day calm; one of the vessels he covered slightly with paper, the other, being left uncovered, the temperature of the water in the covered vessel sunk many degrees below 32° without freezing, while ice invariably formed upon the surface of the water in the other vessel before a thermometer immersed in it was cooled quite to the freezing point. This difference he accounted for on the supposition that the frozen particles which float in the air, at that temperature, being permitted to come into contact with the water in the uncovered vessel, occasioned the process of congelation to commence. The effect of oil poured upon the surface of water in preventing it from freezing may be ascribed to the same cause.

The beautiful spiculæ, which shoot in different directions at certain angles through water at the commencement of freezing, and the enlargement of bulk produced by the process, prove that it is a species of crystallization, in which the particles are united by certain points or surfaces in preference to others; and the effect of agitation, in facilitating the process, may be explained by supposing that it assists the particles in assuming that position which is most favourable to their solidification; and since this effect is more likely to be produced by internal agitation among the parts of the fluid than by the general motion of the whole, it is found that a sudden jerk of a vessel containing water cooled below 32° is the most effectual kind of motion in promoting congelation. The effect produced by the introduction of a solid particle of the same substance, is supposed to depend upon the attractive power which it exerts upon the contiguous particles, occasioning them to arrange themselves in the manner most favourable for their union with other particles; and the same influence being extended from particle to particle, the solidification proceeds with rapidity.

Many of the circumstances alluded to in relation to the freezing of water may be illustrated by reference to other fluids, the best of which for that purpose is a solution of sulphate of soda.

Ex. A flask of the shape of *fig.* 15, being filled with a saturated solution of sulphate of soda, near the boiling point,

Fig. 15.

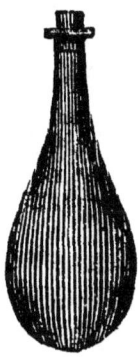

the neck of the flask being then closed so as effectually to exclude the air, by firmly tying pieces of bladder over it, or in any other way, the flask must then be suffered to cool until it attains the temperature of the surrounding air, at which time the surface of the fluid will be much lower in the neck of the flask; a thread being put round to mark its place, and the temperature of the flask having been felt by the hand, a hole may be made with a sharp point through the bladder, so as to admit the pressure of the air. The surface of the fluid will be agitated by the sudden admission of the air, and it is very probable that crystallization will commence at the surface, and proceed rapidly downwards in a beautiful manner, until the whole becomes solid. If crystallization should not take place on the admission of air, which is sometimes the case, the process may be made to commence by letting fall a small solid particle of the same salt into the solution. Sometimes it can scarcely pass below the surface before particles are attracted, which, arranging themselves round the solid nucleus, form beautiful radiating crystals that enlarge rapidly, extending throughout the whole mass, which becomes solid in a very short time. On trying the temperature of the flask with the hand, it will be found quite warm, a considerable quantity of heat being set free in the transition from fluid to solid. A few drops of fluid will probably remain, the surface of which will stand considerably above the thread on the neck of the flask, proving that the new arrangement of the parts necessary to the solid state occupies more room. It has usually been thought that the pressure of the air is essential to enable crystallization to take place in this experiment; but sometimes, as has already been stated; the pressure of the air may be admitted without producing the effect, while the introduction of a solid particle generally succeeds. It is more probable, therefore, that when crystallization happens on the admission of air, that it is occasioned by the agency of solid particles admitted along with the air, which serve as nucleii or points of attraction for crystallization to commence upon.

Dr. Black observed appearances attending the liquefying of other substances which connected them with the doctrines of latent heat, and he was of opinion that the same reasoning which applies to the melting of ice may apply to the melting of all other bodies.

Dr. Irvine, making some experiments, at the desire of Dr. Black, on spermaceti, bees' wax, and some other substances, found that spermaceti absorbed in melting, without becoming sensibly warmer, a quantity of heat sufficient to have rendered the same quantity of melted spermaceti from $141°$ to $148°$ hotter. Bees' wax, in the same way, absorbed $175°$; and it appeared to him that tin absorbed as much heat in melting as would raise its temperature in its solid state $500°$. Dr. Black was of opinion that the softness which takes place in some bodies before they assume the fluid state, depends upon their absorbing a portion of heat, though not in sufficient quantity to produce fluidity. The malleability and ductility of metals were also considered by him as depending upon the absorption of heat. " I therefore consider the metals," says he, " as substances which have the power to retain strongly a certain quantity of latent heat, which gives them their toughness and malleability; but I imagine that heat is driven out of them by the violent agitation, compression, and friction of their parts, in hammering them strongly into another shape. Those called the more perfect metals retain this heat with the greatest force, and retain it in some cases, though extended by skilful hammering, to an amazing degree. Tough iron, which is a purer metal than steel, contains more of it than steel does, and shows a little more power to retain it; from iron it cannot be expelled but by the strokes of the hammer, or violent compression; from steel it can be separated not only by hammering, but also by sudden and violent refrigeration of the steel from a red-hot state. This happens in the operation called the hardening of steel. The steel is made red-hot in the fire, and then suddenly plunged into cold water. Thus it is made excessively hard, but at the same time perfectly inflexible or brittle. We must, therefore, conclude that this sudden and violent refrigeration prevents its retaining a due portion of latent heat, which it would have retained, had it been allowed to cool slowly and quietly. Iron when heated in the same manner loses but very little of its latent heat."—*Black's Lectures*, vol. i, p. 140.

Steam.

Although Dr. Black did not find opportunities for the performance of such experiments as satisfied him completely respecting the quantity of heat which becomes latent in the conversion of water into steam before 1762, he had made many observations as to the fact a considerable time before. He had observed that every addition of heat applied to a fluid produces an elevation of temperature until it arrives at the boiling point, but however violently the fluid may boil, it does not become hotter, nor does the steam that arises from it indicate a greater degree of heat than the water: a large proportion of the heat, therefore, he had no doubt, enters into the steam, and becomes latent. He also observed the great heat imparted to the worm-tub of a still, and was convinced that when vapour is condensed into a liquid, its latent heat is again set free.

The experiments by which these opinions were proved to be correct were simple and convincing. He applied heat to a small quantity of water at 50°, and having noticed what length of time was required to make the water boil, he continued to apply the heat until all the water was converted into vapour, and found that the vaporization of the water required five times as much heat as was requisite to make it boil, or 810°; from which he inferred that 810° of heat had been carried off by the steam. Reversing the experiment, he converted a pound of water into steam, and made it pass through the worm of a still, by which he found that 20° of heat were imparted to 40 lbs. of water in the worm-tub, and inferred from the effect produced that 800° of heat must have been given out by the steam.

A strong phial was half filled with water, close corked, and heated in a vessel of sand; after the water had boiled, and there was a strong pressure within the phial, Dr. Black suddenly withdrew the cork, and was delighted to find, as he had been led to anticipate, that a portion of the water only was converted into vapour, and that the temperature of the remaining water was reduced to the boiling point, and thus ascertained that all the excess of heat was expended in the formation of vapour.

A similar experiment was soon afterwards performed by Mr. Watt, in a more satisfactory manner. " He put three inches of water into a small copper digester, and screwing on the lid, he left the safety-valve open; he then set it on a clear fire of coke, and after it began to boil and produce steam, he allowed it to remain on the fire half an hour with the valve open; then taking it off the fire, he found that an inch of water had boiled away. In the next place, he restored that inch of water, screwed on the lid, and set it on the fire; and as soon as it began to boil, he shut the safety-valve, and allowed it to remain on the fire half an hour, as before. The temperature of the whole was many degrees above the boiling point. He took it off the fire, and set it upon ashes, and opened the valve a very small matter: the steam rushed out with great violence, making a shrieking noise for about two minutes. When this had ceased, he shut the valve, and allowed all to cool. When he opened, it he found that an inch of water was consumed.—*Black's Lectures*, vol. 1, page 160.

The inferences drawn by Dr. Black from these experiments were, that the same quantity of heat entered into the water in the second as in the first, and that as much escaped with the steam which rushed out, as was carried off by the vaporization of the water when the vessel was open.

Under the usual pressure of the air, water cannot be heated above the boiling point; but when exposed to greater pressure, by being confined in the vessel, it may be raised to a much higher degree of heat, and if the excess of heat should be insufficient to convert the whole of the water into vapour, a portion of it would rush out in steam on opening the vessel, and the remaining water would be at the boiling temperature.

The low temperature at which water boils in vacuo, was observed by Dr. Black, and explained upon the same theory. The evaporation of alcohol and ether affords still more striking illustrations. Dr. Cullen found that on wetting the bulb of a thermometer with either of these, and suspending it in the air, its temperature was rapidly reduced. The greater the tendency of the liquid to assume the state of vapour, and the more its evoporation is hastened by blowing a current of air upon it, the greater the degree of cold produced. A glass goblet, containing water, was placed by him upon the plate of an air-pump, a wide-mouthed phial containing vitriolic ether being immersed in it; a thermometer was so suspended to a wire passing through the top of the receiver, that its bulb could be dipped into the ether and taken out at pleasure. On exhausting the receiver, the ether boiled violently, being rapidly converted into vapour, and so great a degree of cold was produced by this evaporation that the water surrounding the ether was frozen, although the temperature of the air in the room was 54°.

By this experiment it was proved that ether is incapable of existing as a fluid when the pressure of the air is removed, and that when it assumes the form of vapour, heat is absorbed in large quantity.

Lavoisier proved by experiment that in cases of combination, where any part of the combining substances assumes the gaseous state, less heat is evolved than in other combinations where no aëriform substance is produced, the heat which would otherwise become sensible being expended in enabling the disengaged substance to assume its expanded form.

In order to prove the disengagement of heat which had been absorbed by water when it returned to the state of ice, Dr. Black exposed pure water and water containing a little salt in solution, in two similar vessels, to the influence of an atmosphere colder than 32°; the pure water began to freeze, and its temperature remained at 32°; the heat set free in the process of congelation being sufficient to counterbalance the abstraction of heat by the colder atmosphere. The temperature of the water which had salt dissolved in it, continued to descend until it was cooled considerably below the freezing point.

But the evolution of heat from a latent state is most strikingly shown when vapour is condensed into water. Dr. Black inferred from his experiments on a still, that the quantity set free is from 774 to 750 degrees. Mr. Watt repeated the experiments with a smaller still, better adapted for the purpose, and obtained as the medium result of many trials 825° as the quantity of heat set free. He adopted another mode of pursuing this enquiry. A metallic cylinder, with a piston accurately fitted to it, was filled with vapour; the air having been previously expelled, the piston was then suddenly forced down, which compressed the steam and occasioned the extrication of a quantity of heat, which, according to the calculation made at the time, would have been sufficient to raise the temperature of an equal weight of a body having the same capacity as water, and which would not evaporate 943 degrees.

In reviewing the progress of Dr. Black in these important discoveries, a predominant feeling of the mind is admiration of the simplicity and clearness with which he explained his opinions, and demonstrated his assertions; for he, instead of affecting the repulsive obscurity of scientific phraseology, still too much in use, stated every thing in such plain language that every pupil of his class must have been able to understand all that he advanced respecting this new department of science; which, in other hands, might have been rendered more than sufficiently difficult and obscure.

Another suggestion that arises in the mind, and which challenges admiration also, is the freedom of this distinguished philosopher from suspicion and jealousy: he had no sooner opened this delightful field of enquiry, than it was eagerly entered by other philosophers, several of whom were encouraged and assisted by Dr. Black himself. Mr. Watt was one of these; and, although he has explicitly denied that any of his most important inventions were suggested by Dr. Black, yet it is obvious to all who are acquainted with the circumstances under which these philosophers were placed with respect to each other, that the very important inventions alluded to were, in all probability, facilitated by the previous discovery of latent heat by Dr. Black.

It is not intended in this essay to enlarge upon the application of these discoveries to the improvement of the steam-engine, but a brief sketch to that effect may not be out of place.

When Mr. Watt's attention was first attracted to the steam-engine, motion was given to it by the introduction of steam below a piston moving, steam-tight, in a cylinder; when the piston was raised by its elastic force, a jet of cold water was made to play into the cylinder, by which the steam was condensed, and a vacuum produced; the air pressing upon the piston above forced it down into the cylinder, raising the weights at the other end of the beam; the steam was then permitted to enter again to elevate the piston, as before.

In this operation it will be obvious that immense quantities of steam must be lost in raising the temperature of the cylinder to the boiling point, every time after being cooled with cold water, and exposure to the atmosphere, and consequently corresponding portions of heat wasted, amounting, according to the calculations of Mr. Watt, to half the quantity used for working the engine.

It was seen by him that the cooling of the working cylinder must deprive the steam of its latent heat, and occasion its condensation, until the cylinder was again heated to 212°. To remedy this, after many experiments, Mr. Watt contrived to condense the steam in a separate vessel without cooling the working cylinder. A communication being established between the cylinder and a separate vessel, called a condenser, exhausted of air and immersed in cold water; the moment the steam had performed its office, a valve was opened, by the working of the engine, which permitted the steam to rush into the exhausted vessel, where it was condensed by the cold temperature of the vessel.

This is decidedly the most important of the numerous inventions of Mr. Watt.

To prevent the cooling effect of the atmosphere, and still further to economize heat, he excluded air altogether from the cylinder, by making the piston-rod work through a collar, steam being introduced above the piston, and afterwards both above and below it; when the steam had pressed the piston to the top it was allowed to escape to the condenser; and steam was admitted above to press it down into the vacuum produced below by condensation, in the same way the steam above escaped into the condenser; and the steam entering below forced the piston up into the vacuum, so produced, thus enabling the engine to exert great power, without the aid of atmospheric pressure.

It is affirmed that Mr. Watt, when he first began to operate on steam, had neither means nor leisure to permit the use of a complicated apparatus, and, therefore, made some of his most important researches with apothecaries' phials. In this way he discovered that a cubical inch of water forms a cubical foot of steam, or 1728 inches; and that the heat evolved by the condensation of that quantity of steam would be sufficient to heat six cubical inches of water from the atmospherical temperature to 212 degrees. It is now usually considered that steam, arising from boiling water, occupies 1800 times as much space as the water from which it was produced.

The apparatus used by Dr. Ure, in his researches on the latent heat of vapours, and which he considered well adapted to the purpose, although exceedingly simple, consisted of a small glass retort, with a short neck, inserted into a globular receiver of very thin glass, and about three inches in diameter. The globe was surrounded with a certain quantity of water, at a known temperature, in a glass basin. A quantity of the liquid, the vapour of which was to be examined, amounting to 200 grains, was put into the retort, and rapidly distilled into the globe, by the heat of an Argand lamp. His experiments were performed when the temperature of the air was 45°, that of the water in the basin being from 42° to 43°; the heat imparted by the condensation of steam to this water, never raised its temperature higher than about four degrees above that of the atmosphere, and each operation generally lasted about five or six minutes. A very delicate thermometer was constantly moved through the water, and its indications were read off, to small fractions of a degree, by the aid of a lens.

The elevation of temperature produced in these experiments being so little above that of the atmosphere, Dr. Ure was of opinion that the influence of the air did not affect the results. The water in the basin weighed 32,340 grains, and the globe was held steadily in its centre by a slender ring round its neck. The experiments were repeated a number of times with corresponding results, which are stated in the following table :—

TABLE of Latent Heat of Vapours.

Vapour of Water at its boiling point	1000
Alcohol, sp. gr. 825	457
Ether, boiling point 112°	312.9
Petroleum	183.8
Oil of Turpentine	183.8
Nitric acid, sp. gr. 1.494; boiling point 165	550
Liquid Ammonia, sp. gr. 0.978	865.9
Vinegar, sp. gr. 1.007	903

Mr. Watt found by his experiments that the latent heat of steam is in proportion to the degree of pressure under which it is produced, being least when the pressure is greatest.

M. Clement connected a small steam-boiler, capable of bearing a high degree of pressure, by means of a pipe with a given quantity of water, at a known temperature, in a bucket, into which he admitted steam at the temperature of 212° for some time, and then measured the increase of heat and of bulk which the water had received by the condensation of steam. Water was next heated in the boiler until the steam had twice the elasticity which it possesses at 212°. This steam being admitted into another quantity of water, equal to the first, until its volume was increased in the same degree, when he found that the same quantity of heat had been imparted. He tried the experiment also with steam, the elastic force of which was equal to three atmospheres, and obtained a similar result.

From these experiments he inferred that equal weights of steam, of whatsoever temperature, contain equal quantities of heat; the latent heat diminishing as the sensible heat increases.

The following TABLE of the elastic force of the vapour of water in inches of mercury, is by Dr. Ure:—

Temp.	Force.	Temp.	Force.
21°	0.170	120°	3.300
32	0.200	125	3.830
40	0.250	130	4.366
50	0.360	135	5.070
55	0.416	140	5.770
60	0.516	145	6.600
65	0.630	150	7.530
70	0.726	155	8.500
75	0.860	160	9.600
80	1.010	165	10.800
85	1.170	170	12.050
90	1.360	175	13.550
95	1.640	180	15.160
100	1.860	185	16.900
105	2.100	190	19.000
110	2.456	195	21.100
115	2.820	200	23.600

Temp.	Force.	Temp.	Force.
205°	25.900	273°.7	91.200
210	28.880	275	93.480
212	30.000	275.7	94.600
216.6	34.400	277.9	97.800
220	35.540	279.5	101.600
221.6	36.700	280	101.900
225	39.110	281.8	104.400
226.3	40.100	283.8	107.700
230	43.100	285.2	112.200
230.5	43.500	287.2	114.800
234.5	46.800	289	118.200
235	47.220	290	120.150
238.5	50.300	292.3	123.100
240	51.700	294	126.700
242	53.600	295.6	130.400
245	56.340	295	129.000
245.8	57.100	297.1	133.900
248.5	60.400	298.8	137.400
250	61.900	300	139.700
251.6	63.500	300.6	140.900
254.5	66.700	302	144.300
255	67.250	303.8	147.700
257.5	69.800	305	150.560
260	72.300	306.8	154.400
260.4	72.800	308	157.700
262.8	75.900	310	161.300
264.9	77.900	311.4	164.800
265	78.040	312	167.000
267	81.900		
269	84.900	Another Experiment.	
270	86.300	312°	165.5
271.2	88.000		

The small steam-boiler a, (fig. 16,) is as convenient as any that has been contrived for experiments on latent heat. The boiler is furnished with two stop-cocks, b and d, to the latter of which is screwed the pipe e: when the latent heat of vapour is to be determined, water is put into the boiler, and made to boil by the application of an Argand lamp f: the end of the pipe e being immersed in a given quantity of water in a vessel g, furnished with a thermometer h. After the water has boiled for some time, the increase of weight of the water in the vessel g may be ascertained, and then the indication of the thermometer will show how much heat has been imparted to the water by the condensation of a quantity of steam equal to the increase of weight. The effect thus produced may be com-

HEAT.

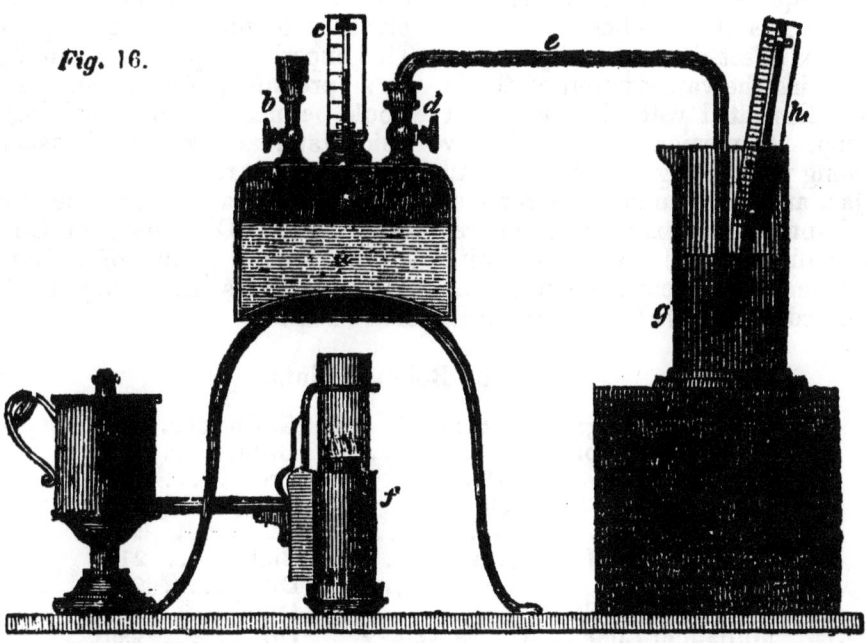

Fig. 16.

pared with that which would result from the addition of an equal weight of boiling water; and it will be found that a given weight of steam, at 212°, has the power of heating water many times more than an equal weight of water at the same temperature. The thermometer c passes through a collar into the boiler a, for the purpose of ascertaining the heat of its contents.

Dr. Ure remarks that it is the greatly superior relation to heat which steam possesses above water, that makes the boiling point of that fluid so perfectly stationary, in open vessels, over the strongest fires; and he found that vapours which have less latent heat are not capable, by their formation, of keeping their respective liquids while boiling at the same uniform temperatures. This he found to be the case with oil of turpentine, petroleum and sulphuric acid, which being heated briskly in common glass phials, they rose from twenty to thirty degrees above the points at which they boiled in hemispherical capsules.

The gases being similar to vapour in their high relation to heat, when they enter into liquid or solid states, heat is copiously evolved. The fixation of gaseous matter in the burning of bodies, occasioning the evolution of heat, was believed by Lavoisier and others to be the sole source of heat in the process of combustion. The cause of ebullition, or boiling, is the formation of vapour at the bottom of a vessel, in consequence of the application of heat there; the vapour being so much lighter than the fluid, bubbles of it continually rise to the surface and escape; the passage of these vapour bubbles through the water produces that agitation which is called boiling, or ebullition. Under the usual pressure of the air, water boils near the level of the sea at 212° of Fahrenheit; but when that pressure is reduced, less heat is sufficient to produce ebullition; as when water is carried up the side of a mountain, the greater the height, the less heat will be required to make the water boil, because a great proportion of the heavy column of air which occasions the pressure is left beneath. Upon this principle the thermometric barometer of the Rev. Mr. Wollaston is constructed, which indicates the elevation of any place above the level of the sea, by the difference in the heat required to make water boil at that elevation. A difference of one degree in the boiling point of water is occasioned by a difference in height, which lowers the barometer 0.589 of an inch, and corresponds very nearly to a difference of elevation amounting to 520 feet.

Saussure found that water boils at the top of Mont Blanc when heated to 187 degrees.

The boiling point of water differs according to the state of the air: when the barometer stands at 31 inches, more heat is required to make water boil than when it is at 28 inches.

Ex. The effect of a reduced pressure in promoting the vaporization of fluids may be illustrated with the aid of an air-pump. A portion of water below the boiling point being put into a small glass jar, and placed under the receiver of an air-pump, on exhausting the receiver ebullition will commence with great violence, and continue until the water is reduced to 70° of Fahrenheit, because, by the action of the pump, the pressure of the air is greatly reduced. This experiment proves the utility of the air's pressure; for without it water would be incapable of remaining in the fluid state, and would all assume the state of vapour.

Dr. Ure has given the following table in his Dictionary of Chemistry, of the boiling points of the most important liquids according to Fahrenheit's scale:—

Table of Boiling Points.

Liquid		Authority	Boiling Point
Ether.... sp. gr. 0.7365 at 48°		G. Lussac..	100
Carburet of sulphur		Ditto	113
Alcohol, sp. gr... 0.813		Ure	173.5
Nitric acid 1.500		Dalton	210
Water			212
Saturated sol. of Glaub. salt		Biot	213½
Ditto Sugar of lead		Ditto	215¾
Ditto Sea salt		Ditto	224¼
Muriate of Lime .. 1 + water 2		Ure	230
Ditto .... 35.5 + ditto 64.5		Ditto	235
Ditto .... 40.5 + ditto 59.5		Ditto	240
Muriatic acid 1.094		Dalton	232
Ditto............ 1.127		Ditto	222
Ditto............ 1.047		Ditto	222
Nitric acid 1.45		Ditto	240
Ditto............ 1.42		Ditto	248
Ditto............ 1.40		Ditto	247
Ditto............ 1.35		Ditto	242
Ditto............ 1.30		Ditto	236
Ditto............ 1.16		Ditto	220
Rectified petroleum		Ure	306
Oil of turpentine		Ditto	316
Sulph. acid. sp. gr. 1.30		Dalton	240
Ditto............ 1.408		Ditto	260
Ditto............ 1.520		Ditto	290
Ditto............ 1.650		Ditto	350
Ditto............ 1.670		Ditto	360
Ditto............ 1.699		Ditto	374
Ditto............ 1.730		Ditto	391
Ditto............ 1.780		Ditto	435
Ditto............ 1.810		Ditto	473
Ditto............ 1.819		Ditto	487
Ditto............ 1.827		Ditto	501
Ditto............ 1.833		Ditto	515
Ditto............ 1.842		Ditto	545
Ditto............ 1.847		Ditto	575
Ditto............ 1.848		Ditto	590
Ditto............ 1.849		Ditto	605
Ditto............ 1.850		Ditto	620
Ditto............ 1.848		Ure	600
Phosphorus			554
Sulphur			570
Linseed oil			640
Mercury (Dulong 662°)			656

The vapours which arise from these liquids, at their boiling points, are capable of balancing a pressure of the atmosphere equivalent to that of thirty inches of mercury, but the vapours arising at inferior temperatures have less elastic power.

HEAT.

Table of the Elastic forces of the Vapours of Alcohol, Ether, Oil of Turpentine, Petroleum, or Naphtha, by Dr. Ure.

Ether.		Alcoh. sp. gr. 0.813.		Alcoh. sp. gr. 0.813.		Petroleum.	
Temp.	Force of Vapour.	Temp.	Force of Vapour.	Temp.	Force of Vapour.	Temp.	Force of Vapour.
34°	6.20	32°	0.40	193.3°	46.60	316°	30.00
44	8.10	40	0.56	196.3	50.10	320	31.70
54	10.30	45	0.70	200	53.00	325	34.00
64	13.00	50	0.86	206	60.10	330	36.40
74	16.10	55	1.00	210	65.00	335	38.90
84	20.00	60	1.23	214	69.30	340	41.60
94	24.70	65	1.49	216	72.20	345	44.10
104	30.00	70	1.76	220	78.50	350	44.86
		75	2.10	225	87.50	355	50.20
2nd Ether.		80	2.45	230	94.10	360	53.30
		85	2.93	232	97.10	365	56.90
105	30.00	90	3.40	236	103.60	370	60.70
110	32.54	95	3.90	238	106.90	372	61.90
115	35.90	100	4.50	240	111.24	375	64.00
120	39.47	105	5.20	244	118.20		
125	43.24	110	6.00	247	122.10	Oil of Turpen.	
130	47.14	115	7.10	248	126.10	Temp.	Force of Vapour.
135	51.90	120	8.10	249.7	131.40		
140	56.90	125	9.25	250	132.30	304°	30.00
145	62.10	130	10.60	252	138.60	307.6	32.60
150	67.60	135	12.15	254.3	143.70	310	33.50
155	73.60	140	13.90	258.6	151.60	315	35.20
160	80.30	145	15.95	260	155.20	320	37.06
165	86.40	150	18.00	262	161.40	322	37.80
170	92.80	155	20.30	264	166.10	326	40.20
175	99.10	160	22.60			330	42.10
180	108.30	165	25.40			336	45.00
185	116.10	170	28.30			340	47.30
190	124.80	173	30.00			343	49.40
195	133.70	178.3	33.50			347	51.70
200	142.80	180	34.73			350	53.80
205	151.30	182.3	36.40			354	56.60
210	166.00	185.3	39.90			357	58.70
		190	43.20			360	60.80
						362	62.40

The low temperature at which water boils in vacuo, may be illustrated by another experiment.

Ex. Adapt a good cork covered on the upper part with a thick coating of sealing-wax, to a glass flask with a long neck *a* (*fig.* 17); put water to the depth of about an inch and a half into it, and apply the heat of a spirit-lamp until it boils; permit the boiling to continue for a short time, and then, having put on a worsted glove, introduce the cork; press it down, and remove the flask from the lamp. The water will boil a little after the heat ceases to be applied. On plunging the flask into the jar *b*, containing cold water, the boiling will recommence with great violence, and will continue until the water in the flask is nearly cold.

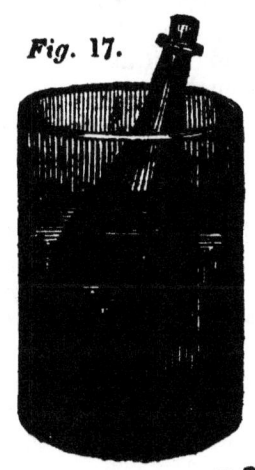

Fig. 17.

If the flask is taken out before the boiling ceases, and is plunged into hot water, it will immediately stop boiling, being re-plunged into the cold water the boiling will begin again.

In this experiment the air is excluded, and the vessel is filled with steam before the cork is introduced. The vessel being removed from the lamp, the water boils a little, because the air of the atmosphere coming into contact with its sides, condenses a portion of the steam within, and thus lessens the pressure upon its surface; so that it is enabled to boil, although its temperature be reduced.

When the flask is plunged into cold water, the steam within, losing its latent heat, is condensed; and the water, being by its condensation freed from pressure, boils with violence.

If the flask be now plunged into water, near the boiling point, it will instantly cease to boil, because the heat will convert a small portion of the water within the flask into vapour, which, occasioning a new pressure, prevents the water from boiling in its cooled state; or being re-plunged into the cold water, this minute quantity of vapour is condensed, and the water in the flask boils again.

When fluids are subjected to a greater degree of pressure than that of the atmosphere, they require higher degrees of heat to make them boil. The apparatus, (*fig.* 18,) is well adapted to illustrate this fact. The hollow globe *a* is composed of two strong hemispheres of brass, screwed together with flanges: some quicksilver is first poured into this globe, which is then about half filled with water; the barometer tube *b* passes through a steam-tight collar, and has its end immersed in the quicksilver: *c* is a thermometer for the purpose of ascertaining the temperature of the water during the experiments; its scale is graduated as high as 400°, and passes through a steam-tight collar; *d*, is the brass frame and stand upon which the globe rests; *e* is a spirit lamp, and *f* is an aperture closed by a stopcock. The stop-cock being closed, and heat applied to this vessel, the temperature of the water soon rises above the boiling point. When the heat arrives at 218 degrees the mercury will be elevated to six inches in the tube, by the elastic pressure of the steam; at 224 the mercury will have ascended twelve inches, rising an inch for every increased degree of heat. At 242 degrees the elasticity of the steam will balance a

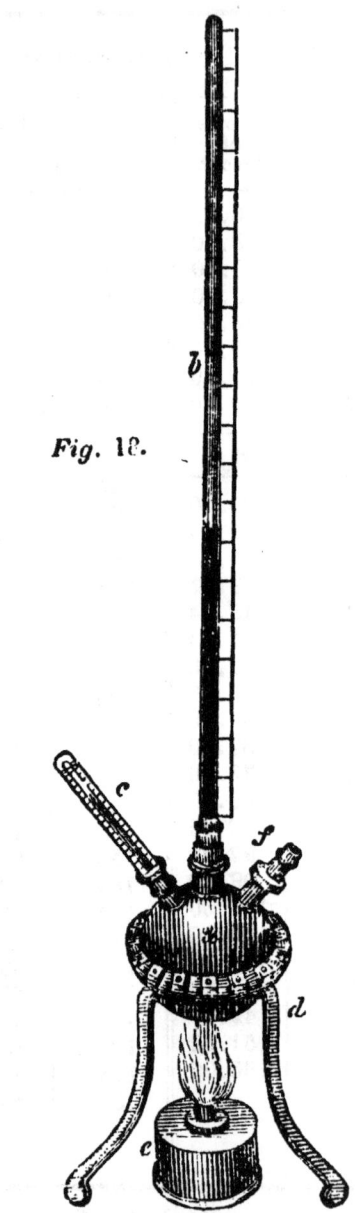

Fig. 18.

column of quicksilver thirty inches high, which is equal to the pressure of one atmosphere.

The facility with which steam imparts its vast treasures of heat to any body colder than itself, fits it admirably for many purposes in domestic life and the arts. Heat applied in this way is much preferable to the heat of a fire, for making extracts of vegetables in pharmaceutical preparations, for heating dyers' and brewers' vats, for the preparation of colours, for warming baths, for drying manufactured goods, for heating apartments, and for culinary operations.

Steam may be applied in two different ways for the purpose of heating large quantities of fluids: in one of these, the end of a pipe conveying steam from the boiler is immersed in the liquid to be heated; the steam issuing from the pipe is condensed, and, its latent heat being set free, raises the temperature of the liquid. When steam is applied in this way to the contents of vessels, they cannot be heated higher than within two or three degrees of the boiling point, although the water seems to boil: the quantity of water must also be greatly increased by the condensation of the steam, in this way of applying it; and this circumstance would be unfavourable to some processes. The other way of applying it is to enclose the vessel, steam-tight, within another, permitting steam to occupy the space between. In this way the water may be brought to a boiling heat, much sooner than if the vessel containing it were placed over an open fire.

Mr. Parkes made an experiment with a vessel of this kind, intended for preparing colours: its diameter, at the top, was twenty inches; it was eighteen inches deep, in the form of an inverted bee-hive, and calculated to hold twenty gallons. Being filled with cold water, at 52° Fahrenheit, steam was admitted into the space between the two vessels. In six minutes the temperature of the twenty gallons of water was raised to 190°, in eight minutes to 200°, in ten minutes to 208°, and in eleven minutes to 212°.—*Parke's Chemical Essays*, vol. v. p. 46.

It is estimated that one gallon of water converted into steam, will heat six gallons at 50° to the boiling point, or eighteen gallons from 50° to 100°, making abundant allowance for waste.

The heat imparted to the air by steam-pipes is peculiarly elegible for warming apartments; diffusing a genial and delightful warmth, combining comfort with cleanliness and safety. Calculations applied to the warming of manufactories by steam, make it appear that one cubic foot of boiler will heat about two thousand cubic feet of space, to the temperature of 70° or 80°; and that one foot of surface of steam-pipe is sufficient to warm 200 cubic feet of space. Cast-iron pipes are considered best for diffusing heat, and they should be placed near the floor.

Steam is a most effectual and convenient agent for preparing food. A close boiler, of any kind, being connected with a range of vessels intended for cooking, steam will rush into them, and heat them to the boiling temperature, and maintain them at the same as long as the water in the boiler is kept in a state of ebullition. Animal food prepared in this way is considered by the best judges to be more nutritious and easier of digestion than the same kind of food boiled in the usual way.

Evaporation.

The doctrine of latent heat is beautifully illustrated by the effects of evaporation. Since fluids, when they evaporate, require that large quantities of sensible heat should enter into them, and become latent, to enable them to assume the expanded state of vapour, all evaporation produces cold. On this account, showers in summer cool and refresh the earth, because the water which is spread over its surface evaporates quickly, and carries away with it the superfluous heat.

Ex. The experiment of Dr. Cullen, already alluded to, by which water was frozen round a phial of ether, under a receiver, exhausted by the air-pump, illustrates the effect of evaporation in producing cold. The experiment is now usually performed by setting a watch-glass containing water upon a stand, under the receiver of an air-pump; a thin metallic cup, containing ether, is placed in the middle of the watch glass. As the exhaustion proceeds the rapid evaporation of the ether makes it boil, and the water to freeze at the same time; so that the metallic cup will, in a short time, be fixed in the centre of a cake of ice.

Fluids evaporate in *vacuo* at degrees of temperature from 120° to 125° below their boiling point, when exposed to atmospherical pressure. Advantage has been taken of this circumstance in Howard's plan for refining sugar, and in plans for preparing pharmaceutical extracts in *vacuo*. The boiler, or evaporating vessel, of Mr. Barry's apparatus for this purpose, is connected by a pipe, having a stop-cock, with a copper sphere, three or four times as large as itself. When the juice or infusion to be inspissated has been introduced into the boiler or still, it is closed air-tight, the stop-cock between the boiler and the copper sphere being shut: steam is then introduced into the latter until it issues out at an aperture uncondensed, when, the aperture being closed, the steam is condensed by permitting it to rush into a refrigerator immersed in cold water. The stop-cock in the pipe leading from the boiler is then opened, and a large proportion of its air rushes into the exhausted sphere. This process is repeated, until the vacuum in the boiler is sufficiently perfect. Heat is applied to the boiler by a water-bath. The peculiarities of this plan are the production of a vacuum without the aid of an air-pump, and the particular methods used for condensation.

By combining the exhaustion of an air-pump, and the absorbent power of sulphuric acid, Mr. Leslie succeeded in freezing water. The experiment was first made in June 1810. A watch-glass, filled with water, was placed over a shallow vessel, filled with sulphuric acid; the air-pump being partly exhausted, vapour was raised abundantly from the water, and absorbed by the acid, which occasioned such a degree of cold as to freeze the water in a very short time. *Fig.* 19, represents an

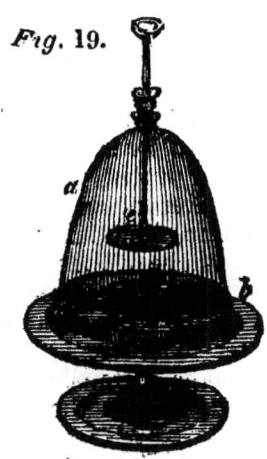

Fig. 19.

arrangement used for this purpose: *a* is the glass receiver; *b* a brass plate furnished with a stop-cock and stand, and capable of being attached to the air-pump; *c*, the flat glass dish for holding the sulphuric acid; *d*, the vessel containing the water to be frozen, supported upon a stand; *e* is a cover attached to a sliding-rod. By this process ice may be readily obtained, in small quantities, at any season of the year. When the water to be frozen has been previously deprived of air by boiling, the process of congelation goes on more slowly, but the ice formed acquires a greater degree of solidity. The process may be stopped by lowering the cover *e*, upon the vessel containing the water; and it proceeds as before, the moment the cover is raised up again. A saucer of porous earthenware is best adapted for holding the water; and other absorbents, such as parched oatmeal, the powder of mouldering whinstone, porous ignited pieces of muriate of lime, and even the dry powder of pipeclay may be used instead of sulphuric acid. A hemispherical porous vessel of earthenware, containing one pound and a quarter of water was placed by Mr. Leslie over a body of parched oatmeal, one foot in diameter, and one inch deep: by working the pump for some time, the whole of the water was frozen.

The natives of India dexterously avail themselves of the combined effects of radiation and evaporation, for the purpose of obtaining a supply of ice, when the temperature of the air is much higher than the freezing point. Excavations, about thirty feet square and two feet deep, are made in the large open plains near Calcutta; these excavations are covered at the bottom, to the depth of about a foot, with the dried stalks of Indian corn or sugarcanes. Rows of small unglazed earthen vessels, about an inch and a quarter deep, are placed upon this bed. Soft water which has been boiled, and suffered to cool, is poured into these vessels; in the dusk of the evening, in December, January, and February, part of the water is usually frozen when the weather is clear. The ice is collected at sunrise, and thrown into a deep pit, which is lined with straw and coarse blanketing; the mouth of the pit is closed up with straw, and sheltered by a thatched roof.

Quicksilver may be frozen by the united influence of evaporation, rarefaction and absorption. A portion of the metal being put into a hollow pear-shaped piece of ice, it must be suspended over a large surface of sulphuric acid; when the exhaustion of the receiver is made as complete as possible, the quicksilver will be frozen, and may be kept in a solid state for several hours. Other modes of effecting the congelation of quicksilver have been adopted with success.

Dr. Ure, in his Lectures at Glasgow, recommended several plans for effecting the congelation of water in considerable quantities. A series of cast-iron plates, ground so as to fit the receivers accurately which were placed upon them, were attached to an air-pump, by screws and stop-cocks, so that all the receivers might be exhausted at the same time. Another and more effectual plan was to fill a cast-iron cylinder or drum, of considerable dimensions, with steam, by boiling a small quantity of water in it; the air being expelled, the steam is condensed by cold water. A vessel of sulphuric acid, and another of water, being placed under a receiver, upon a plate attached to the drum by a pipe with a stopcock, and a communication made with the exhausted drum, the air in the receiver will be rarefied so as to occasion the congelation of the water. If the vacuum in the cylinder could be made nearly perfect, its size being sixty times greater than that of the receiver, the air within the latter would be rarefied sixty times; and the moisture of the cylinder would be excluded by turning the stopcock again, after the communication had been effected.

The effect of evaporation in withdrawing heat is admirably illustrated by the process of perspiration. The natural temperature of the human body is from 96° to 98°; but when we take very active exercise, or when we are exposed to a great degree of heat, there is a tendency to a rise of temperature above that which is conducive to health; and the most injurious effects would ensue, if they were not prevented by perspiration. Whenever this tendency begins to be experienced, a watery fluid is brought to the surface of the skin, that, by its evaporation, the body may be cooled to the healthy temperature.

Examples of the power of the human body to support heat, under apparently dangerous circumstances, have been placed upon record. Sir Joseph Banks and Sir Charles Blagden, being anxious to ascertain the highest degree of heat that the human body can endure without injury, went into an apartment prepared for their reception by Dr. Fordyce. The account given of this experiment by Sir Charles Blagden may be seen in the *Philosophical Transactions for* 1775, pp. 111 and 484. The temperature of the room was gradually raised until it became 52° hotter than boiling water, as indicated by thermometers in different parts of the room. Many persons may feel disposed to doubt the correctness of these indications; but they were abundantly confirmed by other circumstances observed at the time. The gentlemen found that their watch-chains, and all other metallic articles about their persons, were so hot that they could not bear to touch them; eggs placed upon a tin frame were roasted hard in twenty minutes, and a beef-steak was overdone in thirty-three minutes.

Notwithstanding the extraordinary degree of heat to which the experimenters were exposed, the temperature of their bodies was not raised.

It is affirmed that evaporation did not take place from the skin; but it is difficult to imagine that they could have remained so long under the circumstances described without the protecting influence of perspiration, especially as it is well known that copious perspiration is usually the result of exposure to high degrees of heat.

Apartments in India are often separated from the courts by curtains instead of walls; and these curtains, in order to cool the air in the rooms, are continually sprinkled with water, the rapid evaporation resulting occasions a reduction of temperature from 10 to 15 degrees.

The porous vessels of earthenware which are used for wine-coolers act upon the same principle; being dipped in water, they imbibe a quantity of it, which gradually evaporates; and, as a part of the heat necessary to convert the water into vapour will be taken from a bottle of wine placed in it, the wine is considerably cooled.

The people who cross the deserts of Arabia in large parties called Caravans, load camels with earthenware bottles filled with water, and preserve the water at a cool temperature on the principle of evaporation, by wrapping the jars in linen cloths, which they keep moist with water.

According to Athenæus, the Egyptians availed themselves of the same principle. Servants were employed during the night to keep pitchers of water constantly wet, that the water might be cooled by evaporation; and to preserve it at the low temperature to which it was thus brought, the pitchers were bound round with straw in the morning.

Dr. Wollaston has invented an elegant instrument for the purpose of illustrating the effect of evaporation in producing cold, and calls it the *Cryophorus*, or frost-bearer. It consists of a glass tube, from eighteen inches to two feet in length, having an internal diameter of one-eighth of an inch; the tube is bent into right angles near the ends, both of which are terminated by bulbs (*fig.* 20.) One of the bulbs

Fig. 20.

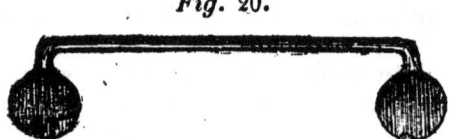

is nearly half filled with water, which being made to boil, the air is expelled from the tube and bulbs, which remain filled with steam; the open bulb is then closed by melting the glass at its capillary termination. The instrument having been thus prepared, is ready for use. When the empty bulb is immersed in a mixture of salt and snow, the vapour existing within it is condensed, a vacuum is produced, which, removing pressure from the surface of the water in the other bulb, enables it to evaporate rapidly; the vapour being condensed as fast as it is produced, the water is therefore speedily frozen, although it may be at the distance of two or three feet from the bulb which is immersed in the cooling mixture.

When the human frame has been exposed to a considerable degree of heat, and the clothes have become moist with perspiration, danger is incurred by sudden and continued exposure to air of a lower temperature, on account of the cold produced by evaporation, by which the body is liable to be too much reduced in temperature.

The bulb of a mercurial thermometer, being surrounded with cotton or tow, kept moist with ether, and exposed to a current of air, the temperature of the quicksilver may be reduced far below *zero* of Fahrenheit's scale.

A small animal would be deprived of its vital heat, in a very short time, by exposure to a current of air, while wet with ether.

Ex. The instrument called a pulse-glass, (*fig.* 21,) is a glass tube with

Fig. 21.

a bulb at each end of the form represented. It is partly filled with coloured spirit of wine, and partly with air; when it was closed by the blowpipe, a portion of the spirit of wine had been converted by heat into vapour, which occasioned a part of the air to be expelled, so that the air remaining within is very thin or rare. When the bulb which contains the liquid is grasped in the hollow of a warm hand, the air above the liquid and the vapour mixed with it are expanded, and pressing upon the liquid, force it over to the other side; the bulk of the liquid having passed over, a rapid bubbling, similar to boiling, instantly commences; a portion of spirit of wine remains adhering to the surface of the bulb; this small portion, being converted into vapour, passes over along with a portion of the expanded air, and rising up through the liquid, occasions the appearance alluded to. There is yet another circumstance attending this experiment which requires to be mentioned and explained. As soon as the bubbling begins, an intense sensation of cold is felt in the hollow of the warm hand, on account of the heat which is suddenly withdrawn, to enable the spirit of wine to assume the state of vapour; for this change cannot be effected until a quantity of sensible heat enters into it, and becomes latent or concealed heat.

The air-thermometer (*fig.* 5, *page* 15) will answer well to illustrate the effect of evaporation in producing cold.

Ex. A little ether being poured upon the bulb of this instrument, heat will be absorbed during the evaporation, to enable the ether to assume the expanded state of vapour; a part of this heat being taken from the air within the instrument, it contracts in bulk, and permits the liquid to rise considerably higher in the tube, indicating the quantity of heat withdrawn.

Distillation.

In the process of distillation for the purpose of obtaining alcohol, that fluid having been produced by fermentation, it is to be separated from the water with which it is mixed; and that distiller is the most skilful who can separate the largest quantity of alcohol at the least expense, and without imparting any disagreeable flavour. The principle upon which the separation is effected is the greater volatility of the alcohol, or spirit of wine, as it is usually called; consequently it assumes the state of vapour more readily than the water with which it is mingled. This vapour

HEAT.

being brought into contact with cold surfaces, is deprived of its latent heat, and condensed into a liquid: this is effected, when the process is carried on upon a large scale, by making the vapour pass through a descending spiral tube, which is technically called a worm, and which is immersed in a large quantity of cold water frequently renewed.

As the varieties in the process of distillation are very numerous, it is not intended to describe them here, but only to explain the general principles. The following experiment will assist in explaining the important but simple process of the distillation of alcohol.

Ex. Into a glass alembic a, (*fig.* 22,) put a mixture, composed of one

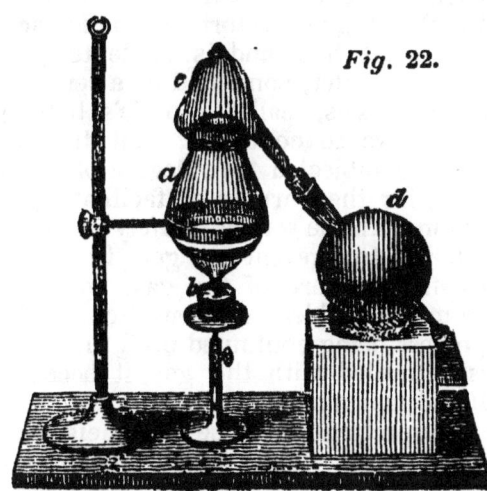

Fig. 22.

part spirit of wine, and seven or eight parts water, coloured with a little tincture of litmus or sulphate of indigo. But before it is put into the alembic, light a piece of paper, and plunge it, while burning, into the mixture; the flame will be extinguished: this will prove that the mixture is uninflammable. Apply the heat of a spirit-lamp b, and in a very short time the lower part of the distillatory apparatus will become dim with moisture; a portion of the alcohol will be raised in vapour, and, coming into contact with the sides of the vessel, will be condensed, but this vessel will very speedily become too hot to condense the vapour; it will then ascend into the capital of the alembic c, and being there condensed by the coldness of its sides, will run down into the groove, and from thence into the receiver d; when the upper part of the apparatus becomes too hot to effect condensation, the vapour will pass into the receiver and be condensed there. In a short time after the coloured mixture boils, a small quantity of a pure, colourless liquid will be accumulated in the receiver; if this liquid be poured into a saucer and a piece of burning paper be applied, it will take fire and burn to dryness. Thus, it will be proved that from a coloured, uninflammable mixture, a pure, colourless inflammable spirit may be obtained by the process of distillation.

A very useful form of still is represented *fig.* 23: a, is the furnace; b, the capital of the copper still; c, a part of the chimney; d, the worm-tub, containing cold water for condensing the vapour that enters the spiral tube.

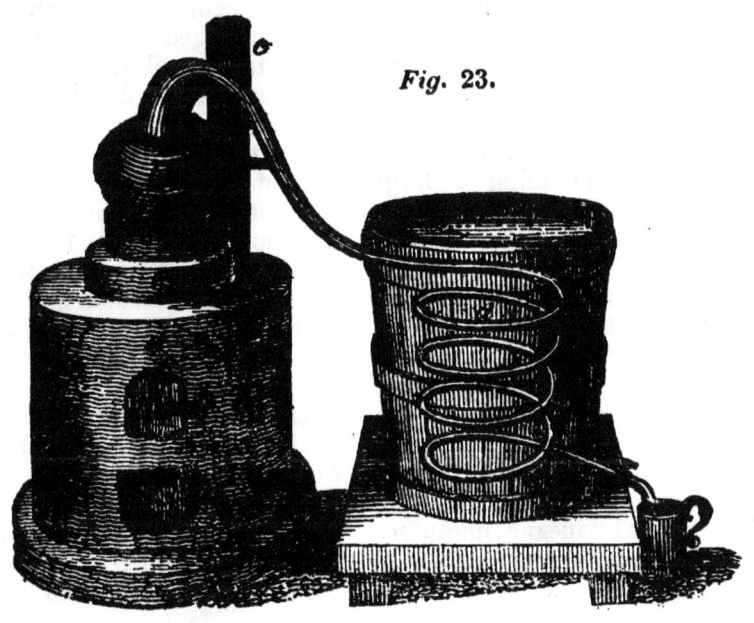

Fig. 23.

Mr. Watt, in the course of his experiments on watery vapours, was led to expect that a temperature of 70° would be sufficient for the distillation of water in a vessel exhausted of air, the refrigerator being immersed in snow. The experiment was tried by him and succeeded; he used a small still, which was about half filled with water and then securely joined to a receiver, having an aperture below. As soon as the water in the still was made to boil, the vapour filled the receiver and expelled the air at the open aperture, which was then closed with a plug. The still was then cooled by being set on ice, which occasioned the condensation of steam in the receiver. On the application of a lamp, steam was again produced; and, on immersing the receiver in cold water, distillation proceeded at a low temperature. The noise of boiling was distinctly heard in the still, although the top of it scarcely seemed warm to the hand. Mr. Watt found from this and other experiments, conducted with greater care, that, although distillation may be effected with very little heat in *vacuo*, no advantage in regard to the saving of fuel can be obtained, as the latent heat of the steam is increased in proportion to the diminution of sensible heat.

Distillation in *vacuo* has, notwithstanding, been adopted in several cases, with great success, where excellence in the products of distillation is the principal object.

This process has been adopted by Mr. Henry Tritton, who uses a still nearly of the common form, which is immersed in hot water, instead of being placed in close contact with fire. The pipe proceeding from the upper part of the still, passes, in the usual way, through a vessel containing a large quantity of cold water, and then communicates with a capacious vessel which is capable of being exhausted of air by an exhausting syringe, or air pump, attached to it. When the water surrounding the still is heated, and the air withdrawn, distillation proceeds rapidly, at a very low temperature.

The same process has been adopted, with great advantage, in the distillation of vinegar, at the extensive and admirably-managed vinegar manufactor of Messrs. Charles Pott and Co., on the Surrey-side of Southwark bridge. Vinegar, subjected to distillation, is freed from its usual colour, and rendered perfectly pellucid. It was found impossible, however, to distil it in the usual way without imparting a disagreeable burned kind of flavour; this is entirely avoided by distillation in *vacuo*, as the heat of the vapour raised is only 130° of Fahrenheit's scale.

The process of distillation by which a gaseous body is set free from one state of combination, for the purpose of making it enter into another, is of a different kind, and requires different management. This may be illustrated by a brief description of the process for obtaining liquid muriatic acid, upon a small scale. Five parts of strong sulphuric acid having been added to six parts of decrepitated sea-salt, in a tubulated glass retort, muriatic acid gas is set free, and is made to pass through water, contained in a series of glass vessels, called Woolfe's bottles, which are so contrived, that the gas may be subjected to a degree of pressure, for the purpose of facilitating its union with the water. Safety tubes are applied to prevent danger from the elastic pressure of the gas, and also from its sudden condensation. The process being continued until the water is saturated with the gas, it becomes liquid muriatic acid.

Respecting the cause of liquefaction, vaporization, and other phenomena which have been described, there have been differences of opinion. Dr. Black believed that those changes are occasioned by the absorption of heat, which remains combined with bodies that have changed from the solid to the fluid state, until they resume the solid state again; and with bodies which have changed from the fluid to the aëriform state, until they resume the fluid state again. Although Dr. Black did not express himself clearly upon this point, there is reason to believe that he considered the caloric, while in a latent or concealed state, to be combined with the bodies, in a way which bears a strong analogy to chemical combination.

Dr. Irvine maintained that when heat is absorbed by bodies, in consequence of a change in their state, it does not enter into combination with them, but exists in them in the same state as the other caloric which they contain; the increased quantity being rendered necessary in consequence of an enlarged capacity for heat which the body acquires on its change of state. Ingenious arguments have been advanced in support of both these opinions; and, perhaps, the preponderance of probability may be in favour of the last mentioned.

Chapter X.

Of Artificial Modes of lowering Temperature.

INTENSE cold may be produced, upon the principle of the rapid absorption of heat by bodies when they pass from the solid to the fluid state. The effects of freezing mixtures depend upon this principle. Solid saline substances are used for this purpose, some of them being much better adapted than others.

A reduction of 17° may be obtained by saturating water at a moderate temperature with nitre. Muriate of ammonia lowers the temperature from 26° to 28°. Nitrate of ammonia dissolved in its own weight of water effects a reduction from 50° of Fahrenheit's scale, to 4° of the same; and a mixture of three parts of muriate of lime with two parts of water, lowers the thermometer from 36° to 1° below zero.

It was discovered by Mr. Walker, that a greater degree of cold may be produced by the solution of several salts at the same time. Five parts muriate of ammonia, five parts nitre, and sixteen parts water, reduce from 50° to 11°, and the salts may be again obtained by evaporation, and will answer equally well a great number of times.

When dilute acid is used instead of water, the solution is effected more rapidly, and the cold produced is therefore greater. Nine parts of phosphate of soda, six parts nitrate of ammonia, and four parts diluted nitric acid, mixed together, cool the thermometer from 50° above zero to 21° below it.

By the action of acids upon snow great degrees of cold are produced. When the acids are used in an undiluted state, Lowitz affirms that the muriatic is the most powerful, then the nitrous, and lastly the sulphuric: but when sulphuric acid is diluted, it is more powerful than the others, a degree of cold equal to 91° having been produced by its agency.

Mr. Walker, by successive cooling of the materials, succeeded with eight parts of snow and ten parts of diluted sulphuric acid, in reducing temperature to 91° below zero of Fahrenheit.

The method most generally used depends upon the mutual action of snow or ice, and solid salts upon each other. Experiments of this kind were made by Fahrenheit, for the purpose of regulating the commencement of his scale. Similar experiments have been made by many others, with greater effect since that time. By mixing solid dry potash with snow, Lowitz obtained a reduction of temperature from 32° to —53°. With a mixture of three parts dry muriate of lime, and two parts snow, he succeeded in freezing 35 pounds of quicksilver.

Fourcroy and Vauquelin produced cold, by mixtures of this kind, 65° below zero of Fahrenheit.

In the course of their experiments, they found that a saturated solution of ammonia in water crystallized at —44° and at —56°, was converted into a semitransparent mass, and lost nearly all its pungent odour. At the last-mentioned temperature nitrous acid crystallized, sulphuric ether became thick and milky at —48°, and at length formed a white mass composed of small crystals. They failed in all their attempts to solidify alcohol.

Ammonia in the form of gas, made as dry as possible, was exposed by Guyton de Morveau, in a glass balloon, to a mixture of muriate of lime and snow, and was condensed into a liquid at the temperature of —56°.

In forming freezing mixtures in which saline substances are used, it is necessary that they should be newly crystallized, neither humid nor efflorescent, and finely pulverized. The materials intended to produce cold ought to be well mixed, and as quickly as possible, in a vessel just large enough to contain it; and the substance to be congealed should be exposed to the freezing mixture in a thin glass vessel. When snow is used it should be light and dry, and, if possible, newly fallen. Before experiments are made, the materials will frequently require to be cooled, which is done by exposing them separately in thin glass or tin vessels to freezing mixtures, care being taken not to cool them below the points at which they act upon each other. To illustrate the necessity of this precaution, it may be mentioned, that snow and common salt have no action upon one another when mixed at the temperature of $-10°$ of Fahrenheit.

Messrs. Allen and Pepys solidified 56 pounds of quicksilver by the use of 13 pounds of muriate of lime, and the same weight of snow. The whole of these were not mixed at once, as one proportion was expended in cooling the other.

To succeed with the experiment upon a small scale, a few ounces of mercury in a thin glass retort may be exposed to a mixture of one pound of crystallized muriate of lime, with the same quantity of snow: when this mixture ceases to reduce the temperature, another similar one should be used, which seldom fails to effect congelation.

Dr. Henry recommends the apparatus represented in section, (*fig.* 24.)

Fig. 24.

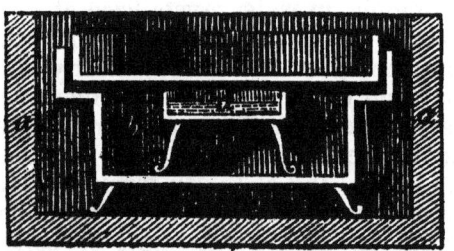

The outer vessel *a a*, he directs to be of wood, about $12\frac{1}{4}$ inches square and 7 inches deep. It should have a wooden cover, rabbeted in, and furnished with a handle. Within this is placed a tin vessel *b*, standing on feet which are $1\frac{1}{2}$ in. high, and having a projection at the top half an inch broad and an inch deep, on which rests a shallow tin pan *c*. Within the second vessel is a third, *d*, made of untinned iron, and supported by feet two inches high: this vessel is four inches square, and is intended to contain the mercury. When the apparatus is used, a mixture of muriate of lime and snow is put into the outer vessel *a a*, so as completely to surround the middle vessel *b b*. Into the latter the vessel *d*, containing the quicksilver to be frozen, previously cooled down by a freezing mixture, is put; and this is immediately surrounded by a mixture of snow and muriate of lime, previously cooled to $0°$ of Fahrenheit, by an artificial mixture of snow and common salt. The pan *c* is also filled with these materials, and the wooden cover is then put in its place. The vessels are now left till the quicksilver is frozen. The solution of muriate of lime may be evaporated, and the salt crystallized for future experiments.—*Henry's Chemistry*, vol. i. p. 94, *and description of plate* 4.

The following Tables exhibit a collective view of all the frigorific mixtures in the publication of Mr. Walker, who made a great many experiments upon the artificial production of cold.

TABLE, consisting of Frigorific mixtures having the power of generating or creating cold without the aid of ice, sufficient for all useful and philosophical purposes in any part of the world at any season.

FRIGORIFIC MIXTURES WITHOUT ICE.

MIXTURES.	PARTS.	Thermometer Sinks.	Degree of Cold produced.
Muriate of Ammonia..............	5	From $+50°$ to $+10°$	$10°$
Nitrate of Potash................	5		
Water	16		
Muriate of Ammonia.............	5	$+50$ to $+4$	46
Nitrate of Potash................	5		
Sulphate of Soda................	8		
Water	16		
Nitrate of Ammonia.............	1	$+50$ to $+4$	46
Water	1		
Nitrate of Ammonia.............	1	$+50$ to -7	57
Carbonate of Soda...............	1		
Water	1		

HEAT.

MIXTURES.	PARTS.	Thermometer Sinks.	Degree of Cold produced.
Sulphate of Soda Diluted Nitric Acid	3 2	From +50° to − 3°	53°
Sulphate of Soda Muriate of Ammonia Nitrate of Potash Diluted Nitric Acid	6 4 2 4	+50 to − 10	60
Sulphate of Soda Nitrate of Ammonia Diluted Nitric Acid	6 5 4	+50 to − 14	64
Phosphate of Soda Diluted Nitric Acid	9 4	+50 to − 12	62
Phosphate of Soda Nitrate of Ammonia Diluted Nitric Acid	9 6 4	+50 to − 21	71
Sulphate of Soda Muriatic Acid	8 5	+50 to − 0	50
Sulphate of Soda Diluted Sulphuric Acid	5 4	+50 to + 3	47

N. B. If the materials are mixed at a warmer temperature than that expressed in the Table, the effect will be proportionably greater; thus, if the most powerful of these mixtures be made when the air is + 85°, it will sink the thermometer to + 2°.

TABLE, consisting of Frigorific Mixtures composed of Ice, with chemical Salts and Acids.

FRIGORIFIC MIXTURES WITH ICE.

MIXTURES.	PARTS	Thermometer Sinks.	Degree of Cold produced.
Snow, or pounded Ice Muriate of Soda	2 1	From any Temperature to − 5°	*
Snow, or pounded Ice Muriate of Soda Muriate of Ammonia	5 2 1	From any Temperature to − 12	*
Snow, or pounded Ice Muriate of Soda Muriate of Ammonia Nitrate of Potash	24 10 5 5	From any Temperature to − 18	*
Snow, or pounded Ice Muriate of Soda Nitrate of Ammonia	12 5 5	From any Temperature to − 25	*
Snow Diluted Sulphuric Acid	3 2	From + 32° to − 23	55
Snow Muriatic Acid	8 5	+ 32 to − 27	59
Snow Diluted Nitric Acid	7 4	+ 32 to − 30	62
Snow Muriate of Lime	4 5	+ 32 to − 40	72
Snow Crystallized Muriate of Lime	2 3	+ 32 to − 50	82
Snow Potash	3 4	+ 32 to − 51	83

N.B.—The reasons for the omissions in the last column of this Table is, the thermometer sinking in these mixtures to the degree mentioned in the preceding column, and never lower, whatever may be the temperature of the materials at mixing.

HEAT.

TABLE, consisting of Frigorific Mixtures selected from the foregoing Tables, and combined so as to increase or extend Cold to the extremest degree.

COMBINATIONS OF FRIGORIFIC MIXTURES.

MIXTURES.	PARTS.	Thermometer Sinks.	Degree of Cold produced.
Phosphate of Soda	5		
Nitrate of Ammonia	3	From 0° to − 34°	34°
Diluted Nitric Acid	4		
Phosphate of Soda	3		
Nitrate of Ammonia	2	− 34 to − 50	16
Diluted mixed Acids	4		
Snow	3	− 0 to − 46	46
Diluted Nitric Acids	2		
Snow	8		
Diluted Sulphuric Acid	3	− 10 to − 56	46
Diluted Nitric Acid	3		
Snow	1	− 10 to − 60	40
Diluted Sulphuric Acid	1		
Snow	3	+ 20 to − 48	68
Muriate of Lime	4		
Snow	3	+ 10 to − 54	64
Muriate of Lime	4		
Snow	2	− 15 to − 68	53
Muriate of Lime	3		
Snow	1	− 0 to − 66	66
Crystallized Muriate of Lime	2		
Snow	1	− 40 to − 73	33
Crystallized Muriate of Lime	3		
Snow	8	− 68 to − 91	23
Diluted Sulphuric Acid	10		

N.B.—The materials in the first column are to be cooled, previously to mixing, to the temperature required, by mixtures taken from either of the preceding Tables.

TABLE of Congealing or Freezing Temperatures of various Liquids, according to Fahrenheit's Scale.

Sulphuric Ether		−46°
Liquid Ammonia		−46
Nitric Acid	sp. gr. 1.424	−45.5
Sulphuric Acid	sp. gr. 1.6415	−45
Mercury		−39
Nitric Acid	sp. gr. 1.407	−30.1
Sulphuric Acid	sp. gr. 1.8064	−26
Nitric Acid	sp. gr. 1.3880	−18.1
Ditto	sp. gr. 1.2583	−17.7
Ditto	sp. gr. 1.3290	− 2.4
Brandy		− 7.0
Sulphuric Acid	sp. gr. 1.8376	+ 1
Pure Prussic Acid		4 to 5
Common Salt	25 + water 75	4
Ditto	22.2 + do. 77.8	7.2
Sal Ammoniac	20 + do. 80	8
Common Salt	20 + do. 80	9.5
Ditto	16.1 + do. 83.9	13.3
Oil of Turpentine		14
Strong Wines		20
Rochelle Salt	50 + water 50	21
Common Salt	10 + do. 90	21.5
Oil of Bergamot		23
Blood		25

HEAT.

Common Salt	6.25	+ water 93.75	25°.5
Epsom Salt	41.6	+ do. 58.4	25.5
Nitre	12.5	+ do. 87.5	26
Common Salt	4.16	+ do. 95.84	27.5
Copperas	41.6	+ do. 58.4	28
Vinegar			28
Sulphate of Zinc.	53.3	+ water 46.7	28.6
Milk			30
Water			30

The rays of the sun constitute the most important natural source of heat. Various opinions have been entertained respecting the cause of this kind of heat. Sir Isaac Newton, influenced by the obvious analogy existing between the sun and terrestrial bodies rendered luminous by heat, believed the sun to be an intensely hot body, having the power of projecting hot particles from its surface, which when they come into contact with other bodies impart heat to them. Another hypothesis was maintained by Descartes and Huygens, and adopted by many other philosophers, which supposes that luminous bodies have the power of propagating vibrations through an extremely rare and elastic fluid that is diffused through all space; and that heat is occasioned by these vibrations.

Several circumstances influence the degree of heat communicated to different parts of the earth's surface by the solar rays; the chief of these are elevation, distance from the sea, and more particularly latitude. The extremes of temperature over the globe, are comprehended within a range of about 160° of Fahrenheit: the heat in the shade having been observed in tropical climates to attain 110°, as at Pekin; at Pondicherry it has risen to 115°; while at Hudson's Bay the spirit thermometer has sunk to —50°, ten degrees lower than the freezing point of quicksilver.

The range of temperature capable of being produced by art is much more extensive. By reference to the preceding tables, it will be seen that the greatest degree of cold, hitherto produced, is 91° below *zero* of Fahrenheit; while the highest degree of heat attempted to be measured, is that of Mr. Wedgwood's small air-furnace, which he considered equal to 21,877° of the same scale. More intense heat may be produced by the agency of a powerful voltaic combination, and by enflaming a condensed mixture of oxygen and hydrogen gases, issuing from a small aperture.

Heat may be artificially produced by electricity, galvanism, condensation, friction, percussion, and chemical action, but the full consideration of these, together with ignition, and the economy of fuel, will afford abundant useful and interesting matter for another treatise.

Chapter XI.

Books relating to Heat.

The books which have been written on this subject are very numerous, and of very various degrees of merit. The following list contains a selection of the most useful.

The Philosophical Transactions contain many important Essays by Black, Blagden, Cavendish, Darwin, Delisle, Count Rumford, Smeaton, Walker, Wedgwood, and others.

The Annales de Chimie are rich in original communications on heat; and many are contained in Nicholson's Journal, the Philosophical Magazine, the Manchester Memoirs, the Annals of Philosophy, the Transactions of the Royal Society of Edinburgh, Gilbert's Journal der Physik, Rozier's Journal de Physique, and the Journal of Science.

Martine on Heat and Thermometers.
Dr. Crawford on Animal Heat.
De Luc's Récherches sur les Modifications de l'Atmosphere.
Dalton's New System of Chemical Philosophy.
Count Rumford's Essays.
Dr. Black's Lectures, by Robison.
Chemical Statics, by Berthollet.
Scheele's Treatise on Air and Fire.

Voyages des Alpes, par Saussure.
Leslie's Experimental Inquiry into the Nature of Heat
Leslie on Heat and Moisture.
Récherches sur la Chaleur, par Prevost.
Elementa Chemiæ, by Boerhaave.
Mémoires de l'Academie des Sciences.
Essais de Physique, par M. Pictet.
Walker on Cold.
Murray's System of Chemistry.
Thomson's System of Chemistry.
Parkes's Chemical Essays, vol. i.

OPTICS.

Chapter I.—Optics.

Definitions—Nature of Light—Its general Properties.

Optics, a term derived from a Greek word, which signifies *seeing*, is the science which treats of vision, and generally of the nature and properties of Light, and the changes which it undergoes in its qualities or in its direction, when passing through bodies of different shapes;—when reflected from their surfaces—or when moving past them at small distances.

The nature of Light has not yet been ascertained; but two opinions of a very opposite kind have been maintained by philosophers respecting its origin and propagation. By some it is supposed to consist of material particles, thrown off from the luminous body with great velocity, and in all directions, while others believe it to be a fluid diffused through all nature, and in which waves or undulations are produced by the action of the luminous body, and propagated in the same manner as sound is propagated through air.

But whatever be the cause of light, and whatever be the manner in which it passes from one point of space to another, it has certain general properties which have been discovered by experiment and observation.

1. *Light is sent forth in all directions from every visible point of luminous bodies.* If we hold a sheet of paper before a candle, or the sun, or a red hot body, or any other source of light, we shall find that the paper is illuminated, or covered with light, in whatever position we hold it, provided that the light is not obstructed by its edge, or by another body. If we examine the illuminated surface, we shall also find that there are no black spaces or intervals destitute of light.

2. *All bodies, whether natural or artificial, which are not luminous of themselves, are rendered visible by light which originally comes from a body luminous of itself, such as the sun, or common artificial lights.* When the sun shines on a plant, the plant is seen in great brilliancy and beauty. If a black cloud covers the sun, the plant is still seen, though with less brightness, but the light which now makes it visible comes from the clouds, which are illuminated by the sun: for when the sun is so far below the horizon as not to illuminate the clouds, the plant ceases to be visible. In like manner, when we read by the artificial light of a candle, the book is generally illuminated by the light which immediately proceeds from it; but we can still read with our back to the candle, in which case the book is illuminated by the light from the candle which falls upon the walls and furniture of the apartment, and which those walls and that furniture again throw off in all directions; for the instant the candle is put out we are left in total darkness.

3. *All bodies, whether natural or artificial, throw off in all directions light of the same colour as themselves, although the light from the sun, which falls upon them and renders them visible, is white.* It has been generally supposed to be a sufficient proof of this important property, to state, that wherever we place our eye it sees those bodies of that colour; but as we consider this unsatisfactory, we shall demonstrate it by an experiment which is both beautiful and instructive. If we hold a white card before a rose bush, the surface of the card will appear of its usual whiteness; but if we place this card at one end of a box shut up on all sides, and if, having made a pin hole in the side opposite the card to admit the light from the rose bush, we look through another hole at the card, we shall see upon the card, and opposite each rose, a patch of red light, and opposite each green leaf a patch of green light. These patches of colour constitute a picture of the rose bush turned upside down, which though not very distinct in the outline, will yet be easily recognised. If we enlarge the small hole opposite the card, the picture will

become more indistinct, and the colours more faint, and when the hole reaches a certain size the red light from the roses will fall upon the same parts of the card as the green light from the leaves, and the card will appear of its original whiteness. The same appearances will be seen in whatever position we hold the box in relation to the rose bush. The reason will be explained in a future Chapter, why the white light of the sun becomes red when thrown off from the rose, and green when thrown off from the leaves.

4. *Light consists of separate parts independent of each other.* If we admit light through an opening into a dark room, we may, by interposing a piece of card, stop a small portion of it, and allow the rest of it to pass; or, if we stop nearly the whole of it, and allow only a very small portion of it to pass, the part which, in both these cases, is allowed to pass, is not affected in any way by its separation from the part which is stopped.

The smallest part of light which we can thus stop, or allow to pass, is called a *ray of light.*

5. *Rays of light proceed in straight lines.* This property may be demonstrated to the eye, by causing light to pass through small holes into a dark room filled with smoke or dust. It is proved also by the fact, that bodies cannot be seen through bent tubes; and it may be inferred from the form of the shadows of bodies. When there is any power on one side of the ray which is not on the other side, it may then deviate from its motion in a straight line, and may even be made to move in a curve line.

6. *Light moves with prodigious velocity, and that of the planets travels at the rate of* 195,000 *miles in a second of time.* If two observers are placed at the distance of 70 or 80 miles, and if one of them strikes a light at a known instant of time, the light will travel to the other observer in such a small portion of time that it cannot be measured by the nicest time-keepers. Astronomers, however, have proved, by observing the eclipses of Jupiter's Satellites when that planet is nearest and farthest from the earth, that light travels from the sun to the earth in seven minutes. Hence, it will move from the one pole of the globe to the other in the 24th part of a second, —a velocity which surpasses all comprehension.

CHAPTER II.—DIOPTRICS.

Refraction of Light—Law of Refraction —Refractive Powers—Table of Refractive Powers.

ALTHOUGH a ray of light will always move in the same straight line when it is not interrupted, yet every person must have observed that when light falls upon a drop of water, or a piece of glass, or a bottle containing any fluid which allows the light to pass, it does not reach the eye, or illuminate a piece of paper, placed behind those bodies in the same manner as before they were put in its way. This obviously arises from the direction of the light being changed by some power which resides in the bodies. The branch of optics which explains the law or rule according to which the direction of light is thus changed, and the results dependent on this law, is called DIOPTRICS, from two Greek words, one of which signifies *through,* and the other *to see,* because the bodies which produce this change are those *through* which we can *see,* or through which light passes.

In order to understand how this change is produced, let M N O P (*fig.* 1.)

Fig. 1.

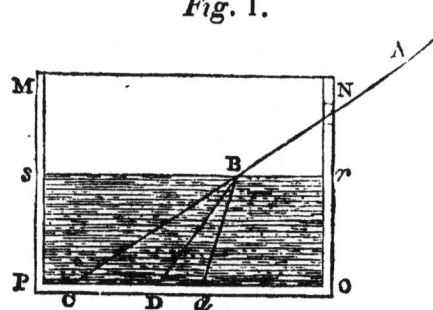

be a vessel, in one of the sides of which, N O, there is a small hole at N. If we place a lighted candle within two or three feet of it, so that its flame may be at A, a ray of light, A N, proceeding from it, will pass through the hole N, and go on in a straight line A N C, till it reaches the bottom of the vessel at C, where it will form a small circle of light. Having put a mark at the point C, pour water into the vessel till it rise to the height *s r,* and you will see that the round spot which was formerly at C is now at D; that is, the ray A N, which, when the vessel was empty, went straight on to C, has been bent at the point B, where it falls on the water, into the line B D. If we mix a little soap with the water, so as to give it a slight mistiness, the ray B D will be distinctly perceived, and it will be seen that it is a straight line, and that the bending or change in its direction has been produced wholly at the point B in the surface of the water. This bending of the ray A N B is called *refraction*, from a Latin word, which signifies *breaking back*, because the ray A B seems to be broken back from its course at B, and the water is said to *refract*, or break back the ray A B.

If, in place of fresh water, we pour in salt water, it will be found that the ray A B is more bent at B. In like manner alcohol will refract the ray A B more than salt water; and oil more than alcohol. If we were to cut a piece of glass of the exact shape of the water *s r* O P, and place it in the same way in the vessel, we should find that it would refract the light still more than oil, and in the line B *d*.

Hence we may conclude in general, that when a ray of light passing through air falls in a slanting direction upon the surface of liquid, or of solid bodies, through which light can pass, it is refracted by them, and by different bodies in different degrees.

If, when the vessel M N O P is empty, we fix at C a bright object, such as a sixpence, and place the eye at A in the straight line A N C, the sixpence will be distinctly seen, because one of the rays C N, which proceed from it, must enter the eye at A. Let water be now poured into the vessel till it stand at *s r*, then the eye at A will no longer see the sixpence; but if we move the sixpence from C to D, it will become visible to the eye at A the instant it comes to D. Now as the ray from the sixpence at D must pass to the eye in a straight line after it comes out of the water, it must pass in the direction B N A; and consequently, the ray from the sixpence D, by which it was seen at A, must have been D B, and this ray, in coming out of the water, must have been bent or refracted at B into the line B A. The same effect will be produced if *s r* is the surface of salt water, alcohol, oil, or glass; but with these substances we must push the sixpence beyond D towards O, in order that it may be seen at A.

Hence we may conclude, that when a ray of light, passing through a liquid or a solid body in a direction slanting or oblique to its surface, quits it, is refracted by that body, and by different bodies in different degrees.

Having thus discovered, by very simple experiments, the nature of the refraction of light when passing out of a rare or thin medium such as the air into a dense medium such as water, and also out of a dense medium into a rare medium, we must now endeavour to determine the law or rule which the refraction follows when it enters or quits the water at different degrees of obliquity.

For this purpose, let us describe (*fig.* 2.) a circle P R Q S upon a piece of

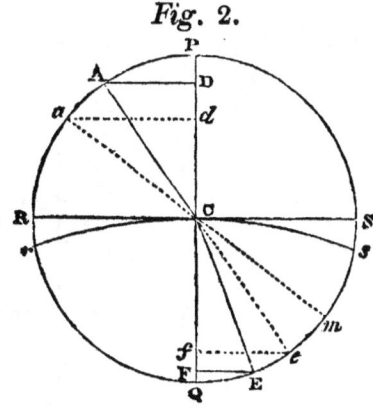

Fig. 2.

slate or metal, and having drawn two diameters P C Q, R C S perpendicular to each other, let a small tube A C be attached to the plate, so that it can move freely round C. The plate P R Q S must now be placed in a vessel of water, and fixed so that the surface of the water coincides with the line R S, and does not touch the lower end C of the tube A C. Let us now bring the tube A C into the position P C, and make a ray of light pass down through the tube, we shall find that the ray, entering the water at C, will pass on in the same straight line to the point Q. Hence it follows, *that a ray of light falling perpendicularly upon a refracting surface undergoes no refraction or change in its direction*. If the tube A C is now placed in the position A C, and a ray of light be made to pass through it, the ray will not pass on in a straight line, but will be bent or refracted at C into the line C E, and strike the circle at E. The angle A C P, which the ray or tube forms with the perpendicular P C Q, is called the *angle of incidence*; and the angle E C Q, which the refracted ray C E forms with the same perpendicular, is called the *angle of refraction*. Let us now take in a pair of compasses the line E F, the shortest distance of the point E of the refracted ray from the perpendicular C Q, and make a scale of equal parts, of which E F is one part. In like manner let us take A D, the shortest distance of the point A of the incident ray from the same perpendicular P C, and setting it upon the above scale of equal parts, we shall find it to be *one* and *one-third* of these parts, or, more accurately, 1.336. If we now repeat this experiment when the tube A C is in any other slanting position, such as *a* C, in which case the refracted ray will be C *e*, and making a scale of equal parts, of which *ef* is one, measure upon it the line *a d*, we shall find that this line is also 1.336. Now the line AD is called the *sine of the angle of incidence* A C P, and E F the *sine of the angle of refraction* E C Q. Hence it follows, that in water the sine of the angle of incidence is to the sine of the angle of refraction as 1.336 to 1, whatever be the position of the ray with respect to the surface; that is, *the Sines of the angles of incidence and refraction have a constant proportion or ratio to one another.*

If we next fix a shining body, as a sixpence, at Q, E and *e* in succession, and place the tube successively in the positions P C, A C, and *a* C, we shall see the sixpence distinctly; that is, when the sixpence is at Q, the ray Q C proceeding from it, passes on to P without refraction; when the sixpence is at E, the ray E C is refracted at C in the direction C A; and when it is at *e*, the ray *e* C is refracted at C into the direction C *a*. In this case the angles E C Q, *e* C Q are the angles of incidence, and A C P, *a* C P, the angles of refraction, and their sines E F, *ef*, A D, *a d*, being the same sines which we formerly measured, will be to one another as 1 to 1.336. Hence it follows, that in refractions from a dense medium, such as water or glass, to a rare medium, such as air, *the sines of the angles of incidence and refraction have a constant ratio or proportion one to another.*

By comparing these two cases of refraction, it will be seen, that when the ray A C passes from air into water, the ray C E is refracted towards the perpendicular C Q, and the sine of the angle of refraction is 1, while the sine of the angle of incidence is 1.336; but that when the ray E C passes from water into air, the ray C A is refracted *from* the perpendicular C P; and the sine of the angle of incidence is 1, while the sine of the angle of refraction is 1.336.

We are now in a situation to determine the direction of any ray after it is refracted by the surface of water. Let it be required, for example, to find the direction of the ray *a* C, *fig.* 2, when it is refracted after falling on the surface R S of water, at the point C. Draw C P perpendicular to R S, and from *a* draw *a d* perpendicular to C P. Take *a d* in the compasses, and make a scale in which this distance occupies 1.336, or 1⅓ parts nearly; then taking one of these parts in the compasses, place one foot in the circle P R Q S, described round C, and passing through *a*, somewhere about *m* in the line *a* C continued, and move that foot towards Q, to *e* for example, till the other foot strikes a point *f* in the perpendicular C Q, and no other point in it, then *e* is the point through which the refracted ray will pass, and consequently the line C *e* must be the refracted ray required.

The number 1.336, which regulates the refraction of water, is called its *index*, or *exponent*, or *co-efficient of refraction*, and sometimes its *refractive power*.

If we now repeat all the above experiments with other fluids and solids, we shall find, that the same law of refraction takes place with all of them, and that the index of refraction, or the refractive power, varies in each. But the refractive power of bodies may be measured more accurately, as we shall afterwards see, by different methods.

The following TABLE contains the index of refraction for a great number of bodies, as determined by different observers, and by different methods; and it is obvious, that by means of the numbers here given, we can, in the way already described, trace the passage of a ray through any plain surfaces by which the body may be bounded.

TABLE OF REFRACTIVE POWERS.

	Index of Refraction.
Chromate of lead, (greatest refr.)	2.974
Ruby silver	2.564
Realgar artifical	2.549
Chromate of lead, (least refr.)	2.500
Octohedrite	2.500
Diamond, Rochon	2.755
Ditto ....Newton	2.439
Blende	2.260
Phosphorus	2.224
Glass of Antimony	2.200

OPTICS.

Substance	Index of Refraction
Sulphur melted	2.148
Ditto native	2.038
Glass, Lead 3, Flint 1	2.028
Tungstate of Lime, gr.	2.129
———————— least	1.970
Carbonate of Lead, gr.	2.084
———————— least	1.813
Calomel	1.970
Zircon, ext.	2.015
——— ord.	1.961
Glass, Lead 2, Sand 1	1.987
Sulphate of Lead	1.925
Glass, Lead 2, Flint 1	1.830
Garnet	1.815
Spinelle Ruby	1.812
Arsenic	1.811
Sapphire, Blue	1.794
——— White	1.768
Pyrope	1.792
Nitrate of Silver, gr.	1.788
———————— least	1.729
Glass, Lead 1, Flint 1	1.787
Ruby	1.779
Feldspar	1.764
Cymophane	1.760
Glass, Lead 3, Flint 4	1.732
——— 1 ——— 2	1.724
Axinite	1.735
Epidote, gr.	1.703
——— least	1.661
Carbonate of Strontites, gr.	1.700
———————— least	1.543
Boracite	1.701
Sulphuret of Carbon	1.678
Peridot, gr.	1.685
——— least	1.660
Arragonite, ord.	1.693
——— ext.	1.535
Calcareous Spar, ord.	1.654
———————— ext.	1.483
Sulphate of Barytes, ext.	1.647
———————— ord.	1.631
Topaz, limpid, ext.	1.620
———————— ord.	1.610
Topaz, Brazil, ext.	1.640
———————— ord.	1.632
Anhydrite, ext.	1.622
——— ord.	1.577
Euclase, ext.	1.663
——— ord.	1.643
Mother of Pearl	1.653
Oil of Cassia	1.641
Balsam of Tolu	1.628
Castor	1.626
Muriate of Ammonia	1.625
Guiacum	1.619
Flint Glass from 1.625 to	1.590
Meionite	1.606
Oil of Bitter Almond	1.603
——— Anise Seeds	1.601
Balsam of Peru	1.597
Gum Ammoniac	1.592
Tortoise Shell	1.591
Pitch	1.586
Balsam of Styrax	1.584
Bottle Glass	1.582
Horn	1.565
Quartz, ext.	1.558
——— ord.	1.548
Mellite, ord.	1.556
——— ext.	1.538
Gum Mastich	1.560
Burgundy Pitch	1.560
Resin	1.559
Turpentine	1.557
Rock Salt	1.557
Sugar melted	1.554
Gum Thus	1.554
Comptonite	1.553
Chalcedony	1.553
Sulphate of Copper, gr.	1.552
———————— least	1.531
Copal	1.549
Canada Balsam	1.549
Amber	1.547
Elemi	1.547
Oil of Tobacco	1.547
Dichroite	1.544
Apophyllite	1.543
Plate Glass from 1.542 to	1.514
Colophony	1.543
Bees Wax	1.542
Olibanum	1.544
Carbonate of Barytes, least	1.540
Crown Glass from 1.534 to	1.525
Caoutchouc	1.530
Oil of Sassafras	1.534
——— Cloves	1.535
Balsam of Capivi	1.528
Lencite	1.527
Citric Acid	1.527
Shell Lac	1.525
Sulphate of Lime	1.525
Gum Myrrh	1.524
Wavellite	1.52
Gum Tragacanth	1.520
Mesotype, gr.	1.522
——— least	1.516
Nitre, gr.	1.514
——— least	1.335
Tartrate of Potash and Soda	1.515
Sulphate of Zinc, ord.	1.507
Bees Wax, 14° Reaum.	1.512
——— Melting	1.450
Gum Arabic	1.502
Sulphate of Potash	1.502
Stilbite	1.508
Oil of Cumin	1.508
——— Nuts	1.507
——— Pimento	1.507
——— Sweet Fennel Seeds	1.506
——— Amber	1.505
——— Rhodium	1.500
——— Beech Nut	1.500
——— Nutmeg	1.497
Balsam of Sulphur	1.497
Sulphate of Iron, gr.	1.494
Oil of Angelica	1.493
——— Caraway Seeds	1.491
Castor Oil	1.490
Obsidian	1.488
Tallow	1.49

Substance	Index of Refraction
Sulphate of Magnesia	1.488 or 1.465
Oil of Hyssop	1.487
Camphor	1.487
Cajeput oil	1.483
Oil of Almonds	1.483
———— Savine	1.482
———— Pennyroyal	1.482
Sulphate of Ammonia & Magnesia	1.483
Carbonate of Potash	1.482
Oil of Lemon	1.379
———— Spearmint	1.481
Opal	1.480
Oil of Thyme	1.477
———— Dill Seed	1.477
Essence of Lemon	1.476
Oil of Turpentine	1.475
———— Rape Seed	1.475
———— Juniper	1.473
———— Bergamot	1.471
———— Olives	1.470
———— Spermaceti	1.470
Fluellite	1.470
Oil of Lavender	1.462
———— Poppy	1.463
———— Camomile	1.457
Alum	1.457
Oil of Wormwood	1.453
Spermaceti, melted	1.446
Fluor Spar	1.434
Sulphuric Acid	1.434
Oil of Rhue	1.433
Phosphoric Acid, fluid	1.426
Nitric Acid, Sp. gr. 1.48	1.410
Muriatic Acid, concentrated	1.410
Nitrous Acid	1.396
Acetic Acid	1.396
Malic Acid	1.395
Alcohol	1.372
Oil of Ambergris	1.361
White of an Egg	1.361
Ether	1.358
Cryolite	1.349
Salt Water	1.343
Human Eye, cryst. lens	1.384
Water, green rays	1.3358
Ice	1.308
Tabasheer	1.1115
Air, *Bradley*. Barom. 29.6, Therm. 50°	1.000,276
Air, *Biot*. Barom. 30.17, Therm. 32°	1.000,295

Table of the Refractive Power of Gases, according to M. Dulong, that of Air being 1.000.

Gas	Index of Refraction
Atmospheric Air	1.000
Oxygen	0.924
Hydrogen	0.470
Azote	1.020
Chlorine	2.623
Oxide of Azote	1.710
Nitrous Gas	1.030
Hydrochloric Acid	1.527
Oxide of Carbon	1.157
Carbonic Acid	1.526
Cyanogen	2.832
Olefiant Gas	2.302
Gas of Marshes	1.504
Muriatic Ether	3.72
Hydrocyanic Acid	1.531
Ammonia	1.309
Oxi-Chloro-Carbonic Gas	3.936
Sulphuretted Hydrogen	2.187
Sulphureous Acid	2.260
Sulphuric Ether	5.280
Carburetted Sulphur	5.179

It will appear from a comparison of the preceding table, with that of specific gravities in HYDROSTATICS, Chap. VI., that in very many cases the refractive power increases with the density of the body. In the case of oily substances, or inflammable bodies, however, such as *hydrogen, phosphorus, sulphur, diamond, bees' wax, amber, spirit of turpentine, linseed oil, olive oil, camphor*, their refractive powers are from *two* to *seven* times greater in respect to their density than those of most other substances. Sir Isaac Newton observed this fact with respect to the last *five* of these substances, which, he says, 'are fat, sulphureous unctuous bodies,' and as he observed the same high refractive power in the diamond, he infers, that it is 'probably an unctuous substance coagulated.' This law, however, at one time seemed to be overturned by an observation of Dr. Wollaston, that *phosphorus*, one of the most inflammable substances in nature, had a very low refractive power; but Dr. Brewster, confiding in the truth of the law, examined the refractive power of phosphorus by forming it into prisms and lenses, and he found it to be nearly as high as diamond, and fully twice that of diamond compared with its density; an observation which re-established and extended the truth of the general principle.

CHAPTER III.—DIOPTRICS *continued.*

Refraction of Rays by Prisms and Lenses—Burning Glasses—Illuminating Lenses.

THE substance which is most commonly used for refracting the rays of light, both in optical experiments, and in optical instruments, is *glass*. For these purposes it is shaped into solids of the following form, a section of which is shewn in *fig.* 3.

OPTICS.

Fig. 3.

1. A *prism*, shown at A, is a solid, having two plane surfaces, A R, A S, inclined to one another.

2. A *plane glass*, shown at B, has two plane surfaces parallel to one another.

3. A *sphere* or *spherical lens**, shown at C, has every point in its surface equally distant from a common centre.

4. A *double convex lens*, shown at D, is bounded by two *convex* spherical surfaces, whose centres are on opposite sides of the lens. It is *equally convex* when the radii of both surfaces (that is, the distances from the centres to the circumferences of the circle they belong to) are equal, and *unequally convex*, when their radii or distances are unequal.

5. A *plano-convex lens*, shown at E, is bounded by a *plane* surface on one side, and by a convex one on the other.

6. A *double concave lens*, shown at F, is bounded by two *concave* spherical surfaces, whose centres are on opposite sides of the lens.

7. A *plano-concave lens*, shown at G, is bounded by a *plane* surface on one side, and a *concave* one on the other.

8. A *meniscus*, shown at H, is bounded by a *concave* and a *convex* spherical surface; and these two surfaces meet, if continued.

9. A *concavo-convex* lens, shown at I, is bounded by a *concave* and a *convex* surface; but these two surfaces do not meet though continued.

The axis of these lenses is a straight line M N, in which are situated the centres of their spherical surfaces, and to which their plane surfaces are perpendicular. If we suppose the sections from B to I to revolve round the line M N, they will generate the different solids which they are intended to represent; but in treating of the refraction of the lenses we shall still use these sections, because, since every section of the same lens passing through the axis M N, has the very same form, what is true of one section must be true of the whole lens.

Refraction through prisms.—Let R S, R' S' (*fig.* 4,) be the faces of a prism of

Fig. 4.

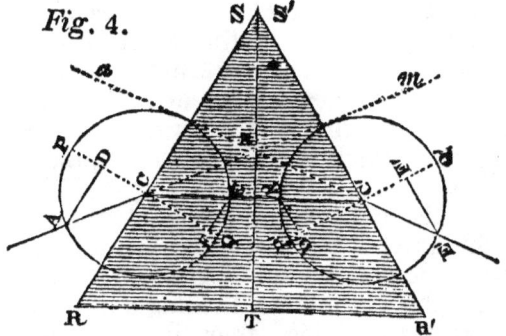

glass having its refractive power 1.525, and A C a ray of light falling upon the face R S at C. Through C draw P Q perpendicular to R S, and from any scale of equal parts take in the compasses 1.525, or 15.25, or 152.5, or 1525 parts, and setting one foot of the compasses on C A, move it along to some point A till the other foot falls only on one point of C P as at D; then upon C, as a centre, describe a circle A P Q passing through A. From the same scale take in the compasses 1.000 or 10.00 or 100.00 or 1000, and setting one foot on the line C Q, move it along till the other falls upon E in the circle A P Q, taking care that the point F is such that, when one foot is placed at E, the other foot can touch C Q in no other point but F. But A D is the sine of the angle of incidence, and E F the sine of the angle of refraction, hence the line C E C' drawn through E will be the refracted ray.

Again, as the ray C C' meets the second refracting surface at C', through C' draw P' Q' perpendicular to R' S', and from any scale of equal parts take in the compasses 1.000 or 10.000, &c. and setting one foot in the line C' A', move it along to some point A' till the other foot falls only on one point of C' P', as at D'. In like manner, take from the same scale 1.525, or 15.25, &c. and setting one foot of the compasses in C' Q', move it towards some point F'

---

* *Lens*, a Latin word signifying a *lentile*, a small flat kind of bean.

till the other foot falls at E′ into a circle E′ Q′ A′ passing through A′, and having C′ for its centre, taking care that the point E′ is such that when one foot is placed there the other foot can touch C′ Q′ in no other point but F′. But as the ray is now passing out of glass into air, A′ D′ is the sine of the angle of incidence, and E′ F′ the sine of the angle of refraction; hence the line C′ E′ drawn through E′ will be the refracted ray. The refraction of the prism has, therefore, bent the ray A C, which would have gone on to *m*, into the line C′ E′, which forms with A *m* an angle E′ *n m*, which is the deviation or change of direction of the ray; so that if the ray A C proceeded from the sun, or from a candle, it would, by an eye placed at E′, be seen at *a* in the direction E′ *n a*, and the angle of deviation will be A *n a* equal to E′ *n m*.

In the case shown in *fig*. 4, the refracted ray C C′, in passing through the prism, is parallel to its base R R′, and when this is the case, the angle of deviation A *n a* is less than in any other position of C C′, and, consequently, of A C, as may be easily proved by constructing the figure for any other position of these rays. If, therefore, we place the eye behind the prism at E′, and turn the prism round, we shall at once ascertain that C C′ is parallel to the base R R′, by the image of the candle at *a* being stationary; for, in every other position of A C and C C′, that image will move towards *a*′. When we have thus placed the prism in this position, or so that the ray C C′ is parallel to R R′, or perpendicular to S T, a line bisecting the refracting angle of the prism R S′ R′, then it is obvious that the angle of refraction at the first surface, viz. E C F, is equal to R S T, half of the angle of the prism. Now, as half this angle is known, and as it is easy to measure at once by a *Goniometer**, or divided instrument of any kind, the angle of incidence A C P, we have, without any further trouble, the angle of incidence, and the corresponding angle of refraction at the surface R′ S′. By making the following proportion, therefore—as the sine of the angle of refraction is to the sine of the angle of incidence, so is unity to the index of refractive power—that is, dividing the sine of the angle of incidence by the sine of the angle of refraction, we obtain the refractive power. This is the simplest of all methods, and the most generally applicable for measuring refractive powers, because soft solids and fluids can be placed in the refracting angles of hollow prisms made by joining two plates of parallel glass.

Refraction through plane glasses.— Let M N, (*fig*. 5.) be a plane glass, and

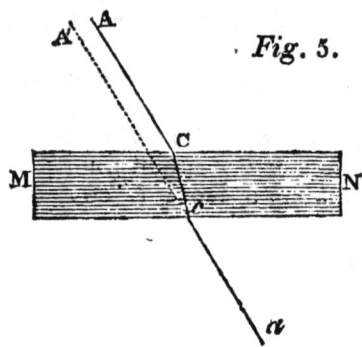

Fig. 5.

A C a ray of light refracted at C on entering the glass, into the direction C *c*, and at *c* on going out of the glass, into the direction *c a*: if we determine the direction of the refracted rays C *c* and *c a* by the method shown in *fig*. 2, we shall find at once that *c a* is parallel to A C; for however much A B is bent out of its direction at the first surface of the glass, it is bent just as much in the opposite direction, at the second surface, so that it is restored to its original direction. It will appear, however, to an eye at *a*, as if it came in the direction A′ *c*. Every person is accustomed to observe that the plane glass of windows does not alter the position of objects seen through it, except in particular parts of the glass, which will be found, upon examination, to be places where the two faces are not parallel.

Refraction through lenses.—Although we have hitherto spoken only of the refraction of plane surfaces, yet most of the refractions we have to consider in optics take place at spherical or other curved surfaces. This circumstance, however, does not add any difficulty to the subject, for the refraction which takes place at a curved surface of any kind is exactly the same as at a plane surface which touches the curve surface at the point on which the ray falls. If, for example, the ray A C (*fig*. 2.) falls upon the curved surface *r* C *s* at C, and if R C touches *r* C *s* at the point C, then the small portion of the curved surface at C, which is concerned in refracting the ray, may be considered as a part of

---

* From two Greek words, signifying *measure of angles*.

the plane surface R S. Although we know that the surface of standing water is a curve of the same radius as the globe, yet no skill could discover this curvature, or prove its existence in a square foot of a lake at perfect rest; and yet this square foot is greater in relation to the radius of the earth than the superficial space occupied by a ray of light is in relation to the radius of a common lens. When we wish, therefore, to determine the direction of the refracted ray at the point C of any curved surface $r C s$, we have only to draw a line R C S perpendicular to the radius C Q, touching the curve at C, and proceed in the very same manner as if we were dealing with a plane surface R S. In order to illustrate this, let us begin with a sphere.

Refraction through a sphere. Let a ray of light A C (*fig. 6.*), fall upon a

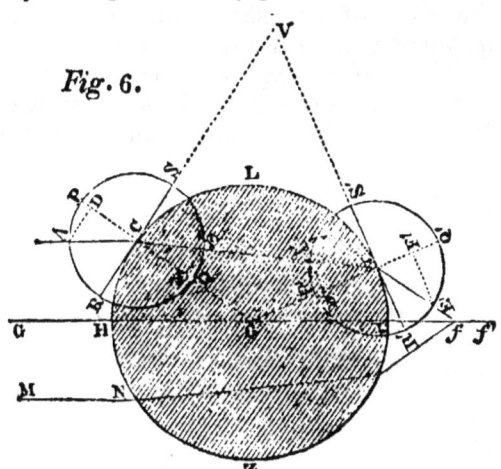

Fig. 6.

sphere of glass L H Z I, at the point C, and parallel to G H O I, the axis of the sphere. Through C draw R S perpendicular to O C, the radius of the sphere. This line will touch the sphere at C, and the ray A C will be refracted as if it fell upon the plane surface R S. By the same process which we have already explained for the prism, find the refracted ray C C′, and through C′ where this ray falls upon the back surface L I Z of the sphere, draw R′ S′ perpendicular to O C′ and touching the sphere at C′. Then, by the same process as before, find the refracted ray C′ f. Another ray M N parallel to A C, and falling on the sphere at N, as far from H I, the axis of the sphere, as C is, will obviously be refracted to f, because the circumstances of the two rays are exactly the same. Hence, these rays will meet at f, which is called the *focus of parallel rays.* If we continue the lines R S, R′ S′ till they meet at V, it will be seen that the refraction of the ray A C through the sphere is exactly the same as it would have been through a prism R V R.

If we determine by the preceding method the focus f upon the supposition that the sphere is *tabasheer, water, glass* and *zircon*, we shall, by measuring I f, the distance of the focus behind the sphere, obtain the following results, the radius O C of the sphere being supposed one inch.

	Index of Refr.	A D	
Tabasheer	1.1145	4 feet	0 inches
Water	1.3358	1	0
Glass	1.500		½
Zircon	2.000		0

When the index of refraction is greater than two, as in diamond, &c. the point f falls within the sphere.

The distance of the focus f from the centre O of any sphere may be found by the following rule:—Divide the index of refraction by twice its excess above one, and the quotient is the distance O f which, in glass, is 1½ the radius of the sphere.

Refraction through convex lenses.—Light is refracted through a convex lens exactly in the same manner as through a sphere, and the progress of the refracted rays may be found by the method already described for a prism and a sphere. Let L L, *fig.* 7, be a double convex lens

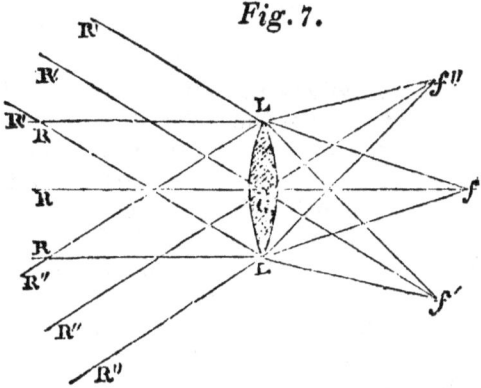

Fig. 7.

whose axis is R C f, and C its middle point, then it will be found that *parallel rays,* R L, R L, will be so refracted by the two surfaces as to meet at f, which is called the *principal focus of the lens.* In like manner it will be found that parallel rays R′ L, R′ C, R′ L, and R″ L, R″ C, R″ L, falling obliquely on the lens, will have their foci at $f′$ and $f″$, at the same distance behind the lens. In these, and all other cases, the rays R C, R′ C, R″ C which pass through the centre C, will be found to proceed to $f, f′$ and $f″$, without changing their direction. The distance C*f* is called the *focal distance* of the lens, and in a *double and equally convex lens* of glass, whose index of refraction is 1.500, it is equal to the radius of the spherical surfaces of the lens. If the lens is a *plano convex lens*, as E, *fig.* 3, it is equal to twice the radius of its spherical surface. If the lens is unequally convex, its focal distance may be found by the following rule:—Multiply the two radii of its surfaces, and divide twice that product by the sum of the radii—the quotient will be the focal distance required.

When *converging rays* or rays which proceed to one point, such as R F, R F, R F (*fig.* 8), are intercepted by or fall upon a convex lens L L, whose principal focus is O, their convergency is hastened, and they will be refracted to a focus *f* nearer the lens. As the point of convergence F recedes from the lens, the point *f* also recedes from it towards O, beyond which it never goes; and as F approaches the lens, *f* also approaches to it. The points F and *f* are called con-

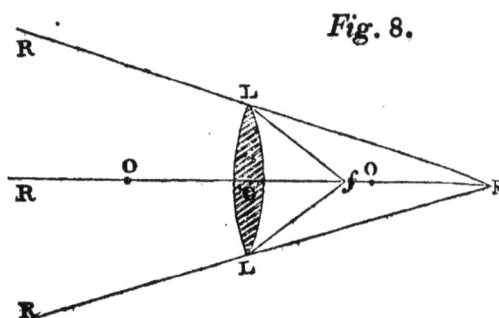

Fig. 8.

jugate foci, because the place of the one varies with the place of the other, and though every lens has only one *principal focus*, yet its conjugate foci are innumerable. The *conjugate focal distance* C*f* may be found by the following rule: Multiply the principal focal distance, or O C by F C, the distance of the point of convergence, and divide that product by the sum of the same numbers. The quotient will be the distance C*f*.

When *diverging rays*, or rays which proceed from one point F, such as R L, R C, R L (*fig.* 9), fall upon a convex

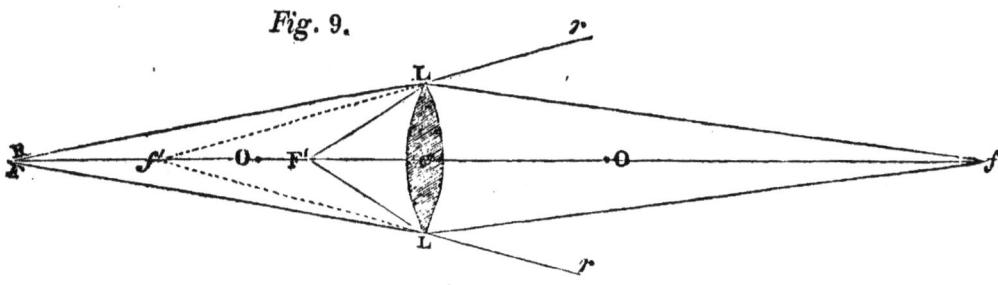

Fig. 9.

lens L L, whose principal focus is O, the refraction of the lens will make them converge to a focus *f* beyond O. As the point of divergence F recedes from the lens, the focus *f* will approach to it, and when F is infinitely distant, *f* will coincide with O, for the rays diverging from F have now become parallel rays. If F approaches to O, the focus *f* will recede from O, and when F coincides with O, *f* will be infinitely distant, or the refracted rays will be parallel. When F is between O and C, as at F', the refracted rays will diverge like L *r*, L *r*, as if they came from a focus *f*' beyond O, and in front of the lens. The points F and *f* are called *conjugate foci* as before, and the *conjugate focal distance* may be thus found:—Multiply the principal focal distance by F C, the distance of the point of divergence, and divide that product by the *difference* of the same numbers. The quotient will be the distance C*f*.

Refraction through concave lenses.

—Light is refracted through concave lenses in the same manner as through prisms, and the direction of the refracted rays may in every case be found by the method already described for a prism. Let L L (*fig.* 10.) be a *double concave*

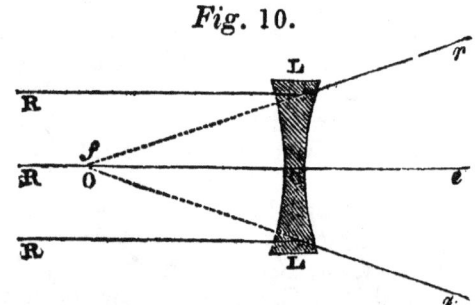

Fig. 10.

lens, whose axis is R*f*C, and C its middle point: then it will be found that parallel rays R L, R L will be refracted into the directions L *r*, L *r*, so as to diverge as if they proceeded from *f*, a point before the lens which is the principal focus of the lens. The principa focal distance Cf is the same as in convex lenses, and when the lens is unequally concave, the focal distance will be found by the rule for unequally convex lenses.

When *converging rays* proceeding to a point F, (*fig.* 11,) beyond the principal focus O of a concave lens, are intercepted by it, they will be made to diverge in lines Lr, Lr, as if they pro-

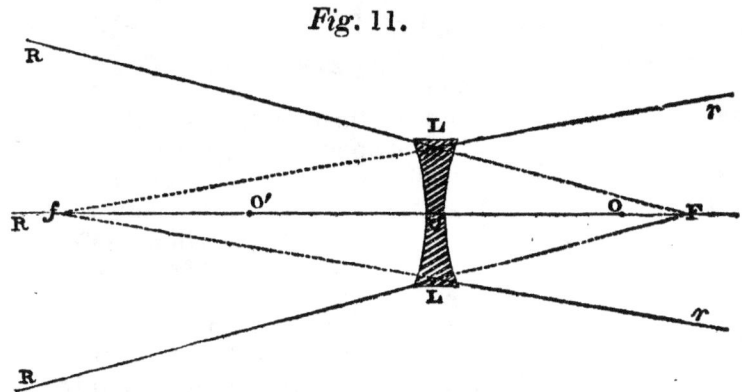

Fig. 11.

ceeded from a focus f in front of the lens beyond O. When F coincides with O, the refracted rays Lr, Lr will be parallel, and when the point F is within O, the refracted rays will *converge* to a focus on the same side of the lens with F, but on the other side of O. These foci, viz. F and f, are called conjugate foci, and the position of one of them, when the other is given, may be found by the rule for converging rays falling on convex lenses.

When *diverging rays* R L, R C, R L, (*fig.* 12.) proceeding from any point F

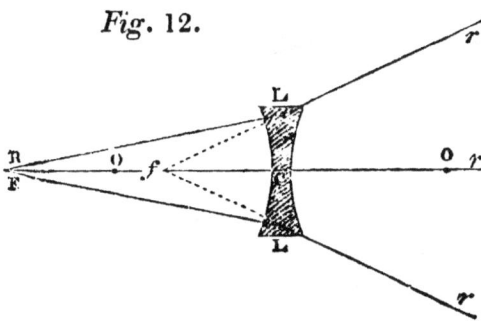

Fig. 12.

without the focus O N, fall upon a concave lens L L, they will diverge in directions Lr, Lr, as if they proceeded from a point f, between O and C; and as F approaches to C, f will also approach to it; and the distances F C or fC will be found when either of them is given, by the same rule as for diverging rays falling upon convex glasses.

Refraction through a Meniscus and a Concavo-convex Lens.—The effect of a meniscus upon light is the same as a convex lens of the same focal distance; and that of a concavo-convex lens is the same as that of a convex lens of the same focal distance. The following is the rule for finding their focal lengths for diverging rays. Multiply double the distance of the point of divergence by the product of the two radii for a dividend; take the difference between the products of the above distances into each of the radii for a divisor, and the quotient will be the focal distance required.

For *parallel rays*, the rule is much simpler. Divide twice the product of the two radii by the difference of the radii, and the quotient is the principal focal distance.

In studying the preceding account of the refraction of light through lenses, we would recommend it to the reader to demonstrate to himself the truth of the different results, by actually projecting the rays in large diagrams, and determining their course after refraction by the method shown in *figs.* 4 and 6. He will thus obtain a knowledge of the progress of light through refracting surfaces, which will facilitate the study of the following chapters.

The property of a *convex lens* of refracting parallel rays to a focus furnishes the principle upon which the *burning glass* is constructed. A burning glass, indeed, is nothing more than a large convex lens, L L, (*fig.* 7.), which collects into a small space, at its focus f, all the rays of the sun R L, R C, R L, which fall upon it.

If the lens L L has a surface of 400 square inches, and if the rays which cover its surface are collected into a space of one square inch, the burning power will be 400 times, provided no light is lost, and all the rays are collected in one spot. It is both difficult and expensive to make large burning glasses; and, on this account, Dr. Brewster has contrived a *built-up* lens, which may be made of any magnitude, and which is superior to a common lens of the same size.

The property of a convex lens, by which rays proceeding from its focus are refracted into parallel directions, enables us in light-houses to throw a strong light to great distances at sea. To this purpose the built-up lens above-mentioned has been applied with great success*.

CHAPTER IV.—DIOPTRICS *continued*.

Formation of Images by Lenses — Vision of Images — Apparent Magnitude — Magnifying Power — Telescopes — Microscopes.

WE have already shown in Chapter I., that a tolerably distinct image or picture of any object may be formed upon a piece of paper, by placing a small pin-hole or other aperture between the object and the paper, and excluding all extraneous light. Thus, if C, (*fig.* 13.) is a small hole in the front of a box, A B *m n*, and M N an object before it, the rays from the end M will pass straight

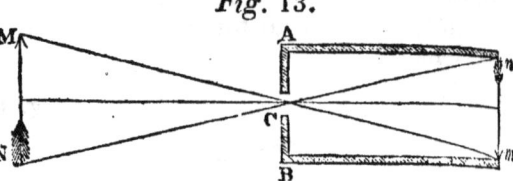

Fig. 13.

through the hole C, and illuminate the point *m* of the back of the box with their own colour; the rays from N will do the same at *n*; and all other points of M N will in like manner throw their rays on points immediately opposite them between *m* and *n*. The effect of the small hole C is to prevent the rays from any one point of the object M N from falling on any other point in *m n*, than the point immediately opposite to it; and hence the smaller that we make the aperture C, the more distinct will be the picture *m n* of the object M N. But from the same cause the picture will be faint, as the hole C admits such a small number of the rays which flow from every point of the object M N. If we enlarge the hole C, and substitute a lens L L, as in *fig.* 14,

Fig. 14.

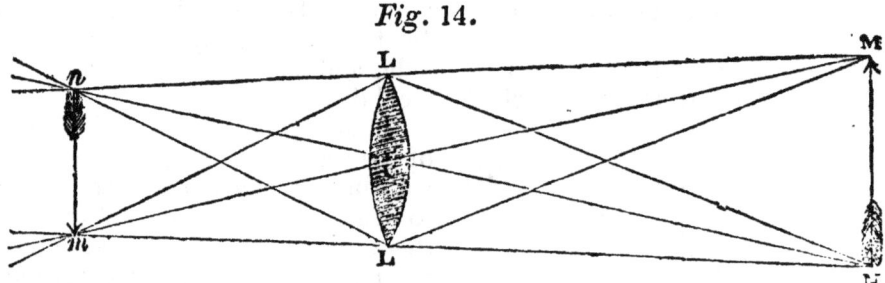

having L *n* for the focal distance suited to the distance of M N, we shall have an image *n m* every way similar to that formed by the hole, but much brighter and more distinct. Since all the rays which flow from M, such as M L, M L, and fall upon the lens L L, will be refracted to a focus at *m*, and all those from N to a focus at *n*, they will there paint a distinct picture of the points from which they come, and consequently of the whole object M N. The superior distinctness of the image *n m* in *fig.* 14, to that formed by the aperture C in *fig.* 13, arises from the circumstance that the rays from one point of the object M N cannot interfere with those from any other point; and its superior brightness arises from the great number of rays from each point which are collected by the lens in the corresponding point of the image.

It is obvious from the figure, that the image *n m* formed by a convex glass must necessarily be inverted, for it is impossible that the rays from the upper end M of the object can be carried by refraction to the upper end of the image at *n*.

As the rays M C, N C are refracted in lines C *m*, C *n*, parallel to C N, C M, the triangles *n* C *m*, N C M are similar, and *m n* is to M N as C *m* is to C M, that is, *the length of the image formed by a convex lens is to the length of the object, as the distance of the image is to the distance of the object from the lens.*

The relative positions of the object and image when the object is placed at different distances from the lens, are exactly the same as the conjugate foci of

---

* See the Chapter on PHOTOMETRY in the next Treatise, where this subject will be resumed.

OPTICS.

rays diverging from a point, as shewn in *fig.* 9. This motion of the conjugate foci is excellently illustrated by the following experiment given by Dr. Smith.

Having determined the focal distance E F, (*fig.* 15,) of a convex lens of glass E, and fixed it in a frame on a stand of wood C E D, placed vertically on a long table or floor A B, draw a line A B perpendicular to the frame, or parallel to the axis of the lens, through the point C, and on this line lay down the focal distance of the lens from C to F, and set the same distance from F to I, from I to II, II to III, &c., and also on the other side of C, from C to *f*, from *f* to 1, from 1 to 2, 2 to 3, &c. Let $\frac{1}{2}$ $\frac{1}{3}$ $\frac{1}{4}$ &c. of the focal distance E F be next set from F towards I, and also from *f* towards 1, and affix the numbers $\frac{1}{2}$ $\frac{1}{3}$ $\frac{1}{4}$ to the points of division. When this is done, darken the room, and set a candle at Q over the mark II, the rays refracted by the lens will converge at *q*, and form an inverted image of the candle upon a paper screen G H, placed at the opposite mark $\frac{1}{2}$. If the candle is removed to III, the inverted image will be seen formed at $\frac{1}{3}$, by advancing the paper to $\frac{1}{3}$, and if the candle is pushed farther in to I, the distinct image will be seen formed at 1, by withdrawing the paper to that point. The effect will be exactly the same if the candle and the paper be made to change places. Hence it will be found by direct experiment, that *f q* varies reciprocally as F Q, that is, it increases in the same proportion as F Q diminishes, and diminishes in the same proportion as F Q increases. If Q is brought forward to F, no distinct image of the candle will be formed at any distance, but the light will be refracted into a parallel beam, of the same diameter as the lens at all distances from it.

If the image *n m* (*fig.* 14.) is received upon ground glass, or upon transparent paper, or upon a plate of glass upon which a layer of skimmed milk has been allowed to dry, and if we place the eye behind it, we shall see the inverted image with as much distinctness as before, provided the eye is distant six inches, the distance at which we view all other near objects. If when the eye is in this position, we take away the glass or paper on which the image is formed, we shall see the image in the air, as it were, as distinctly as before. The reason of this is, that all the rays which are refracted to foci at *n, m*, &c. cross

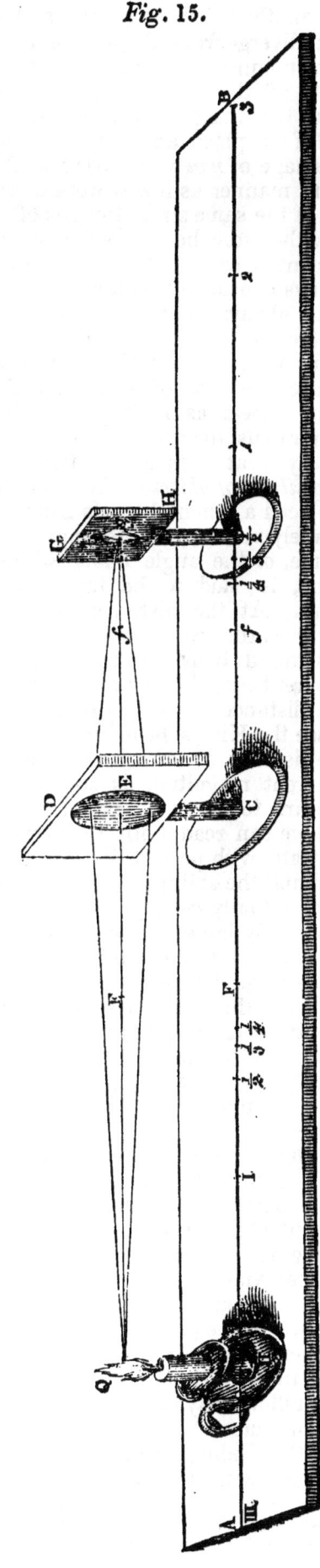

Fig. 15.

one another at these points, and therefore diverge from them in precisely the same manner as they do from the point M N of the object. Hence we may treat the image nm as a new object, and if we place another lens behind it, an image of nm would be formed in the same manner as if nm were a real object of the same size. Images of images may therefore be formed in succession by convex lenses, the last image being always considered as a new object, and being always an inverted picture of the one before.

In order to explain how lenses increase the size of objects, and make them appear as if they were brought nearer to us, the reader must understand clearly what is meant by the *apparent magnitude of objects*. When a shilling is placed a hundred yards from us, it is scarcely visible, and its apparent magnitude, or the angle under which it is seen*, is said to be then extremely small. At the distance of twenty or thirty yards, we can just see that it is a round body; and we see that its apparent magnitude has increased; at the distance of three yards, we begin to see the King's head upon it; and at the distance of six or eight inches, its apparent magnitude is so great, that it appears to cover a distant mountain, and we can read both the legend and the date with perfect distinctness. By bringing the shilling nearer the eye, we have actually *magnified* it, or made it apparently larger; and though its size remains the same, we have thus made all its parts distinctly seen.

When the distance of the shilling is twenty feet, let a convex lens, whose focal length is five feet, be placed half way between the shilling and the eye, that is, ten feet from each: then it is demonstrable that the image of the shilling formed by the lens will be *exactly of the same size* as the shilling, and, consequently, it is not directly magnified by the lens; but, as the image is brought so near us that the eye can view it at the distance of six inches, its apparent magnitude is increased in the proportion of six inches to twenty feet, or as one to forty, that is, forty times. Hence, we have magnified the shilling forty times merely by bringing an image of it near to the eye.

If the shilling, or object, is so remote that we cannot place a lens half way between it and the eye, we can still magnify it by forming a small image of it in the following manner: Let the same lens of five feet focal length, like L L, (*fig.* 14.) be placed in a hole in the window-shutter of a dark room, and let us suppose that the object, such as a church-spire, is distant 5000 feet, or about a mile; then, as the rays from this object will fall nearly parallel on the lens L L, an inverted image nm will be formed in its principal focus, or five feet behind the lens, and the size of this image will be to that of the object as 5 feet is to 5000, or 1000 times smaller than the object. But if we view this small image, so as to see it distinctly, at the distance of six inches, we see it under an angle, or with an apparent magnitude, as much greater than if the same small image were equally far off with the spire, as 6 inches is to 5000 feet, that is, 10,000 times. Hence, though the image is 1000 times less than the spire, from one cause, yet from its being brought near to the eye, it is 10,000 times greater in apparent magnitude; consequently, its apparent magnitude is increased $\frac{10000}{1000}$ or *ten* times, that is, it is actually magnified ten times by means of the lens L L. This magnifying power is always equal to the focal length of the lens, divided by the distance at which the eye sees near objects most distinctly, which in the present example is $\frac{5\text{ feet}}{6\text{ inches}}$ or $\frac{60\text{ inches}}{6\text{ inches}}$ or *ten* times, as before.

When the image nm is received upon any smooth and white surface, such as paper, stucco, ground glass, &c. then the lens, and other apparatus, is called a *camera obscura*, or *dark chamber*; but when the eye is placed behind the lens, and sees the inverted image in the air, the apparatus is a *telescope*, from two Greek words signifying to *see at a distance*, though this name is commonly given only when there are two or more lenses.

But there is another method of magnifying objects, particularly objects within our reach, which is of great importance in optics. We all know that the eye can see objects distinctly when placed at a great distance, that is, when the rays proceeding from the object are parallel, or nearly so. Consequently, if we place an object very near the eye, so as to give it great apparent magnitude, and if we can by any means make the rays which flow from it enter the eye nearly parallel to each other, we must

---

* The angle M C N is the angle under which the object M N is seen to an eye at C, in *fig.* 14.

see it distinctly. This is effected by placing close to the eye a convex lens, and holding the object in its focus; for we have already seen that when rays diverge from f, the focus of a lens L L, *fig.* 7, the refracted rays L R, L R are parallel. By placing the object a little nearer than f, the rays which flow from it may receive that precise degree of divergency which they have when the object is placed six inches from the eye, the nearest distance at which we see minute objects distinctly. If the distance C f is one inch, the object at f will have its apparent magnitude six times greater than when it is seen at the distance of six inches without the lens. It is, therefore, said to be magnified *six* times by the lens L L. This lens is called a *single microscope*, and the magnifying power of such microscopes may be always found by dividing six inches by the focal distance of the lens. A lens, for example, the tenth of an inch in focal length, will magnify 60 times; and one the hundredth of an inch, 600 times.

To the telescope with one lens, which magnified 10 times, when the image *m n* (*figs.* 14 and 16) was seen by the naked eye placed six inches behind it, we may now give additional magnifying power, by bringing the eye O within an inch of the image, that is, by viewing the image *n m* with a lens *l l*, whose focal distance is one inch. This lens will magnify the image six times; but, as the image had been previously magnified ten times, by the lens L L, the magnifying effect of the two lenses will be 10×6, or 60 times. This instrument

Fig. 16.

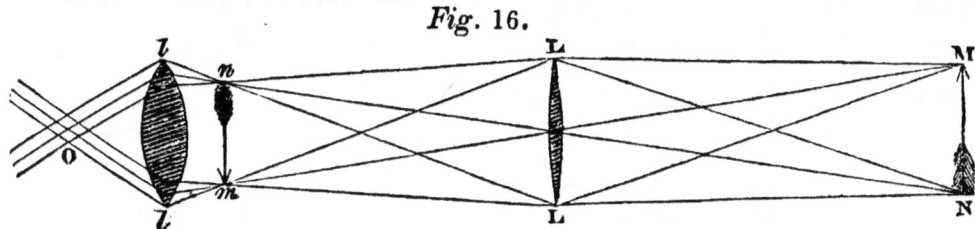

is the *astronomical telescope*, by which objects are seen inverted, and the magnifying power of which is always equal to the focal length of the *object glass* L L, or the lens next the object, divided by the focal length of the *eye glass l l*, or the lens next the eye.

The principle, therefore, of the telescope, is simply this: the object glass forms, in its focus, a distinct image, or picture of the object, which, though very much smaller than the object, is yet seen under a much greater angle, or magnified; and this image, so magnified, is seen under a still greater angle, or still farther magnified by the eye glass, which enables the eye to see it distinctly at a less distance than six inches.

The process of magnifying objects by the single microscope* has been already explained; but, when a very high magnifying power is required, it is necessary to use two lenses, as in the astronomical telescope. The object M N (*fig.* 17.) is placed a little farther from the lens L L than its principal focus, and an in-

Fig. 17.

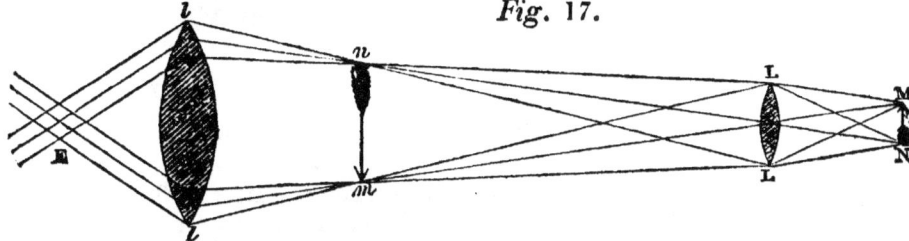

verted image of it is formed at *n m*. This image, being in the principal focus of another lens *l l*, the rays which proceed from it will be refracted into parallel directions, and thus afford distinct vision of it to the eye at E: the lens L L is called the object glass, and *l l* the eye glass, and the instrument is called a *compound microscope*. The object M N is first magnified by the object glass L L in the proportion of L *m* to L M, and this magnified image is again magnified by the eye glass *l l*, in the proportion of *l n* to six inches. Hence, if the focal length of L L is half an inch, L *n* six inches, and the focal length of *l l* one inch, the magnifying power will be $\frac{6}{\frac{1}{2}} \times \frac{6}{1} = 72$ times, or 12 times by L L, and again 6 times by *l l*.

---

* From two Greek words, signifying *to see small things.*

Chapter V.—Catoptrics.

Reflexion of Light—Law of Reflexion— Reflexion from Plane, Concave, and Convex Mirrors.

Hitherto we have considered only the light which is transmitted through transparent bodies; but in every case where light falls upon a body, a portion of it is thrown back or reflected from its surface, according to a regular law. The branch of optics which treats of the reflexion of light is called *Catoptrics*, from two Greek words, one of which signifies *from* or *against*, and the other to *see*, because things are *seen* by light reflected *from* bodies.

When a ray of light, AC, (*fig.* 18) falls upon a polished surface, either plane like R C S, or curved like *r* C *s*, at the point C, it will be reflected in such a direction C B, that the angle A C P, which the ray makes with C P, a line perpendicular to the surface at C, is equal to the angle B C P, which the reflected ray makes with the same perpendicular. The angle A C P is called the *angle of incidence*, and B C P the *angle of reflexion*. When the ray falls in the direction P C, it is reflected back in the same line; and when the ray falls in the direction R C, it is reflected in the direction C S.

These results may be easily proved by reflecting the light of the sun or a candle from a piece of looking-glass; and hence we may consider it as a general law, that *the angle of reflexion is equal to the angle of incidence.*

The bodies which are used to reflect light are called *mirrors*, or *specula*, and are commonly pieces of metal or glass, having their surface highly polished. Those made of glass are generally quicksilvered on one side, so as to reflect more light; but in the following observations it is supposed that the mirror is made of metal. Mirrors are either *plane, concave,* or *convex,* according as they are bounded by plane or by spherical surfaces.

Reflexion of rays from plane mirrors. —When *parallel rays* fall upon a plane mirror they will be parallel after reflexion. If A C, A' C' (*fig.* 18) are two parallel rays falling upon the plane mirror R S', they will be reflected into the parallel directions C B, C' B': since C P, C' P' are both perpendicular to the same plane, they are parallel; and because A C is parallel to A' C', and C P to C' P', the angle A C P will be equal

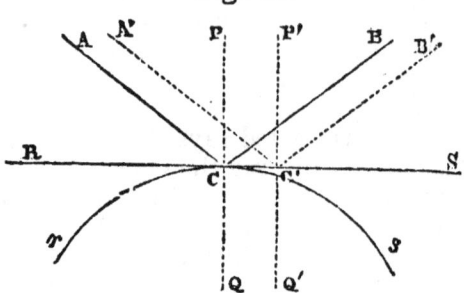

Fig. 18.

to A' C' P'. Hence B C P is equal to B' C' P', and C B parallel to C' B'. The same truth may be easily proved experimentally.

When *diverging rays* fall upon a plane mirror, they will have the same divergency after reflexion. Let the rays A B, A D, A F, diverging from A (*fig.* 19.) fall upon the plane mirror R S;

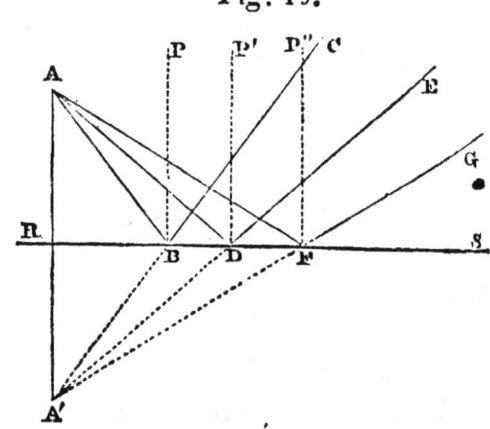

Fig. 19.

draw B C, D E, F G, so as to make the angle C B P equal to A B P; E D P' equal to A D P', and G F P''' equal to A F P''; then by continuing the lines C B, E D, G F backwards, they will be found to meet at A', so that A' B, A' D, and A' F are respectively equal to A B, A D, and A F; and B A F equal to B A' F.

When *converging rays* fall upon a plane mirror they will have the same convergency after reflexion. This is obvious, from *fig.* 19, where the rays C B, E D, and C F fall upon the mirror R S, and would have met in a point at A', if the mirror had not intervened. Since the lines F A, D A, B A form equal angles with the perpendicular at F, D, and B, they will be the reflected rays which will meet at A, in the same manner as they would have done at A', had there been no mirror to reflect them.

Reflexion of parallel rays by concave and convex mirrors.—Let M N (*fig.* 20.) be a concave mirror, of which RCE is the axis, or the line, by a motion round which the section MN

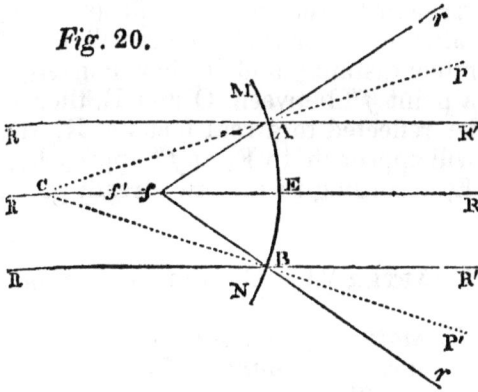

Fig. 20.

would generate a concave mirror. Let C be the centre of its concave surface MEN, and let *parallel rays* RA, RE, RB fall upon it at the points A, E, B; these rays will be all reflected or made to converge to a focus *f*, half way between C and E, so that the *principal focal* distance E *f* is half the radius C E of the concave surface. The ray R E falling perpendicularly at E, will be reflected backwards in the same line E R, and will consequently pass through *f*. In order to find the direction of R A after reflection, draw C A P, which will be perpendicular to the spherical surface at A; then as R A C is the angle of incidence, make C A *f* equal to it, and A *f* will be the reflected ray; in like manner find B *f*, the reflected ray for R B. Now, since R A and R E are parallel, R A C is equal to A C *f*, that is, C A *f* is equal to A C *f*; consequently C *f* is equal to *f* A. But as the point A approaches to E, *f* A will become equal to *f* E, and consequently *f* E to *f* C.

By continuing all the lines in the figure to the other side of the mirror, the very same reasoning may be used to prove, that when parallel rays R' A, R' E, R' B fall upon a convex mirror M A E B N, the reflected rays A *r*, E R', B *r* will diverge as if they came from *f*, which is called their *virtual focus*, and which is the *principal focus* of parallel rays.

Reflexion of diverging rays by concave and convex mirrors. Let M N (*fig.* 21.) be a concave mirror, whose axis is C E, and centre C, and let O be

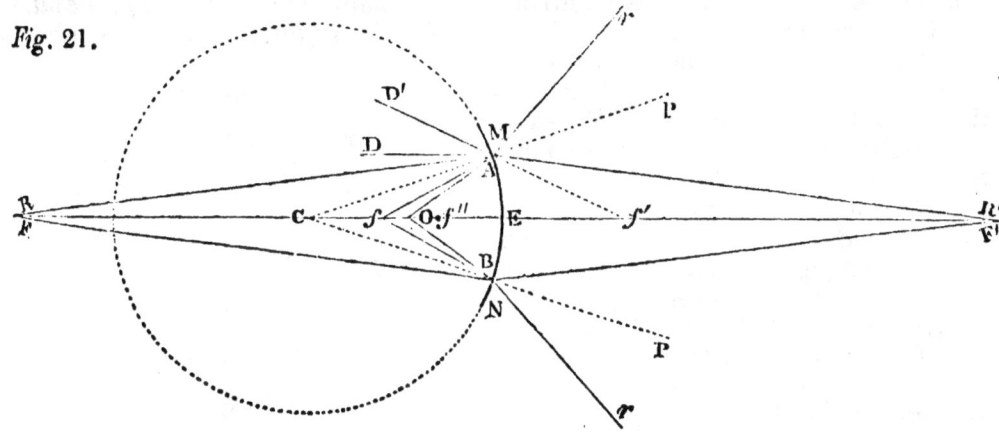

Fig. 21.

its principal focus or focus of parallel rays, such as *f* was in *fig.* 20. Then if rays R A, R E, R B, diverging from F, fall upon it, they will be reflected to a focus *f* between O and C, so that R O is to O C as O C is to O *f*; that is, the distance *f* O is equal to half the radius of the mirror multiplied by itself, and divided by the distance of the divergent point R or F from the point O. Hence by adding *f* O to half the radius O E, we obtain *f* E, the conjugate focal length of the mirror for rays proceeding from F. The truth of this may be easily proved by projecting the reflected rays, and measuring the distances on a scale of equal parts; but the following demonstration of it is so simple, that we shall lay it before the reader. Let A O be the reflected ray, corresponding to the incident ray D A, parallel to the axis C E; then, since D A C is equal to C A O, and since R A C is equal to C A *f*, the remainder D A R is equal to the remainder O A *f*. But in the triangles A R O, A *f* O, the angle A O *f* is common, and A R O equal to D A R, which is equal to *f* A O; hence the triangles are similar, and R O is to O A, as O A is to O *f*; but O A is equal to O C, consequently, R O is to O C, as O C is to O *f*.

From this rule we conclude, and it may be clearly proved by projecting the incident and reflected rays, that when one of the conjugate foci R approaches to C, the other focus f also approaches to C; and when F coincides with C, f also coincides with it; so that it follows, that when rays diverge from the centre of a sphere or a spherical surface, they are all reflected back again to the same point from which they diverged. When R passes C towards O, f will then pass beyond C, and move farther off as R approaches to O. When F coincides with O, f will be infinitely distant, or the reflected rays will be parallel. When R passes O towards E, the reflected rays will diverge like A D', and will have their virtual focus about f' behind the mirror; and as R approaches E, f' will also approach E.

If we continue the lines C A, C E, C B behind the mirror in *fig.* 21, and suppose M E N the surface of a *convex* mirror, upon which rays R' A, R' E, and R' B fall, diverging from R', then it may be proved, by the very same reasoning, that they will be reflected in the directions A r, E R, B r in lines which diverge from a virtual focus f'', whose distance from O or E is found by the rule above given for concave mirrors. As R' recedes from the mirror, f'' will approach to O, with which it will coincide when R' is infinitely distant, and the rays become parallel. When R' approaches to E, f'' also approaches to E.

Reflexion of converging rays by concave and convex mirrors.—It is obvious, from *fig.* 21, that all rays, such as D' A, which fall converging upon the *concave* mirror M N, will be reflected to a focus f'' between O and E, and this focus will approach to E, as the point of convergence f' approaches to E. It may be shown by the same reasoning as for diverging rays, that f' O is to O C, as O C is to O f'', f'' being now between O and E.

When converging rays r A, r B (*fig.* 21.) fall upon a *convex* mirror M N, as if they proceeded to some point f'' between O and E, they will be reflected to R' whose distance from O or E is found by the very same reasoning which we have given for diverging rays. From this it follows, and it may be proved also by projecting the rays, that when they converge to any point between O and C, they will be reflected, as if they diverged from R beyond C. When they converge to C they will be reflected in the same direction as if they came from C; and if they converge to a point beyond C, they will be reflected, diverging as if they proceeded from some point between C and O. When they converge to O, they will be reflected, in parallel lines, or their focus will be infinitely distant; and if they converge to a point f'' between O and E, they will be reflected to a real focus at R, which will approach to E, as f'' approaches to E, according to the law already given.

CHAPTER VI.—CATOPTRICS *continued*.

Formation of Images by Plane, Concave, and Convex Mirrors—Reflecting Telescopes — Reflecting Microscopes.

THE principle of the formation of images by mirrors is exactly the same as by lenses, and the place of the image may be determined from the place of the object, and the radius of the mirror, by finding the foci or points of convergence of the rays, from the rules in the preceding chapter. The application of these rules we shall now exemplify.

Formation of images by plane mirrors. —Let R S (*fig.* 22.) be the surface of a

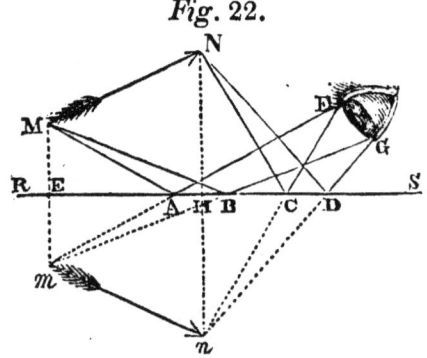

Fig. 22.

plane mirror, and M N any object placed before it, and let the eye of the observer be placed any where before the mirror, as at F G. Of all the rays which proceed in every direction from the points M, N of the object, and are reflected from the mirror, those which enter the eye are few in number and must be reflected from portions A B, C D of the mirror, so situated with respect to the eye and the object, that the angles of incidence of the rays which fall on these portions must be equal to the angles of reflexion of those which enter the eye between F and G. The ray M A, for example, will be reflected in the direction A F, and the ray M B in the direction B G; in like manner, the rays N C, N D will be reflected in the directions C F, D G. Now the rays A F, B G, by which the point M is seen, enter the eye, F G, as if they came from m, as far behind the mirror as M is before it, and the rays C F, D G enter the eye as if they came from a point n, as far behind the mirror as N is before it, that is, E m is equal to E M, and H n to H N. Consequently, if we join $m n$ it will be of the same length as M N, and have the same position behind the mirror as the object has before it. If the eye F G is placed in any other position before the mirror, and if rays are drawn from M and N, which after reflexion enter the eye, it will be found that these, if continued backwards, will meet at the points m and n, and, consequently, in every position of the eye, the image will be seen in the same spot, and of the same size at equal distances from the eye. If the object M N is a person looking into the mirror, he will see a perfect image of himself at $m n$, and hence we have an explanation of the properties of the *looking glass*.

If we place an object M N (*fig.* 23)

Fig. 23.

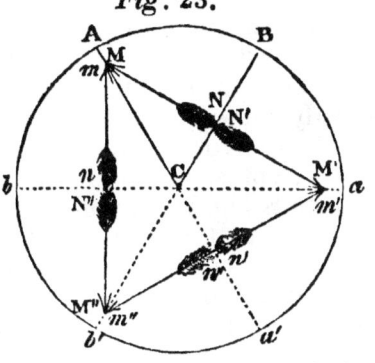

between two plane mirrors A C, C B, inclined to one another, at any angle A C B, several images of the object will be formed, and they will be arranged in the circumference of a circle. This truth may be clearly proved by drawing the image of the object in its proper place behind each mirror, and then considering each successive image as a new object, and drawing its image. By doing this, it will become evident, that the image of M N in the mirror A C is $m n$, while its image in B C is M' N'. In like manner the image of the image $m n$ in B C will be $m' n'$, while the image of the image M' N' in A C will be M" N". It will be found also that $m'' n''$ is the image both of M" N" in the mirror B C, and of $m' n'$ in the mirror A C, so that it consists in reality of two images which will exactly cover one another, if A C B is 60° or the 6th part of a circle, as it is in the figure; but if it is ever so little less or more, the image $m'' n''$ will be seen double. This is the principle of the *kaleidoscope*[*], so far as the multiplication of the images and their general arrangement is concerned; but it has nothing to do with the principle of symmetry which is essential to the kaleidoscope. The above truth is independent of the position of the object and the eye, but the kaleidoscope requires that the object and the eye have certain positions, without which it cannot produce symmetrical and beautiful forms.

Formation of images by convex mirrors.—Let R S (*fig.* 24.) be a convex

Fig. 24.

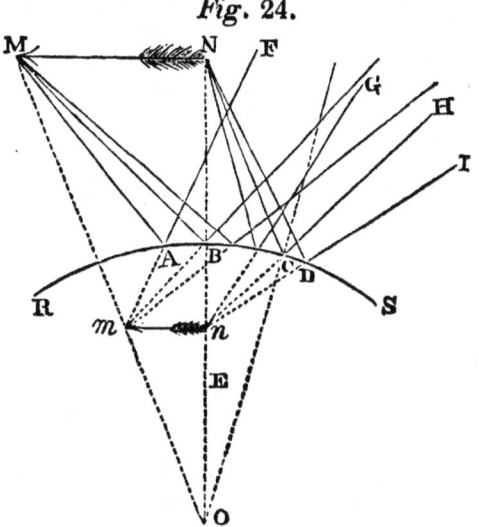

mirror whose centre is O, and M N any object placed before it, then upon the same principles which have been explained for a plane mirror, it will be found that an image of it will be formed at $m n$, the points m, n being ascertained by continuing back the reflected rays A F, B G, till they meet at m, and C H, D I, till they meet at n. By joining the points M, m and N, n, and continuing the lines till they meet, it will be found that they meet at O, the centre of the mirror, whatever be the distance or the position of the object M N. The image $m n$ is always less than the object; and as it must always be contained between lines M O, and N O, which meet at O, its length $m n$ will be to that of the object M N as O n is to O N. When M N approaches to the mirror, $m n$ will also approach to it, and when M N touches the mirror, $m n$ will also touch it, and

---

[*] From two Greek words, signifying *beautiful forms*.

become equal to M N. When M N recedes from the mirror, m n will become less and less, and recede from the mirror also; and when M N is infinitely distant, m n will be at E, the virtual focus of parallel rays. Objects, therefore, are always seen diminished in a convex mirror, unless when they touch it.

Formation of images by concave mirrors.—Let M N (*fig.* 25.) be an object at a considerable distance from a con-

Fig. 25.

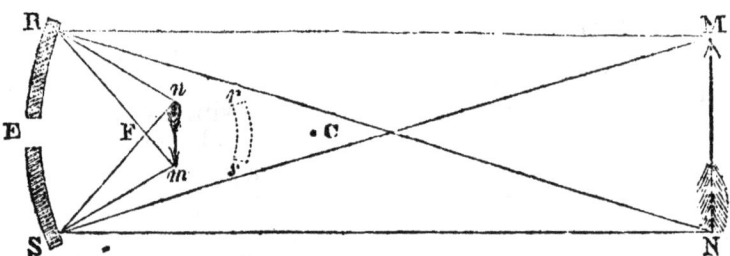

cave mirror R S, whose centre is C and principal focus F: then, as the rays from M fall diverging on the mirror, they will be reflected to a focus at m, a little without its principal focus, and there form a representation of the point m; in like manner the rays diverging from N will be reflected to n, and there form a picture of N; so that there will be an inverted image n m of the object formed a little without the principal focus F. This image seems to be suspended in the air, and has a very singular appearance when it is received on a thin blue smoke from a chafing dish placed below m. As the object M N recedes from the mirror, the image m n approaches to F, with which it coincides when M N is infinitely distant. This is the principle of the *Reflecting telescope*. If we conceive m n to be a small object, then the rays diverging from it will form an enlarged image of it at M N, which may be either viewed by the eye, or, which is better, by a convex lens, in which case it constitutes a *Reflecting microscope*.

If we consider the image m n as a new object, and place a small concave mirror r s behind it, so as to form an enlarged image of that image, the rays of which pass through a hole E, in the large mirror R S; then, this second, or enlarged image, may be either viewed by the eye behind E, or magnified still more by a convex lens. In this case, the combination becomes the *Gregorian reflecting telescope*. If we make the small mirror r s convex, and place it between F and n m, so as to intercept the rays before they actually meet their virtual foci, n m, then an enlarged image of this virtual image will be formed somewhere about E, and may be magnified, as before, with a convex lens. In this case, the combination constitutes the *Cassegrainian reflecting telescope*. The former instrument is called after its inventor, James Gregory; the latter after its inventor, Monsieur Cassegrain. In these telescopes, the magnifying power is determined in the very same manner as for convex lenses, or combinations of them; the size of the image being always to the size of its object, as the distance of the image from the mirror is to the distance of the object.

When the object is placed nearer a concave mirror than its principal focus F, the rays will not have their focus in front of the mirror, but will diverge as already shewn, from conjugate foci behind the mirror, where they will form a correct representation of the object. The image is highly magnified when the object is near the focus, but it gradually diminishes as the object approaches the mirror, and it becomes equal to it when the object touches the mirror.

CHAPTER VII.—*On Spherical Aberration in Lenses and Mirrors.*

IN treating of the refraction of rays at the surfaces of spheres and lenses, we have supposed that all the rays meet exactly in the focus. This, however, is not exactly true; for if, in *fig.* 6, the ray A C is refracted by the sphere L L to the point f, another ray falling upon the sphere nearer the axis, any where between C and H, will have its focus, or will intersect the axis, at a point f' farther from the sphere than f. This is easily proved by actually projecting the refracted rays, and if it is done for those rays farthest from the axis, and for those nearest the axis, the difference ff' between the foci of these rays is called the *spherical aberration*, or the *aberration* or *straying* of the rays from the focus, caused by the *spherical* figure of the lens. That this aberration arises from the curvature of the glass being equal or spherical at C and at H is evident, for if the glass was rounder or more convex at H than it is, it would have a focus nearer the sphere, and the ray which it now refracts only to f' would be refracted to f; or if when H remains the same, the glass were made flatter at C than it is, it would refract the rays to a more distant point than at f. Hence, in order to refract rays at different distances from the axis to the same point, the glass must have different degrees of curvature at different distances from the axis.

By actually projecting the refracted rays for spheres and lenses of different kinds, which we strongly recommend to the student, he will obtain the following results:—

1. In a *plano-convex lens* with its plane side turned towards parallel rays, that is, turned *outwards*, if it is to form an image behind it, as in the object glass of a telescope; or *inwards*, if it is to be used as a single microscope, the aberration is $4\frac{1}{2}$ times its thickness*.

2. In a *plano-convex lens* with its convex side towards parallel rays, the aberration is $1\frac{17}{100}$dths of its thickness. Hence in using a plano-convex lens, the parallel rays should always be incident on its convex surface, or emerge from it.

3. In a *double convex lens* with equal convexities, the aberration is $1\frac{67}{100}$dths of its thickness.

4. In a *double convex lens* whose radii are as 2 to 5, the aberration is the same as in the plano convex lens (§ 1,) if the side with the radius 5 is turned towards parallel rays: and the same as the plano-convex lens (§ 2,) if the side with the radius 2 is turned towards parallel rays.

5. The *lens with least spherical aberration* is a double convex one, whose radii are as 1 to 6, the side whose radius is 1 being turned towards parallel rays. The aberration is then $1\frac{7}{100}$dths of its thickness. When the side with the radius 6 is turned to parallel rays, its aberration is $3\frac{45}{100}$dths of its thickness.

If we call the aberration of the preceding lens 1, Mr. Herschel has shewn

---

* The *thickness* of a lens is the difference between its thickness at the middle, C, (fig. 7,) and at its circumference, L.

that the following are the aberrations of other lenses.

Best form as in § 5 - - 1.00
Double convex or concave 1.567
Plano-convex or concave, curved
  surface towards parallel rays 1.081
Plano-convex or concave, plane
  surface towards parallel rays 4.2

As it is desirable to reduce the aberration below *once* the thickness of the lens, and as this cannot be done by a single one, we must have recourse to two lenses put together. Mr. Herschel has shewn that if two plano-convex lenses are put together as in *fig.* 26, the aberration will

Fig. 26.

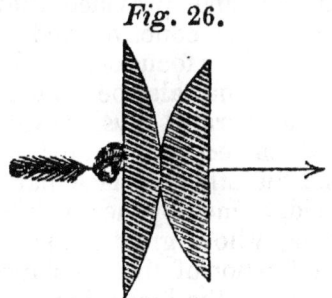

be only 0.2481, or one-fourth of that of a single lens in its best form. The focal length of the first of these lenses must be to that of the second, as 1 to 2.3. If their focal lengths are equal, the aberration will be 0.603, or nearly one half.

The spherical aberration, however, may be *entirely destroyed* by combining a meniscus and double convex lens, as shewn in *fig.* 27 and 28, the convex sides

Fig. 27.

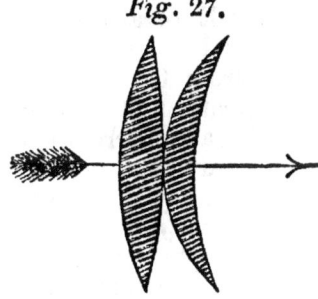

being turned to the eye when they are used as lenses, and to parallel rays when they are used as burning glasses. Mr.

Fig. 28.

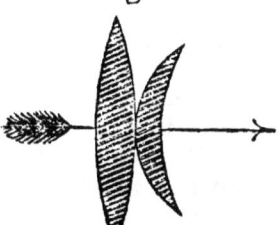

Herschel has computed the following curvatures for these lenses:—

	Fig. 27.	Fig. 28.
Focal length of the *convex lens*	+10.000	+10.000
Radius of its first surface	+ 5.833	+ 5.833
Radius of its second surface	−35.000	−35.000
Focal length of the *Meniscus*	+17.829	+ 5.497
Radius of its first surface	+ 3.688	+ 2.054
Radius of its second surface	+ 6.291	+ 8.128
Focal length of the *compound lens*	+ 6.407	+ 3.474

A single lens may be made free from aberration for parallel rays, provided the surface which receives the parallel rays is part of an ellipsoid, (or prolate spheroid, formed by the revolution of an ellipse round its greater axis,) whose greater axis is the index of refraction of the substance, the distance between its foci being 1; and provided that the second surface is concave, and whose centre is the farther focus of the spheroid.

A single lens may also be made free of aberration for parallel rays, provided the surface which receives parallel rays is plane, and the other surface part of a hyperboloid, formed by the revolution of a hyperbola, whose greater axis is the index of refraction of the substance, the distance between the foci being 1.

Spherical Aberration of Mirrors.— In determining the focus of parallel rays reflected by a concave spherical mirror, M N (*fig.* 20.) it has been proved that the focus f is always so situated in the line C E, that for any ray R A, Cf is equal to fA: but if f' is the focus of rays very near R E, so that Cf' is equal to f' E, then, as f' A is greater than f' E, f' cannot be the focus of the ray R A; and, consequently, its focus must be nearer E, or at f, in order that Cf may be equal to fA. As the ray R A recedes from the axis R E, f' A will become greater and greater in proportion to f' E; and, therefore, the focus f must come nearer and nearer to E, in proportion as the ray R A recedes from R E. The distance ff' for any ray R A or R B; or for a spherical mirror, whose diameter is A B, is called its *spherical aberration*. This aberration obviously increases in the same mirror with the diameter A B of its aperture; and, in mirrors of different curvature, it increases with the curvature, for it is clear that if the surface A E B is more concave, fA will increase faster in proportion to fE. Hence, it is plain, that if we had a curve of such a nature that a line R A parallel to its axis C E, and another line Af drawn from A to a fixed point f, should always form an equal angle with C A, a line perpendicular to the curve at A, we should then have a surface which would reflect parallel rays to a focus or mathematical point f. Now this curve is actually a *parabola*, and hence the specula, or mirrors, of all reflecting telescopes are ground into the shape of a *paraboloid*, or a surface formed by the revolution of a parabola round its axis.

By the same reasoning it may be shewn that when rays fall diverging from any point R (*fig.* 21.) on a concave spherical mirror A B, they will not be refracted to the same focus, as the rays near the axis, such as R E, and that such rays can only be reflected to the same focus with those near the axis, when the surface A E B is such that lines drawn from two points R, f form equal angles with a line C A, perpendicular to the surface at the point where the ray falls. Such a surface is that of an *ellipsoid*, whose foci are R and f; so that when rays diverge from one focus of an ellipsoid, they are accurately reflected to the other focus. Hence, in reflecting microscopes, the mirror should be always a portion of an ellipsoid, in one focus of which is the object, and in the other the image.

CHAPTER VIII.—CHROMATICS.

Decomposition of White Light into Colours—Different refrangibility of differently coloured Rays—Recomposition of white light.

HITHERTO we have considered light as a simple substance, and all its parts or rays as refracted in the very same manner, by the lenses upon which they fall. This, however, is not the case. The *white* light, which comes from the sun, or from any other luminous body, is actually composed or made up of *seven* different kinds of light of different colours, viz., *red, orange, yellow, green, blue, indigo,* and *violet*. These colours often appear by themselves, and the white light from which they are produced is decomposed, or separated into its elements, by different processes, which we shall presently explain.

That branch of optics, which treats of the colours of light, of their physical properties, and of the laws according to which white light is decomposed, and recomposed from its elements, is called CHROMATICS, from a Greek word, which signifies *colour*.

If we were required to decompose a *greenish grey* powder, consisting of fine brass filings, and fine steel filings, we could easily do it by putting into the powder a loadstone, which would instantly attract all the blue steel filings, and leave behind the yellow brass filings, thus decomposing, as it were, the *greenish grey* powder into the *yellow* and *blue* powders, of which it consists. If the *steel* filings were all much smaller than the *brass* ones, we could have separated them still easier, by a sieve, whose meshes or holes would permit all the steel filings to pass, while they retained the brass ones.

The decomposition of light is effected in many cases, by processes somewhat analogous. In the experiments on the refraction of *water*, which are described in Chap. II., and illustrated in *fig.* 2, we used *white* light, and we found its refractive power, which is represented by the line A D, *fig*. 2, to be 1.336. If we now repeat the same experiment, and make the light which passes down the tube, *red, orange, yellow, green, blue, indigo,* and *violet,* in succession, we shall find that each colour has a different refractive power of its own, that of the *red* being the *least*, and that of the *violet* the *greatest*. The following will be the results with water, crown, and flint glass:

	WATER. Index of Refr.	CROWN GLASS. Index of Refr.	FLINT GLASS. Index of Refr
Red	1.3310	1.5258	1.6277
Orange	1.3317	1.5268	1.6297
Yellow	1.3336	1.5296	1.6350
Green	1.3358	1.5330	1.6420
Blue	1.3378	1.5360	1.6483
Indigo	1.3413	1.5417	1.6603
Violet	1.3442	1.5466	1.6711

Hence we may conclude, that the rays of light of different colours have different degrees of refraction, or, as it is expressed, *different refrangibilities*.

The method by which Sir Isaac Newton established this great discovery is shewn in *fig.* 29.

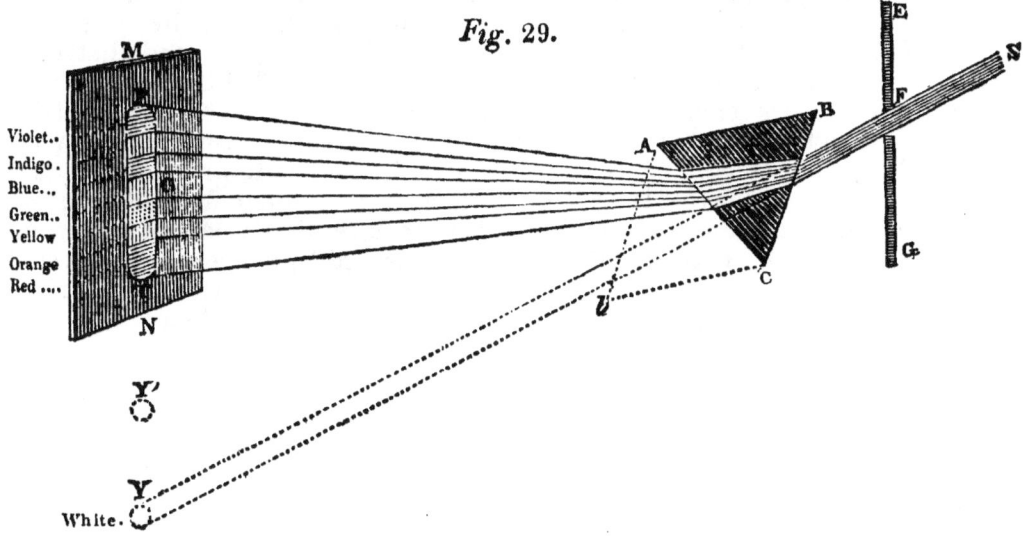

Fig. 29.

In the window shutter E G of a dark room, he made a hole, F, about one-third of an inch broad, and he placed behind it a glass prism A B C, so that the beam of the sun's light S F might enter and leave the prism at equal angles as described in page 8, col. 1.

Before the interposition of the prism, the beam S F proceeded in a straight line to Y, where it formed a round white spot; but being now refracted by the prism, it will form upon the screen M N an oblong image P T, containing seven colours, as enumerated in the figure, the *red* being *least*, and the *violet most* refracted from the original direction S Y of the solar beam. This oblong image is called the *solar,* and sometimes the *prismatic spectrum*. By making a hole in the screen M N opposite any one of these colours, so as to allow it alone to pass; and by letting the colour thus separated fall upon a second prism, Sir Isaac found that the light of each of the colours was alike refrangible, because the second prism could not separate them into an oblong image, or into any other colour. Hence he called all the seven colours *simple* or *homogeneous*, in opposition to *white* light, which he called *compound,* or *heterogeneous*.

With the prism used by Sir Isaac, he found the lengths of the colours and spaces to be as follows:—Red, 45;

orange, 27; yellow, 40; green, 60; blue, 60; indigo, 48; violet, 80: or 360 in all.

But these spaces vary with prisms of different substances, and as they are not separated by distinct limits, but shade gradually into one another, it is almost impossible to obtain any thing like an accurate measure of their relative extents. This difficulty is increased too by the circumstance, that as the spectrum is brightest in the yellow space, and grows fainter and fainter towards the red and the violet extremities, its length increases with the intensity of the light from which it is formed.

Having thus decomposed white light into its seven primary colours, Sir Isaac Newton shewed, that these seven colours, when again put together, or combined, recomposed white light. This may be proved rudely, but yet accurately enough for the purposes of illustration, by mixing together seven different powders, having the colours and proportions indicated above; or, what is better, by painting the rim of a wheel with the seven prismatic colours, and making it revolve rapidly about its axis. In both these cases the mixture of the colours will be a sort of greyish white, because the colours employed cannot possibly be obtained of the proper tints, or laid on in the proper proportions. A more accurate proof is obtained by making the prismatic spectrum fall on a lens or concave mirror, and thus bringing the whole seven colours into a focus, which will be white

Chapter IX.— Chromatics continued.

Dispersion of Light—Dispersive Powers—Table of Dispersive Powers.

In the prismatic spectrum P T, formed by the prism A B C, (*fig.* 29), the green space G is placed in the *middle* between P and T; and hence it has been called the *mean ray of the spectrum:* the index of refraction, which belongs to it, is called the *mean refractive power* of the prism; and the angle, which the green ray forms with the line S Y, the *mean refraction* of the prism.

Although Sir Isaac Newton seems to have made use of prisms of different substances, yet it is strange to say, that he never observed that they formed spectra, whose lengths P T were different, when the mean refraction of the green ray was the same. If, for example, we make a prism of plates of glass, and fill it with oil of cassia, and adjust its refracting angle A C B, so that the middle of the spectrum, which it forms, falls exactly on the point G, where the green space is with the glass prism, then we shall find, that the spectrum of the *oil of cassia* prism will be *two* or *three* times longer than that of the *glass* prism; the oil of cassia is therefore said to *disperse* the rays of light more than the glass, that is, to separate the extreme red and violet rays at T and P more from the mean ray G, and to have a greater *dispersive power*.

In order to obtain a distinct measure of the dispersive power of a body, let us suppose that the prism A B C is filled with water, and that by the methods described in Chap. II. we find the index of refraction for the extreme violet ray P to be 1.330, and that of the extreme red ray T, 1.342; then the difference of these, or 0.012, would be a measure of the dispersive power of water, if it and all other bodies had the same mean refraction; but as this is not the case, the dispersive power must be measured by the relation between the separation of the extremes rays P, T, and the mean refraction; or between the difference of the indices of refraction for the extreme red and the extreme violet, and the difference between the Sines of incidence and refraction, to which the mean refraction is always proportional.

Thus, in *diamond*, the difference between the indices of the red and violet ray is 0.056, nearly *five* times greater than 0.012 which it is in *water;* but then the difference between the Sines of incidence and refraction, viz. 1.439, is also nearly *five* times greater than 0.336, which it is in water; so that the real dispersive power of diamond is not much greater than that of water. The ratio of the dispersive powers will be thus expressed:—

For Water.. $\dfrac{1.342 - 1.330}{1.336 - 1}$ or $\dfrac{0.012}{0.336} = 0.0351$ Dispersive power.

For Diamond $\dfrac{2.467 - 2.411}{2.439 - 1}$ or $\dfrac{0.056}{1.439} = 0.0388$ Dispersive power.

In the following TABLE we have given the dispersive powers of various bodies, as determined by Dr. Brewster. The first column contains the dispersive power; and the second, the difference of the indices of refraction for the red and violet rays, or the part of the whole refraction to which the dispersion is equal. Hence, if we add the half of the numbers in the last column to the index of refraction, we shall have the index of refraction for the extreme violet ray; and if we subtract it, we shall have the index for the extreme red ray. We may, therefore, obtain, by means of the second column in the table, the length of the spectra, formed by prisms of any of the substances it contains, for any refracting angle, for any position of the prism, and for any distance of the screen, upon which the spectrum is received. In doing this, however, it must be recollected, that the measures here given are suited to the ordinary light of the sky; and that when the sun's image is used, and when great care is taken to screen the middle rays of the spectrum, the red and the violet are found to extend to a greater distance from the mean ray.

TABLE of DISPERSIVE POWERS.

	Dispersive power.	Diff. of Index of Refr. for extreme rays.
Chromate of lead, gr. refr. ext.	0.400	0.770
———— ———— least refr.	0.262	0.388
Realgar, melted	0.260	0.384
Oil of Cassia	0.139	0.089
Sulphur, after fusion	0.130	0.149
Phosphorus	0.128	0.156
Sulphuret of Carbon	0.115	0.077
Balsam of Tolu	0.103	0.065
Balsam of Peru	0.093	0.058
Barbadoes Aloes	0.085	0.058
Oil of Bitter Almonds	0.079	0.048
Oil of Anise Seeds	0.077	0.044
Balsam of Styrax	0.067	0.039
Guiacum	0.066	0.041
Oil of Cummin	0.065	0.033
Oil of Tobacco	0.064	0.035
Oil of Cloves	0.062	0.033
Sulphate of Lead	0.060	0.056
Oil of Sassafras	0.069	0.032
Muriate of Antimony, refractive power 1.598	0.050	0.036
Resin	0.057	0.032
Oil of Fennel Seeds	0.055	0.028
Oil of Spearmint	0.054	0.026
Rock Salt	0.053	0.029
Oil of Pimento	0.052	0.006
Flint Glass	0.052	0.026
Oil of Angelica	0.051	0.025
Oil of Thyme	0.050	0.024
Oil of Fenugreek	0.050	0.024
Oil of Carraway Seeds	0.049	0.024
Flint Glass	0.048	0.029
Gum Thus	0.048	0.028
Oil of Juniper	0.047	0.022
Oil of Brick	0.046	0.021
Nitric Acid	0.045	0.021
Canada Balsam	0.045	0.021
Cajeput Oil	0.044	0.021
Zircon, gr. refr.	0.044	0.045
Muriatic Acid	0.043	0.016
Oil of Turpentine	0.042	0.020
Balsam of Capivi	0.041	0.021
Calc. Spar, gr. refr.	0.040	0.027
Sulphate of Iron	0.039	0.019
Diamond	0.038	0.056
Oil of Olives	0.038	0.018
Beryl	0.037	0.022
Alum	0.036	0.017
Castor Oil	0.036	0.018
Crown Glass, very green	0.036	0.026
Water	0.035	0.012
Glass of Borax	0.034	0.018
Crown Glass	0.033	0.018
Oil of Wine	0.032	0.012
Plate Glass	0.032	0.017
Sulphuric Acid	0.031	0.014
Nitre, least refr.	0.030	0.009
Borax	0.030	0.014
Alcohol	0.029	0.011
Sulphate of Barytes	0.029	0.011
Tourmaline	0.028	0.019
Rock Crystal	0.026	0.014
Emerald	0.026	0.015
Calcareous Spar, least refr.	0.026	0.016
Blue Sapphire	0.026	0.021
Bluish Topaz	0.025	0.016
Chrysoberyl	0.025	0.019
Sulphate of Strontites	0.024	0.015
Fluor Spar	0.022	0.010
Cryolite	0.022	0.007

It is obvious, from the preceding results, that different bodies possess very different powers of dispersing, or of separating the coloured rays of light.

If we now proceed to a more minute examination of spectra of equal lengths, by two bodies of very different dispersive powers, such as *oil of cassia* and *sulphuric acid*, we shall observe a very remarkable difference between them. If A B, for example, (*fig.* 30.) is the spectrum, produced by a prism of *oil of cassia*, and C D that produced by a prism of *sulphuric acid*, then we shall find, that the least refrangible colours, *red*, *orange*, and *yellow*, will occupy *less* spaces, or will be more *contracted* in the oil of cassia spectrum than in the sulphuric acid one; while the most refrangible colours, *blue*, *indigo*, and

Fig. 30.

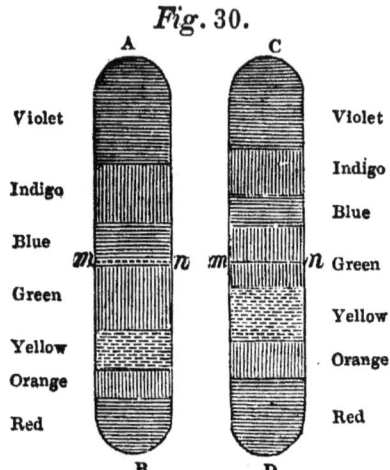

violet, will occupy *larger* spaces, or will be more *expanded*. Hence the coloured spaces have not the same *ratio* to each other as the lengths of the spectrum; and therefore this property is called the *irrationality* of *dispersion*, or of the coloured spaces in the spectrum. This property is distinctly shewn in the above figure, from which it will also appear, that the mean ray, *m n*, is among the *blue* rays in the *oil of cassia* spectrum; and among the *green* rays in the *sulphuric acid* spectrum.

As the examination and measurement of this property of transparent bodies is very difficult, we can give only a list of substances, arranged nearly in the order into which they contract the less refrangible spaces, and expand the more refrangible ones, according to the experiments of Dr. Brewster.

OIL OF CASSIA	Oil of Olives
Sulphur	Calcareous Spar
Sulphuret of Carbon	Rock Salt
Balsam of Tolu	Gum Juniper
Oil of bitter Almonds	Tartrate of Potash and Soda
——— Anise seeds	
——— Sassafras	Oil of Almonds
——— Sweet Fennel seeds	CROWN GLASS
	Gum Arabic
——— Cloves	Alcohol
Muriate of Antimony	Ether
Canada Balsam	Borax
Oil of Turpentine	Tourmaline
——— Hyssop	Beryl
Amber	Topaz
Oil of Caraway seeds	Fluor Spar
	Citric Acid
——— Nutmegs	Malic Acid
——— Peppermint	Acetic Acid
Castor Oil	Muriatic Acid
Diamond	Nitric Acid
Nitre	Rock Crystal
Nut Oil	Ice
Balsam of Capivi	WATER
FLINT GLASS	Phosphoric Acid
Zircon	SULPHURIC ACID.

CHAPTER X.— *Imperfections of the Refracting Telescope — Achromatic Telescope — Dr. Blair's Aplanatic Telescopes.*

THE application of the principles explained in the preceding chapter to the improvement of the refracting telescope, forms one of the most interesting portions of optical science. If we take a prism A *b* C, *fig.* 29, having the angle *b* A C = A C B, and formed of the very same substance as A C B; and if we place it in contact with A C B, it will destroy or correct the spectrum P T, by refracting the whole of the rays separated by the prism A B C to the same point Y, where, by their mixture, they will form white light, the separation arising from the refraction and dispersion of the first prism being exactly compensated or balanced by the refraction of the second prism*. If the angle *b* A C is less than A C B, the second prism will neither correct the refraction nor the dispersion of the first, and a short spectrum will be formed a little above Y; and if *b* A C is greater than A C B, the second prism will more than correct the first, and a short spectrum will be formed below Y. Hence it is manifest, that by combining prisms of the same kind of glass in the manner shown in *fig.* 29, we cannot make the ray S Y deviate from its direction without producing the prismatic spectrum; that is, *we cannot produce refraction without producing colour.* Now, as we have already shown that every lens acts exactly like a prism, it follows also, that we cannot combine a concave and a convex lens of the same glass to refract in opposite directions, without producing colour: for when we succeed in finding two which destroy the colours, we shall find also that the refraction is destroyed, and that the two lenses put together resemble a watch-glass, which has not the property of a lens at all.

In the same manner as we have now reasoned respecting *prisms or lenses of the same glass*, Sir Isaac Newton reasoned respecting *prisms and lenses of all kinds of glass and of all bodies whether solid or fluid*, because he believed that all bodies whatever had the same dispersive power, or produced the same length of spectrum in proportion to their mean refraction. Had this been true, Sir

---

* This is evident also from the consideration that the faces A *b*, B C are parallel, and that the two prisms are nothing more than a plane lens like that shown at B, in *fig.* 5.

Isaac would have been correct in concluding that "*the improvement of the refracting telescope was desperate.*"—(*Optics*, Part I. Prop. VII. Theor. VI.)

Sir Isaac, however, was in this case mistaken, and it was reserved for our countryman, John Dollond, to prove, by direct experiment, that refraction can be produced free of colour, and actually to construct an *achromatic* telescope*, or a *telescope without colour*.

We have already shown that all bodies have different dispersive powers; and it will be seen from our Table, that *flint glass* (the white glass of which drinking glasses are made), and *crown glass* (the glass with which windows are glazed), have different powers of producing colour.

If we now make the prism A B C, *fig.* 29, of *crown glass*, and A *b* C of flint glass, and make the angle *b* A C such that it corrects the colour of A C B, or produces a spectrum of exactly the same length, then since the flint glass does this at a much less mean refraction than the crown glass, it will refract the rays from the prism A C B to a point Y′, above Y, where they will be all collected into a circle of white light. We have, therefore, succeeded in refracting the beam S F Y into a new direction, S F Y, *without* colour.

The application of this to lenses is shown in *fig.* 31, which is drawn so as to admit of comparison with *fig.* 29. In this figure, L L is a *convex* lens of *crown glass*, and *l l* a *concave* one of *flint glass*.

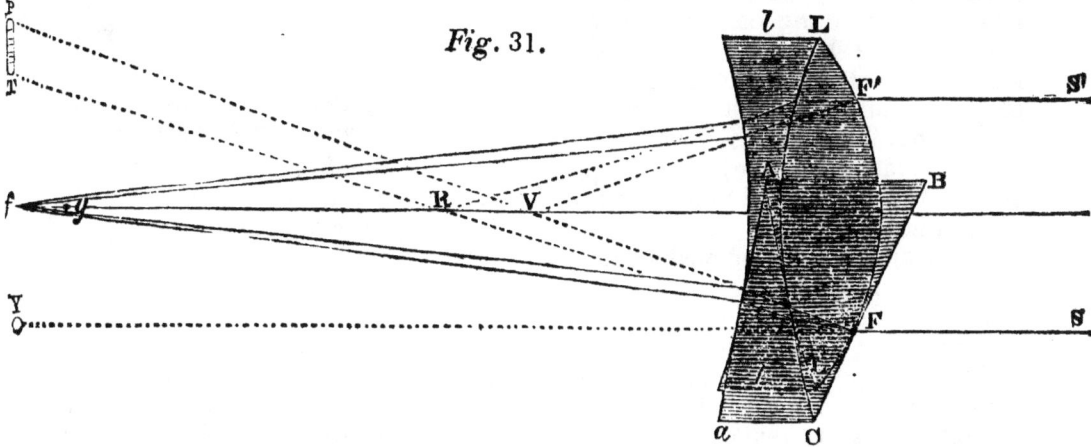

Fig. 31.

A ray of the sun, S, falls at F on the convex lens, which will refract it exactly in the same manner as the prism A B C, whose faces touch the two surfaces of the lens at the points where the ray enters and quits it. The solar ray, S F, thus refracted by the lens L L, or prism A B C, would have formed a spectrum P T on the wall, had there been no other lens, the violet ray F V crossing the axis of the lens at V, and going to the upper end P of the spectrum, and the red ray F R going to the lower end T. But as the flint glass lens *l l* or the prism A *a* C which receives the rays F V, F R at the same points, is interposed, these rays will be united at *f*, and form a small circle of white light, the ray S F of the sun being now refracted without colour from its primitive direction S F Y into the new direction F *f*. In like manner the corresponding ray S′ F′ will be refracted to *f*, and a white and colourless image of the sun will be there formed by the two lenses.

In this combination of lenses, it is evident, that the spherical aberration of the flint lens corrects to a considerable degree that of the crown one, and, by a proper adjustment of the radii of the surfaces, it may be almost wholly removed. This, however, is more perfectly effected in the *triple achromatic object-glass*, which consists of three lenses, viz. a concave flint glass lens placed between two convex lenses of crown glass; but this form of the achromatic object-glass is now generally abandoned, and almost all the large object-glasses which have been recently constructed consist of two lenses only. In the treatise on optical instruments, the reader will find the practical details respecting achromatic object-glasses and eye-glasses.

When we examine with attention the best achromatic telescope, we shall find that it does not show white or luminous objects perfectly free from colour, their edges being tinged on one side with a claret-coloured fringe, and, on the other, with a green fringe. These uncorrected colours, which have been called the

---
* From two Greek words which signify *without colour*.

secondary spectrum, arise from the *irrationality* of the coloured spaces which we have explained in the preceding chapter. The achromatic telescope, therefore, required still further improvement, in order to get rid of these secondary colours; and science is indebted to Dr. Blair of Edinburgh, for a most beautiful method of accomplishing this great object. Having observed that when the extreme red and violet rays were perfectly united, the green were left out, or were the *outstanding* rays, as shown in *fig.* 31, where the red and violet rays F V, F R are perfectly united at *f*, while the green rays are more refracted, and cross the axis at *g*, he conceived the idea of making an achromatic concave lens, which should refract the green less than the united red and violet, and an achromatic convex lens which should do the same; and as the concave lens refracted the outstanding green *to* the axis, while the concave one refracted them *from* the axis, it followed, that by a combination of these two opposite effects, the green would be united with the red and violet.

By means of two fluid media and three glass lenses, Dr. Blair constructed a telescope in which he could not discover any colour by the most rigid test.

As this, however, was a complex combination of lenses, Dr. Blair still sought for some single fluid which should produce the effect when combined with glass, and he fortunately discovered that the muriatic acid mixed with a metallic solution answered his purpose. In the spectrum formed by this fluid, the green were among the most refrangible rays as shown in *fig.* 30; and when its dispersion was corrected by that of glass, there was produced an inverted secondary spectrum, that is, one in which the green was above, when it would have been below with a common medium. He, therefore, placed a concave lens of muriatic acid with a metallic solution between two lenses of glass, as shown in *fig.* 32, and he informs us that with this object-glass the rays of different colours were bent from their rectilineal course with the same equality and regularity as in reflexion. Through telescopes of this description, only 12 and 15 inches long, Professors Robison and Playfair saw double stars with a degree of perfection which astonished them*.

At the time we are writing, Professor Barlow, of Woolwich, informs us, that he has completed a fluid object-glass, six inches in diameter, on a principle different from Dr. Blair's, and which allows him to reduce the length of the telescope from one-third to one-half, without diminishing its focal power†.

CHAPTER XI.—*Physical Properties of the Prismatic Spectrum—Its Heating Power—Invisible Rays—Deoxidating Power—Chemical Rays—Magnetising Power—Illuminating Power—Lines across the Spectrum.*

THE physical properties of the prismatic spectrum, or, more accurately, of the simple rays composing white light, have of late years been studied by the most eminent philosophers, and merit our particular notice.

Heating power of the spectrum.— From the slightest examination of the prismatic spectrum, formed by refraction of the sun's rays, it is evident, that the yellow is the most luminous of all the coloured spaces; and that the degree of light diminishes both towards the red and the violet extremities. Hence it was naturally supposed, that there would be most heat in the yellow rays, less in the red, and least in the violet. Dr. Herschel, however, found, that the heat increased from the violet to the red end of the spectrum, the heat of the orange being greater than that of the yellow, and the heat of the red greater than that of the other colours; but, upon placing his thermometer beyond the red rays, and in the dark, he was surprised to observe that the mercury still rose; and upon repeating this experiment under a variety of circumstances, he established the remarkable fact, that the heat was the greatest at a point beyond the red extremity of the spectrum, and at a spot upon which none of the luminous rays at all fell. Hence he concluded, that *there were invisible rays in the sun's light which had the power*

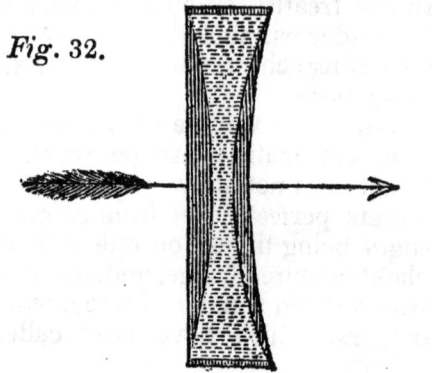

Fig. 32.

---

* See the *Edin. Journal of Science,* No. viii, p. 212.
† Ibid. No. xiv, p. 335.

of producing heat, and which had a less refrangibility than red light. This result was confirmed by the experiments of Sir H. Englefield, and also by Sir Humphry Davy, who repeated the experiments in the rays of an Italian sun, and by means of thermometers with minute bulbs. Sir H. Englefield obtained the following results:—

	Temperature.
Blue	56°
Green	58
Yellow	62
Red	72
Beyond Red	79

The prisms, by which all these experiments were made, were, we believe, of flint glass. It has been recently proved by M. Seebeck*, that the heating power of the colours of the spectrum depend upon the substance of which the prism is made. Thus:—

In Water† the greatest
  heat is in the........Yellow.
Sulphuric Acid‡........Orange.
Crown or Plate Glass....Middle of Red.
Flint Glass............Beyond the Red.

Deoxidating power of the spectrum.—In the year 1801, the late Mr. Ritter, of Jena, discovered that the rays of the spectrum had different chemical properties which resided in the violet end of the spectrum, and existed even beyond the violet light. Muriate of silver, for example, became black beyond the violet rays; a little less black in the violet; and still less in the blue. Dr. Wollaston made the same discovery about the same time. In repeating these experiments, Dr. Seebeck found, that the colour of muriate of silver varied with the coloured spaces in which it was placed. In and beyond the violet, it was reddish brown; in the blue, it was blue or bluish grey; in the yellow, it was unchanged white, or faintly tinged with yellow; and in the red, it was red. With prisms of flint glass the muriate of silver also became red at a spot entirely beyond the red.

Magnetising power of the solar rays.—Nearly 20 years ago, Dr. Morichini, of Rome, found that the violet rays of the spectrum had the property of communicating magnetism; but this result was involved in doubt, and by many philosophers entirely discredited, till it was established by some recent experiments by Mrs. Somerville. Having covered half of a sewing needle, about an inch long, with paper, she exposed the other half for two hours to the *violet* rays. The needle had then acquired north polarity. The indigo rays produced nearly the same effect; and the blue and green rays produced it in a still less degree. In the yellow, orange, red, and invisible rays, no magnetic influence was exhibited, even though the experiment was continued for three successive days. The same effects were produced by inclosing the needle in blue or green glass, or wrapping it in blue and green ribbands, one half of the needle being always covered with paper.

Illuminating power of the spectrum.—Dr. Herschel has represented, by a curve, the gradual shading off of the light from the yellow space to the red and violet extremities of the spectrum. A series of experiments on this subject were made with great care by the late M. Fraunhofer of Munich, and the results of them are exhibited in *fig.* 33.

In this figure A I Q P represents the prismatic spectrum, and the lines A 1, B 2, &c., bounded by the curve line 1, 2, 3, 4, 5, &c., represent the degree of light at the points A, B, C, D, &c. of the spectrum. In numbers they are as follow, the intensity of the light of the brightest point being 1.

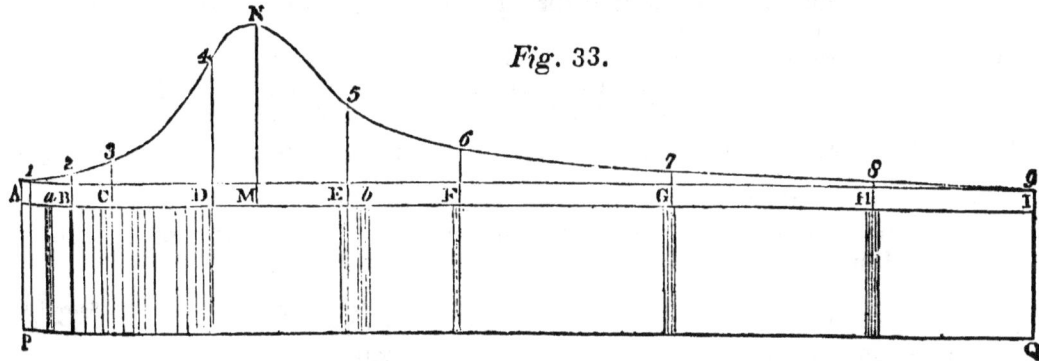

Fig. 33.

* See the *Edinburgh Journal of Science*, No. i. p. 353.
† M. Wunch found that in alcohol and oil of turpentine the greatest heat was in the yellow.
‡ And also in solutions of sal-ammoniac and corrosive sublimate.

The light at A or the line A 1 is 0.000
B.........B 2 ... 0.032
C..........C 3 .. 0.094
D..........D 4 .. 0.64
M ....MN.. 1.00
E..........E 5 .. 0.48
F..........F 6 .. 0.17
G..........G 7 .. 0.031
H ....H 8 .. 0.0056
I ....I 9 .. 0.000

M. Fraunhofer found that D M was nearly $\frac{1}{3}$ or $\frac{1}{4}$ of D E; and hence the most luminous rays of the spectrum formed by the finest prisms, and when all other light is excluded, in place of being situated in the middle of the spectrum, are nearer the red than the violet end, in the proportion of 1 to 4. It appears, also, that the mean refrangible ray lies between the blue and the indigo spaces.

Lines across the spectrum.—One of the most curious discoveries of modern times is that of Fraunhofer, that the spectrum is covered with dark and coloured lines parallel to one another, and perpendicular to the length of the spectrum. In order to observe these lines, it is necessary to use prisms perfectly free from veins, to exclude all extraneous light, and even to stop those rays which form the coloured spaces which we are not examining. It is necessary also to use a telescope, and the light must enter and emerge from the prism at equal angles. In this way the following lines will be seen.

At A a well-defined dark line within the red space............	1
At *a* a mass of 7 or 8, forming together a dark band..........	8
At B there is a thick and distinct one, and one fainter	2
Between B and C, the one at C being broad and black	9
Between C and D...	30
At D two nearly of the same size, separated by a bright one ..	2
Between D and E there are of different sizes	84
The line at E consists of several, the middle one being strongest...	
Between E and *b*	24
At *b* three very strong lines, with a fine clear one between two..	3
Between *b* and F, F being very strong	52
Between F and G...	185
Between G and H, many being accumulated at G	190
In all they amount to..	590

The largest lines occupy a space of 5" to 10" We have inserted only a few in the figure.

One of the most important practical results of this curious discovery of M. Fraunhofer is, that these lines are fixed points in the spectrum, or rather, that they have always the same position in the coloured spaces in which they are found. In flint glass, for example, the distance B C (*fig.* 33.) is greater than B C in crown glass, because the dispersion of the former is greater than the latter. The index of refraction, therefore, for each coloured ray, may be accurately determined by means of these lines. Fraunhofer has done it for several substances, the most important of which are *flint glass, crown glass, water, and oil of turpentine*. The angle of the flint glass prism was 26° 24' 30", and its specific gravity 3.723. The angle of the crown glass prism was 39° 20' 35", and its specific gravity 2.535. The angle of the other prisms was 58° 5' 40"; and the specific gravity of the oil of turpentine was 0.885.

The following were the indices of refraction for the lines B, C, D, E, F, G, H, in *fig.* 33, corresponding with the *red, orange, yellow, green, blue, indigo,* and *violet*.

	B	C	D	E	F	G	H
Flint Glass..	1.627749	1.629681	1.635036	1.642024	1.64826	1.660285	1.671062
Crown Class	1.525832	1.526849	1.529587	1.533005	1.536052	1.541657	1.546566
Water......	1.330935	1.331712	1.333577	1.335851	1.337818	1.341293	1.344177
Oil of Turpentine	1.470496	1.471530	1.474434	1.478353	1.481736	1.488198	1.493674

From these numbers M. Fraunhofer has computed the following numbers, which are the ratios of the dispersive powers of the differently coloured rays in several combinations of the above refracting substances.

	Space B C.	Space C D.	Space D E.	Space E F.	Space F G.	Space G H.
Flint Glass and Water	2.562	2.871	3.073	3.193	3.400	3.726
Flint Glass and Crown Glass......	1.900	1.956	2.044	2.047	2.145	2.195
Crown Glass and Water..........	1.349	1.468	1.503	1.560	1.613	1.697
Oil of Turpentine and Water	1.371	1.557	1.723	1.732	1.860	1.963
Flint Glass and Oil of Turpentine.	1.868	1.814	1.783	1.843	1.861	1.899

In flint glass and water, for example, the ratio of the dispersion for the rays B, C, or for the space B C, which they bound, is as 1 to 2.562. This is found by dividing the differences of the indices of refraction for B and C, in flint glass, by the differences of the same indices for water, as given in the preceding table.

CHAPTER XII.—*Inflexion or Diffraction of Light—Law of Interference—Lengths of a Wave of Light of different colours—Practical consequences.*

ALTHOUGH the subject of the inflexion and the interference of the rays of light is of a somewhat abstruse nature; yet it will not be difficult to convey to the reader some distinct, though general notions of these curious properties of light.

If we make a hole in a window shutter 1-40th part of an inch in diameter, or, what is better, if we fix in the window shutter of a dark room a small convex lens, of a short focus, we shall obtain a beam of divergent light. If we place bodies of *any kind* in this light, and attentively examine their shadows, we shall find that, on both sides of the shadow, there are *fringes of coloured light*, the colours being as follows, reckoning from the shadow:—

First fringe; *violet, indigo, pale blue, green, yellow, red.*

Second fringe; *blue, yellow, red.*

Third fringe; *pale blue, pale yellow, red.*

The distances of these fringes, as well as their intervals, varied as the numbers, 1, $\sqrt{\frac{1}{2}}$, $\sqrt{\frac{1}{3}}$, $\sqrt{\frac{1}{4}}$, &c.

When homogeneous coloured light was used, the fringes were of the colour of the light in which they were held, and their intervals black. Those formed in *red* light were the largest; those formed in *violet* the least, and those formed in the *green* of a *middle* size: the above fringes are called the *external fringes.*—See Newton's *Optics*, B. III. Part 1.

If we now examine the shadow of the body which causes those fringes, we shall find, as was first shown by Maraldi, that the shadow is divided by parallel fringes, which vary in number and in breadth according to the distance from the body that the shadow is examined. These fringes are called the *internal fringes*. The *external* and the *internal fringes* are shown in *fig.* 34, where A B C D is the shadow, and 1, 2, 3, the external fringes.

As the phenomena now described

Fig. 34.

must depend on light, *bent*, somehow or other, into and towards the shadow A B C D, the name *inflexion* has been employed to distinguish them, from a Latin word signifying a *bending*. The name *diffraction* has also been applied to them.

In studying the phenomena of inflexion, Dr. Young found that if an opaque screen was placed either a few inches before, or a few inches behind, one side of the inflecting body, whose shadow is A B C D, so as to intercept all the light on that side by receiving the edge of its shadow B D, then all the fringes in the shadow A B C D instantly disappeared, although the light passed by the other edge of the body corresponding with A C as before. Dr. Young found that this disappearance was not owing to any diminution of the light, and hence he concluded *that the fringes in the shadow* A B C D *were occasioned by the interference of the rays bent into the shadow at one side of the body with the rays bent into the shadow on the other side.* Both Dr. Young and M. Fresnel ascribed the external fringes to the interference of the direct rays which passed at a little distance from the inflecting body with rays which they supposed might be *reflected* from the margin of the inflecting body; but M. Fresnel has since proved that this cannot be the case, and he has, therefore, been under the necessity of supposing that the rays which pass at a sensible distance from the inflecting body deviate from their primitive direction, and concur also in the production of the external fringes.

M. Arago has made some important discoveries on the effects of transparent screens upon the coloured fringes. He found that such a screen had the same effect as the opaque screen used by Dr. Young, and that very thin transparent screens transferred the fringes from the side where they are formed. This result has very important applications, which our limits will not allow us to notice.

The law of interference deduced from Dr. Young's experiment may be thus explained. Let us suppose two minute pencils of light radiating from two points close to another, to fall upon the same spot of a piece of paper, in which case they may be said to interfere with one another (for if the paper were removed they would cross one another at that point). Then if *the lengths of their paths* (or the distances between the paper and the two radiant points) *are the same*, they will form a bright spot or fringe of light, having an intensity greater than that which would have been produced by either portion alone. Now it is found that when there is a certain difference between the lengths of their paths, a bright fringe is produced exactly similar to what is produced when their lengths are equal. Let us represent this difference by the letter d, then similar bright spots or fringes will be formed when the differences in the lengths of the paths are $2d$, $3d$, $4d$, $5d$, &c. But, what is very remarkable, it is clearly proved that if the pencils of light interfere at intermediate points, or at those points in their paths when the differences in the lengths of the paths are $\frac{1}{2}d$, $1\frac{1}{2}d$, $2\frac{1}{2}d$, $3\frac{1}{2}d$, then, instead of adding to one another's intensity, the two pencils of light destroy each other, and produce a black spot or fringe.

This curious property of light has a striking analogy with the beating of two musical sounds nearly in unison with each other, the beats corresponding to the luminous spots or fringes, and the cessations of sound between the beats, to the black spots or fringes.

M. Fraunhofer has found the following to be the values of d for the different colours of the spectrum. The measures are in decimals of an English inch.

Colour.	Lines in Fig. 33.	Values of d, or Breadths of a Wave of Light. Inch.
Red	C	0.00002582
Orange yellow	D	0.00002319
Green	E	0.00002073
Blue	F	0.00001912
Indigo	G	0.00001692
Violet	H	0.00001572

In the theory which supposes light to consist in the vibrations or undulations of a highly elastic medium, and which is now supported by many arguments, the quantity d, or the difference in the lengths of the paths, at which the interfering pencils of light either destroy one another, or unite their effects, that is, at which they produce the black and light fringes, is also the *breadth of an undulation or a wave of light*.

Those who do not adopt the system of undulations, must, as M. Fraunhofer* has remarked, admit that the quantity represented by d is a real, absolute magnitude. Whatever meaning is attached to it, it necessarily follows, that one half of it in reference to the effect is opposed to the other half, so that if the anterior half combines accurately with the posterior half, or interferes with it in this manner under a small angle, the effect of each is destroyed, whereas that effect is doubled if two anterior, or two posterior halves combine, or interfere in the same manner. From this determination of the quantity d some important practical results may be derived.

1. With respect to the influence of the inequalities of polished surfaces in refracting and reflecting light.
2. With respect to the limits of microscopic vision; and
3. With respect to the colours which are most suitable for delicate observations.

1. When we consider how glass is ground and polished, its surface cannot be mathematically correct; but as long as the inequalities, in reference to their distance from each other, are less than the magnitude d, they will not be detrimental either to the light which is transmitted, or to that which is reflected, and no colours of any kind can be produced by them. It would likewise be impossible by any means to render inequalities of such a size visible.

2. Hence, we may deduce the smallest magnitude which can be rendered visible by a microscope. For if any object whose diameter is d, consists of two parts, it cannot be recognised as consisting of more than two parts. In red light, therefore, the limit of microscopic vision is the *thirteen-millionth* part of an English inch, and in violet light the *eight-millionth* part of an English inch.

3. From these considerations, it follows, that since the quantity d is greater in red light than in any other, the imperfections of refracting and reflecting surfaces will have less effect in injuring vision when it is performed by red light, than when it is done by any other rays of the spectrum. On the other hand, if these imperfections are made less than d by skilful workmanship, a close double star, which could not be seen in red light, might be rendered visible in violet light, provided always that there be no want of light.

* *Edinburgh Journal of Science*, No. xiv. p. 213

CHAPTER XIII.— *Colours of Thin Plates—Solids—Fluids—Air—Newton's Table of the Colours of Thin Plates—Theories of the Phenomena.*

EVERY person must have observed that the light reflected from, and transmitted through, transparent and colourless bodies, such as flint glass, and water, &c., is always white, provided that in the case of the transmitted light the two surfaces of the body are parallel. This is true for all the different thicknesses of these bodies which we are in the habit of observing, but if we diminish their thickness more and more, we shall at last arrive at a thickness where both the reflected and the transmitted light becomes coloured.

In *solid bodies*, such as glass, this is not easily accomplished, but in mica, a thin platy mineral, it is easily effected. If we stick one side of a piece of mica to sealing wax, and again tear it away with a jerk, we shall find some very thin films left on the wax, some of which will reflect a brilliant red, others a brilliant yellow, and others a bright blue. We may accomplish the same object, perhaps better, by taking the thinnest film that can be split from gypsum, or sulphate of lime, and immersing it in a vessel of water. The water will dissolve the sulphate of lime most at the edge, so that we shall have the film shading off in thickness to the finest edge. At this edge will be seen fringes of colour corresponding to the different thicknesses of the film. If the film could be made thin enough, we should arrive at a point when it would cease to reflect any light, and when the whole light which fell upon it would be transmitted. This has never been done artificially in solid bodies, and probably never will be.

Accident, however, on one occasion accomplished what was beyond the reach of skill, and exhibited, perhaps, the most curious optical fact that has ever been witnessed. A crystal of quartz, about 2¼ inches in diameter, having been broken in two, the faces of the fracture appeared *absolutely black*, like black velvet. This was ascribed by those who saw it, to a thin film of minutely divided opaque matter which had insinuated itself at a crack in the stone. Upon examining it, however, by various optical methods, Dr. Brewster found that the blackness was owing to a *fine down of quartz, the diameter of the fibres of which was so minute, that they were incapable of reflecting light.* The diameter of these delicate fibres, as will be afterwards seen, could not exceed the *one-third of the one-millionth part of an inch.** This remarkable specimen belongs to the cabinet of her Grace the Duchess of Gordon.

In *fluid bodies* it is much more easy to observe the colours produced when their thickness is greatly reduced. If we blow a soap bubble, and cover it with a clear glass, we shall observe a great many concentric coloured rings round the top of it. As the bubble grows thinner, the rings grow wider, and at last, before the bubble bursts, there will be seen at the top of it a small round *black spot*, which will expand itself to ½ or ¾ths of an inch. The same phenomena may be seen at the mouths of bottles containing oil of turpentine, alcohol, and many of the essential oils, where it is easy to form a film of the fluid, in which the colours will be seen to great advantage. The experiment may be still more easily made by putting a thin film of any evaporable fluid upon a clean plate of glass, and observing the colours at the edges of the film, and just before it is dried up.

The colours of thin films have been chiefly studied when formed by thin plates of air. In order to exhibit them distinctly, two convex lenses, A B, C D, of long focal lengths, are placed the one above the other, so as to touch at their summits. Three pair of screws, *p, p, p,* are used, to keep the lenses together, and to produce a regular pressure at the point where the lenses touch each other. Sir Isaac Newton used a plano-convex lens, the radius of whose convex surface was 28 feet, and a double convex one, the radius of each of whose surfaces was 50 feet. The first was placed, like C D, with its plane side downwards, and the other, A B, was placed above it. By pressing the lenses together there appeared round the point of contact a regular system of circular coloured rings or spectra, having a *black* spot in the centre, each spectrum, or order of colours, consisting of fewer colours as they receded from the centre.

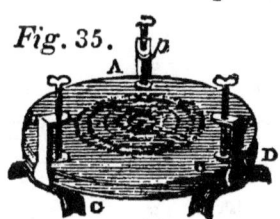

Fig. 35.

Upon examining the light transmitted through the lenses, Sir Isaac ob-

---

* See the *Edinburgh Journal of Science*, No. I, p. 108

served another system of circular coloured rings, in which the colours were quite different from those seen by reflexion. The central spot, for example, was white, and the colour transmitted at any point was always the colour which, when combined with the colour reflected at that point, made white light.

The form of half of the system of coloured rings is shown in *fig.* 36, and the letters in the following table will point out the colours at any part of the system. The relation of the *reflected* and the *transmitted* rays will be understood from the following diagram on the left-hand column, in which A B

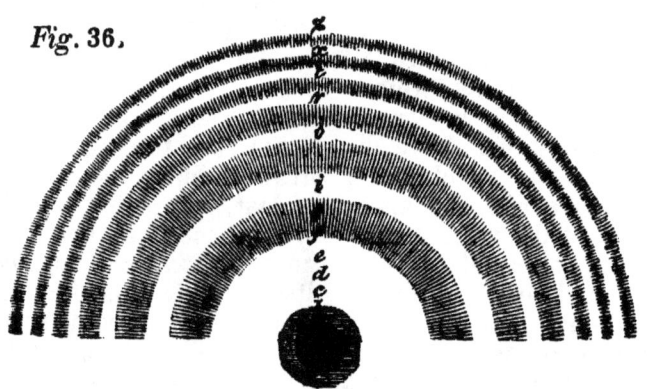

Fig. 36.

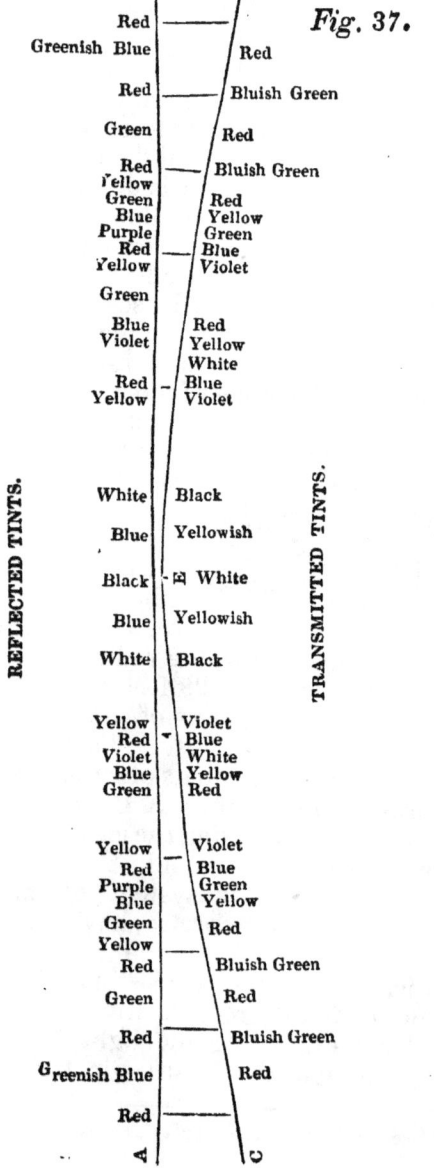

Fig. 37.

and C D represent the surfaces of the lenses which touch at E. The names of the colours engraved on the left hand of the line A B, are those seen by reflexion, and those engraved on the right hand of the line C D, are those seen by transmission.

The following table contains all the results of Sir Isaac Newton's experiments, and, if compared with *figs.* 36 and 37, it will give the reader the most complete information respecting the colours of thin plates. Some of the leading results in it may be thus stated:

1. *Air*—at and below a thickness of *half a millionth of an inch* ceases to reflect light.—At and above a thickness of *seventy-two millionths of an inch* it reflects white, or all the rays of the spectrum. Between these two limits it reflects the various orders of colours contained in the table.

2. *Water*—at and below a thickness of *three-eighths of a millionth of an inch* ceases to reflect light. —At and above *fifty-eight millionths of an inch* it reflects *white*, and between these two limits it reflects the orders of colours contained in the table.

3. *Glass*—at and below a thickness of *one-third of a millionth of an inch* ceases to reflect light.—At and above a thickness of *fifty millionths of an inch* it reflects *white*, and between these limits it reflects the orders of colours contained in the table.

OPTICS.

Sir Isaac Newton's Table of the Colours of thin Plates of Air, Water, and Glass.

Succession of *Spectra*, or *Orders* of Colours.	Letters of Reference to Fig. 36.	Colours produced at the thicknesses in the three last Columns.		Thickness in millionths of an inch.		
		Reflected.	Transmitted.	Air.	Water.	Glass.
First Spectrum, or Order of Colours.	a b c d e	Very Black Black Beginning of Black Blue White Yellow Orange Red	White Yellowish Red Black Violet Blue	$\frac{1}{2}$ 1 2 $2\frac{2}{5}$ $5\frac{1}{4}$ $7\frac{1}{9}$ 8 9	$\frac{3}{8}$ $\frac{3}{4}$ $1\frac{1}{2}$ $1\frac{4}{5}$ $3\frac{7}{8}$ $5\frac{1}{3}$ 6 $6\frac{3}{4}$	$\frac{10}{31}$ $\frac{29}{31}$ $1\frac{2}{7}$ $1\frac{11}{20}$ $3\frac{3}{8}$ $4\frac{3}{5}$ $4\frac{1}{5}$ $5\frac{4}{5}$
Second Spectrum, or Order of Colours.	f g h i k	Violet Indigo Blue Green Yellow Orange Bright Red Scarlet	White Yellow Red Violet Blue	$11\frac{1}{6}$ $12\frac{5}{8}$ 14 $15\frac{1}{8}$ $16\frac{2}{7}$ $17\frac{2}{9}$ $18\frac{1}{5}$ $19\frac{2}{3}$	$8\frac{3}{8}$ $9\frac{5}{8}$ $10\frac{1}{2}$ $11\frac{1}{3}$ $12\frac{1}{5}$ 13 $13\frac{3}{4}$ $14\frac{3}{4}$	$7\frac{1}{5}$ $8\frac{2}{4}$ 9 $9\frac{5}{7}$ $10\frac{2}{5}$ $11\frac{1}{9}$ $11\frac{5}{6}$ $12\frac{2}{3}$
Third Spectrum, or Order of Colours.	l m n o p	Purple Indigo Blue Green Yellow Red Bluish Red	Green Yellow Red Bluish Green	21 $22\frac{1}{10}$ $23\frac{2}{5}$ $25\frac{1}{6}$ $27\frac{1}{7}$ 29 32	$15\frac{3}{4}$ $17\frac{4}{7}$ $17\frac{11}{20}$ $18\frac{6}{10}$ $20\frac{1}{3}$ $21\frac{3}{4}$ 24	$13\frac{11}{20}$ $14\frac{1}{4}$ $15\frac{1}{10}$ $16\frac{1}{4}$ $17\frac{1}{2}$ $18\frac{5}{7}$ $20\frac{2}{3}$
Fourth Spectrum, or Order of Colours.	q r	Bluish Green Green Yellowish Green Red	 Red Bluish Green	24 $35\frac{2}{7}$ 36 $40\frac{1}{3}$	$25\frac{1}{2}$ $26\frac{1}{2}$ 27 $30\frac{1}{4}$	22 $22\frac{3}{4}$ $23\frac{2}{3}$ 26
Fifth Spectrum.		Greenish Blue Red	Red	46 $52\frac{1}{2}$	$34\frac{1}{2}$ $39\frac{3}{8}$	$39\frac{2}{3}$ 34
Sixth Spectrum.		Greenish Blue Red		$58\frac{3}{4}$ 65	44 $48\frac{3}{4}$	38 42
Seventh Spectrum.		Greenish Blue Reddish White		71 71	$53\frac{1}{4}$ $57\frac{3}{4}$	$45\frac{1}{4}$ $49\frac{2}{3}$

The colours in the preceding table are those seen when the light is reflected and transmitted perpendicularly; but as the incident ray deviates from the perpendicular the rings increase in size, the same colour requiring a greater thickness to produce it. Hence, the colour of any film will descend in the scale to one of a lower order, when we view the plate which produces it more and more obliquely. When the thin plate is rarer than the ambient medium, it will reflect at differently oblique incidences all sorts of colours; whereas if it is much denser, the colours are but little changed by a variation of obliquity.

No explanation, entirely free from objections, has yet been given of the colours of thin plates. Sir Isaac Newton supposed that every ray of light in passing through any refracting surface is put into a certain transient condition or state, which in the progress of the ray returns at equal intervals, and disposes the ray at every return to be easily transmitted through the next refracting surface, and between the returns to be easily reflected by it. By means of this principle Sir Isaac has given an explanation of most of the phenomena; but, as it is entirely hypothetical, and is besides of a complex nature, we shall content ourselves with having merely announced it.

In the undulatory theory of light the colours of thin plates are supposed to arise from the interference of the light reflected from the *second* surface of the plate with the light reflected from the *first* surface. This explanation, which may be a true one, even if light should consist of material particles, seems to agree well with the experiments of Sir Isaac Newton.

CHAPTER XIV.—*Colours of Thick Plates—of Double Plates of Equal Thickness—of Double Plates of Unequal Thickness.*

Colours of Single Thick Plates.—The colours produced by glass mirrors, or thick transparent plates, were discovered tand first examined by Sir Isaac Newon. Having admitted a beam of the sun R R (*fig.* 37.) through a hole in

Fig. 37.

his window shutter, *one-third* of an inch in diameter, he threw it in the direction of its axis on a glass mirror M, a *quarter of an inch thick*, concave in front, and convex and quicksilvered behind; the radius of the curvature of both sides being 5 feet 11 inches. When a sheet of paper was held 5 feet 11 inches in front of the mirror, he discovered *four* or *five* coloured rings round the aperture R. These rings had the same colours as those seen by light transmitted through thin plates, and described in the preceding chapter. When the light R R was *red*, all the rings were *red*, and so on with the other colours; the rings being *largest* in *red*, and *smallest* in *violet* light. Upon measuring their diameter in homogeneous light, Sir Isaac found that the squares of the diameters of the most luminous parts were as the numbers 0, 1, 2, 3, 4, 5, &c., and the squares of the diameters of the darkest parts, as the intermediate numbers $\frac{1}{2}$, $1\frac{1}{2}$, $2\frac{1}{2}$, $3\frac{1}{2}$, $4\frac{1}{2}$, &c. When mirrors of greater thicknesses were used, the rings grew less and less, and their diameters were reciprocally as the square roots of the thickness of the mirror. If we rub off the quicksilver from the back of the mirror, the rings become fainter, without altering their magnitude; and if we place a large drop of oil of turpentine on the back of the mirror deprived of its silvering, or any other oil of the same refractive power as the glass, we shall remove entirely the reflective power of that part of the surface, and the part of the rings corresponding to it will disappear. Hence it is manifest, that the back of the mirror is necessary to the production of the rings; an inference which is also proved by the fact, that they never appear when the reflexion is made from a single metallic surface.

However perfectly any surface of glass or metal is polished, it scatters irregularly in every direction a faint light, by means of which the polished surface, when illuminated in a dark room by a beam of the sun's light, may be seen in all positions of the eye. The colours of thick plates are obviously produced by this scattered light. Sir Isaac Newton explains the colours, by the hypothesis of fits of easy reflexion and transmission, mentioned in the preceding chapter; while Dr. Young ascribes them to the interference of two portions of light, one scattered by the front surface of the mirror before refraction, and the other scattered by the same surface when the ray returns to it after reflexion from the back surface.

Colours of Double Plates of Equal Thickness.—In the preceding experiments the rings are produced by a single plate; but they may be more easily seen, and with much more brilliancy, when they are produced by successive reflexions from two plates of equal thickness.—This phenomenon, which was discovered by Dr. Brewster, will be understood from (*fig.* 38.),

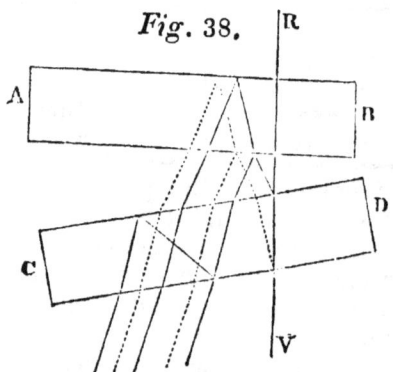

Fig. 38.

where A B, C D are sections of two plates of parallel glass cut out of the same piece. Let the distance of their nearest surfaces be about $\frac{1}{10}$th of an inch; and the eye being placed behind them at V, let the observer look through them in the direction V R at a candle, or, what is better, at a circular disk of light subtending an angle of 2° or 3°. This circular disk will be seen single; but, if one of the plates be gently inclined to the other, as shown in the figure, till one or more of the reflected images are distinctly separated from the bright image seen by transmitted light in the direction R V, the reflected image will be crossed with about 15 or 16 beautiful parallel fringes. The central fringes and the external ones on each side, have the same relation to each other as those formed by thin plates. The direction of the fringes is parallel to the common section of the reflecting surfaces; and Dr. Brewster determined by a series of experiments, *that their production depends upon the action of all the four surfaces of the plate of glass, and that their magnitude is inversely as the thickness of the plates that produce them at a given inclination.*

These results are explicable by the law of interference, the effect of the inclination of the plates being, as Dr. Young has shown, to reduce the vertical thickness of the plate in the ratio of the cosine. See *Edinburgh Transactions*, vol. vii. p. 435—444.

Colours of Double Plates of Unequal thickness. — In using a sextant, Mr. Nicholson observed colours on the glasses employed for the sights, and he regarded them as analogous to those of thin plates. Dr. Young considered them as arising from a slight difference in the thickness of the two plates, and as the same that would be produced by a single plate whose thickness is equal to the difference of the thickness of the plates.

CHAPTER XV.—*Colours of Minute Particles and Fibres—Eriometer.*

If we look at the sun, or a candle, through a plate of glass upon which we have gently breathed, or over which we have scattered particles of dust, or of any fine powder, we shall observe it surrounded with rings of colours. By using the seed of the Lycopodium, or by placing a drop of blood diluted with water between two pieces of glass, the rings of colour will be finely exhibited. Round the luminous body there is seen a light area, terminating in a *reddish* dark margin; this is succeeded by a ring of *bluish* green, and then by a *red* ring,—these two last colours succeeding each other several times when the particles are of an uniform diameter.

As the diameter of the rings thus produced increases when the particles or fibres become smaller, Dr. Young proposed to measure the diameters of such minute bodies, by determining the size of the rings which they produced. For this purpose he selected the limit of the first green ring and the red one, and by means of an instrument which he calls an *Eriometer*,* he was enabled to measure the size of minute particles or fibres. This instrument consists of a plate of brass, having an aperture in its centre of about the sixtieth of an inch in diameter. This aperture is surrounded by a circle of perforations about half an inch in diameter, the perforations being 8 or 10 in number, and as minute as possible. The eye being aided with a lens, the substance to be examined is fixed in a slider, and the instrument being held before an Argand lamp, or two or three candles placed in a row, the slider is drawn out till the limit of the first green ring and the red one coincides with the circle of perforations, and the index shows on the scale the magnitude of the particles or fibres.

In order to find the value of an unit on this scale, Dr. Young availed himself of an observation of Dr. Wollaston, that the seed of the *Lycoperdon Bovista* was the 8500dth of an inch in diameter. This powder gave rings in which the limit of the first green and red indicated $3\frac{1}{2}$ on the scale; so that the value of an unit of the scale was $3\frac{1}{2}$ times 8500, or the 29,750th part of an inch, or, in round numbers, the *thirty thousandth* part of an inch. The leading results obtained by Dr. Young are found in the following Table:

	Parts of the scale
Milk diluted, very indistinct	3
Dust of *Lycoperdon Bovista*, very distinct	3.5
Bullock's Blood, from Beef	4.5
Fibres of crystalline lens	5.5
Smut of Barley, called male ear	6.$\frac{3}{8}$
Blood of a Mouse	6.5
Human Blood diluted with water, 5; after standing some days, 6 or	7
Blood recently diluted with serum only	8
Pus	7.5
Silk, very irregular, about	12
Beaver Wool, very even, (jointed)	13
Angola Wool, about	14
Vigonia Wool	15
Siberian Hare's Wool, Scotch Hare's Wool, Foreign Coney Wool, yellow Rabbit's Wool, about	15.5
Mole's Fur, about	16
Skate's Blood, very indistinct, about	16
American Rabbit's Wool, British Coney Wool, about	16.5
Buffalo's Wool	18
Wool of the Ovis Montana	18
Finest real Wool, mixed, about	18.5
Shawl Wool, 18 or	19
Goat's Wool	19
Cotton, very unequal, about	19
Peruvian Wool, mixed, the finest locks	20
A small lock of Welsh Wool	20
Saxon Wool, a few fibres, 17, some 23, chiefly	22
Wool of an Escurial Ram, at Lord Somerville's show, 23 to	24

* From two Greek words which signify a *measure* and *wool.*

	Parts of the scale
Wool of Mr. Western's South Down, some specimens	24.5
Lioneza Wool, 24 to 29, generally	25
Paular Wool, 24 to 29, generally	25.5
Alpacca Wool, about	26
Farina of *Laurustinus*	26
Ryeland Merino Wool	27
Merino South Down Wool	28
Seed of *Lycopodium*, beautifully distinct	32
Wool of a South Down ewe	39
Coarse Wool, Sussex	46
Coarse Wool, from some worsted	60

In order to find in parts of an English inch the diameter of the particles or fibres of any of these bodies, we have only to multiply $\frac{1}{30000}$ by the number in the table. Thus, *Blood* being 7, we have the diameter of its particles $\frac{1}{30000} \times 7 = \frac{7}{30000}$, or $\frac{1}{4285}$th part of an inch.

CHAPTER XVI.—*Colours and Structure of Mother of Pearl—Colours of the grooved surface of the Lenses of Animals—Mr. Barton's Iris ornaments.*

A VERY interesting class of colours, which have been recently employed in the useful arts, are exhibited by polished surfaces, either of glass or metal, when they are crossed by parallel grooves very near to each other. As these colours have been long ago observed in mother of pearl, we shall begin by giving an account of the very remarkable phenomena which this substance exhibits.

Mother of pearl has in general a very irregular surface, and therefore in order to observe its properties, we must select a piece which is regularly formed, and which in general has an uniform white colour in daylight. When this piece of mother of pearl has been ground on both sides upon a flat stone, or upon a piece of metal with very fine emery, it is ready for use. If we now place our eye near one of its surfaces, so as to see the image of a candle in it by reflexion, we shall observe a reddish dull image S, (*fig.* 39.), free from any of

Fig. 39.

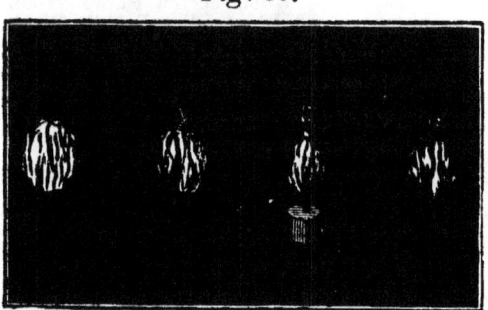

the prismatic colours. This image is formed by the ordinary laws of reflexion, and its dullness arises from the roughness of the surface in which it is seen. On one side, suppose the left of this dull image, there will be seen a brighter image A, which is a real prismatic spectrum of the candle containing the same colours, and dispersed nearly as much as in the spectra formed by a large refracting angle of flint glass, but having its blue extremity *b* nearest the ordinary image. The distance of the red part *r* of this image from the ordinary image, is, in a specimen now before us, 7° 22′. On the outside of this coloured image, and nearly at the same distance beyond it on the one side as the dull image is on the other, will be seen a mass of light, C, of a crimson colour, which becomes green by varying the inclination of the plate. These three images, S, A, C, are all in the same straight line.

If we now *polish* the surface of the mother of pearl, the ordinary dull image S will become brighter, and a *second prismatic image* B *will start up directly opposite to the first, and at the same distance from the common image* S. This *second* prismatic image has exactly the same properties as the first one, with the exception of having its brightness a little diminished by the polishing, and of its never being accompanied with the mass of crimson light. When the polish of the surface is removed by grinding, the second prismatic image B disappears, and the first A is restored to its former lustre. By repeating the preceding experiments on the *opposite surface* of the mother of pearl, the same phenomena are observed; the *first* prismatic image A, and the mass of coloured light S being now on the *right* hand of the ordinary image, and the *second* prismatic image B on the left hand of it.

If when the plate of mother of pearl is sufficiently thin we examine the transmitted light, we shall see the same appearances which we see by reflexion; the image which is brightest by reflexion being faintest by transmission. In this case, too, the blue end *b* of the prismatic image is nearest the ordinary image, and the red end *r* farthest from it.

The communication of the colours of mother of pearl to other substances upon which it is impressed, which was first pointed out by Dr. Brewster, forms, to those who see it for the first time, one of the most surprising phenomena in optics, while to the scientific observer it furnishes the true cause of the origin of the colours. If we take an impression of the mother of pearl upon black wax, when very hot, or indeed upon any other cement, and examine the surface of the wax by looking at the candle in it, we shall see all the phenomena which we saw in the mother of pearl, excepting the mass of crimson light. If the mother of pearl is unpolished, the wax will exhibit only one of the prismatic images, and it will be on the opposite side of the ordinary image from what it was on the mother of pearl; because the impressed surface must be the reverse of the impressing surface.

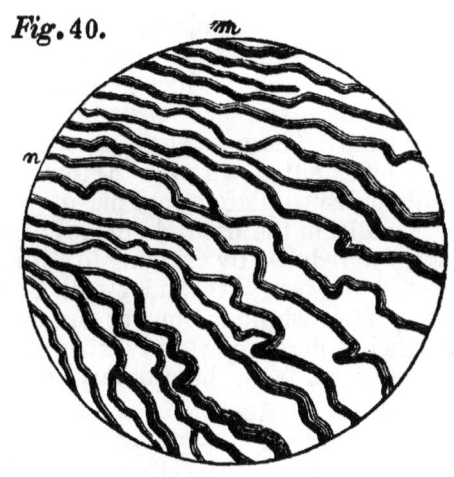

Fig. 40.

We may imitate artificially and more perfectly the action of the mother of pearl, by placing *Isinglass* or *Gum Arabic*, or *Balsam of Tolu* between two surfaces of mother of pearl. When the enclosed substance has dried or cooled, if it is Balsam of Tolu, and is removed from the mother of pearl surfaces, it will display by reflexion from either of its surfaces, and also by transmission, the fine prismatic colours of the natural shell. An impression of mother of pearl may also be taken upon the fusible metal composed of bismuth and mercury; and by hard pressure, or the blow of a hammer, it may also be made upon cold lead. On the fusible metal the play of the colours is singularly fine; but from a gradual change in the crystalline state of the metal, the surface soon loses its polish, and the colours disappear.

From these facts it is obvious, that all the above phenomena of mother of pearl, as seen by reflected and transmitted light, have their origin in a particular configuration of its surface;—that the communication of its properties to other bodies is the necessary consequence of the communication of its superficial structure,—and that none of the light, excepting that which produces the mass of crimson, has penetrated the surface of the mother of pearl.

In order to ascertain what this configuration of surface was, we examined it with very high magnifying powers, and found that every specimen which exhibited these colours had a grooved structure, resembling the delicate texture of the skin at the top of an infant's finger, or the wrinkles which are often seen on surfaces covered with varnish or with oil paint. We have attempted to represent this surface in (*fig.* 40.), a small portion of which, *m n*, has the grooves nearly parallel. In most cases, however, the grooves are irregular, and as the line joining the coloured images is always perpendicular to the direction of the grooves, these irregular specimens give coloured images lying in almost every direction. Upon measuring the distance of these grooves, we found them to vary from 200 to upwards of 5000 in an inch; and in every case the distance of any of the prismatic images from the ordinary image increases as the grooves become smaller and closer. In a specimen with 2500 in an inch, the distance of the prismatic image from the ordinary one is 3° 41′, and in a specimen of 5000 in an inch, the distance is 7° 22′, almost exactly double. For every thousand more grooves that there are in an inch, the prismatic images separate from each other half a degree. Hence in most specimens of mother of pearl, when both the direction and the distances of the grooves are various, we have the prismatic images scattered in various directions, and at various distances from each other.

One of the most remarkable circumstances in mother of pearl, is that when we grind down the natural surface with the finest powders, and polish it to the utmost degree of brilliancy, we shall never be able to grind out the grooved structure which produces the colours. The substance of the shell disappears, but the depressions as well as the elevations on the surface are worn away at the same time. It deserves to be remarked too, as a curious circumstance, that on grinding down the surface after it is polished, one of the sides of the grooves seems to be worn down, while the other is scarcely at all affected by the process.

Mr. Herschel has discovered in mother of pearl another pair of nebulous coloured images, the line joining which is always perpendicular to a sort of veined structure in the shell, which goes through its substance, and cannot be impressed upon wax. These images are seen by light transmitted through a thin and highly polished plate of mother of pearl, cut parallel to the natural surface of the shell, and reduced by grinding to a thickness of between $\frac{1}{70}$th and $\frac{1}{300}$th of an inch. The nebulous images are large, and their different parts have the following distances from the ordinary image.

The Extreme Red Ray ...... 10° 29′
The Mean Ray 6 59
The Extreme Violet 6 16

By measuring with a high magnifying power the width of the veins which produced these images, Mr. Herschel found that there were 7700 of them in an inch.

In examining the laminæ or plate which composed the crystalline lens of a cod newly killed, Dr. Brewster discovered, that their surfaces gave the same colour as mother of pearl, with this difference only, that two and sometimes three prismatic images were seen on each side of the ordinary image. These laminæ communicated their colour to wax; and by measuring the distances of the coloured images at different parts of the laminæ, he found that the fibres diminished gradually from the equator to the pole of the lens, tapering like needles, so as to allow them to pack together into a spherical superficies as they converge to the pole. He discovered also in the lens of the Boneto, the flying fish, the herring, &c. another set of coloured images exactly at right angles to them, and about 16° distant from the ordinary image. These images prove the existence of grooves or divisions across the fibres, whose distance is at least the 11000dth of an inch. When we consider that the crystalline lens of a small fish is thus composed of several millions of separate fibres, and each of them subdivided into several thousand portions, we cannot fail to be struck with the exquisite beauty of such a combination, and with the admirable skill by which it is fitted for performing the several operations of vision.

The principle of the production of colour by grooved surfaces has been elegantly and ingeniously applied by John Barton, Esq., of the Royal Mint, to the manufacture of what he appropriately calls *Iris ornaments*, from their reflecting the brilliant hues of the rainbow. By cutting with a delicate engine parallel grooves upon steel, at the distance of from the 2000dth to the 10,000dth of an inch, he has manufactured imitative jewels and other articles of female ornaments of transcendent beauty; and by stamping these grooves on brass with steel dies, he has manufactured buttons at a moderate expense. In day light, these colours are scarcely distinguishable, excepting when the surface reflects the margin of a dark object upon a light ground; but in strong light, and particularly in that of the sun and of gas flames, the colours shine with extraordinary brilliancy, and the play of tints, which flit about with every luminous image, are rivalled only by the matchless hues of the diamond.

M. Fraunhofer, who has studied the phenomena produced by grooved surfaces, constructed a machine by which he could draw lines in which there are 32,000 in a Parisian inch.

CHAPTER XVII.—*Description of the Eye—Dimensions of the Eye—Formation of Images on the Retina—Direction of Visible Objects—Cause of Erect Vision—Distinct and Indistinct Vision in the same Object—Indistinctness of Vision at the base of the Optic Nerve—Intermission in the Vision of Objects seen Obliquely—Insensibility of the Eye to Faint Light—Seat of Vision—Duration of Impressions on the Retina—Thaumatrope—Single Vision with Two Eyes — Squinting — Accommodation of the Eye to different Distances—Longsightedness — Shortsightedness—Ocular Spectra—Accidental Colours—Colours from the Unequal Action of Light on the Eye.*

IN the application of the principles of optics to the explanation of natural phenomena, the structure of the eye, and the manner in which it performs the functions of vision, claim particular notice.

The human eye, of which we have given a front view in (*fig.* 41.), and

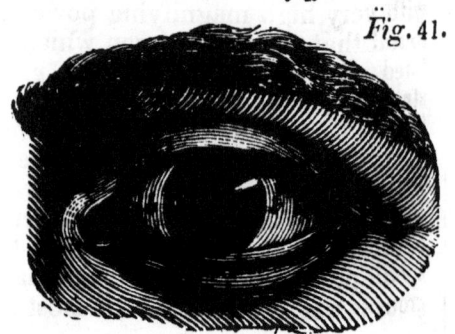

Fig. 41.

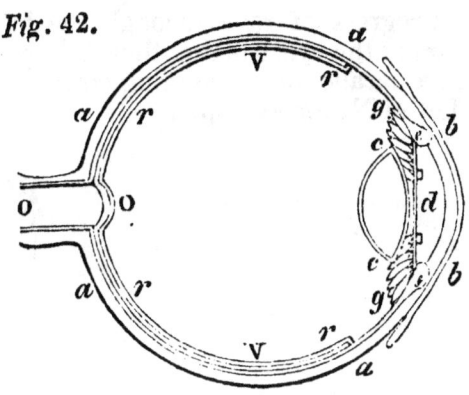

Fig. 42.

a vertical section in (*fig.* 42.), is nearly of a globular form, with a slight elongation or projection in front. It consists of *four* coats or membranes, *viz*. the *Sclerotic*, the *Cornea*, the *Choroid*, and the *Retina*; of two fluids or humours, the *Aqueous* and the *Vitreous*; and of one lens, called the *Crystalline*. The Sclerotic coat, *a a a*, (*fig.* 42.), is the outer and strongest coat, to which the muscles for giving it motion are attached. It constitutes the white of the eye, *a a*, (*fig.* 41.) It is joined to the *Cornea*, *b b*, or the clear and transparent circular membrane through which we see. The *Cornea*, which is equally thick throughout, is very tough, and consists of several layers or folds to give it strength, so as to defend the delicate parts within from external injury. On the inner surface of the sclerotic coat is a delicate membrane, called the *Choroid* coat, which is covered with a black pigment. On the inner side of this lies the *Retina*, *r r r r*, which is the innermost coat, and is a tender reticular membrane, formed from the expansion of the optic nerve, which enters the eye at O, a little more than *one-tenth* of an inch from the axis on the side towards the nose. At the end of the axis of the eye, and in the very centre of the retina, there is a small hole, with a yellow margin. It is called the *foramen centrale*, or central hole, though it is not a hole, but merely a transparent spot, free of the soft pulpy matter of which the retina consists.

A flat membrane of a circular form, *ef*, called the iris, (*c c, fig.* 41.), and seen through the cornea *b b*, divides the interior globe of the eye into two very unequal parts. It has a circular opening, *d, fig.* 41, in its centre, called the *pupil*, which *expands* when the light which enters the eye is *diminished*, and *contracts* when the light is *increased*. The space before the *iris*, called the *anterior chamber* of the eye, contains the *aqueous humour*, from its resemblance to pure water; and the space behind the iris is called the *posterior chamber*, and contains the *crystalline lens*, *c c*, and the *vitreous humour*, which fills all the rest of the eye. The *crystalline lens* is suspended in a transparent *capsule*, or *bag*, by what are called the *ciliary processes*, *g g*. This lens is more convex behind than in front, as the figure shows; and it consists of concentric coats composed of fibres. It increases in density from its circumference to its centre, for the purpose of correcting its spherical aberration. The *vitreous humour*, V V, occupying the largest portion of the eye, lies immediately behind the *crystalline lens*, and fills the whole space between it and the retina, *r r r r*.

The following are the dimensions of the eye, as given by Dr. Young and M. Petit:

	English Inches
Length of the optical axes	0.91
Vertical chord of the cornea	0.45
Versed sine of ditto	0.11
Horizontal chord of the cornea	0.47
Opening of pupil seen through the cornea	0.27 to 0.13
Diminished by magnifying power of cornea to	0.25 to 0.12
Radius of the anterior surface of the crystalline lens	0.30
Radius of the posterior surface	0.22
Principal focal distance of the lens	1.73
Distance of the centre of the optic nerve from the central hole at the end of the axis	0.11
Distance of the iris from the cornea	0.10
Distance of the iris from the anterior surface of the crystalline	0.02
Range of the eye, or diameter of field of vision	110°

Dr. Brewster and Dr. Gordon took the following measures of the crystalline and cornea from the eye of a woman above 50 years of age, a few hours after death.

Diameter of the crystalline	0.378
Diameter of the cornea	0.400
Thickness of the crystalline	0.172
Thickness of the cornea	0.042

The following are the refractive powers of the humours of the eye, according to different observers:

	Aqueous Humour.	Crystalline Lens.			Vitreous Humour
		Outer Coat.	Centre.	Mean.	
Hauksbee	1.33595				1.33595
Jurin	1.3333				
Rochon	1.329				1.332
Young	1.3333				
Brewster	1.3366	1.3767	1.3990	1.3839	1.3394

From the last of these measures we may deduce the following indices of refraction:

	Index of Refraction.
For rays passing from the aqueous humour into the outer coat of the crystalline lens	1.0406
For rays passing from the aqueous humour into the crystalline, taking its mean index of refraction	1.0353
For rays passing from the outer coat of the crystalline into the vitreous humour	0.93

From the dimensions of the eye given above, and by means of the preceding indices of refraction, it will be easy to trace, by the method already described, the progress of rays through the humours of the eye, whether they fall upon it in a parallel or a diverging condition.

Let M N, for example,

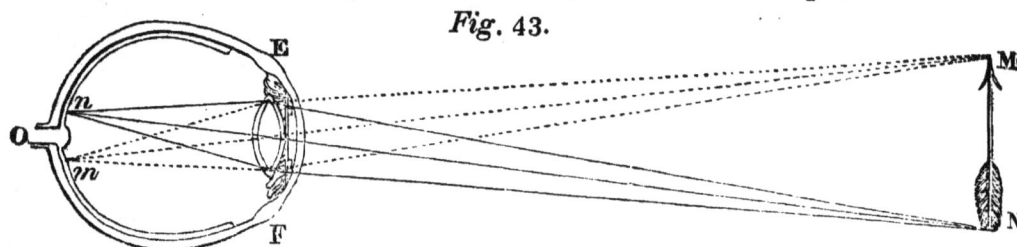

Fig. 43.

be an object at a considerable distance from the eye, E F O. Rays of light diverging from the points M N, will be converged by the refraction of the humours to points m, n upon the retina, where they will form an inverted image of it, in the same manner as an image is formed in a camera obscura. That such an image is actually formed on the back of the eye, may be easily proved by paring away the sclerotic coat of the eye of an ox, with a sharp knife, till it is sufficiently thin to allow the image to be seen through it.

In what manner the retina, thus impressed with a distinct image of an external object, conveys to the mind, through the medium of the optic nerve, of which it is the expanded termination, a knowledge of the existence, the position, and the magnitude of that object, is not known, and probably never will be. Certain facts, however, or laws of vision, have been deduced from observation, and merit our attentive consideration.

1. *On the direction of visible objects.*—When the mind sees the extremity M of any object M N, by means of rays flowing from M and collected at m, the retina receives these rays at different degrees of obliquity, and yet the point M is seen only in one direction, namely, in the direction of the central ray of the cone whose apex is at m. This however does not arise from the ray being the resultant, as it were, or the mean of the directions of all the other rays; for if we close up all the pupil excepting a small opening at its margin, the point M will be represented at m only by the most oblique rays of the conical pencil, and yet it will still be seen in the same directio nas before. Hence we conclude, that when a ray of light falls upon any point m of the retina, in any direction, however oblique to its surface, the object will be seen in the direction of a line perpendicular to the retina at the point m. As the surface of the retina is a portion of a sphere, these perpendiculars must all pass through one point, which may be called the *centre of visible direction*; because every point of an external object will be seen in the direction of a line joining that centre and the given point. The truth of this we have established by marking the perfect stability of the image of any object, when it is seen by different points of the retina when the eyeball alone is moved. Hence the centre of visible direction is a fixed point in the vitreous humour; and, as it never changes its place during the rotation of the eyeball, it must be coincident with the centre round which that rotation is performed. In consequence of this coincidence, and in virtue of the law of visible direction, an arrangement of consummate skill, the great Author of nature has provided for the perfect stability of every point in the images of external objects.

2. *Cause of erect vision.*—As the humours of the eye act exactly like a convex lens of an equivalent focal length, an *inverted* picture of external objects will, for the reasons already assigned (Chap. iv. p. 12), be formed upon the retina. Many philosophers of eminence have perplexed themselves very unnecessarily, in attempting to deduce erect vision from inverted images. The law of visible direction removes at once every difficulty; for as the lines of visible direction must necessarily cross each other at the centre of visible direction, those from the lower part of the image must go to the upper part of the object, and those from the upper part of the image go to the lower part of the object, and hence an erect object is the necessary result of an inverted image.

3. *Distinct and indistinct vision in the same object.*—When we look intensely at any point of an object in order to examine it with care and attention, we direct to that point the axis of

the eye, and, consequently, the image of that point falls upon the central hole in the retina. Every other point of the same object is seen indistinctly, and the indistinctness increases with the distance of the point from that which is seen distinctly. The only perfectly distinct point of vision, therefore, is that where there is no retina; but we are not entitled to ascribe this to the absence of the nervous matter, as the gradual increase of distinctness towards the central hole does not appear to be accompanied with a gradual diminution in the thickness of the retina.

4. *Indistinctness of vision at the base of the optic nerve.*—It was discovered by M. Mariotte, that when the image of any object fell upon the base of the optic nerve, the object disappeared. In order to prove this experimentally, fix on the side of a room, and at the height of the eye, three wafers, two feet distant. Stand opposite to the middle wafer with one eye shut, and, beginning near the wall, retire gradually from it, (looking always at the outside wafer, which is on the same hand as the covered eye,) till the middle wafer disappears. This will be found to take place at about *five* times the distance at which the wafers are placed, and when it does happen, the other wafers will be plainly seen. If we use candles in place of wafers, the middle one will not disappear, but it will become a cloudy mass of light. The base of the optic nerve, therefore, is not insensible to light, it is only unfit for giving distinct vision of those objects whose images fall upon it. M. Le Cat considered the size of this portion of the retina to be about one-third or one-fourth of a line; but Daniel Bernoulli found it to be about *one-seventh* part of the diameter of the eye.

5. *Intermission in the vision of objects seen obliquely.*—The inability of the eye to preserve a sustained vision of objects seen obliquely, was discovered by Dr. Brewster. If when one eye is shut we fix the other upon any point, such as the head of a pin, A, stuck into a green cloth, and continue for some time looking at the pin head, objects, such as a pen, B C, or a strip of paper laid upon the green cloth at a distance from the pin, will occasionally disappear altogether; the impression of the green cloth extending itself over the part of the retina on which the image of the pen, B C, or strip of paper, was formed. In a short time the vanished object will again reappear. The same effect is produced when both eyes are used; and when the object is highly luminous, like a candle, it does not wholly disappear, but expands itself into a mass of nebulous light, which is of a blue colour, encircled with a bright ring of yellow light.

Fig. 44.

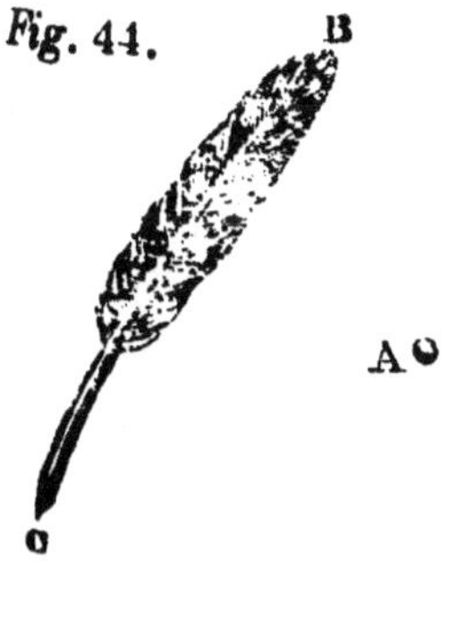

But though objects thus seen indirectly, or obliquely, occasionally disappear, very minute objects, which cannot be seen by direct vision, may be rendered visible by looking a little from them. This has been observed by several astronomers, both with regard to faint stars and to the satellites of Saturn. When the eye is turned full upon the star or satellite, it disappears; but when it is directed to another part of the field of the telescope, the luminous point will become distinctly visible. This superior vision of a small point of light seen obliquely, seems to arise partly from the expansion of its image by indirect vision, which makes its light act upon a greater portion of the retina.

6. *Insensibility of the eye to direct impressions of very faint light.*—When the eye is steadily directed to objects illuminated by a feeble gleam of light, it is thrown into a state nearly as painful as that which is produced by an excess of light. A kind of remission takes place in the conveyance of the impressions along the nervous membrane: the object actually disappears, and the eye is agitated by the recurrence of impressions which are too feeble for the performance of its functions.

"The preceding facts," (§ 5, 6,) says Dr. Brewster,* "respecting the affections of the retina, while they throw considerable light on the functions of that membrane, may serve to explain some of those phenomena of the disappearance and reappearance of objects, and of the change of shape of inanimate objects, which have been ascribed by the vulgar to supernatural causes, and by philosophers to the activity of the imagination. If in a dark night, for example, we unexpectedly obtain a glimpse of any object, either in motion or at rest, we are naturally anxious to ascertain what it is, and our curiosity calls forth all our powers of vision.

* *Edinburgh Journal of Science*, No. vi. p. 290.

This anxiety, however, serves only to baffle us in our attempts. Excited by a feeble illumination, the retina is not capable of affording a permanent vision of the object, and while we are straining our eyes to discover its nature, it will entirely disappear, and afterwards reappear and vanish alternately. The same phenomenon may be observed in daylight by the sportsman, when he endeavours to mark upon the monotonous heath the particular spot where moor-game has alighted. Availing himself of the slightest difference of tint in the adjacent heath, he keeps his eye steadily fixed upon it as he advances; but whenever the contrast of illumination is feeble, he invariably loses sight of his mark; and if the retina is again capable of taking it up, it is only to lose it a second time."

7. *Seat of vision.*—The inability of the base of the optic nerve to perform the same functions as the parts of the retina which surround it, led Mariotte to suppose that the choroid coat, which lies immediately below the retina, is the seat of vision. This opinion was confirmed by the fact of the transparency of the retina, which rendered it unfit for the reception of images, and by the opacity of the choroid.

In the eye of the cuttle-fish, Dr. Knox* has shown that there is interposed between the vitreous humour and the retina an excessively dark and opaque pigment of considerable consistency, assuming the form of a membrane. Hence, if the retina performs any part in vision, the impressions made by the images on this dark membrane must be conveyed by vibration to the retina *behind it.* In like manner in the human eye, the impressions on the choroid coat may be conveyed to the retina *before it,* by the vibrations of the choroid. This view of the matter, which is however not without its difficulties, reconciles the opposite sentiments which have been so long entertained. The choroid coat has generally been supposed to be *black,* and M. Le Cat states that it grows less black with age. I have however observed in young persons, generally below the age of twelve, that it reflects a brilliant crimson colour, similar to what we observe in the eyes of dogs and other animals. Hence it would follow, that if the retina is affected by rays which fall upon it, the young persons above mentioned ought to see the crimson light reflected by the choroid and falling upon the retina, in its progress out of the eye. I have ascertained, however, that this is not the case; and consequently we obtain a strong argument in favour of the opinion, that the retina is affected only by the vibrations communicated to it by its contact with the choroid coat.*

8. *Duration of the impressions of light upon the eye.*—Every person must have observed that when we whirl in the hand a burning stick, a circle of light is seen marking out the paths described by its burning end. As the burning extremity can only be in one point of the path at the same instant, it is manifest that the impression of its light continues some time on the eye. M. D'Arcy found that the light of a live coal, placed at the distance of 165 feet, continued its impressions on the eye during the *seventh part of a second.* This affection of the eye has been ingeniously used by Dr. Paris in constructing a toy called the *Thaumatrope,* from two Greek words which signify to *turn wonders.* It is shown in

Fig. 45.

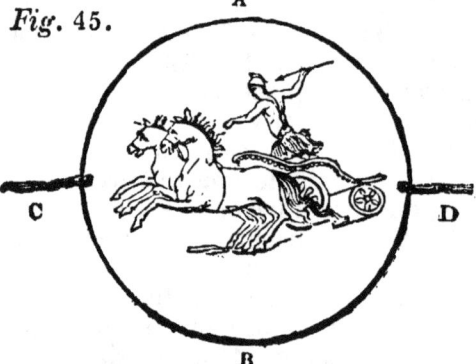

where A B is a circle cut out of card, and having two silk strings, C D, fixed to it, by twisting which with the finger and thumb of each hand it may be twirled round with considerable velocity. On one side of the piece of card there is drawn any object, such as a chariot, and on the other side of it the charioteer in the attitude of driving, so that when the card is twirled round, we see the charioteer driving the chariot, as in the figure; or, in consequence of the duration of the impressions of light on the retina, we see at once what is drawn on both sides of the card.

* *Edinburgh Journal of Science,* No. vi. p. 199.

* M. Lehot has recently endeavoured to show that the seat of vision is anterior to the retina, and that vision is effected by images of three dimensions formed in the vitreous humour. He considers it probable, that the sensation is conveyed to the retina by small nervous filaments extending from the latter into the vitreous humour.

Hitherto we have considered the eye as a single organ, and as viewing objects at that precise distance when rays diverging from them are converged to points on the retina; but as almost all animals have more than one eye, and have the power of seeing objects distinctly at different distances, we must proceed to the consideration of these two points.

9. *Cause of single vision with two eyes.*—The subject of single vision with two eyes has excited much needless discussion, as it is the necessary consequence of the law of visible direction. By the external muscles of the eyeball we can direct the axis of each eye, so that these axes when prolonged may meet in any point of absolute space beyond the distance of four or five inches. Let us suppose that we are placed at one end of a room, and that we direct the axes of both eyes to a circular aperture in a window shutter at the other end; then, though an image of this aperture is formed in each eye, yet because the lines of visible direction from similar points of the one image meet the lines of visible direction from similar points of the other image, each pair of similar points must be seen as one point, and the aperture seen by one eye will exactly coincide with the aperture seen by the other eye. The same singleness of vision would take place if we possessed an hundred eyes, all capable of having their axes directed to the same point.

If when an object is seen single with both eyes, we press one eye aside, the image formed by that eye will separate from the other image, and the object will appear double. Or, if the axes of both eyes are directed to a point either nearer or more remote than the aperture in the window shutter, then in both of these cases the aperture will appear double; because the similar lines of visible direction no longer meet at the aperture.

A small object may, and sometimes does, appear double with one eye, when the crystalline lens has ceased to be homogeneous, either from age or disease.

10. *Cause of squinting.*—A person is said to squint when both eyes do not seem to be directed to the object at which he is looking. When either of the eyes has a less perfect vision, or a different focal length, or when there is any weakness in its external muscles we are apt to make use only of the good eye; and when we acquire the habit of doing this the imperfect eye is left at rest, and will sometimes cease even to follow the movements of the other. In this case squinting is produced. If the good eye is shut, and the bad one forced to exert itself, the iris will be placed symmetrically between the eyelids, and the squint formerly seen in the eye will disappear. Should the eye in this case still squint, the cause of it must be sought either in the central hole of the retina not being at the extremity of the axis, or in some mal-conformation by which the retina is not perpendicular to the axis of the eye at the point where they meet. Such a case we have never met with. This disease of the eye might, we are persuaded, be frequently cured, even in adults, by those who are thoroughly acquainted with the structure and functions of this organ.

11. *Accommodation of the eye to different distances.*—The narrowness of our limits will not permit us to detail the various theories which have been devised to explain this property of the eye, and the experiments which have been made to support them. The eye is, we conceive, adjusted to very remote objects when it is in a state of perfect repose. When near objects are to be seen, we are enabled by a voluntary action to draw forward the crystalline lens. This action is performed by the contraction of the pupil, or by the expansion of the iris towards the centre of the pupil, and as the base of the iris is connected with the ciliary processes which suspend the lens, the lens will be thus removed from the retina. But while the eye possesses the power of voluntary adjustment, the same effect may be produced involuntarily by the stimulus of light upon the eye. By a combination of the voluntary and involuntary actions, the eye is accommodated to all distances within its range; and for short distances, when the voluntary power of adjustment fails, the adjustment may still be effected by the involuntary stimulus of light. The facts and reasonings by which this view of the subject is supported, will be found in the *Edinburgh Journal of Science*, No. i. p. 77—83.

The accommodation of the eye to any distance is effected at the same time with the convergency of the axes of both eyes to the object to be viewed. These two movements being necessarily called into action at the same instant, cannot easily be performed separately, which has led to the belief that the external muscles which converge the axes, produce also the adjustment by pressure on the eyeball. This, however, is not the case; as we have succeeded in producing, by the involuntary stimulus of light, an adjustment to one distance when the axes were converged to a more remote point.

12. *Cause of longsightedness.*—When the eye loses the power of accommodating itself to near objects, the person is said to be *longsighted*. This change, which generally shows itself by the difficulty of reading small type with candle-light, commonly takes place at the age of forty, and arises from a mechanical change in the state of the crystalline lens, by which its density and refractive power are altered. When every other part of our frame begins to shrink and decay, the eye partakes in the general change. The variation of density takes place most frequently at a particular point in the margin of the lens, and requires some time to complete its circle. At its commencement vision is considerably injured, but when the change has become symmetrical round the margin of the lens, the symmetrical action of a convex lens enables the eye to see as distinctly as before, by converging upon the retina rays flowing from near objects, which the unassisted eye refracted in such a manner that they would meet at points behind the retina.

13. *Cause of shortsightedness.*—When the eye is not able to see distant objects, and requires to bring minute objects very near it in order to be distinctly seen, the person is said to be *shortsighted*. In this case, the rays from distant objects are converged to points before they fall upon the retina, and the evil is removed by using a concave lens, which delays their convergency. This imperfection of the eye often appears in early life, and seems to arise from an increase of density in the central parts of the crystalline lens.

14. *Ocular spectra.—Accidental colours.*—One of the most curious affections of the eye, is that in virtue of which it sees what are called *ocular spectra*, or *accidental colours*. If we place a *red* wafer on a sheet of white paper, and, closing one eye, keep the other directed for some time to the centre of the wafer, then if we turn the same eye to another part of the paper we shall see a *green* wafer, the colour of which will grow fainter and fainter as we continue to look at it. This *green* image of the wafer is called an ocular spectrum, or the *accidental*, or *opposite*, colour of *red*. By using differently coloured wafers, we obtain the following results:

Colour of the Wafer.	Colour of the Spectra.
Black	White.
White	Black.
Red	Bluish Green.
Orange	Blue.
Yellow	Indigo.
Green	Violet with a little Red.
Blue	Orange Red.
Indigo	Orange Yellow.
Violet	Bluish Green.

If we arrange all the colours in a circle in the proportions given in Chap. viii. p. 24, the red and the violet extremities of the spectrum meeting at 0°, then the accidental colour of any other colour will be always found directly opposite that other colour, and for this reason these colours have been called *opposite* colours.

The same thing may be done more easily in the common spectrum A B, (*fig.* 46.) Take half the spectrum A B,

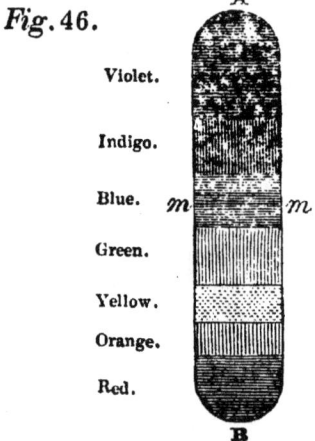

Fig. 46.

viz. A m, or B m, in a pair of compasses, and having set one foot in the colour whose accidental colour is required, the other foot will fall upon the accidental colour. This law of accidental colours, derived from observation, may be thus expressed: *The accidental colour of any primitive colour, is that colour which in the prismatic spectrum is distant from the primitive colour half the length of the spectrum.*

If we suppose the primitive colour to be reduced to the same degree of intensity as the accidental colour, then we shall find that the one is the *complement* of the other, or what the other wants to make it white light, that is, the primitive and the accidental colour when mixed together will make white light. Hence the *accidental colours* have also been called *complementary colours*. Since a mixture of all the colours of the spectrum forms white light, it is obvious, that if one is left out, the mixture of the remainder will not be white but some other tint. This other tint is found to be nearly that which corresponds to the centre of gravity of all the other colours which are left. So that if we arrange the colours in a circle, as in *fig.* 47, which is nothing more than the prismatic spectrum bent round till its two ends A, B meet, we shall see that the centre of gravity of the colours which remain after one colour is omitted, must necessarily be opposite to the omitted colour, that is, the complementary colour is found in the same way as the accidental colour. Thus

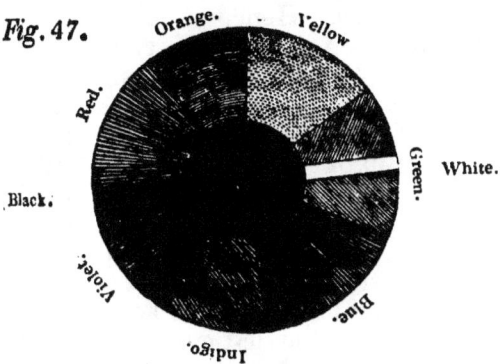

Fig. 47.

if the *red* is omitted, the centre of gravity of the remaining arch will be in the *blue*. We have inserted in the figure a small strip of white, and another of black opposite to it, in order to include all the specimens of accidental colours; but it ought to be remarked, that the tints thus formed from the common prismatic spectrum are not exactly those which experiment gives. The colours which ought to be used are those which are found in a spectrum formed by a prism, when the beam of light is larger than the angular magnitude of the real spectrum. In this case, the centre of the spectrum will be *white* light, passing on one side into *pale yellow, yellow, orange,* and *red,* and on the other side into *greenish blue, indigo,* and *violet*. In such a spectrum there is no unmixed green, though we have inserted it in the figure.

From the preceding facts, the reader will have no difficulty in understanding the common theory of accidental colours. When the eye is fixed for some time on the red wafer, the part of the retina on which the red rays fall is strongly excited by their continued action. Its sensibility to red light must therefore be diminished, in the same manner as the palate when long accustomed to a particular taste ceases to feel its impression. When the eye, therefore, is turned from the red wafer to the white paper, the excited portion of the retina is insensible to the red rays in the white paper, and, consequently, sees that colour which arises from the union of all the other rays but the red, that is, a *greenish blue*. The same explanation applies to all the other colours. If the wafer is *white* and placed upon a dark ground, the accidental colour must be *black;* because the enfeebled portion of the retina is insensible, as it were, to all the colours which compose white light. When the wafer is *black* upon a white ground, the portion of the eye upon which the image falls, in place of being enfeebled, is refreshed by the absence of light, while the rest of the retina around it is enfeebled by the white light of the paper. Hence, when the eye is turned upon a white ground, it will see a portion whiter than the rest, so that the accidental colour of *black* is *white*. La Place's theory of accidental colours, which we cannot pretend fully to understand, is given by Haüy in the following words:—" He supposes that there exists in the eye a certain disposition in virtue of which the *red* rays comprised in the *whiteness* of the ground, are, at the moment when they arrive at that organ, in a manner attracted by those which form the predominant red colour of the circle, so that the two impressions become blended into one, and the *green* colour finds itself at liberty to act as though it existed alone. According to this method of conceiving things, the sensation of the red decomposes that of the whiteness, and while the homogeneous actions combine together, the action of the heterogeneous rays which are disengaged from the combination produces its effect separately." *

When a strong impression of white light is made upon the eye, a succession of remarkable spectra is visible. When the sun was near the horizon, M. Æpinus fixed his eye steadily upon it for fifteen seconds. Upon shutting his eye he saw an irregular, pale, *greenish yellow* image of the sun surrounded with

---

* Dr. Gregory's translation of Haüy's *Traité de Phys.* vol. ii. p. 424.

a faint *red* border. When he opened his eye and turned it to a white ground, the image of the sun was *brownish red*, and its border *sky blue*. With his eye again shut, the image appeared *green*, and the border a *red* different from the last. On opening his eye, and turning it to a white ground as before, the image was *more red* than formerly, and the border a *brighter sky blue*. His eye being again shut, the image was *green*, approaching to *sky blue*, and the border a *red* still differing from the former. When his eye was again opened upon a white ground, the image was still *red*, and its border *sky blue*, but with different shades from the last. At the end of four or five minutes, when his eye was shut, the image was a *fine sky blue*, and the border a *brilliant red*; and upon opening his eye as formerly upon a white ground, the image was a *brilliant red*, and the border a *fine sky blue*.*

Experiments of a similar kind were made by Dr. Brewster, by looking at a brilliant image of the sun's disk formed by a concave reflector. With his right eye tied up, he viewed this luminous disk with the left through a blackened tube, to prevent any extraneous light from falling upon the retina. When the retina was highly excited by this intense light, he turned his left eye to a white ground, and perceived the following spectra by alternately opening and shutting the eye.

Spectra with the left Eye open. Spectra with the left Eye shut.
1. Pink surrounded with Green, Green.
2. Orange mixed with Pink Blue.
3. Yellowish Brown............Bluish Pink.
4. Yellow ....Lighter Blue.
5. Pure Red......................Sky Blue.
6. Orange ....Indigo.

These spectra were always surrounded with a ring of the accidental colour.†

The phenomena above described, prove that the common theory of accidental colours is true only with weak degrees of light, for in the preceding experiments the spectrum ought to have been black.

If when one of these spectra is visible we press the eye to one side, the spectrum will appear to be absolutely immovable, if the experiment is not made with much attention; and upon this imperfect observation, Dr. Wells and others have founded strange theories. It will be found, however, by pressing both the eyes at once, and by due attention to their corresponding motions, that the spectrum does move, and that it is seen by the eye in the same manner as if it were the image of an external object, conformably to the law of visible direction.*

By means of pressure upon the eyeball, ocular spectra may be produced; and when spectra produced by external impressions of light are seen by the eye, their colours are changed by pressure on the eyeball. The pressure of the blood vessels on the back of the eye often produces spectra, in particular states of the stomach. In slight affections, these spectra are floating masses of blue light, which appear and disappear in succession; but in severe ones, they become green, and sometimes rise to yellow. Hence it follows, that pressure upon the retina creates the sensation of light and colours.

15. *Colours produced by the unequal action of light upon the eyes.*—If we hold a slip of white paper vertically about a foot from the eye, and direct both eyes to an object at some distance beyond it, so as to see the slip of paper double, then when a candle is brought near the right eye, so as to act strongly upon it, while the left eye is protected from its light, the left-hand slip of paper will be of a tolerably bright *green* colour, while the right-hand slip of paper seen by the left eye will be of a *red* colour. If the one image overlaps the other, the colour of the overlapping parts will be white, arising from a mixture of the complementary *red* and *green*. When equal candles are held equally near each eye, each of the images of the slip of paper is white. If when the paper is seen *red* and *green* by holding the candle to the right eye, we quickly take it to the left eye, we shall find that the left image of the slip of paper gradually changes from *green* to *red*, and the right one from *red* to *green*, both of them having the same tint during the time that the change is going on. This beautiful experiment was first made by Mr. Smith, surgeon in Kinguissie,† and seems to confirm the observation made by Dr. Brewster, in the article on accidental colours already quoted, that in certain highly excited states of one eye, the reverse im-

---

* See *Nov. Comment. Petrop.* tom. x. p. 283.
† *Edinburgh Encyclopædia,* Art. *Accidental Colours,* vol. i. p. 90.

* *Edinburgh Journal of Science,* No. iii. p. 1, and No. x. p. 265.
† *Edinburgh Journal of Science,* No. ii. p. 52.

pression may be conveyed from the one eye to the other. In order to ascertain if this was the case, we placed a blue glass in front of the unexcited eye that gave the red colour, and the effect of this was to convert the green image seen by the other eye into a greenish sulphur yellow colour. In this case, the right eye must have had its image modified by the image in the left eye. If in the preceding experiment we substitute a candle in place of the slip of paper, the green image of the candle seen by the excited eye, will appear to be surrounded with a bright blue margin.

16. *Insensibility of certain eyes to particular colours.*—Various cases have been described, in which persons capable of performing the most delicate functions of vision, are unable to distinguish particular colours, and, what is certainly a remarkable fact, this imperfection runs in families. Mr. Huddart mentions in the *Phil. Trans.* for 1777, the case of one Harris, a shoemaker at Allonby, in Cumberland, who could only distinguish *black* and *white*. He was unable, when a child, to distinguish the cherries on a tree from the leaves, by any other means than their shape and size; and was surprised to find that his companions could discern them at a much greater distance than he could, although he saw objects in general as well as they did. He had two brothers, almost equally defective, one of whom constantly mistook orange for grass green, and light green for yellow. He had two other brothers and sisters who, as well as their parents, had no such defect.

Another case of a Mr. Scott is described by himself in the *Phil. Trans.* for 1778. He did not know any green colour: a pink colour and a pale blue were perfectly alike to him. A full red and a full green were so alike, that he often thought them a good match; but yellows, light, dark, and middle, and all degrees of blue, except pale sky blue, he knew perfectly well, and he could discern, with particular niceness, a deficiency in any of them: a full purple and a deep blue, however, sometimes baffled him. Mr. Scott's father, his maternal uncle, and one of his sisters, and her two sons, had all the same defect.

Our illustrious countrymen, Mr. Dugald Stewart, Mr. Dalton, and Mr. Troughton, experience the same inability to distinguish certain colours. Mr. Stewart, we believe, first perceived this defect when one of his family was calling his attention to the beauty of the fruit of the Siberian crab, which he could not distinguish from the leaves, but by its form and size. Mr. Dalton cannot distinguish blue from pink by daylight; and in the solar spectrum the red is scarcely visible, the rest of it appearing to consist of two colours, yellow and blue. Mr. R. Tucker, son of Dr. Tucker, of Ashburton, mistakes orange for green, like one of the Harrises. He cannot distinguish blue from pink, but always knows yellow. He describes the colours of the spectrum as follows:

1. Red, mistaken for ....Brown.
2. Orange................................Green.
3. Yellow generally known, but sometimes taken for ....Orange.
4. Green, mistaken for ....Orange.
5. Blue...................................Pink.
6. Indigo ....Purple.
7. Violet ....Purple.

Mr. Harvey has described in the *Edinburgh Transactions* the case of a tailor, now alive, and aged sixty, who could distinguish with certainty only white, yellow, and grey. On one occasion he repaired an article of dress with *crimson*, in place of black silk; and on another occasion he patched the elbow of a blue coat with a piece of crimson cloth. He regarded *Indigo* and *Prussian blue* as black; he considered *purple* as a modification of *blue;* and *green* puzzled him extremely. The darker kinds he considered to be *brown*, and the lighter kinds as pale *orange*. He experienced no difficulties with good yellows. His notions of orange were imperfect. The reddish oranges he termed brown, and the lighter kinds yellow. He considered carmine, lake, and crimson to be blue. The solar spectrum he regarded as consisting only of yellow and light blue. None of the family of this person had the same defect.

Dr. Nicol has recorded a case in the *Medico-Chirurgical Transactions*, where a person who was in the navy, purchased a blue uniform coat and waistcoat, with red breeches to match the blue; and he has mentioned a second case, in which the defect was derived through the father; and a third, in which it descended through the mother.

In the case of a gentleman in the prime of life, on whom we have ourselves made experiments, only two colours were perceived in the spectrum of four colours, in which there was only red, green, blue, and violet. The colours which he saw were *blue* and *yellow*. Whenever the colours of the spectrum were absorbed by a reddish glass, excepting red and dark green, he saw only one colour, *viz.* yellow or orange, which he could not distinguish. When the middle of the red space was absorbed by a blue glass, he saw the black line, with what he called the yellow on each side of it.

In these various cases the persons *are insensible to red light, and all the colours into which it enters.* Mr. Dalton thinks it probable, that the red light is, in these cases, absorbed by the vitreous humour, which he supposes may have a blue tint. If, which is probable, the choroid coat be essential to vision, we may ascribe the loss of red light, in certain eyes, to the retina itself having a blue tint. If the dissection of the eye of any person who possesses this peculiarity shall not establish any of these two suppositions, we must content ourselves with supposing that the retina is insensible to the colours at one end of the spectrum, just as the ear of certain persons has been proved, by Dr. Wollaston, to be insensible to sounds at one extremity of the scale of musical notes, while it is perfectly sensible to all other sounds.

Chapter XVIII.

Explanation of Natural Phenomena—1. Rainbow—2. Halos and Parhelia—3. Phenomena of the Mirage, or Unusual Refraction — 4. Colours of Natural Bodies—5. Colours of the Atmosphere—6. Coloured Shadows — 7. Converging and Diverging beams.

1. *On the Rainbow.* — The rainbow consists of two bows, or arches, extended across the part of the sky which is opposite to the sun, and glowing with all the colours of the prismatic spectrum. The principal rainbow, or the innermost of the bows, which is most commonly seen by itself, is part of a circle whose diameter is $82°$, and is nothing more than an infinite number of prismatic spectra of the sun arranged in the circumference of a circle; the colours being the very same, and occupying the same space as in the spectrum produced from the sun's light. The *red* rays form the *outermost* portion, and the violet rays the *innermost* portion of the bow. The *secondary*, or external bow, is much fainter than the other, and has the violet outermost, and the red innermost: it is part of a circle $104°$ in diameter.

As this interesting phenomenon is never seen unless when the sun is shining, and when rain is falling between the spectator and the part of the horizon where the bow is seen, it has been universally ascribed to the decomposition of the white light of the sun by the refraction of the drops of rain, and their subsequent reflexion within the drops; and this supposition is sufficiently proved by the fact, that rainbows are produced by the spray of waterfalls, and may be made artificially, by scattering water with a brush or syringe when the sun is shining.

In order to explain the production of the rainbow, let us suppose that the observer, placed at E, *fig.* 48, is looking through a shower of rain at the part of the sky opposite to the sun when he is free from clouds. Let A be a drop of rain, and S R a ray of the sun falling upon the upper side of it, A R. Those rays which pass through the middle of the drop will fall upon it, and form an image of the sun in the focus of the drop, as explained in Chap. iii. p. 9, and therefore we consider only those which fall obliquely on the drop. Some of the rays of the beam S R will suffer reflexion at R, but the greater number will enter the drop, and suffer refraction. The violet light of the beam will be refracted in the direction R v, and the red in the direction R r, all the intermediate colours lying between these two. Some of these rays will pass out of the drop at v and r, being refracted a second time; but none of them can reach the eye at E. Those, however, which suffer reflexion at v r will return through the drop, the *red* ray R r in the direction r r', and the violet ray R v in the direction v v', and experiencing a second refraction at the points r' v', they will issue from the drop, and proceed to the eye of the observer at E; who will then see all the prismatic colours between r' E and v' E projected on the opposite sky. Those drops of rain which are directly between the observer E, and the point of the sky opposite to the sun, will form the upper part of the coloured arch; those drops which are to the right hand of the observer, and near the ground, will form the right-hand extremity of the bow; and those to the left hand of the observer, and near the ground, will form the left-hand extremity of the bow. Drops having an intermediate position, and an intermediate height, will form the intermediate parts of the bow. If

OPTICS.

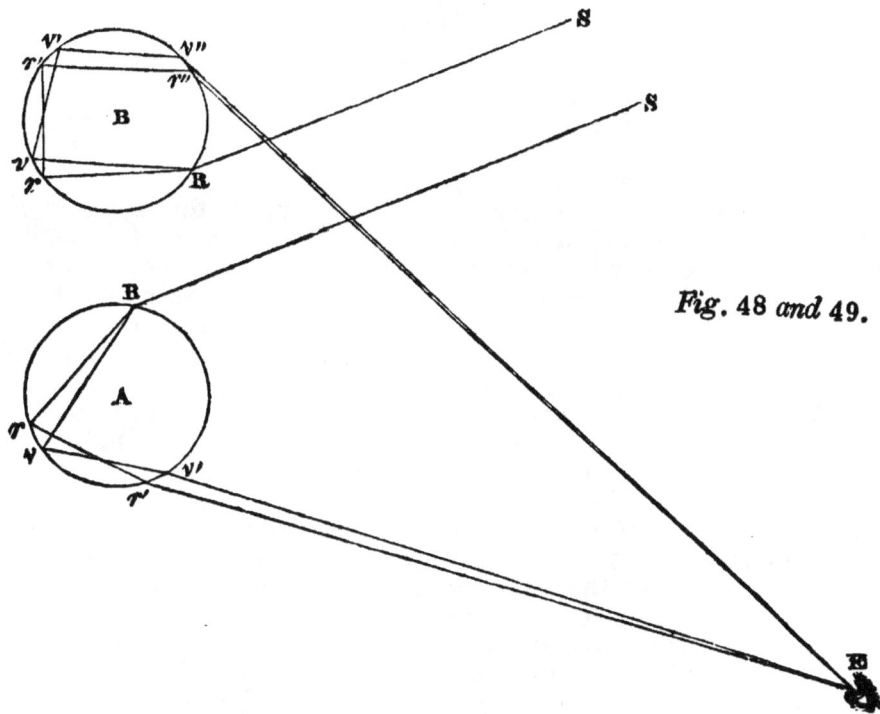

Fig. 48 *and* 49.

there were no ground to intercept the rain and the view of the observer, the rainbow would form a complete circle, the centre of which is diametrically opposite to the sun. It will be found, either by calculation or projection, that the inclination of the red ray r' E to the violet ray S R is 42° 2′, while that of the violet ray v' E to S R is 40° 17′; so that the breadth of the rainbow is 42° 2′ − 40° 17′ = 1° 45′, or about $3\frac{1}{2}$ times the sun's diameter. The bow thus formed is called the *primary rainbow*, and it is produced by *one reflexion and two refractions* of the sun's rays by the drops of rain.

If the rays r' E, v' E were to be a second time reflected at the points r' and v', they would suffer their second refraction a little below R, and would entirely escape from the observer at E. But though this is the case with rays S R that enter at the side of the drop

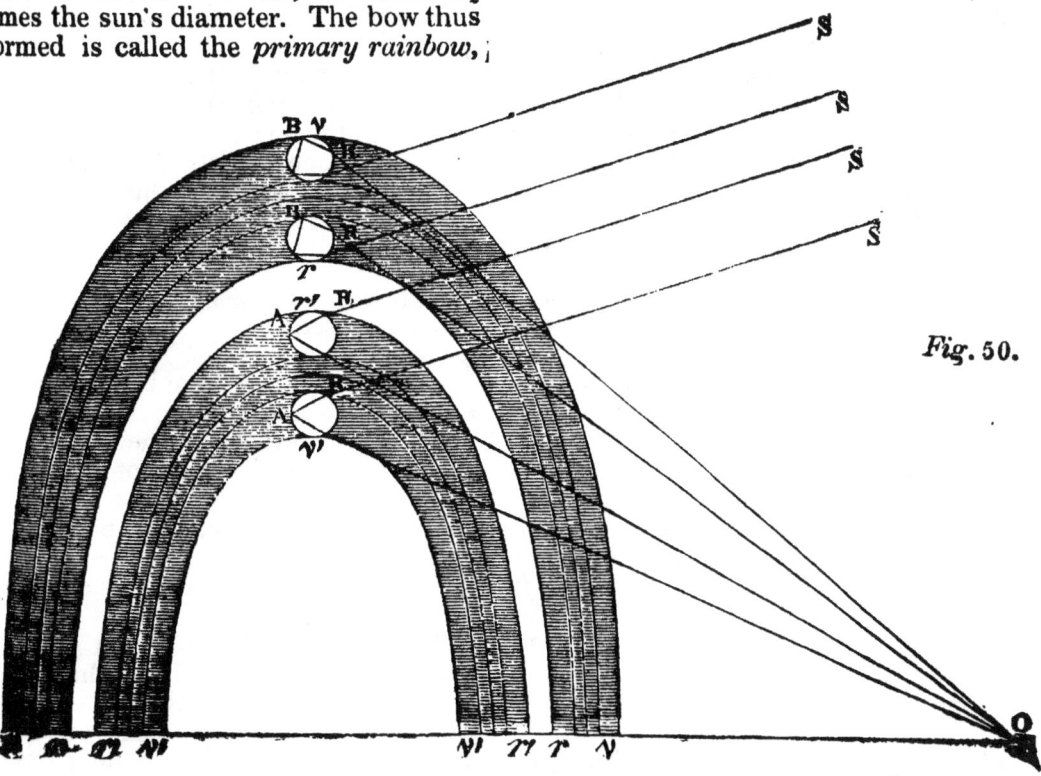

Fig. 50.

farthest from E, yet it is otherwise with those that enter on the side nearest E, as shown in *fig.* 49. The ray S′R refracted at R, and suffering reflexion at r, v and r', v', will emerge at r'', v'', and reach the eye of the observer at E. The inclination of the violet ray v E, to S R will now be 54° 10′, and that of the red ray 50° 58′; and hence the breadth of the bow will be 54° 10′ − 50° 58′ = 3° 12′. This bow, which is called the *secondary rainbow*, will be without the primary one, and will have the colours reversed, the violet being uppermost and the red undermost. The breadth will be nearly *twice* as great as that of the primary bow; but its light will be much less intense, in consequence of the rays by which it is formed having suffered two reflexions within the drop, the effect of which is often to render the outer bow invisible. This *secondary rainbow*, consequently, is formed by *two reflexions and two refractions* of the drops of rain.

The two rainbows are shown in *fig.* 50., where $r' r' r'$ is the red, and $v' v' v'$ the violet circle of the first bow; and $r\ r\ r$ the red, and $v\ v\ v$ the violet of the secondary bow.

If we suppose the rays $v' v'', r' r''$, *fig.* 49, to suffer a *third* reflexion, it may be shown that a third bow will be formed, but it will be between the observer and the sun, with a diameter of 80° 40′, and it will be formed by drops of rain *between the observer and the sun*. In like manner, if we suppose the rays to be four times reflected within the drop, they will form a *fourth* bow, whose diameter will be 91° 6′. None of these bows, however, have been seen; both on account of the faintness of the light which forms them, and from the circumstance of their light being more overpowered by the sun's rays than if they were opposite to that luminary. The following Table shows at one view the proportions of these rainbows.

	No. of Reflexions.	Mean Diameter of the Bow.	Position.
Primary Rainbow	1	82° 18′	Opposite the Sun.
Secondary Rainbow	2	105° 8′	Opposite the Sun.
Tertiary Rainbow	3	80° 40′	Round the Sun.
Quaternary Rainbow	4	91° 6′	Round the Sun.

When no rain is falling between the observer at O, and the part of the sky through which the bow passes, a part of the bow will be wanting at that place; so that portions of rainbows are frequently seen, particularly near the horizon.

When the prismatic spectrum is formed from a very narrow pencil of light, the *yellow* and *blue* colours disappear almost wholly; and when it is formed from a broad disk or band of light, whose breadth exceeds the angular separation of the red and violet rays, the green will disappear, and there will be two primary coloured arches, separated by an arch of white light. Hence in summer, when the sun's diameter is least, the colours of the rainbow are more condensed and homogeneous than in winter; when, from the size of his disk being a maximum, the yellow and blue will be more copious. If a rainbow should appear when the sun is eclipsed, the colours of the bow would be more homogeneous in one part than in another.

The following will be the character of the primary rainbows seen in the different planets.

Colours.

MERCURY.—Red, orange, yellow, *white*, greenish blue, indigo, violet.
EARTH.—Red, orange, yellow, blue, indigo, violet.
SATURN.—Red, orange, green, indigo, and violet.

Within the primary rainbow, and immediately in contact with it, there have been seen what are called *supernumerary rainbows*, each of these bows consisting of red and green. On the 29th July, 1813, we were fortunate enough to see four of these. The red of the first supernumerary bow was in contact with the violet of the primary bow, and this was followed by green, red, green, red, green, red, green, red. M. Dicquemarre observed similar supernumerary rainbows on the *outside of the secondary bow*. These bows have not been satisfactorily explained.

Lunar rainbows have been occasionally seen; but they differ in no respect from those formed by the solar rays, excepting in the faintness of their light. In the autumn of 1814 we saw in a dense fog, near Berne, a fog-bow, which resembled a nebulous arch, in which the separation of the colours could not be distinguished.

2. *Halos and Parhelia.*—A *halo* is a circle, (either composed of white light, or consisting of the prismatic colours,) which is occasionally seen round the sun or moon. When one or more halos are seen round the sun, they are gene-

OPTICS

rally accompanied with *parhelia*,* or *mock* suns, which appear at the places where two halos, or arches of luminous circles, intersect each other.

The large white halo, called in Scotland a *brough*, generally appears round the moon in cold weather, when the sky is of an uniform misty tint; and the prismatic halos, generally called *coronæ*, which are seen round the sun and moon, are commonly seen in fine weather, when white, thin, fleecy clouds float in the atmosphere. Owing to the dazzling effect of the sun's rays, the halos which surround his disk may be seen to most advantage when he is seen by reflexion in a pool of water.

One of the most curious and best described combinations of halos and parhelia was observed by Hevelius, at Dantzic, on Sunday, the 20th February, 1661, New Stile. It is represented in *fig.* 51, and has been thus described by Hevelius.*

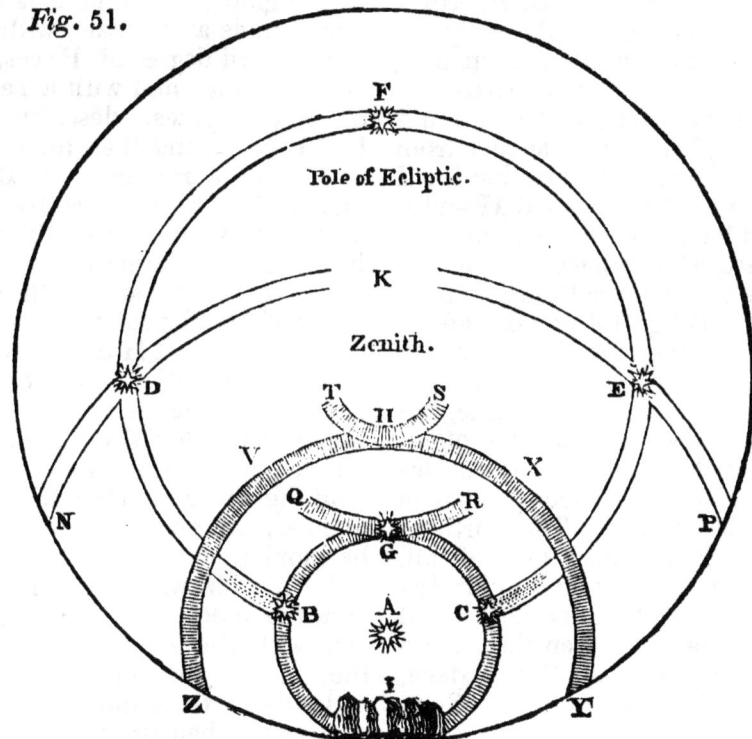

Fig. 51.

"A little before eleven o clock, the sun being towards the south, and the sky very clear, there appeared seven suns together, in several circles, some white and some coloured; and these with very long tails, waving and pointing from the true sun, together with certain white arches crossing one another. 1st. The true sun at A, being about 25° high, was surrounded almost entirely by a circle whose diameter was 45°, and which was coloured like the rainbow, with purple, red, and yellow, its under limb being scarcely 2½° above the horizon. 2d. On each side of the sun, at B and C, towards the west and east, there appeared two mock suns coloured, especially towards the sun, with very long and splendid tails, of a whitish colour, terminating in a point. 3d. A far greater circle, Y X H V Z, almost 90° in diameter, encompassed the sun, and the former lesser circle, G B I C, and extended itself down to the horizon. It was very strongly coloured in its upper part, but was somewhat duller and fainter on each side. 4th. At the tops of these two circles, at G and H, were two inverted arches, whose common centre lay in the zenith, and these were very bright and beautifully coloured. The diameter of the lower arch, Q G R, was 90°, and that of the upper one, T H S, was 45°. In the middle of the lower arch at G, where it coincided with the circle B G C, there appeared another mock sun; but its light and colours were dull and faintish. 5th. There appeared a circle, B C E F D, much bigger than the former, of an uniform whitish colour, parallel to the horizon, at the distance of 25°, and 130° in diameter, which arose, as it were, from the collateral mock suns B and C, and passed

---

* From two Greek words signifying *near the Sun*.   * Appendix to his *Mercurius in Sole Visus*, p. 174.

through three other parhelia, of an uniform whitish colour, like silver: one at D, almost 90° from the true sun, towards the east; another at E, towards the west; and a third at F, in the north, diametrically opposite to the true sun, all of the same colour and brightness. There passed also two other white arches, E N, D P, of the greatest circle of the sphere, through the eastern and western mock suns E, D, and also through K, the pole of the ecliptic. They went down to the horizon at N and P, crossing the great white circle obliquely, so as to make a white cross at each parhelion; so that seven suns appeared very plain at the same time; and if I could have seen the phenomenon sooner from an eminence, I do not question but I should have found two more at H and I, which would have made nine in all; for there remained in those places such marks as made this suspicion not improbable.

"This most delightful and extraordinary sight lasted from 30 minutes past 10 to 51 minutes past 11; though it had not the same appearance all that while, but sometimes one and sometimes another. It appeared in the perfection of this description at about 11 o'clock, and then degenerated by degrees. The northern mock sun at F vanished first of all, together with a part of its circle; the other parhelia, with their arches, lasted till 10 minutes past 11; then the eastern mock sun, and after that the western, vanished, with both the crosses. Soon after this the collateral parhelia C, D suffered several changes; sometimes one was brighter than the other, in light and colours, and sometimes fainter and darker. For at 18 minutes past 10 the eastern parhelion at C vanished, while the western parhelion at B remained very conspicuous; and at 24 minutes past 11 the eastern one was very bright again, and remained so, while the western one disappeared at 40 minutes past 11; although this western one had almost always the longer tail. For the tip of it was frequently extended for 30 degrees, and sometimes 90, as far as the parhelion E; but the tail of the eastern one C was scarcely above 20 degrees. At 30 minutes past 11 the great vertical circle, Y X H V Z, was destroyed; but the inverted arches H and G, together with the collateral parhelia B and C, continued to the last.

"The figure of this phenomenon is drawn in the same manner as the constellations are drawn upon an artificial globe, to be viewed by the eye on the outside of it. For by this means every thing is represented much clearer and distincter. Nevertheless, the place of the observer was nearly under the zenith within the circle, parallel to the horizon; so that the true sun appeared to him in the meridian, the mock sun F in the north, and the other two at D and E on each hand. But if you desire to have this extraordinary phenomenon represented a little plainer; upon an artificial globe, whose pole is elevated to our latitude at Dantzic, with the centre A in the 2d degree of Pisces, where the sun then was, and with a semidiameter of $22\frac{1}{2}$ degrees, describe the circle G B I C; 2. and then the circle Y X H Y Z, with a radius of 45 degrees; 3. and with the same centre and semidiameter of 90 degrees, draw the circle N E K D P through the two white mock suns E, D; 4. and with a semidiameter of $22\frac{1}{2}$, the zenith being the centre, draw the arch I H S; 5. and also the arch Q G R, with a radius of 90 degrees, upon the same centre; 6. and, lastly, the circle B E F D C parallel to the horizon, with a radius of 90 degrees. And the draught being finished in this manner, will appear very beautiful and harmonious."

In the drawing of this phenomenon, the halos are represented as circles, with the sun in their centre; but they are in general of an oval form, wider below than above, and having the sun nearer their upper than their lower extremity. This is an optical illusion, depending on the apparent figure of the sky. When the halo touches the horizon, its apparent vertical diameter has been estimated by Dr. Smith as divided by the moon in the proportion of about two to three, or four, and is to the horizontal diameter drawn through the moon as four to three nearly.

A halo of a different kind, and exhibiting all the prismatic colours, was observed by Mr. Huygens on the 13th of May, 1652. "I observed," says he, "a circle about the sun as its centre: its diameter was about 46°, and its breadth the same as that of a common rainbow. It had also the same colours, though very weak, and scarcely discernible, but in a contrary order; the red being next the sun, and the blue being very dilute and whitish. All the space within the circle was possessed by a vapour duller than the rest of the air; of such a texture as to obscure the sky with a sort of continued cloud, but so thin that the colour of the blue sky appeared through it. The wind blew very gently from the north."*

Our limits will not permit us to give any farther description of individual halos; but the inquiring reader will have his curiosity amply gratified by consulting the article *Halo*, in the *Edinburgh Encyclopædia*, vol. x. p. 612; and he will find in the accounts of the recent voyages of Captains Ross, Parry, and Scoresby, descriptions of several which have been observed since the publication of the above article.

The explanations which have hitherto been given of this class of phenomena, are by no means so satisfactory as might have been expected in the present improved state of optical science. It seems, however, to be satisfactorily proved, that they owe their origin to the crystals of ice and snow floating in the atmosphere, and in some cases to the action of drops of rain of different sizes.

That crystals of ice do float in the atmosphere is well established. Sir Charles Giesecké, who lived seven years in Greenland, describes this phenomenon in the following words: " Previous to that operation of nature, (*viz*. the freezing of the sea,) the sea smokes like burning turf-land, and a fog or mist arises, called *frost smoke*. This cutting mist frequently raises blisters on the face and hands, and is very pernicious to the health. It appears to consist of small particles of ice, and produces the sensation of needles pricking the skin."†

The existence of such crystals in the arctic regions being thus proved, there can be little doubt that they occur in the upper part of our own atmosphere, where the cold is sufficient to freeze the watery particles of which the clouds and vapours are composed. That a number of transparent crystals placed between the eye and a luminous body, will produce halos round that body, whose diameters will depend on the refractive power, and the refracting of the crystals, may be proved by the following experiment, described by Dr. Brewster in the article *Curiosities of Science*, in the *Edinburgh Encyclopædia*, vol. xvii. p. *590. If we spread a few drops of a saturated solution of *alum* over a plate of glass, it will quickly crystallize, covering the glass with an imperfect crust, which consists of flat, octohedral crystals scarcely visible to the eye. When this plate is held between the sun or any other luminous body and the observer, whose eye must be kept close behind the smooth side of the glass plate, he will see *three* fine halos encircling the luminous body at different distances. The *innermost halo*, which is the whitest, is formed by the refraction of the rays of the sun through the pair of faces of the octohedral crystals which are least inclined to each other. The *second halo*, which is more coloured, having the blue rings outwards, is formed by refraction through a pair of faces more inclined to each other; and the *third halo*, which is very large and highly coloured, is formed by a pair of faces constituting a prism, with a still greater refracting angle. Now each individual crystal of the alum forms, by means of three of the similar prisms which it includes, three images of the sun, placed at points 120° distant from one another, and in the circumference of a circle of which the sun is the centre; and as the numerous minute crystals with which the plate of glass is covered, have their refracting faces turned in every possible direction, the whole circumference of each halo will be filled up as it were with images. Similar effects may be obtained with other crystals; and when they have the property of double refraction, (which alum has not,) each halo will be either doubled when the double refraction is considerable, or rendered broader when the double refraction is small.

Having thus shown how circles of light may be formed by viewing a luminous body through a number of minute crystals, we shall proceed to give a brief sketch of the leading opinions which have been entertained respecting the cause of halos.

Although Descartes had stated that halos were produced by crystals of ice, yet it was Huygens who first investigated the form of the crystals, or rather masses of hail, which was necessary to produce the observed phenomena. He supposes that there are globular particles of hail not larger than turnip seed, the outer portion of which is melted and in the state of water, while the inner part or kernel is opaque like snow. These globules, he thinks, were first globules of soft snow, which are rounded by a continual agitation in the air, and thawed on the outside by the

* Hugenii *Opera Posthuma*, p. 366.
† Article *Greenland*, in the *Edinburgh Encyclopædia*, vol. x. p. 489, col. 2.

heat of the sun. He then shows, by calculation, that when the shadows of the globule is to the radius of the opaque kernel or nucleus, as 1000 to 480, a halo 45° in diameter will be produced; and that when the proportion of the same radii is as 1000 to 680, a halo of 90° in diameter will be produced.

In order to explain the more complex phenomena, similar to that shown in *fig.* 51, Huygens resorts to half thawed cylinders of snow, differing only in form from the globules above described. He considers the large white circle, B E F D C, (*fig.* 51.) as formed by the reflection of the sun's rays from the outer surface of these cylinders, which he supposes to have an upright position. The lateral parhelia, B, C, he ascribes to two refractions of the sun's light through the watery cylinder, and he regards the halos which pass through the parhelia as produced by the round ends of the upright cylinders. He considers the inverted arches T H S, Q G R, as produced by two refractions in those cylinders whose axes are parallel to the plane of the horizon though not to one another; the parhelia which appear in the middle of these arches being nothing else than the brightest parts of them.

The subject of halos occupied likewise the attention of Sir Isaac Newton. He considers the halo of 45° in diameter as different from the smaller prismatic ones, and as "made by refraction in some sort of hail or snow floating in the air in an horizontal posture, the refracting angle being about 58° or 60°." Sir Isaac explains the small prismatic halos by the fits of easy reflexion and transmission in small drops of water, and he concludes that the rings will be greater or less according as the globules are greater or smaller.

M. Mariotte and Dr. Young ascribe halos to two refractions of equilateral prisms of snow having angles of 60°, a supposition which is the more probable, as ice actually crystallizes in six-sided prisms. Mariotte, indeed, observed, that the filaments of hoar frost had three equal faces, and exhibited rainbows when placed in the sun; and he calculated that they would produce a halo whose diameter was 45° 40′, which is very near 45° 50′, the mean of five accurate observations. Dr. Young accounts for the halo of 90°, by supposing that a considerable portion of the light may fall, after passing through one prism, upon a second prism, so that the effect will be doubled, and a halo of 90° produced. Mr. Cavendish has suggested, that this large halo may be produced by the refraction of the rectangular termination of the crystals, which would give a halo of 90° 28′, if the index of refraction for ice be 1.31.*

3. *Phenomena of the Mirage, or unusual refraction.*—The elevation of coasts, ships, and mountains above their usual level, when seen in the distant horizon, has been long known and described under the name of *Looming.* The name of *Mirage* has been applied by the French to the same class of phenomena; and the appellation of *Fata Morgana* has been given by the Italians to the singular appearances of the same kind which have been repeatedly seen in the straits of Messina. When the rising sun throws his rays at an angle of 45° on the sea of Reggio, and neither wind nor rain ruffle the smooth surface of the water in the bay, the spectator on an eminence in the city, who places his back to the sun and his face to the sea, observes, as it were upon its surface, numberless series of pilasters, arches, and castles, distinctly delineated; regular columns, lofty towers, superb palaces with balconies and windows; extended valleys of trees, delightful plains with herds and flocks; armies of men on foot and horseback, and many other strange figures, in their natural colours and proper actions, passing one another in rapid succession. When vapours and dense exhalations, rising to the height of about twenty feet, accompany the state of the atmosphere above described, then the same objects are seen depicted as it were in the vapour and suspended in the air, though with less distinctness than before. If the air be slightly hazy, and at the same time dewy and fitted to form the rainbow, the above-mentioned objects appear only at the surface of the sea, but they are all brilliantly fringed with the prismatic colours. This description of the Fata Morgana, given by Antonio Minasi so recently as 1793, is no doubt a little overcharged, but there can be no hesitation in believing that the objects and movements which existed on the opposite coast, were occasionally displayed in all the grandeur of aerial representation.

* Since writing the above, we have found quadrilateral prisms of ice with angles of 90°, so that it is through these faces that the halo of 90° is produced.

The phenomena of the Mirage are most frequently seen in the case of ships when they are just beginning to appear above the visible horizon. Mr. Huddart, Dr. Vince, and Capt. Scoresby, have described various appearances of this kind, of which the following are the most interesting.

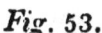

On the 1st of August, 1798, Dr. Vince observed at Ramsgate, a ship which appeared as at A, (*fig.* 52.), the topmast being the only part of it that was seen above the horizon. An inverted image of it was seen at B immediately above the real ship A, and an erect image at C, both of them being complete and well defined. The sea was distinctly seen between them, as at *v w*. As the ship rose to the horizon the image C gradually disappeared, and while this was going on the image B descended, but the mainmast of B did not meet the mainmast of A. The two images B, C were perfectly visible when the whole ship was actually below the horizon.

While navigating the Greenland sea on the 28th of June, 1820, Captain Scoresby observed about eighteen or nineteen sail of ships at the distance of from ten to fifteen miles. He saw them from the mast-head, beginning to change their form. One was drawn out, or elongated, in a vertical plane; another was contracted in the same direction: one had an inverted image immediately above it, as at *a*, (*fig.* 53.), and two, at *b* and *c*, had two distinct inverted images in the air: along with these images there appeared images of the ice, as at *b* and *c*, in two strata, the highest of which had an altitude of about 15′.

In a later voyage, performed in 1822, Capt. Scoresby was able to recognise his father's ship, when *below the horizon*, from the inverted image of it which appeared in the air. "It was," says he,

Fig. 53.

"so well defined, that I could distinguish by a telescope every sail, the general 'rig of the ship,' and its particular character; insomuch, that I confidently pronounced it to be my father's ship, the *Fame*, which it afterwards proved to be; though in comparing notes with my father, I found that our relative position, at the time, gave our distance from one another very nearly 30 miles, being about 17 miles beyond the horizon, and some leagues beyond the limit of direct vision. I was so struck by the peculiarity of the circumstance, that I mentioned it to the officer of the watch, stating my full conviction that the *Fame* was then cruising in the neighbouring inlet."

One of the most curious phenomena of this kind was seen by Dr. Vince on the 6th of August, 1806, at 7 P. M. To an observer at Ramsgate, the tops of the four turrets of Dover castle are usually seen over a hill between Ramsgate and Dover. Dr. Vince, however, when at Ramsgate, saw *the whole of Dover castle* as if it had been brought over and placed on the Ramsgate side of the hill. The image of the castle was so very strong and well defined, that the hill itself did not appear through the image.

In the sandy plains of Egypt the Mirage is seen to great advantage: These plains are often interrupted by small eminences, upon which the inhabitants have built their villages, in order to escape the inundations of the Nile. In the morning and evening objects are seen in their natural form and position, but when the surface of the sandy ground is heated by the sun, the land seems terminated at a particular distance by a general inundation; the villages which are beyond it appear like so many islands in a great lake, and between each village an inverted image of it is seen.

Our limits will not permit us to give any farther examples of these curious phenomena. We shall, therefore, attempt to give a popular explanation of their cause.

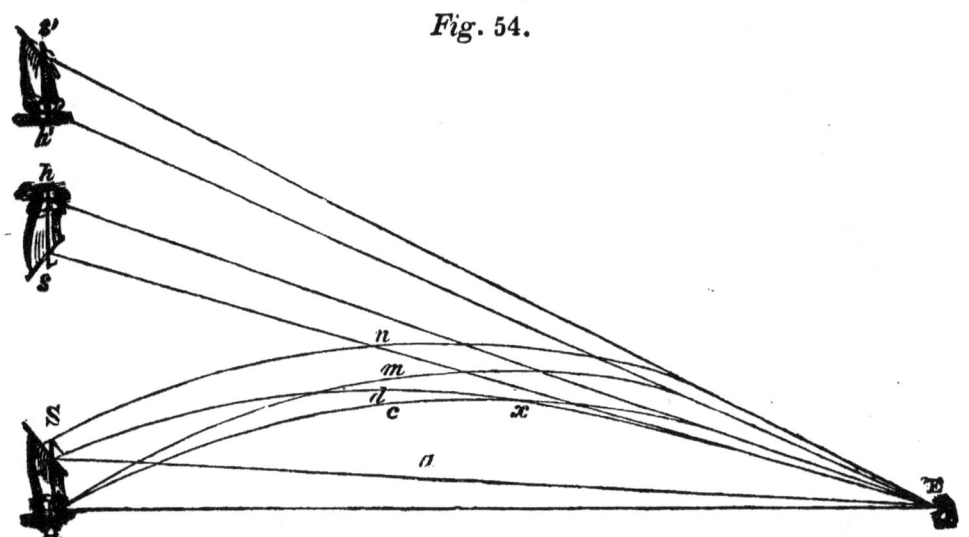

Fig. 54.

Let S H (*fig.* 54.) be a ship in the horizon, and visible to the eye at E, by rays S E, H E proceeding in straight lines to E, through a tract of the atmosphere in its usual state.* If we suppose, what is known to be sometimes the case, that the refractive power of the atmosphere, or air, above the line S a E varies, so as to be less at c than at a, then rays S d, H c proceeding upwards from the ship, and that never could in the ordinary state of the air reach the eye at E, will be refracted into curve lines H c, S d; and if the variation of refractive power is such, that these last rays cross each other at x, then the ray S d, in place of being the uppermost, will now be the undermost, and, consequently, will enter the eye as if it came from the lower end of the object.

If we now draw lines E s, E h tangents to these curve lines at E, these lines will be the direction in which the ship will be seen by the rays H c, S d, and the observer at E will see an inverted image s h of the ship S H considerably elevated above the horizon. The refractive power of the air still continuing to diminish, other rays, H m, H n, that never could reach the eye at E in the ordinary state of the atmosphere, may likewise be bent into curves which will not cross each other before they reach the eye at E. In this case, the tangent E s' to the upper curve S n E will be uppermost, and the tangent E h' to the lower curve S m E lowermost, so that the observer at E will see an erect image s' h' of the ship above the inverted image. It is possible that a third, and even a fourth image may be seen.

If the variation of refractive power takes place only in the tract of air through which the rays H c, S d pass, then there may only be an inverted image; and if it takes place only in the tract through which S m, S n pass, there may only be an erect image. It is also obvious, that if the variation of refractive power commences at the line joining the eye and the horizon, the ordinary image S H will not be seen; and, in like manner, it is clear that the inverted and erect images s h, s' h' may be seen even if the real ship S H is below the visible horizon.

In the case of Dover castle, the rays from the top and bottom of the castle passed above the hill in curve lines, and the top of the hill was seen by the observer at Ramsgate, by means of a curved ray which reached the eye

---

* We do not here consider that rays of light moving through the atmosphere are bent into curve lines when the atmosphere is in its usual state; because the effect is very small, and the consideration of it would tend only to make the present explanation more complex.

between the rays of the top and bottom of the castle.

That the phenomena of the Mirage are produced by such variations in the refractive power of the atmosphere as we have mentioned, may be proved by actual experiment: All the phenomena may be represented artificially to the eye, and we may even venture to predict new phenomena which have not yet been witnessed. If the variation of the refractive power of the air takes place in a horizontal line perpendicular to the line of vision, that is, from right to left, then we may have a *lateral* Mirage, that is, an image of a ship may be seen on the right or left hand of the real ship, or on both, if the variation of refractive power is the same on each side of the line of vision.* If there should happen at the same time both a vertical and a lateral variation of refractive power in the air, and if the variation should be such as to expand or elongate the object in both directions, then the object would be *magnified*, as if seen through a telescope, and might be seen and recognised at a distance at which it would not otherwise have been visible. If the refractive power, on the contrary, varied, so as to contract the object in both directions, the image of it would be diminished as if seen through a concave lens.

In order to represent artificially the effects of the Mirage, Dr. Wollaston views an object through a stratum of spirit of wine lying above water, or a stratum of water laid above one of syrup. These substances, by their gradual incorporation, produce a refractive power diminishing from the *spirit of wine* to the *water*, or from the *syrup* to the *water;* so that, by looking through the mixed, or the intermediate stratum at a word or object held behind the bottle which contains the fluids, an inverted image will be seen. The same effect Dr. Wollaston has shown may be produced by looking along the side of a red-hot poker at a word or object ten or twelve feet distant. At a distance less than three-eighths of an inch from the line of the poker, an inverted image was seen, and within and without that an erect image.

The method employed by Dr. Brewster† to illustrate these phenomena consists in holding a heated iron above a mass of water bounded by parallel plates of glass: as the heat descends slowly through the fluid, we have a regular variation of density which gradually diminishes from the bottom to the surface. If we now withdraw the heated iron, and put a cold body in its place, or even allow the air to act alone, the superficial stratum of water will give out its heat, so as to produce a decrease of density from the surface to a certain depth below it. Through the medium thus constituted, the phenomena of the Mirage may be seen in the finest manner.

We have no doubt that some of the facts ascribed in the Western Highlands of Scotland to second sight, have been owing to the unusual refraction of the atmosphere, and that the same cause will explain some of those wonders which sceptics discredit, and which superstitious minds attribute to supernatural causes. The beacon keeper of the Isle of France, who saw ships in the air before they rose above the visible horizon, may now recover his good character in the eyes of the former, while the latter may cease to regard him as a magician.

4. *On the Colours of Natural Bodies.*—There are few of the applications of science to explain natural phenomena so extremely simple, and at the same time so beautiful, as that of the colours of thin plates, to account for all that variety of splendid tints, which colour the animal, the mineral, and the vegetable kingdom. To Sir Isaac Newton we owe this explanation; and we have no hesitation in saying, that none of his discoveries exhibit more penetration and sagacity.

The colours of bodies may be deduced from those of thin plates, as explained in Chap. xiii., in the following manner, and without ascribing any new property to the particles of matter.

1. *Those surfaces of transparent bodies reflect the greatest quantity of light that have the greatest refractive power, or that separate two media which differ most in their refractive power. When two media have the same refractive power, no light is reflected at their separating surfaces.*

This proposition may be proved by many facts: *chromate of lead* and *diamond*, and the other bodies which are placed at the head of our table of refractive powers in Chap. ii., reflect

---

* M.M. Jurine and Soret observed a fact of this kind in the lake of Geneva. See *Edinburgh Encyclopedia*, Art. OPTICS, vol. xv. p. 620.

† See *Edinburgh Encyclopædia*, Art. HEAT, vol. x. p. 675.

much more light than any of the other bodies which follow them in the table; and *water, ice,* and *tabasheer,* at the foot of the table, reflect much less light than any of the bodies which precede them. In like manner, if we pour *castor oil* upon *crown glass,* which have nearly the same refractive power, there is almost no light reflected from their separating surface. If we pour *sulphuric acid* on the same glass, the reflective power of the surface is increased. With *alcohol* it is still farther increased; with *water,* still farther; and when the glass is placed in *air,* the reflective power is a maximum.

2. *The smallest parts of almost all natural bodies are, in some degree, transparent, and the opacity, or imperviousness to light, of these bodies, arises from the multitude of reflexions produced in their internal parts.*

Gold and silver leaf are both transparent; and as metallic salts, and the solutions of all metals are perfectly transparent, we may regard the proposition as established for the most opaque of all substances. The blackest and most opaque of stones, &c. become translucent, and even transparent, when a strong light is transmitted through the sharp edges of small fragments of them.

3. *Between the parts of opaque and coloured bodies there are many spaces, which are either empty or are filled with media of different densities;* as water, *for example, between the particles with which any liquor is coloured;* — air *between the aqueous globules that constitute clouds and mists; and for the most part* space *without either water or air, but yet perhaps not wholly without any substance, between the parts of hard bodies.*

The truth of this proposition may be deduced from the two preceding ones; for, by Prop. 2, there are many reflexions made by the internal parts of bodies, which, by Prop. 1, would not happen if the parts of those bodies were continuous without any interstices between them, and of the same refractive power. Besides, many transparent bodies, such as minerals and salts, become opaque when their water of crystallization is driven off by heat; and many opaque bodies become transparent by filling their pores with water or oil. *Hydrophane* and opaque *tabasheer* are perfectly transparent; the former when it has absorbed water, and the latter when it has absorbed oil.

Paper, vellum, and *linen* become transparent in oil; and *iodine,* a dark, metallic, and opaque substance, when driven off in vapour by heat, forms a transparent, purple coloured gas.

4. *The parts of bodies and their interstices must not be less than of some definite size, to render them opaque and coloured.*

The experiments in Chap. xiii., on thin plates, completely prove, that below a certain degree of thickness bodies have no power to reflect light; that is, are *black;* and this is finely illustrated by the black down of quartz mentioned in the same chapter. Hence it is clear, that if the particles of all terrestrial bodies were so small as, or smaller than, the *eight millionth part* of an inch, ($\frac{8}{1000000}$), every object in the animate and inanimate world would be absolutely black, and consequently invisible; for the sun, planets, and stars could only show us their own individual positions in the sable firmament. The transparency of water, glass, &c., Sir Isaac Newton conceives to arise from this — that though they are as full of pores, or interstices, between their parts as other bodies are, yet their parts and interstices are too small to cause reflexion at their common surfaces.

5. *The transparent parts of bodies, according to their several sizes, reflect rays of one colour and transmit those of another, for the same reasons that thin plates, or minute particles of air, water, and glass, reflect or transmit those rays; — and this is the cause of all their colours.*

If a body, such as a film of mica, appears all over of one uniform colour, *blue,* for example; then, if it is cut into threads, or broken into fragments, these portions will still be *blue;* and, consequently, a heap of these blue portions will constitute a mass, or powder, of a blue colour. And as the parts of all natural bodies are like so many fragments of a thin plate, they must, for the same reasons, exhibit the same colours.

This conclusion appears also, by examining the similarity between the colours of natural bodies and those of thin plates. The finely coloured feathers of the humming birds, and those of peacocks' tails, appear in the very same part of the feather of different colours in different positions of the eye; the colour descending in the scale as they are seen more obliquely, as is the case with the colours of thin plates. Hence

Sir Isaac Newton concludes, that their colours arise from the thinness of the transparent parts of the feathers; that is, from the slenderness of the very fine hairs which grow out of the sides of the grosser lateral branches of the feathers. The finer webs of spiders, and the transparent capillary crystals of *apophyllite*, *mesolite*, and *scolezite*, are often so minute as to appear coloured. Gold and silver leaf reflect one colour and transmit another; and the infusions of various coloured woods appear *blue* by reflected, and *yellow*, *orange*, and *red* by transmitted light.

6. *The parts of bodies on which their colours depend are denser than the medium which pervades their interstices.*

This will appear from the considerations, that the colour of a body depends not only upon the rays incident perpendicularly on its parts, but also on those incident at all other angles; and that a very little variation of obliquity changes the reflected colour when the thin plate, or particle, is *rarer* than the surrounding medium; insomuch that such a small particle will, at different oblique incidences, reflect all sorts of colours in so great a variety, that the colour resulting from them all, confusedly reflected from a heap of such particles, will be a greyish white. Whereas, if the thin plate or particle is much denser than the surrounding medium, the colours are so little changed by the variation of obliquity, that the rays which are reflected least obliquely may predominate over the rest; so much, as to cause a heap of such particles to appear intensely of their colour.

7. *The size of the component parts of natural bodies may be conjectured from their colours.*

In order to do this we must suppose that the particles have a given refractive power, such as that of air, water, glass, or diamond. For example, if a body which is likely to have the same refractive power as glass reflects a *green* of the third order, its thickness will be found, by the Table in page 35, to be $16\frac{1}{4}$ millionths of an inch. The difficulty however consists in determining to which order the particular colour belongs. The following rules are given by Newton.

Scarlets and other *reds*, *oranges*, and *yellows*, are most probably of the second order, if they are pure and intense. Those of the first and third order may be pretty good, only the yellow of the first order is faint, such as that of dry straw; and the orange and red of the third order have a great mixture of violet and blue. The red of different kinds of roses belongs to the third order.

Purest *greens* are of the third order, though there may be good ones of the fourth order. The greens of all vegetables seem to belong to the third order; for when they wither they turn to a greenish yellow, or to a more perfect yellow or orange, or perhaps to a red, passing through all these intermediate colours. These changes may arise from the exhalation of the moisture, which may leave the colouring particles more dense. These last colours are too full and lively to be of the fourth order, and consequently the green through which they have passed is likely to be of the third order.

The best *blues* and *purples* are of the third order, though some of them may be of the second. The colour of violets Newton considers as of the third order, because acids change the syrup of violets into a fine red, and alkalis into a beautiful green.

The *azure* colour of the purest and most transparent sky he supposes to be of the first order, and to arise from particles of vapour before they have attained the size requisite to reflect other colours.

The most intense and luminous *whites* are of the first order, and those which are less strong and luminous are a mixture of colours of several orders. Of this last kind is the whiteness of *froth,** *paper*, *linen*, and most white substances. The colour of white metals seems to be of the first order. The colours of gold and copper are of the *second* or *third* order. The colour of mercury is probably of the first order.

Blackness requires a smaller size of particles than any colour, for at all greater sizes there is too much light reflected to constitute this colour. If the particles are a little less than what is necessary to reflect the white and very faint blue of the *first* order, they will reflect so very little light as to appear

---

* We have retained *froth* in this list, though we think it demonstrable that *froth* owes its whiteness, like the powder or minute parts of all transparent bodies, to its reflecting an immense number of images of the luminous objects above and around it. In the open air each of the little spherical vesicles or bubbles of which froth is composed, reflects an image of the sky, and all these accumulated images constitute its *white* colour. Pounded glass, snow, and other bodies which are transparent, owe their whiteness to the same cause.

intensely black, and yet may, perhaps, refract it within themselves so long, until it happen to be stifled and lost, by which means they will appear black in all positions of the eye without any transparency.

Having thus stated, as clearly as we can in such a small compass, Newton's celebrated theory of the colours of natural bodies, we shall lay before the reader several illustrations and confirmations of it drawn from the discoveries of modern science, together with such facts as may be of use either in modifying or extending the views of our great philosopher.

1. One of the most curious facts of this description was discovered by M. Thenard. Having obtained some very pure *phosphorus* by repeated distillations, he melted it in hot water, when it became of a whitish yellow colour as usual. When it was allowed to cool slowly, and become solid, it preserved this colour unchanged, and was semi-transparent; but when it was thrown in its melted state into cold water, it became *suddenly opaque and absolutely black*. Its nature, however, remained the same, for when it was melted again it became yellow and transparent as before. In repeating this experiment, M. Biot observed a very curious fact. When the melted phosphorus was thrown into cold water, some little globules of it remained yellow and liquid, but the instant they were touched with the end of a piece of glass tube they became solid and absolutely black. As the same piece of phosphorus can thus be made opaque or transparent at pleasure, it affords a fine example of the influence of the arrangement of the particles, and of a change in their size in producing the opposite conditions of yellowish white and black.

2. That remarkable substance called *tabasheer*, which is a siliceous concretion found in the joints of the bamboo, exhibits some curious phenomena relative to its colour and its porosity. The pure varieties which have their index of refraction so low as 1.1114 between water and air, reflect a delicate azure colour, and transmit a sort of straw yellow colour. When a small drop of water is put upon it, the wetted spot becomes instantly *milk white and opaque*, although the water is absorbed and enters its pores; but when more water is added so as to fill its pores, it recovers its transparency, ceases to reflect the azure tint, and transmits a yellow less intense than before. The cause of this singular property has been explained in the following manner by Dr. Brewster, who first observed it. Let X Y, *fig.* 55,

Fig. 55.

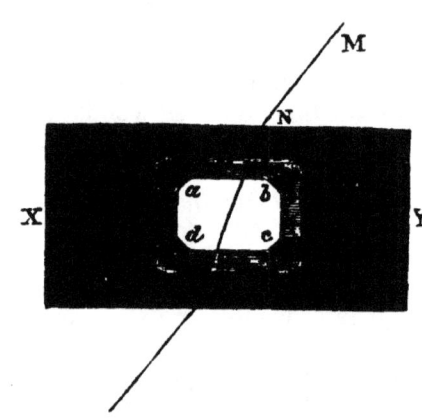

be a plate of tabasheer, and A B C D one of its pores highly magnified. We know that this pore is filled with air, and that when a ray of light M N enters the separating surface A B at E, and quits it at H, it suffers so little refraction, and is therefore so little scattered, that the tabasheer appears transparent, and allows us to see objects through it distinctly. This coexistence of a high degree of transparency with a high degree of porosity is unexampled in material bodies, and arises from the slight difference between the refractive power of air and tabasheer. Let us now suppose that a *small* quantity of water is introduced into the pore A B C D, so as not to fill it, but merely to line its circumference with a film contained between A B C D and *a b c d*. Then the light which was formerly scattered by the slight refraction at E and H, in passing from tabasheer into air, will now be a little less scattered at these points, since it passes from tabasheer into water, where the difference of refractive power is less; but while the light passes from the film of water into the air at F, and enters the water again at G, the scattering of the rays will be very considerable, owing to the great difference of refractive power between air and water. In passing through every pore therefore the light is refracted, and consequently scattered no less than four times, and hence the piece of tabasheer when slightly wetted with water must appear opaque. If we now saturate it with water, the pore A B C D will be completely filled: the two great refractions which took place at F and G will no longer exist, and the light will suffer only a slight refraction at E and H, by which it will be less scattered than when the tabasheer was dry, a result which is perfectly conformable to observation.

An analogous effect is produced with opaque tabasheer and oil. This opaque variety, which retains its opacity when its pores are filled with water, acquires the most beautiful transparency by the absorption of oil of beech nut. Having saturated a large piece of this variety with oil of beech nut coloured red with anchusa root, it was laid on a mass of lead of a lower temperature than that of the room. The oil instantly appeared to retire from the surface into its interior, and the transparent mass became opaque like a piece of red brick. Upon removing it into its former temperature the tabasheer resumed its transparency. In this experiment the oil seems to have quitted the centre of the pores in consequence of its contraction by cold, and collecting itself by capillary attraction round the solid parts, left the pores in the state shown in *fig.* 55. The application of heat, by expanding the oil, causes it to fill the pores and resume its transparency. If when the tabasheer is saturated with oil, it is carried into a warmer place, a part of the oil will be discharged by expansion.

Tabasheer presents us with a still more remarkable property relative to the three conditions of solid bodies, *viz.* transparency, and black and white opacity. If we wrap a transparent piece in paper, and burn the paper, and repeat this operation twice or thrice, the tabasheer will become perfectly black and opaque, with a sort of pitchy lustre. A red heat will restore it to its primitive state; but if the heat is considerably below redness, some specimens acquire a slight transparency, and a dark slaty blue colour, shading in some places into whiteness. When slightly wetted in this state it becomes chalky white; with a greater portion of water it becomes black, and with a still greater portion it becomes again transparent.*

3. Several curious phenomena of colour are presented by mineral bodies.

* See the *Philosophical Transactions* for 1819, p. 292.

The yellow *Brazil topaz* loses its yellow colour entirely by heat, without suffering any change in its other properties. Some specimens thus become nearly colourless, while others are left with a fine pink colour, which is much prized. The yellow phosphate of lead grows green when heated. The balas ruby in some specimens becomes *green* by heat; the *green* fades into *brown* as the cooling advances, and the *brown* rises to its original *red* colour,

4. *Tincture of turnsole*, which becomes *orange* after being long corked up in a bottle, an effect ascribed to deoxidation, becomes *red* in a few minutes, and then *violet blue*, by opening the bottle and shaking the fluid, the colour thus passing from the first to the second order. The *Cameleon Mineral*, which is a bright *green* of the third order, is a solid formed by heating pure and solid oxide of manganese with potash. When dissolved in much warm water, it is rapidly disunited and separated from the oxide; but if a little water is used, and if the mineral is well made, the separation becomes progressive, the solution changing its colour from *green* to *bluish green*, *blue*, *purple* and *reddish purple*, the last descending in the order of the rings, as if the particles became smaller. M. Biot conceives, that the proportion of potash united to the oxide, is successively dissolved by the action of the water, till it is all carried off, and the oxide alone left in the liquor; and hence he concludes, that the brown (*brun-marin*) colour of the oxide is a reddish orange, of the *second* order, rendered excessively sombre by the absorption of a great quantity of light.—Another chemical fact of much interest was observed by M. Claubry. He mixed oil of sweet almonds with soap and sulphuric acid. The combination which is at first *yellow*, soon passes to *orange yellow* and to *deep orange*, and thence to *red* and to *violet*, which, as M. Biot observes, is precisely the order of colours as they advance from the *first* to the *second* order. In the passage from the *orange* to the *red*, there is an instant when the absorption of the incident rays is so strong, that the mixture appears almost black. The same interruption is observed, if in place of oil of almonds we use oil obtained from alcohol, treated with chlorine. The colours then pass through the following gradations; *pale yellow* of the first order, *orange*, *black*, *red*, *vio-*

let, and finally a beautiful blue of the second order. Hence, as M. Biot remarks, we observe that the extinction to which the intensity is accidentally subject, does not prevent the tints from following the same order as that of the rings.

A great number of the metallic oxides exhibit a momentary change of tint by being heated, and resume their primitive tint by cooling. This arises from the increase of size in the particles, and consequently the new colours thus developed should rise in the order of colours.* A phenomenon of the opposite kind was observed by M. Chevreul in volatilizing indigo spread upon paper. During vaporization the indigo colour passes into a *poppy red*, highly brilliant, which seems to prove that the particles have become less in the act of evaporation. The same eminent chemist noticed an analogous fact in the new substance, which he calls *hæmatine*. This substance, when pure and solid, has a *greyish* tint. When dissolved in water, containing some drops of acetic acid, it produces a fluid, whose colour is a slightly greenish yellow of the second order. If the fluid in this state is introduced into a tube filled with mercury, and heated by surrounding it with a hot iron, it becomes successively *yellow*, brilliant *orange*, brilliant *red*, *purple*, and *bluish purple*; and, what is very remarkable, if it is afterwards left to cool, it returns gradually to its primitive tint, which it requires some days to do, if the quantity used is about the one-third of a cubic inch.

The progressive steps by which bodies attain their definite tints, are well seen in the crystallization of a saturated solution of super-oxygenated muriate of potash during its slow cooling. As the temperature falls, the salt is precipitated in thin rectangular scales which unite to one another, and whose thinness is such, that they are differently coloured, according to the obliquity of the incident light, or the thickness of the scales. The thickest are of an uniform white colour, and the thinnest, by uniting themselves to others, become white in their turn. Sometimes they do not apply themselves exactly to one another, and then they do not cease to reflect the tints which they exhibit individually, even though they form part of a plate too thick to produce these colours. Similar variations are seen in the small scales of acidulous tartrite of potash precipitated from a warm and saturated solution of this salt.*

5. The vegetable kingdom presents many curious illustrations of Newton's theory, as he himself observed, and as we have noticed in Prop. 7. M. Biot is of opinion, that the colours descend† in the order of rings, as the force of vegetation developes itself, and ascend during its decay. The young buds of the oak and of the poplar, for example, are at first of a *red* colour, bordering on *orange*; from this they pass to a reddish orange, and soon to a green, through a kind of reddish yellow, extremely fugitive. When the flower of the honeysuckle blows, its colour is a pure white of the first order, and in decaying it passes into pale yellow, yellow, orange, and deep orange. The flower of the *geranium sanguineum*, whose colour is a violet red, intermediate between the *first* and *second* order, becomes blue in withering. *Pinks* of a bright red of the second order pass as they decay into a poppy red, and a violet purple. The same thing happens to certain species of *roses*, but there are others whose colour appears to be red of the third order. While these grow old upon their stalk, they lose by degrees the brilliancy of their red, and the blue and violet of the fourth order, acquiring a greater influence over their tints, they rise to a bluish red. The *tigridia*, which blows and withers in a few hours, appears, even when it is not quite open, of a bright *reddish orange*, from which it rises to a *deep red* of the first order, and in withering it rises to the *violet red* of the second order. The *cobæa* when it opens is at first of a pale and imperfect *yellowish green* of the second order; but it is soon spotted with violet, and in a few hours it becomes wholly violet, without passing through the intermediate blue. In withering, however, it descends from violet to blue. M. Decandolle ascribes the sudden change of colour at the first period to the fecundation, which he considers as the cause which modifies rapidly the colour of a great many flowers.‡

---

* The tints described by M. Gay Lussac in the *Ann. de Chimie*, follow the order of the rings.

* See Biot's *Traité de Physique*, tom. iv. p. 135.
† In quoting the opinions of this eminent philosopher, it is necessary to state, that when he uses the word *ascend* in the order of rings, we use *descend*, because the colours fall from a higher to a lower order. M. Biot's term ascend, indicates a local ascent in the printed table, the first order being at the top of the table, and the last order at the bottom.
‡ Biot's *Traité de Physique*, tom. iv. p. 133.

6. The animal kingdom also contributes its aid in support of the same theory. The choroid coat of the dog and other animals, which produces the *blue, green,* and *red* reflexions from the eye of the living animal, retains the same faculty after death. When the choroid coat dries, it becomes black, and the colours disappear. We have found, however, that after remaining dry for nearly ten years, their colours could still be developed by moisture. The *black* passed instantly into a *brilliant blue,* the *blue* into *green,* and the *green* into *greenish yellow.*

5. *Colours of the atmosphere.*—As the earth is surrounded with an atmosphere varying in density from the surface of the globe, where it is a maximum, to the height of about 45 miles, where it is extremely rare, and just able to reflect the rays of the setting sun, the rays of the sun, moon, and stars are refracted into curve lines, unless when they are incident upon it perpendicularly. Hence the apparent altitude of the celestial bodies is always greater than their real altitude, and they appear above the horizon when they are actually below it.

But while the solar rays traverse the earth's atmosphere, they suffer another change from the resisting medium which they encounter. When the sun, or any of the heavenly bodies, are considerably elevated above the horizon, their light is transmitted to the earth without any perceptible change; but when these bodies are near the horizon, their light must pass through a long tract of air, and is considerably modified before it reaches the eye of the observer. The momentum of the red, or greatest refrangible rays, being greater than the momentum of the violet, or least refrangible rays, the former will force their way through the resisting medium, while the latter will be either reflected or absorbed. A white beam of light, therefore, will be deprived of a portion of its blue rays by its horizontal passage through the atmosphere, and the resulting colour will be either orange or red, according to the quantity of the least refrangible rays that have been stopt in their course. Hence the rich and brilliant hue with which nature is gilded by the setting sun; hence the glowing red which tinges the morning and evening clouds; and hence the sober purple of twilight which they assume when their ruddy glare is tempered by the reflected azure of the sky.

We have already seen that the red rays penetrate through the atmosphere, while the blue rays, less able to surmount the resistance which they meet, are reflected or absorbed in their passage. It is to this cause that we must ascribe the blue colour of the sky, and the bright azure which tinges the mountains of the distant landscape.

As we ascend in the atmosphere, the deepness of the blue tinge gradually dies away; and to the aeronaut who has soared above the denser strata, or to the traveller who has ascended the Alps or the Andes, the sky appears of a deep black, while the blue rays find a ready passage through the attenuated strata of the atmosphere. It is owing to the same cause, that the diver at the bottom of the sea is surrounded with the red light which has pierced through the superincumbent fluid, and that the blue rays are reflected from the surface of the ocean. Were it not for the reflecting power of the air, and of the clouds which float in the lower regions of the atmosphere, we should be involved in total darkness by the setting of the sun, and all the objects around us would suffer a total eclipse by every cloud that passed over his disk. It is to the multiplied reflections which the light of the sun suffers in the atmosphere, that we are indebted for the light of day, when the earth is enveloped with impenetrable clouds.

From the same cause arises the sober hue of the morning and evening twilight, which increases as we recede from the equator, till it blesses with perpetual day the inhabitants of the polar regions.

The cause which we have assigned for the blue light of the sky, and which was, we believe, first given by Bouguer, though a very probable one, still required the evidence of demonstration. In examining this light, Dr. Brewster found that a great portion of it was polarized; and hence it follows, that it has suffered reflexion. M. Saussure found that the intensity of the blue colour increased with the height of the observer above the sea; and it has been observed by others, that the intensity diminishes as the quantity of aqueous vapour is increased. In order to measure this intensity, M. Saussure contrived an instrument called a *Cyanometer.** A circular band of thick paper or pasteboard is divided into 51 parts, each of

---

* From two Greek words signifying a *measure* and *blueness.*

which is painted with a different shade of blue, decreasing gradually from the deepest blue, formed by a mixture of black, to the lightest, formed by a mixture of white. This coloured zone is held in the hand of the observer, who notices the particular tint which corresponds to the colour of the sky. The number of this tint, reckoned from the greatest, is the intensity at the time of observation. Saussure, Humboldt, Depons, and other travellers, have made observations with this instrument. The following are some of their results:

General intensity in Europe .... 14°
General intensity in the Caraccas ... 18
General intensity at Cumana 24

6. *Coloured Shadows.*—The shadows of bodies placed only in one light, and at a distance from all other bodies capable of reflecting light, must necessarily be black. In a summer morning or evening, however, the shadows of bodies formed either by the light of the sun, or by that of a candle, have been observed to be *blue;* this obviously arises from the shadows being illuminated with the light of the blue sky. The colours thus produced vary in different countries, and at different seasons of the year, from a pale blue to a violet black; and when there are yellow vapours in the horizon, or yellow light reflected from the lower part of the sky, either at sunrise or sunset, the shadows have a tinge of green arising from the union of these accidental rays with the blue tint of the shadow.

If the light of the sun, or of the candle, be faint, then the shadow of the body formed by the light of the sky will be visible also, and the two shades will be the one *blue* and the other a *pale yellow*, two colours which are complementary to each other. This fact has been ascribed to the circumstance of the light of the candle, and that of the rising and setting sun, being of a yellowish tinge; but though this will increase the effect it is not the main cause of it, as one of the shadows would be yellow, even if the light of the sun and the candle had been perfectly white.

The phenomena of coloured shadows are sometimes finely seen in the interior of a room; the source of one of the colours being sometimes the blue sky, and the other the green window blinds, the painted walls, or the coloured furniture.

The best method of observing and studying this class of phenomena is to use two candles, and to hold before one of them a piece of coloured glass, taking care to remove to a greater distance the candle before which the coloured glass is not placed, in order to equalize the darkness of the two shadows. If we use a piece of green glass, one of the shadows will be *green*, and the other a fine *red;* if we use blue glass, one of the shadows will be *blue,* and the other a pale *yellow,* and so on; the one colour being always complementary to the other, as explained in page 46. The light from the candle with the green glass obviously illuminates the shadow formed by the other candle, and hence it is easy to understand why that shadow is green; but as the other shadow is illuminated only by the common light of the candle which is not red, it appears difficult to discover the origin of the red light. The explanation of this must be sought not among optical, but among physiological principles. We have already seen, when treating of accidental colours, that when a portion of the retina was strongly impressed with any one colour, such as red, that same portion tinged *green* the images of white objects that fell upon it. In like manner, when nearly the whole retina is impressed with any one colour, such as red, a portion of it not impressed with that colour will tinge white objects green,—or, to speak more generally, every excitation of the retina by one colour is accompanied by an excitation of its accidental colour, just as in Acoustics every fundamental sound is actually accompanied by its harmonic sound. Hence, when we see red we at the same time see green, but its impression is less forcible, and the tendency of this double vision of colours is to weaken the original impression, *viz.* the red; because the union of complementary colours produces whiteness. This may be proved by looking for a considerable time at a red wafer, which will appear less and less red the longer we view it; because the green which the retina is seeing at the same time, produces a whiteness which dilutes the red. This we conceive to be the true theory of accidental colours. Its application to coloured shadows is very obvious: When the eye is impressed with the green colour of the light transmitted through the green glass, it at the same time sees red, which, of course, appears only on the shadow upon which a green light falls.

7. *Converging and diverging beams.* —When the sun is descending in the west, through masses of open clouds, the divergency of his beams, rendered visible by their passage through numerous openings, forms frequently a very beautiful phenomenon. It is sometimes accompanied, however, with one of an opposite kind, *viz. the convergency of beams to a point in the eastern horizon opposite to the sun, and as far beneath the horizon as the sun is above it,* as if another sun, throwing out divergent beams, were about to rise in the east. This phenomenon is rarely seen in perfection. Dr. Smith, who observes that he *once* saw this phenomenon on Lincoln heath, describes it as 'an apparent convergence of long whitish beams towards a point diametrically opposite to the sun, and, as nearly as he could estimate, as much below the horizon as the sun was then elevated above the opposite point of it.'

On the 9th of October, 1824, we had the satisfaction of seeing this curious appearance in unusual splendour. The sun was considerably elevated, and was throwing out his diverging beams in great beauty through the interstices of the broken masses of clouds which floated in the west. The eastern portion of the horizon, where the converging lines were seen, was occupied with a black cloud, which seems necessary as a ground for rendering visible, by its contrast, such feeble radiations. The converging beams were very much fainter than the diverging ones, and their point of convergence was as far below the horizon as the sun was above it. About ten minutes after the phenomenon was first seen, the convergent lines were *black*, or very dark. This arose from the real beams having become broad, and of unequal intensity, so that the eye took up, as it were, the spaces between the beams more readily than the beams themselves.*

In order to explain this phenomenon, which is a case of perspective, let us suppose a line to join the eye of the observer and the sun. Let beams issue from the sun in all possible directions, and let us suppose that planes pass through these beams, and through the line joining the eye of the observer and the sun, which will be their common intersection, like the axis of an orange, or the axis of the earth, through which there pass all the septa of the former, and all the planes passing through the meridians of the latter. An eye, therefore, situated in this line, or common intersection of all the planes, will, when looking at a concave sky, apparently spherical, see them diverging from the sun on one side, and converging towards the opposite point, just as an eye in the axis of a large globe would perceive all the planes passing through the meridians diverging on one side, and converging on another.*

CHAPTER XIX.—*Partial Reflexion of Light—Absorption of Light—Light reflected at different angles from Water — Glass — Metals — White opaque Bodies—from both surfaces of Glass—from a number of Glass Plates.*

FROM the phenomena described in the preceding chapters, the reader must have observed, that when light falls upon the most transparent bodies, such as water, glass, &c. a certain portion of it is reflected from their surfaces. When we measure the quantity *reflected* and the quantity *transmitted,* we invariably find that the sum of these quantities is less than the light which falls upon the body. Hence it follows, and the fact is a very important one to remember, that *light is always lost in passing through the most transparent bodies.* This light is lost in two ways: a portion of it is absorbed or stopped by the body and forms heat, and another portion is scattered in all directions by irregular reflexion. When light falls on metallic bodies, such as polished silver, or speculum metal, about one half of it is reflected, and the other half lost. The part lost consists, as in the former case, of two portions; one of which, and by far the largest, being absorbed, and the other scattered by irregular reflexion.

No complete set of experiments has yet been made from which the laws of

---

* This disposition of the eye is a very curious one, and has, we believe, never been observed. When we look steadily at a carpet having figures of one colour, green for example, upon a ground of another colour, suppose red, we shall, sometimes, see the whole of the green pattern, as if the red one were obliterated; and, at other times, we shall see the whole of the red pattern, as if the green one were obliterated. The former effect takes place when the eye is steadily fixed on the green part, and the latter, when it is steadily fixed on the red portion. It is easy to conceive that when the retina is in a state of irritation or excitation with red light, it will more easily take up, as it were, the vision of a red object than of any other.

† See Smith's *Optics*, vol. ii. Remarks. p. 57, 58; and *Edinburgh Journal of Science*, No. iii. p. 135.

these phenomena can be determined. The principal facts which have been ascertained, we owe to the ingenuity of M. Bouguer and M. Lambert, and these we shall now lay before the reader :—

Number of Rays reflected out of 1000.

Angles of Incidence.	Water.	Glass.	Quick-silver.	Silver.	Plaster.	Dutch Paper.
89½°	721	..	721	..	..	..
89	692	..	..	..	..	..
88½	669	..	..	..	..	..
88	639	..	..	..	..	..
87½	614	584	..	..	..	..
85	501	543	..	..	..	..
82½	409	474	..	..	..	..
80	333	412	..	..	..	..
77½	271	356	..	..	..	..
75	211	299	..	209	194	203
72½	178	222	..	..	..	..
70	145	210	..	..	..	..
65	97	156	..	..	..	..
60	65	112	..	319	352	332
50	34	57	..	..	..	..
45		41	..	455	529	507
40	22	34	704	..	..	..
30	19	27	..	640	640	..
20	18	25	..	..	..	..
15	18	25	..	802	762	971
10	18	25	..	..	..	..
0	18	25	666	1000	1000	1000

From these results we may draw the following conclusions :—

1. That in *fluids, transparent solids* and *metals*, the quantity of light reflected increases with the angle of incidence reckoned from the perpendicular; whereas in white opaque bodies the quantity of light reflected decreases with the angle of incidence.

2. That at great angles of incidence water reflects more light than even both the surfaces of plate glass.

The following very accurate results were obtained by M. Lambert, who measured the quantity of light reflected both at the first and the second surfaces:

Angles of Incidence.	No. of Rays out of 1000 reflected at *first* surface.	No. of Rays out of 1000 reflected at *second* surface.
70°	158	320
60	77	165
50	47	105
40	34	71
30	26	59
20	22	50
10	20	45
0	20	45

Lambert does not seem to have observed the law of these results. Upon carefully comparing them, we have found that the quantity of light reflected at either surface is inversely as the square of the cosine of the angles of incidence. It is a most curious fact which Lambert has established, that the light reflected at the second surface of a plate of glass is at all angles of incidence more than double of the quantity reflected by the first surface.

M. Lambert likewise obtained the following results for different numbers of very transparent plates of glass at a perpendicular incidence.

No. of Plates of Glass.	No. of Rays reflected out of 1000.	Light transmitted.
1	62	938
2	117	883
3	165	835
4	209	791
5	248	752
6	284	715
7	316	684
8	345	654

When the glass which he used was less transparent, he obtained the following results, the quantity of light lost being given in the last column.

No. of Glass Plates.	No. of Rays reflected out of 1000.	No. of Rays transmitted out of 1000.	No. of Rays lost out of 1000.
1	52	811	137
2	86	660	255
3	108	537	355
4	123	438	449
8	147	195	659
16	152	39	809
32	153	2	846

From the preceding facts it is obvious, that in all the various operations by which we distribute or concentrate light for economical purposes, a considerable portion of it is lost. This portion is much greater in metals than in glass; and hence, when other circumstances are the same, *lenses* are preferable to *mirrors* or *specula*, either for concentrating the solar rays for the purposes of combustion, or for producing in light-houses an intensely brilliant column of light capable of reaching to a great distance, and penetrating the fogs of the ocean. For the same reason a *Refracting* telescope gives far more light than a *Reflecting* one of the same aperture; and if we could manufacture glass as easily as we can cast metallic specula, the Reflecting telescope would disappear from among optical instruments in actual use.

ON THE
DOUBLE REFRACTION AND POLARISATION
OF
LIGHT.

PART I.

ON THE DOUBLE REFRACTION OF LIGHT.

INTRODUCTION.

Simple Refraction—Double Refraction in Iceland Spar described—Ordinary and Extraordinary Ray—Double Refraction possessed by various Mineral, Animal, and Vegetable Bodies.

In explaining the various optical phenomena which arise from the transmission of light through transparent bodies, it is always supposed that these bodies are perfectly homogeneous, and have the same temperature and density throughout their mass.

In such substances as pure *water*, and well annealed *glass*, the minutest point, or the finest line, will appear *single* when seen in any direction or through any thickness, provided that the mass is bounded by parallel faces. If the *water* or the *glass* have a prismatic shape, a luminous point or a luminous line will still appear single through the prism, if the light, which issues from the point or the line, is homogeneous or simple. But if the light is white, there will be a *red, orange, yellow, green, blue, indigo,* and *violet* image. In like manner, if the mass of water or glass, when bounded by parallel surfaces, is heated unequally so as to produce strata of different density, and consequently of different refractive power, then, if the luminous point or line is seen in the direction of the strata, a double, and sometimes a triple image of it will appear, as in the phenomena of the mirage or unequal refraction.

In all these cases, however, whether the object is seen double, treble, or quadruple, the phenomena are those of *single* or *simple refraction*, because they are all produced by the same attractive force, varying only in the degree of its intensity; and are all regulated by the simple *law of the sines* discovered by Snellius. The existence of more than one image is not a proof of the existence of more than one force, unless the substance is perfectly homogeneous, of equal density throughout, and bounded by parallel faces.

A substance called *Iceland spar, calcareous spar*, or *carbonate of lime*, has been long known to mineralogists. It is found in masses often larger than one's head. It is composed of 56 parts of *lime*, and 44 of *carbonic acid*, and has a specific gravity of 2.714. It is perfectly transparent and colourless, and is susceptible of taking a fine polish. When broken, it occurs in pieces of the form shown in *fig.* 1., which is a solid

Fig. 1.

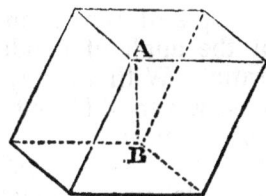

called a *rhomb* or *rhomboid*, bounded by parallel faces which are inclined to each other, at an angle of 105° 5'. These natural faces are often even and perfectly polished; and as the mineral cleaves or splits parallel to any of its six faces, it is easy to replace an imperfect face by a new one.

Having obtained a rhomb of Iceland spar with smooth faces, place it, as shown in *fig.* 2, above a sharp line, and look through it with the eye about R. The line will appear doubled like *m n, p q*. In like manner a black dot, or a luminous point or aperture will appear double, as *e, o*. If we cause a ray or pencil of light R *r* to fall upon the surface of the rhomb, it will be separated into two rays or pencils *r o, r e*, each of which will emerge from the rhomb at *o* and *e* in the directions *o o', e e'* parallel to R *r*. The ray R *r* has therefore suffered

B

double refraction in passing through the rhomb, and as the very same phenomena will take place by making the ray R*r* fall at the same incidence and in the same direction relative to the summit A upon any point of any of the faces, it is manifest that the double refraction cannot arise from any difference of density in different parts of the rhomb.

Fig. 2.

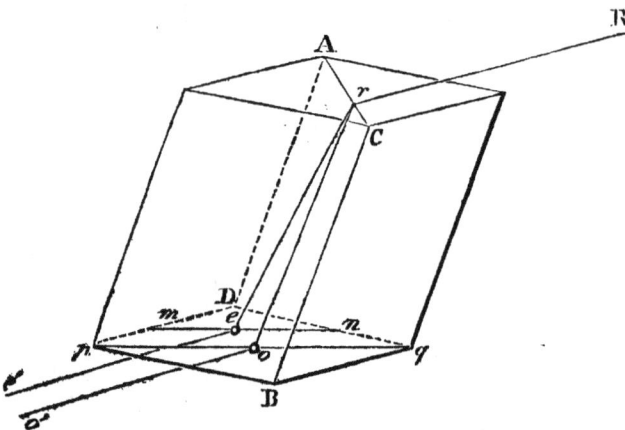

In order to prove this, however, by direct experiment let the angles of refraction of the ray *r o, r e* be measured corresponding to the different angles of incidence of R *r*, beginning at a perpendicular incidence or 0°. It will then be found that at 0° the ray *r o* has suffered no refraction, and that at 10°—20°—30°, &c. its refraction is such as it should be by the ordinary law of the sines; the sine of the angle of refraction being to the sine of the angle of incidence in a constant ratio. With the ray *r e*, however, the case is very different; at 0° its angle of refraction, in place of being 0°, is 6° 12'; and at 10°—20°—30°, &c. it is such as not to follow the constant ratio of the sines. Hence it follows that Iceland spar has a double refraction, separating a pencil of light into two, one of which is refracted according to the *ordinary law*, and the other according to a new or *extraordinary law*.

Def. 1. The ray *r o* is therefore called the *ordinary ray*, and *r e* the *extraordinary ray*.

The property of double refraction is possessed by a very great number of minerals and artificial salts. It is found also in various animal and vegetable bodies, and it may be communicated either transiently or permanently to substances in which it does not naturally reside.

Def. 2. In all doubly refracting substances there are *one* or *more lines*, or *one* or *more planes*, along which there is no double refraction, or along which no doubly refracting force exists.

Def. 3. Those substances in which there is only *one* such line or plane, are called crystals or bodies with *one axis*, or *one plane of axes of double refraction*, and those which have *two, three, four*, &c. such lines are called crystals or bodies with *two, three, four*, &c. *axes*, or *planes of axes, of double refraction*.

Def. 4. When the doubly refracting force does not exist in any of these axes or planes of axes, the axis is called a *real axis* of double refraction; but when the disappearance of double refraction arises from the existence of two opposite and equal doubly refracting forces which destroy one another, the axis or plane of axes are called a *resultant axis* or plane of double refraction, or an *axis or plane of compensation*.

Def. 5. If the ray which suffers the extraordinary refraction is refracted *towards* the axis or plane of axes of a doubly refracting body, the axis is called a *positive axis of double refraction*; and if it is refracted from the axis, it is called a *negative axis of double refraction*.

Chapter I.

Crystals with one Axis of Double Refraction — List of such Crystals — Law of Double Refraction in those with a Negative Axis—Law of it in those with a Positive Axis — Crystals with two Axes of Double Refraction — Crystals with one Axis for one Coloured Light, and two for another Coloured Light — Crystals with many Planes of Double Refraction—Circular Double Refraction—

DOUBLE REFRACTION.

On the Double Refraction produced by Heat and Pressure.

1.—*Crystals with one Axis of Double Refraction.*

From the examination of a great number of crystallised bodies, Dr. Brewster found that all those bodies which crystallised in the form of the *rhomboid*, the *regular hexahedral prism*, the *octohedron with a square base*, and the *right prism with a square base*, have one axis of double refraction, and he has arranged them as follows:—The sign − indicating that the axis is *negative*, and the sign + that it is *positive*.

Table of Crystallised Bodies having one Axis of Double Refraction.

i.—*Rhomb with an Obtuse Summit.*
Fig. 3.

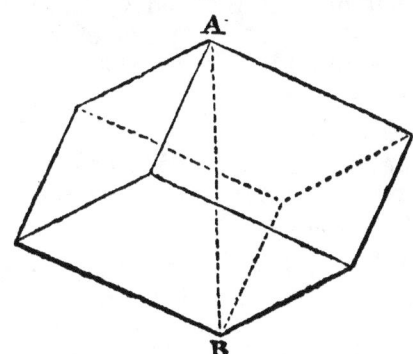

- − Carbonate of Lime (*Iceland Spar.*)
- − Carbonate of Lime and Iron.
- − Carbonate of Lime and Magnesia.
- − Carbonate of Zinc.
- − Nitrate of Soda.
- − Phosphate of Lead.
- − Phosphato-Arseniate of Lead.
- − Levyne.
- − Tourmaline.
- − Rubellite.
- − Ruby Silver.
- − Alum-stone.
- + Dioptase.
- + Quartz.

ii.—*Rhomb with Acute Summit.*

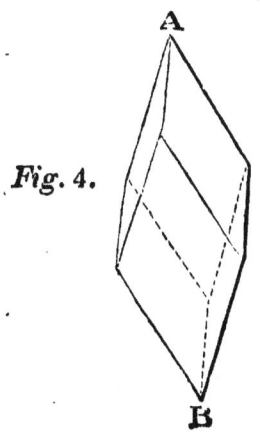

Fig. 4.

- − Corundum.
- − Sapphire.
- − Ruby.
- − Cinnabar.
- − Arseniate of Copper.

iii.—*Regular Hexagonal Prism.*
Fig. 5.

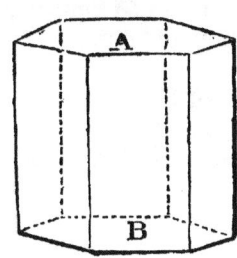

- − Emerald.
- − Beryl.
- − Phosphate of Lime.
- − Nepheline.
- − Arseniate of Lead.
- + Hydrate of Magnesia.

iv.—*Octohedron with a Square Base.*
Fig. 6.

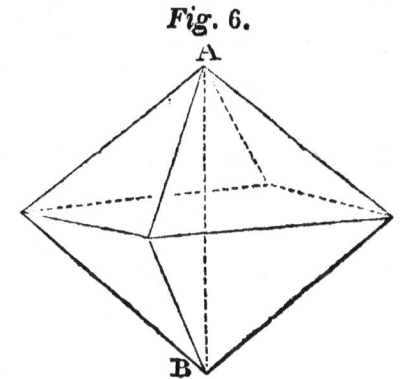

- + Zircon.
- + Oxide of Tin.
- + Tungstate of Lime.
- − Mellite.
- − Molybdate of Lead.
- − Octohedrite.
- − Prussiate of Potash.

v.—*Right Prism with a Square Base.*
Fig. 7.

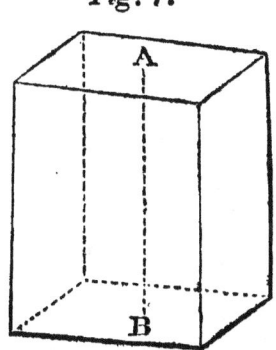

- + Titanite.
- − Idocrase.
- − Wernerite.
- − Paranthine.
- − Meionite.
- − Subphosphate of Potash.
- − Edingtonite.
- + Apophyllite of Uton.
- + Superacetate of Copper and Lime.
- − Phosphate of Ammonia and Magnesia.
- − Hydrate of Strontites.
- − Arseniate of Potash.
- − Sulphate of Nickel of Copper.
- − Somervillite.
- + Oxahverite.

In all these crystals the axis of double refraction coincides with the line A B, which is the axis of the geometrical solid.

The following crystals, whose primitive form has not been perfectly determined, have also *one* axis of double refraction.

Position of the Axes.

- − Mica from Kariat . . . Perpendicular to the Laminæ.
- − Mica with Amianthus . Perpendicular to the Laminæ.
- − Muriate of Lime . . Axis of Hexagonal Prism.
- − Muriate of Strontian . Axis of Hexagonal Prism.
- − Hyposulphate of Lime Axis of Hexagonal Table.
- + Boracite . . Axis of Rhomb of 90°.
- + Apophyllite surcomposée . Perpendicular to the Plate.
- + Sulph. of Pot. and Iron Axis of Hexagonal Prism.
- + Ice . . . . Axis of Hexagonal Prism or Rhomb.
- − Cyanuret of Mercury . . . Axis of Square Prism.

Having thus given a list of those regular crystals which have one axis of double refraction, we shall now proceed to describe the phenomena which they exhibit, and to explain the law by which the phenomena are regulated. In doing this, we shall begin with crystals which have one negative axis, such as Iceland spar, a mineral which is peculiarly adapted for investigating the phenomena of double refraction.

2.—On the Law of Double Refraction in Crystals with one Negative Axis.

If we grind down and polish the two opposite summits A, B, *fig.* 1, of a rhomb of Iceland spar, so that the faces are perpendicular to the axis A B, we shall find that a ray of light transmitted parallel to A B is not divided into two pencils. This will be the case whether the ray is incident perpendicularly upon the two faces, or obliquely upon any face not perpendicular to A B, provided that in the latter case the refracted ray is parallel to A B. If, in this latter case, we measure the index of refraction of the Iceland spar, we shall find it as follows:—

Index of refraction along the axis. { 1.6543 ordinary ray. 1.6543 extraor. ray.

If we measure the indices of refraction in a direction perpendicular to each of the six faces of the rhomb (which are all inclined 44° 36′ 34″ to the axis) so that the plane of incidence passes through A B, we shall find them as follows:—

Indices of refraction perpendicular to the faces of the rhomb. { 1.6543 ordinary ray. 1.5720 extraor. ray.

If we now grind a face parallel to A B, and measure the indices of refraction in a plane of incidence perpendicular to A B, we shall find them to be the same all round the axis, and to be as follows:—

Indices of refraction perpendicular to the axis. { 1.6543 ordinary ray. 1.4833 extraor. ray.

From these results it follows that the double refraction, or the force which produces it, disappears, or is nothing when the ray acted upon passes along the axis of the crystal; that it increases with the angle which the ray forms with the axis; and is a *maximum* when the incident ray is perpendicular to the axis.

In order to discover the precise law by which the doubly refracting force increases as the inclination of the incident ray with the axis increases, Huygens measured the double refraction at different angles, and found that the reciprocal of the index of refraction of the extraordinary ray was measured by the radius of an ellipse whose lesser axis is to its greater as $\frac{1}{1.6543}$ is to $\frac{1}{1.4833}$ the reciprocals of the greatest, and the least index of extraordinary refraction.

In order to make this plain, let us suppose that the rhomb of calcareous spar is turned in a lathe to an exact sphere A B C D, *fig.* 8, whose centre is

Fig. 8.

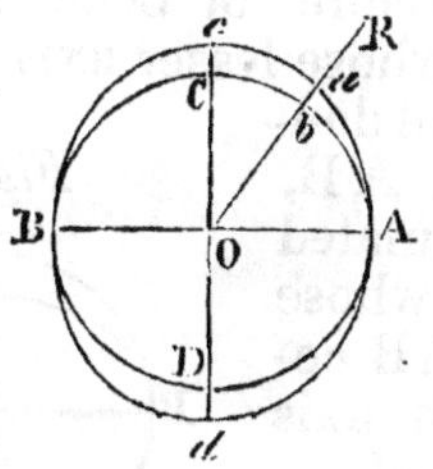

O, and whose axis A B corresponds with the axis of the rhomb A B, *fig.* 3. Through O draw cOd at right angles to the axis A B, and set off O c, O d, so that O A or O B is to O c or O d as $\frac{1}{1.6543}$ is to $\frac{1}{1.4833}$, or as .6045 is to .6742, and through the points A, B, c, d draw the ellipse A c B d. Then, if R ab is a ray of light incident on the rhomb at b, at an inclination to A B of R O A or 44° 36′ 34″, the radius O a of the ellipse will be found either by projection or calculation to be .6361 or $\frac{1}{1.5720}$. Hence, the index of refraction for the extraordinary ray formed by R b will be 1.572.

As the reciprocal of this index increases from A to C, it will itself diminish, and consequently, though the successive increments ab, C c of its reciprocal increase also, the successive decrements of the index (viz. C c = .1710 and ab = .0823) will be *negative*, or to be subtracted from the maximum index 1.654.

If we now call m' the index of extraordinary refraction, (or the velocity of the extraordinary ray,) and φ the inclination of that ray to the axis, then it may be shown that

$$m'^2 = 1.6543^2 + 0.536510 \sin^2 \varphi$$

that is, the square of the index of extraordinary refraction at any inclination φ is equal to the square of the greatest index of extraordinary refraction (or the index of ordinary refraction) *diminished* by a quantity varying with the inclination to the axis.

Hence, we see the propriety of calling such crystals *negative*, because the term which expresses the influence of the doubly refracting force is always *negative*.

The above formula becomes—

$$m' = \sqrt{2.736693 - 0.53610 \sin^2 \varphi}.$$

Having thus explained the law which regulates the variation of the variable index of extraordinary refraction, we shall proceed to illustrate some of the other properties of double refraction as they appear in calcareous spar.

Let A C B D, *fig.* 9, be a section of the rhomb passing through the axis A B (see *fig.* 3). This and every section passing

Fig. 9.

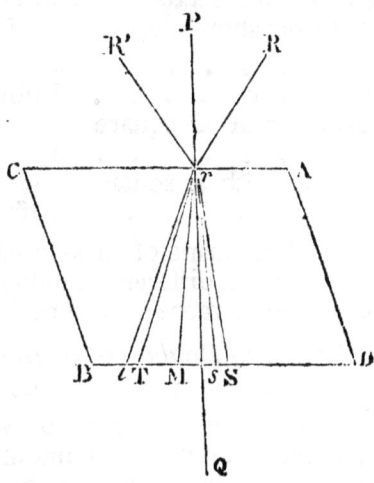

through the axis is called *a principal section* of the crystal. Draw PQ perpendicular to the surface AC at r. A ray, P r, incident perpendicularly at r, will be divided into two rays, the ordinary one r Q, which goes straight on, and the extraordinary ray r M. Then, if two rays R r, R′ r, fall on the same point r at equal inclinations to P r, or at equal angles of incidence, but in the plane of the section A C B D, the extraordinary rays of each, viz. r T, r S, will be so refracted that T M = S M, and these refracted rays, as well as the ordinary ones rt, rs, will be all in the same plane.

The force which produces the extraordinary refraction exerts itself as if it emanated or proceeded from the axis A B of the rhomb; for when the plane of incidence passes through the axis, the extraordinary ray is always in the same plane. But if the plane of incidence is inclined at any angle to the axis, the extraordinary ray is pushed out of that plane by the force proceeding, as it were, from the axis; and hence it is tedious, either by a graphic projection or by calculation to determine, in that case, the position of the extraordinary ray.

When the plane of incidence is perpendicular to the axis, or is in what may be called the *equator of double refraction*, where the force is a maximum, the extraordinary ray is always in the plane of incidence, and its position may be determined at all angles of incidence in this plane, in the same manner as if it were acted upon with an ordinary force whose index of refraction is 1·6543.

All these observations are equally applicable to all the other crystals with one negative axis.

The following are the number of principal sections, or planes of refraction, passing through the axis in the different primitive forms shown in *figs*. 3 to 7.

Rhomb 6
Hexagonal prism . . . . Infinite.
Octohedron, with a square base 4
Right prism, with a square base . . . . Infinite.

The secondary forms of these crystals have, of course, a different number of such planes, some more and some less.

3.—*On the Law of Double Refraction in Crystals with one positive axis.*

The mineral called *quartz*, or *rock crystal*, crystallizes most commonly in six-sided prisms, terminated with six-sided pyramids, as shown in *fig*. 10. If we grind down and polish the summits A and B, we shall find that there is no separation of the images, or no double refraction when the refracted ray passes along the axis AB. Hence AB is the axis of double refraction.

Fig. 10.

If in this case we measure the index of refraction, we shall find

Index of refraction at any axis $\begin{cases} 1\cdot5484 \text{ ordinary.} \\ 1\cdot5484 \text{ extraordinary.} \end{cases}$

If we measure next the indices of refraction in a direction perpendicular to any of the faces E of the pyramid (which are all inclined 38° 20′ to the axis), so that the plane of incidence passes through AB, we shall find them as follows:—

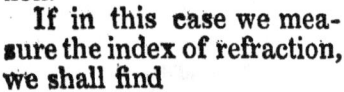

Index of refraction perpendicular to the faces of the pyramid . . . $\begin{cases} 1\cdot5484 \text{ ordinary ray.} \\ 1\cdot5544 \text{ extraord. ray.} \end{cases}$

In like manner, we shall find that the indices of refraction through CD, *fig*. 11, and in a plane perpendicular to the axis AB, are

Indices of refraction perpendicular to the faces of the prism $\begin{cases} 1\cdot5484 \text{ ordinary.} \\ 1\cdot5582 \text{ extraordin.} \end{cases}$

From these results it appears that the index of extraordinary refraction of quartz increases from the axis to the equator, whereas in Iceland spar it diminishes. In place, therefore, of being regulated by an ellipse whose lesser axis coincides with the axis of double refraction, AB, *fig*. 8, it is regulated by an ellipse whose greater axis AB coincides with the axis of double refraction, as shown in *fig*. 11.

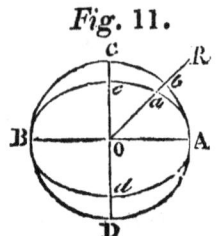

Fig. 11.

In this case OA will be to O*c* as $\frac{1}{1\cdot5484}$ to $\frac{1}{1\cdot5582}$, or as ·6458 is to ·6418.

If we, therefore, call m' the index of extraordinary refraction (or the velocity of the extraordinary ray,) and φ the inclination of that ray to the axis, it may be shown that

$$m'^2 = 1\cdot5484^2 + \cdot030261 \sin.^2 \varphi ;$$

that is, the square of the index of the extraordinary ray m' at any inclination φ is equal to the square of the index of ordinary refraction *increased* by a quantity varying with the inclination to the axis.

Hence, we see the propriety of calling such crystals *positive*, because the term which expresses the influence of the doubly refracting force is always *positive*. The above expression becomes

$$m' = \sqrt{2\cdot3975 + \cdot030261 \sin.^2 \varphi}.$$

The existence of a *positive* axis of double refraction in quartz was discovered by M. Biot.

4.—*On Crystals with two Axes of Double Refraction.*

The great body of crystals, whether they are mineral or chemical substances, have two axes of double refraction. This discovery was made by Dr. Brewster, who traced the double image through the crystals, and found the double refraction to diminish as the ray approached two lines or axes, and at last to disappear wholly when the ray passed along either of these two axes. He found also that these lines were not coincident with any prominent lines in the crystalline form, and that they formed various angles with each other from the smallest angle in *glauberite* up to 90° in *sulphate of iron*.

After examining more than one hundred of these crystals, Dr. Brewster also found that all crystals which belong to the prismatic system of Mohs, or whose primitive forms are the *right prism* with its base a rectangle, a rhomb, or an oblique parallelogram; the *oblique prism*, with its base a rectangle, a rhomb, or an oblique parallelogram, or the *rectangular* and *rhomboidal octohedron*, have two axes of double refraction.

In these cases the double refraction follows a very complicated law (see Chap. VIII.); and M. Fresnel has made the important discovery that both the rays follow a law of extraordinary refraction.

5.—*On Crystals which have two Axes for the most refrangible, and one Axis for the least refrangible rays.*

This singular property was discovered by Dr. Brewster in *Glauberite*, in which he found two resultant axes inclined to one another at an angle of 5° when red light was used, and only one negative axis when violet light was used. In this case, however, it may be shown, by principles which will afterwards be explained, that glauberite has more than one real axis even for the violet rays*.

6.—*On Crystals with many Planes of double Refraction.*

In all the crystals hitherto mentioned the double refraction is related solely to one or more lines or axes; but Dr. Brewster has found that *analcime* has its double refraction related to various planes within the crystal, in all of which the double refraction disappears. This remarkable structure will be more particularly described in a subsequent part of the treatise.

7.—*On Crystals with circular double Refraction.*

M. Fresnel has discovered that a ray of light passing along the axis of quartz where its ordinary double refraction vanishes, is divided into two rays which have remarkable properties. The law of variation of the doubly refracting force is not known, but the properties of the two rays to which it gives rise will be afterwards described.

8.—*On Bodies to which double Refraction may be communicated by Heat and Pressure.*

Bodies with one or more axes of double refraction may be formed artificially out of glass, &c. either by pressure or by the transmission of heat, or by rapid cooling. In these cases the double refraction depends on the external form of the body, and changes with a change of form. If the body is a cylinder, it may be made to have one *negative* or one *positive* axis of double refraction. If it is a cylinder whose section is an ellipse, or if it is a parallelopiped, it will have more than one axis; and if it is a sphere it will have an infinite number of axes of double refraction. In all these cases the double refraction may be accurately calculated, as will be shown in a subsequent part of this treatise.

PART II.

ON THE POLARISATION OF LIGHT.

"The Phenomena of the Polarisation of Light," to use the language of one of our most eminent mathematicians and natural philosophers†, "are so singular and various, that to one who has only studied the subject of physical optics under its ordinary relations, it is like entering into a new world, so splendid as to render it one of the most delightful branches of experimental inquiry; and so fertile in the views it lays open of the constitution of natural bodies, and the minuter mechanism of the universe, as to place it in the very first rank of the physico-mathematical sciences."

When light emitted from the sun, or from any self-luminous body, is reflected from the *surface*, or *transmitted* through the *substance* of any homogeneous uncrystallised body, the property of the reflected or transmitted light continues the same when we turn round the body, so that the light falls on the first surface always at the same angle; that is, the different sides of the rays exhibit no different properties in relation to the plane of its incidence. Such light is called *common light*.

A kind of light, however, has been discovered which, when *reflected* from the *surface*, or *transmitted* through the *substance* of homogeneous uncrystallised bodies, exhibits different properties when the body is turned round in the manner above described. Hence it follows that different *sides* of the rays of such light must have different properties in relation to the plane of their

---
* *Edinburgh Journal of Science*, No. XIX.
† Mr. Herschel, in his Treatise on Light.

incidence, and hence this light is called *polarised light*, because its rays have *poles*, or sides with different properties.

Polarised light is never emitted from any self-luminous body, or from any artificial flame produced by combustion. Whenever it is obtained, it must have previously existed in the state of common light, from which it may be procured in three ways:

1. By *reflexion* from the surfaces of transparent and opaque bodies.

2. By *transmission* through a number of plates or planes of uncrystallised bodies.

3. By transmission through bodies regularly crystallised, and possessing the property of double refraction.

CHAPTER II.—*Polarisation of Light by Reflexion—Discoveries of Malus—Dr. Brewster's Law of the Tangents—Table of the polarising Angles of bodies—Polarisation of Light at the second surfaces of bodies—Polarisation of Light at the separating surfaces of two media—By successive Reflexions—State of partially polarised light—The polarising angle used to measure refractive powers.*

In order to explain the difference between *common* and *polarised* light, let A, *fig.* 12, be a plate of glass placed at the end of the tube M N, so that a ray of light R A, incident at A, may be reflected along the axis of the tube M N.

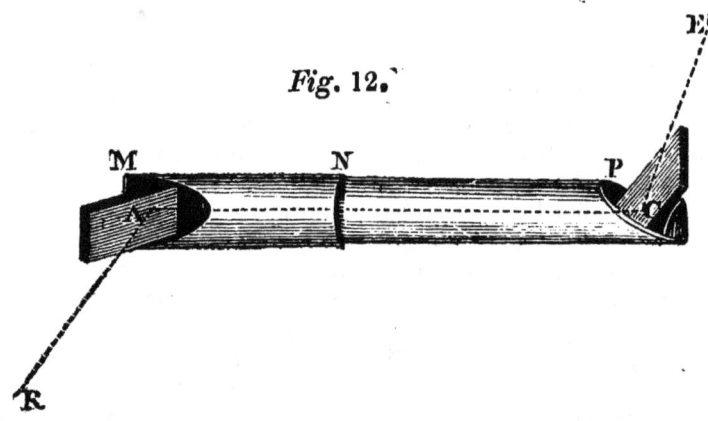

Fig. 12.

At the end of another smaller tube N P, which can turn round within MN, place a similar plate of glass, capable of reflecting a ray A C to the eye at E.

Let a ray of light R A fall upon the vertical plate of glass A at an angle of incidence of 56°, so as to be reflected in the direction A C; and let this reflected ray A C fall at the same angle of incidence of 56° upon a plate of glass C, and be reflected from it to E. Then in the position shown in the figure, where the *first* reflexion is made in a *horizontal* plane RAC, and the *second* in a *vertical* plane ACF, the ray C E will be so weak as to be scarcely visible, the plate of glass C E having almost no power to reflect the light A C. If we now turn round the tube N P within N M, without shifting the tube M N, and reflector A, the ray C E will become stronger and stronger till it has been turned round 90°, or so that the plane of reflexion A C E is horizontal like R A C. In this position the light in the beam C E is the greatest possible. If we continue to turn the tube, C E will become fainter and fainter, till after being turned round 90° more, when the plane of reflexion ACE is again vertical, the ray CE will almost cease to be visible. After a farther motion of 90°, the ray C E will recover its strength; and by 90° more, which brings the plate C back into its first position, as shown in the figure, the ray C E will cease to be visible.

From this experiment it clearly follows, that when the *upper* or the *under* side of the ray A C is towards or nearest the reflecting plate C, the plate is incapable of reflecting it, whereas when the *right* or *left side* of the ray is towards or nearest the reflecting plate, the plate reflects it as it would do common light; and at intermediate positions intermediate degrees of light are reflected. The ray A C has, therefore, properties different from common light; and as the common light R A, from which it has been obtained, has suffered no other change but that of reflexion, we are entitled to conclude that *light becomes polarised by reflexion at an angle of 56° from glass*. The simple test, therefore, of polarised light is, that it refuses to be reflected by the surface of a transparent body when it is incident at an angle of about 56°, and in two positions at right angles to one another, which will be discovered by turning the reflecting surface round the polarised ray.

This beautiful property of light, in virtue of which it is polarised by reflexion, and refuses to be again reflected under the circumstances above described, was discovered, in 1810, by M. Malus, a French philosopher of distinguished eminence.

In continuing his researches, Malus found that *black marble, ebony*, and other opaque bodies, polarised the light by reflexion like transparent ones; and that when the light RA was incident on A at an angle *below* or *above* 55°, only a part of the reflected ray was polarised; and that the light which fell upon the second surface of the glass plate was polarised at the same time with that which fell upon the first surface. He found the angle of incidence upon water, at which it polarised the light most completely, to be 52° 45', and the angle for glass to be 55°; and he concluded that the property by which bodies polarised light was independent of the other modes of action which they exert upon light.

The experiment represented in *fig.* 12 is susceptible, as Dr. Brewster has shown, of a singular and pleasing variation. If, in the position shown in the figure, when the ray AC is not reflected, and the body from which it proceeds therefore not seen to an eye at E, we breathe gently upon the glass E, the ray CE will be, as it were, revived, and the candle or body from which RA proceeds will become instantly visible. The reason of this is, that a thin film of water is deposited upon the glass by breathing; and as water polarises light at an angle of 52° 45', the glass C should have been inclined at an angle of 52° 45' to AC, in order to be incapable of reflecting the polarised ray; but as it is inclined at an angle of 56°, it has the power of reflecting a portion of AC.

If we now place the glass C at an angle of 52° 45' to AC, then it will reflect a portion of the polarised ray to the eye at E; but if we breathe upon the glass C, the reflected light will disappear, because the reflecting surface is now water, and is placed at an angle of 52° 45', the polarising angle for water. If we, therefore, place beside each other two sets of reflectors, arranged as above described, we may, by breathing upon two adjacent plates of glass, exhibit the paradoxical phenomenon of recovering and extinguishing a luminous image by the same breath.

While repeating the experiments of Malus, Dr. Brewster measured the polarising angles of a great number of transparent bodies, and found, from a careful comparison of them, that they led to the following simple law:—

The index of refraction for any transparent body is the tangent of its angle of polarisation.

The following are the observations by which this law is confirmed.

	Observed Polarising angle.	Calculated Polarising angle.
Air	45° or 47°	45° 0' 32"
Water	53° 14'*	53° 11'
Fluor spar	54 50	55 9
Obsidian	56 3	56 6
Sulphate of lime	56 28†	56 45
Crown glass	56 12	56 45
Rock crystal	57 22	56 58
Sulphate of barytes	57 47 ⎫ 58 0 ⎬ 58 29 ⎭	58 33
Topaz	58 40 ⎫ 59 0 ⎭	58 34
Mother of pearl	58 47	58 50
Iceland spar ‡	58 51	58 51
Spinelle ruby	60 16	60 25
Zircon	63 8	63 0
Glass of antimony	64 45	64 30
Sulphur	64 10	63 45
Diamond	68 2 ⎫ 67 13 ⎬ 67 0 ⎭	68 1
Chromate of lead	67 48	68 3

If the original beam of light R A has considerable intensity, it will be observed that the reflected pencil C E does not wholly vanish, and that the remaining portion is coloured. This effect is finely seen when we use *oil of cassia*, which has a great dispersive power, or *diamond* or *chromate of lead*. With *glass* it is of a *purple* colour, and with oil of cassia it is a fine *blue*; these colours varying according as the angle of reflexion is above or below the polarising angle. This unpolarised light Dr. Brewster ascribed to the circumstance, that as the different rays had in every substance different indices of refraction, they would have also by the general law dif-

---

* This is a mean of four observations by M. Malus, M. Arago, M. Biot, and Dr. Brewster.
† Mean of six observations.
‡ This and other crystals with powerful double refraction give different polarising angles in different azimuths.

ferent angles of polarisation, and upon making the experiment with homogeneous light he found that the unpolarised portion disappeared. When the blue light, therefore, is polarised, and disappears to an eye at E, *fig.* 11, the red light is not polarised, and consequently is partly reflected to the eye at E. In like manner, when the angle is such as to polarise the red, the blue is not polarised, and is consequently partly reflected to the eye at E. This will be obvious from the following table:—

WATER.

Indices of refraction.	Polarising angle.	Variation.
1·330 red rays —	53° 4′ ⎫	
1·336 mean rays —	53 11 ⎬	15′
1·342 violet rays —	53 19 ⎭	

PLATE GLASS.

1·515 red rays —	56 36 ⎫	
1·525 mean rays —	57 45 ⎬	19′
1·535 violet rays —	57 55 ⎭	

OIL OF CASSIA.

1·597 red rays —	57 57 ⎫	
1·641 mean rays —	58 39 ⎬	1° 24′
1·687 violet rays —	59 21 ⎭	

A number of important conclusions may be drawn from the law of the tangents now explained. Let MN, *fig.* 13, be a surface of any transparent body, and having drawn EAK perpendicular

Fig. 13.

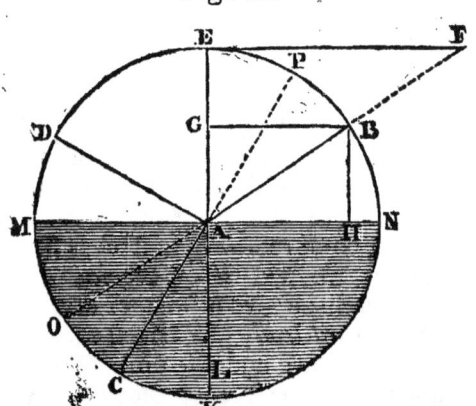

to MN, describe round A as a centre the circle MENK. Draw EF a tangent to the circle at E, and making AE =1, set the index of refraction of the body MN, 1·525 for glass, from E to F, and join FA, which will be the direction of a ray which will be polarised after reflexion from MN in the direction AD. The angle EAB = EAD = 56° 45′ is the *polarising angle* of the substance MN, or it might be found at once by finding the angle in a table of natural tangents corresponding to 1·525 in the column of tangents. If we now calculate the angle of refraction CAK corresponding to the index 1.525, and to the incident ray BA, we shall find it to be 32° 15′, or equal to the complement BAN of the angle of incidence, and, consequently, to DAM. Hence, since MAK is a right angle, DAC will be a right angle, or the reflected ray is perpendicular to the refracted ray. That these properties are general may be thus shown :—

Since tang. BAE = m, or index of refraction, we have $CL = \dfrac{BG}{m} = \dfrac{BG}{EF}$. But $HB = \dfrac{BG}{EF}$, because in the similar triangles ABH, AEF, AH or BG : HB = EF : Rad. consequently CL = HB, and BAN = CAK, that is,

The complement of the polarising angle is equal to the angle of refraction.

But since EAB + BAN = 90°, we have EAB + CAK = 90°, that is,

At the polarising angle the sum of the angles of incidence and refraction is a right angle.

And since DAM = BAK = CAK, the angle DAC = MAK, that is,

When a ray of light is polarised by reflexion, the reflected ray forms a right angle with the refracted ray.

Polarisation of Light at the second Surfaces of Bodies.

Hitherto we have considered only what takes place at the first surface of bodies; but we shall find that the same law is applicable also to the *second surfaces* of bodies.

Let MNPQ, *fig.* 14, be a plate of glass, AB a ray incident on the first

Fig. 14.

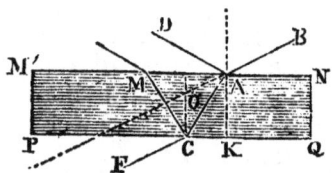

surface at the polarising angle, AD the polarised ray; and AC the refracted ray. It is found by experiment, that the ray CM reflected at the second surface is polarised. In this case, too, the angle MCF formed by the refracted and reflected ray is a right angle. For since DAC is a right angle, MN parallel to PC, and BA to CF, the angle FCP is equal to DAM, but MCP is equal to MAC : hence the whole MCF is equal to the whole DAC or to a right angle.

Polarisation of Light at the separating surfaces of two media.

When a ray of light is incident at the separating surface of bodies of different refractive powers, it is polarised at angles whose tangent is equal to the index of refraction. In this case, if m is the index for the most refracting body, and m' that of the least, such as *glass* and *water*, then the index for the separating surface will be $\frac{m}{m'}$ or $\frac{1.525}{1.336} = 1.1415$, which is the tangent of 48° 47′. This case is shown in

Fig. 15.

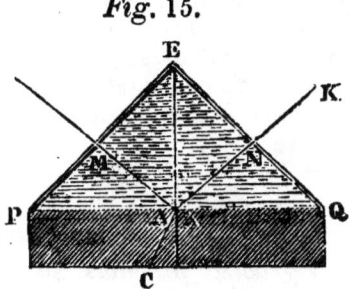

fig. 15, where P Q is the separating surface of the water M N, and the glass beneath, R A the ray incident on the separating surface, A M the ray reflected at the separating surface, and A C the ray refracted by it. In this case the ray A C may be shown to be at right angles to A M by the same reasoning already used.

From this law a curious consequence is deducible, which Dr. Brewster verified by experiment. If the water is laid in a parallel stratum upon the surface of the glass, there is no angle of incidence upon its first surface at which it can fall that will give an angle of incidence upon the separating surface P Q, capable of polarising the pencil. In short, the polarising angle would, by the law, be greater than 90°. The polarisation of the incident pencil increases from 0° of incidence up to 90°, where it is nearly complete.

Hence we see the reason of giving the water in *fig.* 15 the form of a prism.

If glass is used in which $m = 1.508$, then the angle of incidence or the stratum of water, which would permit the polarisation to be complete at the separating surface of the water and the glass, would be exactly 90°.

Polarisation of Light by successive Reflexions.

Although there is only one angle at which incident light can be completely polarised at any surface, viz. an angle whose tangent is equal to the refractive index, yet by reflecting a ray of light a sufficient number of times, it may be polarised at any angle of incidence. This property of light was established by Dr. Brewster by the following experiments made with glass, whose index of refraction was 1.525.

When the Angles of Incidence are GREATER than the maximum Polarising Angle or 56° 45′.		When the Angles of Incidence are LESS than the maximum Polarising Angle or 56° 45′.	
Number of Reflexions necessary to Polarise the Incident Light.	Angles at which the Incident Light is wholly Polarised.	Number of Reflexions necessary to Polarise the Incident Light.	Angles at which the Incident Light is wholly Polarised.
1	56° 45′	1	56° 45
2	62 30	2	50 26
3	65 33	3	46 30
4	67 33	4	43 51
5	69 1	5	41 43
6	70 9	6	40 0
7	71 5	7	38 33
8	71 51	8	37 20
9	72 30	9	36 15
10	73 4	10	35 18
27	77 40	27	26 39
64	80 41	64	20 52
100	81 57	100	18 11
125	82 32	125	16 58
1000	86 15	1000	8 46

The numbers in the preceding table were computed by a formula deduced from the observed results for eight reflexions.

In the preceding experiments the successive reflexions were made between two plates of glass placed parallel to each other; but Dr. Brewster obtained the same results by arranging the different glass plates so as to form the circumference of a polygon, each plate receiving the ray reflected by the one before it.

It is not necessary that the reflexions should be all made at the same angle. Some of them may be above and some below the polarising angle: for example, two reflexions at an angle of 62° 30', which is above the polarising angle, and 50° 26', which is below it, will also polarise the incident ray, or it may be done by several reflections, each reflection being made at a different angle. Dr. Brewster likewise determined that the same law prevailed at the separating surface of glass and water.

On the State of Light partially Polarised by Reflexion.

When a ray of light is incident on a polarising medium, at an angle greater or less than the angle of complete polarisation, a portion of it is completely polarised, and this polarised portion diminishes from the polarising angle on one side to 0° of incidence; and on the other to 90°, when it disappears. The other portion of light has been regarded by Malus, Biot, Arago, Fresnel, Dr. Young, and others, as in the state of common light, and this opinion has been deduced from speculative views and some insulated experiments, the results of which are incompatible with the preceding facts respecting the polarisation of light by successive reflexions. The character of common light is, that it cannot be polarised by one reflexion at any other angle of incidence than one, *viz.*, the maximum polarising angle, which for glass is 56° 45'. But the light under our consideration has received a physical change, which enables it to be polarised by a second or a third reflexion at a greater and a less angle than 56° 45'. For example, a pencil of light reflected from glass at an angle of 70°, contains a small quantity of polarised light, which we may call *p*, and a large quantity of other light, which we may call P. The light P will, after six reflexions, have suffered such a physical change, *that it is capable of being wholly polarised* by ONE reflexion at 70°, whereas such a reflexion is not capable of polarising one-fifth of common light. The original pencil of common light has suffered a change at every successive reflexion, which brings it, at the sixth reflexion, into the state of polarised light.

Determination of refractive Powers by the Polarising Angle.

The law of the polarisation of light above explained enables us to measure the refractive powers of bodies which are not transparent, and which could not, therefore, be submitted to the ordinary process, and of small fragments of minerals and other substances. If the substance has a plane and polished surface, we have only to place it on a goniometer, and measure the angle of maximum polarisation, and the tangent of this angle will be the index of refraction. If the substance is soft or fusible by heat, we may impress upon it a plane surface with a flat piece of glass; or if a surface cannot be obtained, as in the case of animal or vegetable membranes, we may press them with great force between two prisms of glass, and measure the polarising angle at the separating surface of the membrane and the glass. In the case of fluids, which do not assume a level surface, or which exist in too small quantities to be put into a vessel, or to be exposed to evaporation, we have only to place them on the lower surface of a prism, and measure the polarising angle at the separating surface. The tangent of this angle will give $\frac{m}{m'}$, and *m* being known for glass, we shall have $m' = \dfrac{m}{\text{tang. A}}$.

Light refracted previous to its Reflexion, and Polarised by bodies at an angle of 45°.

There is one important result of the law of the tangents which Dr. Brewster has deduced, namely, that the force which produces refraction extends beyond that which produces reflexion, and therefore that light is polarised after it has suffered refraction, and that the real angle of polarisation in every body is 45°. Let M N, *fig.* 16, be the surface

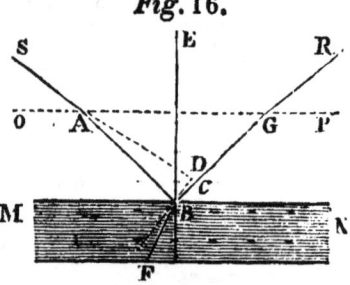

Fig. 16.

of the body, O P the termination of the attractive force which produces refraction, and let us suppose that the reflecting power is exerted at or very near the surface M N, and after the attractive force has produced one half of the whole deviation due to it. Let a ray R G be incident at G at the polarising angle; let G B be the refracted ray subsequently reflected at B to A, and refracted again at A S. Continue S A to C, and F B to D. Then, since half of the refraction is supposed to be performed before the ray reaches B, and half of it after it enters the body M N, we have B A C equal to D B C, or to half the angle of deviation. But A D B is a right angle; hence A B C is likewise a right angle, and the angles A B E, G B E, each half a right angle, or 45°. The effect of the refracting force consequently has been merely to bend the ray of light R G, so as to make it suffer reflexion at the particular angle of 45°.

Chapter III.

Polarisation of Light by ordinary Refraction—Experiments of Malus—of Dr. Brewster—Law of the Polarisation of Light transmitted through a Number of Plates—Condition of the Light transmitted through one or more Plates.

Hitherto we have paid no attention to the state of the ray A C, *fig.* 13, refracted by the transparent surface after the part separated from it by reflexion had been polarised. It might naturally have been expected that it had suffered some change in its properties; but it was not till 1811 that it was discovered that it contained a portion of polarised light*.

This property will be better understood if we make use of a bundle of glass plates, A B, C D, *fig.* 17, placed parallel to one

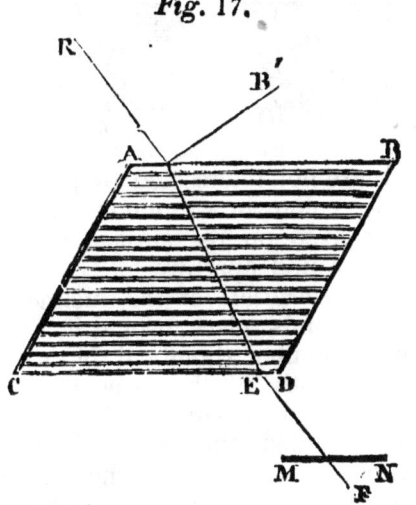

Fig. 17.

another. Let a ray R A, therefore, fall upon the first plate, A B, of this bundle, at the polarising angle, so that the reflected ray A B' will be polarised. The transmitted ray E F, emerging at E, will be found to be completely polarised; but if we receive it upon a plate of glass M N at the polarising angle of 56° 45′,

---

* This discovery was made by Malus. M. Biot made the same discovery about the same time; and in 1813 Dr. Brewster discovered the same fact by a different method, and his Paper on the subject was read to the Royal Society of London before he knew that Malus had anticipated him in the discovery.

we shall find that it will refuse to be reflected; whereas A B' does not refuse to be reflected, unless the plate M N is turned round 90° into a plane at right angles to the plane of refraction B A E. Hence we conclude—

That when a ray of light is incident at the polarising angle upon any transparent body, the whole of the reflected ray is polarised; and a nearly equal portion of the transmitted ray is polarised in a plane at right angles to the polarisation of the reflected ray*.

If we now take two bundles of glass plates A B, C D, *fig.* 18, and place them in a similar position, so that the planes

Fig. 18.

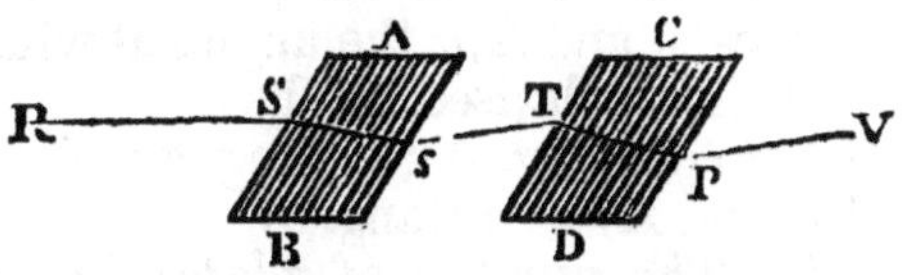

of refraction in each are parallel to one another, then a ray of light R S, incident at the polarising angle, and polarised at *s* T by the first bundle, will penetrate the second bundle as at T P; and not a single ray of it will be reflected by the plates of the second bundle C D. If we now turn C D round its axis, the transmitted light P V will gradually diminish, and more and more light will be reflected by the plates of the bundle, till, after a rotation of 90°, the ray P V will disappear, and all the light will be reflected. By continuing the rotation of C D, the pencil P V will again appear, and be a maximum at 180°, a minimum at 270°, and again a maximum at 0°, when it has returned to its first position.

In order to determine the law of the phenomenon, Dr. Brewster provided himself with 47 plates of crown glass, and, having formed them in succession into bundles of 47, 44, 41, &c. plates, he measured the angles at which the transmitted ray was wholly polarised, and obtained the following results:—

No. of Plates in each Bundle.	Calculated Angles.	Observed Angles at which they polarised the Light.
8	78° 52′	79° 11′
10	76. 24	76. 33
12	74. 2	74. 0
14	72. 15	71. 30
16	69. 40	69. 4
18	66. 43	66. 43
21	63. 39	63. 21

---

* According to an experiment by M. Arago, the one portion is *exactly* equal to the other; but though this is probable, we think the experiment requires to be repeated under a better form.

No. of Plates in each Bundle.	Calculated Angles.	Observed Angles at which they polarised the Light.
24	61° 0′	60° 8′
27	56. 58	57. 10
29	54. 50	55. 16
31	53. 16	53. 28
33	51. 0	51. 44
35	50. 23	50. 5
39	46. 50	47. 1
41	45. 49	45. 35
44	44. 0	43. 34
47	42. 0	41. 41

From a comparison of the numbers in the second column, it will be found that the cotangents of the polarising angles are to one another as the number of plates by which the polarisation is effected. Hence if N, n represent the number of plates in any two parcels, and A, a the angles at which the pencil is polarised, we have

N : n = cotang. A : cotang. a and
N (tang. A) = n (tang. a)

that is, *The number of plates in any bundle, multiplied by the tangent of the angle at which it polarises the transmitted pencil is a constant quantity.* For crown glass, this constant quantity is 41.84, when the light is that of a good wax candle, placed at the distance of about 12 feet. Hence we have

tang. A = $\frac{41.84}{n}$: that is, divide the constant quantity by any given number of plates, and the quotient will be the natural tangent of the angle at which light will be polarised by that number of plates. The constant quantity diminishes with the refractive power of the plates.

When light is transmitted through one plate of glass, or through several, at an angle of incidence less than that which polarises the whole parcel, the transmitted light will consist of two parts: one P wholly polarised, and another p which has suffered a physical change, approaching, more or less, to that of complete polarisation. According to the preceding Table, 16 are required to polarise completely a pencil of light at an angle of incidence of 69°; and 12 plates will not polarise the whole pencil at 69°, but leave a portion p unpolarised. Now, if the light p were wholly unpolarised like common light, they would require to pass through other 16 plates, at an angle of 69°; but the fact is, that they require only to pass through other 8 plates at an angle of 69°, in order to be completely polarised. They have, therefore, been half polarised by the first 8 plates, and the polarisation completed by the other 8.

Chapter IV.

Polarisation of Light by Double Refraction—Malus's Formulæ for the Intensity of the Pencils.

In treating of the double refraction of light by Iceland spar, we alluded only to the separation of the two images; but when we examine the light which forms the two pencils e e′, o o′, *fig.* 2, we find that they are both composed wholly of polarised light, the light of the one being polarised in a plane at right angles to that of the other, in the same manner as the pencils A B, E F, *fig.* 16, reflected from, and transmitted through, a bundle of glass plates.

The discovery of the opposite polarisation of the two pencils was made long ago by Huygens, and the leading phenomena accurately described in his "Treatise on Double Refraction." Take two rhombs of Iceland spar M N, *fig.* 19,

Fig. 19.

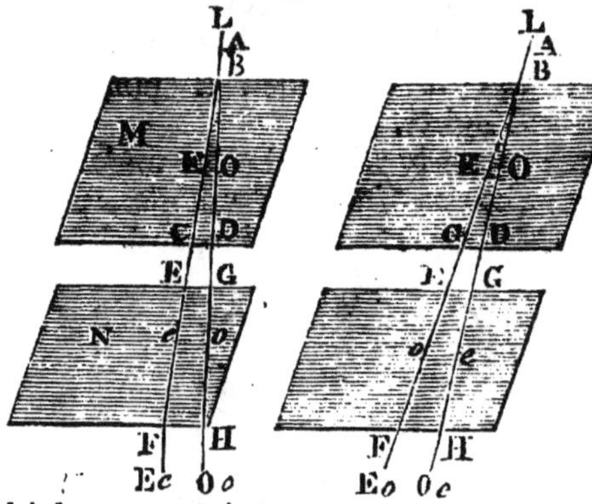

which are not intersected by planes that produce colour in a luminous body, and, having fixed on the surface of one of them a round aperture at B, not more than *one twentieth* of the thickness B D of the rhomb, place behind it, or close to it, a similar rhomboid N, similarly situated, with all the faces of the one parallel to all the faces of the other, as if they formed one piece. The single rhomb M will separate the images as shown at A, *fig.* 20; but if the eye is placed behind the two at F H, it will see two distinct round apertures, separated from one another and of equal brightness, as shown at B, *fig.* 20. If we now turn the rhomb N nearest the eye, from left to right, two faint images will appear as shown at C; continuing to turn, the four images will be all equally luminous as at D; they will then become as at E; and when the crystal N has turned round 90°, there will be only two images of equal brightness as at F. Continuing to turn, other two faint images will appear as at G; farther on

POLARISATION OF LIGHT.

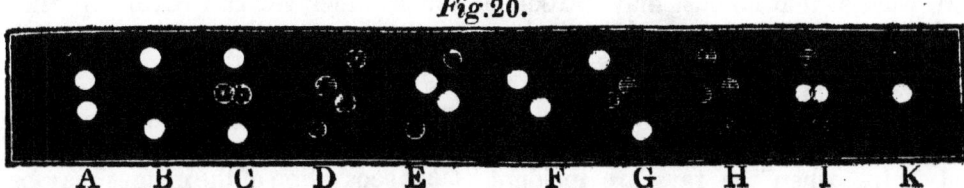

Fig. 20.

A B C D E F G H I K

the four images will be all equal, as at H; farther on at I, they will become unequal; and at 180° of revolution, they will all coalesce into one bright image, as at K.

From these results, it follows, that in the position of the two rhombs shown in *fig.* 19, which are separated a little, and where the planes of the principal sections are parallel to each other, *the pencil D C, which was regularly or ordinarily refracted by the first rhomb* M, *has not suffered double refraction by the second rhomb* N, *but has only suffered ordinary refraction* in the line G H, and emerges as a single pencil corresponding to one of those at B, *fig.* 20; while the pencil C E, which was extraordinarily refracted by the first rhomb M, is now only extraordinarily refracted by the second rhomb N, and emerges as a single pencil corresponding to the other at B, *fig.* 20. After a rotation of 90°, when the planes of the principal sections are at right angles to one another, two images are only seen as at F; but in this case *the ray* D G, *which proceeds from the ordinary refraction, suffers only the extraordinary refraction in* G H; *and the ray* C E, *which proceeds from the extraordinary refraction, suffers only the ordinary refraction in* E F. In all other positions beside these, in which the planes of the principal sections of M and N are *parallel* and *at right angles* to each other, each of the rays C E, D G, are divided into two, as shown at D, C, G, H, I, E, *fig.* 20.

The four images thus described may be expressed in the following manner:—

O the pencil refracted ordinarily by the *first* rhomb.

o the pencil refracted ordinarily by the *second* rhomb.

E the pencil refracted extraordinarily by the *first* rhomb.

e the pencil refracted extraordinarily by the *second* rhomb.

Then the pencils which actually emerge at F, H will be thus expressed:—

O o the pencil refracted *ordinarily* by both rhomboids.

O e the pencil refracted *ordinarily* by the *first*, and *extraordinarily* by the *second*.

E o the pencil refracted *extraordinarily* by the first and *ordinarily* by the *second*.

E e the pencil refracted *extraordinarily* by both rhombs.

Then, according to Malus, if we suppose L to be the intensity of the light incident at B, and a the angle formed by the principal sections, and set aside the consideration of the light lost by reflexion and absorption, we shall have

$$O o = \tfrac{1}{2} L \cos^2 a = E e$$
$$O e = \tfrac{1}{2} L \sin^2 a = E o, \text{ and}$$
$$O o + O e + E o + E e = L.$$

CHAPTER V.

Description of Apparatus for Experiments on Polarised Light.

Having thus described the various ways by which common light may be polarised, we must now describe the different kinds of apparatus which are necessary for investigating the wonderful phenomena which next demand our attention. There are two different kinds of apparatus—one for *polarising* light, and another for *analysing* polarised light.

1. *Single Reflecting Planes.*—Light may be conveniently polarised by a *single plate* of any transparent body without double refraction, such as *glass, obsidian, ebony;* or by a single surface of *water, oil, treacle,* any varnished body, or any ordinary crystallised surface. But in selecting any plate or surface, it should be one which has a low dispersive and refractive power; for it is only in this case that the reflected light will be completely polarised. *Glass of antimony, oil of cassia, flint glass* of high refractive power, *coloured* or *stained glasses,* are all unsuitable for this purpose. A plate of thin well-annealed crown glass (if with parallel surfaces, so much the better) will answer for ordinary experiments.

2. *Reflecting Bundles of Glass Plates.*—When a great deal of light is required, which is frequently the case, especially when we use the microscope for examining imperfectly transparent bodies, from *one* to *sixteen* plates of the *clearest* and thinnest annealed glass should be placed in a frame, having their surfaces well washed and cleaned with fresh chamois leather. Their edges must then be covered with some cement or

with wax, so that no dust may introduce itself between the plates. If the glass is thin and with little colour, the light reflected from its surface will be as bright as that reflected from a quicksilvered mirror, and will consist wholly of polarised light, when the rays are incident upon it, at the polarising angle. The light transmitted may be also used.

3. *Reflecting Bundles of Blown Glass.*—As it is extremely difficult to obtain thin plates of clear and colourless glass, even if we take flint glass, which is not desirable from its high dispersive power, we may substitute in their place films of glass blown to the utmost thinness, and place them in a trough between two plates of the thinnest glass. The light transmitted through this bundle may be also used.

4. *Reflecting Bundles of Mica.*—Take a piece of clear and transparent mica, as colourless as possible, and cut it into the form of a right angled parallelogram, whose sides are parallel and perpendicular to the plane passing through its resultant axes*. Hold it by an edge in a powerful vice, and with a lancet, or a thin-bladed knife, split it into ten or twelve laminæ, or more if necessary. Before taking it out of the vice, cover all its edges with a coating of wax or strong cement, so that, after the laminæ are separated from one another, they may have the same relative position as before their separation. This bundle of mica films, when taken out of the vice, is one of the best means of polarising light that can be used; but the light must be polarised by reflexion in a plane parallel to either of the sides of the bundle.—The best is that which is *perpendicular to the plane passing through the resultant axes*. The light transmitted through this bundle being also perfectly polarised, may be used with great advantage.

5. *Doubly-refracting Crystals of great Thickness.*—When we can obtain a thickness of from *three* to *six* or more inches of colourless calcareous spar, it forms one of the most valuable pieces of polarising apparatus. We have only to place on one of the sides that contains the greatest thickness, a circular aperture just as large as that the two images of it may not overlap each other. We shall thus have two circular areas of light which are polarised, the one in one plane, and the other in a plane at right angles to it; and by means of a screen or a black wafer we can cover up the one circular space, when we require only one kind of polarised light.

6. *Doubly-refracting Prisms of Iceland Spar.*—As it is not easy to procure large and pure masses of Iceland spar, a sufficient separation of the images may be obtained, by selecting a piece with one good natural surface, and grinding down the other, so that the common intersection of the two faces of the prism may be perpendicular to the axis or the plane of refraction, coincident with the plane of its principal section. The colour of the images may be nearly corrected by a prism of crown or flint glass*. By increasing the refracting angle of the prism, the separation of the images may be increased at pleasure. The objection so often made to the use of prisms of Iceland spar is not well founded; for it is capable of taking an admirable polish, equal indeed to its original surface; and even if the operator is not skilful in the art, the polish may be made perfect, and the surface preserved from injury, by cementing, on the two surfaces of the prism, two pieces of pure and parallel glass. When the prism is rendered achromatic, indeed, by a glass prism, the latter serves for one of the plates of glass, and one plate only is required for the other surface. We have had prisms of this kind which have lasted fifteen years, though exposed to constant use. The separation of the images will be a maximum with the same refracting angle if the faces of the prism, or their common intersections, are parallel to the axis of double refraction.

7. *Doubly-refracting Prisms of Rock Crystal.*—The following ingenious me

Fig. A.

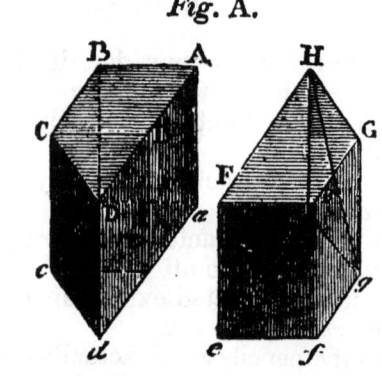

---

* This will be understood after perusing the next chapter.

* In the Annals of Philosophy for March, 1818, p. 175, Dr. Brewster has described a method of completely correcting the two dispersions of the two images of Iceland spar, by using two prisms of crown glass of different refracting angles, and making the rays which form one image pass through one prism, and the other rays through the other prism.

thod of getting over the small double refraction of rock crystal has been used by Dr. Wollaston.

"Let A B C D *a b c d* E F G H *e f g h* (*fig.* 20.) be two halves of a hexagonal prism of quartz (the form it affects), produced by a section parallel to two of the sides. In the vertical face A D *d a* draw any line L K parallel to the sides, and therefore to the axis of the prism, (which is also that of double refraction,) and join C L, *c k*.

"Then a plane C L *k c* will cut off a prism C L K *d c* D, having L *k*, D *d*, or C *c*, for its refracting edges, either of which is parallel to the axis. Again, in the other half of the prism join E *f* and H *g*, and cut the prism by a plane passing through these lines; then, regarding either portion as a double refracting prism, having for refracting edges the lines E H, *fg*, *these* will have the axes of double refraction perpendicular to their refracting edges; and, in particular, the axes will lie *in* the faces H E *e h*, or F G *g f* at right angles to H E or *fg*. If, then, we take care to make the refracting angle C L D of the prism C L K *d c* D equal to that of the edge H E of the prism H E *e f g h*; and if we make these two prisms act in opposition to each other, placing the edge H E opposite to D *d*, and the edge *h e* opposite to K L; and having thus brought the two surfaces D L *k d* and H E *e h* in contact, cement them together with mastic, or Canada balsam, it is evident that their principal sections will be at right angles to each other; and therefore only two images will be formed, the whole of the extraordinary ray of the one prism passing into the ordinary image of the other, and *vice versâ*.—Now, to see how this acts to double the separation of the images, let us conceive *m n* to be a luminous line viewed through one of the prisms, with its edge downwards and horizontal. It will be separated into two images, *e* and *o*, the one more raised than the other. Suppose the ordinary image to be most refracted. Then, if we interpose the other prism with its edge upwards, both these images will be refracted downwards; but the ordinary image *o*, which was before *most* raised, now undergoing extraordinary refraction, is *least depressed*, and comes into the position *o e*, while the extraordinary one *e*, which was before *least raised*, is now *most depressed*, and comes into the situation *e o*; and it is evident, that (the refracting angles being equal, and the double refraction of the two prisms the same) the line *o e* will fall as far short of the original line *m n*, as *e o* surpasses it, viz. by a quantity equal to the distance between the two first images *o* and *e*; so that the distance between the twice refracted images, is double that of those which have undergone only one refraction*."

8. *Single Image Prisms of Iceland Spar.*—Prisms of this kind were first used by Dr. Brewster. The method of making them is to roughen as much as possible the two surfaces, or even one surface, of a prism of Iceland spar, and to cover it with grooves. A fluid or balsam with the same refractive index as the ordinary ray, is then placed between the rough surface of the spar and a plate of glass. This polishes, as it were, the surface for the ordinary ray, and allows it to pass through uninterrupted, in consequence of the spar and the fluid having the same index of refraction for that ray. The extraordinary ray, on the other hand, is scattered in all directions by reflection at the separating surfaces of the grooves and the fluid, and totally disappears, leaving only the ordinary image. But as there is no proper oil or fluid of such a high refractive power as 1.654, it is better to take an oil of the same refractive index as that of the extraordinary ray, for the surface which is roughened. If the oil does not exactly suit the surface, a slight inclination of the prism one way or another, will produce the adjustment. When this is done, we shall see the extraordinary image quite distinct, while the ordinary image has wholly disappeared. For ordinary purposes this prism is perfectly sufficient, but for others it will not answer so well, as the nebulous light seen all round, is polarised in a plane opposite to that of the extraordinary image.

9. *Agate Plates and Microscopes.*—Among the bodies of the mineral kingdom, Dr. Brewster found *agate* to be one which gave only one distinct image, all the light of which is polarised in one plane. He therefore used it in his experiments. Agate microscopes, or plates of agate placed close to a single microscope, may be very advantageously used.

10. *Tourmaline Plates.*—M. Biot and M. Seebeck discovered that certain yellowish tourmalines, that is, those which are yellowish by refracted light, transmitted only one pencil polarised in the same

---
* Mr. Herschel's *Treatise on Light*.

plane, when cut parallel to their axis. It has been much used in experiments on polarisation; but owing to the colour which it produces, it is of no use whatever in researches where the phenomena of colour are to be studied. When two plates of tourmaline or agate are placed in rectangular positions, not a ray of light is transmitted through them, not even the light of the meridian sun.

By using any of these pieces of apparatus, we can at all times produce either a ray, or a broad beam of polarised light; but when the structure of crystallised or organised bodies is examined by observing their affections under polarised light, the light transmitted through their substance requires to be analysed by a reflecting plate, or a doubly refracting prism, or a plate of tourmaline or agate which has the property of reflecting or transmitting one portion of the polarised, and allowing another portion to be seen which was in a state of combination with the first portion. The use of these analysing plates in prisms will be better understood from the following chapter.

Chapter VI.

Colours produced by the Action of Crystallised Bodies upon Polarised Light—Systems of Rings produced by Crystals with one Axis of Double Refraction—Negative System of Rings—Positive System of Rings—List of Crystals of the Negative and Positive Class—Method of calculating the Tints—Transformation of the Rings.

The phenomena of colour produced by the action of crystallised bodies upon polarised light, are the most splendid within the whole range of optics. The colours themselves were first seen in Iceland spar by Huygens, and studied by subsequent philosophers, but they knew nothing of their origin or nature. They were discovered, by independent observation, by M. Arago and Dr. Brewster, and the subject has been successfully pursued by these two authors, and also by M. Biot, Dr. Young, M. Fresnel, M. Herschel, and Professor Mitscherlich, from whose labours, to use the words of a distinguished author, " it has acquired

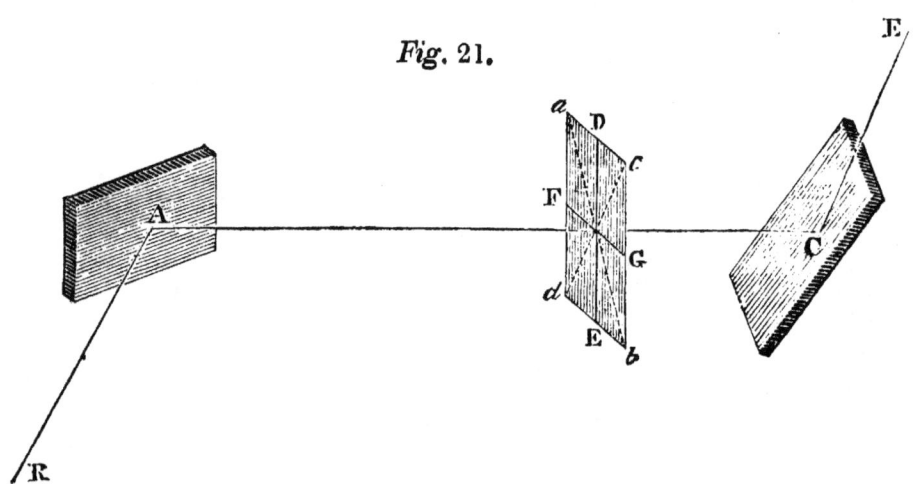

Fig. 21.

a developement, placing it among the most important, as well as the most complete and systematic branches of optical knowledge." In order to exhibit these colours in the simplest manner; let two plates of glass, A, C, *fig.* 21, be arranged, as shown in *fig.* 12, so that the light polarised by the *first* plate A, (or the *polarising plate*,) refuses to be reflected by the *second* plate C, (or the *analysing plate.*) If the light R A, be that of the sky, which will do very well for ordinary purposes, the proper adjustment of the glass plates will be known, by looking at C in the direction E C, and observing a dark undefined spot, in the image of the part of the sky reflected by A. The glass plates should be adjusted till this spot is as dark as possible. In order to increase the quantity of polarised light, and to have a larger surface, it would be desirable to use the bundle of glass plates described in the last chapter, in place of the single plate of glass A.

Having placed the polarising plates A,

so as to reflect the brightest part of the sky, take a thin film or slice D G E F, of *sulphate of lime* (or *mica*, if sulphate of lime cannot be had) between the 20th and 60th part of an inch in thickness, and hold it, as shown in the figure, between the polarising and the analysing plates. When, previous to the interposition of the crystallised plate, the eye E, looked into C, it saw only the dark spot above-mentioned; but it will now observe the whole surface of the polarizing plates at A, covered with colours of the richest and most varied hues, and following one another, according as the sulphate of lime is more or less inclined, or according as the light passes through thicker or thinner portions of the film. If the plate is equally thick, which with a little care may be effected, and if it is held perpendicular to the polarised light, there will be found two lines D E, F G, which have the property, that when either of them is parallel or perpendicular to the *plane of primitive polarisation* R A C, or to the plane A C E, no colours are seen, and the black spot appears exactly as if the film were not interposed. These two lines may be called the *neutral axes* of the crystallised film. If the film D G E F is turned round in its own plane, there will be found in all other positions the phenomenon of a single colour; but this colour will be most brilliant, when either of the lines ab, cd, perpendicular to one another, and each inclined 45° to the neutral axes, is in the plane of primitive polarisation R A C,—the brilliancy or intensity of the colour gradually diminishing from the position of no colour, to the position where the colour is a maximum. The two lines $a\,b$, $c\,d$, may be called the *depolarising axes of the film*.

If we suppose the plates A and C, to be fixed, and the film D G E F, to revolve round the ray A C, from a position where no colour is seen, it will then be found, that the colour which we may suppose *red*, is a maximum at the azimuths, or angles of revolution, of 45°, 135°, 225°, and 315°, while it disappears altogether at azimuths of 0°, 90°, 180° and 270°. If we now suppose the film D G E F, to be fixed in any of the positions 45°, &c. or where it produces the brightest *red*, and if we cause the *analysing* plate C, to revolve round the ray A C, its inclination to A C remaining invariable, we shall observe the following phenomena. The brightest *red* being visible at 0°, or where the plate C begins to move, the brightness of this colour will gradually diminish till C has turned round 45°, when the red colour will disappear. Beyond 45°, a faint *green* will appear, and will gradually increase in intensity till it reaches its maximum brightness at 90°. Beyond 90° the *green* becomes paler and paler, till it disappears at 135°, where the *red* again comes in, and reaches its maximum brightness at 180°: the very same changes are repeated between 180° and 360° or 0°. Hence it follows, that when only the film of sulphate of lime revolves, a *single colour* merely is seen; while, when only the plate C moves, *two colours* are seen during its revolution.

By repeating the above experiment with films of sulphate of lime that give different colours, it will be found that the two colours are always complementary to each, or that the two together make up white light. This curious property may be ocularly demonstrated by the following experiment. Instead of analysing the light transmitted by the sulphate of lime by the plate C, substitute a prism of calcareous spar, that gives two images, and when the plane of the principal section of the prism (or rather of the crystal of which it is composed) is in the plain of primitive polarisation, the one image will be *red*, and the other image *green;* and if the two are made to cross one another, the overlapping portions will be perfectly white. Instead of a prism, it will be simpler to use a complete rhomb of spar, having on one of its faces a circular aperture, so large that the two images of it seen through the spar overlap each other: by substituting this for the prism, the right hand portion of the one image will be *red*, and the left hand portion of the other *green*, while the intermediate or overlapping parts will be perfectly *white*.

If we reduce the thickness of the film of sulphate of lime to 0.00046 of an English inch, it will produce no colour at all, having no more action upon polarised light, than a plate of common glass. A film 0.00124 of an inch thick, gives the white of the first order in Newton's scale of colours (see OPTICS, p. 35); and a plate 0.01818 of an inch thick, and all thicker plates, give a *white* composed of a mixture of all the colours. Plates having a thickness intermediate between 0.00124 and 0.01818 of an inch, produce all the different orders of colours contained in Newton's table; and the colour which any given thickness will exhibit may be calculated from the last column of Newton's table, under Glass, because glass and sulphate of lime have nearly the same refractive power. Since the *white* in the column of reflected tints is produced at a thickness of 0.00124, and the white or end of the seventh spectrum is produced at a thickness of 0.01818, and since the numbers in the table opposite to these tints are $3\frac{2}{3}$ and $49\frac{1}{3}$, we have the following proportion: as 0.01818—0.00124 or .01694 is to $49\frac{2}{3}$ or $3\frac{2}{3}$, or 46 nearly, so is the excess of any thickness of a plate of sulphate of lime above 0.0124 to a fourth number, which when added to $3\frac{2}{3}$, will give a sum to enter the last column, and opposite to it will be found the two complementary colours which such a plate will produce.

As the colours of polarised light are proportional to the thickness of thin plates, which give the same colours, the superposition of two films will have the same effect as one film, equal to their united thicknesses, provided they are laid together in the same manner as they lie in the crystal. But if the films are placed transversely, that is with any one line of the one at right angles, to a similar line in the other, they will produce a tint equal to the difference of their thicknesses. If the plates are therefore perfectly equal, they will, when thus crossed, destroy each other's action, and produce blackness. Hence, also, the colours may be produced by crossing two plates of very considerable thickness, which give no colour when taken separately, provided that the difference of their thickness does not exceed 0.01818 of an inch*.

The different phenomena which we have now described, may be seen in a more instructive manner, in the following experiment made by Dr. Brewster. Having taken a plate of sulphate of lime of equal thickness, and about $\frac{1}{25}$th of an inch thick, he ground down one of its faces, so as to make its thickness vary from $\frac{1}{25}$th of an inch, down to the thinnest edge that could be made. He then placed the plate in water, which slowly acted upon it, making its edge thinner, and giving a slight polish to its surface. By placing this film between the polarising and analysing plate, its surface was covered with coloured fringes parallel to the thin edge, $a\,d$, *fig.* 22, and including

Fig. 22.

all the colours in Newton's Table, thus showing to the eye how the different tints are produced by different thicknesses. When the film $a\,d$, was cut into two $a\,b$, $c\,d$, and crossed as in *fig.* 23, a

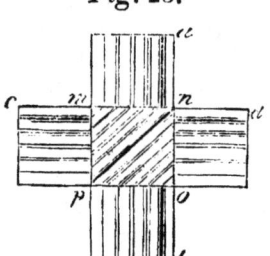

Fig. 23.

new set of fringes was produced parallel to a black line $n\,p$, extending from the point where the two thinnest edges meet to the point where the two thickest sides meet.

On the Colours and Systems of Rings produced by Crystals, with one Axis of Double Refraction.—The phenomena of the colours of polarised light had been examined under very unfavourable circumstances, till 1813, when the systems of rings round the axis of double refraction, were discovered by Dr. Brewster.

If we take a rhomboid of calcareous spar, whose principal section is represented by A B C D, *fig.* 24, and cement upon its surfaces A B, C D, two

Fig. 24.

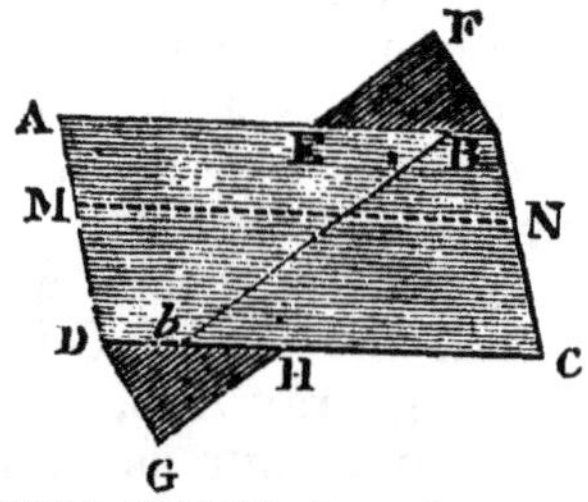

prisms BEF, DEH, having their refracting angles EBF, GDH about 45°, we shall be able to see along the axis B b, of double refraction of the spar. Let the spar be now substituted in the apparatus *fig.* 21, in place of the film D F E G, so that the polarised ray A C, *fig.* 21, may pass along a line parallel to the axis B b; then whatever be the position of the spar, there will be seen along its axis A B, a most beautiful system of coloured rings, intersected in the direction of their diameters by a black cross A B C D, *fig.* 25.

---

* The preceding interesting results were first obtained by M. Biot.

POLARISATION OF LIGHT.

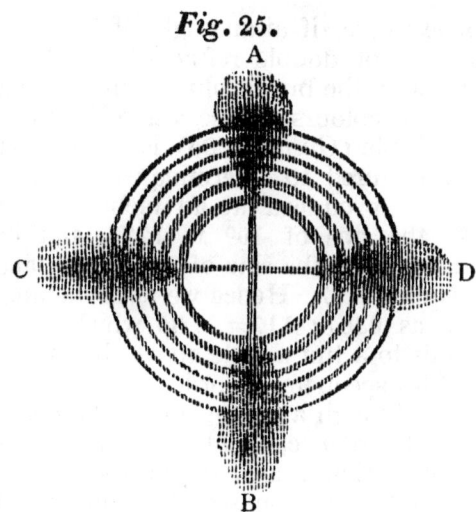

Fig. 25.

No change whatever will take place in this system of rings, by turning the spar about its axis; but if we turn the analysing plate C, *fig.* 21, round, as formerly described, then in the azimuths 0°, 90°, 180° and 270°, the same system of rings will be seen, while at the azimuths 45°, 135°, 225°, and 315°, another system will be seen like that shown in *fig.* 26.

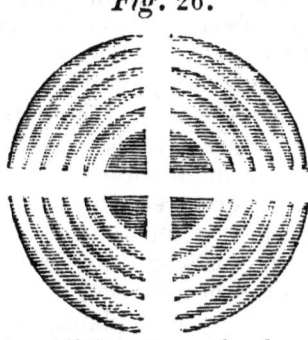

Fig. 26.

This system differs from the former in no other respect than this, that all the colours in the one are exactly complementary to those in the other, so that the superposition of the two, if it could be effected, would completely obliterate both systems.

If the rhomboid of calcareous spar is now cut into two plates by any line MN, and if the rings produced by each plate be examined separately, it will be found,

1. That the rings given by each plate are larger in diameter than those produced by the whole rhomboid previous to its division.

2. That the rings in the thickest of the two plates are less in diameter than those produced by the thinnest; or in general,

3. The squares of the diameters of the rings produced by the same plate are proportional to the number which represents the corresponding tint in Newton's Table; and in plates of different thicknesses, the squares of the diameters of similar rings are reciprocally proportional to the square roots of their thicknesses.

The phenomena now described may be seen, with equal advantage, by cutting off the solid angles of the rhomb by surfaces FN, HM perpendicular to the axis B *b*; but as the mineral does not cleave parallel to those planes, and is difficult to polish, we cannot, in this way, make the comparative experiments mentioned above with the same facility.

In examining, in the same manner, other crystallised bodies that have one axis of double refraction, we discover in all of them a system of rings similar to that in calcareous spar, and the axis of this system invariably coincides with the axis of double refraction. In those crystals, however, which have *positive* double refraction, the system of rings, though the same in appearance, has a very different property. If we take a system of rings, for example, formed by *ice* or *zircon*, and combine it with a system of the same diameter formed by Iceland spar, we shall find that the two systems destroy one another; and hence we conclude that the system of rings produced by these crystals are *positive*, or opposite in character to the *negative* system of rings in calcareous spar. In the following Table will be found all the different crystals which give a *negative* and a *positive* system of rings.

Crystals that give a Negative System.

Carbonate of Lime.
Carbonate of Lime and Magnesia.
Carbonate of Lime and Iron.
Carbonate of Zinc.
Corundum.
Sapphire.
Ruby.
Emerald.
Beryl.
Phosphate of Lime.
Idocrase.
Wernerite.
Paranthine.
Tourmaline.
Rubellite.
Mica from Kariat.
Molybdate of Lead.
Phosphate of Lead.
Phosphato-Arseniate of Lead.
Hyposulphate of Lime.
Hydrate of Strontites.
Arseniate of Potash.
Muriate of Lime.
Muriate of Strontian.
Nitrate of Soda.

Subphosphate of Potash.
Sulphate of Nickel and Copper.
Ruby Silver.
Mellite.
Somervillite.
Octohedrite.
Phosphate of Ammonia and Magnesia.
Nepheline.
Arseniate of Lead.
Arseniate of Copper.
Gmelinite.
Oxahverite.
Edingtonite.
Levyne.
Cyanuret of Mercury.
Alunite.

Crystals that give a Positive System.

Zircon.
Quartz.
Oxide of Tin.
Tungstate of Lime.
Titanite.
Boracite.
Apophyllite.
Sulphate of Potash and Iron.
Superacetate of Copper and Lime.
Hydrate of Magnesia.
Ice.
Prussiate of Potash, certain specimens.
Dioptase?

If we combine two plates of two crystals of the positive class, such as *Calcareous Spar* and *Beryl*, the system of rings will be the same as would be produced by two plates of calcareous spar, one of which is the plate employed, and the other, a plate which gives rings of the same size as the plate of beryl. But when a positive system of rings is combined with a negative system, such as those produced by zircon or ice with those produced by calcareous spar or beryl, the resultive system of rings, in place of being the sum of their separate actions, will be their difference; that is, it will be equal to the system produced by a thin plate of calcareous spar, whose thickness is equal to the difference of the thicknesses of the plate of calcareous spar employed, and another plate of calcareous spar that would give rings of the same size as those given by the zircon above.

By comparing the numerical values of the tints produced at different angles of inclination to the axis, it follows from experiment, that if the thickness of the mineral is invariable, the numerical value of the tints will always vary as the square of the sine of the angle which the refracted ray forms with the axis of the crystal. For example, if at an angle of $10°$ with the axis of double refraction, we have the tint of the bright blue of the second order of colours, whose value, in Newton's Table (*Optics*, p. 35), is 9; then let it be required to determine what will be the tint produced at an inclination of $20°$: the sine of $10°$ is .1736, and its square .0301; the sine of $20°$ is .342, and its square .117. Hence we have the analogy, as $.0301 : .117 = 9 : 35$, which corresponds to a tint a little above the *red* of the fifth spectrum or order of colours.

But though a tint of 35, or the *red* of the fifth order, can only be produced at an inclination of $20°$, the thickness of the crystal being supposed the same at all inclinations, yet, if we suppose the thickness of the crystal at an inclination of $10°$, to be increased in the proportion of 9 to 35, we should then have at $10°$ the same tint as we have at $20°$, with a smaller thickness. In any given crystal, any tint may be produced at any given inclination. If we require to produce a very low tint, such as 4, or the *yellow* of the first order, at an inclination of $80°$, where the polarising force is very strong, we must then reduce the substance to a very thin film; and, on the other hand, if we wish to develope a high tint, such as 45, or the *greenish blue* of the seventh order, at the inclination of $5°$, we must then take a very great thickness of crystal to make up for the low polarising force which exists so near the axis.

The system of polarised rings, like the rings formed by thin plates, may be increased in number by viewing them through a prism; and at inclinations to the axis of a crystal at which they cease to become visible, they may be readily developed by the opposite action of a crystal, but which does not exhibit them separately.

The phenomena exhibited by a single system of rings undergo curious and beautiful transformations, by interposing thin crystallised films of sulphate of lime, or mica, between two plates, each of which give a system of rings. If, for example, in the split rhomboid shown in *fig.* 24, we insert a thin and equal film of mica, a very singular effect will be produced upon the ring; but when the two rhomboidal plates AMNB, DMNB, are equal, the effect is still more beautiful, and the character of the system changes, not only by the revolution of the analysing plate, but during the revolution of the rhomboid. In order to show all the varieties of this beautiful class of phenomena, Dr. Brewster took a plate of the *Spath Calcaire basée*, which has a natural face perpendicular to the axis, and having cut it into two pieces, and placed them parallel to one another, with a sufficient interval between them to admit the interposition of different films, he was enabled to see in succession all the modifications which they underwent, but of which it is not easy to convey any idea without numerous drawings.

Chapter VII.

Double System of Rings produced by Crystals, with two axes of Double Refraction—Phenomena exhibited by them—Table of the Inclination of the resultant Axes of Crystals—General Law of the Tints.

The double system of coloured rings was discovered in 1817, by Dr. Brewster, who described them in the Philosophical Transactions, as seen in *Topaz*, where they appear with unusual splendour; but the axes or lines along which each system is seen, are so much inclined to one another, that we shall first describe them as seen in *Nitre*, where they were soon after discovered by the same author.

Nitre or *Saltpetre* crystallizes in six-sided prisms, with angles of about 120°, and its principal axis of double refraction is coincident with the axis of this prism. Having detached with the edge of a knife and the assistance of a smart blow of a hammer, a small piece from the end of the prism, grind it down upon a file or coarse freestone till it is reduced to the eighth or tenth of an inch; and having smoothed its parallel faces, which should be as nearly as possible perpendicular to the axis of the prism, wet each of them slightly with the tongue, and having dried them quickly, place the plate thus formed between two plates of glass, so that a thin layer of Canada balsam may cement them to the glass. This will produce the effect of the most perfect polish, and will preserve the plate of nitre for years without injury.

Let the nitre thus prepared be placed in the apparatus of *fig.* 21, the eye looking into the plate C, and seeing the black undefined space already mentioned. When the plane of the axis of nitre is parallel or perpendicular to the plane of primitive polarisation, there will be seen the beautiful system of rings shown in *Fig.* 27. This system is intersected with a black cross, one of whose arms passes through the centres of the two systems of curves, while the other arm of the cross, which is always less defined, is at right angles to the former, and equi-distant from the centres of the two systems.

If we now turn the plate of nitre round its axis, the revolution commencing at 0°, the black cross will open, as shown in *Fig.* 28. As the revolution advances, it

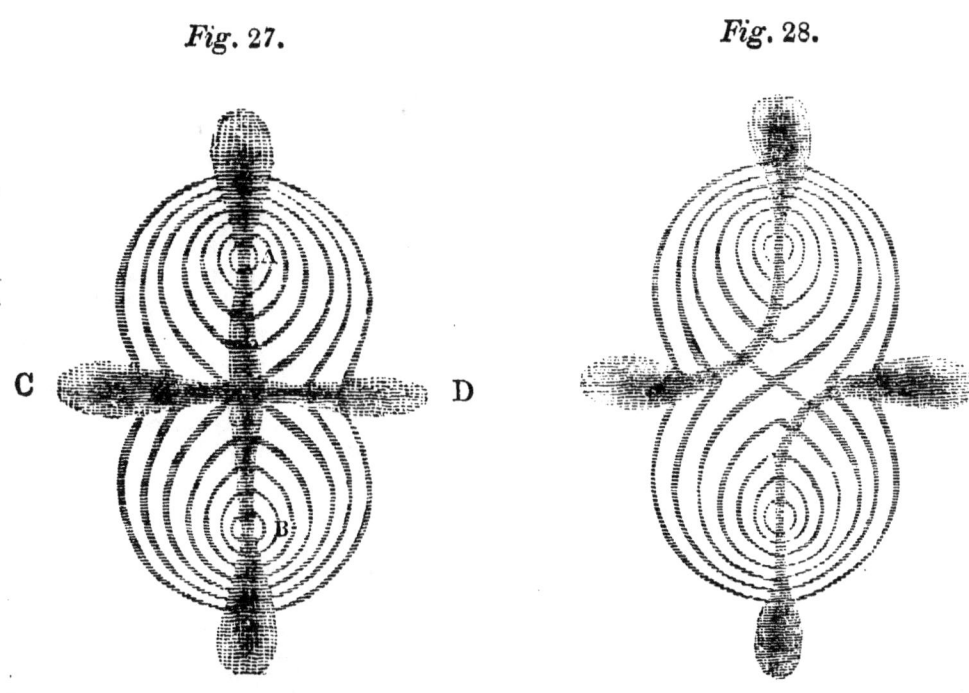

Fig. 27. Fig. 28.

opens more, as shown in *Fig*. 29; and at

Fig. 29.

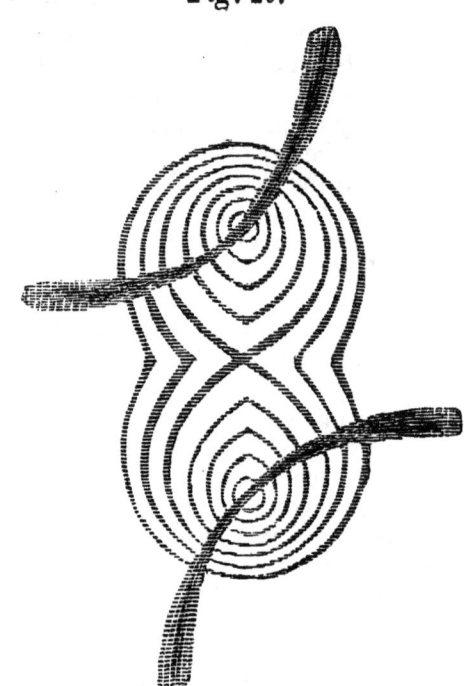

45°, it has the form shown in *Fig.* 30, where the form and colour of the rings are much more distinctly seen than in

Fig. 30.

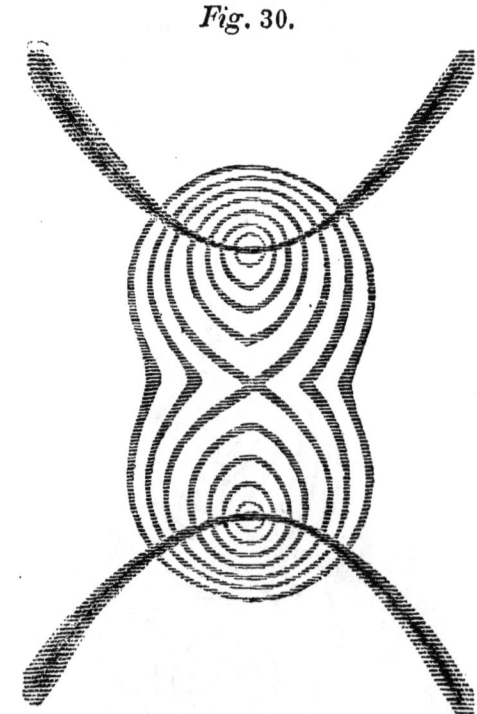

fig. 27. The black cross has now separated into two hyperbolic curves, the branches of one curve being parallel and perpendicular to those of the other.

The form of the rings has a general resemblance to that of the ellipse. A certain number of them surround each separate centre, which seems to be nearly in one of their foci; but after the outermost of them meet at the point of intersection of the black cross, some of the rings have points of contrary flexure, and they afterwards surround the two centres, as if each centre were one of their foci. We shall presently be able to give a more accurate description of the form of these *isochromatic curves*, or lines of equal tint. By continuing the revolution of the plate, the phenomena of *fig.* 27 will occur at 90°, 180°, and 270°, and that of *fig.* 30 at 135°, 225°, and 315°; but during all these changes, the form, and the colours of the rings themselves, suffer no change.

If we now examine the colours of the rings, it will be found that they have a general resemblance to those of Newton's Table, and that the *zero* of the different orders of colours is at or near the poles or centres, A B, *fig.* 27, and they increase outwards, as in the *uniaxal* system of rings already described. The rings themselves increase in diameter as the plates of nitre become thinner, and diminish when they become thicker; but at all thicknesses the poles A and B are the centres where the colours of the rings originate, and, generally speaking, never suffer any displacement.

But if we reduce the plate of nitre to a great degree of thinness, so that the colour or tint produced at the intersection of the arms of the black cross, or at a point half way between A and B is not perceptible, the whole system of rings will appear to be like the uniaxal system, and the black cross will not exhibit the appearance above described. By thinning the plate of nitre, we have, as it were, destroyed the action of the second axis at small inclinations (as will be presently better understood); but at greater inclinations this axis will still modify the character of the rings.

As these poles, viz. A, B, *fig.* 27, are points where there is no polarisation, the lines passing through them may be called the *lines or axes of no-polarisation*, a long but an expressive name, and we think better than the vague one of *optical axes**, which has been given to them. The angle subtended by the poles A, B is

---

* All axes in crystals are *optical* axes; but all axes are not axes of *no-polarisation*. An expressive and useful name, which contains a fact, ought never to be discarded, till a better one is obtained.

in nitre about 8° at the eye; but within the substance of the crystal the axis forms an angle of only 5° 20′.

In crystals such as *Nitre, Carbonate of Lead, Arragonite*, where the inclination of the *axes of no polarisation*, or of the *resultant axes*, as they will afterwards be found to be, is small, we can easily see at once the two systems of rings surrounding their two poles, and the two poles themselves surrounded by the same ring; but when the inclination of the resultant axes is great, as in *Topaz, Mica, Feldspar, &c.* we can only see at once the system of rings round each pole. In order to do this advantageously, it is convenient to grind and polish a face perpendicular to the axis passing through that pole. In mica and topaz, however, this is not necessary, owing to the facility with which these minerals cleave in planes equally inclined to the two resultant axes.

If A B, for example, (*fig.* 31,) is a plate of topaz cut or split perpendicular to the axis of the prism; then if we

Fig. 31.

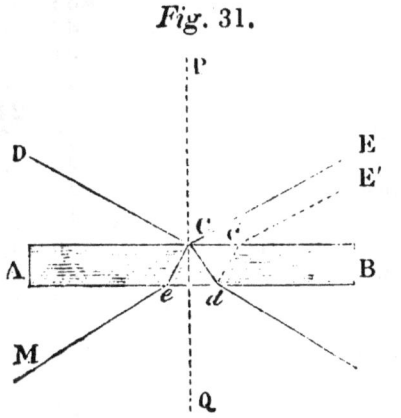

place this in the apparatus, *fig.* 21, so that the ray of polarised light passes along D C d N, we shall see a system of rings like that in *fig.* 32.

In like manner, by transmitting the polarised light along E C e M, so that D C P = E C P, we shall see the very same system. Hence D C, E C are the resultant axes or lines of no polarisation, and the angle D C E is equal to 121° 16′; but the real inclination of the resultant axes within the crystal, or e C d, is about 65°.

Hitherto we have supposed that the analysing plate, C, *fig.* 21, is fixed, while the plate of nitre or topaz revolves. But if we suppose the nitre or topaz fixed in any of the positions which give the phenomena shown in *fig.* 27—30, and then turn round the plate C, we shall see in the azimuths of 90° and 270°, a complementary system of rings, in which the *black* cross is *white*, the *dark* parts *light*, the *red green*, and so on, as described in our account of the Uniaxal System of Rings.

The crystals which possess a double system of rings, are very numerous; and we must refer the reader to the long list of them given by Dr. Brewster in the article Optics, in the Edinburgh Encyclopædia. He found that all crystals have a double system of rings, which belong to the prismatic system of Malus, or whose primitive forms are:—

Right Prism . . .	Base a Rectangle
——— . . .	Base a Rhomb
. . .	Base an Oblique Parallelogram
Oblique Prism . . .	Base a Rectangle
——— . . .	Base a Rhomb
. . .	Base an Oblique Parallelogram
Octohedron . . .	Base a Rectangle
——— . . .	Base a Rhomb

The following is a list of crystals, with a double system, in which Dr. Brewster measured the inclination of the resultant axes within the substance of the crystal. The measures were carefully made, but some of them are only approximate results, and will admit of considerable correction by employing better specimens than he was able to procure. Many of the measures, indeed, were taken with very

POLARISATION OF LIGHT.

small fragments of minerals placed between prisms, in order to permit the polarised ray to pass along the resultant axes.

List of Minerals and Crystals, with the Character of their principal Axis and the Inclination of their Resultant Axes.

Names of Minerals.	Character of Principal Axis.	Inclination of Resultant Axes.	
Glauberite	Negative	2° or 3°	
Sulphate of Nickel, certain specimens	Positive	3	
Nitrate of Potash	Negative	5	20'
Mica, certain specimens	Negative	6	0
Carbonate of Strontites	Negative	6	56
Talc	Negative	7	24
Carbonate of Lead	Negative	10	35
Sulphato-carbonate of Lead	Negative	10	35
Mother of Pearl	Negative	11	28
Hydrate of Barytes	Negative	13	18
Mica, certain specimens	Negative	14	0
Arragonite	Negative	18	18
Prussiate of Potash, certain specimens	Positive	19	34
Cymophane	Positive	27	51
Borax	Positive	28	42
Anhydrite	Positive	28	7
———— (*Biot*)		44	41
Apophyllite, *biaxal*	Negative	35	8
Sulphate of Magnesia	Negative	37	24
———— Barytes	Positive	37	42
Spermaceti	Positive	37	40
Tincal, or Native Borax	Negative	38	48
Nitrate of Zinc, estimated at about		40	0
Heulandite	Positive	41	42
Sulphate of Nickel	Positive	42	4
Carbonate of Ammonia	Negative	43	24
Mica	Negative	45	0
Lepidolite	Negative	45	0
Benzoate of Ammonia	Positive	45	8
Sulphate of Zinc	Negative	44	28
———— Magnesia and Soda	Positive	46	49
Hopeite	Negative	48	0
Sulphate of Ammonia	Positive	49	42
Brazilian Topaz	Positive	49 or 50°	
Sugar	Negative	50	0'
Sulphate of Strontites	Positive	50	0
Murio-sulphate of Magnesia and Iron	Negative	51	16
Sulphate of Ammonia and Magnesia	Positive	51	22
Phosphate of Soda	Negative	55	20
Comptonite	Positive	56	6
Sulphate of Lime	Positive	60	0
Oxynitrate of Silver	Positive	62	16
Dichroite	Negative	62	50
Feldspar	Negative	63	0
Topaz, Aberdeenshire	Positive	65	0
Sulphate of Potash	Positive	67	0
Carbonate of Soda	Negative	70	1
Acetate of Lead	Negative	70	25
Citric Acid	Positive	70	29
Tartrate of Potash	Negative	71	20
Tartaric Acid	Negative	79	0
Tartrate of Potash and Soda	Positive	80	0
Carbonate of Potash		80	30
Kyanite	Positive	81	48
Hyper-oxymuriate of Potash		82	0
Muriate of Copper		84	30
Epidote, about		84	29
Peridot		87	56
Crystallised Cheltenham Salts		88	14
Succinic Acid, estimated about		90	0
Sulphate of Iron, about		90	0

POLARISATION OF LIGHT.

Having thus given a general account of the phenomena exhibited by the double system of rings, we shall now proceed to explain the law which regulates the polarised tints in this class of crystals.

In all crystals without axes, the axis coincides with some prominent line in the crystals such as the axis of the rhomboid, the axis of the octohedron with a square base, &c.; but as the resultant axes, above described, do not always, or even frequently, coincide with any fixed line in the crystals, Dr. Brewster conceived that they were not the real axes of the crystals, but only the resultants of the real axes, or lines, in which the opposite actions of the two real axes compensated each other. Various other considerations rendered this opinion almost certain, and still more recent discoveries have established it upon an impregnable basis. Hence, he was led to consider all the phenomena of the rings and all those of double refraction as the result of two rectangular axes, the principal one of which was equally inclined to the two resultant axes round which the rings are formed.

It is easy upon this principle to determine what will be the tint developed at any given inclination, by each of the axes acting separately, after we have ascertained the relative inclinations of each axis. For this purpose, let $ACBD$, fig. 33, represent any crystal, with two axes or systems of rings; and let us suppose it turned into a sphere. Let P

Fig. 33.

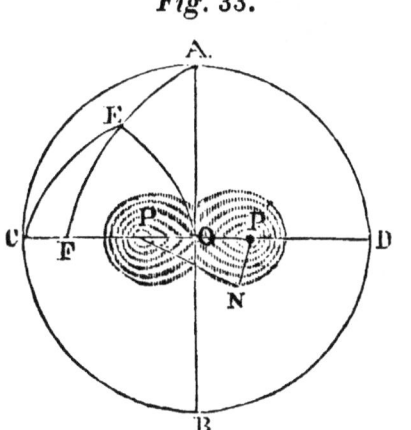

be the pole or centre of one of the systems of rings, and P′ the pole of the other system. Join PP′, and bisecting PP in O, draw AOB at right angles to PP′, and continue PP′ to C and D. We shall call the axis or diameter passing through the point O of the sphere Oo, and the diameters drawn through P and P′, Pp and $P'p'$ respectively. Now the double system of rings round P, P′ may be produced by means of an axis Oo, and another axis AB, or CD perpendicular to Oo. If Oo is a *negative* axis, which we shall suppose it to be, then the axis AB must also be a *negative* one; but if we suppose the two axes to be Oo, and CD, then CD must be *positive*. We shall suppose, then, that the two axes are Oo and AB, both *negative*.

Since the action of the axis AB, or the tint which it produces at P, 90° from A, is destroyed or compensated by the action of the axis Oo or the tint produced by it; and it is evident that the ratio of the intensities of the axes A,B must be that of 1 to $\frac{1}{\sin.^2 OP}$. For, as the tint produced at P by AB is equal to the tint produced at the same point by C; and as the tint produced at P by AB is its maximum tint, AP being an arch of 90°, then the maximum tint produced by Oo will be found by the analogy, $\sin.^2 OP : \text{rad.}^2 :: 1 : \frac{1}{\sin.^2 OP}$. Hence, the maximum tint of AB will be to the maximum tint of Oo as $\sin.^2 90°$ or $1 : \frac{1}{\sin.^2 OP}$, the maximum tint which any axis produces being a proper measure of its intensity.

From a great number of observations made at all points of the sphere, and from measurements of the projected rings, Dr. Brewster found that all the phenomena of the rings, with all their varieties of form, were represented by the following law:—

The tint produced at any point of the sphere, by the joint action of two axes, is equal to the diagonal of a parallelogram, whose sides represent the tints produced by each axis separately, and whose angle is double of the angle formed by the two planes passing through that point of the sphere, and the respective axes.

In order to explain the application of this law, let it be required to determine the tint produced at E, fig. 33, by the two axes Oo, AB, whose relative intensities are as 1 to $\frac{1}{\sin.^2 OP}$. Through the given point of the sphere E draw three great circles A E F, C E, and O E: then let

T = Tint required at the point E
θ = E O

φ = E C
a = Tint produced separately at E by the axis O o
b = Tint produced separately at E by the axis A B
ψ = The angle of the parallelogram of forces
π = The angle C E F
ω = The angle O E F
A = The arch F O
D = The arch F E
ζ = Half the difference of the angles of the base at the diagonal of the parallelogram of forces

We have then, by spherical trigonometry,
$$\cos \theta = \cos A \times \cos D$$
$$\varphi = 90^\circ - D$$
$$\cos \omega = \frac{\tan D}{\tan \theta}$$
$$\cos \pi = \frac{\tan D}{\tan \varphi}$$
$$2 \, A\,E\,O = \psi = 2\,(180^\circ - \omega) = 2\,\omega.$$

Now, since the tints produced by each axis O o, A B at E, are as the squares of the sines of inclination to the axis, or as $\sin.^2 O E$ and $\sin.^2 A E$, and as the relative intensities of the axes are as 1 to $\frac{1}{\sin.^2 OP}$, we shall have $a = \sin.^2 O E$, and $b = \sin.^2 A E \times \sin.^2 O P$.

Having thus found a and b the sides of the parallelogram of forces, whose angle is ψ, the diagonal T of this parallelogram will be thus obtained:—

$$\tan \zeta = \frac{a - b}{a + b} \tan \tfrac{1}{2}\psi$$

$\zeta + \tfrac{1}{2}\psi$ = Greater angle at the base.
Hence,
$$T = \frac{a \sin \psi}{\sin \zeta + \tfrac{1}{2}\psi}$$

When $a = b$, then
$$T = 2\,a\,(\overline{\cos \pi + \omega}).$$

When $a = b$, and the axes O o, A B, of equal intensity, then $\pi = \omega$ and
$$T = 2\,a\,(\cos 2\pi), \text{ or } T = 2\,a\,(\cos 2\omega).$$

When twice the angle, formed by the planes O E, A E, is 90°, or $\psi = 90^\circ$, we have
$$T = \sqrt{a^2 + b^2}$$
When $\psi = 180^\circ$ $T = a - b$
When $\psi = 0^\circ$ or 360° $T = a + b$

Such is the method of determining the tints and the form of the rings, in relation to the *real axes* from which the forces emanate; but in relation to the poles P, P, the law may be expressed more simply by the formula:
$$T = t\,\sin.\,P\,E \times \sin.\,P\,E, \text{ where } t \text{ is the maximum tint.}$$

This result was deduced mathematically by M. Biot from Dr. Brewster's law; and, by independent observations, it was established experimentally by Mr. Herschel, who found, also, that the curves belonged to the class called Lemniscates, which have this property, that the rectangles under two lines drawn from the poles P, P′ to any point in the periphery N, for example, is invariable throughout the whole curve—that is, P N × P′ N is a constant quantity.

If the axis O o, *fig.* 33, is exactly equal to the axis A B in intensity, it is obvious that the points of compensation P, P′, where the tints of each axis are equal and opposite, and therefore destroy one another, will be at C and D, the extremities of an axis C D, at right angles to the two axes O o and A B; and as there cannot be any other points of compensation, the phenomena will now be related to one axis C D, and this axis will be of an opposite character to O o and A B—that is, it will be *positive* if they are *negative*, and *negative* if they are *positive*. Dr. Brewster has demonstrated that a single system of rings will be seen by looking along C D, and that all the phenomena produced by the two equal axes will be mathematically the same as in crystals with a single axis. Hence he ascertained that a single system of rings did not necessarily indicate the action of a single axis, but that certain physical circumstances might occur which would determine that the system of rings might be the result of two equal axes, or even of three axes which are not all equal. Such circumstances in the condition of the rings have been discovered by him; and it is therefore an undoubted fact that crystals, with apparently *one* axis, have in reality a greater number.

System of Rings produced by Common Light.—Hitherto we have considered the system of rings as produced by polarised light; but under certain circumstances they may be produced by common light, and it was indeed by common light that they were first discovered in topaz by Dr. Brewster. If, for example, *fig.* 31, A B, be a plate of topaz, and if common light is incident in the direction D C of one of the resultant axes, and is reflected from the posterior surface of the plate at *d* so as to reach the eye in the direction C′ E′ of the other resultant axis, we shall see, by the analysing plate, the system of rings shown in *fig.* 32; or if D C is polarised light, the rings will be seen at E′ without an analysing plate. Other curious phenomena are seen when the rings are viewed in this way, but our limits prevent us from enlarging on the subject.* In the first of these cases, even when the rings are produced by common light, the light is polarised by reflexion at d, and the rings are formed by the action of the part $d\,C'$ of the crystal; but in the second case where polarised light is used, the rings are formed by the action of the thickness $C\,d$, and the reflexion at d performs the function of an analysing plate. These effects are owing to the property of topaz, by which its angle of maximum polarisation is almost the same as the angle which each of its resultant axes forms with a line $P\,C$ perpendicular to the plate.

The system of coloured rings, produced by the interrupting films of calcareous spar which will be described in a subsequent chapter, may be seen by a proper method of observation, without any polarising or analysing plate. Dr. Brewster found certain crystals of nitre which exhibited their rings in the same manner; and Mr. Herschel subsequently found that the same property was common in carbonate of potass. This last author has given to such crystals the name of *idiocyclophanous*, which indicates that they *show their own rings*.

Chapter VIII.
Connexion between the Polarisation and the Double Refraction of Light—Law of Double Refraction in Crystals with two Axes—Combination of Axes of Double Refraction—Intensity of the Polarising and Doubly Refracting Forces in different Crystals.

By comparing the phenomena of the polarised rings with the intensity of the doubly refracting force in the various crystals which produced them, it was obvious that, in crystals with one system of rings, the polarising and the doubly refracting force increased and diminished together; but long after the complicated tints in mica were discovered, and for several years after the publication of Dr. Brewster's paper on the double system of rings in *topaz, nitre*, &c., it was confidently maintained by the French philosophers *that the crystals which gave two systems of rings had only one axis of double refraction*, and it consequently followed that there was no connexion between the two classes of phenomena.

In order to decide this question by direct experiment, Dr. Brewster prepared prisms of topaz so as to allow the incident ray to be powerfully refracted along the resultant axis, and also along the axis supposed to be that of the crystal; but along this latter axis he found a distinct double refraction, while along the two resultant axes there was none at all; thus establishing, beyond a doubt, the intimate and necessary connexion between the two classes of phenomena. In order to make this result more general, Dr. Brewster prepared plates of carbonate of potash, which has a great double refraction, and he observed and measured the separation of the images in different planes near the resultant axes. He had thus the satisfaction of seeing the two images overlap each other along the two resultant axes, and again separate; such separation being always proportional to the numerical value of the tint at the point of incidence.

In this way he was enabled to determine the law of extraordinary refraction, and to confirm it by direct measures of the separation of the images. This law may be thus expressed:—

The increment of the square of the velocity of the extraordinary ray produced by the action of two *axes of double refraction is equal to the diagonal of a parallelogram, whose sides are the increments of the square of the velocity produced by each axis separately, and calculated by the law of Huygens, and whose angle is double of the angle formed by the two planes passing through the ray and the respective axes.*

This law is now admitted as the universal law of refraction for the extraordinary ray; and M. Fresnel has shown that it coincides rigorously with the results deduced from the theory of waves*.

This distinguished author, whom a premature death has recently cut down in the middle of the most brilliant career, has discovered that the ordinary ray in crystals with two axes is not, as was supposed, under the influence of the ordinary refracting force, but is regulated by a law analogous to that of the extraordinary ray.

When the *two* axes are of equal intensity, and are both negative or both positive, the law above described gives identically the same results, as the law of Huygens does, for a single axis of double

---
* See the *Philosophical Transactions*, 1814, p. 203–211.

* "This consequence of the theory of waves," says M. Fresnel, "translated into the language of emission, where the ratios of the velocities attributed to the rays are inverse, is precisely the law of the difference of the squares of the velocities which Dr. Brewster had deduced from his experiments, and which was afterwards confirmed by those of M. Biot, to whom we owe the simple form of the product of the two sines."—*Annales de Chim. et de Phys.* 1825.

refraction, of an opposite character, placed at right angles to the other two, and having the same intensity as either axis singly.

If there are *three* axes, two of which, either both positive or both negative, are of equal intensity and in the same plane, while the *third* is at right angles to the other, then the resultant of these *three* axes will be a single axis coincident with the latter axis. Thus, in *fig.* 33, if the two equal axes are A, C, and the third axis O, then since A = C

If their characters are $+A+C-Oo$, we shall have

The single axis at Oo, which we shall call x
$$x = -(Oo + A).$$
If their characters are $-A-C-Oo$, then
$$x = -(Oo - A), \text{ if } Oo > A$$
$$x = +(A - Oo), \text{ if } Oo < A.$$
If their characters are $+A+C+Oo$, then
$$x = +(Oo - A), \text{ if } Oo > A$$
$$x = -(A - Oo).$$
If their characters are $-A-C+Oo$, then
$$x = +(O + oA).$$
If all the axes are equal, and have the same signs; that is, if $A = C = Oo$, then
$$x = 0.$$
That is, the three equal axes destroy one another, when they are all of the same character.

In the preceding combinations of axes we have supposed two of them to have the same intensity and the same character, so that the resultant is a single axis, or system of rings, in the direction of the strongest; but when the axes are three in number, and the resultant is a double system of rings, we must combine them in a different manner.

Let A B C, for example, *fig.* 34, be the

Fig. 34.

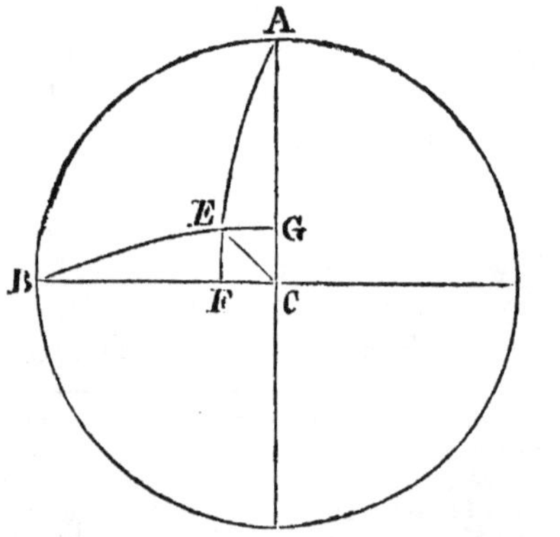

three axes the resultant of which is required; then, if we combine A and C by the general law given in the preceding chapter, we shall have the resulting tint:
$$T = \frac{a \sin. \psi}{\sin.(\zeta + \frac{1}{2}\psi)}$$
But in order to combine this tint, arising from the united action of A and C, we must know the direction of it. When we consider that ψ is the double of the real angle of the planes in which the forces from A and C act, we shall find that the direction of the new plane in which A and C are united forms an angle with the real direction of C, or the lesser force, whose complement is
$$\frac{\frac{1}{2}\psi + \zeta}{2} \text{ or } \frac{\psi}{4} + \frac{\zeta}{2}$$
or it forms with the real direction of A, or the greater force, an angle, whose complement is
$$\frac{\frac{1}{2}\psi - \zeta}{2} \text{ or } \frac{\psi}{4} - \frac{\zeta}{2}.$$
Hence it follows that, since the direction of the resultant, in relation to C E, is known, its direction in relation to B E, or the force with which it is to be combined, is also known; and, using accented letters to express the same parts of the new parallelogram of forces, we shall have
$$T' = \frac{a' \sin. \psi'}{\sin.(\zeta' + \frac{1}{2}\psi')}).$$

In order to illustrate this in a simple case, where the truth of the result will be immediately recognised, we shall take the case of three equal axes, where the resultant of all the three is 0 or *zero*. Let E, *fig.* 34, be the point of the sphere where we require to know the tint produced by the three equal axes — A — B — C, and let

A E = 70°	A G = 66° 44′
B E = 60	C G = 23 16
E G = 30	C E = 37 17
E F = 20	Sin.² A E = .883104 = a
Sin.² BE = .75000 = b	= {237° 16′ / 122 54}
Sin.² CE = .36694 = c	ζ = 37 12
ω = 40′ 41	a + c = 1.25004
π = 77 52	a − c = 0.51616

Hence, if we combine A and C, we shall have
$$T = .7500,$$
which will be + or positive, because ψ is greater than 180′.

Now, we have $\dfrac{\psi}{4} + \dfrac{\zeta}{2} = 49°\ 19'$, which gives 40° 21′ for the direction of the new plane in which the two forces, emanating from A and C, produce the resultant force of .7500; but the angle π or CEG = 40° 41′, so that the resultant lies in the plane B E G; and hence if we combine with this resultant, or +.7500, the force −.7500 produced by the axis B, the result will be 0 *.

The same method is applicable to the combination of axes of double refraction; the numbers corresponding to a, b, c being in this case the difference between the squares of the velocities of the ordinary and extraordinary rays, as produced by each axis separately.

Intensity of the polarising force in different crystals.—As the force of double refraction, which depends on the angular separation of the ordinary and extraordinary images, is proportional to the intensity of the polarising force, it would be extremely interesting to possess a complete list of doubly refracting crystals with numerical measures of the two forces. M. Biot determined these intensities for a few crystals; but the following list, which is much more complete than his, has been given by Mr. Herschel.

As these numbers form the most valuable mineralogical characters *, it would not be difficult for a mineralogist to acquire the art of making such minerals. To do this he has only to obtain the maximum or equatorial tint of crystals with one axis, or the tint perpendicular to the two resultant axes in crystals with two axes, and reduce the measures to a given thickness of the mineral. Now the equatorial tint T, in the first case, may be found by the rule given in p. 22, col. 2, or by the formula $T = \dfrac{t}{\sin^2 \phi}$, where t is the tint expressed numerically at any angle ϕ with the axis; and in the second case, by the formula $T = \dfrac{t}{\sin \phi \times \sin \phi'}$ where ϕ and ϕ' are the angles which the refracted ray forms with the resultant axes of the crystal.

Table of the Polarising Intensities of some Crystals.

I.—Crystals with one Axis.

	Values of T for yellow light.	Values of $\dfrac{1}{T}$
Iceland Spar	35801	0.000028
Hydrate of Strontia, assuming the Index of Refr. = 1.25	1246	0.000802
Tourmaline	851	0.001175
Hyposulphate of Lime	470	0.002129
Quartz	312	0.003024
Leucocyolite, Uniaxal Apophyllite, 1st variety	109	0.009150
Camphor	101	0.009856
Vesuvian	41	0.024170
Uniaxal Apophyllite, 2nd variety	33	0.030374
——————— 3rd variety	3	0.366620

II.—Crystals with two Axes.

Nitre	7400	0.000135
Anhydrite (Inclination of axis 43° 48′)	1900	0.000526
Mica (Inclination of axis 45°)	1307	0.000765
Sulphate of Barytes	521	0.001920
Heulandite (White; inclination of axis 54° 17′)	249	0.004021

---

* The preceding very general explanation of the combination of *three* axes has been rendered necessary by the following remark in Mr. Herschel's able *Treatise on Light* recently published:—

"It appears to us that the *rule for the parallelograms of tints, as laid down by Dr. Brewster*, becomes inapplicable when a third axis is introduced; for this obvious reason, that when we would combine the compound tints arising from two of the axes (A,B), with that arising from the action of the third (C), although the sides of the new parallelogram, which must be constructed, are given (viz. the compound tint T, and the simple tint t''), yet the *wording of the rule* leaves us completely at a loss what to consider as its *angle*—inasmuch as it assigns no single line which can be combined with the axis C in the *manner there required*, or which, *quoad hoc*, is to be taken as a resultant of the axis A, B." We humbly conceive that the distinguished author of this passage has committed an oversight in supposing that Dr. Brewster has given any *rule* for the combination of three axes. This rule or law, which is distinguished by italic printing, as in page 27, col. 2, of this treatise, relates solely to the combination of the two axes. In the paragraph following the rule given in the *Philosophical Transactions*, 1818, Dr. Brewster remarks that " if the crystal has three or more axes, the resulting tint produced from any two of them may, in like manner, be combined with the third, and this resulting tint with the fourth, till the general resultant of all the forces is obtained." Here he obviously states no rule, but merely that the third axis may be combined in like manner with the resultant of the other two. This manner he did not think it necessary then to point out, as he conceived it would occur to any person who studied the subject. We have, therefore, felt it necessary to show that the rule or law is perfectly applicable in all cases.

* *Edin. Phil. Journ.* vol. vii. p. 13.

Chapter IX.

Deviation of the polarised tints from those of Newton's scale—Mr. Herschel's discovery of the different positions of the optic axes in the same crystal for differently coloured rays—Deviation in crystals with one axis—Rings of Apophyllite, &c.—Phenomena of Glauberite.

Having considered in the preceding chapter the form of the rings and the law of their production, we come now to consider the colours of which they consist. M. Biot had taken it for granted, in all his investigations, that they were the same as the colours of thin plates; but in 1813, Dr. Brewster showed, in his table of the colours of the rings in topaz*, not only that they varied in different azimuths, but that there were even colours developed at the extremity of the two resultant axes. In his paper on the laws of polarisation, written in 1817, he remarks, "that in almost all crystals with two axes, the tints in the neighbourhood of the resultant axes, when the plate has a considerable thickness, lose their resemblance to those of Newton's scale, as will be more minutely described in another paper;" (*Phil. Trans.*, 1818, p. 243,) and in April, 1817, he communicated to the Royal Society of Edinburgh, his discovery of the extraordinary system of rings in the apophyllite from the Tyrol, in which the colours had not the slightest resemblance to those which appear in carbonate of lime, apatite and beryl. In the prosecution of the subject, he found that in biaxal crystals the deviation was strong, as in tartrate of potash and soda, and in acetate of lead; and that the crystals in which it was found might be divided into two classes; viz.—1st. those that had the *red* ends of the rings inward, or *within* the resultant axes, and the *blue* ends *outwards*, or without the resultant axes; and 2nd. those that had the *red* ends *outwards*, and the blue ends inwards. Those crystals in which the deviation is very striking, are given in the following table:—

Class I.—*Red ends inwards.*
Nitre.
Sulphate of Strontia.
——————— Baryta.
Phosphate of Soda.
Tartrate of Potash.
Hyposulphite of Strontia (Herschel).
Sugar (Herschel).
Arragonite.
Carbonate of Lead.
Sulphato-bi-carbonate of Lead.

Class II.—*Red ends outwards.*
Topaz.
Mica.
Anhydrite.
Tartrate of Potash and Soda.
Native Borax.
Sulphate of Magnesia.
Arseniate of Soda.

Crystals unclassed.
Chromate of Lead.
Muriate of Mercury.
——————— Copper.
Oxynitrate of Silver.
Sugar.
Crystallised Cheltenham Salts.
Nitrate of Mercury.
——————— Zinc.
——————— Lime.
Superoxalate of Potash.
Oxalic Acid.
Sulphate of Iron.
Cymophane.
Feldspar.
Benzoic Acid.
Chromic Acid.
Nadelstein.

This curious branch of the polarisation of light attracted the particular notice of Mr. Herschel, who, by examining the phenomena in homogeneous light, discovered that *the resultant axes differ in situation within one and the same crystal for the differently refrangible homogeneous rays.* "To make this evident," says he, "to popular inspection, take a crystal of Rochelle salt (tartrate of potash and soda), and having cut it into a plate perpendicular to one of its optic axes, or nearly so, and placed it in a tourmaline apparatus, let the lens be illuminated with the rays of a prismatic spectrum, in succession, beginning with the *red*, and passing gradually to the *violet*. The eye being all the time fixed on the rings, they will appear for each colour of perfect regularity and form remarkably well defined, and contracting rapidly in size as the illumination is made with more refrangible light; but, in addition to this, it will be observed that the whole system appears to shift its place bodily, and advance regularly in one direction as the illumination changes; and, if it be alternately altered

---

* *Phil. Trans.* 1814, p. 204 207.—The phenomena were represented in coloured drawings now in the possession of the Royal Society.

from *red* to *violet*, and back again, the pole, with the rings about it, will also move backwards and forwards, vibrating, as it were, over a considerable space. If homogeneous rays of two colours be thrown at once on the lens, two sets of rings will be seen, having their centres more or less distant, and their magnitudes more or less different, according to the difference of refrangibility of the two species of light employed."

This description will be understood by referring to *fig.* 27, where we may suppose the rings round A to be those viewed by the observer. In *violet* light, they will approach towards CD, and within 28° of it, while, in *red* light, they will recede from CD as far as 38°, the rings formed by intermediate colours having intermediate positions, the centres of all these systems of rings lying in one plane, viz. that of the principal section of the crystal passing through AB. These results will be still better seen by using a crystal, in which both the systems of rings round A and B are seen at once. The centres AB of the two systems will approach to, and recede from, each other, according as violet or red light is used; so that, when white light is used, all the systems, when seen at once, will form a most irregular system.

In the rings of topaz, and of other crystals, Dr. Brewster observed the tints to commence from black, at points which he called *virtual poles*, because they were different from the real poles. These virtual poles lie between the resultant axes in crystals of the first class, and beyond them in those of the second class, and are easily explained by the compensation which takes place in consequence of the displacement of the rings for different colours.

In crystals where the displacement of the rings is very great, the two oval central spots shown in *fig.* 32 are drawn out, as Mr. Herschel observes, into long spectra or tails of *red, green,* and *violet* light, and the extremities of the rings shown in the same figure, are distorted and highly coloured, exhibiting the appearance shown in *fig.* 35. If we examine these spectra with coloured media, which absorb different colours, they will be found to consist of well defined spots of the several simple colours, arranged on each side of the principal section, as shewn in *fig.* 36. The length of the spectra within the crystal is, in Rochelle salt, no less than ten degrees.

Fig. 35.

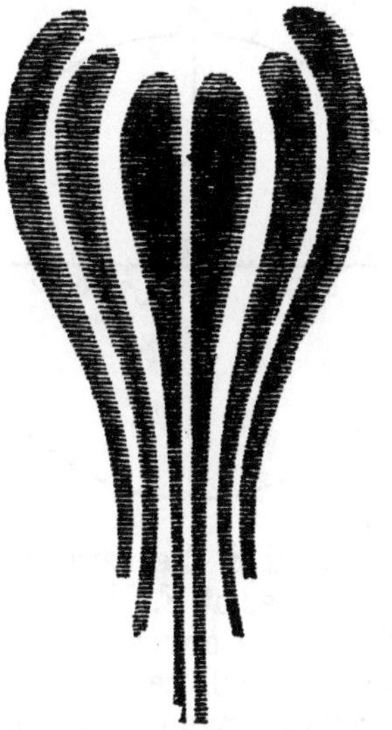

The discovery of Mr. Herschel, which we have now explained, is a complete proof, if any were wanted, of Dr. Brewster's theory, that all the tints are related

Fig. 36.

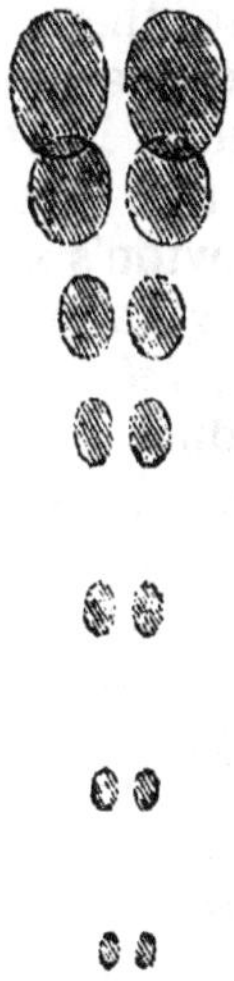

Red.
Orange.
Yellow.
Green.
Blue.
Indigo.
Violet.

to two rectangular axes, and that the two apparent axes passing through the centres of the systems of rings, are merely axes of compensation, or resultant axes. If this were not the case, Rochelle salt would have two axes for each different ray of the spectrum, and the axes of crystals would have no definite position, and no relation to the crystalline form of the substance.*

In order to explain the cause of the displacement of the systems of rings in homogeneous light, let the rings be produced by two negative axes C, A, *fig.* 37, of which C is of such strength, that it

---

* See Mr. Herschel's original paper, in the *Mem. Camb. Phil. Soc.*, vol. i.

Fig. 37.

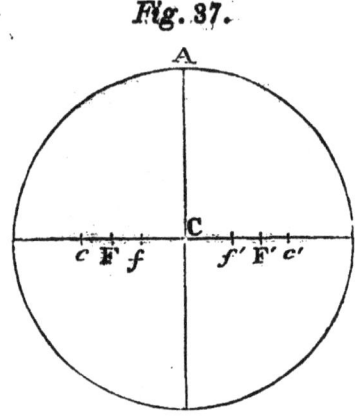

will produce at F the same tint of red light that A does at F. In this case, the tints will destroy one another, and the black spot at F will be the pole of one of the systems of rings of *red* light. If C and A had the same proportional action on the *violet* and other rays, as on the red rays, which is the case in bi-carbonate of ammonia, then F would also be the point of compensation for violet or other light, and the pole of the violet or other rings. In this case, there would be no virtual poles, no displacement of the rings in homogeneous light, as in Rochelle salt; and the tints would be exactly those of Newton's scale. But, if the axis C has a greater proportional action upon the *violet* and other rays than A, it will produce a higher tint at F than that produced by A; and the point of compensation will now be at f, which will become the centre of the violet system of rings. The centres of the other systems of rings for yellow and green light will occupy intermediate points between F and f, and FF′ will be the inclination of the resultant axes for red light, and ff' for violet light. This is the case with all the crystals in Class I. of the preceding Table. On the other hand, if the axis C had a less proportional action upon the violet rays than A, the points of compensation would be at c and c', and cc' would be the inclination of the axes for blue light, which is the case with all the crystals in Class II. Here, then, we have a complete explanation of all the phenomena observed by Mr. Herschel, and are able to calculate them in the most rigorous manner, by supposing the real axes to be at A and C, and to have an invariable position coincident with fixed lines in the primitive form of the mineral.

The most remarkable example of deviation from the tints of Newton's scale occurs in *apophyllite*, which has generally *one* axis of double refraction. In the Tyrol apophyllite, according to Dr. Brewster, the system of coloured rings with which its axis is surrounded, is composed of unusual tints, the only colours being *bluish violet* and *greenish yellow*, separated by a ring of white light. By examining the apophyllite, however, in homogeneous light, Mr. Herschel succeeded in determining that some specimens exercise a *negative* or *repulsive* action upon the rays at one end of the spectrum, a *positive* or *attractive* action upon the rays at the other end of the spectrum, and *no action at all* upon the mean refrangible rays. In one case the doubly refracting action ceased in the *yellow* rays, and in another in the *indigo* rays. The following were the tints observed in these two cases.

FIRST SPECIMEN.—*First Order.* Black, sombre red, orange yellow, green, greenish blue, sombre and dirty blue.

Second Order. Dull purple, pink, ruddy pink, pink yellow, pale yellow, (almost white) bluish green, dull pale blue.

Third Order. Very dilute purple, pale pink, white, very pale blue.

SECOND SPECIMEN.—*First, and only Order.* Black, sombre indigo, indigo, indigo inclining to purple, pale blue purple, very pale reddish purple, pale rose red, white, white with a hardly perceptible tinge of green.

In these two specimens the rings increase in diameter with great rapidity from the red end of the spectrum;—they become infinite in diameter in the *yellow* rays in *Specimen first*, and in the *indigo* rays in *Specimen second*; after which they again become finite and continue to contract up to the violet end of the spectrum, where they have still a considerably larger diameter than in the red rays.

In other specimens of apophyllite, which Mr. Herschel calls *leucocyclite*, from the rings being white and black, the action of the doubly refracting force was so equal upon all the rays of the spectrum, that the diameter of the rings was nearly alike for all colours. If this were accurately the case, the system of rings formed in white light by the super-position of all these rings would be simple alternations of perfect black and white. This equality was so nearly the case in one specimen, that Mr. Herschel counted thirty-five rings. Under a more careful examination, however, he found that they had the following colours.

First Order.—Black, greenish white, bright white, purplish white, sombre violet blue.

Second Order.—Violet almost black, pale yellow green, greenish white, white, purplish white, obscure indigo inclining to purple.

Third Order.—Sombre violet, tolerable yellow green, yellowish white, white, pale purple, sombre indigo.

Fourth Order.—Sombre violet, livid grey, yellow green, pale yellowish white, white, purple, very sombre indigo.

Mr. Herschel likewise found a remarkable deviation of the tints in *hypo-sulphate of lime*, and in *Vesuvian**.

The explanation of such remarkable deviations from the usual tints, as exhibited in apophyllite, was deduced by Dr. Brewster from his Theory of Rectangular Axes, and by means of it, all the preceding phenomena are capable of the most rigorous computation. In the *Phil. Trans.* 1818, p. 249, he has shown "that a single positive axis (*fig.*38) may be represented by three rectangular positive axes (C, A, and B) provided two of them (A, B) are equal, and the third (C) has a less intensity than the other two." The same author has also shown (*Phil. Trans.* 1813) that double refracting crystals have also two dispersive powers; and he concluded that in crystals with two axes, each axis has a different action upon the differently coloured rays.

In the case of apophyllite, then, the two positive axes A, B, (*fig.* 38) will produce a negative resultant axis at C; and as the real axis at C is positive, the apparent or finally resultant axis at C will be a single axis, *negative* if the *negative* be the strongest, and *positive* if the *positive* axis be the strongest. Now let us suppose that in the apophyllite the two axes at C have equal intensity, viz. $+C$ and $-C$, ($-C$ being the resultant of $+A$

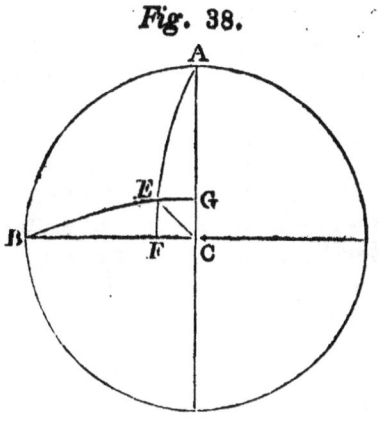

Fig. 38.

and $+B$,) for *yellow* light, and that $-C$ acts more powerfully upon the *red* rays, than $+C$, while $+C$ acts more energetically upon the *violet* rays. In this case the two axes $+C$ and $-C$ will compensate one another exactly for yellow light, or there will be no double refraction and polarisation for yellow rays, or the diameter of the rings will be infinite. In *red* light the predominance of $-C$ will leave a single negative axis of double refraction for red rays, and will consequently produce a *negative* system of rings. In violet light, on the contrary, the predominance of the action of $+C$ will leave a single *positive* axis of double refraction for violet rays, and will consequently produce a positive system of rings. The compensation here described is exactly analogous to that of a compound lens, consisting of a convex and concave lens of equal curvatures, of such glass that their indices of refraction for yellow rays is equal, while the index of refraction for the *violet* rays is *greater* in the *convex* lens, and the index for the *red* rays *greater* in the *concave* lens. Such a lens will *converge* the *violet* rays, *diverge* the *red* rays, and produce no deviation at all in the *yellow* ones. That is, the same *compound* lens will be a *plane* lens in *yellow* light, a *convex* one in *blue* light, and a *concave* one in *red* light.

In this view of the subject each order of colours in apophyllite is, as it were, a secondary residual spectrum arising from the opposite action of the negative and positive axes, and the tints of which these orders are composed will consequently vary according to the locality of the ray of compensation.

From the circumstance of some specimens of apophyllite exercising a negative action upon light, Dr. Brewster states, that he had no doubt that apophyllites

---

* "Among crystals with one axis," says Mr. Herschel, "Dr. Brewster has enumerated the *Idocrase* or *Vesuvian*, and correctly. Had he noticed, however, in the specimens examined by him, the very striking inversion of the tints of Newton's scale exhibited in the rings of that now before us, he would doubtless have made mention of it." Treatise on Light, § 1125. Dr. Brewster examined *only one* specimen of Vesuvian, which was a large and valuable crystal lent to him for the purpose, and which he was not allowed to cut. It was of a nutbrown colour, sufficient to mask completely any peculiarity in its tints; and was in other respects quite unfitted for the observations made by Herschel.

would yet be found in which the axis is negative in all the rays of the spectrum[*]; and some years afterwards he discovered the remarkable mineral of *oxahverite*, which is an apophyllite with this property.[†]

These views have been confirmed and illustrated by a more recent observation of the same author, who has found that *glauberite* has *two axes for red light and only one negative axis for violet light*. In this case the single *negative violet axis* C is the resultant of two *positive* axes at A and B of equal intensity, while the same two axes have different intensities for *red* and the other rays of the spectrum.

Hence in *apophyllite* the single system of rings is the resultant system of *three* rectangular axes, while in *glauberite* the single system of *violet* rings is the resultant of two rectangular axes.

CHAPTER X.

Cause of the Colours of Polarised Light—Biot's Theory of moveable Polarisation—Laws of the Interference of Polarised Rays—their application to explain the Colours of Polarised Light.

HAVING thus described, as briefly and perspicuously as we can, the general phenomena of the colours of polarised light as produced by doubly refracting crystals, we shall proceed to consider the explanations which have been given of them. We have already shown, in Chap. VI. p. 19, that the thin plate of sulphate of lime, D E F G, divides white light into two coloured pencils, complementary to each other, as, for example, *red* and *green*. These are the *extraordinary* and *ordinary* images pro-

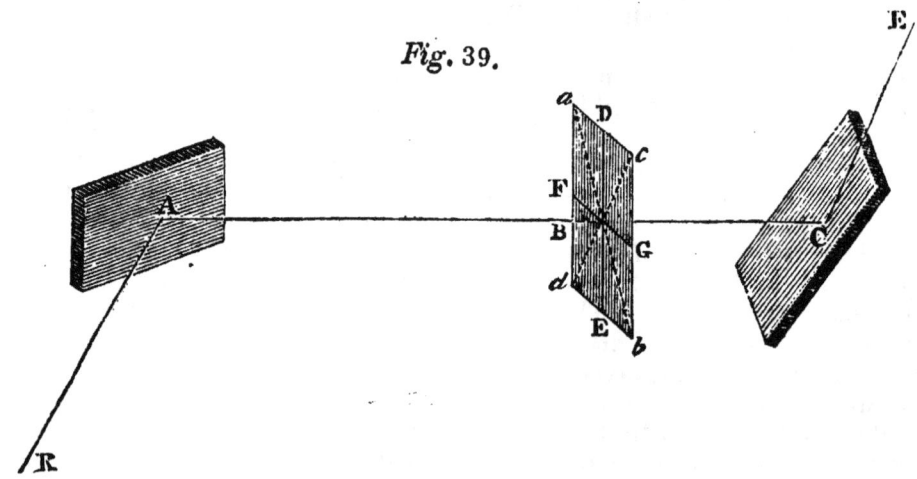

Fig. 39.

duced by double refraction; and we shall distinguish them by the letters E and O. In doubly refracting plates or crystals of considerable thickness, the two pencils, O and E, are perfectly white and equal, and are polarised in planes at right angles to each other, as already explained; but in thin plates, where O and E are coloured, they are polarised in a different manner.

Since the extraordinary pencil, namely, the *red* one or E, is reflected by the analysing plate C, and is a maximum when C is in the azimuths of 90° (the one shown in the figure) and 270°, its polarisation must be different from that of the ray A B; and since no part of the ordinary pencil, or the *green* one O, is reflected, this last must have the same polarisation as the pencil A B. Hence the action of the plate of sulphate of lime, D E F G, upon the polarised ray A B, is to divide it into two pencils, O and E, *green* and *red*, the former having the same polarisation as A B, and the latter a different polarisation. Let us now suppose the plate D E F G to revolve round the ray A B, and let *a* be the angle of azimuth which the axis F G of the crystal or plate of sulphate of lime forms with the plane of primitive polarisation R A B: then we have already seen that when $a = 45°$, the *red* rays are reflected at C, when the azimuth of C is 90° and 270°, and is not reflected at all when its azimuth is 0° and 180°. Hence the red pencil or E must have been polarised in a plane at right angles to that of A B, or the change of polarisation effected by the plate must have been $90° = 2 \times 45° = 2a$. By making *a* o-

---

[*] Edin. Encycl. art. Optics. Vol. XV. p. 597.
[†] Edin. Journal of Science. No. XIII. p. 115.

various magnitudes, M. Biot determined that the change of polarisation of the pencil E was always equal to 2 *a*, and he thus established his doctrine of *moveable polarisation* in a double azimuth, in contradistinction to *fixed polarisation*, or that which takes place in thick crystals. Hence it follows that in thin plates the pencils O and E are not polarised at right angles to each other, as in thick plates; but no attempt was made to determine by what changes the moveable polarisation passed into the fixed polarisation, or at what limit a plate ceased to be a thin one, or began to be a thick one.

Upon this doctrine M. Biot attempted to explain all the colours of polarised light by his theory of the "oscillation of luminous molecules," a theory of great boldness and ingenuity. He supposed that as soon as a polarised ray penetrated a thin crystalline plate, its plane of polarisation oscillated alternately in two different planes, one its original plane of polarisation, and the other the plane of 2 *a*. The frequency of these alternations, like Newton's fits, varied with the refrangibility of the ray, being greatest in the red and least in the violet, and are supposed to take place at equal intervals, while the ray is passing through the plate. Upon this hypothesis M. Biot has founded his explanation of the colours of polarised light; and it might have remained long as a monument of the author's ingenuity and as a hypothetical expression of a great number of phenomena, had not M. Fresnel sapped its foundations by a beautiful analysis of the phenomena on which it rests, and a reference of all the colours of polarised light to the general principle of interference. This explanation, indeed, was first given by Dr. Thos. Young, but it was the discovery of M. Fresnel alone that established it upon an impregnable basis.

The general principle of the interference of common light has been explained in the Treatise on Optics, Chap. XII. p. 31. We shall therefore proceed to give some account of the experiments of M. Fresnel, who was associated with M. Arago in this inquiry. The following is a brief view of the leading results which they obtained.

1. *When two rays, polarised in the same plane, interfere with each other, the phenomena of their interference are identically the same as with two rays of common light.*

This law may be easily verified by repeating the experiment in Chap. XII. p. 31, in polarised instead of common light, when it will be found that the fringes polarised by interference, and shown in *fig.* 34, are exactly the same as there represented.

2. *Two rays of light polarised at right angles to each other exhibit none of the phenomena of interference.*

In order to prove this, M. Fresnel bisected a rhomboid of Iceland spar, so that each piece at the line of bisection must have had exactly the same thickness. He then placed the one above the other, so that their principal sections formed an angle of 90°. In this state the emergent pencils will only be double, as shown at F, *fig.* 20. These two pencils, therefore, differ only in being polarised at right angles to each other, and when any body is placed in this light no phenomena of interference are visible.

M. Arago obtained the same result by transmitting light diverging from a luminous point through two fine slits in a thin piece of copper. When these slits were viewed by a lens in the manner employed by Fresnel, the fringes produced by interference were distinctly visible. He then prepared two bundles of pieces of thin mica, or films of blown glass, by dividing one bundle into two with a sharp cutting instrument. These bundles were placed so that they could revolve; and when they were so arranged as to polarise light in parallel planes, distinct fringes were produced by the slits, in the same manner as if the bundles of mica were removed; but when they were placed so as to polarise the light in rectangular planes, no fringes were produced. A still more elegant and convincing experiment was employed by M. Fresnel. He placed a film of sulphate of lime before two narrow slits. Two images of each slit were thus produced, which may be called R O, R E, and L O, L E, *viz.* right ordinary ray, right extraordinary ray, &c., according as they come from the right or left hand slit. In observing carefully the results of the experiment, it is found that R O and L O, and R E and L E, similarly polarised, produce by their interference distinct fringes; while R O and L E, and L O and R E produce no fringes at all. This experiment admits of a beautiful variation by bisecting the film, and turning one half a quadrant round in its own plane;

but we have not space for continuing the subject.

3. *Two rays originally polarised in rectangular planes may be afterwards reduced to the same plane of polarisation, without acquiring the property of interference.*

If in the experiment with the film of mica we place between the eye and the sheet of copper a doubly refracting crystal, having its principal section inclined 45° to either of the planes of polarisation of the interfering pencils, each pencil will be divided by the crystal into two of equal intensity, and will be polarised in two rectangular planes, one of which is the principal section of the crystal. In this state of things there are no fringes seen in the union of R O with L O, nor in that of L E with R E.

4. *Two rays polarised in opposite planes, and afterwards brought into similar states of polarisation, interfere like common light, provided they belong to a pencil, the whole of which was originally polarised in one and the same plane.*

5. *In the phenomena of interference produced by doubly refracted rays, a difference of half an undulation must in certain cases be admitted.*

These two last results are deduced from experiments analogous to those already described; but it would occupy too much of our limited space to describe them as they deserve. We must therefore refer the reader to Mr. Herschel's Treatise on Light, Part IV., § viii., No. 960—973.

The doctrine of interference was first employed by Dr. Young, in an article in the Quarterly Review for 1814, to explain the colours of polarised light. In that article he maintains "that such colours are perfectly reducible, like all other cases of recurrent colours, to the general laws of the interference of light which have been established in this country; and that all their apparent intricacies and capricious variations are only the necessary consequences of the simplest application of these laws. They are, in fact, merely varieties of the colours of mixed plates, in which the appearances are found to resemble the colours of simple thin plates, when the thickness is increased in the same proportion as the difference of refractive densities is less than twice the whole density: the colours exhibited by direct transmission, corresponding to the colours of thin plates seen by reflection, and to the extraordinary refraction of the crystalline substances, and the colours of mixed plates exhibited by indirect light to the colours transmitted through common thin plates, and to those produced by the ordinary refraction of the polarising substances." According to these views, colours ought to be produced in common as well as in polarised light, and it was therefore left to MM. Fresnel and Arago to show how the production of such colours was dependent on the primitive polarisation of the pencil, and its subsequent analysis before entering the eye.

The second of the preceding laws explains at once the reason why no colours are exhibited by the transmission of light through a thin plate possessing double refraction. The two pencils are polarised in opposite planes, and therefore incapable of producing the periodical colours by their interference.

In order to explain how the polarised tints are produced by interference in ordinary cases, let us take the case shown in *fig.* 21, pp. 18, 19, where the neutral axes are inclined 45° to the plane of primitive polarisation.

Let R A, *fig.* 40, be the polarised ray

Fig. 40.

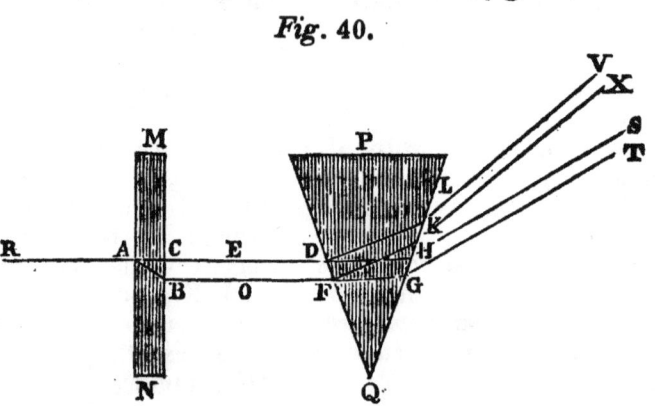

incident on the crystallised plate M N, having its principal section or one of its neutral axes inclined 45° to the plane in which R A is polarised. This ray will be divided by double refraction into two rays oppositely polarised, *viz.* the extraordinary ray C D or E, and the ordinary ray B F or O. As these rays differ in velocity, the one ray will be behind the other, and they will consequently interfere, being polarised +45° and −45° to the plane of primitive polarisation. Let these rays be now received on a doubly refracting prism of calcareous spar P Q, having its principal section in the plane of primitive polarisation, and they will be again doubled, forming the four pencils D L, F K, D H, F G, all of equal intensity, of which H S and G T are parallel, and L V, K X. The compound pencils, H G T S and L K X V will consist of two systems of ray, O e and E e, and O o and E o, the one of each system following the other at a given distance, the distance between O e and E e being d, and by law 5, the distance between O o and E o being $d \pm \frac{1}{2}$ undulation. But as each of the rays of these two systems have similar polarisations, they will by law 1, p. 38, interfere and produce the complementary colours corresponding to the intervals d and $d + \frac{1}{2}$ undulation. If the ray R A is polarised in a plane at right angles to what it was in the preceding case, it will suffer exactly the same division; but the intervals of retardation will now be $d - \frac{1}{2}$ undulation and d, so that the two pencils will exchange colours.

Chapter XI.

New Species of Double Refraction in Analcime.

The remarkable mineral called *Analcime*, or *Cubizite*, has been ranked by mineralogists among those which have the cube for their primitive form; and hence, if this were the case, we should expect to find it without double refraction. By attentive observation, however, no distinct cleavage planes can be observed, and the remarkable optical structure of the mineral confirms us in the opinion that its crystallographic structure is still unknown.

The most common form of this mineral is the icosatetrahedron shown in *fig.* 41. This solid is contained by twenty-

Fig. 41.

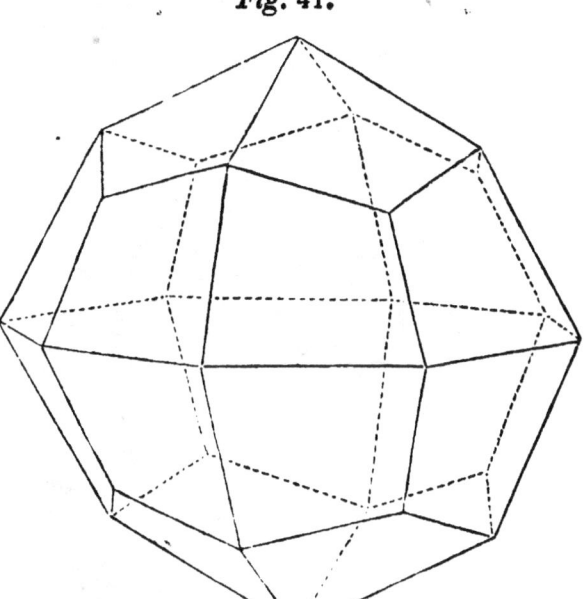

four equal and similar trapezia, and may be considered as derived from the cube by three truncations on each of its angles, inclined 144° 44′ 8″ to each of its faces, and 146° 26′ 33″ to one another.

If we suppose the original cube to be divided by planes passing through all the *twelve* diagonals of its six faces, it will be reduced, as shown in *fig.* 42, into twenty-four irregular tetrahedrons. The same planes will divide the icositetrahedron, *fig.* 41, into twenty-four similar pentahedrons, two of whose planes are placed at right angles to each other, having for their common section one of

Fig. 42. 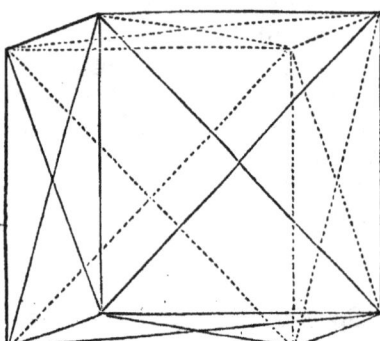 *Fig.* 43.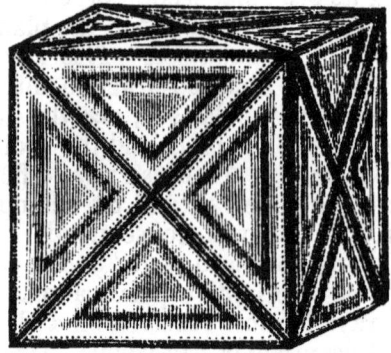

the axes of the solid, while a third, equally inclined to those two, and forming an angle of 45° with the common section, passes through the centre of the icosatetrahedron. The other two planes of the pentahedron are halves of two of the adjoining trapezia which form the surface of the general solid.

If we suppose the crystal to have a cubical form, and expose it to polarised light, incident perpendicular to any of its faces, we shall find that all the planes passing through the diagonals are planes of no double refraction and polarisation, as shown in *fig.* 43. The black lines at right angles to one another show the planes where there are no polarised tints, and the intermediate shades represent the different orders of colours which of course depend on the thickness of the crystal. This effect is produced when any of the two axes of the cube, or those lying in a plane perpendicular to the polarised ray, are inclined 45° to the plane of primitive polarisation. When any of these two axes, however, are in the plane of primitive polarisation the tints disappear, and continue invisible while the crystal is made to revolve round that axis; but when the axis is inclined to that plane, the tints re-appear, and reach their maximum intensity when the inclination becomes 45°.

In order to convey an idea of the structure of the complete crystal we have represented the icosatetrahedron in *fig.* 44, with its planes of no double refraction and polarisation, and the tints of the in-

Fig. 44.

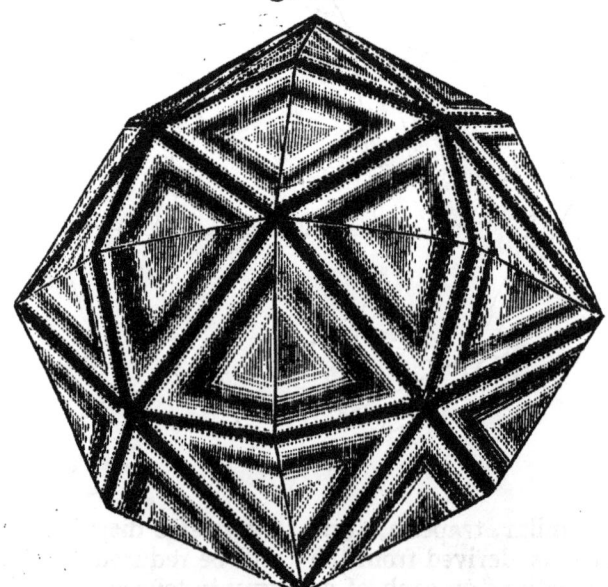

termediate solids. The dark shaded lines represent the planes in which there is no double refraction and polarisation, and the fainter shadings represent the tints. The appearances, however, shown in this figure, and in *fig.* 43, can never be seen by the observer at once.

The tints polarised by analcime are those of Newton's scale, and they are negative in relation to each of the four axes of the icosatetrahedron. This remarkable structure produces a distinct separation of the ordinary and extraordinary images of a minute luminous object when the incident ray passes through any pair of the four planes which are adjacent to any of the three axes of the solid. The least refracted image is the extraordinary one, and consequently the doubly refracting force is *negative* in relation to the axis to which the doubly refracted ray is perpendicular.

The phenomena of the tints exhibited in any individual sector, C O B, *fig.* 45,

Fig. 45.

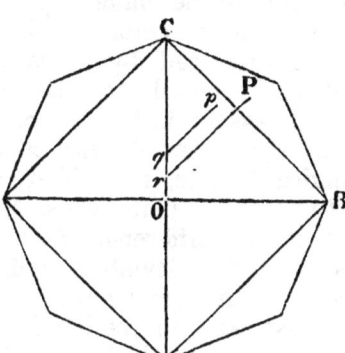

have no relation to the axis of the icosatetrahedron passing through O, considered as an axis of double refraction. The direction of polarisation of every portion in each sector as C O B, is, on the contrary, perpendicular to the line C B, or parallel to one of the rectangular axes of the icosatetrahedron which is perpendicular to the axis passing through O. The tint at any point, p for example, does not depend upon its distance pO, from any point O, but upon its distance pq, from the nearest plane of no polarisation taken in a direction perpendicular to C B. Calling T the tint as determined by experiment at any point p whose distance Pr, taken in the manner now mentioned, is D, we shall have the tint t at any other point p whose distance pq is d, by the following formula, $t = \dfrac{Td^2}{D^2}$, the thickness of the crystal being supposed equal at both these points. One of the most important results of these experiments is the singular distribution of the doubly refracting force. In all other crystals in which the laws of double refraction have been studied, the axis to which the doubly refracting force is related, has no fixed locality in the mineral. It is a line parallel to a given line in the primitive form, and every fragment of a crystal, however minute, possesses this axis, and all the optical properties of the original crystal, however large. The property of double refraction, in short, in regularly crystallised substances, resides in the ultimate particles of the body, and does not depend upon the mode in which they are aggregated to form an individual crystal. In analcime, on the contrary, we have planes of no double refraction, having a definite and invariable position, and we may even extract a portion of each separate pentahedron which has no axis at all*.

Chapter XII.

Circular Polarisation— in Quartz— Right and Left handed Quartz—Magiedral Crystals—Both these structures united in Amethyst—Circular Double Refraction—Circular Polarisation in Fluids.

In the year 1811, M. Arago observed along the axis of quartz, when exposed to polarised light, certain colours, which descended in the scale when the doubly refracting prism by which the emergent light was analysed, was made to revolve round its axis. He observed also that the two images displayed the complementary colours. In this state of the subject, M. Biot directed to it his particular attention, and was enabled to analyse the phenomena with his usual sagacity.

We have already seen that in crystals with one axis the system of rings is traversed by a black cross at the intersection of whose rectangular branches there is neither double refraction nor polarisation, as shown in *fig.* 25, p. 21. In rock crystal, however, the black cross is obliterated by colours which fill up the first ring, and encroach upon the rest, as shown in *fig.* 46. These colours vary with the thickness of the plate of quartz; but they

Fig. 46.

* See Edinburgh Transactions, vol. x. part i. pp. 187—194, where Dr. Brewster first described the phenomena contained in this chapter.

suffer no change by turning the plate round its axis.

Let us now suppose the plate of quartz to be placed, at D F E G, in the polarising apparatus shown in *fig.* 39, p. 36, and let us suppose that to an eye at E the colour in the centre of the rings is red. Let the analysing plate C be turned round from *right to left*, keeping its inclination to A C invariable, and the *red* colour will change successively to *orange, yellow, green* and *violet*, the plate C acquiring, as it were, by its rotation, the power of reflecting these colours in succession, a result which is perfectly explained by supposing that the rays of each of those colours are polarised in different planes. Upon trying various specimens of quartz, M. Biot found several in which the very same phenomena were produced by turning the plate C from *left to right*. Hence in reference to this property some specimens of quartz are *right handed* and others *left handed*.

In order to analyse this remarkable property we must use homogeneous light. When this is done, we find that the ray, *yellow*, for example, is reflected by the plate C, but when C is turned round, the yellow ray becomes more and more faint, and after a certain angle of rotation it disappears. The homogeneous red disappears at a less angle of rotation, and the homogeneous violet at a greater angle.

By employing plates of quartz of various thicknesses, M. Biot found that for the same ray the arcs of rotation, after which it disappeared, were proportioned to the thicknesses of the plates; and that in the same plate they were reciprocally proportional to the squares of the lengths of their fits or to the squares of the length of an undulation.

Supposing the thickness of the quartz to be one millimetre or 1-25th of an inch, the following were the arcs of rotation for the different rays.

	Arc of rotation for *one* millimetre of quartz.
Extreme red	17°.4964
Mean red	18.9881
Limit of red and orange	20.4798
Mean orange	21.3968
Limit of orange and yellow	22.3138
Mean yellow	23.9945
Limit of yellow and green	25.6752
Mean green	27.8606
Limit of green and blue	30.0460
Mean blue	32.3088
Limit of blue and indigo	34.5717
Mean indigo	36.1273
Limit of indigo and violet	37.6829
Mean violet	40.8828
Extreme violet	44.0827

From these curious facts it follows that polarised light transmitted along the axis of quartz comports itself as if the planes of polarisation of its different rays revolved in the interior of the crystal, in some crystals from left to right, and in others from right to left.

If we combine two plates of right-handed or two of left-handed quartz, the deviation of the plane of polarisation of any ray will be equal to that which would be produced by a plate whose thickness is equal to the sum of their thicknesses; but if we combine a plate of right-handed with a plate of left-handed quartz, the effect will be equal to that of a plate whose thickness is equal to the difference of their thicknesses, and the deviation will be to the right if the right-handed plate is the thickest, and to the left if the left-handed plate is the thickest. If the two plates are equal, the tints will be entirely obliterated, and if their axes coincide rigorously, the black cross, though obliterated in each of them separately, will appear in their combination.

In examining the *Amethyst*, Dr. Brewster discovered that it possessed the power in the same specimen of turning the planes of polarisation both to the left and to the right; and upon a close inspection, he found that this curious mineral was actually composed of alternate layers of right and left handed quartz. This singular structure is seen by cutting a plate out of a crystal of amethyst, by planes perpendicular to its axis; and when such a plate is exposed to polarised light in the apparatus *fig.* 39, it has the appearance shown in *fig.* 47. The three sets of veins here represented correspond to the alternate faces of the

Fig. 47.

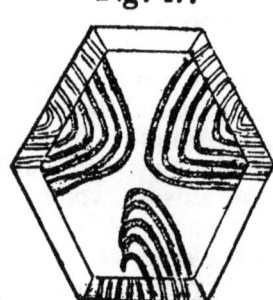

six-sided pyramid. The shaded veins turn the planes of polarisation from right to left, while all the intermediate unshaded veins, and the three unshaded sectors turn the planes of polarisation from left to right. The line or narrow space where these two structures meet, has no action on the planes of polarisation; and the action increases on each side of it to the centre of the shaded veins where it is a maximum. Hence it is obvious, that the amethyst is not, in the ordinary sense of the word, a compound mineral, in which dissimilar faces of the crystal are brought into mechanical contact: for in this case we should have a dark line of junction, and the intensity of the polarising force would be the same in every part of the combined layers. In the present case, the right-handed passes gradually into the left-handed polarisation, and there is no appearance whatever of cleavage in the direction of these planes. We must, therefore, consider the amethyst as a mineral in which, like the analcime, the ether is distributed in an unusual manner, or in which the structure has been regulated by laws of crystallisation which have not yet been recognized by mineralogists. In some specimens, these opposite layers are so minute, that the maximum intensity of the force which turns the planes of polarisation is nearly reduced to nothing, so that the black cross in the centre of its rings is seen with nearly the same distinctness as in calcareous spar. Hence, in the veins of amethyst 1 millimetre thick (1-25th of an inch) we find them of very different intensities, the arc of rotation for the mean yellow ray varying from $0°$ up to $23°.9945$.

The colouring matter of the amethyst is arranged in a very remarkable manner in relation to these veins. The lilac tints often reside in the veined structure; and in some specimens Dr. Brewster found the red colouring matter arranged in veins corresponding with the dark spaces where the two structures meet. In another specimen the *right-handed veins* were *lilac*, the *left-handed veins brownish red*, and their lines of junction *yellowish white*. In other crystals, the colouring matter affects the largest masses of the crystal, such as those left white in *fig.* 47.

When an amethyst is perfectly formed, its structure is symmetrical, as shown in *fig.* 48, which represents the section of part of the pyramid and part of the

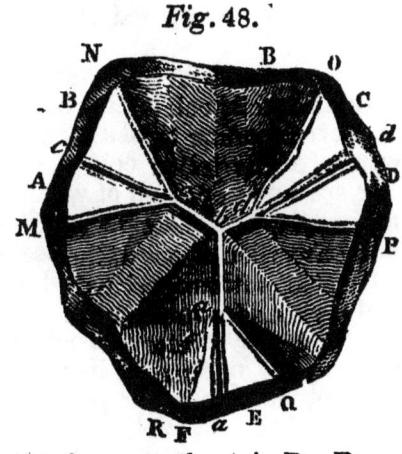

Fig. 48.

prism of an amethyst in Dr. Brewster's possession, measuring nearly *two inches and three-tenths* across. "On the three alternate sides of the prism," says he, "viz. M N, O P, and Q R, are placed sectors M *c* N, O *d* P, Q *a* R, which are divided into two parts by dark lines, *c c'*, *d d'*, *a a'*, which separate the direct structures of A, C, and E from the retrograde structures of B, D, and F. On the other three alternate faces of the prisms are placed the three veined sectors M *c b a* R, N *c b d* O, and P *d b a* Q, which meet at *b* in angles of $120°$, and consist of veins of opposite structures, alternating with each other, and so minute, that in many places the circular tints are almost wholly extinguished by their mutual action. The direct sectors, A, C, and E, are all connected together by the three radial veins *b a*, *b c*, *b d*, and are therefore to be considered as the expanded terminations of those veins. The retrograde sectors B, D, and F, are expansions of the first retrograde veins next to *b d c*, *d b a*, and *a b c;* and the lines *c c'*, *d d'*, and *a a'* are continuations of the dark or neutral lines which separate the first retrograde vein from the direct radial veins.

All the sectors A, B, C, D, E, and F, are of a *yellowish brown* colour, and all the rest of the crystal is of a *pale lilac* colour, the lilac tints being arranged in the manner previously described. The phenomena which I have now mentioned as existing in this specimen are very common in the amethyst; and I have never yet found a specimen in which the yellow tints were not confined to those portions which formed the expanded terminations of veins; a fact which indicates that this would have been the colour of the crystal, whether its actions were direct or retrograde, and that the lilac colour affects in general those portions which are composed of opposite veins."

In a large amethyst the veined portions were perfectly colourless, while the sectors corresponding to M c N, &c. *fig.* 48, were of a pale yellow colour, and in another specimen, one half of which was *yellow*, and the other *lilac*, the yellow was obviously a portion of one of the sectors; while the lilac portion consisted wholly of alternate veins, so minute as to destroy almost wholly the rotatory structure.

The property of quartz, in virtue of which it produces circular polarisation, was supposed, by M. Biot, to reside in the ultimate particles of silex; but if this were the case, the same property would be possessed by silex in all its forms, which Dr. Brewster found not to be the case, after a minute examination of opal, tabasheer, and other siliceous minerals. He likewise found that the rotatory property was not possessed by quartz, which had been deprived of its crystalline structure by fusion; and Mr. Herschel sought for it in vain in a solution of silica in potash, though the silex previously exhibited circular polarisation.

Conceiving that this property might be related to some crystalline structure in quartz, Mr. Herschel examined different crystals of the quartz *Plagiedre* of Hauy, which possesses unsymmetrical faces, x, x, x, x', x', x', (see *fig.* 10. p. 6,) which always lean in one uniform direction round the summit A, but sometimes to the *right* and sometimes to the *left*. After an examination of fifty-three different crystals, he found that the direction in which they turned the planes of polarisation was invariably the same as the direction in which the plagiedral faces x, x, leant round the crystal; so that even, if these faces were microscopic, the sight of one of them would enable us to predict the direction of rotation in a plate cut from it. Hence Mr. Herschel concluded *that whatever be the cause which determines the direction of rotation*, the same has acted in determining the direction of the plagiedral faces. Apatite and some other crystallised minerals exhibit also plagiedral and unsymmetrical faces; but as they do not possess circular polarisation, we must infer that the latter is not a necessary consequence of the structure which exhibits the former.

In order to determine if the colours of circular polarisation were produced by the interference of the rays formed by double refraction, M. Fresnel made the following experiment. He took a prism of *right-handed* quartz, A B C, (*fig.* 49,)

Fig. 49.

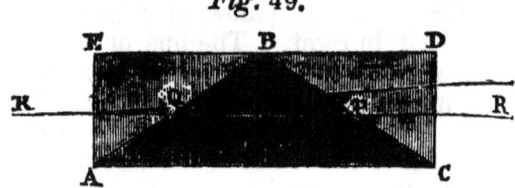

having its faces A B, B C equally inclined to R R, the axis of the prism, along which the circular polarisation is seen. The refracting angle A B C was 150°. As the ray R R, incident at Q, could not emerge from the face B C, he cemented on the faces B A, B C, two halves of another prism exactly similar to the first, but cut from a crystal of *left-handed* quartz. These two halves are shown at A B E, C B D, and are distinguished by the sign —. As the ray R R will pass through all these three prisms in a line parallel to their axes of double refraction, it cannot be separated into two by the ordinary refracting forces; but if it is influenced by another doubly refracting force belonging to circular polarisation, it will be first divided into two pencils by the left-handed prism A E B: but when these two pencils enter the right-handed prism A B C at Q, their angular separation will be doubled, owing to the prism A B C having an opposite circularly polarising structure. When the two rays come to P, and enter the prism B C D, their angular separation will be again doubled, so that the ray will finally emerge in two pencils. By this ingenious contrivance, M. Fresnel succeeded in separating the two pencils produced by the force of circular polarisation.

When either of these pencils is examined by a doubly refracting prism, it is doubled like common light, and none of the two pencils ever vanish during the revolution of the doubly refracting prism; but that they differ from common light M. Fresnel proved by the following experiment: (*fig.* 50.) If the two pencils R P produced along the axis of quartz are made to fall perpendicularly on the face A B of a parallelopiped of crown glass, A B C D, whose refractive index is 1.51, and whose angles A B C, A D C, are each 54½°, they will suffer total reflection at Q and S, and will emerge in the direction S T. The two emergent pencils will now be found *completely polarised*,

POLARISATION OF LIGHT.

the one in an azimuth 45° to the right of the plane of reflexion, and the other 45° to the left.

If one of the two circularly polarising rays is transmitted through a thin crystallised film, and parallel to its axis, it will be divided by the double refraction of the film into two pencils, exhibiting the complementary colours; and these colours differ by an exact quarter of a tint, or order, from those that would have been produced by the same film with common polarised light.

M. Fresnel had the good fortune to discover another method of producing a pencil possessing all the properties of one of those formed along the axis of quartz. He allowed a common polarised ray, R P, (*fig.* 50) to suffer two total reflexions at Q and S in a glass parallelopiped: then if the plane of reflexion P Q S is in-

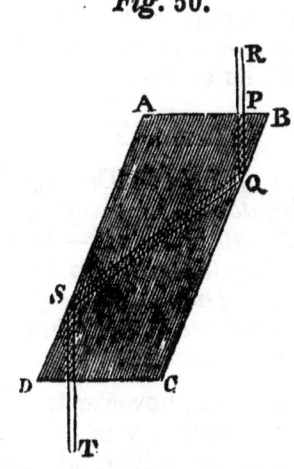

Fig. 50.

clined 45° to the plane of primitive polarisation of the ray R P, it will emerge at T, possessing all the properties of one of the rays formed along the axis of quartz.

Circular Polarisation of Fluids.

THE property of circular polarisation is not confined to quartz. M. Biot and Dr. Seebeck discovered it nearly about the same time in certain fluids which possessed it in a feeble degree. If we fill a tube, six or seven inches long, with oil of turpentine, and expose it to polarised light in the apparatus, (*fig.* 39,) the observer will perceive the complementary colours similar to those in rock crystal. Some fluids turn the plane of polarisation from right to left, and others from left to right. The following Table shows the results of M. Biot's experiments.

Right to Left.	Arc of Rotation for 1 millimetre of thickness.	*Left to Right.*	Arc of Rotation for 1 millimetre of thickness.
Rock crystal	+ 18°.414	Rock crystal	− 18°.414
Oil of turpentine	+ 0.271	Essential oil of lemons	− 0.436
Ditto another kind	+ 0.251	Concentrated syrup of sugar	− 0.554
Ditto purified by repeated distillation	+ 0.286		
Solution of 1753 parts of artificial camphor in 17359 of alcohol	+ 0.018		
Essential oil of laurel			
Vapour of turpentine			

M. Biot found that when oil of turpentine was mixed with sulphuric ether, which has not the rotatory property, it gave, when mixed, the very same tints which it would have produced alone in the same tube; and that when a right-handed was mixed with a left-handed fluid, in quantities reciprocally proportional to the intensity of their action, they neutralised each other. He likewise found that oil of turpentine required to have a thickness of $68\frac{1}{2}$ millimetres to give the same polarised tint as a single millimetre of quartz; that a thickness of 38 millimetres of oil of lemons was equal to a thickness of 66 millimetres of oil of turpentine, and that a thickness of $4\frac{1}{2}$ millimetres of concentrated syrup of sugar was equal to one millimetre of quartz.

The very remarkable phenomena above described might, at first sight, be attributed to certain polarities in the particles of fluids, in virtue of which they assume some regular arrangement analogous to that of crystalline structure; but Dr. Brewster has remarked that this cannot be the case, for the same phenomena are seen in whatever direction the polarised ray is transmitted through the fluid, so that the structure of the particles of a circularly polarising fluid must be exactly the same along every one of its diameters, that is, the structure must be symmetrical round the centre of the particle, or a structure analogous to that which takes place in common polarisation, when a sphere of glass has its density regularly increasing or regularly diminishing towards its centre.

Chapter XIII.

Absorption of Light in Doubly Refracting Crystals — List of absorbing Crystals with one Axis — List of absorbing Crystals with two Axes — Properties of Dichroite — Influence of Heat in modifying the Absorption of Light by Crystals.

Every substance, however transparent, possesses the property of *absorbing* a portion of the light which falls upon it[*]; and the quantity of light absorbed by homogeneous fluids and solids that have single refraction is the same, whatever be the direction in which the ray is transmitted. In doubly refracting crystals, however, the absorption is of a different kind. They not only possess the power of absorbing light like other bodies, but they possess another absorptive force which is related to the axis of the crystal, and intimately connected with its doubly refracting and polarising forces. In order to analyse this phenomenon, Dr. Brewster, who discovered this property in crystals, took a rhomb of yellow carbonate of lime, of such a thickness as to give two distinct and separate images of a small circular aperture placed before it and illuminated with white light. In this case, he found that the two images differed both in colour and intensity, the extraordinary image having an *orange yellow* hue, while the colour of the ordinary image was a *yellowish white*. Along the axis, the two images had the same colour and intensity; at different inclinations to the axis, the difference in the colour and intensity of the two pencils increased, and was a maximum at 90°. When the two images were made to overlap at different inclinations with the axis, their combined colour was always the same, and was of course the same with the natural colour of the mineral, which appeared to be the same in all directions. When the rhomb is exposed to polarised light, the following effects are produced. In the position where the ordinary image O vanishes, the extraordinary image E is *orange yellow*, exactly the same as it appeared by common light; and in the position where E vanishes, O is a *yellowish white* as before.

The property now described was found by Dr. Brewster in the following crystals with one axis, in most of which the two images O and E exhibited two different colours.

List of Crystals with one Axis that absorb different Colours.

Names of Crystals.	Colour when its principal section is in the plane of primitive Polarisation.	Colour when its principal section is perpendicular to that plane.
Zircon	Brownish white	A deeper brown
Sapphire	Yellowish green	Blue
Ruby	Pale yellow	Bright pink
Emerald	Yellowish green	Bluish green
Emerald	Bluish green	Yellowish green
Beryl Blue	Bluish white	Blue
Beryl green	Whitish	Bluish green
Beryl yellow green	Pale yellow	Pale green
Rock crystal almost transparent	Whitish	Faint brown
Rock crystal yellow	Yellowish white	Yellow
Amethyst	Blue	Pink
Amethyst	Greyish white	Ruby red
Amethyst	Reddish yellow	Ruby red
Tourmaline	Greenish white	Bluish green
Rubellite	Reddish white	Faint red
Idocrase	Yellow	Green
Mellite	Yellow	Bluish white
Apatite, lilac	Bluish	Reddish
Apatite, olive	Bluish green	Yellowish green
Phosphate of lead	Bright green	Orange yellow
Calcareous spar	Orange yellow	Yellowish white
Octohedrite	Whitish brown	Yellowish brown

The absorptive property is not possessed by every specimen of the minerals contained in the preceding list. Even when they have the same colour as those above described, the ordinary and extraordinary pencils which they produce

---

[*] See Optics, chap. xix. p. 67.

have sometimes the very same tint, and they exhibit no peculiarities in their absorptive properties when exposed to polarised light.

Some of the preceding crystals exhibit different colours, even when *common light* is transmitted in directions parallel and perpendicular to their axes. A specimen of sapphire had a *deep blue* colour in one direction and a *yellowish green* in the transverse direction. Tourmaline is often *green* along the axis, and of a deep *red* in a transverse direction; and Mr. Herschel has mentioned a variety of sub-oxysulphate of iron, which is of a *light* green colour across the axis, while in the direction of the axis its colour is a deep blood *red*, so intense that a thickness of 1-20th of an inch scarcely allows any light to pass. The potash muriate of palladium was observed by Dr. Wollaston to be of a *deep red* along the axis, and a vivid *green* in a transverse direction.

The phenomena of absorption in crystals with two axes are extremely interesting. The two colours which appear in the ordinary and extraordinary pencils are seen diverging from the resultant axes when exposed to common light, as shown in *fig.* 51, which represents the phenomena in *Iolite* or *Dichroite*.

Fig. 51.

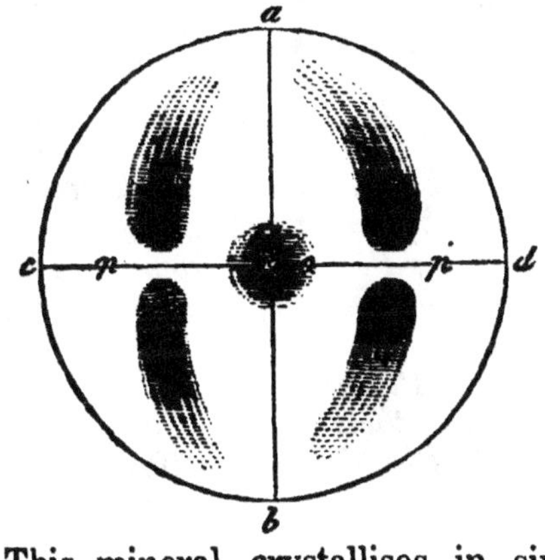

This mineral crystallises in six or twelve-sided prisms, which appear of a deep blue colour when seen along the axis, and of a *yellowish brown* when seen in a direction perpendicular to the axis of the prism.

If $a\,b\,c\,d$, Fig. 52, is a section of a prism of iolite by a plane passing through the axis of the prism, the transmitted light will be *blue* through the faces $a\,b$, and $d\,c$, and *yellowish brown* through $a\,d$, $b\,c$, and in every direction perpendicular to the axis of the prism. If we grind down the angles, a, c, b, d so as to replace them with faces $m\,n$, $m'\,n'$, and $o\,p$, $o'\,p'$, inclined 31° 41' to $a\,d$, or to the axis of the prism; then, if the plane $a\,b\,c\,d$ passes through the resultant axis of double refraction, we shall observe, by transmitting polarised light through the crystal in the directions $a\,c$, $b\,d$, and subsequently analysing it, a system of rings round each of these axes. The system will exhibit the individual rings very plainly if the crystal is thin; but if it is thick, we shall observe, when the plane $a\,b\,c\,d$ is perpendicular to the plane of primitive polarisation, *some branches of blue and white light, diverging in the form of a cross from the centre of the system of rings*, or the poles of no polarisation, as shown at p and p', *fig.* 51, where the shaded branches represent the blue ones. The summits of the blue masses at p and p' are tipped with purple, and are separated by whitish light in some specimens and yellowish light in others. The white light becomes more blue from p and p' to o, where it is quite *blue*, and more yellow from p and p to c and d, where it is completely *yellow*. When the plane $a\,b\,c\,d$ is in the plane of primitive polarisation, the poles $p\,p'$ are marked by spots of white light, but everywhere else the light is a deep blue.

In the plane $c\,a\,d\,b$, *fig.* 52, the mi-

Fig. 52.

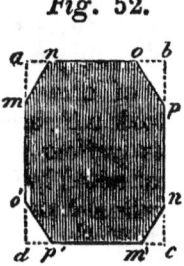

neral, when we look through it at common light, exhibits no other colour but yellow, mixed with a small quantity of blue, polarised in an opposite plane. The ordinary image at c and d is yellowish brown, and the extraordinary image faint blue; the former acquiring some blue rays, and the latter some yellow ones from c and d to a and b, where the difference of colour is still highly marked. From a and b towards p and p' the yellow image becomes fainter, till it changes into blue, and the weak blue image is reinforced by other blue rays till the intensity of the two blue images is nearly equal. The faint blue image increases in intensity as the incident ray approaches from c and d to p and p', and the yellow one, acquiring an accession of blue light, becomes bluish white. From p and p' to o, the ordinary image is whitish, and the other deep blue; but the whiteness gradually diminishes towards o, where they are both almost equally blue.

The following Table contains the crystals with two axes, in which Dr. Brewster discovered the absorptive property.

List of absorbing Crystals with Two Axes.

Names of Crystals.	Plane of the Resultant axes in the plane of Primitive Polarisation.	Plane of Resultant axes perpendicular to the plane of Primitive Polarisation.
Topaz blue	White	Blue
——— green	White	Green
——— greyish blue	Reddish grey	Blue
——— pink	Pink	White
——— pink yellow	Pink	Yellow
——— yellow	Yellowish white	Orange
Sulphate of barytes.		
——— yellowish purple	Lemon yellow	Purple
——— yellow	Lemon yellow	Yellowish white
——— orange yellow	Gamboge yellow	Yellowish white
Kyanite	White	Blue
Dichroite	Blue	Yellowish white
Cymophane	Yellowish white	Yellowish
Epidote, olive green	Brown	Sap green
——— whitish green	Pink white	Yellowish white
Mica	Reddish brown	

The same author has given (*Phil. Trans.* 1819, p. 19) a list of various other crystals which possess the property, but our limits will not permit us to pursue the subject any farther.

The influence of heat in modifying the absorptive action of crystals he found to be very remarkable. Having selected several crystals of Brazilian topaz which displayed no change of colour by exposure to polarised light, he brought them to a red heat, and thus communicated to them the power of absorbing polarised light. He then took a topaz in which one of its pencils was *yellow* and the other *pink*. A red heat acted more powerfully upon the extraordinary pencil than upon the ordinary one, discharging the yellow colour entirely from the one, and producing only a slight change on the pink tint of the other. When the topaz was hot, it was perfectly colourless, and acquired the pink tint gradually while cooling. By exposing it repeatedly to the action of a very intense heat, he was unable either to modify or remove this permanent tint.

From several experiments which have not yet been published, Dr. Brewster has discovered that the colouring matter itself, both in crystals with one and two axes, possesses the property of double refraction — that this matter exhibits hemitropism in crystals that are not themselves compound—and that the colouring matter has in some rare cases two axes of double refraction, while the crystal itself has only one. The prosecution of this curious subject is likely to throw much light on the constitution of bodies.

For an account of various interesting phenomena relative to the distribution of the colouring matter in topaz, the reader is referred to the *Transactions of the Cambridge Philosophical Society*, vol. ii.—See also Chap. XVI.

Chapter XIV.

Double Refraction communicated to Glass by Heat—to Cylinders—Rectangular Plates—Chromatic Thermometer—Effects of Crossed Plates—Spheres of Glass — Tubes — Unannealed Plates of Glass—Effects of altering their Form—Chromatic Vernier—Double Refraction produced by Induration—Lenses of Fishes.

The various phenomena described in the preceding chapters were ascribed to some unknown structure in the bodies which produced them; and it was never even imagined that the power of producing double refraction could be communicated artificially to glass and other bodies. On the 8th April 1814, Dr. Brewster communicated to Sir Joseph Banks the remarkable fact that double refraction could be imparted to glass by the transient passage of heat through its substance, and the letter containing this fact was read at the Royal Society on the 19th of May of the same year. This letter was followed by a series of papers containing an elaborate inquiry into the laws which regulate this new class of optical phenomena. A brief and general view of these facts will constitute the subject of this chapter.

1. *On Cylinders of Glass with one axis of double refraction.*—If we take a cylinder of glass about half an inch thick and an inch in diameter, and transmit heat from its circumference to its centre, it will exhibit when exposed to polarised light in the apparatus, *fig.* 39, a system of rings traversed by a black rectangular cross exactly like those shown in *fig.* 25; and by turning round the analysing plate, C, 90°, we shall see the complementary set shewn in *fig.* 26. As the cylinder must be held at a distance of at least six inches from the eye, the rings and cross will appear as it were in the interior of the glass. If we cross the rings with a plate of sulphate of lime, we shall find that they exhibit the same phenomena as the rings formed by *calcareous spar*, and therefore the double refraction is *negative*, or repulsive. When the heat is uniformly distributed over the glass, the system of rings entirely disappears, and the doubly refracting structure no longer exists.

If the same cylinder of glass, when cold, is immersed in boiling oil, or equally and strongly heated in any other way, and is made to cool rapidly by applying a cold and good conductor to its circumference, it will exhibit a similar system of rings which will also disappear when the glass returns to an uniform temperature. This system of rings, however, is *positive*, like those produced by *zircon* and *ice*.

By comparing the value of the tints with their distances from the axis of the cylinder, Dr. Brewster found that if T is the tint corresponding to any distance D, t the tint corresponding to any other distance, d, it will be thus expressed: $t = \dfrac{T d^2}{D^2}$, that is, *the values of the tints vary as the squares of their distances from the axis of the cylinder.*

If the polarised light is transmitted through the circumference of the cylinder when the system of rings is complete, a system of fringes will be seen parallel to the base of the cylinder, and similar to those which are next to be described.

2. *On Rectangular Plates of Glass with two series of axes of double refraction.*—Take a well annealed rectangular plate of glass, E F C D, *fig.* 53, which exhibits no tints whatever when examined in the apparatus, *fig.* 39, and place its edge C D on a bar of iron A B

Fig. 53.

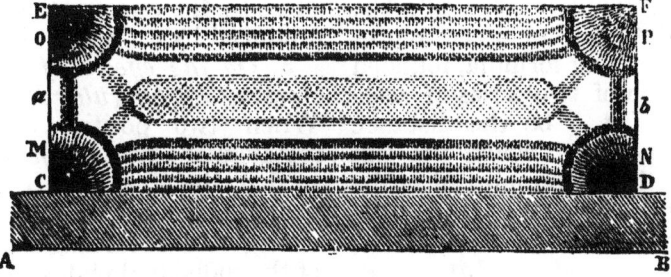

nearly red hot. Let the glass plate resting on the iron be placed at D E, in *fig.* 39, so that the polarised light, A C, may pass through every part of it. The moment that the heat of the iron enters the surface C D, fringes of brilliant colours will be seen parallel to C D, and *nearly at the same instant, and before a single particle of heat has reached the upper edge* E F, *or even* a b, *similar fringes will appear at the edge* E F. Light at first white and then yellow, orange, &c., will appear at *a b*, and these colours will be separated from the other two sets of fringes by two dark lines M N, O P, in

which there is neither double refraction nor polarisation. Between M N and O P the double refraction and polarisation is *negative*, like that of calcareous spar, while, on the other side of M N and O P, the double refraction is *positive*. Similar fringes are seen through the thickness of the plates and also in the direction of their lengths. When the plate of glass is of a square form, as in *fig.* 54, and the thickness through which the polarised light passes about one-third the length of one of the sides, the tints have the form shown in *fig.* 54.

When the thickness is increased so as

E

Fig. 54.

to be about three times that of ab, *fig.* 55, the tints have the form shown in *fig.* 55.

Fig. 55.

In all these cases beautiful complementary systems of fringes are produced by causing the plate C, *fig.* 39, to revolve 90°; but we cannot find room for figures of these phenomena, of the beauty of which it is impossible to form any idea without coloured drawings. When the heat is uniformly distributed over these plates of glass, the colours all disappear.

The tints in all these phenomena are similar to those polarised by crystallised bodies, and are regulated by the very same laws, *mutatis mutandis*.

By comparing the values of the tints with their distances from the central line ab, of the plate in *fig.* 53, Dr. Brewster found that they were represented by the following formula, founded on the supposition of two series of rectangular axes. Let d be the distance from ab of the point at which the tint t is required, T the maximum tint in the centre ab of the plate, and D the distance of either of the black lines M N, O P from ab: then $t = T - \frac{Td^2}{D^2}$. The term $\frac{Td^2}{D^2}$ represents the tint which would be produced by the principal axis perpendicular to the plate, and passing through its centre; but as the axis in the plane of the plate would produce an uniform tint, T, in every part of the plate, which acts in opposition to the other tint, the real tint t will be equal to the difference of these, or to $T - \frac{Td^2}{D^2}$; or, making T and D equal to unity, we have $t = 1 - d^2$.

In order to find the tint at any point in terms of the shortest distance of that point from the lines of no double refraction MN, OP, let δ, δ' be the distances of the point from MN, OP: then since d is the distance of that point from the central line ab, we have $\delta = 1 - d$, $\delta' = 1 - d$, and $\delta\delta' = 1 - d^2$: that is, *the tint t at any point varies as the product of the distances of that point from the lines of no double refraction.* Calling v the velocity of the extraordinary ray, and V that of the ordinary ray, we shall have $v = \sqrt{V^2 + a\delta\delta'}$ a formula which represents the extraordinary refraction in rectangular plates of glass. In circular plates the expression will be $v = \sqrt{V^2 + a\delta^2}$.

If the plate of glass, highly and uniformly heated, is placed upon a cold piece of iron A B, it will exhibit similar fringes; but the double refraction between MN, OP, will now be *positive*, and the extreme fringes *negative*: and in this case $v = \sqrt{V^2 - a\delta\delta'}$.

Analogous effects are produced in plates of rock salt, fluor spar, obsidian, semiopal, rosin, copal, amber, &c.

As the heat of the hand is sufficient to develope a faint system of fringes in a plate of glass, the number of fringes and tints may be increased indefinitely by increasing the number of plates, and hence the foundation of Dr. Brewster's *Chromatic differential Thermometer*, by which differences of heat may be measured by the numerical value of the tints produced by a bundle of glass plates.

3. *On the effects of combining and crossing Rectangular Plates of Glass.*—When two positive or two negative rectangular plates of glass are combined, so that the lines M N, O P, *fig.* 53, are parallel, the combination will be *positive* or *negative* according to the character of the individual plates, and the tints will be equal to what would have been produced, by using a plate equal to the sum of their thicknesses; when a *negative* and *positive* plate are similarly combined, the effect will be equal to the difference of their action. If their actions are equal, the effect of the combination will be to destroy the double refraction altogether.

If two negative or two positive rectangular plates are crossed, as in *fig.* 56, the tints in the square of intersection are raised where the negative crosses the positive structure, and depressed where the negative crosses the negative,

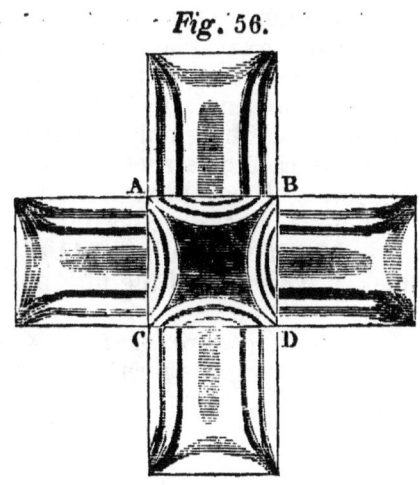

Fig. 56.

or the positive the positive structure. By determining the tint at any given point in each plate by the preceding formula, and combining these tints according to the rules already given, it will be found that the lines of equal tint, which we may call the *isochromatic* lines in the square of intersection A B C D, are *hyperbolas*, which will be *equilateral* when the breadths of the two plates and their maximum tints are the same*. The beauty of this combination surpasses all description.

When a *positive rectangular plate crosses a negative rectangular plate*, it will be found, by the same method, that the isochromatic lines in the rectangle of intersection are *perfect circles* when the breadth of the plate and the tints in each are the same: this effect is shewn in *fig.* 57. But when the breadth of the plates is different, the isochromatic lines will be *ellipses*.

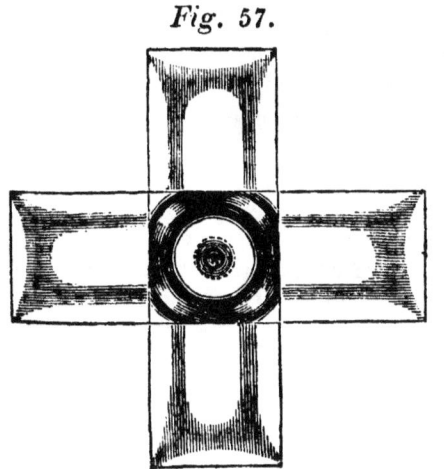

Fig. 57.

4. *On the distribution of the doubly refracting force in spheres, spheroids, and tubes of glass.*—If we take a cold

* See *Edin. Transactions*, vol. viii. p. 357.

sphere of glass and immerse it in a trough of hot oil placed in the polarising apparatus *fig*. 39, we shall observe, when the heat has reached its centre, a black cross with four sectors of polarised light like the inner circle of *fig*. 25. The maximum tint is not at the edge, but nearly half way between the centre and the circumference of the sphere. If in this state the sphere is turned round in the trough, it will exhibit in every position the very same figure. If we now suppose the trough to be filled with such spheres, they will exhibit the same phenomena in whatever direction the polarised light is transmitted through the fringes, and even if the spheres were in a state of motion in the trough. A fluid composed of such spherical particles would exhibit the same polarising structure in every possible direction, and even if it were in a state of rapid gyration. If the particles possessed the structure that produces circular polarisation, the fluid would develope the phenomena exhibited by oil of turpentine and the other fluids already mentioned in Chapter XII, p. 5.

If a spheroid is used in place of a sphere, the structure will be symmetrical only round its axis of revolution, *viz*., the shorter axis, if it is oblate, and the longer axis, if it is prolate. If the polarised ray A C, *fig*. 39, passes along any of these axes, we shall observe a black rectangular cross, and four luminous sectors, which will remain unaltered during the motion of the spheroids round the axis of revolution. But if this axis is inclined to A C, the symmetry of the figure is deranged, and the black cross will sometimes open at the centre. If an equatorial diameter of the spheroid is parallel to A C, then the black cross will be complete when the plane of the equator is parallel or perpendicular to the plane of primitive polarisation, but it will open at the centre, in other positions, like the system of rings in crystals with two axes.

If heat is applied to the circumference, A C B D, *fig*. 58, of a glass tube, whose diameter is A B, and the diameter of whose bore is *ab*, the black cross AB, C D, will be seen, and there will be observed a dark circle, *m n o p*, of no double refraction, having in the outside the positive doubly refracting structure, and in the inside the negative doubly refracting structure. The breadth of the negative annulus is less than that

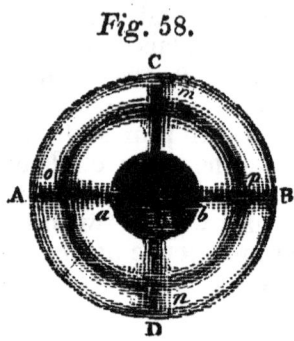

Fig. 58.

of the positive one. As the bore of the tube becomes smaller the circle of no double refraction approaches to the axis of the tube.

5. *On the communication of a permanent doubly refracting structure to Glass.*—In March 1814, Dr. Brewster found that glass melted and suddenly cooled, such as Prince Rupert's drops, possessed a permanent doubly refracting structure. In December 1814, Dr. Seebeck published experiments of a similar kind, with cubes of glass, and Dr. Brewster, who had extended his experiments to plates of glass of all forms, analysed the various phenomena which they produced, and published an account of them in the Philosophical Transactions for 1816.

In order to form cylinders, or plates, or spheres, with a permanent doubly refracting structure, we have only to bring the glass to a red heat, and cool it rapidly at its circumference or its edges. When the cylinders or plates have been thus rapidly cooled, they will produce the very same phenomena which are exhibited by plates that have only transiently the doubly refracting structure during the propagation of heat through the mass. The maximum tint developed at the edge of a plate of crown glass 0.44 of an inch thick, was the red of the fifth order of colours.

6. *On the effects produced by subdividing or altering the form of Plates and Cylinders of doubly refracting Glass.*—In doubly refracting crystals, the phenomena which they produce are quite independent of the form of the crystal or portion of a crystal employed. The case, however, is quite different with plates and cylinders of glass, as the effect depends, in a great measure, on their external shape. If we divide the plate E F C D into two, by a diamond cut, in the direction *a b*, and separate the two pieces, they will, when exposed to the polarised light, no longer exhibit the fringes which appear in *fig.* 53, on each side of *a b*, but *each half of the plate will have the same structure as the whole plate had originally*, with this difference only, that the tints are all much lower in the scale. This remarkable effect is shewn in *fig.* 59, in which *a b* corresponds with *a b* in *fig.* 53. Each half of the plate has now two lines of no double

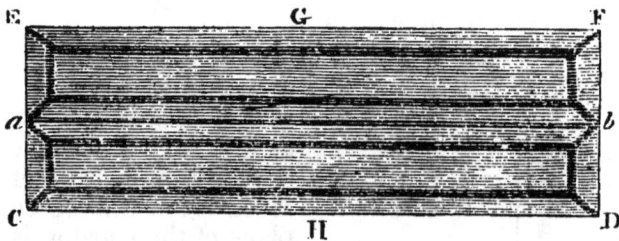

Fig. 59.

refraction, with one negative structure between them, and two positive structures without them. If the plate had been divided in the direction G H, the angular structure at E, as in *fig.* 53, would have appeared at the four new angles.

In like manner, if, in the glass cylinder shewn in *fig.* 57, we cut a notch through it, by means of a file, two lines of no double refraction will appear, a negative structure being interposed between two positive ones.

The optical figures produced by unannealed plates and cylinders of glass exhibit very curious variations, by grinding them into new forms. A cylinder, for example, which gives a circular system of rings, with a black cross, as in *fig.* 25, will, if its section is made elliptical, give the black cross only when the greater and lesser axis of the ellipse are in the plane of primitive polarisation. When they are inclined 45° to it, the black cross opens in the centre, exhibiting the influence of a new axis developed by the elliptical form of the cylinder.

7. *Description of a Chromatic Vernier for subdividing tints.*—If we take a plate of glass of considerable thickness,

and grind it into the form of a wedge, as shewn at A B, *fig.* 60, and then give it

Fig. 60.

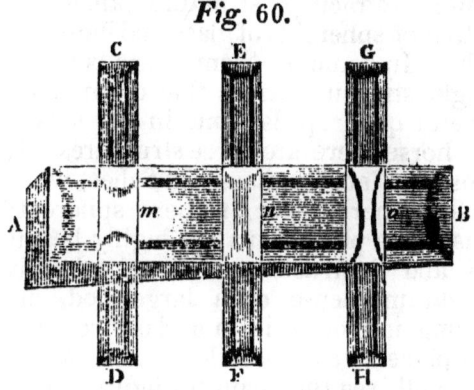

the doubly refracting structure, both its positive and negative tints will increase gradually from B to A, so that if the maximum tint near A, is yellow of the first order, it will shade off gradually, and terminate in white near B. In a wedge of this kind, two inches long, and having an angle of 8°, the highest tint is between the *blue* and the *white* of the first order, corresponding to 2.20 in Newton's scale of colours, and the lowest tint is between the *black* and the *blue*, corresponding to about 0.8. We have consequently a scale nearly two inches long to measure a variation in the tints amounting to $2.2 - 0.8 = 1.4$. The method of using this wedge is shewn in *fig.* 60. If it is required to ascertain very exactly the tint of a plate of crystallised glass C D, it must be held as in the figure, and moved gradually from A to B. When it has the position C D, the intersectional figure *m* is opened horizontally, which proves that the tints of the wedge A B, at the point *m*, are higher than those of C D. In the position G H, the figure at *o* is open vertically, and therefore the tints of the wedge at *o* are lower than those of the plate. But in the intermediate position E F, a dark cross is produced, which indicates the perfect equality between the tints of the wedge at *n* and those of the plate E F. By a scale of equal parts, one of which may be the one tenth or the twentieth part of an unit in Newton's scale, all tints may be compared with each other, and referred to their exact place in the scale of colours. This wedge is particularly suited as a vernier for the chromatic thermometer already mentioned.

8. *On the production of the doubly refracting structure by evaporation and gradual induration.*—In the beginning of 1814, Dr. Brewster discovered that the structure which produces double refraction could be communicated to soft substances by gradual and unequal induration ; and he afterwards published some of his results in the *Phil. Trans.* for 1816.

When isinglass is dried in a circular glass trough, and is placed in the polarising apparatus *fig.* 39, it exhibits the black cross and four luminous sectors like *negative* crystals with one axis of double refraction. When a thin cylindrical plate of isinglass is indurated at its outer edge, it gives the black cross and four luminous sectors like *positive* crystals with one axis of double refraction.

A thin cylinder of isinglass, with a hole in its centre like the glass tube shown in *fig.* 57, gives exactly the appearance there represented, but both the structures are, in this case, positive.

When jelly is evaporated in rectangular troughs of glass, as A B C D, *fig.* 61,

Fig. 61.

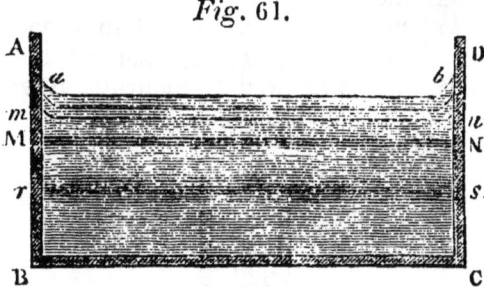

the induration commences at the surface *a b*, and fringes *m n* are formed parallel to the surface, having the same structure (viz. positive) as the external fringes in plates of unannealed glass. The surface *a b* sinks as the induration advances, but at last the jelly adheres so firmly at *a* and *b* to the sides of the trough, that the surface *a b* becomes fixed. Hence, as the induration proceeds, the softer jelly about *r s* is expanded or drawn, as it were, towards *a b*, in consequence of its moisture escaping slowly through *a b*, and its adherence to the more indurated structure above it. The consequence of this is, that an opposite or negative structure is developed at *r s*, and this structure is necessarily separated from the negative structure at *m n* by a black neutral line M N, in which there is no double refraction.

If the glass trough is open at its bottom B C, so as to allow the induration to take place there also as in *fig.* 62, positive fringes are formed at *o p*, and negative ones at *r s*, and these are sepa-

Fig. 62.

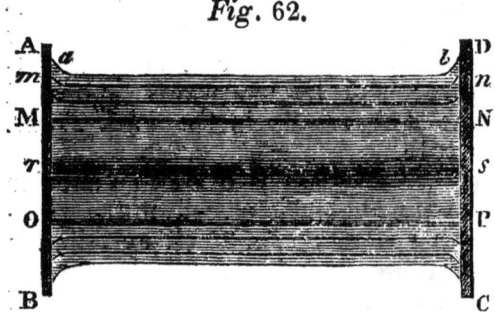

rated by the line O P of no double refraction. This system of fringes is exactly the same as that produced by a rectangle of glass heated and then rapidly cooled, and when it was crossed by a rectangle of glass having the system of fringes developed by the passage of heat across it, the intersectional rectangle exhibited the elliptic fringes mentioned in p. 51. A plate of jelly one-third of an inch thick, and one inch and two-thirds long, produced at *r s* a green of the second order on the day after it was coagulated.

When isinglass is placed in a cylinder A B of glass, *fig.* 63, open at both ends, and is allowed to indurate, it ap-

Fig. 63.

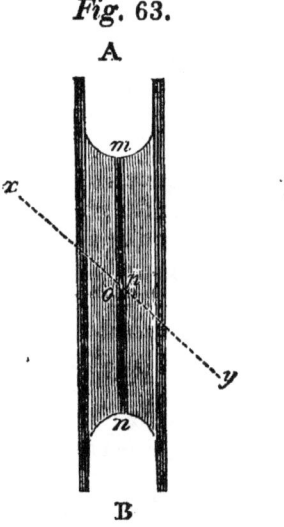

pears to be divided into two structures *o, p*, by a dark line *m n*, when A B is parallel or perpendicular to the plane of primitive polarisation. The tints of *o* descend in the scale, while those of *p* ascend, when the axis, *x y*, of a plate of sulphate of lime crosses them as in the figure.

If we take a sphere or spheroid of transparent jelly and allow it to indurate, it will exhibit the same phenomena as a sphere or spheroid of glass that has received the doubly refracting structure,

All the lenses of animals which are formed of albuminous matter exhibit a doubly refracting structure analogous to that of spheroids of glass and indurated jelly. In some of them there is only a single structure, as in that of man and several quadrupeds; but in the lens of the horse there are three structures, like those in plates of glass. In fishes, which have spherical or rather spheroidal lenses, the phenomena are highly beautiful and instructive. If we take the crystalline lense of a large cod, and having immersed it in a glass trough of oil, place its axis parallel to A C, *fig.* 39, we shall see the beautiful figure shown in *fig.* 64, which will never vary while

Fig. 64.

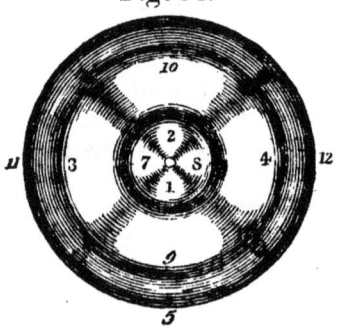

the lens is turned round upon its axis. The figure consists of twelve luminous sectors 1, 2, 3, 4, 5, &c., separated from each other by a black cross, and two dark concentric circles, which are circles of no double refraction. The interior sectors, 1, 2, 7, 8, are small, and exhibit a white tint of the first order, increasing in brilliancy towards the centre where the black cross is very sharp. The middle sectors, 3, 4, 9, 10, which are very large, are separated from the interior by a broad dark circle, and display a white tint of the first order. The outer sectors, 5, 6, 11, 12, are extremely faint, and are seen with considerable difficulty in this position of the lens. If the axis of the lens (or the axis of vision of the eye) is inclined to the polarised ray in a plane passing through 1 and 2, the sectors 1 and 2 will diminish, and 7, 8 will increase in size, and an additional luminous space will appear at the centre, till, by increasing the inclination, the sectors 1, 2 and the luminous space will completely disappear, leaving the sectors 7, 8 much enlarged, and of a bluish white tint. If the lens is inclined in a plane passing through 7 8, the sectors 1, 2 will increase, and 7, 8 diminish in the same manner

When the polarised light is transmitted in a direction perpendicular to the axis, or in the plane of the equator, the black cross will be complete, and the figure symmetrical when the plane of the equator is parallel or perpendicular to the plane of primitive polarisation; but out of these planes the black cross changes its form, and only two luminous spaces appears in place of 1 2, 7 8, separated by a single black line passing through the centre. The middle and outer sectors of the crystalline had the same structure as that of a sphere of glass placed in hot oil, and the middle sectors had an opposite structure*.

Chapter XV.

Double Refraction communicated to Plates of Glass by Mechanical Force—Combination of such Plates with each other and with Plates of Glass made Doubly Refracting by Heat—Chromatic Dynamometer — Manner in which Heat and Pressure produce Double Refraction.

On the 3d of January, 1815, Dr. Brewster discovered that the property of double refraction could be communicated by simple pressure to soft animal substances, such as isinglass and calves' foot jelly. He took a cylinder of calves' foot jelly, so small that it could scarcely support its own weight, and having no action whatever upon polarised light; and by pressing this between the finger and the thumb, or even touching it gently, it received the structure of doubly refracting bodies as exhibited in their action on polarised light. During subsequent experiments in October, 1815, he found that *compression* produced a *negative* polarising structure, and *dilatation* a *positive* structure, and by dilating isinglass in a certain state of toughness, he communicated to isinglass a much more powerful doubly refracting structure than that of beryl. On the 1st of November of the same year, he extended these experiments to plates of solid glass.

This remarkable property may be easily shown by taking a strip of glass cut merely with a diamond, and bending it slightly by holding one end of it in each hand. When the strip of glass is held in the apparatus, *fig.* 39, so that its length is inclined 45° to the plane of primitive polarisation, it will exhibit two separate doubly refracting structures shown in *fig.* 65, separated by the dark neutral line M N. Each of these struc-

Fig. 65.

tures is covered with coloured fringes parallel to M N, and those between the concave side C D and M N are *positive*, while those between the convex side, A B and M N, are *negative*. The tints vary as their distance from M N. If we slacken the bending force, the fringes will become less numerous, descending to the white of the first order, and then disappearing altogether when the force is reduced to nothing.

When two slips of glass of the same thickness and size, and similarly bent, are crossed, as shown in *fig.* 66, the tints in the intersectional square are rectilineal, and are parallel to the line of no double refraction *m n*, which forms the diagonal of the square, which joins the intersection of the two concave sides with that of the two convex sides.

When one of these bent strips of glass crosses a rectangular plate of glass with the two structures, the fringes in the intersectional square are *parabolas*.

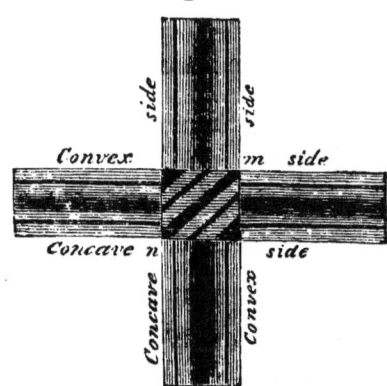

Fig. 66.

Effects of a similar kind were produced by applying mechanical force to various other bodies destitute of double refraction; and the system of rings in separate crystals, and the uniform tints pro-

---

* See *Phil. Trans.* 1816, p. 311, where Dr. Brewster first described these appearances.

duced by thin plates of crystals were modified by compression and dilatation, according to laws, of which the reader will find a full account in the *Phil. Trans.* for 1816, and the *Edin. Trans.* vol. viii. The principles thus developed have been applied by Dr. Brewster to the construction of a *chromatic dynamometer*, a *chromatic hygrometer*, and a *chromatic thermometer*, different from the one formerly mentioned. In these cases, either direct force, or force arising from expansion, is to be measured; and in the instruments under consideration the force is measured and indicated by the tints developed in a plate of glass bent by the force to be measured. The perfect elasticity of glass gives it a vast superiority over steel, as it will invariably return to its original state after being bent; and as the tints of polarised light have a precise numerical value, and may be subdivided and read off by the chromatic vernier described in p. 53, the results of such instruments will merit great confidence.

It is not difficult to form an idea of the manner in which heat and pressure produce that mechanical change in the condition of the glass which gives rise to the very singular phenomena above described. When Dr. Brewster first saw the extraordinary phenomena of a doubly refracting structure produced at parts of the glass where the heat had not arrived, he was struck with its analogy to the phenomenon in magnetism in which the production of south polar magnetism at one end of a needle instantly creates north polar magnetism at the other end, and he was disposed to believe that the phenomena might be owing, as in magnetism, to the action of a fluid. This opinion, however, was soon abandoned, after he was better acquainted with the influence of compression and dilatation in developing the doubly refracting structure, and he gave the following explanation of the phenomena. Let C D F E, *fig.* 67, be an

Fig. 67.

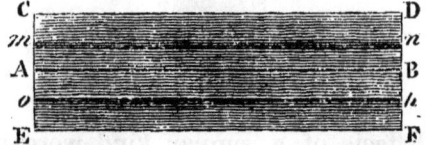

elastic transparent substance like caoutchouc or isinglass in a particular state of induration, and let it be dilated or drawn out in the direction A B by forces applied at A and B: the obvious effect of this is to shorten the sides C D, E F; or, what is the same thing, to produce a compression along these lines. There will consequently be neutral lines *m n*, *o p* separating the dilated from the compressed portions, and if the plate is exposed to polarised light, we shall have a positive structure A B between two negative structures C D, E F. If, on the other hand, we compress C D and E F, the effect of this will be to cause a protrusion at A and B, or to dilate the substance in the direction A B. If we apply the compressing force only to E F in a hard elastic substance like glass, this will necessarily produce a protrusion at A and B, or a dilatation in that direction, and this dilatation will produce a compression at C D, though no force is applied there. Hence it is obvious why tints appear at C D when the edge E F of a piece of glass C D F E is laid upon a piece of hot iron.

In the experiment shown in *fig.* 65, with the bent plate of glass, the particles of the glass are compressed on the concave side C D and in the direction C D, whereas, on the convex side, A B, they are dilated in the same direction as that of A B: hence there must be some neutral line M N in which there is a line of particles neither compressed nor dilated.

From these principles, it is easy to understand how the structure of unannealed glass, as indicated by the optical figure which it produces, changes by dividing it in two, or by altering its form. The structure of the optical figure depends on the form of the glass as a whole, and it is easy to conceive how portions kept in a state of compression by dilating forces in another part of the glass, should lose their state of compression by the removal of the dilating forces which occasioned it, or should even be thrown into a state of dilatation by the influence of the remaining compressing forces.

Mr. Herschel has, in his Treatise on Light, given an analogous view of the subject as a theory of the phenomena. We regard the views given above as the result of direct experiment.

Chapter XVI.

Structure of composite Doubly Refracting Crystals — Brazilian Topaz — Sulphate of Potash — Remarkable formation of tesselated Apophyllite.

In examining the phenomena exhibited by doubly refracting crystals, the reader cannot fail to have observed that the forces which produce them have the same character and the same intensity in all parallel directions. The tints or the systems of rings, or the separation of images, are identically the same through whatever portion of a crystalline plate the ray is transmitted, provided it has always the same inclination to the axis or axes of the crystal.

In composite or hemitrope crystals there is an apparent deviation from this law. If one crystal adheres to another, so that their axes are not parallel, the system or systems of rings seen through a plate formed out of the adhering crystals will not have the same position, nor will the tints, or the separation of the images, be the same in parallel directions. This kind of composite structure sometimes presents very curious phenomena, as in *nitre, arragonite, calcareous spar, harmotome, arseniate of iron, aplome, scolezite, feldspar, sulphato-tricarbonate of lead*, and various minerals; but it is particularly beautiful in *Brazilian topaz* and certain crystals of *sulphate of potash*.

A very particular account of the compound structure of Brazilian topaz has been given by Dr. Brewster in the *Cambridge Transactions*, vol. ii. It consists of a central rhomb inclosed within four other crystals, as in *fig*. 68. The whole

Fig. 68.

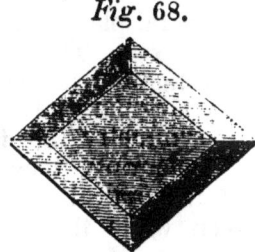

have often the same colour, but very often the central rhomb is of one colour, while the external tesselæ are of a different colour; and in some rare cases one of the external tesselæ has been pink while the other three were yellow. These external tesselæ are often divided into a number of minute laminæ, whose principal sections are not parallel, the principal section of the innermost being inclined no less than 10° or 11° to that of the outermost.

The bipyramidal sulphate of potash, in place of being a simple crystal, as Count Bournon supposed, has been shown by Dr. Brewster to be a compound one, and when a plate is cut out of it perpendicular to the axis of the pyramid, it exhibits the tesselated structure shown in *fig*. 69, when placed in the apparatus

Fig. 69.

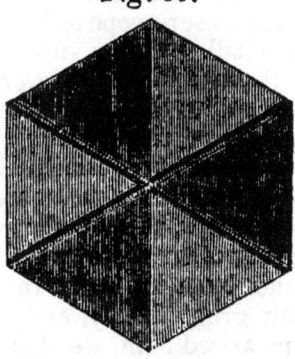

fig. 39. By inclining the plate the tesselæ give different tints, which have a very fine effect.

In all these cases, and in many others that might be adduced, each of the tesselæ have all the properties of separate crystals. They have all the same polarising force, and exhibit the same properties at equal inclinations to the axes of each, so that their optical structure and properties are exactly such as might have been predicted from a knowledge of their crystallographic structure.

From all these structures that of the *tesselated apophyllite* differs in a very remarkable manner. The doubly refracting force varies in different parts of the crystal, and this variation takes place with such admirable symmetry in relation to the faces of the crystal, that it produces, when exposed to polarised light, the most beautiful phenomena that have ever been witnessed.

The apophyllite from Faroe most commonly crystallises in right-angled prisms like C D, *fig*. 70. If we remove the

Fig. 70.

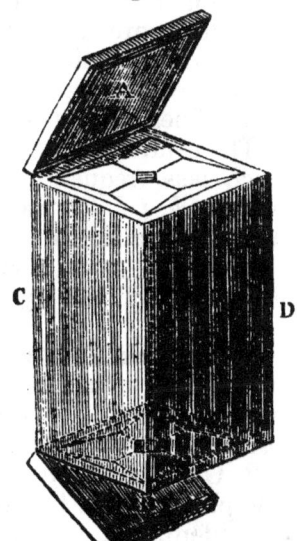

slices A, B, which form the summit and base of the prism to the thickness of about the 100th of an inch, and examine it either by the miscroscope or by polarised light, we shall perceive no difference between them and ordinary crystalline plates, excepting that the colour of the single system of rings which they produce are peculiar, as described in Chap. IX. p. 34. A number of veins merely appear at the edges, as shown in the figure. By removing other slices, which may be easily done by a knife, as the mineral splits with great facility, and exposing them to polarised light, we shall observe that they exhibit the beautiful tesselated figure shown in *fig.* 71. The outer case,

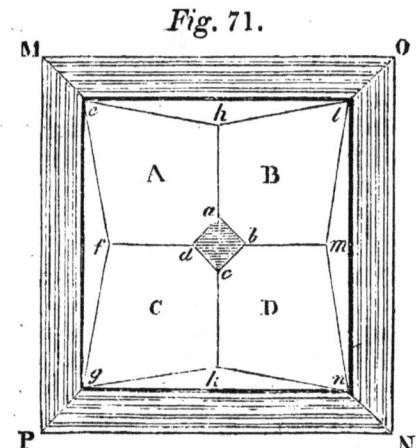

Fig. 71.

M N O P, which, as it were, binds the interior parts together, is composed of a great number of parallel veins or plates which, from their minuteness, display the colours of striated surfaces. Within this frame are contained no fewer than *nine* separate crystals, *viz.* the central lozenge *a b c d*, the four prisms A, B, C, D with trapezial bases, and the four triangular prisms *e h l*, *l m n*, and *g f c*, all of which are separated from one another by distinct lines or veins. By means of the microscope we can easily see the lines *e h l*, *l m n*, *n k g*, and *g f e*. The central lozenge *a b c d* is is seen much less frequently, and the radial lines *h a*, *c k*, *f d*, *b m* can only be recognized by a particular mode of throwing the light upon the plates, though they are easily seen by polarised light.

But the most remarkable circumstance in this composite structure is, that *the central lozenge a b c d has only* ONE *axis of double refraction, while the four prisms* A, B, C, D, *have* TWO *axes.* In A and D the planes of the two resultant axes are coincident, and lie in the direction of the diagonal M N; and in like manner the planes of the resultant axes of B and C lie in the other diagonal O P. This combination of crystals with one and two axes, may be very easily recognised by holding the plate M O N P in the position D E F G of *fig.* 39, and turning it about its axis. In every position of the plate the lozenge *a b c d* will be dark, while the crystals A, B, C, D will be luminous when the sides M O, O N are parallel or perpendicular to the plane of primitive polarisation.

Beautiful as this structure is, it is yet far surpassed by that of another variety of Faroe apophyllite, the extraordinary organisation of which is thus described by Dr. Brewster.

" Among the various forms in which the apophyllite occurs, there is one from Faroe of a very interesting nature. The crystals have a greenish-white tinge, and are aggregated together in masses. The quadrangular prisms are in general below one-twelfth of an inch in width; they are always unpolished on their terminal planes; they have the angles at the summit more deeply truncated than the other quadrangular prisms from Faroe; they are always perfectly transparent, and may sometimes be detached in a complete state, with both their terminal summits.

" In examining this variety of apophyllite, I was enabled, by the perfection of the crystals, to study their structure, through the natural planes, and at right angles to their axes. The phenomena which this investigation presented to me were of a very singular and unexpected nature. In symmetry of form and splendour of colouring, they far surpassed any of the optical arrangements that I had seen, while they developed a singular complexity of structure, and indicated the existence of new laws of mineral organisation.

" When a complete crystal of this variety of apophyllite is exposed to polarised light, with its axis inclined 45° to the plane of primitive polarisation, and is subsequently examined with an analysing prism, it exhibits, through both its pair of parallel planes, the appearance shown in *fig.* 72. In turning the crystal round the polarised ray, all the tints vanish, re-appear, and reach their maximum at the same time, so that they are not the result of any hemitropism, but arise wholly from a symmetrical combination of elementary crystals possessing different primitive forms and different refractive and po-

POLARISATION OF LIGHT.

Fig. 72.

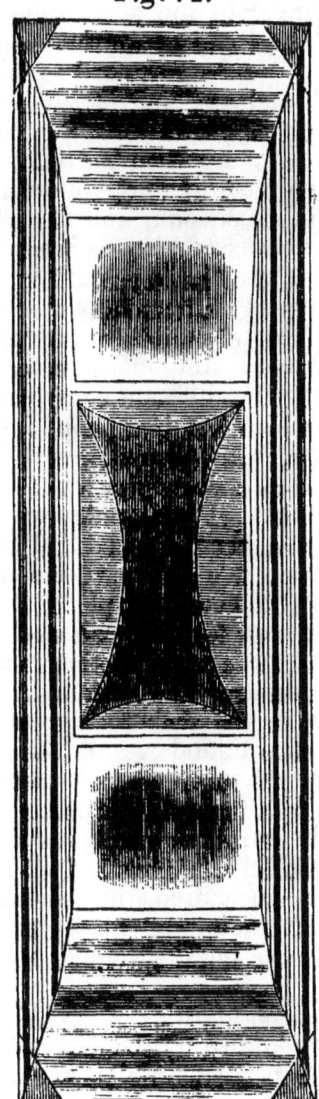

larising powers. The difference in the polarising powers is well shown by the variation of tint; and the difference of refractive power may be observed with equal distinctness by examining the crystal with the microscope under favourable circumstances of illumination, when the outlines of the symmetrical forms shown in *fig.* 72 will be clearly visible.

"In examining the splendid arrangements of tints exhibited in the figure, the perfect symmetry which appears in all its parts is particularly remarkable. The existence of the curvilineal solid in the centre;—the gradual diminution in the length of the circumscribing plates, in consequence of which they taper, as it were, from the angles of the central rectangle to the truncated angles at the summits; but, above all, the reproduction of similar tints on each side of the central figure, and at equal distances from it, cannot fail to strike the observer with surprise and admiration.

"The tints exhibited by each crystal vary, of course, according to its thickness, but the range of tint in the same plate, and at the same thickness, generally amounts in the largest crystals to three of the orders of colours in Newton's scale. The central portion, and the two squares above and below it, have in general the same intensity, while the four segments round the central portion, and some of the parts beyond each of the squares, are also isochromatic. In the central part the colours have a decided termination; but towards the summit of the prism their outline is less regular, and less distinctly marked; though this irregularity has also its counterpart at the other termination. A part of these irregularities is sometimes owing to the longitudinal striæ on the natural faces of the crystal, so that by carefully grinding these off, the beauty and regularity of the figure is greatly improved.

"In order to ascertain the order of the colours polarised by the crystal, and observe in what manner they passed into one another, I transmitted the polarised light in a direction parallel to one of the diagonals of the quadrangular prism, and thus obtained, as it were, a section of the different orders of colours, from the zero of their scale. The result of this experiment, which is shown in *fig.* 73,

Fig. 73.

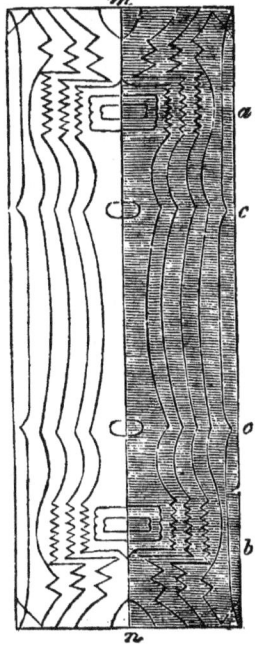

was highly interesting, as it displayed to the eye not only the law according to which the intensity of the polarising forces varied in different parts of the crystal, but also the variation in the nature of the tints, and the connection between these two classes of phenomena. At the points in the diagonal $m\ n$, opposite to a and b of the crystal, the tints rose to the *seventh* order of colours; at other two places, opposite to c and d, they rose only to the *sixth*; while near the summits, at m and n, they descended so low as the *fourth* order. Hence it follows that the four curvilineal segments, *fig.* 72, are next to these in intensity; that the central portions of the squares are again inferior to these; and that the weakest polarising force is near the summits of the prism. At a and b, the fourth, fifth, and sixth fringes have a singularly serrated outline, exhibiting in a very interesting manner the sudden variations which take place in the polarising forces of the successive laminæ.

"Having thus described the structure and properties of the tesselated apophyllite, it becomes interesting to inquire how far such a combination of structures is compatible with the admitted laws of crystallography. The growth of a crystal, in virtue of the aggregation of minute particles endowed with polarity and possessing certain primitive forms, is easily comprehended, whether we suppose the particles to exist in a state of igneous fluidity or aqueous solution. But it is a necessary consequence of this process that the same law presides at the formation of every part of it, and that the crystal is homogeneous throughout, possessing the same mechanical and physical properties in all parallel directions.

"The tesselated apophyllite, however, could not have been formed by this process. It resembles more a work of art, in which the artist has varied, not only the materials, but the laws of their combination.

"A foundation appears to be first laid by means of an uniform homogeneous plate, the primitive form of which is pyramidal. A central pillar, whose section is a rectangular lozenge, then rises perpendicularly from the base, and consists of similar particles. Round this pillar are placed new materials, in the form of four trapezoidal solids, the primitive form of whose particles is prismatic, and in these solids the lines of similar properties are at right angles to each other. The crystal is then made quadrangular by the application of four triangular prisms of unusual acuteness. The *nine solids*, arranged in this symmetrical manner, and joined by transparent veins, performing the functions of a cement, are then surrounded by a wall, composed of numerous films, deposited in succession, and the whole of this singular assemblage is finally roofed in by a plate exactly similar to that which formed its foundation.

"The second variety of the tesselated apophyllite is still more complicated. Possessing the different combinations of the one which has just been described, it displays, in the direction of the length of the prism, an organization of the most singular kind. Forms, unknown in crystallography, occupy its central portion; and on each side of it particles of similar properties take their place, at similar distances, now forming a zone of uniform polarising force, now another increasing to a maximum, and now a third, descending in the scale by regular gradations. The boundaries of these corresponding though distant zones are marked with the greatest precision, and all their parts as nicely adjusted as if some skilful workman had selected the materials, measured the spaces they were to occupy, and finally combined them into the finest specimen of natural mosaic.

"The irregularities of crystallisation, which are known by the name of *Macle*, or *Hemitrope* forms, and those compound groups which arise from the mutual penetration of crystals, are merely accidental deviations from particular laws, which govern the crystallisations in which they occur. The aberrations themselves testify the predominance of the laws to which they form exceptions, and they are susceptible of explanation, by assuming certain polarities in the integrant molecules. The compound structure of the apophyllite, however, cannot be referred to these capricious formations. It is itself the result of a general law, to which there are no exceptions, and when more deeply studied and better understood, it must ultimately lead to the introduction of some new principle of organisation, of which crystallographers have at present no conception.

"The difficulty of accounting for the formation of apophyllite is in no way diminished by giving the utmost licence to speculation. We cannot even avail ourselves of the extravagant supposition of a crystalline embryo, which, like that of animal and vegetable life, gradually expands to maturity. The germ of plants and animals is nourished by a series of organs, of which, however recondite be the operation, we yet see the action, and witness the effects; but in the architecture of apophyllite no subsidiary organs are seen. The crystal appears only in its state of perfection; and we are left to admire the skill which presided at its formation, and to profit by the instruction which is so impressively conveyed by such mysterious organisations."*

Chapter XVII.

Multiplication of Images in Calcareous Spar—caused by oppositely crystallised Veins—Explanation of the Phenomena—Method of imitating them by artificial Combinations.

Those who have been in the habit of making experiments with calcareous spar cannot fail to have observed that various specimens, while they produce only two images through two faces of the rhomb, produce great numbers of coloured images, by transmitting the light through the other faces of the rhomb. Upon examining such specimens, it will be seen that there are one or more planes passing through the specimen, and that light is reflected from these planes, so as to produce more than two images by reflection. This multiplication of images was observed by Bartholinus and Huygens, and was afterwards described by Benjamin Martin, Dr. Robison, and Mr. Brougham.

The crystals of Iceland spar, which possess this curious property, are intersected with one or more planes, A B C D,

Fig. 74.

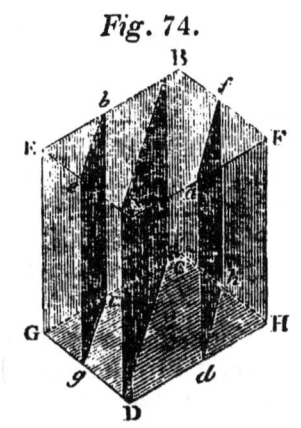

* *Edinburgh Transactions*, vol. ix. p. 323.

fig. 74, *e b c g, a f h d,* perpendicular to the long diagonals EF, GH of the rhomboidal faces, and parallel to the edges E G, F H. When we look perpendicularly through the faces A E B F, D G C H, the light will not pass through the above planes, and consequently we shall see only the two images of the object formed by double refraction. But if we look through any of the other faces, we shall observe the two common images very close together, then two secondary images at a much greater distance, one on each side of the two common images; sometimes there are *four*, and sometimes six secondary images, the secondary images being in two lines, one on each side of the common images, and perpendicular to the line joining the common images. Sometimes the secondary images are double, triple, and quadruple, so that when the interrupting planes are numerous, the images are multiplied to such a degree that heaps of them are visible, sometimes varying in the intensity and colour of the light, sometimes vanishing, and sometimes re-appearing by the inclination of the plate. These phenomena are still further varied, if the luminous object consist of polarised light. The images are in general highly coloured, exhibiting the complementary tints of polarised light, but in some specimens there are no colours at all excepting a prismatic tinge at the edges arising from refraction. We have now a large specimen before us, in which the rhomb is so intersected with planes, that it throws up a floating light like the finest specimens of moon stone, but produces none of the complementary colours of other specimens.

Malus has explained the general phenomena above described, by supposing that the planes A B C D, &c., are fissures within the crystal, and that the colours are those of a plate of air similar to the Newtonian colours of thin plates.

In this state of the subject Dr. Brewster was led to the examination of the phenomena. As the planes A B C D, &c., are almost always extended to all the four faces of the rhomb, and give exactly the same colour at every part of their surface, it was obvious that if a fissure occasioned the phenomena, it must be equally wide at every part of its surface, an effect so extraordinary, that it could not possibly take place. As the supposed fissure extended to every surface of the rhomb, it necessarily followed that the slightest blow would produce a separation of the two portions of the crystal between which it lay. Dr. Brewster, therefore, tried to produce such a cleavage; but he found this impracticable, and upon grinding down the crystal, and removing the calcareous spar with a sharp knife, till he reached the supposed fissure, he found that there was no such breach of continuity in the mineral, but that the adhesion of the molecules was exceedingly powerful at the very place where the fissure was supposed to exist. Upon more minute examination he found that the phenomena were all owing to veins or thin crystals of calcareous spar, which interrupted the regular formation of the minerals, or, what is the same thing, that the rhombs which produced the multiplication of images were hemitrope crystals of calcareous spar. This opinion is capable of the most rigid demonstration. If we cleave the crystal, *fig.* 74, in the direction A E B F or D G C H, we shall find that the edges A B *e b, a f* of the thin crystal are not coincident with the general surface, but present each a face inclined 141° 44′; while a cleavage parallel to all the other faces exhibits no such crystalline face, the cleavage of the veins being coincident with the cleavage of the general crystal. These facts determine the exact position of the axis of the vein, and by cutting two faces on the crystal, perpendicular to this axis, we shall observe the system of rings belonging to the vein itself.

The cause of the multiplication of the images will be understood from *fig*. 75, where M N is the section of the vein or crystal of calcareous spar placed within a

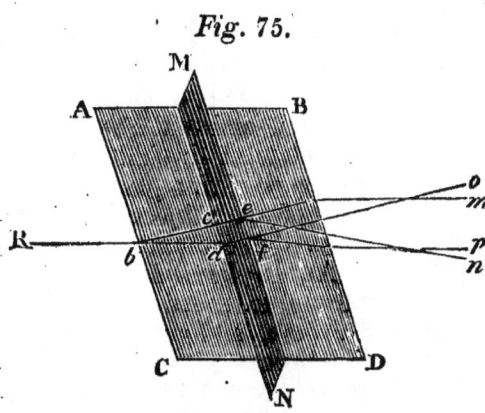

Fig. 75.

rhomb whose principal section is A B C D. A ray, R *b*, incident at *b*, being refracted doubly at *b*, will enter the plate of spar at *c d*, where each pencil will suffer double refraction a second time, because the vein M N is not in the position where double refraction does not take place*; but as the vein is so thin as to produce colours by polarised light, each of the pencils *c e* and *d f* will consist of two complementary colours, depending on the thickness of the vein, and the inclination of the polarised rays, *b c, b d* to the axis of the vein. These double pencils will emerge at *e, f* from the vein, and be divided, as in the figure, into the rays *e m, e n, f o, f p*, the colour of the pencils *e n, f o*, being complementary to those of *e m, f p*.

The rhomb of calcareous spar, shown in *fig.* 75, is equivalent to the polarising apparatus shown in *fig*. 39, the light being first polarised by the rhomb A M N C, the vein M N being the thin crystallised vein shown at D E F G in *fig*. 39, and the light transmitted through it being analysed by the rhomb, M B D N. When the vein M N is very thin, and the rays *b c, b d* not much inclined to the axis of M N, the colours are recognised as portions of the system of coloured rings which surround the axis of M N.

In order to give ocular proof that the multiplication and colour of the images are produced by the causes above explained, Dr. Brewster divided rhombs of calcareous spar, and inserted between them, or into grooves cut in them, plates of calcareous spar, or thin films of sulphate of lime and mica, and was able to reproduce all the phenomena displayed by the natural compound crystal. The phenomena admit of many interesting variations, by interposing several thin films in different azimuths round the polarised pencils *b e, b d*, and at different inclinations to the axis of the principal rhomb. Some of these phenomena have been already referred to in p. 22, at the end of Chapter VI.

Chapter XVIII.

Influence of an uniform Heat upon doubly refracting Crystals—upon Calcareous Spar — Sulphate of Lime—Curious experiment with Sulphate of Potash and Copper, with the Hydrous Sulphates of Magnesia and Zinc—Remarkable effect of Heat on Sulphate of Lime—and on Glauberite.

The very curious subject of the influence of heat upon double refraction has been recently investigated by Professor Mit-

---

* See Chap. iv. fig. 19, p. 14.

scherlich of Berlin; but we regret that it is out of our power to give any thing more than a meagre account of some of his results.

In uncrystallised bodies, and in all crystals which have no double refraction, a rise of temperature throughout the whole mass produces an equal expansion in all directions, without any change of figure. With doubly refracting crystals the case is different. When calcareous spar is heated, it dilates in the direction of its axis of double refraction; but Professor Mitscherlich found that *in all other directions at right angles to this axis it contracts*, so that there must be a line inclined to the axis in which there is neither dilatation nor contraction. Hence the angles of the crystal are changed by heat, being diminished (by a heat from the freezing to the boiling point) 8' 30" in the dihedral angle at the extremities of the axis. Its form being thus brought nearer to that of the cube, which has no double refraction, its double refraction, as might have been expected, is diminished. M. Fresnel found that heat dilates sulphate of lime less in the direction of its principal axis of double refraction (in the plane of the laminæ) than in a direction perpendicular to it, a difference analogous to that of calcareous spar, but of a contrary character, as might have been anticipated from the opposite nature of the double refraction of these two minerals.

These results being obtained by very nice experiments, which but few persons are able to repeat, Mr. Herschel has given the following experiment as an ocular demonstration of the truth of the general fact of unequal change of dimension by change of temperature. " Let a small quantity of the *sulphate of potash and copper* (an anhydrous salt easily formed by crystallising together the sulphates of potash and of copper) be melted in a spoon over a spirit lamp. The fusion takes place at a heat just below redness, and produces a liquid of a dark green colour. The heat being withdrawn, it fixes into a solid of a brilliant emerald green colour, and remains solid and coherent till the temperature sinks nearly to that of boiling water, when all at once its cohesion is destroyed; a commotion takes place throughout the whole mass, beginning from the surface, each molecule, as if animated, starting up and separating itself from the rest, till in a few moments the whole is resolved into a heap of incoherent powder, a result which could evidently not take place had all the minute and interlaced crystals of which the congealed salt consisted contracted equally in all directions by the cooling process, as in that case their juxtaposition would not be disturbed."

When Professor Mitscherlich was examining the double refraction of the *hydrous sulphate of magnesia* when heated in oil, he observed that it suffered no change till the temperature reached 126° of Fahrenheit. The crystal then *became opaque*, and on being broken, it shewed the structure of a pseudo-morphous crystal, consisting of a number of individual crystals, beginning at the surface and meeting in the inside of the original crystal. The same effect was produced at the same temperature on the *hydrous sulphate of zinc:* hence he infers that a movement of the particles of a solid body may take place, by which the particles take a new symmetrical arrangement, and form a new mineral species.

The most extraordinary fact, however, discovered by Professor Mitscherlich relates to the influence of heat on the double refraction of *sulphate of lime*. In this mineral, which has two resultant axes in the plane of the laminæ inclined 60°, these two axes, P, P, *fig*. 33, gradually approach with heat till they unite at O, and when further heated they again open out on each side of *o* towards A and B.

An analogous fact of equal interest has been recently observed by Dr. Brewster, in *Glauberite*. This crystal, at ordinary temperatures, has one axis of double refraction for violet, and two axes for red light. By applying a heat below that of boiling water *the weaker axis for red light disappeared altogether* in consequence of the two resultant axes P, P, *fig*. 33, uniting in O. By a slight increase of heat, the resultant axes again opened out in the plane A B, indicating the creation of a new axis for red light. By the application of artificial cold the single axis for violet light at O opened out towards P and P, producing two resultant axes in the same plane as that of the two axes for red light at ordinary temperatures. At a certain temperature the violet axis also opened up in the plane A B. *

---

* *Edinburgh Transactions*, vol. xi.

Conclusion.

We have thus endeavoured to lay before the reader a general view of the facts and laws which constitute this new and curious branch of Optical Science. In so far as the exclusion of mathematical illustration can accomplish it, these treatises will be sufficiently intelligible to ordinary readers; though the author feels that the subject is susceptible of being treated in a still more popular form. This, however, could only have been accomplished, either by diffuse illustration totally incompatible with limitation of space, or by an imperfect view of the subject, which would have excited, without gratifying, scientific curiosity. His object has, therefore, been to condense into two Treatises the most important phenomena, and to explain them with as much perspicuity as he could, within such narrow limits.

Those who wish to study the subject more deeply are referred to Biot's *Traité de Physique*, tom. iv.; the article Optics in Dr. Brewster's *Encyclopædia*; the Art. Polarisation in the Supplement to the *Ency. Brit.*; Mr. Herschel's *Treatise on Light*; and to the various papers published by Dr. Brewster in the *Philosophical Transactions*, from 1813 to 1819; in the *Edinburgh Transactions*, vols. vii. viii. ix. and x.; and in different Numbers of the *Edinburgh Journal of Science*.

EXPLANATION OF SCIENTIFIC TERMS

MADE USE OF IN THIS VOLUME.

ABERRATION (Latin *aberrare*, to stray) is simply any wandering of a body from the path in which it is expected to move. In Natural Philosophy, the term is used with respect to the rays of light. In Astronomy, for example, the apparent place of a star differs from the true; because, light not being instantaneous in its progress, the earth will have moved so far in her orbit while the particle of light which renders the star visible is passing to the eye; and, hence, the tube through which we view the luminary must be directed forward, on a similar principle as the fowler points his gun *before* the bird which he would shoot in its flight.

——————, SPHERICAL. The intention of spherical lenses, or of concave mirrors, is that the rays of light should, in the former case, be refracted, and in the latter reflected, so as to converge and meet in a single point or *focus*. In practice, the rays are generally found to deviate from that point, and this deviation is termed the *Spherical aberration* of the lens, or of the mirror. These aberrations proceed from two causes: from the form of curvature of the lens, or of the reflector, and from the different refrangibility of the rays of light.—See *Refrangibility*.

ABSCISSA.—See *Conic Sections*.

ACCELERATION is an increase in the rapidity of the motion of a moving body. Thus it being found, by experiment, that a stone, or other body, falling to the earth, moves faster and faster as it descends, the motion is said to be *continually accelerated*.

ACCELERATED FORCE is the increased force which a body exerts in consequence of the acceleration of its motion.

—————— MOTION.—See *Acceleration*.

ACCIDENTAL COLOURS. If we look intensely with one eye upon any coloured spot, such as a wafer placed on a sheet of white paper, and, immediately afterwards, turn the same eye to another part of the paper, we shall see a similar spot, but of a different colour. Thus, if the wafer be red, the seeming spot will be green; if black, it will be changed into white; and, in the same manner, every colour has a corresponding one into which it is transformed. These corresponding spots are termed *Accidental Colours*, or *Ocular Spectra*.

ACHROMATIC (from the Greek *a* privative, and *chroma*, colour) signifies *without colour*. Objects, when viewed through an ordinary telescope, appear to be coloured round their edges, on account of the different refrangibility of the rays of light; and *telescopes* which are constructed so as to counteract, or prevent, this aberration, are denominated *Achromatic*.

ACTING POINT.—See *Machine*.

ACTION is that motion which one body produces, or endeavours to produce, in another. *Mechanical Action* is exerted either by percussion or by pressure; and, in either case, the force exerted by the acting body is repelled in an equal degree by the body on which it acts. Thus, in driving a nail with a hammer, the stroke acts as powerfully against the face of the hammer as against the head of the nail; and, in pressing the hand upon a stone, the pressure upon the stone is equally impressed upon the hand. In each of these cases the impulse is counteracted by what is termed the *Re-action*; and that "Action and Re-action are always equal" is not only laid down as an axiom in mechanics, but is understood to be a general law of nature.

ACTIVE FORCE.—See *Force*.

ACUTE ANGLE.—See *Angle*.

ADAMANTINE SPAR.—See *Corundum* and *Spar*.

ADULARIA.—See *Feldspar*.

AERIFORM BODIES, or AERIFORM FLUIDS.—See *Gas*.

AGATES are not simple stones, but aggregates of different species, such as quartz, flint, amethyst, &c.; all differing in colour and transparency, but sliding into one another by almost imperceptible gradations. The *Mocho-stones*, which appear as if they contain little stems of *moss*, are Agates; and so are the variegated *Scotch pebbles*.

AIR, IN A POPULAR SENSE, is that transparent invisible fluid which surrounds the earth, and in which we move and breathe. It is also termed *Common Air*, and *Atmospheric Air*, to distinguish it from the other gases.—See *Gas* and *Atmosphere*.

——, IN A GENERAL SENSE, is any permanently elastic fluid which is so similar, in this and other qualities, to common air, as to be properly classified under the same general name.—See *Gas*.

——, CONDENSED, is air rendered more dense by being subjected to pressure.

——, ETHEREAL, or ETHER, is an imaginary fluid, supposed by some to fill all space beyond the atmospheres of the earth and other planets.

——, PRESSURE OF, a term sometimes

used in place of the *weight* or the *pressure* of the atmosphere. — See *Atmosphere*.

AIR, RAREFIED.—See *Rarefaction*.

AIR-TIGHT, that degree of closeness in any vessel or tube which prevents the passage of air.

AIR-VESSEL, a vessel in which air is condensed by pressure, for the purpose of employing the re-action of its elasticity as a moving power.

AMETHYST.—See *Corundum*.

ANALCIME is a stone which is found " in grouped crystals, deposited by water, in the fissures of hard lavas." It melts under the blowpipe into a semi-transparent glass. It is also called *Cubizite*.— See *Polarisation of Light*, page 39.

ANGLE. When two straight lines, not lying in the same direction, as A C and B C, meet in a point, as at C, the opening between them is, in common language, called a nook, or corner; and, in Geometry, an *angle*. Thus, the opening at C is called the angle A C B.

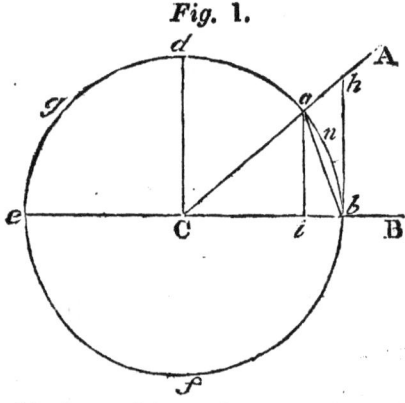

Fig. 1.

Mathematicians have modes of expressing the comparative extent of such openings, or angles. Thus, in figure 1, draw, round C, as a centre, a circle $b\,n\,a\,d\,g\,e\,f$, extending the line B C until it meet the circle, which will be thus cut into two equal parts, or *Semicircles*. Let the circumference of this circle be divided into **360** equal parts (for all circles are supposed to be so divided) and the number of those parts that are contained in the portion $a\,n\,b$, which is called an *Arc*, is the measure of the angle A C B. As the figure is here drawn, the number of parts are forty, and, therefore, A C B is said to be an angle of forty *Degrees*, and thus marked $40°$. Every degree is supposed to be subdivided into sixty equal parts, called *Minutes*, and those again into sixty still more minute parts termed *Seconds*, and even *Thirds*, each a sixtieth part of a second, are calculated by astronomers. Such subdivisions, however, can refer only to circles of a large diameter, and are measured by means of instruments.—See *Vernier*.

A whole circle containing $360°$, the semicircle will contain $180°$; and if, at the point C, we draw a straight line C d, so as to cut the semicircle into two equal parts, or *Quadrants*, each of these quadrantal arcs, $d\,a\,b$, and $d\,g\,e$, will contain $90°$, being the measure of the angles d C B and d C e, which, being equal, are each termed a *Right angle*; and the line C d, neither inclining to the right hand nor the left, is called a *Perpendicular* to the line $e\,b$, the *Diameter* of the circle. Any line from the centre C to the circumference, as C e, C d, C a, and C b, for they are all equal, is the *Radius*. When an angle is less than $90°$, it is called an *Acute angle*, such as A C B first mentioned; but when it exceeds a right angle, as A C e does, it is said to be *Obtuse*.

If, on the same figure, we draw a line $b\,h$, perpendicular to C B, touching the circle at b and the line A C at h; then $h\,b$ is termed the *Tangent*, and h C the *Secant* of the angle A C B; that is, they are the *tangent* and the *secant* of an angle of $40°$, when C b is the radius.—See *Tangent*.

Again; if, from the point a, we draw another line $a\,i$, also perpendicular to C B, this line ($a\,i$) is termed the *Sine* of the same angle A C B; and the part $i\,b$, (cut off from the semidiameter or radius C b) is the *Versed Sine*. A straight line $a\,b$ drawn from a to b is called the *Chord* of the arc $a\,m\,b$. It is the *cord* or *string* of the *bow* (the Latin *arcus*). These lines are the *sine*, *tangent*, &c. of the arc or angle of the circle here represented; but were it increased ever so much, the number of degrees would still be the same, though larger, and the lengths of the sine, tangent, &c., would bear the same proportion to the new radius as they now do to C B.

ANGLES of INCIDENCE, REFLEXION, and REFRACTION.—See *Reflexion* and *Refractive Power*.

——— of DRAUGHT. When a power is applied to drag or roll a body over a plane surface, it has to overcome two obstacles: one is the friction of the surface over which the body slides or rolls; and the other is the weight of the body itself. There is, in every case, a certain direction of the drawing power which is best adapted to overcome these conjoined obstacles; and the angle made by the line of direction with a line upon the plane over which the body is drawn, and perpendicular to that line of direction, is termed the *Angle of Draught*. Calculations on this subject may be seen at pp. 19—26 of *Mechanics*, Treatise iii.

ANHYDROUS.—See *Hydrate*.

APEX.—See *Cone*.

APOPHYLLITE, or FISH-EYE-STONE, is a scarce mineral, having a pearly lustre, like to the species of feldspar called moonstone. Its crystals are various, and often tessellated with thick tables irregularly piled and grown together. It has a white milky colour, but in its divided portions it is usually transparent. This mineral is found in the iron mines of Uto, in Sudermania, a province of Sweden.

AQUEOUS VAPOUR (Latin *aqua*, water) is the vapour of water.—See *Vapour*.

ARC OF A CIRCLE.—See *Angle*.

ASYMPTOTES OF AN HYPERBOLA.—See *Conic Sections*.

ATMOSPHERE (Greek *atmos*, vapour, and *sphaira*, a globe) is that sphere of air which surrounds and includes the earth, and is the common receptacle of all its vapours and exhalations. Its height, taken as that to which the vapours are supposed to ascend, or that where the rays of light cease to be reflected, is generally understood to be between forty and fifty miles.

ATMOSPHERE, PRESSURE AND WEIGHT OF. The atmosphere, like other bodies, gravitates towards the earth. It has consequently *weight* and *pressure*. The pressure upon every square inch of the earth's surface is equal to the weight of a column of the whole height of the atmosphere, an inch square. This weight varies with the elevation of the ground and the fluctuating density of the air; but it is found, at an average, at the level of the sea, to be about fifteen pounds; and, as fluids press equally in all directions, according to their heights, the same pressure is exerted on the square inch of the surface of every body, on this globe, to which the atmosphere has access.

ATMOSPHERES, ONE, TWO, THREE, &c. The elasticity of air increases with its condensation; and, the ordinary pressure being fifteen pounds on the square inch, a condensation which produces a pressure of thirty pounds on the inch is termed *two atmospheres*; that which gives forty-five pounds pressure is three atmospheres, and so on. Pressures arising from other causes, such as the weight of liquids and the force of steam, are also frequently counted by atmospheres.

ATTRACTION (from the Latin *attrahere*, to draw to) is a name given to that tendency which bodies have to approach one another, when no obvious cause is recognised. It differs from gravity in being a more general term; gravity is a species of attraction.—See *Gravity*.

——————— CAPILLARY.—See *Capillary Attraction*.

——————— CHEMICAL.—See *Chemical Attraction*.

——————— of COHESION.—See *Cohesion*.

AXIS OF AN ELLIPSIS, PARABORA, &c.—See *Conic Sections*.

AXIS OF REFRACTION.—See *Refractive Power*.

AXIS OF A CONE.—See *Cone*.

BALANCE is a lever, turning on a *pivot* or *fulcrum*, constructed for the purpose of finding the weight of different bodies. The lever, or rod, of a balance is termed the *beam*, and the parts of the beam on each side of the pivot on which it turns are its *arms*. When those arms are equal, it is the common balance; and its ends, to which the body to be weighed and its equivalent counterpoise are hung, are called the *points of suspension*. Other kinds of balances, as the *Roman balance*, or *steelyard*, the *Danish balance*, &c. are described in *Mechanics*, Treatise ii. chap. v.

BAROMETER (Greek *baros*, weight), an instrument for measuring the varying weight of the atmosphere. It is particularly described at pp. 6—14 of the Treatise on *Pneumatics*. The vacant space at the top of the tube is called the *Torricellian vacuum*, from *Torricelli*, the inventor of the instrument.

BERYL.—See *Emerald*.

BODY is any determinate part of matter.

BOILING is that rolling, bubbling appearance which water and some other liquids assume, when they are converted, by means of heat, into steam or vapour. It is also termed *Ebullition*.

BOILING-POINT. When a thermometer is immersed in any particular fluid that is in a state of ebullition, the point of the scale of the thermometer which marks the measure of heat, in that boiling fluid, is its *boiling-point*. This point varies with the nature of the fluid and the pressure of the air under which it boils; but the boiling-point of a fluid, generally speaking, is that degree at which ebullition is produced under the medium weight of the atmosphere.

BURNING-GLASS is a glass lens which refracts the rays of the sun into a focus. The solar rays may be also brought to a focus by reflexion from a concave mirror, then called a *burning mirror*.

CAIRNGORM, a species of quartz.—See *Quartz*.

CALCAREOUS SPAR is a crystallized *carbonate of lime*. One of the purest varieties has the name of *Iceland spar*, though it is not peculiar to that island.

CALORIC (Latin *calor*, heat) is an imaginary fluid substance supposed to be diffused through all bodies; and the sensible effect of which is termed *heat*. With chemists, *caloric* is, properly, the matter producing the sensation, and *heat* the sensation itself. The terms, however, are often confounded, the word *heat* being used both for the cause and the effect. Caloric produces other effects besides the sensation, namely, the expansion, rarefaction, and liquefaction of bodies.

——————— CONDUCTORS OF.—See *Conductors of Caloric*.

CALORIC, LATENT, is that portion of the fluid matter of heat which exists in any body without producing any effect upon another; what produces an effect being termed *free* or *sensible Caloric*.

────── **SPECIFIC.** Although all bodies possess some quantity of Caloric which is *latent*, yet the quantity in each varies with the nature of the body. The relative proportion that any body retains without the effects being sensible, is termed the *Specific Caloric* of that body; and its power of retention is called its *Capacity for Caloric*.

CALORIFIC RAYS are those rays or emissions from the sun, or any burning body, which impart the sensation and other effects of heat.

CAPACITY FOR HEAT.—See *Caloric, Specific*.

CAPILLARY TUBE. A hair (Latin *capillus*) is a tube; and hence tubes, which are so small as to be likened to hairs, are termed *Capillary Tubes*.

────── **ATTRACTION.** If an open capillary tube be placed upright, with its lower end immersed in a vessel of water, the liquid will rise in the tube, to a greater height than the surface of that which surrounds it. This is not in conformity with the commonly observed laws of the ascent of fluids; and, therefore, the cause of the phenomenon is denominated *Capillary Attraction*.

CATOPTRICS, that part of the science of optics which treats of the Reflexion of Light.

CENTIGRADE THERMOMETER.—See *Thermometer*.

CENTRE OF GRAVITY.—See *Gravity*.

────── **OF GYRATION.**—See *Gyration*.

────── **OF PERCUSSION.**—See *Percussion*.

────── **OF PRESSURE.**—See *Pressure*.

CENTRIFUGAL FORCE is that by which the parts of a body moving round a centre endeavour to recede from that centre. Thus, if a stone be tied to one end of a string, and swung round in a circle while the other end of the string is held by the hand, as the centre of motion, the stone will be felt pulling the hand as if endeavouring to escape; and, in fact, if allowed, would fly off in a tangent to the circle in which it moves. It is thus that a stone is projected from a sling.

CHEMICAL COMBINATION is that intimate union of two substances, whether fluid or solid, which forms a compound differing in one or more of its essential qualities from either of the constituent bodies.

CHORD OF AN ARC.—See *Angle*.

CHROMATICS (from the Greek *chroma*, colour) is that division of the science of Optics which treats of the colours of light, their several properties, and the laws by which they are separated.

CHROMATIC VERNIER.—See *Vernier*.

CIRCLE OF GYRATION.—See *Gyration*.

CIRCUMFERENCE.—See *Perimeter*.

COHESION (Latin *cohærere*, to stick together) is that relation among the component particles of a body, by which they are found to cling together, requiring more or less effort to force them asunder.

────── **ATTRACTION OF,** is a name given to the unknown principle which makes the particles of a body *cohere*, or stick together.

COLOUR is a general name for those modifications of *Light* (whether direct or reflected from other bodies) by which it is distinguished into species that affect the eye with separate sensations. The colour of a body is designated by the species of light which is reflected from its surface.

COLOURS, ACCIDENTAL.—See *Accidental Colours*.

────── **PRIMARY.** These are *red, orange, yellow, green, blue, indigo,* and *violet*, being the seven different colours into which a solar ray of light, which is *white*, may be decomposed or separated. *White* is, therefore, a compound of those seven, and *black* is the absence of all colours.—See *Prismatic Spectrum*.

COMBINATION OF BODIES.—See *Chemical Combination*.

COMMENSURABLE.—See *Ratio*.

COMPOSITION OF FORCES.—See *Forces, Composition of*.

COMPRESSIBILITY is that quality of a substance, whether solid or fluid, which allows it to be pressed, or rather squeezed, into a less bulk than it naturally occupies. The ultimate particles of all bodies are supposed to be incompressible.—See *Hardness*.

CONCAVE MIRRORS.—See *Mirror*.

────── **LENSES.**—See *Lens*.

CONDENSATION is causing a mass of matter to occupy less space by means of the closer approach of its particles. When this is done by outward force, it is *compression*. The term is commonly used with regard to *air, gas,* and *vapours*. The two former are *condensed*, and their elasticity increased by compression; and the latter are condensed into liquids and solids by cold.

CONDUCTORS OF CALORIC, OR OF HEAT, are bodies which, when heated in one part, communicate the effects to the other parts. This is the case with most natural bodies, but some have that power in a much greater degree than others: thus a rod of dry wood may be burned at one end, while the other end shall be little affected.

CONE. A cone is a solid with a circular

base, and tapering equally upwards until it terminates in a point. Were the base a right-lined figure, the solid would be called a *Pyramid*; and, in either case, all lines drawn from the *Periphery*, or bounding line of the base, to the top, (which is termed the *Apex* or *Vertex*,) are straight lines.

The surface of a cone may be conceived as formed by the angular motion of a straight line, one end of which moves along the *Circumference*, or outline of the circular base, while the other end continues either to touch, or to pass through a fixed point above that base. The following explanation is applicable to each of the annexed figures:—

Let the straight line A B (*fig. 2.*) be

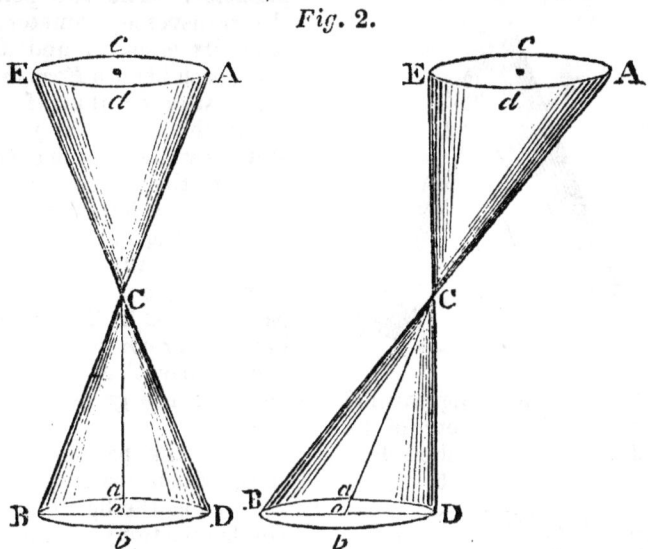

Fig. 2.

so placed as to rise above the circle B *a* D *b*, which it touches at B. Let the end, B, of this line be moved along the whole of the circumference B *a* D *b*, while the same line always touches the fixed point C. The line C B will then have marked out the surface of a cone C B D, similar to the paper cones in the grocer's shops. While the line C B has thus traced the cone C B D, the other portion of the line, C A, will have described an *inverted cone* A C E, with its circular top E *c* A *d*. These opposite cones are similar, having the angles E C A and B C D, at the common apex C, equal. Had the line A B been unequally divided at C, the two cones would have still been similar, but not equal. A right line, C *o*, drawn from the vertex C to the centre of the base *o*, is termed the *axis* of the cone. When this axis is at right angles to the base, the solid is termed a *Right cone*; otherwise, as in the right-hand figure, it is an *Oblique*, or *Scalene cone*. In the former case, the sides C B and C D are of equal length; in the latter, they are unequal.

CONGELATION is that state of certain fluids in which they thicken and become partially or wholly solid. Thus water, at a certain temperature, is converted into ice, and the skins of animals, when dissolved in water by boiling, *congeal* in cooling, and become glue.

CONIC SECTIONS. Sections are *cuttings*; and Conic Sections is a name for that science which treats of the properties of certain curves that are formed by the cutting of a cone. If a cone be cut by a plane parallel to the base, the section (or flat surface of the cut) will be a circle; and if it be cut by a plane passing through the vertex, the section will be a triangle. But neither the circle nor the triangle are treated of, under the head of Conic Sections; because they belong to ordinary Geometry. There are, however, three other sections,—the Ellipsis, the Parabola, and the Hyperbola.

I. 1. If the cone (*fig. 3.*) be cut by a plane which passes through both the

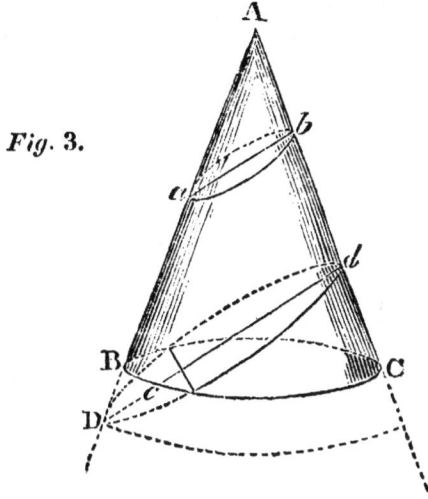

Fig. 3.

sides A B and A C, the outline of the section will be an ellipsis. Or, if it be cut in the direction *c d*, which cuts the base, it will still be a portion of an ellipsis; because this plane would meet the side A B at D, were the cone extended in size downwards, and the ellipsis would be completed as in the dotted part of the figure.

2. If the cone (*fig.* 4.) be cut by a plane *a b*, parallel to one of the sides A B, the outline of the section will be a Parabola. This curve never returns upon itself; that is, it never completes its round like the circle and ellipsis. On the contrary, it would spread out wider and wider, were the cone extended; because, the plane being parallel to A B, will always cut the diameter of the base at an equal distance from the side.

Fig. 4.

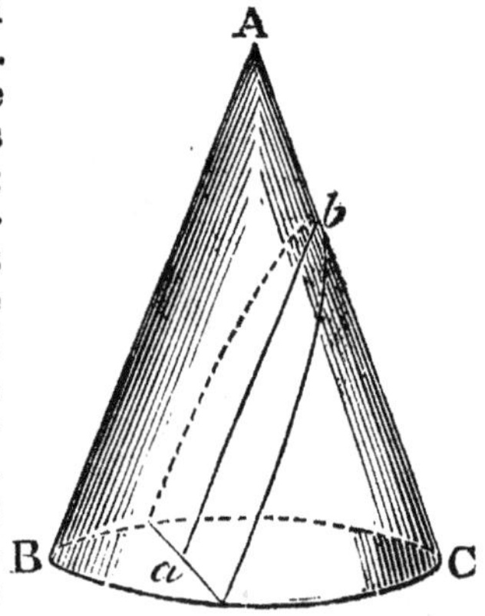

3. If the cone ABC (*fig.* 5.) be cut by a plane *a b*, which, if extended, would cut the opposite cone A D E in *c*, passing through to *d*, the sections of both cones will exhibit curves expanding continually, like the parabola, but with different properties. They are termed Hyperbolas.

Fig. 5.

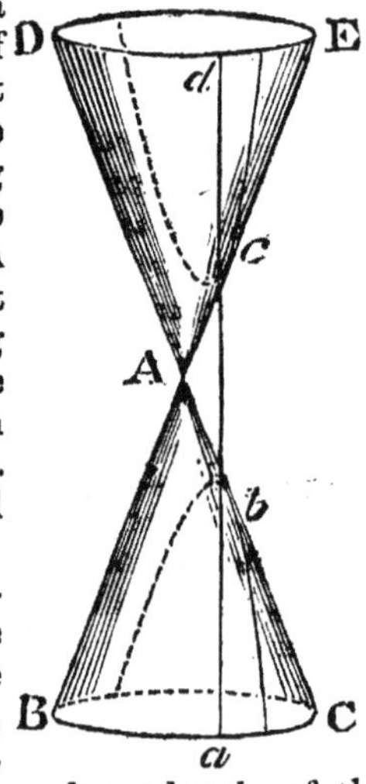

II. The distinction between those curves will be more easily perceived, when they are exhibited on a plane, independently of the cone.

1. *Fig.* 6. is an ellipsis, of which the

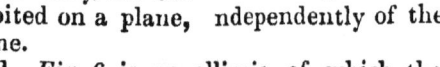

Fig. 6.

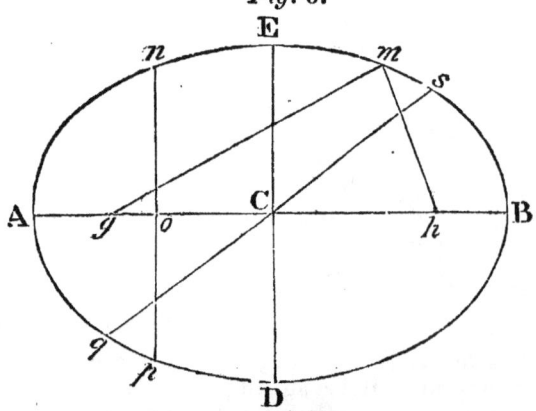

longest diameter, A B, is called the *Transverse diameter*; and the shortest, D E, is the *Conjugate diameter*. These lines are at right angles to each other; are both equally divided at the centre C, and cut the ellipsis into four equal and similar portions: they are also termed the *greater* and the *lesser Axis*. Any other line (as *q s*) which passes through the centre C, and terminates in opposite points of the circumference, is also said to be a *diameter*. The two points, *g* and *h*, in the transverse diameter, equally distant from its ends, A and B, are called the *Foci*, each being a *Focus*; and these points are so situated, that, if we take any point *m*, in the circumference of the ellipsis, and draw the lines *m g* and *m h* from that point to the two foci, the length of these lines, when joined together, will always be the same, at whatever part of the circumference the point *m* may be taken. Any line, *n o p*, drawn across the ellipsis, parallel to C D, is a *double Ordinate*, its half, *p o*, or *o n*, being called an *Ordinate*; and the part A *o*, which the ordinate cuts off from the greater axis A B, is an *Abscissa*.

2. In the parabola (*fig.* 7.), the line A B, which, passing through the vertex A, divides the figure into two equal and similar portions, is the *axis* of the parabola. Any line within the curve, drawn parallel to the axis (as well as the axis itself), is termed a *diameter*, and has its vertex, where it meets the curve line.

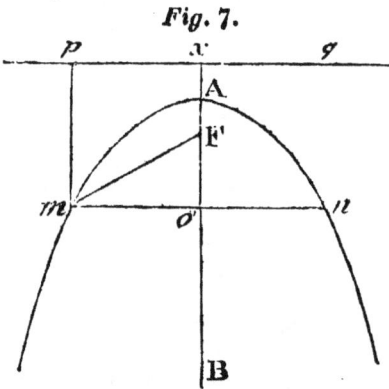

Fig. 7.

The point F, in the axis A B, is the *focus* of the curve; and a line, *p q*, at right angles to the axis when produced to *x*, (the points *x* and F being equally distant from the vertex A) is called the *Directrix*. The focus, F, is so situated, that, if we take any point, *m*, of the parabolic curve, and from that point draw the right line *m* F,—and also another right line, *m p*, perpendicular to the directrix, and meeting it at *p*, the two lines, *m* F, and *m p*, will be always of equal length. As in the ellipsis, any straight line, *m o n*, crossing the axis at right angles, and terminating at both ends in the curve, is a *double ordinate*; *m o* and *o n* are *ordinates*; and A *o*, the part of the axis which is cut off, is the *abscissa*.

3. *Fig.* 8. shews two opposite hy-

perbolas, such as we may conceive to have been cut from the opposite cones, represented in *fig.* 5; the line *d a* in both

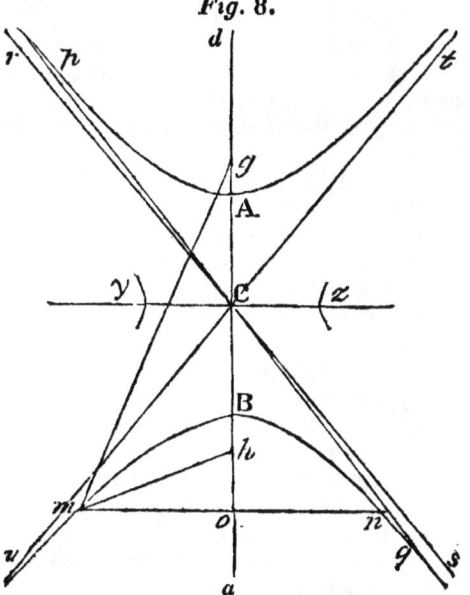

Fig. 8.

figures being different views of a single line in the cutting plane; and the part *c b* cut off by the cones is here represented by the line A B, which joins the vertices of the curves. Bisecting A B in C, any right line (as *p q*) drawn through C (which is called the *centre*), and terminating in both curves, is a *transverse diameter*, and of all these diameters the *axis* A B is the shortest.

Two points *g* and *h*, in the line of the *Axis*, equally distant from either vertex of the hyperbolas, are their *Foci*, and these are so situated that, if we take any point *m*, in either of the curves, and draw the straight lines *m g* and *m h*, the difference of the lengths of those lines will be always equal to A B, the shortest transverse diameter. Again, as in the ellipsis and parabola, any straight line *m o n*, in either hyperbola, crossing the axis at right angles, and terminating at both ends in the curve, is a *double Ordinate*; *m o* and *o n* are *Ordinates*, and *o* B is the *Abscissa*.

The conic sections have certain properties in common, but the hyperbola possesses a peculiar one, which is often alluded to, and usually considered as paradoxical: two right lines, *r s* and *t u*, may be drawn through the centre C, which will pass alongside of the different legs of the two hyperbolas; and although continually approaching nearer and nearer, these curves and straight lines, however much produced, would never meet each other. These lines are called the *Asymptotes*. The opposite hyperbolas, here described, fill two angles of the cross formed by these asymptotes: and the two blank angles might be filled with two other hyperbolas, of which *y z* would

be the axis; and the same lines, *r s* and *t u*, would also be asymptotes to the new curves. In such a case each opposite pair would be *Conjugate hyperbolas* to the other, and the shortest *Transverse diameter* of the one pair would be the *Conjugate diameter* of the other. A very curious account of coloured rings, crossed by opposite hyberbolic curves, is given at pp. 24, 25, of the Treatise on the *Polarisation of Light*.

It will be observed, that in every conic section, we have pointed out two lines, at right angles to each other, called the *Ordinate* and the *Abscissa*. At whatever point of the axis (in the same sort of curve) the ordinate may be drawn, these two lines will have always the same relation to one another; and the algebraic expression which points out that relation, in each figure respectively, is termed the *Equation of that curve*. From any one general property of a curve, all its other properties may be ascertained; and the reasoning that enables us to do so, in the *Ellipsis*, the *Parabola*, and the *Hyperbola*, constitutes the whole of the doctrine of *Conic Sections*.

CONJUGATE DIAMETERS.—See *Conic Sections*.

CONJUGATE HYPERBOLAS. — See *Conic Sections*.

CONOID. A conoid is a solid which may be conceived as generated by the motion of a parabola or of a hyperbola round its axis. Some have included the spheroid in the class of conoids, but they are more usually limited to the *Paraboloid* and the *Hyperboloid*.—See *Spheroid*. Conoids are of various thicknesses in comparison with their height, according to the proportions of the parabola, or hyperbola, by which they are generated. The *Solid of least resistance*, spoken of at page 22 of the *Preliminary Treatise*, is a Conoid.

CONVERGING RAYS are rays of light, the direction of which is such that they will meet or cross one another at, or near to, a common centre. Their divergence from that centre is termed their *aberration*.—See *Aberration*.

CONVEX LENSES—See *Lens*.

———— MIRRORS.—See *Mirror*.

CORUNDUM, or CORINDON, a stone found in India and China, which, when crystallized, has usually the form of a six-sided prism. The diamond was formerly called *Adamant*; and the crystals of corundum, being next in hardness, have the name of *Adamantine Spar*. The *Amethyst, Ruby, Sapphire,* and *Topaz* are considered as varieties of this spar, differing from one another chiefly in colour. The *amethyst* is of a reddish violet colour; the *ruby* is red; the *sapphire* is blue, and the *opaz* is yellow. These are termed *oriental* gems; but stones having the same names are found in other countries. *Topazes*, in particular, are of all colours.—See *Quartz*.

CRYSTALLIZATION is that state of certain bodies in which, when passing from the fluid to the solid form, they separate into portions, each portion (or *crystal*) assuming the same determinate and angular shape. It is a species of congelation, but this last does not necessarily include the idea of separate crystals. Ice was called crystal (*crystallos*) by the Greeks. An account of certain crystals will be found under their several names in this Glossary; but to have included all that are mentioned in the volume, would have been to have written a work on Crystallization.

CUBIZITE.—See *Analcime*.

CURVATURE.—See *Curve*.

CURVE. A straight (or *stretched*) line is the measure of the shortest distance between two points. A *curve* or *curved* line is that of which no portion, however small, is straight. A *crooked line* may be either a curved line or the junction of two or more straight lines drawn in different directions. The varieties of curve lines are innumerable; that is, they have different degrees of *bending* or CURVATURE. The curves most generally referred to, beside the circle, are the *Ellipsis*, the *Parabola*, and *Hyperbola*, to which we may add the *Cycloid*.

CURVES, *Evolutes* and *Involutes* of. Let a thread be wound round the curve

Fig. 9.

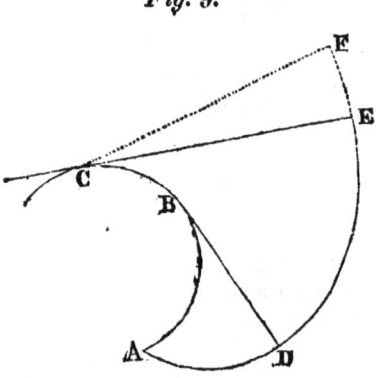

C B A, fixing one end at C, and carrying the other round to A. If we unwind this thread, keeping it tight upon the convexity of the curve, its end A will describe another curve A D E, passing further and further from the former curve C B A, as the string gradually lengthens, until it reaches the point C, where it is supposed to be fixed. If carried further on to F, the length of the thread would continue the same, and the arch E F would be part of a circle. The primary curve C B A, that round which the thread was wound, is called the *Evolute*, and the secondary curve A D E, formed by the unrolling of the thread (now stretched out in the line C E) is termed the *Involute*. The thread, during the progress of unwinding, is, at every point, a tangent to the Evolute; thus, at the point D, it is a tangent to C B A at B. The *Involute of a Circle* is described, with its use, in Mechanics, Treatise ii. page 29. It is a *spiral*.—See *Spiral*.

CURVES, EQUATION OF.—See *Conic Sections*.

CURVILINEAL, or CURVILINEAR, designates figures that are bounded by curve lines. Thus a *Curvilinear* surface is that which can be touched by a plane only in one point.—See *Tangential Plane*. A cone and a cylinder are rightlined surfaces in the direction of their length. A sphere and a spheroid are wholly curvilinear.

CYCLOID. If we conceive the circle *b n a c d* to roll along the line A B; the point *a* being first at A, and ending at B, this point (*a*) will describe, or pass through the curved line A *h p a k* B, which curve is termed a *Cycloid*. Seeing that the circle rolls over the whole line, it is obvious that the length A B is equal to its circumference, and the general properties of the curve are these: that taking any point *h* and drawing the line *h g* (parallel to the line on which the circle rolls) to meet the circle, when in the middle of its motion, at *g*; and joining *g a*, the line *h g* is always equal in length to the circular arc *g n a*; and the portion of the cycloidal arc *h p a* is always double the length of the chord *g a*. Further, the area of the whole cycloidal space A B *k a p h* is equal to thrice that of the circle *g n a c d*, by which it is formed.—See *Preliminary Treatise*, p. 21

Fig. 10.

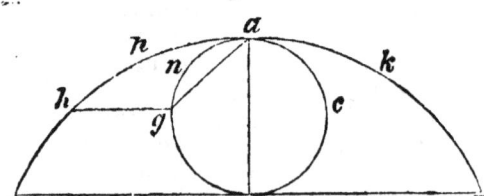

CYLINDER. A cylinder is a solid having a circular base, and which base may be considered as carried upwards in a straight line, and continuing the circle in a parallel direction. It is a circular prism, as a cone is a circular pyramid. When the base is elliptical, it is a *Cylindroid*. When the sides are perpendicular to the base, it is a *Right cylinder* or *cylindroid*; otherwise it is an *Oblique* one.

D'ALEMBERT'S PRINCIPLE.—See *Principle D'Alembert's*.

DEAD LEVEL.—See *Level*.

DEGREES AND MINUTES.—See *Angle*.

DENSITY (Latin *densitas*, closeness) is a relative term, and denotes the comparative quantity of matter, in different bodies, which is contained in the same space. (See *Volume*.) Gravity is understood to act in proportion to the relative quantity of the matter of bodies; and, hence, the specific gravities of bodies are presumed to be the measure of their densities.—See *Gravity*.

DE-OXYDATION is the depriving a substance of the oxygen, or vital air which it contains. Concerning the *de-oxydating power* of the solar rays, see *Optics*, p. 29.

DIAMETERS, TRANSVERSE AND CONJUGATE.—See *Conic Sections*.

DIGESTER, a strong vessel of iron, or other metal, having a screwed-down and air-tight lid, into which substances, either fluid or solid, are inclosed, and are therein submitted to a much higher degree of heat than they could be subjected to in the open air.

DIOPTRICS is that division of the science of Optics which treats of the *Refraction of Light*.

DIRECT PROPORTION, or DIRECT RATIO.—See *Ratio*.

DIRECTION, LINE OF.—See *Force, Direction of*.

DIRECTRIX OF A PARABOLA.—See *Conic Sections*.

DISTILLATION is a process by which a fluid, or portion of a fluid, is converted into vapour by means of heat, and that vapour returned into a state of fluidity by cold, or, as the chemists say, by the abstraction of caloric. Distillation is *Evaporation*, that is, raising a fluid to the state of vapour, but the latter term does not include the idea of preserving that vapour and condensing it again into a fluid.—See *Vapour*.

DIVERGING RAYS are the opposite of *Converging* (which see.) They separate in their progress further and further asunder, as the radii of a circle do from its centre.

DODECAHEDRON.—See *Rhombus*.

DOUBLE REFRACTION.—See *Refraction*.

DYNAMICS (Greek *dynamis*, force) is that division of the science of mechanics which considers bodies as acted upon by forces which are not *in equilibrio*. It therefore treats of bodies in motion.—See *Equilibrium*.

EBULLITION.—See *Boiling*.

ELASTICITY (from a Greek word signifying to *push*, or drive back) is that quality of a substance, whether solid or fluid, by which, when compressed, or when forcibly expanded, it endeavours, in either case, to re-assume its former bulk.

ELASTIC FLUIDS.— See *Fluids*, and *Gas*.

ELLIPSIS.—See *Cone*, and *Conic Sections*.

ELLIPSOID.—See *Conoid*, and *Spheroid*.

EMERALD. The emerald is ranked among the gems, and is now found only in Peru. It is of a green colour, rather harder than quartz, and always in crystals, which are translucent and generally transparent. What is called *Oriental emerald* is a *green* sapphire. The *Beryl* is a variety of the emerald, of a paler green, frequently passing into blue, and is much less prized. It is found in various countries, sometimes in Scotland. The *Emerald* of Brazil is a *Tourmaline*, which see.

EMPIRICAL (Greek *en* and *peirao*, I try) designates any assertion or act which is made or done, merely as an experiment, without any past experience or known principle to direct the choice.

EQUATION OF A CURVE.—See *Conic Sections*.

EQUILIBRIUM. When two or more forces, acting upon a body, are so opposed to each other that the body remains at rest, although either would have moved it if acting alone, those forces are said to be *in equilibrio*, which is a Latin term signifying *equally balanced*.

ETHER.—See *Air, ethereal*.

EVAPORATION; the state or action of a fluid when its particles are so far separated by caloric as to assume the form of vapour. Evaporation, or (as it is sometimes called) *vaporization*, is often, but not always, preceded by ebullition.—See *Boiling* and *Vapour*.

EVOLUTE OF A CURVE.—See *Curves*.

EXHAUSTED RECEIVER. — See *Vacuum*.

EXPANSIBILITY is that property of a substance which renders it capable, under certain circumstances, of occupying more space than it usually requires. The grand agent in the expansion of bodies is *caloric*.

FAHRENHEIT'S THERMOMETER is that arrangement of the scale of the instrument, in which the space between the freezing and the boiling points of water, under a medium pressure of the atmosphere, is divided into 180 parts, or degrees: the freezing being marked 32° and the boiling 212°. This scale was adopted by Fahrenheit, because he supposed, erroneously, that 32 of those divisions below the freezing-point of water (which was therefore (0) on his scale) was the *zero*, or greatest degree of cold.—See *Thermometer*.

FELDSPAR is, next to quartz, the most abundant stone that exists; being a constituent in granite and other rocks. It scratches glass, and gives out sparks with steel; but all its varieties are inferior to quartz in hardness. The transparent laminæ of its crystals have a double refraction; and one of the species, *Adularia*, or *Moonstone*, exhibits a pearly lustre. It is the famous *Petuntse* of the Chinese, being the vitrifying ingredient in their porcelain.

FIRST, or PRIME MOVER, in mechanics.—See *Machine*.

FLUIDITY (Latin *fluere*, to flow) is that state of a substance in which its constituent particles are indefinitely small; and so slightly cohesive, that they are moveable in every direction, passing over one another with the least impulse. There is a partial fluidity, in which the particles are condensed or thickened into a coherent though tremulous mass. Jellies are of this kind, and may be considered as holding a middle place between liquids and solids.

FLUIDS are substances, or rather masses of particles, which have the quality of fluidity; and, in consequence, have no fixed shape, but assume that of the vessel by which they are contained. They are usually divided into two kinds; *gaseous* and *liquid*.

——— ELASTIC.—See *Gas*.

——— NON-ELASTIC.—See *Liquid*.

FLY-WHEEL is an addition to certain machines, for the purpose of equalizing the effect of the moving power. If this power act irregularly, there will be moments in which it will exert more force than is required. This excess is employed in giving motion to the *fly-wheel*, and *part* of this communicated excess is returned upon the machine when the power is too languid. In the former case it is a retarding, and in the latter an impelling power.

FOCUS. The Latin *focus* is a hearth or fire-place; and hence the word has been employed to denote any point in which light, and consequently heat, is concentrated. In optics, it is the point where several rays are collected, whether in consequence of refraction or of reflexion. For the situation of the *foci* of the ellipsis, parabola, and hyperbola, see *Conic Sections*.

FORCE is the name of any exertion which, if applied to a body, has a tendency to move that body when at rest; or to affect, or to stop its progress, if already in motion. This is sometimes termed *Active force*, in contradistinction to what merely *resists* or *retards* the motion of another, but is itself, apparently, *inactive*. The degree of resistance to any motion may be measured by the *active force* required to overcome that resistance, and hence writers on mechanics make use of the terms *Resisting forces* and *Retarding forces*.

FORCE, CENTRIFUGAL.—See *Centrifugal Force*.

——— LINE OF DIRECTION OF, is the straight line in which any force tends to make a body move.

FORCES, COMPOSITION OF. When two forces act on a body in the same *line of direction*, the resulting force (or *Resultant*, as it is called) will be the sum of both. If they act in opposite directions, the body will remain at rest if the forces be *equal*; or, if *unequal*, it will move with a force equivalent to their difference, in the direction of the greater. If the *lines of direction* make an angle with each other, the *resultant* will be a *mean* force in an intermediate direction. Any number of forces may be thus resolved into one resulting force, the effect of which is the absolute motion; and any motion may be assumed to be the result either of a single force, or of a combination of many. This is what writers on mechanics call the *Composition and Resolution of forces*.

FORCES, ACCELERATED.—See *Acceleration*.

FREEZING POINT. That point in a thermometer at which the included fluid stands, when the instrument is immersed in another fluid that is in the act of freezing, is the *freezing point* of the latter.

FRICTION (Latin *fricare*, to rub) is the rubbing or grating of the surfaces of bodies upon one another. In mechanics, it is considered as one of the causes of the hinderance or stopping of motion,—as a *retarding force*.

FRIGORIFIC, having the quality of producing extreme cold, or of converting liquids into ice:—from the Latin *frigus*, coldness.

FULCRUM.—See *Lever*, and *Balance*.

FUSIBILITY (from the Latin *fusus*, melted or poured out) is that quality of a solid which renders it capable of being brought to the state of a liquid by heat.

FUSION is the state of melting, or softening into a liquid.

GAS is an old Teutonic word, equivalent to the Greek *pneuma*, air, or spirit, and has been adopted by the modern chemists to denote permanent aëriform (or airlike) fluids generally, for the purpose of distinguishing them more clearly from common air, which is a mixture of two species of gas. *Gases* are distinguished from *liquids* by the name of *Elastic fluids*; while liquids are termed *non-elastic*, because they have, comparatively, no elasticity. But the most prominent distinction is the following:—*liquids* are compressible to a certain degree, and expand into their former state when the pressure is removed; and in so far, they are *elastic*: but *gases* appear to be in a continued state of compression; for when left unconfined, they expand in every direction, to an extent which has not hitherto been determined. Thus, a small portion of common air, inclosed in a thin bladder, will, when the pressure of the atmosphere is removed, expand so as to inflate the whole cavity, stretching out every part of the surface. The expansion of a liquid, under such circumstances, would not be perceptible. *Gases* retain their elasticity in all temperatures, and in this they differ from *vapours*.—See *Vapour*.

GASEOUS signifies that the substance spoken of has the nature of *gas;* and thus *gaseous fluids* are distinguished from other fluids.

GLAUBERITE is a crytallized salt composed of nearly equal parts of sulphate of lime and sulphate of soda, both *anhydrous*, or nearly so. It was so called, in honour of Glauber, whose name is also given to Glauber salts, or sulphate of soda. Glauberite is found among the pieces of rock salt brought from South America.

GONIOMETER (from the Greek *gonia*, an angle) is an instrument for measuring angles. Such an instrument is particularly requisite in measuring the solid angles of crystals. That of the late Dr. Wollaston is peculiarly ingenious.

GOVERNOR, an addition applied to certain machines for the purpose of equalizing their motion. It is a centrifugal power, like that of the *fly-wheel*, and is described at large at page 52, MECHANICS, Treatise ii.

GRAVITY (Latin *gravitas*, heaviness) is a name given to that tendency which bodies have to fall to the earth,—or rather towards its centre. The abstract power, or unknown cause, by which these phenomena are produced, is termed *Gravitation*,—and this power is supposed to act throughout nature, so that all bodies, as well as the particles of the same body, have a tendency to approach each other, in proportion to their masses, but lessening in force as the squares of the distances between the centres of the several masses are increased. *Gravity* and *Attraction* are often used synonymously. Both are abstract names for the same unknown power; but the latter is applied more generally: we speak, for example, of *capillary attraction*, and *magnetic attraction*, but not of capillary or magnetic *gravity*.

GRAVITY, CENTRE OF, is a point in a body from which, if that body could be suspended, the whole body would remain at rest, (with respect to its tendency to the earth,) in whatever respective position the surrounding parts may be turned. Thus, the *centre of gravity* of a globe is its common centre, and that of a balanced beam is the pivot on which it turns.

———— RELATIVE.—See *Gravity, Specific*.

———— SPECIFIC. The *comparative* or *relative gravities* of different bodies towards the earth are measured by a general standard termed *weight*; and one substance is said to have a greater *specific gravity* than another, when a less portion of its bulk is of equal weight to that other. Thus, a cubic inch of platina is nearly twice the weight of a cubic inch of silver; and, therefore, is said to have double its specific gravity,—the specific gravity of platina is to that of silver as 2 to 1.

GRAVITY, LINE OF DIRECTION OF, is that line which passes through the centre of gravity of a body in a direction to the centre of the earth.

GYRATION (Latin *gyrus*, a circle) is the action of turning round in the manner of a wheel.

———— CENTRE OF.—See *Oscillation*.

———— CIRCLE OF.—See ditto.

HALO, " a luminous, and sometimes coloured circle, appearing occasionally around the heavenly bodies, but more especially about the sun and moon."—See *Parhelia*.

HARDNESS is the resistance to impression. It is *incompressibility*, but limited to solids.—See *Compressibility*.

HEAT.—See *Caloric*.

———— CAPACITY FOR.—See *Caloric, Capacity for*.

———— CONDUCTORS OF.—See *Conductor*.

———— LATENT.—See *Caloric, Latent*.

———— RADIATION OF.—See *Radiation*.

———— SPECIFIC.—See *Caloric, Specific*.

HERMETIC SEAL. The origin of chemistry has been ascribed to the Egyptian Hermes, and, therefore, termed the *Hermetic Art*. When the neck of a glass vessel, or tube, is heated to the melting point, and then twisted with pincers until it be air-tight, the vessel, or tube, is said to have received the *seal of Hermes*—to be *Hermetically sealed*.

HETEROGENEOUS. — See *Homogeneous*.

HEXAHEDRON.—See *Rhombus*.

HOMOGENEOUS (from the Greek *homos*, alike, and *genos*, kind) designates such substances as have their particles all of the same nature, and, consequently, possessing the same properties. *Heterogeneous*, on the contrary (Greek *heteros*, different) denotes that the substance which it denominates is made up of parts that have different qualities. Thus, in minerals, the diamond is a *homogeneous*, and granite is a *heterogeneous* body.

HYACINTH.—See *Zircone*.

HYDRATES. Chemical compounds (particularly salts) which contain water as one of their ingredients, have been termed *hydrates*. If water be not a constituent, they are said to be *Anhydrous*, which signifies *without water*; from the Greek privative *a* and *hydor* water.

HYDROUS, watery, or containing water in its composition.

HYPERBOLA. — See *Cone*, and *Conic Sections*.

HYPERBOLOID.—See *Conoid*.

ICELAND SPAR.—See *Calcareous Spar*, and *Spar*.

ICOSAHEDRON.—See *Rhombus*.

IDOCRASE, a name sometimes given to *Vesuvian*, which see.

IMPENETRABILITY. In the popular acceptation every substance is *penetrable*, that is, another substance may be introduced, or made to pass through it, provided a sufficient force be applied; but the presently received system of philosophy holds all matter to be *impenetrable*, and that what is supposed to be *penetration* is merely the admission of one substance into the *pores* of another.

IMPULSE (Latin *impulsus*, a push or stroke) is the direct action of one body upon another in the production of motion. Bodies are impelled, or driven forward, either by *percussion*, or by *pressure*,—by a *stroke*, as with a hammer, or a *push*, as by a spring, or a living power. The former is instantaneous, and the latter continuous. In both cases the moving body flies *from* the power; in the action of pulling (or attraction) it does the reverse.

INCIDENCE, POINT OF.—See *Refractive Power*.

INCIDENCE, ANGLE OF.—See *Reflexion*, and *Refractive Power*.

INCOMMENSURABLE.—See *Ratio*.

INCOMPRESSIBILITY.—See *Compressibility*.

INSTRUMENT.—See *Machine*.

INDEX OF REFRACTION.—See *Refractive Power*.

INERTIA.—See *Vis Inertiæ*.

INSULATION. When a body, containing a quantity of free caloric, or of the electric fluid, is surrounded by non-conductors, so as to cut off the communication with other bodies, it is said to be *insulated*; a metaphor taken from the Latin *insula*, an island.

INVERSE PROPORTION, or RATIO.—See *Ratio*.

INVOLUTE OF A CURVE.—See *Curves*.

ISOCHROMATIC. The Greek *isos* signifies *equal*, and is prefixed to many scientific words which are derived from that language. *Isochromatic* is, having the same colour. *Isoperimetrical* is, having the same length of perimeter, or bounding line. *Isochronous* is what passes in equal times, as the vibrations of pendulums of the same length, &c.

JARGON.—See *Zircone*.

LATENT HEAT.—See *Caloric*.

LAW OF THE SINES.—See *Refractive Power*.

LENS (Latin *lens*, a bean) is properly a small roundish glass of the figure of a *lentil*. The meaning, however, is now extended. Lenses are not now necessarily glass, nor shaped like a bean, but may be made of other forms, and of any transparent substance. Their essential characteristic is, that they shall refract the rays of light, so that the divergence, or convergence, of those rays shall be equally produced after their passage. For this purpose the surfaces must be polished. Their usual forms and names are shown and explained at page 7, OPTICS.

LEVEL. Two points on the surface of the earth are said to be on the same *level* when they are equally distant from its centre. A level surface, therefore, is not a plane, but a portion of a spherical surface; and this is the form which a sheet of water, or any other liquid, naturally assumes. There are various instruments used in *levelling*, which are called *levels*. These all give a *horizontal level*, that is, a tangent to the earth's surface; and in the case of a *drain*, or *canal*, the bottom of the excavation must be carried lower than the level indicates, otherwise the water would not run. The declivity must be in a circle equivalent to that of the earth's circumference before the water could reach it, and this would then be termed a *dead level*.

LEUCOCYOLITE, a name given to a variety of *Apophyllite*, which see.

LEVER (Latin *levare*, and French *lever*, to lift, or raise) is one of the mechanical powers. It is an inflexible bar, supported and moveable in one point of its length on a pivot, or prop, called the *Fulcrum*. One end of the lever is applied to the weight to be raised, while a force is applied to the other end. The power of this instrument depends on the proportion between the lengths of the parts of the lever on each side of the *fulcrum*.—See *Balance*.

LIGHT is the cause of those sensations and colours which we refer to the eyes, or sense of seeing, as their source. The essence of light is unknown: whether it consists of emanations from the substance of the luminous body, or is propagated, by impulse, through the medium of an universally diffused and subtile ether, has not yet been determined. The knowledge of the laws which regulate the phenomena of light constitutes the science of *Optics*;—the investigation of its action upon the structure of bodies belongs to *Chemistry*.

——— **PENCIL OF.**—See *Light, Ray of*.

——— **RAY OF,** is considered as an evanescent element of a stream of light; and a *pencil* as a collection of such rays accompanying each other.

——— **REFLEXION AND REFRACTION OF.**—See *Reflexion* and *Refraction*.

LIMIT. A limit is literally a boundary, from the Latin *limitare*, to bound. There are certain effects in Natural Philosophy, as well as quantities in Mathematics, which we cannot determine with minute accuracy; but, in many such cases, we

EXPLANATION OF SCIENTIFIC TERMS.

can fix a *point* which that *effect* or *quantity* must certainly exceed, and another to which it cannot possibly arrive. These *points* are the *limits* of the problem. We cannot, for instance, predict the exact height at which the mercury will stand (at the level of the sea) in a barometer, on any future day; but we may assert, from past experience, that it will be somewhere between twenty-eight and thirty-one inches. Again, we cannot determine exactly the length of the circumference of a circle; but we are certain that it is greater than that of any inscribed polygon, and less than that of any circumscribed one, however numerous their sides may be.

LIQUIDITY, the state of being liquid.

LIQUIDS. The medium between the solid and the gaseous states is that of *liquidity*. Liquids are fluids whose elasticity is inactive, and the cohesion of whose particles is less towards each other than their individual gravities; so that they separate by their own weight, and may thus be divided drop by drop. It is hence that the slightest pressure on the surface of a liquid,—even that of the thinnest stratum of its own body,—presses the lower portion of the fluid equally in all directions, sideways as well as downwards: and even upwards, into any vessel to which it may have access, if there is no other way of escape.

MACHINE (Latin *machina*, a frame or contrivance). Any complication of artificial bodies acting upon one another by contact, through the medium and motion of which any effect is produced, is a machine. The initial force which puts the machine in motion is called the *First* or *Prime mover*. The *point* at which that force is applied is the *Acting point;* and that in which the effect is produced is the *Working point:* the machine being the medium through which the power is transferred, and by which it is modified so as to answer the intended purpose. When a simple body is the medium between the *acting* and the *working points*, it is an *Instrument*.

MASS (of matter).—See *Volume*.

MAXIMUM. In a variable *quantity* or *effect*, that quantity or effect which is *the greatest possible*, under the circumstances in which it is placed, is termed a *maximum*. Thus, in respect to the sails of a windmill, they may be placed at any angle; but there is one angular direction on which the wind will have more power than on any other, and this is, therefore, termed a *maximum*. There are other cases in which we seek for a *Minimum*, that is, *the least possible*.

MECHANICS is that science which investigates the nature, laws, and effects of motion and moving powers.

MECHANICAL POWERS are the simple instruments or elements of which every machine, however complicated, must be constructed: they are the *Lever*, the *Wheel* and *Axle*, the *Pulley*, the *Inclined Plane*, the *Wedge*, and the *Screw*.

MELTING POINT. That point of the thermometer which indicates the heat at which any particular solid becomes fluid, is termed the *melting point* of that solid.

MENISCUS (Greek *mene*, the moon), a lens which is concave on one side, and convex on the other; and so called because it resembles the appearance of the new moon.

MINIMUM.—See *Maximum*.

MIRROR (French *mirer*, to look at), any surface from which light is reflected, so as to exhibit the images of objects placed before it. It is sometimes (especially when formed of polished metal) termed a *Speculum*, the Latin term for a looking-glass.

—————— PLANE, has a *plane* surface, such as the common looking-glass.

—————— CONCAVE, has a hollow surface, which collects the rays and reflects them to a focus, in front of the mirror, thereby enlarging the image of the object.

—————— CONVEX, disperses the rays, and, in consequence, diminishes the image of the object. These *concave* and *convex* surfaces are formed of different curves, according to the purposes intended.—See *Burning-Glass*.

MOCHO STONE.—See *Agate*.

MOMENTUM, or MOMENT, is the impetus, or force of a moving body. The comparative *momenta* of bodies are in a compound ratio of their quantity of matter and their velocity: that is, they are in proportion to the products of the matter and velocity, *when expressed in numbers*. Thus a ball of four pounds weight, moving at the rate of eighteen feet in a second, would have double the momentum,—that is, it would strike against an object with twice the force that a ball of three pounds weight, moving at the rate of twelve feet per second, would do; because the first product (4 multiplied by 18) is double that of 3 multiplied by 12. *Momentum* is the *force of percussion*.—See *Percussion*.

MOONSTONE.—See *Feldspar*.

MOTION is the passing of a body, or any parts of a body, from one place to another: we say *parts* of a body, because in the cases of a globe turning on its axis, or a wheel revolving on a pivot, the parts of the body change their situation, while the bodies themselves are stationary.

MOVING POWER.—See *Power*.

NON-ELASTIC FLUIDS.—See *Gas* and *Liquids*.

NONIUS.—See *Vernier's Scale*.

OBLATE AND OBLONG SPHEROIDS. —See *Spheroid*.

OBTUSE ANGLE.—See *Angle*.

OCTAHEDRON.—See *Rhombus*.

OCULAR SPECTRA.—See *Accidental Colours*.

OPACITY (Latin *opacus*, dark), a state impervious to light.

ORDINATE, of an *Ellipse*, *Parabola*, and *Hyperbola*.—See *Conic Sections*.

OSCILLATION (Latin, *oscillatio*, swinging) is particularly applied to designate the motion of a pendulum.

——————— CENTRE OF. A pendulum, when oscillating, has one point in which its whole moving force is concentrated; and at which, if it meet with resistance, it will instantly stop, without vibration or strain of its other parts: that point is called the *centre of oscillation*.

A wheel in motion may be considered as an indefinite number of pendulums, each of which has its own *centre of oscillation*. If the wheel be nearly balanced, those several points of oscillation will accommodate themselves, so as to form, in their continued motion, a set of points equally distant from the rim. These are *Centres of gyration*, and in their junction will form a *Circle of gyration*.

OVERSHOT WHEEL.—See *Waterwheel*.

PARABOLA.—See *Cone* and *Conic Sections*.

PARABOLOID.—See *Conoid*.

PARALLEL LINES. When two straight lines in the same plane are so directed, that, however much they might be lengthened, they would never approach nearer to, nor recede from, one another, they are said to be *parallel*.

PARHELIA, PARHELIUM, or PARHELION (Greek *para*, near, and *helios*, the sun), is a *mock sun*; an appearance similar to the sun, which occasionally accompanies *halos* (See *Halo*). There have been sometimes seen six or seven of these *mock suns* at the same time, which, in that case, are denominated by the plural, *Parhelia*.

PENCIL OF LIGHT.—See *Light, Ray of*.

PERCUSSION, CENTRE OF. Percussion is a forcible stroke given by a moving body. In taking any particular body, such as a rod of equal thickness, held at one end, and swung forcibly by the hand, so as to strike upon a resisting object, the force of the stroke will be greater or less, according to the part of the rod that shall hit the object. There is one point of the rod in which the whole force of the stroke is concentrated, and the resistance to which would neutralize the blow. That point is termed the *centre of percussion*, which always coincides with that of oscillation.

——————— FORCE OF.—See *Momentum*.

PERIMETER. The length of the whole bounding line of any plane figure, of whatever parts or shapes that line may consist, is termed the *perimeter* of the figure. The length of the bounding line of a circle (or perhaps of any curve which returns upon itself) is its *Circumference*.

PERPENDICULAR.—See *Angle*.

PETUNTSE.—See *Feldspar*.

PISTON, a short plug, or block, exactly fitted to the bore of a tube, so as to slide outwards and inwards by means of a rod. The *piston* (with its *piston-rod*) is a necessary part of the apparatus of a pump. It serves the purpose of exhausting the air from the tube, and is hence commonly called the *Sucker*.—See *Suction*. A piston is generally accompanied with a valve, otherwise it is a *Plunger*.

PLANE, TANGENTIAL.—See *Tangent*.

PLUNGER.—See *Piston*.

POINT, ACTING.—See *Machine*.

——————— BOILING.—See *Boiling point*.

——————— FREEZING.—See *Freezing point*.

——————— OF INCIDENCE.—See *Refractive Power*.

——————— WORKING.—See *Working point*.

PORES (of matter).—See *Volume*.

POWER is that principle which is capable of effecting a change in the state or condition of a body. When power is exerted, as in mechanics, it is force, applied for the purpose of producing or preventing motion. In the former case it is termed a *moving power*, or *force*, and in the latter a *sustaining power*, or *force*. Power is latent force.

——————— ANIMAL, or ANIMATE, is the power of a man, or other animal.

——————— INANIMATE, is that of *air*, *fire*, *water*, or other inanimate bodies.

——————— MECHANICAL.—See *Mechanical Power*.

——————— IN OPTICS expresses the effect producible by lenses, or other instruments, as *magnifying power*, *heating power*, &c.

PRESSURE is the application of force to a resisting body, when that force is in continued contact with the body upon which it is exerted.—See *Impulse* and *Percussion*.

——————— ATMOSPHERIC.—See *Atmospheric Pressure*.

——————— CENTRE OF. When a fluid presses upon a surface, there is a *point* in that surface, at which, if a force be applied in the same line with the pressure of the fluid, and equal to the whole of that pressure, but in a contrary direction,—this counter-force will exactly balance the whole pressure of the fluid, —and that *point* is called the *centre of pressure*.

PRIME MOVER.—See *Machine*.

PRIMARY COLOURS.—See *Colours, primary*.

PRINCIPLE, D'ALEMBERT'S, *in Mechanics*, is this:—If several *non-elastic* bodies have a tendency to motion, with velocities, and in directions which they are constrained to change, in consequence of their reciprocal action on each other, then these motions may be considered as composed of two others;—one which the bodies actually take; and the other such, that, had the bodies been acted on by such alone, they would have remained in equilibrium. — See *Equilibrium* and *Forces, composition of.*

PRINCIPLE OF VIRTUAL VELOCITIES. "When a system of material points, solicited by any force, is in equilibrium, if the system receive a small alteration in its position, by virtue of which every point describes an infinitely small space, the sum of each force multiplied by the space described by the point to which it is applied, according to the direction of the force, is always equal to *zero.*" This is the *general principle of virtual velocities,* referred to at page 2 of MECHANICS, Treatise ii.

PRISM. A prism is a solid contained by plane figures, of which two are parallel, and the rest are parallelograms.

PRISMATIC SPECTRUM is the various coloured *appearance* (Latin *spectrum*) which a ray of white light exhibits when separated by refraction through a glass prism. The prism of the opticians is triangular; that is, its two ends are parallel, equal and similar triangles, and consequently its other faces are three parallelograms.

PROPORTION, DIRECT AND INVERSE.—See *Ratio.*

PROPORTIONALS.—See *Ratio.*

PYRAMID.—See *Cone.*

PYROMETER.—See *Thermometer.*

QUADRANT.—See *Angle.*

QUARTZ is a hard sparkling stone, extremely abundant in nature, from the common pebble to large mountain veins, and even entire rocks. It is found in crystals with various degrees of transparency, which, when pure, have the name of *Rock crystal*: of this, the Scotch *Cairngorm* (denominated from a mountain where they were once plentiful) is a variety. The purple-coloured rock crystals are commonly called *amethysts*, and the yellow-coloured have the name of *topazes.*—See *Corundum.*

RADIATION (Latin *radiare*) is the shooting forth, in all directions, from a centre. The Latin *radius* was a *shoot* or *rod*, and its plural *radii* (rays) was used both literally and metaphorically: they were the spokes of a wheel, or the *beams* shot from the sun. In natural philosophy, whatever sends emissions in all directions, is said to *radiate;* and hence we have not only radiations, or rays of light, but of heat and of sound. Each of these *radii* is a *ray.*—See *Ray.* It may here be observed, that the *radiant heat* of the sun passes through glass; but it is otherwise with *terrestrial heat.*

RADIUS.—See *Angle.*

RAREFACTION is the act of causing a substance to become less dense; it also denominates the state of this lessened density. The term is more particularly applicable to elastic fluids, which expand so as to fill the vessel in which they are contained after part is extracted. The gas becomes *rarefied* in consequence of the partial exhaustion. Liquids are expanded by means of heat, and thence become *thinner* or more *rarefied.*

RATIO. In comparing two subjects, with regard to some quality which they have in common, and which admits of being measured, that measure is their *ratio.* It is the *rate* in which one exceeds the other. *Proportion* is the *portions*, or parts of one magnitude that are contained in another. When the ratio is *commensurable* (that is, when it is reducible to numbers), it is equivalent to *proportion;* but the latter term is usually employed in the comparison of *ratios,* in which case, two equal ratios are said to be *proportionals.* Thus 3 has to 4 a certain *ratio,* or *proportion;* but the expression 3 is to 4 in the same proportion as 6 to 8, denotes that the ratios of 3 to 4 and 6 to 8 are equal; 3 being the same proportion of 4 as 6 is of 8, that is, three fourths.

——— DIRECT AND INVERSE. When two quantities, or magnitudes, have a certain ratio to each other, and are, at the same time, subject to increase or diminution; if, while one increases, the other decreases in the same ratio, or, if while the one diminishes, the other diminishes in the same ratio, the *proportions,* or comparisons of ratios, remain unaltered, and those quantities, or magnitudes, are said to be in a *direct* ratio or proportion to each other. Thus, if a yard of cloth be worth a pound, ten, or any number of yards will be worth so many pounds, and the proportion of value continues unaltered.

But, if the magnitudes are such, that, when one increases, the other necessarily diminishes; and *vice versa,* when the one diminishes the other increases, the *ratio,* or proportion, is said to be *inverse.* Thus, there is, at any moment, a certain ratio of the length of the day to that of the night; but this is an *inverse ratio;* for, in proportion as the length of either *increases,* that of the other must *diminish.*

RAY is a single radiation from a body which sends out emissions in all directions.—See *Radiation,* and *Light.*

RAYS, ABERRATION OF.—See *Aberration.*

——— CALORIFIC.—See *Calorific Rays.*

——— COLOURED.—See *Colours,* and *Prismatic Spectrum.*

RAYS, CONVERGENT.—See *Reflexion, Laws of.*
——— DIVERGENT. — See *Reflexion, Laws of.*
——— PARALLEL. — See *Reflexion, Laws of.*
——— REFLEXION OF. — See *Reflexion.*
——— REFRACTION OF.—See *Refraction.*
——— ORDINARY AND EXTRAORDINARY.—See *Refraction, Double.*

RE-ACTION.—See *Action.*

REAUMUR'S THERMOMETER (so called from the name of its inventor) is that in which the space between the freezing and the boiling points of water is divided into eighty parts, or degrees; the freezing point being marked 0, or *zero*, and the boiling point eighty. The degrees are continued of the same size, below and above these points; those below being reckoned negative.

REFLEXION (from the Latin *reflectere*, to bend back) is a term generally used in natural philosophy to denote the rebound of the rays of light, heat, or sound, from an opposing surface. Polished surfaces reflect the light to the eye, and are, therefore, more generally termed *reflectors* or *mirrors*. Heat and sound are reflected without relation to the eye, and are returned from more rugged objects.

——— LAWS OF. The reflexions of *light*, *heat*, and *sound*, are found to obey the same laws as the rebound of elastic balls projected upon elastic surfaces. It is, therefore, that the particles of light and air have been treated as being reflected by virtue of their *elasticity*; although, on this principle, we cannot well account for the reflexion of light from both surfaces of a glass mirror.

——— ANGLE OF. The law of reflexion is generally expressed by the assertion that "the angle of incidence is always equal to the angle of reflexion," and is thus explained:—

If A B (*fig. 11.*) be a plane surface, and a ball, at D, be impelled towards C, perpendicular to that surface, in the direction D C, it will rebound, from the point C, back towards D, in the same line C D; but if the ball be projected to the same point C, from any point E, in a direction not perpendicular to A B, it will rebound on the other side of D C, towards F, in such a manner that E C D, which is termed "*the angle of incidence*,"

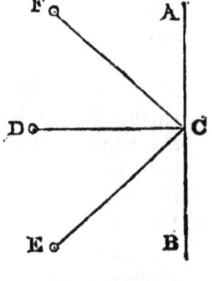
fig. 11.

shall always be equal to F C D, "*the angle of reflexion.*"

If, instead of a ball, we suppose a ray of light to emanate from E, and fall upon C, it will be reflected in the same manner to the eye at F, along the line C F; in which direction only could an object, reflected from the point C, be visible. A pulse of air, which is sometimes called a "*ray of sound*," follows the same law, and, if proceeding from E, would be reflected from C, directly in the line C F, in the points of which it would be heard (if sufficiently strong), as a reflected sound, or *echo*. Some authors call E C B the angle of incidence, and A C F that of reflexion; but the misnomer is of little consequence, for they, too, are equal.

When the reflexion is made from a *concave*, or from a *convex* surface, the angles of incidence and reflexion are still equal; but they are measured by the *tangent*, or rather *tangential plane*, which touches the curve at the point on which the incident ray falls. By this, we shall account for the several cases at pages 15—18 in *Optics*. We may add, that all terrestrial rays are *divergent*, as proceeding from a point; but those of the sun are, on account of his immense distance, considered as *parallel*. *Convergent* are such as meet in a *focus*, which they can only do by *reflexion*, or by *refraction*.

REFLECTING MICROSCOPES AND TELESCOPES are such as carry a magnified image of the object to the eye, by means of rays *reflected* from a concave speculum.

REFRACTION. When we immerse one end of a rod, in a slanting direction, in a vessel of water, the part immersed appears as if it were bent, or *broken*, at the surface of the liquid. This phenomenon is the consequence of the rays of light (by which the rod is rendered visible) being bent in their course; the straight-lined direction, in which they originally issued, being changed (Latin *refractus*, broken) by falling on another medium. Refraction is, therefore, used in natural philosophy as the denomination of that deviation from its course, which a body invariably experiences, when passing, in an oblique direction, from one fluid medium to another of a different density. The term is chiefly applied to the rays of light as they pass through transparent bodies.

REFRACTIVE POWER. The various transparent media *refract* the rays of light in different degrees. Let A B *a b* (*fig.* 12.) be a transparent body on which a ray, C D, *incides* from a luminous point C, upon the plane surface, A B, at D. Were this ray to preserve its rectilinear direction, it would pass on to the point

E: but, meeting with another medium at the point D, it is reflected to F; so that the luminous point, C, would be seen by the eye at F, and not at E. Draw the right line, GDH, perpendicular to AB, through the *point of incidence* D, which line, G D H, is termed the *Axis of Refraction*.

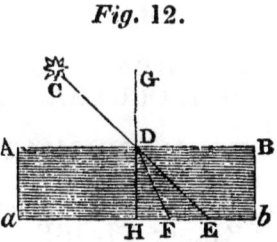

Fig. 12.

The angle, C D G, is the *angle of incidence*, and H D F is the *angle of refraction*. These angles have a fixed relation to each other, in the same transparent body, whatever the angle of incidence may be, but that proportion is different in some bodies from what it is in others; and hence those bodies are said to have a greater or a less *refractive power*. When the *incident ray* is perpendicular to the surface on which it falls, (as in the direction G D H,) there is no refraction. In every other direction, the ratio between the *sines* of the angles of incidence and of refraction is constant, and is termed the *Index of Refraction*. Thus, in water, if the sine of the angle of refraction be taken as unity, that of incidence will be about $1\frac{1}{3}$; and, therefore, the index of refraction in water is marked in the comparative Tables as being 1.336. This is called the *Law of the Sines.*—See *Angle*.

In the passage of a ray of light from a *dense* to a *rarer* medium, the refraction is reversed. The angle of incidence (at the point D, where the two media meet) is then the lesser one; and a luminous object at F, would be seen by an eye at C.—See *Tangent*.

REFRACTION, DOUBLE. The refraction last mentioned is now termed *Simple Refraction*, because a theory has been formed of the laws of that *Double Refraction*, which was long ago observed in Iceland spar, but has since been found to take place in many other crystals, and may be even artificially communicated to glass: the ray, or pencil of light, when falling on a crystal of double refraction, produces a double image. It separates into two parts or rays; one of which follows the *ordinary* law of the sines, and the other is refracted " according to a new, or *extraordinary* law." These two pencils of light, into which the ray is divided, are termed by Dr. Brewster the *ordinary ray*, and the *extraordinary ray*.

REFRACTING MICROSCOPES AND TELESCOPES are such as show a magnified image of an object, by means of rays of light refracted and collected into a focus through lenses.

REFRANGIBILITY is the capability of being refracted, and has been employed to designate the degree of that property which is possessed by the several divisions of a ray of light. It is owing to their various *refrangibilities* that the threads or rays separate from each other in passing through the prism, and thereby form the coloured *spectrum*.

RELATIVE GRAVITY.—See *Gravity*.

REPULSION (Latin *repellere*, to drive back) is the name of a power or principle in the particles of natural bodies, by which, under certain circumstances, they refuse to meet one another. It is the opposite of attraction, and equally inexplicable. The elasticity of bodies has been referred to this principle, which is merely giving us another name for an unknown cause.

RESISTING FORCE.—See *Force*.

RESULTANT.—See *Forces, Composition of*.

RHOMBUS. A rhombus is a surface having four equal sides, but of which the angles are unequal; it is a square pressed out of shape until it assumes the form of the diamond of a pack of cards. If the opposite sides only are equal, it is called a *rhomboid* or *rhomboides*. It is a compressed parallelogram, its opposite angles only being equal. In describing crystals, some are termed *rhombs* or *rhomboids*, because they are solids whose faces have those figures. They are *rhomboidal* solids. Others are described by the number of their sides (Greek *hedra*) or faces. Thus a solid with four faces is called a *tetrahedron*; with six, a *hexahedron*; with eight, an *octohedron*; with twelve, a *dodecahedron*; with twenty, an *icosahedron*; and, generally, a solid having many sides, is a *polyhedron*. All these have their adjectives *tetrahedral, hexahedral*, &c. equivalent to the English four-sided, six-sided, &c.—*A* cube is a *hexahedron*.

RIGHT ANGLE.—See *Angle*.

RIGHT LINE. The same as a straight line.—See *Curve*.

RIGIDITY OF CORDAGE. One of the properties, which is useful in ropes and cordage, when applied to machinery, is flexibility, so that they may be easily bent, and apply easily to wheels and pulleys. The opposite of this property is termed *rigidity*.

ROCHELLE SALT is a chemical preparation, used in medicine; the tartrate of potash and soda. It crystallizes in large regular eight-sided prisms.

ROCK-CRYSTAL.—See *Quartz*.

RUBY.—See *Corundum*.

SAFETY-VALVE (a necessary appendage to a steam-engine) is a valve opening outwards from a boiler, and *loaded with a weight* sufficient to withstand the elastic pressure of the steam until it rise to a certain height; but which would be f ed open before the strain could burst he boiler.

SAPPHIRE.—See *Corundum.*

SATURATED SOLUTION.—See *Solution.*

SCALE, a line divided into a marked number of small and equal parts, which is applied to the measure of other lengths that are not so divided; and thereby to ascertain their relative dimensions. The common measures of length are divided into feet, inches, &c., but are not termed scales; this being the scientific designation. The scales of thermometers have a certain point from which the heat is counted upwards and downwards, that point being marked with a cypher, and termed *zero.* The Latin plural, *scalæ,* is a ladder which is descended by *degrees* (*degressus*) or steps.

SCREW, one of the mechanical powers.—See *Mechanical Powers.*

SEAL, HERMETIC.—See *Hermetic Seal.*

SECANT.—See *Angle.*

SILEX is an opaque stone, sufficiently hard to scratch glass,—sparkling, but never crystallized. Common flint and light-coloured pebbles are wholly of this earth, which are termed *Siliceous.* It also forms the basis of *chalcedony, cornelian, jasper,* and many other stones.

SINE.—See *Angle.*

SINES, LAW OF THE.—See *Reflective Power.*

SOLIDS are bodies, the cohesion of whose particles are so strong, that they are moveable only as a combined mass.—See *Fluids,* and *Liquids.*

SOLID OF LEAST RESISTANCE.—See *Conoid.*

SOLUTION. A solution, in chemical language, is any fluid which contains another substance dissolved and intimately mixed with it. When the fluid will dissolve no more of the substance, but allows the excess to deposit on the bottom of the vessel, it is said to be *saturated* (Latin *satur,* full), and the mixed fluid is then a *Saturated Solution* of the substance which it contains.

SOUND, a sensation communicated through the ear, by means of the particles of air (and, occasionally, other fluids) which are impelled by the vibrations of the sounding body.

——— RAYS OF.—See *Reflexion.*

SPAR. There are a great number of stones, the broken surfaces of which present polished shining plates, placed so as to cover each other, like horizontal beds. Most of these have been called *spars;* and this form is termed the *sparry* texture.

SPAR, ADAMANTINE.—See *Corundum.*

——— ICELAND.—See *Calcareous Spar.*

SPECIFIC denominates any property that is not general, but is confined to an *individual* or *species.*

——— GRAVITY.—See *Gravity, Specific.*

——— HEAT.—See *Caloric, Specific.*

SPECTRA, OCULAR.—See *Ocular Spectra.*

SPECTRUM, PRISMATIC.—See *Prismatic Spectrum.*

SPECULUM.—See *Mirror.*

SPHERE, or GLOBE. A sphere is a solid, every point of the surface of which is equally distant from a single point within it, which is its centre. It is conceived to be formed by the motion of a semicircle round the diameter.

SPHERICAL ABERRATION.—See *Aberration, Spherical.*

SPHEROID. There are two species of spheroids, the *oblate* and the *oblong,* both of which are understood to be formed from the circular motion of a semi-ellipsis round its axis. The oblate spheroid is shaped like an orange, and the oblong like a lemon. The former is generated by the motion of the semi-ellipsis round its lesser axis, and the latter by the ellipsis divided longwise, and turned round the greater axis. These solids are generally called *ellipsoids,* and sometimes *conoids,* though they have no resemblance to single *cones,* and but little to double ones. The earth is an *oblate spheroid,* being flattened at the poles.

SPIRAL. A spiral is a curve which turns round like a circle, but instead of ending where it began, it continues to revolve, receding farther and farther from the centre. There are various species of spirals. The power that moves a watch is a spiral spring.

STATICAL.—See *Statics.*

STATICS is that division of the science of mechanics which considers bodies as influenced by forces that are in equilibrium. It is formed from the Greek *statas,* standing still.—See *Force* and *Equilibrium.* What belongs to *Statics* is *Statical.*

STEELYARD, OR ROMAN BALANCE.—See *Balance.*

STEAM is the vapour of water raised to a high degree of elasticity by means of heat, so as to be applied, in mechanics, as a moving power. In ordinary language, it is confounded with *vapour.*

STEAM-TIGHT denotes such a degree of closeness as prevents the escape of steam.

STRAIGHT LINE, the same as a right line.—See *Curve.*

SUCTION. The action of sucking is performed by the child's making a vacuum in its mouth, which exhausts the air from the pores of the nipple; and the milk is consequently ejected from the breast by the unresisted elasticity of the air within. The raising of liquids through a tube, by means of a piston which lifts and sustains the weight of the atmosphere from that part of the well which is covered with the tube, leaving it to press on the other parts of the surface, is also, metaphorically, termed *suction*.

TABASHEER. This substance, which has been long famous as a medicine in many parts of the East, is, originally, a transparent fluid in the jointed cavities of the bamboo cane. This fluid thickens, spontaneously, until, by degrees, it is converted into a white, or a bluish white solid, something like a small fragment of a shell. It is almost wholly composed of *Silica* (the material of common flint), but is easily crumbled between the fingers. By imbibing water, it becomes transparent: the white bits in a low degree, but the bluish nearly as much so as glass.—See OPTICS, p. 62. Similarly formed concretions are not uncommon. Humboldt discovered Tabasheer in the bamboos of South America; and Sir Joseph Banks found " a solid pebble, about the size of half a pea,—so hard as to cut glass,"—in a green bamboo that was reared in a hothouse at Islington!

TANGENT, TANGENTIAL. A straight line touching, but not cutting, a curve is termed a *Tangent*, from the Latin *tangere*, to touch. Thus A B, *fig*. 13, which touches the circle D E C F at C, is a tangent at that point; and, in mechanics, a force acting upon a wheel in the direction of the line A B, is said to be *Tangential*. It is in this direction that motion is communicated between wheels and pinions, or from one wheel to another. A plane which touches a curvilineal solid is, in like manner, termed a *tangential plane*. It is this tangential plane from which we measure the *angles of incidence* on the point C, whether the impinging ray be *reflected* or *refracted*.—See *Reflexion*, and *Refractive Power*.

Fig 13.

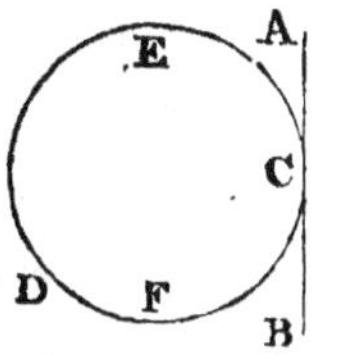

TANGENT *of an Angle.*—See *Angle*.
TELESCOPE, ACHROMATIC.—See *Achromatic*.
TEMPERATURE. The temperature of a body is the comparative degree of active heat accumulated in that body, as measured by an instrument, or generally, by its effects on other bodies.
TETRAHEDRON.—See *Rhombus*.
THERMOMETER (from two Greek words, signifying *a measurer of heat*) is an instrument which serves to compare the degree of active heat existing in other bodies. This comparison is made by marking the effect of the heat; and generally by its power in expanding a fluid, confined in a glass tube hermetically sealed. The fluid is chiefly contained in a bulb, and rises, or falls, in a very narrow tube, supplied from the fluid in the bulb, which contained fluid expands or contracts when immersed in, or applied to, the body whose heat is to be measured. The upper part of the tube is freed from air, to allow the fluid to expand. The fluid capable of sustaining the greatest degree of heat without boiling, is mercury. Higher degrees are measured by other instruments called *Pyrometers* (Greek for *fire-measurers*); but these are all very imperfect, so much so, that a good pyrometer is yet a desideratum.

THERMOMETER, CENTIGRADE, FAHRENHEIT'S AND REAUMUR'S—See those several articles.

TORRICELLIAN VACUUM is the vacuum at the top of the column of mercury in a barometer, and so called from *Torricelli*, the inventor of that instrument.

TOURMALINE. This stone is hard enough to scratch glass, and becomes electric by heat. It is of various colours and forms; it is transparent when viewed across the thickness of a crystal, but perfectly opaque when turned in the opposite direction.

TRANSVERSE DIAMETERS.—See *Conic Sections*.

VACUUM (Latin *vacuus*, empty) is literally an empty place, but is generally used to denote the interior of a close vessel, from which the atmospheric air and every other gas has been extracted.—See *Torricellian*. The *vacuum* produced by means of an air-pump is always imperfect; the vessel is, nevertheless, termed an *Exhausted Receiver*.

VALVE, a close lid affixed to a tube, or opening in a vessel, by means of a hinge, or some other sort of moveable joint, and which can be opened only in one direction.

VAPOUR is any liquid expanded into an elastic, or gaseous fluid, by means of heat. It differs from gas in its want of permanency; for it returns into the liquid state, when exposed to a diminished temperature.

VELOCITY is the comparative celerity of motion in a moving body.

VERNIER. A Vernier (so called from the name of its inventor) is a small moveable scale, running parallel with the fixed scale of a quadrant or other instrument, and having the effect of subdividing the divisions of that instrument into more minute parts.—See *Scale*.

Let A G, *fig*. 14, be any proportion of the limb (or circular part) of a quadrant: for example, half a degree divided into six parts, A B, B C, &c. of five minutes each. Let H I be another limb of equal extent, divided into five parts. In consequence of the relation of these divisions, we see that the line *f b* will be further advanced than N by a fifth part;

g c by two-fifths; *k d* by three-fifths; *m e* by four-fifths; and I S by five-fifths, or a whole division. By this means each

Fig. 14.

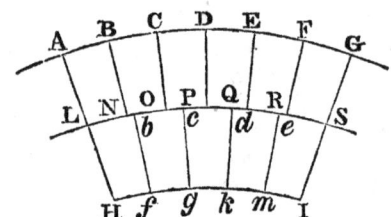

of the divisions, A B, B C, &c. may be divided into five parts, or minutes, by shifting the moveable limb (or *vernier*) H I, to any part of the quadrant where the subdivision is required. This appendage is also added to right lined scales, as may be seen commonly on barometers, by which the inch is first divided into tenths, and a sliding vernier applied so as to subdivide the inch into hundredths. The vernier was invented about the year 1630, and was long termed a *Nonius*; because it was considered as merely an improvement of the method of subdivision adopted by *Nunnez*, a Portuguese, who lived about a century previous. The method of *Nunnez* was, however, different. He drew upon the quadrant a number of circles (46) concentric with the limb, each of which he divided differently:—thus, the limb had 90 parts; the first circle 89; the second 88, &c. When he made his observation he marked the division on which it fell, (it mattered not on what circle,) and proportioned this division to that of 90 on the limb. Thus, if it cut the twenty-third division of the quadrant which was divided into 82 parts, he said, if quarter of a circle divided into 82 parts has given 23 divisions, how many would it have given in a quadrant of 90 parts? and by this calculation he satisfied himself that the real angle was 25 degrees, 14 minutes, and 38 seconds, the exactitude of which must have depended much upon the size and the accuracy of the construction of his instrument.

VERNIER, CHROMATIC, is an instrument so called and invented by Dr. Brewster, for the purpose of measuring, by comparison, the very minute variations of tints. We must refer to page 53 of the treatise on *Polarisation of Light* for the description of this vernier, as we find it impossible to give a simpler explanation.

VERSED SINE.—See *Angle*.

VERTEX.—See *Cone*, and *Conic Sections*.

VESUVIAN, or IDOCRASE, is a stone generally of a reddish-brown colour, similar in appearance to common *garnet*. It is found, crystallized, among substances thrown out by volcanoes; and, as its name indicates, particularly by Mount Vesuvius.

VIS INERTIÆ. According to Newton, every body perseveres in the same state, either of rest or of uniform motion, in a right line, unless it be forced to change that state by a foreign force. This *inertness*, or principle of inactivity, is called by the Latin name *Vis inertiæ*.

VOLUME. The *apparent* space which a body occupies is termed its *volume*; the *effective* space which the same body occupies, or its real bulk of matter, is its *mass*; the relation of the *mass* to the *volume* (or the quotient of the one by the other) is its *density*; and the empty spaces or voids, which render the volume larger than the mass, are its *pores*.

WATER-TIGHT is that degree of closeness in a vessel, or tube, which prevents the passage of water.

WEIGHT is the comparative measure of the gravity of bodies at the earth's surface.

——— OF THE ATMOSPHERE.—See *Atmospheric Pressure*.

WIND is air in perceptible motion.

ZERO (nothing) is with us applied only as a scientific term; but by the French, generally, to denote a cypher (0); while, in that language, *un chiffre* denotes any of the digits, or arithmetical figures. Both words appear to be of similar origin; and probably from the Arabic *tsaphara*, empty or void. In this literal sense, it fills the blank between the ascending and descending numbers in a series.—See *Scale*. In common language, *to cypher* is to calculate; and *to write in cyphers* is to write in secret or unknown characters, such as were the Arabic numerals when first introduced into Europe.

ZIRCONE is a heavy, hard, sparkling, and transparent stone, susceptible of a fine polish, and having a strong double refraction. It is usually divided into the two varieties of *Hyacinth* and *Jargon*; the former having a yellowish-red colour, and the latter being most esteemed when colourless.

Erratum—BLAKE, p. 9, lines 20, 27, and 39, *for* Guernsey, *read* Jersey.

GENERAL INDEX.

The references are given to the treatise, or treatises in which the article is to be found. Of the contractions, PREL. TREAT. stands for *Preliminary Treatise*; HYDROST. for *Hydrostatics*; HYDRAUL. for *Hydraulics*; PNEUM. for *Pneumatics*; MECH. t. i., MECH. t. ii., MECH. t. iii., for the first, second, and third *treatises on Mechanics*, respectively; and POLAR. OF LIGHT, for the treatises on the *Polarisation of Light*.

		Page
Aberration of light, spherical, in lenses	OPTICS	20
.. .. in mirrors	———	22
Absolute heat in bodies of different temperatures	HEAT	39
Absorbing crystals with one axis, list of	POLAR. OF LIGHT	46
.. .. with two axes	———	48
Absorption and reflection of heat	HEAT	33
.. of light in doubly refracting crystals	POLAR. OF LIGHT	46
.. .. influence of heat in modifying	———	48
Acceleration of motion in falling bodies	MECHANICS, t. i.	9
Accidental colours, or ocular spectra	OPTICS	46
.. .. experiments on	———	47
Achromatic telescopes, principles and description of	———	27
Action of crystallized bodies upon polarised light in producing colours	POLAR. OF LIGHT	18—20
Active and passive forces explained and distinguished	MECHANICS, t. iii.	1
Aërostats, or air-balloons, principles of	PNEUMATICS	28
Air, description and properties of	———	2
.. condensed, experiments on	MECHANICS, t. i.	26
.. elasticity of	PNEUMATICS	11, 14
.. atmospheric, its capacity for caloric	HEAT	38
.. pressure of	PREL. TREAT. 19, 26. PNEUM.	13
.. table of its expansion by heat	HEAT	13
.. a mechanical agent	MECHANICS, t. i.	23
.. weight of	HYDROST. 1. PNEUM.	4
Air-balloons, principle of	PNEUMATICS	28
.. *bladder* of fishes, use of	PRELIMINARY TREAT.	24
.. *gun*, description of	PNEUM. 28. MECH. t. i.	26
.. *thermometer*, description of	HEAT	15
.. *pump*	PNEUMATICS	14
.. *vessel* of birds described	PRELIMINARY TREAT.	24
.. .. in machinery	HYDRAUL. 13. PNEUM.	25
Alcohol, distillation of, described	HEAT	56
.. elastic force of its vapour	———	51
Algebra, or universal arithmetic, defined	PRELIMINARY TREAT.	3
Amethyst, circular polarisation in	POLAR. OF LIGHT	42
.. structure of the perfectly formed	———	43
Analcime, new species of double refraction in	———	39
Anatomy, separate and comparative, its uses	PRELIMINARY TREAT.	12
Animal electricity, or galvanism, explained	———	20
.. strength, experiments on	MECHANICS, t. i.	27
Angle of draught, having the least friction	——— t. iii.	19—26
.. of polarisation of different substances, table of the	POLAR. OF LIGHT.	9
Ants, description of the economy of	PRELIMINARY TREAT.	28
Apophyllite, extraordinary system of its coloured rays	POLAR. OF LIGHT	34
.. tesselated, its remarkable formation	———	58
Apparatus for experiments on polarised light described		15—18
Approach of the earth to meet a falling body	MECHANICS, t. i.	8
Applications of the expansion of solids to the arts	HEAT	8
Arago and Fresnel, their experiments on the interference of polarised light	POLAR. OF LIGHT	37
Archimedes' screw, description of	HYDRAUL. 7. MECH. t. ii.	54
Areometer, principle and use of	HYDROSTATICS	13—16
.. Parcieux's	———	15

GENERAL INDEX.

		Page
Arithmetic, its nature and use	PRELIMINARY TREAT.	3
Arnold's compensation balance described	HEAT	10, 19
Arts, expansion of solids applied to the	HEAT	8, 9
Astronomy, physical, its objects and use	PRELIMINARY TREAT.	17
Astronomical telescope, description of	OPTICS	15
Atmosphere, capacity of, for caloric	HEAT	38
.. colours of, accounted for	OPTICS	65
.. weight of	PNEUMATICS	6, 14
Atmospheric pressure, effect of . . HYDRAUL. 11.	PNEUM. 21. MECH. t. i.	24
Attraction, capillary, account of	HYDROSTATICS	24
Atwood's Machine for discovering the law of descent in falling bodies	MECHANICS, t. i. 12.	t. iii. 6
Axes of refraction, explanation of the term	POLAR. OF LIGHT	2
.. rectangular, theory of	————	35
.. negative and positive	————	2
.. of double refraction, combination of	————	29, 30
Axle in wheel, principles of	MECHANICS, t. ii.	21—25
Balance, general principles of the	———— t. ii.	13
.. Arnold's compensation, described	HEAT	10, 19
.. bent lever described	MECHANICS, t. ii.	20
.. Brady's	————	21
.. Danish	————	20
.. fraudulent, description of, and means of detecting	————	17
.. hydrostatic, description and use of	HYDROSTATICS	14
.. philosophical description and representation of a good one	MECHANICS, t. ii.	17
.. Roman, or common steel-yard, method of graduating	————	18
.. sensibility of,—mathematical principles of	————	15
Balloons, principles of	PNEUMATICS	28
Banks's calculations respecting water-wheels	HYDRAULICS	27
Barker's centrifugal mill described . . HYDRAUL. 30.	MECH. t. ii.	55
Barlow, Professor, his improvement of the telescope	OPTICS	28
Barometer, principle and construction of	PNEUMATICS	6
.. diagonal and wheel	————	9
.. uses and application of	————	10, 16
Barton's Iris ornaments, account of	OPTICS	40
Beavers, economy of those animals described	PRELIMINARY TREAT.	29
Bees	————	28
.. curious structure of their cells	————	25
Bejuco, large quantity of water contained in that plant	————	32
Bellows, hydrostatic, description of	HYDROSTATICS	8
Bent-lever balance, description of	MECHANICS, t. ii.	20
Bevelled wheels, description and application of	————	30
Biot, Brewster, &c., their experiments on the polarisation of light	POLAR. OF LIGHT	13
Biot's theory of the colours of polarised light	————	37
Birds, description of the eyes and eyelids of	PRELIMINARY TREAT.	23
.. the air-vessels of	————	24
Black, Dr., character of	HEAT	46
Blair's achromatic telescope described	OPTICS	28
Block and sheaves, their application	MECHANICS, t. ii.	33
Bodies, component parts of	OPTICS	60
.. absolute heat of, at different temperatures	HEAT	39
.. expansion of, by heat . . HYDROST. 17.	MECH. t. i.	29
.. .. experiments on	MECHANICS, t. i.	30
.. falling, laws of their descent	————	10
.. .. experiments on	————	12
.. gravity of, reciprocal	————	6
.. in motion, forces of	————	7
.. .. experiments concerning	————	8
.. natural, investigation of the colours of	OPTICS	59
.. transparency the cause of	————	60
.. zero of, the heat of, investigated	HEAT	40
.. to which double refraction may be communicated by heat and pressure, concerning	POLAR. OF LIGHT	7
.. crystallised, colours produced by their action on polarised light	————	18—20
.. not transparent, method of measuring their refractive powers	————	12
.. polarisation of light at their second surfaces	————	10
.. .. at their separating surfaces	————	11

GENERAL INDEX.

		Page
Boiling, phenomenon of explained	Hydrostatics	18
.. point of water under different pressures	Heat	49
.. points of various fluids, table of	Heat	50
.. of water in vacuo, and under very high pressure	———	50, 51
Botany, definition of, and objects of the science	Preliminary Treat.	12
Brady's balance, description of	Mechanics, t. ii.	21
Bramah's fire engine described	Hydraulics	16
.. hydrostatic press, principle of	Hydrost. 8. Mech. i.	23
Brazilian topaz, structure of	Polar. of Light	57
Breast, water-wheel described	Hydraul. 25. Mech. t. i.	21
Brewster's general law of the phenomena of coloured rings	Polar. of Light	27
.. theory of rectangular axes	———	35
Bucket engine described	Hydraul. 9. Mech. t. i.	21
Built-up lenses for burning-glasses	Optics	12
Burtons, Spanish, a species of pulleys	Mechanics, t. ii.	36
Calcareous (or Iceland) spar, its composition and refractive qualities	Polar. of Light	1
.. multiplication of images in	———	61
.. .. explanation of this phenomenon	———	61
.. .. imitation by artificial combinations	———	62
.. influence of heat upon	———	63
Calculation of the discharge of pumps	Hydraulics	16
.. velocity of rivers	———	5
Caloric, definition of	Heat	1
.. specific, explanation of	———	33
Calorimeter, an instrument for measuring heat	———	34
Camel, peculiarity in the hoofs of that animal	Preliminary Treat.	30
Camera obscura, principle and description of	Optics	14
Camus's machine for moving sieves described	Mechanics, t. ii.	64
Capacities for heat, experiments on	Heat	34
.. caloric, of elastic fluids, tables of	———	36
Capillary attraction, effects of described	Hydrostatics	24
Capstans, descriptions of various kinds of	Mechanics, t. ii.	23-25
Carriages, loading of, observations on	Mechanics, t. i.	19
Cassegrainean telescope described	Optics	20
Catenary, a description of that curve	Preliminary Treat.	7
Catoptrics, the name and objects of the science defined	Optics	16
Causes of erect vision ascertained	———	42
.. long-sightedness	———	46
.. short-sightedness	———	46
.. single vision with two eyes	———	45
.. squinting	———	45
Cells of bees, construction of described	Preliminary Treat.	25
Centre of gravity, explained and calculated	Hydrost. 18. Mech. t. i.	16
.. gyration	Hydraulics	28
.. oscillation	———	28
.. percussion	Hydrostatics	29
.. pressure	———	11, 28
Centigrade thermometer, the scale of explained	Heat	4
Centrifugal mill, Barker's, described	Hydraul. 30. Mech. ii. 55,	102
.. pump, description of	Hydraulics	19
Chain of buckets, a water engine described	Mechanics, t. i.	21
.. pump	Hydraulics	9
Changes on various substances by heat, table of	Heat	20
Character of Dr. Black	———	46
Charcoal, its relation to the diamond	Preliminary Treat.	37
Chemical properties of the prismatic spectrum	Optics	29
.. science, its connection with heat	Heat	1
Chemistry, definition and objects of	Preliminary Treat.	11
Chromatic Vernier for subdividing tints, described	Polar. of Light	52
Chromatics, definition and objects of	Optics	22
Chronometers, useful rules for makers of	Mechanics, t. iii.	16
Circle, definition of	Preliminary Treat.	6
.. involute of, applied to mechanics	Mechanics, t. ii.	29
Circular and rectilinear motions reciprocally converted into one another	———	54—63
.. polarisation in general	Polar. of Light	41

Circular polarisation in quartz	POLAR. OF LIGHT	41
.. .. in amethyst	———————	42
.. .. in fluids	———————	45
.. double refraction, concerning	———————	44
Classes of science discriminated	PRELIMINARY TREAT.	2
Classification of machinery	MECHANICS, t. ii.	3
Cochlion, or Archimedes' screw described	HYDRAUL. 7. MECH. t. ii.	54
Cohesion, quantity of its effect on friction determined	MECHANICS, t. iii.	10
Coloured rays of light, remarks on	PRELIMINARY TREAT.	23
.. rings, double system of	POLAR. OF LIGHT	23
.. .. positive and negative systems of	———————	21
.. .. general law of the phenomena	———————	27
.. .. system of, produced by common light	———————	28
.. .. of the Apophyllite, extraordinary system of	———————	32—36
.. .. splendour of, as seen in the topaz	———————	23
.. .. of topaz, virtual poles of	———————	33
.. .. in Rochelle-salt	———————	33
.. .. hypo-sulphate of lime	———————	35
.. .. leucocyclite	———————	34
.. .. Vesuvian or idocrase	———————	35
.. shadows, explanation of	OPTICS	66
Colours, accidental, phenomena of	———————	46, 48
.. .. theory of	———————	66
.. of bodies changed by heat	———————	63
.. .. .. light	———————	64
.. the atmosphere and sky accounted for	———————	65
.. mother of pearl accounted for	———————	38, 40
.. .. communicable by impression	———————	38
.. natural bodies, cause of	———————	59
.. indistinguishable by certain eyes, curious account of	———————	49
.. thin plates and films, causes of	———————	33
.. .. of air, water, and glass, tables of	———————	35
.. thick and of double plates	———————	36
.. the original particles and fibres of bodies	———————	37
.. primary of the rays of light	———————	23
.. produced by the action of crystallised bodies upon polarised light	POLAR. OF LIGHT	18—20
.. and systems of rings produced by crystals	———————	20—23
.. of polarised light, cause of	———————	36
.. .. Biot's theory of moveable polarisation	———————	37
Combination of frigorific mixtures, tables of	HEAT	62
.. forces, concerning the results of	MECHANICS, t. i.	3
.. wheels and axles, different	———————— t. ii.	27
.. of axes of double refraction	POLAR. OF LIGHT	29, 30
.. of doubly refracting glass plates, effects of	———————	55
.. of rectangular glass plates, effects of	———————	50
Common balance, principles of	MECHANICS	14
.. light distinguished from polarised	POLAR. OF LIGHT	8
.. .. system of coloured rings produced by	———————	28
Communication of double refraction to glass by heat	———————	48
.. .. to glass plates by mechanical force	———————	55
.. of a permanent doubly refracting structure to glass	———————	52
Comparative anatomy, objects of	PRELIMINARY TREAT.	12
.. temperature of the prismatic rays, table of	OPTICS	29
Comparison of the centigrade and Fahrenheit scales of thermometers	HEAT	4
Compensation balance, Arnold's account of	———————	19
Complex wheelwork, concerning	MECHANICS, t. ii.	26
Component parts of bodies, investigation concerning	OPTICS	60
Composition of forces, the effects of	MECHANICS, t. i.	2
.. of motions	———————	4
.. of calcareous or Iceland spar	POLAR. OF LIGHT	1
Compound levers, principles of	MECHANICS, t. ii.	10
.. microscopes	OPTICS	15
Compressibility in general, concerning	PNEUMATICS	1
.. of water	HYDROSTATICS	1
Condensed air, experiments on	MECHANICS, t. i.	26
Condenser, its use described	PNEUMATICS	20
Conducting powers of different kinds of wood, tables of	HEAT	22

GENERAL INDEX.

		Page
Conducting power of various fluids, tables of	Heat	25
Conductors of heat, concerning the	———	21
.. various experiments on	———	23, 24
Connexion between the polarisation and the double refraction of light	Polar. of Light	29
Constellations, remark on the	Preliminary Treat.	16
Converging and diverging beams of light, phenomena of	Optics	67
Convex and concave mirrors, concerning	———	16
.. .. lenses	———	9
.. and concave screws	Mechanics, t. ii.	44
Cooling effect of perspiration, experiments on	Heat	55
.. heated bodies, table of	———	32
Cordage, remarks on the rigidity of	Mechanics, t. iii.	16, 18
.. experiments and tables on the rigidity of	———	26, 29
Correspondence between the different scales of thermometers, table of	Heat	17
Coulomb compared with Vince as an experimentalist	Mechanics, t. iii.	11
.. his experiments on friction detailed	———	4—12
Cow tree, description of that curious tree	Preliminary Treat.	33
Crank, applications of	Mechanics, t. ii.	50, 59
.. , triple, described	Hydraulics	12
Crichton's metallic thermometer, described	Heat	19
Crown, Hiero's, account of the detection of its alloy	Hydrostatics	16
.. wheels described, with their application	Mechanics, t. ii.	30
Cryophorus, or frost bearer, account of that instrument	Heat	55
Crystal (rock) its refraction	Polar. of Light	6
Crystals of ice float in the atmosphere	Optics	55
.. different axes and planes of their refraction	Polar. of Light	7
.. having one axis of double refraction, list of	———	3
.. law of double refraction	———	4—7
.. absorbing, lists of	———	46, 48
.. doubly refracting, absorption of light by	———	46
.. .. influence of heat upon	———	48
.. having two axes, law of their double refraction	———	29
.. regular, effects of pressure upon	———	56
.. composite doubly refracting, effects of pressure upon the structure of	———	56
.. rhomboidal, formation of	———	1
.. table of, with character of their axes	———	26
.. .. of their different polarising intensities	———	31
.. colours produced by their action on polarised light	———	18—20
.. .. and systems of rings produced by	———	20—23
.. possessing a double system of coloured rings	———	23—25
.. of Rochelle salt, spectra in	———	33
Ctesebes's pump, description of	Hydraulics	15
Cubezite, new species of double refraction in	Polar. of Light	39
Cuckoo, some account of that bird	Preliminary Treat.	31
Curious experiment with sulphate of potash and copper	Polar. of Light	63
Curvature of lenses, table of	Optics	22
Cyanometer (Saussure's) description of	———	65
Cycloid, description of that curve, and its application to pendulums	Preliminary Treat.	21
D'Alembert's principle	Mechanics, t. ii.	2
Danish balance, description and principle of	———	20
Decomposition of white light, experiments on	Optics	22
Definite proportions, remarks on that chemical doctrine	Preliminary Treat.	15
De la Hire's pump, description of	Hydraulics	15
De-oxydizing power of the prismatic spectrum	Optics	29
Descent of falling bodies, investigation of the laws of	Mechanics, t. i.	10
.. table of	———	11
Description of a chromatic Vernier for subdividing tints	Polar. of Light	52
Deviation of the polarised tints from those of Newton's scale	———	32
Devonshire, account of a remarkable intermitting spring in	Hydrostatics	22
Diagonal barometer, description of	Pneumatics	9
Diamond, its relation to charcoal	Preliminary Treat.	37
Differential thermometer, Leslie's, description of	Heat	29
Diffraction of light, account of	Optics	31
Dilation of solids by heat, table of	Heat	7
Dioptrics, definition and objects of the science	Optics	6
Direction of gravity, line of	Mechanics, t. i.	18

GENERAL INDEX.

		Page
Direction of motions, various modes of altering	Mechanics, t. ii.	53—59
.. visible objects, concerning	Optics	42
Discharge pipes, proper form of described	Hydraulics	3
.. of pumps, calculations on the	———	16
Dispersion of light, concerning	Optics	24
Dispersive powers of bodies with regard to light, table of	———	25
Distillation, process of, described	Heat	56
.. of fluids in vacuo	———	58
Distinct and indistinct vision in the same object, cause of	Optics	42
Diverging and converging beams of light, phenomena of	———	67
Dollond's achromatic telescope, description of	Prel. Treat. 23. Optics	27
Double axle and wheel, described	Mechanics, t. ii.	24
.. rack	———	51
Double refraction of light, general account of	Polar. of Light	1
.. laws of, in crystals	———	3—7
.. circular	———	7
.. communicable by heat and pressure	———	48
.. .. to glass plates by mechanical force	———	55
.. productive of polarisation of light	———	14
.. its connexion with polarisation	———	29
.. law of, in crystals with two axes	———	29
.. combination of axes of	———	29, 30
.. new species of in Analcime	———	39
Doubly refracting crystals, absorption of light in	———	46
.. .. structure of	———	56
.. .. influence of heat upon	———	62
.. force in spheres, spheroids, and tubes of glass, distribution of	———	51
.. glass plates, combination of	———	55
.. structure rendered permanent in glass	———	52
.. .. produced by evaporation and induration	———	53
Double system of coloured rings produced by certain crystals	———	23
.. possessed by certain crystals	———	25
Draught, angle of, considerations on	Mechanics, t. iii.	19—26
Drill-bow, manner of its motion	——— t. ii.	59
Driving piles, machine for, described	———	51
Duck, description of its bill	Preliminary Treat.	31
Duration of the impressions of light on the eye ascertained	Optics	44
Dynamics, definition of the science	Prel. Treat. 12. Mech. t. i.	1
Earth, concerning its approach to a falling body	Mechanics, t. i.	8
Eccentric, a machine for producing parallel motion, described	——— t. ii.	59
.. pump, description of	Hydraulics	16
Echoes, the cause of described	Pneumatics	30
Eckhardt's capstan, description of	Mechanics, t. ii.	24
Economical application of Steam	Heat	52
Economy of ants and bees, description of	Preliminary Treat.	28
.. of beavers	———	29
Effect, of light on vegetables	———	27
.. in changing the colours of bodies	Optics	64
.. different kinds of, produced by machinery	Mechanics, t. ii.	1
.. of velocity upon friction	——— t. iii.	31
.. of combining and crossing rectangular plates of glass	Polar. of Light	55
.. produced by altering the form of glass plates	———	52
.. of pressure on regular crystals	———	56
Efficacy, mechanical, of machines in general, observations on	Mechanics, t. ii.	13
.. .. of pulleys	———	33
.. .. of wheels and axles	———	24
Egg-sucker, or toucan, description of that bird	Preliminary Treat.	32
Elastic fluids defined	Pneumatics	1
.. .. their capacities for heat investigated	Heat	36
.. .. .. compared with atmospheric air, table of	———	38
... force of vapour and steam of water, tables of	———	48
.. .. of different vapours, compared with each other, table of	———	51
Elasticity of air, concerning the	Pneumatics	11
.. .. shewn to be equal to the weight of the atmosphere	———	14
.. of fluids in general	Hydraulics	1

GENERAL INDEX.

		Page
Elasticity of water, illustrated by experiments	HYDROSTATICS	1, 2
Electricity, definition and effects of	PRELIMINARY TREAT.	20
Ellipsis, description of that curve	———	7
Ellipsoid, the proper form for mirrors of reflecting microscopes	OPTICS	22
Endless chain of buckets for drawing water	MECHANICS, t. i.	21
Engine for driving piles, description of	——— t. ii.	51
Equilibrium, mechanical, defined	——— t. i.	1
.. of pressure explained	HYDRAULICS	2
.. its effects in modifying friction	MECHANICS, t. iii.	18
Erect vision, cause of	OPTICS	42
Eriometer, an instrument for measuring minute fibres, described	———	37
Errors in the construction of pumps pointed out	HYDRAULICS	11
Ether, elastic force of its vapour	HEAT	51
Evaporation, cause of it explained	———	58
.. of fluids in air and vacuo	———	53
.. observations on the effects of	MECHANICS, t. i.	31
.. productive of a doubly refracting structure	POLAR. OF LIGHT	53
Exhaustion of air, degree of it measured by the barometer	PNEUMATICS	16
Expansion of bodies by heat generally	HYDROSTATICS 17. HEAT	6
.. of air at different heats, Table of	HEAT	13
.. of liquids, Table of	———	10
.. of water peculiarity in	———	12
.. of solids, application of to the arts	———	8
.. of bodies by heat, particular experiments on	MECHANICS, t. i.	29
Expansive force of water on freezing	———	12
Experiment, curious, with sulphate of potash and copper	POLAR. OF LIGHT	63
Experiments on accidental colours	OPTICS	47
.. on animal strength	MECHANICS, t. i.	27
.. on the capacities of bodies for heat	HEAT	34
.. on conductors of heat	———	23
.. on the expansion of liquids	———	11—18
.. on condensed air	MECHANICS, t. i.	26
.. on falling bodies	———	10—12
.. on the cooling effects of perspiration	HEAT	55
.. on the refraction of light	OPTICS	2
.. on reflected heat	HEAT	30
.. on the polarisation of light by Biot, Malus, &c.	POLAR. OF LIGHT	13
.. on polarised light, apparatus for, described	———	15—18
.. on the interference of polarised light by Arago and Fresnel	———	37
.. on quartz by Fresnel	———	44
.. on Vesuvian, &c. by Herschel	———	34, 35
Explanation of the multiplication of images in calcareous spar	———	61
.. of the law of the sines	———	2
.. .. of the tangents	———	10
Extraordinary and ordinary rays of light distinguished	———	2
Eye, anatomical description of	OPTICS	40
.. accommodates itself to different distances	———	45
.. refractive powers of its different humours	———	41
.. colours produced by the unequal action of light upon	———	48
.. insensibility of to faint light	———	43
.. of birds, description of	PRELIMINARY TREAT.	23
.. of the horse	———	24
Eyes, causes of single vision with two	OPTICS	45
.. insensibility of some, to certain colours	———	49
Fahrenheit's thermometer compared with other thermometers	HEAT	19
. scale compared with the centigrade	———	4
Faint light, insensibility of the eye to	OPTICS	43
Falling bodies, laws of their descent	MECHANICS, t. i.	10
Feeding pipe of pumps, error in the construction of	HYDRAULICS	11
Ferguson, James, remarks on his genius	HYDROSTATICS	8
Fibres, minute, the colours and comparative measures of	OPTICS	37
Films, the colours of, displayed	———	33
Fire-engines, description and representation of HYDRAUL. 15. PNEUM. 26 and MECH. t. i.		26
.. Bramah's described	HYDRAULICS	16
First-mover, explanation of the term	MECHANICS, t. i.	2
Fishes, account of their air-bladders	PRELIMINARY TREAT.	24

		Page
Fixed pulleys, description of	MECHANICS, t. ii.	33
Flies, means by which they are enabled to walk on window-panes and ceilings	PREL. TREAT. 26. PNEUM.	5
Float-boards in water-wheels, proper proportions of	———— t. i.	22
Fluidity caused by heat	HEAT	42
Fluids definition of	HYDRAUL. 1. PNEUM.	1
.. elastic and inelastic distinguished	PNEUMATICS	1
.. friction of	HYDRAULICS	2
.. circular polarisation in	POLAR. OF LIGHT	45
.. evaporation of in air and vacuo	HEAT	53
.. pressure of, exemplified	HYDROSTATICS	2, 10
.. their power in motion	HYDRAULICS	22
.. spouting, laws of	————	4
.. transmission of their pressure	PNEUMATICS	5
.. experiments on their expansion by heat	HEAT	14
.. table of their comparative expansions by heat	————	11
.. table of their several powers of conducting heat	————	25
.. (elastic) table of their several capacities for caloric heat	————	36
Fly-catcher, or *Fly-trap*, singular apparatus in the leaves of that plant	PRELIMINARY TREAT.	32
Fly-wheel, principle and power of	MECHANICS, t. ii.	49
Foot of the camel, construction of	PRELIMINARY TREAT.	30
.. horse	————	31
.. rein-deer	————	31
Force, different definitions of	MECH. t. i. 1. MECH. t. iii.	1
.. degree of required to work pumps of different constructions	PNEUMATICS	22—25
.. expansive, of water by heat	HEAT	12
.. of gravity, investigations of	MECHANICS, t. i.	6
.. of vapour of different fluids, table of	HEAT	51
.. and lift pump described	HYDRAULICS	11
Forces of two species, active and resisting	MECHANICS, t. iii.	1
.. composition and resolution of	———— t. i.	2
∴ of equal masses are proportionate to their velocity	————	7
Forcing pumps, descriptions of	HYDRAUL. 11. PNEUM.	24
Form, proper, of the teeth in wheel-work	MECHANICS, t. ii.	28
Formation of images by lenses	OPTICS	12
.. by a plane mirror	————	18
.. by concave and convex mirrors	————	19, 20
.. remarkable, of tesselated apophyllite	POLAR. OF LIGHT	57
.. of rhomboidal crystals	————	1
Formulæ (Malus's) for the intensity of pencils of light	————	15
Fracture of a crystal of quartz, peculiar appearance of	OPTICS	33
Fraudulent balances, calculations on	MECHANICS, t. ii.	17
Freezing temperature of various liquids, table of	HEAT	62
.. of quicksilver, phenomenon of	————	54—60
.. of water in large quantities, Dr. Ure's plan	————	54
.. of water in the receiver of an air pump	————	54
Fresnel and Arago, experiments on light by	POLAR. OF LIGHT	37
Fresnel's experiments on right and left-handed quartz	————	44
Friction, its general laws and effects as found by experiments	MECHANICS, t. iii.	1—32
.. of bodies in motion and at rest	————	10
.. .. sliding	————	3
.. .. rolling	————	11
.. .. revolving on each other without rolling	————	12
.. .. turning on pivots	————	14
.. of fluids	HYDRAULICS	2
.. comparative, of different kinds of wood	MECHANICS, t. iii.	30
.. an uniformly retarding force	————	6
.. a producer of heat	HEAT	3—5
.. modified by equilibrium	MECHANICS, t. iii.	18
.. affected by velocity	————	30
.. tables of experiments on	————	26—30
.. works written upon, referred to	————	31, 32
Friction-rollers, Garnet's	———— t. ii.	40
Frigorific mixtures, combinations of	HEAT	62
.. .. table of	————	60
Frost-bearer, Dr. Wollaston's, described	————	55
Frost-smoke of Greenland, Giesecke's description of that phenomenon	OPTICS	55
Fulcrum, or pivot, defined	PRELIMINARY TREAT.	18

		Page
Galvanism, or animal electricity, explained	PRELIMINARY TREAT.	20
Garnet's friction rollers described	MECHANICS, t. ii.	40
Gases, distillation of	HEAT	58
.. table of the refractive power of	OPTICS	6
Gastric juice, account of the	PRELIMINARY TREAT.	27
General law of the phenomena of coloured rings	POLAR. OF LIGHT	27
Genius of Ferguson, remarks on	HYDROSTATICS	8
Geology, definition and objects of that science	PRELIMINARY TREAT.	12
Geometry	———	3
Glass lenses, different kinds of	OPTICS	7
.. panes, how flies are enabled to walk upon	PREL. TREAT. 26. PNEUM.	5
.. refraction of light through	OPTICS	8
.. table of the colours of thin plates of		35
.. double refraction communicated to, by heat	POLAR. OF LIGHT	48
.. plates, effects of combining and crossing	———	50
.. .. double refraction communicated to by mechanical force	———	55
.. .. combination of doubly refracting ones	———	55
.. on the communication of a permanent doubly refracting structure to	———	52
.. spheres, tubes, &c., distribution of the doubly refracting force of	———	51
Glauberite, influence of heat upon	———	63
.. phenomena of	———	33
Glow-worm, the purpose of her shining light	PRELIMINARY TREAT.	31
Goniometer, an instrument for measuring angles	OPTICS	8
Governor, a machine for equalizing motion, described	MECHANICS, t. ii.	52
Gradual induration, a method of producing a doubly refracting structure by	POLAR. OF LIGHT	53
Gravity, definition and laws of	PRELIMINARY TREAT.	13—17
.. distinguished from impulse	MECHANICS, t. i.	9
.. causes all bodies to descend with equal velocity	———	10
.. of bodies reciprocal	———	7
.. line of direction of	———	18
.. force of	———	6
.. centre of explained and calculated	HYDROST. 18. MECH. t. i.	16
.. specific, explanation of	HYDROSTATICS	13
Gravities, specific, of various bodies, tables of	———	19—21
Gregorian telescope, description of	OPTICS	20
Gridiron pendulum (Harrison's), described	HEAT	10
Gyration, centre and circle of, explained and calculated	HYDRAULICS	28
Haloes and parhelia, causes of these phenomena	OPTICS	52—56
Harrison's gridiron pendulum, described	HEAT	10
Haw, the third eyelid of a horse, described	PRELIMINARY TREAT.	24
Heat, nature and cause of	HEAT	1
.. absorption of	———	33
.. absolute, in bodies at different temperatures	———	39
.. its connexion with chemical science	———	1
.. conductors of	———	21
.. .. experiments on	———	23, 25
.. capacities for, experiments on	———	34
.. .. tables of	———	36
.. change of colours of bodies by	OPTICS	63
.. expansion of bodies by	HEAT, 6. MECH. t. i.	29
.. .. air by, table of	———	13
.. .. liquids by, table of	———	10
.. .. .. experiments on	———	14
.. .. solids by, application to the arts	———	8
.. .. .. table of	———	7
.. general agency of	———	1
.. considered as a mechanical agent	MECHANICS, t. i.	29
.. .. the cause of fluidity	HEAT	42
.. latent, experiments concerning	———	41
.. .. in vapours, table of	———	48
.. .. weight of, attempt to ascertain the	———	2
.. produced by means of friction, experiments of	———	3—5
.. radiant, velocity of its motion	———	28
.. radiation of, its laws explained	———	26

Heat, reflected rays of, experiments concerning	HEAT	29, 30
.. specific, explanation of	———	33
.. .. of different metals, table of	———	39
.. of the sun's rays, cause of	———	63
.. .. separated by a prism	———	28
.. supportable by the human body, experiments on	———	55
.. works on referred to	———	63, 64
.. zero of, according to Dr. Irvine	———	40
.. communicates double refraction to certain bodies	POLAR. OF LIGHT	48
.. .. to glass	———	48
.. its influence in modifying the absorption of light by crystals	———	48
.. .. upon doubly refracting crystals	———	62
.. .. upon Glauberite	———	63
.. .. upon calcareous spar	———	63
.. .. upon sulphate of lime	———	63
Heated bodies, table of the times of cooling	HEAT	32
Heating power of the prismatic spectrum	———	28
Heights, measured by means of the barometer	PNEUMATICS	10
Herschel's table of the curvature of lenses	OPTICS	22
.. experiments on leucocyclite, Vesuvian, &c.	POLAR. OF LIGHT	34, 35
Hiero's crown, method of detecting its alloy	HYDROSTATICS	16
High-pressure steam-engine described	MECHANICS, t. i.	32
Highlanders of Scotland, their second sight accounted for	OPTICS	59
History, definition and utility of	PRELIMINARY TREAT.	3
.. of the steam-engine	MECHANICS, t. i.	32
.. Natural, definition and objects of	PRELIMINARY TREAT.	12
Hooke's universal joint described	MECHANICS, t. ii.	62
Horizontal water wheels, observations on	HYDRAULICS	29
Horse, observations on the eyes of	PRELIMINARY TREAT.	24
.. .. the limbs and feet of	———	31
.. strength of, compared with that of a man	MECHANICS, t. i.	29
Howard's thermometer described	HEAT	19
Human body, experiments on the degree of heat endurable by	———	55
.. strength average value of	MECHANICS, t. i.	28
.. .. compared with that of a horse	———	29
Humours of the eye, refractive powers of	OPTICS	41
Hungarian machine, description of	HYDRAULICS	17
Hunter's screw, described	MECHANICS, t. ii.	46
Hunting cog, description of	———	30
Hydraulics defined	PREL. TREAT. 19. HYDROST. 1. HYDRAUL. 1	
Hydraulic machines, account of various	HYDRAULICS to end.	
.. works on referred to	———	32
Hydrodynamics, definition of	PREL. TREAT. 19. HYDROST. 1	
Hydrometer, principle of	HYDROSTATICS	13—15
Hydrostatics, defined	PREL. TREAT. 19. HYDROST. 1. HYDRAUL. 1	
.. mathematical illustrations of	HYDROSTATICS	27—30
.. works on, referred to	———	31, 32
Hydrostatic balance described	———	14
.. bellows	———	8
.. paradox	———	5
.. press, Bramah's	HYDROST. 8. MECH. t. i. 23	
Hyperbola, description and properties of that curve	PRELIMINARY TREAT.	7
Hypo-sulphate of lime, tints in the rings of	POLAR. OF LIGHT	35
Ice, crystals of, float in the atmosphere	OPTICS	55
.. method of procuring in India	HEAT	54
.. tables of frigorific mixtures with and without that ingredient	———	60
Iceland spar, its double refraction and composition described	POLAR. OF LIGHT	1
Idocrase, tints of its coloured rings	———	35
Illuminating power of the prismatic spectrum	OPTICS	29
Illustrations, mathematical, of hydrostatics	HYDROSTATICS	27—30
Images formed by lenses	OPTICS	12
.. by plane mirrors	———	18
.. by concave and convex mirrors	———	19, 20
.. multiplication of, in calcareous spar	POLAR. OF LIGHT	61
.. .. explanation of the phenomena	———	61
.. .. imitation by artificial combinations	———	62
Impenetrability of air asserted	PNEUMATICS	2, 3

GENERAL INDEX.

		Page
Imperfections of refracting telescopes	Optics	26
Impregnation of vegetables, remarks on	Preliminary Treat.	27
Impression of mother of pearl on wax, &c. producing colours	Optics	38
.. of light, direction of, on the eye	———	44
Improvement of telescopes proposed by Mr. Barlow	———	28
Impulse distinguished from gravity	Mechanics, t. i.	9
Inclined plane, its power and experiments on	——— t. ii.	40—42
Independent parts in the composition of light	Optics	2
India, method of procuring ice in	Heat	54
Indistinct and distinct vision in the same object	Optics	42
Induration, productive of a doubly refracting structure in bodies	Polar. of Light	53
Inelastic fluids, observations on	Pneumatics	1
Inertia, an universal property of matter	———	3
Inflexion, or diffraction of light, observations on	Optics	31
Influence of heat in modifying the absorption of light by crystals	Polar. of Light	48
.. upon doubly refracting crystals	———	62
.. upon Glauberite	———	63
.. upon calcareous spar	———	63
.. upon sulphate of lime	———	63
Insensibility of the eye to faint light accounted for	Optics	43
.. of certain eyes to particular colours	———	49
Intellectual philosophy defined	Preliminary Treat.	2
Intensity of pencils of light, Malus's formulæ for	Polar. of Light	15
Intensities, polarising, of different crystals, table of	———	30
Interference of the rays of light, laws of	Optics	31
.. of polarised light, experiments upon	Polar. of Light	37
Intermission in the vision of objects seen obliquely	Optics	43
Intermitting springs, explanation and cause of	Hydrostatics	21
.. .. peculiar one in Devonshire	———	22
Involute of a circle, its application in mechanics	Mechanics, t. ii.	29
Iris ornaments, account of	Optics	40
Irvine's supposed zero of heat in bodies	Heat	40
Java, the swallow of, account of its edible nests	Preliminary Treat.	32
Juice, gastric, its properties	———	27
Kaleidoscope, principle of its construction	Optics	19
La Garousse's lever, described	Mechanics, t. ii.	55—63
Lantern-wheel, description and application of	———	30
Latent heat, experiments on	Heat	41
.. .. in vapours, tables of	———	48
.. .. weight of	———	2
Latitude, in geography, explanation of the term	Preliminary Treat.	17
Law of descent in falling bodies investigated	Mechanics, t. i.	10
.. of the sines explained	Polar. of Light	2
.. of double refraction in crystals	———	4—6
.. of the tangents explained	———	10
.. of the phenomena of coloured rings, by Dr. Brewster	———	27
.. of double refraction in crystals with two axes	———	29
Laws, general, of light	Optics	16
.. of interference of rays of light	———	31
.. of spouting fluids	Hydraulics	4
Least resistance, the solid of, observations on	Preliminary Treat.	22
Leucocyclite of Herschel, systems of its coloured rings	Polar. of Light	34
Lenses defined and severally described	Optics	7
.. refraction of light through	———	8
.. images formed by	———	12
.. magnifying power of	———	14
.. spherical aberrations in	———	20
.. table of the curvatures of	———	22
Level, spirit, described	Hydrostatics	10
Lever, principles of, explained	Preliminary Treat.	18
.. as a mechanical power	Mechanics, t. ii.	3
.. account of different forms of	———	6—8
.. of La Garousse, described	———	55—63
.. perpetual	———	22
.. rectangular described	———	11

Levers, compound, observations on	Mechanics, t. ii.	10
Lift, or lifting pump, construction of	Hydraul. 10. Pneum.	23
.. and force pump	———	4
Light, nature and properties of	Optics	1
.. consists of separate and independent parts	———	2
.. coloured rays of, observations on	Preliminary Treat.	23
.. its effects on vegetables	Prel. Treat. 27. Optics	64
.. its effects on changing the colours of bodies	Optics	64
.. beams of, converging and diverging, cause of	———	67
.. diverging rays of, reflected from plane, concave, and convex mirrors	———	16
.. decomposition of white	———	22
.. diffraction of, explained	———	31
.. dispersion of	———	24
.. dispersive powers of, by different bodies	———	25
.. duration of its impressions on the eye	———	44
.. reflected from bodies of their own colour	———	1
.. reflexion of, general laws of	———	16
.. reflexion of, from different forms of mirrors	———	16
.. refraction of, through different lenses	———	8—11
.. .. experiments on	———	2, 3
.. rays of, proceed always in straight lines	———	2
.. .. primary colours of	———	23
.. .. their different refrangibility	———	23
.. .. their interference	———	31
.. .. partially lost by reflexion	———	67
.. .. .. table of	———	68
.. .. velocity of, described	———	2
.. .. undulations of, account of that theory	———	32
.. .. waves of	———	31
.. absorption of, in doubly refracting crystals	Polar. of Light	46
.. common, may produce systems of coloured rings	———	28
.. pencils of, formulæ for their intensity	———	15
.. refraction of, its connexion with polarisation	———	29
.. polarisation of, description of the phenomena	———	7
.. .. at the second surfaces of bodies	———	10
.. .. at the separating surfaces of two bodies	———	11
.. .. by successive reflexions	———	11
.. .. by ordinary refractions	———	13
.. .. experiments on, by Biot, Malus, &c.	———	13
.. .. by double refraction	———	14
.. .. Malus's researches on	———	9
.. polarised, in what it differs from common light	———	8
.. .. how obtained	———	8
.. .. partially, by reflexion, state of	———	12
.. .. after it has suffered refraction	———	12
.. .. colours produced by the action of crystallised bodies upon	———	18—26
.. .. cause of the colours of	———	30
.. .. theory of	———	37
.. .. apparatus for experiments upon	———	15—18
.. .. (interference of) experiments upon	———	37
.. polarisation of, list of works on	———	64
Lime, hypo-sulphate of, tints of its rings	———	35
.. sulphate of, influence of heat upon	———	63
Line of direction of gravity	Mechanics, t. i.	18
Lines crossing the prismatic spectrum	Optics	30
Liquefaction and evaporation, causes of	Heat	58
Liquids, table of their expansion by heat	———	10
List of absorbing crystals with one axis	Polar. of Light	46
.. with two axes	———	48
Loading of carriages, observations on	Mechanics, t. i.	19
Logarithms, nature of those factitious numbers	Preliminary Treat.	4
Longitude, in geography, explanation of the term	———	17
Longsightedness, cause and remedy of	Optics	46
Lowering of temperature, modes of	Heat	59
Low-pressure steam-engines, construction of	Mech. t. i.	32
Lunar rainbow, cause of the phenomenon	Optics	52

Machine, definition of	Mechanics, t. i.	2
.. Atwood's, for experiments on falling bodies	Mech. t. i. 11. Mech. t. iii.	6
.. Camus's, for moving sieves	Mechanics, t. ii.	64
.. Hungarian, for raising water	Hydraulics	17
.. weighing, described	Mechanics, t. ii.	12
.. mechanical efficacy of	———	13, 24
Machines, hydraulic	Hydraulics	9
Machinery, classification of	Mechanics, t. ii.	3
.. kinds of effects produced by	———	1
Magnetizing power of the solar rays	Optics	29
Magnifying power of lenses, cause of	———	14
Magnitude, smallest, visible by a microscope	———	32
Malus, M., his researches on the polarisation of light	Polar. of Light	9
.. his formulæ for the intensity of pencils of light	———	15
Marquis of Worcester's steam-engine	Mechanics, t. i.	32
Masses, equal, have forces proportionate to their velocities	———	7
Mathematics, definition and objects of	Preliminary Treat.	2
.. mixed	———	11
Mathematical truths distinguished from physical	———	7
.. illustrations of hydrostatics	Hydrostatics	27, 30
Measuring of heights by the barometer	Pneumatics	10
.. exhaustion of air by ditto	———	16
Mechanical philosophy, its objects	Preliminary Treat.	11
.. powers described	———	18
.. agency of air	Mechanics, t. i.	23—27
.. .. of heat	———	29—32
.. .. of water	———	19—23
.. efficacy of machines	——— t. ii.	13, 24
.. .. of pulleys	———	33
.. force communicates double refraction to glass plates	Polar. of Light	55
Mechanics, practical, its objects	Prel. Treat. 17. Mech. t. i.	1
.. works on, referred to	Mechanics, t. ii.	64
Meniscus, a species of lens, described	Optics	7
.. refraction of light through	———	11
Metals, specific heat of	Heat	39
Metallic thermometers described	———	19
Method of procuring ice in India	———	54
.. of measuring the refractive powers of opaque bodies	Polar. of Light	12
Micrometer-screw, described	Mechanics, t. ii.	48
Microscope, principles of	Optics	15
.. compound	———	15
.. reflecting	———	20
.. smallest magnitude, visible by	———	32
.. reflecting, proper form of their mirrors	———	22
Milky-way, causes of its light	Preliminary Treat.	16
Mill, Barker's centrifugal, described	Hydraul. 30. Mech. t. ii.	55
Mind of man distinguished from his body	Preliminary Treat.	33
Mineralogy, objects of the science	———	12
Minerals and crystals, table of, with character of their axes	Polar. of Light	26
Mirage, description and cause of that phenomena	Optics	56—59
Mirrors, reflection of rays of light from	———	16—17
.. formation of images in	———	18—20
.. of reflecting microscopes, proper form of	———	22
.. .. telescopes	———	22
.. spherical aberrations in	———	22
Mixed mathematics defined	Preliminary Treat.	11
Mixtures, frigorific or freezing, different	Heat	59
.. .. temperatures of	———	62
.. .. tables of	———	60
Moment or momentum, definition of	Mechanics, t. ii.	5
Moon, mountains in, capable of being measured	Preliminary Treat.	17
Moral philosophy, definition and objects of	———	2
Morveau's pyrometer described	Heat	21
Mother of pearl, prismatic colours of, communicable by impression	Optics	38
.. structure of	———	39
Motion of falling bodies, acceleration of	Mechanics, i.	9
.. of fluids, power of	Hydraulics	22

GENERAL INDEX.

		Page
Motion of friction of bodies in	Mechanics, t. iii.	10
.. methods of changing its direction	——— t. ii.	53—64
.. parallel, described	———	59
Motions, composition of	——— t. i.	4
Moveable pulleys	——— t. ii.	33
.. polarisation of light, Biot's theory of	Polar. of Light	37
Mover, first, explanation of the term	Mechanics, t. i.	2
Moving bodies, ratio of their powers	———	7
.. experiments on	———	8
Mountains in the moon, their height capable of being measured	Preliminary Treat.	17
Multiplication of images in calcareous spar	Polar. of Light	61
.. .. cause of	———	61
.. .. explanation of	———	61
.. .. artificial imitation of	———	62
Murray's (Dr.) proposed scale for thermometers	Heat	18
Muscipula, or fly-catcher, description of that plant	Preliminary Treat.	32
Naphtha, elastic force of its vapour	Heat	51
Natural bodies, colours of	Optics	59
.. history, objects of	Preliminary Treat.	12
.. philosophy	———	2—8
Nature, or cause, of heat	Heat	1
.. and properties of light	Optics	1
Nautilus, description of that curious shell-fish	Preliminary Treat.	31
Negative and positive axes of refraction explained	Polar. of Light	2
.. systems of coloured rings	———	21
Nepenthes distillatoria, a singular plant	Preliminary Treat.	32
New species of double refraction in Analcime	Polar. of Light	39
Newcomen's steam-engine described	Mechanics, t. i.	32
Newton's table of colours of thin plates and films	Optics	35
.. scale, its deviation from that of the polarised tints	Polar. of Light	32
Objects, intermission in the vision of, when seen obliquely	Optics	43
.. of mechanics	Mechanics, t. i.	1
.. visible, duration of	Optics	42
Oblique ropes with pulleys, concerning	Mechanics, t. ii.	39
Ocular spectra, or accidental colours	Optics	46
Oil of turpentine, boiling point of	Heat	51
Opaque bodies, method of measuring their refractive powers	Polar. of Light	12
Optic axis, different positions of, for different coloured rays	———	32
Optics, definition of	Prel. Treat. 20. Optics	1
Ordinary and extraordinary rays distinguished	Polar. of Light	2
.. refraction, polarisation of light by	———	13
Ornaments, iris	Optics	40
Oscillation, centre of	Hydraulics	23
Ostrich, mode of hatching its eggs	Preliminary Treat.	31
Overshot water-wheel	Hydraul. 24. Mech. t. i.	19
.. proper velocity of	Mechanics, t. i.	21
Pala de vaca, or cow-tree, account of	Preliminary Treat.	33
Panes of glass, how flies are enabled to walk upon	———	26
Parabola, description and properties of that curve	———	6
Paraboloidal surface, proper for the mirrors of reflecting telescopes	Optics	22
Paradox, definition of the term	Hydrostatics	6
.. hydrostatic, explanation of	———	5
Parallel motion, description of	Mechanics, t. ii.	59
Parcieux's areometer described	Hydrostatics	15
Parhelia, phenomena and causes of	Optics	52
Paris's (Dr.) thaumatrope, a curious optical toy	———	44
Particles, minute, of bodies, colours of	———	37
Passive forces. See Active forces.		
Pearl, mother of, its structure explained	———	38
.. its colours communicable by impressions	———	39
Peculiarity in the expansion of water	Heat	12
Pencils of light, formulæ of M. Malus for their intensity	Polar. of Light	15
Pendulum, application of the cycloid in its construction	Preliminary Treat.	21
.. gridiron, by Harrison, account of	Heat	10
Percussion, centre of, explained	Hydrostatics	29

GENERAL INDEX.

		Page
Percussion, force of, applied to the wedge	Mechanics, t. ii.	43
Permanent doubly refracting structure to glass, on the communication of	Polar. of Light	52
Perpetual lever, or axle in wheel	Mechanics, t. ii.	22
.. screw, a mechanical power	———	47
Persian wheel, description of that machine	Hydraulics	22
Perspiration, curious experiments on its cooling effect	Heat	55
Petrolium, elastic force of the vapour of	———	51
Phenomenon of boiling explained	Hydrostatics	18
.. of freezing of water	Heat	43
.. of the mirage	Optics	56—59
Phenomena of the polarisation of light described	Polar. of Light	7
.. of coloured rings, general law of	———	27
.. of Glauberite	———	33
.. of images in calcareous spar explained	———	61
Philosopher, the term defined	Preliminary Treat.	39
Philosophical balance described	Mechanics, t. ii.	17
Philosophy, moral and natural, distinguished	Preliminary Treat.	2
.. mechanical, objects of	———	11, 12
Physics, or natural philosophy, objects of	———	8, 11
Physical astronomy defined	———	17
.. and mathematical truths distinguished	———	7
.. properties of the prismatic spectrum	Optics	28
Physiology, animal and vegetable, explanation of the terms	Preliminary Treat.	11, 12
Piles, machine for driving, described	Mechanics, t. ii.	51
Pinions and wheels, systems of	———	27
Pipes, discharge, proper form of	Hydraulics	2
.. velocity of water in	———	5
.. table for calculating their contents	———	22
.. suction or feeding, in pumps, proper size of	Pneumatics	21
Pivots, friction of bodies turning on, considered	Mechanics, t. iii.	14
Plane, inclined, a mechanical power, considered	——— t. ii.	40
Planet and sun wheel, Watt's, described	———	63
Planets, description of their orbits, &c.	Preliminary Treat.	13—17
Plates, thin, thick, or double, the colours of	Optics	33—37
.. .. .. Newton's tables of	———	35
.. of glass, combination of different doubly refracting	Polar. of Light	55
Pneumatics, definition and objects of	Prel. Treat. 19. Hydrost. 1. Pneum. 2	
.. works on, referred to	Pneumatics	31, 32
Point, working, in machinery, explained	Mechanics, t. i.	2
Points, boiling, of water under different pressures	Heat	49
.. .. table of	———	50
.. of suspension in a balance, concerning the	Mechanics, t. ii.	14
Polarisation of light, list of works on	Polar. of Light	64
.. .. phenomena of, described	———	7
.. .. researches on by M. Malus	———	9
.. .. moveable, Biot's theory of	———	37
.. .. angle of in different substances	———	9
.. .. at the second surfaces of bodies	———	10
.. .. at the separating surfaces of two bodies	———	11
.. .. by successive reflections	———	11
.. .. by ordinary refractions	———	13
.. .. experiments on	———	37
.. .. by double refraction	———	14
.. .. and refraction, difference between	———	29
.. circular	———	41
.. .. in Quartz	———	41
.. .. in Amethyst	———	42
.. .. in fluids	———	45
Polarised light, in what it differs from common light	———	8
.. .. how obtained	———	8
.. .. after it has suffered refraction	———	12
.. .. apparatus for experiments on	———	15—18
.. .. colours produced by the action of crystallised bodies upon	———	18—20
.. .. cause of the colours of	———	36
.. .. Biot's theory of	———	37
.. .. the interference of, experiments upon	———	37

Polarised tints, their deviation from Newton's scale		Polar. of Light	32
Polarising intensities of different crystals, table of		——————	31
Poles, virtual, of the rings of topaz		——————	33
Position proper for the sails of a windmill		Mechanics, t. i.	25
.. of the optic axis for different coloured rings		Polar. of Light	32
Positive and negative axes of refraction		——————	2
.. .. systems of coloured rings		——————	21
Power of the pressure of water		Hydrostatics	7
.. requisite to work pumps		Hydraulics	21
.. of conducting heat in different sorts of wood		Heat	22
.. .. .. of fluids		——————	25
.. and weight distinguished		Mechanics, t. ii.	1
.. illuminating, of the prismatic spectrum		Optics	29
.. magnetizing, of the solar rays		——————	29
Powers, mechanical, described		Prel. Treat. 18. Mech. ii.	8
.. refractive of non-transparent bodies, method of measuring		Polar. of Light	12
Practical mechanics, defined and illustrated		Preliminary Treat.	17
Prediction of the weather by the barometer, rules for		Pneumatics	11
Press, Bramah's hydraulic explained		Hydrost. 8. Mech. i.	23
Pressure of air, particular effects of		Preliminary Treat.	19, 26
.. .. numerous experiments on		Pneumatics	13, 21
.. .. considered as a mechanical agent		Mechanics, t. i.	24
.. centre of		Hydrostatics	11, 28
.. equilibrium of		Hydraulics	2
.. of fluids		Hydrostatics	2, 10, 11
.. .. transmitted in all directions		Pneumatics	5
.. high and low, steam-engines, described		Mechanics, t. i.	32
.. of water, immense power of detailed		Hydrostatics	7
.. communicates double refraction to bodies		Polar. of Light	7
.. its effects upon regular crystals		——————	56
Primary colours of rays of light		Optics	23
Principle, D'Alembert's, in mechanics		Mechanics, t. ii.	2
.. of virtual velocities, explained		——————	2, 28, 42
Prism, neat of the sun's rays when separated by a		Heat	29
Prisms, refraction of light through		Optics	7
Prismatic rays, comparative temperature of		——————	29
.. spectrum de-oxydizing and illuminating power of		——————	29
.. .. physical properties of		——————	28
Proper position of sails in a windmill		Mechanics, t. i.	25
.. velocity of water-wheels		Hydraulics	27
Properties and nature of air		Pneumatics	2
.. .. of caloric		Heat	1
.. .. of light		Optics	1
Proportions, definite, or mathematical chemistry, concerning		Preliminary Treat.	15
Pulley and rope, a mechanical instrument		Mechanics, t. ii.	31
Pulleys, fixed and moveable, their efficacy		——————	33
.. systems of, described		——————	34, 37
.. White's pulley, double moveable, described		——————	35
.. Spanish Burtons, described		——————	3
.. with oblique ropes		——————	39
Pulse-glass, principle of		Heat	56
Pump, air, described		Pneumatics	14
Pumps, air-vessel for		Hydraul. 13. Pneum.	25
.. calculations for the discharge of		Hydraulics	16
.. .. of the power requisite to work		Hydraul. 21. Pneum.	22, 25
.. Ctesebes and De la Hire's		Hydraulics	15
.. centrifugal		——————	19
.. chain, and Vera's rope pump		——————	9
.. eccentric pump		——————	16
.. force pump		Hydraul. 11. Pneum.	24
.. lifting		————— 10 ——————	23
.. lift and force		————— 14	
.. suction pump		Pneumatics	21
.. suction pipes for their action		——————	21
.. .. errors in the construction of		Hydraulics	11
Pyrometer, general account of		Heat	19
.. comparison of Wedgewood's with the scale of Fahrenheit's thermometer		——————	20

GENERAL INDEX.

		Page
Pyrometer, Morveau's and Dr. Ure's proposed one	HEAT	21
Quantity of cohesion in friction determined	MECHANICS, t. iii.	10
Quartz, curious fracture of a crystal of	OPTICS	33
.. its refraction	POLAR. OF LIGHT	6
.. circular polarisation in	———	41
.. experiments on, by Fresnel	———	44
Quicksilver, account of its freezing	HEAT	54, 60
Rack, double, effect of	MECHANICS, t. ii.	56
Radiant heat, velocity of	HEAT	28
Radiating power of heat of different substances in atmospheric air, table of	———	32
Radiation of heat, laws of	———	26
Rainbow, account of, and cause of	OPTICS	50
.. lunar, described	———	52
.. secondary	———	52
.. colours of the primary, as seen at the different planets	———	52
Ram, water, description of that machine	HYDRAULICS	20
Rays of light proceed in straight lines	OPTICS	2
.. primary colours of	———	23
.. reflected from bodies of the colours of those bodies	———	1
.. reflexion of, the general laws of	———	16
.. interference of	———	31
.. refraction of	———	2
.. refrangibility of	———	23
.. velocity of	———	2
.. of the sun, their heat when refracted	HEAT	28
.. prismatic, comparative temperature of	OPTICS	29
.. solar, magnetizing power of	———	29
.. ordinary and extraordinary, distinguished	POLAR. OF LIGHT	2
Reciprocating springs, cause of	HYDROSTATICS	21
Reciprocal gravities of bodies	MECHANICS, t. i.	3
Rectangular axes, Brewster's theory of	———	35
.. lever, description of	——— t. ii.	11
Reflected rays of heat, experiments on	HEAT	29
Reflecting microscope and telescope, principles of	OPTICS	20
.. and refracting telescopes compared	———	68
Reflexion, light lost in consequence of	———	67
.. of rays of light	———	16
.. of sounds, laws of	PNEUMATICS	30
Reflexions, successive, produce polarisation	POLAR. OF LIGHT	11
.. state of light partially polarised by	———	12
Refracting (double) crystals, effect of heat upon	———	62
.. telescopes, imperfections of	OPTICS	26
Refraction of rays of light	———	8—11
.. through prisms	———	7
.. simple, described	POLAR. OF LIGHT	1
.. double, general account of	———	1
.. of Iceland spar	———	1
.. axes of, explained	———	2
.. in crystals, laws of	———	4—7
.. double, communication of	———	7
.. connexion between, and polarisation of light	———	29
.. double, in crystals, laws of	———	29
.. new species of, in Analcime	———	39
.. double circular, account of	———	44
.. ordinary, polarisation of light by	———	13
.. double	———	14
Refractive power of opaque bodies, method of measuring	———	12
.. powers of the humours of the eye	OPTICS	41
.. .. of different bodies, table of	———	6
Refrangibility of the rays of light	———	23
Regular crystals, effect of pressure on	POLAR. OF LIGHT	56
Reindeer, peculiar structure of its hoofs	PRELIMINARY TREAT.	31
Researches of M. Malus on the polarisation of light	POLAR. OF LIGHT	
Resistance, solid of the least	PRELIMINARY TREAT.	22
Resisting forces, observations on	MECHANICS, t. iii.	

GENERAL INDEX.

		Page
Resolution of forces	MECHANICS, t. i.	3
Retarding force, friction from	——— t. iii.	6
Revolving bodies without rolling, friction of	———	12
Rhomboidal crystals, formation of	POLAR. OF LIGHT	1
Right and left-handed quartz, experiments on	———	44
Rigidity of cordage, observations on	MECHANICS, t. iii.	16
.. mathematical theory of	———	16—18
.. tables of	———	26—30
.. works on, referred to	———	31, 32
Rings, coloured, systems of, produced by crystals	POLAR. OF LIGHT	20—23
.. splendour of, in topaz	———	23
.. possessed by certain crystals	———	25
.. general laws of their phenomena	———	27
.. produced by common light	———	28
.. positions of the optic axes for	———	32
.. of the Apophyllite, extraordinary system of	———	34
.. virtual poles of, in topaz	———	33
.. systems of in leucocyclite	———	34
.. tints of, in Vesuvian, &c.	———	35
Rivers, rule for calculating the velocity of	HYDRAULICS	5
Rochelle salt, spectra in crystals of	POLAR. OF LIGHT	33
Rock-crystal, its refraction	———	6
Rollers, friction, account of Garnet's	MECHANICS, t. ii	40
Rolling bodies, friction of	——— t iii.	11
.. Colomb's experiments on	———	12
Roman balance, description and principles of	——— t. ii.	18
Rope and pulley, effect of	———	31
Rope-pump of Vera described	HYDRAULICS	9
Ropes, oblique, and pulleys, their effect	MECHANICS, t. ii.	39
Rules for predicting the weather by the barometer	PNEUMATICS	11
Runner, or single moveable pulley, effect of	MECHANICS, t. ii.	33
Sails of a windmill, best position of	——— t. i.	25
Satellites, or moons, description of	PRELIMINARY TREAT.	16
Saussure's cyanometer described	OPTICS	65
Savery's steam-engine, description of	MECHANICS, t. i.	32
Saw-mill, Taylor's	——— t. ii.	27
Scale for thermometers proposed by Dr. Murray	HEAT	18
.. of Fahrenheit's thermometer compared with Wedgewood's pyrometer	———	20
Scales of different thermometers compared	———	16
Science defined and classified	PRELIMINARY TREAT.	1
Screw, Archimedes's, described	HYDRAUL. 7. MECH. t. ii.	54
.. Hunter's, described	MECHANICS, t. ii.	46
.. as a mechanical power, principle of	———	44
.. micrometer, description of	———	48
.. perpetual, description of	———	47
Seat of vision investigated	OPTICS	44
Second sight of the Highlanders accounted for	———	59
Sensibility of a balance, remarks on	MECHANICS, t. ii.	15
Shadows, coloured, the phenomena accounted for	OPTICS	66
Sheaves and block, observations on	MECHANICS, t. ii.	33
Shortsightedness, cause and remedy of	OPTICS	46
Simple refraction described	POLAR. OF LIGHT	1
Sines, law of the, explained	———	2
Single vision, with two eyes, accounted for	OPTICS	45
Sketched account of the solar system	PREL. TREAT.	13—15, 40
Sky, cause of the colour of, investigated	OPTICS	65
Sliding, friction occasioned by	MECHANICS, t. iii.	3
Smalle. magnitude visible by a microscope	OPTICS	32
Snipe, curious network upon the bill of that bird	PRELIMINARY TREAT.	32
Solar rays, magnetizing power of	OPTICS	29
.. system, sketch of	PREL. TREAT.	13—15, 40
Solid of least resistance, remarks on	———	22
Solids, definition of	HYDRAUL. 1. PNEUM.	1
.. application of their expansion to the arts	HEAT, 8. MECH. t. i.	30
.. table of their expansion by heat	———	7
Sounds, reflexion of, concerning the	PNEUMATICS	30

GENERAL INDEX.

		Page
Sounds, transmission of	Pneumatics	29
Spanish Burtons, pulleys	Mechanics, t. ii.	36
Spar, Iceland, (or calcareous) its composition, &c.	Polar. of Light	1
.. multiplication of images in	———	61
.. influence of heat on	———	63
Species (of double refraction, new) in Analcime	———	39
Specific caloric, observations on	Heat	33
.. gravity	Hydrostatics	13
.. .. tables of in different bodies	———	19—21
.. heats of various metals ascertained	Heat	39
Spectra, ocular, or accidental colours, accounted for	Optics	46
.. in crystals of Rochelle salt	Polar. of Light	33
Spectrum, prismatic, described	Optics	23
.. de-oxydizing power of	———	29
.. heating power of	———	28
.. illuminating power of	———	29
.. lines crossing it accounted for	———	30
.. table of temperature of its rays	———	29
Sphere of glass, refraction of light through	———	9
Spheres and spheroids of glass, of the double refracting force in	Polar. of Light	51
Spherical aberration of light in lenses	Optics	20
.. in mirrors	———	22
Spiral spring in watch-work, a mechanical power	Mechanics, t. ii.	26
Spirit-level, description of	Hydrostatics	10
Spirit of wine, manufacture of	Heat	56
Splendour of coloured rings as seen in topaz	Polar. of Light	23
Spouting fluids, laws of	Hydraulics	4
Springs, spiral, in watch-work, power of	Mechanics, t. ii.	26
.. intermitting and reciprocating cause of	Hydrostatics	21
.. .. curious one in Devonshire	———	22
Spur-wheel, form and application of	Mechanics, t. ii.	30
Squinting, cause of	Optics	45
Stars, fixed, their immense number	Preliminary Treat.	15
State of light partially polarised by reflection	Polar. of Light	12
Statics, definition of	Mechanics, t. i.	1
Steam-boat wheels, observations on	Hydraulics	24
.. experiments on	Heat	39
.. engine, history of	Mechanics, t. i.	32
.. economical uses of	Heat	52
.. engine, Watt's improvements on	———	46
.. .. high and low pressure	Mechanics, t. i.	32
.. .. Marquis of Worcester	———	32
.. .. Newcomen's and Savery's	———	32
Steel-yard mode of graduating	——— t. ii.	18
Still, different forms of	Heat	57
Straps, combination of, with wheels and axles	Mechanics, t. ii.	27
Stream, how to measure the velocity on	——— t. i.	22
.. wheels, observations on	Hydraulics	23
Strength, animal, computation of	Mechanics, t. i.	27
.. .. experiments and calculations on	———	28
.. human, compared with that of the horse	———	29
Structure of mother of pearl	Optics	39
.. of composite doubly refracting crystals	Polar. of Light	56
.. of the Brazilian topaz	———	57
.. of sulphate of potash	———	57
.. doubly refracting, communicated to glass	———	52
.. of the perfectly-formed amethyst	———	43
Successive reflexions, polarisation of light by	———	11
Suction pipe and pump, described	Pneumatics	21
Sulphate of lime, influence of heat upon	Polar. of Light	63
.. of potash and copper, curious experiment with	———	63
Sun and planet wheel, Watt's, described	Mechanics, t. ii.	63
Sun's rays, heat of when separated	Heat	28
Surfaces of bodies, polarisation of light at the	Polar. of Light	10, 11
Suspension, points of in a balance	Mechanics, t. ii.	14
Swallow of Java, account of its nest	Preliminary Treat.	32
Syphon, principles of	Hydrost. 2. Pneum.	26
.. Wirtemberg	Pneumatics	27

GENERAL INDEX.

		Page
System, solar, account of	Prel. Treat.	13—15, 40
Systems of pulleys, concerning	Mechanics, t. ii.	34—36
.. of coloured rings produced by crystalline refractions	Polar. of Light	18—32
.. .. of the apophyllite	———	32—36
.. .. produced by common light	———	28
.. of rings in leucocyclite	———	34
Tabasheer, remarkable properties of	Optics	62
Table of the boiling points of different liquids	Heat	50
.. of changes of different substances by heat	———	20
.. for calculating the contents of pipes	Hydraulics	22
.. of colours of thin plates of water on glass	Optics	35
.. of comparative capacities for caloric in elastic fluids	Heat	38
.. .. expansions	———	11
.. .. measures of particles and fibres	Optics	37
.. .. elastic force of different vapours	Heat	51
.. .. friction of different kinds of wood	Mechanics, t. iii.	30
.. .. scales of thermometers	Heat	17
.. .. temperature of the prismatic rays	Optics	29
.. of the conducting powers of caloric of different kinds of wood	Heat	22
.. of the cooling of heated bodies	———	32
.. of the descent of falling bodies	Mechanics, t. i.	11
.. of the dispersive powers of certain bodies respecting light	Optics	25
.. of the linear dilation of solids by heat	Heat	7
.. of the elasticity of vapour and steam	———	48
.. of experiments on friction and rigidity of cordage	Mechanics, t. iii.	26—30
.. of expansion of air by heat	Heat	13
.. .. of liquids by heat	———	10
.. of frigorific mixtures	———	60
.. of freezing temperature of various liquids	———	62
.. of latent heat of vapours	———	48
.. of light lost by reflection	Optics	68
.. of the radiating heat of different substances in atmospheric air	Heat	32
.. of the refractive of power of different bodies	Optics	4
.. .. .. gases	———	6
.. of specific gravities	Hydrostatics	19—21
.. .. heat of metals	Heat	39
.. of crystals having one axis of double refraction	Polar. of Light	3
.. of angle of polarisation of different substances	———	9
.. of crystals with positive and negative systems of coloured rings	———	21—22
.. of minerals and crystals, with character of their axes	———	26
.. of the polarising intensities of different crystals	———	31
.. of the angle of polarisation of different substances	———	9
Tangents, law of the, explained	———	10
Tapioca-tree, its great value as food	Preliminary Treat.	33
Taylor's saw-mill, description of	Mechanics, t. ii.	27
Teeth of wheel-work, proper form of	———	28
Telescope, description and principles of	Optics	14
.. astronomical	———	15
.. achromatic, Dollond's	Prel. Treat. 23. Optics	27
.. .. Blair's	Optics	28
.. .. Barlow's improvement	———	28
.. Cassograinean	———	20
.. Gregorian	———	20
.. reflecting and refracting, difference of light in	———	68
.. .. observations on	———	20
.. .. proper form of the mirrors of	———	22
Temperature, modes of lowering	Heat	59
.. of freezing point of various mixtures	———	62
Tessellated Apophyllite, remarkable formation of	Polar. of Light	58
Thaumotrope, an ingenious toy described	Optics	44
Theory of accidental colours	———	66
.. of rigidity	Mechanics, t. iii.	16—18
.. (Biot's) of the cause of the colours of polarised light	Polar. of Light	37
.. of rectangular axes	———	35
Thermometer, principles of	Heat	15
.. air	———	15
.. experiments with	———	15

GENERAL INDEX.

		Page
Thermometer, Crichton's metallic ones	HEAT	19
.. Howard's	———	19
.. Murray's proposed scale	———	18
.. various experiments with	———	18
Tide-wheel described	HYDRAULICS	23
Tides, cause of, described	PRELIMINARY TREAT.	16
Tints, chromatic Vernier for subdividing	POLAR. OF LIGHT	52
.. polarised, their deviation from those of Newton's scale	———	32
.. of the rings in hypo-sulphate of lime	———	35
.. .. Vesuvian, or Idocrase	———	35
Topaz, splendour of its coloured rings	———	23
.. virtual poles of its rings	———	33
Torricellian vacuum, experiments on	HEAT	2
Toucan or egg-eater, its curious bill	PRELIMINARY TREAT.	32
Trammel, an instrument for drawing ellipses	———	7
Transmission of pressure of fluids	PNEUMATICS	5
.. of sounds	———	29
Transparency of bodies, cause of	OPTICS	60
Triple crank, description of	HYDRAULICS	12
Trundles of the lantern wheel	MECHANICS, t. ii.	30
Truths, mathematical and physical distinguished	PRELIMINARY TREAT.	7
Vacuo, boiling of water in, account of	HEAT	51
.. distillation of gases, vinegar and water in	———	58
.. freezing of water in	———	53
Vacuum, Torricellian	———	2
Vanilla, peculiarity of the growth of that plant	PRELIMINARY TREAT.	27
Vaporization, cause of it explained	HEAT	58
Vapours, definition of, as distinguished from gases	PNEUMATICS	2
.. table of the latent heat in	HEAT	48
.. .. the elastic force of, and of steam	———	48
Vegetables, effects of light on	PREL. TREAT. 27. OPTICS	64
.. impregnation of, remarks on	PRELIMINARY TREAT.	27
Velocity of descent by gravity equal in all bodies	MECHANICS, t. i.	10
.. its effects on friction	——— t. iii.	39
.. of light calculated	PREL. TREAT. 17. OPTICS	2
Velocity of falling bodies, accelerated in their descent	PRELIMINARY TREAT.	10
.. of radiant heat computed	HEAT	23
.. of a stream or river, methods of calculating	HYDRAUL. 5. MECH. t. i.	22
.. proper for water-wheels generally	HYDRAULICS	27
.. .. an overshot wheel	MECHANICS, t. i.	21
.. of water in pipes, calculated	HYDRAULICS	5
.. virtual, principle of	MECHANICS, t. ii.	2
Vera's rope-pump described	HYDRAULICS	9
Vernier, chromatic, description of	POLAR. OF LIGHT	52
Vesuvian, tints in its rings	———	35
Vince's experiments on friction	MECHANICS, t. iii.	7—9
Vince and Colomb compared as experimenters	———	11
Vinegar, distillation of, in vacuo	HEAT	58
Virginia creeper, peculiarity in the tendrils of that plant	PRELIMINARY TREAT.	27
Virtual velocities, principle of, and applications	MECHANICS, t. ii.	2, 22, 28, 42
Virtual poles of the rings of Topaz	POLAR. OF LIGHT	33
Visible objects, duration of	OPTICS	42
Vision, causes of its being erect	———	42
.. distinct and indistinct in the same object	———	42
.. of objects, intermission in	———	43
.. seat of, investigated	———	44
.. seen single with two eyes, reason of its being	———	45
Undershot wheel, descriptions of	HYDRAUL. 23. MECH. t. i.	22
.. proper form and number of its float-boards	MECHANICS, t. i.	22
Undulations of light, account of the theory of	OPTICS	32
Universal joint, Hooke's described	MECHANICS, t. ii.	62
Uses, economical, of steam particularized	HEAT	52
Watchwork, concerning the spiral spring of	MECHANICS, t. ii.	26
Water boiling in vacuo, concerning	HEAT	51
.. .. under high pressure	———	52
.. considered as a conductor of heat	HEAT	25
.. .. as a mechanical agent	MECHANICS, t. i.	19

GENERAL INDEX.

		Page
Water, compressibility of, experiments on	HYDROSTATICS	1
.. distillation of, in vacuo	HEAT	58
.. force and peculiarity of its expansion	———	12
.. elasticity of, experiments on	HYDROSTATICS	1, 2
.. freezing, phenomenon of	HEAT	43
.. .. in vacuo and in large quantities	———	54
.. pressure of, its power and effects	HYDROSTATICS	7
Water-pressure engine described	HYDRAULICS	29
Water-ram, description of that machine	———	23
Water-wheels, various kinds of	———	6—29
.. power of, calculations on	———	27
.. overshot, proper construction of	——— 24. MECH.	19
.. undershot	——— 23. ———	22
.. velocity of their motion, observations on	——— 27. ———	23
.. of steam-boats	HYDRAULICS	24
Water-with, a plant valuable for its contained water	PRELIMINARY TREAT.	32
Watt's improvements on the steam-engine detailed	HEAT	47
.. sun and planet wheel described	MECHANICS, t. ii.	63
Waves of light, description of the phenomenon	OPTICS	31
Weather-glass, or barometer, its construction	PNEUMATICS	10
.. .. Rules for predicting the weather by the	———	11
Wedge, described as a mechanical power	MECHANICS, t. ii.	43
Wedgewood's pyrometer, account of	HEAT	19
.. .. scale of, compared with Fahrenheit's	———	20
Weighing machine, construction of	MECHANICS, t. ii.	12
Weight, definition and cause of	——— i.	6
.. comparative, of bodies at the sun and different planets	PRELIMINARY TREAT.	40
.. of air, concerning the	HYDROST. 1. PNEUM.	4
.. of the atmosphere	PNEUMATICS	6, 14
.. of latent heat investigated	HEAT	2
.. distinguished from power	MECHANICS, t. ii.	1
Wheel. See Water-wheel.		
.. and axle, single	———	22
.. .. double	———	24
.. .. combinations of	———	27
Wheel-barometer, construction of	PNEUMATICS	9
Wheels, bevelled, crown, lantern and spur, described	MECHANICS, t. ii.	30
.. and pinions, concerning	———	27
Wheel, Persian, description of	HYDRAULICS	6, 22
Wheel-work, complex	HANICS, t. ii.	26
.. proper form of the teeth in	———	28
Wheel, sun and planet, described	———	63
White, a mixture of all colours	PRELIMINARY TREAT.	37
.. light, decomposition of	OPTICS	22
White's pulley described	MECHANICS, t. ii.	35
Wild-pine, its curious water-reservoirs	PRELIMINARY TREAT.	32
Windlass, description of that mechanical power	MECHANICS, t. ii.	23
Wind-mills, proper angles of their sails	——— i.	25
Wine-coolers, their effect in diminishing heat	HEAT	55
Wine, spirit of, how manufactured	———	56
Wirtemberg syphon, description of	PNEUMATICS	27
Wollaston's Cryophorus or Frost-bearer, described	HEAT	55
Worcester's (Marquis of) steam-engine	MECHANICS, t. i.	32
Working-point of a machine, defined	———	2
Works on friction and rigidity of cordage, referred to	——— iii.	32
.. heat, referred to	HEAT	63, 64
.. hydraulics	HYDRAULICS	32
.. hydrostatics	HYDROSTATICS	31, 32
.. mechanics	MECHANICS, t. ii.	64
.. pneumatics	PNEUMATICS	31, 32
.. polarisation of light	POLAR. OF LIGHT	64
Ximenes' experiments on friction	MECHANICS, t. iii.	4, 5
Zero of heat in bodies, according to Dr. Irvine	HEAT	40
Zoology, definition and objects of the science	PRELIMINARY TREAT.	12
Zureda's method of producing converted motions	MECHANICS, t. ii.	57

www.ingramcontent.com/pod-product-compliance
Lightning Source LLC
Chambersburg PA
CBHW062123160426

43191CB00013B/2186